DICTIONARY OF THE SOCIAL SCIENCES

Dictionary
of the
SOCIAL
SCIENCES

Edited by

CRAIG CALHOUN

OXFORD
UNIVERSITY PRESS
2002

OXFORD
UNIVERSITY PRESS

Oxford New York
Auckland Bangkok Buenos Aires Cape Town Chennai
Dar es Salaam Delhi Florence Hong Kong Istanbul Karachi Kolkata
Kuala Lumpur Madrid Melbourne Mexico City Mumbai Nairobi
São Paulo Shanghai Singapore Taipei Tokyo Toronto
and an associated company in Berlin

Published by Oxford University Press, Inc.
198 Madison Avenue, New York, New York 10016
www.oup.com

Library of Congress Cataloging-in-Publication Data

Dictionary of the social sciences / edited by Craig Calhoun.
p. cm.
Includes bibliographical references.
ISBN 0-19-512371-9 (hardcover : alk. paper)
1. Social sciences—Dictionaries. I. Calhoun, Craig J., 1952– II. Oxford University Press.

H41 .D53 2001
300'.3—dc21 00-068151

EDITORIAL AND PRODUCTION STAFF
Executive Editor: Christopher Collins
Assistant Project Editor: Abigail Powers
Copyeditors: Martha Goldstein, Mary Jacobi
Manufacturing Controller: Genieve Shaw
Book Designer: Joan Greenfield
Managing Editor: Matthew Giarratano
Publisher: Karen Day

3 5 7 9 8 6 4

Printed in the United States of America
on acid-free paper

CONTENTS

DICTIONARY OF THE SOCIAL SCIENCES

EDITORIAL BOARD

EDITORS AND CONTRIBUTORS

Karen Albright, New York University

Parama Chaudhury, New York University

Alvis E. Dunn, University of North Carolina–Chapel Hill

Pushan Dutt, University of Alberta

Vibha Gaba, University of Oregon

Saran Ghatak, New York University

Brunson Hoole, Independent Researcher

James Ingram, New School for Social Research

Taylor Sisk, Independent Researcher

Triadafilos Triadafilopoulos, New School for Social Research

Guobin Yang, University of Hawaii

PREFACE

From seventeenth- and eighteenth-century roots, the social sciences have grown enormously. They have flourished in conjunction with the growth of modern states, long-distance trade, and new communications media. They have responded to urbanization, to class division, and to shifts in fertility, life expectancy, family composition, education, religion, and labor markets. At the same time, the social sciences have become both global and culturally diverse. They have reflected not only the West's changing ideas about itself but also the shifting currents of nationalism and international relations, as well as the creation of new kinds of knowledge in widely varying cultural idioms and on diverse social bases.

The rise of universities in the nineteenth century and the successive transformations and expansions of higher education and research institutions in the twentieth have also left their mark. Among other things, they have supported both the division of the social sciences into separate disciplines and the generation of interdisciplinary fields. The expansion of the social sciences, proliferation of new research programs, and generation of new specializations all continue—so do changes in the social world that demand innovations in social science. Colonialism gave way to national independence, for example, but independent nations also became increasingly interdependent participants in new forms of globalization. New media transformed communication.

With this proliferation of fields and subfields, with internationalization, and simply with innovation itself, have come new terms, new usages, and difficulties of communication among scholars. Jargon too has proliferated, sometimes bringing precision but always a need for interpretation. The conceptual vocabulary of social science overlaps substantially with ordinary language, but this does not make social science usage transparent; indeed, it often increases the chances for confusion. It is easy, for example, to think that everyone knows what "class" or "community" or "capitalism" means. Likewise, the two words in the concept "collective action" are clear enough that a casual reader may not recognize the phrase as a term of art carrying reference to a specific analytic problem and sometimes also an implicit distinction from "collective behavior."

The expansion of the vocabulary of social science not only divides researchers from one another, it is a barrier between social science and the broader public. The purpose of this dictionary is to mitigate both divisions. We have tried to make it clear enough that it can be used profitably by those with no specialist background in any specific academic discipline or field, yet precise and substantial enough that it will be genuinely clarifying and enriching for social scientists. Reading outside of his or her own specialty, almost every scholar quickly becomes a lay person. We have oriented this dictionary to the educated lay person, who may sometimes be an anthropologist reading work in psychology or a journalist trying to grasp a technical concept in economics.

Dictionaries have been published specific to each of the social science disciplines. Their quality and reliability varies dramatically, but some—like the *New Palgrave: A Dictionary of Economics* (1987)—are serious scholarly works. In each case, however, trying to understand the terminology of social science entirely from within the usage of one discipline can lead to confusion. Our *Dictionary* will help to reduce that, not only by including the full range of social sciences but also by explicitly relating the different disciplinary usages to one another. We imagine that researchers in fields like political science or sociology will find the *Dictionary* especially useful because their fields are notable for both their internal diversity and the porousness of their boundaries. Such diversity and such porousness are characteristic in varying degree of all the social sciences, however, which is one reason a dictionary like this is needed. We expect that economists will seldom consult the *Dictionary* for definitions of terms in economics, thus, but that the *Dictionary* will be useful if they want to know how the word "institution" is used in other disciplines or what anthropologists mean by "acephalous societies" or who Max Weber was anyhow.

No one commands the whole vocabulary of social science. Not only are there terms that escape our awareness until we encounter them in something we read, thus creating a need for definition we had not known before. In addition, terms we use regularly have different nuances of meaning in different contexts. They are often shaped by trajectories of which we may not be aware. The term "civil society," for example, shaped the notion of "society" long before it returned to English-language usage to denote a more specific concept in the 1980s and 1990s. Its meanings shifted under the influence of different Scots, English, French, and German theoretical traditions, and then when it was mobilized as part of the intellectual struggle under communism both to understand and to resist the domination of the political over social life. Its meanings shifted further when the term was taken up in India and Africa, and they have shifted again when put to work as part of a critique of American individualism and the destruction of "social capital."

Not only do specific fields generate their own distinctive terminologies, they give apparently identical terms different meanings. This is true especially for broad, formative concepts like "culture" or "institution" that have many dimensions of meaning, though they may be linked. Sometimes there is a common root meaning to a word—as a part of ordinary language—but it has come to refer to distinct concepts in different social science contexts. "Representation" means one thing, thus, as part of an account of the production of meaning ("cultural representations of evil") and another in theories of democratic politics ("no taxation without representation"). In sociology and psychology, "sanctions" may be positive or negative, rewards or punishments; in international relations, the word almost always carries the negative meaning. "Pluralism" can refer to the coexistence of different ethnic or national groups in a single society, regardless of whether they share power or one subordinates the others, or to the vesting of political power in multiple and shifting groups, regardless of whether any is ethnic.

These clashes of meaning challenge readers of social science literature, and they have challenged us in writing this dictionary. We hope it has value as a resource for overcoming obstacles. We do not, however, imagine that this dictionary can or even should eliminate all the clashes. While some may reflect mistaken readings or historical ignorance, many arise from differences in topics of analysis and theoretical orientations; they are not simply confusions to be eliminated but contrasting perspectives to be understood. Indeed, the struggle to make concepts and conceptual frameworks adequate to perceived social reality is one of the main ways in which social science advances (albeit one not given appropriate recognition in the dominant model of theories, propositions, and verification). Moreover, quite a few social science terms fit the designation of "essentially contested concepts," coined by the philosopher Wilfred B. Gallie in his *Philosophy and Historical Explanation* (Oxford, 1967). These are terms whose meaning can never be fully settled by a single definition because they are a part of history and practical struggles. Not only can meanings change, the struggle over meanings is a part of different projects of practical social action. Social scientists can define the word "democracy" clearly, thus, but never quite exhaustively and beyond dispute so long as there are political consequences to calling one system or policy democratic and another not. For the purposes of any one research project, an operational definition may be rendered clear and precise—but the relationship of the operational definition to the broader concept will always be problematic. In addition, opposing usages reflect not only competing theories, but the fact that the terms of social science do not merely describe the world but shape it.

Faced with the many sources of diversity and even contradiction in usage, we have developed a set of guidelines for the *Dictionary*. First, we have faced the situation that there is no clear and standard definition of the *social sciences*. The idea of this "family" of disciplines took shape only in the late nineteenth century. For some, being part of the "human sciences" as distinct from the natural or physical was basic. For others, the ideal of the unity of science remained crucial, and the designation "social science" meant no deep difference in kind, only a specification of topic. In the United States especially, those who would emphasize the second word in social *science* often also emphasize a distinction from the humanities. Some contest this explicitly with a notion of "humanistic social science." Others, in Europe especially, use the term *science* in a way that includes much of what Americans call "the humanities." In some settings law is counted among the social sciences; we did not include it, although some legal concepts are covered. This issue cannot be addressed in detail here, let alone settled. For the purposes of the *Dictionary*, however, an operational definition was needed. Our approach was to cover all of some academic fields and some interdisciplinary fields, and only parts of others where these seemed to fit only ambiguously into the social sciences. Here, we have stressed the first word in *social* science, emphasizing coverage of those fields that most clearly focus on social phenomena and relations.

The result is this. Economics, politics, and sociology are covered in their entirety. Social and cultural anthropology are covered along with some (but not truly thorough) treatment of linguistics and some (but much less detailed) coverage of archaeology and physical anthropology. Human and social geography (and its subfields like political geography and population geography) are included, but physical geography is not, save for a necessary minimum of terms and concepts. History and historiography are covered, but with an emphasis on analytical concepts rather than factual domains, and with less systematic detail than economics, politics, social and cultural anthropology, or human geography. We have made special efforts to cover the interdisciplinary fields of cultural studies, communications and media studies, Marxism, and psychoanalysis, each of which has an intellectual existence at least partly distinct from the various social science disciplines yet with relatively broad influence in social science. Likewise, we have included core concepts from the philosophy of social science. We have also included major ideas, orientations, and thinkers from philosophy, generally, insofar as these are integral to the intellectual heritage of the social sciences. We have included concepts from statistics and research methods in only a rudimentary fashion and where they had a distinct relationship to social science. Psychology was perhaps for us the most ambiguous field, and we exercised judgment in the inclusion of terms, always conscious that our selection and presentation might be less than perfect. The issues were the predominance of work in psychology focused on individuals without explicit attention to social contexts, as well as the large parts of the field oriented more to the natural sciences (e.g., to neuroscience and/or psychopharmacology). We have not tried to cover all dimensions of "behavioral science," a term that has grown in prominence, referring to an intellectual orientation and set of disciplines that overlap with but are not included by "social science." We do include social psychology, which has developed in close relationship to other social science disciplines, and in somewhat less detail political psychology, cultural psychology, and environmental psychology. All these fields explicitly have social as well individual foci of analysis. Likewise, we have addressed parts of developmental psychology and cognitive science where they intersect with social science most broadly.

With the qualifications mentioned above, we have tried to be thorough. Selectivity is inevitable in an enterprise such as this, but we have tried to limit it to the criteria of importance and currency (by the latter we mean not novelty, but continuing utilization and significance). We have tried to avoid taking stands on the merits of different intellectual approaches, or even different usages of terms, but rather attempted to explain what they are. Our aim throughout has been to present an authoritative account that will enable readers to understand both the specific meanings of terms and the intellectual issues at stake in their use. We thus go beyond definitions to locate concepts in relation to theories and to explain something of their analytic significance.

Inevitably, perhaps, but more than we would like, our account is based on English-language sources and thus describes mainly social science as it is conducted in English. We do present ideas that originated in other languages, but generally only insofar as they have been translated into English or appropriated by English-language social scientists. A variety of German and French terms appear, thus, because they have been appropriated as part of the jargon of English-language social science; the *Dictionary* is not in itself a guide to translation or to terminology in other languages. This suggests a further unfortunate fact: the *Dictionary* is not a guide to the distinctive social science traditions that have developed around the world but mainly reflects these when they have contributed to English-language social science. The *Dictionary* is, however, international, and is produced by many people for whom English is not a first language. It would not only be valuable to have companion dictionaries addressing social science in other languages (some of which do exist) but also to examine the trajectories of terms and concepts as they move in and out of different scholarly and cultural communities.

In a more positive sense, we have embraced writing in English. That is, we have tried to write clearly and accurately, and also to make our accounts of terms, concepts, and thinkers as inviting—as genuinely readable—as possible. Jargon can be useful, and indeed our project consists largely in making it intelligible. But we have tried to do this through the considerable resources of ordinary English—not by referring bits of jargon to one another. We do not expect readers to curl up with the *Dictionary* on a long winter's evening, but we have tried to make reading it pleasurable. Good writing serves clarity and accuracy, but it is not their only servant. For all of the social sciences—and most especially for economics—mathematics and/or formal logic are also crucial. These are valuable tools; they are the normal means by which economic theory is typically presented. To bypass them altogether would be to do violence to the nature of contemporary economics; the formulae and the mathematics are part of the field. Accordingly, we have presented them here, but we have chosen to do so as infrequently as possible, relying as much as we could on the rendering of mathematical notation into English. Also in the interests of accessibility, we have kept references to a minimum throughout and presented them in a straightforward (if not quite standard) manner. We have referred to major books by title and date of original publication (supplemented, when needed, by date of more recent republication), and these were compiled into a bibliography, presented at the back of the book. For the most part, references are intended to guide readers to major work, not to indicate sources.

The goal of accessibility has also shaped the scale of the project—the whole was kept to one substantial volume, although more could be written on almost every entry. While many readers might have preferred a more detailed account of one or another term, we reasoned, few would prefer a heavier or more expensive book. The pressure of selectivity has been especially acute in deciding which biographies to include. The presence of the biographies is important, and not just as a "human interest" context for the social sciences. Access to social science knowledge is organized not only through common nouns referring to concepts (or empirical facts). It is organized by proper nouns that not only designate historical individuals and their work but also identify scholarly orientations and serve as signposts on the paths of exploration. "Weberian," "Boasian," and "Keynesian" are significant keys to interpreting contemporary social science—just as "behavioral," "reflexive," and "autopoetic" are. We have restricted ourselves, however, to identifying twenty to thirty of the most important figures from the formation of each of the disciplines, plus another three dozen "at large" entries that include pivotal philosophers. As an arbitrary limit on the temptation to include contemporaries who may or may not loom large in the future, the biographies have been limited to those whose work was already widely influential before the 1970s. In selecting the figures for biographical entries, as in developing our lists of entries generally, we began with the major scholarly reference works in each field. We then consulted textbooks, bibliographic indices, the Social Science Citation Index, and other sources. We created preliminary lists, each of which was reviewed and revised by members of the *Dictionary* 's editorial board and sometimes by other scholars in relevant fields. Further research frequently suggested still more revisions. While our list of entries—some 1,800 of them—is by a considerable margin the most comprehensive of any social science dictionary, it does not yet contain the totality of terms emerging in the rapidly expanding fields. That must be left to revised editions.

Many colleagues have contributed in various ways, and deserve credit for a share in any accomplishment, though I deserve the blame for failings. Not least are those who have compiled other reference works. We stand on the shoulders not only of the social scientists who developed powerful conceptual tools, as well as of those who labored to make them as clear and precise as possible. It is true that quality was highly variable among the disciplinary dictionaries, encyclopedias, and textbooks we surveyed. We winced when some authors confused their personal views for authoritative definitions, and resolved to avoid this error. But we were also often impressed. The high quality of the *Encyclopedia of the Social Sciences* edited by David Sills remains evident after three decades, for example. Overall, however, we admire and appreciate the accomplishments of the authors of major reference works.

When the editorial "we" is used in this preface, it refers to the team composed of the editor-in-chief and his two associate editors, Joe Karaganis and Paul Price, who worked long, hard, and extraordinarily well. As fine scholars and fine writers, many of the good qualities of the overall product are due to their efforts. All three of us benefited from the working environment of the Social Science Research Council and the contributions of many colleagues to the contents of the *Dictionary*. My three editorial board colleagues—James Peacock in anthropology, Andrew Schotter in economics, and Aristide Zolberg in political science—were especially helpful in ensuring appropriate coverage of their fields. We also relied on a range of colleagues who reviewed lists of terms in interdisciplinary fields or specialized subfields. Not least of all, we want to acknowledge the work of the many scholars who either contributed entries or checked the presentation in the final drafts. We made the decision at the outset that entries would remain unsigned, but the work is not unappreciated.

I am grateful to Chris Collins, my editor at Oxford University Press, for sponsoring the project. Chris honored me by seeking me out for this project, although he deceived me into thinking it would be much easier than it has been. I forgive him, because he has in fact made it easier—and better—than I think any other editor would have done. I also thank the editorial/production team of Matt Giarratano, Martha Goldstein, and Abigail Powers for their care and concern over each entry and element of this volume. Oxford University Press has established itself as the premier publisher of academic reference works—a considerable service to scholarship—and I am pleased that this *Dictionary* will appear on its list.

I would like to dedicate the *Dictionary of the Social Sciences* to Robert K. Merton. Of all social scientists, he is perhaps the most careful writer and editor and as a result a model for those who would think and communicate clearly.

Craig Calhoun
New York, New York
November 2001

DICTIONARY OF THE SOCIAL SCIENCES

A

ability-to-pay principle A principle of taxation based on the *theory of equal sacrifice*, which holds that each taxpayer should make the same sacrifice of UTILITY that he or she obtains from income. The magnitude of a person's sacrifice depends not only on the size of the tax payment but also on the person's income and other circumstances. This principle is often used to justify progressive taxes. The ability-to-pay principle leads to two corollary notions of equity: vertical equity and horizontal equity. Vertical equity states that a person with a greater ability to pay taxes should contribute a larger amount. Horizontal equity states that taxpayers with the same ability to pay should contribute the same amount in taxes. To determine whether two taxpayers or families are similar in terms of ability to pay requires making INTERPERSONAL UTILITY COMPARISONS (i.e., comparing how much different people's welfare would decline if they had to give up the same amount of their income), a practice considered difficult, if not impossible, under most circumstances. See also TAXES AND TAXATION; and WELFARE ECONOMICS.

aboriginal Describes populations that inhabited a region before the arrival of European or other modern settlers. When capitalized, "Aborigine" refers specifically to the native population of Australia.

absolute advantage See COMPARATIVE ADVANTAGE.

absolute income hypothesis See CONSUMPTION FUNCTION.

absolutism The theory and practice of unlimited, legitimate state power and authority, typically concentrated in the person of a monarch. The theoretical basis of the doctrine was developed by Jean BODIN and Thomas HOBBES in response to the political upheavals of the sixteenth and seventeenth centuries. They argued that power should be absolute and undivided in order to maintain social order. In practice, absolutism is associated with the consolidation of the state in early-modern Europe. The "Age of Absolutism" lasted from 1648 to 1789, and was personified by Louis XIV of France and Frederick II of Prussia, although czarist Russia retained many absolutist features until its collapse in 1917. The term itself emerged at the end of the eighteenth century in the context of early discussions of constitutionalism (see CONSTITUTION AND CONSTITUTIONALISM) and LIMITED GOVERNMENT (e.g., in the U.S. Declaration of Independence). But absolutism should not be equated with more general and exclusively negative terms, such as TYRANNY and despotism (see DICTATORSHIP), nor with specifically modern forms of rule, such as AUTHORITARIANISM or TOTALITARIANISM.

absorbing barrier A barrier that prevents the spread of innovations and cultural forms. Usually it is a strongly entrenched competing form of cultural activity; sometimes it is a legal barrier to importation. Absorbing barriers are distinct from *permeable barriers*, which permit passage. See also DIFFUSION AND DIFFUSIONISM.

abstinence In economics, the phenomenon of refraining from or postponing current consumption in order to facilitate capital accumulation. Abstinence typically requires a reward or payment, which in economic terms is generally the rate of interest (or other increase). It thus provides a theory of the supply of savings.

acceleration principle The principle that the demand for captial goods accelerates following a rise in the demand for output. The theory therefore emphasizes the role of demand, not the role of input prices and interest rates, in explaining investment.

The acceleration principle is central to theories of the supply of capital goods. It has played an important role in models of BUSINESS CYCLES and in theories of economic growth, where it has been used to explain both aggregate investment and investment decisions by individual firms.

The idea of investment acceleration has been criticized, however, for neglecting expectations of future demand, technological change, and the effects of expected changes in output and input prices over time. Moreover, the theory assumes optimal adjustment in each period, which, given the irreversibility of many investments, is too strong a requirement. A decrease in the aggregate capital stock would often be limited by the rate of depreciation, and thus firms might have excess capacity prior to a positive demand shock. In such a situation, there would not necessarily be any increase in investment. More recent variations on the model have addressed some of these shortcomings by generalizing the simple accelerator model and by using a flexible accelerator (also called the distributed lag accelerator). While these models also assume an optimal relationship between output and capital stock, they allow for a slow adjustment of the capital stock toward the optimal level.

accessions tax Tax levied on gifts and inherited property. Inheritance taxes are the primary form and are usually designed to mitigate the inequalities of wealth that develop over generations. Certain kinds of accessions taxes target acquisitions at a progressive rate, which reduces the benefit of parceling out a large bequest over time. See also TAXES AND TAXATION.

accommodating transactions Capital transactions undertaken by monetary authorities in order to reestablish equilibrium in a country's BALANCE OF PAYMENTS (the sum total of transactions between a country and its trading partners). Such transactions are essentially monetary in nature: there is no accompanying movement of goods, services, or fixed assets—only money (gold or foreign exchange) and/or short-term liquid claims. In this respect, accommodating transactions differ from AUTONOMOUS TRANSACTIONS, or transactions carried out for the purpose of profit. Accommodating transactions tend to ease the pressure on the exchange rate that arises when the autonomous component is in deficit or surplus.

accommodation The process of adaptation that allows groups or individuals to coexist in spite of basic conflicts or underlying differences. Accommodation occurs because all sides gain from the avoidance of open hostility, even if structural inequalities and other sources of tension persist. The concept is significant in a number of theories of race relations in the United States—notably in the work of Chicago school sociologist Robert Ezra PARK (see CHICAGO SCHOOL OF SOCIOLOGY). It has also been used to describe the process by which whole societies adjust to their environments, analogous to biological adaptation. This usage draws on an earlier use of the term in experimental psychology, where it described how individual behavior changes to meet the requirements of the external environment.

acculturation The adoption of new cultural patterns following contact between groups—often used synonymously with, or as a more voluntarist substitute for, *assimilation*. Acculturation is frequently invoked in the context of immigration, where the cultural and linguistic practices of the dominant culture exercise a powerful normative influence upon newcomers. Acculturation can include exchanges between generations, although the terms ENCULTURATION and SOCIALIZATION are more commonly used in these cases.

accumulation of capital One of the fundamental topics in ECONOMICS is the process by which the CAPITAL stock is accumulated. Labor productivity—the primary determinant of economic well-being—depends in large part on the stock of complementary inputs, of which capital and land are the two most important classes. The process of industrialization and economic development involves building productive capital in order to increase living standards.

Capital accumulation is a function of INVESTMENT, which is the share of an economy's aggregate output that is not used for current consumption or government expenditures. In the simplest formulation, the capital stock depreciates slowly over time, and the rate of capital accumulation is the rate of investment less the rate of depreciation. Economists have focused on two aspects of the capital stock: the expansion of productive potential and the transformation of the technical and productive organization of the economy. Capital accumulation is studied within the framework of GROWTH THEORY, from the early Solow model, which posited that, in equilibrium, growth would just equal population growth, to the more recent endogenous growth models, in which the technology embedded in capital is a catalyst for further growth, allowing for continued per-capita growth and CAPITAL DEEPENING.

Because investment requires forgoing current consumption in favor of future growth and increased living standards, the accumulation of capital is linked to the degree to which individuals discount the future. Investment in capital (and other productive assets) will occur as long as the marginal return on the investment is as least as great as the discount or interest rate, which equals the OPPORTUNITY COST of current consumption. Modelers of economic development have always been concerned that poor countries would have difficulty generating growth through investment, because of the high cost of deferred consumption.

For Marxists, accumulation has a different significance. Karl MARX argued that accumulation is the basic imperative of capitalism and refers not only to the form that competition takes among individual capitalists (individual accumulation) but more generally to the progressive concentration of capital over time and its alienation from individual ownership. Marx also used the concept to divide the history of capitalism into different dominant regimes or ways of organizing the means of production. The first historical phase is that of primitive accumulation, in which the conditions of labor are first separated from the laborers themselves, chiefly through the emergence of wage-labor. The second phase is dominated by industrial manufacturing and the vast increase in the means of production, especially those embodied in new technologies. The third phase is the emergence of monopoly capitalism, in which individual capitalists gradually lose control of the means of production to financiers and corporate powers. The fourth and last phase was the anticipated reunification of labor with the means of production under COMMUNISM, which was to mark an age in which the accumulation of wealth would no longer depend on its separation from the workers who produced it.

A crucial feature of the accumulation of wealth within capitalism, according to Marx, was its tendency to lose its relative value if not reinvested continually in more production capacity. A factory owner who does not renew facilities and innovate in technology will face rising costs of production and loss of market share, and will eventually see the original investment lose value. Since accumulation depends on continually increasing productive capacity, the system is prone to recurring crises of overproduction. See also CAPITALISM.

acephalous society A society "without a head" or formal leadership. Pastoral societies, band societies, and other small-scale groups are frequently acephalous. When, in addition, these societies possess few distinctions of rank, they are considered *egalitarian societies*.

achieved status Social distinction that is earned or attained, either through merit or by way of acquired credentials (e.g., by education). Achieved status is distinguished from ASCRIBED STATUS, or status accorded at birth (such as nobility or other elite distinctions). Max WEBER distinguished premodern from modern societies on this basis, although modern class relationships continue to transmit de facto ascriptive status to a considerable degree. See also STATUS.

action anthropology Like APPLIED ANTHROPOLOGY, action anthropology describes a commitment to use anthropology to achieve social and policy goals, especially in communities facing serious threats. It is associated with Sol Tax's work of the 1950s and 1960s and became popular in the United States and in Germany.

action group and action set Terms from political anthropology that designate a group of actors organized by a common purpose or activity, but without a strong sense of corporate identity derived from that activity—for instance, shopping, or participating in a political campaign. See also NETWORK ANALYSIS.

action theory A major orientation within sociology and related disciplines that privileges the analysis of the intentional behavior of individuals, or *action*. Action, in this narrow sense, is behavior that takes into account the reactions or interpretations of others, and is therefore directed toward a social context in which expectations, norms, and values come into play. Action theory is especially associated with Max WEBER's analysis of action and his methodological emphasis on VERSTEHEN, or the need to understand the motives and intentions of social actors. Weber distinguished four IDEAL TYPES of action: *traditional action*, which is justified as a repetition of the past; *affective action*, which is geared toward the expression of emotion; *value-oriented action*, in which the performance is taken as an end in itself; and *instrumental action* or means-ends rationality, in which actors choose from among possible courses of action in pursuit of their interests.

Weber's emphasis on action and the generality—even vagueness—of his account of *verstehen* have opened the door to a variety of sociological approaches. A strong tradition of RATIONAL-CHOICE THEORY, drawing on Weber's concept of instrumental action and more directly on economic theories about the profit-maximizing behavior of individuals, has provided one methodological framework, rooted in questions about the nature of optimal choice under diverse or constraining conditions.

SYMBOLIC INTERACTIONISM and related areas of sociological inquiry, on the other hand, have privileged the interpretations and negotiations of meaning that structure interpersonal encounters. Phenomenological approaches have privileged the prior structure of disposition and experience that individuals bring to social encounters (see Alfred SCHUTZ).

One of the challenging issues for action theory is the relationship between individual action and larger SOCIAL STRUCTURES, which many social theorists (although generally not action theorists) accord a broadly determining role in social interactions. This marks a major, but by no means exclusive, perspectival divide in the social sciences—especially in ANTHROPOLOGY and SOCIOLOGY. Talcott PARSONS's emphasis on the *action frame of reference* is one of the most influential efforts to reconcile the notion of rational action and social structure. Parsons treated social structure as a set of abstracted and aggregated norms rooted in patterns of individual interaction. These norms, in turn, contextualize and inform subsequent interactions. Individuals benefit, Parsons suggested, from the recognition by others that normative action bestows. Anthony GIDDENS (in his theory of STRUCTURATION) and Pierre BOURDIEU (with practice theory) have based their research largely on this same analytical challenge, privileging the ways in which individuals draw on and—in acting—reproduce rules and norms, while leaving a margin for deviation or improvisation. Alain Touraine's *actionalism* has a similar ambition in privileging the role of individuals (and sociologists) as agents in the reproduction and contestation of existing social structures. See also AGENCY.

adaptation   The range of genetic, physiological, and cultural changes through which individuals and societies respond to their environment. One of the earliest and most enduring theories of adaptation was Charles Darwin's evolutionary theory, which posited that advantageous biological adaptations to the environment tend to dominate over time. This schema has been extended to explain cultural change and the diversity of cultural forms, variously as a response to different environmental challenges, internal constraints, or challenges from other groups. The analysis of *adaptive strategies*—implicit or explicit attempts on the part of groups to respond to environmental or social challenges—continues to be one of the main methodological perspectives of contemporary anthropology, especially in the United States.

adaptive expectations   Also known as the *error learning hypothesis*, the term refers to expectations about the future based on past information and experience. In economics, it has a more precise meaning in the prediction of the value of variables based on past values. According to the standard method, a variable's future value will be an average of all previous values, which are themselves weighted to emphasize the greater importance of the recent past. Work on INFLATION and MACROECONOMICS in the 1960s drew heavily on this hypothesis. Among the advantages of the adaptive expectations rule was that it had the appearance of being an application of classical statistical inference; also, it was empirically easy to implement and achieved a high degree of explanatory power. The model was eventually abandoned, however, in the 1970s in favor of the RATIONAL EXPECTATIONS hypothesis, which proved more satisfactory on logical grounds. Adaptive expectations implied that it was possible to systematically fool economic agents over time—a position the rational expectations hypothesis denies.

Addams, Jane   (1860–1935) A prominent pacifist, feminist, and sociologist, Addams is perhaps best known as the founder of Hull House, a *settlement house* that pioneered the provision of welfare services in Chicago, especially to indigent and immigrant women. By the turn of the century, Hull House had become a center of radical political and sociological activity, and exerted a powerful influence on the generation of University of Chicago urban sociologists that came to prominence in the 1920s (see CHICAGO SCHOOL OF SOCIOLOGY). Addams herself was deeply interested in sociological research as a means of reforming society. In recognition of her efforts on behalf of pacifism, Addams received the Nobel Peace Prize in 1931. Her major works include *Democracy and Social Ethics* (1902), *New Ideals of Peace* (1907), and *Twenty Years at Hull House* (1910).

additional member system   See ELECTORAL SYSTEM.

adjustment costs   Costs that economic agents incur when decision variables are changed. High adjustment costs will result in a low rate of change in response to changing conditions (as in the case, for example, of capital investment in response to changes in demand). Low costs will have the opposite effect. In either case, adjustment costs are central to attempts to measure optimizing behavior by economic agents (optimization of PROFITS, cost, or UTILITY) and to explain lags in the process of adjustment.

Adjustment costs may be classified as either external or internal. Internal adjustment costs refer to the output that the firm forgoes in diverting resources from production to investment activities. These include planning and installation costs. External adjustment costs arise when the firm has a *monopsony* in the market for capital goods—that is, the demand for capital by the individual firm is a significant proportion of the total market demand for that particular type of capital. In this case, the firm faces a rising supply price of capital. Therefore, the larger the rate of its investment, the higher the prices it must pay for the capital goods.

administered prices   Prices established by an administrative process rather than by a standard market-clearing Walrasian adjustment, or TATONNEMENT process. Such practices generally require the participation of government or some official regulatory body. Administered policies may establish upper limits, as in rent controls, or lower limits such as a minimum wage. They also play a prominent role in the agricultural policies of many countries.

administrative law   The area of public law governing the exercise of power by the EXECUTIVE branch. It spells out the powers, organization, and procedures of particular administrative bodies, as well as the means by which citizens may appeal their decisions. In continental Europe, where public and private law are sharply distinguished, administrative law has long been a separate and distinct practice with its own codified rules, courts, and procedures. COMMON LAW countries such as England and the United States did not begin to develop a separate body of administrative and private law until the dramatic expansion of the state in the twentieth century. See also LAW.

Adorno, Theodor   (1903–1969) A German philosopher and cultural theorist associated with the FRANKFURT SCHOOL. Adorno was a prolific and influential writer on a range of topics, from dialectical theory to critiques of the "CULTURE INDUSTRY," PSYCHOANALYSIS, and musicology. He wrote literary criticism and studies of major philosophers (including Georg HEGEL, Søren Kierkegaard, Edmund Husserl, and Martin HEIDEGGER), contributed to the empirical work of the Frankfurt school on political attitudes and prejudice, and was coauthor of the most provocative of these studies, *The Authoritarian Personality* (1950). He had a long and productive collaboration with Max HORKHEIMER, whom he succeeded as director of the Institute for Social Research in the 1960s, and close relationships with Walter BENJAMIN and Bertolt Brecht, with whom he engaged in productive exchanges on aesthetics and negation.

Born Theodor Wiesengrund, Adorno adopted his mother's maiden name in the late 1930s, after he and the Frankfurt school had moved to the United States. In addition to philosophy, he received a strong education in music and studied composition in Vienna for two years. Musicology and philosophical studies occupied much of his attention in the 1930s, although as the decade passed he became more closely involved in the forms of social critique pursued by Horkheimer and Herbert MARCUSE. With Horkheimer, he authored one of the essential texts of Frankfurt school cultural critique, *The Dialectic of Enlightenment* (1944), which exemplified the Frankfurt school turn from the Marxist terms of class struggle and liberation to a strongly Nietzschean account of the classical origins and modern apotheosis of instrumental reason. The endpoint of this tendency, Adorno argued, was a "totally administered society" that integrated culture, the state, and the economy into a seamless totality that structured individual behavior and expression in increasingly fine detail.

Although much of Adorno's later work confirms this pessimistic appraisal of the chances for social change, it also manifestly struggles to recast dialectical thinking as a source of radical alterity—what Adorno called "negative dialectics." Adorno tended to locate this potential in modernist art; the atonal music of Schönberg is his most famous example, which he repeatedly contrasted to allegedly commodified musical forms such as jazz. This controversial view earned Adorno a not undeserved reputation as a cultural elitist, although it should be noted that he recognized elements of utopian desire in even the most degraded cultural forms. Adorno remains a vexed figure in this regard, but the problems he posed continue to challenge social theory and CULTURAL STUDIES. His other major works include *Minima Moralia* (1951), *Prisms* (1955), *Negative Dialectics* (1966), and *Aesthetic Theory* (1970).

ad valorem tax   A tax on the value of a transaction, assessed as a percentage of price at the retail, wholesale, and manufacturing stages. Examples of ad valorem taxes include the retail sales tax in the United States, the value-added tax employed in Europe, and the purchase tax levied in the United Kingdom. These are different from *specific taxes* or unit taxes, which specify a flat sum per unit of product. Ad valorem taxes are often preferred to unit taxes because they are considered less regressive. Moreover, their real value is not eroded by inflation, whereas the unit tax remains constant as prices rise. See also TAXES AND TAXATION.

adversarial system   A judicial or political system that produces outcomes based on the rule-governed struggle between two or more opposed parties. Most commonly, the term refers to a criminal justice system in which the state and the accused, each represented by counsel, contend before a presumably impartial judge who interprets the rules under which evidence is presented. The adversarial system is found in Britain, the United States, and their former colonies and dependencies. The *inquisitorial system*, in which the court conducts its own investigation based on the practice of Roman or Napoleanic law, is found in the countries of continental Europe, their former colonies, and (for independent historical reasons) much of the rest of the world. A less common usage of the term refers to political systems, particularly the parliamentary system, in which the party in power confronts an officially recognized and institutionalized opposition. See also GOVERNMENT.

adverse selection   The name given to a problem of asymmetric information in the marketplace, in which economic agents on one side of an exchange lack important information possessed by agents on the other side. The best known model of adverse selection is George Akerlof's "market for lemons." Here buyers and sellers trade used cars, but only sellers are aware of the quality of the cars—buyers simply know the average quality of cars in the market. If both buyers and sellers were aware of the quality of the cars, all cars would be exchanged and the market would be efficient. In the presence of asymmetric information, however, the buyers will be willing to pay a price corresponding to the average quality. In such circumstances, from the perspective of the seller, the value of the higher quality cars exceeds their price and these will not be put up for sale. Rational buyers recognize that only "bad" cars will be sold, but these cars are not worth the "average" at which they are offered. In the extreme case, no transactions take place. In general, not all trade is eliminated under conditions of adverse selection, but the market allocation is inefficient. GRESHAM'S LAW and some credit-rationing models are other instances of adverse selection.

affect control theory   (ACT) A social psychological model for explaining emotions and the expressive aspects of action. Developed largely by David Heise, ACT argues that individuals seek to achieve consistency between long-term *fundamental sentiments*—determined by processes of socialization—and *transient impressions* occasioned by specific events. The gap between the two is known as *deflection*. Individuals minimize deflection by managing external events, their interpretations of those events, and their emotional responses. This process involves not only shifts in interpretation but also shifts in individuals' perceptions of social identities (see LABELING THEORY) and an active process of steering events to conform to their fundamental sentiments. This active role, in turn, reproduces larger social norms and values. Where this is not possible, ACT holds that fundamental sentiments may change. In this regard, ACT draws on Erving GOFFMAN's view that impressions are actively generated through conduct—not merely produced through passive reflection on it. These impressions serve to maintain the identities, or faces, that people have in diverse social situations. ACT also builds on BALANCE THEORY when it suggests that people seek to maintain stable emotional states by managing internal as well as external responses and by seeking cognitive consistency.

ACT relies heavily on the categorization of sentiments into three distinct registers: evaluation, potency, and activity (together known as

EPA). These, in turn, are dichotomized into positive and negative forms or mapped onto scales of intensity—in both cases yielding a range of empirical techniques for measuring and analyzing affective responses.

affinal relations Relations through marriage rather than descent (or CONSANGUINEAL RELATIONS). See also KINSHIP.

affirmative action The policy of favoring members of historically disadvantaged groups, such as women or ethnic minorities, as a way of compensating for current underrepresentation and past or present discrimination. This may be advanced by QUOTAS, which reserve a certain number or ratio of positions for members of specified groups, or by preference systems, which favor members of less advantaged groups in choices between two otherwise equal candidates. Such policies are almost always presented as temporary and are frequently controversial, resulting in claims of reverse discrimination by members of groups purportedly displaced by affirmative action policies. Although the term originated in the United States during the 1970s, similar practices have developed in a variety of polities and organizations around the world.

age Although the process of aging is a biological fact, the significance accorded different ages or stages of life is a cultural one and strongly reflects cultural differences. Age is a basic social category that shapes perceptions and nearly all forms of interpersonal interaction. Social research on the question of age reflects this centrality and shows a corresponding diversity. It deals with such issues as the historical evolution or cultural specificity of concepts of childhood; correlations between age and wealth, status, or power; gender-dependent forms of age stratification; occupational shifts; studies of youth cultures and delinquency; and the question of generational transmission of knowledge, cultural practices, and authority.

Many of these issues have important historical components: premodern societies especially tend to be highly structured by distinctions in occupation and status associated with age (divided into *age grades* or *age sets*), and often possess elaborate rituals of passage from one to the next.

The age distribution of a population is one of its most important demographic features. It influences fertility and mortality rates, the dependency ratio (the proportion of those who are too old or two young for productive labor), the openness of a society to change, and, according to some researchers, its propensity for political instability.

Although this diversity makes it difficult to generalize about research on aging, there have nonetheless been historical trends in the attention focused on different aspects of age and aging. Age, for instance, was central to much of the work on KINSHIP in early- and mid-twentieth century anthropology, which generally focused on societies in which the generational transmission of authority and property was of paramount importance. The last fifty years have seen a tremendous increase in sociological interest in the question of youth cultures—first through major work on delinquency and DEVIANCE, and later in studies of the diverse youth subcultures that emerge in the margins of dominant cultural norms and values. More recently still, there has been growing sociological interest in the roles, treatment, and cultural specificity of the elderly, from historical inquiries into the evolution of the category to investigations of age discrimination (*ageism*) and changes in the prevailing forms of care.

age-area hypothesis A corollary to the theory of cultural diffusion first proposed by Clark Wissler (*The Relation of Nature to Man in Aboriginal America*, 1926). The hypothesis suggests that cultural traits can be dated in relation to their spatial diffusion from a center point or origin. It implies that diffusion occurs at a known speed. See also DIFFUSION AND DIFFUSIONISM.

agency The capacity for autonomous social action. Agency commonly refers to the ability of actors to operate independently of the determining constraints of SOCIAL STRUCTURE. The origins of the term lie in the legal and commercial distinction between principal and agent, in which the latter is granted the capacity to act autonomously on behalf of the former. An agent in this sense may sign contracts or manage property autonomously, while still bound to serve the interests of a principal. The nature of such relationships continues to be a subject of considerable interest in sociology, economics, and political science, where it draws strongly on rational choice models of individual and firm behavior and is generally referred to as AGENCY THEORY. See also RATIONAL-CHOICE THEORY.

More generally, however, social science usage has shifted toward an emphasis on the problem of autonomy itself. In this context, agency raises questions about the importance of human intentions, the nature and social construction of free will, moral choice, and political capacity. In common usage, agency places the individual at the center of analysis. However, collectivities may also be said to possess greater or lesser capacity to exercise agency or autonomous action. In both cases, agency suggests not merely the ability to act, but to act in ways that demand the recognition and/or response of others. This distinction is sometimes described as that of action from mere behavior (see ACTION THEORY).

Debates about agency commonly oppose it to SOCIAL STRUCTURE, although some scholars also study the structural conditions for agency. A variety of schools of sociological analysis have addressed the question of the extent to which individuals may operate autonomously from social structure. Much sociology and anthropology is structural in the sense that it attempts to explain the identity or behavior of individuals on the basis of positions in social structure or culturally assigned roles. In opposition to this approach, some symbolic interactionists (such as Herbert Blumer) argue that social structures (or social systems) are abstractions that do not exist apart from human construction, and that individuals consequently have a great deal of agency whether they recognize it or not. From this perspective, human agency is central and everything else in social life—including social systems—stems from it. Some critics have argued that such a notion does not adequately grasp agency because it presents individuals as determined by a constant, pervasive process of social construction. These critics place more emphasis on the capacity to reflect on one's social circumstances and self in order to rise above the more general process of social construction.

The *agency-structure debate* came to the fore in sociology in the 1970s and 1980s, in the context of increased attention to practice or action and an increased concern for the analysis of power relations and conflict. The framing of this debate was influenced by French STRUCTURALISM—associated initially with the anthropology of Claude LÉVI-STRAUSS and later with the work of scholars who sought to pay greater attention to practical action (notably Pierre BOURDIEU). Following this lead, Anthony GIDDENS argued that structure and agency should be seen as inextricably linked, with neither altogether ascendant over the other. Other theorists of the middle ground between agency and structure include Peter Berger and Thomas Luckmann, who argue for a dialectical relationship between the two.

agency theory The economic analysis of contractual relationships. An agency relationship is defined through an implicit or explicit contract in which one or more persons (the principals) engage another person (the agent) to take actions on their behalf. An example of an agency relationship is the delegation of decision making authority from the shareholders of a firm (the principals) to a manager (the agent). The total costs of structuring, administrating, and enforcing such contracts are called agency costs—also referred to as TRANSACTION COSTS, MORAL HAZARD costs, and information costs.

Traditional economic analysis treats the FIRM either as a black box or as a production function that transforms raw materials into final output. The actual process through which such inputs are organized and coordinated is ignored. As a result, questions concerning the organization of firms (partnerships vs. individual proprietorship vs. corporations), the financing of firms (equity vs. debt), employee compensation plans (wages vs. stock options; hourly wages vs. piece-rate wages), and accounting procedures have received little attention. Agency theory, with its emphasis on contractual relationships, provides a framework for the study of such questions. Within agency theory, *principal-agent* studies apply optimization and mathematical techniques to study the effect of preferences and asymmetric information. Studies rooted in the *positive theory of agency*, on the other hand, take a more empirical approach and concentrate on the effects of the contracting technology and the specific human and/or physical capital involved. See also FIRM, THEORY OF THE.

agenda setting In its narrow sense, the power to determine the order in which a LEGISLATURE will consider various proposed bills and other business. The power to set agendas is typically held by the parliamentary leader of the majority party—for instance, the prime minister in parliamentary systems or the Speaker in the U.S. Congress. SOCIAL-CHOICE theory has demonstrated that the order in which issues are considered can significantly alter outcomes. More broadly, agenda setting refers to efforts by any political actor to introduce or remove issues from the public sphere or specific party programs.

agent See AGENCY THEORY; and PRINCIPAL AND AGENT.

agglomeration Refers to the concentration of specialized forms of economic activity—for instance, single industries—in localized areas. Agglomeration factors include the proximity of production to markets, the need for skilled labor, and the lower costs of shared infrastructure. The concept dates back to early-twentieth-century work on industrial development by the geographer Alfred WEBER and remains important to the study of economic DEVELOPMENT, INDUSTRIALIZATION, and URBANISM.

aggregate demand function Expresses the relationship between the general price level and the aggregate quantity of goods and services demanded, composed of aggregate consumption, government expenditures, investment, and net exports. While demand functions for individual goods are downward sloping in price because of the substitution away from other goods as prices fall, an aggregate demand function is downward-sloping because of the relationship between its components and the interest rate. An increase in the price level increases the demand for money, which in turn increases interest rates. Consumption, investment, and net exports all decrease as the interest rate rises; thus aggregate demand drops as the price level rises. See also DEMAND THEORY; and KEYNESIANISM.

aggregate production function See PRODUCTION FUNCTION.

aggregate supply function Traces the aggregate output supplied at each general price level, given the wage rate, technology, the degree of competition, and static price expectations. In the short run, with static expectations, the function's positive slope reflects the fact that an increase in nominal wages that accompanies an increase in prices is mistaken for a rise in real wages. In the short run, higher prices encourage a rise in output, which can be achieved by offering higher wages to secure additional labor. The rise in nominal wages, however, does not match the rise in prices, and as a consequence real wages fall—a necessary condition for increased employment. In the long run, however, an increased supply of labor can be sustained only if real wages rise. Over time, workers revise their expectations to take the movement of prices into account, the aggregate supply curve moves up, and output and employment fall back to their previous level. In the long run, the aggregate supply curve is vertical at the full-employment level of output.

aggregation problem The problem of combining microeconomic variables and the behavior of microeconomic agents—individuals and firms—into macroeconomic aggregates such as the gross domestic product, INFLATION, UNEMPLOYMENT, and so on. Under certain circumstances, aggregate behavior can be predicted by the behavior of a *representative agent*—that is, aggregate and individual behavior are viewed as consistent but different in scale. However, statistical and experimental evidence suggests that under a wide range of circumstances, aggregate behavior does not conform to this logic.

agnates Persons related solely through the male line. See also KINSHIP.

agricultural revolution A transformation in the productive capacity of agriculture and the size of the population it can support. Anthropologists and other specialists on agricultural development generally distinguish among several different agricultural revolutions, beginning with the shift from hunting and gathering to the domestication of plants and animals. Most specialists believe this revolution first occurred in the Middle East some ten thousand years ago, in the region known as the Fertile Crescent. There is also a significant consensus among cultural geographers that the spread of agriculture in early human societies followed a pattern of independent development, emerging at different times from the separate cultural hearth areas of the Americas, the Middle East, and Asia.

The technological developments that permitted regular agricultural surpluses in Europe in the 1700s are usually considered a separate agricultural revolution, as are the emergence of genetically manipulated crops (also known as the *green revolution*) and the replacement of family-organized agriculture by large-scale agribusiness in recent decades. Although these late revolutions are subjects of considerable interest, the early agricultural revolutions are virtually coterminous with the emergence of complex, sustainable civilizations, and therefore provide a strong explanatory perspective on broader historical and social change.

alien See CITIZENSHIP.

alienation A social or psychological state of separation from self, others, social life generally, or the products or processes of one's labor. The term enters modern thought with Jean-Jacques ROUSSEAU's account of the emergence of society, which divorces man from an idyllic state of nature. Georg HEGEL developed the concept into a more complex theory of history, and Karl MARX offered the most influential account. Marx describes how the capitalist labor process subjects workers not only to the appropriation of their labor by others, but to a systematic reduction in their capacity to realize their full human potential. Because Marx defined humanity largely through its capacity for creation—for making both things and social relations—this alienation of labor represented a fundamental estrangement from the world.

Other sociological inquiries have extended this more general sense of the term, removing alienation from its strict relationship to the conditions of capitalist labor. Thus, alienation finds its way into descriptions of the breakdown of almost any form of social integration or participatory process: voter apathy, oppositional youth cultures, artistic distance from the cultural mainstream, and so on. The term is also used loosely to denote a more purely psychological feeling of separation and/or dissatisfaction. Although this usage also has roots in Rousseau and Marx, it is important to see that it misses much of their more complex social meaning. PSYCHOANALYSIS makes a somewhat deeper use of the term, closer to the original, but still more heavily intrapsychic and less social. Existentialist philosophers and social scientists, including Jean-Paul SARTRE, made it a central part of their understanding of the human situation in general, although again in a way much less tied to the analysis of historical social change and specific relations of production.

Within MARXISM, alienation became especially important to the "Western Marxist" current that emphasized consciousness and action more than objective class structure and productive relations. The split between Marxist traditions was sharpened by the fact that Marx's principal discussion of the concept occurs in *The Economic and Philosophic Manuscripts of 1844*—a document that Marx never published and which became widely available only in 1932. Critics of Soviet orthodoxy

and deterministic versions of historical materialism made much of the newly available "early writings," especially the concept of alienation. Debate ensued over whether it was possible for the members of socialist societies to suffer alienation—a controversy in which governing elites in the socialist countries provided the strongest voices of denial.

Through Marxist and existentialist channels, alienation acquired great currency in the student protest movements of the 1960s—now refashioned to meet the demands of a critique of affluence and consumer culture. This was the case in much of the postwar work of Erich FROMM, Herbert MARCUSE, and others associated with *critical theory*, for whom the concept of alienation formed a bridge between psychoanalysis and Marxism, and a link to the broader agenda of Marxist cultural critique.

alignment The relationship between underlying social CLEAVAGES and support for political parties in liberal democracies. Political scientists have provided a variety of explanations for why some cleavages—such as those based on class, religion, region, and ethnicity—become salient to partisan politics while others do not. Seymour Martin LIPSET and Stein Rokkan's *Party Systems and Voter Alignments* (1967) points to a number of factors, including the "freezing" of certain party alignments at the historical moment when parliamentary democracy and a functioning PARTY SYSTEM were achieved, the strategic action of party elites, and the advantages and opportunities afforded by particular types of state institutions, especially ELECTORAL SYSTEMS.

A relatively swift change in party alignment is referred to as *realignment*. Beginning in the 1960s, most Western party systems underwent rapid realignment: long-stable patterns of class and religious support eroded; single-issue VOTING increased dramatically; and noneconomic issues grew in importance. Debate persists over whether this fluctuation has given way to a new, relatively stable pattern of party identification, or whether these symptoms herald a deeper trend toward "dealignment," that is, toward patterns of party support unrelated to deeper social cleavages.

Allais, Maurice (1911–) A French economist best known for the *Allais paradox*, which illustrates how people weigh risks and benefits in the decision-making process. He has also published widely in general equilibrium theory, capital and GROWTH THEORY, monetary theory, and risk analysis. He was awarded the Nobel Prize in 1988 for his work on markets and efficient utilization of resources.

Allais was born in Paris and educated as an engineer. Later, motivated by the crisis of widespread unemployment during the Great Depression, he taught himself economics. Allais was chiefly responsible for contributing a quantitative dimension to French economics. Although he wrote two major books on the efficiency of markets and had students who became famous in their own right (such as Gerard Debreu), his work began to be published in English only late in his career—a fact that limited his influence among Anglo-American economists.

A la recherche d'une discipline economique; Première partie: l'economique pure (1943) was a major contribution to the study of general EQUILIBRIUM. Allais formally proved that equilibrium prices are efficient in the sense that departures from equilibrium prices cannot make anyone better off without correspondingly making someone worse off (a condition also known as PARETO OPTIMAL). One of the achievements of this book was the explicit modeling of intertemporal markets in which transactions extend over time. *Economie et intêret* (1947) is Allais's other contribution to this field and includes his work on capital, interest, and growth theories. He was one of the first economists to derive the GOLDEN RULE of accumulation, which states that in order to maximize national income, the interest rate should equal the growth rate of that income. Allais also analyzed the process by which investment in primary inputs today yields gains in national income in the future.

The Allais paradox describes the way in which people make decisions under conditions of uncertainty. According to the standard theory—John von NEUMANN and Oskar Morgenstern's *independence axiom*—people decide between two alternatives based on the difference in expected payoff, and not on the basis of other factors internal to the choices. Allais showed that internal factors do play a determining role when the two payoffs are dependent on an identical but unknown variable.

Allais's work on general equilibrium compares favorably in importance to John R. HICKS's *Value and Capital* (1939) and Paul SAMUELSON's *Foundations of Economic Analyses* (1947).

alliance theory An approach to the study of KINSHIP relations that looks to marriage and the rules that govern it to explain social organization, primarily in preindustrial societies. It is often contrasted to approaches that privilege descent or CONSANGUINEAL RELATIONS. The key figure in the development of alliance theory was Claude LÉVI-STRAUSS, whose *Elementary Structures of Kinship* (1969) challenged the traditional priority given descent relations and introduced a number of concepts into the study of marriage systems. These include the function of marriage EXOGAMY in relation to a fundamental INCEST TABOO, and the distinction between systems in which marriage choice is governed by positive injunctions (such as favoring the marriage CROSS COUSINS) and those structured only by restrictions on certain kin relations (such as banning marriage between close relations). The former, Lévi-Strauss argued, constitute elementary structures of marriage; the latter are complex structures. See also ELEMENTARY STRUCTURES OF KINSHIP.

Debates between proponents of alliance theory and descent theory tended to polarize in the wake of Lévi-Strauss's work of the 1950s and 1960s and overlap other divisions between Anglo-American and French anthropologists. Recent work has tended toward a less categorical approach to kinship that emphasizes the diversity of kinship systems and thus calls into question the existence of universal kinship structures. This turn has largely deflated the stakes of the alliance–descent debate in contemporary anthropology.

allophone A difference in sound within a language that does not produce a difference in meaning. Often compared with PHONEMES, which designate the minimum difference in sound that does produce a difference in meaning.

Allport, Gordon (1897–1967) An American social psychologist best known for his theory of personality and studies of the social and psychological construction of ATTITUDES. Allport developed a theory of human motives that permitted them relative independence from psychological depth models, especially theories of the instincts. He also distanced himself from the antipsychological tendencies of BEHAVIORISM, which relied heavily upon external, mechanistic models of motive and action. Choices and actions, rather, had to be conceived as following from personality structures or *traits*, but these traits were generally dynamic and forward looking rather than determined by past action. They worked to synthesize experience and render it consistent, and thereby shaped attitudes and beliefs. Allport put these conceptual tools to work in a widely read study of prejudice, *The Nature of Prejudice* (1954). He was also the author of *Personality and Social Encounter* (1953) and *Pattern and Growth in Personality* (1961).

Althusser, Louis (1918–1990) An influential French Marxist philosopher who challenged the two dominant strains of twentieth-century Marxist thought: the Hegelian tradition of Western MARXISM (exemplified by Georg LUKÁCS and Alexandre Kojève) and the scientific Marxism of the Communist Parties. In two works published in 1965, *For Marx* and *Reading "Capital"* (the latter written with Etienne Balibar), Althusser rejected the prevailing understanding of Marxism as a teleological system—an inevitable and unilinear logic of historical development. This critique applied both to revolutionary assumptions about intensifying class conflict and the victory of communism, and to the diverse theories of ALIENATION and reconciliation rooted primarily in Karl MARX's early work.

Instead, Althusser insisted on a decentered conception of SOCIAL STRUCTURE, a nonteleological understanding of historical change, and an open-ended notion of Marxist theory that acknowledged the need for further development and revision. Against Communist doctrine, Althusser saw Marxism neither as a natural science (as in claims for DIALECTICAL MATERIALISM), nor as a blueprint for the social structure that clearly linked political and cultural life to class conflict and class conflict to economic determinants. Although he held to the Marxist principle of economic determination "in the last instance" in the context of capitalist society, he argued that other eras were subject to other dominant logics and that no universal law determined their specificity. Moreover, rather than trace a simple line of determination from the economic *base* to the political, social, and religious *superstructure* of society, he recognized a much more complex set of relationships among the economic, political, ideological, and theoretical practices that structured social life. Althusser accorded these practices a RELATIVE AUTONOMY from one another. By the same logic, contradictions within society were always overdetermined by a range of social factors and causes, and did not always line up neatly with prescribed class positions. When they did, however, revolution became possible.

Althusser produced an influential account of IDEOLOGY, which argued that the social order is reproduced and enforced not only through coercive forces—primarily the law, the police, and the military—but at a much broader and unconscious level through what he called IDEOLOGICAL STATE APPARATUSES (ISAs), which included religion, the family, the media, schools, and political parties. Persons, Althusser argued, did not exist as autonomous individuals who adopt particular beliefs or roles, but as subjects whose identity and even individuality is a product of these various systems. These forms of self-knowledge, he argued, are ideological in a very broad sense: they are the network of ideas and beliefs that structure a person's experience of transpersonal, "real" history and society. Marxism could claim a scientific character insofar as it analyzed this process. This strong constructivism was also the basis of Althusser's claim that Marxism was not humanism and that history was a "process without a subject."

Althusser characterized his work as a return to the fundamentals of Marx—although such claims disguised a number of dramatic revisions and elaborations of key source concepts. His radical critique of existing Marxism and, notwithstanding, his adherence to the obstinately Stalinist French Communist Party made him a controversial figure on the left. This controversy took on a much more personal character after he murdered his wife in 1980. Few would dispute that his work of the 1960s and early 1970s had an enormous impact on a generation of younger scholars, and in part paved the way to POSTSTRUCTURALISM. His writings of the 1970s took on an increasingly self-critical tone, however, and in many respects deliberately cast doubt on his earlier claims.

Althusser was born in Algeria, spent nearly all of World War II in a German prisoner-of-war camp, and studied and taught at the Ecole Normale Supérieure in Paris. His other major works include *Lenin and Philosophy* (1971), *Essays in Self-Criticism* (1976), and a posthumously published autobiography, *The Future Lasts Forever* (1992).

altruism Concern for the welfare of others has been a recurring subject of interest for social philosophers, social scientists, and more recently behavioral scientists. The origin of the term, however, lies with the nineteenth-century social theorist Auguste COMTE, who opposed the positive social values of altruism to the negative values associated with egoism. Although nearly all observers agree that human beings exhibit altruistic behavior, there is less agreement about the sources and specific nature of such acts.

Research has differed on the question of whether altruism is a learned, innate, or developmentally acquired trait. Many animals, for instance, display altruistic behavior in caring for their young. Human beings, however, demonstrate clear variations in altruistic behavior, leading many social psychologists and sociologists to investigate the conditions under which altruism is reproduced or favored. The psychologist Jean PIAGET developed a different position, arguing that altruism is one of the final stages in human psychological and cognitive maturation, which not everyone achieves.

The relationship between altruism and collective or group behavior has also been a subject of considerable research, ranging from behavior in classic divide-the-dollar games, where interests are directly opposed (ZERO-SUM GAMES), to studies of responses to emergencies or calls for help. Altruism has been of renewed interest to economists, as economic experiments have consistently demonstrated that certain kinds of situations lead to cooperative and altruistic behavior. The source of individual altruistic behavior has been modeled in several ways: as a distaste for unequal outcomes (difference aversion), as generalized reciprocity, and as utility derived from the well-being of others.

amortization An accounting term that refers to the allocation of a cost over several installments. Amortization is analogous to depreciation, with the difference that the former typically refers to intangible assets and the latter to tangible assets. The gradual write-off of a debt is an example of amortization. Similarly, an amortized loan is one in which the principal amount is paid back in installments over the life of the loan.

anarcho-syndicalism See ANARCHY AND ANARCHISM; and SYNDICALISM.

anarchy and anarchism Anarchy is the absence of centralized authority or government. The term was first formulated negatively by early modern political theorists such as Thomas HOBBES, who regarded it as a condition of chaos, terror, and violence. In the nineteenth century, however, it came to be seen as an alternative to state coercion and economic exploitation. Historically, anarchism is based on the assertion that people are capable of harmony but are deformed and oppressed by political and economic institutions. Its most active early promoter was Pierre-Joseph PROUDHON, whose influential

What is Property? (1840) argued that "property is theft" and proposed that small associations of free producers replace CAPITALISM and the STATE. In the next generation, the more radical Mikhail BAKUNIN propsed the complete replacement of private property by COLLECTIVISM. Anarchism gradually lost ground to SOCIALISM and particularly COMMUNISM during the late nineteenth and early twentieth centuries. Revolutionary anarchism peaked in the West with a wave of assassinations around 1900. *Anarcho-syndicalism*, which drew on Proudhon's ideas and advocated the DEVOLUTION of power to workers' councils, played an important role in the short-lived Spanish republic of the 1930s. Contemporary anarchism plays a role in opposition to GLOBALIZATION and NEOLIBERALISM on the world stage.

ancestors Ancestors are an important source of authority and legitimation in many cultures and are consequently an enduring topic of anthropological research. Exactly which ancestors a society memorializes is closely related to the form of descent that organizes that society. In PATRILINEAL societies, for example, the significant ancestors are those of the male line, while in matrilineal societies the key figures descend along the female line. The number of generations that count in the calculation of ancestors also varies greatly from one culture to the next.

In his theory of the developmental stages of religion, nineteenth-century anthropologist Edward Burnett TYLOR described ancestor worship as a form of ANIMISM, in which the persistence of the spirits of the forebears obliges respect or appeasement. More recent anthropology, however, has observed enough diversity regarding ancestors to call into question broad generalizations about their significance and uses across cultural lines.

In SEGMENTARY-LINEAGE SYSTEMS, groups of kin are identified by descent from a common ancestor, and distinguished by differences in collective ancestry.

animal spirits Refers to investment demand driven by the whims or "animal spirits" of investors. The term was introduced into economics by John Maynard KEYNES in *The General Theory of Employment, Interest and Money* (1936). The essence of Keynes's proposition was that general optimism among investors (reflecting higher expectations of return) raised the demand for investment, whereas pessimism depressed it. Keynes believed that economic fluctuations can be partly explained by spontaneous (or exogenous) shifts in moods (whether optimism or pessimism). The causal chain from the change in moods to economic fluctuations does not pass through changes in the expected utility of different consumption or investment alternatives, but through the degree to which investors choose action or passivity in the face of investment opportunities.

animatism The belief that an impersonal supernatural force pervades everything. The term was introduced by R. R. Marrett in *The Threshold of Religion* (1900) as a criticism of Edward Burnett TYLOR's 1871 evolutionary theory of religion, which held that the earliest manifestation of religion was the belief in personal or individual spiritual forces such as the soul—a belief Tylor called ANIMISM. Marrett's most prominent counterexample was the Polynesian concept of MANA, which he claimed was developmentally prior to animism.

animism The belief that a spiritual element or vital principle animates living bodies and can persist after death, either as a ghost or by inhabiting material objects. Animism was introduced into anthropology by Edward Burnett TYLOR (1832–1917) in an attempt to explain the origins of religion, but the concept was widely criticized by later anthropologists who challenged either Tylor's particular evolutionary schema (such as R. R. Marrett) or evolutionary schemas in general (such as Franz BOAS and his students). The term is also often used to describe African tribal religions.

A related term is *eidolism*, which refers to the belief in disembodied spirits.

anisogamy Marriage between partners of different social statuses. Hypergamy is a variant in which the woman is typically of lower social status than the man, and generally corresponds to cultures in which the wife is given as a gift, accompanied by a dowry. Hypogamy designates the opposite relationship: the man is typically of lower social status than the woman, and the bride's family is compensated for the marriage. Marriage between partners of equal status is called ISOGAMY.

Annales school A group of French social historians affiliated with the journal *Annales d'histoire economique et sociale*, founded in 1929 by Lucien Febvre and Marc BLOCH. The Annales school—composed of Febvre, Bloch, Fernand BRAUDEL, and Emmanuel Le Roy Ladurie, most prominently—developed an interdisciplinary model of historiography that emphasized the long-term evolution of social systems in relation to cultural, economic, demographic, and ecological change. This perspective challenged the chronological and narrative conventions of contemporary historical writing, which tended to privilege the political and military history of nations—what Braudel dismissed as *histoire événementielle* (event history).

Instead, the Annales school historians focused their attention on long-term forces such as imperialism, industrialization, and the transition from feudalism to capitalism. For Braudel, this involved treating history as a series of layers of temporality, differentiating among processes that belonged to the *longue durée* of centuries or millenia, medium-term shifts in economic or cultural patterns, and the shorter-term miscellany of events. Classic works such as Bloch's *Feudal Society* (1961) and Braudel's *The Mediterranean and the Mediterranean World in the Age of Philip II* (1949) combined attention to material and psychological factors and examined the relationship between everyday life and patterns of social structure as these changed at different rates and rhythms. This emphasis on the underlying structures of history drew on the economic history of François Simiand and carried forward Emile DURKHEIM's ambition of a unified social science. Later Annales historians such as Ernest Labrousse explored the affinity of Annales history and MARXISM, although for most of the major Annales figures the relationship to Marxism was remote. The Annales school was a major influence on the growth of social history in the post–World War II period and contributed to a wide range of accounts of modernization and capitalist development, including Immanuel WALLERSTEIN's WORLD-SYSTEMS THEORY.

anomie Emile DURKHEIM introduced the term into sociology with his studies *The Division of Labour* (1893) and *Suicide* (1897). For Durkheim, *anomie* referred to the absence of governing rules, norms, values, and identities in a society, leading to feelings of isolation and uncertainty. Durkheim stressed that anomie is a *social* state of disrupted meanings and values, although it has consequences for individuals. The earlier of the two studies traced this phenomenon to industrialization, the resulting breakdown of traditional social frameworks of work and family, and the general absence of newer, stable norms and structures of social regulation. Under such circumstances, rapid modernization creates a *pathological* division of labor and widespread anomic feeling. The later work argued that anomie may be a more general result of social instability, which tends to diminish the limiting and stabilizing role of social networks and norms on individual desires. This unchanneling of desire from existing forms of fulfillment similarly leads to anomic feeling and, Durkheim argued, higher rates of suicide.

Robert K. MERTON provided an influential revision of Durkheim's notion of anomie in his analysis of patterns of DEVIANCE (*Social Theory and Social Structure*, 1949). Anomie, Merton argued, was not necessarily a generalized pattern of breakdown, but could also result from local disjunctions between widely held social values and the means of realizing them. The American emphasis on success, he argued, conflicted with unevenly distributed opportunities for social advancement. Those who have aspirations but not the means to achieve them experience a psychological strain that leads to four potential responses: *innovation*, by which Merton meant criminal activity, cheating, or other unsanctioned means of achieving success; *ritualism*, typified by bureaucratic ossification and superconformity; *retreatism*, on the part of those who drop out of the "rat race"; and *rebellion* or other movements to effect social change.

Both Durkheim's and Merton's definitions have been central to studies of deviance and social discontent—especially during the post–World War II boom in sociological research on these subjects. The term anomie has also entered common usage well beyond such specific conceptualizations, coming to designate feelings of isolation in general and overlapping the notion of ALIENATION.

ANOVA   See VARIANCE.

anthropology   Broadly speaking, anthropology is as old as the earliest attempts to describe human nature and the diversity of human societies, examples of which date back to antiquity. Modern anthropology, however, has its roots in the explosion of interest in "PRIMITIVE" societies encountered in the course of European exploration, conquest, and colonial rule. As a discipline, anthropology was not invented so much as

formalized, professionalized, and ultimately institutionalized around a range of inquiries into tribal cultures—a process that in Britain, France, and the United States occurred in the second half of the nineteenth century. This consolidation took place in the context of the increasing complexity of colonization and empire, including growing needs to rationalize and legitimate colonial rule. Much of nineteenth-century anthropology was shaped by these ethnocentric and imperial priorities, and largely amounted to an extension of the field of ETHNOLOGY (the study of ethnic origins) to the inevitably comparative context of empire. The major national exceptions to this tendency were Germany and Austria, where the ethnological tradition remained strongest and imperial concerns were comparatively distant. In these countries, anthropological research remained focused on local, folk traditions.

The colonial situations of the major Western powers impacted anthropology in diverse ways. The field was shaped not only by differences among the populations available for study but also by differences in the ways that COLONIALISM affected those societies. Early French and British anthropology, for instance, was largely limited to the African colonies of the two nations, and took place under conditions in which the social organization of tribal societies was often substantially intact. In the United States, on the other hand, anthropological study focused primarily on the displaced and frequently disrupted Native American societies. Such differences produced deep methodological divisions—American anthropologists privileged, in general, a more integrated study of CULTURE and LANGUAGE than their British counterparts.

The consolidation of anthropology was also driven by the growing pressures placed on primitive societies by the direct expropriation of land by imperial enterprises, and by contact with modern cultures more generally. In the United States, in particular, this recognition fostered a broad program of "salvage ethnography" intended to document Indian tribal cultures.

By the turn of the century, anthropology had begun to gain acceptance as an academic field. In the United States, this occurred largely by way of the FOUR-FIELDS APPROACH, which subdivided anthropology into archaeology, physical anthropology, linguistic anthropology, and cultural anthropology. British anthropology did not reproduce this division, but like American anthropology slowly separated physical anthropology from the study of SOCIETY and culture. This separation reflected, above all, the progressive marginalization of racial determinism in the social sciences in the early twentieth century.

The importance of different national contexts to the development of anthropology is visible in the way that a number of major theoretical debates played out along national lines. Preeminent among these was the division between British "social" anthropology and American "cultural" anthropology, although both traditions contain many exceptions and points of commonality. Although the meaning, relevance, and even existence of the distinction continues to be a matter of debate, the two forms are most often differentiated by their major emphases: social anthropology has tended to concentrate on isolating systems or structures of social relations—LAW, STATUS, and most prominently, KINSHIP. Cultural anthropology, on the other hand, has tended to avoid formulating hypotheses about basic social structures; it has taken a more integrative approach to characterizing cultural experience by admitting a broader range of elements into its descriptive practice. These include not only kinship and political structures but also folklore, language, technology, and childrearing.

The division between the two has roots in the emergence of a strong American school of anthropology centered around the figure of Franz BOAS in the early part of the century. Boas militated for a more holistic notion of culture and an appreciation of the incommensurability of different cultures. He argued for abandoning the universal and often racist evolutionary models that dominated nineteenth-century anthropology, as well as against the narrowness of many comparativists' focus on certain dimensions of social and political organization. Boas's work generated a range of synthetic and interdisciplinary theories of culture, and perhaps more importantly a strong commitment to ethnographic fieldwork within anthropology.

Continued interest in SOCIAL STRUCTURE in French and especially British anthropology led to the consolidation of FUNCTIONALISM—a theoretical orientation that describes cultural forms in terms of their utility in promoting various basic social features, such as social integration or more generally the material survival of the community. Emile DURKHEIM in France and A. R. RADCLIFFE-BROWN in England were the early innovators in

this area. Although strong versions of functionalism have been criticized for their tendency to reduce human behavior to a simple and even singular framework of explanation, functionalism has not been rejected so much as diffused into the larger matrix of anthropological thought. More flexible versions of functionalism continue to be central to a range of anthropological and sociological approaches.

In addition to the still vital cultural and social traditions, the postwar period has seen the emergence of a number of other interpretive paradigms—too numerous to cite here with any thoroughness. These include Claude LEVI-STRAUSS's structuralist anthropology (see STRUCTURALISM), which undermined the distinction between social and cultural perspectives by positing a linguistic basis for both social structure and social variation. The more general problematic of POSTMODERNISM has also had a significant impact on anthropological discourse—particularly in regard to assumptions about scientific objectivity and neutral description. These issues have been directly addressed in the SYMBOLIC ANTHROPOLOGY of Clifford GEERTZ and others. Finally, contemporary anthropology has vigorously taken up the relation of everyday practices to the reproduction and transformation of larger cultural forms: the question of what Pierre BOURDIEU has called practice (see PRACTICE AND PRACTICE THEORY).

anthropometry The study of the physical proportions of different human populations. Anthropometry played an important role in nineteenth- and early-twentieth-century social science, which had not yet clearly separated questions of CULTURE from biological determination. Measuring different body parts was a fundamental method of such studies, used in asserting or disproving correlations between physical and moral or intellectual qualities, in investigations of bodily averages, and in attempts to classify the races.

anthropomorphism The attribution of human qualities to nonhuman things, such as animals or deities.

anticlericalism The conviction that the church should have a lesser role in politics and public life. Anticlericalism has often been a central feature of liberal and socialist movements in the Roman Catholic world, particularly in France and

Latin America, and can be a major source of political instability in secularizing societies.

anti-psychiatry A loosely organized movement of the late 1950s and 1960s that critiqued the institutions and practices of psychiatry and analyzed the social construction of mental illness. A broad range of scholars and clinicians in the United States and Europe were associated with the movement, including Ronald David LAING, Thomas Szasz, Félix GUATTARI, Erving GOFFMAN, and Michel FOUCAULT. Goffman's analysis of TOTAL INSTITUTIONS, such as the asylum, and Foucault's histories of the connection between madness and social control played significant roles. On a practical level, the movement targeted practices of widespread institutionalization and hard therapeutic treatments. It played a part in the broad turn toward the deinstitutionalization of mental health care in Western countries in the 1970s.

appeasement Offering concessions to a political adversary, most often in international affairs, in order to preserve peace. The term was used favorably after World War I by those who argued against imposing punitive terms and demands for reparations on the war's losers. After British Prime Minister Neville Chamberlain used the term in reference to his concessions to Adolph Hitler in 1938, appeasement became a term of opprobrium—disavowed in principle, if not always in practice, as a morally unsound and usually ineffective means of postponing confrontation.

applied anthropology The application of anthropological methods to social problems and the shaping of policy. Early versions of applied anthropology focused on colonial policy, including the training of colonial administrators, and later privileged approaches to third world development issues. After World War II, however, the traditionally close links between anthropological research and the colonial mission became subject to increasing scrutiny and challenge, consistent with the postwar process of decolonization. More recently, Marxist and poststructuralist anthropologists have called into question the distinction between "pure" and applied anthropology, emphasizing the political and epistemological ambiguities of academic research. But applied anthropology (and the more recent equivalent, *practicing anthropology*) has continued to expand and develop into a variety of areas and subfields, including medical, legal, educational, and urban anthropology.

apportionment In a legislative context, the allocation of seats in representative bodies to various states or electoral divisions, usually on the basis of population (see ELECTORAL GEOGRAPHY). In an administrative context, the EXECUTIVE's responsibility, after a budget has been passed by the LEGISLATURE, to reconcile available revenue with program spending.

arbitrage Buying in one market and immediately selling in another at a higher price. Simultaneous lending and borrowing at two distinct rates of interest is an example of arbitrage. The arbitrageur aims to profit from the discrepancy, but such action will have the effect of driving the rates toward each other. Over time and in the aggregate in a perfectly competitive market, arbitrage opportunities are zero.

Most modern finance theory is based on either an intuitive or explicitly theorized exclusion of arbitrage—an assumption analogous to the zero-profit condition for a firm. One implication of this exclusion is the assertion that two perfect substitutes (e.g., the spot exchange rates for a currency in Tokyo and London) must trade at the same price. This implication is referred to as the *law of one price*. Similarly, in discussions of purchasing power parity in international trade, it is the arbitrage possibility that forces the spot exchange rate between currencies to equal the relative prices of traded goods.

archaeology The study of the past through the recovery and interpretation of artifacts and their surroundings. Traditionally, archaeology has focused on classical and prehistoric societies, but archaeological analysis has also been applied to the remains of more recent groups and peoples. Consequently, archaeology is often distinguished more by the range of research techniques that have developed around the study of ancient civilizations—excavation, laboratory dating, *stratigraphy* (the study of layers), and *seriation* (the use of evolutionary theories to separate artifacts)—than by attempts to assign it a particular object.

In universities in the United States, archaeology is most widely taught as a subfield of ANTHROPOLOGY (one element of the FOUR-FIELDS APPROACH to anthropology). In Europe it is associated with history—particularly that of ancient civilizations that possessed written languages. Civilizations that did not possess writing are typically the subject of a separate field of research called *prehistory*. This distinction reflects archeology's origins in the renewal of interest in ancient Greece and Rome during the Renaissance and Enlightenment, in which the recovery of texts was a fundamental objective.

During the nineteenth century, archaeology expanded its purview to include other civilizations and older periods of human habitation. Archaeological investigation became central to the development of theories of cultural evolution, particularly to theories of the necessary stages of societal development. As the nineteenth century ended, these theories proved congenial to nationalist and ethnic ideologies, and the focus of much archaeological work shifted toward establishing or proving theories of national origins. See DIFFUSION AND DIFFUSIONISM; and *KULTURKREIS*.

Post–World War II archaeology has largely eschewed these investments. In the 1950s, Lewis Binford and David Clarke inaugurated a mostly Anglo-American movement known as New Archaeology, which promoted a strongly positivistic approach that emphasized scientific proof, statistical study, and functional analysis over the descriptive tradition of cultural or historical archaeology. Many of the differences between the New Archaeology and its cultural/historical counterparts have been taken up again in the contemporary debate between the somewhat loosely termed *processualist* and *postprocessualist* positions. Post-processualism, by and large, is responsible for bringing to archaeology the ideological and epistemological challenges to POSITIVISM that have figured so prominently in other disciplines.

archetype   In Jungian psychology, archetypes are images or symbols thought to be universal to human culture. For Carl JUNG, they were the elements of a COLLECTIVE UNCONSCIOUS—the deepest layer of memory shared by humanity in general or, he sometimes suggested, differentiated by different race. According to Jung, archetypes are visible in religion and mythology, which preserve and condense the most significant human experiences. At the individual level, they are accessible through dreams.

areal differentiation   Simply, the question of how one area differs from another. Areal differentiation has remained at or near the center of most debates about the proper subject of GEOGRAPHY since the turn of the century. Its most influential adherent was Richard Hartshorne, who reinterpreted the tradition of geography in light of the concept in his seminal work *The Nature of Geography* (1939). In the course of subsequent disciplinary debates, Hartshorne became dissatisfied with the concept's lack of specificity. Nonetheless, it continues to provide explanatory purchase on the work that most geographers do today.

area studies   The concentration of scholarship on specific regions of the world. Underlying area studies is the view that cultural, political, geographic, and other factors unify the peoples and societies of a region in significant ways and impede cross-regional generalizations. Within comparative politics (see COMPARATIVE GOVERNMENT AND COMPARATIVE POLITICS), area studies tended to define itself against the broad, multiple-case methods associated with BEHAVIORALISM and structural FUNCTIONALISM of the 1950s and 1960s. Area studies approaches have themselves been criticized for exaggerating the internal unity of areas, for reifying linguistic, cultural and historical "roots" of regions, and for reflecting unacknowledged factors like the COLD WAR in the definition of areas. They have been vital, however, to research efforts to grasp the full diversity of forms of social organization and culture, and to seeing how these interact with broad political, economic, and other forces.

Arendt, Hannah   (1906–1975) A political theorist and philosopher best known for her highly original analyses of political action, the public sphere, and TOTALITARIANISM. Arendt was born in Germany and studied philosophy with Martin HEIDEGGER and later Karl Jaspers. With the rise of the Nazis to power, she became an activist on behalf of Jewish causes, especially Zionism. She was arrested by the Gestapo and released; the threat of further persecution prompted her flight to France, where she spent several years until she was trapped by the Nazi invasion in 1940. She escaped from internment, however, and made her way to the United States, where she remained after the war, teaching at the University of Chicago and the New School for Social Research.

In the 1940s, Arendt became part of the New York intellectual circle centered around the journal *Partisan Review*. She also completed the work that would establish her as a major political theorist, *The Origins of Totalitarianism* (1951).

Here, Arendt drew parallels between the methods of NAZISM and Stalinism. Both, she argued, were structured by the goal of total control over all aspects of life; both relied on strong ideological accounts of their historical role and on terror to enforce them. Both, she argued further, emerged out of the breakdown of traditional structures of authority and tradition in Europe. Arendt pursued some of the same themes—and courted more controversy—in her journalistic account of the Adolf Eichmann trial, *Eichmann in Jerusalem* (1963). Contrary to the conventional depictions of Nazi evil, Arendt emphasized the bureaucratic mentality that fostered duty and efficiency at the expense of self-reflection and personal responsibility. Eichmann was an example, in the now famous phrase, of "the banality of evil."

Arendt's philosophical and historical work focused more broadly on the nature of politics and political life. *The Human Condition* (1958) is the most important exploration of these themes, and constitutes in part a critique of the Marxist emphasis on labor as the chief human capacity. Rooting her inquiry in a distinctive interpretation of ancient Greek philosophy, Arendt differentiated between labor (needed for survival) and work (or the form of human expression invested in things), and subordinated both to the *vita activa*—a vision of human life as realized most fully in its public, political dimension. POLITICS was not an instrument for achieving certain social goals, she argued, but a form of creative activity through which human beings defined their relations to one another.

In *On Revolution* (1963), Arendt explored these values in the context of the American and French revolutions—the former initially structured by a republican political ethos that valued the political as such; the latter by the rise of the "social" (the problem of reducing human misery) that subjected politics to instrumental ends. Arendt's idealization of a pure form of political activity has been influential (and also controversial) for contemporary social theorists, especially those with an interest in exploring the nature and possibilities of the contemporary public sphere (see PUBLIC SPHERE AND PRIVATE SPHERE). Arendt was pessimistic that much margin for true political action remained in the highly social, mediated political sphere of modern democratic societies. Nonetheless, she insisted that the future remained fundamentally open—a belief expressed in her concept of *natality*, or the possibility for the new embodied in each human life. Her other major works include *Between Past and Future* (1968), *Men in Dark Times* (1968), and *The Life of the Mind* (1978).

aristocracy   Literally, "rule by the best," generally associated with the nobility or highest social class. According to ARISTOTLE's influential account of types of regimes, the aristocracy is selected and rules on the basis of virtue; where this fails, aristocracy degenerates into OLIGARCHY. Most often, the term refers not to a type of regime but to a hereditary class determined by the possession of land, the conferral of title by a monarch, or both. Aristocracies of one form or another have existed throughout the world, predominantly in agricultural societies with some level of urban and state development and where military structures intersect with political authority. The feudal system visible in medieval Europe and in parts of Asia brought together many of these features and continues to underlie the remnants of aristocratic distinction today (see FEUDALISM). The European feudal aristocracy in particular consisted of an elaborate and sometimes overlapping hierarchy of titles and privileges (e.g., duke, earl, baron, count). The rise of absolutist monarchies, however, generally limited the autonomy of aristocrats (especially in western Europe) and tied them more closely to the central state. It also involved creating new aristocratic titles as rewards for nonmilitary service to the state.

The elimination of formal aristocratic privileges was one of the major political objectives of the Enlightenment and a central feature of the early wave of LIBERALISM and DEMOCRATIZATION in the nineteenth century. Such privileges have all but disappeared in the modern world, although aristocratic titles still often imply a degree of social prestige and sometimes wealth. Great Britain was one of the last countries to accord limited political privileges to members of the aristocracy, where until 1999 membership in the House of Lords was based on peerage.

Aristotle   (384–322 BCE) Greek philosopher, student of PLATO, and teacher of Alexander the Great. Aristotle set the terms for much of the metaphysical, scientific, literary, and political thought of the next two thousand years. Beyond specific ideas, he developed a systematic and empirical approach to knowledge that profoundly informed the natural and social sciences. He distinguished between different forms of knowledge, separating "scientific" and "practical" knowledge (including politics) from the technical arts and qualities of intelligence (wisdom and rational intuition), and grounding empirical thought in a thoroughgoing critique of Platonic metaphysics and ethics. In particular, he emphasized empirical observation far more than Plato did and argued for attention to processes of historical and natural development (*physis*) that were not graspable in terms of timeless ideal forms. Aristotle's method commonly involved the careful definition of terms—often opposed pairs—followed by the search for a moderate path or sense of just proportion between them. This was also his method of determining the good life—a central but not always consistently defined concept in Aristotle's work, sometimes defined as the exercise of the soul's faculties in conformity with excellence or virtue (as in the *Nicomachean Ethics*) and sometimes subordinated to the good of the state (as in *Politics*).

Politics is perhaps the most influential of Aristotle's writings; it provides a broad analysis of the social order, the origin and types of states, a justification of mixed government, and a partial sketch of the ideal state. The basis of Aristotle's social thought is the claim that human beings are fundamentally "political animals"—fulfilled and capable of pursuing the good life only in organized social relations (ideally, as citizens of a state). Aristotle dismissed any notion of an originary social contract and argued that the state is merely the culmination of the human need to congregate, visible also at the level of households and villages. The state, in this context, is an organic entity developed and reinforced by customary and written law, which in turn constrains its members and shapes its idea of the good. The state achieved an ideal form, he argued, in the self-sufficient polis, or city-state, in which the political realm retained a basis in face-to-face relations. Without this immediacy, the good life of the citizen becomes impossible.

CITIZENSHIP—defined as eligibility for office—is the foundation of this political life. Aristotle restricted this privilege to male landowners, reflecting his view of the social order as rooted in the natural inequality of persons. This was the basis of his defense of slavery, the subordination of women, and the special treatment of children. These classes of person belonged to the "household" (*oikos*, the realm of economic production), but they were not citizens or in any sense "free." Within the economic realm, private property—not the communalism of Plato's *Republic*—provided the necessary basis of the social order. The state, too, exercised broad authority over household matters, principally through the regulation of marriage and the education of children.

Politics is perhaps most concerned with the problem of political stability and, for this reason, includes a lengthy analysis of the virtues and defects of different types of states. Aristotle distinguished three pure types of state: kingship, ARISTOCRACY, and timocracy or constitutional government (reflecting rule by the one, the few, and the many, respectively). He further recognized three degenerate versions of these types, in which the interests of all are sacrificed to the interests of the ruling power: TYRANNY, OLIGARCHY, and DEMOCRACY—the last associated with demagoguery and mob rule. Because the chief threat to stability, Aristotle argued, was the inequality of rich and poor, he advocated a "mixed" government that included elements of both aristocracy and timocracy. In such a state, all citizens could hold office and no class would enjoy a monopoly of power.

Aristotle undertook a comparative analysis of one hundred fifty Greek constitutions and political systems. All but one, the *Constitution of the Athenians*, has been lost. His other major works include *Metaphysics* and *Eudemian*.

Much of the history of Western philosophy has been shaped by the shifting proportionate influence of Plato and Aristotle. Plato dominated scholarship during late antiquity. Many of Aristotle's works, in comparison, were lost to western Europeans until the Middle Ages, when they were rediscovered in Arabic scholarship. Aristotle, consequently, proved far more influential to late medieval and Renaissance thought than to earlier periods. More recently, his thought has influenced social theory from Georg HEGEL to Martin HEIDEGGER and various advocates of COMMUNITARIANISM, who assert a strongly social conception of the person, knowledge, and the good life in opposition to Cartesian or Kantian individualism. Aristotle's idea of excellence and virtue inform the work of Alasdair MACINTYRE, among other ethicists and social philosophers. Pierre BOURDIEU has drawn on Aristotle's idea of bodily *hexis* in explaining his notion of HABITUS and embodied knowledge.

arms control   The effort to mitigate or reverse the risk and expense of an ARMS RACE by political means. Arms control may be (1) unilateral, as in the decision of countries to dismantle certain weapons without reciprocal commitments from adversaries; (2) bilateral, as in the strategic weapons reductions negotiated periodically between the United States and USSR during the COLD WAR; or (3) multilateral, as in the international agreements between many countries restricting chemical weapons and nuclear proliferation.

arms race The competition between two or more powers to develop and build more and newer weapons. The prototype was the competition between the British and German navies in the late nineteenth century, whereas the most extreme case was the development of vast nuclear arsenals by the United States and USSR during the COLD WAR. The latter was based on the logic of mutually assured destruction (MAD), whereby any act of nuclear aggression by one party would trigger a retaliation that would destroy both.

Aron, Raymond (1905–1983) A leading French sociologist and political philosopher of the postwar period. Aron addressed a wide range of issues in his career, producing sociological accounts of industrial society, studies of the German sociological tradition, and analyses of international relations and political systems. He is perhaps best known, however, as a defender of LIBERALISM and Western democracy and in this context is often juxtaposed to Jean-Paul SARTRE, the dominant existentialist and later Marxist thinker of his day. Both Aron and Sartre studied at the elite Ecole Normale Supérieure in the 1930s; both were highly visible public intellectuals who engaged prolifically in journalism and political commentary.

Aron played a large role in disseminating the German social theory of Wilhelm DILTHEY, Ferdinand TÖNNIES, George SIMMEL, and Max WEBER in France—primarily through the publication of *Contemporary German Sociology* (1936). He met considerable resistance, however, from a postwar intellectual culture enamored with the social theories of Karl MARX and Emile DURKHEIM. Aron disagreed with the historical DETERMINISM of the former and the strong FUNCTIONALISM of the latter, relying instead on Weber's more pluralistic conception of social domains and human motivations. He argued strongly against the reduction of historical development to any singular or privileged explanatory variable, and critiqued as dogmatic those political philosophies that did. Aron

made this case pointedly in *The Opium of the Intellectuals* (1955). More generally, Aron translated Weberian pluralism into a positive theory that underwrote his belief in the relative independence of the political from the economic realm. This, in turn, contributed to a valorization of the political realm that justified his defense of political liberalism—in spite of acknowledged faults—against its economic critics.

Aron described his own intellectual trajectory as leading from Marx to Alexis de TOCQUEVILLE—beginning in the critique of capitalism and discovering, eventually, the greater need for an inquiry into the nature of democratic society. This was the basis of his sociology of industrial society and in particular his *Eighteen Lectures on Industrial Society* (1963), which stressed the pluralism and social mobility of the Western countries and developed a critique of the Soviet form. Aron's comparative approach carried over into his studies of class structures and elites. Again, class structures were most important for the political differences they produced: the competing, plural elites of the Western democracies made for a better system, less capable of tyranny, than the monolithic ruling class of the USSR.

Aron also wrote prolifically on international relations and war in *Peace and War* (1967), *Clausewitz, Philosopher of War* (1976), and other works. His other writings include the influential *Main Currents in Sociological Theory* (1967), *Democracy and Totalitarianism* (1965), and *Progress and Disillusion* (1969).

Arrow, Kenneth (1921–) An American economist and social-choice theorist. There are few fields in economics that do not acknowledge a fundamental contribution from Arrow. He has also contributed significantly to POLITICAL SCIENCE and POLITICAL SOCIOLOGY. While his best known publications deal with social choice and general equilibrium theory, his research has also engaged issues as diverse as the analysis of RISK and the accumulation of human capital through work experience. Arrow was awarded the Nobel Prize for economics in 1972, together with John R. HICKS.

Arrow graduated from City College, New York, and studied statistics at Columbia University under Harold HOTELLING. Arrow's reputation was established with the publication of his doctoral dissertation, *Social Choice and Individual Values* (1951), which addressed the question of whether there is a reliable way of inferring the true interests of society from the interests of individuals—regarding, for example, the distribution of wealth. Arrow was interested in how voting systems might transform individual preferences into social preferences, which would then provide policy makers with a mechanism for social choice. He concluded that there was no logically infallible way of aggregating the preferences of disparate individuals in a pluralistic society—a result known as ARROW'S IMPOSSIBILITY THEOREM.

Arrow also examined the possibility of general equilibrium in an economy with multiple markets. Leon WALRAS believed that the existence of such an equilibrium could be proved by showing that the number of demand-supply equations in the economy is equal to the number of unknown variables. However, it was left to Arrow and coauthor Gerard Debreu to derive the formal proof (known as the ARROW–DEBREU MODEL). They discovered that, under perfect competition, the existence of a general equilibrium requires the existence of forward markets, in which an agent can pay today in exchange for delivery in the future. This finding casts doubt on the practical importance of general equilibrium, but Arrow later argued that general equilibrium theory is robust even if forward markets are missing.

Arrow's other important contributions include his analysis of the implications of RISK AVERSION in sectors such as medical insurance. He also integrated "learning by doing" into the theory of growth by showing how experience can lead to greater efficiency. Finally, he introduced the constant elasticity of substitution (CES) production function ("Capital-Labor Substitution and Economic Efficiency," 1961, coauthored). See also EQUILIBRIUM; PARETO OPTIMAL; SOCIAL-CHOICE THEORY; and WELFARE ECONOMICS.

Arrow–Debreu model A general equilibrium framework for addressing questions about the viability and efficiency of competitive markets, developed by Kenneth ARROW and Gerard Debreu. The great achievement of the Arrow–Debreu model was to state the conditions under which a price system must always be possible that, like the invisible hand, can guide diverse and independent agents to make mutually compatible choices. One of these requirements, they argued, was the existence of forward markets, in which an agent can pay today in exchange for delivery in the future.

The three crucial results of the Arrow–Debreu model are the demonstrations of the existence, optimality, and local uniqueness of a competitive general EQUILIBRIUM. Arrow and Debreu spelled out the precise microeconomic assumptions that the general equilibrium model required and also used their findings to demonstrate the fundamental theorem of welfare economics: the Pareto optimality of competitive markets (see PARETO OPTIMAL).

This axiomatic approach to the formulation of general equilibrium has been enormously influential, and it is now taken for granted that a model is not properly defined unless it is logically consistent and has a firm microeconomic foundation.

Arrow's impossibility theorem Also known as Arrow's theorem or Arrow's possibility theorem, after the economist Kenneth ARROW. The theorem addresses the question of whether there is a reliable way of determining the aggregate interest of society from the interests of individuals. Such a method would, in principle, provide policy makers with a mechanism for social choice. The theorem states that *no social-choice mechanism exists* that satisfies certain minimal reasonable conditions:

- *Universality*: The mechanism should accommodate all possible individual preferences.
- *Pareto criterion*: If everyone prefers alternative *x* to *y*, then the social preference should be *x* over *y*.
- *Independence of Irrelevant Alternatives*: If *x*, *y*, and *z* are available choices and the society chooses *x* over *y* (and *z*), then the society must also prefer *x* to *y* when *z* is *not* available. The intuition is that the decisions made should not depend on the existence of options that are not chosen.
- *Nondictatorship*: Arrow ruled out any method for social choice in which one individual's preferences were always decisive. Arrow's theorem demonstrated that the only social-choice mechanism that satisfies the above three conditions is one of dictatorship.

The theorem proved that no mechanism exists for making a decisive social choice in a society where all preferences are to be considered, according to the criteria Arrow postulated. A broad literature has developed around variations and modifications of this theorem, without substantially challenging its conclusions. See also PARETO OPTIMAL; and SOCIAL-CHOICE THEORY.

articulation A key concept in the neo-Marxist theory of culture developed by Antonio GRAMSCI in the 1930s, elaborated by Stuart HALL in the 1970s, and widely adopted by CULTURAL STUDIES in the 1980s. Articulation refers to the process through which practices, texts, and discourses are assigned or produce particular meanings. It plays on the two connotations of the word: articulation as expression and articulation as a point of connection or contact between things. This double signification reflects the Gramscian (and more broadly, structuralist) principle that meaning does not merely inhere in texts or actions—in other words, it is not strictly *intentional*—but results from the place of a text or act within a specific historical context in which meaning is always contested by different groups. In a related sense, articulation is often used to refer to the relationships between different registers of social identity—for instance, race, gender, and class. This, too, has been central to the cultural-studies agenda. A different usage was important in the structuralist Marxism developed by Louis ALTHUSSER and colleagues in the 1960s. Here, articulation linked different MODES OF PRODUCTION in historically specific social formations.

ascribed status STATUS attributed by birth, such as being a member of the nobility or another social elite. Ascribed status is distinguished from ACHIEVED STATUS, which is based on accomplishment and/or acquired credentials (such as education). For Max WEBER, the two formed one of the major axes of difference between premodern and modern societies.

Asiatic mode of production In Marxist political economy, the Asiatic mode of production describes the relationship between a highly centralized, bureaucratized state and small agricultural villages without private ownership of land. These were typically HYDRAULIC SOCIETIES located in river valleys, where the management of irrigation, flood control, and other infrastructural concerns formed the basis of political authority. Because the maintenance of a complicated system of waterways required highly centralized control, such authority tended toward despotism. These arrangements were often referred to as ORIENTAL DESPOTISM, although this term has older roots. The concept acquired importance in late nineteenth-century evolutionary perspectives on societal development and has been widely debated since as the diversity of hydraulic societies has begun to be better understood. German historian Karl Wittfogel provided one of the most important accounts of such societies in *Oriental Despotism* (1957).

association The activities and goals that link people together in associations have been a primary subject of sociological and anthropological research. In English, the term has been used to translate Ferdinand TÖNNIES's influential distinction between *Gesellschaft* (association) and *Gemeinschaft* (community). A broad current of social research adopted Tönnies's characterization of association as large in scale and constituted by impersonal or contractual bonds. A variety of other definitions and theoretical tools address group identity and interpersonal networks. The most common variable in such studies is the degree to which the members of a group are abstracted from personal contact with one another. A number of theories view associations as basic to the stable functioning of DEMOCRACY, PLURALISM, and CIVIL SOCIETY, especially when these mediate between the individual and the state. See also NETWORK ANALYSIS.

asymmetrical exchange See SYMMETRICAL EXCHANGE AND ASYMMETRICAL EXCHANGE.

asymmetric information A situation in which economic agents have different or unequal access to information about economic variables. George A. Akerlof's "lemons" model of ADVERSE SELECTION is a prime example of an asymmetric information problem, as are MORAL HAZARD models. Usually, the term refers to information privately held by an agent on one side of a market (a buyer or a seller), which would not be advantageous to reveal or cannot be revealed *credibly* to agents on the other side. In some circumstances, parties can reveal information through signaling behavior (for example, a college degree might serve as a signal of ability to employers), which may allow markets to function but only in a costly way. In the presence of asymmetric information, the first fundamental theorem of welfare economics—that no agent can be made better off without making some other agent necessarily worse off—breaks down. Put differently, competitive equilibria are no longer guaranteed to be PARETO OPTIMAL.

atomistic competition A market characterized by numerous individual actors on both sides, all without *market power*. The independent actions of these actors aggregate to the functioning of the market as a whole, but no single actor can influence market outcomes. The concept is one common condition for a competitively functioning market.

attitudes Clusters of beliefs or values that influence evaluations of persons or situations. Attitudes have been a major subject of research in SOCIOLOGY and SOCIAL PSYCHOLOGY, as well as in the related areas of marketing, recruitment, and political polling. Some research treats attitudes as synonymous with opinions—a person may have different attitudes regarding different subjects. Other research emphasizes the strong affective dimension of attitudes, which mobilize emotions as well as beliefs. In both cases, attitudes form proclivities to act or judge in a certain way, although the strict relationship between the two is a matter of considerable debate.

There are many qualitative and quantitative methods for studying attitudes. Large-scale social analysis frequently relies on *attitude scales* of various kinds, which quantify data from survey questions or interviews into singular registers that represent large social phenomena, such as—in two prominent examples—racism or authoritarian tendencies. Members of the FRANKFURT SCHOOL who investigated the latter issue produced the well-known *F-scale*, which measured authoritarian sentiments on the basis of opinion information gathered from surveys. The Likert, Guttman, and Thurstone scales are commonly used general methodologies for measuring and classifying attitudes. The *Bogardus social distance scale* is used especially in relation to social distinctions such as race and class. See GUTTMAN SCALE; and LIKERT SCALE.

The chief difficulty in all such studies is the sensitivity of respondents to minor differences in the methodology or nature of the questioning. Respondents also often underreport negative or socially unacceptable attitudes.

auctioneer, Walrasian An analogy introduced by Leon WALRAS to explain the formation of equilibrium prices in a market. EQUILIBRIUM is reached by what Walras called a *TATONNEMENT process*: the auctioneer announces a price; buyers and sellers then announce their net trades at this price; if the total demand equals total supply, then trading commences. If the total demand exceeds (or is less than) the total supply, then the auctioneer announces a higher (or lower) price. The process continues until total demand equals total supply and no actual trading occurs during the process. Under certain conditions, this method of calculation will lead the auctioneer to an equilibrium.

auctions A form of market in which buyers and sellers bid for goods and services. Auctions can be classified according to the different institutional rules that govern the exchange. These rules typically reflect variations in the form of bidding incentive. There are four primary types:

1. *English Auction*: The auctioneer first asks for a bid from potential buyers, or announces the reservation price of the seller. Any higher bid, once recognized by the auctioneer, becomes the standing bid, and the item is ultimately sold to the highest bidder. Auctioning of antiques at Christie's and Sotheby's follows the English model.

2. *Dutch Auction*: Here the auctioneer starts by announcing a price level thought to be higher than any buyer is willing to pay. The auctioneer then decreases the price in decrements until the first buyer accepts by shouting "mine." The name derives from the auctioning of flowers in Holland many years ago.

3. *First-Price Sealed Bid Auction*: Here bidders make their bids simultaneously and put them in sealed envelopes. The highest bidder is then awarded the item. The weekly auction of U.S. treasury securities uses this procedure.

4. *Second-Price Auction*: This is an auction in which the item is awarded to the highest bidder, who then pays the price of the second highest bidder. The London stamp auction uses a close variant of the second-price auction.

Augustine, Saint (354–430) An early Christian philosopher who shaped much of the ethical, social, and political thought of the Middle Ages through his theological and autobiographical writings. Among the most important of these was *Confessions* (397–400), an account of Augustine's libertine youth, his exploration of religious and philosophical systems, and his ultimate conversion to Christianity. Augustine joined the priesthood and rose quickly to the position of Bishop of Hippo (in North Africa) and to increasing fame as a teacher and theologian. Influenced by the Stoics, he was one of the first philosophers to emphasize the place of introspection in human life. His *Confessions* was one of the first real autobiographies of note and was innovative in exploring the sense of interior space within the person—a mansion of many rooms, in his phrase. This contributed to the development of the modern notion of the individual, even where it departed from the religious framework of Augustine's thought.

The chief document of Augustine's political and social thought is *On the City of God* (413–426)—conceived as a reply to those who regarded the abolition of pagan worship as the primary cause of the sacking of Rome by the Goths in 410. In this work, Augustine described disaster and human suffering as the products of an inscrutable divine will whose punishments were always just in light of man's sinful nature. He critiqued the worldliness and self-love of Roman culture, and the rational ethos that informed Greek and Roman concepts of worldly JUSTICE. He viewed the state as a necessary and divinely sanctioned means of preserving peace rather than justice. In principle, obedience to God's laws might make for a just state—indeed the Church had a responsibility to pursue this—but humanity's failings would prevent its realization in the worldly "City of Man."

Augustine fundamentally refused to valorize the transitory City of Man over the eternal, perfect City of God. Membership in the latter was by no means guaranteed, however. People were chosen, but their status was not visible. Despite this uncertainty, Augustine argued that grace was in all cases mediated by the church. This formed the basis for subsequent Catholic proselytism and universalism, and for the assignation of the state and church to different realms: the one to the City of Man and the other to the City of God. As elaborated by subsequent thinkers, the Church was accorded superiority over the state but prohibited from intervening in secular matters.

Augustine wrote influentially on other issues, including his conception of the human mind as an image of the trinity, divided into memory, intellect, and will (*On the Trinity*, 399–412). His other writing includes *On Genesis According to the Letter* (401–415).

autarky Self-sufficiency in economic terms. A country is said to be autarkic if it is closed to international trade. Similarly, individual agents are said to be in autarkic equilibrium when they are self-sufficient and do not trade with one another.

authoritarianism Government distinguished by a high degree of state power and discretion and, most often, the absence of procedures for popular consent or for guarding individual rights. A modern term, it does not refer to anything more precise than DICTATORSHIP. During the COLD WAR, some Western political theorists and international affairs experts developed a distinction between authoritarianism and TOTALITARIANISM. Authoritarian states were held to be less severe, less intrusive, and less durable than totalitarian states, such as Hitler's Germany or Stalin's USSR. The examples cited were Western rather than Soviet allies. Most current research on authoritarianism centers on the question of why certain states evolve in a democratic direction while others do not. See also AUTHORITARIAN PERSONALITY; and DEMOCRATIZATION.

authoritarian personality A rigid character formation characterized by ethnocentrism, a desire for clear order in social relations, and a worldview centered on dominance and submission. The psychologist and FRANKFURT SCHOOL member Erich FROMM developed the concept in the 1930s in the context of empirical and philosophical work on antisemitism in Germany. In his view, the authoritarian personality was a sadomasochistic formation that reflected the collective weakening of the ego in modern society. The concept became much better known after the publication of a Frankfurt school study of prejudice in the United States by Theodor ADORNO and colleagues, *The Authoritarian Personality* (1950). This study made much more ambitious claims about the relationship between social attitudes and authoritarian tendencies, and went so far as to propose an *F-scale* on which such tendencies could be measured. Ultimately, their empirical work proved controversial and was widely criticized—as was their tendency to treat authoritarianism as solely a phenomenon of the right. The broader Frankfurt school analyses of the development of authoritarian regimes and the psychological makeup of their subjects, however, continue to have an influence on contemporary social theory.

authority POWER that is recognized as legitimate by both those who possess it and those who are subject to it. Because of this normalization, authority generally relieves the need for direct coercion. Authority is deeply related to the structures of LEGITIMACY, consent, and social hierarchy in a given society, and generally reflects at least a partial consensus regarding those structures.

The most influential conceptualization of authority in the social sciences is that of Max WEBER, who distinguished three types. *Traditional authority*, Weber argued, is rooted in beliefs and practices that have been passed down over time. Particular forms of power are accepted and obeyed because of custom or because social institutions have come to seem part of the natural order. This type of authority is most common in societies based on KINSHIP and descent—generally premodern societies. Leadership, in such cases, generally depends upon occupying a traditionally sanctioned office, such as that of king or chief.

Charismatic authority, in contrast, rests solely on the personal qualities of individual leaders and on the receptivity of followers. Because the loyalties of followers can be fickle, charismatic authority is comparatively unstable and difficult to sustain. Charismatic leadership is frequently a threat to traditional authority and often emerges in the context of changing social conditions in which traditional authority may be unresponsive or ineffectual. Charismatic authority is thus frequently an agent of social change, capable of mobilizing persons outside the existing structures of power. Over time, however, charismatic movements either die out or succumb to a process of *routinization*, in which the movement codifies its principles and establishes a bureaucratic structure in order to pursue them beyond the range of singular charismatic leadership. When successful, charismatic authority evolves into traditional and/or rational-legal forms.

Rational-legal authority is a function of explicit laws or rules that define the legitimate uses of power. Instead of depending upon particular individuals or sacred practices or traditions, rational-legal power is vested in offices or positions alone. Weber viewed the trajectory of the West as largely defined by the shift from traditional to rational-legal authority. This shift was facilitated, he argued, by charismatic authority—especially during periods of radical rebellion against traditional forms, such as the Protestant Reformation.

The three types of authority, for Weber, were IDEAL TYPES—rarely if ever encountered in their pure forms. Weber took particular interest in the social consequences that followed from these different forms, and in their combinations, which tended to entrench support for a particular regime of power. He focused, too, on the transitional situations in which one form gave way to another, and on the role of charismatic leadership as a means of breaking, if only temporarily, the hold of modern legal-rational and bureaucratic structures of power.

Still more generally, authority refers to legitimate claims to the correct interpretations of texts, to the representation of scientific knowledge, and to the power to make law or resolve legal disputes. All usages derive some of their meaning from the root "author" and the implication that creators have special claims over the meaning or use of their products. In poststructuralist thought, the notion of the death of the author (echoing Friedrich NIETZSCHE's assertion of the death of God) is part of a general critique of authority.

autocorrelation See CORRELATION.

autocracy Rule by a single individual, a specific subtype of AUTHORITARIANISM or DICTATORSHIP.

autonomous transactions Those transactions recorded in a country's BALANCE OF PAYMENTS that occur for reasons of profit or satisfaction of wants (both public and private). These are contrasted with ACCOMMODATING TRANSACTIONS that arise from the overall surplus or deficit in the autonomous transactions.

autonomy Self-rule or self-determination. In politics, autonomy generally refers to the right or ability of a group or institution to govern itself. Thus, regions or cultural groups may be accorded limited autonomy under FEDERALISM, a nation-state may be said to have more or less autonomy from the pressures of other states or social forces, and institutions (for instance universities or private bodies) may be said to be autonomous if they are not subject to government or other external control. In POLITICAL THEORY, Immanuel KANT identified autonomy as the ability of individuals to govern themselves according to reason, rather than according to whim or appetite. This notion has remained the basis of the more rationalistic varieties of LIBERALISM, in contrast with utilitarian accounts of the collective good (see UTILITARIANISM).

The term is also used in sociology to refer to fields of human activity such as art or politics, where the criteria of judgment or value have acquired independence from other fields.

autopoiesis A key term in Niklas LUHMANN's theory of social subsystems. Autopoiesis refers to the self-contained and self-moving nature of subsystems (such as law, economics, or even intimacy). Subsystems generate their own operating logics based on binary oppositions (property and non-property; legal and illegal), and these cannot be applied to other subsystems—although attempts to do so are common and generally result in conflict, or *dislocations*.

Averch-Johnson effect Describes the response of profit maximizing firms that face a fixed allowed rate on the return on capital. Such regulation may cause the firm to select excessively capital-intensive techniques of production, choosing a higher CAPITAL-LABOR RATIO than would have been chosen in the absence of a set rate of return—the cost minimizing ratio. In such a case output is not produced at the minimum social cost (see SOCIAL COSTS AND SOCIAL BENEFITS).

avunculate A pattern of KINSHIP in which the uncle—usually the mother's brother—has important responsibilities toward the sons of a family. This pattern is widespread in matrilineal societies, particularly those of southern and western Africa.

B

Bachelard, Gaston (1884–1962) A philosopher of science and a literary theorist who played a key role in the emergence of STRUCTURALISM and POSTSTRUCTURALISM in France. Bachelard trained in mathematics, taught chemistry and physics, earned his doctorate in philosophy, and ultimately spent most of his career at the Sorbonne. He wrote voluminously on physics, but become best known for his theories of the relationship between scientific and humanistic knowledge and the larger question of scientific progress. In his seminal *The New Scientific Spirit* (1934 [1985]), Bachelard argued that the twentieth-century revolutions in physics—relativity and quantum mechanics—had profound implications for knowledge in general. At one level, the new physics broke with the subject–object relationship that had underwritten scientific inquiry and many other areas of knowledge. No longer could observation be strictly distinguished from the thing observed. At a deeper level, however, Bachelard argued that this revolution challenged the notion that science progressed through the accumulation of facts. As twentieth-century physics made clear, what was at stake was not simply a new fact, but an "epistemological break" with the reigning structure of knowledge. Scientific change was not steady, therefore, but disruptive—a struggle between orthodoxies and new conceptual frameworks. Bachelard thereby anticipated Thomas KUHN's notion of scientific PARADIGM shifts.

Such breaks, Bachelard contended, demonstrated the power of the imagination to step beyond the prevailing network of facts. Bachelard's many inquiries into the creative power of the intelligence emphasized the dynamic relationship between thought and fixed conceptual structures—a constant interplay of "rational" and "imaginative" faculties. These inquiries led him toward explorations of the creative dissonance between language and its objects, and also toward analyses of imagery—the basis of imaginative thinking—in literary texts. He thus opened the door to a range of poststructuralist concerns with LANGUAGE and EPISTEMOLOGY that informed the work of Jacques DERRIDA, Michel FOUCAULT, and others. Bachelard's other major works include *The Psychoanalysis of Fire* (1938) and *The Poetics of Space* (1957).

backwardation A fee paid by sellers of stocks for the privilege of deferring delivery to the buyer. Backwardation assumes that the future price will be less than the spot price of immediate delivery. "Contagio" is the opposite relation, in which the buyer pays a fee to postpone delivery on the assumption that the future price will exceed the current price.

backward linkages The relationship between a firm or industry and the suppliers of its inputs, or raw materials. An increase in the output of the firm or industry is transmitted backward, yielding an increase in the demand for inputs. DEVELOPMENT planners usually prefer to target industries with significant backward linkages, so that investments have additional multiplier effects in generating benefits for other sectors and in helping to further growth in input industries.

bad In economic terms, a commodity or product that is disadvantageous to its consumer. Pollution and congestion are examples of "bads," the opposite of "goods."

Bahktin, Mikhail (1895–1975) A Russian philosopher and literary theorist whose theories of LANGUAGE have influenced the study of communication and popular culture. Bahktin's concept of language and individual acts of communication is resolutely social. It relies on the interpersonal context for meaning and is sensitive to differences of power. In Bahktin's terms, language is *dialogic*—inherently conversational, shaped by give and take, and not simply the monological description of the world or a mirror of speakers' intentions. Language forms at the intersection of dominant ideologies and new unauthorized discourses that continually open new possibilities. *Heteroglossic* textual forms exploit this creative possibility through the juxtaposition of narrative styles and perspectives—quintessentially the case of the novel, Bahktin argued (*Problems of Dostoevsky's Poetics*, 1929; *The Dialogic Imagination*, [1975] 1981). Bahktin's influential concept of the *carnivalesque* also references this contestation and inversion of authoritative discourse (*Rabelais and His World*, 1966).

These concerns placed him at odds with much of the Russian formalist school of LINGUISTICS in the 1920s, as well as with the broader current of structuralist linguistics articulated by Ferdinand de SAUSSURE. Bahktin fell afoul of the Soviet authorities in 1929 and was exiled to Kazakhstan, where he remained until the 1950s. He was belatedly recognized and appointed to the University of Moscow in 1957. Most scholars agree that Bahktin's works include a number of books published under the names of friends, including *The Formal Method in Literary Scholarship* (1928, attributed to P. N. Medvedev).

Bakunin, Mikhail (1814–1876) A Russian anarchist and revolutionary who developed an influential critique of the state and vied with Karl MARX for control of the First International (1864–1876). Bakunin saw authoritarian tendencies in Marx's SOCIALISM and especially opposed Marx's emphasis on the need for a centralized proletarian regime. For Bakunin, the state in any form became a mechanism of mystified power, controlled by an elite. In this respect it mirrored religion—indeed Bakunin saw the two as parallel historical developments. The alternative, Bakunin suggested, was a decentralized federation of communes that guaranteed relative autonomy and control over the means of production at the local level. Bakunin directed a similar critique against scientific elites, the social sciences, and the scientific pretensions of MARXISM.

Bakunin also stressed that the destruction of the old order was a prerequisite for socialism, and thus he strongly opposed Hegelian and liberal reformist notions of progress (see Georg HEGEL; and LIBERALISM). His theory of revolution was contradictory, however, sometimes leaning on the notion of spontaneous action and at other times emphasizing the need for conspiracy and careful direction. The latter, in any event, better characterized his actions during the First International. Ultimately, Bakunin's apocalyptic views and associations with nihilists such as Sergei Nechayev (accused of murdering a fellow conspirator) contributed to a gradual loss of credibility and to his eventual expulsion from the First International.

Although Bakunin's split with Marx fragmented the revolutionary movement in Western Europe, he had a lasting effect on the anarchist movements in Russia, Italy, Switzerland, and Spain. Throughout his career he founded actual and sometimes imaginary revolutionary networks, whose varying degrees of political REALISM often perplexed his followers. Among his more effective organizations was the International Alliance of Social Democracy (founded in 1868), which he conceived as a forward-thinking movement within the First International for advocating "the definitive abolition of classes and the political, economic, and social equalization of the sexes." Bakunin's major work includes *The State and Anarchism* (1873). See also ANARCHY AND ANARCHISM.

balanced budget multiplier A tool for analyzing the changes in aggregate demand and output that accompany changes in government spending or taxation. The multiplier reflects the fact that equal rises in taxes and government spending do not cancel each other out at the level of aggregate demand, but cause demand to rise. This occurs because individuals normally devote a portion of their income to saving, whereas government expenditure will return the full amount to the economy. This effect is extended through multiple rounds of economic activity, leading to a multiplier value higher than the savings rate alone would suggest. The multiplier was a key component of John Maynard KEYNES's advocacy of government spending as a tool of macroeconomic policy—especially in conditions of high unemployment.

balanced growth A principle of coordinated growth and development of all sectors of the economy. The concept is based on SAY'S LAW, which states that "Supply creates its own demand." John Stuart MILL added the important caveat that while production creates specific supply, the income generated via the production process creates general demand, that is, demand for many goods and services. For supply to match demand, and to prevent gluts and bottlenecks in any of the economy's sectors, there has to be simultaneous investment in the economy's various industries—in other words, balanced growth.

The doctrine of balanced growth was influential in the newly independent countries of the post–World War II era, most of which were poor and underdeveloped. Much of development economics in this period emphasized "export pessimism," which held that the low demand elasticities of primary product exports would keep the growth rates of these countries well below those of advanced countries. Trade, in other words, would not suffice as an "engine of growth." These countries, it was felt, should not make development contingent upon trade with developed counties, but rather promote inward-looking development policies that simultaneously developed all sectors. This critique furnished a rationale for programs of rapid and diversified internal development. In the words of Paul Rosenstein-Rodan (1902–1985), a "big push" was needed for such economies to achieve self-sustaining economic growth. While some economists advocated CENTRAL PLANNING to achieve this, others favored indicative planning coupled with incentives such as import protection, tax breaks, and cheap credit. Economists such as Albert Hirschman, on the other hand, stressed that poor countries lacked the resources to undertake such programs, making a balanced growth approach to development untenable. Instead, he advocated a policy of "unbalanced growth," in which only a few projects would be undertaken at any given time. The resulting imbalances would be corrected gradually through a sequential process of project building and market shortages, which would provide incentives for new production. In the long run, the desired balance would be achieved. Such a process would be more in line with the resource constraints faced by developing nations. Generally speaking, policies of import-substituting industrialization and export-led growth are both instances of unbalanced growth. See also DEVELOPMENT; and MODERNIZATION THEORY.

balance of payments   A double entry system of accounting that records all the economic transactions between one country and the rest of the world. The balance of payments table is usually divided into two parts, each with its own subdivisions.

1. The *Current Account* includes all flows that directly affect the NATIONAL INCOME accounts. It includes:

- Exports and imports of goods and services (the difference between the exports and imports is the *balance of trade*).
- Inflows and outflows of investment income.
- Grants, remittances, and transfers.

2. The *Capital Account* includes all flows that directly affect the national balance sheet. Every transaction here is an asset-related flow:

- Direct investment by foreign firms in the home country and by home firms in foreign countries
- Portfolio investments by domestic residents in foreign securities and by foreign residents in domestic securities
- Changes in cash balances held by banks and other foreign exchange dealers resulting from current and capital transactions
- Changes in foreign exchange reserves held by official institutions, arising from intervention in the foreign exchange markets

If official institutions accumulate foreign exchange reserves, then the balance of payments is said to be in surplus; if they run down official reserves, the balance of payments is said to be in deficit.

There are a number of theoretically distinct approaches to predicting the outcome of policy changes on the balance of payments. The *elasticity approach* describes the effects of changes in the exchange rates. It states that, starting from a balanced trade situation, devaluation will improve the balance of payments if the sum of the price elasticities (a measure of how much demand changes in response to a price change) of domestic and foreign demand for imports is larger than one. A devaluation always improves the balance of payments if this condition is satisfied (also termed the *Marshall Lerner condition*)—although it is not a necessary condition of such improvement.

The *absorption approach* is in some respects an alternative to the elasticity approach. It states that a country's trade balance will improve if its output of goods and services increases by more than its "absorption"—the expenditure by domestic residents of goods and services. This approach takes a more macroeconomic view of the balance-of-payments question and looks at production and expenditure for the economy as a whole. It argues that a currency devaluation will be successful only if the gap between domestic output and expenditure widens. The theory has been criticized, however, from a number of directions: first, for ignoring the inflationary effects of devaluation; second, for being inappropriate if the economy is at full employment, in which case output cannot increase; third, for completely ignoring monetary factors; and fourth, for dealing with the balance of trade without taking account of capital movements.

The *monetary approach* emphasizes the interaction between the demand and supply of money to determine the overall balance-of-payments position of the economy. Since, for any economy, the MONETARY BASE equals the sum of the domestic value of international reserves and the domestic asset holdings of monetary authorities, a change in international reserves is reflected in the change in the money supply.

balance of power A situation in which political stability is maintained through the opposition of two or more states, or blocs of states, of roughly equal power. Such situations can be *bipolar*, as in the case of the COLD WAR, or *multipolar*, in the case of three or more distinct powers, as in Europe for most of modern history. According to the realist school of international affairs, a stable balance of power provides the best assurance of peace in the absence of a single dominant power. The term is less commonly used to refer to a parliamentary situation in which two large parties or blocs are unable to form a majority without the help of smaller parties. The smaller parties are said to hold the balance of power. See also DETERRENCE.

balance theory A social psychological theory based on the assumption that individuals have a deep-rooted inclination toward consistency in their relationships and cognitions. It holds that individuals constantly seek to achieve balance where social relationships enter into conflict, either by changing their sentiments or attitudes toward persons or situations, or by subjectively diminishing the importance of the conflict. Balance theory is closely related to the principles of GESTALT THEORY and is used to account for differences in social perception among individuals. See also AFFECT CONTROL THEORY; and COGNITIVE DISSONANCE.

Balkanization The division of a formerly stable and usually united region into a number of small, hostile parts, most often on the basis of cultural or ethnic differences. Although originally applied to southeastern Europe during the dissolution of the Ottoman, Austro-Hungarian, and Russian empires in the late nineteenth and early twentieth centuries, Balkanization now refers to the disintegration of any multinational or multicultural polity.

band societies Small societies that rely primarily on hunting and gathering for subsistence. Band societies have a prominent place in theories of cultural evolution, where they typically describe the first extended group form to supersede the family. They are also distinguished from the larger-scale, more hierarchical organizations of tribe, chiefdom, and STATE. Early scholarly attention to band societies was largely speculative and tended to characterize them as the anarchic "other" to Victorian norms of sexuality, property, and social order. The ethnographic research of Marcel MAUSS and later Julian STEWARD challenged many of these assumptions by emphasizing the stability of ritual, KINSHIP, and self-organization in these groups. Recent research, moreover, has complicated the evolutionary perspective, bringing to light not only the potential advantages of foraging over agriculture in some circumstances, but also tying the existence of modern band societies to the breakup of larger organized foraging societies under the pressure of colonization. Large bands composed of hundreds of members are often called *composite bands*.

bandwagon effect The tendency of persons to join or support a form of collective behavior that has acquired momentum or whose success appears probable. Bandwagon effects are frequently cited in studies of VOTING behavior to explain unexpected shifts in support for candidates. It also describes the tendency of less powerful states to align with rising or dominant powers. In economics, the bandwagon effect refers to a phenomenon of imitation among consumers that increases the demand for a good. This often occurs when a good becomes important for status reasons. The bandwagon effect can defy the usual inverse relationship between price and demand.

bank rate The rate at which the CENTRAL BANK makes short-term loans available to commercial banks. The need for such short-term loans arises when commercial banks face a general shortage of liquidity. In such instances, the central bank (the "lender of last resort") can cover the shortfall.

bargaining theory Examines the possible division of payoffs when there are gains from cooperation or exchange between two or more parties. Typical applications include the gains from trade, wage bargaining between workers and employers, joint business ventures, and treaties and contracts between nations or individuals.

Early bargaining games were characterized by two desiderata: a *feasible set* of all commodity bundles or payoff outcomes that each of the parties could jointly attain, and a *disagreement (or threat) point*, which is the default payoff that each of the parties would receive if they failed to reach a mutually acceptable division. The feasible set is usually constrained to those outcomes that are both *individually rational*—those for which the parties are better off (in terms of UTILITY) than at the disagreement point—and *group rational*, or Pareto efficient, such that there are no possible outcomes that would improve the outcomes for some players without costing others. By applying normative criteria such as proportional or equal division of gains to the bargaining game, an outcome can be characterized as "fair," although different normative criteria can generate conflicting views of fair division.

John NASH first used the conceptual tools developed by John von NEUMANN and Oskar Morgenstern in their *Theory of Games and Economic Behavior* (1944) to provide a *strong bargaining theory*. Key to his analysis were the von Neumann–Morgenstern utility functions, which offered a mathematical formulation of individuals' attitudes toward risk—a critical component of a theory of bargaining. Since the introduction of this theory, many alternative axiomatic frameworks have been put forth, and alternative bargaining solutions have been generated. Variations have also emerged that take into account the effects of such factors as incomplete information among players, the ability to vary threats, and the ability to make offers and counteroffers in a dynamic setting.

barriers to entry   Factors that make it difficult for new firms to enter an existing market. Such barriers tend to reduce the degree of competition in the market and to help perpetuate existing monopolies or oligopolies. They can take the form of legal barriers to entry (such as state monopolies), high initial fixed costs, ECONOMIES OF SCALE, product differentiation, and access to some unique factor of production (including exclusive patent rights).

barter   A system of exchange whereby goods or services are simultaneously traded without the use of money as a medium of exchange. The origin of money has often been traced to the inefficiency of barter systems. As market economies developed both locally and over long distances, the barter system proved cumbersome and inefficient. Above all, it requires "the double coincidence of wants": a cobbler, in order to obtain clothing, must find a tailor who needs shoes. In the absence of such coincidence of wants, not all trades that are desired will be realized. This results in market inefficiencies. Over time, trading via a medium of exchange proved a more practical solution.

Barter has never been the sole means of exchange in a society, but there are societies in which it predominates. It has also often been used as a temporary solution to a problem of exchange. Much of the trade between the West and the former Communist bloc, for instance, took the form of barter. Barter operations are also sometimes undertaken as a means of avoiding or bypassing taxes.

Barthes, Roland   (1915–1980) An influential cultural and literary critic in the post–World War II era. Barthes's abiding interest was the way in which meaning is produced in the encounter between cultural objects or texts and their publics. He was a versatile thinker who moved easily between literature and popular culture, and he formulated a number of interpretive approaches that profoundly marked the emerging field of CULTURAL STUDIES.

Despite the wide array of subject matter that Barthes addressed, he returned consistently to two general issues: first, the ways in which texts or images reference existing cultural codes, shaping the experience of the reader, viewer, or consumer in an essentially conservative process of legitimation of the social order; second, the fundamental dependence of meaning on the always contingent and potentially open-ended encounter with that reader/consumer/viewer. Barthes's best known work, *Mythologies* (1957 [1972]), is primarily an exploration of the first set of issues. In it, he decodes the political and social content of diverse examples of popular culture, from wrestling to advertising to political symbolism. The aspect of popular culture that interested him most was the way in which specific cultural values became naturalized, drawing on larger structures of *myth*. Barthes used the terms *connotative* and *denotative* to refer respectively to these surface and deeper levels of signification. In *Elements of Semiology* (1964 [1967]), he explicitly associated this analytical method with Ferdinand de SAUSSURE's concept of semiology—the science of signs.

In later writing, Barthes increasingly emphasized the encounter between dominant narrative and cultural codes and the space of freedom inherent in the interpretive act. It is in this context that Barthes described the *death of the author*, by which he meant that meaning could no longer be understood as a simple reflection of authorial intention. Barthes continued to pursue this question in a variety of areas, addressing such subjects as love and photography. His later work is increasingly personal in tone, reflecting his distance from the earlier scientific implications of semiology and his wish to write in a manner that avoided the authoritative structures of professional critical discourse. Other major works by Barthes include *Writing Degree Zero* (1953), *S/Z* (1970), and *Camera Lucida* (1980).

base and superstructure   Karl MARX's metaphor for the relationship between material production and economic relations (the base) and the political, legal, and cultural dimensions of society (the SUPERSTRUCTURE). Marx's key claim is that the base determines the superstructure, although this easily simplified relationship requires some qualification: (1) base refers not to a particular economic position (the working class, for instance) but to the entirety of productive relationships; (2) the superstructure is historically variable and frequently unevenly developed across different areas of societal activity—for instance, in art and political culture; and (3) there is an element of reciprocity between base and superstructure—an observation that Friedrich Engels made explicit by claiming that the base determined the superstructure only "in the last instance." This margin of action for individual and group agency assumed increasing importance in the work of twentieth-century Marxists such as Antonio GRAMSCI and Louis ALTHUSSER, as well as in the broad neo-Marxist and CULTURAL STUDIES enterprises influenced by their work. See also MARXISM.

basing point system   A price system in which the price to be charged for a good is calculated by adding the transportation cost to the fixed list price. The transportation cost is related to the distance between the consumer and the nearest of an agreed number of locations known as "basing points." If the basing point is nearer to the consumer than the seller, then the consumer pays less than the "true"

transportation cost. The inverse also holds. This implies that all sellers charge the same "delivered price" to each consumer. The steel industry in the United States has been a notable user of this system. A common objection to this system is that it reduces price competition in the market, introduces geographic PRICE DISCRIMINATION, and results in wasteful cross-hauling and uneconomic location of plants.

basis point   A unit of measure used to express interest rates and bond yields. One basis point is equal to one-hundredth of a percentage point. Given the huge sums of money involved in short-term capital flows and in bond markets around the world, a difference of a few basis points provides sufficient incentives to trade.

Bateson, Gregory   (1904–1980) A scholar of enormous range who made significant contributions to ANTHROPOLOGY, psychology, and zoology. Bateson was born in England and studied natural history before turning to anthropology in the late 1920s. His early career included an appointment to St. John's College and extended fieldwork in New Guinea, where he met his first wife, the anthropologist Margaret MEAD. *Naven* (1936), a remarkable study of ritual and social change, was the main result of this research. He later collaborated with Mead on a photo study, *Balinese Character* (1942).

Bateson spent long intervals teaching in the United States in the 1930s and relocated there permanently after World War II. Like many social scientists, he played an active and rather diverse role in the war effort, working initially on the analysis of German propaganda films at the Museum of Modern Art and later for the Office of Strategic Services, in which capacity he served as an advisor to General MacArthur during the occupation of Japan.

In the late 1940s, he turned his attention toward psychology, particularly to the question of how schizophrenics communicated. This resulted in the famous "double-bind" hypothesis, which suggested that schizophrenics differed from healthy persons not in their mental capacities but in their logical and affective processes. As Bateson himself recognized, this interest in communication and understanding was the thread that linked his work in New Guinea, his studies of schizophrenia, and his later research on dolphin communication. These became the basis of his study of larger structures of communication and information in biological, social, and ecological systems, which contributed greatly to the field of CYBERNETICS. He saw communication and learning as key to "coevolution," a process of active human participation in the evolution of the species, society, and nature. He addressed these underlying issues directly in his major works, *Steps to an Ecology of Mind* (1972) and later *Mind and Nature: A Necessary Unity* (1979). At a philosophical level, these works attempted to reconceptualize the divide between mind and the external world by prioritizing the ways in which the mind brings order to the diverse data of the senses. His notion of an "ecology of mind" refers to this dynamic process of interaction and ordering.

Baudrillard, Jean (1929–) A social theorist associated primarily with his provocative views on the disappearance of the "real" in late-capitalist society—views that generally position Baudrillard at the extreme end of debates about the qualitative social and experiential changes attributed to POSTMODERNISM. Like much of the generation of French theorists that experienced the turmoil of May 1968, Baudrillard's early work was in part a reevaluation of MARXISM in light of both that latest failure of revolutionary action and, over the longer term, the dramatic changes in capitalist society. Chief among these was the dominance of consumer society over the earlier paradigm of industrial production—a shift that implied, for Baudrillard, the obsolescence of Marx's fundamental distinction between use and exchange value. Early works such as *The Consumer Society* (1970 [1998]) and *For a Critique of the Political Economy of the Sign* (1972 [1981]) explore this dynamic and the totalization of the capitalist system it implies. The latter work, in particular, inaugurates the increasingly central theme in Baudrillard's work that consumption no longer bears a significant relationship to "real" needs, but merely responds to an increasingly integrated field of codes that administer symbolic exchange. Satisfaction, under these conditions, is no longer found in having needs met, but in the immersive experience of the system itself. Resistance or negation, under these conditions, is all but impossible, and Baudrillard finds himself in the equivocal and much criticized position of either embracing the system—refusing what for him can only be the nostalgia of negation—or defending a posture of "ironic detachment."

Baudrillard's later work extends these principles toward the concept for which he is best known, the *simulacrum*. The simulacrum is not

a false representation—it is not opposed to the real—but rather reflects the disappearance of the opposition between representation and reality. For Baudrillard, the simulacrum becomes the essential metaphor of society insofar as social activity and the experience of self have become inseparable from their representations. Nonetheless, simulacra are efficacious. The Gulf War, in which television played such a large role in both the conduct and representation of the event, is Baudrillard's most controversial example. Baudrillard's recent work has focused increasingly on the autonomous prerogatives of technology—especially the assimilation of forms of difference into diversified but ultimately homogeneous networks structured by technological reason. His other major works include *The Mirror of Production* (1973 [1975]), *Simulations* (1981 [1983]) and *The Transparency of Evil* (1990 [1993]).

Bayesian inference Bayesian techniques are used in the assessment of probabilities, in particular where additional (if still probabilistic) information can refine estimations of the likelihood of events. Bayes' Rule allows the calculation of *conditional probability*—moving from "the probability that it will rain today" to "the probability that it will rain today given that it rained yesterday." More importantly, Bayes' Rule allows the reverse to be asked: given that it is raining today, how likely is it that it was raining yesterday? As such, the Bayesian techniques provide a solution to the central problem in induction, or *inference*.

Bayesian inference has been widely used in science, law, and economics, as it permits investigators to use both sample and prior information in a logically consistent manner in making inferences. Bayesian inference procedures are used to evaluate economic hypotheses and models, to estimate values of economic parameters, to predict unobserved values of variables, and to solve various decision problems (e.g., portfolio problems, firm and consumer stochastic optimization problems, and economic control and policy problems).

These techniques were developed by Thomas Bayes, an English Presbyterian minister, and are sometimes collectively referred to as the "theorem of inverse probability."

Beard, Charles (1874–1948) One of the most influential American historians of the twentieth century, Beard is best known for *An Economic Interpretation of the Constitution* (1913), which attributed the political stances of advocates and opponents of the Constitution to their economic interests. The Constitution, Beard argued, was largely the product of this clash of economic interests, and advocates often stood to personally gain from ratification. The constitutional debates were not, therefore, primarily a clash of political principles—as historians had almost universally argued before Beard. Although Beard's views were considered scandalous on publication, his views and his methodological focus on economic interests quickly became dominant in American historiography and highly influential in the study of politics more generally. Beard thus played a key role in the emergence of *Progressive historiography*, a term that references the broader values of the American Progressive movement that informed Beard's critique. Beard himself described his approach as "New History," combining the study of events and the motivations behind them with a view toward affecting change in the present. This objective was visible in his reformist study of municipal government, *American City Government* (1912), which he conducted while a member of the New York Bureau of Municipal Research. He also served as an advisor to the city of Tokyo after the devastating earthquake of 1923.

Beard was active on behalf of a variety of political causes. Perhaps most prominently, he resigned from Columbia University in 1917 to protest its attempts to curtail faculty opposition to American involvement in World War I. In the 1920s, Beard moved away from his commitment to the science of history and placed greater emphasis on values. His later work stressed the importance of individuals and individual moral judgments in the shaping of history. These views were widely disseminated in a number of major studies of American society, including the four volumes of *The Rise of American Civilization* (1927–1943) and his influential *A Charter for the Social Sciences in the Schools* (1932). Beard continued to believe in the informed interpretation of history as an agent of social change, but strongly opposed many of the new directions of government interventionism—particularly the New Deal. His other major works include *The Industrial Revolution* (1901), *The Supreme Court and the Constitution* (1912), and *Economic Origins of Jeffersonian Democracy* (1915).

bears   Refers to speculators who expect the prices of stocks, bonds, commodities, or foreign exchange to decline in the near future. Bears act on this belief by selling short in the hope that they can buy the stock, bond, or currency at a lower price. A market where the prices are declining is thus referred to as a bear market.

Beauvoir, Simone de   (1908–1986) A philosopher and novelist best known for *The Second Sex* (1949)—a founding document of twentieth-century feminist thought. Its famous opening statement that "woman is not born, but made" condenses Beauvoir's strong constructivist argument about women's roles, psychology, and ultimately biology, which she argues are the products of historical forces and forms of socialization. The book's indictment of patriarchy and forms of subjugation of women had a major impact on the feminist movement of the 1960s and 1970s, especially in the United States.

Beauvoir's earlier work, primarily *Pyrrhus et Cineas* (1944) and *The Ethics of Ambiguity* (1948), drew heavily on Sartrean existentialism in exploring the ethical dimension of FREEDOM. Her later work, on the other hand, took a sharp turn toward fiction and memoir—namely *The Mandarins* (1954), *Memoirs of a Dutiful Daughter* (1958), *The Woman Destroyed* (1968), and *All Said and Done* (1974). Collections of letters to Jean-Paul SARTRE and Nelson Algren have also been published.

Beauvoir's life itself has become iconographic—partly for her accomplishments in the male-dominated field of philosophy, partly for her political activism, but more generally because of her lifelong relationship with Sartre, which has been the object of intense publicity and extended treatment (on several occasions by Beauvoir herself) as a source, performance, and sometimes contradiction of her FEMINISM.

Becker, Gary   (1930–) A prominent economist who pioneered the application of economic analysis to social phenomena as varied as divorce and discrimination. His work has helped shape NEOCLASSICAL ECONOMICS and RATIONAL-CHOICE THEORY approaches in other areas of the social sciences.

Becker was educated at Princeton University and the University of Chicago. He received the John Bates Clark medal and, in 1992, the Nobel Prize. In his doctoral dissertation, published as *The Economics of Discrimination* (1957), Becker showed that the pay differentials between black and white workers could be explained by a "taste" for discrimination. This theory was controversial and spawned a broad literature on pay differentials based on racial and sexual difference. He used a similar methodology to suggest that crime was just another occupation that reflected the calculation of expected benefits, the costs of getting caught, and individual risk preferences.

Some of Becker's most innovative work concerns how human capital is accumulated through schooling and on-the-job training—a topic he explored in *Human Capital* (1964). In recent years, Becker has studied the mechanics of family consumption, which is often taken as the basic unit of consumption in economic theory. His first contribution on this question explored the division of labor among family members. He later expanded this investigation to include other family decisions: marriage, childbearing, education, and divorce.

Becker has been accused of trying to explain all social phenomena with economic methods. He has frequently ventured into areas usually left to sociologists, anthropologists, and psychologists. In so doing, he has contributed to a rich and highly contested set of debates concerning economic analysis, rational choice, and the nature of human behavior. See also CHICAGO SCHOOL OF ECONOMICS; and HUMAN CAPITAL.

Becker, Howard S. (1928–) An American sociologist associated primarily with SYMBOLIC INTERACTIONISM, the study of DEVIANCE, and the sociology of art. Becker became well known with the publication of *Boys in White* (1961, with Blanche Greer, Everett Hughes, and Anselm Strauss), an account of the socialization of a group of medical students into the medical field. The book established Becker's reputation as a scholar of subcultures and an innovative practitioner of PARTICIPANT OBSERVATION.

Becker's *Outsiders* (1963) is a classic study of deviance in the broad sense that American sociology gave it after World War II, encompassing the formation and transgression of a wide array of social norms. It was also one of the central works of LABELING THEORY—a major orientation within American sociology in the 1950s and 1960s. Building on accounts of the significance of the perceptions of others in the formation of the self (a key principle in the symbolic interactionism of Charles Horton COOLEY and George Herbert MEAD), as well as on earlier accounts of labeling and juvenile delinquency by Frank Tannenbaum, Becker argued that deviance has little to do with the nature of specific acts and much to do with how society defines those acts. These definitions often follow lines of class, race,

or other social distinction. He suggested further that deviance is not an individual impulse but a learned one, sustained by the environment in which it is practiced. Becker drew an important distinction between *primary deviance*, representing the first instance of transgressive behavior by an individual, and *secondary deviance*, or the process of socialization to a deviant lifestyle, subculture, or career. His work inspired a range of accounts of the processes by which social institutions and actors draw and maintain the boundaries of deviant behavior, often in their own interests.

Becker's *Art Worlds* (1982) developed a similar critique of artistic production—a set of practices traditionally assumed to be individual in character or isolated from broader social networks. Becker emphasized the degree to which art—even in such individualistic forms as painting or writing—is implicated in a broad social context that includes education, training, mentoring, technology, the manufacturing of the materials involved (canvases, musical instruments, costumes, theaters, and so on), and audiences. Creativity, Becker argued, is a highly collaborative effort.

Becker's other works include *The Other Side* (1964), *Making the Grade* (1968, with Blanche Geer and Everett C. Hughes), and *Tricks of the Trade* (1997).

beggar-thy-neighbor Tactics designed to improve a country's trade balance (exports minus imports) in order to increase its level of employment and output—generally at the expense of other countries. In an underemployment situation, an increase in the trade balance is equivalent to an increase in investment and can move the economy toward full employment of resources. Examples of such tactics include currency devaluation, wage restrictions, import quotas and tariffs, and subsidies for exports. All can increase the output of both the import-competing and the exporting sectors. All will simultaneously reduce the levels of employment and output of the country's trading partners. For any of these measures to succeed, therefore, the trading partners must not retaliate. If they do, an international beggar-thy-neighbor game ensues and total world trade shrinks, eventually leading to a decline in world output. In such a scenario the tactic causes more harm than good. To avoid such harmful tariff or subsidy wars, international institutions such as the IMF and GATT (now the WTO) were created after World War II.

behavioral economics A field concerned with the empirical validity of neoclassical assumptions about human behavior and, where these assumptions are found to be invalid, with describing behavior more adequately. The standard neoclassical assumptions hold that individual preferences can be described by a utility function (reflecting tastes and notions about individual welfare) and that individuals seek to obtain the highest utility possible (optimization behavior). Departures from these assumptions take a number of forms, including SATISFICING, inconsistency of choice over time, habit formation, and concern for relative social status. A large branch of behavioral economics explores the concept of BOUNDED RATIONALITY, which acknowledges and specifies the limits on information and analytical ability that structure most economic decision making.

Much of the field of behavioral economics has been shaped by controlled experiments designed to test individual behavior in economic environments. A related research goal involves supplying empirical evidence about the shape and content of the UTILITY FUNCTION so as to strengthen predictions about economic behavior.

behavioral geography A field that attempts to account for human interaction with the environment in terms of behavioral models, particularly regarding how decisions are made that respond to or affect the environment. Behavioral geography therefore deals not just with the study of various empirical environmental pressures, but with the diverse ways in which those pressures are perceived by actors, including how they interpret information and how their responses are shaped by political or social contexts. MENTAL MAPS and environmental perception have been popular topics of research in this area, based on the recognition that decision making is influenced as much by perceptions as by the reality of place or environment. Behavioral geography thus integrates a range of concerns about social structure and cognition more commonly associated with ANTHROPOLOGY, and has been entangled in many of the same disputes surrounding theories of action, decision making, and methodologies of gathering and interpreting data. See also GEOGRAPHY; and LOCATION THEORY.

behavioralism The empiricist tenet that science should be based exclusively on externally observable phenomena. Behavioralism has played a central role in the development of sociology,

political science, psychotherapy, economic theories of decision making, and theories of training and management. In the social sciences, behavioralism's longest lasting and perhaps most pervasive influence has been in political science (discussed below). For its influence in other fields, see BEHAVIORISM, which generally refers to the theory of learning by conditioning. The common root of both terms is visible in the work of seventeenth-century political philosopher John LOCKE.

As the dominant tendency within political science from the late 1940s to the early 1970s, behavioralism represented an effort to make the study of politics more scientific by focusing on the observable behavior of individuals and groups, particularly through quantitative survey research. As early as 1908, Arthur F. Bentley in *The Process of Government* declared that political science should be concerned with observable facts. Of wider influence, though, was Charles Edward MERRIAM. From his several positions during the 1920s and 1930s as president of the American Political Science Association, president of the Social Science Research Council, and leading figure of the Chicago school of political science, Merriam advocated breaking with what many had come to feel was the moralism, formalism, and legalism of earlier political science. Emulating the "harder" social sciences of economics and psychology, behavioral political science embraced a new methodology that sought to derive testable generalizations from empirical data. Social scientific methods were to be based, as closely as possible, on those of the natural sciences, and were to provide objective knowledge, which in turn would inform policy decisions from a value-free vantage point.

Behavioralism was slow to take hold in political science prior to the end of World War II. From the late 1950s to the early 1970s, however, the behavioral perspective effectively dominated the discipline. Behavioralists expanded the explanatory range of political science by looking beyond institutions to the processes and structures that affect politics (e.g., class, ethnicity). They broadened the conception of the political by expanding their focus beyond government to the "authoritative allocation of values." They also introduced a number of methodological innovations to political science, including the application of survey research and quantitative methods. The "behavioral revolution" began to slow, however, in the late 1960s, in the face of growing criticism that:

(1) its emphasis on methodological sophistication blinded it to its own agenda of shedding light on the sociopolitical problems of the day; (2) its version of scientific methodology did not take into account the role of values in the entire process of research, from selecting what to study to interpreting "facts"; and (3) its search for scientific laws to explain the behavior of individuals or states failed to yield results (measured by predictions of political behavior), while it obscured the possibilities of human agency by reducing states and individuals to passive intersections of abstract processes. Although the term figures less prominently, many elements of the behavioral agenda were rediscovered in the late 1980s and in the 1990s. See also POLITICAL SCIENCE; and POSITIVISM.

behaviorism Strictly speaking, the empiricist tenet that science should be based exclusively on externally observable phenomena. Behaviorism acquired enormous importance in early-twentieth-century psychology, SOCIAL PSYCHOLOGY, and related areas of sociological inquiry. In these contexts, behaviorism referred above all to the study of the observed behavior of individuals at the expense of consideration of internal states and feelings, which behaviorists generally regard as unmeasurable or irrelevant. It also represented a turn away from the study of social structures and other comparatively abstract concepts divorced from specific, observable situations.

Behaviorism has a long history. John LOCKE and other seventeenth- and eighteenth-century psychological empiricists made profound contributions to economics and social theory by examining the ways in which external conditions—especially pleasure and pain—shaped individual behavior. Debates about the line between free will (or more generally human potential) and environmental and biological constraints continued throughout much of the nineteenth century. The emergence of modern behaviorism in turn-of-the-century psychology represented the fusion of strongly deterministic views of human behavior with scientific methodologies and mechanistic models of cause and effect. In this period, behaviorism became associated with learning theory and especially with the idea of *operant conditioning*—the practice of behavior modification through rewards and punishments. This dimension of the behaviorist tradition emerged from experimental research with lower animals. Ivan Petrovich Pavlov's experiments with dogs are by far the best known work of this kind. He demonstrated that biological responses such as salivation could be manipulated through training and repeated association with secondary stimuli, such as the ringing of a bell.

The American psychologist James Watson was especially influential in the early extension of scientific behaviorism to the study of human behavior. B. F. SKINNER, however, is perhaps its most prominent social theorist. Although Skinner similarly used positive and negative reinforcement to train animals to perform complex actions, he was much more interested in the consequences of behaviorism for human society. In this direction, Skinner argued not only that responses could be conditioned—a principle that has become the basis of innumerable therapeutic and learning methodologies—but also that conditioned behavior could become a stimulus to further behavioral change. Skinner outlined his goals for such social conditioning in a utopian novel, *Walden Two* (1948), which presented a thoroughly ordered society based entirely on principles of positive reinforcement rather than punishment.

Because of its emphasis on environmental determinants and its general opposition to "depth" psychology and introspective accounts of mental life, behaviorism is frequently contrasted with methodologies that privilege the interpretation of social meaning and the investigation of social structures. Nonetheless, the strong empirical bent of behaviorism—especially in regard to the primacy of externally observable phenomena—has had a profound impact on sociology, economics, and political science (where its basic principles informed BEHAVIORALISM). Behaviorism has influenced economic theories of decision making; it has opened the door to a broad sociology of incentives and punishments—as in George HOMANS' comparatively supple *social behaviorism*; and it has become the basis of a broad range of techniques in psychotherapy (e.g., aversion therapy and desensitization).

belief system Although "belief" is notoriously resistant to precise definition, "belief system" generally refers to the fundamental assumptions, ideas, and expectations that underlie a culture and that generate the range of practices and NORMS within it. The concept has a long and varied history within a number of anthropological subfields, including social anthropology, where it sometimes serves to distinguish the realm of "CULTURE"—beliefs and values—from that of

"SOCIETY," defined by roles, SOCIAL STRUCTURE, and institutions. Recent work has tended to complicate the notion that societies possess a single and uniform belief system, recognizing that individuals experience such systems only partially and always mediated by factors such as class, gender, and age. This more complex presentation of belief has tended to approximate the Marxist concept of IDEOLOGY.

Bell, Daniel   (1919–) A sociologist and journalist whose books have had a significant impact on public debates about the political, economic, and cultural transformations of the post–World War II era. Three of Bell's works have been especially important in this regard: *The End of Ideology* (1960), *The Coming of Post-Industrial Society* (1973), and *The Cultural Contradictions of Capitalism* (1976). In the first, Bell articulated a strong version of the CONVERGENCE HYPOTHESIS, the belief that ideological differences would give way before the shared technical and administrative needs of modern societies. Bell argued that the major ideologies of the nineteenth century—MARXISM and LIBERALISM—had both failed to deliver on their utopian promises, and that a compromise form, epitomized by the social-democratic welfare state, was the probable future course of industrialized societies. This general thesis proved popular in the 1960s and received new attention after the fall of the Communist bloc.

The Coming of Post-Industrial Society is in some respects an extension of *The End of Ideology* and is probably Bell's most celebrated book. In this later work, he predicted the emergence of a global society driven by services and information rather than the production of goods, and increasingly dominated by scientists and technocrats. The United States, he argued, was the front-runner in this new global economy, although he was optimistic about the global prospects of prosperity more generally. In such a world, the majority of the work force would be white-collar, class conflict would dissipate, and information and technological expertise would become the chief commodities.

With *The Cultural Contradictions of Capitalism* (1976), Bell offered a darker account of these transformations. He now foresaw lingering tensions in POSTINDUSTRIAL SOCIETY between the competing demands of economic efficiency, the social-welfare state, political equality, and libertarian self-expression. He viewed modern CAPITALISM as locked into the hedonistic demands of consumer culture, and those demands as ultimately destructive of the underlying ethic of capitalist achievement (here strongly echoing Max WEBER). Perhaps most controversially from the perspective of theorists of postindustrialism and POSTMODERNISM, Bell argued that culture, and especially its avant-garde manifestations in modern art, had replaced the economy as the primary determinant of social organization and experience. In so doing, he articulated a powerful (if by no means unique) fall narrative of postmodern culture that continues to influence popular and scholarly debates.

In the 1950s and 1960s, Bell was a member of a group known as the "New York Intellectuals," which included Irving Howe, Nathan Glazer, and Irving Kristol and was centered around the City College of New York. He has taught at the University of Chicago and Columbia University and is now professor emeritus at Harvard University. He has also had a long career in magazine journalism, serving as an editor at *Fortune*, *Common Sense*, and *The New Leader*. His other works include *History of Marxism in the United States* (1952), *The New American Right* (1955), *The Radical Right* (1963), *The Reforming of General Education* (1966), and *Communitarianism and Its Critics* (1993).

Bendix, Reinhard   (1916–1991) A sociologist and political scientist who brought a comparative approach to a range of topics in organization theory, social stratification, political systems, and intellectual history. Bendix's best-known work, *Work and Authority in Industry* (1956), is a comparative, historical examination of the evolution of bureaucracy and managerial ideology from the preindustrial models of the early nineteenth century to the large-scale industrial societies of the twentieth century. In other studies, Bendix addressed the relationship between political rights and working class integration into the national community (*Nation Building and Citizenship*, 1964), and the comparative development of the modern state (*Kings or People*, 1980). He was also a prominent interpreter of the work of Max WEBER and worked for closer links between German and American sociology—a goal that shaped his first book, *Social Science and the Distrust of Reason* (1951). Bendix emigrated to the United States from Germany in 1938 and spent most of his career at the University of California, Berkeley. His other published works include *Social Mobility in Industrial Society* (1959), *Max Weber: An Intellectual Portrait* (1960), and *Embattled Reason* (1970).

Benedict, Ruth Fulton (1887–1948) A prominent cultural anthropologist and folklorist, Benedict was an enormously popular theorist of patterns of cultural difference and one of the key contributors to the CULTURE AND PERSONALITY MOVEMENT of the late 1920s. Born Ruth Fulton, she attended Vassar College, the New School for Social Research, and later Columbia University, where she studied with Franz BOAS. She completed her doctoral work on the "guardian spirit" in American Indian religions in 1923 and taught part-time at Columbia until her appointment to a permanent position in 1931. She remained there until her death in 1948 and became one of the first women at Columbia to reach the rank of full professor. Between 1925 and 1940, she also edited the *Journal of American Folk-Lore*.

Benedict's most influential work was *Patterns of Culture* (1934), which drew on theories of personality to describe more general patterns of cultural development and difference. Different cultures, she argued, were characterized by different patterns of belief and values, and varying resistances and proclivities to change that played themselves out at the level of individual personality. The book played an important role in promoting cross-cultural research, including the search for a basic personality type—one of the principal goals of Culture and Personality researchers. It also contributed significantly to relativizing the notion of CULTURE and to challenging cultural and scientific defenses of racism.

Benedict defended this position in her study of ethnocentrism and racism, *Race: Science and Politics* (1940), and later extended it in the analyses of foreign cultures that she produced for the Office of War Information during World War II. This work led to her landmark study of Japanese culture, *The Chrysanthemum and the Sword* (1946), and to her unfinished study of the more general features of "national character." Begun during the restrictions of wartime, these studies expanded and tested the limits of what could be learned about other cultures without actual fieldwork, relying instead on a range of techniques from expatriate interviews to literary analysis.

Benedict's other major works include two folklore compilations, *Tales of the Cochiti* (1931) and *Zuni Mythology* (1935), and *The Races of Mankind* (1943, with Gene Weltfish).

benefit-cost analysis See COST-BENEFIT ANALYSIS.

benefit principle of taxation Dating back to Adam SMITH and other earlier writers, the benefit principle of taxation holds that a truly equitable tax structure is one in which the costs of government services are apportioned among individuals according to the benefits that each enjoys. However, there are often difficulties in determining the benefits received by any particular taxpayer, and the principle cannot accommodate taxes needed to finance transfer payments and other redistributional objectives. This is a serious shortcoming since, at the limit, there is no separation between taxes used to finance public services and taxes used to redistribute income. Application of this theory is therefore limited, but it underlies the thinking behind highway tolls and property taxes. See also TAXES AND TAXATION.

Benjamin, Walter (1892–1940) A German literary critic and cultural theorist associated with the FRANKFURT SCHOOL. Benjamin brought an eclectic fusion of MARXISM and Jewish mysticism to bear on a range of issues in aesthetics, literary history, and the history of modernity. He had strong ties to Theodor ADORNO and Bertolt Brecht, with whom he shared an interest in the problem of negating the ideological codes of mass culture, and he had a profound impact on the CULTURAL STUDIES movement, which drew on his interdisciplinary inquiries into the relationship between technology and art.

Benjamin was the most atypical of the Frankfurt school critical theorists. Where Adorno, Max HORKHEIMER, and Herbert MARCUSE privileged a distinction between instrumental and objective reason, Benjamin championed a rather different distinction between authentic and inauthentic existence. He approached this division primarily through the question of aesthetic experience. Authenticity, for Benjamin, was deeply rooted in a sense of the wholeness expressed in premodern artistic modes, such as the "aura" of presence he associated with singular artwork and storytelling. The development of mass-produced cultural experience abolished this aura, substituting a fetishized commodity for the socially embedded work of art. Through this process, it opened art to forms of political manipulation. Benjamin's response mixed revolutionary Marxism with a sense of messianic historical rupture to envisage the radical intrusion of authentic experience into daily life. Materialism, in this context, meant recovering the full social and productive dimension of experience, thereby breaking the fetishized autonomy of the commodity. More generally, it signified a break with the empty, linear time imposed by the rhythm of mechanized cultural forms—quintessentially, the cinema. This all or nothing proposition sustained both Benjamin's gnosticism and his poetic, imagistic explorations of radical alterity. It sustained, too, Benjamin's hope that Brechtian theater provided the method for fostering reflection on the condition of art. Unlike other members of the Frankfurt school, but like Brecht, Benjamin saw the politicization of art as an opportunity for its radicalization.

Although the rest of the Frankfurt school moved to New York in 1934, Benjamin spent the years before World War II in Paris, where he worked on his great, incomplete history of the bourgeois era and the modern city, *Arcades* (1999). With the French defeat and German occupation, however, Benjamin fled for Spain. Fearing imminent capture by the Germans, he committed suicide at the Spanish border. Benjamin's other major works include two collections of essays, *Illuminations* (1968) and *Reflections* (1978), and *Understanding Brecht* (1977).

Bentham, Jeremy (1748–1832) A reformer, political philosopher, legal theorist, and economist often regarded as the founder of UTILITARIANISM. Bentham based much of his thinking on the classical model of rational self-interest promoted by Adam SMITH, and on the broader problem of whether the general good is achieved when individuals are left free to pursue those interests. On the one hand, Bentham argued forcefully against the aristocratic position that accorded some individual interests more importance than others—a highly controversial view among the British governing classes at the time. On the other hand, he thought—here against Smith—that freedom of individual interest was no guarantee that the general good would follow. Instead, Bentham emphasized the role of social, political, and moral institutions in shaping individual behavior and individual contributions to social welfare. Interventionist approaches were justified when they promoted, in the essential utilitarian phrase, "the greatest good for the greatest number."

In this context, Bentham proved a tireless reformer in a wide range of areas. His interest in criminology led to lifelong contributions to legal and penal reform, including innovative work on penal architecture and organization. Chief of these was his scheme for the PANOPTICON, a model prison built on the principle of constant (and ultimately, internalized) surveillance. Michel FOUCAULT credits Bentham with thus formulating the basic principle of modern SOCIAL CONTROL, eventually extended to schools, factories, and other areas of social life. Nonetheless, Bentham made a practice of questioning authority and institutions, and subjected the British constitution to unaccustomed scrutiny. He was a proponent of representative democracy and an advocate of universal suffrage. He strongly supported open forms of government and criticized French revolutionary radicalism for its emphasis on natural rather than legal RIGHTS—a doctrine he viewed as unfounded. Because Bentham argued that legislation could be used to good effect in remedying social ills and in ensuring equality and prosperity, some regard his activist liberal constitutional philosophy as an anticipation of the modern welfare state. Bentham also championed the minimum wage, free schooling, and the free provision of care for the sick.

Because the question of marginal utility—the point at which the costs of an action exceed its benefits—informed most of his inquiries into law, punishment, and the determination of the general good, Bentham sought a quantitative measure of happiness (conceived rather narrowly in terms of pleasure and pain). In this, he came up against the problem of INTERPERSONAL UTILITY COMPARISONS—the comparison of inevitably complex evaluations of individual happiness, especially as it relates to changes in wealth. Few thought Bentham succeeded in this effort, but he did launch the search for a quantitative model of UTILITY that proved a major preoccupation for economists well into the twentieth century. Bentham's ideas became the cornerstone of work on marginal utility, and many of his utilitarian principles continue to underlie modern economic analysis. With the exception of *An Introduction to the Principles of Moral Legislation* (1780), Bentham's major work was collected, edited, and published by others—in many cases posthumously. These include works of legal scholarship such as *The Limits of Jurisprudence* (1945) and *Indirect Legislation* (1802), as well his unfinished *The Constitutional Code* (1822–) and *A Fragment on Government* (1776).

Berkeley school of cultural geography See CULTURAL GEOGRAPHY.

Berlin, Isaiah (1909–1997) One of the most influential political philosophers and historians of ideas of the twentieth century. Berlin was an articulate defender of political and philosophical LIBERALISM—perhaps most famously in his essay "Two Concepts of Liberty" (1959). Here Berlin drew the classic distinction between *negative liberty*, consisting of freedom from constraint by others, and *positive liberty*, the power to pursue a particular vision of self-realization. Berlin recognized that the two were to a degree inextricable, but that the latter often justified forms of tyranny and arbitrary judgments about the value of human life. This distinction underwrote Berlin's anticommunism and framed his belief in the fundamental pluralism of human values. Human values, he argued, were diverse, shaped by history and context, and consequently in frequent tension both at the level of societies and within individuals themselves. No single solution to humanity's problems existed; no underlying forces determined the course of human history; and finally no unanimity was possible regarding the nature of the good life. In this context, liberal principles of government provided individuals the maximum freedom to pursue their inevitably complex negotiations of values and notions of the good.

Much the same distinction animates another of Berlin's well-known essays, "The Hedgehog and the Fox" (1953). Here Berlin used the work of Tolstoy as an occasion for exploring the distinction between two worldviews: one characterized by the pursuit of many ends (the fox), and another that "relates everything to a single central vision" (the hedgehog).

Berlin was a skilled and accessible writer, although not a prolific one: he limited himself primarily to essays. He was perhaps more famous as a lecturer and conversationalist, however, and occupied a central place in British (and more generally Western) intellectual life from his post at Oxford University.

Berlin was born in Latvia and moved with his family to London in 1921. His education and later career at Oxford culminated in his role as founding president of Wolfson College. Berlin's writing includes *Karl Marx* (1939), *The Age of Enlightenment* (1956), *Four Essays on Liberty* (1969), *Vico and Herder* (1976), *Russian Thinkers* (1978), *Against the Current* (1979), *Personal Impressions* (1980), and *The Crooked Timber of History* (1990).

Berry, Brian (1934–) One of the leading urban and environmental geographers of the past thirty years. Berry was born in England but spent most of his career in the United States, primarily at the University of Chicago. He was one of the principal figures in the quantitative revolution that transformed geography from a humanistic to a largely mathematical discipline in the 1960s, and in particular contributed to the spatial analyses of cities, drawing on Walter CHRISTALLER's CENTRAL-PLACE THEORY and broader theories of optimizing behavior. Berry's later work extended these considerations toward the experiences of developing countries, especially India, and problems of regional development more generally, including the difficulties of American inner cities and long-term patterns of migration. Although Berry has continued to work in these areas, his research has focused more recently on longer-term trends and rhythms of economic change. His major works include *Geography of Market Centers and Retail Location* (1968), *Geographic Perspectives on Urban Systems* (1970), and *The Human Consequences of Urbanization* (1973).

Bertrand duopoly   See DUOPOLY.

best linear unbiased estimator (BLUE)   See REGRESSION ANALYSIS.

bias   Distortion in research and analysis, especially due to preconceptions of the researcher, but also as a function of unanticipated relationships of dependence among the variables under study or in the methods of gathering data. Certain kinds of bias have become well known in the social sciences. The sex of the interviewer, for instance, may introduce a persistent bias in responses to certain kinds of questions. In statistics, bias has a strict meaning that refers to systematic, nonrandom error that separates a "true" value from the average value obtained through repeated investigative research (there is, however, considerable debate about whether "true" values exist independent of the measuring process itself). Bias, like random error, introduces numerous problems for researchers because of its potential to distort data, but random error can be estimated and adjusted for if the appropriate statistical methods are employed. See also EXPERIMENTER EFFECTS.

bicameralism   See LEGISLATURE.

bifurcation   Refers to the terminological distinction between the mother's and father's sides of the family in the study of KINSHIP. The use of different terms for maternal and fraternal uncles is a common example.

bigman   The pidgin-English term for *leader* in Melanesian society. Unlike other forms of political authority located in a chief or headman, the bigman typically owes his prestige to economic accumulation and largesse—to his role, in other words, as the center of an economic system of production and distribution. The bigman's authority is informal, nonhereditary, and open to challenge from other men. The general use of the term dates to Marshall SAHLINS's 1963 essay on political authority in Melanesia.

bilateral descent   Refers to KINSHIP systems that acknowledge descent through both sexes, as opposed to UNILINEAL systems that privilege one or the other sex. Also known as *cognatic descent*. See also DESCENT THEORY.

bilateralism   Agreements or joint policies between two states, most often with regard to trade and security. With the end of the COLD WAR and the emergence of new forms of GLOBALIZATION, bilateralism has given way to increasingly pervasive *multilateral* arrangements, such as the European Union and the World Trade Organization. Bilateralism can still offer advantages, however, where collective agreements are hard to achieve, as in the Arab-Israeli peace process. See also MULTILATERALISM.

bilateral monopoly   A market characterized by one agent, a *monopolist*, on the supply side, and one agent, a *monopsonist*, on the demand side. A firm bargaining with a union that represents the entire labor force employed by the firm is an instance of a bilateral monopoly.

Bion, Wilfred   (1897–1979) A British psychoanalyst and contributor to OBJECT-RELATIONS THEORY. Bion's most innovative work lies in the areas of group psychology and the study of thought processes—the latter in particular relation to his work on schizophrenia. Like Melanie KLEIN, Bion argued strongly for the centrality of the mother-infant relationship—especially the mother's role in teaching techniques to moderate the paranoid and depressive positions of thought identified by Klein. When successful, this results in the relatively complete socialization of the child. Absent that socialization, the movement between the two poles potentially falters, and with it the key capacity to link and integrate thought. The radical dissociation of

thought that Bion identified in schizophrenics is the consequence of this breakdown. In his work in this area, Bion bridged psychoanalytic theory and more traditional philosophical concerns with *a priori* structures of thought, especially in his psychoanalytic rereading of the distinction between the container and the contained. See also PSYCHOANALYSIS.

Bion also pioneered group research and group therapy. In *Experience in Groups* (1961) and other writings, he argued that group life possessed collective mental characteristics different from those of individual life, and that these were essential to human development. He gave particular emphasis to the ways in which members of a group passed through stages of resistance and bonding that reflected inner needs and patterns of object-relations, including what he called a general "hatred" of learning or making adjustments from experience. He saw the study of group dynamics as a necessary complement to the traditional psychoanalytic focus on the individual.

Bion's later work departed from the strongly scientific ambition of his early research on groups and schizophrenia. Increasingly, he reconceived psychoanalysis in creative, even literary terms, and set the psychoanalyst in a position akin to the artist. Psychoanalysis, he argued, was dependent on subjective and aesthetically derived methods of observation for capturing the patterns of the unconscious through language. Bion's other major works include *Elements of Psychoanalysis* (1963), *Transformations* (1965), and *Attention and Interpretation* (1970).

Birmingham school   See CULTURAL STUDIES.

black economy   The portion of formal economic activity that is either systematically understated for the purposes of evading taxes or regulation, or simply missed by inefficient data gathering methods. Some definitions of the black economy also include the INFORMAL ECONOMY—the forms of marginal labor and self-employment that fall outside the framework (and thus outside the reporting) of corporate, public, and private-sector employment.

black market   An illegal market established in a context where the government has either regulated prices, or forbidden or rationed the buying and selling of a particular commodity. Black markets are common in wartime when shortages and rationing impact the availability of goods. They also develop in foreign currency trade when the currency market is restricted and the currency is considered overvalued. Black markets have also arisen in situations where CENTRAL PLANNING of the economy creates distortions in market prices for goods. The post–World War II Soviet Union provides a prominent example.

Blau, Peter (1918–) An American sociologist whose contributions touch a number of areas, including the sociology of organizations and BUREAUCRACY, microsociological theories of EXCHANGE, and inquiries into social mobility and SOCIAL STRUCTURE. Much of Blau's work has sought to relate larger structural features of organizations to the patterns of interpersonal behavior within them. This is true of his early study, *The Dynamics of Bureaucracy* (1955), and it underwrites his examination of the basic forms of interpersonal relationships in *Exchange and Power in Social Life* (1964). The latter focused on simple patterns of reciprocity, obligation, and deference to authority. It is widely regarded as a foundational work in EXCHANGE THEORY.

Blau was a preeminent researcher and theorist of formal organizational structure. In this context, he addressed the question of how the size of an organization affects its bureaucratic structure, productivity, and avenues of personal advancement. With Otis Dudley Duncan, Blau undertook a much broader study of the last issue that resulted in the classic study, *The American Occupational Structure* (1967). This empirically rigorous account of social mobility in the United States found a high degree of intergenerational mobility (reflecting the dominance of meritocratic or ACHIEVED STATUS), and accorded relatively little influence to ascribed status. It launched a wave of statistically grounded research on social mobility, collectively referred to as STATUS-ATTAINMENT THEORY.

In the 1970s, Blau turned to the development of a formal, general theory of social structure. Drawing inspiration from Georg SIMMEL, Blau was especially attentive to the significance of numbers on structure. He took interaction rates as an elemental variable, examining how these provided an empirical index of the salience of different population categories. First published in his presidential address to the American Sociological Association, this theory was elaborated in *Inequality and Heterogeneity* (1977) and extended to a more detailed investigation of social integration in *Cross-Cutting Social Circles* (1984, with Joseph Schwartz).

Like many other major American sociologists of the 1950s and 1960s, Blau was an emigré (from Austria) who arrived in the United States just before the outbreak of World War II. He received his Ph.D. from Columbia University and has taught mainly at the University of Chicago, Columbia University, and the University of North Carolina at Chapel Hill. Other works by Blau include *Formal Organizations: A Comparative Approach* (1962, with Richard Scott) and *The Structure of Organizations* (1971, with Richard Schoenherr).

bliss point In economics, a bundle of consumption that marks the level of consumer satiation, in the sense that either increasing or decreasing consumption would reduce well-being or UTILITY.

Bloch, Marc (1886–1944) A French historian who specialized in Medieval Europe and cofounded (with Lucien Febvre and Fernand BRAUDEL) the ANNALES SCHOOL of social history. Against the dominant political and military historiography of his day, Bloch articulated a much more comprehensive program of research into social and historical processes—one that integrated politics, economics, sociology, demographics, cultural and artistic production, and geography, and that above all was sensitive to the *longue durée*, or historical change over long periods of time that might not be perceptible in specific events. This perspective developed through contact with a number of other prominent scholars who, like Bloch, were located at the University of Strasbourg. This group included Febvre and Maurice Halbswachs. In 1929, Bloch and Febvre founded the journal, *Annales d'histoire économique et sociale*, which brought together a broad range of practitioners of the new historical methods and lent its name to the movement.

Much of this methodology was in place by the time Bloch wrote *French Rural History: An Essay on Its Basic Characteristics* (1931)—a work that reopened the long neglected topic of peasant life in France, and accorded to peasants a much more active role in the shaping and contesting of social life than earlier accounts had done. His most celebrated work, however, is the two-volume *Feudal Society* (1939, 1940), which like his earlier research de-emphasized the history of specific events in favor of the *longue durée* and the depiction of *mentalités*—the general structure of beliefs and concerns of individuals, in this case during the medieval period.

Bloch was a decorated soldier and officer in World War I and became an active member of the resistance during World War II. He was captured and executed by the Gestapo in 1944. Bloch's account of the German invasion and occupation, *Strange Defeat*, was published posthumously in 1946. His other works include *The Royal Touch* (1924), a study of the healing powers attributed to the French and English monarchs, and *The Historian's Craft*, an overview of his theories of comparative history, also published posthumously (1949).

blockmodeling   A key technique in NETWORK ANALYSIS for establishing points of equivalence between social structures. Developed by Harrison White and colleagues (including Scott Boorman and Ron Breiger), it relies on complex computer algorithms to model both the presence and absence of possible relationships, and thereby creates a basis for the comparison of different structures.

blue chip stocks   Equities that have a very low risk of depreciation of earnings. Shares of large established companies with strong market positions are regarded as blue chip shares.

Boas, Franz   (1858–1942) One of the founding figures of modern ANTHROPOLOGY, Boas directed the field away from evolutionary theories, armchair analysis, and assumptions of racial determinism, and toward a fieldwork-intensive approach to the study of CULTURE. He was a prolific writer and perhaps more significantly a masterful teacher and promoter of research. Together with his students, Boas defined the dominant methods and objectives of American anthropology for much of the twentieth century, and collected anthropological data of extraordinary breadth and value.

Born in Germany, Boas began his studies in science and mathematics. He completed his doctorate in physics at the University of Kiel in 1881, and accepted a position in geography at the University of Berlin. In this capacity, he conducted field research among the Inuit Eskimos, intending to demonstrate the effects of environment on Inuit culture. His experience, however, led him toward the conclusion that culture operated in relative autonomy from environmental determinants. Over the next fifteen years, Boas devoted himself primarily to ethnographic study, focusing on the Indian tribes of the Pacific Northwest (see ETHNOGRAPHY). He conducted twelve research expeditions in this period, collecting and publishing numerous accounts of Indian material culture, rituals, language, and mythology. Much of this material was published without accompanying analysis, and thereby furnished a valuable and often unexploited body of data for future researchers. Prominent among these researchers was Claude LÉVI-STRAUSS, who relied heavily on Boas's work in developing his theory of STRUCTURALISM.

Boas himself made several major attempts to analyze the patterns of cultural diffusion and contact among the Northwestern tribes, beginning with *The Social Organization and Secret Societies of the Kwakiutl Indians* (1897) and culminating with *Kwakiutl Culture as Reflected in Mythology* (1935). These were notable not so much for the patterns they revealed, which proved enormously complex, as for the long-standing anthropological assumptions they debunked, namely, clear correlations between race, culture, and language. These findings challenged the linear evolutionary models of culture and physiology that had dominated nineteenth-century anthropology, as well as the broad cross-cultural generalizations that such models encouraged. Boas thereby opened the door to the much more flexible and relativistic concept of culture that would become the basis of twentieth-century anthropological research.

Much of Boas's agenda was driven by the urgency of documenting Indian cultures that were being rapidly driven to extinction. This became known as "salvage ethnography"—the attempt to reconstruct the traditions and practices of cultures that had already suffered radical losses of integrity. Salvage ethnography, therefore, relied largely on reminiscences of the past rather than on observations of existing practice. Boas's own prolonged immersion in Indian cultures, however, meant that this salvage work was almost always informed by PARTICIPANT OBSERVATION.

Boas's vast opening of the field was consolidated and extended by his students at Columbia University, many of whom became prominent anthropologists in their own right. They included Alfred L. KROEBER, Edward SAPIR, Ruth Fulton BENEDICT, Margaret MEAD, Clark Wissler, and Melville J. HERSKOVITS. Boas also played an active part in a wide range of political and social debates, opposing racism in the United States, and the claims of racial science more generally, and defending the independence of scholarly work in the face of the wartime politicization of the university.

Other important works by Boas include *The Mind of Primitive Man* (1911), *Primitive Art* (1927),

General Anthropology (1938), and *Race, Language, and Culture* (1940).

Bodin, Jean (1529–1596) A prominent early-modern jurist, political theorist, economist, and demonologist best known for his theories of SOVEREIGNTY and money, and his comparative studies of legal systems. Bodin predates Thomas HOBBES in theorizing monarchical absolutism. Breaking with rationalist views of LAW and AUTHORITY, he argued that the source of law lay in the sovereign's will and that social order was dependant upon the sovereign's absolute authority. Bodin also challenged the notion of the divisibility of sovereignty implicit in mixed constitutionalism and other mechanisms for balancing power. He argued that political authority should be unshared and absolute, though moderate. Only then could a state achieve unified governance. The principal account of these ideas is his *Six Books of the Commonwealth* (1576), in which he described and analyzed the ideal state.

As a jurist, Bodin broke ground in denying the universality of Roman law. He argued that the comparative study of legal systems was preliminary to any attempt to determine universal legal principles, and that such principles would allow the sovereign to determine the code of law most appropriate to his time and place. As an economist, Bodin was an advocate of trade and an early proponent of the notion that inflation was linked to increases in the supply of precious metals and to the effects of trade barriers. His economic theories are found primarily in *Response to the Paradoxes of Malestroit* (1568). As a demonologist, Bodin developed a number of guidelines for the detection and judging of witches, holding that popular opinion was generally right in such matters and that—curiously—the absence of a visible mark of Satan on the accused was a more definitive sign of guilt than its presence. Despite these sentiments, Bodin became known as a defender of religious pluralism and tolerance after the posthumous publication of *Colloquium of the Seven about Secrets of the Sublime*.

Bodin also wrote an account of his comparative methodology, *Method for the Easy Comprehension of History* (1566).

Bolshevism In 1903, the Russian Social Democratic Party split along doctrinal lines into a *Bolshevik* or *majority group*, led by Vladimir Ilich LENIN, and the more moderate *Menshevik* (minority) contingent—although at the time the Bolsheviks were, in fact, in the minority. The core of Bolshevism was its doctrine of party organization, which demanded active political participation on the part of all members, democratic decision making within the party, and total loyalty in carrying out party objectives. After the Bolshevik revolution of 1917, the term came to designate the Russian Communist Party and its policies more generally, from Stalinist industrialization strategies to the retreat from international revolution. With the discrediting of Stalin in 1952, the term was dropped from official use.

The issue of party organization has been a highly contested subject in socialist party politics since the Bolshevik split, particularly in view of the antidemocratic development of the Bolsheviks themselves. Leon Trotsky was an early opponent of this centralization of authority, as were many of the Marxist parties and intellectuals of the West.

Bonapartism Originally used to describe the REGIME of Napoleon Bonaparte, the term now refers more generally to autocratic, highly centralized regimes dominated by the military. Bonapartism can also include strong elements of meritocratic advancement, expansionist foreign policy, and concern for symbolic gestures toward popular sovereignty. In modern usage, it is sometimes used in connection with fascist and authoritarian regimes.

In *The Eighteenth Brumaire of Louis Napoleon* (1852), Karl MARX developed a distinct analysis of Bonapartism linked to the rule of Louis Napoleon in France. He argued that a stalemate at the level of class struggle permits the state to become autonomous. Bonapartism, in this context, channels popular revolutionary energies away from class struggle by uniting the lower popular classes and sections of the BOURGEOISIE behind a charismatic, nationalistic leader and a strong, militaristic state.

The term *Caesarism* sometimes denotes similar qualities, particularly when popular dictatorship emerges from the disintegration of a weak democracy. Marx disparaged the term Caesarism because he thought it gave too much credit to the leader and disguised class and revolution as central explanatory concepts.

bonds A contract or a written promise to pay a specific sum of money (the principal) at a certain date in the future, with interest paid according to an explicit schedule during the interim. Bonds are issued by governments and corporations to finance deficits or to acquire assets. They differ from other debt instruments such as loans or notes in that they have long maturities, or sometimes none at all (as in the case of *consols*). For some bonds, the issuers have the right to call them in after they have been outstanding for a specified period—these are *callable* bonds. While bondholders have no ownership stake in the issuer's common stock, some corporate bonds have a clause that permits the conversion of the bond to shares in the common stock at a specified conversion value. These are *convertible* bonds. The Black-Scholes option pricing formula is designed to determine the value of such an option.

Bonds are usually negotiable and are traded in an established secondary market. The return from a bond has two components: the sum of the interest payments and the change in its price in the secondary market, which yields capital gains or losses if the bond is sold.

Borda count   A system of voting in which voters rank a set of options or candidates. These rankings are then assigned points, with the first choice receiving as many points as there are options, the second choice one less, and so on down to one. The points are then tallied and the receiver of the most points wins. The system was proposed in 1781 by Jean-Charles de Borda, a French academician. This system of voting avoids the majority-preferred cycles that are associated with the simple MAJORITY RULE of VOTING. While it allows a role for different degrees of preference, it is subject to the criticism that it is not "strategy proof." Voters may find it rational not to vote according to their actual preferences, but according to strategies such as lowering the ranking of the candidate that most threatens their preferred candidate.

boundaries, antecedent and subsequent   A distinction drawn by cultural geographer Richard Hartshorne in the mid-1930s between political boundaries established before significant settlement of an area (antecedent boundaries), and political boundaries established after settlement in an attempt to accommodate cultural differences (subsequent boundaries). Hartshorne also identified two subtypes: *pioneer boundaries*, which precede significant exploration, and *superimposed boundaries*, which ignore cultural considerations. Boundaries were a central preoccupation of political geography in the first half of the twentieth

century, when the two world wars, imperialism, and later decolonization made the viability of state boundaries a major concern of Western governments.

bounded rationality   Most economic models are based on the following neoclassical assumptions: First, individual preferences can be represented in the form of a UTILITY FUNCTION. Second, economic actors choose from among a fixed set of alternatives in such a way as to maximize their UTILITY. Third, the consequences of alternatives are either known with certainty or have (subjectively) known probability distributions of outcomes. While these assumptions provide the basis for a rich and elegant theory of economic behavior, they often do not empirically describe the situations that interest social science. Theories of bounded rationality relax some or all of the above assumptions. They recognize that instead of considering all alternatives, individuals must determine which alternatives to consider. They may spend considerable time searching for alternative courses of action and evaluating their consequences, but this is costly and usually falls short of complete knowledge. Accordingly, individuals bound their searches. Bounded rationality further postulates that the computational abilities and cognitive capacity of humans are limited, and that the assumption of maximization may impose a heavy computational burden upon the decision maker. Rather than predicting choice, bounded rationality is more concerned with the processes that persons use in making choices—that is, what kind of simplifying strategies and heuristic mechanisms they adopt. In this sense, bounded rationality is a procedural theory of decision making.

Bourdieu, Pierre   (1930–) A French sociologist and anthropologist whose work focuses on the reproduction of social patterns of power, the strategic behavior of individuals and groups, and the margin of improvisation implicit within structures of NORMS. Bourdieu's method generally combines the minute exploration of forms of embodied behavior, individual improvisation, and the subtle shadings that distinguish structured from autonomous action, with structural analysis of social fields and systems of distinction. *HABITUS* is his term for the regulated form of improvisation that characterizes daily life—the set of "durable dispositions" that condenses tradition, knowledge, and practices, and which guides choices without ever being strictly reducible to formal rules.

Bourdieu organizes his analyses of diverse fields of knowledge and social activity around the question of practices in order to reconstruct theory from the ground up, reaching conclusions about regularities and social structures on the basis of empirical research. For Bourdieu, this is the advantage of SOCIOLOGY over philosophy, but it is not sufficient by itself. Empirical work must be complemented by careful consideration of the role of the sociologist and the place of sociological knowledge in society, which like all forms of knowledge is produced by interested parties. Only by reflexively making OBJECTIVITY itself an object of analysis is it possible to avoid the "theoretical distortion" associated with objectivity claims—the birds-eye view that reduces all social relations to "decoding operations." This immanent critique of the role of the sociologist, Bourdieu argues, is not a threat to the truth of social science; rather, it makes social science more scientific, capable of accounting, finally, for its constitutive blind spot—the researcher. The self-referentiality of this gesture completes what Bourdieu calls the "autonomization" of the social scientific field—the complete formulation of its own principles—much as, he argued, the doctrine of "art for art's sake" completed the autonomization of the artistic field.

Bourdieu has pursued these themes through studies of a number of different fields of social activity, including education, art, and popular taste. Each, Bourdieu argues, is structured by different forms and hierarchies of value, but each is also in relationship—and to a degree translatable—with other fields. These differences underwrite his distinctions among different kinds of capital—economic, social, and cultural—which constitute the goals and principal resources of social life. SOCIAL CAPITAL refers to the resources provided by personal networks such as families and communities; CULTURAL CAPITAL refers to the value of certain kinds of cultural knowledge or credentials, such as the benefits of an elite education; and economic capital refers to money. Social conflict is structured by all three to different degrees—generally, Bourdieu argues, in close correlation with CLASS.

In *La Misère du Monde* (1993) and other recent work, Bourdieu has drawn attention to the rhetorics that legitimate forms of injustice and inequality. Some critics, however, have found it difficult to see how his account of the *habitus* permits individual behavior to escape the essentially conservative limits of reproduction, or more generally how social transformation occurs at all—except, as in his example of Kabyle society, through intervention from the outside (*Outline of a Theory of Practice*, 1972). Struggles for money, prestige, legitimation, and other forms of capital occur, Bourdieu argues, at all levels of society and across a wide range of differently organized fields. The difficulty is that such contention appears as a universal social feature in his work, only minimally tied to specific historical or economic contradictions, and thus not resolved in any fundamental sense by their development. This has made it difficult to see what basis Bourdieu provides for critiquing particular social arrangements.

Bourdieu's other major works include *Reproduction in Education, Culture and Society* (1970, with Jean-Claude Passeron), *Distinction: A Social Critique of the Judgment of Taste* (1979), *The Logic of Practice* (1980), and *The Field of Cultural Reproduction* (1993).

bourgeoisie The commercial class that emerged during the feudal era and that became the principal protagonist of the transition to capitalism and democratic rule. The bourgeoisie began primarily as merchants but gradually took on the roles made possible by a diversifying and expanding economy—banking, professional activities, and, ultimately, manufacturing. As the principal group actor of the age, the bourgeoisie forms the backdrop to much of the social thought of the period—although nowhere as centrally or explicitly as in MARXISM. For Karl MARX and Friedrich Engels, the bourgeoisie is the capitalist class, defined by its ownership of capital and its control of the means of production. This control, in turn, shapes the societal superstructure—the complex assemblage of state, law, religion, art, family, and other institutions. Capitalist society is therefore a fundamentally bourgeois society, in which the bourgeoisie finds its ideas, interests, and values reflected in and reproduced by social and political institutions. This includes the achievement of political freedom, which Marx viewed as the pinnacle and last instance of bourgeois progressivism.

With the rise of CAPITALISM, the bourgeoisie replaces the feudal aristocracy as the ruling class, drawing its preeminence from industrial production rather than the control of land and agriculture. In the Marxist account of capitalism, bourgeois dominance is, in turn, challenged by the rise of the working class, which, unlike the bourgeoisie, owns only its own labor and which, consequently, finds itself in intractable opposition to bourgeois society. Although Marx believed that this was the primary social division in capitalist society, he also identified a range of marginal or intermediate positions, including the peasantry, the *petite bourgeoisie* or small business owners, and the LUMPENPROLETARIAT, or underclass. Marx theorized that as capitalism developed, the concentration of capital into fewer and fewer hands would intensify the conflict between the working class and the bourgeoisie. The rise of the middle class in twentieth-century Western society has thrown this distinction into considerable disarray, however, challenging the Marxist teleology and directing sociology toward a much closer analysis of different types of work and status. The reconstruction of meaningful class categories remains, however, one of the central concerns of Marxist-oriented political economy.

Braudel, Fernand (1902–1985) A historian and key postwar figure in the ANNALES SCHOOL of social history, founded by Lucien Febvre and Marc BLOCH in the late 1920s. The great contribution of the Annales school was its critique of the dominance of political and military history—what Braudel disparaged as the history of events (*l'histoire évenementielle*). Braudel characterized such events as only the uppermost layer of history, which was underlaid and largely determined by medium- and long-term processes operating at other levels.

The long term or *longue durée* was shaped by structural factors—for Braudel largely environmental and demographic phenomena. Here he included such issues as wind patterns and the relationships between mountain and plains societies. The medium term, Braudel argued, was comprised of broad cultural and economic shifts within those structures, such as economic expansions.

Braudel developed this approach in his magisterial work, *The Mediterranean World in the Age of Philip II*, 2 vols. (1949), an account of the decline of Mediterranean society in the sixteenth century. Not the least exceptional aspect of this work is that it was largely composed during the five years he spent as a prisoner of war in Germany, without the benefit of research materials. Braudel extended his approach further in the three-volume *Civilization and Capitalism* (1979), which traced the global development of these intertwined phenomena from the Middle Ages through the twentieth century. Here Braudel similarly sought to articulate the relationships between three layers of historical experience—a layer of everyday life, a layer of small-market relationships, and an increasingly dominant layer of organized capitalism, which he provocatively viewed as a monopolistic threat to the freedoms, efficiencies, and moderate profits of the market. Although Braudel has been criticized for failing to adequately articulate the relationships among these levels, his approach to multiple historical temporalities has been enormously influential. Braudel had completed two volumes of a projected four-volume study, *The Identity of France*, by the time of his death in 1985.

Bretton Woods agreement See EXCHANGE RATE.

bricolage A metaphor introduced by Claude LÉVI-STRAUSS to describe the improvised construction of mythical thought from the heterogeneous, often recycled materials of earlier myths, stories, and experiences. In French, the term refers to the work of a handyman or jack-of-all-trades. Following Jacques DERRIDA's characterization of bricolage as the condition of all discourse and cultural production (*Writing and Difference*, 1978), it has become a widely used and debated concept.

bridewealth See DOWRY AND BRIDEWEALTH.

broken windows theory A criminological theory associated with James Wilson and George Kelling that holds that criminality operates on a continuum that reflects perceptions about the breakdown of the social order. They argue that the prevention of minor crimes (such as vandalism) and the encouragement of physical maintenance of properties and neighborhoods leads to an effective reinforcement of the social order that deters more serious crime. The broken windows theory has been widely applied in recent community policing projects in American cities and in the turn against "quality of life" crimes. It is often credited with contributing to the decline of crime in American cities since the early 1990s, although this continues to be a matter of debate among sociologists and policymakers.

bubbles In economics, a sharp rise in the price of an asset or a group of assets that cannot be fully explained by economic fundamentals. The initial rise attracts additional buyers who expect a speculative gain through further price increases. The rise is usually followed by a reversal of expectations and a sharp decline in price, often resulting in a financial crisis. Some famous instances of bubbles are Tulipmania in Holland (1636); the South Sea Bubble in London (1721); the Mississippi bubble in Paris (1719–1720); and the Railway mania in England (1846–1847). RATIONAL EXPECTATIONS theory holds that prices cannot diverge from fundamental values, and considerable theoretical work has been devoted to reconciling speculative bubbles with such models. However irrational, bubbles may play a role in helping to finance bursts of technological innovation and other productive outcomes.

budget The statement by a government of its planned income and expenditure for the coming period, usually delivered annually. Formal budgets developed in the nineteenth century with the increasing scale and publicity of state economic activity. In parliamentary systems, they are typically the clearest statement of a government's policies and how it means to achieve them. In less centralized systems, such as that of the United States, budgeting can be an extended process of negotiation between different parties and branches of government. See also BUDGETARY OR FISCAL POLICY; and KEYNESIANISM.

budgetary or fiscal policy Concerns the effects of government expenditure and taxation upon aggregate demand and aggregate output. Since the development of organized state BUDGETs, it has been recognized that forms and levels of taxation and expenditure have effects on the economy. However, fiscal policy acquired its present sense only with John Maynard KEYNES's *General Theory of Employment, Interest and Money* (1936). KEYNESIANISM argued that the net levels of taxes and spending could and should be manipulated by the government in order to mitigate the effects of BUSINESS CYCLEs and reduce the likelihood of economic crises. Apart from the particular programmatic goals of a budget, the net amount of money it added or subtracted from the economy came to be regarded as the government's primary tool to combat INFLATION and UNEMPLOYMENT. Keynes's recommendations were never followed rigorously, and the sustained economic crisis of the 1970s cast doubt on the efficacy of fiscal policy. Keynes's theoretical claims have been hotly contested by MONETARISM, while the growing openness of domestic economies to international trade and currency movements have made his ideas much more difficult to apply in practice.

There are two sides to fiscal policy: public expenditure and taxation. Public expenditure may, in turn, be classified into two components: expenditure on goods or services and TRANSFER PAYMENTS. Because aggregate demand is an increasing function of government spending and a decreasing function of taxation, these instruments can affect economic activity. In periods of recession when aggregate demand is too low in relation to the productive capacity of an economy, a combination of tax cuts and public expenditure may be used to stimulate demand. In times of inflation with excessive aggregate demand, a reversal of these instruments will help to diminish excess demand and to stabilize prices. The magnitude of the change depends on the value of the MULTIPLIER, which measures the secondary spending effects of a change in government expenditure or tax policy.

The government's budgetary position is defined as the difference between tax revenues and public expenditures. If the revenues exceed expenditure, then the budget is said to be in surplus. Expenditure greater than revenues yields a deficit. However, the effect of a government budgetary policy cannot be judged simply by looking at the budgetary position: although government expenditure and revenue affect income, they also depend on the level of NATIONAL INCOME. Moreover, the lower the multiplier, the more powerful these endogenous forces. For instance, high marginal tax rates or lower rates of transfer payments imply that more income and expenditure will find its way into the government coffers. This tends to reduce the multiplier and cushion the effects of an increase in government spending on the levels of aggregate demand and income. As a result, an increase in government expenditure has a proportionally lower impact on aggregate national income. These are referred to as built-in stabilizers, since they moderate the fall in income when public or private spending declines and restrain the increase in income when public or private spending increases. See also TAXES AND TAXATION.

budget set Describes the set of *consumption bundles* a consumer can buy given market prices and a specific income. There are generally several ways in which a consumer can divide his or her income between two goods: five dollars can be used to buy three apples and two oranges at a price of one dollar each, or two apples and three oranges at the same price. Thus, the budget set for two goods is a line, rather than a point. The set is usually restricted to those bundles that fully exhaust a consumer's income.

buffering hypothesis A theory of stress management that holds that individuals who possess certain resources or qualities are better equipped to handle stress or potentially traumatic situations than those who do not—i.e., these resources or qualities provide a buffer against such situations. Social support networks (friends, family) are often cited as resources in this regard. The derivative *Buffy hypothesis* suggests that sheer obliviousness may also reduce stress.

buffer state A buffer state acts as a "cushion" or "crush zone" between two belligerent states or blocs and is generally conceived as providing security against surprise attack. The former Soviet Union, for example, justified its domination of the countries along its western border in part as a defensive buffer against its NATO enemies. Buffer states are coming to play a less crucial role in BALANCE OF POWER calculations as the capacities of modern air forces are better integrated into strategic thinking.

buffer stocks Commodity reserves held in order to even out price fluctuations. The concept is often associated with John Maynard KEYNES, who argued that a stable postwar economic order would require a scheme to stabilize prices. He suggested creating buffer stocks that could increase the supply of certain goods and materials in periods of shortage and price inflation, and absorb excess supply in periods of glut and price deflation. While such mechanisms may help smooth short-term fluctuations, they provide little leverage on long-term price movement, which is often the question of greater concern for economists.

bull A person who believes that prices of commodities, stocks, or foreign exchange are likely to rise and who consequently buys in the hope of selling at a higher price. A market is said to be "bullish" if a significant proportion of the market participants expect it to rise.

bureaucracy The most highly developed and complex type of formal organization and administrative system, involving impersonal, official rules and a hierarchical arrangement of offices or positions. Although most often associated with government administration, bureaucratic structures are far and away the dominant administrative form of large organizations—usually proportionate to the scale, complexity, and stability of their responsibilities. The study of bureaucracy has been prominent throughout twentieth-century SOCIOLOGY and has recently gained renewed attention in the context of globalization, the emergence of flexible forms of capitalist accumulation, the broad turn against the welfare state in the United States and other countries, and the fall (and sometimes bureaucratic persistence) of the highly bureaucratized socialist regimes.

Although the term dates to the mid-eighteenth-century work of the economist Vincent de Gournay, it was Max WEBER who most strongly defined the concept and placed it at the center of studies of modernization—primarily with the publication of *Economy and Society* (1921). For Weber, bureaucracy becomes increasingly dominant in modern societies because it is the purest expression of the principle of legal-rational authority and the most efficient form of administration yet devised. His IDEAL TYPE of bureaucracy consists of a hierarchical authority structure, administration based on written documents and specific procedures, fixed areas of official jurisdiction, appointment on the basis of technical qualification, a fixed salary according to rank, promotion by seniority or rank, and the separation of private and official lives. The defining and legitimating qualities of such organization, Weber argued, are its rationality and predictability: its expression of authority is consistent with the dominant legal-rational values of its members. Bureaucratic systems are therefore extremely difficult to dislodge or transform and are very likely to spread and intensify their control of diverse areas of social life. Weber described the totality of the phenomenon as the "iron cage of bureaucracy"—threatened only by its reduction of social values to purely formal, rationalistic principles that are vulnerable to disruption by charismatic leaders.

Bureaucracy is a central topic within the fields that constitute organization theory—including economic theories of FIRM behavior (see FIRM, THEORY OF THE), studies of personnel management and HUMAN CAPITAL, and AGENCY THEORY, which examines the contractual relationships between buyers and providers of services. Many scholars have revised and expanded Weber's account of bureaucratic forms and tendencies. Robert K. MERTON, among others, has argued that bureaucracies are frequently inefficient, and that their very structure encourages inflexibility and a strong tendency toward self-perpetuation—sometimes at the expense of the social function they are intended to serve. Michael Crozier's *The Bureaucratic Phenomenon* (1964) goes further, defining bureaucracy as an organization that cannot alter its behavior by learning from its errors.

Burke, Edmund (1729–1797) An English Whig politician and political philosopher considered by many to be the founder of modern CONSERVATISM. Burke's conservatism was rooted not in nostalgia for the past, but in an appreciation of society as the product of accumulated customs and practices that root institutions, laws, and behavior in something resembling an organic whole. For Burke, this slow, mostly undirected process was the product of a collective wisdom far greater than that of individual social thinkers. He accorded a positive role to traditions and—provocatively—to prejudice or unreflective views, which he argued provided a stronger guide for behavior than intellectual notions. Burke consequently had little patience for abstract systems of social theory, and outright hatred for the radical activity such systems fostered—especially the French Revolution, which occasioned his most famous statement of principles, *Reflections on the Revolution in France* (1790). Chief among these forms of political abstraction was the liberal tradition of SOCIAL-CONTRACT THEORY, which imagined simplified states of nature on which society was suddenly and decisively imposed. Burke creatively revised the notion of the social contract as a bond between the members of society to accommodate his vision of the collaborative process that linked the generations, and consequently constrained any single generation in what it could, or morally should, change. He argued, too, against the notion of natural RIGHTS. True rights were not natural or in any sense prior to society; rather, they were prescriptive—embedded in society and guaranteed only by LAW.

Burke was nonetheless a political reformer who recognized that healthy political systems needed the means to change themselves over time. Reform, however, was best when it was a piecemeal affair, responding to specific needs or emergencies. The attempt to transform society in accordance with abstract principles, he believed, destroyed the basis for rights and could only lead to chaos or tyranny.

Burke supported a number of the progressive causes of his day. He was an advocate for his native Ireland and a defender of the powers of Parliament over those of the king. As the London agent of the state of New York, he was sympathetic to the American colonies. Unlike the *tabula rasa* approach of the French, Burke supported the colonists' attempts to seek redress in the context of their traditional rights as Englishmen—especially the right to refuse taxation without representation. Burke wrote prolifically on politics, including *Thoughts on the Causes of the Present Discontent* (1769) and *Thoughts on French Affairs* (1791). He also wrote an influential discourse on aesthetics, *A Philosophical Enquiry into the Nature of Our Ideas of the Sublime and the Beautiful* (1757).

business cycle The alternating expansion and contraction of overall economic and business activity. A business cycle consists of a phase of rapid growth followed by a decline in rates of growth—sometimes resulting in "negative growth," or shrinkage of the economy. These changes are tracked through aggregate economic measures, such as gross domestic product, industrial output, investment, consumption, and employment. A vast amount of economic literature deals with the explanation, periodicity, and duration of business cycles—variously describing them as fluctuations around long-term patterns of growth, products of external supply shocks (such as the oil crisis), or adjustments to longer term waves of innovation. In many models of the business cycle, expectations play a key role in propagating trends. Macroeconomic theory is largely devoted to the mitigation of business cycles, whether through Keynesian fiscal measures or monetarist adjustments to the money supply and interest rates.

Political business cycles can develop when parties attempt to secure reelection by actively timing booms and slumps. Once in power, a political party can engineer a noninflationary boom prior to the next elections—although the inflationary consequences of this boom will be felt later. There is some disagreement among economists and political scientists about how effective such manipulation can be, but most acknowledge that business cycles correlate somewhat with electoral cycles.

C

cabinet A committee composed of the most important executive members of government, most often chosen by the prime minister or president. Each member is typically assigned responsibility for overseeing particular ministries or fields of policy. In the parliamentary systems, cabinet members are chosen from among the LEGISLATURE, usually from the majority party, and are called ministers. In the case of COALITION GOVERNMENTS, cabinet appointments are one of the primary means of distributing power among the coalition partners. In presidential systems, cabinet members are called secretaries and have no necessary connection to the legislature or to the PARTY SYSTEM. Generally, cabinets in parliamentary systems are authorized to make executive decisions collectively, either by majority or by consensus, whereas cabinets of the presidential type tend to play a consultative role. A smaller, informal group of advisors to the prime minister or president is often termed a *kitchen cabinet*. A group of legislators in a parliamentary opposition party, each of whom is assigned responsibility for criticizing a particular government minister or ministry, is termed a *shadow cabinet.*

cadastral pattern The pattern of property ownership in a given area, generally represented on a map. Cadastral patterns often diverge from the original *survey pattern*, the term for the delineation of the available plots of land before settlement. The term *field patterns* refers to the way in which farmers divide their land.

Caesarism See BONAPARTISM.

cannibalism Outside the extreme circumstances of human starvation, there have been two main forms of cannibalism. The first is the eating of the flesh of dead relatives, which is associated with some funeral rites and sexual rituals; this is termed *endocannibalism*. The second is the eating of enemies, which is associated with rituals of conquest and purification; this is termed *exocannibalism*. Although charges of cannibalism are a timeworn means of vilifying strangers or foreign populations, the actual practice has been extremely rare among the world's cultures.

capacity utilization The ratio of the actual to the potential output of a firm, industry, or economy. If actual output falls short of potential output, excess capacity is said to exist. Excess capacity is common during times of depression or recession, when it is possible to expand output without putting upward pressure on the price of inputs such as labor and raw materials.

capital The most common meaning refers to the equipment and structures used to produce goods and services, in conjunction with (or in replacement of) other inputs such as labor and land. The central characteristic of capital is that it is a durable stock—accumulating over time with investment decisions and depreciating as it becomes outdated or worn out. (Thus capital is a *produced factor of production*—it is both a means of production and an output from another production process.) Modern economic models of production and economic growth give capital a central role as an input to production in models of firm behavior and, in the aggregate, as one of the major generators of growth in output. However, there have been numerous and basic disagreements about the nature of the concept.

The PHYSIOCRATS were the first to develop a theory of capital, which they conceived as an available pool of money used to finance the lag between expenditure on inputs and receipts from the sale of final output. Because all production took time, all production, the Physiocrats argued, required capital advances. Classical economists such as Adam SMITH (*The Wealth of Nations*, 1776) and James Mill (*Elements of Political Economy*, 1821) defined capital more broadly, as that part of an individual's possessions that is expected to yield an income. Its function was essentially to assist labor in the production process. They also distinguished between fixed capital, which yields income and assists labor without "changing masters" (buildings and machinery are in this category), and circulating capital, such as money and goods, which provides financing advances and needs to be invested in order to be productive. Nonetheless, the Physiocrat's notion of capital as a form of advance remained dominant in this work, and the role of fixed capital was relegated to the background.

Neoclassical economists held a variety of views on the subject. Eugen von Bohm-Bawerk (*Positive Theory of Capital*, 1889) viewed capital as a produced means of production that derived value from its prospective usefulness in future production. J. B. Clark and Phillip Wicksteed, in contrast, rejected the view of capital as essentially a monetary advance and argued that it was a factor of production on equal footing with land or labor. Alfred MARSHALL (*Principles of Economics*, 1890) made the further distinction between capital goods, which produce a surplus over their cost of production if used productively, and money capital, which earns interest. Following Frank Knight's work on economic organization (*The Economic Organization*, 1933), capital came to be seen as a "material entity"—a homogeneous mass created by savings decisions, which could be transferred across industries and given different forms. In Knight's view, not only was capital in itself productive, but when used intensively, it guaranteed higher productivity for other factors of production (i.e., LABOR). Neoclassical economists like John R. HICKS and Paul SAMUELSON dispensed with both the heterogeneity of forms of capital goods and the problem of the duration of production. They developed an atemporal microeconomic theory of production based on a concept of homogeneous capital, the value of which can be expressed in monetary terms. See also NEOCLASSICAL ECONOMICS.

One of the fundamental issues in defining capital concerns how, exactly, capital accumulation occurs (see INVESTMENT). Karl MARX's account of capital in this regard proved highly influential (*Das Kapital*, 3 vol., 1867–1894). In Marx's view, there is a basic distinction between capital accumulation and exchanges of equal value. For example, trading oranges for apples is an exchange of equal value—no new value is produced. The same is true of lending money at interest, which only transfers capital from one owner to another. Investing money in the production process, in contrast, creates new value by combining living labor (work) with capital in the form of tools and other means of production.

Rudolf Hilferding's *Finance Capital* (1910) introduced another dimension to Marx's theory of capital, specific to the massive flows of investment money controlled by tightly integrated banking systems. For Hilferding and later for Vladimir Ilich LENIN and Nikolai Ivanovich Bukharin, financial capital was the mechanism by which banks appropriated control from the capitalists, resulting in yet another stage of monopolization.

The term capital has come to be used in a wider sense to describe any accumulating stock with productive value. Pierre BOURDIEU has proposed the concept of cultural capital, and many theorists (notably Robert Putnam) use the term social capital in order to capture the idea that there are economic payoffs to social networks and knowledge. Cultural capital refers to socially valued knowledge that conveys social status, such as a knowledge of literature or the arts among certain elites; social capital refers to the benefits obtained by belonging to social networks that facilitate cooperation and economic development. As in the case of productive capital in the traditional sense, theorists refer to these as stocks in which individuals and communities can invest to draw future benefits. See also HUMAN CAPITAL, which refers to an individual's stock of education and skills, likewise producing a flow of benefits.

capital account   A national account of overseas transactions in assets markets, including residents' investment in foreign concerns, foreign investment in domestic ventures, and foreign exchange transactions. See also BALANCE OF PAYMENTS.

capital asset pricing model   Also CAPM. A model developed in the 1960s by William Sharpe and John Lintner that addresses the problem of valuing assets. The model gives specific form to the trade-off between risk and return on a portfolio of assets.

capital deepening   Describes the accumulation of capital at a faster rate than the growth of the labor force, which results in a rising ratio of capital to labor ratio.

capital flight   The sudden and large movements of funds out of a country. The impetus for capital flight includes actual or feared monetary instability, confiscatory taxation, war, or revolution. Capital flight can potentially exhaust foreign-exchange reserves and causes national bankruptcy (meaning that foreign credits are frozen and exchange restrictions are introduced). All measures to reverse capital flight have their attendant costs—raising interest rates may trigger a depression and intensify bank failures; devaluation of the currency may provoke retaliation by other countries or lead to a wage–price spiral.

capital formation   See INVESTMENT and ACCUMULATION OF CAPITAL.

capital gains and losses   Profits made from the difference between the purchase price of an asset and its resale value at a later point are termed *capital gains*. If the value of an asset falls during that time, or if inflation exceeds the percentage gained, a capital loss results. Although capital gains are not classified as income in most countries, they do clearly generate a monetary payoff. This provides a rationale for their taxation.

capitalism   The dominant modern form of social and economic organization, generally but not exclusively characterized by private ownership of the means of production and by the use of markets to allocate resources, distribute goods, and generate profits. Most histories of capitalism date its emergence to the beginning of the Industrial Revolution in late sixteenth-century Holland and to the expansion of the mercantile system in England. Both processes created a dynamic new class of entrepreneurs, increased domestic and foreign levels of trade, and provided a model for the exploitation of new colonies. Many historians also draw attention to the role of agricultural capitalism and to broader cultural changes—notably Max WEBER's account of the religious origins of the capitalist ethos and of such features as the practice of reinvesting profits into production (see PROTESTANT ETHIC).

In economic thought, a strong "classical" tradition emerged in response to the growth of capitalism in the eighteenth century. Adam SMITH, David RICARDO, J. B. Say, John Stuart MILL, and Karl MARX produced seminal analyses of the production, distribution, and exchange of goods in a market economy. Smith, in particular, formalized a set of concepts and methods that have since been closely associated with capitalism, specifically his social justification for the "invisible hand" of the market, through which the diverse pursuit of individual goods produces a larger, optimal collective good. This belief in the market as the most efficient and equitable adjudicator of wealth and other resource decisions

furnishes the basis of the liberal doctrine of minimal government—the political counterpart to much capitalist thought in the nineteenth and twentieth centuries. Such thinking has generally assumed a strict division between the economy (including economic rights) and other spheres of human activity, such as government. These assumptions have been challenged on a number of fronts by both defenders and opponents of capitalism—especially as the industrial revolution transformed the relationship between owners and workers and as government took on responsibility for national economic health and public welfare. MARXISM is the most prominent of these challenges.

The Marxist tradition strongly departs from liberal thought in seeing capitalism not simply as an economic system but as a form of society whose larger features can be treated as expressions of the economic base. Capitalism, in this broad sense, is a "mode of production" that determines not only the general organization of the production, distribution, and consumption of goods but also the dominant patterns of social stratification, politics, and cultural life. This was the basis for a revolutionary program that sought to transform society by changing the basic relations of property. The impact of this method extends far beyond its mostly defunct revolutionary tradition. In the wake of Marx's writings, the link between economic and social organization became a virtual axiom of social theory, visible in diverse traditions of Marxist and non-Marxist thought.

Weber provided one of the principal cultural accounts of the emergence of capitalism, notable for departing from the economic determinism of Marxist thought while continuing to subscribe to much of its general interpretation. For Weber, the capitalist values of accumulation and economic competition were rooted in the broad processes of RATIONALIZATION and *disenchantment* of the premodern world. They were specifically fostered, moreover, by the uncertainty of salvation and by the sense of professional vocation implicit in early Protestantism. The association of capitalism with rationalization has been an especially powerful influence on a range of social theorists, including FRANKFURT SCHOOL figures such as Max HORKHEIMER and Theodor ADORNO, and post-structuralist historians such as Michel FOUCAULT.

Modern economic theory has embraced this notion of rationality in narrower terms, conceiving individual economic decisions as strongly guided by rational choices about profit maximization (see RATIONAL-CHOICE THEORY). Economic theory has also generally eschewed integrated definitions of capitalism as a social system, in favor of a narrower focus on the major institutions of capitalist economies: developed LABOR and commodity markets, private INVESTMENT and the ownership of CAPITAL, the growth and concentration of productive capacities, and the development of mechanisms of finance. Marx differs little from most modern theorists of market economics on the first point—he, too, recognized the internal logic of profit maximization in capitalist behavior, although he thought (so far, mistakenly) that this process would rapidly run up against it own limits (see FALLING RATE OF PROFIT). Marx differed by providing a historical account of this behavior that stripped it of its general identification with nature (classically, in Adam Smith's "invisible hand" metaphor) or its specific identification with human nature (visible in much contemporary rational-choice theory). He also provided a context for understanding whose interests were served by such beliefs and how those beliefs were maintained (see IDEOLOGY).

Contemporary analysts of capitalism as a socioeconomic system have had to account for a range of transformations that Marxism did not clearly predict, including the capacity of democratic regimes to regulate economic behavior and redistribute profits, the growth of the middle class, the failure of traditional Marxist expectations of class struggle, the decline of the industrial model of labor, and the emergence of consumer capitalism. This has led to much discussion about a new paradigm of capitalist accumulation—variously described as flexible accumulation, post-FORDISM, or, more generally, POSTMODERNISM—in which capitalism emerges as a strongly global system, marked by a division of labor between rich and poor countries. See also WORLD-SYSTEMS THEORY.

capital–labor ratio The ratio of CAPITAL available per worker, often used as a measure of the degree of industrialization and productivity. Economies with high capital–labor ratios are said to be *labor scarce*.

capital–output ratio The ratio of the amount of capital (such as equipment or structures) to the amount of output (or final goods) produced

by that capital, often used as a measure of the aggregate productivity of capital.

capital widening The process of accumulating capital to keep up with growth in the labor force, so that the capital–labor ratio does not fall.

cardinal and ordinal utility Refers to two ways of measuring UTILITY—the term widely used in economics to describe the satisfaction or well-being of individuals. *Cardinal utility* refers to a meaningful measurement scale for utility (often expressed in *utils*) that would allow for comparison across individuals and for an absolute scale of utility across consumption options (e.g., a choice yielding two utils would be deemed twice as good as a choice yielding one util). This was the original vision of the utilitarians, who argued in favor of maximizing the sum total of individual utilities in society (see UTILITARIANISM). Because the quality of happiness proved difficult either to measure or compare across circumstances and individuals, economists soon preferred to account only for *preference orderings* over outcomes. Individuals could identify their preferences given two choices, and this allowed for an *ordinal* utility comparison—one that was valid only in relative terms. The use of ordinal utility left little foundation for assessing aggregate welfare, however, and much of modern welfare economics refers only to the relatively weak welfare criterion of Pareto optimality, which requires only ordinal information (see PARETO OPTIMAL).

Cardoso, Fernando Henrique (1931–) President of Brazil since 1995, Cardoso first attracted international attention as a political scientist, sociologist, and leading proponent of DEPENDENCY theory. With Chilean historian Enzo Faletto, Cardoso wrote the seminal *Dependency and Development in Latin America* (1967), which argued that the unique cultural, sociological, political, and economic conditions of the third world made first-world development models inapplicable. In the course of development, they contended, third-world countries would necessarily confront obstacles and opportunities that were different from those experienced by developed countries—not least because of the constant influence of the developed countries on the local culture and economy. Such factors would shape the nature and degree of dependency, and they made necessary a "historical-structural" approach to the study of underdevelopment in Latin America.

Born in Rio de Janeiro, Cardoso was a vocal opponent of the Brazilian dictatorships and spent several years in forced exile in the 1960s. In 1986, he was elected to the Brazilian senate and became leader of the Social Democratic party. He served as foreign minister in 1992 and as minister of finance in 1993. In that role, Cardoso championed free-market reforms and the privatization of state-owned industries. He has been widely credited with reversing the decline of the Brazilian economy and with dramatically reducing the rate of inflation (the latter by indexing a new currency, the *real*, to the U.S. dollar). He has also pursued land redistribution as a means of addressing chronic agricultural poverty in Brazil.

Cardoso is a coauthor of *The New Global Economy in the Information Age* (with Martin Carnoy, Manuel Castells, and Stephen S. Cohen, 1993).

cargo cults A type of religious movement associated primarily with Melanesia and the World War II era, when the arrival of military forces brought infrastructural development and modern goods to the islands. Military withdrawal after the war created a situation of scarcity, in which the anticipated arrival of new goods became a powerful symbol of salvation for many islanders. Cargo-cult prophets soon converted this desire into a number of more or less enduring millenarian sects, fusing the question of the delivery of goods with older beliefs about the return of ancestors and often ritualizing the construction of cargo infrastructure—airfields, docks, and radio towers—in the hope of propitiating the deliverers of the goods. See also MILLENARIANISM OR MILLENNIALISM.

The cargo cults have been a rich and well-traveled subject of modern anthropology, since they bring into sharp relief many of the discipline's contemporary concerns: the effects of contact between colonizers and colonized and the cultural response to underdevelopment.

carrying capacity Refers to the maximum population that a given environment and resource base can sustain. Carrying capacity is a crucial issue in any relatively closed ECOSYSTEM; it therefore plays a vital role in economic and ecological research into the sustainability of human life at the global level. There is still little agreement about the planet's carrying capacity or what

consequences approaching or exceeding it would have.

cartels A voluntary agreement among private enterprises to collude in setting output or price levels in their market. Cartel behavior may involve coordinated selling prices (price fixing), output controls, bid rigging, the allocation of buyers among producers, the establishment of trade practices, and a variety of other strategies. Although such coordinated activity may control prices only indirectly, a functioning cartel always implies diminished price competition. Consequently, as with monopolies, cartel prices exceed the marginal cost (a standard condition for competitive markets) and the amount sold falls below the level associated with a competitive market.

A perfect cartel maximizes the sum of the profits of its members, and allocates output among the members to minimize costs. Since some members may be more efficient producers than others, a cartel may employ their capacities at different rates. Side payments between participants are used to induce adherence to the arrangement. Countries that coordinate the production of a shared export commodity—such as the oil-producing countries that make up OPEC—are also considered cartels.

In recent years, the problem of the rational defection of members from a cooperative equilibrium has attracted considerable attention. Such actions can quickly unravel a cartel. Enforcement, therefore, is crucial to the success of cartels and requires the power both to monitor members and to impose sanctions on defectors. GAME THEORY has been used to generate strategies that members of a cartel may adopt to enforce the cooperative outcome.

case study A research method that engages in the close, detailed examination of a single example or phenomenon. In some instances, it may be a version of *ideographic* rather than *nomothetic* investigation—seeking deep and thorough understanding of a phenomenon instead of general laws about classes of phenomena. In other instances, case studies are explicitly intended as part of comparative research, since some element of comparison is always implied, even in the consideration of single case. Advocates for the case-study approach argue that knowledge obtained need not be restricted to the case at hand, since results may be employed both to develop and to test theories and generalizations. In anthropology, Max GLUCKMAN developed an "expanded case-study method" as a way of analyzing the structure of relationships that lay behind the production of a specific event in a specific social situation (see also THICK DESCRIPTION). Case studies are often published by ethnographers, participant-observers, and historical researchers. The study of "classic" cases plays a central role in training in some fields, especially anthropology, law, and psychoanalysis.

cash–reserve ratio   The ratio that banks have to maintain between their holdings of cash and their deposit liabilities. Historically, this has been determined by the liquidity needs of banks. Over time, it has become fixed by law or regulated by the CENTRAL BANK. Control of the cash–reserve ratio is an important instrument of monetary policy because it is a component of the money MULTIPLIER. By changing the cash–reserve ratio, the central banks can affect the magnitude of the change in money supply.

caste   The term that the Portuguese and later the British used to describe the hereditary Hindu system of rank that organizes society in India. In principle, there are four castes—the priests (Brahmin), the warriors (Kshatriya), the merchants (Vaisiya), and the peasants (Sudra). There is also a group below and excluded from the caste system—the untouchables. The exclusivity of the castes was reinforced through rigid norms that governed contact among them and that especially proscribed marriage outside each caste. Traditionally, caste dictated employment possibilities according to a system that ranked occupations by their degree of spiritual pollution.

In practice, in an occupationally complex and modernizing society, the castes are divided into many subcastes, which vary across localities. Certain occupations are open or vied for by more than one caste, and a significant minority in Indian society rejects the system altogether—notably the Muslims.

India has proved a rich and difficult subject of anthropological and sociological interpretation—one that resists simple accounts of caste practices. The study of the Indian caste system has also had an impact on the accounts of divided societies more generally, contributing the notion of the SUBALTERN as a way of thinking about subordination that cuts across lines of class, race, and gender.

Castoriadis, Cornelius   (1922–1997) An iconoclastic thinker and political radical whose work bridged economics, philosophy, and psychoanalysis. Castoriadis was born in Turkey but spent most of his life in France, where he worked as an economist and later as a psychoanalyst. During the 1950s, he was one of the founders of Socialisme ou Barbarie (Socialism or Barbarism)—a radical leftist organization that tried to separate revolutionary practice from the bureaucratic and authoritarian solutions of the Communist party (as well as from its Trotskyite critics). In the course of wide-ranging investigations of capitalist modernity and its revolutionary alternatives, Castoriadis criticized the Marxist reduction of society and social change to a matter of economic arrangements. He advocated a much broader conception of the mechanisms of social reproduction and social change, one that left an important place for sexual and cultural life. He described the significant elements of the social fabric as "social imaginary significations"—the socially invested concepts, values, and objects that played a role in shaping the institutional framework of society. Although these elements are diverse, Castoriadis argued that modernity was divided in general terms between the capitalist enterprise of domination over nature and a counter-value of autonomy, expressed in progressive and liberatory social movements. His ideas had a major influence on the generation of 1968 in France, and he continued to be an important critic of the poststructuralist mainstream of French thought in his later years (see POSTSTRUCTURALISM). His major works include *The Imaginary Institution of Society* (1964–1965 [1987]) and *World in Fragments* (1978–1993 [1997]).

catastrophe theory   A branch of topology—the mathematics of shapes—that attempts to describe discontinuous patterns, including sudden changes in dynamic systems. Catastrophe theory was developed by René Thom in the 1960s, initially for the analysis of biological processes, such as cell division. It has been widely debated and refined in the years since, and has found a place in a wide range of environmental studies and related areas of human geography. It has also been used, to an extent, in economics and sociology and has been partially integrated with recent work on chaos theory.

catch-all party   See PARTY, POLITICAL.

catchmenting   The determination by a government authority of the geographical area(s) that will receive a particular government service.

cattle complex   A term introduced by the anthropologist Melville HERSKOVITS (1926) to describe the system of values that governed native cattle ownership in a large part of East Africa. Herskovits investigated how and why cattle ownership was crucial to the acquisition of prestige and AUTHORITY in a number of those societies—an importance that extended well beyond the apparent economic significance of owning cattle. The term had a relatively short life in anthropology, however, since it was quickly popularized and vulgarized among white settlers in East Africa as a way of denigrating the supposedly "irrational" organization of such societies.

The question of the central place of cattle in East African and other societies has not disappeared, and contemporary research has tended to locate such patterns of ownership within an elaborate network of symbolic and social functions.

caucus   Usually, a closed meeting of political party members to determine party strategy, select candidates, or enforce party discipline. In the United States, the term refers to several kinds of meetings, including those of all party members of one of the houses of Congress, closed party nominating meetings at the local level, and bipartisan meetings of legislators united by an interest in a particular issue. The term is also used to describe groups or factions within a party that attempt to steer the party in a particular direction.

causal inference   A set of statistical methods used to address questions of cause and effect by analyzing how certain variables are produced. Causal inference is used in both cross sectional and temporal contexts.

The principal difficulty in establishing causality between two or more variables is that mere correlation between variables is not sufficient—correlation is a symmetrical relationship ($X = Y$). Causation is an asymmetric relationship (X yields Y, but Y does not yield X). Such asymmetry can be established by any of the following methods: controllability, temporal priority, and outside knowledge.

Controllability shows that X is a cause of Y if by controlling X it is possible to indirectly control Y. Temporal priority holds that an effect cannot precede its cause, thus eliminating symmetrical correlations. Outside information, especially regarding exogenous variables (e.g., variables outside an economic system), can establish causality. For example, a variable like the weather can be shown to have a direct causal effect on certain economic variables.

Many approaches emphasize temporal causality. One prominent approach, termed *Granger causation*, is based on two axioms: (1) that cause precedes effect (temporal priority); (2) that the cause provides predictive information about the event. In this context, X is said to cause Y if taking account of the past values of X provides a better forecast of Y.

census   The process of gathering demographic, social, economic, or other kinds of data on all members of a population, usually distinct from surveys that gather data from a sample of a population. Although the practice is ancient, with notable Roman examples, census-taking developed primarily with the emergence of the modern state, whose functions increasingly relied on the ability to count and categorize the population. These censuses were used for political representation, economic policy and taxation, and as measures of economic or military strength. Today, they underlie most political decisions about the allocation of resources. For this reason, the methodology underlying censuses has been an object of controversy—especially in the United States in recent years. The way that U.S. ethnic groups and other minority groups are labeled and counted has an effect on their political power and economic resources. The recognition that the census routinely undercounts sectors of the poor—especially transient and indigent populations without fixed domiciles—has also been a subject of debate. This concern has led to efforts to integrate sampling methods into the census count in order to better estimate the size of systematically undercounted groups.

center–periphery   and   core–periphery   Describes patterns of unequal relations between relatively developed centers and less developed outlying areas within an economy or other system. Although Marxist theories of imperialism by Vladimir Ilich LENIN and others prefigured these issues in the first decades of the twentieth century, core–periphery models emerged in the late 1950s in an attempt to explain a more narrow set of economic observations: uneven development and relations of dependency within countries, particularly in developing economies where the progress toward a gradual economic equilibrium between areas was patently absent. The pioneering core and periphery models developed by political theorists Gunnar MYRDAL and Albert Hirschman during the period described similar processes, whereby the emergence of growing economic sectors (such as a single industry) not only remained localized and self-reinforcing—often in a core city—but monopolized a disproportionate share of the limited investment resources of a country, resulting in the further deprivation of the periphery. Myrdal termed these secondary deprivations *backwash effects*.

Core–periphery models have also been employed by geographers and historians to describe the relationship between specific heartlands and their hinterlands (e.g., the Paris Basin, Rome and its empire, Beijing and the North China Plain). Less place-specific uses of the concepts are most prominently associated with the WORLD-SYSTEMS THEORY approach to international political economy (see Immanuel WALLERSTEIN), which focuses on the relations between capitalist core economies and those of the semiperiphery and periphery. Most core–periphery models focus on imbalances of power, in which authoritative decision making, communications, cultural activity, industry, and a wide variety of other privileged activities tend to be concentrated in one or a few locations within a political or economic system. The outlying areas within such systems participate in relatively few authoritative decisions, offer less to the overall flow of information, and contribute mostly raw materials or low value-added goods to the general economy.

Over time, center–periphery analysis has been revised to account for more complex relations between the two poles. Claims for the recognition of peripheral local identities, for example, have had a major effect on inter- and intrastate politics. In the cultural sphere, there are many examples of reciprocal exchanges between center and periphery, as content from the core is appropriated by the periphery, transformed through local influences, and exported back to the center.

central bank   A national-level financial institution, usually responsible for discretionary monetary management and for controlling the health of a country's banking system. Central banks have a privileged position in the issuing of notes and as bankers to their governments. In most cases,

the central bank is a public body, although the constitutions of some countries give it a degree of independence from the government.

While some central banks began as private institutions, true central banking was the product of a shift away from competitive, profit-maximizing banking. The powers and precise functions of central banks vary widely from country to country, but essentially include the macro functions related to the overall monetary conditions of the economy and the micro functions related to the health and well-being of the members of the banking system. In the macro realm, the main objective is to maintain the internal and external value of the national currency. In the micro realm, the bank provides a central source of reserves and liquidity to other banks, serving as a lender of last resort as well as undertaking regulatory and supervisory functions. These objectives are generally pursued through:

- Open-market operations, where the central bank sells or purchases securities in the open market. Open-market sales, for example, contract the reserve base and compel a reduction in banks' loans and other assets. This, in turn, contracts the money supply via the money multiplier. Central banks also help finance budget deficits, substituting for and hence controlling the growth of the money supply.
- Setting the discount rate, that is, the rate at which commercial banks can borrow from the central bank.
- Setting the minimum reserve ratio, whereby banks and other financial institutions are required to maintain a minimum ratio between assets held as reserves and deposit liabilities. Varying this ratio influences the money multiplier, which determines how much money the banking system puts into circulation per dollar of reserves.

centralization   Generally refers to the concentration of power or functions in a single location (such as a capital) or organization (such as the EXECUTIVE branch of government or the ruling party). Researchers have studied centralization as a prominent feature of modernization, associated with the development of the nation-state, the expansion of state functions, and the related emergence of bureaucratic forms of organization. Evidence for ongoing centralization in many areas of social and political life is equivocal, however, and decentralization has become a common theme in studies of politics and organizational structures. DEVOLUTION, REGIONALISM, and BALKANIZATION are aspects of this countertendency.

central-limit theorem States that the sum and the mean of a set of random variables will follow a normal probability distribution as the sample size becomes sufficiently large, regardless of the probability distribution from which the individual variables come. Since the mean, variance, and shape of the normal probability distribution are well known, it becomes easy to test hypotheses based on a sample variable. One important use of the central-limit theorem is in the specification of econometric models. In econometric analyses, the regressors explain most, but not all, of the variation in the dependent variable. The unexplained part is called the *error term*. The central-limit theorem justifies the assumption that the error term is normally distributed.

central-place theory Proposed by Walter CHRISTALLER in the early 1930s to explain the geographical distribution of settlements in a given area. Christaller recognized that settlements tend to develop productive specializations according to geographic criteria—the type of available land, for example—and that the spatial distribution of those settlements reflects a compromise between the value of the specialization and its access to a centralized market. In short, the more specialized a good, the farther people are willing to travel for it. According to Christaller's criteria, this dictated a central-market location for highly specialized goods, which could service a wide area, and a more evenly distributed network of markets for basic goods. This spatial model, in turn, was affected by other factors, such as the tendency to minimize the cost of transportation infrastructure and the effects of political borders that cut through optimum market areas. Although Christaller's version of this idea was highly abstract and rarely proved predictive of actual historical situations, it did engender a long and varied tradition of spatial analysis in GEOGRAPHY and ANTHROPOLOGY that continues to be influential.

central planning Refers to the coordination of national economic development by the government, usually through the mandating of levels of production, capital investment, and consumption. The United Nations officially distinguishes between centrally planned economies, private enterprise (market) economies, and mixed economies—although all involve some efforts at macroeconomic control. In this context, central planning may be further differentiated into "direct" forms of control (as in most of the former communist countries), "financial" forms (as in Hungary), and "indicative" forms (as in France). Central planning was first implemented on a large scale in the Soviet Union through a series of five-year national economic plans—the first implemented in 1928.

The chief advantage of central planning over a pure market economy is that it directs economic activity toward specific political and social goals, such as industrialization, forms of social welfare, or militarization. In this context, fewer resources are likely to be wasted on marginally useful or undesirable forms of production. The Soviet Union and other centrally planned societies initially experienced very high growth rates that appeared to validate the practice. In the 1950s, however, the disadvantages of central planning began to be the subject of closer study and more public debate, both by economists and politicians. Perhaps the most difficult problem was that, in the absence of market signals, central planning could not guarantee an efficient allocation of resources. Allocation was made on the basis of information from lower ranked agencies—a mechanism that commonly introduced mistakes and delays and, at worst, systematically distorted information about demand as enterprises sought the largest allocations of resources and the smallest tasks. Moreover, once enterprises gained access to resources, there were no incentives to cut costs, save resources, or enhance productivity. This rigidity and inertia was exacerbated by a bureaucracy that generated *ad hoc* priorities, often at the expense of social sectors such as education, health, and municipal services. From the consumer's point of view, centrally planned economies provided poor quality goods and a limited range of products. The pro-democracy/anti-Communist revolutions in Eastern Europe (1989–1991) have been partially attributed to the failure of the planned systems to deliver consumer goods.

central tendency Refers to the average or middle value in a data set or distribution. There are a number of related measures of the central tendency, which may be more or less appropriate to different data sets; these include the mean, the median, and the mode. The *mean* (or average) is calculated by adding all the values and dividing by the number of values. The *median* is the middle value in a distribution (i.e., there are an equal number of values above and below); it is most useful when a data set contains extreme values (termed outliers), which potentially distort the mean. The *mode* is the value or set of values that appears most frequently in a data set; it may represent, for example, the most popular choice in a series of choices, but it bears no necessary relationship to the overall distribution of values.

centrifugal and centripetal forces Originally terms in physics, these refer, respectively, to forces that push bodies out from or pull bodies toward the center of a space or field. Although the concepts have been used in a number of areas, Richard Hartshorne made influential use of them to distinguish between forces that tend to fragment or weaken the state (centrifugal forces) and those that tend to consolidate or strengthen it (centripetal forces). Natural barriers within a country or competing sources of political legitimacy (such as tribal organization) are examples of centrifugal forces; shared languages and ethnic homogeneity are centripetal forces. The terms are also frequently used by urban geographers to distinguish between forces that encourage movement toward or away from inner cities.

centrism A political tendency that involves finding a middle ground between political forces on the left and the right, either as a matter of principle or as a means of maximizing electoral appeal. Within a particular party, centrism usually involves downplaying ideological appeals in favor of a moderate, pragmatic, or managerial platform.

certainty equivalent The payment a person would accept to forgo a particular risk or gamble. For a risk averse individual, the certainty equivalent will be lower than the EXPECTED VALUE of the gamble—its average return (see RISK AVERSION). The certainty equivalent is thus the value that generates the same UTILITY to the individual as the risky option. (For risk-loving individuals, the certainty equivalent would be higher than the expected value of the gamble.)

CES production function Or *constant elasticity of substitution production function*. The CES function is a production function used to model the relationship between the quantity of inputs used to make a good (such as labor and capital) and the quantity of output of that good. Its key feature is that it assigns a constant value to the substitutability between inputs—the elasticity parameter ρ. ρ can vary from zero to infinity, allowing the inputs to range from perfect COMPLEMENTS to perfect SUBSTITUTES.

Several commonly used production functions can be expressed as special cases of the CES production function. When the elasticity of substitution is infinite, output is a linear function of capital and labor—meaning that labor and capital are perfect substitutes. When the elasticity of substitution is one, the CES production function is equivalent to the COBB-DOUGLAS FUNCTION—probably the most common form in economic analysis. It owes its popularity to the fact that it can be manipulated easily and embodies several theoretically desirable properties. For example, a Cobb–Douglas production function implies that the marginal product of labor (or capital) is positive and exhibits diminishing returns. When the elasticity of substitution is zero, output is determined by the scarcest factor of production (thus the inputs are perfect complements). This is known as a Leontief function. Kenneth ARROW, Hollis Chenery, B. S. Minhas and Robert SOLOW developed the C.E.S. production function in "Capital-Labor Substitution and Economic Efficiency" (1961).

cession The legal transfer of jurisdiction over a territory from one country to another, usually by treaty.

ceteris paribus Latin for "other things being equal." The concept is central to modeling in the social sciences, especially in economics. It is used as a reminder that all things other than the variable(s) under study are assumed to be held constant. Any practicable theory must take the stability of certain background circumstances as given. For this reason, certain forms of variation are taken to be outside the model. In this sense, the *ceterus paribus* assumption is an approximation (a partial equilibrium approximation) to a more general and comprehensive theory or a transitional step in our understanding of a general equilibrium theory.

Chayanov slope Measures the value of labor in land-rich societies as a function of the ratio of consumers to producers. The model was developed by Russian economist A. V. Chayanov in the 1920s and popularized in contemporary Western anthropology by Marshall SAHLINS.

cheap money Traditionally, the short-term interest rate has been referred to as the price of money. In this context, "cheap" money implies a low rate, whereas "dear" money implies a high rate. In contemporary economic terminology, cheap money is used in the context of monetary policy to refer to a fall in real interest rates or to a policy that seeks to provide loans at low rates of interest.

checks and balances A principle of constitutional design in which government powers are divided and shared among different institutions and agencies. This ensures that power cannot be exercised unilaterally for long without being approved or checked by another branch or level of government. Checks and balances have historically been conceived as protections against TYRANNY—whether by individuals, elites, or majority opinion. They are thus fundamental to modern systems of LIMITED GOVERNMENT. The concept itself is credited to both Charles-Louis MONTESQUIEU and John LOCKE but was substantively developed by James Madison in *The Federalist Papers*. Checks and balances can be instituted in a number of ways; the U.S. Constitution implements at least three: the SEPARATION OF POWERS among the judicial, executive, and legislative branches; the division of state and federal authority, known as FEDERALISM; and the bicameralism visible in the two houses of Congress. Few constitutions since 1791 have employed the principle as freely, primarily because it tends to make concerted government action extremely difficult.

Chicago school of economics A broad tendency of neoclassical economic thought that flourished at and became identified with the economics department of the University of Chicago, initially in the 1930s under Frank Knight, Jacob Viner, and Henry C. Simons, and in later years through the work of Milton FRIEDMAN, George Stigler, Gary BECKER, and W. Allen Wallis. Against interventionist, institutionalist, and redistributive economic thought—most especially KEYNESIANISM—the Chicago school consistently emphasized two principles: the power of neoclassical price theory to explain observed economic behavior and the efficacy of free markets to best allocate resources and distribute income. The major Chicago school theorists posited a minimal role for the state in the regulation of economic activity and advocated strict laissez-faire policies. This work has had a lasting impact on economic and social policy in the United States and around the world.

The Chicago school's general model of economic behavior is based on the assumption that individuals maximize their UTILITY, or well-being, in decisions about the allocation of resources, subject to the constraints of market prices and their disposable means. Much of this work derives from research on RATIONAL EXPECTATIONS by John Muth at Carnegie-Mellon University—work warmly received in Chicago by Robert Lucas and Franco Modigliani. The Chicago school has applied the tools and concepts of price theory and rational expectations to diverse situations, from racial discrimination and crime (Gary Becker) to unionization (H. G. Lewis) to the determinants of political activity (George Stigler). Chicago-trained economists played an active role in international development from the 1960s on—most visibly in Chile, where the "Chicago Boys" implemented market reforms under the Pinochet regime (see NEOCLASSICAL ECONOMICS).

Chicago school of sociology The University of Chicago was the dominant center of American sociology for much of the first half of the twentieth century. It was home to Robert Ezra PARK—the longtime chair of the department—as well as to Ernest Burgess, Louis Wirth, William Ogburn, Everett C. Hughes, Edward Franklin Frazier, George Herbert MEAD, and numerous other influential figures in a wide range of sociological subfields. Chicago's Department of Sociology was the first in the United States (1892), and its members played a major role in the larger institutionalization of American sociology through the creation of the *American Journal of Sociology* (1895) and the founding of the American Sociological Association (1905).

The Chicago school is best known for its pioneering work in urban sociology—especially its research on the diverse forms of social stratification visible in Chicago. Robert Park set a strong example in emphasizing the centrality of fieldwork and the interest of questions of social diversity within the complex city environment. Chicago school sociologists produced groundbreaking work on questions of immigration, race, and social status; occupational and professional issues; and poverty, crime, and delinquency. They pioneered numerous qualitative and quantitative methods, from PARTICIPANT OBSERVATION, to surveys and other statistical data-gathering techniques, to the sector and the zone models of LOCATION THEORY. The Chicago school was strongly marked by philosophical PRAGMATISM and empiricism, especially that of John DEWEY, who was also at the University of Chicago at the turn of the twentieth century. George Mead's SYMBOLIC INTERACTIONISM was the major sociological expression of this tradition—notable for its emphasis on the complex relationships that link language, action, the self, and social roles together in collective social processes.

chiefdom   Usually describes a society that possesses strong distinctions of rank based on KINSHIP, culminating in the position of a chief. These features have played an important role in arguments about cultural evolution, including influential work in the 1960s by the anthropologist Elman Service. Service proposed that the chiefdom represents an evolutionary advance over the informal authority and smaller scale organization of the TRIBE. He also distinguished chiefdoms from STATE societies, which possess greater institutionalization of power. This evolutionary schema implies change in the complexity of the organization of power: unlike state power, the chief's power remains largely undifferentiated and includes political, religious, economic, and military functions. More recent research has tended to emphasize the diversity of these arrangements among various groups and has revised or jettisoned hypotheses of strict linear evolution from tribal authority to chiefdom to state.

Chomsky, Noam   (1928–) The most important linguist of the late twentieth century, Chomsky is also one of the foremost leftist critics of American foreign policy and the news media. His main contribution to LINGUISTICS is the influential "transformative–generative grammar"—an attempt to describe mathematically the syntactical processes common to all human language. Chomsky draws a key distinction between the *deep structure* and *surface structure* of languages. The deep structure, he argues, is not culturally determined (and therefore ultimately arbitrary) but rather "hardwired" in the human brain. It constitutes what he terms a *competence*, a set of dispositions to grammatical formation that underlie the surface diversity of human languages. Some of Chomsky's most interesting examples draw on the relatively uniform process of language acquisition among children and their capacity to extrapolate rules (if often incorrectly) from limited linguistic experience.

Transformative–generative grammar thus seeks to move beyond the strongly culturalist position of structural linguistics (as developed by Ferdinand de SAUSSURE, C. S. PEIRCE, Roman JAKOBSON, and others), which had demonstrated that language was a free-floating structure of signifiers that bore no intrinsic relation to the mental concepts signified. If the major thrust of this work was to reveal language as a relatively arbitrary structure of differentiated signs, Chomsky set out to scientifically describe the ground rules of that structure. Although many of his specific claims and mathematical abstractions have been challenged by subsequent work, some version of transformative–generative grammar underlies virtually all of modern linguistics.

Chomsky's prolific criticism of politics and the mass media bears little relationship to his work in linguistics. In this area, he has repeatedly sought to demonstrate the alignment of media coverage with government and corporate interests (which, Chomsky is quick to point out, include the media companies), especially in the area of foreign policy. His major works in linguistics include *Syntactic Structures* (1957) and *Cartesian Linguistics* (1966). In media and political criticism, his writing includes *Manufacturing Consent* (1968, with Edward Herman) and *Necessary Illusions* (1989).

chorology or chorography   The study of AREAL DIFFERENTIATION, or the differences between areas of the earth. Richard Hartshorne's influential *The Nature of Geography* (1939) made the case that GEOGRAPHY should concern itself primarily with chorology, rather than with the problem of spatial distribution (e.g., of settlements or industries) and their geometric patterns. This programmatic statement, although more nuanced than many later geographers credited, touched off a lengthy and often semantically convoluted debate that pitted emphasis on spatial difference against the more integrated understanding of areal relationships. Researchers in latter camp consolidated around the concept of SPATIAL ANALYSIS.

Christaller, Walter   (1893–1969) A German geographer who produced a number of influential theories about the spatial distribution of economic activity. The most important of these was CENTRAL-PLACE THEORY, which sought to explain the geographical distribution of settlements in a given area. Christaller theorized that settlements tend to develop productive specializations according to geographic criteria (e.g., the type of available land) and that the spatial distribution of those settlements reflects a compromise between the value of the specialization and its access to a centralized market. In short, the more specialized a good, the farther people are willing to travel for it. According to Christaller's criteria, this dictated a central market location for highly specialized goods, which could service a wide area, and a more evenly distributed network of markets for basic goods. This spatial model, in turn, was affected by other factors, such as the tendency to minimize the cost of a transportation infrastructure and the effects of political borders that cut through optimum market areas.

Christaller acknowledged a strong debt to other work on location theory, especially that of Johann Heinrich von Thünen and Alfred WEBER, which similarly stressed questions of distance and available resources. He was somewhat less fortunate, at least initially, in his own readers, who included Nazi settlement planners for eastern Europe. Christaller's work fit poorly into existing academic GEOGRAPHY, and he never had a successful academic career; however, he continued to publish and lived to see his ideas become central to the emerging field of quantitative and spatial geography in the 1960s. His key works remain his doctoral dissertation, "Die zentralen Orte in Süddeutschland" (Places in Central Southern Germany, 1934) and *Die ländliche Siedlungsweise im Deutschen Reich und ihre Beziehungen zur Gemeindeorganization* (1937).

Christian Democracy A twentieth-century political movement that was successful in much of the Roman Catholic world. Christian Democracy was initially proposed in 1891 by Pope Leo XIII, who argued that the Roman Catholic church should compete with, rather than oppose, the rising forces of secular democracy and socialism. While the first Christian Democratic parties that formed around World War I were anticapitalist and center-left, their opposition to socialism and statism eventually made them more conservative. In the post–World War II period, Christian Democrats often became the dominant moderate conservative party in the countries of Western Europe and Latin America, emphasizing both stability and progress; traditional values and MODERNITY; and PLURALISM and anticommunism. By the late twentieth century, however, they tended to operate as ideologically indistinct, catchall parties of the center-right, grouping together a wide range of mostly middle-class constituencies and interests.

circular flow of income Refers to the flow of receipts and payments between domestic firms and domestic households. Money passes from the households to the firms as payment for final goods and services, then from firms to households in the form of salaries and compensation. This simple identity between the money value of the output of firms, household income, and household expenditures provides the basis for NATIONAL INCOME accounting.

circumcision The practice of cutting away the foreskin of the penis of male children. Circumcision is a ubiquitous religious ritual among Muslims and Jews, and a common health-based secular practice in North America and Europe. It is also a rite of passage in some cultures (usually a puberty rite). Female circumcision—the cutting away of the clitoris—is today often called female genital mutilation. It exists almost exclusively in Africa, where it is practiced as a part of several religious traditions and takes a number of forms (all to limit or eliminate sexual sensation for women). The most radical of these, INFIBULATION, involves the removal of the clitoris (and often the labia), and the sewing up of most of the genital area, including some of the vagina. For obvious reasons, female circumcision of all kinds has become a subject of intense debate both inside and outside Africa.

citizenship Generally denotes full membership in a political community, comprising a set of rights and/or political obligations. As originally shaped by the values and experience of ancient Greece, citizenship is defined primarily by forms of individual engagement in the political life of the community, such as voting, eligibility for public office, and participation in militias or the military. Until the rise of modern democracies, therefore, citizenship was a concept with little meaningful content. Persons were, rather, the "subjects" of a king or other sovereign authority.

Citizenship became a prominent political concept in the early modern period with the rise of republicanism, and a dominant concept during the American and French revolutions, as it replaced the logic of political "subjects." In the modern system of NATION-STATES, citizenship has become what Hannah ARENDT called the right to have rights. The question of how to accord and how far to extend these rights has been one of the central features of political struggle in the West, as diverse groups have challenged the exclusionary principles that initially restricted citizenship along lines of property, sex, and, in some cases, race, and as the notion of political rights has been expanded to include new economic and/or social rights. The definition and management of citizenship categories have also been important aspects of the development of the modern STATE, especially as the nation-state asserted its primacy over intermediate political identities and as the state became an increasingly extensive provider and manager of services. With citizenship, then, came a range of complementary categories (and associated forms of administration) that identify those who are not entitled to (or, for diverse reasons, are excluded from) full citizenship rights, variously including aliens, immigrants, natives, minors, the insane, felons, and other groups. Beyond the minimum legal conditions for membership in a polity, citizenship also frequently refers to the extent and quality of actual civic participation.

While systems of citizenship differ in their specifics, there are two main traditions that inform citizenship law in the West: *jus sanguinis*, in which citizenship is determined by that of one or both biological parents, and *jus soli*, where it is determined by one's place of birth. France is the classic example of *jus soli*, Germany—until quite recently—of *jus sanguinis*. Most countries also have some provision for naturalization, whereby immigrants or other non-citizens may apply for citizenship after satisfying a number of conditions. An important area of contemporary citizenship debate surrounds those rights accorded to people who are residents but not citizens of a country. These are sometimes linked to supranational political entities, such as the European Union, or are provided for by specific national law. This has given rise to discussions of transnational citizenship, and to the recognition of multiple citizenships in many countries. See also OBLIGATION, POLITICAL.

city A dense zone of human habitation where economic activity is highly differentiated and primarily nonagricultural in character. The earliest cities were found in the hearth civilizations of the Near East—Egypt, the Indus valley, and Mesopotamia—where they were closely linked to the development of agriculture. Early cities were typically dependent on relations with surrounding rural areas, from which they acquired food and other means of subsistence through

some combination of trade and domination. In the case of early HYDRAULIC SOCIETIES, central cities played a more fundamental role, organizing and administering the complex systems of irrigation on which both rural and urban populations depended.

The emergence of cities is historically related to the development of trade—advantageous locations for trade are one of the most frequent determinants of city location. As populations increased and political systems consolidated, cities became centers of administration and culture—the latter in close relation to the growing division of labor and the concentration of wealth (see CENTER-PERIPHERY AND CORE-PERIPHERY).

Rapid urbanization in the industrializing West during the nineteenth century made cities a distinct object of social reflection and ultimately sociological analysis, most notably by the CHICAGO SCHOOL OF SOCIOLOGY in the early part of the twentieth century. Urban sub-specialties now play a prominent part in all the social sciences. With this increased attention has come an extensive and evolving descriptive vocabulary. Geographers, demographers, sociologists, and other students of urban form draw numerous distinctions among types of cities, forms of administration, and dominant functions. There are *nucleated* cities, with one center, and *polynucleatic* cities, with many; there are commercial, industrial, residential, and capital cities, depending on their primary function; the terms *overbounded* and *underbounded* refer to cities that administer greater or smaller areas, respectively, than their principal zone of settlement. Political distinctions between self-governing and administered cities reflect the range of possible degrees of autonomy enjoyed in matters of administration and decision making. Fully autonomous cities, such as those of ancient Greece, are termed *city-states*. *Cosmomagical cities* are designed to reflect or embody sacred principles, as in many Mesoamerican and early Chinese examples. *Primate cities* are cities that dominate the political, cultural, and economic life of their countries, such as London, Paris, or Mexico City. Increasing attention has been paid recently to the phenomenon of *edge cities*—areas peripheral to major cities that have severed much of their connection to the traditional downtown, becoming independent concentrations of residential, work, and retail activity. Finally, the vast merging of urban settlement in some regions of the world has given rise to the concepts of megalopolis and CONURBATION. See also URBANISM.

civil disobedience   See DISSENT.

civil law   Broadly, law that defines relations between citizens, as opposed to criminal law, which concerns relations between citizens and the state. In English, the concept derives from the French *droit civil* or the German *Zivilrecht*. It also describes the codified legal systems that were derived from Roman law and used in most of continental Europe, as opposed to the COMMON LAW systems of the English-speaking world or other systems of law, such as *shari'a*, the religious law used in much of the Islamic world.

civil religion   Originally used by political philosopher Jean-Jacques ROUSSEAU to designate the restriction of the state's legitimate authority in matters of religion to a few minimal common principles. The phrase is more recently associated with Robert Bellah's account of the quasi-religious dimension of American nationalist sentiment and the transcendental meaning that many Americans accord the national experience (*Beyond Belief*, 1970). It also connotes a denominationally and doctrinally nonspecific expectation of some form of religious participation as a dimension of citizenship.

civil society   A realm of free activity and association that is not organized by the state. The idea of civil society has venerable roots, including the freedoms claimed by medieval cities and the distinction of civil from criminal law (governing relations formed voluntarily among individuals and the claims of society against malefactors, respectively). It entered political philosophy and social theory in the early modern period as a way of describing the capacity for the self-organization of political communities outside the state. If society had such a capacity, then "the people" integrated in that society could better be seen as the source of political LEGITIMACY, rather than merely as the object of rule. In some early uses—notably by the Scottish moralists, including Adam Ferguson and Adam SMITH—the notion of civil society referred to all nonstate capacities for social organization. The free market provided a key example. To these early capitalist thinkers, the self-regulating character of markets demonstrated the possibility for social organization without the direction of the state.

As Charles TAYLOR has argued, however, it is crucial to distinguish two different branches of discourse on civil society. While one branch followed Ferguson and Smith in stressing the economic character of civil society, the other branch followed Charles-Louis MONTESQUIEU, Jean-Jacques ROUSSEAU, and Alexis de TOCQUEVILLE in stressing social relations entered into by autonomous agents. In this conceptualization, civil society is a realm of intermediate associations that stand between the individual and the state. Georg HEGEL and later Karl MARX saw these types of associations as intrinsically partial: civil society was an incomplete, bourgeois achievement, immersed in self-interest and fraught with alienation. It fell short of the full ethical and political integration enjoyed by the ancient Greeks or to be enjoyed in a better constituted future society. Antonio GRAMSCI, however, conceived of civil society as a terrain upon which partial identities were contested and capitalist logics confronted, thus opening a rich vein of neo-Marxist theorizing on civil society, CULTURE, and IDEOLOGY, and preparing the way for critical theory's grounding of a discursive public sphere in civil society (see FRANKFURT SCHOOL). Thinkers of pluralist and communitarian persuasion (see COMMUNITARIANISM) from Tocqueville onward have pointed out that it is in such partial social units as churches, clubs, party precincts, and even bowling leagues that people find the capacity for a collective voice and the possibility of differentiated, directly interpersonal relations. Such intermediate associations are also seen as a crucial defense of distinctive identities imperiled by MASS SOCIETY and of democracy against OLIGARCHY and TOTALITARIANISM.

The concept of civil society has received heightened attention in recent years. The post-1989 discourse on transitions to democracy employed the term to account for the various resources outside direct state control that offered alternatives to the state organization of collective life. Indeed, the slogan "the revival of civil society" was a rallying cry for East European groups that opposed communism in the years leading up to the revolutions of 1989. In both populist and academic discourses, however, the role of more or less self-regulating markets was infrequently distinguished from the roles of networks of interpersonal relations, social movements, and public discourse. A similar ambiguity characterizes the literature on international civil society (see NONGOVERNMENTAL ORGANIZATION). A predominantly nonmarket sense of civil society has played a crucial part in the revival of

COMMUNITARIANISM and in developments in critical theory and theories of the public sphere (see PUBLIC SPHERE AND PRIVATE SPHERE; and SOCIAL CAPITAL).

clans Generally the largest category within a society in which membership is constructed on the basis of descent. Clans typically have a strong corporate identity and often an important social or political function. They can be defined through bilateral descent (descent via both male and female ancestors) or, more commonly, through unilineal descent along either the male line (PATRILINEAL DESCENT) or the female line (MATRILINEAL DESCENT). Clans generally practice EXOGAMY (marriage to a person of another clan).

The term has also been used to describe an assemblage of large groups claiming common descent, which may be organized individually according to different logics. Unlike lineage membership, which is rooted in a network of specific, demonstrable kinship relations, clan membership in this context is understood as the direct membership of the individual in the larger collectivity.

class Commonly refers to large social groups defined by persistent, shared economic conditions, although other shared factors such as prestige, power, or culture can also play determining roles. Class is a central differentiating feature of modern society and has consequently been of enormous interest to social scientists. The most widespread understanding of class derives from Karl MARX's account of society as fundamentally divided between groups that bear different relationships to the *means of production* (such as tools and material resources). Historical eras, Marx argued, are distinguished largely by the dominance of different modes of production, characterized by different primary social divisions: masters and slaves, lords and serfs, and, in the capitalist era, the BOURGEOISIE (or capitalists) and workers (the PROLETARIAT). Marx recognized other classes at the periphery of this basic social division within industrial society—remnants of the ARISTOCRACY and landed gentry, as well as an underclass (the LUMPENPROLETARIAT) that was totally excluded from the relations of production. In Marx's account, consequently, economic criteria hold the determining place, explaining "in the final instance" the particularities of social organization, political power, and cultural forms. His

view has maintained a powerful hold on the concept of class despite both the failure of Marxist expectations of class struggle in the twentieth century and transformations of the dominant forms of labor and ownership.

The Marxist criteria imply that clear, objective class interests follow from an individual's relationship to CAPITAL. The tremendous challenge of achieving broad-based large-scale mobilization on this basis, however, confronted Marx and subsequent Marxists with the dilemmas of class factionalism, insufficiently developed CLASS CONSCIOUSNESS, FALSE CONSCIOUSNESS, reactionary peasant and worker movements, the complex role of intellectuals and other nonworker vanguards, and other sources of diversity and divergent perceived interests.

Part of the difficulty lay in reconciling different forms of power and status with the fundamental test of ownership of capital, as well as the fundamental demand for conformity of interests among different groups. Max WEBER was largely responsible for freeing the analysis of class from these requirements. Weber argued against the notion of strict economic determination of society and for a more flexible understanding of group organization based on multiple, overlapping criteria. Economic criteria remained central to the understanding of class divisions, but he distinguished these from questions of status (or prestige) and political power, which were subject to their own, not always identical, hierarchies. Class, in this sense, referred less to a group's relationship to the means of production than to its ability to successfully control its LIFE CHANCES (access to goods, future prospects, etc.) in the marketplace. This control depended on a variety of factors—income, to be sure, but also status and access to the power of such large organizations as government, corporations, and associations.

A vast amount of scholarship has drawn on Marx and Weber as sources, seeking answers to the failure of Marxist predictions of class development (Georg LUKÁCS and the FRANKFURT SCHOOL) and exploring the contemporary waning of class identity rooted in industrial labor models. André Gorz's *Farewell to the Working Class* (1982) and Alain Touraine's *Post-Industrial Society* (1971) are prominent examples. A large body of American sociology exploited the flexibility of the Weberian model to account for the relative disorganization of class divisions in the United States (see C. Wright MILLS), and even to replace the conventional understanding of class with one based more narrowly on occupation, income, and prestige. Pierre BOURDIEU's work, from this perspective, represents an attempt to find a common measure (SYMBOLIC CAPITAL) for the Weberian divisions of class, status, and political power, as well as a sociological method for evaluating the forms of convertibility that structure them. Recent scholarship, too, has sought to redress the historical neglect of women in class analysis, who as workers in the home were often excluded from consideration except as dependents of their working male partners. The changing place of women in the workforce has fostered and necessitated this change, as have Marxist attempts to reexamine the contemporary possibilities of class struggle.

class consciousness In Marxist analysis, a class is defined by its objective relationship to the means of production, either as workers or owners of capital (the BOURGEOISIE). Nonetheless, Karl MARX argued, such objective conditions only define a class *in-itself*—as a structurally determined object within capitalist society. A class becomes a class *for-itself* (a Hegelian distinction of the active from the passive subject) when it comes to consciousness of the fundamental nature of the capitalist division of society and of the common interests that class members possess in seeing it overthrown. Class consciousness became a central subject of Marxist and revolutionary theory and a principal dividing line between those who held that class polarization and consolidation were inevitable and those (such as Vladimir Ilich LENIN and Mao Tse-tung) who saw a strong need for active class formation and external guidance in the form of the party.

classical economics Refers to the work and assumptions that dominated economic thought from the mid-eighteenth to the mid-nineteenth century. During that period, a group of primarily British economists produced a number of innovative analyses of the production, distribution, and exchange of goods in a market economy. Its principal figures were Adam SMITH, David RICARDO, J. B. Say, John Stuart MILL, Thomas Robert MALTHUS, and Karl MARX (a German in London). The classical economists made a number of basic theoretical innovations that opened the door to modern economic thought. These included the development of the LABOR THEORY OF VALUE, Malthusian population theory, SAY'S LAW, and the quantity theory of money. These propositions were predominantly oriented toward

the issues of economic growth, especially capital accumulation, the expansion of markets, and the DIVISION OF LABOR. Microeconomic problems such as price determination were also subject to close attention for the first time. In contrast to contemporary economic theory, where the same forces (supply, demand, production, and cost functions) determine all prices, the classical economists argued that prices were determined by fixed production and cost coefficients, independent of demand. They argued that real wages were determined by "subsistence requirements" and that the profitability of land was determined by scarcity and fertility. In the classical economic world, profit is simply the residual left after paying for all factors of production (such as labor and tools). In all these instances, the classical economists failed to recognize the role of aggregate demand—an issue that marks one of the major discontinuities with modern economic thought.

In terms of methodology, classical economists can be divided into two camps. Some, such as Smith, followed an inductive method—formulating premises on the basis of EMPIRICISM, deriving empirical laws, reasoning on the basis of those laws, and testing the result against other empirical data. The second group, notably Ricardo, based its reasoning on deductive principles—deducing conclusions from hypothetical premises and making little attempt to verify the results.

Reinterpretations of classical economics form the basis of much modern economic theory, including development economics, GROWTH THEORY, general equilibrium theory, and Sraffan analysis. See also NEOCLASSICAL ECONOMICS.

classification The ways in which human beings organize perception, experience, and social life by making distinctions, recognizing commonalities, and naming. The centrality of these activities is basic to the arguments that philosophical idealists posed against radical EMPIRICISM, in holding that knowledge is based not only on induction but also on the human capacity to give order to sensory impressions and to the world itself. Immanuel KANT held classification to be grounded in inherent categories of mind, such as a grasp of spatial relationships and temporal sequence. Emile DURKHEIM and Marcel MAUSS famously argued that even the most basic categories of classification are not innate but products of society. Accordingly, systems of classification and knowledge vary across societies, although some of the most basic categories seem, according to Durkheim, to be reflections of the experience of society as such. Claude LÉVI-STRAUSS took up the latter argument, drawing on linguistics and suggesting that certain basic classificatory oppositions lie at the root of social organization. For Lévi-Strauss, classification does not simply reflect society but helps to create it. Pierre BOURDIEU added to this argument the notion that struggle over classification constitutes a basic social process. Classification is an exercise of power as well as a basis for knowledge, he contends, and people struggle both individually and in groups to remake systems of classification (through usually without a view of the operations of any system as a whole). Here Bourdieu's argument is close to that of Michel FOUCAULT, although distinguished by a greater emphasis on the positive achievements of struggles over classification (e.g., in the creation of new fields of knowledge and social action) rather than on simple resistance to classificatory power.

Cognitive anthropology has approached classification from the opposite direction, seeking universal structures of cognition as the underpinning of both classification in general and cross-cultural variations in particular. Much of this work has focused on conceptual differentiation within specific fields, such as KINSHIP or color terminology. It is part also of the more interdisciplinary development of cognitive studies, which shares Kant's presumption of universal structure of mind, but seeks a more empirical basis in psychology and neurology.

class struggle   In MARXISM, class struggle is the driving force of history, transforming social relations in response to oppression on the one hand and opportunities created by new forces of production on the other. Class struggle, in these terms, reflects the structural tension between those on opposite sides of the means of production—in Karl MARX's analysis, the BOURGEOISIE (or capitalist class) on one side and the PROLETARIAT (or workers) on the other. Just as the earlier struggle between the aristocracy and the bourgeoisie led to the emergence of CAPITALISM, the contemporary struggle between the bourgeoisie and the proletariat leads, classical Marxism held, to the establishment of SOCIALISM. Modern sociological work on class (and even some of Marx's work), however, generally recognizes the complexity and diversity of class positions, and consequently the difficulty of making broad generalizations about class struggle—although

in some Marxist circles efforts continue to reconstruct viable contemporary models of class identity.

clay-clay   Describes production technology that does not permit the capital-to-labor ratio in production to be varied, either before or after investment is carried out. On the opposite end of the spectrum is *putty-putty* technology, which allows the capital-to-labor ratio to be continuously reshaped both before and after the actual investment. Putty-clay technology is a compromise between perfect substitutability and fixed coefficients. This allows substitution between labor and capital before investment is carried out but not after the machines have been installed.

cleavage   Deep and persistent differences of political opinion and behavior within a polity, most commonly along lines of class, religion, language, nationality, ethnicity, and/or gender. Many political scientists, such as Seymour Martin LIPSET and Stein Rokkan, argue that the stability of democratic regimes often depends on salient, crosscutting cleavages—where individuals' various memberships and identifications with groups create cross-allegiances to different political positions or support for catchall, large political parties. When cleavages are reinforcing rather than crosscutting, the probability of mass conflict and political instability increases. Arend Lijphart, drawing on observations of cooperation and accommodation between elites in Europe, argued for CONSOCIATIONALISM as a means of overcoming the politically disintegrative tendencies of reinforcing cleavages. See also ALIGNMENT.

clientalism   A political system based, usually informally, on the ability of political leaders (patrons or "bosses") to provide jobs, local investment, or services for their supporters (clients). Unlike corruption, *clientalism* is not necessarily negative and describes a durable system of relations. It is typical of democracies in which the formal, bureaucratic political apparatus is relatively underdeveloped. Clientalism is most often associated with the urban "machine politics" of the Gilded Age in the United States or with Southern Italian politics, but it can often be found in traditional, colonial, and transitional societies as well.

cliometrics   A set of methods that uses advanced statistical analysis and econometrics to study historical problems. It is also known as "new economic history" or "econometric history." Much of the work in cliometrics has relied on *counterfactual* speculation—a technique familiar to economists but generally eschewed by historians. For instance, in studying the role of railroads in nineteenth-century America, Robert Fogel and Albert Fishlow speculated on what would have happened to the American economy if the railroads had not been built. They attempted to measure the difference between the actual rail costs and the hypothetical costs of a rail-less economy. Other cliometricians rely on large scale quantitative data collection and analysis—again in contrast to traditional narrative history.

closure or cloture A mechanism for ending debate on a particular matter in a LEGISLATURE, typically by majority vote. Closure rules developed in most Western systems in the late nineteenth century, in response to the prevalence of filibusters and other forms of parliamentary obstruction.

coalition government A government formed by the cooperation of two or more parliamentary parties. Coalition governments are rare in two-party and plurality electoral systems, but common in systems that use proportional representation (see PARTY SYSTEM; and ELECTORAL SYSTEM). Under special circumstances, such as when no party wins a convincing plurality of votes or if a gesture of united national purpose is felt to be needed, major parties sometimes form a "grand coalition." Coalition theory, first developed by William RIKER in *The Theory of Political Coalitions* (1962), attempts to apply the methods of game theory to coalition building. Its most enduring hypothesis is that the smallest necessary majority will be the likeliest result.

coalition theory See COALITION GOVERNMENT.

Coase, Ronald (1910–) An economist who innovated in a number of areas, including the study of TRANSACTION COSTS, the purpose of firms, the role of EXTERNALITIES such as pollution, and the relationship between social and private costs. The last is the subject of the COASE THEOREM, which holds that in the absence of transaction costs, private and social costs are equal. Among other well-known inquiries, Coase has asked why firms exist—why their internal operations are not organized by markets instead. The answer lies, he argued, in

the reductions of transaction costs that can be achieved by relying on direction from managers rather than markets. This raises the further question of how to assess this efficiency (a theme pursued by Oliver Williamson and some of Coase's followers).

A strong proponent of the free market, Coase contributed to the emergence of the LAW AND ECONOMICS MOVEMENT, which is concerned with predicting the efficiency of legislation and regulation. Coase was also a critic of mathematical economics, and he argued that the field had become too abstracted from the real behavior of markets and economic actors. He attributed many of his own theoretical insights to his first-hand observation of firms and he refused to couch his theories in numbers or logical notation. Coase spent most of his career at the University of Chicago.

Coase theorem Ronald COASE first articulated his "theorem" in "The Problem of Social Cost" (1960), which addressed the possibility of privately negotiated solutions to the market inefficiencies that result when economic activities affect third parties (market externalities). The Coarse theorem holds that if property rights (to pollute, or to clean water) are well established and if there are no barriers to private negotiation (zero transaction costs), then the parties involved will be able to negotiate a Pareto-improving trade, in which some people benefit and none suffer a loss in welfare. The key insight was not that property rights could be traded in a market environment but that an efficient outcome could be had regardless of the party to whom the property rights were assigned. For example, assigning a smoker the right to smoke in public places leaves the burden to offer compensation for a smoke-free environment on the nonsmoker. If it is worth more to the nonsmoker to be smoke-free than to the smoker to smoke, there is room for welfare-improving trade (e.g., a payment to the smoker not to smoke). Coase's theorem showed that it is equally efficient for nonsmokers to be given a right to smoke-free public spaces, leaving smokers to offer compensation in order to smoke (the offer would have no takers if, as assumed above, the value is greater to the nonsmoker). Thus the designation of property rights has distributive consequences but should not have efficiency consequences—both situations result in a smoke-free public space. For these welfare-improving transactions to occur at all, and therefore produce efficient outcomes, the costs of negotiation must be minimal. The higher the barriers to trade, the greater the impact of the initial designation of property rights on the outcome. The Coase theorem also highlights the imperative that property rights be well-defined—an insight that has underwritten the extension of property rights to new domains, such as the establishment of tradable pollution permits to solve environmental externalities. See also PROPERTY AND PROPERTY RIGHTS.

Cobb–Douglas function   A special case of the CES PRODUCTION FUNCTION, the Cobb–Douglas function is the most common form of production and utility functions. It owes its popularity to the exceptional ease with which it can be manipulated and to the fact that it possesses the minimum properties that economists consider necessary to derive reasonable implications about the behavior of economic agents. The Cobb–Douglas utility function is based on the empirical observation that individuals spend a constant fraction of their income on items like food and clothing. A Cobb–Douglas production function implies that marginal products of labor (or capital) are positive and exhibit diminishing returns as more labor (or capital) is used.

cobweb theorem   Developed to explain persistent fluctuations in certain agricultural markets—a problem that attracted the attention of economists in the 1930s. In its simplest form, the model holds that the supply of a good in a given year is a function of the price in the previous year, but that demand is related to current prices. In other words, there is a lag in the supply side of the market. Depending on the elasticities of the demand and supply functions, the model can generate fluctuating prices that may either converge on the equilibrium price, oscillate around the equilibrium price, or exhibit explosive and increasing fluctuations with time. In the last instance, price and output fluctuates in what is termed a *cobweb cycle*, so called because of the uneven outline of a graph of prices. At the time, estimates of supply and demand elasticities suggested that agricultural markets had a strong tendency toward explosive price behavior, but long-term observations of price cycles in agricultural markets have not generally supported this conclusion.

code switching   One of the forms of linguistic variation studied within SOCIOLINGUISTICS. Code switching describes the shift from one linguistic style (or code) to another, as dictated by social circumstances. Selectively dropping a dialect in favor of an official or mainstream linguistic style is a common example.

co-determination   The joint management of business enterprises by owners and labor unions. Co-determination is most strongly associated with Germany, where union participation is required by law in certain industries, but similar arrangements exist in many advanced industrial countries. See also CORPORATISM.

cognates   Persons related through a secondary line of descent or kinship, either male or female. This is distinguished from a primary agnatic line, in which descent passes only through the male line. Cognatic descent, in such cases, generally refers to the mother's family, to which an individual may be recognized as connected, without the full significance of membership in the father's family. See also AGNATES; and KINSHIP.

cognitive anthropology   Concerns itself with the search for patterns and variations in human cognition from one culture to another. It emerged as a distinct subfield in the 1950s with the development of techniques of COMPONENTIAL ANALYSIS, which enabled researchers to map systems of CLASSIFICATION across different cultures. Such work has argued for revision of the notion, derived from Franz BOAS, that while the structure of human perception was universal, the cultural forms that interpreted perception were highly variable, and that individual cognition largely reflected this variability (a position also known as the SAPIR-WHORF HYPOTHESIS). Cognitive anthropology has shown, rather, that certain patterns of cognition are widespread, if not universal. The best-known example of this type of work is Brent Berlin and Paul Kay's *Basic Color Terms* (1969), which demonstrated striking regularities in the classification of colors across cultures. Similar work has been done with respect to other classificatory schemes: plants, animals, diseases, subsistence techniques, and kinship relations. Particularly in its early phase, this work was known as ETHNOSCIENCE and later as ethnographic semantics.

More recently, cognitive anthropology has expanded into a range of other, less easily schematized forms of cognition, for example, the study of systems of logic and sense in different cultures (known as DISCOURSE ANALYSIS), the study of how consensus develops and spreads, and the analysis of patterns in folk tales and myths.

It has also become linked to interdisciplinary cognitive science, drawing on neurology and related brain research, and increasingly uses techniques of computer modeling.

cognitive dissonance The state of tension or displeasure that follows from the experience of contradictory or difficult to reconcile beliefs, perceptions, or thoughts—in short, cognitions. In such cases, according to most versions of cognitive dissonance theory, the least resistant cognition is sacrificed or modified in order to relieve cognitive stress. First elaborated by social psychologists Leon Festinger and J. M. Carlsmith in *A Theory of Cognitive Dissonance* (1957), the concept has become a research subfield unto itself and has had a significant influence on other fields. Fredric Jameson's concept of *cognitive mapping*, developed in his analysis of the disorienting and fragmented character of postmodern experience, draws upon a similar assumption that people work to overcome inconsistencies.

There are several distinct theories in social psychology that share the underlying principles of cognitive dissonance theory but that vary slightly regarding the source or consequences of the inconsistency. These include Fritz Heider's BALANCE THEORY, Theodore Newcomb's symmetry model, M. J. Rosenberg's affective cognitive consistency theory, Charles Osgood and Percy Tannenbaum's congruity principle, and Milton Rokeach's Values-Attitudes-Behavior model.

cohort Any group of persons defined by a common, time-specific situation, such as college entrance or retirement. Birth cohorts refer specifically to people born in the same year, or within a small number of consecutive years; the *baby boomers*, born in the years following the end of World War II, are a prominent example. By virtue of their common situation, members of a cohort will respond to many of life's experiences in similar ways. This has made cohorts a frequent subject of sociological interest, although disagreements abound about the degree to which generalizations about cohort behavior hold true (c.f. Karl MANNHEIM).

Cohort analysis is generally distinguished from age or LONGITUDINAL ANALYSIS, which studies changes related to aging, such as patterns of childbirth.

Cold War Sustained competition and conflict between states that stop short of major military confrontation. In practice, the term is used almost exclusively to refer to the standoff between the United States and the Soviet Union in the post–World War II era. This rivalry took place on several levels: ideology; economic competition; a massive conventional and nuclear ARMS RACE; and proxy wars and other "limited" military conflicts in client states.

Two views of the origins of the Cold War have been prominent in academic discussions. *Traditionalists* place the onus for the Cold War on the Soviet Union and its expansion into Eastern Europe. In the face of this aggression—and in the light of calls for worldwide communist revolution—traditionalists hold that U.S. foreign-policy leaders were forced to abandon their isolationist tendencies. By 1947, they had responded with the Truman Doctrine, which announced U.S. intentions to counter communist insurgencies around the world, and the Marshall Plan, which provided massive relief to war-torn (and potentially Left-leaning) European allies. This was the "official" U.S. version of Cold War history, written by diverse participants and scholars from George Keenan to Jean Kirkpatrick to, more recently, Stephen Ambrose.

Revisionist accounts emerged in the wake of the Vietnam War, in the context of a larger questioning of the U.S. role in world affairs. These assigned more responsibility for the Cold War to the United States and cited a range of U.S. efforts to isolate and confront the Soviet Union well before the end of World War II. From this perspective, the Soviet Union's occupation of Eastern Europe had a defensive rationale as an attempt to avoid encirclement by the United States and its allies. Some post-Soviet Russian scholarship supports this account of Soviet perceptions. Many scholars now speak of a more nuanced "post-revisionist" moment in Cold War scholarship, less interested in choosing sides than in contextualizing U.S. and Soviet actions and perspectives.

At the peak of the Cold War, relations between the United States and the Soviet Union approached direct warfare. In 1962, the United States responded to the installation of nuclear missiles in Cuba with a naval blockade—a game of brinksmanship that brought the world close to nuclear war. Over the next decade and a half, the two antagonists pursued a less direct form of competition characterized by DETERRENCE and CONTAINMENT. This entailed conflicts in peripheral zones and client states—most prominently in Vietnam (1959–1976) and in Afghanistan (1979–1989).

For the United States, the Cold War brought a definitive end to its episodic commitment to isolationism. (In 1938, the United States was without military alliances and had no troops stationed in non-U.S. territory; by 1989, military alliances were in effect with 50 countries, and 1.5 million U.S. troops were posted in 117 countries.) It also institutionalized the wartime commitment to a huge MILITARY-INDUSTRIAL COMPLEX.

In the Soviet Union, the arms race arguably hastened its economic decline, leading to complete disintegration in 1991. Many scholars, however, date the end of the Cold War to 1989, when the East German communist regime collapsed and the Cold War partition of Germany came to an end.

The Cold War had a variety of collateral impacts on the social sciences. Defense dollars shaped the growth of AREA STUDIES into a field devoted to "national security concerns." They underwrote the growth of universities, laboratories, institutes, and "think tanks." More narrowly, they sponsored the development of mathematical modeling and other formal techniques of analysis.

Coleman, James S.   (1926–1995) A prominent American sociologist who shaped much of the debate over public education, achievement, and inequality in the 1960s and 1970s. He was a leading figure in the use of computers and the development of mathematical sociology, as well as one of the key developers of RATIONAL-CHOICE THEORY within SOCIOLOGY.

Coleman was educated as a chemist and initially employed in that field; he turned to sociology in his mid-twenties, enrolling at Columbia University and working closely there with Robert K. MERTON, Paul LAZARSFELD, and Seymour Martin LIPSET. Coleman's early research dealt primarily with adolescent subcultures and related issues of educational achievement—most prominently in *The Adolescent Society* (1961). His growing reputation in that area earned him the leading role in a major government study of educational inequality, ultimately published as *Equality of Educational Opportunity* (1966), but known more generally as the Coleman Report. Coleman concluded—very controversially—that educational achievement depended more on the home environment than on the level of school funding; this ran counter to much of the current thinking about educational opportunity and reform. His conclusions, however, have earned greater acceptance over time.

Throughout the 1970s and 1980s, Coleman continued his empirical research on youth culture and passages to maturity, with particular attention to peer-group subcultures and conflicts with the institutionalized goals of the educational system—*Youth: Transition to Adulthood* (1973) and *Becoming Adult in a Changing Society* (1985) are the principal examples. *High School Achievement* (1982) and *Public and Private High Schools* (1987) further examined the role of schools on the development and education of children; they demonstrated Coleman's continued concern with the importance of external factors on scholastic achievement, such as family, community, and religion.

Coleman also contributed to the study of processes of collective decision making and collective action in *Introduction to Mathematical Society* (1964) and *The Mathematics of Collective Action* (1973); these showed a strong interest in the formal analysis of basic social processes. His late work—especially *Foundations of Social Theory* (1990)—developed a rational-choice approach to understanding individual and collective behavior, and to overcoming the divide between theoretical and empirical work. *Foundations* has proved to be an influential, if also controversial, entrant into debates about the virtues and limitations of rational-choice theory. Among the most comprehensive and wide-reaching studies in the field, it is perhaps best known for its arguments on the origins of NORMS.

Coleman's research touched a number of other areas, including an early contribution to Lipset's *Union Democracy* (1956), the monographs *Community Conflict* (1957) and *Medical Innovation* (1966), and studies of games as tools for socialization, again primarily in education. Coleman was a prolific author of some twenty-eight books and three hundred articles. He led the Johns Hopkins University sociology department in a particularly creative and influential phase and was connected for much of his later career with the University of Chicago. He also served as president of the American Sociological Association in 1991–1992.

collective-action problem   Occurs in situations in which the uncoordinated action of individuals is less beneficial or efficient than coordinated action. This becomes a problem for rational choice–based approaches when self-interested individuals fail to choose beneficial coordinated action. Collective-action problems often arise in relation to PUBLIC GOODS, which attract FREE RIDERS who do not contribute to production or conservation of the goods. These persons are, in a limited way, acting rationally in their self-interest. They can, however, hamper the ability of interest groups and social movements to organize sufficient numbers of people to attain the good in question, thereby undermining the whole. A wide variety of political problems can be restated as collective-action problems; GAME THEORY, RATIONAL-CHOICE THEORY, and social choice paradigms have all contributed to this area of research. Mancur OLSON's *The Logic of Collective Action* (1965) pioneered a number of these approaches by showing under what formal conditions actors were more or less likely to cooperate. Small groups and short-term problems are more likely to lead to cooperation; less cooperation can be expected from those with limited resources, because of the higher relative costs of participation. Olson also proposed that groups succeed, in part, by offering members selective incentives beyond the goals of the group itself, such as the satisfactions of solidarity or participation in festive public events. Collective action is usually defined as an organized, self-conscious, and relatively nonroutine response to events and shared interests. See also SOCIAL MOVEMENTS; COLLECTIVE BEHAVIOR.

collective bargaining Refers to the variety of methods used to regulate the relationship between employers and representatives of employees, who act as agents for the larger body of workers. The distinctive feature of collective bargaining is that it clearly acknowledges and structures the role of LABOR UNIONS. Although it can encompass any aspect of the management–labor relation, collective bargaining most commonly addresses issues of pay and working conditions. Because collective bargaining replaces individual or *ad hoc* contract arrangements, such agreements are generally binding upon all employees. The relative bargaining power of the two parties depends on a range of factors, including the place of the firm in its respective product market, the nature of the labor market, and the space of action permitted to management and labor by the state.

collective behavior The way people congregate and behave in groups—especially in crowds, mobs, and riots but also extending to fads, rumors, panics, mass publics, and the emergence of organized social movements. Collective behavior has been a prominent subject of research in SOCIOLOGY and SOCIAL PSYCHOLOGY. Crowds and mobs have also played an important role in

democratic political thought, inasmuch as they have always been one of the chief outlets of political and social discontent. Mobs have been celebrated by some as a form of direct democracy, but feared by others—especially by many of the liberal thinkers of the late eighteenth and nineteenth centuries, who viewed mobs as a threat to the social order. The first major examination of the dynamics of crowd behavior was Gustave LE BON's *The Crowd: A Study of the Popular Mind* (1895). Le Bon set the tone for several decades of research by emphasizing the way that crowds submerge individual identity into the "collective mind" and incite primitive, destructive, and antisocial feelings that are normally suppressed in social life. He also discussed the process of *social contagion*, through which information or sentiments spread from one person to the next.

The sociologist Herbert Blumer sought to account for the obvious differences between types of crowds, based on the different occasions and different ends that motivate them. Blumer differentiated four types: *casual crowds*, which form spontaneously when something unusual occurs, such as a fire; *conventional crowds*, which gather for a specific purpose and follow relatively clear norms of behavior, such as audiences and sporting-event publics; *expressive crowds*, which are characterized by intense feeling that itself becomes the goal of the members, as at religious revivals or rock concerts; and *action crowds*, which include angry mobs. Action crowds, Blumer noted, are motivated primarily by indignation, anger, and a desire for rapid protest or redress ("Collective Behavior," 1939). Blumer also revised Le Bon's theory of social contagion to account for the phenomenon of mass hysteria on the part of dispersed publics. The capacity of the media to mobilize and, in many instances, create such collective phenomena has also been a subject of considerable attention.

Neil J. SMELSER made one of the most influential contributions to this field with *Theory of Collective Behavior* (1963). He stressed three features of collective behavior: the role of *structural conduciveness*, or the economic and social conditions that legitimate collective and potentially extralegal behavior; *precipitating factors*, which crystallize collective sentiment, as in the case of the police beating that preceded the Los Angeles riots in 1992; and the *counteraction* by forces of SOCIAL CONTROL. More recent research into collective behavior has broadly challenged the assumption that mobs and rioters are fundamentally irrational and unorganized. Some of this work has focused on the process of decision making and the emergence of provisional norms in crowd contexts (see Ralph Turner and Lewis Killian, *Collective Behavior*, 1972). These also emphasize goal-directed rational action and argue that crowds (and more sustained movements) usually act reasonably in accord with particular objectives, resources, and opportunities.

collective consciousness The English translation of Emile DURKHEIM's term *conscience collective*, which he defined in *The Division of Labor in Society* (1893) as "the set of beliefs and sentiments common to the average members of a single society." In French, however, the word *conscience* refers to both "consciousness" and to "conscience"; thus the *conscience collective* relates to both the cognitive and moral dimensions of experience. Durkheim called specific instances or aspects of the collective consciousness *collective representations*. The concept plays a role in Durkheim's account of the emerging division of labor in modern societies, described in part by the transition from MECHANICAL SOLIDARITY to ORGANIC SOLIDARITY as the dominant social bond. Collective consciousness, Durkheim argued, is a far more significant determinant of individual behavior where mechanical solidarity is the norm—reflecting in part the absence of a strong social basis for INDIVIDUALISM.

collective consumption Refers to education, mass transportation, and other "collectively consumed" goods that are typically provided by the state. The concept was introduced by the urban sociologist Manuel Castells in his analysis of the role of the state in the modern reproduction of the labor force—especially in areas that private capital considers too unprofitable to service (*The Urban Question*, [1972] 1977). Although not precisely equivalent, it is similar to the economic concept of *collective goods*.

collective security A structure of international relations among states that assures the security of each through the potential for collective action by the international community, especially in cases of aggression or war. Collective security represents a departure from traditional mechanisms of international security, such as the BALANCE OF POWER. It is typically implemented through such institutions as the United Nations Security Council. Broad

collective-security arrangements face considerable challenges from the multiplicity of interests inherent in a heterogeneous international community. On this basis, advocates of the "realist" tendency in international relations are pessimistic about their effectiveness and think that peace is better maintained through traditional or regional alliances or through the maintenance of a balance of power among dominant states. Those of the "liberal" school are somewhat more sanguine about the creation of durable international regimes under certain circumstances. See also INTERNATIONAL RELATIONS; and REALISM.

collective unconscious The psychologist Carl Gustav JUNG distinguished between the *personal unconscious*, formed through the repression of the impulses, experiences, and wishes of daily life, and the *collective unconscious* of deep-seated, inherited personality structures—in Jung's view a kind of "racial memory"—that reproduced age-old life patterns and forms of behavior. For Jung, the collective unconscious is composed of *archetypes*—basic situational, behavioral, and imaginative elements that provide the continuity of human existence. These are represented in condensed form, he argued, in mythology and religion.

collectivism A political or moral principle that asserts the priority of the group over the individual. The term was originally associated with the late-nineteenth-century anarchism of Mikhail BAKUNIN, who advocated a society based on *collectives*—small, self-governing communities that hold property in common (see ANARCHY AND ANARCHISM). Since that time, collectivism has come to refer to any political movement or policy that tends to place the good of the community and communal bonds over personal freedom. In the sphere of property arrangements, collectivism entails state or group ownership and management of the means of production, particularly land. The former Soviet Union, China, Cuba, Yugoslavia, and Israel have all relied on collectives as productive enterprises, with varying degrees of success. See also COOPERATIVES.

collectivization The appropriation and consolidation of private property by the state—most notably in relation to agriculture. Collectivization, in this context, is often associated with the disastrous policies of the Soviet Union in the late

1920s and the 1930s, where it resulted in famine and the deaths of millions of peasants. See also COLLECTIVISM.

collusion The coordination of economic activities (or strategies) by individuals, firms, or actors, usually in the context of collective agreements. See also CARTELS.

colonialism A system of control, exploitation, and occupation of one territory or country by another. While often used interchangeably with *imperialism*, colonialism differs in emphasis: since the ancient Roman *colonia*, or "estate," colonial rule has usually been associated with settlement of a dominated territory, whereas imperialism simply connotes rule *per se*. The colonial period or "Age of Empire" refers to the European conquest and domination of much of the rest of the world between the early sixteenth and the mid-twentieth century. Colonial practices varied widely, from plunder (the Iberian conquest of the Americas), to elaborate extractive bureaucracies (British India and Africa), to the displacement and/or destruction of the original inhabitants and imitation of the mother country (North America and Australia/New Zealand), to attempted integration with the mother country (French Algeria and most of the territories annexed by Russia).

Much of the colonial system was dismantled by the mid-1960s, but the colonial period has two noteworthy legacies. First, most former colonies remain poorer than the advanced capitalist West and are often under the economic and political domination of the former imperial powers, a situation often described as "neocolonialism." Second, colonialism had enormous effects on both the dominant and dominated cultures and polities, resulting in large-scale cultural diffusion and SYNCRETISM, and important patterns of MIGRATION toward the colonial powers. See also DIFFUSION AND DIFFUSIONISM; IMPERIALISM AND EMPIRE; and POSTCOLONIALISM.

commensality The practice of eating together, often strongly defined by societal rules and conventions.

commercial policy The policy rules adopted by a particular country to regulate its foreign trade, usually consisting of some combination of tariffs, subsidies, quotas, and exchange controls. Commercial policy generally operates between the extremes of strict free trade, which implies no restrictions on the importation or exportation

of goods, and AUTARKY, or complete economic autonomy and isolation from international trade.

commodities See GOOD.

commodity fetishism A commodity is a product of human LABOR that is entered into a relationship of exchange. *Commodity fetishism* is the term that Karl MARX used to designate the way that the dominance of exchange relationships in capitalist society destroys people's sense of the world as the product of their own labor. Since in capitalist society almost all dimensions of human productivity are mediated through exchange, Marx argued, including not only the purchase of goods but the sale of one's labor, the material world comes to be perceived as independent of human labor—as a set of relationships between things rather than persons. The abstract workings of the market, rather than the concrete relationships between persons, become the locus of agency in human affairs. For Marx, this represents a major mystification of the relationships of production; one of the principal goals of communist society was to restore this sense of productive connection to the material world. See also GOOD; and MARXISM.

common law Law based on judicial decisions rather than on statutes written by a LEGISLATURE. The term also refers to the legal systems of Britain and the United States, as opposed to the Roman-derived civil-law regimes of continental Europe. Common law is, for the most part, uncodified and depends on a history of precedent and custom dating back to medieval England. While judicial precedent continues to drive legal rulings in Anglo-associated countries, statute-derived law is gaining ground in such key areas as administrative, commercial, and criminal law.

common-property rights As distinct from private property rights, common-property rights imply no exclusive use, no right of transfer, and, in the limit case, no net gain of income. This last condition follows from an economic proposition termed the *dissipation of rent*, which holds that in the absence of exclusive-use rights (i.e., private property rights), competition among individuals will reduce the rental value or net worth of the property to zero.

Typical examples of property subject to common-property rights include public beaches, marine fisheries, and common grazing grounds for cattle. Here, the dissipation of rent implies that excessive use of the common resource may have deleterious effects. Such a situation is referred to as the "tragedy of commons." As a result, common property is usually regulated to ensure the long-term viability of the resource. See also PROPERTY AND PROPERTY RIGHTS.

Commons, John R. (1862–1945) A sociologist, historian, and economist interested primarily in the labor movement and the role of institutions. The starting point of Commons's analysis was the conflict of interest between different groups in society—principally the producers and consumers of wealth. Commons divided these groups into classes that engage in collective action according to their particular interests. Their differences generate conflict but also an eventual harmony of interests, which underlies the fragile social order.

Commons spent most of his career at the University of Wisconsin. He became active in progressive politics and wrote legislation for workers' compensation, unemployment benefits, and the regulation of utilities. He also played a role in resolving labor disputes through collective bargaining and undertook a major history of the labor movement, *History of Labor in the United States* (1918).

Commons defined institutions as structures of collective action that formed to overcome the weakness of individual action. The government, Commons argued, has a role in recognizing the sovereignty of these collective bodies, mediating among them, and working to regulate and direct their behavior at the individual and group level. Commons's belief in institutions as the basic vehicle of social and economic power led him to defend LABOR UNIONS as a means of expressing the collective will of workers. Much against the prevailing sentiment about the limits of government action, Commons suggested that the state step in to protect the property rights of workers and their right to bargain, just as it protects the property rights of businesses.

Commons' radical tendencies were controversial and cost him his position at several universities. In addition, his work was overshadowed by that of Thorstein VEBLEN, a contemporary who pursued a number of similar interests. Nonetheless, Commons was ahead of his time in many regards; his progressivism, particularly in relation to property rights, eventually became the norm, as did much of his work on state regulation and intervention. His major publications include *Legal Foundations of Capitalism* (1924), *Institutional Economics* (1934), and an autobiography, *Myself* (1934).

commonsense knowledge A key concept in Alfred SCHUTZ's phenomenological sociology. Commonsense knowledge refers to the level of practical, routine, naturalized knowledge that underlies everyday activity. A distinction between commonsense and theoretical or sociological knowledge is basic to much sociological inquiry and is at stake in certain Marxist debates over ideological forms of knowledge and the role of intellectuals in securing popular support for radical struggles (see Antonio GRAMSCI).

communalism Common usage refers to the practices of a COMMUNE. The term also describes a political system in which each ethnic, linguistic, or religious community is represented separately—synonymous, in this respect, with CONSOCIATIONALISM. A third and common usage refers to the tendency of people to identify primarily with their own community, regardless of the political structure. In this context, communalism is most frequently applied to the rise of religious or ethnic movements in India and to ethnonationalism in the recently independent republics of the former Soviet Union, where it is associated with SEPARATISM or with intolerance toward other groups.

commune Generally, a group of people larger than a family who live together and hold productive property in common. Communes take many forms, from the Israeli *kibbutz* to traditional village organizations in many parts of the world. In France and in some of its former colonies, the term refers to the smallest unit of local government. "The Commune" also denotes the Revolutionary government of Paris from 1792 to 1794, and more famously, the radical government that gained control of Paris during the Franco-Prussian War of 1870–1871.

communicative action A key concept in Jürgen HABERMAS's work on discursive ethics and the public sphere, communicative action is oriented toward reflective understanding and the creation of social relations—as distinct from *instrumental action*, which is guided by an efficiency principle and embodied in the integrated, large-scale systems of the economy and state (see PUBLIC SPHERE AND PRIVATE SPHERE). Communicative action is basic to the realm of everyday social life that Habermas calls the LIFE-WORLD, in which social relations are guided by mutual understanding. For Habermas, clarifying the structures of communicative action requires the development of a *universal pragmatics*—an account of the basic structures of human linguistic competencies. This would identify the set of validity claims or normative presuppositions inherent in all speech (e.g., truthfulness), which are, in turn, the bases for both concrete attempts to improve understanding and for larger hope that improved communicative competencies will lead to better social organization. For this to happen, Habermas argues, life-world organization through communicative action must resist "colonization" by systems based on the nonlinguistic steering media of money and POWER. This can be accomplished partly through reliance on highly specialized communicative action in the legal realm and partly through the reinvigoration of genuine political discourse, understood as a process of unimpeded consensus formation or "communicatively achieved understanding." See Habermas's *Theory of Communicative Action* (vol. 1, 1984; vol. 2, 1987).

communism A form of social organization in which property is held in common. Communism was a relatively common feature of premodern agricultural societies and represented a particular solution to limits of technology and social complexity. This is often termed *primitive communism*. Communism figures prominently in the Western tradition as an explicit alternative to private ownership, dating back to Plato's proposal that the ruling class share property as a way of ensuring public-spiritedness. Communism has been practiced by a variety of groups since then, including early Christian communities that sought to cultivate selflessness and devotion to God.

Since the 1840s, communism has been primarily associated with MARXISM, although Karl MARX himself had relatively little to say about the nature of an eventual communist society. Nonetheless, in *The Communist Manifesto* (1848), Marx and Friedrich Engels outlined a communist future of universal freedom and equality, underwritten by shared control of the means of production. This was an explicitly forward-looking communism—distinct from nostalgic, pastoral visions. It incorporated and depended upon industrialism and the political and social achievements of bourgeois society.

Marx and Engels's assertion that the "specter" of communism haunted Europe proved premature in 1848 but increasingly valid as the nineteenth century drew to a close. Revolutionary

movements were coordinated through a series of international congresses—the "Internationals"—the first in 1864, the second in 1889, and the third in 1919. Until the Bolshevik revolution in Russia in 1917, the term *socialism* was used interchangeably with and often in preference to communism—partly reflecting divergences of opinion among revolutionaries, reform-minded socialists, and anarchists of different stripes. These divisions undermined organizing efforts and were responsible for the dissolution of the First International. The Third International, or Comintern, followed the Bolshevik victory and definitively severed relations with reformist and less radical socialist movements. Henceforth, communism was associated primarily with the revolutionary program of the Marxist–Leninist Communist parties.

In practice, communism—or "actually existing socialism," as it came to be known among Western socialists—loosely resembled Marx's transitional stage to communism, characterized by the "dictatorship of the proletariat." After a brief period of experiments in local control, productive property was seized and centrally managed by the state. This reflected Vladimir Ilich LENIN's party-centered version of Marxist doctrine and resulted in oligarchic and bureaucratic rule by the party, rather than by members of society.

Although authoritarian and sometimes tyrannical communist regimes scarcely resembled the Marxist ideal (where the state, under communism, "withered away"), they spread quickly after World War II. Communist regimes were imposed on Eastern Europe in 1948 by the Soviet Union and instituted by popular (if also party-led) revolutions in many countries of the developing world. In China, Vietnam, and Cuba, communism was seen as a popular, egalitarian alternative to oppression by traditional ruling elites and to Western imperialism. Communist parties in Western Europe—especially in France and Italy—were supported by large numbers of working-class voters. By the 1970s, most of these parties had jettisoned the Leninist elements of their platforms in favor of a more moderate "Eurocommunism," which accepted the institutions of liberal democracy.

While some communist regimes succeeded in rapidly industrializing and equalizing wealth on a broad basis, by the 1980s it was generally apparent that communism was neither economically competitive with capitalism nor progressing toward greater freedom and democracy. Party regimes in the Soviet Union and elsewhere had calcified into corrupt, inefficient bureaucracies with little popular support. Most of Europe's communist regimes collapsed in 1989, followed by the Soviet Union in 1991. Most of those that remain (such as China) have begun integrating elements of market capitalism into their economies, although they continue to resist political change.

communitarianism A diverse current of political and social thought that emphasizes the social nature of the individual against the atomistic individualism of LIBERALISM. Communitarianism argues for communally defined norms for politics and society rather than those based on the aggregation of individual preferences or interests (see INTEREST). While communitarianism often looks back to premodern forms of social organization, its theoretical foundation was laid by the early nineteenth-century philosopher Georg HEGEL, who argued, against Immanuel KANT and other liberals, that an ethical community based on shared substantive values (*Sittlichkeit*) was possible under modern conditions. This vision of a community united around common norms informs disparate strands of modern thought, including SOCIALISM (in its prioritizing of the bonds of *fraternité*), anarchism (in its emphasis on communities that occur naturally, without the coercive intervention of the state), and various concepts in social science (e.g., Ferdinand TÖNNIES's *Gemeinschaft* and Emile DURKHEIM's *mechanical solidarity*).

During the 1980s, communitarianism became a distinctive political position and strain of social theory. Political theorists such as Alasdair MACINTYRE, Michael Sandel, Michael Walzer, Charles Taylor, and sociologist Robert Bellah diverged on many points but shared a critique of liberal orthodoxy, centered on its assumption of socially disembedded individuals as the basic units of analysis and on its failure to ascribe value to community as such. In the 1990s, under the leadership of Amitai Etzioni (*The New Golden Rule: Community and Morality in a Democratic Society*, 1996), many communitarians took their arguments more aggressively to public venues, contending that a pervasive corrosion of norms was fostering a destructive, anarchic individualism in contemporary society. They attributed this in the main to liberal overemphasis on the rights of individuals against state and community and on a commensurate neglect of individual responsibilities and obligations to communities

and the family. While this version of communitarianism has had some success in contemporary policy circles (e.g., the Democratic party in the United States and the Labour party in Great Britain), its promotion of a consensus around core community values has proved difficult to reconcile with the increasing MULTICULTURALISM of advanced industrial democracies, even as communitarians have stressed balancing the rights of minorities against majoritarianism. Communitarianism's relative neglect of economic causes in accounting for societal dysfunctions has also caused critics to question its explanatory power.

communitas A term introduced by Victor Turner (*The Ritual Process*, 1969) to designate the feeling of heightened solidarity produced during the "liminal" moments of RITUAL, in which participants step outside their prescribed social roles.

community Many sociological and anthropological definitions exist, but most tend to privilege some combination of small-scale, relative boundedness, strong affective ties, traditionalism, and face-to-face contact. These qualities distinguish community from larger and more impersonal forms of relationship such as SOCIETY or association. Such distinctions between traditional communities and modern, generally urban industrial societies lie at the foundation of much of the modern sociological tradition—as in Ferdinand TÖNNIES's seminal distinction between GEMEINSCHAFT AND GESELLSCHAFT (community and association). Community became not only a yardstick by which sociologists measured modernization and other forces of social change but also a receptacle of values, sometimes nostalgically defended against the perceived threats of MODERNITY. The modern political signification of community draws heavily on this sense of nostalgia and fear of loss of the personal dimension of many social relationships. A great deal of twentieth-century sociology follows in this tradition, from Georg SIMMEL's classic essay "The Metropolis and Mental Life" (1902–1903 [1950]) to Louis Wirth's efforts to link the anonymity of urban life to diverse social and psychological problems. Work by Herbert Gans and other urban sociologists have emphasized, in contrast, the persistence of personally structured communities within urban settings. The subject continues to be of considerable sociological and political interest, particularly as long-distance communities (via the Internet or other technologies of communication) become increasingly widespread. Contemporary COMMUNITARIANISM, the movement represented by Alasdair MacIntyre, Michael Sandel, Michael Walzer, Amitai Etzioni, Charles Taylor, and others, has addressed this set of issues directly and has become a major voice for reconciling the values of community with the large-scale, technological demands of modern society.

Benedict Anderson's influential concept of *imagined community* (*Imagined Communities*, 1983) illustrates a different approach to the question. Anderson emphasizes the practices and technologies that permit the creation of affective bonds that extend beyond the face-to-face contact of traditional communities. NATIONALISM is his primary example—built, he argued, on a print culture that created a sense of common space and purpose in an otherwise dispersed, large-scale society. National communities, in other words, reproduce something of the affective identification with the collectivity characteristic of small communities, without the need for immediate contact with or knowledge of the other members. The sociologist Talcott PARSONS approached similar issues through the concept of *societal community*. The related issue of mass identification—again facilitated by a range of technologies of communication—has been central to the critical theory and CULTURAL STUDIES traditions. See also FRANKFURT SCHOOL.

compadrazgo In Spain and Latin America, *compadrazgo* is a widespread and elaborate form of "godparenting," or ritual kinship, organized around Roman Catholic ceremonies of baptism, confirmation, and marriage. The term is also used to describe some more general forms of patronage or sponsorship.

compage A concept introduced into regional geography by Derwent Whittlesey as a way of encompassing the diverse aspects of geographical research. The term designates all the features of the physical, biological, and social environment that are functionally associated with human habitation of the earth.

comparative advantage First articulated by David RICARDO in 1817, the principle of comparative advantage provides the basic explanation of "gains from trade." Although its logic applies equally to interpersonal, interfirm, and interregional trade, Ricardo stated and proved it in the context of international trade.

As Ricardo argued, any enduring two-way flow of goods between countries must reflect international differences in the structure of costs and prices: things cheaper to produce at home will be exported to other countries, whereas things cheaper to produce abroad will be imported from other countries. This generalization is the principle of *comparative advantage*—in a world of competitive markets, trade will occur and be beneficial whenever there are international differences in the relative costs of production. *Relative* is the crucial term, since Ricardo showed that even if a country has an absolute cost advantage in all commodities, it will specialize in the production of those commodities where its advantage is greatest.

From a positive standpoint, the principle of comparative advantage yields predictions about the direction and terms of trade. From a normative standpoint, it implies that citizens of both countries benefit from trade, with the benefits depending on the extent to which the international price ratio differs from the domestic opportunity cost ratio in each country. This last point is very sensitive to the model assumptions of perfect competition, the mobility of the labor force and the relative size of the two countries.

The two-good, two-country model has been extended to many countries and many goods, but the underlying logic remains much the same.

comparative dynamics See COMPARATIVE STATICS.

comparative government and comparative politics A principle subfield of POLITICAL SCIENCE that focuses on the comparative study of constitutions, systems of government, and political developments. Comparative political study has a long history in Western thought, beginning with ARISTOTLE's study of Greek constitutions and running prominently through the Enlightenment tradition of Charles-Louis MONTESQUIEU, Jean-Jacques ROUSSEAU, and Alexis de TOCQUEVILLE. Historically, the field has relied heavily upon systems of classification and generalization to frame its analyses—although the term comparative politics is sometimes used more broadly to designate the study of foreign countries *per se*.

In modern political science, the methodologies and objects of study of comparative politics have tracked closely with other developments in the field. In the early twentieth century, researchers typically followed Aristotle's example in comparing the governmental institutions of different countries and tracing their histories. The midcentury rise of BEHAVIORALISM focused on making this process scientific by using more cases and measurable empirical data to develop testable causal theories. Since the fragmentation of behavioralism in the late 1960s, the leading approaches include a revitalized historical-institutionalism, this time with the aim of identifying limited, context-specific causal relations; rational-choice studies, which seek the underlying logic behind political behavior; more-restricted varieties of behavioralism; and approaches that emphasize culture and ideology. Little consensus now exists within the field as to whether comparative politics should work toward broad generalizations or the explanation of particular cases. See also AREA STUDIES; and CASE STUDY.

comparative method   The benefits, risks, and methods of comparative study have been a subject of wide debate in the social sciences since the turn of the twentieth century—perhaps most actively in SOCIOLOGY and ANTHROPOLOGY, where objectively measurable social variables are difficult to establish. In its classic form, this debate opposes cultural particularism (the belief in the incommensurability of cultural differences) to cross-cultural or international comparativism (quintessentially the study of nations, which bear much of the weight of modern political and social identity). Emile DURKHEIM recognized that the comparison of cultures and nations merely extrapolated a comparative process basic to all social analysis—the drawing of generalizations from diverse, endlessly particular social data. Nonetheless, the tendency to think in terms of unitary cultures or societies has left a strong imprint on comparative work, and produced an equally strong reaction.

Debates about comparativism profoundly shaped the development of modern anthropology, which relied heavily on the concept of individual, unified societies. In anthropology, *comparative method* refers specifically to the methodology used in constructing the broad evolutionary typologies of the nineteenth century, which tried to derive laws of social development from apparent similarities among cultures. In 1896, Franz BOAS delivered an influential critique of this methodology that set the terms for much of American anthropology in the next decades. Boas emphasized the potentially arbitrary nature of such comparisons, the distortions

inherent in stripping cultural features from larger contexts, and the power of diffusion as an alternative theory of social development (see DIFFUSION AND DIFFUSIONISM). Nonetheless, cross-cultural comparison continues, and more carefully circumscribed cultural evolutionary schemes have been developed by Julian STEWARD, Marshall SAHLINS, and other anthropologists.

comparative politics   See COMPARATIVE GOVERNMENT AND COMPARATIVE POLITICS.

comparative statics   A method of analyzing the impact of change in the parameters of a model by comparing the new equilibrium position with the original one. The limitation of this method is that it does not explain the transitional forces involved in the adjustment from one equilibrium position to the next. When such analysis is conducted on dynamic economic models, economists use the term *comparative dynamics*.

compensation principle   In economics, a method used to determine whether one set of economic or social conditions constitutes an improvement over another. The compensation principle addresses the problem of diverse outcomes: while some may be better off under new arrangements, others may be worse off. It defines improvement by asking whether, hypothetically, the winners under a new set of conditions could compensate the losers for their losses and still be at least as well off as in their original state. The principle has been used in a variety of contexts—especially those relating to policy changes and events with major economic impact. Examples include the differences between perfectly and imperfectly competitive systems, free and restricted trade, prewar and postwar economies, the effects of economic depression, and changes in technology.

competition   See PERFECT COMPETITION.

complements   In economics, complements are goods that are consumed in conjunction with one another, as opposed to SUBSTITUTES, which are consumed in place of one another. *Perfect* complements are goods that are useless without each other, such as left shoes and right shoes. More generally, *complementarity* refers to the degree to which goods are consumed together—measured by *cross-price ELASTICITY*. An increase in price for one good (for example, butter) leads to a decrease in demand for the other (for example, bread) when the goods are complements.

complex society Complexity has been an important variable in evolutionary models of societal development since the late nineteenth century. Evolutionary theories of that period tended to posit a singular trajectory from simple, undifferentiated, family-based societies to their complex modern counterparts—an interpretive formula that was adopted by many of the pioneer researchers of turn-of-the-century social theory. Political authority, the DIVISION OF LABOR, KINSHIP relations, and LANGUAGE have all been modeled in terms of complexity and transformed into indexes that can measure a society's degree of stratification, the differentiation of its concepts, and the extent and nature of its relations beyond the immediate family. The term *structural differentiation* is sometimes used to describe this process.

Newer evolutionary models continue to address the question of complexity, particularly in regard to political authority and the development of the state. However, categorical claims to linear societal development and many of the implied contrasts with "simple societies" have been largely abandoned in the face of more comprehensive anthropological data. The term *complex society* remains most widely in use as shorthand for designating highly differentiated, large-scale societies with developed systems of political authority and widespread use of technology in economic production. See also EVOLUTION AND EVOLUTIONISM.

componential analysis A method of linguistic analysis used to establish definitions within a relatively finite set of terms or elements. Componential analysis has been widely used in the study of KINSHIP in order to establish which terms in a given language designate which relations—for example, whether separate terms exist for parallel and CROSS COUSINS, or for the mother's and father's brothers. Cultural differences in the classification of colors has been another active area of componential research, revealing cross-cultural similarities in the cognitive framework of perception. This finding has allied componential analysis with the more recent and broader research agendas of COGNITIVE ANTHROPOLOGY and cognitive science.

Within componential analysis, the terms *denotata* and *significata* mark, respectively, the difference between existing terms within a particular language and their objective, abstracted meanings.

comprador Or *comprador bourgeoisie*. A term used in theories of economic globalization to designate groups in developing countries who align themselves with multinational capital and promote its interests, sometimes (although not necessarily) in the belief that such development will benefit their society. The term literally means "buyer" in Portuguese.

Comte, Auguste (1798–1857) A French philosopher who, with Claude-Henri SAINT-SIMON, founded POSITIVISM as a philosophy of science, an ideology of progress, and a humanist religion. Comte also coined the term *SOCIOLOGY*, which he argued would become the "queen of the sciences." This did not mean that it would rule over the others but that it would integrate knowledge from all. In his six-volume *The Positive Philosophy* (1830–1842), Comte divided sociology into distinct areas: economics, politics, individuality, familial organization, labor, language, and religion. Each area implied the study of both "social statics" and "social dynamics"—the former necessary for social order and the latter decisively affecting social change. Each area also played a necessary functional role in the maintenance of the social whole.

Comte's positivism stressed the unity of science, which meant that there was no essential break in method between the natural sciences and the social sciences. All progressed by identifying, confirming, and accumulating truth. Each had a distinct level of reality as its object, and those—like physics—that addressed the most basic reality developed faster. Sociology, he argued, developed more slowly because its subject matter was more complex.

The longer trajectory of human knowledge, Comte claimed, involved progress through three stages: theological, metaphysical, and positive knowledge. In the first, natural phenomena were explained in terms of the actions of supernatural beings; in the second, these explanations gave way to notions of abstract forces ordered by Nature; in the third, societies accepted that there was no reality beyond this world and the rational laws that organized its observable facts. Science described the world with increasing exactitude and on that basis developed predictive laws. Each person, each branch of human knowledge, each society, and ultimately all of humanity developed according to this "law of the three stages." In this context, the role of scientists was not limited to discovering the laws that governed existence; they were also called to use this knowledge to organize society in accordance with scientific principles—including family life, politics, and even religion. To this end, Comte founded a positivist religion, complete with a collection of humanist "saints" and specific forms of worship.

Comte had relatively few followers for his religious program, although congregations existed in Britain and France well into the twentieth century. Comte's theory of progress was more influential and contributed to the development of evolutionary thought, although progress in biology rapidly outstripped his work. His conception of science as a combination of description and prediction was still more significant. Comtean positivism joined with British empiricism in shaping UTILITARIANISM, political economy, and evolutionary theory—notably in the work of Jeremy BENTHAM, John Stuart MILL, and Herbert SPENCER. Mill, in particular, was an avid Comtean for several years. Comte's work also had profound influence on Emile DURKHEIM, and through him the tradition of FUNCTIONALISM.

Comte disapproved of the French revolutions of 1789, 1830, and 1848. He thought that revolutionaries acted out of passions and metaphysical ideas, rather than on the basis of science. For this reason, they (and the Enlightenment thinkers generally) underestimated both the interconnectedness and positive social effects of the institutions of the old regime. Social institutions needed to change gradually, guided by scientific knowledge. Substantively, Comte's social theory focused on how social integration was achieved. Like many observers of the rapid changes wrought by industrialization and modern science, he both praised innovation and feared disruption. These two sides of his thought are reflected in his motto "Order and Progress." Similar principles linked his thought to later technocratic and sometimes authoritarian political movements; his influence in this regard was especially great in Latin America, where positivism became a major political force and ideology of national development.

concentration ratio   A standard measure of the degree of oligopolistic control of an industry or market. The concentration ratio measures the proportion of the total industry size accounted for by the principal firms in the industry. The four-firm ratio is commonly used (the market share of the top four firms), but any number of firms can be used. See also HERFINDAHL INDEX.

concentric zone theory   A theory of patterns of urban land use developed by Robert Ezra PARK, Ernest W. Burgess, and R. D. McKenzie in the mid-1920s—all members of the CHICAGO SCHOOL OF SOCIOLOGY. The theory divides the city into a series of concentric rings characterized by different land uses: prototypically a central business district (often abbreviated CBD), surrounded by a zone dominated by wholesaling and trucking, then a transitional low-income and light-manufacturing zone, a working-class and immigrant residential zone, an upper-class residential zone, and finally, a zone of commuters. Alternative models of urban land use include the MULTIPLE-NUCLEI THEORY and SECTOR THEORY.

concubinage   A form of authorized sexual relationship outside marriage, distinct from POLYGYNY insofar as it does not typically include rights of inheritance.

Condorcet criterion   See PARADOX OF VOTING.

Condorcet, Marie-Jean-Antoine-Nicolas de Caritat, Marquis de (1743–1794) A French mathematician and political philosopher who pioneered the study of voting systems and promoted the extension of scientific reason to matters of public life. Born an aristocrat, Condorcet broke with convention in pursuing a career as a mathematician—a field in which he produced innovative work in calculus and probability. He eventually became one of the chief contributors to the *Encyclopédie* in the 1750s and 1760s and an important figure in the Académie des Sciences.

When the French Revolution began, Condorcet took an active role in the Revolutionary assemblies and in devising schemes for "rational" government. He believed that government had to reflect the "public mind," as the king had once ostensibly done, but that rule by the elite was preferable to broad-based democracy. He imagined that society's problems could be best handled by a mathematically inclined bureaucratic elite, capable of determining the probabilities of actions and outcomes in the social world. Condorcet carried these ideas furthest in *Sketch for a Historical Picture of Progress for the Human Mind* (1795)—an argument for the limitless potential of science and mathematics and an anticipation, in some respects, of positivist claims for SOCIOLOGY (see POSITIVISM).

With Enlightenment figures such as Voltaire, Condorcet was active in legal reform that sought to end the persecution of religious dissidents. His mathematical approach to voting systems generated a number of important concepts and observations, from the *jury theorem*, regarding the power of majority decisions, to *Condorcet's paradox*, which identified the potentially circular outcome of certain types of sequential voting (see PARADOX OF VOTING). Condorcet ultimately sided with the moderate Girondin faction during the Revolution. When the extremist Jacobins came to power, Condorcet went into hiding. He was later captured and thrown into prison, where he died in circumstances that remain obscure.

configurationism A theoretical perspective that applied the insights of psychology to the study of CULTURE. Configurationism is associated with the CULTURE AND PERSONALITY MOVEMENT of the late 1920s and the 1930s in anthropology, and particularly with Ruth Fulton BENEDICT's influential book *Patterns of Culture* (1934). It is also closely associated with the holistic perspective of GESTALT THEORY. The core of configurationism is the proposition that culture is structured and integrated in ways analogous to individual personality, such that culture can be treated as an integrated whole with more or less unique and consistent patterns of perception and thought—hence the concept of a "cultural configuration." While many of the particulars of Benedict's approach have been challenged or discarded, the basic framework of configurationism still has considerable currency in the study of culture, as demonstrated in the work of Clifford GEERTZ and Norbert ELIAS.

conflict studies A subfield of INTERNATIONAL RELATIONS that tries to understand and prevent or ameliorate conflicts in world politics. It differs from strategic studies in that it deals with nonstate as well as state actors, and also in that it generally refuses to concede that conflict is inevitable. Conflict studies has grown since the end of the Cold War, as negotiated settlements of international and domestic conflicts have become more common.

conflict theory Loosely describes a body of sociological and anthropological work produced in the 1950s and 1960s that emphasized (1) the role of coercion in maintaining the social order in the face of conflict and (2) the occasions when group relations are mediated by persistent conflict, resulting not in the disintegration of social order but in a different form of order. In this context, the anthropologist Max GLUCKMAN argued that there was "peace in the feud" because stabilized relationships developed even amid ongoing conflict.

Conflict theory emerged as a critique of the main tendencies of structural FUNCTIONALISM—the dominant theoretical perspective of the period. Structural functionalism emphasized mechanisms of integration and consensus in the reproduction of the social order and tended to minimize the role and severity of social conflict. Conflict theorists rarely rejected structural functionalism, however, and often described their work as a revision or extension of structural-functionalist principles toward the recognition of potential divergences of interests among different social actors and the limitations of normative or consensus-building structures. This work drew on Marxist notions of structural differences in class interests, and still more on Georg SIMMEL's theory of conflict and Max WEBER's notions of multiple registers of social power and social interests. Major contributors to conflict theory include Ralf Dahrendorf, David Lockwood, Lewis Coser, and Randall Collins.

conformity Adherence to the norms, patterns, or standards of society and/or to the legitimate means of achieving sanctioned societal goals. As a subject of research, conformity is the reverse side of the longstanding sociological interest in DEVIANCE and forms a key part of Robert K. MERTON's seminal work on the subject. Social psychology has also explored the subject in some detail at an experimental level; these studies generally focus on the pressures that encourage conformity among individuals or groups (e.g., Stanley MILGRAM's studies of OBEDIENCE to authority) or, alternatively, on the social resources and individual capacities that facilitate resistance or unconventional behavior (see Solomon E. Asch's experiments on creativity and resistance to "wrong" answers). Conformity has also been widely lamented as one of the features of MASS SOCIETY, especially where individual autonomy visibly gives way to larger forms of homogenized behavior and collective identification.

congestion A general term in economics for the degradation or additional cost imposed by the overuse of a service or facility—classically, the highways. Congestion occurs under conditions where pricing is lower than the costs imposed, often when property rights are not well defined. The economic analysis of congestion seeks to design policy measures that minimize such costs (e.g., the design of highway tolls) and plays an important role in public-policy arenas. See also PROPERTY AND PROPERTY RIGHTS.

conjectural equilibria A concept in the analysis of economic decision making that takes into account individuals' perceptions of the market environment. Under conditions of PERFECT COMPETITION, the market environment of any single economic agent is independent of his or her market actions. If the economy is not perfectly competitive, however, an agent may have to take into account the effect of his or her decision on that environment. Changing output decisions, for example, may cause rivals to change their output decisions as well. This, in turn, may affect the market price. These effects are generally not known with certainty and are therefore subject to conjecture.

In an imperfectly competitive world, agents act only if those conjectures are deemed advantageous. A conjectural equilibrium is said to exist when every agent conjectures that unilaterally altering his or her control would be *disadvantageous*. For economists, conjectural equilibria require that conjectures be correct or "rational," although they are always subject to revision.

connotation and denotation A distinction between primary and secondary meanings that became important in structural LINGUISTICS and literary criticism in the 1920s and 1930s. *Denotation* refers to the literal or given meaning of a word; *connotation* to the secondary meanings or associations the word also carries.

consanguineal relations Relations by descent rather than marriage (also known as AFFINAL RELATIONS). See also KINSHIP.

conservatism As a political philosophy, conservatism is usually credited to the English social theorist and politician Edmund BURKE, who developed a strong critique of abstract social theories, the perfectibility of man, and radical social engineering in response to the French Revolution. Modern usage, however, refers to a wide range of political tendencies and positions that often have little connection to Burke's principles or rationales, although his work continues

to inform an important tradition of conservative thought. Perhaps the key point of divergence is Burke's rejection of nostalgia for the past and, consequently, of conservative utopianism rooted in forms of TRADITION. Instead, Burke took a progressive view of society as the product of accumulated customs and practices, which connect institutions, laws, and behavior in an organic whole. This slow, mostly undirected process, Burke argued, was the product of a collective wisdom far greater than that of individual social thinkers. Tradition and even prejudice, in this context, play a positive role in restraining radical change.

Burke's animosity to abstract social theories extended to the liberal tradition of SOCIAL-CONTRACT THEORY. His own version of the social contract involved not an imaginary bond between individuals and society, but a collaborative process that linked the generations and, consequently, constrained any single generation (much less individual) in what it could, or morally should, change—this was perhaps the most influential of Burke's ideas. Nonetheless, Burke was a political reformer who recognized that healthy political systems needed incremental change over time.

Subsequent conservative thought took a variety of paths, including nostalgic retreats from modernization, DEMOCRATIZATION, and social change (Thomas Carlyle), as well as theories of the necessity or virtue of elite rule (José ORTEGA Y GASSETT). A number of Alexis de TOCQUEVILLE's criticisms of democratic society—especially regarding the deleterious effects of equality on individualism—became touchstones of modern conservatism, especially after World War II.

The British philosopher Michael OAKESHOTT was perhaps the leading voice of twentieth-century Burkean conservatism, a revised version that addressed itself to the new horrors of TOTALITARIANISM and large-scale social engineering. Oakeshott argued that nearly all politics in post-Renaissance Europe had committed the rationalist error of trying to improve the human condition through the application of formulas based on abstract ideas. Such schemes left little margin for the transmission of practices from generation to generation, which for Oakeshott defined a responsible political tradition. Like many conservatives, Oakeshott argued for a much narrower conception of politics—one limited to working within the margins of a legitimate political order based on law and tradition.

Most modern conservatism reproduces this commitment to sharp limits on the scope of the political sphere, especially in regard to government involvement in areas of social welfare. In modern society, consequently, conservatism has acquired a range of associations that were foreign to its early forms, which were often anticapitalist and overtly paternalistic. Twentieth-century conservatism, especially the neoliberal and neoconservative varieties of the last few decades, has in many cases become indistinguishable from the defense of CAPITALISM and market principles, which are frequently identified with the space of human freedom and achievement. Friedrich von HAYEK and Milton FRIEDMAN are among the leading theorists of this type of conservatism (see NEOLIBERALISM).

consociationalism Institutional measures designed to protect or ensure fairness to minorities in deeply divided societies. Where political cleavages are durable and salient, simple majority rule threatens to turn smaller groups into permanent minorities with no control over their political fates. Some highly pluralist societies, such as the Netherlands, Canada, and Malaysia, have tried to solve this problem through a variety of means, including guaranteed representation in the government, forms of autonomy for different groups, and minority vetoes in sensitive areas of public policy. While such measures are typically constitutionally defined in consociational regimes, they also sometimes develop in strongly majoritarian polities as a means of stabilizing minority relations.

conspicuous consumption Introduced by Thorstein VEBLEN in *Theory of the Leisure Class* (1899), the term refers to the ostentatious display of wealth by which members of the elite demonstrate and enhance their social prestige. Veblen's commentary was directed largely against the new capitalist leisure class of the late nineteenth century, although his argument was couched in anthropological terms and developed parallels to tribal POTLATCH practices. Veblen also identified a more general human need for "invidious comparison" with one another.

constant elasticity of substitution production function See CES PRODUCTION FUNCTION.

constituency Generally, the supporters of a politician or political movement. In Britain and several other countries, it refers more specifically to an electoral district. See also ELECTORAL GEOGRAPHY.

constitution and constitutionalism The basic LAW or set of fundamental rules and principles that govern a polity. In most countries, these rules are recorded in a single written document (the constitution), although basic rules may also reside in accumulated custom, practice, judicial precedent, and ordinary law (see COMMON LAW). A few countries, such as Britain, Israel, and Saudi Arabia, do not have written constitutions; instead they rely on convention and precedent to regulate ordinary politics. In these cases, the parliament or monarch is technically sovereign, although ordinarily they are bound by informal rules.

Constitutionalism can refer to politics under either a written or an unwritten constitution, and means simply that the rule of law is respected. Political scientists usually distinguish between ancient and modern forms. Under ancient constitutionalism, the sovereign was bound by a multitude of particularistic agreements with different social actors; these could be written or purely conventional. This practice was widespread in Europe in the Middle Ages and exemplified by England after the *Magna Carta* (1215). The age of modern constitutionalism arguably began as early as the English Glorious Revolution of 1688 and took hold with the American and French constitutional conventions of 1787 and 1791, respectively. Thereafter, governance and sovereignty tended to be general, uniform, formalized, and entrenched in written constitutions.

Although written constitutions vary widely, nearly all include certain basic elements: (1) a statement of ideological principle, usually in a preamble; (2) an account of the form of government, particularly the nature of and relations among its main institutions and the procedures by which it is to make laws; (3) an enumeration of RIGHTS, setting out what the government cannot restrict (e.g., speech or association) or must provide (e.g., food or employment) to individuals or groups; (4) the means by which the constitution may be amended, which is invariably more difficult than the passage of ordinary legislation. Over two centuries of constitution-making, constitutions have tended to become longer and more detailed, both in their assignation of governmental powers and in their provision of individual rights. In most countries, constitutions are ordinarily interpreted and enforced by some form of JUDICIAL REVIEW.

Ultimately, constitutions are only as strong as the constitutionalism—the collective faith in the priority of constitutional law—that underlies them. The conditions under which constitutions are legitimately instituted, broken, amended, or temporarily suspended have been a persistent concern for political theory, beginning with the social contract tradition of Thomas HOBBES and John LOCKE (see SOCIAL-CONTRACT THEORY). As the Abbé Sieyès noted in his contribution to the drafting of the first (short-lived) Revolutionary French constitution, the creation of a constitution is itself almost always "unconstitutional." Sieyès called the creation of a new constitution the "constituent power" (*pouvoir constituant*), an exceptional political moment in which the people act directly, whereas the government created by that function was the "constituted power" (*pouvoir constitué*), which acts within the realm of ordinary politics. Although new constitutions are still being written, several new democracies, including Poland and South Africa, have succeeded in reinventing the political order by amending the rules of the old constitution, thereby avoiding any break in the rule of law.

constructionism   A broad theoretical orientation in sociology that regards social facts—including especially social identities—as the products of socially and historically situated practices. Within this context, social constructionism is used to designate several different sociological agendas, including Peter Berger and Thomas Luckmann's well-known sociology of knowledge (*The Sociological Construction of Reality*, 1966), Alfred SCHUTZ's study of the phenomenological and symbolic shaping of ordinary daily experience—termed the *social construction of reality*—and a variety of studies of education, labeling, and DEVIANCE. Although social construction usually refers to broad, diffuse patterns of activity and influence, analysts sometimes limit the term to more specific historical acts of cultural creation.

Social constructionists challenge the positivist notion that social reality is given or unproblematically objective. They argue that observed social realities cannot be understood by disengaging them from the observers or from cultural and historical circumstances. Taken to the extreme, such a position is open to the criticism that it denies the possibility of transcultural and historical understanding. Social constructionism does generally reject the possibility of a strongly objectivist, externally scientific concept of truth in the study of society, but few social constructionists argue that social realities are so divergent as to provide no points of commonality, avenues of insight, or understanding among different perspectives.

As a general doctrine, social constructionism is often opposed to *essentialism*—the belief that the major features of social reality or identity lie in inherent, inalienable qualities. These principles are at stake not only in the study of society or human activity, which is often held to require different methods or standards than the natural sciences, but also in science studies, where the term "constructivism" refers to the notion that descriptions of reality are the active creations of scientists (in turn shaped by the broader culture) and not simply transcriptions of material facts or observations. See Thomas KUHN.

The use of "constructivism" in the psychology of Jean PIAGET and in other social psychological research covers similar ground—in Piaget's case with a strong emphasis on the way that social life affects the formation of basic cognitive faculties and categories. The resulting mental constructs, he argued, are responsible for filtering information and thus for shaping experience at a fundamental level.

consumer   The unit of microeconomic analysis on the demand side of goods markets. Analysis of consumer choice is the basis for deriving market demand, savings behavior, and labor-supply decisions.

consumer surplus   A measure of the net benefit to the consumer from purchasing in a market. If a consumer would pay up to $10 for a good when the market price is $7, then the consumer is said to have a "utility" surplus of $3 in purchasing the good. Consumer surplus is effectively a measure of welfare and provides a convenient way of evaluating the impact of various types of public policies. One of the simplest versions was introduced by Alfred MARSHALL, who argued that the impact on welfare of a price change can be measured by the area under the demand curve for the good between the initial and the terminal price. Two more popular measures of consumer surplus are termed the *compensating variation measure* and the *equivalent variation measure*. Compensating variation measures the amount of income that can be taken from an individual who benefits from the price change without diminishing that individual's well-being. The opposite can be done with losses. Equivalent variation is the minimum amount that someone who gains would be willing to accept to forego the change. For the loser, it is the maximum they would be willing to pay to prevent the change.

consumption function An economic model of the proportion of income spent on consumption. John Maynard KEYNES pioneered in this area with the *absolute income hypothesis*, which states that consumption is solely a function of current disposable income. Divergence between Keynes's predictions and subsequent empirical data, especially over the long run, has led to a number of other theories of consumption—most prominently, those based relative income (Duesenberry), permanent income (Milton FRIEDMAN), and life-cycle income (Modigliani and Brumberg).

Keynes argued that any change in income results in a smaller change in consumption—i.e., the marginal propensity to consume is less than one. He also argued that the marginal propensity to consume is less than the average propensity to consume, which implies that consumption declines as a percentage of income as income rises. Short-run studies broadly support a consumption function of this form, but long-run data suggest that the average and the marginal propensities to consume are roughly the same.

The *relative income hypothesis* conceives consumption in relation to the income of other households and past income. The first implies that the proportion of income consumed remains constant provided that a household's position on the income distribution curve holds constant in the long run. This is consistent with long-run evidence. Higher up the income curve, however, there is a lower average propensity to consume. The second part of the hypothesis suggests that households find it easier to adjust to rising incomes than falling incomes. There is, in other words, a "ratchet effect" that holds up consumption when income declines.

The measurement of permanent and lifetime income has become a central issue in recent attempts to specify the consumption function. The *permanent income hypothesis* postulates that consumption depends on the total income and wealth that an individual expects to earn over his or her lifetime. The *life-cycle hypothesis* assumes that individuals consume a constant proportion of the present value of lifetime income as measured in a number of financially distinct periods of life, such as youth, middle age, and old age. Empirical research in this area has proved challenging, because theories of consumption generally include the long-term "use" of durable goods. Consumption data, however, focus primarily on current purchases, or consumption expenditure.

consumption taxes Direct or indirect taxes on consumable goods. Indirect consumption taxes include excise taxes, wholesale or retail taxes, and value-added taxes. Their rates often vary according to the commodity and may be progressive or regressive in effect. Direct consumption taxes, in contrast, resemble income taxes in that they are based on the amount that individual consumers spend. No major country has yet adopted a direct consumption tax, although provisions that shelter savings from income taxes perform a similar function.

Consumption taxes are often used as policy tools, as in the cases of cigarette taxes and gasoline taxes. They are sometimes preferred by policy-makers because it is often easier to measure consumption than income, especially in an inflationary setting where distinctions between real and nominal income come into play. See also TAXES AND TAXATION.

contact conversion Refers to the spread of *proselytizing religions* (primarily Christianity, Islam, and Buddhism) through the contact between believers and nonbelievers. See also DIFFUSION AND DIFFUSIONISM.

contact hypothesis The argument that contact among members of different groups will reduce existing prejudice and improve social relations between them. This common-sense proposition was first systematically investigated by social psychologist Gordon ALLPORT in the 1950s. Allport recognized that simple contact alone was no guarantee of the positive integration of different groups and might in practice create more prejudice and potential for conflict. A strong condition for the positive integration of different social groups, he argued, was *equal status contact*, in which individuals cooperate to achieve common goals in an institutional environment structured by integrationist policies.

contagious magic Introduced by anthropologist James FRAZER in *The Golden Bough* (1890) to designate magic in which power is a function of past proximity to an object. He contrasted contagious magic to *homeopathic magic*, in which power is based on resemblance between things. See also MAGIC.

containment   In INTERNATIONAL RELATIONS, the policy of preventing an adversary from expanding without engaging in direct conflict. First articulated in 1947 by U.S. diplomat George Keenan, containment was the pillar of U.S. strategy against the Soviet Union and its allies for much of the COLD WAR. Because containing communism entailed a practically unlimited commitment of U.S. military forces around the world, however, Kennan later qualified his position to emphasize political rather than military containment and the commitment of major resources only in the world's strategically sensitive areas, particularly Europe. Despite this shift, Keenan provided the theoretical underpinnings for the Truman Doctrine and essentially overturned the long-held, if inconsistently observed, tradition of U.S. isolationism in foreign affairs: in 1938, the United States was without military alliances and had no troops stationed overseas; by 1989, it had military alliances with fifty countries and 1.5 million troops posted around the world.

content analysis   A group of formal and, especially, statistical techniques used to analyze texts. Content analysis began as a method for analyzing propaganda during World War II; it consisted mostly of evaluations of the relative significance of subjects, as based on the incidence of particular words or phrases. This counting and sorting of words was one of the first applications of computers in the social sciences. In the postwar decades, content analysis became a popular form of analyzing texts and large bodies of related documents, growing more accessible as computing power increased and as experience with such techniques grew. Content analysis eventually expanded to include the study of a range of qualitative issues, including stylistic, thematic, and ideological aspects of texts, as well as other media and genres (e.g., photography and advertising).

contestable markets   Markets in which the potential entry of other firms exercises strong competitive pressures on the behavior of incumbents. In such a market, it makes little difference whether monopolistic or oligopolistic structures exist: it is the competition from potential entrants rather than competition among active suppliers

that effectively constrains the equilibrium behavior of the producing firms. The characteristics of such a market are free entry and costless exit by entrepreneurs who face no disadvantages vis-à-vis the incumbents.

Perfectly contestable markets serve as a benchmark for analyzing industry structure. They provide an idealized limit case that has desirable welfare properties. Perfectly contestable markets are also sometimes used as a substitute for perfect competition, for example, in cases where ECONOMIES OF SCALE would theoretically imply the dominance of a single large firm.

contingency theory   A body of research in economic sociology that revised many of the prevailing assumptions of SCIENTIFIC MANAGEMENT regarding optimal management techniques and firm organization. Where scientific management generally pursued the goal of describing the most efficient method of organizing production for a wide range of situations, contingency theory placed greater emphasis on the ways in which specific technological and market demands shaped organizations. Among the most important of these contributions was the argument, advanced by Tom Burns and George Stalker, that industries with rapidly changing technologies and markets (such as electronics) were better served by relatively flexible organizational structures with multiple internal avenues of communication and feedback, and by the ability to redefine and redistribute tasks as the need arose. Drawing on Emile DURKHEIM, Burns and Stalkner opposed this *organic* organizational style to a *mechanical* organizational structure, characterized by centralized decision making and comparatively rigid internal hierarchies. Their work—and the work of other contingency theorists such as Paul Lawrence and Jay Lorsch—dramatically changed the character of organization theory, theories of leadership, and theories of the firm in the 1960s (see FIRM, THEORY OF THE).

contingent commodities   A way of conceiving commodities applicable to cases in which uncertainty exists regarding the availability of resources, consumption, or production possibilities. Contingent commodities thus address a limitation of the theory of general competitive equilibrium, which was originally developed for environments in which economic agents experienced no uncertainty. Introduced by Kenneth ARROW and Gérard Debreu, the concept takes into account both the standard characteristics of commodities and environmental events that may impact their availability. The theory is useful, too, in that it requires no theory of probabilities and, therefore, allows for the calculation of equilibrium in a manner similar to the classical general equilibrium models.

contradiction A state of logical opposition between two ideas. Social science usage derives primarily from the critique of eighteenth-century. Enlightenment social thought, which tended to understand social development and human history in terms of the constant progress of reason and rationality. In the nineteenth century, a strong countertradition of social theory emerged that viewed human history as a contradictory process that generated opposing tendencies and progressed by overcoming those oppositions. This notion of contradiction underlay Georg HEGEL's dialectical system of logic and later his philosophy of history. Sometimes associated with Johann Gottlieb Fichte's triad of thesis, antithesis, and synthesis, Hegel's account turned especially on the relationship between the whole and its parts. This informed the influential Marxist conception of history as a struggle between irreconcilable classes and of CAPITALISM as a system that contained within it its own fatal contradictory tendencies (such as the FALLING RATE OF PROFIT). See MARXISM.

If the progressive view of history continues to be reproduced in positivistic and scientific modern worldviews, the question of contradiction has been central to the Marxist and dialectical tradition of social critique. One of the chief virtues of the latter is that it need not turn a blind eye to (or treat as an aberration) the horrific and dangerous aspects of modernity that have accompanied the extraordinary increase in human power. Disaster, for this reason, has provided the occasions for many of the major theoretical considerations of the contradictions of modernity. For Hegel, the French Revolution's reign of terror played this role, reflecting not the absence of reason but its terrifying extreme—its emergence as an institutionalized, murderous logic of unanimity. Similarly for FRANKFURT SCHOOL critical theorists, Nazism was not a monstrous exception to human progress but a product of an increasingly rationalized society freed from traditional structures of authority. Similar notions of a deeply contradictory modernity play a prominent role in French POSTSTRUCTURALISM and in debates over POSTMODERNISM, even as the Marxist concept of contradiction embodied in existing social actors

becomes more tenuous. Such issues continue to inform a wide and vigorous debate among social theorists. See also DIALECTICS; and MODERNITY.

conurbation An early term in geography that describes the emergence of continuous urban zones, such as that between Washington, D.C., and Boston. The term was introduced by the Scottish geographer and urban planner Patrick Geddes (*Cities in Evolution*, 1915). Jean GOTTMANN's more recent term, *megalopolis*, is a near synonym.

convergence hypothesis The theory that SOCIALISM and CAPITALISM will, over time, become increasingly alike in economic and social terms. Convergence theory was popular in the 1950s and 1960s, when Raymond ARON, John Kenneth GALBRAITH, and Jan TINBERGEN, among others, argued that the functional requirements of a technologically advanced society acted to diminish the differences between capitalist and communist countries. Both, convergence advocates argued, were becoming mixed economies administered by a meritocratic, managerial elite. Over time, this would be reflected in diminished political differences and foreign policy tensions.

Recent work on modernization in the United States, the former Soviet Union, and Japan has tended to challenge the technological determinism that underwrote much of convergence theory, especially by emphasizing the role of other causes and outcomes of social change. The collapse of the Soviet block has become a pivotal, if equivocal, example in this debate, variously held as proof of convergence or as evidence of the crucial role of other factors in social change. The dominance of NEOLIBERALISM and market economies since 1991 has rendered the convergence hypothesis somewhat moot, although the different types and specific qualities of mixed economies continue to be important subjects of research.

Economists often make more general use of the term as well. Most economic models predict that unless market systems are completely isolated, the interaction of economies will lead to the gradual equalization of economic variables. Wage convergence is a prediction of migration flows; price convergence is a prediction of increased trade. Most notably, many neoclassical growth models predict that the countries that are the furthest behind (in per-capita income) will grow the fastest, generating a convergence of national incomes over time. Evidence for such income convergence is weak for the global economy, but quite strong for states within countries, as in the United States. See also AUTARKY; and MARKET ECONOMY.

conversation analysis An area of ETHNOME-THODOLOGY and SOCIOLINGUISTICS associated primarily with the research of sociologist Harvey Sachs. Conversation analysis examines the habits, patterns, and structures of speech, as well as forms of nonverbal communication that enable conversations—such as the habit of taking turns speaking, the periodic indications of assent or engagement on the part of the participants, and the pressure to avoid long pauses or interruptions. These structures can differ among social groups, as Deborah Tannen suggests in her work on differences in the conversational habits and goals of men and women (*You Just Don't Understand*, 1990).

Cooley, Charles Horton (1864–1929) A major figure in early twentieth-century American sociology who laid much of the groundwork for SYMBOLIC INTERACTIONISM. Cooley refused the methodological individualism of many of his contemporaries and instead insisted that the self develops in and through social relations—that self and society are "twin-born." Like Max WEBER, he concluded that sociology was fundamentally concerned with understanding the meanings that persons attribute to their actions. It was, therefore, an interpretative field allied with the humanities, rather than a science restricted to the observation and description of behavior.

Cooley developed several important concepts that describe aspects of this process. His term, the *looking-glass self*, emphasizes that personality is formed, maintained, and developed through the real and perceived judgments of others, which the self progressively integrates. He held that this process exists primarily in the mind—an idealism that would be criticized by George Herbert MEAD and other interpretive sociologists.

The formation of the self occurs, Cooley argued, through "primary groups"—the family, schools, the immediate community, and so on—that consist of face-to-face and sustained interactions that weave the individual into a larger community. These primary groups are, in turn, responsible for creating the values and sense of SELF that the individual carries into the larger "secondary groups" that form society and

that are characterized by mediated or impersonal relationships.

Central to Cooley's work was his belief that society is an organic arrangement in which individuals are inextricably part of a whole. The complete understanding of any society, in this context, requires the interdisciplinary analysis of demographics, economics, politics, religion, and other dimensions of social life. Cooley was optimistic about this possibility and believed that sociological understanding was part of a larger social dialectic that led to a more compassionate society.

Among his most important works are *Human Nature and the Social Order* (1902), *Social Organization* (1909), *Social Progress* (1918), and *Life and the Student* (1927).

cooperative games GAME THEORY usually refers to *noncooperative* game theory, in contrast to what has become known as *cooperative* game theory. In noncooperative games, individual participants have defined strategy options, with payoffs determined by the uncoordinated choices of all players in the game. Cooperative game theory is neither cooperative nor a game, but has come to be associated with cooperation because it sets aside the internal dynamics of the group of players. Cooperative game theory developed as a tool for assessing the proper allocation of costs or benefits in a situation where the individual or group contribution depends on the others involved.

Consider the following simple production problem: Andrew by himself can bake three loaves of bread. Barbara can produce two, and Connie can produce just one. If Andrew and Barbara are working together, they can produce six loaves, Barbara and Connie together can produce four, and Andrew and Connie can produce six. If all three work together, they can produce ten loaves. There are evident gains to cooperation, but how should the ten loaves be divided? The CORE solution is the set of allocations that satisfies each individual's and each coalition's *rationality constraint*. That is, Andrew needs to be given at least three loaves, or he could do better baking on his own. Likewise, the sum of the shares to Barbara and Andrew must be six loaves, or they could work together and produce more, leaving Connie out on her own. The root of the cooperative label on these production games is that it is always assumed that if a coalition can benefit from forming, it will do so, ignoring strategic threats, failure of negotiations over division of gains, and other hurdles.

The core is rarely a unique allocation; choosing among possible solutions is a problem parallel to choosing solutions in a bargaining problem (see BARGAINING THEORY). The *Shapley value* allocates production according to an individual's expected marginal contribution but is not guaranteed to be in the core. (Note that the marginal product of an individual depends on the size and identity of the coalition to which he is added.) The *nucleolus* establishes equal gains to all coalitions, as nearly as possible. Other solutions include the *kernel*, the *yolk*, and the *equal allocation of non-separable costs*.

Cooperative games have provided a way to analyze many problems of interest in the social sciences, from the allocation of airport fees among airlines to voting behavior in legislatures.

cooperatives   A model of economic organization that involves the voluntary association of producers or consumers for the purposes of sharing profits and managing the collective interests of the group. The term, in this sense, emerged in the nineteenth century and was closely associated with the social theory and reform projects of Robert Owen. Resisting capitalist competition, many cooperatives limited themselves to the task of uniting consumers in order to maximize buying power. Others assumed productive roles, and some sought self-sufficiency. When properly managed, "co-ops" provide access to the economies of scale characteristic of large organizations, such as corporations. They have been successful in the United States and in some parts of Europe—particularly in the areas of agricultural production and distribution, as well as housing and banking. They tend to experience difficulties in areas that require highly differentiated, specialized, or full-time management.

core   A *solution concept* in cooperative game theory, originally proposed by D. B. Gillies and later developed by Lloyd Shapley. It describes the set of equilibrium outcomes of a cooperative game in which actors join coalitions to pursue winning strategies. The core solution implies that no group or coalition of agents can improve upon its result by using the means available to that group. By the same token, no subset of players can obtain more by acting by themselves. See COOPERATIVE GAMES.

This concept of optimal solutions provides the foundation for an important noncooperative-equilibrium concept—the competitive equilibrium. In a competitive equilibrium, every good has a price and every agent makes decisions independently. The price system coordinates these decisions in such a way as to clear all markets. At the limit, where there is either a large number of agents or the economy is enlarged by "replication," the set of allocations of goods and resources among individuals that constitutes competitive equilibria is a core solution.

core–periphery models   Describe situations in which centralized economic and political power—such as that of a capital city—dominates a surrounding, often rural, area. Core–periphery models were used in the late 1950s to explain uneven development and relations of dependency within countries, particularly in developing economies where the gradual achievement of economic "equilibrium" between areas was patently absent. The pioneering core and periphery models developed by Gunnar MYRDAL and Albert Hirschman explained this imbalance in terms of a vicious circle, whereby the emergence of a growing economic sector, such as a single industry in a core city, not only remained localized but also monopolized a disproportionate share of the limited investment resources of the country, resulting in the further deprivation of the periphery. Myrdal termed these deprivations *backwash effects*. Both Hirschman and Myrdal recognized possible mitigating factors, such as the rise in price of raw materials, which would benefit the periphery, but the experience of developing economies led them to believe that market forces alone would not resolve such inequalities.

Core–periphery models continued to attract attention in the 1960s and 1970s, both in the service of theories of development in the third world and as an element of the larger analyses of global capitalism developed by Marxist-influenced researchers, such as Immanuel WALLERSTEIN and André Gunder FRANK. Here, the *core* referred to high-productivity centers (also commonly centers of political and military power) in global systems of unequal exchange. Instead of cities and hinterlands, core and periphery expressed relationships between countries.

corporate group   A group (often a KINSHIP group) that shares control of property or other resources over time. Corporate groups are usually conceived as the basis of social and political organization by proponents of DESCENT THEORY and structural-functionalism in anthropology. The essential feature of corporateness is that it conceives the group as a whole, distinct from its members. See also CORPORATISM.

corporation The dominant form of capitalist ownership and activity in the modern era. As an organizational form, the corporation has roots in earlier forms of business association—notably the joint-stock company—and in the tradition of chartering certain kinds of public institutions, such as universities and guilds. Many not-for-profit organizations are also corporations—and indeed, states are a special kind of corporation.

The modern business corporation developed in the nineteenth century as a means of facilitating large-scale investment while limiting the financial liability of owners. In part, this was a response to the limitations of individual ownership and small partnerships in funding and managing large-scale entrepreneurial and productive activity. In economics, the rise of the corporation led directly to theories of the firm, which examined the conditions under which hierarchical, bounded organizations were more efficient than markets in organizing economic activity (or more effective for other purposes) (see FIRM, THEORY OF THE). Although there are national differences in laws governing corporations, incorporation generally provides certain key advantages over other forms of ownership. For example, except in cases of gross malfeasance by management, the corporate entity protects investors, management, and employees from liability. Investors are not held responsible for debts or legal judgments exceeding the amount of their investment.

In many respects, corporations operate as "fictive persons." They have rights and duties similar to "natural persons"; they can own property, sue or be sued in court, and enter into binding contracts. An important debate centers on whether corporations are basically creatures of contract (and thus essentially private) or are made possible by state charters and other legal provisions that grant limited liability and other special privileges (in which case they are essentially public). Legally, a corporation exists separately from its owners and employees, and corporations are designed to persist as these change. Ownership and management are therefore commonly (although not necessarily) separate. Corporations are generally owned by shareholders, which may include both individuals and other firms. They are managed, however, by specialized employees—indeed their rise was closely tied to the emergence of the managerial middle class in the late nineteenth century.

Successful techniques of large-scale capitalization and internal management have enabled corporations to grow tremendously, to the point where the largest now rival some countries in wealth and output. They are also no longer tied to particular national jurisdictions—a feature that many see as a driving force of GLOBALIZATION and as a potential threat to the SOVEREIGNTY of nations over economic activity. These are called MULTINATIONAL corporations, or MNCs.

corporatism A usually formal arrangement whereby decisions of state agencies are made in consultation with interest groups, which in turn guarantee the cooperation of their membership in implementing policy. Interests may be economic (e.g., owners or producers) or socially or politically based (e.g., the church or the armed services). Corporatism contrasts sharply with LIBERALISM and PLURALISM in that it assigns interests to groups rather than simply to individuals; it also departs from parliamentary systems that organize representation on the basis of territory or population.

Like Christian Democracy, corporatism can be traced back to Pope Leo XIII's 1891 call for a Roman Catholic response to SOCIALISM. As an alternative to class struggle, workers, industrialists, and farmers could be organized by sector and negotiate with one another and the state. This principle was interpreted in fascist Italy as "coerced cooperation": free-trade unions and other independent associations were banned and replaced with state-dominated associations. Because of this and similar patterns in other European dictatorships (Salazar's Portugal, Franco's Spain) and some Latin American dictatorships, corporatism was often associated with FASCISM.

The concept of corporatism was rehabilitated in the 1970s to describe the policy-making practices of some European countries, including Austria, Sweden, and West Germany, which featured tripartite negotiation among business associations, labor unions, and government. These democratic examples were referred to as "societal corporatism" or "neocorporatism" in contrast to fascist "state corporatism." Neocorporatist authors, such as Philippe Schmitter, argued that these countries seemed better able to fight inflation and maintain employment than their liberal counterparts. Even pluralist countries such as the United States and Britain have corporatist arrangements in particular sectors (see QUANGO). Some theorists have suggested that corporatism is a logical successor to representative democracy in complex technological societies, where key decisions require a great deal of technical expertise. It has also been advocated as a way to offset inequalities of power and resources by guaranteeing parity between groups in decision making. Critics have objected that corporatist arrangements are involuntary for many individuals, and that those who are outside major labor groups or business associations go entirely unrepresented. Moreover, corporatism has an ongoing legitimation problem, insofar as it favors functional over territorial representation, administrative agencies and councils over legislatures, and technocrats over citizen amateurs. These features are difficult to justify to democratic and liberal critics. In addition, its focus on technical economic issues such as employment, wages, and prices hampers its response to other social concerns, such as identity issues and quality of life. One key empirical question is whether policy arenas where corporatism has been practiced have become so fragmented that effective negotiation among organizations is no longer possible.

correlation   An observable relationship between two variables in which changes in one are accompanied by predictable changes in the other. If variables move together in the same direction, the correlation is *positive*. If an increase in one is accompanied by a decrease in the other, the correlation is *negative*. Correlation is often expressed in terms of a decimal number between zero and one, in which one represents a perfect, positive relationship. This is termed the *coefficient of simple correlation*. Where two or more independent variables affect a dependent variable, statisticians calculate the *coefficient of multiple correlation*. Correlation implies neither a causal relationship between variables nor a strict one-to-one correspondence between the changes. The causes of an apparent correlation may lie in another factor or variable, and the magnitude of change may itself be a variable.

Serial correlation and *autocorrelation* refer to statistical problems in which the current value of a variable (or the error term in a regression) is correlated with its own past values. *Serial correlation* implies the use of data over time, or time-series data; *autocorrelation* implies observations from cross-section data. Under autocorrelation, the residual for one observation is correlated with the other observations. As a result, the ORDINARY LEAST SQUARES estimate no longer has desirable properties in terms of efficiency (i.e., it no longer has minimum variance). Special tests (such as the Durbin–Watson test) exist for determining serial correlation, and econometric procedures may be used to restore the efficiency of the estimates. See also REGRESSION ANALYSIS.

One of the principle risks of any research methodology is the possibility of illusory or spurious correlations that stem either from coincidences in the data or from the prior expectations of the observer. MULTIPLE-INDICATOR MODELS and multiple operationalism provide strategies for minimizing such risks.

cosmology   A set of beliefs or theories about the origin and nature of the universe. Cosmological systems have been a subject of considerable interest to ANTHROPOLOGY and to researchers who theorize general relationships between beliefs, needs, and social structures. The relationship between Judeo-Christian cosmology and the "scientific" mind-set has, for example, been a rich subject of historical and sociological research. The projection of Western cosmological distinctions onto other cultures has also been a topic of interest in a range of subfields in contemporary anthropology and CULTURAL STUDIES.

cost, insurance, freight   Also CIF. Describes the pricing or valuation of a good, including all the transfer costs involved in bringing the good to its place of consumption. Excluding transfer costs yields the FOB (free on board) value of a good.

cost and cost functions   In microeconomic theory, the cost function is the primary means of describing the economic possibilities of the FIRM (see MICROECONOMICS). Cost is a measure of what needs to be given up in order to obtain something by means of purchase, exchange, or production. Economists, when they speak of costs of production, include not only the explicit or money cost but also the implicit or OPPORTUNITY COST, which reflects alternative uses of the time or resources. They also tend to distinguish between the private costs to a producer or a consumer and the social cost imposed on the community as a whole (see SOCIAL COSTS AND SOCIAL BENEFITS).

The cost function of a firm is simply the outlay on factors of production, including wage costs, rental costs of capital, the interest cost of loans, and so on. It is derived from an exercise whereby the firm minimizes its cost or outlay subject to the output that it wishes to produce. The cost function, therefore, indicates the cheapest way to produce a specified output, given certain factor prices. It holds true in the long run, where all the factors can be varied. In the short run, however, some of the factors of production are fixed, limiting the freedom of the firm to optimize them. These functions, together with the production technology, form the basic unit for the analysis of firm behavior.

cost-benefit analysis A conceptual framework for evaluating and choosing investment projects in the government sector, especially in the context of planning, although it can be extended to any private sector project as well. Cost-benefit analysis differs from a financial appraisal in that it considers all gains and losses irrespective of how or to whom they accrue. The underlying rationale of the approach is that market prices are subject to distortions that arise from various forms of market imperfection. In addition, private profitability considerations may be misleading as an indicator of the desirability of a project where broader or more complex issues of social welfare are at stake. Cost-benefit analysis takes both present and future effects into consideration by discounting the future at an appropriate rate. Government projects are generally discounted to reflect evaluations of the social benefits provided (or *social rate of return*), while private projects are discounted at the private rate of return (generally profit).

Cost-benefit analysis provides a method of collecting relevant data at the project level and helps distinguish projects that are socially desirable from those that are marginal or potentially harmful. Many of the specific techniques for calculating costs and benefits, however, remain objects of serious disagreement, especially where matters of subjective well-being are at stake. These areas of uncertainty include the social rate of return and the correction of market prices in the presence of EXTERNALITIES and distortions. Moreover, it is difficult to measure costs and benefits when the choice involves INDIVISIBILITIES (cases in which investment must be of a minimum size or greater) or where there are interindustry linkages (as when a project harms a single industry that is an important supplier to others).

cost–push inflation A type of inflation attributed to situations of market disequilibrium or market shock. Supply shocks that raise the price of certain commodities—for example, the oil-price shocks in the 1970s—are one prominent example. Wage gains attributable to labor union activity, especially when unemployment is high, are sometimes considered another. The circular relationship between wages and prices, however, makes it difficult to identify instances of pure cost–push inflation. Cost increases will be reflected in product prices that raise the cost of living; this will stimulate further demands for wage increases.

Economists, especially monetarists, are skeptical that cost–push inflation is a distinct form. They distinguish between inflation as an ongoing rate of price increases and singular wage increases or supply shocks, which prompt one-time increases in prices. Moreover, a rise in the price of one commodity can be accompanied by a fall in others, so that the aggregate price level remains unchanged.

cottage industry A pre-industrial, often rural mode of manufacturing, in which products are made in individual homes, usually with the part-time labor of the resident(s) and for local consumption.

counterfactual reasoning A method for evaluating claims of causation by exploring what might have happened had the causal event not occurred. Such reasoning is a common test of the validity of claims in the social sciences and in historical studies. The claim, for example, that the American military build-up in the 1980s caused the downfall of the Soviet Union could be counterfactually challenged by asking whether the Soviet Union would have fallen without that build-up. It might also identify other significant factors that modify or refute the claim. The weakness of counterfactual arguments is that they are inevitably speculative.

countervailing power Refers to the power of major interest groups in pluralistic societies to check or restrain the actions of other groups. The term is most often associated with John Kenneth GALBRAITH's analysis of modern industrial democracy in *American Capitalism: The Concept of Countervailing Power* (1952). Galbraith argued that modern economies were no longer strictly competitive but were based on a balance of power among corporations, unions, consumer groups, and government. This worked to check the dominance of corporate interests in American society.

Cournot, Augustin (1801–1877) A French economist remembered primarily for his pioneering study of MONOPOLY, and especially DUOPOLY. Rather than analyze the conditions of perfect competition that concerned most of his contemporaries, Cournot concentrated on what was later termed *imperfect* competition. He found that when only two firms dominate a market, each firm adjusts the quantity it produces based on its rival's output. Price and production stabilize between the levels indicated by monopoly and perfect competition.

Cournot's major work was *Researches into the Mathematical Principles of the Theory of Wealth* (1838). Here, Cournot provided the first definition of a *demand curve* and stated unambiguously that sales of a good diminish as its price rises. This assertion was based on observation rather than derived from any theory of value, however. Cournot went on to show that the change in total revenue following a rise in prices depends on the degree to which demand falls. This concept later came to be termed the *price elasticity of demand*.

In regard to the theory of monopoly, Cournot demonstrated that, for the monopolist, profit is maximized if production is increased up to the point where marginal cost (the cost of one more unit of production) equals marginal revenue (the profit from that unit). This became one of the foundations of neoclassical microeconomics. Cournot then moved on to the theory of duopoly, where he characterized the continuum between one seller (monopoly) and many sellers (perfect competition) as one in which price falls and output rises as the number of sellers increases.

Cournot's book was largely ignored in its day. The mid-twentieth-century revolution in the analysis of monopoly led by Joan ROBINSON and Edward Chamberlin, and the popularization of GAME THEORY, led to a recovery of Cournot as an important figure in the history of mathematical economics. See also MARGINAL ANALYSIS.

couvade A ritual of "sympathetic pregnancy" in some preindustrial cultures, in which the father-to-be mimics aspects of pregnancy and childbirth.

crawling-peg system See EXCHANGE RATE.

creative destruction Joseph SCHUMPETER's term for the constant internal renewal of the economic structure under CAPITALISM, which relentlessly destroys the old in favor of new methods of production. In his view, the competitive character of capitalism was determined mainly by this process and far less by price competition among entrepreneurs.

credentialism In general, the practice of requiring specific educational credentials for certain occupations—a practice closely related to the consolidation of professions (see PROFESSION AND PROFESSIONALIZATION). In a number of contemporary sociological studies, however, credentialization refers to the form of social stratification that restricts occupational mobility by limiting it to persons who have had the advantages of extended education—a group that strongly correlates with CLASS. In addition, many industrialized societies have undergone a process of creeping credentialization that has steadily raised educational requirements for the performance of certain job categories—notably those that have been traditional avenues of occupational mobility, such as low- and midlevel managerial positions. In many such instances, education no longer functions as a form of training for particular positions but as a mechanism that controls access to employment. Credentialization, in this sense, is sometimes viewed as a way of perpetuating the class system, although proponents of functional integrationism argue that the needs of a modern, highly technological society with a mobile population justifies the practice. *Diploma disease* describes much the same phenomenon. See also SOCIAL MOBILITY.

credit Credit generally signifies a transfer of the right to a given object (e.g., a sum of money) in return for payment at a future point in time. Credit markets regulate exchange over time; INTEREST RATES set the relative price of such exchange. Credit markets are important, above all, in permitting consumption and investment decisions by individuals or firms to occur relatively independently of short-term income flows or cash reserves, which results in more efficient allocation of resources over time.

A credit market will function efficiently provided the future payment capacity of debtors is known with certainty and social institutions exist that ensure that debtors meet their future payment obligations. The first requirement is seldom met, since the borrower has a better estimate of repayment ability than the lender—a case of ASYMMETRIC INFORMATION. The recognition of the existence of a moral hazard/adverse selection problem in this context has given rise to a literature on "credit rationing," or the inadequate supply of credit in the face of high demand.

Credit rationing implies a number of conditions. A lender who cannot determine the reliability of borrowers is forced to charge an interest rate that reflects the repaying capacity of the "average" borrower. In such cases, "good" customers may be faced with higher interest rates, causing them to leave the market while "bad" customers stay—an instance of ADVERSE SELECTION. Alternatively, individual customers may be forced by the higher interest rates to choose riskier investment projects—an instance of MORAL HAZARD. In either case, the average "quality" of the loan customer is reduced. If adverse selection dominates, then the optimal policy of the lender may be to hold the interest rate steady, even in the face of excess demand for loans. The interest rate then remains below the market-clearing level, resulting in rationing.

The two main functions of credit institutions are (1) risk consolidation (or spreading the risk by dealing with a large number of lenders and borrowers) and (2) reducing transaction and information costs, by providing a convenient venue for borrowers and lenders and better evaluation of credit risks.

credit multiplier   See MULTIPLIER.

creole   A cultural hybrid, most often in the context of contact between a colonial and an indigenous population. Creole can refer to both languages and peoples: in the former case it is distinguished from a pidgin language by its complexity and its use as a primary language; in the latter it refers to the local descendants of colonial families and came into particularly widespread use in Latin America and the Caribbean islands.

crime   The violation of laws, or more precisely those social norms that have become subject to state control and legal sanctions reliant on punishment. Crime is thus distinct from DEVIANCE, which describes any violation of social norms, including those that are merely subject to societal or group disapproval. The definition of crime consequently plays a strong role in social integration, determining the essential boundaries of behavior in society. This is the core principle of a broad range of functionalist accounts of crime and deviancy, which recognize the enormous social power of expelling or punishing the transgressor.

Criminal law focuses on transgressions against the social order as such—as distinct from CIVIL LAW, which regulates relationships among private individuals (contract law is an example). A variety of historical approaches have invigorated the study of crime and transgression more broadly in recent years. The work of Michel FOUCAULT, in particular, has elevated the organizing and policing of social boundaries, especially regarding criminality and insanity, into a major subfield of research.

Definitions of crime are culturally determined and, in many instances, highly culturally and historically specific. In societies where the dividing line between religion and the state is thin or indistinct, for example, notions of crime may overlap notions of the sacred—a characteristic of nearly all premodern legal systems. Blasphemy against official or dominant religions has often been the subject of criminal law (and still is in a number of Islamic societies). Criminality has also been a tool of authoritarian regimes, which often relabel political dissent as individual transgression.

Modern sociologists and criminologists have generally opposed individualistic concepts of criminal behavior, which tend to view crime as a reflection of individual immorality or failure. Instead, they have emphasized the degree to which patterns of criminal behavior reflect larger structural social and economic issues, such as access to jobs, the strength of social institutions such as schools and communities, age factors, forms of policing, and widespread transformations of family structure. This has been the subject of a vast amount of sociological research on deviancy and youth culture, as well as more recent debates over the cultural reproduction of POVERTY and related criminal behavior.

There is also frequently a large gap between the perceptions of crime and its actual incidence—an important issue insofar as fear of crime can exercise a major influence on people's behavior. In cities, crime is often highly localized in poor neighborhoods; additionally, violent crime is frequently domestic or committed by persons known to the victim. Nonetheless, the news media often contributes the perception of generalized, random danger (see DEVIANCE AMPLIFICATION). Moreover, certain kinds of crime go severely underreported, such as white-collar crime committed in the context of legitimate business—fraud, misuse of funds, or bribery are examples. Sexual abuse and domestic crime—largely directed against women and children—are also notoriously underreported, although the norms and institutions governing these crimes are changing rapidly.

In the United States, violent crime and property crime strongly correlate with age and sex: offenders are overwhelmingly young men between the ages of fourteen and thirty—although this too is subject to historical variation and has recently exhibited a tendency toward younger criminality. Higher rates of crime, too, have been correlated with poverty and race—the subject of a large and contentious body of urban sociology and CRIMINOLOGY that focuses especially on the high rates of violent crime among young African-American men. As many have observed, this group is often treated as a de facto criminal population, subject to "profiling" and discriminatory treatment by the police and the courts. Long-term imprisonment, including for nonviolent crimes like drug possession, has emerged as the dominant American response to crime, and has resulted in a vast expansion of both prisons and the prison population since the 1970s—disproportionately young, black, and male—even as crime decreased in the 1990s. Similar tendencies affect the application of the death penalty in the United States.

There are a variety of important subcategories of crime: the term *victimless crime* is often used to designate illegal activities that do not directly harm other persons, such as prostitution, drug use, and gambling. *Organized crime* involves the coordination of criminal activity, often on a large scale, by mobs or syndicates. *Corporate crime* refers to illegal acts committed by employees on behalf of a corporation, for which the corporation itself is held responsible. *Hate crime* has become an increasingly visible category, used in cases where the motive is prejudice against ethnic, racial, religious, or sexual minorities.

criminology The study of CRIME and criminal behavior. Criminology is an interdisciplinary field associated with SOCIOLOGY. Criminologists focus on a range of issues, including the definition of crime; patterns and demographics of criminal activity; the cultural, socioeconomic, and psychological dimensions of criminal behavior; and different types of crime; and methods for its control. These factors are frequently subject to large historical and cultural variation—a fact that thwarted early efforts to establish general theories of criminal behavior.

The study of crime is closely related to, but in some important ways distinct from, the study of DEVIANCE, which examines the violation of social norms, whether or not those norms are codified into criminal law. Criminology has also overlapped with work on LABELING THEORY and other strongly constructivist accounts of social transgression. A large body of criminological research, however, has avoided the problem of constructivism in favor of practical, applicable research—often in formal or informal coordination with the justice system. Criminological research in this tradition takes a number of forms, from measuring crime to examining the impact of specific laws to evaluating strategies of social control.

As a field, criminology has been enriched since the 1970s by a range of new approaches. Many of these challenge the classical perspective of criminality as a reflection of individual immorality and individual choice—looking instead to structural and group features of social life that underlie patterns of criminal behavior. Most modern criminology similarly challenges theories of criminal types, such as the early physiological studies of Cesare LOMBROSO, which correlated criminality with allegedly atavistic physical characteristics. Nonetheless, biological and genetic explanations periodically resurface in theories of extra "sociopathic" chromosomes and other physical indicators of criminal tendencies.

The fusion of criminology with broader theories of MODERNITY, modernization, and SOCIAL CONTROL is associated with the variety of Marxist approaches that emerged in the 1970s, and also with the enormously influential work of French poststructuralist Michel FOUCAULT. A number of feminist approaches have addressed the traditional neglect of women in criminological studies; in particular, the ways in which sexual crimes such as rape have been managed and redefined over the years (see Susan Brownmiller's *Against Her Will*, 1975).

The related field of *penology* deals with the issues of punishment, DETERRENCE, and reform of criminals and criminal behavior. See also LAW.

crisis management In INTERNATIONAL RELATIONS, the term refers to efforts to avert large-scale conflict in volatile or unpredictable situations. The 1962 Cuban Missile Crisis is perhaps the most conspicuous example in recent decades.

During the COLD WAR, a branch of strategic studies emerged that analyzed such situations with the tools of GAME THEORY and decision theory. These approaches presupposed a small number of unitary, rational actors and sought to clarify the conditions under which actors would escalate or retreat from conflict. Such methods tended to be highly abstract, however, and rarely offered meaningful purchase on complex, evolving, real-world crises.

critical-path analysis A generic name for a set of techniques that allow people to manage large projects and their interrelated constituent activities. The analysis consists of specifying the activities necessary for completing a project, establishing a precedence ordering of these activities, identifying the critical activities, and determining the cost–time trade-offs for the entire project. With this list of priorities, analysts work to expedite the project by allocating greater resources to activities deemed "critical." The 1960s saw the emergence of two such techniques: the PERT (Program Evaluation and Review Technique) and CPM (Critical Path Method). The former was developed to manage the development of the weapons system for Polaris submarines; the latter was developed to manage large construction projects.

critical theory Social theory that seeks to avoid the ideological assumptions of conventional worldviews and more traditional theories. In particular, it seeks to grasp the underlying conditions of possibility for social life, and thus for change in existing conditions. It also critically examines the categories of thought incorporated into theories and the dependence of theoretical perspectives on historical and cultural contexts. The term is most famously associated with the FRANKFURT SCHOOL.

cross cousins Cousins related through the parents' opposite-sex siblings—that is, through the father's sister or the mother's brother. They are distinguished from PARALLEL COUSINS (related through same-sex sibling bonds), and play a crucial part in the marriage customs of some societies. Marriage between a man and his mother's brother's daughter is considered the ideal in some cultures. Cross-cousin marriage is central to Claude LÉVI-STRAUSS's theory of elementary kinship structures.

cross-sectional analysis The statistical analysis of a population or set of data at a specific instant or "snapshot" of time. Such methods are often used to isolate important relationships in situations in which dynamic change over time adds an unmanageable degree of complexity to the process of data gathering.

Cross-sectional analysis is distinct, in this regard, from LONGITUDINAL ANALYSIS—the analysis of changes over time. The terms *synchronic* and *diachronic* are used in analogous fashion in ANTHROPOLOGY and CULTURAL STUDIES.

crowd See COLLECTIVE BEHAVIOR.

crowding out The fall in private consumption or investment resulting from a rise in government expenditure. An increase in government expenditure either raises output and income (if the economy is in an underemployment equilibrium) or raises prices (if the economy is at full employment). In the first case, it increases the *transaction demand for money*; in the second case, it reduces the real-money supply. In either case, it reduces the real-money supply available to meet the *speculative demand for money*. This reduces bond prices and raises interest rates, which in turn leads to a fall in private investment and/or consumption. In the case of full employment, a rise in government expenditure is fully crowded out by the subsequent fall in private investment and consumption. With underemployment of resources, the crowding out is only partial.

cult of domesticity An idealization of "home and family" as a space of moral purity protected from the harsher world outside. This Western cultural ideal centered on the belief that women were responsible for the moral affairs and everyday activities of the domestic sphere. The cult of domesticity was a development of the Victorian age and was primarily directed at middle-class and upper-class women who could afford to stay at home to tend to household affairs, instead of joining the work force.

cults No hard-and-fast definition distinguishes cults from religions, but studies of cults tend to privilege a fairly small set of issues: marginality with respect to larger established religions, simplicity of organization, and charismatic leadership. As vehicles for redemptive hopes or other expectations of divine intervention, cults can be powerful social actors, especially in times of crisis when the legitimacy or efficacy of established religions and institutions is weak. Cults that manifestly respond to social disintegration are often called *revitalization cults*—a term originally applied to Native American spiritual movements of the nineteenth century.

cultural capital Educational credentials or other resources that an individual controls by virtue of evidencing greater attainment of knowledge, sophisticated taste, or other attributes of CULTURE. As developed by Pierre BOURDIEU, the concept extends Max WEBER's analysis of status and adds a cultural component to Marxist and other economic analysis of social life. Bourdieu sought to show first of all that culture is not a realm of "disinterest" but of interests and struggles carried out according to different logics and drawing on distinctive resources. Educational systems are not simply devoted to pure learning; nor are they perfect meritocracies. They are institutions that apportion cultural capital in an unequal fashion. Bourdieu's second point is that the different forms of capital (economic, symbolic, and cultural) are convertible. One student may get more education—or a more prestigious education—because his parents can pay for it. The conversion of capital from one form to another is thus part of strategies of social reproduction. The conversion may privilege one or another form of capital, depending on the way that a society is organized: symbolic capital is valued more in aristocratic society; cultural capital serves more in bureaucratic states; and economic capital provides extra advantages when more areas of social life are commercialized. Lastly, different social fields are dominated by specific forms of capital and maintain their autonomy by controlling conversion. If money alone could buy the best educational credentials, they would lose their distinctive value as cultural capital. See also CAPITAL.

cultural geography Perhaps the most important conceptual turn in twentieth-century GEOGRAPHY, cultural geography concerned itself with the question of human interaction with and transformation of the landscape. Cultural geography initially privileged inquiry into the impact of new technologies or techniques on local or regional ecology, the spread of those techniques through cultural diffusion, the effects of different models of settlement and urban development, and ultimately, the framework of beliefs and attitudes that shape a culture's relationship to its environment. The chief (and earliest) exponent of this perspective in Europe was the French geographer Paul VIDAL DE LA BLACHE, whose writing and institutional presence had an enormous influence on the practice of geography around the turn of the century. In the United States, the principle figure was Carl SAUER, at the University of California, Berkeley. Through his scholarship and founding role at the Berkeley

school of cultural geography, Sauer set the agenda for much of the field in the 1930s, 1940s, and 1950s. Among other things, this involved a diminished role for strict "environmental determinism" in accounts of human culture and behavior, and greater attention to the study of premodern cultures.

The humanist orientation of cultural geography came under growing pressure in the 1960s from a range of quantitative approaches to spatial analysis, which gave new impetus to the study of economic activity and modern societies. This spelled the end of the disciplinary dominance, if not the intellectual influence, of the Berkeley school, which had to a large degree specialized in the study of premodern societies. The culturalist perspective that Sauer championed, however, is more flexible than some of its critics have allowed, and continues to be a major orientation within the field—especially as reconfigured in the "new cultural geography" of the 1980s. Current work, in general, stresses the spatial distribution of cultural patterns and practices, without positing integrated and bounded cultures.

The term *cultural ecology* has been used to describe much the same set of preoccupations—although it often refers specifically to the work of anthropologist Julian STEWARD, who used the term in his inquiries into the variety of forms of cultural adaptation to the environment among the Shoshone and Paiute desert tribes of the American Southwest. See also CULTURE.

cultural materialism Associated in anthropology primarily with the work of Marvin HARRIS, cultural materialism is rooted in the proposition that culture is strongly determined by material conditions. Although it bears a relationship to Marxist HISTORICAL MATERIALISM, cultural materialism departs from it on many key points, especially in marginalizing or abolishing the Marxist concern with ideology and dialectics. Instead, Harris favors the idea that culture is an adaptation to material conditions that largely reflects rational individual evaluations of the least costly or most beneficial action. For Harris, material conditions are primarily environmental and geographic, but they also include certain kinds of societal feedback, such as technology, modes of subsistence, and population pressure. For him, these constitute the *infrastructure* on which social and political organization (*structure*)—and ultimately broader areas of belief and cultural production (*superstructure*)—are based. Cultural materialism has been an influential point of convergence for ANTHROPOLOGY, ecology, and CULTURAL GEOGRAPHY since the 1960s.

The term has also been used by Raymond WILLIAMS and other social theorists to describe the work of locating texts and other cultural products within the larger material, social, and economic fabric of a historical period. Michel FOUCAULT's emphasis on the interpenetration of discourse, institutions, and power shares this analytical perspective. In literary studies, some of this work is referred to as "New Historicism."

cultural studies A field most closely associated with the study of popular culture in industrialized societies, although a comprehensive description would include a much wider range of subjects and approaches to the problem of CULTURE. Part of the difficulty of describing cultural studies is due to the resistance of many of its practitioners to its consolidation as a discipline, which might informally limit the field to a particular set of objects or methodologies. Instead, cultural studies has developed at the intersection of a range of disciplines, drawing on techniques of textual analysis from literary criticism, ethnography and empirical research from the social sciences, and studies of colonial and postcolonial societies.

The origins of cultural studies are usually traced to a group of scholars that gathered in the 1960s at the Centre for Contemporary Cultural Studies in Birmingham, England, founded by Richard HOGGART in 1964. The Centre's intellectual orientation was shaped by the scholarship of several key figures—including, especially, Raymond WILLIAMS and Edward Palmer THOMPSON, who in different ways examined the development of popular culture in the context of a Marxist theory of social organization and collective struggle. Although the work of these three figures is quite diverse in subject and methodology, the cultural studies movement tended to cohere around their commitment to exploring the cultural resources and resourcefulness of the English working class. Their work endorsed what might be said to be the cardinal point of cultural studies: the proposition that culture is a divided field and an object of struggle between different groups. Much of the subsequent history of cultural studies has involved elaborating this notion of struggle, both by enabling it to recognize and account for other forms of cultural subordination (primarily those articulated by race, gender, or subcultural status) and by exploring models of

how groups construct meaning. This latter question has been the subject of a wide range of work in media and reception studies, the main thrust of which has been to problematize or reject earlier FRANKFURT SCHOOL visions of the public as passive consumers of views formulated by a cultural elite. Most cultural studies today favor a model of active and varied interpretation by cultural actors engaged in a struggle for hegemony over meaning. This approach has drawn considerable support from Antonio GRAMSCI's neo-Marxist theory of cultural struggle, which Stuart HALL helped place at the front of the cultural-studies agenda during his tenure as head of the Centre in the late 1960s and 1970s. See also RECEPTION THEORY AND READER-RESPONSE THEORY.

Cultural studies flourished in the United States, especially during the 1980s and 1990s. While in Britain it had strong roots in Marxism, history, and sociology, in the United States it grew primarily out of literature and other fields in the humanities. It also absorbed ideas and perspectives from French poststructuralist thought. As a result, American cultural studies has been less oriented toward social theory.

One point of wide agreement among advocates of cultural studies is that its specificity lies (or should lie) in a commitment to social engagement—to intervening in the field under study. The precise nature of that engagement, however, remains a subject of considerable debate. The widespread influence of STRUCTURALISM and POSTSTRUCTURALISM has tended to undercut the models of agency that would legitimate conventional political and/or social struggle. The tendency of cultural studies to equate issues of representation and cultural production with political struggle both reflects and complicates this issue, while also providing an avenue for academic scholarship to graft itself into the hegemonic field.

Antonio GRAMSCI's concept of hegemony has been a major influence on politically engaged cultural studies because it emphasizes the need to articulate the relationships between the diverse forms of exclusion experienced by different groups. The work of intellectuals, Gramsci argued, involves aligning these forms against the dominant group or class. Consistent with this ambition, cultural studies has been closely associated with ethnic studies, gay studies, and FEMINISM, and it is deeply marked by explorations of cultural diversity. Some critics, however, see the retreat from existing channels of political engagement as a surrender of the terrain of the state to a romanticized and often, in practice, merely symbolic form of opposition. These are not issues that cultural studies is likely to resolve; they are perhaps better thought of as the constitutive tensions of a field that both resists and profits from its entrenchment in a politically isolated academy.

culture   The term has acquired a wide range of meanings since its original association with the cultivation of land, but two modern significations stand out: the humanistic definition that emerged in eighteenth-century Europe in reference to the arts, music, and letters, and the anthropological definition that developed in the nineteenth century to describe the sum total of human activities. This second meaning initially referred to humanity as a whole, but it increasingly developed a discrete and pluralist sense that asserted the existence of separate and different cultures. Edward Burnett TYLOR is usually acknowledged as the originator of the anthropological definition of culture, arguing in 1871 that "Culture or civilization, taken in its wide ethnographic sense, is that complex whole which includes knowledge, belief, art, morals, law, custom, and any other capabilities and habits acquired by man as a member of society." Tylor's notion of culture, however, remained essentially singular—a variable on an evolutionary scale along which different societies could be located. The modern sense of multiple and discrete cultures derives primarily from Franz BOAS's turn-of-the-century critique of evolutionary models such as Tylor's and the widespread derivation of culture from race that frequently accompanied them.

Boas emphasized that cultures developed not according to evolutionary stages, but in response to particular historical circumstances, including the diffusion of ideas or cultural traits from other cultures. He argued that cultures had to be approached largely independently and on their own terms. This articulation of the goals and methods of ANTHROPOLOGY proved enormously influential in the United States, if less so in France and Great Britain. There, Emile DURKHEIM and A. R. RADCLIFFE-BROWN, respectively, succeeded in defining the agenda of anthropology (and in Durkheim's case, of sociology as well) as the study of social structures and organization. Radcliffe-Brown summed up the views of many British anthropologists in arguing that the holistic approach to culture, incorporating components as diverse as language, myth, child rearing, psychology, and technology, was a "vague abstraction." This divide would be more or less formalized and routinely debated in the distinction between cultural and social anthropology.

The question of how, precisely, cultures are integrated set the terms of much of the debate about culture in the first half of the twentieth century. The FUNCTIONALISM of Durkheim and Radcliffe-Brown provided one influential answer, arguing that particular cultural forms developed and survived according to their utility in achieving social integration. The CULTURE AND PERSONALITY MOVEMENT developed by Boas's students Edward SAPIR, Ruth Fulton BENEDICT, and Margaret MEAD provided another answer that relied on analogies between individual psychology and the culture that produces it. Social theorists from Antonio GRAMSCI to Talcott PARSONS and Clifford GEERTZ, in contrast, emphasized the role of shared norms in the social bond. In an important qualification of many of these assumptions, the sociologist Pitirim SOROKIN argued that integration should not be assumed but studied as an empirical variable.

Postwar anthropology has been characterized by a variety of attempts to move beyond the social–cultural divide—Claude LEVI-STRAUSS's STRUCTURALISM can be said to have attempted a synthesis—and more generally by challenges to both sides: to the hegemony of culture as an explanatory term, and to the possibility of an objective framework in which social organization might be deciphered. The question of whether cultures can be viably described as integrated wholes has prompted the rise of a range of other interpretive tools that attempt to account for the diversity and conflict within cultural formations. Interest in IDEOLOGY, discourse, and hegemony reflects some of this suspicion of earlier notions of cultural integration.

The rise of CULTURAL STUDIES, first in England and more recently in the United States, is an indication of this shift and has carried some of the challenges of POSTMODERNISM, discourse theory, and interdisciplinarity to the door of traditional social science. Whether this constitutes a crisis or an opportunity for the social sciences remains a subject of considerable debate.

Culture and Personality movement   An interdisciplinary movement in ANTHROPOLOGY and psychology that emphasized the reciprocity between psychological development and social formations. It was the first explicit attempt to integrate the insights of Freudian psychology and perspectives on child development with anthropological observations of cultural varia-tion. The movement was defined more by this intersection of interests than by any specific positions or methodologies. Although it had no leadership or organization *per se*, it coa-lesced in the late 1920s around the work of anthropologist/linguist Edward SAPIR and the anthropologists Margaret MEAD and Ruth Ful-ton BENEDICT. Mead's and Benedict's case studies of the relationships between psychological and social development in different societies consti-tuted a challenge to universalizing assumptions about human psychology. Their work led to attempts to find a universal psychological struc-ture that underlies observed societal variations, notably in Abram Kardiner and Ralph LINTON's proposition of the "basic personality structure" in *The Individual and His Society* (1939). While initially focused on premodern societies, Cul-ture and Personality methods were popularized by the study of national character during and after World War II—most famously in Benedict's study of Japanese culture, *The Chrysanthemum and the Sword* (1946).

By the 1950s, the development of more sophis-ticated theories of cognition and the recognition of the psychological reductivism of many of the Culture and Personality approaches signaled the effective end of the movement. Continued inter-est in the phenomena and relationships that the Culture and Personality movement identi-fied, however, led to a reorganization of the field under the banner of psychological anthropology in the 1960s and, later, to the emergence of the contemporary field of cultural psychology.

culture area or culture region   A geographi-cal region defined by certain shared cultural traits, such as similar languages or forms of social orga-nization. The concept has been central to theories of cultural diffusion, which postulate the outward movement of cultural innovations from a single source. Tracing the geographical distribution of particular cultural traits has found applications in a wide range of projects within anthropology and geography, from the study of religious groups to subsistence patterns, sports cultures, and patterns of speech.

Geographers often distinguish between *formal* culture regions based on shared cultural traits and *functional* cultural regions based on systems of coordinated economic or social activity, such as farming or church-going. Geographers also recognize *vernacular* cultural regions, based on the perception of shared identity among inhabitants

of a given area. The concept of culture regions was important in the emergence of modern ANTHROPOLOGY and CULTURAL GEOGRAPHY at the turn of the twentieth century, although the identification of specific culture regions quickly proved (and has remained) a highly subjective issue that has generated major disagreements among scholars working in the same areas. See also DIFFUSION AND DIFFUSIONISM; and *KULTURKREIS*.

culture industry   The key descriptive term in Max HORKHEIMER's and Theodor ADORNO's account of the development of mass culture in capitalist society. Elaborated primarily in *The Dialectic of Enlightenment* (1944), the term refers to a variety of changes in the nature of cultural production and reception: especially the merger of culture with big business (quintessentially the movie studios) and the abolition of the pleasure and emancipatory impulses that once character-ized art in favor of palliating entertainments. For Horkheimer and Adorno, culture is increasingly harnessed and rationalized by capitalism in order to provide an anesthetic for the brutalizing effects of work and a means of integrating desires into the capitalist economy. The public, on the other side, is reduced to a position of passively consum-ing carefully manipulated imagery and meaning. Horkheimer and Adorno provide, in short, an analysis of the totalitarian direction of consumer society, in which much of the register of political and social freedom has been reduced to choices between superficial brands or styles.

This came to be the dominant position on popular culture of the FRANKFURT SCHOOL, and was often signaled in the distinction that Adorno and other Frankfurt critics drew between "high" and "low" art—the former retaining vestiges of the original values of artistic production. CULTURAL STUDIES emerged, in part, as a critique of the Frankfurt school's assumption about the passivity of consumers of popular culture.

culture region   See CULTURE AREA OR CUL-TURE REGION.

currency board   An institution that stands ready to exchange domestic currency for a foreign-reserve currency at a specified and fixed rate. To make this promise credible, the board needs reserves of the foreign currency equal to the value of the outstanding domestic currency. Because of the vulnerability of currency to speculative attacks—especially in developing countries—currency boards now survive in only a handful of countries, including Hong Kong, Singapore, and Brunei.

custom At its most general, a custom is any practice or tradition that is characteristic of a social group. Early ANTHROPOLOGY and ETHNOLOGY focused largely on the description of customs, but the concept has been largely superseded by and subsumed into the study of CULTURE, cultural formations, and the historical issues implicit therein.

customary law LAW passed on by unwritten tradition. The term came into use with the codification of indigenous laws and customs by colonial administrations.

customs union A type of agreement between countries that abolishes trade barriers among its members and establishes a common external tariff on trade with nonmember countries. The European Union is a customs union. Customs unions stand in contrast to free-trade associations such as NAFTA (the North American Free Trade Agreement), in which the member countries have no tariff barriers among themselves but retain separate commercial policies toward countries outside the association.

Jacob Viner provided the first rigorous analysis of customs unions and identified two ways in which they can affect trade patterns and resource allocation. He focused primarily on the concepts of *trade creation* and *trade diversion*. Trade creation occurs when the removal of tariffs on intra-member trade shifts a member country's demand from high-cost domestic producers to lower-cost producers in a partner country. Trade diversion occurs when the abolition of the tariff shifts demand from outside the customs union to a higher-cost union source. Viner demonstrated that the removal of tariff barriers is a move toward free trade only when trade creation dominates trade diversion. If the opposite occurs, then the union may reduce the welfare of its members, as well as the welfare of other countries outside the union. Viner's theory exemplifies the "theory of the second best," which suggests that an incomplete move toward the optimum (here, the abolition of some trade barriers) might make matters worse.

Viner's analysis launched a broader literature that sought to establish whether customs unions created or diverted trade and to analyze the subsequent welfare effects on members and nonmembers. Such questions are open to an almost infinite variety of historical particulars, however, and no significant consensus exists regarding their effects.

cybernetics The study of self-organizing and self-regulating systems, generally in terms of flows of information and mechanisms of control. Developed by mathematician Norbert Weiner in the 1940s as a general theory of complex systems, cybernetics was widely adapted to the study of politics and society. In sociology, it is associated with the FUNCTIONALISM of Talcott PARSONS, for whom the notion of self-regulation was central, and (mediated by later developments) with the SYSTEM(S) THEORY of Niklas LUHMANN. In anthropology, the principal figure was Gregory BATESON, who studied the larger question of human interaction with the biosphere and human consciousness as an informational problem of ordering and categorizing. Karl DEUTSCH brought cybernetics to the study of politics in the 1960s and early 1970s, emphasizing the question of the linkages among different organizations, issues, and ideas in decision-making processes, as well as the value of negative FEEDBACK in aiding organizations to adapt to their environments.

D

Dahl, Robert (1915–) An American political scientist who has made major contributions to the study of democratic political processes and to the theory of democratic PLURALISM. The problem of political power sharing in democratic societies has been central to a number of Dahl's inquiries, including his *Preface to Democratic Theory* (1956), which focused on the structures of conflict and compromise through which groups with divergent interests exercise power.

For Dahl, conflicting interests were essential to good democratic government. Rather than centralizing power in the hands of a single majority, contested elections ensure that various, not necessarily like-minded minorities determine who holds power. In practice, he suggested, the chief issue in democracy is not the tyranny of the majority, but the ways in which minority blocks accommodate or frustrate one another's demands. Dahl's influential *Who Governs?* (1964) is an empirical study of these processes at the level of city government in New Haven, Connecticut. He revised and extended this theory in several works, including *Polyarchy, Participation and Opposition* (1971).

In more recent works—*Dilemmas of Pluralist Democracy* (1982) and *Preface to Economic Democracy* (1985)—Dahl has looked more closely at the effects of money on the political process, especially on the power of special interests and big business. He has also written extensively on American foreign policy and on issues surrounding nuclear power and weaponry. Dahl's other major works include *After the Revolution? Authority in a Good Society* (1970), *Size and Democracy* (1973; with Edward Tufte), *Democracy and its Critics* (1989), and *On Democracy* (1999).

Davis, Kingsley (1908–1996) An American sociologist and demographer known primarily for his work on population dynamics and social stratification in modernizing societies. Davis's major achievement was the theory of the DEMOGRAPHIC TRANSITION—a shift from high birthrates and high mortality rates to low birthrates and low mortality rates that has occurred in many industrializing societies. Davis was particularly interested in the fact that the decrease in mortality rates preceded the decrease in birth rates, resulting in a "transitional" period with rapid population growth—a situation common in developing countries. He conducted numerous empirical studies of this phenomenon and coined the term *population explosion*.

Throughout, Davis tied demographics to the broader analysis of social systems and to the question of human habitats. He also worked toward a general theory of the social sciences in *A Crowding Hemisphere* (1958) and *World Urbanization 1950–1970* (1969 and 1972; 2 volumes).

Davis's other claim to notoriety derives from a paper written with Wilbert E. Moore on the positive aspects of class stratification and inequality in modern Western societies, entitled "Some Principles of Stratification" (*American Sociological Review*, 1946). Davis and Moore argued that class inequality is of functional benefit to society, insofar as the most important occupations receive the greatest rewards. This position launched a major debate within the sociology of occupations and stratification, known as the DAVIS-MOORE DEBATE. Davis was elected president of the American Sociological Association in 1959. His other publications include *Human Society* (1949) and *The Population of India and Pakistan* (1951).

Davis–Moore debate A controversy surrounding the theory of the functional role of inequality in society, as proposed by the sociologists Kingsley DAVIS and Wilbert Moore ("Some Principles of Stratification," 1945). Davis and Moore argued that inequality in income and other incentives reflects the fact that some jobs are more important than others for the functioning of society, and that society is best served by placing a premium on those jobs in order to attract the most talented individuals. While the theory intuitively describes some of the broad features of social stratification, it was criticized by those who considered CLASS and power relations significant in the maintenance of social inequality, as well as by those who objected to comparing the importance of different jobs on the basis of salary.

dealignment   See ALIGNMENT.

dear money   See CHEAP MONEY.

decision analysis   A method for organizing sets of choices under conditions of uncertainty in order to ascertain the expected payoffs of various courses of action. Decision problems are broken down into possible outcomes, the uncertain events that may effect the outcomes, and actions that may be taken. Usually, outcomes are assigned values and uncertain events are assigned probabilities of occurrence, so that the expected value of each course of action can be determined. Decision analysis is common in ECONOMICS and in areas of public policy.

decoding   See ENCODING AND DECODING.

deconstruction   A method of philosophical and linguistic criticism originally associated with the work of Jacques DERRIDA but now widespread in the humanities and—to a lesser degree—the social sciences. The goals of deconstruction generally involve illuminating the process of construction of binary oppositions within texts and philosophical systems. The method extends the structuralist understanding of LANGUAGE as a system of differential relationships, in which concepts acquire significance only in relation to other concepts, toward a consideration of the limits of structure itself. This is the core of Derrida's elaborate critiques of metaphysical claims to truth and the concept of an adequate or fully "present" language that underwrites them. Derrida insists on the diverse ways in which meaning is a partial, never fully achieved act, both divided internally and deferred in time. He coined the term *différance* to describe this articulation between spatial and temporal difference, although it is only one of many Derridean operating terms that express the divided nature of the linguistic sign. This insistence on the fundamental insufficiency of language to anchor itself in any transcendental reality marks deconstruction as a form of POSTSTRUCTURALISM.

At its philosophical core, deconstruction is an inquiry into what language makes possible—in other words, what kinds of operations it performs, first and foremost the always incomplete generation of identity and difference. Derrida does not deny the importance of strategies that legitimize these distinctions—such as hierarchical claims of truth and falsehood, or value systems that anchor structures of thought or action—so much as reveal and contextualize those strategies. Much of his writing demonstrates how texts construct their authority by marginalizing or eliding certain differences, and how one might invert the values that underlie that authority. Derrida's well-known assertion of the priority of writing over speech is such an exercise. In many quarters, deconstruction has become identified with this style of criticism rooted in metaphysical skepticism, reliant on the close analysis of slippages and errata in texts, and expressed through a punning and labyrinthine style that serves to highlight the circularity and openness of signifying processes, as well as the vulnerability of truth claims.

As a method of analyzing texts, deconstruction has had its greatest impact in literary studies, where its general linguistic critique has diffused to the point of ubiquity. Yet deconstruction has also been central to poststructuralist analyses in the social sciences—especially ANTHROPOLOGY—as well as to innumerable recent debates over the socially and linguistically constructed character of categories of gender, race, and other markers of difference.

de facto and de jure   Latin for "in fact" and "in law." The terms refer to the potential difference between the actual and official condition of a thing or a practice. In politics, it sometimes refers to the inefficacy of law to dictate a situation—as in the case of many antidiscrimination laws. It can also, however, reflect a double intention, as when a government confers de facto but not de jure recognition on another government, in order to express disapproval without impeding business or other political relationships. The United States' de facto relations with the People's Republic of China after 1972 are an example. De jure recognition was conferred in 1979.

deficit financing   Government budget deficits and the means of financing them have been an important focus of planning and economic analysis since John Maynard KEYNES's studies of fiscal policy in the early twentieth century. Both have potentially large effects on aggregate demand in the economy. A fiscal deficit arises either through changes in government expenditure or through a reduction in taxes. Both of these raise aggregate demand—the first directly and the second indirectly—by raising the level of disposable income. Keynes showed that the initial effect of deficit spending on demand is amplified by the resulting higher levels of income, which enable subsequent rounds of individual and firm spending. This is the MULTIPLIER effect, which accounts for the general rise in income and employment above the level of the original fiscal stimulus.

This logic, however, is subject to the following qualifications: (1) if the economy is at full employment, deficit spending will only serve to increase prices; (2) the effect of fiscal policy depends on monetary policy as well—the fiscal stimulus will raise interest rates if monetary policy is unchanged and the CROWDING OUT of private sector spending will occur; and (3) permanent and temporary fiscal changes have different effects. The RICARDIAN EQUIVALENCE THEOREM, posited by David RICARDO and developed by Robert Barro, addresses this question. It states that deficits bring about an offsetting change in private saving that negates the effect of the fiscal stimulus. Empirical research suggests that partial offsetting does occur in such situations.

definition of the situation Sociologist William Isaac THOMAS's phrase for the way in which persons subjectively construct the meaning of social situations. It refers to the process by which people determine what roles they are to play in a given situation and, therefore, how they will behave. Social reality, Thomas argued, is primarily the product of these subjective constructions, and might have little to do with the "objective" facts of a situation. To paraphrase Thomas, if persons define a situation as real, then it is real in its consequences.

The definition of the situation may vary from actor to actor and change with circumstances. Different definitions of the situation can develop as social cues are interpreted in different ways and as people bring different resources to bear. The "objective" factors are not, however, dismissable in defining a situation; there must be some agreement between individuals as to the nature of the interaction. This margin has been of considerable interest to sociologists, especially in relation to ROLE theory and Robert K. MERTON's subsequent work on SELF-FULFILLING PROPHECY.

de jure See DE FACTO AND DE JURE.

Deleuze, Gilles (1925–1995) One of the major philosophers of the latter half of the twentieth century and, with Michel FOUCAULT and Jacques DERRIDA, a leader of French POST-STRUCTURALISM. Deleuze has had a significant and, in the Anglo-American world, still growing impact on social theory. Much of his work is devoted to reconstructing a philosophical tradition organized around the concept of *becoming* rather than *being*—i.e., around the refusal of static systems, transcendental truths, and restrictive theories of the subject and psychology. This perspective is basic to his numerous studies of philosophers (Friedrich NIETZSCHE, David HUME, Immanuel KANT, Henri-Louis Bergson, Baruch Spinoza, Foucault, and Gottfried Leibniz), literary figures (Marcel Proust, Franz Kafka, Leopold von Sacher-Masoch), and the history of the cinema—the art form of temporality par excellence. In the Anglo-American world, he is best known for his two-volume collaboration with the psychoanalyst Félix GUATTARI, *Capitalism and Schizophrenia: Anti-Oedipus* (vol. 1, 1972) and *A Thousand Plateaus* (vol. 2, 1980). The first book presented subjectivity as an infinitely variable and constantly renewed process of construction of "desiring-machines." It also critiqued the Oedipal model as a violently normalizing schema of desire that operates in the service of CAPITALISM. The second book is a more loosely organized and experimental extension of these principles into a range of topics in history, politics, art, and the natural sciences.

Deleuze and Guattari's larger account of capitalist development centers on around two processes: the *deterritorializing* effect of market principles (such as money) on previously unconvertible realms of value in premodern societies; and the simultaneous need to *reterritorialize*, or recode, the social world around new principles, desires, differences, and institutions in order to maintain the flow of socially productive desire and exchange.

Both books were products of the heated social and theoretical climate of 1968 and, in particular, of the organized resistance to the hard psychiatry of the 1950s and 1960s (see ANTI-PSYCHIATRY). Although they are sometimes criticized for their reductionism and obscurity, neither was conceived as a sustained exposition of a system of thought—anathema to Deleuze. Rather they extended a principle that organizes much of Deleuze's work: the continuous provocation to thought and the pragmatic redeployment of concepts and traditions in the service of other, more useful, critical projects. Deleuze's other major works include *Difference and Repetition* (1969 [1994]), *The Logic of Sense* (1960 [1990]), and *What is Philosophy* (1994).

deliberative democracy A school of political thought that argues that DEMOCRACY should be organized in such a way as to promote reasoned debate among citizens. Like advocates of PARTICIPATORY DEMOCRACY, deliberative democrats seek not only to expand the scope of current democracies but also to improve its quality in two ways. First, they argue that wider and more informed debate will result in better, more rational, more inclusive decisions. Second, they suggest that wider debate will improve citizens' moral reasoning, cognitive abilities, and public spiritedness. Advocates such as James Fishkin have proposed a variety of specific measures to enhance deliberation. Deliberative polling, for example, replaces attempts to discern citizens' already-formed opinions with a series of polls interspersed with provision of additional information and occasions for discussion. Deliberative democracy draws on a long tradition of inquiry into the nature of political participation and republican government. The most prominent modern advocate of such deliberative mechanisms (and critic of existing structures of mass democracy) is Jürgen HABERMAS.

delinquent drift   A state of limbo for some adolescents in which there is no strong attachment to either conventional or criminal lifestyles. As developed by David Matza (*Delinquency and Drift*, 1964), the concept attributes delinquency to a general weakening of the moral ties of society, rather than to a conscious criminal drive or strong determination by other social forces. According to Matza, delinquents "neutralize" or exempt themselves from the moral constraints of law or social norms and, for this reason, act without strong feelings of responsibility, guilt, or remorse.

demand for money   The determinants of the demand for money are among the fundamental issues in macroeconomic theory. In modern economics, MONEY has generally been understood to serve three functions. It is a medium of exchange that is accepted in payment for commodities. It is the economy's medium of account—i.e., prices are quoted in terms of money. And it is a store of value, which may be used to transfer purchasing power from the present to the future. These roles give rise to the demand for money.

One of the earliest approaches to the theory of money demand is the *quantity theory of money* attributed to Irving FISHER (*The Purchasing Power of Money*, 1911). Fisher argued that the more transactions an individual undertakes, the more

money he or she will want to hold as money balances.

John Maynard KEYNES modified this view in his account of the speculative motive for holding money. In this case, money and bonds are viewed as alternative assets. Since bond demand is sensitive to interest rates, and since individuals must allocate their wealth portfolio between bonds and money, money demand also responds to changes in the interest rates. Keynes termed this interest sensitivity of money the *liquidity preference*.

Keynes's speculative motive was, in turn, reformulated by James Tobin in terms of portfolio-allocation decisions under conditions of uncertainty. According to Tobin, people allocate wealth between riskless assets (money) and assets with an uncertain return expected to exceed that of money. Tobin showed that the optimal portfolio mix depends on an individual's degree of RISK AVERSION and wealth, and on the mean variance of the risky asset's return distribution.

Milton FRIEDMAN's restatement of the quantity theory of money dispensed with the individual motives posited by Keynes and treated money like any other asset that yields a flow of services. This view emphasizes the impact of levels of wealth and expected INFLATION on the demand for money. Still other theories of money demand address the effects of inflation and capital accumulation in a dynamic context, in which individuals solve dynamic optimization problems of portfolio allocation and wealth accumulation.

demand-pull inflation   See COST-PUSH INFLATION; and INFLATIONARY GAP.

demand theory   The main purpose of demand theory in economics is to explain observed consumer choices regarding commodities or commodity bundles. Market parameters—mainly prices and income—determine the level and composition of demand. The model that maps these market parameters onto a given bundle of commodities is termed the *demand function*.

Demand theory endows the consumer with preferences over some group of commodities—representing tastes and desires—which together define the consumption set. These preferences are used to establish an ordering or ranking of these bundles, which in turn can be graphically represented as INDIFFERENCE CURVES, which show the different combinations of commodities that yield the same utility.

If the preferences satisfy certain rational-choice criteria then they may be represented by a UTILITY function, which similarly graphs the ranking of choices (see RATIONAL-CHOICE THEORY). The consumer then chooses a preferred commodity mix from the feasible consumption set (feasibility being defined by the consumer's budget). The results are called the (Marshallian) demand function for the individual (see Alfred MARSHALL). Extending similar analyses to all consumers and adding the individual demand functions yield the market-demand function for a particular commodity. See also AGGREGATE DEMAND FUNCTION.

democratization   The transition from undemocratic to democratic regimes, or, more generally, the expansion of access to decision making and power within societies, organizations, or associations. Democratization is one of the major features of Western modernity, first in the transition to popular, democratic forms of rule and then in the extension of the franchise and related forms of social empowerment to excluded groups—principally women and racial and ethnic minorities.

According to Samuel Huntington's widely used, although contested, typology, democratization has occurred in three broad waves at the global level. The first (but least distinct) began with the American and French Revolutions of the late eighteenth century and continued until the 1920s. Its principle effect was the creation of lasting democracies in northern and western Europe and in the independent former British colonies, as well as some short-lived attempts in other parts of the world. The second wave, lasting from 1943 to 1962, extended democracy to the defeated Axis countries, to many Latin American countries, and to some of the newly independent former European colonies in the developing world. The majority of democratic regimes in the latter two groups did not survive. The third wave began in southern Europe after 1974, swept across Latin America and parts of Asia in the 1980s, and by 1990 included most of the former Soviet bloc, as well as some African countries.

Theories of democratization tend to privilege two main questions: What makes democratization possible? And what allows democracy to endure? The diversity of cases makes a definite answer unlikely, but important factors seem to include defeat in war (by a democratic power); social and economic development, including the emergence of a viable middle class; a broad consensus on the desirability of democracy, especially among political elites; and the "demonstration effect" of other successful democracies.

democracy   Rule by the *people* (in ancient Greek, the *demos*), generally at the level of the state, but also including small-scale forms of governance and decision making. The earliest formal experiments with democracy were in ancient Athens, where citizen-rule flourished for extended periods in the fifth century BCE. Greek political philosophy laid the basis for much of the tradition of democratic thought, although the most influential philosophers—PLATO and ARISTOTLE—were critical of democracy on a number of grounds. Plato believed that rule by an enlightened elite was preferable; Aristotle viewed democracy as rule by the lower orders of society, and therefore as a form of government that needed to be mixed with aristocratic or monarchical elements in order to guarantee that no one group held a permanent monopoly on power. Both associated democracy with mob-rule, corruption, and chronic instability. Neither thought democracy feasible in large states, where face-to-face public life was difficult or impossible. The Aristotelian account—especially the small-republic thesis—was rediscovered during the Renaissance and informed early discussions of democracy and popular sovereignty in the eighteenth century.

Modern democracy draws on a range of developments of the medieval era, including the emergence of legal regimes that guaranteed certain individual rights and that bound the sovereign to enumerated customary laws—initially in England's *Magna Carta* (1215) and later in the constitutional and social contract traditions of social thought (see SOCIAL-CONTRACT THEORY). The emergence of formal processes of consultation between the sovereign and other defined sectors of society also played a large role (most notably involving the three *estates*: the commoners, the aristocracy, and the clergy). Another crucial factor was the developing matrix of modern individuality, including new conceptions of the self, new social values, and new spaces for collective social processes (such as the marketplace) that together underwrote a shift in sovereignty from monarchs to the "people." The social contract tradition of Thomas HOBBES, John LOCKE, and Jean-Jacques ROUSSEAU investigated the meaning of political legitimacy in this changing social order.

For much of the seventeenth and eighteenth centuries, the English constitutional monarchy was the most acclaimed model of political participation—balancing popular, aristocratic, and monarchical elements in a relatively stable and prosperous structure of government. The American and French revolutions carried the democratic principle further in placing sovereignty entirely on a popular basis—even when, in the American case, it included a complex SEPARATION OF POWERS between branches and levels of government.

Modern democracy at the state level relies on the concept of *popular sovereignty*: ultimate political authority rests with the citizens, but routine decision making is delegated to officials. At the local level, direct participation is possible, and in fact traditions of local democratic governance greatly predate the state-level democratic revolutions of the eighteenth and nineteenth centuries. The nature of these arrangements continues to be of interest to democratic theory and activism, especially in the face of the growth of centralized state power and systems of bureaucratic administration. Communitarians are among the strongest advocates of reinvigorated democratic participation (see COMMUNITARIANISM). A variety of counterpositions exists, from advocates of TECHNOCRACY (or rule by experts) as society grows more complex, to theories of the inevitability of elites (see ELITE AND ELITISM). Other long-standing debates within democratic theory and practice continue to play a role in contemporary discussions, including the risk that minority groups (political, religious, ethnic, or racial) will have little power in systems that privilege MAJORITY RULE.

Debates over the meaning of REPRESENTATION also have a long history, rooted in the question of whether officials are elected to make their own decisions or to enact the collective opinion of their constituents. Current efforts to strengthen democracy often turn on increasing popular participation, for example, through the use of referenda and other forms of direct citizen action. DELIBERATIVE DEMOCRACY refers to efforts to increase the space for the consideration of key issues by ordinary citizens. Such concerns are closely related to analyses of the formation of PUBLIC OPINION, generally understood as the sum of private opinions, and to the more collective understanding produced through discourse in the public sphere (see PUBLIC SPHERE AND PRIVATE SPHERE).

Popular sovereignty implies no particular set of institutions and has, in the modern era, become the dominant rhetoric of state power more generally. It is also closely tied to the roughly concurrent development of NATIONALISM, especially those aspects that directly implicate individuals in the collective national body without regard to the mediating or representative institutions that enable self-governance. Political science has nonetheless devoted considerable attention to specifying those forms of democratic infrastructure, particularly the types of democratic society they sustain. Institutional guarantees of the peaceful transition of power and open, contested political arenas figure prominently in this research, as do the mechanisms and practice of elections.

Many scholars posit DEMOCRATIZATION as one of the major axes of MODERNITY. Democratization refers to the transition to democracy from other forms of rule, as well as to the processes within democratic societies that extend political participation to new arenas and new communities. In this way, the originally narrow franchise of most Western democracies was replaced by more inclusive forms of suffrage, extended toward the propertyless, racial and ethnic minorities, women, and young adults.

Since the late eighteenth century, democratization has been a profoundly international process—exported to other countries and linked to patterns of globalization, development, and domination by the Western powers. The fall of Soviet-bloc communism, some have argued, removed the last major challenge to the progress of global democratization, although again the meaningful content of that process is a subject of much disagreement.

One key debate involves the distinction between economic and political democracy. The principle of one person–one vote implies an equal share of POWER for each citizen, yet all modern democracies exhibit a highly unequal distribution of economic resources, which correlates with political influence. Marxists have traditionally argued that political democracy serves to obscure (and thus legitimate) the lack of economic democracy in most societies, while conservatives and neoliberals have argued that the redistribution of economic resources undermines the principles of personal liberty, meritocracy, and economic efficiency. The extension of democratic practices to aspects of economic life constitutes another dimension of this debate—especially in the workplace. See also ELECTORAL SYSTEM; and PARTICIPATORY DEMOCRACY.

demographic transition Refers to the shift that has occurred in many industrialized countries from a condition of high birth rates with high mortality rates to low birth rates with low mortality rates. Since the pioneering work of Warren Thompson in the late 1920s and Kingsley DAVIS in the 1940s, the demographic transition has been correlated with the process of industrialization and the range of social transformations that accompany it in many countries, including the entry of women into the workplace and the lowering of child mortality. In most cases, the decrease in mortality rates precedes the decrease in birth rates, resulting in a "transitional" period of rapid population growth—a situation now common in underdeveloped countries. Many developed countries (such as Germany, Italy, and Japan) now have birth rates below the mortality rate, leading to predictions of long-term population decline.

demography The study of human populations in terms of size, growth, movement, composition, and other variables. Demographic analysis became a possibility as increasingly organized methods of documenting populations were implemented in the nineteenth century. These allowed for the first accurate measures of birthrates, mortality, and the analysis of subdivisions of the population (age, marital status, educational level, and so on). Data of this kind quickly found a place in a wide range of social science research. The term *population studies* is often used to describe the application of demographic data to investigations of social organization and change. See also MIGRATION; and MORTALITY.

denotation See CONNOTATION AND DENOTATION.

dependency Often used to describe the inequality of power and forms of economic domination that characterizes the relations between rich and poor countries. Dependency theory emerged from the work of André Gunder FRANK and the United Nations Economic Commission on Latin America under Raul PREBISCH. Reacting against theories of DEVELOPMENT and modernization that contended that poor countries would inevitably follow the stages of Western economic development, dependency theorists argued that these countries faced systematic "underdevelopment" within the world economy. This resulted from patterns of collaboration between first-world and THIRD-WORLD political and business elites, which enriched multinational corporations and their local clients but left a majority of third-world populations with declining standards of living. Drawing on broad analyses of imperialism, dependency theorists observed that poorer countries had to rely on the sale of primary products to the developed core countries, generally on disadvantageous terms, and on the importation of manufactured goods from them. To counter this structural imbalance and the domination of development by multinationals and local elites, dependency theorists tended to be advocates of SOCIALISM, PROTECTIONISM, and import-substitution. Economic programs of this kind were implemented in a number of developing countries in the 1960s and 1970s. While the programs were often successful in promoting industrialization, they did not in most cases create balanced growth or improve terms of trade with the West. Under pressure from Western governments, multinational corporations, and international institutions, and faced with the example set by East Asian "newly industrializing nations," these policies were generally replaced in the 1980s by free trade and by decreased government involvement in the economy. Critiques of unequal international economic relations continue, however, often integrated into Center–periphery theory and WORLD-SYSTEMS THEORY.

depreciation The decline in the value of assets as a result of aging and use. This reduction in value comes from both diminished productivity as the asset ages and from the decrease in the remaining expected life of the asset. Depreciation is important in capital accounting because dividends are calculated as the amount of surplus over costs as a fraction of the current (undepreciated) value of the asset. The two conventional methods of calculating depreciation are the straight-line method and the declining-balances method. In the former, the cost of the asset minus the scrap value is divided by the years of its expected life, yielding an annual figure. In the latter, the figure employed is a constant proportion of the value of an asset, thereby yielding an annually diminishing amount.

The term *depreciation* is also used in the context of a decline in the value of a country's currency against other currencies or gold. See also EXCHANGE RATE.

depression Economic growth is subject to disturbances and cyclical episodes of rapid and slower (or declining) growth—termed BUSINESS CYCLES. While diminished and even negative growth often reflect the contractionary phase of such business cycles, particularly severe and longer periods of adversity are generally termed *depressions*. The extended downturn of 1873–1896, the Great Depression of the 1930s, and, for some economists, the downturn following the oil shocks of 1973 belong in this category. Shorter severe periods are often called "panics," and less severe periods are called "recessions."

deprivation Closely related to and often inclusive of the concept of POVERTY, deprivation can refer to the lack of any number of social goods and resources. Precise definitions of deprivation depend largely on context but, as with poverty, social scientists tend to distinguish between absolute and relative deprivation. *Absolute deprivation* refers to the absence of the basic requisites for survival: food, water, and shelter belong in this category. Most sociological attention to the question, however, focuses on *relative deprivation*, which refers to the discrepancy between people's expectations and their actual condition.

Relative deprivation exists under a variety of circumstances, but it almost always involves comparison with a more privileged group. This can be an observation by researchers or something perceived by the deprived population. Considerable research in the United States has been devoted to the issues of SOCIAL MOBILITY and rising expectations of the quality of life—a virtual article of faith of much of postwar American society. When real gains fail to meet expectations or when prosperity is perceived as passing over a group, the sense of relative deprivation can become acute. The perception of relative deprivation can be strongly linked, too, to the availability of legitimate avenues of social mobility or success. Here, Robert K. MERTON's work on structural strain, ANOMIE, and DEVIANCE has been a defining influence. Where the sense of relative deprivation is high, individuals and groups may turn to delinquency or form social movements as a way of expressing their frustration and changing their situation. Relative deprivation thus plays a significant role in studies of both CRIME and COLLECTIVE BEHAVIOR.

Where different forms of deprivation coincide, sociologists use the term *multiple deprivation*.

derived demand The idea that the demand for raw materials or other factors of production is derived from the demand for the final good that they help produce. The main application of derived-demand research is in the area of labor markets.

Derrida, Jacques (1930–) A French philosopher whose critique of metaphysics and linguistics is one of the cornerstones of POSTSTRUCTURALISM and a major influence on cultural and literary studies. If Derrida has been less easily adopted into the social sciences, it is largely due to the textual focus of his work and its oblique relationship to historical, political, and social concerns. Derrida's thinking turns on a structuralist understanding of language as a system of differential relationships, in which concepts acquire significance only in relation to other concepts. No concept is autonomous or exists independent of the generative process of differentiation. This is the core of Derrida's elaborate critiques of metaphysical claims to truth and of the concept of an adequate or fully "present" language that underwrites them. Instead, Derrida has insisted on the diverse ways in which meaning is a partial, never fully achieved act, both divided internally and deferred in time. Derrida coined the term *différance* to describe this articulation between spatial and temporal difference, although it is only one of many Derridean operating terms that express the divided nature of the linguistic sign.

One of the early targets of Derrida's critique was the structuralist tradition—particularly as represented by Ferdinand de SAUSSURE and Claude LÉVI-STRAUSS—which he accused of linguistic sleight of hand in attempting to metaphysically "ground" its own concepts of structure. Fundamentally, Derrida argued, all such efforts at grounding involve acts of violence upon a heterogeneous and shifting body of conceptual adequations. Privileges have to be won and enforced, such as the superiority of *speaking* to *writing*, which Derrida traces through the philosophical tradition. Nonetheless, Derrida does not so much challenge the necessity of such legitimizing strategies as reveal and contextualize them. Many of his analyses are demonstrations of how texts construct their authority by marginalizing or eliding certain differences, as well as of how one might invert the dominant structure of values—insisting, in one prominent example, on the priority of writing to speech.

Derrida's metaphysical skepticism and his method of close analysis of inconsistencies and slippages in texts became known as DECONSTRUCTION. Always wary of the traps of systematizing thought, he has cultivated a sometimes poetic, often punning, and always labyrinthine writing style that serves to highlight the circularity and openness of signifying processes and the vulnerability of truth claims. His recent work on Karl MARX suggests an attempt to reexamine the social implications of deconstruction by revealing the processes of endless deferral at the heart of the dialectical project. Derrida's major works include *Writing and Difference* (1967), *Of Grammatology* (1967), *The Margins of Philosophy* (1972), and *Spectres of Marx* (1994).

Descartes, René (1596–1650) A French mathematician and philosopher who inaugurated a long tradition of inquiry into mind–body dualism and the conditions of knowledge. Descartes's search for a set of principles that would provide certain knowledge about the world marked him as a rationalist, although not all of his work fit easily into this category. Descartes was born in France but spent much of his career in Holland, where he pursued his interest in mathematics—especially geometry—and where he undertook to develop a unified and rigorous philosophical system. His first major effort in this direction was an elaboration of Copernicus's physics and cosmology, entitled *Le Monde*. When Descartes learned that Galileo had been condemned by the Inquisition for similar efforts, he suppressed the work and turned to the question of knowledge.

Much of Descartes's method was based on the apparent certainty and universality of mathematics—a topic he addressed in *Discourses on the Method* (1637). There he introduced the famous notion of *Cogito ergo sum* ("I think, therefore I am"), which he asserted was the kernel of certainty that underlay all subsequent claims to knowledge. In response to criticisms of his positions, Descartes undertook a much more thorough elaboration of his method and epistemology in *Meditations on First Philosophy* (1641). There, he proposed a systematic solution to the problem of uncertainty and offered a response to empiricist claims that knowledge was limited to what was received by the senses. The certainty that one is conscious provides the starting point, he suggested, from which other assertions can be proved. He ran into difficulty, however, in

acknowledging that all other knowledge might be illusory. Descartes worked around this problem by developing a notoriously flimsy proof of the existence of God to establish the validity of further knowledge claims, based on God's gift to man of "clear and distinct" concepts, such as mathematics.

The difficulties raised by Cartesian dualism—the distinction of mind and body (or thought and action)—have been among the main preoccupations of the philosophical tradition and can be said, in many respects, to have inaugurated philosophical modernity. The body was the province of the physical sciences—the study of extension and movement—and Descartes's work gave impetus to that scientific project. The mind, in contrast, belonged to the realm of theology and metaphysics. In later years, Descartes sought to work around some of the difficulties that his ideas had raised, such as the need for some connection between the mind and body (which he thought might reside in the pineal gland). As the leading philosopher of the day, his *Meditations* (1641) were critically engaged by his contemporaries, including Thomas HOBBES, Pierre Gassendi, and Antoine Arnauld.

Descartes recapitulated and expanded on his philosophy in *The Principles of Philosophy* (1644). He also wrote a more eclectic study of psychology, physiology, and morals, entitled *Passions of the Soul* (1649).

descent theory Descent or lineage theory explores the ways in which consanguineal (or blood) relations are structured in various societies. It is a central aspect of the study of KINSHIP and has been fundamental to a large body of anthropological work on social organization. Observed kinship patterns include systems of PATRILINEAL DESCENT and MATRILINEAL DESCENT, in which inheritance is recognized exclusively through the male or female lines, respectively; there are also cognatic or multilineal systems, which designate descent from a common ancestor along either the male or female line or both (i.e., BILATERAL DESCENT). Anthropologists such as A. R. RADCLIFFE-BROWN, E. E. EVANS-PRITCHARD, and Meyer FORTES viewed descent as the primary determinant of social structure in relatively low-technology, stateless societies. They took procreation and inheritance to be basic and emphasized the role these play in the formation of the CORPORATE GROUP. Descent, in these societies, frequently governs domestic arrangements, the transmission of property, and political authority. This perspective became central to the British tradition of social ANTHROPOLOGY from the 1920s on.

By the 1950s, descent theory was under attack for marginalizing the importance and functions of marriage relations. This led to a long-running division within kinship studies over the relative importance of AFFINAL (marriage or alliance) RELATIONS—a subject associated most strongly with the work of Claude LÉVI-STRAUSS. ALLIANCE THEORY, as it was called, emphasized patterns in interpersonal relations over the formation of corporate groups. Arguments between descent and alliance theorists occupied center stage in social anthropology for much of the 1960s. Progressive recognition of the limits of the universalistic claims of both sides, however, has drained the debate of much of its competitive animus and focused research on the specificity of kinship structures in particular societies. Despite this general deflation of its claims, the major classifications of descent continue to play an important role in anthropological research.

deskilling The process of replacing skilled labor with unskilled labor as technological innovation makes complex tasks unnecessary or redundant. Deskilling is the central feature of Harry Braverman's account of the social impact of technological change (*Labor and Monopoly Capital*, 1974), which was part of a major sociological debate in the 1960s and 1970s over the changing character of modern CAPITALISM. Braverman anticipated a continuing "degradation" of work toward low-paying, unskilled jobs. The evidence to support this claim in many industrialized countries, however, is ambivalent: although the boom in service-sector employment and the decline of skilled industrial labor are frequently cited as the primary engines of deskilling, the enormous growth of information technologies and related industries has called for substantial investment in new and high-level skills by a significant part of the workforce. More recent work on post-FORDISM and FLEXIBLE SPECIALIZATION has explained this countertendency by postulating that workers need higher-level skills to perform the many different roles that they will likely perform in their careers.

determinism At its extreme, determinism describes the view that chance occurrences and voluntary choices play no independent role in causal analysis—that externally ascertainable causes explain everything. More loosely, it describes any theory that attributes causal priority to one factor over all other factors. In the social sciences, determinism underlies many debates about SOCIAL STRUCTURE and CULTURE, and major doctrinal lines have been drawn according to whether or where causal priority is assigned. There are numerous examples: ENVIRONMENTAL DETERMINISM plays a large part in many anthropological and ecological accounts of cultural development, which view culture as primarily a process of adaptation to environmental conditions. Economic determination is basic to the Marxist tradition, which refers cultural forms to the MODE OF PRODUCTION underlying given societies. The early anthropological tradition placed considerable stock in theories of racial determinism.

Social theory today has tended to complicate strongly deterministic accounts of cultural development, both by emphasizing the relative autonomy of different fields of human activity and by tracing the reciprocal relationships that obtain between them—between, for example, culture and the natural environment. Many social theorists also insist on limiting the scope of determinism by making a place for human agency and chance.

deterrence A general principle of raising the cost of certain actions to the point where actors refrain from undertaking them. Deterrence is a widely invoked objective of criminal law and is often linked to forms of punishment, as in the case of the death penalty in the United States. The impact of such penalties on the incidence of crime, however, has been notoriously hard to measure and remains subject to considerable debate. In INTERNATIONAL RELATIONS, deterrence is a form of political engagement or confrontation between countries, in which the threat of punishment or retaliation maintains the status quo. It was the central policy of both nuclear SUPERPOWERS during the COLD WAR and has been the subject of theoretical research within strategic studies. Deterrence provides one of the classic political instances of a cooperative, nonzero-sum game, in which greater benefits result from cooperation than from the pursuit of narrow individual interests (see GAME THEORY).

Deutsch, Karl (1912–1992) Widely regarded as the founder of the cybernetic study of politics—especially the study of patterns of communication and control in international and intranational political systems (see CYBERNETICS).

As such, Deutsch was also a pioneer of the behavioralist approach in political science that flourished after World War II (see BEHAVIORALISM). In *The Nerves of Government* (1963), Deutsch argued that studying patterns of communication opened the door to new ways of understanding a wide range of political functions and forms of political activity, from the acquisition of power, to the making and implementation of decisions by governments, to the maintenance or loss of social order. Equally practical and humanistic in his scholarship, Deutsch believed that the goal of such analysis was to respond to the political dangers and social disparities of the modern international order.

Although he argued for the utility and even the necessity of the NATION-STATE, Deutsch warned against the dangers of excessive NATIONALISM. He suggested that improved forms of international communication and cooperation among nation-states was a viable means of regulating and minimizing these dangers, and he advocated such measures as an international income tax to address disparities between rich and poor countries.

Deutsch was born in Prague and emigrated to the United States in 1938, just before the outbreak of war. He received his Ph.D. from Harvard University in 1951 and taught at the Massachusetts Institute of Technology (MIT) and at Yale University, before returning to Harvard, where he finished his career.

Deutsch's other major published works include *Nationalism and Social Communication* (1953), *Political Community at the International Level* (1954), *The Analysis of International Politics* (1968), *Politics and Government* (1970), and *Tides among Nations* (1979).

development Change identifiable as the fulfillment of possibilities inherent in an earlier state—whether in reference to organisms, psyches, or societies. Hence, *developmental psychology* focuses on the processes through which humans mature as they progress through the life course. Development is usually associated with progress and may be contrasted with directionless or regressive change.

In social science, *development* refers most often to economic and social change that brings qualitative improvement in the conditions of life. Although economic development dominates these discussions, and is sometimes narrowly identified with rising per capita incomes, broader usage often encompasses the full range of social,

political, and cultural transitions that accompany and (some argue) condition economic growth. This includes the emergence of democratic institutions and an efficient and responsive state apparatus. It sometimes includes the growth of INDIVIDUALISM, rationalism, PLURALISM, secularism, and other attributes of modern industrialized societies.

Although a long tradition of social theory deals with processes of social and historical change, research on the social and economic conditions of development emerged in the 1950s. MODERNIZATION THEORY was among the first bodies of research to analyze the mechanisms of the transition from subsistence agriculture to modern, industrialized society. W. W. ROSTOW and others conceived this transition as a linear progression through which all societies passed. While most emphasized the development of markets and physical infrastructure, some argued that effective legal and political infrastructures were also essential components of development.

Since the 1950s, there has been considerable debate over whether this path of transformation is appropriate or even possible for developing countries. Three main schools of thought have argued that it is not. The first, associated with DEPENDENCY theory and WORLD-SYSTEMS THEORY, holds that development cannot be understood simply as a process internal to individual countries; rather, global social and economic systems play a large role in determining the opportunities that countries have for economic growth and other forms of development. Rather than an invariable progression, they suggest that the early economic development of some countries may grant them an insuperable advantage over latecomers—one that changes the terms on which subsequent development occurs. Such arguments seek to explain why development produces distorted forms of "dependence" in poor countries and why the poorest societies face systematic "underdevelopment" through their subordinate positions in international systems of trade and security.

The second critique asserts that economic growth is an excessively narrow goal and that development must take into account other factors, such as social equity, economic independence, and environmental sustainability. The economist Amartya Sen is among the most prominent figures to link economic development to more general ideas about human potential and its opportunities for fulfillment. This holistic approach to societal welfare has gained adherents in recent years, although it creates additional challenges for researchers and policy makers.

The third critique contends that Western societies are unworthy of emulation and that poor societies should instead seek to preserve and build upon their traditional strengths. Mohandas Gandhi was perhaps the most forceful proponent of this view. This rarely implies a categorical rejection of MODERNITY, but rather an emphasis on combining economic and technological development with traditional social and cultural forms.

Although arguments about basic values continue, there has been considerable research and practical experimentation with alternative development strategies. One approach has involved disengagement from the world economy in favor of internal development strategies. On the whole, this has not proved successful. DEPENDENCY theorists often recommended IMPORT SUBSTITUTION policies as a way of promoting INDUSTRIALIZATION and autonomy, but over time these generally harmed economies more than they helped. The contrast with free-trading, fast-growing East Asian economies is stark (see Stephan Haggard, *Pathways from the Periphery*, 1990). Nonetheless, the historical record is complex, and few simple recipes for development have proved viable across regional, cultural, and historical divides.

Comparative research on the different developmental paths of Latin American, Asian, and African countries suggests that economic growth depends on a more complex variety of factors than earlier thought. Economists focusing on endogenous GROWTH THEORY have shown that a relatively egalitarian distribution of assets—wealth, but also health and education—favors economic growth. Economists, political scientists, and sociologists increasingly recognize that SOCIAL CAPITAL and social institutions are central to understanding the markedly different rates of economic development among seemingly similar groups. Research has also focused on the social dislocations and new forms of inequality that accompany success in some developing economies.

Recognition of the significances of different levels of analysis also plays an important role in contemporary research—especially in regard to local institutions and other local resources. Community development, banks, health clinics, schools, local administrations, kinship networks, and neighborhoods all play a part in development, both in their own right and as mediators of larger-scale forces of change (see Eric Hershberg, "Social Science and Development," 2001).

deviance   Behavior that is perceived to violate a widely held social norm or value. Deviance is thus a broad category that includes criminality (the violation of norms that are invested with the force of law) but that also extends to forms of behavior that are the objects of more modest forms of social reprobation or dissuasion. Such norms structure a vast array of daily activities and forms of interaction, from manners to practical knowledge to large ethical and moral questions. Norms (and consequently deviance) are not only culturally specific, but may vary within cultures on the basis of class, gender, race, or other social difference. This diversity points to a significant division within sociological research on deviance that separates those who treat deviance as a departure from the shared norms of a well-integrated society from those who see norms as objects of contention among social groups and deviance as a tool of stigmatization and SOCIAL CONTROL.

The sociology of deviance emerged largely in opposition to the criminological theories of the nineteenth and early twentieth centuries, which tended to be highly individualistic and legalistic in their understanding of criminal behavior. Studies of deviance have tended to emphasize the social and contingent character of norms and the structural factors that encourage or lower the cost of deviant behavior. Robert K. MERTON's work on structural strain and ANOMIE established the Durkheimian functionalist framework for much of this research. Merton emphasized the breakdown of normative integration when legitimate opportunities for success (in social terms) are unavailable. Others have emphasized the stronger point made by Emile DURKHEIM that deviance can positively reinforce society by establishing the "permissive zone of variation" for behavior—or more directly through the creation of scapegoats. Durkheim also emphasized that deviance is part of the process of social change: successful deviant groups establish new norms.

The formation of norms by and within deviant groups is a logical extension of this question. Many forms of deviant behavior are not merely the accumulation of individual acts but are activities that occur in the context of subcultures and deviant groups (see SUBCULTURE). Reinforcing mechanisms, such as processes of learning or socialization to deviance, play a role in establishing patterns of deviant behavior. Edwin Sutherland's DIFFERENTIAL-ASSOCIATION THEORY pioneered research in this area by emphasizing the process of peer or group reinforcement of delinquent behavior. His work inaugurated a long tradition of sociological interest in deviant careers.

The terms *primary deviance* and *secondary deviance*—introduced by Edwin Lemert in 1951—also describe this process of reinforcement. Primary deviance refers to an individual's first act of deviant behavior. Secondary deviance refers to multiple or habitual acts. LABELING THEORY provides an account of this transition in some contexts: an individual progresses from primary to secondary deviance by virtue of the labels that society assigns that behavior. Deviant labels can become self-fulfilling prophecies. Characterizing groups of youths as a gang or protesters as rioters may corner groups into the forms of behavior that are attributed to them—especially where such distinctions involve forms of social control. These labels can be and often are applied in ways that favor the dominant social groups. For example, similar behavior on the part of rich kids and poor kids may be described differently. This was Karl MARX's point in arguing that labels and norms are the prerogatives of the ruling class and serve its interests. Concepts of *resistance* and *struggle* also continue to inform a wide array of research on deviance, often in the context of efforts to counter the stigmatization of sexual minorities and to resist the extension of systems of social control (see Michel FOUCAULT).

deviance amplification A strong version of LABELING THEORY that suggests that media coverage and police action not only distort perceptions about the nature and incidence of deviant behavior but indirectly shape that behavior through stereotypes and systematic harassment. Minor deviancy, in this context, can be amplified by the mechanisms designed to control it. Deviance amplification was proposed by Leslie Wilkins and integrates elements of SYSTEM(S) THEORY.

devolution The transfer of powers and functions from a higher to a lower level of government without constitutional change. Devolution is often used by governments to satisfy regional demands for AUTONOMY without the surrender of sovereignty involved in establishing or deepening FEDERALISM. It may be used selectively to appease particularly restive regions, as in the cases of separatist provinces in Spain or Canada, or generally to strengthen LOCAL GOVERNMENT, as in France. Because the devolved powers are not constitutionally guaranteed, however, they may be retracted at the discretion of the central government, as Britain demonstrated in 1972 by abolishing the parliament of Northern Ireland.

Dewey, John (1859–1952) A philosopher, social theorist, and educator who was arguably the leading American public intellectual of the 1910s, 1920s, and 1930s. With William JAMES and C. S. PEIRCE, Dewey founded the philosophical approach known as PRAGMATISM, which sought to replace the long tradition of metaphysical speculation about ultimate truths with a future-oriented, instrumental, and always provisional conception of knowledge and reflection. Dewey was also one of the leading educational theorists of the day, and his ideas continue to shape educational curricula and research in the United States. He was politically active and a prolific writer on a number of contemporary issues, including women's rights, class relations, labor unions, and, in the 1930s, the formation of a third party. Dewey also found time to speak and write on world peace and the social and political transformations of Mexico, China, and Russia.

Dewey studied philosophy at Johns Hopkins University, worked at the University of Michigan, and in 1894 became chair of the Department of Philosophy, Psychology, and Education at the University of Chicago. There, he founded the famous Laboratory School, where many of his ideas on education were put into practice. In 1904, he moved to Columbia University, where he stayed until his retirement in 1929. Retirement, for Dewey, only accelerated the pace of his writing, political activism, traveling, and public speaking.

Dewey's pragmatism and much of his educational theory were rooted in a rejection of the "spectator theory of knowledge," which he viewed as underwriting the search for metaphysical truth in Western philosophy. Philosophy of this kind, Dewey argued, had abstracted the experience of consciousness from its involvement in the world. At its worst, it had reduced knowledge to a series of unverifiable abstractions. Dewey insisted, on the contrary, that knowledge was primarily a guide for action—that thought and concepts were ways of addressing contingent problems rather than of fixing truths. In that context, Dewey refused the sharp distinction between knowledge and action, or between facts and values. His instrumental conception of knowledge integrated both into the fold of purposive action. It was less concerned with testing the validity of a hypothesis through experiment (as in empirical science) than with evaluating the usefulness of a theory in light of the results of the action it recommended.

Throughout his work, Dewey stressed the need for critical reflection on received ideas and habits. This, he argued, was the basis for individual autonomy from larger social determinants and forms of irrational authority. Similar priorities run throughout his theories of education, which emphasize the teaching of critical thinking over particular content. Both education and philosophy, as Dewey conceived them, should serve the goals of democratic society, understood as a space of maximal freedom to create. He coupled this with a strong faith in social science and scientific government (again conceived in pragmatic rather than narrow positivistic terms), the development of which, he argued, lagged far behind the natural sciences.

Dewey's major works include *Democracy and Education* (1916), *Reconstruction in Philosophy* (1920), *The Quest for Certainty* (1929), *Art as Experience* (1934), and *Freedom and Culture* (1939).

diachronic Refers to change through time, such as historical or evolutionary change, and more generally to analytical perspectives that privilege historical development. Diachronic analysis is often distinguished from synchronic analysis, which treats a subject (a society, for example) as a cross section at a single instant. The distinction was important in LINGUISTICS, notably in early twentieth-century debates between philology, which was based on the historical explanation of language patterns, and STRUCTURALISM, which explained language in terms of internal structures of differentiation. This debate resulted in an enduring opposition between two explanatory logics: historical (sometimes called genetic) analysis and structural analysis.

dialect A variant form of a language still intelligible to speakers of other variants, such as standard British and American English. Dialects may differ in semantics, syntax, vocabulary, or other features and be stably reproduced.

dialectical materialism The theory of knowledge that certain post-Marxist thinkers (notably Georgy Plekhanov and Vladimir Ilich LENIN) extrapolated from the work of Karl MARX and Friedrich Engels—especially Engels's *Anti-Duhring* (1877–1878). The term describes a commitment to both the priority of matter over thought or spirit—with particular reference to Marx's critique of Georg HEGEL's idealism—and to the concept of dialectical change over deterministic or mechanistic models. It emphasizes very general laws of contradiction, negation, and synthesis that are ostensibly applicable to both the natural and social worlds. In this respect, dialectical materialism is distinct from HISTORICAL MATERIALISM—the direction of Marxist thought given over to the "science" of history.

In the communist world, dialectical materialism became the philosophical orthodoxy and, more generally, a synonym for "correct thinking." Partly in response, the scientific claims made for the dialectical process largely dropped out of the theoretical tradition of Western MARXISM, eventually leading to a selective recovery of the Hegelian roots of Marxist critique in the writing of Georg LUKÁCS and others. This has continued to be an area of significant interest and debate among theorists working in or around the Marxist tradition.

dialectics Has roots in pre-Socratic Greek philosophy, where it designated a mode of reasoning and argument. It received its strongest Classical-era articulation, however, in the Socratic account of dialectics as a method for discovering truth. Socratic dialectics presupposed the existence of opposing views on a subject; it arrived at the truth through the discovery of CONTRADICTION within one of the positions. The Socratic method has survived in the fields of logic and analytical philosophy, where contradiction is the sign of a false answer. Much of the modern legacy of dialectical thought, however, draws on the tradition of Hegelian dialectics and on the Marxist critique of that position.

For Georg HEGEL, truth lay not in the logical superiority of one position, but in the relationship that joined two ostensibly opposed concepts or positions. This relationship is sometimes represented by way of a third position that transcends the two, or, by some writers, simply as a synthetic awareness that encompasses them, comprehends their relationship, and measures their distance. In this sense, there is a dialectical relationship between dispersed parts and the whole that unifies them. For Hegel, this process was inscribed at all levels of the social and natural worlds, forming a single yet internally differentiated process that expressed and embodied the larger evolution of "Spirit." Johann Fichte's conceptual triad of thesis, antithesis, and synthesis is sometimes used in the same sense—although not by Hegel.

Marx's famous "inversion" of Hegelian dialectics attacks Spirit as a mystification of concrete, historical processes—in particular, the historical development of successive MODES OF PRODUCTION. The logic of those processes, for Marx, is immanent and material rather than transcendental and spiritual; the economic base, for Marx, determines the realm of ideas, and not the other way around. Much of Marx's early work in the *German Ideology* (1845) and in *The Economic and Philosophical Manuscripts* (1844) is an effort to work through the consequences of this position, which later came to be known as DIALECTICAL MATERIALISM. His inversion in no way dispenses with the dialectical method; indeed the concept of contradiction and overcoming underwrites not only Marx's logic of historical development (most explicitly in the concept of CLASS STRUGGLE) but also many of his key analytical tools—preeminently the contradiction between use value and exchange value, which underlies much of his account of CAPITALISM.

These intertwined traditions of dialectical thought have been central to twentieth-century philosophy and social theory—from the Marxist tradition running through Georg LUKÁCS, Antonio GRAMSCI, and the FRANKFURT SCHOOL to the predominantly Hegelian tradition visible in PHENOMENOLOGY and STRUCTURALISM. In the context of the setbacks and disappointments dealt Marxist historical dialectics during the twentieth century, the term has come to be associated mostly with theories of social critique—especially those that seek an antagonistic or exterior position from which to analyze the totalizing ideological system of late capitalism. A prominent example of this shift in emphasis is Theodor ADORNO's concept of *negative dialectics*.

dictatorship Absolute rule by a person or small group unrestricted by law. The term dates back to the Roman Republic, where the dictator was a magistrate authorized by the senate and the assembly to rule by decree for a fixed term during a period of emergency, after

which he was held accountable to democratic institutions. Dictatorship acquired its present meaning in reference to such later figures as Oliver Cromwell and Napoleon Bonaparte, who, unlike traditional monarchs, based their authority on the popular will, however symbolically or cursorily consulted. This tradition continues among both right-wing and left-wing dictatorships of the present era, which almost always seek or claim legitimacy through the people and frequently justify themselves as a means of preserving popular sovereignty from internal or external threats. Dictators differ further from monarchs in that their authority is generally personal or charismatic, rather than divine, dynastic, or bureaucratic.

Political theory has tended to differentiate among types of dictatorial regime, beginning with ARISTOTLE's influential distinction between TYRANNY and despotism. The former refers to the lawless and coercive rule of a usurper, whereas the latter describes a more enduring and sometimes lawful system of rule (a notion developed further in the concept of ORIENTAL DESPOTISM, or in Voltaire's qualified endorsement of the "enlightened despotisms" of the eighteenth century).

Many democratic constitutions revive the Roman precedent by permitting the EXECUTIVE to declare a constitutional dictatorship in times of crisis, through special EMERGENCY POWERS. Karl MARX similarly invoked the classical precedent in referring to the dictatorship of the proletariat, which would seize control of the state after the revolutionary overthrow of capitalism.

differential-association theory A theory of criminal and delinquent behavior that emphasizes the importance of socialization to such behavior. Differential-association theory stresses that CRIME is essentially learned and reinforced through contact with individuals who define criminality favorably, or through experiences in which criminal behavior is not stigmatized. The theory was proposed by Chicago school sociologist Edwin Sutherland in the 1930s as a critique of hereditary and biological accounts of criminality; it had a significant impact on subsequent research on DEVIANCE and delinquency. Differential-association theory has proved more useful in describing repeat or career criminal behavior than other types of relatively isolated individual criminality, such as embezzlement—although Sutherland and others revised it continuously in the light of criticism. It was also criticized for promoting an overly simplified view of the way that individuals choose models for their behavior, although again, subsequent work has paid more attention to the specific mechanisms of positive and negative reinforcement of criminal norms. The function of role models has also been explored in this context, under the name *differential-identification theory.*

differential-opportunity theory   A theory of delinquency and delinquent subcultures developed by Richard Cloward and Lloyd Ohlin in *Delinquency and Opportunity* (1960). Cloward and Ohlin made use of Robert K. MERTON's observations that legitimate opportunities to pursue culturally approved goals are socially structured and unevenly distributed—especially by CLASS. Differential-opportunity theory extends this notion of socially structured unequal access to delinquency and criminality. Drawing on Edwin Sutherland's work on forms of delinquent and criminal socialization, Cloward and Ohlin suggested that the SOCIAL STRUCTURE of a community determines access to both the learning and performance structures that underwrite career delinquency and criminal subcultures.

diffusion and diffusionism   Diffusion refers to the spread of a trait or innovation outward from a source or from one CULTURE to another. Diffusionism is the theory that cultural and technological innovation, in general, has spread outward from a small number of sources (or in extreme versions, from one source). Theories of diffusion emerged in the late nineteenth century as a way of explaining the commonality of certain cultural features that were found in a wide range of primitive societies. Diffusionism thus competed with evolutionary accounts of cultural development, which tended to emphasize the importance of incremental stages through which each society necessarily passed. Diffusionism similarly posed a challenge to later functionalist theories, whose accounts of societal development viewed innovation as a response to particular historical conditions (see FUNCTIONALISM).

Although diffusion was originally promoted by Franz BOAS as a way of contesting racial theories of societal development, the term later became associated with an updated set of racial and ethnocentric agendas that sought to trace civilization to particular racial homelands. Such theories reached a popular audience but proved marginal to anthropological debates, which had largely abandoned the link between

RACE and culture, as well as the related problem of ranking human creative capacity. Contemporary work on cultural change has tended to integrate diffusion into a more synthetic perspective that includes flexible models of evolutionary processes and functionalist adaptations. See also ACCULTURATION; EVOLUTION AND EVOLUTIONISM; and *KULTURKREIS*.

Dilthey, Wilhelm   (1833–1911) A German philosopher and historian known primarily for his inquiries into the goals and methods of what he collectively termed the *human sciences* or *Geisteswissenschaften.* Dilthey was concerned to distinguish these fields—including philosophy, history, psychology, literature, politics, and economics—from the positivistic ambitions and methods of the natural sciences, which sought to isolate phenomena and the laws that governed them. Dilthey argued that the human sciences were fundamentally interpretive sciences, devoted to understanding human motivations, beliefs, and actions. His work in this regard had a profound influence on Max WEBER's emphasis on *verstehen* ("understanding") in sociology.

Dilthey rejected general laws of history, but he believed that smaller regularities could be determined with some certainty—in fact, he argued that the human sciences have an advantage over the natural sciences in that they deal with perceptible phenomena rather than hypothetical elements, such as atoms. Knowledge in these areas might well aspire to a kind of objectivity, for Dilthey, but it could not be a scientific objectivity—a closure of inquiry around the concept of truth. Because knowledge in the human sciences depended on a web of ongoing social and historical relationships, it remained necessarily open and subject to revision. Moreover, because knowledge was historically and culturally contingent, and because the knower was implicated in the context of the thing known, philosophies of consciousness (such as Immanuel KANT's) were of limited value. Dilthey moved, in this respect, toward a descriptive psychology that influenced the phenomenological theories of Edmund Husserl. More generally, his work played an important part in the broader turn-of-the-century German debate about the nature of the social and natural sciences, known as the *METHODENSTREIT*.

Dilthey was a prolific writer but not a systematic one. Much of his work, including the second volume of his influential *Introduction to Human Sciences* (1883), remained unfinished.

His other major writing includes *The Essence of Philosophy* (1907), *The Construction of the Historical World in the Social Sciences* (1910), and *The Meaning of History* (1961, edited by H. P. Rickman).

direct democracy   Direct involvement of the people in political decision making. In small polities, from the ancient Greek city-state to the New England town meeting, direct democracy was achieved by frequent face-to-face meetings of all citizens, who debated and voted on public issues. It contrasts with representative democracy, in which citizens appoint or elect representatives to legislative bodies or other offices of government. Political philosophers since ARISTOTLE have recognized the limitations of direct democracy as the size of the polity increases. The question of whether democracy is viable in large states was a prominent subject of debate during the Enlightenment, and remains a concern for communitarian political philosophers and other critics of the oligarchical tendencies of modern democratic systems (see COMMUNITARIANISM).

Many modern states possess means of allowing citizens to make decisions directly. Referenda or plebiscites, in which all citizens vote on a particular question, are the most common of these devices. These are sometimes sponsored by a petition system that amounts to a parallel legislative track in some states; in other cases, they are held at the discretion of the LEGISLATURE; in still others, the national constitutions require that certain issues be put directly to the people (e.g., constitutional amendment in Australia). Because referenda and plebiscites can be a basis for political legitimation outside the existing structure of government, they are frequently associated with extra-legal changes in power. The absence or limited role of deliberative bodies in plebiscitory systems has been criticized by democratic theorists as particularly vulnerable to manipulation and demagoguery, and destructive of the diverse local structures of power that form and inform citizens. Nonetheless, the face-to-face quality of older models of direct democracy continues to serve as an ideal for some democratic theorists (for example, the communitarians and Hannah ARENDT), who prioritize the task of strengthening the public sphere (see PUBLIC SPHERE AND PRIVATE SPHERE).

With the notable exception of Switzerland, few countries hold national referenda with any frequency. In Swiss cantons, some of the U.S. states, and other subnational political units, they are more common: citizens can raise issues directly by gathering a certain number of signatures, which places a proposition on the ballot for consideration in the next election. Finally, petitions provide a means in several American, Swiss, and Italian districts to "recall" representatives and compel new elections.

directly unproductive profit-seeking activities   Also DUP activities. DUP activities use resources and generate profits but produce zero output, in the sense that they produce neither goods and services for consumption nor inputs that may be used in a production process. DUP activities include lobbying for tariffs, for a greater share of government resources, or for the creation of an artificial monopoly. They also include illegal activities such as smuggling. See also RENT-SEEKING ACTIVITIES.

discourse analysis   Generally refers to approaches to the study of language that examine the conditions of possibility of particular statements and their effects. Discourse analysis, in this sense, situates specific instances of language use within larger discursive formations, which define the limits, variations, and effects of what can be said or written in a given context. These can be treated in various ways—as ideological constraints, for example, or as the set of assumptions that organizes a given field.

Much of this work lies at the border of LINGUISTICS and philosophy, and explores language as the medium of construction of both the social world and the SELF. The work of Emile Benveniste figures prominently in this area; for Benveniste, discourse is the dimension of language that localizes, contextualizes, and situates the speaker. His account thus strongly contrasts with the impersonal structure of language emphasized by Ferdinand de SAUSSURE and later proponents of structural linguistics. There is also a related Anglo-American tradition of SPEECH-ACT THEORY, represented by J. L. Austin, that focuses on the performative effects of speech in everyday situations. In addition, the term *discourse analysis* has a technical meaning in linguistics that refers to the study of elements of language larger than a sentence.

The term *discourse* was also strongly marked by Michel FOUCAULT, who introduced many of the major concepts of modern discourse analysis in the 1970s, especially in *The Archaeology of Knowledge* (1972). Foucault recovered much of the impersonal character of discourse, locating specific instances of language (and even individuals) within larger discursive fields. For Foucault, discursive fields were always closely linked to institutions and other forms of POWER, such as the law; these relationships not only determined the criteria of truth for various kinds of statements (scientific statements, for example) but also tended to reproduce the social order that underlay those institutions.

This conception of discourse has profoundly influenced the social sciences, philosophy, and literary studies, where it has been central to the broad reflexive turn toward the construction of fields and the position of the intellectual and scholar within them. Much of this work continues to draw on the POSTSTRUCTURALISM of Foucault and other European social theorists.

discrete-choice models Sometimes termed *qualitative-response models*, these are statistical models that specify the ways that discrete decisions may be explained by means of independent variables. For example, individual economic agents frequently have to make discrete choices—whether to enter the labor market, the choice of occupation, whether to enter a particular foreign market, and so forth. Although aggregating individual cases causes discrete variables to behave like continuous variables (that therefore may be subject to standard regression analysis), the econometric models that make use of aggregate data cannot accurately explain or predict individual-level phenomena. Economists started using such models extensively following the rapid development of computer technology (which facilitates the accurate estimation of such models) and the widespread availability of disaggregated firm and individual-level data.

discriminating monopoly A situation in which a monopolist practices PRICE DISCRIMINATION; the practice of charging different prices to different groups of buyers or of charging the same consumer different prices for different units of the same good.

Perfect discrimination exists when the monopolist is able to charge the full price that each buyer is willing to pay. In such a case, the monopolist extracts the entire consumer surplus.

discrimination Most social-science usage refers to the unequal treatment of groups based on their particular identities—generally, racial and ethnic groups but also extending to nearly any distinguishable identity category, including age (*ageism*) and gender (*sexism*). The term is often associated with prejudice, although that refers primarily to individual attitudes rather than to social actions and structures. The term *positive discrimination* is sometimes used synonymously with AFFIRMATIVE ACTION, to describe programs that favor traditionally deprived or marginalized groups.

disequilibrium analysis An area of economics that abandons the axiomatic assumption that supply and demand clear the market, and seeks a consistent theory of the functioning of decentralized economies. Under disequilibrium conditions, transactions on the market no longer reflect the intersection of supply and demand. Most often, disequilibrium analysis examines situations of supply scarcity, as in the case of a monopoly supplier who rations goods or resources. In such cases, transactions take into account quantity signals as well as price signals. The equilibria that emerge in such an analysis are termed *rationed equilibria*.

disguised unemployment The economy is said to exhibit disguised unemployment when part of the labor force may be withdrawn from employment without affecting aggregate output—that is, their productivity is essentially zero. Disguised unemployment on a significant scale is usually attributed to the existence of an informal labor market, where redundant workers either seek forms of self-employment or sell their services as domestic servants, odd jobmen, porters, and the like. Another source is the traditional agricultural sector, which can absorb large quantities of labor. Urban disguised unemployment is often the result of migration from rural areas—a feature common to many developing economies. While some migrants are able to secure proper jobs, a significant fraction spends their time in the search for appropriate jobs. In the meantime, they work in the marginally productive informal sector.

disintermediation Funds usually flow between savers (or lenders) and borrowers through a financial intermediary such as banks. Disintermediation is said to occur when government intervention lessens the advantages of financial intermediaries in the provision of such services, in order to drive funds into other channels. In some cases, the funds are routed directly from savers to borrowers. Reintermediation is the opposite process, in which a direct flow of funds is rerouted through banks and other intermediaries.

displacement In PSYCHOANALYSIS, a means of disguising an inadmissible or traumatic thought. Sigmund FREUD first described the process in relation to dreams, in which one thing can stand for another and thereby provide an acceptable substitute (*Interpretation of Dreams*, 1900). In this context, displacement is a function of a censoring mechanism that mediates between social norms and libidinal wishes.

Social scientists also use the term *displacement effect* to describe a change in the distribution of something (e.g., crime among different categories or neighborhoods) that is unaccompanied by a change in the total amount of that thing. The arrest of prostitutes in one neighborhood, for example, may simply displace prostitution to another.

dissaving Consumption in excess of current income. Such consumption is financed out of wealth (savings) or by borrowing against expected future income.

dissent In politics, open opposition to a government or its policies. Tolerance of dissent is commonly viewed as the *sine qua non* of open government, and DEMOCRACY has been described as a system that institutionalizes dissent within certain limits. The peaceful turnover of power from one group to another that democratic government facilitates requires institutionalized channels of dissent, whether in the form of multiparty systems, provisions for freedom of political speech, or other protections of political pluralism. The limits of this tolerance have been a recurring subject of debate within democratic societies, especially when political dissent aims at changing the system of government itself. The varying responses of democratic regimes to communist and fascist parties illustrate that there is no simple solution to this question or means of guaranteeing pluralism in the face of political crises.

Dissent frequently operates outside "authorized" political channels, through petitions, demonstrations, noncompliance with certain laws, or other forms of civil disobedience. Large-scale, organized dissent has played a major role in twentieth-century social and political movements, including Mohandas Gandhi's "Quit India" campaign against British occupation in the 1940s and the Civil Rights movement in the United States in the 1950s and 1960s.

distance decay The attenuation of a process or effect over distance. Distance decay is fundamental to theories of cultural diffusion and has applications in a range of other areas (see DIFFUSION AND DIFFUSIONISM). With respect to cultural diffusion, distance decay refers to the decrease in the impact or spread of a cultural trait or innovation as the distance from the center of innovation increases. *Time–distance decay* incorporates the concept of diminution of effects over time.

distribution theory An economic theory that addresses the distribution of national income among individuals and groups, particularly the division of wages and profits. There are four broad categories of distribution theory: classical, Marxian, post-Keynesian, and neoclassical.

The classical economists from Adam SMITH to David RICARDO distinguished between two components of national income: (1) the amount necessary for the reproduction of the economy, including the subsistence level of wages of workers and the replacement of depreciated capital and other resources; and (2) the surplus over and above the subsistence requirements. They maintained that wages are determined solely by subsistence needs and that profits are a residual after wages have been paid. An important consequence of this relationship is that an increase in profits can come about only through a fall in wages. See CLASSICAL ECONOMICS.

Karl MARX held similar views, although he was much more interested in the long-term tendencies of this relationship and believed it contained the principle of its own destruction. He argued that historical conditions, not just biological subsistence, establish a "customary" wage. Monopoly power leads to a rising surplus and a rise in the share of profits. With this surplus, capitalists are compelled to consolidate capital, expand foreign markets, and invest in ever more costly technical improvements. Over the long term, Marx argued, these methods yield a FALLING RATE OF PROFIT and, ultimately, stagnation and decay. In the final stage, inequities in income distribution lead to the collapse of CAPITALISM and to social revolution. See MARXISM.

Several post-Keynesian models—most notably, those of Roy F. Harrod, Evsey D. Domar, Nicholas KALDOR, and Luigi L. Pasinetti—draw upon and extend the Marxian analysis. In their models, the different economic or social classes have different saving rates, and the distribution of income among them adjusts so that the total amount of savings in the economy equals planned investment. In this case, the distribution of income is not a function of residual profit, as the classical economists believed, but of a more dynamic process that provides for a more complex model of income stratification. See KEYNESIANISM.

Neoclassical distribution theory departs from the above assumptions. Neoclassicists emphasize that the pricing of both goods and the factors of production (labor and raw materials) is determined by the interaction of demand and supply. The demand for each factor, in turn, depends on its marginal product. Neoclassical distribution theory therefore differs from most other perspectives by claiming that the optimal distribution of income is determined by the conditions of production, rather than by external factors like subsistence or history. See also NEOCLASSICAL ECONOMICS.

distributive justice Distributive justice is concerned with how goods, honors, and obligations are distributed within a community. Distributive claims can be (and have been) justified on the basis of need, moral standing, precedent, rights (especially property rights), and aggregate social welfare, among others. See JUSTICE for more discussion.

district or districting See ELECTORAL GEOGRAPHY.

division of labor The degree and nature of the specialization of work in a society, whether distinguished by task, profession, or stratified according to class or gender. The concept dates back to Greek philosophers such as PLATO, ARISTOTLE, and Xenophon, who devoted considerable attention to the advantages and disadvantages of a differentiated social body. It became a basic concept in the modern social sciences with the work of Adam SMITH (*The Wealth of Nations*, 1776), who made the division of labor central to his analysis of economic growth and progress. For Smith, specialization was the result of the freedom provided by the free market to exploit natural advantages; it brought about a more efficient use of labor and resources. In his famous example, a pin-maker who made pins individually from start to finish (drawing out the wire, cutting and pointing it, etc.) would make only a few in a day. Dividing

the production process into discrete steps allows for the specialization of skills, increased labor productivity, and greater innovation. The limit on specialization was primarily the size of the market.

Romantic social theorists, Karl MARX, and much of the subsequent sociological tradition accepted this inherent link between the free market and the division of labor, but they located this process within the larger social process of modernization. The division of labor became a major index of the modern and, for many social theorists, a major cause of unhappiness in modern society as human powers were narrowed and channeled into minute, repetitive tasks. The development of industrial labor only accentuated this aspect of work. It was further rationalized by turn-of-the-century SCIENTIFIC MANAGEMENT and by the humanizing (if still rationalizing) tendencies of organizational theory and personnel management.

The possibility of a reunification of the fragmented world of labor, experience, and pleasure played a strong role in nineteenth-century social theory and visions of social change. Marx's vision of communist society offered an explicit challenge to the regimentation and division of labor—a person might fish in the morning, farm in the afternoon, and write poetry in the evening, moving between intellectual and physical labor and remaining unrestricted in the types of activities he or she pursued. Emile DURKHEIM similarly treated the strong class character and extreme differentiation of modern labor as a source of unhappiness. For Durkheim, the modern division of labor outstripped the bonds of interdependence that linked individuals together and yielded a condition of ANOMIE or social disintegration.

The division of labor continues to be an important subject in many areas of the social sciences, which now include research on the diverse forms of stratification (by gender, age, race, and so on) that influence the distribution of occupations and roles in modern societies. See also MODERNITY.

Dobb, Maurice (1900–1976) Dobb was one of the most prominent Marxist economists of the twentieth century. His interests ranged from economic theory (*Political Economy and Capitalism*, 1937) to economic history (*Studies in the Development of Capitalism*, 1946). Outside the academy, Dobb was also concerned with policymaking and especially planning for DEVELOPMENT. Much of his popular writing dealt with these practical issues.

Dobb was born in London and studied economics at the University of Cambridge. One of the striking features of his approach is that he subscribed to the LABOR THEORY OF VALUE, which had been abandoned by both neoclassical economists and their critics. This stemmed from his belief that the description of the production process in terms of labor had implications beyond the determination of relative prices and distribution, insofar as it focused on those directly involved in the production process (as opposed to managers and capitalists). Dobb believed that neoclassicists obscured the nature of profit and of income distribution by ignoring their connections to institutions of property and social relations. Dobb's opposition to the utility theory of value favored by the neoclassicists was based on the high priority they attached to individual choice; he also rejected the move from the subjective utility approach to a "revealed preference" approach, because the latter reduced the psychological dimension of choice to what is observed in the market.

Dobb's openness to non-Marxist traditions allowed for a notable flexibility in his work. In this vein, he criticized the theory of socialist pricing developed by Oscar Lange, Abba Lerner, and others in the 1930s, by pointing out the efficiency of the price mechanism. He was also among the first to appreciate the conflict between the demands of efficiency and equality in a competitive price mechanism—one of the main issues in the theory of resource allocation. Another of Dobb's criticisms of Marxist economics was the failure of market socialism to pay sufficient attention to intertemporal issues.

Dobb was also interested in the problems of development in economies with large labor surpluses. He showed that growth in such economies required policies that targeted not only savings and investment rates but also the choice of techniques, sectoral imbalances, and pricing. In sum, by incorporating insights—both practical and theoretical—from other economic traditions, while still adhering to key Marxist concepts, Dobb was instrumental in rekindling interest in the classical approach to economics and in providing an alternative to neoclassical theory. See also CLASSICAL ECONOMICS; and MARXISM.

domestic group   Used as an alternative to the terms *family* or *household* to describe the basic unit of a society, especially in societies where activities such as the preparation of food are not organized at the level of family groups or where immediate kin do not reside together.

domestic labor   See LABOR.

domestic mode of production   A theory of peasant economies proposed by the anthropologist Marshall SAHLINS, in which production and consumption are organized at the level of and for the purposes of the household. The model therefore implies the absence of community production or significant exchange. These features have been a subject of debate among anthropologists. See also CHAYANOV SLOPE.

double coincidence of wants   The necessary condition of barter that stipulates that the goods or services each party is willing to exchange must be exactly what is demanded by the other party. The double coincidence of wants becomes unnecessary where there exists an accepted medium of exchange (money) that permits the complete convertibility of goods and the accumulation of buying power over time.

double consciousness   A concept developed by the American sociologist and intellectual W. E. B. DUBOIS to describe the felt contradiction between social values and daily experience for blacks in the United States. Being black, DuBois argued, meant being deprived of a "true self-consciousness," insofar as blacks perceived themselves through the generalized contempt of white America. To be black and American thus implied a range of contradictions between American social ideals, which blacks shared, and the experience of exclusion from American life. The term has entered into more general use in CULTURAL STUDIES to describe conflicting and/or overlapping forms of identification—especially in Paul Gilroy's work on trans-Atlantic culture. Most sociological usage involves the opposition between the dominant culture or set of beliefs into which persons or groups are socialized and the different perspective they may acquire through daily experience.

The term *dual consciousness* is also sometimes used in reference to persons or groups who hold two sets of inconsistent beliefs, primarily in the context of research on the working class in Europe.

Douglas, Mary   (1921–) A prolific and wide-ranging British anthropologist best known for a series of studies of the common under-lying structures of human societies. Douglas obtained her doctorate at the University of Oxford in 1951, where she studied with Max GLUCKMAN, Meyer FORTES, and E. E. EVANS-PRITCHARD. Her early work in the Belgian Congo shared the structural-functionalist orientation of this group—especially that of Evans-Pritchard. Her most influential study, however, *Purity and Danger: An Analysis of Concepts of Pollution and Taboo* (1966), reflects a turn toward the more fundamental structural oppositions identified by Claude LÉVI-STRAUSS. The principal claim of this work—that "dirt," broadly conceived, is an essen-tial boundary concept in the moral systems of all societies—proved highly influential. Douglas elaborated this notion in *Natural Symbols* (1970), which advanced a general model of social organi-zation that distinguished between *grid* (a measure of the degree and intensity of internal social differentiation) and *group* (the intensity of dif-ferentiation from external others). More recently, Douglas has turned her attention to related sub-jects, from Western individualism to her widely read study of environmental movements, *Risk and Culture* (1982, with Aaron Wildavsky). Other major works include *Witchcraft: Confessions and Accusations* (1970), *The World of Goods: Towards an Anthropology of Consumption* (1978, with Baron Isherwood), and *How Institutions Think* (1986).

dowry and bridewealth Forms of marriage payment. *Dowry* is a practice in which the bride's family gives the bride property (the dowry) to bring to the marriage. In *indirect* dowry, the recipient is still the bride, but the donor is the groom's family. In societies that practice *bridewealth*, the groom gives property or service (also known as bride service) to the bride's family, in exchange or in compensation for their daughter. These terms have largely replaced the older term *bride price*, following disagreements between anthropologists over the economic logic at stake. Both practices are symbolically complex and enable a range of transactions, as well as conversions of goods and prestige. See also EXCHANGE.

dramaturgical approach A sociological per-spective that holds that social interactions usually follow familiar and predicable scripts, much like theatrical productions. In this context, individu-als are understood as creating, interpreting, and "playing" particular social roles. The dramatur-gical approach was developed primarily by the American sociologist Erving GOFFMAN, although it goes back at least to William Shakespeare ("All the world's a stage") and to such Enlight-enment thinkers as Denis Diderot and Jean-Jacques ROUSSEAU, who commented on (and in Rousseau's case, condemned) the artful perfor-mance of social roles.

For Goffman, the scripts of many types of interaction outline in basic terms what roles are available and what is generally supposed to occur. However, in contrast to the theater, individuals in real life negotiate among themselves to determine who will play which role and exactly how events will transpire. Individuals must also work to convince others that their roles are genuine; in doing so, they use the props appropriate to the role and enlist the tacit support of other actors to control the events that occur.

Goffman used such theatrical terms as *frontstage* and *backstage* to refer to the staged sets of real life. Frontstage is where the act is put on, where all actors are engaged in the production and the script is followed. Backstage is where the performers can take off their various masks and specified identities and safely abandon the per-formance for a time. By monitoring the effects of their roles on others, individuals engage in what Goffman termed *impression management*.

Dravidian kinship A system of KINSHIP prevalent among the cultures of Southern India (home of the Dravidian language group) but also identified in the Americas and in the Pacific. An important element of Dravidian systems is the designation of available marriage partners. In general, such systems prescribe symmetrical marriage alliance (the exchange of marriage partners of both sexes between two groups) and privilege the marriage of cross cousins (cousins related through the opposite-sex parent).

dual consciousness See DOUBLE CONSCIOUS-NESS.

dual economy Describes perceived differences of economic structure between the rural agricul-tural sector and the urban manufacturing sector in developing economies. The process of economic development has traditionally been seen as a transformation from the former type of economy to the latter. The two sectors remain fundamen-tally distinct until the process of transformation is complete, a process that is slowed by any barriers to the equilibrating forces of labor migration and capital accumulation.

W. Arthur LEWIS elaborated on the concept in his 1954 work *Economic Development with Unlimited Supplies of Labor*. Lewis postulated that the key difference between the sectors was the way in which wage income was allocated. Agricultural workers were paid their average product—a sharing of available resources—and marginal productivity was near zero because of universal employment. In the capitalist sector, workers were paid their marginal product, and higher wages pulled surplus labor from the rural areas. Thus, in rural areas, social norms prevailed to treat wage income as a social support system, whereas the modern sector behaved according to neoclassical economic predictions. Over time, as the surplus labor left the rural areas, agricultural wages would rise and workers would be paid according to productivity, and the two sectors would no longer be distinct with respect to wage allocations. Lewis was awarded the Nobel Prize in economics for his contributions in this area.

More generally, the term *dual economy* has come to represent any disequilibrium across sectors in which the market forces at play in one remain steadfastly inoperative in the other. Thus enclaves of economic stagnation (such as the urban informal sector) are seen as distinct from economic activity that may be occurring in the same physical location, but through very different institutions (such as the export sector). The idea has been extended across countries, where the divisions of national borders and policies represent potential barriers to economic integration between the "surplus labor" economies of the developing world and the capitalist economies of the developed world.

DuBois, W. E. B. (1868–1963) DuBois was a public intellectual, sociologist, and activist on behalf of the African-American community. He profoundly shaped black political culture in the United States through his founding (and directing) role in the NAACP (National Association for the Advancement of Colored People), as well as internationally through the pan-African movement. DuBois's sociological and historical research on African-American communities and culture broke ground in many areas, including the history of the post–Civil War Reconstruction period. More generally, he was a relentless and prolific critic of racial inequality at home and of the colonial system abroad. Beginning in the 1920s, and more so after his visit to the Soviet Union in 1927, he came to view the race question in terms of a broader

Marxist critique of CAPITALISM. In this context, he abandoned the goal of racial integration in favor of a separate economy for blacks organized on socialist principles. By the mid-1930s, he had cut his links to such moderate organizations as the NAACP. After World War II, DuBois's radicalism and his efforts on behalf of anticolonial activities made him a target for harassment by the U.S. government. He was a hero in Africa, however, and spent his last years in Ghana.

DuBois earned his Ph.D. at Harvard University and obtained a two-year fellowship for study in Berlin. The influence of his teacher William JAMES is visible in DuBois's well-known theory of black DOUBLE CONSCIOUSNESS. DuBois's early views on education and political activism brought him into conflict with the most prominent leader of the black community, Booker T. Washington; DuBois had argued against Washington's restrictive program of practical, trade-oriented education, at least for that "Talented Tenth" of the black population that Dubois viewed as ready to receive higher learning. More directly, he challenged Washington's role in discouraging social and political organization by the black community. Many of these views are gathered in DuBois's classic *The Souls of Black Folks* (1903)—a wide-ranging set of commentaries, ethnographies, and analyses of African-American life. DuBois also wrote novels, autobiographical accounts, innumerable editorials and journalistic pieces, and several works of history, including *Black Reconstruction* (1935). His other major works include *Darkwater* (1920), *Dusk of Dawn* (1940), and the *Encyclopedia of the Negro* (1931–1945).

dummy variables Qualitative or categorical variables that are introduced into REGRESSION ANALYSIS to utilize information that cannot be measured on a numerical scale.

Dumont, Louis (1911–1999) A French anthropologist and sociologist, best known for his studies of the caste system in India—a body of work that strongly marked anthropological debates about South Asia in the 1970s and 1980s. Chief among these is *Homo Hierarchicus* (1967), which argues that caste is rooted in a binary system of religious values that distinguish "pure" from "impure." Generalizing from this work, Dumont proposed a basic opposition between the static and holistic qualities he identified in this system and the egalitarian and individualist values of the West. This line of inquiry is developed in the comparative study *Homo Aequalis* (1977, translated as

From Mandeville to Marx: The Genesis and Triumph of Economic Ideology). Although influential, these generalizations and the specifics of his analysis of caste society have provoked controversy and opposition on a number of fronts—mostly related to his strong methodological debts to British and French STRUCTURALISM.

Dumont addressed a number of other subjects in his wide-ranging career, including peasant festivals, KINSHIP systems, and TOTALITARIANISM. His other major works include *A South Indian Subcaste* ([1957] 1986), *Affinity as a Value: Marriage Alliance in South India, with Comparative Essays on Australia* (1983), and *Essays on Individualism: Modern Ideology in Anthropological Perspective* ([1983] 1986).

dumping   In economics, *dumping* refers to export sales that occur at a price low enough to cause significant harm to economic interests in the importing country (usually firms that produce similar products). A more technical definition is that dumping occurs when the export price of a good is lower than the cost of production or when the export price is lower than the price of the same good sold domestically in the exporting country. Dumping is therefore a form of PRICE DISCRIMINATION, in which the producer charges a higher price in one market than in the other. Dumping can be consistent with maximizing profits or can be used as an oligopolistic tactic to deter the entry of competitors into a market, eliminate competition, or enforce a cartel. The multilateral trade institutions—GATT and now WTO—have provisions that allow countries to lodge formal complaints against dumping, which is considered an unfair trade practice.

duopoly   A market in which two firms dominate. In duopoly models, each duopolist makes rational decisions and takes into account the impact that its actions will have on the decision of the other duopolist. This is in marked contrast to the competitive market model in which agents' decisions are independent of one another.

Augustin COURNOT (1838) pioneered in this area by studying the decision-making problems of duopolists for a homogenous product market in a static setting. Under these conditions, each firm's optimal output is a function of the output chosen by its rival—a concept termed the *reaction function* of the firm. The Cournot–Nash equilibrium (as generalized by John NASH) is reached when neither firm can increase its profit by unilaterally choosing some other output level.

This equilibrium concept is the cornerstone of noncooperative GAME THEORY.

The Cournot equilibrium underlies much subsequent work on duopolies, from Joseph Bertrand's (1883) analysis of price competition between duopolists (rather than output decisions), to Francis EDGEWORTH's (1897) work on supply constraints. In the late 1920s and early 1930s, Harold HOTELLING and Edward Chamberlin made a related contribution to the equilibrium analysis of firms that sell similar but nonidentical products and that compete on prices.

One criticism of the Cournot equilibrium is that firms will collude to achieve MONOPOLY-like profits. Yet in the absence of binding agreements, such collusion faces the classic problem of cartels—the profitability of defection. Tacit collusion breaks down because each of the firms can profit by violating the agreement. In this case, the only acceptable agreement is a price level (or an output level), at which neither can gain through unilateral deviation, thereby returning to the original Cournot equilibrium.

Collusion can, however, arise in a dynamic setting in which there are repeated interactions between the firms. Game-theory models show that if firms play an infinitely repeated Cournot game, then they can use the threat of future punishment to deter deviant behavior and enforce collusion, even in the absence of binding agreements. Here, a firm's strategy is defined as choosing its output in each period as a function of the output chosen by its rival in all previous periods. This is, in essence, a noncooperative equilibrium strategy but it results in a cooperative outcome.

durable good   Goods that perform their intended function over a long period, rather than being immediately consumed. The analysis of durable goods takes explicit account of the distinction between the stock of the good and the flow of services derived from it. Since the services are derived over the lifetime of the product, the decision to purchase a durable good involves comparing the current cost to current and future benefits. For example, buying a car involves weighing its price against the expected future benefit from the use of the car, whereas buying ice cream, a perishable, involves balancing its price against the immediate utility that can be derived from it.

Durkheim, Emile (1858–1917)   A founding figure of both modern SOCIOLOGY and

ANTHROPOLOGY, Durkheim succeeded in dramatically changing the ways in which social scientists think about the relationship between individuals and SOCIETY. Most fundamentally, Durkheim argued that society constitutes a reality distinct from the individuals who compose it. It obeys rules and logics that are not reducible to psychology or other individual factors—indeed he argued that society shaped those factors and the even more basic cognitive experiences of time and space. His views ran counter to much of the contemporary anthropological focus on customs and behavior, which followed an inductive path from individuals to larger social values and institutions.

Chief among these social logics, Durkheim argued, was the principle of FUNCTIONALISM—the claim that institutions, practices, and customs exist because they contribute to the reproduction and integration of society. Society, from this perspective, is a self-organizing, self-reinforcing unity of diverse elements and features. These self-reinforcing processes include the broad range of norms and normative practices that define a society's legitimate goals and forms of activity, as well as the acceptable limits of those activities.

In *The Rules of Sociological Method* (1895), Durkheim laid out his vision of a distinct science of SOCIAL FACTS—aspects of society that are objectified, and therefore analyzable, through their effects. Social facts, he argued, are enduring and external to individuals; moreover they exercise a coercive function. Although they could not be analyzed with the methods of the natural sciences, as some proposed, a true and rigorous social science was possible that could guide and shape society. One cardinal principle of this science was that social facts could be explained only in terms of other social facts. Here again, Durkheim broke with the psychologizing and/or racializing tendencies of much early anthropological and sociological research, which tended to fall back on notions of human nature or instinct. Instead, Durkheim insisted that a crucial feature of social facts was their potential for "internalization."

Durkheim relied on the comparative study of societies, especially the study of small premodern societies, as a way of isolating the principles at work in contemporary Western society. In the process, he developed a number of influential analytical concepts that distinguished simple from complex societies. These include the well-known but somewhat counterintuitive distinction, articulated in *The Division of Labor in Society*

(1893), between MECHANICAL SOLIDARITY and ORGANIC SOLIDARITY: the former describes the high degree of social uniformity present in societies with a limited division of labor; the latter describes modern, highly differentiated societies, in which social solidarity derives primarily from the interdependence of functionally different parts. In societies with a high degree of mechanical solidarity, Durkheim argued, individual behavior is shaped by what he termed the "collective consciousness" (Fr., *conscience collective*)—the set of naturalized rules and norms that determine the scope of individual action. This natural order, he held, progressively break downs in modern society.

Durkheim produced two other studies that were crucial to the development of the social sciences. The first is *Suicide* (1897), in which he argued that this quintessentially individual act could be explained in terms of larger social patterns. He also developed a typology of modern and traditional forms of suicide and introduced the concept of ANOMIE—the societal and/or individual loss of purpose that follows a breakdown or conflict in the moral order. The second of these works is *The Elementary Forms of Religious Life* (1912), which approached the study of religion in terms of basic functional prerogatives and simple structural relationships. Based on his study of primitive Australian religions, Durkheim argued that all religions organized collective beliefs by dividing the world into the sacred and profane, and that the sacred operated as a form of collective social restraint. Centrally, Durkheim sought to show the social origin of the basic categories of human consciousness (conceived in otherwise Kantian fashion).

Durkheim dominated the social sciences in France in the late nineteenth and early twentieth centuries—in no small part through the network of researchers he fostered and the prominence of his flagship journal, *Année Sociologique*. He trained a generation of major scholars in France, including MAUSS (his nephew), and profoundly influenced the development of social anthropology in Britain (largely through the work of A. R. RADCLIFFE-BROWN) and sociology in the United States (principally through Talcott PARSONS). These figures extended his insights into long, productive, and often overlapping traditions of functionalism and STRUCTURALISM that continue to set the parameters of much social science research. Durkheim also produced a vast body of empirical research in a number of areas (some of which has been challenged), but his greater legacy lies in the perspectival and methodological revolution of the social sciences that he made possible. Durkheim's other major works includes *Primitive Classification* (1903, with Marcel Mauss) and *Moral Education* (1925).

Duverger's law   See ELECTORAL SYSTEM.

dynamic inconsistency   See TIME INCON-SISTENCY.

dynamic programming   A mathematical technique for analyzing multistage or sequential decision-making processes. It is particularly useful in solving complex optimization problems over a period of time. For example, an economic agent who lives for n periods must decide how much of her current wealth she should save and how much she should consume. After she makes her consumption decision, she invests the remaining wealth during each period and earns some return (which may not be known with certainty) on her savings. The agent's goal is to choose a level of consumption in each period that will maximize her lifetime utility (more accurately, she maximizes the expected present discounted value of lifetime utility). This is a complex n variable optimization problem. Dynamic programming facilitates its transformation into n single-variable optimization problems that may be solved and analyzed more easily.

dysfunction   A social activity that either disrupts the functioning of other social activities or impairs the larger functioning of society. The concept is a component of functionalist accounts of society, although it is not always adequately emphasized. See also FUNCTIONALISM.

E

Easton, David (1917–) An American political scientist best known for his application of SYSTEM(S) THEORY to the analysis of political systems. Easton devoted much of his career to arguing the need for, and later developing, a "unified theory of politics" capable of analyzing the general problems common to all political systems—in Easton's view, survival, reproduction, and adaptation. Easton conceived all political systems as means of processing *inputs* (external and internal demands on the system—the latter termed *supports*) into *outputs*, or decisions. Through this process, the political system "authoritatively allocated" the values of a society.

Easton argued that the persistence of political systems in the face of changing stresses was the central fact of political life and the question most in need of explanation. Systems, he argued, were always at risk of breakdown. The systems approach allowed for certain insights into this process; it defined the boundaries of the political and the nature of exogenous variables. It was less well adapted to examining the internal nature of the political process, insofar as it worked at a high level of abstraction and deliberately avoided the concrete specifics of the interplay of interests and groups.

Easton pursued these ideas in a number of important works during the 1950s and 1960s, including *The Political System* (1953), *A Framework for Political Analysis* (1965), and *A Systems Analysis of Political Life* (1965). Other of his works developed empirical illustrations of this method, including *Varieties of Political Theory* (1966) and *Regime and Discipline: Democracy and the Development of Political Science* (1994).

ecological fallacy A specious correlation between two sets of population data, such as when individual characteristics are inferred from aggregate statistics.

ecology The study of organisms in relation to each other and their environment. Ecology includes a range of issues, from population change to environmental adaptation and specialization.

Although the field of ecology developed out of biology—especially the study of plant life—the holistic implications of the concept resonated in the social sciences and strongly influenced a number of research traditions, from the CHICAGO SCHOOL OF SOCIOLOGY to the Berkeley school of cultural geography. Particularly for Chicago school sociologists such as Robert Ezra PARK and E. W. Burgess, ecology suggested a range of analogies between natural systems and social systems that provided insight into the organization of city life.

The *cultural ecology* of Julian Steward is perhaps the most influential social science appropriation of ecological models. Steward privileged the question of cultural adaptation in the struggle for subsistence and introduced a multi-lineal conception of cultural evolution that avoided many of the deterministic tendencies of earlier work. Ecological models are still used in research on the interactions of culture and the environment and have integrated methods and perspectives from SYSTEM(S) THEORY, environmentalism, and DEVELOPMENT theory.

economic-base theory Introduced by the economic geographer John Alexander in the mid-1950s, the theory proposes that regional economic growth is largely a function of exports, whether of goods or services. Economic activity, accordingly, is divided into two categories: *basic* activities, directed toward external markets; and *nonbasic*, or local, activities, directed toward the internal regional market. The two are linked by a multiplier effect that specifies that a proportionally greater increase in the former will lead to an increase in the latter.

economic man In Latin, *homo economicus*. Refers to the neoclassical portrayal of economic agents or individuals as rational actors who maximize their profits or welfare in the marketplace. NEOCLASSICAL ECONOMICS often posits that individuals possess complete and fully defined preferences, or tastes, perfect information, and no limit to their abilities to calculate advantage and disadvantage. This scenario can be made more complex either by introducing other agents or by introducing RISK, whereby actions may have several possible outcomes. In case of the former, strategic interactions need to be taken into account; in the latter, agents make assumptions about the expected utility and possible consequences of a course of action. *Homo economicus* is a stylized ideal, defended as an element of economic modeling not on the presumption that individuals really do behave so precisely, but that their learned behavior over time approximates that of the rational economic actor.

economics A field of study that consolidated in the late eighteenth century around inquiry into the generation of wealth, the growth of trade and markets, the division of labor, and other features of incipient CAPITALISM. This attention reflected growing awareness of the economy as an organized system that obeyed general laws, and growing interest in the role of the state in enhancing national wealth. The mercantilists and PHYSIOCRATS were among the earliest schools of economic thought—the former emphasizing the relationship between trade and national wealth (see MERCANTILISM); the latter, the relationship between agriculture and the extraction of RENT, or profit. The classical tradition, inaugurated by Adam SMITH, built on and revised these ideas (see CLASSICAL ECONOMICS). Until the mid-nineteenth century, *POLITICAL ECONOMY* was the preferred term for this field, reflecting the strong connection between economic analysis and the activities of the state. As scholars adopted an increasingly abstract approach to modeling markets and economic behavior—especially following the *marginalist* revolution—the notion of a distinct and autonomous field of economics gradually took hold.

The history of economic thought is marked by a number of major paradigm shifts. Classical economics refers to the work and assumptions that dominated economic thought from the late eighteenth to the mid-nineteenth century. Its principal figures were Smith, David RICARDO, J. B. Say, John Stuart MILL, and Karl MARX. The classical economists made a number of basic theoretical innovations that opened the door to modern economic thought, including the development of the LABOR THEORY OF VALUE, Malthusian population theory, SAY'S LAW, and the quantity theory of money. Questions of

international trade and NATIONAL INCOME were central. Microeconomic problems such as price determination were also subject to close attention for the first time (see MICROECONOMICS).

The refinement of MARGINAL ANALYSIS in the mid-nineteenth century extended some classical assumptions while breaking with others. Marginalism—now more generally known as NEOCLASSICAL ECONOMICS—formalized assumptions about the maximizing behavior of economic actors, the ideal behavior of competitive markets, and the importance of demand in determining prices. It became the dominant tradition of economic thought for most of the twentieth century, especially in the United States, and continues to play a major role in advocating minimal government intervention in the marketplace.

Sustained attention to the role of government in managing the economy developed in the 1930s—especially with the groundbreaking work of John Maynard KEYNES. KEYNESIAN ECONOMICS emphasized the ability of fiscal policy to moderate the BUSINESS CYCLE—stimulating aggregate demand during economic downturns and reining it in during upturns. With respect to the field, it consolidated a disciplinary division between research on the aggregate features of the national or world economy (MACROECONOMICS) and research on individual or firm-level decision-making (microeconomics). MONETARISM emerged in the 1960s as a critique of the fiscal orientation of Keynesianism, and of the possibility of effective government management of the economy. Marxist accounts of the role of the state in facilitating the transition to SOCIALISM have also generated a strong tradition of economic thought—and more generally a mode of social analysis that accords preeminence to economic factors (see MARXISM).

Additionally, subdisciplines have emerged that often bridge the macro/micro division and extend the neoclassical paradigm. Among these, BEHAVIORAL ECONOMICS studies the psychological foundations of individual choices in market and nonmarket environments; LABOR ECONOMICS seeks to understand the dynamics of employment, wages, income inequality, and related issues; GAME THEORY investigates the strategic behavior of decision-makers; and GROWTH THEORY analyzes processes of investment, capital accumulation, and increasing income and wealth.

economies of scale A situation in which the average cost of production decreases as production increases. Large fixed costs, such as factories, are the usual sources of such economies. The term is sometimes extended to business activities other than production, such as managerial, marketing, and financial activities. Economies of scale that appear at the individual or firm level are called *internal* economies of scale; economies that appear at the aggregate level are described as *external* economies. For example, external economies of scale exist where an increase in the size of an industry facilitates the specialized training of the labor force, thereby reducing the costs of all firms in the industry. Diseconomies of scale are also possible in situations where average cost rises with output.

Economies of scope is a related concept that refers to variations in costs as the output mix changes.

ecosystem Describes the complex relations among all organisms in a given area as a single biological system linked by flows of energy (such as the food chain). Ecosystems are the basic subject of ECOLOGY and play an important role in human geography, particularly that of the Berkeley school of CULTURAL GEOGRAPHY, as well as in recent research on changes in the environment.

Edgeworth, Francis (1845–1926) An economist who considered himself a follower of Alfred MARSHALL, although he influenced Marshall on a number of technical issues. Edgeworth made several contributions to NEOCLASSICAL ECONOMICS, introducing IN-DIFFERENCE CURVES, clarifying the law of diminishing returns, and developing the definition of the *core* of an economy. Many of his ideas, particularly the last, were ahead of their time and not sufficiently appreciated by his contemporaries. They are, however, among the central tenets of economic theory today, and most economists rate Edgeworth as one of the most important members of the neoclassical school.

Edgeworth was educated at Trinity College, Dublin, and at the University of Oxford. After practicing law and teaching English literature, he turned to lecturing in logic at the University of Cambridge and later took up a professorship in POLITICAL ECONOMY. When the *Economic Journal* was first published in 1891, Edgeworth became its editor. Together with John Maynard KEYNES, he continued to edit the journal well into his retirement.

One of Edgeworth's most important contributions was the introduction and use of indifference curves, which describe all combinations of two goods that yield the same utility (or well-being). Edgeworth's description of the "core" of an economy was even more significant, in that it affirmed the validity of equilibrium results from a perfectly competitive price system regardless of combinations among participants. Modern-day game theorists have used this result in order to prove the existence of Walrasian general equilibrium (see Leon WALRAS).

Edgeworth made several other contributions to neoclassical theory. He was the first to postulate that the *marginal product* of a variable factor of production (such as labor or raw materials), rather than its average product, falls as more of the factor is used. He also introduced a generalized UTILITY FUNCTION—in which the utility derived from a good depends not only on the quantity consumed but also on the quantity of other goods consumed. This allowed for the analysis of substitution and complementary effects in consumption. See also DUOPOLY.

effective demand Demand for goods and services that is backed by purchasing power and adequate resources. Effective demand is distinguished from *notional demand*, which is simply the desire for goods and services unrelated to available purchase power. The difference between the two is sometimes a source of market disequilibrium, since market prices signal only effective demand.

efficient market hypothesis An economic theory about the degree to which prices (typically of securities or stocks) reflect available information about those items. A capital market is said to be efficient if the prevailing security prices reflect all relevant information and are the best estimates of their real value. This notion has given rise to three forms of efficient market hypothesis. One is the *random walk hypothesis*—a weak form of which states that current prices fully reflect the information contained in the past history of prices. In such a case, strategies based on the analysis of past prices cannot yield exceptional profits, because such strategizing is already incorporated into current prices. According to the random walk hypothesis, prices tomorrow are expected to be the same as prices today, unless some random event occurs in the interim.

A medium-strength form of the hypothesis asserts that current stock prices reflect not only all historical price information but also all publicly available information. Under these conditions, a more substantial analysis of company balance sheets, profit statements, and announcements of dividends will similarly fail to yield exceptional profits. Financial econometric research has justified both the weak and medium-strength hypotheses with widespread evidence of both the integration of the history of prices and of the rapid adjustment to new information. The strong version of the efficient market hypothesis asserts that share prices will have fully taken into account all information known to any market participant, whether this information is publicly available or not. Therefore, even those with privileged information cannot use this to secure superior investment results. The evidence for this is mixed. The profitability of insider trading presents one problem. Yet some studies show that randomly selected portfolios or unmanaged portfolios do as well as (and sometimes better than) professionally managed portfolios. Moreover, studies have shown that professional fund managers are generally inconsistent in their performance: managers who do exceptionally well in one period are just as likely to underperform in the next period.

egalitarianism   A social doctrine that emphasizes the goal of equality among all members of a society—or, indeed, all humanity. Eighteenth-century Enlightenment thinkers closely linked egalitarianism to the appreciation of common humanity, based on the capacities for language use and reason. The concept underlies most efforts to redistribute wealth or reduce social inequality, and it is the core value underlying socialist programs for the large-scale reorganization of economic life. Two versions are usually distinguished: equality of opportunity and equality of condition. The former is more closely associated with LIBERALISM, the latter with SOCIALISM and COMMUNISM, although there are many admixtures. While liberal advocates of egalitarianism are concerned to provide an equal basis for competition among individuals in society—which may imply the intervention of the state in matters of social welfare—many consider inequality of outcome to be a positive good that provide incentives for talent and effort. Most modern liberal democratic societies pursue a mix of the two, seeking to moderate social inequality in order to assure greater equality of opportunity. Welfare policies, public education, and progressive taxation are among the most common forms of support for such goals.

Beyond the primarily economistic referents of the term, egalitarianism also refers to the equal political rights of citizens and the equal entitlement to respect. The nineteenth-century French political philosopher Alexis de TOCQUEVILLE famously addressed the latter, as well as what he viewed as the tension between FREEDOM and EQUALITY in democratic societies.

ego   One of the three core elements of the psyche postulated by Sigmund FREUD. The *ego* (or "I") embodies the *reality principle*: it tests reality against the instinctual demands of the *id* and enables the practical adaptations to the environment that ensure survival. In some accounts, the ego is therefore represented as the choice-making, rational part of the psyche. It serves as a mediator of conflict between the *id*—the mass of instinctual drives that demand immediate satisfaction—and the *superego*, which represents internalized parental and social authority. It therefore exercises a powerful censoring function. The development of a healthy ego is a central concern of much of the psychoanalytic tradition, including EGO PSYCHOLOGY and OBJECT-RELATIONS THEORY. See also PSYCHOANALYSIS.

ego focused   In kinship studies, the term describes a kinship network that is traced from a living person, as opposed to an ancestor-focused network.

ego psychology   One of the major branches of the psychoanalytic tradition to emerge from Sigmund FREUD's research, ego psychology generally accepts Freud's theory of the instincts but emphasizes the development of capacities to manage the conflicts and contradictions that characterize the mature, socialized psyche. As developed by Anna Freud (Freud's daughter), Heinz Hartmann, Edith Jacobson, and others, ego psychology analyzed the capacity of the ego to defend itself against external and internal threats (forming "ego defenses") and to accommodate itself to societal demands as the individual matures. It had a strong therapeutic focus that emphasized the efficacy of the relationship with the therapist in facilitating those accommodations.

Ego psychology's stress on the psychological dimension of SOCIALIZATION proved highly congenial to the sociologist Talcott PARSONS, who saw an active role for the individual in meeting social demands for conformity and integration. For many of the same reasons, ego psychology was criticized by members of the FRANKFURT SCHOOL (such as Max HORKHEIMER and Herbert MARCUSE), who saw such pressures for conformity as a mechanism of control and more generally as a refusal of the burden of critical reason. Jacques LACAN—in his own version of the return to Freudian orthodoxy—similarly opposed the contradiction-resolving tendencies of ego psychology on the grounds that those contradictions constituted human subjectivity.

Ego psychology was the dominant tradition of PSYCHOANALYSIS in the United States in the post–World War II decades, and it continues to exercise a powerful influence on clinical practice. Its most direct competitor in this regard is modern OBJECT-RELATIONS THEORY, derived from the work of Melanie KLEIN.

elasticity A measure of the percentage change in one variable due to a percentage change in another variable. Elasticity most commonly measures economic responses to price changes, especially the change in demand for a good due to a price change—the *price elasticity of demand*. More precisely, the price elasticity of demand is the *percentage* change in demand for a good due to a *percentage* change in its price. Other common elasticities include the *income elasticity of demand* and the *cross-price elasticity of demand*. Demand is considered elastic if demand changes (in percentage terms) by more than the change in price. Demand is inelastic if the change in demand is less than the change in price. An equally large demand response to a price change is referred to as *unit elasticity*.

electoral geography The study of the spatial aspects of elections. With the notable exception of Israel's Knesset (parliament), nearly all electoral systems rely on territorial divisions to translate votes into seats. In some cases (e.g., U.S. districts, French *circonscriptions*, British constituencies), these territories have no other political or administrative significance; in others, they correspond to units of local government. Generally speaking, majority and plurality electoral systems tend to elect one or two members per district per election, whereas systems of proportional representation tend to elect several. Where electoral divisions are not determined by historical territories, the drawing of boundaries (districting or apportionment) can become an object of political contestation. In the United States, the reapportionment of districts in the majority

party's favor is termed *gerrymandering*. To avoid this, many polities rely on politically insulated boundary commissions.

Electoral geography was first studied in France to determine the relationships between social groups and voting behavior. "Ecological association" was one common early form of reasoning that inferred the political tendencies of social groups from electoral results—for example, inferring that farmers were generally conservative based on the results from rural districts. Subsequent research showed that this was too crude a measure to determine precisely who was voting and for what reasons, and the practice waned as more sophisticated survey methods were developed in the 1950s. Nonetheless, culturally or economically distinct groups frequently live in identifiable areas, and many important political cleavages take a corresponding spatial form.

electoral system The rules according to which citizens' votes determine which candidates and parties win public office. Political scientists usually distinguish three basic types.

1. Plurality or first-past-the-post systems award the office to the candidate with the most votes in a district, and therefore strongly emphasize the territorial aspect of representation. Primarily used in Britain and its former colonies (including the United States and India), plurality systems tend to lead to two-party systems, as voters will be disinclined to vote for parties or candidates with little chance of winning. As the examples of India and Canada illustrate, however, this tendency may be overcome by the advantage these systems give to parties whose support is regionally concentrated. Plurality systems have the advantage of being most likely to produce clear legislative majorities, but they have the disadvantage of allowing governments to be elected with a minority of the popular vote.

2. Majority systems attempt to correct for this disadvantage by ensuring that the winning candidate commands at least 50 percent of the vote. They are employed by many countries for electing a chief executive, and by Australia and France for legislative elections. Australia uses an alternative vote system in which voters rank the candidates, while France and a number of other countries hold a second ballot between the top candidates if no candidate wins a majority on the first.

3. Proportional representation (PR) systems are used in most other countries. They employ various means to ensure that a party's representation in the legislature is proportional to its share of the

popular vote. There are three main varieties of PR: party-list methods, single transferable votes, and additional-member systems. In party-list systems, voters choose between parties; a number of candidates from each party's list, commensurate with the party's share of the popular vote, are thereby elected to the legislature. In single transferable vote (STV) or Hare systems, voters rank a number of candidates equal to the number of seats to be filled; all candidates whose vote equals or exceeds the Droop quota (the total vote cast divided by the number of seats plus one) are elected, and all votes cast for other candidates are transferred to the next round of counting, until all seats are filled. In additional-member systems (AMS), voters select candidates within constituencies, as in the plurality system, but extra members are added either from party lists or from constituencies with the narrowest margins of victory, in order to make the total number of representatives proportional to the popular vote. While PR systems more closely represent actual voter preferences, they tend to encourage multiple-party systems and coalition governments. Variations of each of these systems also exist, as do a variety of other possible rules for electoral systems. Voting, for example, may be voluntary or required by law. In nearly all modern political systems, each citizen's vote is equally weighted, but elections held in other kinds of organizations sometimes follow other rules. In elections to corporate boards of directors, for example, shareholders have different numbers of votes based on the number (and sometimes the kind) of shares they own. See also ELECTORAL GEOGRAPHY; and VOTING.

elementary structures of kinship   Claude LÉVI-STRAUSS's term for an approach to KINSHIP systems that sought to identify the simplest and most basic variations as keys to the entire phenomenon. In the manner of Emile DURKHEIM's *Elementary Forms of Religious Life* (1912), Lévi-Strauss found these elementary structures in societies where the choice of marriage partners is carefully circumscribed—for example, limited to cross cousins. By contrast, the term *complex structures of kinship* describes those that proscribe marriage with close kin but leave the choice of marriage partner open to other factors, such as economics, status, or love. This distinction laid one of the foundations of Lévi-Strauss's STRUCTURALISM and marked a departure from kinship theories that privileged descent or lineage as the basis of social organization. In later

work, Lévi-Strauss acknowledged that there was a "complex" dimension to all kinship systems.

Elias, Norbert   (1897–1990) A Polish-born, German-educated historical sociologist whose work is increasingly recognized as one of the most original contributions to twentieth-century sociological and historiographical thought. This recognition has been slow in coming: Elias's two-volume study of the political and psychological dimensions of the "civilizing process" in medieval Europe (*The Civilizing Process*, 1978 [1939]) barely circulated in the years after its publication and remained largely unknown until the 1960s. Only in the 1980s did a serious appreciation of his work begin to emerge in British and American SOCIOLOGY.

Elias was an interdisciplinary thinker who insisted that the study of *sociogenesis*—the development of society—could not be separated from *psychogenesis*—changes in personality structures, notions of SELF, and other psychological developments. In *The Civilizing Process*, Elias emphasized the interrelations between the development of behavioral restraints in medieval society (for example through moral codes and systems of etiquette) and the rise of the STATE as an agency for social regulation. *The Court Society* (1969) explored a similar question, treating the development of ceremony in the royal court of pre-Revolutionary France as an index of the decline of the aristocracy and the rise of the bourgeoisie. Elias's scholarship engaged a remarkable range of topics: emotional and psychological life, attitudes toward sexuality and the body, sports and leisure, self-discipline and social control, the growth of the state and emergence of national identities, and the historical meaning of childhood, to cite the most central. A major factor in the neglect of his work was that these issues, and the historical, interdisciplinary methodology that connected them, ran counter to the tendencies of mid-twentieth-century sociology—especially the functionalist tradition of Emile DURKHEIM and Talcott PARSONS. Elias was highly critical of what he perceived as the reification of social phenomena in functionalist and structuralist accounts. He insisted, rather, on the need to place historical change at the center of social analysis. He also insisted on seeing society in terms of shifting relationships of power, instead of static situations or capacities. Elias recognized the impact of the sociologist on the objects of study and advocated constant work at emotional detachment from one's research. The broad sociological turn toward these themes in the 1960s had much to do with the growth of interest in his work.

In *What Is Sociology* (1970), Elias explored the theoretical underpinnings of his approach. He argued that society was rooted neither in individuals nor in external social systems, but in the web of interactions that defined both. He termed these patterns of relationships *figures* and his work *figurational analysis*.

Elias fled Germany in 1933 for Paris and later England, where he spent some twenty years. His other writing includes *The Loneliness of the Dying* (1982), *An Essay on Time* (1984), and *Involvement and Detachment* (1986).

elite and elitism A minority that possesses a disproportionate share of resources or POWER within a group or society. The study of elites, their composition, and their behavior is a major focus of POLITICAL SCIENCE and POLITICAL SOCIOLOGY. Elitism is the belief that the existence of an elite is either desirable or inevitable. This view was common in Classical political thought—PLATO advocated rule by a select caste of guardians and philosopher kings in his *Republic*—and it continued well into the nineteenth century. *Classical elite theory*, however, generally refers to the work of Italian sociologists Gaetano MOSCA and Vilfredo PARETO around the turn of the twentieth century. Mosca's *The Ruling Class* (1896) argued that all societies come to be dominated by a relatively small, more or less cohesive group that possesses some crucial skill or attribute. Against MARXISM, elitists hold that domination is not fundamentally economic; against PLURALISM, they contend that although elites may be replaced, their existence is inevitable. Robert MICHELS's *iron law of oligarchy* draws the same conclusion about political parties. Elite theories of democracy, deriving especially from Joseph Schumpeter's *Capitalism, Socialism, and Democracy* (1942), argue that stable democracies are those that are governed by competing elites.

embedded and disembedded A key distinction in the FORMALIST–SUBSTANTIVIST DEBATE within economic anthropology, initially proposed by Karl Polanyi. The terms describe the degree of separation of the economy from other social institutions, such as KINSHIP or religion. Modern capitalist economies are said to be disembedded, and are thus interpretable, Polanyi argued, in terms of market rationality. Premodern economies are embedded in other institutional structures and are subject to other logics of behavior—in Polanyi's example, logics of *reciprocity* and/or *redistribution*.

embourgeoisement The spread of bourgeois or middle-class values and lifestyles into sectors of the traditional working class and, concomitantly, the loss of working-class support for class-based or radical political movements. The term has Marxist roots in accounts of the ideological domination of the working class by the BOURGEOISIE. It came into broader use in the 1950s and 1960s to describe the expansion of the middle class and the social consequences of the shift away from traditional industrial labor toward a service and informational economy. In the United States, in particular, the expansion of access to home ownership and consumer goods after World War II—and the homogenization of lifestyles implied therein—gave impetus to the concept. Accounts of widespread cultural homogenization, however, were eventually challenged by a range of generally more subtle inquiries into persistent class differences and their cultural markers among "affluent workers"—especially in England in the 1960s. Nonetheless, embourgeoisement continues to be studied in SOCIOLOGY and POLITICAL SCIENCE as the traditional structures of working-class political and social identity continue to deteriorate.

emergency powers The right of the executive to suspend ordinary constitutional procedures and protections in order to respond quickly and effectively to war, civil strife, or other crises. Emergency powers allow the executive to bypass the legislature, to suspend certain rights of citizens, and to govern by decree—a situation sometimes termed a *constitutional* dictatorship. Most democratic constitutions have some provision for emergency powers, typically subject to review by the LEGISLATURE (in Britain) or the JUDICIARY (in the United States). Their use is considered dangerous to DEMOCRACY and the rule of law because they can normalize extraordinary police and military powers (as in France during the Algerian crisis of 1961 or in British Northern Ireland after 1973). Over time, they can erode the legitimacy of democratic regimes.

emergent norms Provisional norms that develop in the context of spontaneous groups, such as crowds, mobs, rioters, and mass publics. Associated with the work of Ralph Turner and Lewis Killian (*Collective Behavior*, 1972), *emergent* *norms* describes a process of decision-making and rational action that runs counter to much of the classical work on crowd behavior. See also COLLECTIVE BEHAVIOR.

emergent properties In the functionalist tradition of Auguste COMTE, Emile DURKHEIM, and Talcott PARSONS, emergent properties are those aspects of social organization that cannot be reduced to the attributes or actions of individuals. Comte held that each science must analyze a distinct order of phenomena. Those of psychology were not reducible to biology, nor were biological facts reducible to those of physics. Similarly, many (but not all) social scientists hold that social facts cannot be explained except by other social facts. In this sense, properties of social organization, like language or normative integration, are termed *emergent*. This distinguishes them from collective properties formed by the mere addition of individual attributes or actions into larger statistical bodies. The concept of emergence plays a similar role in the SYMBOLIC INTERACTIONISM of George Herbert MEAD and Herbert Blumer, where it describes the synthesis of new patterns of behavior in the course of social interactions.

emic and etic The term *emic* describes an insider's perspective on cultural practices or forms; it refers to the self-description or reflexivity possible within any culture, as well as to the conformity of such description to the categories, values, and terms of that culture. The term *etic*, in contrast, describes an account of practices or forms based on external criteria—the perspective of an outsider. The tension between the two is a subject of constant interest and concern to anthropologists and ethnographers—and predates the formal introduction of the terms in Kenneth Pike's *Language in Relation to a Unified Theory of the Structure of Human Behavior* (1954). The distinction between emic and etic has been challenged, however, as part of the broader poststructuralist attack on objective observation and the neutrality of language as a descriptive medium.

eminent domain The right of the state to take private property for public use without the owner's consent, but usually with fair compensation. The term is primarily used in the United States, where it is spelled out in the Fifth Amendment to the Constitution. The doctrine of eminent domain evolved in the seventeenth and eighteenth centuries as natural law theorists, such as Hugo GROTIUS and John LOCKE, attempted to reconcile state SOVEREIGNTY with what they perceived as a natural right to private property. See also PROPERTY AND PROPERTY RIGHTS.

empire See IMPERIALISM AND EMPIRE.

empiricism A broad philosophical orientation associated with the emergence of modern science and the scientific method. Empiricism stresses that human knowledge is limited to what can be observed and tested; it is therefore highly critical of theoretical abstractions, speculative philosophy, and most forms of psychology. The eighteenth-century British philosophers John LOCKE, George Berkeley, and David HUME were the major innovators of this tradition.

Empiricism and the nature of scientific truth have been fundamental issues in the evolution of the social sciences—particularly in the context of early debates about whether the social sciences were different from the natural sciences (see *METHODENSTREIT*). Empiricism continues to occupy a prominent place in social-science methodologies. It is sometimes loosely coupled with POSITIVISM, but in strict usage in the philosophy of science it represents a different position.

employment, theories of There are two basic theories of employment—the neoclassical and the Keynesian (developed by John Maynard KEYNES). The neoclassical theory applies standard demand-and-supply analysis to labor markets and treats unemployment as a disequilibrium phenomenon that arises from the persistence of wages at a level higher than that which clears the labor market. Minimum wage legislation, union bargaining, and *efficiency wages* (where higher wages produce better workers or draw better workers from the employment pool) are some of the reasons that labor markets may not adjust to full employment. Further, some level of unemployment is to be expected—the *frictional* unemployment that occurs when people transition between jobs. Neoclassical models predict that trying to increase employment by too much will cause INFLATION. Estimates of the *nonaccelerating inflation rate of unemployment (NAIRU)* for the United States in the late twentieth century have been between 5 percent and 6 percent (see NAIRU).

Keynesian theories, formulated in the context of the Great Depression, postulate that unemployment results from the equilibrium of aggregate demand and supply at a level too low to require the productive services of the entire labor force. The remedy is to raise aggregate demand by a combination of fiscal and monetary measures, such as lower taxes, increased government spending, or accelerated monetary growth. Protective measures in the realm of international trade, such as tariffs and subsidies, can also help alleviate the problem by switching demand from foreign to domestic goods and services.

enclave and exclave The term *enclave* refers to an autonomous political district or state surrounded by another state, such as the Vatican in Italy or Lesotho in South Africa. The term *exclave* refers to a piece of national territory separated from the rest of the nation, such as Alaska. Enclaves and exclaves were the subject of considerable attention in political geography between the 1930s and 1960s, when questions about the nature and viability of state boundaries were closely tied to debates about empire and decolonization.

encoding and decoding Key terms in Stuart HALL's influential 1973 theory of the production and reception of television. *Encoding* is that part of the production process related to the formation of specific, intentional meanings—for example, a particular account of an event that bolsters an official governmental position; *decoding* is related to reception and refers to the process of interpretation through which that text acquires meaning. In this work, Hall challenged the notion that viewers are passive consumers of opinions fabricated by a CULTURE INDUSTRY—a view associated with the Frankfurt school. As subsequent research has shown, interpretations of the same televised story can vary widely, although they break down in fairly consistent ways according to social position and education.

enculturation The process of learning and incorporating basic cultural roles, knowledge, and beliefs, generally during childhood. Enculturation is central to the work of Melville J. HERSKOVITS, who distinguished it from *acculturation*, in which the learning involves contact between cultures. Herskovits gave the term several additional inflections, using it to refer to the process of conscious adaptation to social change and thereby distinguishing it from the process of

SOCIALIZATION embodied in formal systems of social integration, such as education.

end-of-ideology theory A prominent sociological attempt to link the transformations of modern capitalism to broad shifts in political culture, generally associated with Daniel BELL's *The End of Ideology* (1960) and related work by Seymour Martin LIPSET and other political scientists. The term *end-of-ideology* refers to the decline of the great nineteenth-century systems of political and social ideals—principally LIBERALISM and SOCIALISM—in the face of a variety of social, political, and economic changes. These include the failure of the liberatory promises of those ideologies; the broad shift away from industrial labor (with its structural social conflicts) toward a service and communication-oriented economy (with more consensual management techniques); and the emergence of a stabilizing democratic welfare state in most industrialized countries.

Although a number of the specific claims by Bell and other end-of-ideology proponents have been debated or revised in the face of later events, many of the theory's broader traits have been reproduced in debates about POSTMODERNISM and postindustrial capitalism. With the recent fall and/or capitalist transformation of the socialist regimes, the tendency to declare the definitive victory of some version of the liberal democratic state has become still more commonplace in popular and, to a lesser degree, academic political discourse. Recent versions of this argument, such as Francis Fukuyama's end-of-history thesis, tend to reflect the neoliberal revival of the 1980s and 1990s, with its accompanying decline of faith in the administered welfare state.

endogamy The practice of marriage within a given group, whether defined in terms of KINSHIP or larger group structures. Marriage outside the group is called *exogamy*.

endogeneity and exogeneity Properties of variables in an economic or econometric model. A variable is *endogenous* (from the Greek for "produced from within") if it changes in response to changes in the other variables in the model. In other words, its causal forces are included in the model. Otherwise, it is *exogenous*—the factors that cause the variable to change are outside the model.

Engel's law Named after the nineteenth-century German statistician Ernst Engel, Engel's law states that the share of food in the total expenditure of a household is inversely related to its income—in other words, the income elasticity of demand for food is less than one. Households spend a smaller percentage of their budget on food as their incomes rise. Engel's Law has been empirically established in both cross-sectional studies and time-series analysis.

entitlement   A claim or right, usually rooted in some broader social value or precedent. In political theory, entitlement generally refers to justifications for the right to private property. For example, in both John Locke's *Second Treatise on Government* (1690) and Robert Nozick's *Anarchy, State, and Utopia* (1974), the individual's right to property is based on the doctrine of original acquisition, which posits that at some point in the past the property in question was legitimately acquired and that its title has been passed to its present owner. More broadly, individual or group claims on the state, particularly for resources, are often termed *entitlements*, although here the justification is more typically based in claims for social justice or EGALITARIANISM.

entry structure and market structure
Models of firm behavior often pay close attention to the decisions of firms to enter and exit markets. The degree of competition in a market hinges in large part on the number of firms active within it. In the perfectly competitive neoclassical model of a market, long-run equilibrium requires that no potential entrant finds entry profitable and that no incumbent finds exit profitable. The first condition requires that price be no greater than the minimum average cost; the second condition requires that price be no less than the minimum average cost. Hence, in long-run competitive equilibrium, price equals the minimum average cost.

For monopolistic and/or oligopolistic market models, the limit-pricing work of Joe Staten Bain and Paolo Sylos-Labini (the Bain–Sylos model) has been the focal point of research. Bain's *Barriers to New Competition* (1956) and Sylos-Labini's *Oligopoly and Technical Progress* (1956) describe how potential rather than actual competition can constrain the ability of the established firm to exploit its monopoly power. In order to keep out potential entrants into the market, the incumbent firm can threaten to produce at a level that would put the entrant at risk of earning no profits.

The work of Bain and Sylos has since been extended to address the problem of the credibility of such threats. In many instances, the established

firm has the opportunity to take actions or establish a position that would dramatically affect any entrant's chances—over and above the production decision. These include the acquisition of excess capacity, advertising, brand proliferation, patenting, strategic location of retail outlets, and so on.

envelope theorem   A fundamental theorem of modern economic analysis that shows the relationship between an unconstrained optimization problem with at least two parameters and the constrained problem when a subset of the parameters is held constant. Holding one parameter of a function fixed (for example, labor in a production function) while varying another (for example, capital) will generate an output function whose maximum value is necessarily bounded by the production function maximum when both parameters are allowed to be chosen optimally. As the quantity of labor is held fixed at various levels, the solutions to these constrained optimization problems trace out the envelope of the unconstrained function. The implication of the theorem is that, at the margin, the impact of a change in one parameter—labor as a production input—is merely the direct change in production due to an increase in labor. At the margin, there is no indirect effect through a change in the optimal capital choice.

environmental determinism   Also sometimes termed *environmentalism*, the assumption that the physical environment is the primary determinant of cultural forms. The concept played a large part in nineteenth-century comparative studies of civilizations, which often placed the explanatory burden on correlations between climate and diverse aspects of human activity and ability—creativity, state forms, religious belief, and so on. Twentieth-century social scientists, however, have tended to temper claims of environmental determinism by emphasizing the relative autonomy of the various areas of human activity, especially in developed societies. They have also stressed the diversity of possible responses to environmental factors—a doctrine known in human geography as *possibilism*. Strong environmental determinism, however, continues to be prominent in the work of the anthropologist Marvin HARRIS (an approach that he terms *cultural materialism*). Possibilism has been variously refined and revised, both by geographers such as O. H. K. Spate, who insist that certain outcomes are nonetheless much more probable than others (*probabilism*), and within anthropology by such researchers as Julian STEWARD, who study the diversity of human adaptations to the environment under the rubric of cultural ecology. More generally, cultural geography has defined itself around the reciprocal impact of the environment on culture and culture on the natural environment, preferring to think in terms of a unified cultural landscape.

environmental perception A critique of rational-choice approaches to environmental decisions that emphasizes the subjective construction of people's relationship with the environment and the way in which those perceptions, images, and attitudes shape culture. Environmental perception became an important subject in human GEOGRAPHY in the 1950s and 1960s, and it continues to be a central element of the larger field of behavioral geography—the study of human choices with respect to the environment.

One of the earliest and most prominent statements on the subject was J. K. Wright's 1947 description of human perceptions of the landscape as a *terra incognita*—an "unknown territory" for geographical study. Subsequent of inquiry in this area led to the concept of the *mental map*, introduced in the 1960s by Peter Gould as a way of representing people's images and impressions of the places around them.

envy Used in SOCIAL-CHOICE THEORY as a possible measure of the equity of distributive choices in a society. One criterion that has been proposed for an equitable distribution is that it be *envy-free*, in that individuals have no wish to exchange their assigned shares for anyone else's shares. If every individual has identical preferences, then an egalitarian division is the only envy-free solution. But if individuals have differing preferences, there may exist other envy-free allocations in which all individuals are better off.

episteme A historically specific organization of knowledge, including the conditions of its production, its nature, and its uses. *Episteme* is a key term in Michel FOUCAULT's historical inquiry into the structure of knowledge, where it forms part of a challenge to the idea of the continuous accumulation of knowledge throughout history. Instead, Foucault sees discontinuities and ruptures in the ways that knowledge is organized in different epochs. In *The Order of Things* (1971), he distinguishes between the classical and modern

epistemes: the former structured by resemblances between things—analogies, sympathies, juxtapositions; the latter by a principle of classificatory reason that anchors the concept of *man* within a singular framework of order and relation—a network of signs that have approximal relationships to things. Foucault suggested that our modern episteme may already be over, although he only began to speculate about a postmodern organization of knowledge.

epistemology Literally "the study of knowledge," epistemology is the inquiry into the conditions, paradigms, and limits of knowledge, including the nature of truth claims and the historical contexts that have shaped human inquiry. These questions have been central to the philosophical tradition since Socrates, which has systematically investigated the grounds of its own inquiries. Accounts of human knowledge have proceeded on a number of bases, from early modern attempts to ground knowledge in consciousness—Descartes' "I think, therefore I am" inaugurates this tradition—to empiricist arguments that the knowable is rooted in (and limited to) the experience of the senses.

Debates over the nature, condition, and limits of social knowledge have recurrently divided social scientists. The most famous of these arguments is the late nineteenth-century METHODENSTREIT, which revisited many of Immanuel KANT's arguments about the structures of consciousness and judgment, and which raised a variety of questions about the distinction between the natural and social sciences—including the contrast between *ideographic* inquiry into particulars with the *nomothetic* pursuit of generalizations. Disputes continue over POSITIVISM, the status of interpretation, objectivity, and concept-formation, and the nature of scientific explanation and its relationship to practical understanding. POST-STRUCTURALISM renewed such debates with challenges to scientific positivism, objectivity, and assumptions about the linear growth of knowledge. The related term EPISTEME, popularized by Michel FOUCAULT in *The Order of Things* (1970), refers to the historical specificity of particular sets of epistemological principles.

At the same time, realist philosophies of science have sought to overcome the weaknesses of positivism without abandoning the pursuit of generalizable causal explanations. A key divide running through many arguments over epistemology distinguishes those who approach social life externally, as a matter of objective knowledge, and those who approach it internally, with an effort at understanding the meaning that social actors give cultural phenomena. There have been many attempts to overcome this division or to combine the two perspectives, but none has commanded general assent. See also *VERSTEHEN*.

equality   The concept of human equality is one of the pillars of Enlightenment social thought and, consequently, the focus of a long tradition of debate and struggle over competing visions of government and social justice. The centrality of the concept to Western social theory reflects the secularization of the Christian notion of equality before God—as well as a challenge to the Christian belief in the inevitability of worldly inequality. Early social-contract theorists, such as Thomas HOBBES, John LOCKE, Jean-Jacques ROUSSEAU, admitted the inequality of natural gifts (although they sometimes minimized them) but insisted upon the equality of individuals before the institutions of civil and political society (see SOCIAL-CONTRACT THEORY). This effectively invested the state with the responsibility for maintaining equality, and much of the modern political history of the West has been an extended struggle over what that role entails. This is the context of ongoing efforts to eliminate the various corporate divisions of society (the ranked "estates" of feudalism, slavery, the special status of the church, the subordinate status of women), as well as debates over the difference between (and desirability of) equality of opportunity and equality of outcome.

Three relatively distinct meanings of equality inform most debates over social justice in the West and furnish many of the dividing lines of Western political life: (1) *equality* before the law; (2) *equality* of opportunity (often linked to MERITOCRACY); and (3) *equality* of results or condition (see EGALITARIANISM). Equality before the law implies that an individual's identity, status, and origins are irrelevant in matters of justice and public life: the law treats individuals abstractly, whether as plaintiffs seeking redress or as defendants accused of criminal behavior. Equality of opportunity implies that all economic actors have the same chance to occupy various positions in society; in principle, position is accorded by talent and effort rather than by inherited social status or wealth. Equality of results refers to the equal distribution of goods in society—long the ideal, if not the practice, of communist societies. The first two are commonly seen as basic to democracy and liberal economics; there is considerably more disagreement over the role of the third.

Economic stratification by some combination of CLASS, RACE, GENDER, region, religion, and ETHNICITY remains a central feature of nearly all societies and a strong determinant of life outcomes. While all societies accept some inequality, they differ in the type and degree that are considered appropriate. Societies differ also in the degree to which they accept inheritance as the basis for inequality. In general, inherited inequality has been discouraged in modern societies in favor of an emphasis on merit-based rewards. Although the meritocratic model is now ascendant, a vast amount of research in the social sciences has been devoted to understanding the mechanisms that produce patterns of wealth and poverty over time—especially those that inhibit social mobility in spite of social policies designed to create access to wealth (chiefly, public education). The term *equity*, in this context, often refers to the "fair distribution of opportunities and rewards."

The emergence of discourses of positive difference on the part of numerous minority groups (especially in the United States) has shifted the terrain of equality from the older concept of equal treatment to new models of cultural equality and redistributive justice. Support for such measures reflects a strong disillusionment with the state's ability to guarantee a meritocratic society, although such measures are frequently articulated as ways of making possible a more genuinely meritocratic future.

equilibrium   A balance of forces, or the center value toward which many dynamic systems tend. Equilibrium can also be described as a point of rest from which there is no internally generated (*endogenous*) tendency to change. Such situations are termed *steady* or *stationary states*. The concept has been useful in a number of kinds of analysis of social systems—particularly the structural-functionalism of Talcott PARSONS and others, who see social structures, laws, and norms as internal regulating mechanisms that provide societies with continuity and stability.

Equilibrium analysis is also the foundation of modern economic theory. Economists distinguish between Marshallian partial equilibrium (see Alfred MARSHALL) and Walrasian general equilibrium (see Leon WALRAS). In partial equilibrium theory, only a specified part of the economy is analyzed. In defining this relationship, Marshall introduced the hallmark concept of the partial equilibrium approach—the *ceteris paribus* condition, which signifies that all other things are held constant, including influences from other sectors of the economy. In contrast, the general equilibrium approach of Walras holds constant only noneconomic influences—those considered to be beyond the range of economic analysis. This does not guarantee that these influences will remain constant when the economic factors change; the predictive power of the analysis may depend on the extent to which the noneconomic factors are truly independent of the economic variables.

Both methods of equilibrium analysis study markets, consisting of economic agents who buy and sell goods and services to one another. The specificity of partial equilibrium theory (to a particular industry, for example) means that the study proceeds in terms of particular market demand curves and supply curves, setting aside agents acting in other markets. In general equilibrium analysis, multiple markets are analyzed simultaneously. True general equilibrium includes all individual agents, as well as all markets and industries.

Equilibrium analysis raises three general questions about the specified system: the existence of an equilibrium, its stability, and its uniqueness. For markets to function well, equilibrium should not only exist but also be both stable and unique—and thus both predictable and durable. In some markets, demand and supply curves do not intersect, in which case equilibrium cannot exist. Even in markets where demand and supply do overlap, there may be no set of prices that clears all markets simultaneously—especially if preferences and quantities are not "well-behaved." The stability of equilibrium depends on the dynamics out of equilibrium: a system is said to be stable if it returns to its equilibrium position after a disturbance. Finally, even if an equilibrium is stable, it may not be unique: demand curves and supply curves can intersect more than once, and systems can consist of multiple equilibria which are only locally stable. Absent a unique equilibrium, it is difficult to argue that market prices represent the true economic value of commodities, since there is potential for several equilibrium prices.

Equilibrium is also an important concept in the theory of noncooperative games. As in models of markets, the idea of a stable outcome lends weight to the predictions of the theory. The earliest version of equilibrium applied to games was suggested by John NASH. A NASH EQUILIBRIUM is reached when each agent has no incentive to unilaterally alter his strategic choice, given what the other players have done. For finite games composed of multiple strategic decisions, *subgame-perfect equilibrium* is often the standard. This requires that strategies chosen and played in any subset of the game are also in equilibrium. Subgame-perfect equilibrium cannot be characterized for infinite games, although there are a number of alternative equilibrium concepts that do apply. See also GAME THEORY.

equity The fair distribution of opportunities and rewards and the fair imposition of costs and punishments. *Horizontal equity* refers to treating similar individuals similarly: e.g., those earning the same income should pay the same level of income tax, or those committing the same crime should receive the same sentence. *Vertical equity* refers to distribution according to differences in relevant circumstances: e.g., those who earn more in income should pay more in taxes, or more severe crimes should result in more severe punishment. See also JUSTICE.

Erikson, Erik (1902–1994) Born Erik Homberger in Frankfurt, Germany, Erikson was a psychoanalyst and psychiatrist noted for his work with children and his multistage theory of human psychological development. Erikson argued that the well-adjusted personality passed through eight sequential stages between infancy and old age. Each stage was dependent on the prior one, and each consisted of a crisis that reflected the social and interpersonal challenges of different moments of life. He called this schema of progressive integration the *epigenetic principle*. The stages begin with (1) infancy, which is defined by the problem of the infant's trust and/or mistrust of caregivers; (2) the development of autonomy; (3) initiative; (4) industriousness; (5) the consolidation of ego identity, based on social roles (source of the term *identity crisis*); (6) the capacity for intimacy; (7) *generativity*, or an outward focus for one's activities; and (8) the mature acceptance of old age. Erikson's work was especially influential in the study of adolescence and adult development in that it challenged the notion that personality formation was completed in childhood.

Many of these questions took Erikson into the field of SOCIOLOGY, where interpersonal relations are paramount and social roles and expectations are explored. In this context, he introduced a theory of "mutuality" that highlighted the influence that children have on the development of their parents. Erikson also conducted well-received studies of adolescence and young manhood in the Dakota tribe, a Native American context in which traditional culture was vanishing and values were being redefined. He also wrote prominent psychobiographies of Martin Luther and Mohandas Gandhi.

Erikson's major works include *Childhood and Society* (1950), *Young Man Luther: A Study in Psychoanalysis and History* (1958), *Identity: Youth and Crisis* (1968), *Gandhi's Truth* (1969), and *The Life Cycle Completed* (1982).

essentially contested concept   As developed by W. B. Gallie, topics on which continued disagreement is a normal and even desirable state of affairs. Aesthetics, theology, and democracy provide Gallie's main examples of concepts in which fixed definitions exclude some positions or actors. Participants, therefore, have an interest in maintaining the open status of the concept. Gallie's proposition challenged the necessity of consensus or agreement on subjects of fundamental importance, including scientific knowledge. The act of definition, he argued, belongs to the debate and is neither prior to nor neutrally outside it.

estimation   The statistical determination of the parameters of models. Estimation usually involves applying statistical techniques to a small sample of data in order to extract information about the characteristics of the entire population. For example, data on consumption expenditures and income can be analyzed by linear regression techniques to estimate the saving rate in the population (saving equals income less consumption). A good estimator is unbiased—i.e., its value equals the value of the parameter of interest and has low variance, so that we can be confident that the true value of the parameter lies close to the expected value of the estimate. ORDINARY LEAST SQUARES is one of the common methods of estimating parameters.

ethnicity   A highly elastic concept applied to groups who say they share or are perceived to share some combination of cultural, historical, racial, religious, or linguistic features. Ethnicity also often implies shared ancestral origins; thus there is thematic overlap with the older concept of *peoples* and some modern notions of RACE.

Ethnicity is distinct from KINSHIP groups, such as tribes, in that the connection between members is not conceived as a familial bond, even in a very extended sense; it is further distinct from the divisions of class that may traverse it. Particularly in the context of American immigration, ethnicity has been seen as a set of bonds that dissolve over successive generations as ethnic groups assimilate into mainstream American culture. Much of this logic has relied on an implicit contrast to racial difference, understood as a form of unassimilable difference. Early work on this subject was centered around the CHICAGO SCHOOL OF SOCIOLOGY in the 1920s, which conducted the first ethnographic studies of assimilation. The rise of MULTICULTURALISM and the valorization of both ethnic and racial identities since the 1960s has required a more sophisticated approach to the processes of formation and dissolution of ethnic identities. Where ethnicity was once seen as inevitably giving ground to processes of modernization and social integration, there is evidence that the reverse is true in many circumstances—that new or revitalized ethnic formations are a response to the dislocating or disempowering effects of modernization.

ethnocentrism   The tendency to judge or interpret another culture by the standards of one's own. Although ethnocentrism is generally condemned as an obstacle to understanding other cultures, especially in ANTHROPOLOGY, the degree to which one can escape or bracket one's cultural assumptions is by no means clear. This has been the subject of considerable debate in the wake of poststructural critiques of knowledge, subjectivity, and ethnographic practices. James Clifford's *The Predicament of Culture* (1988) has been particularly influential in recent discussions of this subject.

ethnocide   The attempt to eliminate a culture, generally through forced assimilation to a colonial or imperial culture. Ethnocide is distinguished from GENOCIDE, the attempt to exterminate a people, although in practice the two may be linked. Ethnocide is sometimes invoked to criticize programs of imposed social change—particularly programs of modernization and industrialization in underdeveloped countries that destroy premodern or local patterns of culture. See also MODERNIZATION THEORY.

ethnogenesis   The process by which a distinct ethnic or group identity emerges out of other, potentially diverse, identities. The concept places an emphasis on processes of *syncretism*, or cultural blending, and consequently critiques the notion of authentic, unchanging cultures. The term is not widely used in British and American anthropology, but it has considerable currency in Latin American anthropology.

ethnographic present The convention of presenting ethnographic research in the present tense—now largely abandoned in favor of more explicit historical contextualization.

ethnography The study of the culture and social organization of a particular group or community, as well as the published result of such study (*an* ethnography). Ethnography refers to both the data-gathering of ANTHROPOLOGY and the development of analyses of specific peoples, settings, or ways of life. In both cases, it is generally distinguished from the subsequent comparative and historical analyses of ethnographic data. Because of this priority, the history of ethnographic methods forms a large part of the history of anthropology as a field. Two distinct ethnographic methods emerged in the late nineteenth century: one based on survey and travel data gathered by missionaries and other amateur observers; and another based on direct observation by the trained anthropologist. To a great extent, the survey model was a product of the immaturity of the field—still largely a gentleman's pursuit in the late nineteenth century—and of the broad comparative interests of most of the early anthropologists. As anthropologists were trained in universities, grew in number, and improved standards of research, the direct model largely replaced the indirect one, and the speculative, comparative, "armchair" approach was discredited. Direct observation meant different things in the context of different cultural situations, however. It was given a particular inflection within American anthropology by the situation of the American Indians, where the primary early ethnographic goal was to "salvage" information about disappearing cultural practices. In more intact cultures, however, the British anthropologist Bronislaw MALINOWSKI and others elaborated an ideal of participant observation that emphasized cultural immersion over the interview style that dominated much of the salvage work. By the 1920s, participant observation became the dominant mode of anthropological research (see Margaret MEAD). Its complex relationship to the question of objectivity has, however, made it a source of continuing debate and controversy, particularly

since the 1970s in the context of poststructural and postcolonial challenges to the anthropological enterprise.

ethnohistory Refers both to the study of a people's history from their own written and oral accounts and to a particular direction within historical anthropology that examines the histories of groups marginalized in Western historiography. Written accounts by travelers, traders, missionaries, government agents, and the like are often central to such research.

ethnology In its contemporary form, ethnology refers to the comparative study of cultures. The term is often used instead of ANTHROPOLOGY in Eastern Europe, where there exists a strong continuity between the early ethnological tradition and more modern culturalist perspectives. In British and American anthropology, however, the term is usually associated with the early, pre-anthropological field of that name, which took culture to be the expression of distinct peoples or ethnic groups. By the mid-nineteenth century, ethnology had become part of a complex and, for anthropology, formative debate among British researchers over the unity of humankind. Ethnology and anthropology came to designate competing views on the subject—ethnologists defending the "monogenist" position that humanity was a single species; anthropologists advocating a "polygenist" account of separate and unequal races. Although the monogenist position eventually dominated, the resulting field retained the name "anthropology." Ethnology is also sometimes used to designate the comparative side of anthropological study, as opposed to the culture-specific work of ETHNOGRAPHY.

ethnomethodology The study of the implicit, taken-for-granted rules and forms of knowledge that structure and give order to people's everyday interactions. This subject is indicated by the provenance of the term, which signifies "the study of people's methods." Ethnomethodology was developed primarily by the sociologist Harold GARFINKEL in the late 1960s. He presented it as a direct critique of conventional sociology, which he argued generally ignored people's own understandings of social order in favor of abstracted conceptual schemata. In this regard, ethnomethodology emphasized the processes by which individuals interpret and thereby constitute their social realities—primarily through conversation and direct interactions, which Garfinkel termed *reflexivity*. Ethnomethodology thus places considerable emphasis on the ground rules that structure conversations in a variety of contexts: e.g., the diverse signs of assent or interest that maintain a conversational flow or the habit of speaking in turn. Many of these issues were explored in detail by Garfinkel's colleague Harvey Sachs, a pioneer of *conversation analysis*.

Without these tacit rules, conversations and other aspects of underlying social consensus break down. Garfinkel tested these limits in a series of *breeching experiments*, which examined reactions when common social understandings, such as the norms governing child–parent relations, were deliberately thwarted. In general, Garfinkel found that social order is dependent upon a high degree of *indexicality*—the ability of persons to furnish a commonly understood context for statements or actions. Without this arbitrary halt to the problem of interpretation, language reveals its infinitely regressive character, in which concepts are defined in terms of other concepts.

Because sociologists are equally creators of methods of interpreting the social order, ethnomethodology also addressed itself to the study of sociological categories. It constituted one of the strong critiques of sociological POSITIVISM that emerged in the 1960s—rejecting the idea that sociologists stand outside or above the social processes they study. Like much of the contemporary work in poststructuralist theory, ethnomethodology reflected the linguistic turn of modern philosophy, which placed a strong emphasis on the role of language in mediating and structuring human experience.

Because of its nearly categorical critique of sociological methods, Garfinkel's *Studies in Ethnomethodology* (1967) was controversial and provoked a number of strong critical responses—in no small part from sociologists who regarded the concept of social structure as necessary to analyzing any substantive social or political issue. The minimal consensual rules underlying conversations or face-to-face interactions, by comparison, seemed relatively distant from questions of larger social transformations. Many of the central concerns of ethnomethodology have been taken up in elements of mainstream sociology (as the work of Anthony GIDDENS and Pierre BOURDIEU demonstrates), where they contribute to contemporary investigations of questions of interpretation, the nature of meaning, and the status of sociological knowledge.

ethnoscience   Initially, the study of differences in systems of classification among cultures, later sometimes called the New Ethnography and now more generally a part of cognitive anthropology. Ethnoscience emerged out of the postwar convergence of ANTHROPOLOGY and LINGUISTICS. It proposed that a rigorous analysis of the systems of classification used by different cultures was not only possible but analytically necessary to ethnographic observation, insofar as cultural practices and forms were rooted in variations in the organization of the basic categories that people used. In practice, ethnoscience relied heavily on the linguistic method of COMPONENTIAL ANALYSIS, and it made its most compelling claims in those areas in which classificatory structures were relatively easy to isolate—for example, the naming of kin relations, colors, diseases, plants, and animals.

ethology   The study of the biological bases of human behavior or, more precisely, of the line between inherited and learned forms of behavior. The great cultural turn of twentieth-century social science went far toward marginalizing ethology, shrinking the vast space that nineteenth-century science accorded the instincts in explaining human behavior. Much of the behavior that such accounts ascribed to biology has been shown to be subject, in greater or lesser ways, to environmental influences—although debates continue regarding the degree of autonomy that can be attributed to CULTURE. Ethnology has traditionally involved the study of animal behavior as a basis for comparison. Contemporary work on the biological sources of behavior and culture generally fall to SOCIOBIOLOGY.

ethos   From the ancient Greek, signifying the character, way of life, or moral purpose of an individual or group. Whereas the ancients tended to assume that the individual's *ethos* conformed to that of his or her community, subsequent political and social theory (beginning with the Stoics) has made the ethical differences between the individual and the community (and between different communities) a central problem. The broad sense of the original term—which encompassed habits, dispositions, values, and sentiments—persisted well into the eighteenth century, when it suggested to Charles-Louis MONTESQUIEU the irreconcilable plurality of morals and ways of life. The term's modern derivative, *ethics*, is usually restricted to general theories of right or moral conduct. The older term is retained to demonstrate how these are rooted in social practices and values.

etic See EMIC AND ETIC.

eufunctional Social activity that reinforces or "positively" contributes to society (*eu* means "good" in Greek). Eufunctional is nearly synonymous with the more recent and much more widely used term *functional* in social analysis—although the earlier term retains a more direct opposition to *dysfunctional* activity, a dimension sometimes lost in modern FUNCTIONALISM.

evaluation research Research that seeks to evaluate the implementation and consequences of social programs. Drawing on a range of disciplines and methodologies, evaluation research became prominent in the context of the Great Society programs of the 1960s in the United States and has remained ubiquitous. It is particularly important for those social programs that lack clearly defined indicators built into their operations—as profit, for example, is a built in (if imperfect) indicator for business.

Evans-Pritchard, E. E. (1902–1973) A seminal figure in post–World War II British ANTHROPOLOGY, Evans-Pritchard was the author of several major ethnographic studies of African societies, primarily those in Sudan. He was also an influential theorist and teacher at the University of Oxford, where he trained many of the leading British anthropologists of the postwar generation.

A decade of research among the Azande and Nuer peoples in Sudan provided Evans-Pritchard with the material for a number of groundbreaking studies, beginning with *Witchcraft, Oracles and Magic among the Azande* (1937). This work constituted a major revision of the anthropological understanding of MAGIC and was, in particular, a theoretical departure from Emile DURKHEIM's functional approach. Durkheim, in emphasizing the socially integrative function of magic, allowed for its basic irrationality. In contrast, Evans-Pritchard proposed that magic is generally a coherent, rigorous, and internally rational system of thought. Among the Azande, Evans-Pritchard contended, magic does not replace mundane cause-and-effect rationality so much as provide a framework for explaining the arbitrary dimension of good and bad fortune.

Influential as this work has been, his reputation owes even more to his trilogy on the Nuer, comprising *The Nuer* (1940), *Kinship and Marriage among the Nuer* (1951), and *Nuer Religion* (1956). Together, these studies demonstrate an orientation shaped by the need to comprehend social and political structures, a commitment to understanding the rationality of primitive social and religious practices, and a highly descriptive methodology that holds that rationality to be fundamentally accessible and translatable into Western terms. *The Nuer* stands as perhaps the foremost example of a comprehensive ethnographic account of SOCIAL STRUCTURE—a model of clarity in combining abstract and empirical analysis. It is, however, frequently criticized for exaggerating the extent to which individual societies may be understood as discrete, bounded, and integral. His works on the Nuer also provide ample evidence of his position in a major disciplinary argument with advocates of a more "scientific" conception of anthropology, such as A. R. RADCLIFFE-BROWN and Bronislaw MALINOWSKI. For Evans-Pritchard, anthropology remained fundamentally one of the humanities, akin to comparative history. Although the historical sensitivity of some of his early work has been called into question, his commitment to historicism has remained one of his most important legacies.

Evans-Pritchard produced a number of other important works, including a study of a family of Islamic scholars in Libya, entitled *The Sanusi of Cyrenaica* (1949), *African Political Systems* (1940, edited with Meyer Fortes), and several other studies of African religious and social systems.

event-history analysis A method of sociological analysis that focuses on events rather than on persons or groups. Typical life events, such as retirement or graduation, are the most frequent objects of study, although the field also includes the analysis of historical events. Event-history analysis is very similar to the life-history method developed by the CHICAGO SCHOOL OF SOCIOLOGY. It tends to emphasize the way in which significant events function as transitions to new stages of life, implying new statuses and expectations. Event-history research, consequently, has a strong longitudinal character.

evolution and evolutionism Evolution denotes qualitative change, whether at the biological level (species) or the historical level (societies). Eighteenth-century studies of social and population change influenced the rise of evolutionary theory in biology. In turn, biological theories of evolution played a formative role in nineteenth-century social science. Charles Darwin's theory of the struggle for existence (1858) and the origins of species (1859) was pivotal in this regard. Its influence in social science was mediated by Herbert SPENCER, who contributed to both biology and SOCIOLOGY, and who coined the phrase "survival of the fittest."

Perhaps the most influential contribution of Darwinian evolutionary theory to social thought was the idea that species adapt to their environments by way of a process of *natural selection*, whereby individual members with advantageous characteristics lived longer and bred more successfully, thus changing the whole species through inheritance. The key to these natural adaptations was the spontaneous generation of variations—the adequate explanation of which had to await Gregor Mendel's work in genetics. The possibility of planned evolution was not new (as horticulture and animal breeding evidenced), but it strongly impressed early social scientists—not least because they could see the human capacity to shape society and the environment as a planned source of variation rather than as spontaneous mutation.

For the emerging field of ANTHROPOLOGY in the late nineteenth century, the salient point of Darwinism was that evolution implied the increasing differentiation of species. This challenged the efforts of Victorian social scientists to explain the common outcome of evolutionary processes—the variously modern, technological, and monotheistic societies that, in their view, stood at the top of the human evolutionary ladder. Diversity in human society, they argued, was a matter of historical location along an evolutionary continuum that stretched, variously, from savagery to civilization, animism to monotheism, primitive to modern, or from the leaderless band to the state. Such linear models were at the heart of the polemic waged by Edward Burnett TYLOR, John Lubbock, James FRAZER, and other early anthropologists against *polygenism*—the theory that humanity was composed of different and unequal species.

The high point of nineteenth-century social evolutionary theory was Herbert Spencer's attempt to explain all evolution (biological as well as social) in terms of movement from simpler to more complex forms. According to this view, human beings represent a higher level of biological evolution than earthworms, and modern industrial states a higher level of social evolution than bands of hunters and gatherers. While Darwin's theory of evolution had emphasized only adaptation and survival (on which grounds the cockroach is a success), Spencer's included a clear notion of progress or advancement. His emphasis on differentiation, combined with a focus on individual fitness, helped produce the widely popularized perspective called SOCIAL DARWINISM—the view that both societies and individuals are locked into competitive, unequal struggles for existence, and that progress comes about through the survival of the fittest. This view was influential in the social sciences in the late nineteenth and early twentieth centuries, but it exercised a greater and much longer-term effect on political and economic ideologies.

As early as 1896, Franz BOAS's sweeping and influential critique of nineteenth-century anthropology took issue with many of the assumptions of evolutionist thought. He attacked the selectivity of the criteria invoked in such comparative approaches (the COMPARATIVE METHOD), the lack of rigorous first-hand observation, the rigidity of the proposed unilinear trajectories, and the implicit association of evolution and progress with the social norms of Victorian England. He also defended the alternative theory of diffusion as an explanation of cultural change (see DIFFUSION AND DIFFUSIONISM). Boas's rejection of comparative and cross-cultural generalizations held sway in American anthropology until the 1930s, when renewed interest in evolutionary models began to emerge. The new evolutionists tended to accept the Spencerian proposition that societal evolution consisted of greater complexity and differentiation. These included Leslie A. WHITE, who proposed a theory of increasing energy utilization; Julian STEWARD, who described a process of multilineal evolution; and the work of Marshall SAHLINS and Elman Service. These more complex accounts of societal change have reestablished a role for evolutionary perspectives in the social sciences, if no longer in such definitive and totalizing terms.

ex ante and ex post   Designate different perspective on an event: *ex ante* ("from before") and *ex post* ("from after"). *Ex ante* analysis is conducted based on the information available before an event; *ex post* analysis is based on information available after the event. *Ex ante* and *ex post* play a major role in the study of economic variables—especially where expectations have an impact on the variable's value and where there is a high degree of uncertainty. In economics, this set of issues was elaborated in the 1930s by Gunnar MYRDAL, Eric Lindahl, Bertil Ohlin, and other economists of the Stockholm school.

exchange A human activity so generalized that it can be said to be universal and, therefore, an activity of broad interest to social scientists. CLASSICAL ECONOMICS is the source of the notion that exchange is subject to the "rational choices" of individuals, who act to maximize their gain in any given situation. This remains the structuring assumption of modern economics, and it has had a major influence on theories of social behavior more generally.

In ANTHROPOLOGY, exchange serves as the core of a number of theories about the origins and structure of human society. Outside the variety of things that can be exchanged, anthropology has recognized different types of exchange based on the degree of relationship between the participants and the different expectations that follow. One of the early and most influential contributions to this line of inquiry is Marcel MAUSS's description of "gift exchange" as the source of social solidarity. In gift exchange, social bonds are formed through the exchange of goods, but only provided that the economic content of the exchange is suppressed. The ritual exchange of sea shells in Melanesia (the KULA RING) is a prominent early example, as is the exchange of women as marriage partners—a practice that Claude LÉVI-STRAUSS described as the origin of KINSHIP systems and, consequently, of society.

Forms of exchange in which the economic character dominates—particularly in modern commercial relations—is more generally termed *commodity exchange*. Here, the personal relationship between the participants is comparatively insignificant and often anonymous, although Karl MARX argued influentially that this trivialization performs the ideological function of masking the true relations between social actors. Even economic and self-interested exchange, however, is guided by norms—for example, what Alvin Ward GOULDNER called "the norm of reciprocity," which requires that any social act, from a morning greeting to a gift, be returned in kind. As Peter BLAU and other American sociologists have demonstrated, being able to give more than one receives can be a source of power in a wide variety of relationships.

Descriptions of exchange have been a site of contention between those who argue that social actors make rational decisions based on reasonable expectations of gain or loss (as Bronislaw MALINOWSKI argued for gift exchange and as RATIONAL-CHOICE THEORY often holds to be universal) and those who argue that the structure of exchange is itself the bearer of social identity—prominently, Marx, Emile DURKHEIM, and Mauss. This difference is the basis of a loose opposition between British-American and the European traditions of exchange theory. The former is dominated by the rational-choice framework and by analyses of the specifics of rational choice in diverse social contexts. It frequently confronts questions about actors' priorities faced with multiple outcomes, or the relative convertibility of one type of gain into another—for example, money into prestige. The European tradition is characterized by a greater emphasis on the social context that precedes and structures exchange, as well as on the often layered symbolic content of forms of exchange.

It is possible and increasingly common in contemporary social science to read the rational-choice vision of individuality as a development related to the modern conditions of market exchange. In anthropology, the distinction between gift and commodity exchange has been both revised and relativized in the wake of research that emphasizes the persistence of mixed economies that integrate aspects of both.

exchange rate Designates the price of one currency in terms of another. The exchange rate of a given country is sensitive to its monetary policies—especially the money supply and prevailing interest rates. Exchange rates may be fixed, floating, or integrate some measure of both positions. In the case of a fixed (or pegged) exchange rate, the monetary authorities commit themselves to maintaining the exchange rate at a certain value on a quasi-permanent basis. For instance, in countries where the exchange rate is pegged to the U.S. dollar, this parity is underwritten by the willingness of the monetary authorities to exchange the national currency for dollars at the declared exchange rate. The gold standard, prior to 1914, was such an arrangement: currency units were defined in terms of a particular quantity of gold that was unalterable under ordinary circumstances. A flexible or freely floating exchange rate, in contrast, is one in which authorities not only refrain from fixing the exchange rate but also from intervening in the foreign-exchange market in order to influence the rate. Indirect impact on the exchange rate, however, continues through the influence of fiscal, monetary, and other policies on exchange-market participants.

A variety of possible arrangements lie between these polar cases: the "adjustable peg," the "dirty float," the "crawling peg," and others. Under the "adjustable peg" of the postwar Bretton Woods system, currencies were pegged to gold or to the dollar (which, in turn was given a par value in terms of gold) but these values could be altered if the country faced a "fundamental disequilibrium" in its balance of payments. Some arrangements oblige monetary authorities to make frequent though small changes in the exchange rate—a system called the "crawling peg." Finally, a "dirty float" refers to a system in which the exchange rate floats but authorities still attempt to manage the rate through extensive intervention in the foreign-exchange market.

exclave   See ENCLAVE AND EXCLAVE.

executive   The branch of government responsible for carrying out government policy. With the growth of the modern STATE, the executive has become difficult to define: few commentators take it to include the entire administrative apparatus; most focus on the cabinet and sometimes also on the very highest levels of the bureaucracy. Another conceptual difficulty arises from the fact that even those executive branches that are entirely distinct from the legislature, such as the U.S. presidency, in practice play a considerable role in shaping rather than simply executing policy. They do so by influencing, proposing, or vetoing legislative bills, and by making extra-legislative decisions on a host of administrative matters.

In authoritarian regimes, power is usually concentrated in the hands of the executive. In liberal democracies, observers usually differentiate between two principal types of executive. In the parliamentary systems employed in most European countries, the prime minister (or chancellor in Germany) and the cabinet are drawn from the majority party or from the ruling coalition in the legislature. In theory, this promotes responsible government by making the executive directly accountable to the people's representatives, who may dissolve a government by a vote of non-confidence; in practice, it places executive and legislative power in the same hands. In presidential systems, found in the United States and several Latin American countries, the president is usually elected directly by the people, and

typically does not name legislators to the cabinet. Presidential systems create the possibility of divided government in which the executive and legislature are controlled by different parties.

During the twentieth century, there has been a broad trend toward the growth of the power of the executive relative to the other branches. There are a number of reasons for this: the president or prime minister is usually a country's most visible politician and thus can potentially command the most popular legitimacy; the growth of the scale and complexity of state activity has made administrative and regulative decisions more important; the executive or its appointees typically direct fiscal and especially monetary policy, which have become highly visible and politicized; and the traditional executive discretion over foreign policy has, in many cases, underwritten an expansion of executive power. This last trend is exemplified by the development of the "imperial presidency" in the United States since World War II.

exit   The ability of members of a political organization or community to leave if its decisions seriously violate their preferences or interests. In Albert Hirschman's *Exit, Voice, Loyalty* (1970), it is one of three choices that members have when at odds with their group or community. When exit is not a viable option—as in the case of citizenship in a state—it can reduce the bargaining power of minorities who wish to redirect public policy. See also VOICE.

exogamy   Refers to marriage outside a given group, either with reference to certain family relations (kin-group exogamy) or distinctions between acceptable marriage partners (alliance exogamy). The practice of marriage within a group is called ENDOGAMY. See also KINSHIP.

exogeneity   See ENDOGENEITY AND EXOGENEITY.

expectations   Beliefs or views about the future state of economic variables or the actions of individuals or governments. Given that the future is inherently uncertain, agents need to form expectations about the magnitudes of economic and other variables in the future when making decisions. Further, when trying to make decisions, beliefs about the actions of others will influence strategic behavior. In economics, the analysis of expectations is fundamental to theories of intertemporal consumption, saving and labor supply decisions, theories of firm supply, investment and price decisions, theories of financial markets and money, and noncooperative games, where payoffs or player utilities are uncertain. Mathematical expectations are the most commonly used representation of economic expectations. Variables are drawn from a probability distribution that is presumed to be common knowledge. The mathematical expectation of a random variable is the mean value of its distribution (see EXPECTED VALUE).

Two major theories of expectations underlie much of the research in this area: adaptive expectations and rational expectations.

Adaptive Expectations: agents form expectations about the future values of variables using the previous, or lagged, values of the same variable—i.e., regardless of new information available, agents rely on past information, updating their beliefs in a form of moving average. The adaptive-expectations approach dominated work on INFLATION and MACROECONOMICS in the 1960s. It was intuitively plausible, tractable both mathematically and empirically, and successful in terms of yielding sensible parametric estimates of models. In the 1970s, however, this hypothesis fell into disfavor following the work of John Muth, who demonstrated that the optimality of using adaptive expectations (in the sense of delivering unbiased and efficient estimates of a variable) was confined to a limited class of variables.

Rational Expectations: John Muth introduced and applied the concept of rational expectations. Economic variables are often influenced by the behavior of actors acting on their expectations of these variables. The stock market is a prominent example, where expectations of an increase in the value of equities will lead to buying, which in turn increases the price of equities. Rational expectations require that actors take all of these interactions into account, so that their actions are based on an expectation that is, in turn, realized as a result of their actions. The rational expectations model assumes that economic agents know the structure of the economy and that they can compute optimal forecasts that represent their expectations, much like econometricians making use of all available and relevant information. In the extreme, when information is complete and there is no uncertainty, the rational-expectations hypothesis becomes a model of perfect foresight. Indeed, in games of strategic interaction, it is often the case that there is only one rational-expectations equilibrium, so

that applying a rational-expectation assumption to agents' behavior produces a unique prediction.

The most basic criticism of rational-expectation models is that they make implausible demands on the computing abilities of economic agents. Moreover, forecasting is a costly activity. The structure of the economy constantly changes; agents may not be able to deal with these changes in statistical terms; and changes may occur faster than the speed at which people assess the economy. In all cases, their forecasts will diverge from optimal forecasts. Even if it were plausible that agents "learn" to form rational expectations, such learning would proceed very slowly given the complexity of the economy and the large amounts of data that they need to sift through. This criticism is perhaps more valid for rational-expectations models in the macroeconomy, where interactions are highly complex. For interaction among a few firms or individuals, it is more plausible that actions can be predicted.

expected utility theory Initially developed by John von NEUMANN and Oskar Morgenstern as a way of defining preferences for—and therefore decision-making power over—uncertain outcomes. Because individuals are often risk-averse, the utility they derive from an uncertain prospect (e.g., a lottery ticket) is not the same as the utility they receive from the expected value of the lottery ticket. That is, declining marginal utility for money (and for most goods) means that the utility function is concave—thus the utility of $10 is higher than the average of the utility of $0 and $20. The theory postulates that individuals, when faced with risky choices, do not merely choose the option with the highest expected value, but evaluate the utility payoffs of all the possible outcomes of each decision and weight them according to their probability. For example, a lottery with a 50 percent chance of winning nothing and a 50 percent chance of winning $20 has an expected value of $10. Expected utility is calculated in the same fashion: p(losing) × Utility($0) + p(winning) × Utility($20). The theory predicts that individuals will maximize expected utility and, in so doing, make choices that take into consideration their tolerance for risk as well as the utility derived from the possible payoffs. See also RISK AVERSION; and UTILITY.

expected value From probability theory, the mathematical averaging of the value of uncertain prospects, weighted by their likelihood. For example, in one year, a stock could be worth $5, $10, or $30, with the probability of each price estimated at 10 percent, 30 percent, and 60 percent, respectively. The *expected* value of the stock is $0.10 \times (\$5) + 0.30 \times (\$10) + 0.60 \times (\$30) = \$21.50$.

experimental economics   The systematic evaluation of economic theories under controlled laboratory conditions. Like most sciences, economics is observational, and economists have traditionally evaluated theories with statistical data from existing markets. For a variety of reasons, however, real-world data sometimes fail to allow tests of theoretical propositions. These reasons can include (1) the infrequency or unpredictability of the historical circumstances that a given model studies or (2) the dependence of the theory on intricate behavioral assumptions, such that there is little practical possibility of obtaining evidence from naturally occurring markets (game theoretic models are a good example).

The chief advantages of experimental economics are replicability and control. *Replicability* refers to the capacity of other researchers to replicate any experiment and verify its findings independently. *Control* is the capacity to manipulate laboratory conditions so that observed behavior can be used to evaluate theories and policies. Such control is usually missing in natural data. Laboratory situations also make it possible to ensure that the environment is consistent with the structural assumptions of the relevant theory.

In addition to market simulations, there are two categories of problems that have attracted the vast majority of economic experiments; they have in common the persistent failure of individuals to behave according to their economic self-interest. *Public-goods games* are often set up under experimental conditions to assess how much individuals will contribute for the provision of such goods. A classic, simple experiment involves asking individuals to contribute any amount of money to a common pool. The total contributed will be doubled by the experimenter, then distributed equally to all players. The more the group contributes, the better they fare, but the expected payoff to an individual is always negative, since every dollar put in will be doubled but divided among all players. The economic prediction is that individuals will each contribute nothing, expecting to free-ride off the contributions of others. Experiments usually find that people are cooperative (and trusting) in

putting in their own money and can be induced to higher levels of cooperation over time if others are doing their part.

The second category of experiments involves two-player games such as the PRISONER'S DILEMMA or divide-the-dollar. In these games, an individual's behavior will directly impact the payoff of the other player, and their interests are in direct conflict. Standard economic theory predicts that players will do as well for themselves as possible, at the expense of the other player. But players in experiments routinely demonstrate cooperative or altruistic behavior. Conversely, when their opponent fails to cooperate, they will often inflict punishment, even when it is personally costly.

Because of the consistency of the behavior observed during experiments—behavior that is surprisingly durable to alternative settings—experimental economics has become an important partner in the development of the field of BEHAVIORAL ECONOMICS, which seeks to understand the deviation of individual choices from those predicted by the standard theory.

experimenter effects   Refers to the impact of the experimenter's presence on the results of a study. There are a wide variety of experimenter effects that can occur in research. These are troubling because they raise questions about the validity and reliability of results. Some effects involve issues of interpretation on the part of the experimenter, while others are due to the interaction between the experimenter and the subject. These effects can be intentional but are most often unintended; they occur when certain characteristics or actions of the experimenter alter the perceptions, beliefs, or responses of the subject. See also BIAS; and HAWTHORNE EFFECT.

ex post   See *EX ANTE AND EX POST*.

extensive form games   Extensive forms are one way to illustrate the available actions and payoffs in a noncooperative game. Extensive forms take the form of trees, with nodes that indicate where each actor must make a strategic decision and lines drawn to subsequent nodes, indicating the choices that follow. The end nodes generally list payoffs. Extensive forms are used to illustrate non-simultaneous games; simultaneous games with few players may be represented in *normal form*—a payoff grid. See also GAME THEORY.

externalities   The indirect effect of one agent's consumption activity or production activity on the well-being or economic activities of other agents. Pollution generated from the production of electricity or loud noise arising from the consumption of music are examples of externalities in markets. These effects may be negative or positive—they may cause disutility or costs to third parties in some cases and provide benefits in others. Thus in markets where an externality exists, *social* benefits or costs (the well-being of all) are different from *private* benefits or costs—defined as those that accrue only to the original parties in the market activity. In the absence of externalities, private marginal costs or benefits coincide with social ones; in this case, the market equilibrium is PARETO OPTIMAL. A positive externality implies that the economic activity benefits society more than it benefits the individual who undertakes it, in which case social marginal benefits are larger than private ones. Under such conditions, market equilibrium leads to underproduction. Analogously, a negative externality leads to overproduction.

A distinction is usually drawn between technological and pecuniary externalities. The price effects among firms or consumers are termed *pecuniary externalities*. For example, a firm that increases its purchase of inputs raises the price of those inputs and imposes a pecuniary externality on other firms. Pecuniary externalities, however, do not drive a wedge between private and social marginal returns. For this reason, economists are generally more interested in nonpecuniary externalities as a source of deviation from Pareto optimality. Examples of technological externalities include changes in the risk of flooding for farmers or in the catch of fishermen following the building of a dam by a hydroelectric power company, or the creation of a broad market for skilled labor resulting from the growth of a particular industry.

extraterritoriality The right of a state under INTERNATIONAL LAW to exercise legal jurisdic-

tion within the territory of another state. Extraterritoriality originated in the European practice of granting immunity to the officials and embassies of foreign countries. This practice was dramatically expanded during the period of European imperialism to ensure that European expatriates were subject to the law of their home country, rather than to local law. Today, in addition to diplomatic immunity and embassy rights, it is also frequently applied to military personnel and officials outside their home countries, and sometimes to those working under the mandate of the United Nations or other international organizations.

Eysenck, Hans (1916–1997) A prolific psychologist who contributed, often controversially, to a number of debates about intelligence and behavior. Eysenck was also a great popularizer of psychology: he is credited with dozens of books and hundreds of articles, many of which were directed toward the general public. A strong behaviorist in orientation, Eysenck disliked PSYCHOANALYSIS and attempted to disprove its therapeutic value (see BEHAVIORISM). He believed in the biological determination of human behavior and intelligence—a view that led him into a controversial argument about the average differences in intelligence between blacks and whites. He also achieved notoriety with a study that claimed to have found a psychological basis for higher cancer rates among cigarette smokers. In other research, Eysenck devoted considerable energy to defining and measuring personality types, including criminal personalities.

Eysenck was a German emigré who fled to England with the rise of fascism. He became a fixture of British SOCIAL PSYCHOLOGY in the latter part of the century, authoring, among other works, *Crime and Personality* (1964), *The Biological Basis of Personality* (1967), *Race, Intelligence and Education* (1971), and *The Structure and Measurement of Intelligence* (1979).

F

Fabianism A socialist progressive movement in English politics that advocated the reform and development of the welfare state. Fabianism was organized around the Fabian Society, formed in 1884. It was an analytic and advisory group rather than a political party—although at its high point in the 1940s it dominated the Labour party. Fabianism opposed the revolutionary agenda of MARXISM and other utopian political tendencies, focusing instead on policy studies and the progressive implementation of egalitarian policies.

factor analysis A set of statistical techniques used to determine underlying correlations and commonalities within complex bodies of data. Where several different variables correlate—for example, attitudes about race, social-welfare programs, and party preferences—it may be possible to identify an implicit common *factor* (such as CONSERVATISM or LIBERALISM) that explains and predicts such variations. To the extent that variables correlate with the broader factor, they are said to *load on* that factor.

The techniques of factor analysis were developed in the 1940s by Charles Spearman, who sought a means of relating the results of different intelligence tests. Factor analysis is most prominent in psychology, but has played an important role in POLITICAL SCIENCE and SOCIOLOGY, especially in the analysis of ATTITUDES and personality. There are a number of different techniques within factor analysis for identifying factors and for measuring their internal reliability and explanatory capacity.

Factor analysis is most important in the exploration of data. Statistical techniques and computer algorithms are used to identify factors—clusters of mutually correlated variables—within a large inventory of survey responses or other data. A problem with factor analysis lies in the necessity of interpreting the meaning of the statistical factor produced—that is, turning it into a theoretically meaningful object of analysis. When complex factors are given labels

(such as racism or liberalism) there is a tendency to focus on the label—not the underlying data—in subsequent analysis. Approaches to confirmatory factor analysis exist, but they exert less influence than exploratory factor analysis. Other methods may be used for further specification of what lies behind factor formation.

factor of production Any material goods or services used to make other goods. Factors are equivalent to *inputs* in the production process, although the term is usually used for broader categories, notably land, LABOR, and CAPITAL.

factor-price equalization A prediction common to most theories of international trade that holds that the free movement of goods—even without free movement of factors of production—will equalize the absolute and relative prices of factors across countries. Movement of the factors—LABOR and CAPITAL—will only accelerate the process, assuming that they are moving to locations of relative scarcity (and therefore higher return). See also HECKSCHER-OHLIN TRADE THEORY.

factor-price frontier A term introduced by the economist Paul SAMUELSON to indicate that changes in wage rates and profits are inversely related—a rise in one necessitates a fall in the other. The relationship has also been referred to as the "wage frontier" by John R. HICKS (*Capital and Growth*, 1965).

fact–value distinction A distinction between what can be known with certainty (facts) and knowledge of what is important or desirable (values). The distinction is usually attributed to David HUME and reflects both his EMPIRICISM with regard to the natural world and his skepticism about the possibility of rationalizing human affairs. The latter, Hume argued, are based on values and beliefs that are not subject to rational analysis.

Versions of the fact–value distinction can be found in much of modern Western thought. It plays a formative (and, to a degree, ongoing) role in the social sciences, as researchers and social theorists seek to understand the status of their knowledge. POSITIVISM in social science comes down strongly on the side of factual knowledge and generalizable laws of behavior. Interpretive approaches tend to privilege the context of action and the role of human motives and beliefs. Early twentieth-century theorists such as Max WEBER and Emile DURKHEIM tried to have it both ways—legitimizing knowledge about society and human action while separating that knowledge from the methodologies of the natural sciences. For Weber in particular, the role of the social scientist as a disinterested observer was not a given fact but a highly desirable value—one that underwrote the production of objective social knowledge. Fact–value distinctions continue to be a prominent topic of debate in the social sciences—especially in the context of poststructural and postmodern challenges to claims of objectivity. See also Pierre BOURDIEU; POSTMODERNISM; and POSTSTRUCTURALISM.

falling rate of profit For Karl MARX, an economic law that underlies historical changes in the forms of capitalist accumulation. Although the competitive logic of capitalism requires constant efforts to increase profits, Marx argued that the two principal strategies for doing so faced internal limits that over time produced a decline in profits. One of these is the natural limit to the extension of the workday, which for a time had provided the most direct way of increasing profits; the second is the growing cost of investments in productivity in the form of larger factories, greater mechanization, and new technologies. Marx argued that the concentration of capital was the most economical means of combating this tendency, but that over time even this reaches a point of diminishing returns. In the process, he argued, CAPITALISM becomes prone to worsening crises that ultimately bring about social revolution.

false consciousness Originally employed by Karl MARX to explain why the PROLETARIAT did not always act in accordance with its real material interests. False consciousness, for Marx, describes the continued investment of the proletariat in mystified accounts of its relationship to the MODE OF PRODUCTION—classically to bourgeois accounts of property and labor, from which the proletariat had little to gain, but also visible, for many Marxist critics who witnessed the rise of FASCISM, in the acquiescence of significant parts of the working class to theories of race and national destiny.

falsificationism A doctrine associated with the philosopher of science Karl Raimund POPPER, which holds that the testing of theories is the means by which science advances. To be testable and thus scientific, Popper claimed, a theory must be potentially "falsifiable." He argued that although scientific theories are formulated and may be more or less powerful in enabling predictive statements, this has little to do with their truth. No amount of evidence will guarantee the truth or universality of a scientific theory; a theory may, however, be falsified or proven incorrect on the basis of specific evidence. Popper thereby circumvented a persistent dilemma in the philosophy of science: the difficulty of justifying the process of induction from specific evidence to universal laws. Popper's theories challenged the logical POSITIVISM of the Vienna Circle (although they were indebted to it) and were themselves challenged by the PARADIGM model elaborated by Thomas KUHN and other historical critics of the scientific method.

family Most commonly, a social group defined in some combination by parentage, KINSHIP (including marriage), and coresidence. Historically, the family has been taken to be the basic unit of social organization, but the latter half of the twentieth century has seen a widespread breakdown of consensus about the meaning of the term. Once presumed to be a universal feature of human societies (subject to certain variations), both structural definitions of the family based on the kin relations that compose it and functionalist definitions based on the functions that it performs (e.g., reproduction) have failed to meet the challenge of the observed variety of forms of collective, small-group life in human societies (see FUNCTIONALISM). This is true, in particular, of the distinction between nuclear families (composed of father, mother, and children) and extended families.

Putting aside the problems of formulating a precise universal definition, however, the distinction between family (based on kinship) and HOUSEHOLD (based on domestic functions—shelter, food preparation, etc.) remains in common use. The term *DOMESTIC GROUP* is also often used as a substitute for either family or household. Extended families composed of distinct nuclear family units are often referred to as *joint families*.

Fanon, Franz (1925–1961) A psychiatrist and revolutionary whose major work examines the psychology of COLONIALISM and racial subordination. *Black Skin, White Masks* (1952) and *The Wretched of the Earth* (1961) became fundamental texts of the anticolonial movements in the 1960s, and Fanon remains an important point of reference in studies of revolutionary action, colonialism, and the psychology of subordination.

While practicing psychiatry in Martinique, his birthplace, Fanon became convinced that many of the pathological conditions he encountered were traceable to social causes, and that the "cures" for these conditions were less a matter of medical practice than of social change. Fanon focused in particular on the process of internalization of the colonial order by the black population—a process that resulted, he argued, in a crippling sense of inferiority among most blacks and a permanent contradiction between the "white mask" of universal subjectivity and the very different social reality imposed by skin color. This was the subject of *Black Skin, White Masks*—a work that challenged the official universalism of French society and critiqued Jean-Paul SARTRE's existential account of self and other as a relatively fluid dialectical relationship. Fanon placed special emphasis on the role of the colonizer's language in securing the psychological subordination of the oppressed group—particularly the stigmatization of creole French.

From 1953 to 1956, Fanon practiced psychiatry in Algeria, where he treated patients who had been tortured by the French special forces. There, Fanon began to argue more strongly for the necessity of violent revolution, both as a political and psychological antidote to colonialism. Expanding on ideas visible in *Black Skin, White Masks*, Fanon presented "absolute violence" as a form of psychological catharsis that could break the binary classifications of the racial order and the value structure associated with them. Violence would result in a "new man." This program of psychological liberation was the most controversial and extreme of Fanon's claims. Drawing on his experience of the psychological complicity of the more privileged members of subordinated groups, Fanon argued that the peasantry was the only possible revolutionary group—the "wretched of the earth" who had

nothing to lose. The urban middle class, by contrast, would inevitably compromise.

In 1956, Fanon left Algeria for Tunisia, where he played an active role in organizing and supporting the Algerian revolution. He served briefly as the new Algerian government's ambassador to Ghana before developing and quickly succumbing to leukemia. His other published works are *A Dying Colonialism or Year Five of the Algerian Revolution* (1959) and *Toward the African Revolution* (1964).

fascism An extreme right-wing nationalist ideology, revolutionary political movement, and type of authoritarian regime that developed in Europe between the two world wars. Its roots lie in Benito Mussolini's National Fascist party, which ruled Italy from 1922 to 1944 and adopted the *fasces* (an ancient Roman symbol of unity and authority) as its emblem. Fascist parties appeared across Europe during the 1920s and 1930s, but came to power independently only in Italy and Germany. Local fascist forces were also installed or given a free hand during the Axis occupation of Austria, Hungary, Romania, Bulgaria, and Yugoslavia during World War II. The Fascist Falangists also played an important role in the Spanish civil war of 1936–1939.

Fascism emerged as a broad-based rejection of the existing political orders, including LIBERALISM, DEMOCRACY, COMMUNISM, and, somewhat more tentatively, monarchism. In opposing the rationalism and materialism of such systems, fascism praised the vitalism of the organic community and called for a radical assertion of national will. Fascism is perhaps best seen as a combination of conservative belief in the racial nation with modern faith in technology and social organization—often of socialist inspiration. Fascists argued that the national community should be unified, pure, and strong. Toward this end, fascist regimes repressed dissent and minorities while pursuing aggressive, usually expansionist foreign policy. Fascism did not entail a specific economic policy but usually maintained capitalist ownership, with a corporatist organization of interests under bureaucratic state control (see CORPORATISM). Fascism was less defined by its policies, however, which were often *ad hoc*, than by its ideology, organization, and style. Ideologically, it celebrated youth, vigor, order, discipline, violence, and hierarchy. Organizationally, it was based on a revolutionary mass movement led by a charismatic absolute leader. Stylistically, it cultivated a combination of archaic, mystical, and militaristic symbolism.

Social scientists most often interpret fascism as a response of the lower middle classes to economic crisis, defeat in World War I, and the threat of communist revolution, although it also received support from the bourgeoisie and some sectors of the working class. Fascist ideals were largely discredited by military defeat in 1945, and the use of fascist symbols and language is now illegal in many European countries. Some postwar European movements—notably the French National Front, the German Republicans, and the Italian Social Movement—have sought to revive them in diluted form, often through veiled appeals to race and national renewal. Although the term *fascist* has been applied to a variety of extreme right-wing phenomena, latter-day examples are more usually and accurately called "neofascist."

federalism A model of political organization that divides sovereignty between national and regional governments. Federalism is a compromise between a unitary state, where local governments are created by the center and may be dissolved or overruled by it, and *confederation*, where the central government is the contingent creation of a league of independent states. Federal arrangements are usually set up by a constitution that divides powers, jurisdictions, and sources of revenue between two levels of government. Federalism was first developed in the U.S. Constitution to preserve regional autonomy and pursue the goal of LIMITED GOVERNMENT. It was subsequently adopted by a number of countries with traditions of separately governed territories. It has also been utilized by countries composed of historically and culturally distinct communities, such as Brazil, Germany, India, Mexico, Nigeria, and the former Yugoslavia and Soviet Union. As the last examples suggest, however, federalism is an intrinsically dynamic arrangement, capable under different conditions of CENTRALIZATION, decentralization, and even disintegration.

feedback The process by which knowledge acquired from past experiences informs and alters actors' choices when they encounter similar situations. It is a central concept of CYBERNETICS and information theory.

femininity The forms of behavior associated with the female sex, as opposed to the biological difference that defines the sexes. Feminity

is primarily a cultural product that exhibits a great deal of variation among cultures and often within cultures, where its specific requirements and normative power can vary widely. Femininity has historically been attributed to or considered inseparable from biological facts—such as childbearing and smaller size and strength compared to men—even by many early feminists, who sought to provide a greater social scope for the feminine virtues. Similar arguments appear in SOCIOBIOLOGY. The exact line between biological and cultural sources of behavior, as well as the effects and variability of biological factors, remains a subject of interest and heated debate among scholars in many fields.

Study of the cultural production and social meaning of femininity is basic to recent interest in SEXUALITY and GENDER, as well as important to FEMINISM. These issues have had an enormous impact on a wide range of social science research since the 1960s.

feminism Both a social movement and a perspective on society. As a social movement, it has challenged the historical subordination of women and advocated political, social, and economic equality between the sexes. As a social and sociological perspective, it has examined the roles that sex and gender play in structuring society, as well as the reciprocal role that society plays in structuring sex and gender.

The origins of feminism are usually traced to Mary Wollstonecraft's *A Vindication of the Rights of Women* (1792), written in answer to Thomas Paine's famous revolutionary appeal, *The Rights of Man* (1791). Feminist activism remained strong throughout the nineteenth century, most notably in the context of campaigns for woman suffrage rights but also in regard to occupational and educational equality. More generally, feminism intersected (although not always easily) the range of other social issues in which women played an instrumental role—primarily abolitionism and temperance. Prominent nineteenth-century American feminists include Susan B. Anthony, Elizabeth Cady Stanton, and Jane ADDAMS, founder of the first social services agency in the United States.

The chief victory of this era of feminist struggle was the achievement of the right to vote (1920 in the United States, 1928 in Britain). In the 1960s, a "second wave" of feminism emerged which drew on the larger context of social and political unrest and a number of specifically intellectual influences from the post–World War II period. The contemporaneous sexual revolution, made possible in part by the availability of the contraceptive pill, brought related pressures on the norms of female sexuality and behavior. Second-wave feminism is associated with a number of prominent critiques of the subordination of women and the cultural construction of femininity. Betty Friedan's *The Feminine Mystique* (1963) is a powerful example of the former, critiquing the limited sphere of activity and limited aspirations of middle-class women in the United States. Simone de BEAUVOIR's *The Second Sex* (1949) is the source of the famous statement that "woman is not born, but made." Beauvoir's strong constructivist argument about women's roles, psychology, and biology, as well as her indictment of patriarchy, had a major influence on the growth of feminism in Europe and the United States.

If much of the animus for second-wave feminist scholarship arose out of the sense that women had been systematically marginalized in accounts of society written by men, much of the more recent debate about feminism involves the degree to which it, too, was structured by universalistic claims to speak about and for all women. A range of modern feminist approaches have sought to reintroduce the salient distinctions that divide the experiences of women and, in particular, move it away from its foundations in white middle-class progressivism. Modern feminism deals with issues of class, race, ethnicity, and sexual orientation as well, leading some scholars to posit the need for larger alliances between subordinated groups that escape the potentially infinite regress of particularism. The recent SUBALTERN studies movement is one attempt to provide an intellectual focus for such activities, especially in relation to third-world societies, where the most primary forms of social and economic equality are often absent. Feminism has been changed, too, by its own successes—not least in relation to long-term shifts in professional opportunities, domestic norms, and attitudes toward women in the public sphere, although significant inequalities remain. Structural economic factors, such as the massive entry of women into the workforce, are both a cause and a consequence of these changes. At the other end of the economic spectrum is the *feminization of poverty*, a term that describes the growing proportion of women and children among the poor in the United States.

Modern feminism contains many tensions with regard to policy goals, tactics, operating categories, and practices. There are important distinctions between liberal orientations, which emphasize blocked opportunities and legal barriers to equality, Marxist critiques, which associate women's oppression with the hierarchical nature of the capitalist system, and radical accounts, which trace the subordination and oppression of women to the patriarchal organization of society. Recent years, too, have seen a dramatic diversification of the ways in which social movements and research are organized by the question of sex, gender, and, perhaps most significantly, the related question of sexual preference. Gay and lesbian studies and studies of masculinity bring to bear many of the tools of feminist scholarship and have addressed similar gaps in the understanding of sexuality and social organization.

fetish The term has currency in a range of fields, from the study of primitive religion, where it denotes an object that is sacred or attributed special power, to psychology, where it refers to a sexual fixation on a part of the body or other object, to MARXISM, where the concept of *commodity fetishism* refers to the way that commodities are attributed autonomous, intrinsic value divorced from their connection with human labor and their usefulness as objects. The Freudian account of fetishism, in particular, has found its way into numerous forms of cultural and postcolonial criticism.

feudalism A social, political, and economic system based on contractual relationships between a lord and the other members of an aristocratic class—most typically in the form of an exchange of land rights for military allegiance and service. Feudalism dominated Western Europe between the ninth and thirteenth centuries. Similar patterns emerged in parts of the Islamic world and Asia and in some cases continued far longer. The term derives from the Latin *feudum* ("fief")—the land granted to a member of the aristocracy by the lord. The relationship between lord and vassal included an array of rights and obligations, including the vassal's right of rule over the inhabitants of the fief. A web of financial obligations to the lord was also frequently implied, both for the maintenance of the court and the diverse ceremonies and undertakings that the lord might require.

Some historians characterize feudalism as pertaining only to the relations of lordship and vassalage within the aristocracy and, therefore, primarily to the pyramidal political structure they sustained. The economic arrangements of serfdom and other forms of peasantry are not considered intrinsic to the feudal order. The Marxist account differs on this point and informs much of the view of feudalism as a complete social and economic system. For Karl MARX, the role of land as the basic unit of wealth and serf labor as the main source of value was fundamental. Feudalism was above all a MODE OF PRODUCTION that produced a profoundly hierarchical social order and that was progressively undone by the emergence of CAPITALISM.

Most modern historians regard this as an incomplete view. Feudalism is generally held to have arisen in response to the breakdown of trade after the early Middle Ages and to the constant threat of marauders from Europe's periphery. By the fourteenth century, the feudal order in Europe began to be undermined by the growth of commercial relations and towns, increasingly complex networks of inheritance and allegiance, and the concentration of power in absolutist monarchies. These broke the economic and political bases of feudalism. Transformation of the religious and intellectual structures of the feudal order took longer but gathered speed in the fifteenth and sixteenth centuries.

Feyerabend, Paul K. (1924–1994) An Austrian-born philosopher of science who challenged the possibility of universal scientific methods. His critique was broadly directed against POSITIVISM in science and particularly against those who sought to save the scientific method from the flaws of positivism—especially Karl Raimund POPPER and the doctrine of *falsifiability*. Feyerabend drew instead on the PARADIGM theory of Thomas KUHN and the late work of Ludwig WITTGENSTEIN; he argued that science generated an inevitably plural set of doctrines, methodologies, and theories, which were often in competition and incommensurable with one another. For Feyerabend, this implied that scientists should resist the temptation to characterize their work as in any sense definitive or true. It implied, more broadly, that society should resist the attempts of scientists to promote themselves as the experts and arbiters of truth. Rather, all members of society participate in a consensual process of determining the status of competing claims to knowledge. Feyerabend's major works include *Against Method* (1975) and *Science in a Free Society* (1978).

fiat money   Money whose status derives from legal enactment—as with all modern currencies. Fiat money is "legal tender" in that the law will recognize the offer of such money as evidence of an intention to settle debt. It is distinguished from commodity money in that it is of virtually no worth beyond its legal status. Commodity money (e.g., gold), in contrast, has worth as a commodity even outside its legal declaration as tender.

fictive kinship   Describes intense and usually ritualized interpersonal bonds that draw on KINSHIP as a model, such as godparenting, brotherhoods, and forms of religious or political adherence.

fieldwork   Research conducted by social scientists among specific groups or communities, although its classic and strongest reference is to long-term anthropological research in face-to-face settings. As the primary tool of ANTHROPOLOGY, fieldwork has been a subject of long and continuing debate regarding the limits and potential distortions of direct and indirect observation. These range from the original formulations of PARTICIPANT OBSERVATION by Bronislaw MALINOWSKI to the highly scientific claims made for anthropology by A. R. RADCLIFFE-BROWN, the humanistic focus of E. E. EVANS-PRITCHARD, and the SYMBOLIC ANTHROPOLOGY made popular by Clifford GEERTZ and others in the 1960s.

financial crisis   A sharp deterioration of a group of financial indicators, such as short-term interest rates and asset prices, potentially also accompanied by failures of financial institutions. Such crises have been a long-term subject of interest in ECONOMICS and have begun to generate a broader body of interdisciplinary research in the social sciences as economies become more financially interdependent.

A financial boom or bubble is characterized by a shift of wealth out of money holdings and into real and long-term financial assets—stocks or bonds, for instance—and sustained on the basis of expectations of capital gains. A financial crisis, on the other hand, is characterized by the liquidation of such assets into money, based on expectations of a decline in their prices. Between these two events, there may be a period of "distress" in which the expectation of continued capital gain has been eroded but the opposite expectation of imminent capital losses has not formed. Whether financial distress culminates in a crisis depends, among other things, upon the speed of the reversal of expectations, the erosion of confidence produced by spectacular financial failures, and whether the financial community believes that in extreme conditions, the domestic lender of the last resort will play a rescuing role. An international financial crisis is one in which foreign investors dump assets and money denominated in a country's domestic currency for stronger currencies. In such cases, there is a well-known risk of *contagion*, as international investors become risk-averse and pull money out of economies that may be sound.

financial ratios Ratios between a particular segment of a firm's assets and liabilities and the corresponding totals of assets and liabilities. Financial ratios are indicators of the strength and prospects of a firm's financial performance. Examples include the *price–earning ratio* (the ratio of current equity price on the stock market to the declared dividend per share) and the ratio of debt finance to the sum of debt and equity finance (called the *gearing ratio*).

firm The unit of economic analysis on the production side of a market, similar to "producer" but with a connotation of internal structure. A producer may be an individual, but a firm is generally assumed to hire labor.

firm, theory of the The economic study of firms and firm behavior encompasses many areas. Most basic is the question of why firms exist at all—why, in other words, economic activity is not simply carried out by individuals. The neoclassical answer to this question is that firms minimize the "transaction costs" that accompany the exchange of goods and services in the market. Ronald COASE ("The Nature of the Firm," 1937) described firms as subsets of the larger economy, where allocation proceeds by direction and command rather than through the price system. He argued that some procedures, such as the allocation of workers within a firm to particular tasks, can be accomplished more cheaply by command than by price. Oliver Williamson (*Modes of Bounded Rationality*, 1980) added that under conditions of BOUNDED RATIONALITY and uncertainty, the command structure of firms allows them to economize on expensive contracts.

In the absence of a price system, monitoring and internal incentives become significant issues. Armen Alchian and Harold Demsetz argue that the problem of monitoring itself provides a rationale for the capitalist firm. More recent approaches have suggested that because not all resources within a firm have their prices determined in external markets, the distribution of rewards is determined through bargaining. Actors within a firm play a cooperative game in which different types of obligations (such as those concerning shareholders and workers) can be adjudicated separately, according to different methods (see COOPERATIVE GAMES).

A great deal of work on firm behavior concerns the optimal allocation of resources and the distribution of income among the different factors of production, such as LABOR and CAPITAL. Among the earliest theoreticians in this area was Alfred MARSHALL, who provided a fairly complete analysis of the short-run equilibrium conditions of a firm in a perfectly competitive market. Marshall demonstrated that in the long run, QUASI RENT (rewards in excess of OPPORTUNITY COSTS) would be eaten away by the entry and exit costs of competition, resulting only in normal levels of profit. Joseph SCHUMPETER denied that quasi rent would be lost through competition, but rather that new innovations would displace existing sources of quasi rent—a process he referred to as *creative destruction* (*Theory of Economic Development*, 1934).

The current neoclassical consensus on firm behavior holds that a firm endowed with a given technology is an optimizing agent that maximizes profits or optimizes some other managerial objective functions. Such an approach is analytically tractable and thought to have important predictive power. Yet it places major demands on the computational capacity and informational requirement of firms as evaluations of the market become complex. In fact, firm-level studies by Richard M. Cyert and James G. March suggest that firms do not optimize very well and commonly adopt *mark-up pricing* routines, that is, they set price at an arbitrary number that exceeds costs (*A Behavioral Theory of the Firm*, 1963). Nonetheless, two arguments support the optimizing model. One is the biological analogy of the survival of the fittest. Firms that maximize will prosper, while those that do not will perish by a process akin to natural selection. The second argument is that a firm can maximize through simple feed-back algorithms that imply no elaborate analytical powers. Richard Day and Herbert Tinney demonstrated that a firm can maximize its profits simply by repeating actions that raise profits and by retreating from those that do not. Such mechanisms work only if they converge fast enough relative to the stability of the environment in which the firm operates.

Two important developments have greatly impacted the neoclassical model of the firm: the theory of RISK and the development of AGENCY THEORY. Risk theory suggests that a risk averse competitive firm will produce less than a risk neutral firm or one that knows with certainty that price will equal its expected value. Agency theory examines the separation of ownership and control in firms. The owner (the *principal*) assigns a task to a worker (the *agent*) and assumes responsibility for monitoring that task—always at some cost. The most expedient solution is to design contracts that provide the agent with incentives to act in the principal's interest. See also NEOCLASSICAL ECONOMICS.

first-past-the-post   See ELECTORAL SYSTEM.

Firth, Raymond William (1901–1999) A prominent British anthropologist whose career spanned much of the twentieth century. Firth was a wide-ranging ethnographer and theorist who made major contributions in the areas of economic anthropology and the study of social organization. Initially trained as an economist, his encounter with Bronislaw MALINOWSKI at the London School of Economics prompted his transition to ANTHROPOLOGY and his turn to ethnographic fieldwork. Firth published a number of studies based on work among South Pacific islanders in the late 1920s and 1930s, including the seminal *We, the Tikopia: A Sociological Study of Kinship in Primitive Polynesia* (1936). Greatly influenced by Malinowski, Firth nonetheless recognized many of the limitations of both FUNCTIONALISM and structural-functionalism in dealing with individual behavior and social change. His attention to models of individual decision-making (particularly related to economic activity) and his influential distinction between SOCIAL STRUCTURE and SOCIAL ORGANIZATION attempted to make functionalism a more flexible tool. With the latter distinction, in particular, Firth sought to differentiate the durable and relatively consistent pattern of social relations (structure) from the realities of individual variation and disruptive events (organization). Beyond *We, the Tikopia*, his major works include *Malay Fishermen: Their Peasant Economy* (1946), *Elements of Social Organization* (1956), *Social Change Among*

the Tikopia (1959), *Essays on Social Organization and Values* (1964), and *Themes in Economic Anthropology* (1967).

fiscal federalism   Refers to the question of the efficient governmental location of taxation and expenditure decisions. Local governments may offer certain efficiencies in the provisions of goods and services and in tax collection, but there may exist offsetting equity considerations, opportunities for risk reduction, and EXTERNALITIES that tilt the balance toward national-level control over fiscal policy. Theoretical and empirical work in this area seeks to determine which dimensions of fiscal programs are best located at the state or local level and which are better handled nationally.

fiscal policy   Refers to political decisions about taxes and government spending. At issue is not only the size of government—how much to tax and how many services and/or transfer payments to provide—but also the use of these tools—spending and taxes—to change variables like employment and output in the larger economy. See BUDGETARY OR FISCAL POLICY for a complete discussion.

Fisher, Irving (1867–1947) An economist known primarily for reformulating the classical quantity theory of money in order to find a way to stabilize prices. Toward this end, Fisher ultimately advocated a banking system based on 100 percent reserves. His theories are exposed primarily in *The Nature of Capital and Income* (1906), *Stabilizing the Dollar* (1920), and *100% Money* (1936).

According to the quantity theory of money, the level of prices depends on the volume and velocity of currency in circulation, the volume and velocity of checking deposits, and the volume of trade. In particular, prices rise as either the quantity of money (currency plus deposits) or its velocity rises, but fall as the volume of trade rises. Fisher postulated that deposits are a multiple of currency, and that the velocity of circulation and the volume of trade are constant. In the short run, with full employment in the economy, the currency in circulation is the determinant of the price level. This proposal is also known as the *neutrality of money*: if the quantity of money doubles, the price level also doubles.

It follows from this argument that the price level can be controlled by controlling the quantity of currency in circulation. One way of doing this is to establish a paper currency that cannot be redeemed in gold. Prior to 1929, Fisher was suspicious of this method, since he felt that public mistrust of a paper currency would lead to speculation. He advocated making paper money redeemable in a quantity of gold that represented a constant level of purchasing power. In this way the purchasing power of a dollar would remain constant.

After the stock market crash of 1929, however, Fisher came to regard the growth of debt as the cause of the Depression. Specifically, he thought that the fluctuations in demand deposits were the chief cause of business fluctuations. This meant that his earlier stabilization program no longer made sense: the volume of checking deposits relative to the volume of gold backing them was so high that small changes in the price of gold would no longer affect purchasing power. Fisher's new plan was to back all deposits with 100 percent reserves, thus halting the credit creation power of banks. This would eliminate bank runs and bank failures, thereby moderating both booms and depressions.

While Fisher's analysis was constrained by his belief that business cycles were merely monetary phenomena (and not inherent in the economy), his use of the quantity theory was a pioneering attempt to theorize macroeconomic stability. He also contributed significantly to econometrics and economic statistics. See also DEMAND FOR MONEY; and MACROECONOMICS.

fixed factors   Factors of production that cannot be varied or changed in quantity, such as the size of the plant (see FACTOR OF PRODUCTION). This usually applies in the short run, where some paths of adjustment are barred to the firm. Over the long run, most factors of production can be adjusted.

fixprice models and flexiprice models   The economist John R. HICKS (1965) developed two methods of studying production and exchange: the fixprice and the flexiprice models. The fixprice models assume that prices are given at the beginning of each period and that they remain fixed at that level. Transactions occur at nonequilibrium prices and differ from planned demand and supply. In this case, prices and wages do not move smoothly to clear markets. Later versions of these models are sometimes referred to as *disequilibrium analyses* and *rationing equilibria*.

In flexiprice models, prices adjust immediately within each period in response to excess demand or supply. Transactions therefore take place at prices for which the excess demand is zero.

Supply and demand are balanced through the TATONNEMENT process of adjusted bidding (see Leon WALRAS).

flexible specialization   A theory about the reorganization of economic production that emphasizes the decline of Fordist principles of large-scale, centralized, homogenized production in favor of the proliferation of small-scale niche manufacturers. Flexible specialization theory implies that improvements in technology make economies of scale possible among a range of interlocking small firms, which enjoy a competitive advantage in tailoring goods to specific markets. It often includes assumptions about the social consequences of such production, including the need for higher-skilled and computer-proficient workers and—as the pressures for an extreme division of labor diminish—a corresponding improvement in labor relations and the character of work.

Advocates of flexible specialization point to evidence of these tendencies in a number of industries and geographic locales—Silicon Valley in California and the manufacturing districts of Northern Italy often figure in these accounts. Yet evidence for a broad industrial shift toward flexible specialization is less clear. Big Fordist-style industries have also integrated new technologies and forms of vertical and horizontal subcontracting, blurring the distinction between production paradigms. The social claims made on behalf of flexible specialization are even more uncertain. Many sociologists of labor and production view technology as primarily a force for DESKILLING workers, as computers take over more specialized tasks. See also FORDISM.

folk devils   A concept widely used in the study of DEVIANCE, folk devils are social types that unite the negative qualities of which a society or group disapproves. They are used as indicators of the boundaries of acceptable behavior and often as means of stigmatizing and policing persons who deviate from those norms. The term is associated with Stanley Cohen's work on British youth cultures, *Folk Devils and Moral Panics* (1972).

folk fortress   Refers to a nation or the core area of a nation bounded by natural defenses, such as mountains or water.

folklore   Primarily the cultural products and traditions of peasant or other premodern societies. Folklore entered the English language in the mid-nineteenth century as a translation of the

German *Volkskunde*, and much of the early study of folklore followed the German example in searching for the premodern origins and authentic cultural traits of national ethnic groups. These agendas have faded from the mainstream of anthropological research, and subsequent theories of folklore have tracked with most of the major variations and shifts in twentieth-century anthropological thought, from Franz BOAS's views of folklore as social allegory, to Bronislaw MALINOWSKI's FUNCTIONALISM, to psychoanalytical approaches. Folklore has been a particularly important subject in the emergence of STRUCTURALISM, particularly in the work of Vladimir Propp and Claude LÉVI-STRAUSS. Recent American scholarship has broadened the focus of folklore to include areas of MATERIAL CULTURE. It has also shifted away from the taxonomic studies of narrative elements and types of myth that characterized structuralist approaches, and toward the examination of the construction of claims for cultural authenticity.

folk–urban continuum   A model of societal development that places small, isolated "folk" societies, dominated by KINSHIP bonds, at one end of an analytical spectrum and large, modern, urban societies at the other. The model was introduced by Robert REDFIELD in *Folk Cultures of the Yucatan* (1941). REDFIELD proposed that development proceeded through the diffusion of cultural and technological innovation from the urban end of the spectrum to the folk.

folkways   Introduced in *Folkways* (1909) by William Graham SUMNER, the term refers to the body of informal traditions, habits, and sanctions of a particular community.

foraging   Used interchangeably with "gathering" to describe the common mode of subsistence of small, seminomadic bands. See also BAND SOCIETIES.

forced saving   Most commonly refers to government-established savings plans with compulsory participation. Taxes withheld for future retirement payments are one example, provided that the funds collected are put in a personal account. Singapore currently uses such a system. Forced savings may also refer to voluntary actions of individuals to put a share of their income out of reach, such as payroll deductions for retirement funds. Further, the term can refer to the saving that occurs when consumers are unable to

spend their money because consumption goods are unavailable. In a free-market economy, such a situation is usually quickly corrected, as producers either increase prices or supply. In planned or rationing economies, however, such increases may not take place, either because production priorities lie elsewhere (as, for example, in wartime) or because of policy decisions that favor faster ACCUMULATION OF CAPITAL and INVESTMENT.

Forde, Daryll   (1902–1973) A wide-ranging British anthropologist whose fieldwork took him to Welsh villages, the Yuma and Hopi tribes of the American Southwest, and the Yakö of Nigeria. Forde was a dominant figure in the crowded field of African anthropology in postwar Britain. He was a prodigious producer and facilitator of Africanist work, publishing several studies of Yakö society and becoming editor of the journal *Africa* in 1944. Methodologically, Forde was a strong advocate of a unified approach to ANTHROPOLOGY that took account of the interrelations between the ecological, political, linguistic, and biological dimensions of society—this at a time when increased disciplinary specialization and the dominance of structural-FUNCTIONALISM had greatly narrowed the field of legitimate anthropological subjects. This generalist approach and the impetus he gave to the field of African studies is the core of his considerable legacy. Forde's major works include *Habitat, Economy and Society* (1934), *Marriage and Family among the Yakö* (1941), *The Context of Belief* (1958), and *Yakö Studies* (1964).

Fordism   A system of production based on mass standardization and especially the use of assembly lines. It is named after Henry Ford, who revolutionized automobile production with these techniques at the turn of the twentieth century. The term was introduced by the Italian Marxist Antonio GRAMSCI around 1930 to characterize what he saw as a distinctively new form of capitalist production. Gramsci associated Fordism with a new form of capitalist discipline called "Taylorism"—the system of SCIENTIFIC MANAGEMENT developed by Frederick Taylor at the turn of the century for Ford and other industrialists, which studied and maximized the efficiency of workers' movements. Later writers, especially those of the Marxist REGULATION SCHOOL, emphasized the extent to which Fordism was the basis of a broader "regime of accumulation" accompanied by a set of social relations in which workers were placated by mass consumption, labor unions worked as partners with business and government, and the Keynesian welfare state ensured social peace. In this broader usage, Fordist institutions and practices can still be found in many parts of the world, but in the West they have been increasingly supplanted by post-Fordist arrangements that include the fragmentation of the labor movement, neoliberal social policies, FLEXIBLE SPECIALIZATION, and the growing importance of "knowledge workers." See also NEOLIBERALISM; and POSTINDUSTRIAL SOCIETY.

forecasting Methods used to predict certain parameters of the economy or the future state of markets. There are three distinct types of forecasting situations: *event timing*, which attempts to determine when a particular event will occur; *event-outcome forecasting*, which tries to forecast the outcome of an uncertain event; and *time-series forecasts*, which use past and present values of a variable to forecast its future value. The difference between the predicted value of a variable and the actual outcome is termed the forecast error.

Event-timing forecasts usually make use of *leading indicators*, that is, other events that generally precede the event of interest. Examples of event-timing forecasts include shifts in interest rates or the turning point of a business cycle.

Time-series forecasts can provide either point forecasts (the most likely future value of a variable) or interval forecasts (in which one uses the mean and the variance of the forecast to construct an interval within which the future value of the variable is likely to fall). A frequently used class of models is the ARMA (autoregressive-moving average), which assumes that the future values of a time series depend on its past values. These techniques have also been extended to modeling vectors, termed VAR (vector autoregression) models. While these methods have proved successful in providing short-term forecasts of macroeconomic variables, they have less success in long-term forecasts.

The main alternatives to these methods are econometric models that describe the variable under study as endogenous and determined within a system of variables. These models often use EQUILIBRIUM theory as a starting point. Forecasts are then made by taking into account interactions with other economic and relevant noneconomic variables. Often, forecasts are based on a combination of these two methods: forecasts of endogenous variables are obtained from econometric methods, while those of exogenous variables are better derived from the ARMA or VAR models.

foreign aid The transfer of resources from industrialized countries to poor countries, mainly for the purposes of economic development. Foreign aid excludes quasi-commercial transactions as well as resource transfer for nondevelopmental purposes, such as military assistance and private charity. From the recipient's perspective, foreign aid adds to the resources available for investment and increases the supply of foreign exchange to finance necessary imports. From the donor's point of view, foreign aid is an instrument of foreign policy, and often comes with implicit or explicit expectations of reciprocity in areas where the recipient can be of assistance. Aid packages frequently restrict the recipient, moreover, to purchase from producers in the donor country.

The two major types of aid are *project aid* and *program lending*. The former is intended to increase efficiency and output in specific industries or sectors. The latter aims at supporting the recipient country's macroeconomic policies and its need for foreign exchange during periods of structural economic change.

foreign-trade multiplier An indicator of how national income changes in response to a change in exports, especially in regard to the feedback mechanism that equilibrates a country's BALANCE OF PAYMENTS when trade levels change. In abbreviated form, an increase in exports increases NATIONAL INCOME; an increase in national income, in turn, increases consumption and therefore imports—although to a lesser degree. The inverse relationship holds in importing countries.

The foreign-trade multiplier also offers an explanation for the spread of international booms and depressions. A decline in one country's income will lower its imports, which in turn lowers the exports of some other country. The second country will suffer a corresponding decline in income and imports, which may affect other countries. Booms in international trade obey much the same principle.

formalist–substantivist debate A debate within economic anthropology about the validity of Western, capitalist models of rational economic behavior in non-Western and/or noncapitalist societies. The formalist position, advocated by Raymond FIRTH and Robbins Burling among others, holds that the forms of rational choice attributed to market relations are fundamental to human behavior and widely generalizable across cultures and periods of history (see RATIONAL-CHOICE THEORY). *Substantivism* was a critique of this position, which argued that the economic model had little value in cultures where KINSHIP relations predominated or where market economies were absent. Karl Polanyi coined the two terms in his 1957 case for substantivism in *Trades and Markets in Early Empires* (Polanyi, Arensberg, and Pearson, eds.), sparking a debate that lasted through the early 1970s.

formal sociology   Most often associated with Georg SIMMEL, formal sociology is an attempt to determine the basic forms of social interaction that underlie more complex forms and contexts of social behavior. Theorizing on neo-Kantian grounds, Simmel sought to reduce social encounters to their simplest arrangements, such as the different possibilities that arise in the transition from two-person relationships (dyadic) to three-person relationships (triadic). Exploring these differences—such as the possibility of alliance and mediation that emerges in triadic situations—Simmel elaborated what he termed the *geometry* of human relations. Central to this project were distinctions between the basic modes of interaction that inform group situations, such as cooperation, competition, and conflict.

There have been a number of subsequent attempts to create a sociology of fundamental forms or processes, including work by Robert Ezra PARK (who was influenced directly by Simmel), as well as in some versions of FUNCTIONALISM and SYMBOLIC INTERACTIONISM. In this last case, *pragmatism* has also been a major philosophical influence. Other neo-Kantian approaches, such Ernst Cassirer's study of symbolic forms, have also been important.

Perhaps the most influential formal sociologies today have arisen on different grounds—although still influenced by Simmel. These are primarily attempts to develop "pure" theories of social structure that distinguish themselves from the analysis of the content of communication, interaction, or relationships. NETWORK ANALYSIS is the most prominent, especially as developed by Harrison White and his students. Another example is Peter BLAU's theory of SOCIAL STRUCTURE, which extends Simmel's

interest in the effects of numbers. See also NEO-KANTIANISM.

Fortes, Meyer   (1906–1983) One of the British social anthropologists responsible for the dominance of structural-FUNCTIONALISM and DESCENT THEORY in the 1930s, 1940s, and 1950s. Fortes was born in South Africa and trained in psychology. He turned to anthropology only in the early 1930s, under the influence of Bronislaw MALINOWSKI and others at the London School of Economics. In that period, he conducted ethnographic work among the Tallensi of West Africa, which provided him material for a series of studies of KINSHIP patterns and religion. Fortes did pioneering work on filiation, descent, and ancestor worship, and ultimately became a strong partisan in the battle for priority between descent theorists and alliance theorists, who privileged horizontal relations such as marriage (see ALLIANCE THEORY). His work, along with Max GLUCKMAN's and Siegfried Frederick NADEL's, paved the way for the development of NETWORK ANALYSIS in its emphasis on webs of relationships and solidary groups. Fortes followed strongly in the functionalist tradition developed by Malinowski and A. R. RADCLIFFE-BROWN, and he shared Malinowski's emphasis on individual psychology and the importance of fieldwork. With E. E. EVANS-PRITCHARD, he edited the influential *African Political Systems* (1940). Fortes's other major works include *The Dynamics of Clanship* (1945), *The Web of Kinship* (1949), *Oedipus and Job in West African Religion* (1959), *Kinship and the Social Order* (1969), and *Time and Social Structure and Other Essays* (1970).

forward markets   A type of foreign-exchange market, forward markets trade in agreements that specify that a particular amount of a particular currency is to be delivered at a future date. Unlike currency FUTURES, forward contracts generally do not have margin requirements that require an explicit commitment of funds. Forward markets provide a way of protecting agents against changes in the exchange rate during a given period. They are also commonly used by currency speculators.

There are two principal kinds of contracts in such a market: spot and forward contracts. The rate at which foreign exchange is traded in the forward market is called the forward rate; this rate may vary with the maturity of the contract. If the agents expect prices to rise in the future, the forward rate is higher than the spot rate. See also SPOT MARKETS.

Foucault, Michel (1926–1984) Possibly the most influential philosopher and historian of the latter part of the twentieth century, Foucault's work is characterized by a persistent concern with the relationship between knowledge and POWER, particularly in the context of the treatment of marginal social groups. Foucault undertook several major studies of the ways in which marginal social groups were constituted as objects of science and targets of techniques of isolation, control, and correction. He analyzed the history of mental illness in his first book, *Madness and Civilization* (1963 [1971]), criminality and incarceration in *Discipline and Punish* (1974), and questions of GENDER and sexual practices in a number of works, including the multivolume *History of Sexuality* (1978–1988).

Although these studies demonstrate a significant evolution of Foucault's interests, methods, and understanding of power, there are three general observations about modernity that underwrite much of his work. First, modern society is shaped by normative processes that operate largely by exclusion—of the criminal, the insane, the sexually deviant, and so on. Second, these processes have become increasingly integrated, extensive, and scientific in the modern era, bringing to bear a vast technological apparatus on the classifying and disciplining of persons. (Foucault frequently juxtaposed modernity, in this respect, to the heterogeneous social logics of early modernity, which neither admitted this principle of totalization nor sublimated the violent display of power into subtler forms of domination.) Third, human subjectivity is nothing other than the product of these processes. This is the content of Foucault's anti-humanism, his rejection of the existence of an intrinsic human self that precedes power or action.

The growth of classificatory reason informs Foucault's magisterial study of modernity, *The Order of Things* (1966), as well his reflections on epistemology and historical method in *The Archaeology of Knowledge* (1969). *The Order of Things* treats the emergence of classificatory reason in the course of the eighteenth century as an epochal shift in the constitution of the human subject. Refusing the temptation to naturalize the modern perspective, Foucault took as his object the paradigm of knowledge in which the modern individual came to power—an epistemological system that anchored the subject "man" in a singular and universal concept of order and relation. For Foucault, this system presided over the 150-year history of man and oriented thought toward the goal of technical mastery over nature. This logic, however, in Nietzschean fashion, eventually encounters its own limits. Artistic modernism (paradigmatically, for Foucault, that of Antonin Artaud and Raymond Roussel) marks the symbolic end of this paradigm by breaking the sign-object structure of truth and identity—signs are no longer assumed to correspond to things. These artistic tendencies, Foucault argued, tracked closely with a larger socioeconomic, political, scientific, and metaphysical retreat from the claims of truth. Foucault then envisioned, somewhat tentatively, another paradigm transition: "since man was constituted at a time when language was doomed to dispersion, will he not be dispersed when language recovers its unity?" Will he not disappear "like a face drawn in sand at the edge of the sea?"

Foucault's sense of the end of the modern era has aligned him with POSTMODERNISM, although not all of his work suggests the same opportunity for radical change. His 1974 book *Discipline and Punish* is probably the most pessimistic in this regard, imagining an inevitable and ubiquitous relationship between resistance and power that serves, in the end, to reconsolidate power on more efficient grounds. Foucault's later work on *biopower*—the growing societal and state administration of sexuality and reproduction—explores another register of this intensification. His excursions into the organization of sexuality in classical Rome and Greece, although generally less gloomy regarding the significance of resistance, nonetheless go farther in universalizing his concept of power.

Foucault's radical historicization of the structures of knowledge, his expansion of the analysis of power beyond questions of agency and the state, and his thorough social constructivism have had an enormous impact on a wide range of fields, including history, SOCIOLOGY, literary criticism, and gender studies. Unlike many other major poststructuralist figures, Foucault's writing is accessible and in some cases reached a popular audience. Foucault was also prolific outside his major studies. Numerous collections of his interviews and essays have been published, perhaps most significantly in *Power/Knowledge* (1980). See also POSTSTRUCTURALISM.

four-fields approach   Refers to the division of ANTHROPOLOGY into archaeological, socio-cultural, biological/physical, and linguistic sub-fields, as envisioned by Franz BOAS in the early twentieth century at Columbia University. This organization of the field is prevalent (although declining) in American universities, whereas in Europe these subfields tended to be institutional-ized as separate disciplines.

Frank, André Gunder   (1929–) One of the pioneers of DEPENDENCY THEORY and a wide-ranging comparative and historical scholar of the global economy. Frank's *Capitalism and Underde-velopment in Latin America* (1967) set the terms for much subsequent work on the relationship between developed and underdeveloped coun-tries; it emphasized the persistent patterns of exploitation of peripheral, third-world nations by central, first-world nations. His subsequent work extended this paradigm to second-world socialist countries and their relationship to the capital-ist economies. Frank also wrote extensively on the global character of the economic crisis of the 1970s, predicting the retreat from Keynesian policies and the decline of national control over economic cycles. He has also undertaken much broader historicizations of the global develop-ment and organization of CAPITALISM—first in *World Accumulation 1492–1789* (1978) and more recently in *ReORIENT* (1998), a study of the long-term economic trajectories and interrelationship of East and West over five hundred years. These share ground with other recent attempts to cap-ture the complexity of long-term world economic DEVELOPMENT by Fernand BRAUDEL, Immanuel WALLERSTEIN, and others.

Frank was born in Berlin but was educated and has taught primarily in other countries, including Chile, the Netherlands, and the United States. His published works include *Latin America: Underdevelopment and Revolution* (1969), *Dependent Accumulation and Underdevelopment* (1978), and *Reflections on the World Economic Crisis* (1981).

Frankfurt school   A group of German social theorists who were members of the Institute of Social Research, founded in 1923 in Frankfurt, Germany. The name came to designate the more general set of concerns with TOTALITARIANISM, CAPITALISM, and mass culture that the major Frankfurt theorists shared—an orientation they often described as *critical theory*. In 1930, Max HORKHEIMER became the director and driving force of the institute. At various times in this early

period, it counted among its members and asso-ciates Theodor ADORNO, Herbert MARCUSE, Erich FROMM, Fredrich POLLACK, Walter BENJAMIN, Franz Neumann, and Leo Lowenthal. The victory of Nazism in 1933 forced the institute to relo-cate to the United States, along with most of its members, including Horkheimer, Adorno, and Marcuse. Much of the best work of the Frankfurt school was produced in this period, including Horkheimer and Adorno's *Dialectic of Enlighten-ment* (1947, written in Hollywood). In 1950, the institute moved back to Frankfurt. Horkheimer and Adorno presided over this reopening and were perhaps the most prominent Jews to return to Germany after World War II. In the wake of this return, however, their work took on an increasingly conservative tone shaped by their fear that popular political movements tended toward FASCISM. In the 1960s, a younger gen-eration began to extend the analysis of capitalist modernity in new, although related, directions. This group included Jürgen HABERMAS, Albrecht Wellmer, and Alfred Schmidt. Younger scholars such as Oskar Negt, Claus Offe, and Axel Honneth continue this tradition.

The Frankfurt school of the 1930s was defined by the growth of totalitarianism and the corresponding crisis for Marxist theory. With the victories of Stalinism and Nazism, Marxist social theorists were confronted with incontestable evidence that the working class—long held to be the vehicle of social emancipation—had played an instrumental role in the rise of totalitarianism. Much of Horkheimer, Adorno, and Marcuse's work, then, is an attempt to reconcile MARXISM with this failure, reconceiving the history of capitalism without the radically oppositional social position previously represented by the working class. The result was a group of theories of the total system: the combination of capitalism with the instruments of mass culture to create a situation in which genuine opposition, much less emancipation, was nearly impossible. Horkheimer and Adorno termed this combination the CULTURE INDUSTRY. Instrumental reason, bureaucratization, and the ongoing specialization of labor and knowledge provided other points of reference for these critiques.

This was the essence of Horkheimer and Adorno's attack on Hollywood and the culture industry in *Dialectic of Enlightenment*, and of Marcuse's later vision of *one-dimensional* soci-ety. Yet various qualifications of this grim vision can be found throughout their writing: Adorno's retreat into modern art, Marcuse's hopes for the youth culture of the 1960s, and Benjamin's attention to the possibility of historical ruptures. The work of Habermas is perhaps the dominant contemporary articulation of this vision, extending the analysis of the systemic integration of modern society, while reestablishing the serious consideration of emancipatory human agency and ethics. Similarly, CULTURAL STUDIES, while deeply indebted to the Frankfurt school, has done much to complicate the picture of the production and reception of mass culture, emphasizing the space of interpretation and struggle (if also domination) implicit in the cultural field.

Frazer, James (1854–1941) A gifted classicist, historian of religion, and anthropologist, Frazer is best known for *The Golden Bough* (1890–1915), an elaborately documented evolutionary account of religious rituals, practices, and myths. Frazer devoted much of his life to editing and expanding this work, which grew from two volumes in 1890 to twelve by 1915. As successive editions became more detailed and comprehensive, Frazer refined the evolutionary argument at its center. With clear and deliberate implications for contemporary religion, Frazer argued that human thinking followed a linear pattern of development from magic to religion to science. He thereby reformulated and stood by a concept of SECULARIZATION that had wide currency in nineteenth-century anthropology and social thought.

Unfortunately for Frazer's academic reputation, early twentieth-century ANTHROPOLOGY grew increasingly dissatisfied with such evolutionary models and the wide-ranging comparativism they fostered. By the 1920s, a new generation of anthropologists, led in Britain by Bronislaw MALINOWSKI (one of Frazer's few protégés) and Franz BOAS in the United States, was in the process of radically reorienting the field away from evolutionary models, "armchair" research, and ethnocentric hierarchies of civilizations. The new paradigms of social and cultural anthropology would have little to do with vast syntheses, and very much to do with intensive, culture-specific study.

Despite this academic marginalization and the diverse criticisms of Frazer's comparative conclusions, *The Golden Bough* achieved great popular success, especially after World War I. Frazer's accounts of primitivism and savagery, his apparent proof of the decline of religion, and his vast documentation of myths became a touchstone for a generation of writers and intellectuals who were absorbing the implications of PSYCHOANALYSIS and the horrors of World War I.

free disposal A condition often used in economic models that states that individuals or firms will be caused no disutility (or negative impact on welfare) from an excess of goods, because they can rid themselves of excess at no cost.

freedom Liberty; the absence of constraint; self-determination. Freedom is, with JUSTICE and DEMOCRACY, one of the most venerated and least agreed-upon ideals in modern politics. In Western political discourse, freedom refers, often simultaneously, to at least two traditions in political thought. The first derives from the ancient Greek *eleutheria*, the right and ability to rule oneself as a full member of a political community. This notion was revived by Niccolò MACHIAVELLI and the republican tradition of the early modern period and was more fully expressed in Jean-Jacques ROUSSEAU's account of freedom in *The Social Contract* (1762). There, Rousseau imagined a society in which freedom was perfectly realized through obedience to laws that people made for themselves. *The Social Contract* highlights the difficulties of such a formulation: where individuals disagree with the law, they might have to be "forced to be free." As Benjamin Constant noted in "Liberties of the Ancients Compared to Those of the Moderns" (1819), Rousseau's attachment to the ancient ideals of CITIZENSHIP and democracy blinded him to the fact that in an individualistic society, freedom often meant liberty from the constraints of the state or other citizens. For this reason, Thomas HOBBES rejected the political liberty of the ancients and declared that freedom consisted of "the silence of the law" (*Leviathan*, 1651). This second tradition of freedom as *nonobstruction* accords most closely with classical LIBERALISM and is found, for example, in the U.S. Bill of Rights and in John Stuart MILL's argument that the only restraint on individual liberty should be the risk to the liberty of others. In "Two Concepts of Liberty" (1969), Isaiah BERLIN explored this tension by distinguishing between *negative liberty*, consisting of freedom from constraint by others, and *positive liberty*, the power to pursue a particular vision of self-realization. Berlin recognized that the two were to a degree inextricable, but that the latter often justified forms of TYRANNY and arbitrary judgments about the value of human life. Other theorists, such as Charles Taylor, have made stronger cases for positive liberty.

Contemporary debates generally accept some version of the negative, liberal understanding of freedom, but most recognize that it fails to resolve a number of problems. Negative freedom can be meaningless if it is the freedom to do something one does not want to do, has no ability or opportunity to do, or lacks the resources to do. These considerations underwrite projects of redistribution of wealth and opportunity, and have informed John RAWLS's revision of social contract and utilitarian notions of freedom—leading to his assertion that the widest liberty is a like liberty for all (see SOCIAL-CONTRACT THEORY; and UTILITARIANISM). Although liberal debates tend to revolve around questions of redistribution, more radical critics have argued that freedom necessarily has social, psychological, and normative components. These have fueled a succession of Marxist, feminist, communitarian, and other challenges to the liberal view (see COMMUNITARIANISM; FEMINISM; and MARXISM). Even among liberals, there is very little agreement on whether and how to evaluate the quality of liberty. While most philosophers have been reluctant to dictate exactly what freedom should mean, they have tended to define and defend it in light of other values, distinguishing between liberty and mere license, for example, by associating it with rationality, morality, or the development of human capacities. However it is conceived, freedom has played a key role in Western social and political discourse. Orlando Patterson (*Freedom*, 1991) has argued that freedom gains its central place in Western thought from the counterexample of SLAVERY—an opposition more categorical in the West (both ancient and modern) than in most other civilizations, where freedom was conceived in less essential or more gradational terms. See also LIBERTARIANISM.

free goods Goods sufficiently abundant such that all economic agents can have them at no *social-opportunity cost*—no sacrifice of an alternative use of the good or resource. Air is the closest example to a free good. Free goods are distinguished from goods whose price is zero but that have opportunity costs, such as medical care in certain countries or a "gift of nature" like clean water. In both these cases, a real cost is involved in their consumption, insofar as they make use of resources that may be used elsewhere (their opportunity cost) or that create pollution

that imposes a cost on society (in the case of the consumption of some "free" natural resources).

free riders Persons who use public or collectively provided goods, services, and benefits without paying the costs. In economic terms, free riding is an effect of the *nonrival* characteristic of such goods—a situation in which one individual's consumption of the good does not directly diminish the supply of that good to other individuals. Highways, national defense, and public parks are all public goods that fall into this category.

There is also a free rider problem related to collective action and public policy decisions to provide nonrival goods or services. In regard to the former, participation in collective action often demands that an individual be ready to sacrifice his or her immediate well-being for the long-term good of the entire group. If too many free riders exist—for example, in union negotiations—there will be resistance to sacrifice and the group's objectives will be more difficult to achieve. In terms of public policy, when potential consumers are asked to state their willingness to pay for a nonrival public good, they have an incentive to understate their true willingness to pay in the belief that they will still receive the good. Often, such a phenomenon leads to the underprovision of the good or underservicing of an area. Such situations are frequently the objects of government action or regulation.

free trade and protectionism Free trade means that there are few—and ideally, no—barriers to the international exchange of goods and services. Protectionism refers to policies that restrict trade, either through taxes on trade (tariffs) or through numeric control (bans and quotas). Trade has been a prominent subject of economic theory since the classical discussions of COMPARATIVE ADVANTAGE by David RICARDO and others. The subject, however, has grown in importance for social scientists of all kinds, as the well-being of individual societies comes to depend increasingly on the structure and health of the world economy. The theoretical advantages of free trade are straightforward: each country can import goods that would be costly to produce domestically, while exporting goods that would be costly for other countries to produce. In principle then, each country can acquire a set a goods and services with fewer resources than if it tried to produce them all domestically. Under such reasoning, free trade is PARETO OPTIMAL—leaving no one worse off and at least some better off—and leads to the most efficient allocation of resources on a world scale.

While it may be true that a country gains from trade on average, opening up an economy has differentiated effects across sectors. Notably, labor-scarce countries that move toward freer trade will likely see a decline in wages and jobs in labor-intensive sectors. This sort of consideration is often the source of government reluctance to implement true free trade. There are also a range of situations in which a country may benefit from a strategically chosen restrictive trade policy. In theory, free trade is the best policy for countries that exercise little to no control over world prices. Since they cannot affect prices to their own benefit, free trade allows them to achieve the maximum national consumption. However, if a country possesses some degree of monopoly power in exports, it can increase its own welfare through trade restrictions. Most evidence suggests that domestic interests and political concerns are more often the source of protectionism than such "optimal tariff" considerations.

One argument often made in favor of protection concerns *infant industries*, or those that are deemed essential to the national interest, which may not be able to compete on an international level. Such protections are often associated with national fears of dependency on the international economy—above all, in such areas as agriculture and defense. National defense is an area in which political priorities almost wholly shape the marketplace—often to the point of ignoring the principles of free trade, competition, or the efficient allocation of resources. Programs of modernization are sometimes another, in which developing countries attempt to recoup the competitive advantage gained by countries that were quicker to achieve a given technological or infrastructural level. Modern trade theory, however, postulates that in such cases, output subsidies are a better welfare-increasing policy than the more commonly used tariff, particularly since tariffs often provoke retaliation.

free-trade area   See CUSTOMS UNION.

Freud, Sigmund   (1856–1939) An Austrian physician who revolutionized Western thinking about human behavior, sexuality, and mental life. The central elements of his thought became PSYCHOANALYSIS, which he conceived as a form of therapy for mental illness. Freud broke with traditional psychology on many issues. He was the first to systematically explore the role that sexuality plays in the development of personality (to an excessive degree, according to some critics). He also posed a radical challenge to the priority that philosophy since René DESCARTES had accorded consciousness in accounts of the SELF. Instead, Freud developed a theory of the self that was internally conflicted and complex. More radically, it was subject to processes and influences that remained fundamentally obscure to conscious thought.

Freud's ideas and methods evolved dramatically during the course of his career. He often changed his mind on issues or introduced new models of psychological processes that are difficult to reconcile with earlier ones. Some of these shifts reflected changes in the empirical problems or data at his disposal; others reflected shifts in his interests, such as his late turn toward the psychological bases of broader social phenomena such as law, religion, and civilization.

Freud was born in Freiburg but spent nearly his entire life in Vienna. Trained as a medical doctor, he specialized first in neurology. His interest in psychology developed during a brief period spent observing Jean-Martin Charcot's work with hysterics in Paris. Upon returning to Vienna, Freud opened a clinic that specialized in nervous disorders. Initially, Freud made use of Charcot's hypnotic techniques, but he gradually moved toward conversation-based therapeutic sessions—first through the questioning of patients (the cathartic method) and later through *free association*, which became the centerpiece of the psychoanalytic method. His theories about the sources of hysteria similarly evolved—initially focusing on the repressed sexual traumas he identified in many of his female patients (often at the hands of their fathers) and later moving toward a more generic developmental theory of sexuality and personality, which culminated in what he called the OEDIPUS COMPLEX. Freud also conducted a lengthy self-analysis in order to investigate the general processes of repression and the relationship between what he came to see as distinct levels of mental activity—the conscious and the unconscious. *The Interpretation of Dreams* (1900) was the first major exploration of this set of issues. Among other key concepts, it introduced the mechanisms of distortion (*displacement* and *condensation*) that transform unconscious needs and unacceptable wishes into acceptable, if cryptic, forms within dreams. Later works such as *The Psychopathology of Everyday Life* (1904) and *Jokes and Their Relation to the Unconscious* (1905) built on this principle by exploring the unconscious impulses and wishes that underlie slips of the tongue, forgetting, jokes, and other common forms of behavior.

Freud increasingly focused on the role that sexuality played in human motivations and in the development of the human psyche. He came to consider neuroses and sexual perversions as two forms of expression of the breakdown of the process of normal sexual development—here conceived as heterosexual, genital, and procreative. Stripped of its sexual narrative, the famous Oedipus complex was an attempt to explain the emergence of an autonomous personality from the situation of childhood dependency. For Freud, this involved a radical disruption of the close (for Freud, conceptually "incestuous") link between mother and son. This disruption was represented, in his account, by the paternal threat of castration, which led to the ultimate reproduction of the paternal role. As many critics have observed, Freud never found a satisfactory analog of this process for daughters, although female patients were in many respects the center of his clinical practice.

In related work, Freud argued that Oedipalization built upon an earlier process of psychological and motor development in infants, which expressed itself as a passage through anal and oral phases of pleasure on its way toward a more restrictive genital sexuality. Together, these models were the basis of much of Freud's research and many of his case studies through the late 1910s. With *Beyond the Pleasure Principle* (1920), *The Ego and the Id* (1923), and other work in the early 1920s, however, Freud began to revise his model of the psyche and of the deeper drives that mediate between psychological and biological needs. Where he had earlier described the drives as fundamentally sexual in nature and oriented toward survival, he now introduced a complicated and evolving distinction between the life instincts and the death drive—Eros and Thanatos—that implied competing creative and destructive tendencies within the psyche and, more broadly, within civilization. Where he had previously mapped the psyche in terms of conscious, preconscious, and unconscious process—distinct from

the developmental drama of the Oedipus complex—he now introduced a new three-part division into the id, ego, and superego. The *id* was the reservoir or matrix of the instinctual drives; the *ego* described the reality-testing, choice-making part of the psyche; and the *superego* was the censoring mechanism that embodies internalized familial and social norms. The Latin terminology was introduced by Freud's English translators; the German original refers to the "it," the "I" and the "over-I."

Freud's later work became increasingly social in scope and pessimistic in tone. He characterized society as an uneasy process of *sublimation* or rechanneling of instinctive drives, and politics as a form of psychological domination of weak egos. *Group Psychology and the Analysis of the Ego* (1921) and *Civilization and Its Discontents* (1930) belong to this category. FASCISM realized many of Freud's fears, and he fled Vienna for London in 1938, following the Nazi takeover. Freud's other major works include *Three Contributions to the Theory of Sexuality* (1905), *Totem and Taboo* (1913), *The Future of an Illusion* (1928), and *Moses and Monotheism* (1938). See also EGO PSYCHOLOGY; and SOCIAL PSYCHOLOGY.

Friedman, Milton (1912–) A strong advocate of both LAISSEZ FAIRE and MONETARISM, Friedman has influenced macroeconomic theory more than any economist since John Maynard KEYNES. Friedman's fame initially derived from his critique of Keynesian theory and policy, and only later from the widespread application of his own monetarist theories.

Friedman earned his Ph.D. from Columbia University, but his strongest institutional attachment was to the University of Chicago, where he obtained an M.A. in 1933, served as research assistant to Henry Schultz, and later taught. Over time, Friedman has become all but synonymous with the CHICAGO SCHOOL OF ECONOMICS, particularly in the post–Frank Knight era. One of the chief characteristics of Friedman's work is its engagement with empirical research. His first published paper proposed a way of using the separability of the utility function to measure price elasticities from budgetary data. Under the influence of Harold HOTELLING and others, he also contributed to the literature on econometrics. Two noted examples are his proposal to use rank-order statistics to avoid normality assumptions in the analysis of variance and his work on what later came to be termed *sequential sampling*.

Most economists consider *A Theory of the Consumption Function* (1957) to be Friedman's greatest theoretical contribution. Here Friedman broke with the Keynesian assumption that an increase in autonomous expenditure (such as government spending) leads to a more than proportionate increase in income through a MULTIPLIER effect. Cross-sectional data, Friedman observed, was inconsistent with the Keynesian conclusions. Friedman explained this by postulating that people increase their consumption only in response to changes in their long-term income, thus rendering negligible the effect on demand of short-term government spending. This seminal contribution came to be termed the *permanent income hypothesis*.

Friedman felt that economic uncertainty would be reduced if the U.S. Federal Reserve Bank followed simple rules instead of relying on discretion. Among other steps, he suggested that the money supply should be increased to finance higher budget deficits during recessions and reduced during booms. Empirical evidence later convinced him, however, that fixed and predictable increases in the money supply were preferable to countercyclical changes in stabilizing the economy.

In *Studies in the Quantity Theory of Money* (1956), Friedman and his coauthors asserted that the demand for money is a stable function of the money income of a household, and that the cost of holding money depends on both the interest rate and the inflation rate. Armed with this theory of money demand, Friedman undertook a major revision of macroeconomic theory (see MACROECONOMICS). In reply to Keynesian claims for the potency of fiscal policy, Friedman showed that a higher fiscal deficit has a temporary effect on nominal income, while a higher rate of money growth leads to a permanently higher inflation rate. Moreover, in the long run, higher money growth affects the inflation rate but has no effect on the level or growth rate of output. Finally, Friedman showed that in the long run, there is no tradeoff between UNEMPLOYMENT and INFLATION.

Friedman's theories proved enormously influential on both academic economists and policymakers worldwide. As both inflation and unemployment rose in the OECD (Organization for Economic Cooperation and Development) countries, it seemed that Friedman's view of the long-run PHILLIPS CURVE (the tradeoff between

unemployment and inflation) was vindicated. Friedman and Anna Schwartz wrote an influential history of the money-supply process and its relation to exchange rates, called *A Monetary History of the United States, 1867–1960* (1963). His advocacy of strict monetarism, however, has been controversial in view of later events—especially the fiscal expenditures required to escape the recession of the 1980s, and the relatively low inflation that has accompanied the expansion of the money supply in advanced economies during the 1990s. Also controversial was his association with the "Chicago Boys," Friedman's students who worked closely with the Pinochet regime in Chile. Friedman was awarded the Nobel Prize in economics in 1977.

Frisch, Ragnar (1895–1973) Generally credited with founding the modern field of econometrics, Frisch sought to make economics a more precise science. He also devoted much of his time to applied economics and acted as an adviser to several developing countries, including India and Egypt. He received the first Nobel Prize in economics in 1969 (with Jan TINBERGEN).

Frisch studied and taught in Norway. His early work was in the field of mathematical statistics, but it was his contributions to the methodology of economics that earned Frisch his international reputation. His demand theory, in which utility functions are not postulated but derived from basic axioms, has been widely used—notably in Norwegian government planning. Frisch was also a pioneer of production theory, providing it its first rigorous formulation and application to practical problems. As early as 1934, he showed how a capitalist economy might falter when two groups cannot buy each other's goods. This anticipated certain elements of John Maynard KEYNES's theory of recession. Frisch's interest in the laws of economic dynamics also led him to analyze the intertemporal structure of production processes.

Frisch's greatest contribution was the development of *econometrics*, which he argued represented the unification of economic theory, mathematics, and statistics. He was one of the founders of the Econometric Society and the first editor of *Econometrica*, the society's journal. His theoretical work in econometrics dealt mostly with linear models, the analysis of multiple-data systems, and estimation when there are several correlated explanatory variables. Frisch's commitment to the belief that economists should not be deterred by the complexity of social problems helped make economics a more rigorous enterprise, while his concern about real world problems encouraged economists to stay engaged with practical realities.

Fromm, Erich (1900–1980) A German psychoanalyst and social theorist, Fromm was a member of the Institute for Social Research (the FRANKFURT SCHOOL) during the 1930s, where he played an important role in the group's effort to integrate PSYCHOANALYSIS and MARXISM. In this capacity, Fromm directed the research and publication of *Studies of Authority and the Family* (1936)—one of the institute's major empirical studies of the relationship between CLASS, social and political views, and the structure of family life. Based on this work, Fromm developed an account of the psychological basis of authoritarianism—which he characterized as anal retentive and sadomasochistic. These views informed his well-known study, *Fear and Freedom* (1941), which argued that social and economic instability had frightened the bourgeoisie and elements of the working class into accepting the reassurances of authoritarianism.

In the course of the 1930s, Fromm became increasingly critical of Freudianism and raised concerns about its historical specificity to turn-of-the-century bourgeois Viennese society. He challenged its libido-centered theory of civilization, which viewed society as the product of repression and sublimation. Fromm progressively discarded Sigmund FREUD's pioneering work in this area, in favor of his own theory of the broad human capacity for harmonious, loving relationships within society. These views put him into conflict with other major Frankfurt theorists, who increasingly relied on Freud's concept of the OEDIPUS COMPLEX and libido theory to ground their accounts of TOTALITARIANISM and theories of revolutionary action. These differences led to Fromm's departure from the institute in 1939.

Although Herbert MARCUSE accused Fromm of an accommodationist view of society, consistent with the therapeutic orientation of American EGO PSYCHOLOGY, Fromm distanced himself from ego psychology and continued to describe his work as both Marxist and fundamentally informed by the problem of ALIENATION. In the course of his prolific career, he turned this sensibility toward a variety of topics, from consumer society to love and personal identity. He achieved best-seller status with *The Art of Loving* (1956) and was the author of, among other works, *The Crisis of Psychoanalysis* (1971) and *The Anatomy of Human Destructiveness* (1974).

frontier thesis Frederick Jackson Turner's 1894 argument that the central determining fact of American national and social development was the continued availability of land in the West. This land, Turner argued, served to absorb successive waves of immigration and acted as a "safety valve" for social discontent. Turner posited a model of progressive settlement and expansion, and he claimed that by his day the frontier was already effectively closed. This interpretation of U.S. history has been criticized from a number of perspectives—most recently, perhaps, by revisionist accounts of the American West that challenge the assumption of steady westward expansion. At the time, however, Turner's thesis crystallized much early thinking about diffusion and settlement, as well as considerable cultural anxiety about urbanization and immigration. See also DIFFUSION AND DIFFUSIONISM.

frustration–aggression hypothesis One of the principle sociopsychological explanations of aggression. The frustration–aggression hypothesis emphasizes how the frustration of goals or productive behavior produces aggression as a response. It contrasts with explanations that postulate an innate aggressiveness that society represses or socializes away. It is also distinct from theories that suggest that aggression is the result of some forms of socialization, as in gangs, armies, or other collectively aggressive groups. The frustration–aggression hypothesis has been widely used in explaining outbreaks of social or collective violence—primarily those rooted in DEPRIVATION and/or forms of social oppression. Both *frustration* and *aggression*, however, remain highly subjective and often culturally specific terms that resist easy comparison from one context to the next.

full-employment budget surplus An economic measure of what a government's budget surplus would be if the economy were at full employment. It is used to determine whether a government's expenditure is increasing (or its tax revenue is decreasing) because of changes in national income. It does not measure changes in the budget surplus due to fiscal policy, however, such as efforts to correct for recession or INFLATION. Compared to an analysis of the budget surplus alone, the full-employment budget surplus offers the advantage of distinguishing the effects of discretionary budgetary policy from the autonomous effects on the budget of variations in economic activity.

function Most generally, the existence of any single variable or phenomenon as a product of its relationship to others. More substantively, the contribution of any social practices or institutions to others with which it is interdependent or in which it plays a part. See also FUNCTIONALISM.

functionalism Functionalism and the closely related term *structural functionalism* form one of the basic orientations to the study of society in twentieth-century SOCIOLOGY and ANTHROPO-LOGY. At its simplest, functionalism asserts that any social practice endures because it performs useful functions. This is true not only of materially beneficial practices—farming, for example—but also, functionalists argue, of symbolic and cultural practices, as well as of the larger organization of society.

Much of the modern sociological and anthropological tradition followed Emile DURKHEIM in positing social integration as the elementary function of cultural practices. Durkheim emphasized that cultural practices and social structure were shaped at their most basic level by the need to reproduce society: reproduction *was* the function of such practices, in the most general sense. Thus, religious rituals might yield no material results, but they play an important part in maintaining community solidarity. Durkheim tended to treat society as an integrated whole, on the analogy of a biological system. In this, he drew on the work of Herbert SPENCER, who had theorized universal tendencies toward the functional differentiation of parts in both biological organisms and societies—the basis of many subsequent arguments about societal evolution and complexity. The key notion was that parts could only be understood in relation to the whole—that is, social analysis had to privilege the ways that parts were connected to one another and the role they played in the life of the whole.

In the 1920s, a strong functionalist orientation developed in British anthropology—again drawing heavily on Durkheim's work. A. R. RAD-CLIFFE-BROWN, Meyer FORTES, E. E. EVANS-PRITCHARD, and Max GLUCKMAN led a generation of fieldwork-driven anthropology—generally operating under the banner of *structural functionalism*—which privileged the analysis of KINSHIP and political structure. In general, this work was conducted in the relatively stable tribal societies of West Africa, and great emphasis was placed on structures of filiation. Critics, including some within this group, noted that stability was sometimes enforced by the colonial powers and that functionalism tended to underemphasize the role of POWER. Although never a unified doctrine, structural functionalism was the theoretical orientation that loosely distinguished British social anthropology from American cultural anthropology.

In sociology, functionalism is associated primarily with the work of Talcott PARSONS, Robert K. MERTON (again under the name of structural functionalism) and their followers. Parsons, in particular, sought to join functional analysis to ACTION THEORY, while retaining a strong emphasis on the integrative function of social systems. He famously identified four functional prerequisites to the survival of any cultural practice or structure: *adaptation, goal attainment, integration,* and *latency* (signifying the tendency toward an equilibrium)—together known as the AGIL model. In contrast, Merton made a concerted effort to develop a more flexible mode of functionalist analysis, arguing that the study of society must accommodate different levels of analysis: the cultural, social, and psychological. Merton distinguished, in particular, between manifest (intentional) and latent (unintentional) functions, and he allowed for practices that were dysfunctional or destructive of social equilibrium.

Strong versions of functionalism have been criticized since the 1960s on a variety of counts, especially for their difficulty (or general lack of interest) in accounting for historical change. Among British social anthropologists, some of this bias was endemic to the subject matter: generally stable societies with intact institutions and other structures of social reproduction. Radcliffe-Brown was probably the most vulnerable in this regard. Nonetheless, many functionalists and structural functionalists recognized the challenge of reconciling relatively horizontal accounts of social structure to the problem of historical change—especially sudden or radical change from inside. In fact, this complementarity had been important in Durkheim's inaugural work. Another criticism of much functionalist research is that it does little to explain the genesis of social differentiation: the function in itself is not a sufficient cause of the phenomenon. Last, but not least, is the recurrent charge of inattention to power.

Through the 1970s and 1980s, these criticisms greatly diminished the status of functionalism in the social sciences. In the 1990s, however, there was a renewal of interest in functionalist approaches on the part of sociologists such as Jeffrey Alexander and Niklas LUHMANN—the latter especially through a return to the work of Parsons. It is worth noting, too, the complex relationship between Marxist and functionalist approaches. Although MARXISM provides a major impetus to the analysis of historical and transformative social change—whence its strong criticisms of the status-quo bias of functionalism—it also tends to treat cultural practices in functional terms, as extensions of the deeper, determining MODE OF PRODUCTION.

Whatever the future of functionalism as an explicit methodology or theoretical school, the idea of *function* remains one of the key concepts and analytic tools of the social sciences.

functional zonation   Refers in urban studies to the pattern of land use in a city, whether with regard to types of economic activity or the geographical segregation of groups along ethnic or class lines. See also URBAN MORPHOLOGY.

fundamentalism   A movement that asserts the primacy of religious values in social and political life and calls for a return to a "fundamental" or pure form of religion. In the Protestant world, and especially the United States in the late nineteenth and early twentieth century, it was associated primarily with religious movements that asserted the literal truth of the Bible (not only against unbelievers but also against "sophisticated" theological interpretation). Since the 1960s, fundamentalism has referred to a network of well-organized American political organizations, such as the Moral Majority and the Christian Coalition, that has exerted a strong conservative influence on the Republican party. In such usage, it is important to keep fundamentalism distinct from *evangelicism*, the commitment to spreading Christian faith and the message of salvation—which is not necessarily tied to biblical literalism, notions of a purer, simpler faith, or to any particular politics.

The term *fundamentalism* has been extended to other religions, as in Hindu fundamentalism or Islamic fundamentalism. In such usage, it remains marked by its origins in Christian Protestant polemics and is limited as an analogy. In the Islamic world, the term fundamentalism has been used to describe clerical and populist reaction against the modernizing, secular, and nationalist movements of the immediate postcolonial period. Whereas reformist leaders since the 1950s have argued that their countries could best recover from Western domination by pursuing state-led development and imitating Western institutions, the fundamentalists have tended to pursue community organization and have called for the imposition of *Shar'ia* (Islamic law), as well as a return to traditional social organization. Especially with the defeat of the Arab coalition by Israel in 1967 and the failures of social and economic development in many Islamic countries, Islamic fundamentalism grew dramatically in the 1970s and 1980s—overthrowing the Westernizing monarchy in Iran in 1979, defeating the Soviet-imposed government of Afghanistan in the 1980s, and seriously threatening the secular governments of Egypt and Algeria.

Many commentators reject the term *Islamic fundamentalism* as pejorative and suggestive of false analogies to Christian fundamentalism. "Islamism" or "Islamicism" are among the suggested alternatives. In India, the resurgence of Hindu religiosity and communalism in the 1980s and 1990s came to be linked both to anti-Muslim violence and to a political program. There, too, the term *fundamentalism* points to some commonalities but little in the way of a strict common definition.

fundamental theorems of welfare   These theorems prove two basic welfare consequences of competitive markets. The first fundamental theorem demonstrates that the market equilibrium of a perfectly competitive world is always PARETO OPTIMAL, meaning that there is no redistribution of resources and goods that could make at least one person in the economy better off without hurting someone else. The second welfare theorem states that *any* Pareto optimal allocation of goods can be achieved at the competitive market equilibrium with the proper distribution of initial endowments. The implication of these theorems is that if markets are functioning competitively, there is no way to improve welfare through intervention without causing some individuals to be worse off. If markets are imperfect, however, because of imperfect information or EXTERNALITIES (such as a polluting byproduct), then there is no guarantee that the market outcome will be welfare-efficient. In such cases, government intervention may be able to achieve a *Pareto-superior* outcome.

futures   Often used interchangeably with the term *forward contracts*, although futures are a modern derivative of the latter. Generally speaking, a forward contract details a transaction in which a good will be delivered at a specific time in the future. Such contracts have been in use since the earliest days of organized trade and commerce. In modern markets, they have a high degree of liquidity and are typically bought and sold many times during the contract's lifetime. Futures have still greater transparency and liquidity compared to most forms of forward contract. They are therefore more effective at reducing risk and collecting and disseminating information. In futures transactions, buyers and sellers normally have no dealings with each other; the contract is guaranteed and executed by a clearing house that collects security deposits from all parties. Futures contracts are of two types: (1) traditional contracts that provide for actual delivery of merchandise or financial instruments like currency; and (2) cash-settlement contracts that are settled by calculating traders' gains and losses from a known price—for instance, an index of equity prices.

G

Galbraith, John Kenneth (1908–) Economist, journalist, adviser to U.S. President John F. Kennedy, and later U.S. Ambassador to India. Galbraith was born in Canada and received his Ph.D. in agricultural economics from the University of California. He spent much of his career as a professor of economics at Harvard University and also served as president of the American Economic Association.

The two books that established his considerable reputation were *The Affluent Society* (1959), which called for a new economics that dealt less with material accumulation and more with the quality of life, and *The New Industrial State* (1962), which questioned prevailing orthodoxies about advanced industrial economies. The positive role of government has been a recurrent theme in Galbraith's writings. *The Affluent Society* argues forcefully that the unregulated market tends to create private affluence and public misery—a splendid private yacht on a polluted public river, in one provocative image. Government must step in to reverse the large-scale irrationality that results from unmitigated self-interest. *The New Industrial State* highlights the strategies that big firms employ in dominating advanced industrial economies, including the "capture" of political favor. Although he argued that modern economies were oligopolistic, Galbraith doubted that this necessarily led to high prices and slow innovation, a common claim against oligopolies and a rationale for government antitrust actions. Instead he saw them as beneficial—if faced with sufficient countervailing power from oligopolistic customers (such as LABOR UNIONS) and government, and if managed by a technostructure concerned with long-term growth. Galbraith argued that the main value added by large dominant firms was their ability to undertake fundamental research and development, without which innovation and associated improvements in the quality of life could not occur.

Galbraith's contribution to economics was to attract attention to the role that government can play in a modern industrial society by empowering the powerless and by balancing the provision of public goods against the excesses of self-interested behavior. He has been prolific on a range of subjects in contemporary politics and economic history. He also played a prominent role in shaping the economic and social policies of the Democratic administrations of the 1960s. Many of Galbraith's views are finding increasing acceptance in mainstream economics, notably in PUBLIC-CHOICE THEORY and in studies of the firm by New Institutionalists (see FIRM, THEORY OF THE). Galbraith's other works include *American Capitalism, the Concept of Countervailing Power* ([1952] 1956), *Money, Whence it Came, Where it Went* (1975), and *The Age of Uncertainty* (1977).

Gallup, George (1901–1984) The inventor of modern political and opinion polling. Gallup was trained in psychology and worked in advertising before founding the American Institute of Public Opinion (1935) and the private firm Gallup and Robinson, which still lends its name to the Gallup polls. The Gallup poll is usually a survey of a random sampling of the public designed to gauge PUBLIC OPINION on issues of public interest.

Gallup's first major electoral survey correctly predicted the 1936 victory of U.S. President Franklin Delano Roosevelt. Electoral polling has since become a ubiquitous part of democratic political processes worldwide, and Gallup's methods arguably provide the dominant means of representing the modern public. Gallup's signal contribution to the social sciences was to prove the value of (and establish a methodology for) random sampling. His writing includes *The Pulse of Democracy* (1940).

game theory Investigates the strategic behavior of decision makers who are aware that their decisions affect one another. While any social and/or economic interaction may be termed a game (with rules and a finite group of players), game theory is distinguished by its analysis of the rationality and strategic behavior of the players—especially the rationality of beliefs about what other players will do. The abstract nature of game theory makes it testable under controlled or laboratory conditions, which has fostered the field of EXPERIMENTAL ECONOMICS. The real-world application of strategic analysis has also had a profound impact on the social sciences. Game theory underlies a wide-ranging body of work on cartel behavior, conflict resolution, the management of public resources, and COLLECTIVE BARGAINING, among other topics.

John von NEUMANN and Oskar Morgenstern's *The Theory of Games and Economic Behavior* (1947) is generally considered the foundational text of game theory. However, a number of game theory's main ideas and principles were anticipated by economists such as Augustin COURNOT and Francis EDGEWORTH in the nineteenth century, and by mathematicians such as Émile Borel and Ernst Zermelo in the early twentieth century. The earliest theorem of game theory is named after Zermelo and asserts that in a game of chess with perfect players, depending on the initial conditions, there are three possible outcomes: either white wins, black wins, or the players draw. In this respect, Zermelo argued, chess is strictly determined. The proof does not provide "correct" strategies of play, nor is it known which of the above three is the unique "correct" outcome. The theorem applies, rather, to two-person, ZERO-SUM GAMES conducted under conditions of "perfect information," including chess, checkers, go, and Chinese checkers. In all such games, one player's victory is the other player's loss. This is the *zero-sum* condition, which can also represent situations in which the prize is limited but divisible in greater or lesser portions. Perfect information refers to the fact that all relevant information, including payoffs and the possible strategies of all players, is known to all players. Zermelo's theorem does not extend to games such as poker, bridge, and kriegsspiel, where important information is not shared.

Von Neumann and Morgenstern investigated two distinct approaches to game theory. The first is the strategic, or noncooperative, approach, which generally disallows coordination among individuals, except when it is in each of their own interests. The second is the coalitional, or cooperative, approach (see COOPERATIVE GAMES), which sets asides issues of credible commitments among individuals in favor of examining the possibilities for agreement and the division of available payoffs among members of coalitions, based on individual and group contributions to the pie.

The noncooperative approach emphasizes the individual player and concentrates on searching for strategies that are *optimal* for each player. Many of these are *nonzero-sum games*, in which agreement among players offers the opportunity to enlarge the total prize. Two widely used types of games are the PRISONER'S DILEMMA and the *Battle of the Sexes*, so named for their well-known illustrations. The first case presents two prisoners with incentives to turn evidence against each other. The pursuit of strictly individual maximizing strategies will produce a *pareto-inferior* outcome (see PARETO OPTIMAL). If each remains silent, each will serve minimal time; if each implicates the other, both serve a longer sentence. If one turns evidence and the other remains silent, the former goes free, while the latter serves a long sentence. Strategically, *regardless* of the actions of the other prisoner, the best choice dictates turning evidence. However, when both prisoners confess, the outcome is worse for both of them than if they had each kept quiet. The classic Prisoner's Dilemma game and its multiplayer extension, the *Tragedy of the Commons*, are widely used by economists and sociologists in the study of collective action problems and the question of ALTRUISM.

The Battle of the Sexes game—coined in a less politically correct era—is an *asymmetrical coordination game*. Both players do better to agree on a common strategy, but they disagree over the best strategy to play. The classic example is of a man and woman who must agree on an evening's entertainment. Each prefers to be with the other rather than remain alone, but the woman receives a higher payoff from the theater, while her male companion prefers a football game. There are thus two outcomes with high payoffs, but each involves a suboptimum outcome for one of the players. Symmetric coordination games, in contrast, involve no such trade-off. Selecting a side of the road on which to drive is an example. Presumably no one cares if we all drive on the left or all drive on the right, but clearly the payoffs are higher for all if we can agree on a common strategy.

Garfinkel, Harold (1917–) An American sociologist who pioneered the field of ETHNO-METHODOLOGY in the 1960s, and thereby launched a major debate about the nature and validity of sociological methods. Ethnomethodology literally signifies "the study of people's methods," by which Garfinkel meant the implicit, taken-for-granted rules and forms of knowledge that structure and give order to people's everyday interactions. In *Studies in Ethnomethodology* (1967) and other writing, Garfinkel developed a broad critique of conventional sociology, which, he argued, generally ignored people's own understandings of the social order in favor of the abstracted conceptual schemata to of sociologists. In this context, ethnomethodology emphasizes the processes by which individuals interpret and thereby constitute their social realities—primarily through conversation and direct interactions. Garfinkel called this process *reflexivity*. He placed considerable emphasis on the ground rules that structure conversations in a variety of contexts: the diverse signs of assent or interest that maintain a conversational flow, or the habit of speaking in turn. Many of these issues were explored in detail by Garfinkel's colleague Harvey Sachs under the rubric of CONVERSATION ANALYSIS.

Without these tacit rules, conversations and other aspects of underlying social consensus break down. Garfinkel tested these limits in a series of *breeching experiments* that examined reactions when common social understandings, such as the norms governing child–parent relations, were deliberately thwarted. In general, Garfinkel found that social order is dependent upon a high degree of INDEXICALITY—the ability of persons to furnish a commonly understood context for statements or actions. Without this arbitrary halt to the problem of interpretation, language reveals its infinitely relative character—concepts are defined in terms of other concepts.

Studies in Ethnomethodology was controversial and provoked a number of strong critical responses, in no small part from sociologists who regarded the idea of an externally existing social structure as necessary to analyzing any substantive social or political issue. The minimal consensual rules underlying conversations, by comparison, seemed relatively distant from questions regarding larger-scale social phenomena. In recent decades, however, this debate has faded. Many of the central concerns of ethnomethodology have shaped more general developments in sociological theory, notably in the work of Anthony GIDDENS and Pierre BOURDIEU. Sociologists now regularly investigate questions of interpretation, the nature of meaning, and the status of sociological knowledge. Garfinkel

continued to explore forms of basic interaction and elaborate ethnomethodological methods in his later writing, including *Ethnomethodological Studies of Work* (1986).

gatekeeper In sociological terms, an individual who occupies a position that allows him or her to control access to goods, information, and services. Such power often extends well beyond the formal authority of the gatekeeper's official position. Gatekeepers are common in bureaucratic settings and other hierarchical organizations.

gaze A central concept in Jacques LACAN's psychoanalytic theory that has proved useful to a number of projects in cultural and feminist studies. The principle quality of the gaze, for Lacan, is its "desubjectifying" effect. It is not a look that recognizes another person as a subject—but a look through the person that calls into question the recognition of his or her own subjectivity. Lacan explored the diverse sexual and social connotations of the concept—theorizing in particular the way in which society (for Lacan, the collective "Other") is invested with the sexualized, generically male gaze. This dimension of his work was adopted in a number of early feminist theories—notably the feminist film theory of Laura Mulvey ("Visual Pleasure and Narrative Cinema," 1975).

GDP Gross Domestic Product. See NATIONAL INCOME.

Geertz, Clifford (1926–) One of the most influential contemporary American anthropologists and a leading proponent of SYMBOLIC ANTHROPOLOGY—the study of individual cultures as unique and autonomous "systems of meanings." This approach is similar to Claude LÉVI-STRAUSS's linguistic STRUCTURALISM, but without its universalistic claims. Rather, Geertz emphasizes the particularity of cultures and concludes that the best that anthropology can achieve is the imaginative translation of one culture's "system of meanings" into a different cultural idiom—not the strict codification of CULTURE into rules or patterns. Geertz's notion of system was influenced by the functional theories of Talcott PARSONS, but he moved gradually away from assumptions of functional coherence and beneficence. He produced major comparative work but is better known for promoting a turn to internal cultural interpretation. He did his best to set the example for such interpretation in his own ethnographic work—especially through a number of highly influential essays published as his methodology coalesced in the late 1960s. This methodology involved a literary and openly subjective style of ethnographic writing that placed the burden of interpretation squarely on the anthropologist. His interpretive style, which he called "thick description," has been a source of considerable controversy within ANTHROPOLOGY and has had a broad impact on areas of literary criticism and history where the relation of author to object is a subject of contention.

Geertz's fieldwork in Java, Morocco, and Bali resulted in a number of important ethnographies published in the 1960s and 1970s, including *The Religion of Java* (1960), *Agricultural Involution* (1963), and *Islam Observed* (1968). The most significant theoretical statements of his position, however, can be found in two volumes of collected essays, *The Interpretation of Cultures* (1973) and *Local Knowledge* (1983). His more recent works include *Work and Lives: The Anthropologist as Author* (1988) and *After the Fact* (1995).

Geisteswissenschaften and Naturwissenschaften German terms designating the human, or social, sciences and the natural sciences, respectively. The terms played a central role in the METHODENSTREIT, a late nineteenth-century debate about the distinction between the two subjects of inquiry and their proper methodologies.

Gellner, Ernest André (1925–1995) A scholar of great breadth who passed easily between ANTHROPOLOGY, philosophy, and POLITICAL SCIENCE, Gellner's work is unified primarily by a persistent concern for EPISTEMOLOGY and a strong historical sensibility. His early critique of analytical philosophy in *Words and Things* (1959) established both of these preoccupations, locating the universalizing claims of analytical philosophy within the historical and social context of its production and opening the way toward the broadly comparative and often sweeping historical analyses that characterized his later work on MODERNITY, NATIONALISM, and Islamic society. Turning to fieldwork in the 1960s, Gellner wrote *Saints of the Atlas* (1969), a study of the Berber peoples of Morocco, and subsequently three broader works on Islamic society that attracted considerable attention: *Arabs and Berbers*

(1973), *Patrons and Saints* (1977), and *Muslim Society* (1981).

Gellner was also an influential theorist of modernization and nationalism. He contended that nationalism was not primordial but closely tied to industrialization and the development of modern states. *Nations and Nationalism* (1983) is the most influential of his many writings on the subject. He also worked to develop contacts and intellectual exchanges with social scientists in the Eastern Bloc countries and the Soviet Union. This included the sponsorship of Soviet anthropology in the West and later close attention to the transition from communism in the late 1980s. This transition became the subject of his last book, *Conditions of Liberty* (1994). In the early 1990s, he headed the new Central European University in Prague, returning to his native Czech homeland after a career spent mostly in Britain.

Gemeinschaft and Gesellschaft An influential sociological distinction between traditional forms of "community" (*Gemeinschaft*) and more modern and impersonal form of "society" (*Gesellschaft*, sometimes translated as "association"). The distinction was developed by the German sociologist Ferdinand TÖNNIES in 1887 and was one of a number of influential turn-of-the-century attempts to theorize the specificity of the modern. For Tönnies, *Gemeinschaft* is defined by common values, aspirations, and roles—and sometimes common ancestry. Individuals are embedded in and supported by a strong social network of friends and relatives, with whom they build close emotional ties through face-to-face interactions; status is usually ascribed at birth, geographic mobility is often limited, and individuals associate their identity with their place within the community. *Gesellschaft*, in contrast, reflects the turn to urban, industrial styles of life and to the patterns of calculated, rationalized behavior that increasingly underlie daily activity; relationships between individuals tend to be more superficial, impersonal, and anonymous—reflecting the diminished role of shared values, backgrounds, norms, and attitudes. Nor do work roles provide a common ground, since urbanization calls for greater specialization and increased mobility. Individual experience in modern societies, Tönnies argued, tends to be much more fragmented and compartmentalized.

The attempt to define and explain the transition from the traditional to the modern was one of the founding projects of modern SOCIOLOGY. As with many typologies of this kind, however, few if any societies exhibit their qualities in pure form. They are better conceived of—following Max WEBER—as IDEAL TYPES, bundles of associated characteristics that may admit of more or less correspondence and admixture in different societies. See also COMMUNITY; MODERNITY; and TRADITION.

gender The culturally constructed forms of behavior that roughly correlate with sexual difference. Traditionally, differences in behavior and roles have been assumed to "naturally" reflect sexual difference. Modern social science, however, has become careful to distinguish between *gender* and *sex*; it has generally laid the burden of explaining behavior, practices, roles, and social organization on the former.

In most societies, gender difference is accompanied by gender inequality—almost always the subordination of women. This is perhaps the major axis of gender research, and it has led to a wide range of speculations about the relationship of sex and reproduction to other social domains, such as economic production, warfare, distinctions between nature and culture, the differentiation of public and private spheres, and a range of other forms of social organization that produce or materialize conditions of gender inequality. As the question of gender attracted growing interest in the 1960s and 1970s, the preponderance of research showed a remarkable variety of gender roles in different cultures. This diversity has raised serious obstacles to formulating a single satisfactory account of gender formation. Other work (notably that of Michel FOUCAULT) has demonstrated the historical contingency of what counts as sexual difference and has investigated the process through which sex became a distinct and independent object of study in the nineteenth century. Such work has problematized the distinction between sex and gender but has hardly dispensed with it, and questions of gender roles, gender inequality, and gendered institutions remains firmly entrenched in the agenda of the social sciences. See also FEMININITY; FEMINISM; and MASCULINITY.

general equilibrium See EQUILIBRIUM.

generalized other In George Herbert MEAD's theory of the development of the self, the generalized other represents the organized attitudes of the community that children extrapolate from their experience and role-playing of specific others, such as parents and other authority figures. By taking on the role of the generalized other, children learn to think about what people in general will think about their actions. For Mead, human behavior is thus always under a certain internalized supervision, regardless of the presence or absence of specific others.

general will Jean-Jacques ROUSSEAU's term for the expression of a community's essential common interests and values. Rousseau's work is pivotal to a long tradition of inquiry into how the opinions of individuals can be aggregated and how legitimate, collective decision making can be achieved. In this, he distinguished between the aggregation of individual opinions or interests ("the will of all") and the *general will*, which he argued was unitary in nature. He held that the general will not only transcended the differences of individuals and expressed what was best for the community but was also what revealed it as a community. Like PLATO and a number of other classical thinkers, he sought to specify how the true and false forms of collective will might be distinguished. Unlike Plato, he discounted the role of political discourse in forming this will, holding instead that the general will could be grasped through direct insight.

According to Rousseau, few people were enlightened enough to recognize the general will, partly because of the inequality and differentiation introduced by social development. This raises a number of well-known difficulties in Rousseau's work: in order to lead the people to recognize the general will, Rousseau posited the need for an enlightened lawgiver—a legislator—who would play a founding role in creating national institutions. Thus, while the people were sovereign, this sovereignty was necessarily exercised, at least transitionally, by an individual who grasped their needs at a higher level than the play of interests normally permitted. For Rousseau, acting in accordance with the general will was the only criterion of political legitimacy. While this elevated the concept of the sovereignty of the people, it counterposed a notion of transcendent higher truth to majority votes and other practical procedures of democratic political life.

This becomes clearer in Rousseau's assertion that a government might be right in disregarding a community's apparent or even majority interest, if by doing so it served the true interests of the people. Under these circumstances, individuals or groups might be "forced to be free"—a formulation that found violent application in Robespierre's dictatorship of virtue during the French Revolution and, later, as some commentators have suggested, in twentieth-century TOTALITARIANISM.

In addressing the distinction between the particular and general will, Rousseau also inaugurated an important philosophical conversation on the nature of FREEDOM—understood here (and in related accounts by Immanuel KANT and Georg HEGEL) as an escape from subjection to individual desire into a rational and universal law of one's own making (either individually or as a member of a community). Jürgen HABERMAS's theory of the public sphere attempted to reconcile Rousseau's notion of the general will with the classical emphasis on dialogue; it suggested a procedure whereby individuals might overcome their focus on mere interests through a rational-critical discourse that could identify truth with the standpoint of the whole (see PUBLIC SPHERE AND PRIVATE SPHERE). Rousseau's contrast between the general will and the distorted collective opinions of actually existing societies also helped shape the distinction of *community* from SOCIETY, in which the former represented natural ties and/or true legitimacy, and the latter, artificial and unequal social arrangements (see *GEMEINSCHAFT* AND *GESELLSCHAFT*). Emile DURKHEIM's concept of society as a whole greater than the sum of its parts owes a clear debt to Rousseau, as does modern NATIONALISM more generally, which draws on Rousseau's vision of an unmediated relationship between the individual and the nation.

genitor and genetrix The *genitor* is the biological father of a child, as distinct from the socially recognized father, or *pater*. *Genetrix* is the analogous term for the biological mother.

Gennep, Arnold van (1873–1957) Born in Germany and educated in France, van Gennep was an anthropologist and folklorist with a strong interest in LINGUISTICS and comparative religion. His early work focused on totems, taboos, rituals, and myths as systems of classification and mechanisms of social integration. This work developed ideas closely related to the FUNCTIONALISM of Emile DURKHEIM but included a number of strong criticisms of Durkheim's scholarly practices and methods that assured him the hostility of the then-dominant Durkheimian school. Abandoning this uphill battle, van Gennep pursued a living as a translator and turned toward the study of folklore in rural France—a subject scarcely

touched by French social science. The publication of seven volumes of collected folklore and then his nine-volume *Manuel de folklore français contemporain* (1943–1958) brought him considerable public recognition and, for the first time, scholarly appreciation of his careful integration of folklore and ETHNOGRAPHY. Outside France, he achieved posthumous fame with the 1960 translation into English of his early *Rites of Passage* (1909). The concept of *liminality* developed in this work—signifying a temporary reversal of or expulsion from the social order during ritual practices—had a major influence on a new generation of anthropological studies of ritual, especially those of Mary DOUGLAS and Victor TURNER.

genocide The attempt to destroy a population on the basis of racial, religious, ethnic, ideological, or cultural criteria. First used by the U.S. jurist Raphael Lemkin in 1944, the concept was central to the prosecution of Nazi leaders during the Nuremberg trials that followed World War II. It was later incorporated into a United Nations resolution (1946) and convention (1948) that made genocide a crime under INTERNATIONAL LAW. The term has been applied to a variety of instances of systematic massacre, including the ancient practice of murdering entire enemy populations, the decimation of populations that accompanied certain phases of European imperialism (see IMPERIALISM AND EMPIRE), mass killing as an instrument of state building (notoriously, the Turkish massacre of 1.5 million Armenians, 1915–1922), and coordinated "ethnic cleansing" in Rwanda and the former Yugoslavia (1990s).

genotype The genetic potential of an organism which, in combination with environmental factors, produces the *phenotype*, or actual living example.

gens Lewis Henry MORGAN (1877) distinguished between matrilineal CLANS and patrilineal *gens* in describing early societies, but the terminological distinction is no longer widely used.

gentrification A process of neighborhood change that involves the influx of middle-class and upper-class residents into poor neighborhoods, with the accompanying renovation of the housing stock. Gentrification is associated with the revitalization of urban centers, many of which suffered long-term economic decline in the context of suburbanization and other demographic shifts, beginning in the 1950s. In the United States, gentrification often has racial overtones insofar as the central-city neighborhoods most often involved are generally home to minority populations. As prices rise, low-income groups may be forced to relocate.

gentry See ARISTOCRACY.

geography Has roots in the age-old human interest in other places, most often expressed since the Classical period in travel narratives. The emergence of geography as a physical and social science, however, is generally traced to the early nineteenth century. *Physical geography* is largely the achievement of the German naturalist and explorer Alexander von HUMBOLDT. Humboldt produced not only vivid, highly detailed descriptions of the natural environments he explored in Latin America, but he also pioneered a strong scientific approach to the causes of natural phenomena. In the same period, another German, Carl RITTER, began to articulate a different set of goals for geography organized around the study of the human interaction with nature and of differences in the uses of space. In so doing, Ritter outlined the major concerns of what would be called *human geography*, setting it the task of spatially analyzing human activity and its effects on the land.

Much of the German human geography of the nineteenth century was predicated on the notion of ENVIRONMENTAL DETERMINISM, which held that human choices about land use were directly related to spatial and environmental factors. Chief among these factors was distance, which soon occupied a central place in accounts of land use and economic development. Another salient development in the field was the integration of geography into geopolitical and imperial planning. Particularly in the late nineteenth and early twentieth centuries, geography played an important role in debates about the integrality and viability of nation-states (visible in the vast production of research on the question of borders) and in the area of strategic policy—most notably Halford J. MACKINDER's HEARTLAND THEORY, which postulated an ostensibly natural opposition between the interior, *heartland* powers of eastern Europe and Asia and the *rimland* nations that relied on naval power, namely Britain.

Environmental determinism came under attack on a range of fronts in the 1920s and 1930s—in France through the influence of Paul VIDAL DE LA BLACHE, whose concept of POSSIBILISM cautioned that there was more than one possible response to given environmental conditions; and in the United States through the work of Carl SAUER and the Berkeley school of cultural geography, which he founded and led. Sauer advocated a predominantly qualitative approach to the question of human interaction with the environment, centered around the concept of the cultural LANDSCAPE. In broader terms, the culturalist and possibilist orientations emphasized the analysis of "place" over the study of "space," or spatial relationships, and privileged the question of differences in cultural relationships to the environment—an issue that became known as ENVIRONMENTAL PERCEPTION. Other major preoccupations of cultural geography have included human migration, the diffusion of ideas and techniques, and processes of adaptation to social and environmental change (see DIFFUSION AND DIFFUSIONISM).

In the 1950s and 1960s, a new generation of quantitative researchers revived and elaborated the tradition of spatial analysis; Torsten Hägerstrand was prominent among this group. This work found numerous applications in economic geography—the spatial analysis of economic activity. It also created a rather sharp disciplinary divide between cultural geographers and spatial/quantitative geographers—a struggle that quantitative geography ultimately dominated in the 1970s. The 1970s, however, was also a period of rapid assimilation of new or newly appreciated theoretical perspectives in the social sciences. David HARVEY led the way in bringing Marxist accounts of historical development to the fore of spatial analysis—particularly concerning the question of *uneven development*. He also advocated the integrated cultural, political, and economic study of the use of space—again with a Marxist emphasis on the priority of changes in the economic base. The 1980s saw a renewed interest in cultural geography—largely prompted by theoretical challenges to the positivism underlying research into laws of spatial distribution and aided by the growth of CULTURAL STUDIES and the prevalence of methods of textual and discursive analysis. See also BEHAVIORAL GEOGRAPHY; and CULTURAL GEOGRAPHY.

geopolitics A theory and school of INTERNATIONAL RELATIONS that treats global politics primarily in terms of the competition between states. Developed in the late nineteenth century by Friedrich RATZEL and other German political geographers, early geopolitical theory tended to present the STATE as a natural organism that grew or died in Darwinian struggle with other states. In the formulation of foreign policy, it called for close attention to matters such as climate, population, and natural resources. British versions of geopolitical theory, such as Halford J. MACKINDER's influential HEARTLAND THEORY, continued this tradition. Especially in Germany, geopolitics was associated with expansionism and ultimately served as a justification for the two twentieth-century German war efforts. Although discredited in this form, it continued to inform the global military strategy of the SUPERPOWERS during the COLD WAR. The term still refers to approaches to international relations that privilege the global struggle between states.

gerontocracy   A form of government or rule in which power is held by the oldest members of society. The term came into use in the context of anthropological research on sub-Saharan tribal societies, where age and status were closely related. It has also been widely used in East Asia.

gerontology   The study of aging and the elderly. Social research into the problems and needs specific to the elderly emerged in the 1960s in the context of policy studies—especially of welfare and health services disproportionately used by the elderly. Gerontology is becoming an increasingly significant field of study as many industrialized countries—especially in Europe—confront declining birth rates, longer life spans, and the consequent rising numbers of elderly citizens as a percentage of total population. This demographic shift has serious implications for the future provisioning, prioritization, and funding of social services.

Gerth, Hans   (1908–1978) A German expatriate sociologist who played a major role in the dissemination and interpretation of Max WEBER's work in the United States. Gerth also made significant contributions to the field of SOCIAL PSYCHOLOGY and was instrumental in the emergence of community studies—a field shaped by several of his graduate students, including Joseph Bensman and Arthur Vidich. Most prominent, perhaps, were his collaborations with C. Wright MILLS. Together, they translated and edited *From Max Weber* (1946), which opened the way to the translation of most of Weber's major works into English in the late 1940s. Gerth translated several other books by Weber, including *Religion of China: Confucianism and Taoism* (1951), *Ancient Judaism*

(with Don Martindale, 1952), and *The Religion of India: Buddhism and Hinduism* (with Martindale, 1958).

As a social psychologist, Gerth opposed BEHAVIORISM—the dominant paradigm of his time—and instead sought to bridge the gap between the sociological notion of SOCIALIZATION and the psychological emphasis on the development of personality. He contended that the modern individual is subject to a complex process of socialization that includes the internalization of mechanisms for social control. He argued further that "master trends" generated at the societal level shape psychological development; these include a number of macro-level tendencies such as bureaucratization and the polarization of international politics. Collectively, he argued, these shape the social roles occupied by individuals and thereby directly affect individual psychology. These ideas were developed primarily in *Character and Social Structure* (1962, with Mills).

Gerth fled Germany in 1938 and subsequently taught at a number of American universities—longest at the University of Wisconsin. He returned to Germany in 1971. His other important works include "The Nazi Party: Its Leadership and Composition" (*American Journal of Sociology*, 1940) and "A Marx for Managers" (*Ethics*, 1942, with Mills).

Gesellschaft   See GEMEINSCHAFT AND GESELLSCHAFT.

Gestalt theory   A psychological theory of perception and social understanding that emphasizes the degree to which individuals understand phenomena as wholes, greater than the sum of their individual parts. Gestalt theory posits that coherent psychological patterns of perception and understanding shape our knowledge of social interactions and social processes. It emerged in early twentieth-century psychology in opposition to empirical accounts of the "given-ness" of reality and to the particularism that underlies attempts to understand social phenomena in isolation. Gestalt theory shares much with PHENOMENOLOGY and phenomenological approaches to SOCIOLOGY. It also informed interdisciplinary movements such as Culture and Personality, which analyzed cultural difference in terms of differences in cognitive and psychological development (see CULTURE AND PERSONALITY MOVEMENT).

ghetto   Distinguished from other kinds of ethnic neighborhoods by the role that discrimination plays in their formation—the original was the mandated Jewish quarter of Venice in the 1600s. Today, residents of a ghetto may have diverse reasons for living there, but the overriding reason is the lack of alternatives. Discriminatory pressures have subsided for many ethnic groups—southern and eastern Europeans in American cities are prominent examples. What were once characterized as Irish or Italian ghettos are more accurately described today as ethnic neighborhoods. Ghettos are at the center of a range of debates about historical and contemporary patterns of economic development and the reproduction of POVERTY.

Gibrat's law   States that regardless of the size and past growth of a firm, the probability of a given proportional change in its size is the same as that for all firms in its sector. Thus, small firms are at no disadvantage for growth, and all are equally likely to double in size during a given period. This generalization describes the most typically observed size distribution of firms in the real world and, hence, serves as a useful first approximation. It is often used to predict the "natural" state of an industry, without factors such as monopolistic concentration or antitrust behavior.

Giddens, Anthony   (1938–) A British sociologist whose STRUCTURATION theory is one of the major contemporary approaches to overcoming the analytical divide between SOCIAL STRUCTURE and AGENCY. Giddens is also a prominent public intellectual in Britain, director of the London School of Economics, and a cofounder of the Polity Press. In the early part of his career, he owed his reputation to a number of strong exegetical readings of classic social theory, including *Capitalism and Modern Social Theory* (1971), *Politics and Sociology in the Thought of Max Weber* (1972), and *Emile Durkheim* (1978).

Giddens's theory of structuration emerged in the course of a number of works of the late 1970s and early 1980s, including the essays collected in *New Rules of Sociological Method* (1976) and *Central Problems in Social Theory* (1979). It was summarized more systematically in *The Constitution of Society* (1984). Structuration theory steps back from the long debate within the social sciences over the relative priority accorded social structure and individual agency. Rather than choose sides, Giddens argues that structures and agency cannot be conceived of apart from one another. Structures are neither independent of actors nor determining of their behavior. Rather, they are a set rules and competencies on which actors draw and which, in the aggregate, they tend to reproduce over time. Put differently, social structures are not simply "facts" that constrain human action; they exist only insofar as they are recognized by agents. Giddens also drew attention to what he described as the dialectical relationship between sociological theories and the everyday interpretations of actors—a situation he described as the necessary "double-hermeneutic" of social research.

Giddens acknowledges the importance of historical change and the difficulty of integrating it into an account that seems to accord individuals only a margin of improvisation within a relatively stable set of rules. Although some recent works (*The Nation-State and Violence*, 1985; *Modernity and Self Identity*, 1991; *The Transformation of Intimacy*, 1992) contain many elements of a historical sociology, a full account of how societies change remains elusive in his writing, and structuration continues to produce skeptics on this point. Giddens has also emerged as a strong critic of POSTMODERNISM, arguing that the present is best understood as a continuation of the longer-term trajectories of modernization and GLOBALIZATION. His other works include *The Consequences of Modernity* (1990) and *The Third Way and Its Critics* (1998), the latter of which outlines an ostensibly new accommodation of global capitalism and the social-welfare functions of the state.

Giffen goods   Also Giffen's paradox. Giffen goods are goods for which the demand rises as the price rises, thereby inverting the usual negative relationship between price and demand. The existence of such goods was postulated by the economist Robert Giffin, who observed that, under some circumstances, the poor consume more bread as its price rises. Such change reflects two interacting effects of a price rise. First, as the price of a good rises, the consumer's purchasing power declines; for *inferior goods*, this income effect is positive—the consumer will tend to consume more of the good because superior alternatives are less affordable. Second, when the price rises relative to other goods, the substitution effect shifts demand toward relatively cheaper alternatives. These two forces act in opposite directions, making the change in demand theoretically ambiguous. In most circumstances, the substitution effect would be expected to predominate, so that a price increase results in a reduction in quantity purchased. But in circumstances where one inferior good makes up a very large share of the budget (e.g., bread for the poor), consumption of the good may increase due to a price increase.

Although potatoes during the Irish potato famine are a commonly cited example of a Giffen good, there is debate about whether they actually exhibited upward-sloping demand—and more generally whether Giffen goods exist at all.

gift-exchange   See EXCHANGE.

Gini coefficient   A measure of the inequality of income among households. The Gini coefficient can vary between zero and one. It is derived from the LORENZ CURVE, which graphs the percentage share of income against the percentage share of the population (i.e., the bottom 20 percent of households may receive only 5 percent of all income). The Gini coefficient is the ratio of the area above the Lorenz curve (and below the 45-degree line) to the total area below the 45-degree line. The graph below is labeled such that the Gini coefficient equals A/(A + B). Thus a Gini coefficient of 1 indicates that all of the wealth is held by a single household, while a coefficient of 0 indicates perfect equality.

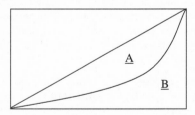

glass ceiling   An unofficial and metaphorically invisible barrier to women's advancement at the highest levels of many career paths. The glass ceiling is one aspect of widespread gender bias in employment. Although the percentage of women in high-level management positions has slowly risen since the early 1980s—the moment when discussion of the glass ceiling became widespread—their representation in the upper ranks of many careers remains in the single digits.

globalization   A catch-all term for the expansion of diverse forms of economic, political, and cultural activity beyond national borders. At the economic level, globalization involves the emergence of a complex system of multinational

CAPITALISM, in which corporations conduct business and locate production at locations worldwide. This includes the development of a system of international finance capable of rapidly shifting large amounts of investment capital from one place to another, as economic or political conditions dictate. Such conditions have produced rapid growth in some parts of the world, as well as new forms of economic dislocation and inequality as businesses relocate to exploit lower labor or regulatory costs. The fluidity of capital movement has also proved highly unstable and subject to speculative, contagious booms and busts. These features are of great interest to economists and specialists in INTERNATIONAL RELATIONS—particularly as institutional structures emerge that can conduct economic and development policy on an international level.

Economic globalization is closely tied to political developments that are intended to facilitate and control international trade. The emergence of the International Monetary Fund as a regulator of international economic stability and the creation of a World Trade Organization with sovereign authority over trade disputes among its members are prominent examples. There are other spaces of international cooperation and governance, however, that suggest the potential of civil society across national borders. These include the formulation of internationally applicable norms of JUSTICE, multinational participation in large-scale police and humanitarian actions, and the collective management of immigration and refugee issues.

Globalization also has a cultural dimension, as international capitalism homogenizes consumer goods and services. The term MCDONALDIZATION is sometimes used to describe this process (notably by George Ritzer). Equally important in this context is the ongoing communications revolution, as the Internet, phone services, and other means of international communication become ubiquitous and affordable—at least for those who are privileged enough to participate in the global economy. This raises a last dimension of globalization that touches simultaneously on cultural, economic, and political issues: the emergence of an international capitalist class whose culture, economic interests, and political allegiances are broadly defined by loyalty to and dependence on the system (see COMPRADOR).

To date, capitalist globalization has produced a strong geographical division of labor that separates the powerful core industrial nations (the United States, most of Western Europe, and Japan) from semiperipheral and peripheral nations. *Semiperipheral nations* include newly industrializing countries, such as Mexico and Malaysia. *Peripheral nations* are those that primarily supply raw materials to the industrial nations, on terms largely determined by the multinational companies and their national proxies. WORLD-SYSTEMS THEORY and MODERNIZATION THEORY provide divergent accounts of this process of uneven development and the difficulties such countries face.

Despite a number of broad and informative approaches, the problem of developing valid qualitative and quantitative models for the study of different aspects of globalization presents a tremendous challenge for the social sciences. Comparative accounts of many aspects of social and political life, such as the quality of life or degree of political democracy, have proved problematic and frequently normative in character. Common economic measures, such as gross national product (GNP) or per capita income, are often of little value in countries with large, subsistence-level populations.

Although many theories of globalization present it as a nearly inevitable process, the nature of that process may be more open to change than is sometimes assumed. There are many forms of resistance to the currently dominant model of capitalist globalization. There are also alternative visions of what globalization might entail, including the reinvigoration of smaller cultural, religious, or national identities (FUNDAMENTALISMS have played a significant role in this respect); the mobilization of the NATION-STATE in defense of old or new prerogatives; INTERNATIONAL ORGANIZATIONS that promote alternative visions of the global future; and SOCIAL MOVEMENTS that utilize new communications technologies to mobilize individuals and groups across national boundaries.

glottochronology   See LEXICOSTATISTICS.

Gluckman, Max   (1911–1975) A South African anthropologist who became director of the Rhodes–Livingston Institute in Rhodesia and later the leading figure of the Manchester school of ANTHROPOLOGY in postwar Great Britain. At the University of Manchester in the 1950s and 1960s, Gluckman gathered together a group of anthropologists (including Victor TURNER and J. C. Mitchell) who shared an interest in reconciling the claims of SOCIAL STRUCTURE with the problems of individual psychology and social change. Collectively, their work reexamined, challenged, and in certain respects extended the structural-functionalist approach that dominated postwar British social anthropology. Among the most important developments were pioneering studies of process (complementing structural analysis) and of social networks.

Like most of the Manchester group, Gluckman's fieldwork focused on central and southern Africa. In the course of several studies of the Bantu and Zulu, Gluckman developed innovative analyses of land tenure, ritual, and legal processes. His studies of Barotse law were particularly influential in revealing the complexity, flexibility, and capacity for sophistication in "customary" law. Writing about the concept of the *reasonable man* in Barotse jurisprudence, for example, he showed the centrality of a concept shared with much modern Western law.

In methodological terms, Gluckman made a concerted effort to expand the functionalist model of social structure to better account for conflict (see FUNCTIONALISM). On the one hand, he argued that conflict often provides a release for tensions in ways that reinforce the existing social structure. On the other hand, he recognized that conflict often was not contained and that, under those circumstances, it led to social change. The relationship between social reproduction and change was the subject of many of Gluckman's analyses, as was differentiating this dynamic from the effects of COLONIALISM and external pressure. His major works include *Custom and Conflict in Africa* (1955), *Order and Rebellion in Tribal Africa* (1963), and *Politics, Law and Ritual in Tribal Society* (1965).

GNP   (Gross National Product). See NATIONAL INCOME.

Goffman, Erving   (1922–1982) An American sociologist who specialized in the analysis of everyday behavior, symbolism, and interactions. Drawing on an analytical tradition as old as Shakespeare, Goffman developed a DRAMATURGICAL APPROACH to social relations, using stage metaphors to illustrate the roles people play when interacting in various settings and conditions. For Goffman, many types of interaction are structured by scripts that outline, in basic terms, which roles are available and what is generally supposed to occur. Unlike the theater, however, individuals in real life negotiate among themselves to determine who will play which role and exactly how events will transpire. Individuals must also work to convince others that their roles are genuine. By monitoring the effects of their roles on others, individuals engage in what Goffman called *impression management*. He laid the groundwork for this approach in *The Presentation of Self in Everyday Life* (1959)—building on the study of a sharecropping community in the Shetland Islands of Scotland. His work contributed profoundly to ROLE theory and, also, to the analysis of strategy—conscious or unconscious—in the construction of self and social relations. This was an important influence on later researchers such as Pierre BOURDIEU.

Goffman made innovative contributions to the study of other types of social relationship and structures. In several studies, including "Deference and Demeanor" (1956), he sought to complement Emile DURKHEIM's understanding of normative social order with an analysis of the ways NORMS are embedded in everyday actions. Elsewhere, he extended the analysis of RITUAL from sacred settings to the whole range of such action. In one of his best-known works, *Asylums* (1961), Goffman pioneered the analysis of what he termed TOTAL INSTITUTIONS—bureaucratic systems that achieve near complete domination of those subjected to them, such as prisons. Goffman placed particular emphasis on how such institutions structure life around principles of bureaucratic control. He focused on the processes of adaptation and resistance among the persons subject to such systems, and especially on the emergence of internal cultures among inmates. *Asylums* was influential in fostering debates over institutionalization, and it became aligned with arguments in favor of decarceration.

Goffman's work on STIGMA, which he defined as visible or invisible social distinctions that disqualify individuals or social groups from full social acceptance, also drew upon and extended his microsociology of everyday life. He distinguished between physical stigmas like obesity or handicaps, moral stigmas like homosexuality, and tribal stigmas that affect ethnic or national groups. This work contributed to the large body of sociological research in the 1950s and 1960s on labeling and DEVIANCE (see LABELING THEORY).

Among Goffman's strongest dramaturgical studies are *Encounters* (1961), *Behavior in Public*

Places (1963), and *Relations in Public* (1971). His later work turned toward other concerns: PHENOMENOLOGY in *Frame Analysis* (1974) and SOCIOLINGUISTICS in *Forms of Talk* (1981). His idea of *frame* has proved especially influential and shapes a large body of work on the ways in which social movements present templates and models that both enable participants to understand issues in their lives and orient them toward movement participation. The most common criticisms of Goffman's work focus on his relatively unsystematic methodology and minimal attention to fieldwork. Nonetheless, his work resonates with much contemporary research on performative and constructed subjectivity, and his influence remains considerable. Although he is often presented as part of the heritage of SYMBOLIC INTERACTIONISM and did influence later work in this tradition, he resisted being classified in those terms and identified other sources for his work.

golden rule   In economics, a general principle of capital accumulation that states that the optimal growth path in a closed economy—one that provides maximum per capita consumption over time—is a growth path in which national consumption equals the national wage bill, or the sum of wages of everyone in the economy. Equivalently, it can be shown that the growth path that maximizes consumption is one in which the competitive rate of interest (the rate of return to saving and investment) is equal to the natural rate of growth (usually the rate of growth of the population).

gold standard   A monetary system in which currency is convertible to a fixed quantity of gold at specified rates. In the nineteenth century, the gold standard largely replaced the bimetal systems of silver and gold currency that most countries had used for centuries. England led the way in basing its currency on a gold standard—taking its first steps in the early eighteenth century and definitively establishing the singular monetary framework in 1821. As an international system of monetary exchange, the gold standard dates to the 1870s, when first Germany and then other industrialized nations joined England in guaranteeing currency convertibility at fixed rates. This facilitated trade by stabilizing exchange rates and reducing the risk of holding currency.

The international gold standard collapsed during World War I under the pressures of wartime spending and borrowing. It enjoyed a short renaissance from 1928 until the Great Depression, when it collapsed again.

The *gold-exchange standard* emerged after World War I as an alternative system of exchange, and dominated the international monetary system between 1958 and 1970. Under the gold-exchange standard, countries peg the value of their currency to another currency, which is itself convertible into gold. Initially, the U.S. dollar and British pound functioned as the central currencies; these, in turn, remained convertible into gold. In the post–World War II era, the dollar alone served this purpose. This system allowed weaker economies to avoid the problem of inadequate gold reserves while preserving some of the stability associated with a guaranteed currency. In 1971, the United States abandoned gold convertibility. Since then, currency values have floated on the currency market, backed only by the credibility of the monetary institutions and the strength of the economies of their respective countries. In this context, gold became a commodity whose price fluctuated on the open market. Despite this change, some countries continue to peg their currencies to the dollar as the currency of highest international confidence.

good   In economics, a *good* refers to any physical object from which individuals derive positive UTILITY, or well-being. (Objects generating negative utility are termed *bads*.) A good does not have to be a commodity—that is, it may be something that is not bought or sold—but should be distinguished from factors of production, such as land and labor.

good Samaritan problem   Refers to the response (or lack of response) of bystanders in cases of emergencies. The determinants of such behavior have been of interest to sociologists, and laws governing individual responsibility in such cases have become increasingly common. The term comes from one of Jesus' parables in the Bible, in which most passersby failed to help a man who had been robbed and beaten. Only the good Samaritan did so—significant because he was a complete stranger and therefore the one who might have been least expected to help.

Gottmann, Jean   (1915–1994) A political and urban geographer, Gottmann was born in the Ukraine, spent his youth in France, and, after fleeing to New York during the Nazi occupation, split his professional life between France and the United States. He wrote prolifically on the subjects of central cities, capitals, and urban growth, from both spatial and political perspectives. He is best known for coining the term *megalopolis*, which he used to describe the emerging zone of continuous urban development that stretched from Boston to Washington, D. C. Gottmann's major works include *A Geography of Europe* (1951), *Megalopolis: The Urbanized Northeastern Seaboard of the United States* (1961), and *Metropolis on the Move: Geographers Look at Urban Sprawl* (1967, with R. Harper).

Gouldner, Alvin Ward   (1920–1980) An American sociologist and critical theorist who diagnosed the "crisis" of post–World War II FUNCTIONALISM and explored the potential for radical politics in the modern era. Gouldner was heavily influenced by Max WEBER, the FRANKFURT SCHOOL, and the radical sociology of C. Wright MILLS. Weber's influence is visible in early works such as *Patterns of Industrial Bureaucracy* (1954) and *Wildcat Strike* (1955), which theorize the potential for radical labor action in the context of bureaucratic intervention. Gouldner's *Notes on Technology and the Moral Order* (1962) extended Weber's sociology of religion toward an analysis of technological progress, which he argued depended on the strength of "Apollonian" moral orders that stressed order, reason, and activism.

Gouldner's most influential work is *The Coming Crisis of Western Sociology* (1970), which synthesized his criticisms of the abstract systems and strong functionalism of the postwar American sociological tradition (identified principally with Talcott PARSONS). Gouldner was especially critical of the deliberate isolation of SOCIOLOGY from political engagement, on the basis on its ostensibly scientific status. He was similarly critical of the scientific pretensions of Soviet-style MARXISM. Gouldner's advocacy of critical rather than scientific Marxism and his hopes for progressive change in the absence of a revolutionary labor force were the subjects of two subsequent books, *Two Marxisms* (1980) and *The Future of Intellectuals and the Rise of the New Class* (1979). *Two Marxisms* was also part of an extended historical and critical study of social theory that began with *Enter Plato* (1965) and ended with the posthumously published *Against Fragmentation: The Origins of Marxism and the Sociology of Intellectuals* (1985). Gouldner's works show an increasing concern with the role that intellectuals and sociologists play in enabling and planning social change.

Gouldner founded *Theory and Society*—a journal devoted primarily to critical approaches to Marxism and society. His other major work includes *The Dialectic of Ideology and Technology* (1976).

governability   The relative efficacy of government in meeting economic, social, and political challenges, especially with reference to liberal democracies. Governability became a major concern during the 1970s, when critics on both the left and the right argued that a combination of factors (including the expansion of the welfare state, rising citizen expectations, the increased politicization of special-interest groups, weakening public authority, and slower economic growth) made it increasingly difficult for democratic governments to respond to citizens' demands. This proposition fueled arguments on the left for social and economic reorganization, and on the right for the strengthening of the STATE. The governability debate mostly ended in the 1980s, as the United States and other industrialized nations experienced renewed growth and as conservative governments in a number of Western countries succeeded in cutting public services with relatively high levels of public support. Governability continues to be a concern in the developing world, where CIVIL SOCIETY is often weak and where governments often have little leverage over national (and international) economic conditions.

government   The agency that exercises political direction or control over a group of people—usually the state considered as a set of institutions. In other contexts, the term designates the political party currently in power, as distinct from the state as an enduring whole.

Since the foundational political analyses by PLATO and ARISTOTLE, political scientists have developed various systems of classification to distinguish and meaningfully compare systems of government. Perhaps the most influential methodology draws on Aristotle in prioritizing the relationship between the government and the governed—or the STATE and SOCIETY. For Aristotle, this relationship offered a finite set of possibilities based on the size of the ruling group and the breadth of its interests. Rule by a single person in the general interest yielded MONARCHY; where this degenerated into rule in the sole interest of the ruler, there was TYRANNY. Analogous distinctions separated ARISTOCRACY from OLIGARCHY (both forms of rule by the few) and republicanism from DEMOCRACY (both forms of rule by the many). This model dominated political thinking well into the eighteenth century and is reflected in modern classificatory systems that privilege the question of popular SOVEREIGNTY and the RULE OF LAW. This is a common basis for distinguishing between constitutional or democratic regimes (where popular sovereignty and the rule of law are respected) and authoritarian or totalitarian counterparts (where they are not). See also AUTHORITARIANISM; and TOTALITARIANISM.

The second set of classificatory schemata privilege the relationships between governmental institutions within constitutional systems. These include inquiry into the diverse possible connections between branches of government and their corresponding primary functions—quintessentially, the EXECUTIVE, legislative, and judiciary. One major axis of difference involves the nature of the "horizontal" relationship between the executive and legislature. In parliamentary systems, the executive is drawn from and is responsible to the legislature; in presidential systems, the SEPARATION OF POWERS is more strictly observed and the branches have greater autonomy.

Under parliamentary systems it is common to speak of the party in power as "the government," because the two most active governmental powers are joined. Under presidential systems, the elected executive and his or her CABINET are more often called "the administration."

A related set of classificatory issues involves "vertical" relations between different levels of government. In unitary systems, power rests entirely with the central government. FEDERALISM designates a principle of shared and overlapping power between the central and local governments. Confederation is a more dispersed principle of association: states unite to create a common government but retain sovereign power.

gradualism   The introduction of political or social change slowly and by degrees. Unlike INCREMENTALISM, which is usually applied to relatively narrow administrative or policy questions, gradualism tends to refer to the general direction of government policy with respect to the political or economic system as a whole—for example, the expansion of rights, DEMOCRATIZATION, or changes to the basic structure of the economy.

grammar   The system that underlies the relationship between sound and meaning in a given

LANGUAGE or dialect; alternatively, the attempt to formalize that implicit system. The study of grammar is divided into *phonology* (the study of the relationships between sound and meaning), *semantics* (the study of differences in meaning), and *syntax* (the rules governing the organization of meaning).

Gramsci, Antonio (1891–1937) Best known as a Marxist theorist of CULTURE and of social struggle as a battle for consent (in Gramsci's terms, *hegemony*). Gramsci was also an important political activist who helped found the Italian Communist party in 1921. He later led it for two years until his imprisonment by the Fascist government in 1926. In prison, Gramsci filled some thirty-four notebooks with reflections on Marxist theory, social struggle, and the task facing Marxism in Western democratic countries. He also wrote at length about Italian history, religion, philosophy, art, and literature. These writings were assembled and posthumously published as the *Prison Notebooks* (1991).

In his prison writings, Gramsci argued against the strict economic determinism of orthodox MARXISM; he proposed instead a more flexible account of the BASE AND SUPERSTRUCTURE relationship that insisted on the dialectical relationship between the two and the difference—within the superstructure—between CIVIL SOCIETY and the STATE. Both points served to emphasize the role that culture and leading cultural actors—intellectuals—played in reinforcing or challenging the social order. The working class, Gramsci held, was oppressed not merely by its relationship to the means of production and its vulnerability to the coercion of the state but also by the fabrication of consent to the dominant ideology through education and other cultural means. Gramsci concluded that social struggle had to be conducted at the level of ideas and that effective rule was based on the ability of a group to spread its ideas among groups who did not share its economic interests. This, Gramsci argued, was the struggle for hegemony.

One of the consequences of this analysis, for Gramsci, was that struggle had to proceed by way of alliance and extension, rather than through the ideological purification characteristic of LENINISM. The appropriate strategy was a "war of position," in which the party or other activists seek to change the dominant culture, gain allies, extend democracy, and strengthen their capacity to deliver concrete benefits to workers. While occasions might arise for revolutionary conflict or other sharply defined struggles—which Gramsci called a "war of maneuver," this was not the case when the capitalist class had secured the consent of large sectors of the working class and where political systems were relatively open—as in the Western democracies. This was of immediate relevance in Italy, where economic and religious differences between north and south had made achieving a broad working-class front difficult. The working class had to overcome such divisions and secure its ideological autonomy from the ruling class—in part, through the cultivation of "organic intellectuals" rooted in the working class rather than in traditional elites. Ultimately, Gramsci believed, it had to extend its influence into the group of official or academic intellectuals that normally defended the social order. Gramsci's ideas foreshadowed and influenced the Eurocommunism of the 1980s, in which the Italian and other Communist parties shed Soviet-style tactics and organization and began to embrace democratic participation.

Gramsci became seriously ill in prison and was released in 1937. He died within a week. Gramsci's letters from prison have also been collected and published.

Granger causality See CAUSAL INFERENCE.

gravity model An extension of Isaac Newton's formula for gravity to the analysis of movement between places, such as traffic flows, migration, or trade. The pull of gravity is positively related to the size of the object and inversely related to the distance between objects; thus, in most models, flow increases with size and decreases with distance. This model has been useful in predicting counterfactual world-trade patterns—those that would exist in the absence of restrictive policies—and has helped assess the impact of protective policies like tariffs and quotas. The gravity model was first proposed by James Stewart, a Princeton astronomer.

Great and Little traditions A distinction between the elite or dominant records of cultural or religious tradition (including literature and art) and the local, informal, and often oral manifestations of those traditions by peasant groups. The distinction was first introduced into ANTHROPOLOGY by Robert REDFIELD in *Peasant Society and Culture* (1956), to explain the interaction between mechanisms that formalize and institutionalize practices within a culture (usually in the service of an elite) and the constant reinterpretation and modification of those practices at the local level.

green revolution   Usually refers to the introduction of new hybrid strains of wheat, corn, and rice in the 1960s, which dramatically increased the agricultural production of many developing countries. More generally, it has been used to describe rapid changes in agricultural technologies, especially the introduction of new strains of crops. Using this criterion, there have been several green revolutions in the past centuries. See also AGRICULTURAL REVOLUTION.

Gresham's law   Usually expressed as "bad money drives out good," Gresham's law predicts that if two types of money circulate simultaneously and their intrinsic relative values (say, their weight in ounces of gold) diverge from their legally determined values, then the money with the higher intrinsic value will be hoarded and withdrawn from circulation. Suppose gold and silver coins circulate simultaneously. If the money value of the silver coin as a fraction of the money value of the gold coin is different from the price of the silver contained in the coin relative to the price of the gold in the gold coin, then people will melt the gold coins, hold them as gold, and continue to use the silver coins as currency. The law is credited to British financier Thomas Gresham (1510–1579).

gross domestic product and gross national product   See NATIONAL INCOME.

Grotius, Hugo   (1583–1645) Dutch jurist, man of letters, and statesman, most often remembered for his work in the area of INTERNATIONAL LAW and for contributions to the theory of natural RIGHTS. A child prodigy, Grotius entered the University of Leiden at eleven and graduated at fourteen. A year later, he received a doctorate in law from the University of Orleans. For the next two decades, Grotius practiced law at The Hague and rose quickly through the administration at the Royal Court. He became well known as a scholar, poet, playwright, and historian. His involvement in religious and political disputes, however, led to his imprisonment. Grotius eventually escaped and spent the rest of his life outside Holland—primarily in Paris.

Grotius's *The Law of War and Peace* (1627) was a formative statement on international law and INTERNATIONAL RELATIONS. It was rooted in a theory of natural law that recognized both competitive and sociable dimensions to human character. Grotius argued that natural law derived from reason rather than God, and on this basis argued that relations between states must be structured by mutually agreed-upon contractual obligations. He based legitimate state power on a version of the social contract—valid as long as government protected and improved the lives of its citizens—and drew an important distinction between perfect (or enforceable) rights and imperfect ones, which are more difficult to state and defend. In other work, Grotius made an innovative and influential case for the freedom of the seas and uncoerced trade. He also developed a definition of *just war* based on the enforcement of legal contracts between nations.

Grotius' other major works include *Commentary on the Law of Prize and Booty* (1605) and *True Religion Explained and Defended against the Archenemies Thereof in the Times* (1632).

group   At its simplest, a small number of people who interact with one another and share an identity. The study of groups is fundamental to the social sciences, and a very broad vocabulary and set of theoretical tools has evolved for speaking about different types of group affiliation and formation. At the most fundamental level, a group requires some form of social interaction and boundedness; this distinguishes it from a social category, which may nominally include persons in similar social positions or with similar traits. Early work on this subject included William Griffith SUMNER's investigations of the way *in-groups* and *out-groups* are reciprocally formed. Other models distinguished *corporate groups* (which control a property or valuable skill) from *noncorporate groups*; *primary groups* (whose members are closely connected) from *secondary groups* (whose members are not; see Charles Horton COOLEY); and *action groups* (whose members come together to perform a specific task) from those organized by more enduring criteria.

The question of how groups organize themselves internally and interact is of central interest to many social scientists. This is often referred to as the study of *group dynamics*, and embraces questions of internal power structures, forms and limits of individual adhesion, degrees of group consciousness (at the low end, yielding "quasi-groups"), hierarchical relationships between groups, forms of leadership, and the way these issues vary with group size. The SOCIAL PSYCHOLOGY of small groups has influenced studies of organizational behavior, informed management techniques, and developed into an approach to therapy.

Groves–Clark mechanism   A solution to the problem of soliciting individual valuations of PUBLIC GOODS, developed independently by Theodore Groves and Edward Clarke. (William Vickrey is also sometimes credited for his development of a similar solution concept for a different class of problems.) The mechanism addresses two related phenomena: (1) the incidence of FREE RIDERS in the provisioning of nonexcludable public goods and (2) the tendency for individuals to overstate the valuation of a public good that they can obtain freely. Groves and Clarke recognized that the most efficient level of provision of public goods occurs where the marginal cost equals the sum of all marginal utilities (see UTILITY). They proposed that each individual be charged according to his or her stated marginal utility, thus making each individual pivotal in the mechanism and without incentive to misrepresent his or her preferences. The shortcoming of the mechanism is that the sum of the payments can exceed the cost of production.

growth theory   Economic growth has been one of the fundamental subjects of ECONOMICS since its origins. The history of economics generally recognizes three dominant theories of growth:

1. The *Classical growth models* consist primarily of the eighteenth-century pioneering work of Adam SMITH, David RICARDO, and Thomas Robert MALTHUS. Together, these three provided the foundations of modern growth theory. For the classical economists, interest in growth developed out of the philosophical question of progress—a basic tenet of Enlightenment thought that applied equally to ideas, scientific innovations, social norms, and more generally the material bases of society. On this basis, they sought a general account of the forces and mechanisms that influenced economic growth. They recognized productive investment and capital accumulation as the principal impetuses to growth—processes that, under capitalism, involved the reinvestment of profits (see ACCUMULATION OF CAPITAL). They also emphasized the contributing effects of technological change, visible in the growing DIVISION OF LABOR and in changes in methods of production. Malthus, in particular, also took into account population growth as providing both an increase in the supply of labor and an escalating risk of profit erosion, as population

outstripped economic growth. This was one version of their general view that growth produces countervailing tendencies that undermine it and that ultimately yield a condition of stagnation. The classical economists were also sensitive to the interrelations among exchange, production, distribution, and accumulation in the growth process. Consequently, there was no sharp distinction between the analysis of economic growth and other key areas of POLITICAL ECONOMY.

2. *Keynesian growth models* derive from a number of John Maynard KEYNES's twentieth-century insights on employment and economic stability (see EMPLOYMENT, THEORIES OF). They tend to emphasize the difficulty of fine tuning the economy to achieve full employment or optimal growth. Roy HARROD (1939) and Evsey Domar (1946, 1947) developed the most influential of these theories, which demonstrated that long-term full employment requires that two fundamental conditions be met: the ratio of investment to income must equal the *full-employment savings ratio* (the savings ratio that would result if all resources were fully employed) and the economy's rate of growth must equal the *natural rate of growth* (the rate of growth of the labor force plus labor productivity).

An economy can achieve full employment only if its rate of growth equals both the natural and the *warranted rate of growth* (the rate of growth that balances the increase in capacity with the increase in demand). They showed that because the determinants of these rates are exogenous, equality between them is a matter of chance and is inevitably unstable—a feature termed the *knife-edge problem*. As a consequence, continuous full employment is virtually impossible to achieve—a characteristically Keynesian result. Instead, the economy moves between two distinct conditions: (1) when the rate of growth is slightly less than the warranted rate, there is excess production capacity and the capital stock grows faster than what entrepreneurs would prefer. Firms respond by cutting investment so that effective demand and growth begin to fall. In this case, the actual rate of growth diverges further from the warranted rate of growth. A similar reinforcement occurs when the actual growth rate exceeds the warranted growth rate; (2) the economy becomes increasingly short of capital, and capital investment rises. These two forms of divergence correlate with unemployment and INFLATION, respectively. The limitations of this model became visible in the 1950s, when many countries achieved almost full employment with little or no inflation.

3. *Neoclassical growth models* tend to emphasize the ease of substitution among factors of production (labor, capital, land, or other essentials in the production of commodities), which permits the economy to achieve *steady-state growth* (a constant proportionate rate of growth of all real variables). Neoclassical theory predicts the long-run equilibrium of a competitive economy, with particular attention paid to the accumulation of capital goods, growth in population, and technological progress. Because factor prices are flexible and substitution among factors possible in such a model, the natural and warranted rates of growth are equal. Neoclassical growth models thus avoid the problem of instability inherent in the Harrod–Domar model. Operating under the assumption that population grows at a constant geometric rate and that a constant proportion of real income is saved, economies approach a unique steady state over time. Such models also assume that technological progress is an exogenous (or external) variable and that new techniques can be incorporated into both new and old machines—the latter a departure from *vintage growth* theory, which assumes that in order to take advantage of new technology, a firm must buy new machines. One of the much debated and researched predictions of neoclassical growth models concerns the CONVERGENCE HYPOTHESIS— the argument that in the long run, the growth rates of different countries tend to converge toward the same steady state.

GSS General Social Survey. An ongoing, large-scale survey of attitudes and social practices in the United States, begun in 1972. It is now conducted biennially by the National Opinion Research Center (NORC).

Guattari, Félix (1930–1992) A French psychoanalyst and philosopher best known for his prominence in the ANTI-PSYCHIATRY movement in France, his political activism on behalf of left-wing causes, and two major collaborations with Gilles DELEUZE, *Anti-Oedipus* (1972) and *A Thousand Plateaus: Capitalism and Schizophrenia* (1980). Anti-psychiatry drew on Ronald David LAING's work on schizophrenia and mental illness. It took a position against the "hard" forms of treatment prevalent in French mental hospitals and against the larger psychiatric tendency to treat mental illness as an individual (as opposed to social)

pathology. Guattari's work with Deleuze developed a broad social and philosophical context for these arguments. They articulated a strong critique of the rigid socialization of human desire at work in the OEDIPUS COMPLEX, the psychiatric orthodoxy that championed and reproduced it, and the imperatives of capitalism that it served. Deleuze and Guattari called this broad anti-Oedipal project *schizo-analysis*—a term that referred to the goal of constantly breaking away from socially channeled desire. Both *Anti-Oedipus* and *A Thousand Plateaus* reflect something of the anarchic sense of possibility and the explosion of social desires visible in the events of May 1968, in which Guattari was deeply involved. Guattari's other major works include *L'inconscient machinique* (1979), *Molecular Revolution: Psychiatry and Politics* (1984), and *Les trois ecologies* (1989).

Gurvitch, Georges (1896–1965) An important institutional figure in French sociology, Gurvitch founded the Centre d'Etudes Sociologiques de Paris, directed the Ecole Pratique des Hautes Etudes, and edited a number of major journals and sociological collections. Gurvitch wrote prolifically on a range of topics, including the sociology of LAW, theories of group and class organization, and the nature of social science inquiry. Much of his writing is highly philosophical in nature and structuralist in orientation. He was a builder of theories on a large scale, and he attempted to ground the social sciences in an account of the fundamental categories and varieties of social experience. Gurvitch's STRUCTURALISM was pluralistic and, in its categorical rejection of *a priori* assumptions and theories, positivistic—the object alone constituted the source of knowledge. His work grew from phenomenological roots toward an EMPIRICISM that he described as *hyperempiric dialectics*—a method that he argued permitted the analysis of the purely intuitive experience of phenomena. In practice, this generally meant dividing phenomena and objects into multiple types. Where Georg HEGEL and Karl MARX relied on a relatively singular notion of dialectical process, Gurvitch distinguished five distinct forms. Where the ANNALES SCHOOL historians distinguished three or four different scales of social time, Gurvitch identified eight. "The true task for the dialectical method," he wrote in *Dialectics and Sociology* (1962), "is to demolish all established and crystallized concepts."

Gurvitch's best-known works are *Sociology of Law* (1942), which emphasized the social processes and values that underlie the development of law (against legal positivism and other statist accounts of the origins of law) and *The Spectrum of Time* (1958). Most of his other writing, including *Karl Marx et la sociologie du XIXe siècle* (1948) and *Déterminisme sociaux et liberté humaine* (1955), remains untranslated.

Guttman scale A technique for measuring attitudes in survey research. The Guttman scale arranges preferences or values along a cumulative, unidimensional scale, so that by accepting or agreeing with a particular item, the subject implicitly accepts or agrees with all items below it. This has the advantage of allowing researchers to compare attitudes along a continuum. It does not, however, measure the intensity of each, unlike the LIKERT SCALE.

H

habeas corpus Latin phrase meaning "you have the body," habeas corpus is a legal procedure for challenging the legality of police (or other official) detention of individuals. It involves (and is limited to) a petition to the court to determine if the arrest was made according to the law. Habeas corpus originally developed in medieval English COMMON LAW and plays an important part in all legal systems derived from the English model. In principle, it allows the judiciary to supervise the EXECUTIVE's use of police power. In practice, its efficacy depends on the power and independence of the judicial branch.

Habermas, Jürgen (1929–) The most influential theorist of the public sphere in the past thirty years and the most significant inheritor and interpreter of the FRANKFURT SCHOOL tradition of critical theory. Like earlier Frankfurt school scholars, he has sought to analyze the systemic integration of capitalist society and the modes of rationality that propel and legitimize it. However, he has been careful to distance himself from the pessimistic conclusions that Max HORKHEIMER and Theodor ADORNO drew in regard to the possibility of social transformation, as well as from the revolutionary utopianism of Herbert MARCUSE's work. Instead, he has conducted a sustained and ultimately quite varied inquiry into the nature of public political discourse—particularly what he identified as "rational-critical discourse" directed toward the public scrutiny of the state, social organization, and societal goals.

On these terms, Habermas set out to restore the "practical" value of critical theory. In his early work, this project took two directions. One was the attempt to analyze the historical institutions in which rational critical discourse achieved political significance—classically, in eighteenth-century republicanism. In so doing, he explored the possibility of reproducing or at least leveraging those values against the mechanisms of fabricated consent that he considered dominant in modern democratic societies. This was his ambition in *The Structural Transformation of the Public Sphere* (1963 [1989])—a work that had an impact on Anglo-American social theory only after its long-delayed translation. The second direction involved the critique of the tradition of social theory itself as a way of identifying its resources and limitations. Habermas's most important work in this regard is his recent *The Philosophical Discourse of Modernity* (1987).

Legitimation Crisis (1975) and other writings of the 1970s carried public sphere issues further in exploring the modern rapprochement of society and state—a tendency that for Habermas undermined the autonomy of public discourse. Habermas emphasized two major characteristics of the late-capitalist system: (1) the growth of state intervention to maintain the system's stability; and (2) the growing interdependence of research and technology, which ultimately makes the sciences the dominant factors in economic growth. The former creates a compact between workers and the state, which increasingly assumes responsibility for their welfare. This process, Habermas argues, "depoliticizes" the population, reducing politics to matters of technical administration, such as the maintenance of economic growth and the buying off of the economy's structural victims. The second characteristic—the systematic pursuit of technological progress and efficiency—becomes the official ideology of this state of affairs.

Habermas reconceptualized these problems in his recent distinction between *system* and *lifeworld* and in the corresponding distinction between *instrumental* and *communicative action*. Where earlier critical theory had effectively consigned the possibility of a privileged oppositional social force (quintessentially, the working class) to an indeterminate future, Habermas reinscribed that opposition into existing arenas of social activity. Communicative action—action oriented to reflective understanding and the creation of social relations—could provide a resource against instrumental action, which is embodied in the integrated economic, state, and cultural networks of the system world. Communicative action could furnish the basis of genuine consensus about public affairs, free from the impersonal "steering mechanisms" of money and scientific reason. In *Theory of Communicative Action* (v. 2, 1987), Habermas tried to clarify the structure of communicative reason by developing an account of the basic structures of human linguistic faculties—a "universal pragmatics." This inquiry continues to inform his more recent discussions of ethics, LAW, CAPITALISM, and the philosophical tradition.

Habermas's linguistic turn has been greeted with skepticism from many sides, as much for the strict separation it seems to imply between lifeworld and system as for its explicit idealization of speech and consensus. This work has departed from his earlier emphasis on institutions by locating an immanent basis for critique in universal potentials of communication rather than in historically specific social arrangements. Nonetheless, Habermas has set the terms for much of the current discussion of both the failings and the potential of public life.

In the late 1980s and 1990s, Habermas turned his attention to developing discourse ethics as a basis for analyzing law. He approached law as mediating not only between the realms of normative values and empirical facts but also between the distinctive forms of reason and judgment characteristic of each. In *Between Facts and Norms* (1998), he argues that law is both basic to the social order and an exemplary, if special, case of the capacity for communicatively achieving social integration—even where values are diverse. Habermas's other major works include *Towards a Rational Society: Student Protest, Science and Society* (1970), *Knowledge and Human Interests* (1971), *On the Logic of the Social Sciences* (1988), and *The Inclusion of the Other* (1999).

habitus The capacity to generate new social actions without explicitly thinking them through, based partly on the internalization of objective social structures through experience (including the success or failure of previous actions). Habitus is a central concept in Pierre BOURDIEU's influential sociological theory, where it represents an attempt to theorize the space in which individual agency meets larger social determinants (norms, rules, and/or structures). Describing neither complete determination by social factors nor individual autonomy, the habitus is a set of "durable and transposable dispositions" (*Outline of a Theory of Practice*, 1972 [1977]) that mediates between "objective" structures of social relations and the individual "subjective" behavior of actors. In

different terms, it is the sum of determining structures (such as class, family, and education) that nonetheless provide the practical skills and dispositions that define "improvisation" within a given field or set of fields—sports, professional life, art, and so on. At the same time, the habitus is constantly remade by these improvisations. The concept has proved highly portable to a range of projects in contemporary ANTHROPOLOGY and especially SOCIOLOGY. See also PRACTICE AND PRACTICE THEORY.

Hall, Stuart (1932–) A prominent social critic and major figure in modern CULTURAL STUDIES, Hall was born in Jamaica and attended Oxford University on a Rhodes scholarship. In the late 1960s, he succeeded Richard HOGGART as director of the influential Centre for Contemporary Cultural Studies at the University of Birmingham (also known as the Birmingham school)—a position he held until his retirement in 1997. He was also a founding professor of sociology at the Open University, reflecting his commitment to opening higher education to nontraditional students.

Hall is a prolific writer and public intellectual of considerable stature in Great Britain. He has been active in a variety of public and intellectual debates on the left, especially during the Thatcher years, which occasioned some of his most insightful analyses of British political culture. It was Hall's interest in MARXISM, however, that led to what is perhaps his most significant contribution to cultural theory: a reworking of Antonio GRAMSCI's concepts of hegemony and IDEOLOGY that focused on popular culture and practices of interpretation. Hall's model of the production and reception of mass culture (through processes of ENCODING AND DECODING) is perhaps the best known of this work, which has in general emphasized the active role that consumers of mass culture play in constructing the meaning of cultural objects (television programs, texts, and so on). Hall has also been one of the principle theorists and interpreters of the larger trajectory of cultural studies, from the humanist class analyses of Richard Hoggart, Edward Palmer THOMPSON, and Raymond WILLIAMS, to the engagement with structural Marxism, POSTSTRUCTURALISM, and the turn toward RACE, GENDER, and SUBCULTUREs in the late 1960s and 1970s. He has worked in recent years to ensure that analyses of identity and cultural studies more generally maintain a strong commitment to social engagement. Hall's major works include *The Hard*

Road to Renewal (1988), *Resistance through Rituals* (1976, ed. with Tony Jefferson), and a number of important essays, including "The Television Discourse—Encoding/Decoding" (1973) and "Cultural Studies: Two Paradigms" (1980).

Hare system   See ELECTORAL SYSTEM.

Harris, Marvin   (1929–2001) A prominent American anthropologist of the post–World War II era, Harris's most influential and controversial contribution involves his claim for CULTURAL MATERIALISM, which asserts that cultural forms are strictly determined by material conditions, such as the environment or subsistence needs. Harris's work is mostly an extended and remarkably diverse elaboration of this notion, carried into different fields and applied to different subjects. The primary theoretical statements of his position are *Cannibals and Kings* (1977), an evolutionary account of human society, and *Cultural Materialism* (1979), although he has also written on racial paradigms, American social history, food taboos, and world population growth. Other major works include *Patterns of Race in America* (1964), *The Rise of Anthropological Theory* (1968), *Good to Eat: Riddles of Food and Culture* (1985), and *Theories of Culture in Postmodern Times* (1999).

Harrod, Roy   (1900–1978) The first economist to reconcile Keynesian economics to models of steady state economic growth—the latter a major topic of economic inquiry since Adam SMITH. This work—especially *The Trade Cycle* (1936)—was the first step in the revival of GROWTH THEORY.

Harrod was educated at the University of Oxford, but also spent time at Cambridge University, where John Maynard KEYNES was among his teachers. The main innovation in what came to be known as the Harrod–Domar growth model was the *moving equilibrium growth path*. Keynesian macroeconomics required that, at equilibrium, savings are continually turned into investment. Harrod used the ACCELERATION PRINCIPLE to show that the growth rate at which a firm's level of investment equals savings was equal to the ratio of the savings rate to the change in investment due to a change in output. If the actual growth rate is above this equilibrium or *warranted growth rate*, then there will be a continual acceleration of growth. If the actual growth rate falls short of the warranted rate, the economy decelerates. This finding is known as *Harrod's knife-edge problem*.

Further research specified the circumstances under which Harrod's knife-edge could be avoided: a high marginal propensity to save and largely autonomous investment, so that investment responds less than proportionately to an increase in output. Most of Harrod's work in the 1940s focused on exploring the differences between the warranted growth rate with the natural growth rate, which he viewed as a function of population dynamics and technical change. He later argued that the rate of technical progress could be derived by measuring the increase in labor productivity that does not change the value of the capital coefficient at a given rate of interest. This concept has since become known as *Harrod-neutral technical change*. See TECHNOLOGICAL PROGRESS, BIASED AND UNBIASED.

Harrod pointed out that equilibrium growth was not possible when the warranted rate and natural rate were unequal. Later developments in neoclassical growth theory (for example, the Solow–Swan model) suggested that the warranted rate and the natural rate could be equalized at an appropriate rate of interest (see Robert SOLOW). Harrod disagreed with this and remained a stalwart Keynesian in most respects—despite Keynes's own misgivings about growth theory. Harrod felt that only persistent government intervention could reconcile the warranted and natural growth rates, and thereby ensure equilibrium growth.

Harrod–Domar model   See GROWTH THEORY

Harvey, David   (1935–) A prominent geographer and social theorist, Harvey studied and taught in England before moving to Johns Hopkins University, where he has spent much of his time since 1969. His first major work was *Explanation in Geography* (1969)—an analysis of the goals of geography in light of the confrontation between cultural geographers and advocates of new quantitative methodologies.

Harvey's subsequent writing, however, turned sharply away from this set of concerns and drew increasingly on the urban sociology of Henri Lefevre and other Marxist-oriented geographers and social critics. With *Social Justice and the City* (1973) and *The Limits to Capital* (1982), Harvey combined spatial analysis and POLITICAL ECONOMY with a predominantly Marxist account of historical development—often in a highly technical form. With *The Condition of Postmodernity* (1989), Harvey integrated a much more developed cultural analysis into these themes and clarified some of the major elements of his account of modern capitalist society. Very much in a classical Marxist vein, Harvey argued that POSTMODERNISM is essentially the broad cultural expression of a transformation in the dominant form of organization of CAPITALISM—no longer Fordist and state regulated, but highly flexible and mobile; no longer concentrated around the urban centers of industrialized nations, but spatially dispersed to suburban peripheries and underdeveloped countries. This put Harvey at odds with other theorists of postmodernism (Jean BAUDRILLARD, for example), who emphasized its aesthetic and culturally autonomous dimensions.

For geography in particular, Harvey's Marxist postmodernism implied a turn away from abstract models of optimum spatial relationships and toward the question of the political, cultural, and economic determinants of uneven development. Due in large part to Harvey's influence, uneven development became one of the major areas of geographical research and debate in the 1980s and 1990s. He has also put his ideas to work in practical political engagement, especially in Baltimore. Harvey's recent works include *The Urbanisation of Capital* (1985) and *Justice, Nature and the Geography of Difference* (1996).

Hawthorne effect Describes the changes in behavior that result from being the subject of a behavioral study. The term derives from experiments carried out in the mid-1920s by the sociologists Fritz Roethlisberger and William J. Dickson at the Hawthorne Western Electric Company in Chicago. They set out to test theories of scientific management by measuring the impact of changes in working conditions on worker productivity—particularly variations in such factors as lighting, breaks, and compensation. They found that productivity increased no matter what they changed—a result attributed to the effect of the attention the researchers paid to the workers, which workers ostensibly interpreted as a sign of management concern and engagement. This research had a profound impact on the theory and practice of supervision and management, and led to Elton Mayo's development of the HUMAN RELATIONS MOVEMENT. See also EXPERIMENTER EFFECTS.

Hayek, Friedrich von (1899–1992) Hayek was the best known proponent of the Austrian school of economics and won the Nobel Prize in 1974. His research interests ranged from the role of knowledge in market processes to the critique of KEYNESIANISM.

Hayek was educated in Vienna and later lectured at the London School of Economics and the University of Chicago. His most fundamental contribution was the analysis of the intertemporal structure of capital. In *The Pure Theory of Capital* (1941), Hayek pointed out that since individual producers must precommit to a level of investment, production plans must be revised if there is a shortfall in a necessary raw material. The degree to which this revision is possible depends on how easily a capital good can be moved from one use to another. Economy-wide coordination of production therefore depends on the specificity of capital.

At the time, the traditional view of monetary policy dealt with the relationship between the quantity of money and the aggregate level of prices. According to Hayek, this disregarded the fact that when money is injected into the economy, relative prices are temporarily distorted, conveying false information about preferences and resources. The resulting misallocation of resources implies that any boom powered by a monetary injection must eventually lead to a bust. Hayek's theory of the trade cycle is based on this monetary theory. Since resources are allocated optimally to the different stages of production, and since production has an inherently intertemporal structure, the demands and supplies of resources at various stages of the production process react differently to changes in interest rates. A central bank–induced change in the interest rate distorts relative prices, and results in a misallocation of resources.

Hayek's critique of Keynesian economics has similar foundations. He accused John Maynard KEYNES of ignoring the intertemporal complementarity between the stages of the production process. As a medium of exchange, money is a "loose joint" in the price mechanism, which may prevent it from reaching equilibrium. By focusing on money as a liquid asset, Hayek argued, Keynes ignored the effects of active monetary policy on the rest of the price mechanism—again resulting in the misallocation of resources.

From a methodological point of view, much of Hayek's work was based on the premise that the economy involves a basic coordination problem. The lack of coordination among producers at different levels and between producers and buyers usually provides producers with an incentive to change their plans as necessary.

However, capitalist economies sometimes experience widespread and prolonged coordination failures. Hayek's research was aimed at discovering the events and circumstances that cause these failures.

Hayek was among the few economists who were wary of directly transporting the methods of the physical sciences into ECONOMICS. One reason for this was his belief that the "given" institutions in an economy are the result of human action. Hayek's own methodology supported both subjectivism and methodological individualism. Where classical economists focused on the objects being valued, and tried to specify the determinants of value, the Austrians—Hayek prominent among them—changed the focus to the subjects who attach value to an object. Hayek's views on methodology in the social sciences are spelled out in his 1952 book, *The Counter-Revolution of Science: Studies on the Abuse of Reason*.

Hayek's main achievement was to formulate theories of price, capital, and money, and to integrate them into a coherent framework capable of analyzing and interpreting the economic history of the nineteenth and twentieth centuries. He also strongly influenced the neoliberal turn in political and economic thought beginning in the late 1970s: his aversion to government intervention in the economy is reflected most prominently in the thinking of Milton FRIEDMAN. See also LIBERTARIANISM; and NEOLIBERALISM.

headman A local leader of a tribe or group, often subordinate to a chief or larger political organization.

hearth areas Refer to the locations of the five earliest urban civilizations. These are, in order of emergence, Mesopotamia, the Nile river valley, the Indus river valley, the Yellow river valley, and Mesoamerica. Hearth areas have been at the center of anthropological debates about the diffusion of cultural traits and innovations, and what has often been a competing logic of cultural evolution, which treats innovation as a relatively independent process linked to internal or environmental factors (see DIFFUSION AND DIFFUSIONISM; and EVOLUTION AND EVOLUTIONISM). One of the classic topics of research on hearth areas is the emergence of urban civilization—especially the question of whether it diffused from a single source or evolved spontaneously in multiple locations. A broad consensus among contemporary geographers favors

the latter. See also HYDRAULIC SOCIETIES; and *KULTURKREIS*.

heartland theory A geopolitical theory first proposed by British geographer Halford J. MACKINDER in 1904. Mackinder argued that the *heartland*, referring to the interior of Eurasia, benefited from a number of strategic advantages over the *rimland*, or coastal areas of Europe, the Mediterranean, and Asia. These benefits included a central location and relative immunity to Western naval power, from which he concluded that world domination could be achieved by a Eurasian power that was capable of unifying the heartland. For Mackinder, this meant Russia, which by the turn of the century had accomplished much of this task of unification. The Bolshevik Revolution in 1917 and the later German interest in heartland theory guaranteed Mackinder's work a wide audience and long shelf life, despite what many geographers came to see as its overreliance on environmental and technological determinism.

Heckscher–Ohlin trade theory A theory of international commodity trade patterns that stresses the importance of the comparative availability of factors of production (such as labor, land, or capital) in different countries. The theory also explains the consequences of international trade for the distribution of income within countries. Two Swedish economists, Eli Heckscher and Bertil Ohlin, produced the most influential version of this analysis, although the underlying insights originated with David RICARDO. Most economists now recognize four component theorems in this area.

The *Heckscher–Ohlin* theorem suggests that countries privilege the exportation of commodities that exploit comparatively abundant factors of production—again labor or capital are prime examples. In this context, labor abundant–capital poor countries export labor-intensive goods and import capital-intensive goods. Capital-intensive countries do the opposite. All the Heckscher–Ohlin trade theories assume that these specializations apply to different goods and that the production of any good requires more than one factor of production. In other words, no specialization is complete.

The *factor-price equalization theorem* was developed by Heckscher and Ohlin but only rigorously proved by Paul SAMUELSON in 1948. Samuelson argued that free international trade will substitute for the free mobility of factors of production. In a free trade context, factor prices will thereby be equalized among the countries in both relative and absolute terms.

The *Stolper–Samuelson theorem* (1941) predicts the relationship between the return on an intensely used factor of production and a change in the domestic price of a relevant good. According to the theorem, a rise in the price of such a good draws resources from the production of goods that depend on other, less intensively utilized and less abundant factors. In this case, the marginal productivity of labor (and therefore real wages) rises in both sectors.

Finally, the *Rybczynski theorem* (1955) focuses on the relationship between comparative endowments in factors of production and commodity outputs. It holds that an increase in the availability of a factor increases production of the commodity that uses it intensively, while the production of other commodities decreases.

Subsequent work on Heckscher–Ohlin trade theory has sought to relax its restrictive assumptions and to improve its ability to analyze multiple factors, commodities, and countries.

hedging   In finance, the purchase of an asset or portfolio of assets in order to insure against fluctuations in wealth due to other factors. For example, individuals may hedge against political or currency turmoil by buying gold; a producer uncertain about the future price of a raw material may buy a forward contract for that material; a pension fund may hedge against capital losses by buying stock index options.

Hegel, Georg Wilhelm Friedrich (1770–1831) A German philosopher who built a powerful and encompassing philosophical system on Greek, Enlightenment, and Romantic foundations. His work paved the way for MARXISM and a variety of contemporary approaches in the social sciences. Some of his other contributions, such as his work on logic, were highly influential in the nineteenth century but have less resonance today.

Hegel's most distinctive innovation was to approach knowledge and thought as inherently social and historical. He broke with a philosophical tradition that equated thought with individual cognitive processes, and instead relied on a dynamic conception of history as a process in which universality, truth, and full human subjectivity were progressively realized. Underpinning this system was a theory of DIALECTICS that took contradiction and transcendence as the basic

operations of logic, history, mind, and nature. In order to understand any specific actuality, it was necessary to approach it from the standpoint of the totality. Otherwise, one risked treating fragmentary, contingent truth as permanent and complete.

Hegel's system carried a number of important implications for later social science. First, both knowledge and knowing subjects had to be conceived as inherently social. People are not individuals first and then social to the extent that they engage others. Rather, Hegel argued, they are social insofar as they are human, and they are never capable of being real subjects except in and through social relations. Second, Hegel emphasized the processes of ALIENATION through which people confront other people, the products of human action, and sometimes themselves as objects rather than subjects. Third, he insisted that relations with others involve contradictions and tensions: the social realm is not harmonious but a space in which people gain self-awareness partly from conflict and opposition. The social whole becomes greater insofar as it incorporates and unifies complex differences. Fourth, social life as we know it is subject to change; we need to understand its internal contradictions and limits to understand the direction of change. Fifth, simply generalizing facts from the world as we see it around us will not yield deep or enduring truth about society as such; what actually exists at any one time is only a relatively arbitrary moment in history—and needs to be understood as such.

In spite of this dynamism, Hegel did hold out the prospect of an end to history and thought that he lived near the point at which contradictions would be resolved into a stable whole. Few of Hegel's successors believed that he had identified the end of history, although many were deeply marked by his thought and dialectical method. Karl MARX, for one, wrote that his own work sought to stand Hegel on his feet. By this he meant that Hegel had made a great advance in conceptualizing history and human existence as a dialectical process but had undercut his achievement by conceiving the starting point as mind or spirit rather than material existence. Twentieth-century critical theorists such as Max HORKHEIMER and Theodor ADORNO pursued this connection further and, in some respects, reintroduced key Hegelian problematics such as the dialectical character of thought.

Hegel's political theory, developed most fully in *The Philosophy of Right* (1821), placed great emphasis on the notion that freedom could be realized adequately and stably only through the state. This influenced a variety of later thinkers on both the left and right, including especially corporatists (see CORPORATISM). It was the state, Hegel suggested, that embodied universality and thus overcame the limits of egotism and family relations. Hegel's account of CIVIL SOCIETY as an important but inherently limited realm of relations among egotistical individuals remains influential. In civil society, passions bring individuals into conflict. The STATE, he argued, unifies these passions at a higher level. This view has seemed authoritarian to many and remains controversial.

A related aspect of Hegel's philosophy joins ideas about individual consciousness to social theory. To achieve consciousness and a strong sense of self, Hegel argued in the *Phenomenology of Spirit* (1807), people seek recognition from others; this is apparent in the desire for acknowledgment that shapes interpersonal relations, but for Hegel it was also more basic. Human beings gain their identities partly by fitting into roles and categories that are recognized as right (that is, as good, just, and appropriate, not merely contingent). They derive this recognition from social processes, including from the state. Hegel held that through fulfilling their roles, people gain the ability to recognize themselves in the state. This challenged SOCIAL-CONTRACT THEORY, with its attempt to base understanding of society and state on egotistical individuals. It has also influenced more recent efforts to understand why identities—national, ethnic, racial, gender, and others—should become basic foci of political contention.

Hegel taught first at the University of Jena and later, for several decades, at the University of Berlin. Many of his works on aesthetics, religion, and history were assembled from his Berlin lectures and published posthumously. Among his other major works are *Science of Logic* (1812–1816) and *Encyclopedia of the Philosophical Sciences* (1817, 1827, 1830).

Heidegger, Martin (1889–1976) A German philosopher who developed a comprehensive critique of Western metaphysics and later of the role of technology as a determinant of how humans understand their existence (in Heidegger's terms, the relationship to *Being*). Initially, his work drew heavily on the phenomenological tradition of Edmund Husserl—especially in *Being and Time* (1927), Heidegger's best-known

work—but he gradually turned toward a more direct engagement with the metaphysical tradition and with cultural issues. Heidegger has had a major influence on a number of traditions within political philosophy and cultural theory, including theories of the public sphere (through Hannah ARENDT, his student) and POSTSTRUCTURALISM, which shares much of Heidegger's sense of the centrality of LANGUAGE to the human relationship with the world. These contributions have been frequently overshadowed, however, by his sympathy for NAZISM during the early 1930s, which earned him an appointment as rector of the University of Freiburg in 1933. The significance of Heidegger's Nazism has been a subject of considerable controversy. Heidegger admitted that he had seen in it a potentially positive response to the crisis of nihilism that he believed threatened Western civilization—although he later came to see it as a symptom of that nihilism.

Throughout his work, Heidegger was concerned primarily with the need to challenge all determinate views of human nature—including classical philosophy's identification of man with nature, the subject–object distinction formalized by René DESCARTES, and the German idealist account of man's alienation and reconciliation with nature visible in Georg HEGEL and Karl MARX. These philosophies reified specific claims about humanity's relationship to Being, Heidegger argued, and set Western societies on an increasingly narrow, dissatisfying, and dangerous course—most particularly through the instrumental relationship toward the world implicit in modern individualism and made explicit through science. Instead, Heidegger sought an ontological conception of freedom, rooted in the capacity to reflect upon and explore one's relationship to Being. An authentic relation to Being, in this context, was indeterminate and open. Heidegger's early work tends to seek external agents for wrenching humanity back to this ontological freedom—poets, rulers, and philosophers. This is often seen as the context for his interest in the aestheticized politics of Nazism. Heidegger's later work turned more meditative—some have argued passive—in its pursuit of inwardness and an undirected notion of "thinking." His later work also portrays technology as the particular form of the modern crisis of Being, understood as a model of instrumental power that takes the world and, ultimately, human beings as materials ready for use. Heidegger also increasingly located the relationship to Being in patterns of language—here setting the stage for the poststructuralist work of Jacques DERRIDA and others.

Heidegger's other major works include *An Introduction to Metaphysics* (1953) and *The Question Concerning Technology and Other Essays* (1977). See also PHENOMENOLOGY.

Herfindahl index   A measure of market concentration and monopoly power. The index is calculated as the sum of the squared values of all firms' shares of a given market. A value of one indicates that a single firm monopolizes the market; lower values imply lower degrees of concentration or inequality among firms. The Herfindahl index is not based on any economic theory that would indicate that actual market power is related to the square of firm concentration. Nonetheless, it provides a shorthand way of comparing markets and the market positions of firms.

hermeneutics   The study of interpretation and the meaning of human action, historically rooted in the problem of determining the original meaning of biblical scripture. The interpretation of cultural artifacts—primarily texts—remains at the center of the hermeneutical tradition, although hermeneutical principles were extended by scholars such as Wilhelm DILTHEY and Karl MANNHEIM, and more recently Hans-Georg Gadamer, Paul Ricoeur, and Charles TAYLOR, to the problem of interpretation more generally. Modern hermeneutics tends to dispense with or marginalize the problem of original meaning as part of a broad challenge to the notion of an objective and scientifically capturable reality. As developed by Dilthey in particular, hermeneutics strongly privileges the question of context and holds that interpretation is shaped by a range of factors, including our position as inquirers, our understanding of the creative process, questions of biography, and the influence of larger social and historical forces. For Dilthey, such issues were inextricably part of the study of society and distinguished the social or human sciences from the natural sciences (see *METHODENSTREIT*). Max WEBER's pivotal notion of *VERSTEHEN* or *understanding* similarly emphasizes the interpretive challenge of understanding the motives of social actors.

Recent hermeneutic theory has focused less on actors' motives than on the ways in which processes of interpretation are constitutive of social phenomena. Practices such as voting or entities such as corporations are made possible by being interpreted as such. Interpretation is thus internal to social action and CULTURE, not a purely external effort to understand. Anthony GIDDENS has characterized the resulting methodological issues as a "double hermeneutic," reflecting the need for social scientists to grasp reality from both an external perspective (enabling structural analysis) and the internal perspective that takes into account the fact that ordinary people are also active interpretants—and thereby potentially shapers—of social reality.

Herskovits, Melville J.   (1895–1963) One of the leading American figures in African anthropology and later in the study of African-American culture. Herskovits's abiding interests were the patterns and processes of transmission of cultural traits within Africa and, in the context of the African diaspora, among the African populations of the New World. He played a major part in promoting Africanist research in the United States and became an active participant in public debates about RACE and CULTURE in the United States—notably with his groundbreaking book *The Myth of the Negro Past* (1941).

Herskovits was one of the group of outstanding anthropologists trained by Franz BOAS in the 1920s. His early research consisted of extensive fieldwork in East and West Africa, which ultimately led to the two-volume ethnography *Dahomey: an Ancient West African Kingdom* (1938). Especially in his early career, he applied himself to the question of the transmission of biological traits, leading to several important studies of the variations of "Negro" features in the United States, patterns of racial mixing, and the relation of skin color to status.

Herskovits developed a number of theoretical concepts to describe the selective transmission and persistence of cultural traits. He distinguished between ACCULTURATION, or contact between cultures, ENCULTURATION, the largely unconscious assimilation of cultural norms and knowledge during childhood, and SOCIALIZATION, or formal processes of social integration, such as education. *The Myth of the Negro Past*, which traced African cultural and linguistic legacies in the Americas, brought together and extended much of this thinking. Herskovits also wrote extensively on art and music, on the economics of primitive societies, and, in the massive *Man and His Works* (1948), on the anthropological study of culture in more general terms. In his later career, he became an important sponsor and ambassador-at-large for

Africanist research, traveling widely and founding the African Studies Program at Northwestern University. His other important works include *The American Negro: A Study in Racial Crossing* (1928, with Frances S. Herskovits), *Acculturation: The Study of Culture Contact* (1938), *The Economic Life of Primitive People* (1940), and *The Human Factor in Changing Africa* (1962, with M. H. Segall and D. T. Campbell).

heterosexism   Informal and institutionalized sets of beliefs and practices that privilege or mandate heterosexuality—the sexual preference for the opposite sex. Deriving from feminist critiques of male privilege, theories of heterosexism tend to emphasize the diverse ways in which it shapes the linguistic, cultural, and physical aspects of social life, as well as the ways in which it marks the private and public spheres. Simple examples include the expectations that families should be based on the sexual union of a man and a woman and that all "normal" adults should seek to marry.

heteroskedasticity   One of the basic assumptions of classical regression models is that the variance of the error term is constant for all observations (see REGRESSION ANALYSIS). This feature of the error term is termed *homoskedasticity*. If the error terms do not share the same variance, they are *heteroskedastic*. The presence of heteroskedasticity implies that the least squares estimates are no longer asymptotically efficient (i.e., they do not have minimum variance) and that the estimated variances of the least squares estimators are biased (the expected value of the estimator is no longer the true value of the parameter). Therefore, the conventional statistical tests are invalid. These deficiencies can be corrected by adopting a weighted or generalized least squares method. This problem arises most often in cross-sectional micro-level data. Regression models are usually used to explain the variation in a variable, or to predict the future value of a variable. Heteroskedasticity implies that the least squares estimator derived from a regression will yield misleading information on both these fronts.

Hicks, John R.   (1904–1989) Hicks was one of the last economic theorists to shape the field as a whole. His contributions touched on or transformed most areas of economic theory. Hicks became well known with the publication of *The Theory of Wages* (1932), which examined the determination of wages in a competitive market. His best known work was *Value and Capital* (1939), which made innovative contributions to consumer and producer theory and popularized the idea of general equilibrium in the English-speaking world.

Hicks studied at the University of Oxford and taught successively at the London School of Economics, the University of Manchester, and the University of Oxford. His interests ranged from the theory of the firm to monetary economics, trade cycles, and WELFARE ECONOMICS (see FIRM, THEORY OF THE). He was first and foremost a value theorist, but his article "Mr. Keynes and the Classics"—an exposition of Keynesian macroeconomics—was probably more directly influential than John Maynard KEYNES's own *General Theory of Employment, Interest and Money* (1936).

In 1972, Hicks was awarded the Nobel Prize (with Kenneth ARROW) for his contributions to general equilibrium and welfare economics. Much of this work is contained in *Value and Capital*. Hicks demonstrated that most results in consumer theory can be obtained from *ordinal utility* (rankings of preferences) and drew parallel conclusions for production theory. It was here, too, that Hicks developed what came to be known as the *Hicks substitution effect*, obtained by changing income as relative prices changed in order to maintain UTILITY at a given level. This book also provided the first attempt to analyze the stability of a system of multiple exchange and devised an influential extension of the static model to allow for the effect of future markets on equilibrium in current markets.

Hicks's most important contribution to welfare economics was the development of a criterion for measuring the benefits of certain kinds of government policies. Known as the *Kaldor–Hicks rule*, it implies that a program is beneficial if the gainers can afford to compensate the losers and still be better off. One of the difficulties with this criterion is that it is unclear whether the compensation must actually be paid for the program to be considered beneficial. Most answers involve value judgments about whether welfare has improved as a result of the program. Hicks, for his part, avoided such judgments.

In response to the publication of Keynes's *General Theory*, Hicks developed the IS-LM model, which has become the staple framework of analysis in macroeconomics textbooks (see IS-LM ANALYSIS). The IS curve shows the inverse relationship between total output and the interest rate in the goods market. As the interest rate falls, output rises. The LM curve describes the same equilibrium relationships in the assets market. As the interest rate rises, it becomes more expensive to hold money. The interaction of the IS and LM curves determines equilibrium interest rates and output. This elegant exposition helped make Keynesian macroeconomics intelligible to generations of economists.

In other works, Hicks made significant contributions to economic history and proposed a theory of trade cycles that emphasized the interaction of the multiplier and the accelerator.

high powered money   See MONETARY BASE.

Hintze, Otto   (1861–1940) A German historical sociologist who wrote innovative studies of administration, state formation, and local government. Hintze developed a strong historical and comparative approach to the study of administrative and constitutional history, tracing the formation of European NATION-STATES from the Middle Ages to the present. Hintze recognized several crucial stages in that process: first, the development of the feudal system, which involved the centralization and institutionalization of state power; second, the rise of planned state development and conscious borrowing from other state systems during the nineteenth century—a shift that underwrote a much more rapid and homogeneous development of the state. Hintze wrote prolifically on Prussian history, which he considered a paradigmatic case of the development of the modern state. He also accorded great importance to foreign pressures and external politics in shaping both state development and the character of internal politics.

After World War I, Hintze's strong nationalist and monarchist sentiments gradually gave way to a more balanced account of the development of democratic regimes. The culmination of Hintze's research—a massive comparative study of constitutions—was, however, lost during World War II. Hintze's work is collected primarily in *Geist und Epochen der preussischen Geschichte* (1943), *Soziologie und Geschichte* (1943), and *Staat und Verfassung* (1962).

historical materialism   Friedrich Engels introduced the term and provided its canonical definition as "that view of the course of history which seeks the ultimate cause and the great moving power of all important historic events in the economic development of society, in the changes in the modes of production and exchange, in the consequent division of society into distinct classes, and in the struggle of these classes against one another" (*Socialism: Utopian and Scientific*, 1880). Historical materialism thus regroups a number of the central themes and analytical claims of MARXISM, emphasizing its scientific, empirically verifiable nature. Like Engels, Karl MARX repeatedly asserted this scientific character of his work, although the heterogeneity of his writing on the subject eventually opened the door to a range of twentieth-century Marxist humanisms. Historical materialism became the global term for the Marxist science of history and ultimately formed a central component of the doctrines of many communist parties. It has been at the heart of enduring debates about the role of revolution, the relationship between the economic base and political or cultural superstructure, the definition of classes in relation to the means of production, and the historical question of stages of development (see BASE AND SUPERSTRUCTURE). The term is sometimes contrasted with DIALECTICAL MATERIALISM, which refers to the larger framework of dialectical thought. At other times it is used as a more general synonym for Marxism.

historical particularism   The central component of Franz BOAS's attack on nineteenth-century evolutionism and the COMPARATIVE METHOD (see EVOLUTION AND EVOLUTIONISM). Historical particularism is rooted in the notion that each culture is unique and intelligible only on its own terms and, consequently, is not readily assimilable to the cross-cultural generalizations and broad evolutionary schemata that were popular in the late nineteenth century. Boas advocated a holistic and descriptive approach to the study of CULTURE, in the process challenging the scientific ambitions that led anthropologists to propose laws of change and social organization. Historical particularism has come to be synonymous with that perspective. Despite the reemergence of evolutionary arguments, historical particularism still underwrites a great deal of anthropological and historical writing, especially in the United States.

historicism   A term with two conflicting but not strictly incompatible meanings: according to the first, historicism is a strong version of historical relativism and holds that historical eras can be understood only on their own terms. At its limit, this view challenges the validity of historical comparisons (see HISTORICAL PARTICULARISM). The second meaning is Karl Raimund POPPER's well-known characterization of historicism as the search for social and historical laws that enable predictions about the future. Popper was critical of such ambitions and targeted in particular the scientific claims of MARXISM, which he argued had been shown to be false. He also extended his critique toward a wide range of teleological theories of MODERNITY and modernization.

Hobbes, Thomas (1588–1679) A British political and moral philosopher of the Early Modern period; generally considered the founder of the social contract tradition in political theory (see SOCIAL-CONTRACT THEORY). Hobbes was active in a number of the major philosophical debates of his day. He produced an important materialist critique of René DESCARTES's account of consciousness (ultimately published as the third set of "Objections" to Descartes's *Meditations on First Philosophy*). He also wrote a number of influential considerations of the nature and origin of LANGUAGE. More generally, Hobbes insisted on the application of the natural laws of mechanics and geometry to moral and political philosophy. He believed the behavior of molecules to be analogous to and ultimately constitutive of human behavior. Hobbes's image of the "Leviathan," or sovereign, as literally composed of the members of society is his most famous extension of this principle and underlies his masterwork of that name.

Leviathan (1651) investigated the nature of the social bond in a time of considerable political and social unrest in England. It was concerned, above all, with legitimating the notion of sovereign power and with providing a rational basis for the social order. Without the bonds of society and family, Hobbes argued, human beings existed in a molecular state of individuality—a *state of nature* in which their rational powers were turned toward self-preservation. Although persons were not universally egotistical, the existence of such motivations on the part of some set the terms for encounters more generally. Despite differences in strength or ability, human life under such conditions was characterized by a broad equality, insofar as each person could potentially kill any other person. Given the constant potential for violence, life was reduced to a "war of all against all"; it was, in Hobbes's well-known words "solitary, poor, nasty, brutish, and short."

Human reason, Hobbes argued, recognized the desirability of peace and the impossibility of achieving it as long as individuals were the arbiters of proper behavior. Rationality, therefore, would lead individuals to give that right to a sovereign invested with absolute and unchallengeable authority, whose law would guarantee the peace. Sovereign power, therefore, was constituted in a one-time, rational act of consent by many individuals. Hobbes recognized no popular right of redress or revolution (unlike later contract theorists, such as John LOCKE and Jean-Jacques ROUSSEAU), although individuals retained an inherent right to defend themselves when their lives were threatened. Although Hobbes devoted much of *Leviathan* to justifying his theory of legitimation in terms of biblical scripture, his theory is fundamentally secular, rooting the social order and sovereign authority in human reason and actions, rather than in divine will. This concept put Hobbes in a complicated political position for much of his life—alternately acceptable to Parliamentarians and Royalists, but deeply at odds with the church.

Hobbes's other major works include *The Elements of Law* (written in 1640, published in 1650), *De Cive* (*The Citizen*, 1642), and *A Dialogue between a Philosopher and a Student of the Common Laws of England* (written in 1666, published in 1681).

Hoggart, Richard (1918–) Hoggart was a key figure in the emergence of CULTURAL STUDIES in the late 1950s and 1960s. He founded the Centre for Contemporary Cultural Studies (1964) at the University of Birmingham (the Birmingham school) and wrote a seminal early analysis of working-class culture, *The Uses of Literacy* (1957). He was one of the first British scholars to develop an integrated approach to the study of popular culture, analyzing the music, magazines, fiction, and the gathering places of the working class and moving easily between personal experience, ethnography, and cultural analysis. Very much the product of an older working-class environment, Hoggart argued that working-class culture had suffered a loss of vitality as newer forms of mass culture, often imported from America, replaced the local, embedded, "lived" forms. *The Uses of Literacy* was, in large part, a study of that transition. It resonated with widespread concern for the fate of the working class in postwar England and achieved both popular and scholarly success.

As head of the Centre for Contemporary Cultural Studies, Hoggart did much to sponsor the study of popular and working-class culture—an interest he shared with the historian Edward Palmer THOMPSON. Hoggart did not share Thompson's (or Raymond WILLIAMS's) Marxist methodologies and leftist political commitments, however, and with his departure from Birmingham in the late 1960s, he became increasingly distant from the politicized mainstream of cultural studies. Hoggart spent several years as Assistant Director of UNESCO before returning to England, where he continued to write and contribute to public policy debates over culture and the arts.

His other major works include *Speaking to Each Other* (1970) and *The Way We Live Now* (1995).

Homans, George (1910–1989) An American sociologist who specialized in the study of individual behavior and interaction within small groups. His early work, *The Human Group* (1950), sought to specify and develop methods for analyzing the three types of variables that he argued informed all group relationships and forms of social organization: *interaction* (the relationships between members of a group); *sentiment* (feelings or emotions related to the group); and *activity* (actions taken as members of the group). These, in turn, were regulated by NORMS and codes and shaped by relationships with other groups.

Homans became best known, however, for his contributions to EXCHANGE theory, initially developed in *Social Behavior: Its Elementary Forms* (1961). Here again he focused on patterns of face-to-face behavior, but conceived them largely in the context of the behavioral psychology developed by B. F. SKINNER and others—especially the notion of *operant conditioning*. Although simple economistic rationales played a part in this work, Homans emphasized conditioning and criticized economistic versions of exchange theory, which placed more stress on conscious strategy. Homans's larger claim for exchange theory—shared by many proponents of ACTION THEORY—was that a microsociological account of small-scale behavior was the necessary foundation of any account of large-scale social behavior. In this regard, he argued against the sociological preoccupation with social structures, which often neglected to account for the individual interactions that compose them. His famous presidential address to the American Sociological Association in 1964 was entitled "Bringing Men Back In."

Homans's other major works include *English Villagers of the Thirteenth Century* (1941), *Sentiments and Activities* (1962), *The Nature of Social Science* (1967), and *Certainties and Doubts* (1987). He also wrote an autobiography, entitled *Coming to My Senses* (1984).

Homo economicus   See ECONOMIC MAN.

homogeneous functions and homothetic functions   A function is said to be homogeneous of degree n if multiplying every argument in the function by the same constant, λ, changes the value of the function by λ^n. A function is said to be linearly homogeneous if $n = 1$. For example, if doubling all the inputs leads to double the output, then the production function is linearly homogenous. A *homothetic function* is simply a monotone transformation of a homogeneous function. In the preceding example, if we changed the specifications of the production function so that an increase in the original function is always accompanied by an increase in the new function, then the new function is homothetic.

homoskedasticity   See HETEROSKEDASTICITY.

Horkheimer, Max (1895–1973) Horkheimer led the Institute for Social Research (better known as the FRANKFURT SCHOOL) from 1930 through the 1960s and was the leading force behind the emergence of *critical theory*—a highly interdisciplinary approach to social critique that sought to address the innovations of PSYCHOANALYSIS, the isolation of philosophy, the inadequacies of scientific MARXISM, and, perhaps most pressingly, the rise of FASCISM. Never a prolific writer, Horkheimer nonetheless articulated many of the fundamental concerns of critical theory in his essays of the late 1930s, particularly in the program statement, "Traditional and Critical Theory" (1937). Although in this period he was still loosely committed to the project of social liberation along Marxist lines, the manifest failures of working-class struggle in Germany and the Soviet Union led Horkheimer (and critical theorists more generally) toward a more encompassing critique of modernity that posited a growing disjunction between instrumental reason and critical reason. The former was exemplified in the cult of efficiency and ease that for Horkheimer diminished the space of traditional bourgeois autonomy. The latter represented the progressive side of Enlightenment thought and foregrounded about questions the goals of human labor and the nature of the good society. If, in general, critical theory sought to recover critical reason in order to break the hold of instrumental reason over human thought and labor, Horkheimer's later work grew increasingly pessimistic about such liberatory possibilities. His most important book, *The Dialectic of Enlightenment* (1947, with Theodor ADORNO), implies the virtual totalization of instrumental reason, realized in the full integration of labor, culture, and the state into a single capitalist process that dominates modern society. Horkheimer's postwar work grew increasingly conservative in this regard and largely abandoned the search for social forces capable of conceiving and carrying out social change. See CULTURE INDUSTRY.

Horkheimer was also a great organizer and facilitator of other work, especially in his capacity as director of the Institute. Although his own work was largely philosophical and cultural in orientation, he sponsored a range of empirical projects, from the *Studies on Authority and the Family* (1936) conducted in Germany to the later *Studies in Prejudice* conducted in the United States. The latter produced, among other results, the well-known account of the "authoritarian personality" (Adorno et al., 1950). As director, Horkheimer also oversaw the exile of the Frankfurt school to the United States after Hitler's rise to power in 1933, and organized its return to Germany after the war. His other major works include *The Eclipse of Reason* (1947) and *Critical Theory: Selected Essays* (1972).

Horney, Karen   (1885–1952) A psychoanalyst best known for her work on neurosis and coping techniques. Horney was a leading figure in the development of a range of nonorthodox psychoanalytic approaches in mid-twentieth-century America. Compared to orthodox Freudians, she emphasized interpersonal relations and minimized the role ascribed to biology (see Sigmund FREUD). Horney was particularly critical of Freud's approach to women.

Horney's theory of personality was based on the identification of a wide range of neurotic needs, from the need for social recognition to that for domination over others, dependence, independence, and personal achievement. These she grouped into three general personality types: a self-effacing or withdrawing personality characterized by the need for independence and perfection; an expansive, aggressive type characterized by the need for power and competitive success; and a compliant, resigning type characterized

by self-sacrifice. The neurotic forms of these needs, she argued, distort one's self-perception and thereby reduce the potential for healthy *self-realization*. Horney assigned great importance to the parental role in the formation of such needs and treated therapy as a way of identifying and overcoming them. Her major works include *Self-Analysis* (1942), *Neurosis and Human Growth* (1950), and *Feminine Psychology* (1967).

horticulture   A form of agriculture that relies on hand-held implements—the hoe or spade, for instance—as opposed to animal-drawn implements such as the plow.

Hotelling, Harold   (1895–1973) An American mathematician who made major contributions to economic theory. Although Hotelling wrote only ten papers that dealt directly with economics, his influence is profound. His paper on locational equilibrium in DUOPOLY is a fundamental text for theoretical economists, and many of the voting models popular in POLITICAL ECONOMY today are inspired by Hotelling's work.

"Stability in Competition" (1929), Hotelling's famous paper on location, developed a game theoretic analysis of duopoly (see GAME THEORY). The game involves two players who first choose a position along a one-dimensional line and subsequently a price. Hotelling claimed to have found a *subgame perfect equilibrium*—conditions under which neither player has any incentive to change position or price. This proposition was later found to be true only if the positions or locations are sufficiently close to each other.

This model has been fruitfully applied to a number of situations, especially in the area of firm behavior and in voting models, where it has been used to analyze stances on political issues in two-candidate elections. Hotelling himself suggested a possible political interpretation of his model, but its potential in this direction has been explored only recently. Hotelling also made contributions to capital theory—notably in defining depreciation as the decrease in the discounted value of future returns—as well as to production theory and WELFARE ECONOMICS.

hot money   Speculative, large-scale movement of short-term capital—i.e., capital that can be shifted between sectors or uses in order to exploit differences in currency values or interest rates. Hot money can be a source of great instability in national economies—especially in small or developing countries—because it produces sudden and sometimes perverse changes in monetary conditions. Large flows of hot money may create self-fulfilling devaluations or revaluations of the exchange rate. In order to combat hot money flows, domestic governments make use of capital controls such as minimum periods before capital withdrawal, dual exchange rates, and sterilization (in which the CENTRAL BANK offsets the effect of foreign reserve changes through OPEN-MARKET OPERATIONS).

household   Often held to be the primary unit of social organization. The concept generally privileges common residence and certain basic economic functions (such as food preparation or domestic production) over reproduction and KINSHIP (quintessentially, the FAMILY). It is useful in describing societies in which households are not organized around nuclear families—and less useful in the context of nomadic or foraging societies that do not possess fixed domiciles. The term *domestic group* is sometimes used as a substitute for both household and family.

human capital   The stock of skills and productive knowledge possessed by people. Among the earliest users of the concept (if not of the term itself) were craft workers during the industrial revolution, who claimed that their skills constituted a form of CAPITAL. Craft workers generally lost such struggles to claim and protect those skills as property, however, as guilds had once done. Economics began to focus extensively on human capital after World War II (the work of Gary BECKER figures prominently). It emphasized not industrial skills per se, but rather the value of formal schooling and the determinants of individual decisions about how much to acquire. More generally, human capital theory extends methods of analysis developed for other forms of capital to questions of investment in training and education, which contribute to productivity. These questions are approached both from the perspective of investment decisions by firms, which must weigh the potential increases in productivity against the cost of training (a question of OPPORTUNITY COSTS) and from the perspective of individual workers, who weigh the future benefits (income, satisfaction, or otherwise) against the cost and deferred earnings.

Considerable work has been done on the nature of these opportunity costs, as well as on the problem of measuring the return on such investment. Benefits, however, are very difficult to quantify or compare across different forms of education and training—particularly in the bottom-line terms desired by analysts of firms and capital optimization. The benefits of investment in human capital depend upon a great number of social and cultural variables, few of which are easily isolated. Nonetheless, economists have had some success in mapping investment decisions against longer-term variables such as life cycles, structural issues such as CLASS and profession, and the related familial stratification by wealth and status (see LIFE-CYCLE HYPOTHESIS). Families themselves are one of the main avenues of investment in human capital, both through formal education and forms of SOCIALIZATION. The patterns of such investment play a large role in the persistence of wealth and poverty over time, and thus enter into public policy decisions about the allocation of resources in education and other areas.

Although the majority of research in human capital theory is framed by rational-choice propositions about behavior and by the question of opportunity cost, significant attention has been devoted in recent years to the larger structural determinants of individual choices, the role of education in reproducing social distinctions, and the convertibility of forms of SOCIAL CAPITAL and CULTURAL CAPITAL into wealth. Much of this attention reflects the influence of the sociologist Pierre BOURDIEU, whose work traces the relationships among diverse forms of capital and analyzes the fields in which they operate.

human ecology   At its most ambitious, human ecology treats social systems as extensions of natural ecological systems, emphasizing the competition for resources by different social groups, processes of adaptation to the environment, the emergence of narrowly adaptive niches, and ultimately the survival of the fittest. This orientation was pioneered by urban sociologists at the CHICAGO SCHOOL OF SOCIOLOGY—especially Robert Ezra PARK, who used the city as his principle example of a human ecological system. Although many of the principles of social adaptation found their way into the broader structural-functionalist mainstream of midcentury SOCIOLOGY—albeit in a form that emphasized the diversity of functional adaptations within society—the strict analogy to natural systems did not. Early human ecology left little room for cultural factors proper, for human agency, or for significant social change. Later research in human ecology generally loosened its account of the relationship between biological and sociological analysis, focusing on narrower instances of social adaptation and on group behavior that tends to restore social equilibrium. Human ecology is especially influential on issues of scale and population density in social organization. It is also the basis for population ecology, an approach to the analysis of organizations that emphasizes the dynamics of whole populations (for example, birth and death rates, or ecological niches) over questions of individual leadership or internal characteristics.

humanitarianism The promotion of basic human welfare in situations of natural disaster or armed conflict—generally through the provision of food, medicine, housing, and other forms of relief, but also potentially including preventive diplomacy and armed intervention. Humanitarian action assumed a large role in international politics in the last twentieth century—in part due to the penetration of the modern media into zones of crisis and the resulting immediacy of mass human suffering to an international audience. Humanitarian aid has not been without controversy, however. European humanitarian missions to the non-European world during the nineteenth century were often associated with religious proselytization among local populations and with furthering the aims of colonial administration. Today, intervention by international bodies such as the United Nations or NONGOVERNMENTAL ORGANIZATIONS (NGOs) such as the Red Cross and Doctors Without Borders sometimes raises complicated SOVEREIGNTY issues in the recipient country. There are also debates over the degree to which the provision of international humanitarian assistance undermines local institutions (for example, when food programs undercut local agricultural production). More generally, most social scientists agree that only longer-term, successful DEVELOPMENT can reduce the frequency and severity of humanitarian crises.

A range of other questions inform humanitarian efforts, such as whether aid to civilian populations during conflicts allows belligerents to devote more resources to fighting. Perhaps most controversial has been the recent trend toward humanitarian military intervention in cases of civil war, the collapse of government, or attempted GENOCIDE. These efforts have often met local resistance and at times have garnered only moderate popular support in the intervening countries.

human relations movement A body of sociological research and management theory that critiqued the principles of labor efficiency promoted by SCIENTIFIC MANAGEMENT. Human relations (or HR) was initially developed by Elton Mayo in the wake of the Hawthorne experiments, which Mayo argued demonstrated the insufficiency of economic incentives for workers (see HAWTHORNE EFFECT). In most factories, Mayo argued, the workplace was an anomic environment that failed to meet the social and emotional needs of workers, resulting in conflictual labor relations and overall inefficiency. Human relations solutions to this problem tended to involve reversing the extreme division of labor posited by scientific management, creating opportunities for teamwork and team solidarity, and fostering closer relations between management and labor. Workplace counseling also played a prominent role.

There has been significant disagreement about whether the Hawthorne studies in fact support Mayo's conclusions, and human relations research has been the subject of a wide range of criticisms, including its generally explicit investment in the logic of productivity and the workplace status quo. With the resurgence of conflict models in SOCIOLOGY in the 1960s, human relations became a much less significant orientation—although some of its major themes returned in the 1980s with the rise of Japanese models of workplace organization.

human rights See RIGHTS.

Humboldt, Alexander von (1769–1859) Humboldt and his associate Carl RITTER are generally considered the founders of modern GEOGRAPHY—Ritter in the area of human geography and Humboldt primarily in physical geography. Nonetheless, Humboldt's influence extended over a broad range of fields, from evolutionary science to literature. Humboldt was a prodigious explorer and naturalist who traveled widely in Latin America and later Russia. Family money funded both his early travels and the subsequent publication of his accounts, which he undertook during his long residence in Paris. Humboldt's achievement lay not only in his vivid descriptions of the locales he visited—descriptions that circulated widely and played a large part in the construction of European perceptions of the New World—but also in his efforts to uncover the history and causes of the phenomena he described. This work did much to legitimize geography as a science, and brought him considerable fame. His major works include the *Personal Narrative of Travels to the Equinoctial Regions of America during the Years 1799–1804*, which eventually comprised some thirty volumes (1805–1834), and the four-volume *Kosmos: A Sketch of a Physical Description of the Universe* (1845–1862).

Hume, David (1711–1776) The principal philosopher of the Scottish Enlightenment, best known for his strong EMPIRICISM and his argument against the possibility of grasping *necessary* causality by induction. The former informed Hume's rejection of speculative philosophy and theology—indeed of all claims to truth that lay outside human experience. The basis for knowledge, he argued, lies only in the experience of the senses. Knowledge cannot be grounded in the abstractions of reason, however logical. Hume's argument against causality—or more precisely, against any necessarily causal connection between two events—follows similar principles. He held that any strict understanding of cause and effect cannot be proved by the senses, but that the impression of causality can and does arise from the repeated experience of two events in juxtaposition. This is the essence of Hume's radical skepticism, which he extended further to cast doubt on knowledge of the independent existence of objects and the world. This in no way implied, however, that causality did not exist or that persons were deprived of practical means of negotiating and acting in the world. It did mean that causes and effects could not strictly be known. For Hume, this implied not only a margin of human freedom but also a moral obligation to act in consideration of the many possible effects of one's action.

Hume put these principles to work in attacks on religion—especially the belief in and cynical uses of miracles. He applied them in a defense of the importance of the passions (which the rationalist tradition in philosophy had subordinated to reason) and in his well-known assertion that, in the moral and political realm, there is no way to logically infer what should be from what is. Hume's most enduring work is *A Treatise of Human Nature* (1739–1740), which presents his philosophical views in detail and advocates the scientific study of human nature as a means of understanding and improving society. Such study, Hume argued, would provide the basis for a secular morality and for a society ruled by justice and reason.

In addition to his philosophical works, Hume wrote extensively on ECONOMICS and English history. His *History of England* (1763) was used as a textbook in English schools for many years. His autobiography, *My Own Life* (1777), is considered a classic. Hume's other writings include *Essays Moral and Political* (1748), *Inquiry Concerning the Principles of Morals* (1751), *Political Discourses* (1752), and *The Natural History of Religion* (1755).

hunting and gathering The basic mode of subsistence throughout most of human history. Groups that rely on hunting and gathering are typically nomadic or seminomadic and are organized in small bands (see BAND SOCIETIES). Hunting and gathering has frequently occupied the bottom rung of schemas of societal evolution, but recent research has challenged these assumptions in a number of regards. First, it has been shown that the pressures of modernization (on land use, especially) have in certain instances forced agricultural groups into nomadic subsistence modes. Second, Marshall SAHLINS and others have argued for the relative ease of hunting and gathering over early agriculture.

Huntington, Ellsworth (1876–1947) A major figure in the development of human geography in the United States in the early part of the twentieth century. Huntington is best known for his advocacy of ENVIRONMENTAL DETERMINISM, particularly in regard to the impact of climate and climate change on civilizations. These positions were both controversial and easily overstated by his critics. In his later work, Huntington adopted a position closer to that of PROBABILISM—the belief that the environment makes certain responses more probable than others. This left a greater margin for human choices and thus for historical differences among civilizations. He was also a strong defender of scientific methods in the study of human geography and a major contributor to the institutionalization of geography in the United States. Huntington's main works include *The Pulse of Asia* (1907), *Civilization and Climate* (1915), and *The Human Habitat* (1927).

hybridity The synthesis that takes place in any encounter between distinct cultures, with the implication that combination, rather than sorting into pure categories, is the norm. The term has been important in a variety of fields, from studies of RACE and ETHNICITY to postcolonial projects that emphasize the processes of survival, ADAPTATION, and resistance of indigenous populations to colonization.

hydraulic societies Societies in which institutions are closely linked to the development and control of systems of irrigation and, sometimes, water-based transport. The term is associated with Karl MARX's concepts of the ASIATIC MODE OF PRODUCTION and ORIENTAL DESPOTISM, although recent research has challenged evolutionary claims about the relation of water management to the emergence of highly centralized, authoritarian regimes. The concept has been deployed most influentially in efforts to explain the importance of the state in China, the impact of dynastic cycles, and the failure of such societies to generate CAPITALISM or another system of self-sustaining growth beyond the limits of the traditional economy.

hypergamy and hypogamy Marriage customs in which the partners are of different social statuses (see ANISOGAMY). In hypergamy, the woman is typically of lower social status than the man; hypogamy is the opposite. ISOGAMY designates marriage between social equals. See also MARRIAGE SYSTEMS.

hyperinflation A condition of rapidly increasing prices for goods and services. Hyperinflation is usually the result of dramatic increases in the printing of money used to cover expanding budget deficits. While this may stimulate economic activity for a short period, the consequent distortion of relative prices quickly overwhelms any benefit. Under such conditions, workers suffer a decline in real wages as nominal wages lag behind the general inflation level, which can involve daily price changes (see WAGES, NOMINAL AND REAL). Hyperinflation also has a strong concentrating effect on wealth, favoring those with concrete assets in land or capital, while rendering worthless money assets such as bank accounts.

Over time, hyperinflation becomes driven by rising expectations of inflation rather than by actual growth in the money supply. It thereby becomes self-perpetuating. Attempts to stop hyperinflation usually involve major increases in interest rates (in order to take money out of circulation) and government commitments to budget austerity, monetary control, and frequently new currencies. The latter measures depend largely on the credibility of the government to maintain them in the face of political pressure and speculative runs on the currency. In situations of political instability, or following repeated episodes of hyperinflation, such credibility can be extremely difficult to establish. Hyperinflation has been a recurring problem in developing countries—especially in Latin America. See also INFLATION.

hypothetico-deductive method Often referred to as the SCIENTIFIC METHOD, the hypothetico-deductive method is an approach to testing and theoretical knowledge based on logical principles of deduction. It postulates a movement from general theories to testable hypotheses and predictions, and finally to empirical observations that support or disprove the theory.

hysteresis A situation in which the equilibrium of a system depends upon the history of the system. The equilibrium is then said to be *path-dependent*.

I

id In Freudian psychoanalytic theory, the id is a reservoir of innate biological drives that demand immediate satisfaction. These drives primarily concern physical pleasure, including sexual pleasure. The id is thus associated with the *pleasure principle* that Sigmund FREUD argued fundamentally shaped human behavior. Freud's later work tended to minimize the biological character of these drives, although the line always remained somewhat vague. The id is part of Freud's tripartite model of the psyche—complemented by the EGO, which is responsible for mediating between instinctual drives and parental (and later social) prohibitions, and the SUPEREGO, which internalizes the latter. See also PSYCHOANALYSIS.

idealism In general usage, the pursuit of or belief in pure or uncompromised ideas or values. The term sometimes stands in pejorative contrast to "realism" or other claims for practical action and realizable goals. In philosophy, idealism refers more specifically to the doctrine that external reality cannot be understood apart from consciousness, or, more radically, that some ideas or categories of understanding exist prior to experience. PLATO's view that all concepts exist separately from their worldly incarnations is the crucial ancient source for radical idealism. His work anchored a fundamental division between idealists and materialists (who generally asserted the completeness of the given world) in Greco-Roman thought. ARISTOTLE, in particular, challenged the static ideals of Platonism with a strongly materialist and empirical philosophy based largely on *physis* (becoming or development). Christian thought was influenced by Platonic idealism, as in the New Testament reworking of Genesis, which asserts that "in the beginning was the word." In turn, Christian thought shaped the idealist tradition in philosophy by developing a more capacious notion of the "interior" mental life of individuals (initially through the writing of Saint AUGUSTINE). Medieval Mysticism (both Christian and Jewish) also contributed to idealism, as did the recovery of advanced mathematics and Greek thought from the Arab world. This set the stage for a formative modern dialectic between idealism and MATERIALISM from the Renaissance forward.

Modern science is shaped in part by the combination of (and tension between) empirical evidence and theory formation. Materialists emphasize the priority of the former; idealists the latter. As a philosophical tradition, modern idealism is most strongly associated with Enlightenment and post-Enlightenment German philosophy. Against the empirical tradition of David HUME and others, Immanuel KANT argued that all knowledge and understanding of the world requires that certain basic categories and ideas are inherent in consciousness (*Critique of Pure Reason*, 1781). Kant's *transcendental idealism* posited a "noumenal" realm of rational ideas distinct from the merely contingent "phenomenal" world of things. A generation later, Georg HEGEL developed a dialectical approach that privileged neither the subject (as had Kant) nor the object (as had the empiricists), but that located both within the historical development of what he termed "Spirit"—an all-encompassing "absolute idealism."

Diverse traditions have built on the Kantian and Hegelian examples—rooting idealism variously in consciousness or history. An important body of political philosophy has demonstrated the vitality of the Kantian concerns—focusing on the human capacity to order the world through knowledge. These include John RAWLS's theory of JUSTICE and Jürgen HABERMAS's theory of COMMUNICATIVE ACTION, as well as a number of French efforts to move beyond POSTSTRUCTURALISM. Habermas, in particular, revises the conventional idealist framework by idealizing *processes* (of knowledge-formation or communicatively achieved agreement) rather than end states. This distances him from static idealisms and deterministic models of history, and allows him to better account for the particularities of empirical political practices and social institutions.

ideal type A hypothetical description of the pure characteristics of a phenomenon or object. Ideal types are strongly associated with the methodological theories of Max WEBER and play a prominent role in his work on BUREAUCRACY. Ideal types are not simple descriptions of real-world phenomena; instead, they are primarily analytical devices that aid in thinking about the constitutive logic or internal tendencies of objects (such as markets or institutions). The ideal types themselves rarely correspond exactly to the complex examples found in reality.

In Weber's account, for example, bureaucracy is defined by several "ideal" qualities—specialization, hierarchy of office, rules, impersonality, and rewards based on merit—that may or may not coincide in any particular bureaucratic system. The economic theory of markets and competition is based almost entirely on ideal types and often comes close to supposing the real existence of the type. Market theories are largely concerned with the imperfections that draw market behavior away from its ideal form, and with methods that can restore or approximate it.

identity politics Political activity organized on the basis of cultural, racial, gender, ethnic, or other claims that prioritize a particular group identity and experience. Usage varies as to whether identities are treated as fixed bases for politics or as themselves products of political struggle or other "identity work."

Although markers of identity have always played a role in politics, the term *identity politics* is most strongly associated with the wave of political organization and contestation launched by black activists in the 1960s and then continued by the women's movement, other minority movements, the gay pride movement, and most recently by conservative identity movements such as the Christian Coalition and white supremacist groups. Identity politics has evolved into a potent rhetorical device for mobilizing members of populations that feel marginalized or mistreated. It generally involves criteria of belonging that are closed to newcomers—for either cultural or biological reasons—and thus also involves a sense of experiential privilege that can be translated into political claims. Identity politics is often presented as a critique of the universalistic and/or liberal forms of political participation that historically promised equal treatment but

practiced discrimination of various kinds. Still, identity politics often operates in uneasy relation to the traditional and still enormously powerful language of liberal redress, sometimes idealizing the identity-blind society of liberal discourse despite its historical failures and sometimes demanding special treatment or a larger share of public and private resources for groups on historical, philosophical, or (in some cases) biological grounds. Identity politics has played a growing—if increasingly institutionalized and less radical—role in U.S. politics since the 1970s. Despite its claims, however, many observers have argued that identity politics reflects the decline of the more coercive structures of discrimination (and privilege) in both public and private life that once anchored most forms of social identity. As a result, these groups are frequently unstable and subject to further internal challenges as new divisions of experience or identity become occasions for mobilization.

ideological state apparatus (ISA) A concept introduced by Marxist philosopher Louis ALTHUSSER in *Lenin and Philosophy* (1971). ISAs are those institutions and systems that legitimate and reproduce the STATE, above all by producing consent to the regime on the part of subordinated groups. For Althusser, religion, education, the legal system, mass culture, and the family are all ISAs—all buttress the ideology of the ruling class by naturalizing its privileges. ISAs are distinguished, however, from what Althusser called *repressive state apparatuses* (RSAs). RSAs include the police and army—the more direct instruments of coercion and violence at the disposal of the ruling class.

Althusser's distinction between the two demonstrates a strong debt to Antonio GRAMSCI's concept of hegemony, which theorizes the relationship between domination and consent in democratic societies. Like Gramsci, Althusser rejected the strict economic determinism of the ideological field, recognizing its "relative autonomy" and therefore the possibility of contestation and struggle within it. This theoretical legacy has been important to contemporary cultural analysis, especially in the area of CULTURAL STUDIES.

ideology A cohesive set of beliefs, ideas, and symbols through which persons interpret the world and their place within it. The term was coined in late eighteenth-century France in reference to a projected science of ideas, but soon came to refer to a view of the world based on irrational beliefs as opposed to objective knowledge. This usage informed the influential account of ideology developed by Karl MARX and Friedrich Engels in *The German Ideology* (1846) and other writings. The term has since carried strong Marxist connotations. For Marx and Engels, ideology was FALSE CONSCIOUSNESS, a distorted understanding of the world that legitimized the domination of the ruling classes.

Twentieth-century Marxism was shaped by a number of influential revisions of the concept, partly in order to accommodate the challenges to revolutionary action posed by uneven development, FASCISM, and the capitalist welfare state. These accounts tend to accord a larger and more complex role to CULTURE—the field of ideological struggle—in relation to the economic determinants of class identity and the political component of revolutionary action. Georg LUKÁCS opened the door to many of these considerations by emphasizing the degree to which revolutionary action depended on proper proletarian consciousness—and thus on overcoming ideological barriers. Antonio GRAMSCI argued that class domination depended heavily on the ideological hegemony of the ruling class, achieved primarily through consent to ruling class ideas and embedded in the commonsense beliefs of day-to-day life. Louis ALTHUSSER expanded this notion by linking the dominant ideology to the social institutions he called IDEOLOGICAL STATE APPARATUSes (ISAs). Like Gramsci, he accorded them considerably more autonomy from the economic substructure than most strict readings of Marx had allowed.

Both Marxist and non-Marxist approaches to ideology distinguish it from objective knowledge. These "critical" views privilege the perspective of the observer and are echoed in the pejorative sense of the term in common speech, caricatured by Clifford GEERTZ: "I have a social philosophy, you have political opinions, he has an ideology." Such reasoning informs indictments of ideologies within the liberal tradition, as well as by writers such as Hannah ARENDT (*The Origins of Totalitarianism*, 1951). It also structures recent work that purports to describe the "end of ideology"—a view popular in the 1960s and again after the fall of the Communist regimes. Marx, however, argued that a belief in the universalism and objectivity of its ideas is the chief ideological support of the BOURGEOISIE and its liberal theories of government. Real

objectivity, in contrast, had to derive from an understanding of the fundamental role of capitalist relations in producing the prevailing ideas. Such reasoning led to a by now familiar dilemma in the philosophy and sociology of knowledge about the authority accorded social knowledge. Karl MANNHEIM's *Ideology and Utopia* (1936) is a prominent attempt to accommodate ideological critique without recourse to an epistemological privilege located in class or social positions. Mannheim argued that the goal of social science is to arrive at a scientific, objective set of principles applicable to all societies that is free from the partialities of ideological perspectives. This requires the reconciling of inevitably diverse and competing worldviews in a "dynamic synthesis," which Mannheim argued was within the reach of the "free intelligentsia" of the world. Sometimes referred to as Mannheim's Paradox, the problem of how a perspectivist account of knowledge avoids implicating itself in its own conclusions (that it, too, is a subjective and partial view) has posed problems for putatively objective, social scientific analyses, for example, that of Talcott PARSONS and Edward Shils.

The latter half of the twentieth century has seen a considerable growth of interest in ideology. One direction of research, based in CULTURAL STUDIES, draws on Gramsci in examining the extent and effect of hegemonic or ruling ideas, particularly through the use of DISCOURSE ANALYSIS. Much of this research examines the ways in which cultural practices and discourses reflect and reproduce ideological formations. Related work traces the ways in which race, ethnicity, gender, nationalism, class, and other identity categories assimilate, contest, and produce ideological codes. In these cases, ideology often no longer makes reference to the material conditions of society's economic base, but refers more generally to the structures and uses of power.

Other scholars, including Geertz, have borrowed from anthropology and semiotics to advance a broader, more inclusive and positive notion of ideology as a meaning-giving symbolic system used by groups to interpret the world. Such neutral uses of the concept of ideology generally underwrite either close, hermeneutic, anthropological studies of particular societies, which focus on symbolic practices, or broad comparative studies of public opinion that use a few conventional, easily recognized ideologies (e.g., liberal, conservative, or social democratic) to differentiate among different groups of opinions.

ideographic science and nomothetic science Distinguishes between science that focuses on the particular and the unique (ideographic science), and science that seeks generalized or universal laws (nomothetic science).

idle balances Money withdrawn from circulation and held as a store of wealth because of uncertainty about the future price of financial assets. John Maynard KEYNES referred to this as the speculative motive for holding money.

imagined community Benedict Anderson's term for large communities (quintessentially nations) in which the collective social bond must be imagined rather than directly experienced through face-to-face interactions. The concept is central to Anderson's account of the rise of modern NATIONALISM and NATION-STATES through the spread of literacy and print-capitalism (*Imagined Communities*, 1983). In the course of this development, newspapers, museums, and other new "technologies" become the means of representing the collective national experience—if only by bringing diverse individual events into spatial association (as in the newspaper). The census, maps, museums, and the novel similarly become sites where the national idea is developed and reproduced. Anderson's approach inaugurated a range of cultural and symbolic approaches to the study of nationalism and the nation-state.

immiserizing growth A model of growth that holds that under certain conditions, economic growth can cause a net reduction in the general welfare of a country (immiseration). Jagdish Bhagwati ("Immiserating Growth: A Geometrical Note" 1958) demonstrated that growth can induce a deterioration in the terms of trade of countries that have some monopoly power in a world market. For such a country, free trade is a suboptimal policy that can potentially produce losses. The country would be better served, in economic terms, by exploiting its monopoly influence. Harry Johnson later demonstrated a similar result for countries that use tariffs in spite of being unable to influence their terms of trade (i.e., countries that hold no monopoly power over an international market). Since the terms of trade cannot be changed, the tariff will simply raise domestic prices, making domestic consumers worse off.

imperfect competition A situation in which some agents in the marketplace have MONOPOLY power—the power to influence the market prices via their actions. This contrasts with perfect competition, in which buyers and sellers approach market prices as given and not subject to influence. Monopoly, oligopoly, and MONOPOLISTIC COMPETITION are examples of imperfect competition. See also OLIGOPOLY AND OLIGOPSONY.

imperialism and empire A system of domination of states and peoples maintained and extended by another state. Imperialism often involves territorial expansion but can also imply less direct forms of economic and political domination. Popular usage of the terms are closely linked and encompass a wide range of historical empires, from Ancient Rome to the European colonial systems to (in some accounts) contemporary American political and economic hegemony. A consensus among scholars on the precise characteristics of imperial systems has been more elusive. Two features emerge in many modern accounts: the development of a complex and often overextended bureaucracy, and the goal of political and economic unification but not cultural or ethnic homogeneity (as distinct from the projects of cultural integration associated with nation-building).

The objectives of imperialism are similarly diverse. Economic gain plays a central role in most, as wealth is extracted from the peripheries and sent to the imperial center. Economic motives are rarely the sole rationale for imperialism, however, and imperial projects develop complex justifying logics of their own. These can be rooted in a variety of material concerns and/or ideological convictions: state security and competition with other states, beliefs about national superiority (including the "civilizing mission" to lesser peoples that rationalized much late-European imperialism), theories of the organic development of the state or the need for world-wide socialist revolution, religious doctrines, and so on.

The term *imperialism* derives from the Latin *imperium*, which described all large territories acquired by force and controlled by a single ruler. It came into widespread modern use in the late nineteenth century in reference to the empire-building ambitions of Louis Napoleon and other European monarchs. This phase—concentrated in the years between 1870 and 1914—was characterized by intense competition among the European powers for control of the world, especially in Africa and Asia. It came to an end with World War I, which destroyed many of the monarchical regimes and devastated others.

Many modern accounts distinguish this "new imperialism" from the earlier phase of European expansion and conquest between 1492 and the late nineteenth century—a period characterized by the consolidation of the major European powers into nation-states and overseas expansion into North and South America, and parts of Africa and Asia. This was often explicitly motivated by the desire for enrichment and capture of resources for the home country—e.g., the Spanish conquest of Central and South America. It also involved the emergence of a trading system through which colonies would provide raw materials to the home country and in return import manufactured goods (MERCANTILISM).

Theories of imperialism arose to explain the latter phase. Most focused on economic factors. John Hobson's *Imperialism* (1902) argued that imperialism was a response to the threat of underconsumption within Western capitalist economies. The development of capital and the poverty of the lower classes forced industrialists to look outside their home countries for markets to absorb excess production. Marxists, including Rudolf Hilferding and Vladimir Ilich LENIN, built on this case to argue that imperialism was the highest (and last) stage of monopoly CAPITALISM. Other theorists, such as Joseph SCHUMPETER and Hannah ARENDT, emphasized the irrationality of imperialism. They saw it as a fundamentally political phenomenon generated as much by state consolidation as by capitalist development. A strong "realist" school of INTERNATIONAL RELATIONS has also sought to explain modern imperialism as broadly equivalent to ancient imperialism—a natural consequence of the fear and ambition of states. See also COLONIALISM; and DEPENDENCY.

import substitution A development strategy designed to foster a particular economic sector by imposing tariffs and other barriers on competing foreign goods. Policies of import substitution were implemented by many developing countries after World War II in an effort to promote INDUSTRIALIZATION. It was hoped that these industries would produce equivalents for imported consumer goods and, eventually, imported capital goods as well. Experience with this strategy has proved disappointing, however; many countries were left with uncompetitive manufacturing sectors, stagnant exports, a resulting BALANCE OF PAYMENTS problem, and an overvalued EXCHANGE RATE. In the absence of competition from abroad, wages and prices remain high. Among other effects, the comparative wage advantage enjoyed in industry contributes to the large-scale migration to cities seen in most developing countries.

impossibility theorem See ARROW'S IMPOSSIBILITY THEOREM.

impression formation The process of formulating impressions of others and events. Impression formation has been a subject of research in SOCIAL PSYCHOLOGY, where it deals primarily with the factors that influence initial impressions and longer-term processes of judgment. The term is also strongly associated with the DRAMATURGICAL APPROACH of American sociologist Erving GOFFMAN, which focuses on the ways in which individuals attempt to control and direct the impressions that others form of them. This involves a constant awareness of the roles that are available to individuals in given social situations, the "props" needed to enhance their acts, and the various manipulative techniques necessary to convince their audience of the authenticity of their performances.

incentive compatibility A concept originally proposed by Leonid Hurwicz ("On Informationally Decentralized Systems," 1972) to describe any set of rules or procedures for which individuals find it in their own best interest to behave *nonstrategically* (in particular, truthfully). This is important in a variety of contexts, such as creating the mechanism for electing representatives or for deciding who receives benefits within a welfare state. In such contexts, individuals must often take action to identify their preferences, their valuation of public goods, their neediness, and so on. A well-designed mechanism is one in which individuals find it best to simply tell the truth—i.e., reveal their preferred candidate or admit their true income. Such a mechanism is called *incentive compatible* because individuals have no incentive to act strategically. More generally, incentive compatibility means that the desired outcome is achievable when individuals act according to their own best interests, without requiring altruistic or uninformed behavior.

incest taboo The social prohibition of sexual relations between certain categories of kin—especially close kin. Incest taboos, whether formal or implicit, have been shown to be universal in human society, although there can be significant variations in their specific formulations. This apparent universality has made incest a prominent subject of anthropological research since the origins of the discipline in the late nineteenth century. For the same reason, it has also been a key subject in debates about the line between biology and CULTURE.

There are many theories about the role of incest in human society. One of the fundamental questions has been—and continues to be—whether there exists a human propensity for incest that would require a strong cultural taboo. This negative model of the incest taboo as the prohibition of a natural desire is widespread, although anthropologists have disagreed about its origins.

As early as 1877, Lewis Henry MORGAN proposed a functionalist explanation of the incest taboo, suggesting that it emerged out of an implicit understanding of the biological danger that incest poses over many generations. Bronislaw MALINOWSKI and others suggested, on the contrary, that it evolved as a means of preserving family peace. More fundamentally, Sigmund FREUD held that incest is the dividing line between nature and culture—between individual propensity and collective prohibition. He viewed the incest taboo as the initial internalization of the concept of LAW. Claude LÉVI-STRAUSS developed a similarly foundational account of incest: the compulsory seeking of marriage partners outside the line of descent, he argued, was the beginning of the process of alliance and exchange that enabled human society.

A natural aversion to incest (as opposed to a social prohibition on incestuous desire) was proposed by Edward Westermark (1891), who argued that close contact between kin inhibits sexual desire. The incest taboo, in this case, emerges as a confirmation or formalization of a natural human disinclination. Westermark's hypothesis has been carried forward in a range of research on human and primate sexual practices, but faces difficulties when confronted by the diverse meanings of incest in different societies.

In the end, incest raises many questions that are far from settled.

income-consumption curve Traces the different possible equilibria between income levels and levels of consumption (or consumption bundles) by showing how the consumer's equilibrium consumption choice varies with income. The income-consumption curve is sometimes also referred to as the *Engel curve*, although most economists use the latter term to designate the relationship between income and the consumption of only one good.

income effect Refers to the effective change in a consumer's purchasing power due to a change in the price of a good. For a *normal good*, a price decrease leads to an increase in the consumption of that good because consumers can afford more. The income effect, in this case, is positive. Conversely, a price increase reduces purchasing power, so that the income effect is negative. For an INFERIOR GOOD, consumption decreases as income rises, so that the income effect of a price decrease is negative. Price changes also induce *substitution effects*, in which the relative changes in price between goods cause the consumer to shift from one to the other. Note that while income effects may be positive or negative, substitution effects always imply more consumption of the good whose relative price has fallen.

income elasticity of demand A measure of the sensitivity of demand for a particular good or service to changes in the level of income. It is usually expressed as the percentage change in the demand for the good divided by the percentage change in income. A *normal good* is one that has a positive income elasticity, such that an increase in income leads to higher demand for the good. INFERIOR GOODS have negative income elasticity of demand, indicating a decrease in demand as income rises.

income taxes See TAXES AND TAXATION.

incomplete markets Exist when certain goods—commodities, as well as financial assets, insurance, and credit—cannot be contracted for, or only partially so. This is often due to information problems (see ASYMMETRIC INFORMATION) or TRANSACTION COSTS. In such cases, markets fail to operate fully, and not all desired transactions between agents take place. As a result, the market allocation is no longer PARETO OPTIMAL. Analysis of incomplete markets is most often pursued in the context of financial markets and in relation to the ability of individuals to manage RISK.

incorporation Most social science usage emphasizes the integration or assimilation of individuals or groups into larger social categories or collectivities. Incorporation can occur through a variety of methods and social processes, including the abolition of differential systems of rights or privileges, the desegregation or dispersal of geographically united groups, the co-optation of social and political issues that structure group differences, or through the forms of social mobility and intermarriage characteristic of immigrant and religious assimilation. The term is commonly used in studies of the decline of working-class and other political and social identity, and generally implies hierarchical relationships between groups. Incorporation is thus among the processes of group identity formation that have been a vital and in many cases defining topic of social science research.

increasing returns to scale A situation in which adding any additional quantity of inputs produces more than that additional quantity of outputs. The concept differs from ECONOMIES OF SCALE in that *increasing returns* generally refers to the type of production function and thus applies regardless of the current level of production. A technology that allows globally-increasing returns implies that there is only one producer in the market, since the cost of production would continuously decrease with quantity produced.

incrementalism The political or administrative practice of making small changes to existing policy rather than undertaking radical or ambitious plans. *Disjointed incrementalism* refers to cases in which such decision making leads to a less desirable outcome than radical action at the outset would have achieved.

independence See AUTONOMY.

indexicality A term used by ethnomethodologists to describe the way in which the meaning of speech and action is dependent upon the context in which they occur (see ETHNOMETHODOLOGY).

indicative planning See CENTRAL PLANNING.

indicator A quantitative measure that provides information about a variable that is difficult to measure directly. Social scientists are often concerned with explaining the causal relationships among independent and dependent variables. Many variables of interest, however, are latent—that is, not directly observable. Social solidarity and job satisfaction, for example, are generally considered latent variables. In these cases, researchers have to choose appropriate indicators of the variables in question (sometimes called *constructs*). These may be couched, for example, in questions designed to elicit feelings that are indicative of, if not identical with, the desired variable. To correct for errors in measurement or in the choice of indicators, researchers use multiple indicators to measure the same variable.

indifference curves A graphical depiction of consumer preferences in regard to a choice between two GOODS. The curve shows the combinations of two goods that yield the same level of UTILITY (or satisfaction) to the consumer; hence the "indifference" among such bundles. Indifference curves are usually downward sloping since an increase in one good must be balanced by a decrease in the other. Higher indifference curves—with more of both goods—indicate a higher level of utility. The complete set of indifference curves (which represents all possible commodity combinations) is called an indifference map.

indirect relationships Social relationships established without directly personal communication—e.g., through bureaucracies, markets, or impersonal information technology. The concept is a refinement of Charles Horton COOLEY's distinction between primary and secondary relationships, introduced by Craig Calhoun in a series of articles in the late 1980s and early 1990s, including "The Infrastructure of Modernity: Indirect Social Relationships, Information Technology, and Social Integration" (1992). Indirect relationships are not likely to be recognized as social relations by the parties they include. Calhoun distinguishes *tertiary* and *quaternary* relationships—the former involving mediation by machines, markets, organizations, or other persons; the latter designating forms of surveillance and monitoring. Scale is the primary obstacle to recognizing the former; POWER obscures recognition of the latter.

indirect taxes See TAXES AND TAXATION.

indirect utility function A function that expresses the UTILITY (or well-being) derived from consumption, but as a function of prices and income rather than as a function of a bundle of goods actually consumed. Given prices and income, a consumer can optimally choose a consumption bundle. Substituting these optimal choices into the original utility function (expressed in terms of quantities of goods consumed) yields the *indirect* utility function.

individualism Most commonly, a political philosophy that takes the individual as the essential unit of the polity, and the polity as existing in large measure to serve and protect the individual. Historically, however, individualism has had a wide range of connotations in the West, where it has generally represented a challenge to strongly integrated concepts of the social order. Conservatives have been mistrustful of individualism on these grounds, as were the early French socialists who first used the term as a means of criticizing resistance to collective social goals. The Romantic movement further inflected the term with its strong commitment to uniqueness and creativity and to the self as a singular work of art constantly in the making.

Underlying many of these perspectives, however, is the close association of individualism with political LIBERALISM. Both became prominent in the early nineteenth century. Together, they contributed to a relatively coherent social vision that prioritized individual autonomy in economic and personal life, privileged individual over social welfare, and sought to minimize governmental involvement in those areas. Following Isaiah BERLIN, these protections are sometimes referred to as *negative freedoms*—freedom from constraints on activity. Individualism also generally includes a strong commitment to the notion of personal responsibility for success, failure, or transgression—beliefs that have contributed to the American idea of the "self-made man" as well as to theories of criminal behavior.

When necessary, individualism generally derives notions of the collective good from the accumulation and maximization of opportunities for individual goods—this is visible in much classical economic thought as well as in the political doctrine of UTILITARIANISM. Such views often clash with collective or egalitarian perspectives that pursue notions of the social good that override or limit areas of individual privilege (see EGALITARIANISM). Progressive taxation and gun control are issues that have contentiously opposed the two visions of the social good in the United States.

Contrary to Europe, where the concept sometimes retains pejorative connotations of disregard for the collective good, individualism is a sacrosanct concept in American political culture—although by no means a simple or unproblematic one to many commentators on American life. Many scholars in the liberal tradition have viewed American individualism as built upon a deep consensus about social values that, paradoxically, contain strong conformist tendencies. From this perspective, individualism is pursued on some levels, as in the celebration of economic self-interest, but ignored or disavowed on others, such as the value of thinking differently about social goals or of pursuing different ways of life. Alexis de TOCQUEVILLE's remarkable *Democracy in America* (1835) inaugurated this deeply ambivalent tradition. It received renewed attention in the postwar historiography of Louis Hartz and other "consensus" scholars. COMMUNITARIANISM—represented by figures such as Robert Bellah, Amitai Etzioni, and Alasdair MACINTYRE—generally takes a stronger position in regretting the excessive individualism of American society, which it views as undermining shared values and the structure of community. Many liberal, Marxist, and critical theorists locate these concerns within the context of the emergence of MASS SOCIETY, in which a denatured individualism becomes a conformist norm associated primarily with fabricated consumer choices (see FRANKFURT SCHOOL).

In the social sciences, the term *methodological individualism* describes perspectives that prioritize the role of the individual in social analysis or seek to reduce notions of social structure to forms of individual behavior or action. For strict methodological individualists, the study of phenomena larger than the single individual must be built upon concepts of individual behavior. RATIONAL-CHOICE THEORY provides the dominant example of such methods. Methodological individualism generally rejects, then, approaches that treat individuals as constructed or determined by social factors or structures; it similarly disputes claims that social systems are more than the sum of their parts or that society exists in any meaningful sense outside the individuals who compose it. These continue to be topics of disagreement in the social sciences. Much of the sociological and anthropological tradition takes these concerns very seriously—particularly as they relate to the division between macrosociological accounts of social structures and microsociological approaches to individual and interpersonal behavior (see MACROSOCIOLOGY AND MICROSOCIOLOGY).

indivisibilities   A commodity is indivisible if it has a minimum size below which it is unavailable. Although economic models often presume that goods are consumable in infinitely divisible quantities, that assumption is less frequent on the production side of the market. Indivisible equipment and other inputs in a production process represent *fixed costs*—the minimum expenditure a firm must incur in order to commence production. Indivisible inputs, consequently, are closely associated with ECONOMIES OF SCALE: the first unit produced requires a more substantial investment than subsequent units, which divide the fixed costs. Moreover, if the indivisible input is not overly specialized, the firm can diversify its line of products at a lower cost than the sum costs of separate specialized enterprises. Indivisibilities thus also permit *economies of scope*.

industrialization   The process underlying the transition from primarily agricultural and craft production to machine-driven mass production organized on the factory model. Industrialization contributes to and correlates with a wide range of other economic, social, cultural, and political transformations, and forms an inextricable part of most theories of modernization and MODERNITY. These broader accounts typically reference the experience of western Europe and the United States, which began to industrialize in the late eighteenth and early nineteenth centuries—at varying rates—and where industrialization accompanied the development of the modern NATION-STATE, CAPITALISM, DEMOCRACY, markets and long-distance trade, urbanization, mass literacy and communication, and a host of other social features. The complex result of this process is often described as *industrial society*.

This experience underwrote a range of theories of modernization that tended to posit relatively coherent trajectories of development based on logics internal to the process. The growing division of labor associated with industrial production was a subject of widespread interest by the late eighteenth century. MARXISM and classical economic theory were quick to understand the competitive advantages of industrialization in the capitalist economy, where machine and factory production provided higher productivity than earlier craft and cottage production (see CLASSICAL ECONOMICS; and COTTAGE INDUSTRY). In this context, profitability alone would speed the development of the industrial model, consign a growing share of the population to the proletariat, and (as Karl MARX argued) transform the structure of ownership as the means of production consolidated in the hands of fewer and fewer owners. Capitalism, especially in the Marxist context, made use of industrialization, but industrialization was not specific to capitalism. Rather it was a set of production techniques that might be organized on the basis of other principles of ownership and other means of distributing wealth. Socialist programs of planned industrialization in the Soviet Union and Eastern Europe, for example, dramatically transformed their respective economies without the pull factors of trade and market signals, although the absence of these mechanisms eventually made these industrial sectors rigid and inefficient.

In a world characterized by radically unequal levels of economic power and access to world markets, industrialization generally remains the most accepted path to long-term growth for underdeveloped countries. Nonetheless, industrialization now requires levels of investment and skill that are beyond the means of many countries. Foreign investment is a common solution, but this has proved unstable in an era of highly mobile capital. Nor can it be counted on to address the broad issues of infrastructure and social development that make industrial society viable in the long term. Large-scale loans by development agencies such as the World Bank have been similarly criticized for neglecting the broad social transformations that make industrialization self-sustaining, and for leaving many countries deeply in debt.

Another major direction of theoretical inquiry on industrialization traces its roots to Max WEBER, who analyzed industrialization as part of the much broader process of *rationalization* of all areas of social activity, including production techniques, forms of administration, belief systems, and social norms. The rationalization hypothesis—integrating aspects of both Marx and Friedrich NIETZSCHE's accounts of modernity—generated a wide range of historical and sociological inquiries into modern society, especially in regard to organizational forms (such as BUREAUCRACY) and social stratification (notably in the STATUS orientation of much occupational sociology).

industrial organization A field of economics concerned with the behavior of firms in imperfectly competitive markets—i.e., those in which one or more firms exercise monopoly power or in which information is either unequally available or too complex to analyze. In general, such markets cannot be analyzed with the standard competitive model. Industrial organization research has devoted considerable attention to exploring the definition of markets, market structure, and the effects of exogenous (noneconomic) variables on both. These questions have important implications in the area of antitrust and regulatory policies, which seek to improve market performance. In this context, one key issue is the degree to which imperfect markets, in certain cases, reflect ECONOMIES OF SCALE that potentially outweigh the higher profits or imperfect decision making of firms. In such cases, TRANSACTION COSTS and economies of scope may be important in determining the relationships among firms. Industrial organization research also examines the competitive strategies of firms in such markets, such as efforts to limit the entry of new rivals through LIMIT PRICING and advertising. This field has been greatly influenced by the emergence of GAME THEORY, with its models of cooperative and non-cooperative rationality.

industry Often divided by economists and geographers into five general categories that encompass all economic activity. *Primary industry* involves the extraction of natural resources, including agriculture; *secondary industry* involves manufacturing; *tertiary industry*, distribution, including utilities and activities related to transportation and communication; *quaternary industry*, a range of producer services from banking to retailing to real estate; and *quinary industry*, consumer services such as education, health care, and government. The relative dominance of the latter three categories over the former two in many industrialized countries has informed discussions of a POSTINDUSTRIAL SOCIETY.

infant-industry argument An economic argument in favor of temporary trade restrictions or production subsidies in order to protect fledgling industries from international competition. In many cases, industries require substantial initial investment and the development of skills and experience—the lack of which can seriously hinder competitiveness. Protectionist arguments generally recognize, however, that free trade provides greater efficiency and a higher overall welfare under most circumstances. In this regard, tariffs and subsidies are usually applied with the expectation that new industries will mature and compete on the international market. There are also a variety of political rationales for restricting trade in favor of domestic industries—especially in the areas of agriculture and military production, where dependence on other countries carries potential risks.

The infant-industry argument is sometimes broadened to include the entire industrial sector of an economy. Especially in newly industrializing countries, a case can be made that the skills and experience acquired by each firm generates benefits for the entire sector, and that by mutual expansion, all firms experience a reduction in production costs. Such assertions played a role in the adoption of IMPORT SUBSTITUTION strategies in many developing countries after World War II. The evidence is strong that a skilled and experienced labor force brings transitive benefits to other developing areas of the economy. The experience of postwar import substitution suggests, however, that such policies become entrenched over time, eventually degenerating into costly supports for static and inefficient industries. In the long run, this strategy may limit the rate of economic growth.

inferior good A good for which, other things being equal, an increase in income leads to a decrease in demand. Inferior goods are contrasted with *normal* goods, for which demand rises as income rises. Inferior goods are often inexpensive but less-preferred foods (such as cassava and millet), public transportation, and low-quality consumer items.

infibulation A radical form of female circumcision (or, as it is often termed, genital mutilation) involving the removal of the clitoris and often the sewing shut of much of the vagina. The procedure is a rite of passage in some societies of northeastern Africa and has become an object of intense controversy both in and outside Africa. See also CIRCUMCISION.

inflation Continuously rising prices or, equivalently, a continuous fall in the value of money. The most common measure of inflation is the rate of change in the gross domestic product deflator—a price index for all goods and services produced in the economy.

Most research on the subject distinguishes between *anticipated* and *unanticipated* inflation. The former refers to a situation in which prices are rising at the rate that all economic agents expect; the latter characterizes situations that agents cannot predict or adjust for in advance, such as supply shocks or the sudden growth of the money supply.

Economists agree that anticipated inflation has a one-to-one effect on *nominal* economic variables such as the nominal interest rate, the nominal wage rate, and the EXCHANGE RATE. An inflation rate of 5 percent will be associated with a 5 percent rise in the nominal interest rate, an equal depreciation of the nominal exchange rate, and a 5 percent faster increase in wages. There is considerably less agreement on the effect of anticipated inflation upon *real* economic variables such as real wages, the real interest rate, and output or gross domestic product. Many economists—especially monetarists—hold to some version of the principle of the *superneutrality* of money, following Miguel Sidrauski's 1967 account, which suggests that inflation has no effect on real variables. Others argue that higher anticipated inflation does have a real impact by raising the opportunity cost of holding *real money balances*. In such circumstances, economic agents will reallocate resources from money to physical capital, leading to a permanent increase in capital stock and output. This is referred to as the Mundell–Tobin effect. A third view (held by Paul SAMUELSON and Robert Clower, among others) inverts the Mundell–Tobin assertion by arguing that inflation leads to lower saving. Since saving is equivalent to investment, this results in lower capital stock and a lower permanent level of income.

While the notion of anticipated inflation permits analysis of the consequences of changes in the inflation rate, unanticipated inflation raises the question of the causes of inflation. Since fluctuations in inflation are accompanied by and associated with fluctuations in the level of economic activity, it is impossible to study unanticipated inflation in isolation. Again, there are three dominant theoretical approaches to unanticipated and cyclical aspects of inflation. One—associated primarily with John Maynard KEYNES—argues that wages and prices are *sticky* and respond sluggishly to demand shocks. As a result, shocks to investment demand or wealth (arising from a sudden change in the money supply) have a significant initial effect on output. Over time, however, wages and prices adjust

to fully reflect the shock to aggregate demand. Keynesian theory also accounts for autonomous price shocks, such as a jump in the price of a basic commodity, or a widespread, unplanned increase in wages (for example, following labor unrest; see KEYNESIANISM). Such a situation leads to STAGFLATION, in which inflation rises while output falls. Some neo-Keynesians have sought a microfoundational account of the stickiness of wages and prices by studying long-term contractual arrangements in labor markets.

The New Classical view was first elaborated by Robert Lucas ("Expectations and the Neutrality of Money," 1972) and assumes that agents are incapable of distinguishing absolute price changes (e.g., a rise in the overall price level) from relative price changes (changes in prices in some sectors only). Thus, a retailer who thinks that the price of his goods has risen relative to the price of other goods will increase his supply. According to Lucas, this is the only channel through which money-supply shocks produce movements in the output level.

Both the Keynesian and New Classical views rely on shocks to the money supply growth rate as the prime driver of inflation and real output. Thus, for both, central banks—the institutions that determine growth in the money supply—are the principle actors. A considerable body of research has examined the behavior of central banks in the face of diverse policy goals (such as the potential trade-off between inflation and employment), available mechanisms, and political and social pressures.

A third view on inflation, known as the *Real Business Cycle Theory*, rejects the primacy of monetary shocks and instead emphasizes technology shocks that generate fluctuations in output and the price level.

Anti-inflationary policies have evolved over time. Wage and price controls have been widely used, although in modern economies these prove highly complex and are prone to perverse effects as agents seek other ways to maximize profits or UTILITY. Reduction of the money supply is a more common method today, although rapid reductions tend to provoke economic downturns, which are often difficult to control. Following the RATIONAL EXPECTATIONS revolution, economists have devoted less attention to finding ways to manipulate these variables, and more to thinking about how different institutional arrangements interact to produce different rates of inflation. For example, the presence of unions makes it hard for firms to cut nominal wages. These firms react differently to a demand shock than firms without a unionized labor force. See also HYPERINFLATION.

inflationary gap A discrepancy between high demand for and limited supply of goods in the economy that gives rise to inflationary pressures—generally termed *demand–pull inflation*. The inflationary gap was theorized by John Maynard KEYNES in *How to Pay for the War* (1940). Prices rise, Keynes argued, because adjustments on the supply side are comparatively slow and because profit-maximizing firms seek additional per-unit profits in order to justify raising output. Over time, the inflationary gap produces its own countertendency, as the reduction in real wages lowers demand. As this happens, the inflationary gap closes.

Keynesian monetary and fiscal policy is largely designed to minimize the inflationary gap by regulating the level of demand. When it succeeds, the economy approaches, but does not exceed, full employment—the optimal level of utilization of resources. Subsequent research has cast some doubt on Keynes's claim that demand–pull is the principle component of INFLATION. Wage–push factors, supply shocks, and monetary changes also play a role. Nonetheless, demand–pull phenomena and the inflationary gap continue to inform research and policy. See also COST-PUSH INFLATION.

inflation tax Inflationary monetary policy can act as a tax because unanticipated (e.g., sudden or one-time) INFLATION decreases the purchasing power of individuals and firms. Purchasing power decreases by precisely the additional amount of money printed (and now held) by the government. In this respect, inflationary policies mimic the effect of an income tax and have frequently been used as a means of paying for government expenditures. Government debt—which is generally owed at a fixed rate—also diminishes in real terms if the rate of inflation increases.

informal economy Economists use the term primarily to describe forms of marginal labor and self-employment that fall outside the framework of corporate, public, and private sector employment. The term was introduced by the anthropologist Keith Hart based on field research in Ghana. Strict definitions vary but frequently include domestic help, day labor, and artisanal work, as well as illegal economic activities such as drug dealing or the sale of stolen merchandise. More generally, all sorts of activities may be kept informal by making transactions in cash or through barter. Informal economic activities leave few records, only occasionally enter into the insurance, occupational safety, and welfare networks of the state, and are therefore rarely or only approximately captured in economic statistics. Much of the research on informal economies has focused on developing countries, where informal work often provides the livelihood for large sectors of the urban population. The term *underground economy* is often used synonymously with informal economy; BLACK ECONOMY, on the other hand, generally refers to the portion of formal economic activity that is systematically understated for the purposes of evading taxes or regulation.

Sociologists use the term to designate similar activities, but more often include the large sector of unpaid labor, such as the majority of household or domestic labor. Because such labor is performed mostly by women, it has been of considerable interest in research on gender roles and gender inequality. Although social scientists generally recognize that domestic labor represents a significant portion of the total productive output of the economy, clear definitions (and therefore accurate statistical measures) of domestic labor have proved difficult to specify and apply. Informal labor is important, however, whenever work is organized on KINSHIP rather than commercial lines, as when it involves children or extended family members.

infrastructure The basic, underlying structure or character of a society. The concept is usually employed in one of two ways. Among Marxists, it refers to a society's fundamental economic structure, the MODE OF PRODUCTION, as opposed to diverse social and cultural phenomena such as the family, law, the state, the arts, and so on (see BASE AND SUPERSTRUCTURE). Among non-Marxist economists and sociologists, it refers to a society's fundamental material and cultural systems, such as communication, transportation, and education—especially those material and cultural attributes necessary for future social and economic development.

initiative See DIRECT DEMOCRACY.

input–output analysis A method of economic analysis that treats the economy as a single system whose operations can be described in terms of basic structural relationships among economic sectors. Pioneered by Wassily LEONTIEF (*The Structure of the American Economy, 1919–1929*, 1941), the standard input–output table contains square arrays of figures. Each row and corresponding column bears the name of a particular sector of the economy. Each individual entry specifies the amount produced in the sector identified by the row and delivered as input to the sector identified by the column. Based on this chart, one can determine the quantity of various inputs required to produce one unit of a good in a particular sector. These *technical coefficients of production* provide the structural matrix of the economy and thus a basis for determining both the total output of the diverse sectors and the intersectoral transactions that such output requires. Input–output analysis has been used with considerable success in the study of labor requirements, wages and prices, and imports and exports. In one notable instance, the U.S. Bureau of Labor Statistics developed an input–output table for the American economy that predicted serious shortages of steel prior to World War II.

inquisitorial system   See ADVERSARIAL SYSTEM.

institutions   Deeply embedded patterns of social practices or norms that play a significant role in the organization of society. Institutions can include diverse areas of social activity, from the family to basic aspects of political life. In some cases they acquire an organized or bureaucratized administrative structure, in which case they become institutions in something closer to the common usage of the term. Institutions are one of the central concerns of the functionalist tradition, insofar as they concretize important social functions (see FUNCTIONALISM). Interactionist perspectives, on the other hand, emphasize the network of shifting interpersonal relations that compose institutions. Erving GOFFMAN introduced the term *TOTAL INSTITUTION* to refer to bureaucratic systems that achieve near complete domination of those subjected to them.

instrumentalism   Refers (especially following Max WEBER) to action conceived as a means to a separate and distinct end, as opposed to action conceived as an end in itself. The difference between instrumental and noninstrumental action has been a recurring subject of philosophical interest and debate since ARISTOTLE, who recognized it as fundamental to considerations of human action. It has consequently been

defined and redefined in a number of ways, and enlisted in a variety of competing and sometimes incompatible contexts. In the twentieth century, the term itself is strongly associated with the PRAGMATISM of John DEWEY, who argued that ideas should be judged not on the basis of truth and falsehood, but rather in terms of the ends they serve. Even where Dewey is concerned, however, certain kinds of ideas escape instrumental reasoning—quintessentially art, the noninstrumental object *par excellence* of the Western philosophical tradition since Immanuel KANT. Certain activities straddle the instrumental–noninstrumental divide; Hannah ARENDT's defense of the intrinsic value of democratic action over the various specific ends that it serves is a prominent example.

As an approach to science, instrumentalism contrasts with theories of knowledge that regard objects as possessing a true or intrinsic nature that science can qualify and categorize. Other users of the term, however, strongly associate it with the scientific and technical mastery of the world rooted in subject–object relations. Instrumentalism, in this context, is deeply embedded in the Western idea of self. The dominance of instrumental reason has consequently been a subject of profound concern for the critical theorists of the FRANKFURT SCHOOL and other critics of Western modernity, such as Martin HEIDEGGER. Here, instrumental reason appears not as a liberatory alternative to static or metaphysical conceptions of truth, but as a pervasive logic of existence, linked to capitalism, the marketplace, and technology, which destroys other sources and forms of value.

instrumental variables   Proxy variables used in statistical research to correct for sample selection bias and unobserved underlying variables in data. For example, employing an Ordinary Least Squares (OLS) regression to measure the impact of schooling on wage income—using years of education to predict earnings—might fail to correct for alternative mechanisms, such as the possibility that workers of higher earning potential may self-select for more schooling. Thus the OLS results might overestimate the impact of schooling. An instrumental variable, in this case, serves as a proxy for schooling choices that are uncorrelated with "earnings potential"—for example, those related to tuition costs or geographical distance to universities. Plausibly, tuition costs could produce variation in schooling choice independent of the earnings potential of individuals.

instruments   See TARGETS AND INSTRUMENTS.

integration   See FUNCTIONALISM.

intellectuals   Persons whose main activity is the production or evaluation of ideas. In most contexts, the term implies a degree of independence from state or official functions. The role of intellectuals has varied tremendously according to time and place. Most often, it reflects the continued legitimacy of the seventeenth- and eighteenth-century tradition of *letters*, in which scientific, literary, legal, and political knowledge belonged to a relatively unified field. Intellectuals play a prominent role in countries where these now-specialized knowledges still provide legitimacy in other areas of public life—as in France and much of Latin America, for example, where intellectual achievement often translates into public authority. This is much less true of the United States, where anti-intellectualism is a powerful political force. The case of African-American and other minority public intellectuals whose role consists partly of representing their group to the majority provides an interesting exception.

Historically, there is a strong tendency to see intellectuals as a de facto opposition group, always ready to challenge traditional values and received ideas. Marxists have been especially interested in this potential and have recurrently debated the role of intellectuals in working-class political movements. They have also recognized the place of official or bourgeois intellectuals, who serve primarily to validate and support the status quo. Antonio GRAMSCI's distinction between "organic intellectuals," who emerge from the working class, and relatively apolitical "traditional intellectuals," such as clerics, teachers, and independent professionals, has oriented much of this debate since the 1930s.

Other social theorists, such as Alvin Ward GOULDNER, have taken a broader view of intellectuals as the principal actors in the extension of rationality and managerial forms of control into new areas of social and economic life (*The Rise of the Intellectuals and the Future of the New Class*, 1977).

intelligentsia   See INTELLECTUALS.

interaction   See SYMBOLIC INTERACTIONISM.

interdependence   At its most general, the notion that what happens to one actor affects others, with the corollary that all may modify their behavior accordingly. Interdependence is a central concept of the neoliberal school of INTERNATIONAL RELATIONS and was developed in particular by Robert Keohane and Joseph Nye in *Power and Interdependence* (1977; see NEOLIBERALISM). Keohane and Nye argue against the "realist" assumptions that states are unitary actors that invariably prioritize security concerns. Instead, they suggest that, at least among the Western democracies, security considerations are diminishing in importance in comparison to economic and social issues. Moreover, because of the growing interconnectedness of advanced capitalist economies, interstate relations are increasingly marked by cooperation and negotiation through INTERNATIONAL ORGANIZATIONS and trade, rather than relations of domination among states. In particular, they argued that interdependence would ensure international peace and stability as U.S. hegemony weakened in the 1970s.

interest   A central concept in liberal political and economic explanations of the actions of unconstrained actors—whether individuals or groups. Individuals (or groups) are identified with a set of interests, which correspond to needs, wants, or, more generally, forms of power. They are expected to act in accordance with their interests whenever possible—indeed, this correspondence underlies broader assumptions about full and responsible individuality in most areas of social life. Combined with theories of rational behavior and calculation, these assumptions form the basis of RATIONAL-CHOICE THEORY. In much of this tradition, and especially in economics, individual or group interest is equated with *expressed* preferences. This follows from the assumption that individuals and groups will naturally express or pursue their interests, except where lack of information or complexity makes such calculations problematic.

The ability of individuals to know their best interests has been a subject of long debate in philosophy and social theory, based on concern that individuals may potentially be misled, misinformed, immature, or, more problematically, irrational. Special statuses exist for categories of persons deemed unable to reliably act in their interests—e.g., children or the mentally incompetent. Differences between individual and group interests, moreover, raise a range of theoretical problems, from the conflict between republican models of virtue (or action in the public interest) and liberal models based on the aggregation of private interests, to COLLECTIVE-ACTION PROBLEMS, where individual and group interests diverge. Many normative political theorists object to the priority that LIBERALISM assigns to individual interests, and instead seek to valorize the common good or the "public interest" (see COMMUNITARIANISM). Liberal approaches to the public interest generally rely on PLURALISM and CORPORATISM to reconcile conflicting interests without privileging a substantive interest common to all.

These complexities form the background of numerous attempts to determine the true or best interests of citizens, groups, or classes. The assumption that a group's "real" interests diverge from its expressed preferences, however, assigns an analytic privilege to the theorist or intellectual that much recent social theory has challenged. Marxist accounts of FALSE CONSCIOUSNESS and the role of intellectuals in working-class movements have struggled with this implied privilege. A large body of empirical political science has found other grounds for rejecting the idea that individual preferences or interests are in any sense "given" or pre-political. These have added the process of "interest formation" to the more visible moment of "interest articulation" in which different groups make themselves heard, as well as a further process of "interest aggregation" in which they organize behind political parties and larger groups in order to affect state decision making.

interest group See INTEREST; and PRESSURE GROUP.

interest rates In economic usage, interest is payment for the use of funds over a certain period of time; the interest rate is the amount paid per unit of time as a fraction of the balance. At any given time, interest rates can vary considerably, based on the risk of the enterprise, the creditworthiness of the borrower, the maturity of the loan, the amount of collateral offered, and so on. Most economic analyses, however, refer to a single interest rate, which assumes that arbitrage will even out these diverse calculations. Lenders, like producers, operate in a marketplace where supply and demand determine the going rate.

Classical economic analysis held that the interest rate was determined by the equivalence between savings and investment. The classical economists postulated that as the interest rate increases, savings increase and investment decreases. The interest rate therefore reflected real output or income. Keynesian analysis takes a somewhat different approach in arguing that the interest rate affects money demand: the higher the interest rate, the more income people place in bonds and the less money they hold. As before, a higher interest rate leads to lower investment as loans become more expensive. In this context, aggregate demand and economic output drop (see AGGREGATE DEMAND FUNCTION). See also CLASSICAL ECONOMICS; and KEYNESIANISM.

intergenerational models See OVERLAPPING-GENERATIONS MODEL.

intermediate good A good that is used in the production of other commodities rather than in final consumption (a final good). Steel and wood are usually intermediate goods. In some cases, goods can be both intermediate and final goods.

internalization The process of acceptance and incorporation of social standards and norms. Internalization is often used as the psychological equivalent of the term SOCIALIZATION, emphasizing the interior processes of psychological life rather than the adoption of externalized forms of behavior. One of the principle sources of the term is Sigmund FREUD's theory of personality development, which stresses the process by which children learn to internalize the standards of others, especially their parents. Sociologists sometimes use the term to describe the process by which individuals learn to identify with social norms or roles and thus develop an interest in their maintenance. Michel FOUCAULT's concept of disciplinary society covers much the same ground. Through this process, individuals regulate their own behavior in conformity with socially approved goals and thereby mitigate much of the need for direct coercion by external authorities. Internalization is thus a crucial aspect of modern systems of SOCIAL CONTROL.

internal rate of return Private investments and government projects are usually assessed by evaluating the flow of resources over time. Costs may come up front, while payoffs are deferred, or costs and benefits may accrue together over time. Net annual benefits (benefits less costs) are discounted at exponentially increasing rates into the future to reflect the OPPORTUNITY COST of tying up resources. The internal rate of return is a measure of the percentage of return on such investments, taking into account their gains over time. It normally needs to exceed the market rate of return on investments in order to justify investment. (Otherwise, greater profits could be had by purchasing another commodity, such as bonds.) Put differently, the internal rate of return on an investment is the rate of interest that sets the net present value equal to zero.

international division of labor See COM-PARATIVE ADVANTAGE.

international law The body of rules and conventions that nominally govern relations between states. Early theories of international law drew on SOCIAL-CONTRACT THEORY and models of NATURAL LAW and, in many cases, assumed that states operated on the same opportunistic principles as individuals in a state of nature. States exemplified the problem of rule of the strongest—no sovereign authority existed to check their actions or guarantee the basic right of the social contract: freedom from violence. Hugo GROTIUS broke ground in this area by conceiving the fabric of international relations as a set of binding contracts. His *On the Law of War and Peace* (1625) combined principles of the Roman law of nations, canon law, and prevailing custom into a system that defined just war as the remedy for breach of contract and set guidelines for wartime conduct. These became a point of reference (if rarely a guide to actual behavior) for states in their conduct of foreign policy. Although international law has traditionally taken states to be the only legal entities (excepting the separate field of international private law), the increased interest in human rights since World War II has created a growing role for individual claims. Recent efforts to establish an international criminal court represent a large step in this direction.

Because international law is not enforced by a sovereign power (in contrast to national law), its significance is often disputed. The "realist" school of INTERNATIONAL RELATIONS, for example, argues that since the international system is always in a state of anarchy, international law in matters of any consequence is simply the law of the stronger. Although the General Assembly of the United Nations passes laws and the International Court of Justice hands down decisions, neither are binding on states unless the states choose to honor them or a powerful state or group of states is prepared to enforce them. However, even realists concede that because states

have an interest in predictable relations based on reciprocity and cooperation, international law is recognized and respected in many areas.

A large body of more or less effective international law exists in the form of treaties, conventions, customs, and principles. Treaties are agreements between states, binding only the signatories. Their enforcement is up to the states themselves, although one party may appeal to the International Court of Justice or seek some other form of arbitration. Broad multilateral treaties are often called conventions; these now cover a diverse range of topics from the conduct of warfare to human rights to the use of the sea and space. When they have been ratified by a large number of countries and nominally direct the conduct of the rest, they are often regarded as customary law, binding even on nonsignatories. Finally, principles of international law are ideas that have emerged through several centuries of custom and jurisprudence. These are generally taken to define the duties of states and to guide the interpretation of international law.

international organization Institutions that transcend national boundaries; also, the study of such institutions. Two types are usually distinguished: intergovernmental organizations created by multilateral treaty or agreement among states, such as the United Nations and the International Monetary Fund; and international NONGOVERNMENTAL ORGANIZATIONS (NGOs) created by private citizens in different countries, such as the Red Cross and Amnesty International. The first international organizations were formed in Europe in the early nineteenth century, usually for the promotion of commerce or science, but they have since proliferated in every field of concern and endeavor. As a subject of POLITICAL SCIENCE, they are of interest insofar as they carry out governance functions—thereby limiting the SOVEREIGNTY and AUTONOMY of states—or, more broadly, insofar as they constitute an international civil society that can influence governments.

international relations The study of political relations between STATES or across state boundaries; one of the main subfields of POLITICAL SCIENCE. Its principal subdivisions include strategic studies, INTERNATIONAL ORGANIZATIONS, and international political economy. International relations grew out of diplomatic history in the early twentieth century. Its profile was clearest in the decades immediately following World War II, as scholars applied methods such as STRUCTURALISM, SYSTEM(S) THEORY, GAME THEORY, and RATIONAL-CHOICE THEORY to derive general propositions about relations between states. This "state-centric" approach has since been contested within the field. Debates have revolved around the question of whether a state can be regarded as a unitary actor, the relative importance of interstate power relations and international organizations, the roles of nonstate actors, and the need to include the study of history, institutions, CULTURE, and other contributing factors. Some scholars therefore call for a more inclusive definition of the field, often under the rubric of "world politics" or "international studies." Nevertheless, three main schools of thought are generally recognized within contemporary international relations:

1. "Realism" or "power-politics," the oldest and still the dominant tradition, claims Thucydides, Niccolò MACHIAVELLI, and Thomas HOBBES as its precursors. It holds that the international system is anarchic; that unitary, sovereign, self-interested states are its key actors; and that power and war are its basic currencies. With no international sovereign power, states must help themselves in the struggle for survival. Peace therefore depends on the BALANCE OF POWER, while foreign policy should be based on the prudent calculation of national interest. While realism has been criticized for its cynicism, its blindness to anything but "high politics," and the vagueness of many of its key concepts, it has dominated the academic study and practice of foreign policy.

2. A "liberal" tradition that descends from NATURAL LAW theorists such as Hugo GROTIUS, John LOCKE, and Immanuel KANT. Often in reaction to realism, liberals argue that states form an international society with the capacity for a rational harmony of interests, including peace, order, and (often) democracy and commerce. They point to the development of international organizations and INTERNATIONAL LAW to demonstrate the possibility of cooperation among states, and prefer forms of COLLECTIVE SECURITY to the balance of power. Contemporary debates between "neoliberalism" and "neorealism" often hinge on emphasis, with each side conceding both the centrality of states and the growth of INTERDEPENDENCE.

3. A number of other approaches contest the priority that both realists and liberals assign to sovereign states, and instead focus on other important determinants of international activity. The most important of these approaches are derived from MARXISM and argue that economic relations are the underlying determinants of the international political order. WORLD-SYSTEMS THEORY, DEPENDENCY theory, and much of the work in international political economy can be characterized in these terms. Other approaches include *constructivism*, which studies how the ideas and institutions of world politics have been socially constructed over time, and *pluralism*, which examines the diverse nonstate participants in international politics.

interpellation Louis ALTHUSSER's term for the process by which persons are "hailed" within an ideologically structured field, and thereby positioned in appropriate social roles. Althusser's classic example is that of being addressed by a policeman—a situation in which recognition on the part of the person hailed positions that person as a subject of legal discourses, penal institutions, and state power more generally. Interpellation, for Althusser, is the work of *ideological* and *repressive state apparatuses*. These include schools, the mass media, unions, the police, social services, and other institutions that produce certain forms of conformance and ultimately identity. The concept is elaborated in Althusser's influential essay "Ideology and Ideological State Apparatuses" (1971).

interpersonal psychoanalysis See PSYCHO-ANALYSIS; and Harry Stack SULLIVAN.

interpersonal utility comparisons Many theories of social welfare recognize that concepts of welfare or well-being (UTILITY in economic terms) differ among persons and societies, but nonetheless require that comparisons between these concepts be possible. UTILITARIANISM is a prominent example: the goal of maximizing the sum of the utilities of all individuals in society requires a quantifiable common measure of well-being; similarly, the Rawlsian concept of justice seeks to maximize the welfare of the most disadvantaged individuals in society (see John RAWLS). Many economists and philosophers argue, however, that welfare is too subjective and variable a concept to measure, much less compare, except in the grossest physical terms. While this leaves a broad margin for interpersonal utility comparisons in areas of manifest suffering or exploitation, it suggests the strong difficulties facing any attempt to quantify forms of satisfaction. There is, consequently, a distinction in economics between theories that rely on cardinal units of utility (termed *utils*) and those that require only ranked (ordinal) preferences (see CARDINAL AND ORDINAL UTILITY). While most branches of economic theory use only ordinal utilities, John von NEUMANN and Oskar Morgenstern (1947) have shown that cardinal utilities play a useful role in the theory of RISK.

intersubjectivity Concerns the relations between people, rather than within them (subjectivity) or beyond them (objectivity or transcendental reality). More generally, it describes a broad trend in twentieth-century philosophy and social science that privileges communication between people and shared understanding over individual consciousness and concepts of objective knowledge. The work of Johann Gottfried von Herder, Wilhelm Humboldt, and Georg HEGEL helped pave the way for this work by critiquing philosophies of autonomous subjectivity—especially Cartesian rationalism and Leibnizian monadology. The "linguistic turn" in modern philosophy continued these developments on a range of fronts, including the work of Ludwig WITTGENSTEIN; Charles Taylor's studies of self, language, and community; and the communication-based philosophy of Jürgen HABERMAS. LINGUISTICS too has moved beyond the referential dimension of language to examine language's structure, use, and performative qualities. Approaches to intersubjectivity have been influential across the social sciences, especially in SOCIOLOGY and ANTHROPOLOGY. ACTION THEORY and SYMBOLIC INTERACTIONISM are among the most prominent of these approaches.

intertemporal equilibrium An extension of the concept of EQUILIBRIUM to determine optimal decisions by HOUSEHOLDS and FIRMS in the present and the future. Many decisions have an intertemporal character in which benefits or profits are deferred, including savings decisions by households, investment decisions by firms, and the decision to acquire skills or education. Decisions require consideration of consumption or production not only for the present but also for all periods in the future. Analyses of intertemporal decision making generally assume that individuals and firms discount the future

to reflect the OPPORTUNITY COSTS of deferred consumption or profit.

investment The use of resources to expand the base of CAPITAL—the goods and resources that are used in production. Although most attention in economics is focused on business investment (in the form of buildings, machinery, and inventories), investment may also be undertaken by consumers and the government. Government construction of roads and bridges, education and training undertaken by individuals, and research and development sponsored by the government or nonprofit institutions may be considered forms of investment activity, although not all are considered as such in national income accounting.

Maintaining a given level of production requires maintenance of the existing means of production. Economic growth, on the other hand, calls for a rise in the rate of output produced. Both of these entail investment on the part of firms to replace depreciated equipment and to add new capital that brings more productive technology to bear. Inevitably, this requires decisions about how resources are allocated between current consumption and investment (which will contribute to future consumption). Investment also plays a role in the achievement of full employment—the optimal condition of an economy in which all resources are being fully utilized. This role was emphasized by John Maynard KEYNES, who correlated insufficient demand for investment with depression and chronic UNEMPLOYMENT. In a depressed economy, Keynes argued, an increase in investment will raise incomes and consumption in both the present and the future. Conversely, excess investment demand can lead to INFLATION. Keynes's views contrasted with those of classical economists, who saw a direct trade-off between investment and consumption in both the short and long term.

Classical and Keynesian economists also disagree on the mechanism that establishes equilibrium between savings and investment in the goods market. The classical economists posited that investment is very sensitive to the rate of interest. If savings exceed investment, the surplus of funds in the credit market will drive the interest rate down, discouraging saving until investment and savings are equal. Keynesians downplay the sensitivity of investment demand to interest rates and believe, rather, that investment is driven largely by expectations about the future.

James Tobin's q-theory extends many of the Keynesian concerns with expectations and the price of capital. Tobin describes investment as a function of the ratio of the market value of capital to its replacement cost, which he termed q. Investment is undertaken if $q > 1$ because the cost of replacing capital is less than the market valuation of the present value of returns from the investment. In general, the greater the value of q, the greater the investment. The market value can be represented by the stock prices of trading shares together with the bonded indebtedness of firms. Predictions based on q-investment equations have not been very successful, however.

Other studies of investment build upon the neoclassical theory of the firm and analyze the means of establishing equilibrium at a desired investment level (see FIRM, THEORY OF THE). In this work, firms follow a *path* of capital accumulation—a dynamic context that depends on expected prices and output over the entire planning horizon. Firms also have to take into account the adjustment costs of changing the capital stock. The best known of these models is the ACCELERATION PRINCIPLE.

invisible hand   A metaphor used by Adam SMITH in *The Wealth of Nations* (1776) to refer to the way in which the unintended consequences of individual action benefit society as a whole. Smith broke this claim into three separate assertions: (1) that human actions lead to unforeseen and unintended consequences; (2) that the sum of these unintended consequences across a large population or over a long period of time produces a social order that appears to be the product of an intelligent planner; (3) that social order is beneficial to participants in ways that they did not intend but nevertheless find desirable.

In modern market economics, the term is more often used to describe the way in which a free exchange and price system within a decentralized market setting coordinates individual decisions and results in an equilibrium that benefits all.

involution   Clifford GEERTZ's term for the relationship in some societies between socio-economic stagnation and increasingly elaborate cultural production.

iron law of oligarchy   Proposed by French sociologist Robert MICHELS in *Political Parties* (1911) to describe the tendency of all organizations or polities to fall under the control of

elites. In Michels's words, "he who says organization, says oligarchy." Oligarchical rule, he claimed, follows from a number of related factors: the impossibility of general political participation by a large number of people; the need for efficient, expert decision making; and the natural human desire for power. The larger the organization, he argued, the narrower the dominant elite. Michels developed this account in the context of his studies of left-wing political movements in Germany, especially the German Social Democratic Party. See also ELITE AND ELITISM; and OLIGARCHY.

iron law of wages   The hypothesis that in a MARKET ECONOMY, wages will always return to the level of subsistence. Usually credited to nineteenth-century German political economist Ferdinand Lasalle, it appears in different forms in the earlier work of Thomas Robert MALTHUS and David RICARDO, for whom it was a necessary consequence of human fertility and the law of supply and demand. Karl MARX accepted it in qualified form but criticized Lasalle for presenting the "industrial reserve army"—the mass of surplus workers that suppresses wages—as a permanent and necessary phenomenon, rather than a product of the capitalist MODE OF PRODUCTION. Many observers have argued that the steady wage gains and decreased population growth of most industrialized countries since the nineteenth century has rendered Lasalle's concept obsolete. Some have suggested it could be retained subject to treating the level of subsistence as historically and culturally variable.

iron triangle   A close and persistent relationship between an interest group, the legislative group or subcommittee that drafts laws that affect it, and the administrative agency responsible for implementing those laws. The term came into use to describe lobbying and legislative practices in the United States.

irredentism   The claim by a government or political movement to a territory lying outside its country's present boundaries. From the Italian *irredenta*, or "unredeemed," it derives from a nationalist Italian political movement of the 1870s that sought to annex certain predominately Italian-speaking parts of Austria. Irredentist claims are typically made on the basis of the ethnicity, language, or culture of the occupants of the disputed territory, or with reference to the state's geographical dimensions at some earlier point in history. It is common where borders were recently shifted or imposed and where populations are mixed.

IS-LM analysis A conceptual tool introduced by John R. HICKS (*Mr. Keynes and the Classics*, 1937) to clarify the relationship between John Maynard KEYNES's macroeconomic theory and those of his predecessors, the classical economists. IS-LM analysis has become the main vehicle for popularizing and teaching Keynesian ideas, and provides the chief conceptual framework for MACROECONOMICS in general.

This basic IS-LM model consists of three components. The IS block (in its simplest form) consists of a consumption or savings curve (as a function of income), an INVESTMENT curve (as a function of the rate of interest), and an equilibrium condition that holds that investment must equal savings in order for the goods market to clear (see CONSUMPTION FUNCTION). The IS curve traces the equilibrium possibilities given differences of income (measured along the horizontal axis) and the rate of interest (measured along the vertical axis). This curve is downward sloping, signifying that an increase in the rate of interest requires a fall in income to clear the goods market.

The second block consists of a money supply curve (usually assumed to be constant) and a money demand curve (as a function of income and the rate of interest). Here the equilibrium condition holds that money demand must equal money supply in order for the money market to clear. The LM curve shows the combinations of income and the rate of interest that clears the money market. This curve slopes upward because a rise in the interest rate requires a rise in income to restore equilibrium. Higher interest rates reduce the demand for money, since they make bonds more attractive. Thus, a rise in income, which raises the demand for money in transactions, is required to clear the money market. The place where the IS and LM curves intersect determines the equilibrium level of income and the rate of interest that clears both the goods and money markets.

IS-LM describes the demand side of the economy. The third component of the Keynesian model is an aggregate production function from which the labor demand curve is derived. The production function (or the labor market equilibrium) describes the supply side of the economy. The IS-LM model plus the supply curve yields the complete Keynesian model.

The IS-LM setting is a very flexible analytical device for studying how the economy responds to a range of possible changes in the goods and money markets. An increase in money supply, for instance, shifts the LM curve to the right, raising income and reducing interest rates. This model underlies the Keynesian revolution in activist budgetary and monetary policies, which sought to moderate the business cycle and achieve steady growth (see BUDGETARY OR FISCAL POLICY; and MONETARY POLICY).

isocost curves Show the combinations of inputs (for example, capital and labor) that yield the same level of *outlay* or *expenditure*. It is similar to the consumer's *budget constraint* in that it demonstrates all combinations of goods at a given level of expense. Unless a firm is a large buyer in the market for inputs, its isocost "curves" will usually be straight lines, reflecting the fact that the firm does not influence market prices by its purchasing decisions.

isogamy Marriage between partners of equal status. See also ANISOGAMY.

isogloss A linguistic border that separates different word usage or pronunciation.

isoquant curves Show combinations of inputs that yield the same level of *output*. They are similar to INDIFFERENCE CURVES for a consumer. The curve is almost always downward sloping: as less of one input is used, it is necessary to use more of the other input to maintain output at its original level. Higher isoquants indicate higher production levels—using more of all inputs. A firm that seeks to minimize the cost of producing a given amount of output will choose to produce that level of output at which the isoquant curve is tangent to the isocost curve (see ISOCOST CURVES).

J

Jacobinism A radical political faction that gained control of the French revolutionary government in 1793–1794. Under Maximilien Robespierre, the Jacobins imposed a reign of terror that sought to enforce equality and political unanimity. The term has subsequently been applied to political movements that advocate strict CENTRALIZATION of power, reject political pluralism, and pursue extremist or violent action in the name of the people; it can also refer to militant ANTICLERICALISM.

Jajmani system The traditional system of division of labor within Indian villages, which assigns certain occupations to certain CASTES.

Jakobson, Roman (1896–1982) The dominant theoretician of structural LINGUISTICS after Ferdinand de SAUSSURE. Jakobson led the Moscow and then Prague linguistic circles in the 1920s and 1930s and became a major influence on the anthropological STRUCTURALISM of Claude LÉVI-STRAUSS. Born in Moscow, Jakobson's early career was marked by his affiliation with Russian formalism—a movement in art and linguistics that sought to isolate the formal, internal rules of artistic composition and expression from questions of content. Jakobson's subsequent work during his years with the Prague linguistic circle and, following the Nazi occupation of Czechoslovakia, in the United States at Harvard University and MIT, extended many of these concerns toward what he argued was a scientific method for analyzing the structure of texts.

Jakobson relied on a strongly Saussurean sense of language as a differential network in which signifiers acquired their meaning only in relation to other signifiers. His interest in *phonemes* (the smallest linguistically significant differences of sound, such as the distinction between /v/ and /b/ in English) and *morphemes* (the basic grammatical components of words that are used consistently, such as prefixes, stems, and suffixes) allowed him to move toward a classificatory system of the components and possible operations of language. At the same time, Jakobson was critical of Saussure's tendency to treat linguistics as a SYNCHRONIC field of study based on the analysis of structural relationships in a snapshot of time. Instead, he insisted on the contextual basis of linguistic acts and on the functions of language that extended beyond the problem of signification. Jakobson emphasized that language was oriented fundamentally toward communication and that communication implied a complex range of functions of language. He identified functions related to the speaker, the addressee, the message itself, the existence of a shared linguistic code, the need for preparatory or context-creating speech (phatic speech), and the larger context to which the message referred (see PHATIC COMMUNION).

Despite this diversity, Jakobson argued, certain types of communication involve some functions more than others. This principle led him toward a basic distinction between poetry and prose, which he aligned with other distinctions in structural linguistics: metaphor and metonym, and the PARADIGMATIC AND SYNTAGMATIC axes of language. At his broadest, Jakobson integrated these distinctions into a general theory of linguistic capacities and language acquisition that supported his scientific claims for structural analysis. His major works are collected in *On Language* (1990) and the four volumes of *Selected Writings* (1962–1990).

James, C. L. R. (1901–1989) One of the leading Caribbean intellectuals of the twentieth century, James wore many hats: historian, journalist, novelist, playwright, cultural critic, political theorist, and constant activist on behalf of radical political causes. He was born in Trinidad but spent most of his life in England and the United States (from which he was deported in 1952 as a communist). James was prominent in the fractious politics of the far left of the 1930s and 1940s and militated on behalf of numerous political causes, including Pan-Africanism, anticolonialism, and workers' struggles in England and the United States. He is best known for two books: *The*

Black Jacobins (1938), a groundbreaking history of the Haitian Revolution, and *Beyond a Boundary* (1963), a cultural and political analysis of cricket. The former became a founding text of contemporary social history through its recentering of historical experience on traditionally marginalized historical actors; the latter helped bring legitimacy to the study of popular culture and thereby contributed to the emerging CULTURAL STUDIES movement. James also devoted several works to the history and theory of revolution, including *World Revolution: 1917–1936: The Rise and Fall of the Communist International* (1937) and *Notes on Dialectics: Hegel, Marx, Lenin* (1948).

James, William (1842–1910) The founder of philosophical PRAGMATISM, an influential scholar of religion, and arguably the dominant figure in psychology before Sigmund FREUD. These roles accorded him a central place in turn-of-the-century intellectual life and a broad influence on a range of disciplines that continues to this day. Throughout his psychological and philosophical writing, James emphasized the plurality of human experience and the processes of choice through which individuals fashion themselves and their lives. He challenged much of the psychological and related philosophical thought of his day, from theories of inherited or socially determined character, to attempts to treat consciousness as the process of association of distinct ideas (*associationism*), to philosophies of consciousness based on abstract and (James argued) unprovable systems of ideas. James suggested instead that human experience was characterized by a "stream of consciousness" that freely mixes feelings and interests, and in which ideas are mobilized toward instrumental ends. This experience of consciousness, James argued, was itself subject to empirical study. Calling himself a "radical empiricist," James tried to establish psychology as a natural science where principles could be proved through experimentation. *The Principles of Psychology* (1890) is his masterwork in this regard, bringing together his views on nearly every contemporary issue in psychology and establishing him as the leading psychologist of his day.

Pragmatism, for James, synthesized and generalized much of this perspective on human experience. Enlisting C. S. PEIRCE's "pragmatic" theory of scientific proof, James argued that the truth of ideas (what James referred to as their "cash value") lies in the degree to which they can be successfully applied to action. In other words,

truth lies in the realm of practices and consequences, not in transcendental realities. In this context, James argued, most of the metaphysical arguments in Western philosophy become unnecessary. *Pragmatism* (1907) is James's most concise and eloquent statement of these views—and for these reasons was a source of controversy at the time. Nonetheless, James had a strong interest in the *belief in truth*, which he accorded enormous power. In *The Will to Believe* (1897), James showed himself to be a defender of religion—not for its access to higher truths but, characteristically, for the intensity of human experience that it fostered. James undertook to present the vast diversity of these forms of belief in *The Varieties of Religious Experience* (1902).

James came from an exceptional family: his father, William James Sr., was a prominent religious philosopher; his younger brother Henry was the celebrated novelist. James's other major works include *A Pluralistic Universe* (1909) and *Some Problems in Philosophy* (1911).

Janowitz, Morris (1919–1988) An American sociologist best known for his studies of structures of social control within institutions, especially in the military. Early in his career, Janowitz was coauthor of one of the studies on prejudice organized by the FRANKFURT SCHOOL, *Dynamics of Prejudice* (1950, with Bruno Bettleheim), which correlated the growth of intolerance in the United States with the breakdown of traditional moral frameworks.

Janowitz later turned toward the analysis of the U.S. military and its organization—often in close collaboration with the Army—on topics related to morale, psychological warfare, leadership, and group structure. His *Professional Soldier* (1960) was a landmark analysis of the development of the military profession and the officers' corps in the twentieth century. Janowitz traced the changes in military organization that occurred as strongly authoritarian forms of domination gave way to other forms of discipline, and as the pool of recruits for the officers' corps grew broader and career paths diversified. These changes went beyond questions of institutional form. As the army, society, and the international scene changed, the relationship between military and civil authority was similarly transformed.

In other work, Janowitz focused on the postwar growth of the welfare state in advanced industrial countries. In *Social Control of the Welfare State* (1976), he explored the new mechanisms of social control enabled by the welfare state and the concurrent changes in the sociopolitical realm. These, he argued, tended to adversely affect political participation in democracies. He continued this theme in *The Last Half Century* (1978) in the context of the development of the postwar American "advanced industrial state." This study was, in large measure, a critique of Daniel BELL's, POSTINDUSTRIAL SOCIETY thesis, which Janowitz thought overstated structural changes in contemporary political economy. In his *Reconstruction of Patriotism* (1983), Janowitz revisited the topic of political participation in democracies by examining the development of civic education in the United States. Janowitz spent most of his career at the University of Chicago.

J curve   A curve tracing improvement after a decline, thus similar to the letter J. In the period following a devaluation of the exchange rate, for example, a country's BALANCE OF PAYMENTS (the net balance of exports, imports, flows of capital, and money) initially deteriorates and then improves. The J curve is explained by the fact that import and export levels are slow to respond to the change in relative prices produced by a devaluation. Consequently, import payments initially rise while export earnings decline in monetary terms. Over time, the volume of exports rises and the volume of imports declines, eliminating the balance of payments deficit and moving it into surplus.

In politics and sociology, a similar curve has been used to describe crisis after a long period of improvement that engenders rising expectations. James Davies argued that this is an important factor in revolutions.

Jevons, William Stanley   (1835–1882) One of the founders of the marginalist school of economics (now largely absorbed by NEOCLASSICAL ECONOMICS). The marginalists opposed the classical orthodoxy by positing demand as the primary determinant of prices. In *The Theory of Political Economy* (1871), Jevons dismissed the LABOR THEORY OF VALUE and asserted that value depends entirely on the UTILITY, or well-being, a good brings to the purchaser—not on the cost of production, as the classical theorists thought. Marginalism is an essential component of modern ECONOMICS, and Jevons's work continues to influence economic analysis.

Jevons studied political economy at University College, London and later returned as a professor of logic, political economy, and philosophy. He believed that the laws of economics could be as exact as those of physical science, and he tried to combine early utility analysis into a coherent theory of value, exchange, and distribution.

The starting point of marginalist theory is the individual and his or her wants. Following Jeremy BENTHAM, the marginalists assumed that each individual's objective is to maximize pleasure (in economics terms, *utility*). In order to do this, an individual increases consumption of a commodity to the point where an additional unit of the good increases utility by less than it costs (the basis of the concept of marginal utility; see MARGINAL ANALYSIS).

Although he recognized the pitfalls of interpersonal utility comparisons (comparing one person's utility with another's), Jevons used them in extending the law of diminishing marginal utility to money. This argument justified redistributing income from the rich to the poor, since the resulting increase in utility for the poor was greater than the decrease in utility for the rich. Jevons's law of diminishing marginal utility also provided an answer to what had become known as the *diamond–water paradox*—the contradiction between the low price of an essential good (water) and the high price of a comparatively useless good (diamonds). Jevons recognized this as reflecting a fundamental difference in their marginal utility.

Although Jevons used the law of diminishing marginal utility as an analytical tool, it was left to John Bates Clark to develop the law fully and formulate a marginal productivity theory of distribution. A more serious problem was Jevons's tendency to generalize from two individuals to many, which obscured the problem of competition.

In spite of the shortcomings of his theories and the fact that he failed to provide a complete alternative to the classical tradition, Jevons's work is important as a break from classical orthodoxy. It set the stage for later proponents of marginalism—most famously Alfred MARSHALL, who developed a comprehensive theory of the economy based on marginal utility.

joint production   The production of more than one product by a single firm. Joint production is often undertaken to maximize *economies of scope*, when production costs may be lowered by sharing materials or capital. It can also be a logical decision where there are relationships among products (as in wool and mutton) or when a production process is flexible enough to permit different forms of production. Finally, firms sometimes choose commodity diversification as a way of reducing risk in an uncertain environment, even when separate production processes are required.

joking relationship   Relationships in which certain kinds of pleasantry or mockery are expected between particular kin: for example, between a son and his father's sister or brother (common in AVUNCULATE societies). Anthropologists since A. R. RADCLIFFE-BROWN have seen this as a way of managing fault lines of potential social conflict. Alternatively, some kin relations in certain societies mandate formality or avoidance, often in the case of a husband and his mother-in-law.

judicial review   The power of the JUDICIARY to decide the legality of the actions of the LEGISLATURE or EXECUTIVE. It is one of the central mechanisms of the SEPARATION OF POWERS in the United States and a common feature of constitutionalism more generally (see CONSTITUTION AND CONSTITUTIONALISM). The power of review is exercised either by the normal court system (as in the United States and most COMMON LAW countries) or by a special constitutional court (as in France and Germany). Particularly in the latter cases, it is common for governments to refer proposed legislation to the court before it is passed. In most common law systems, in contrast, the court judges only those cases that come before it in its routine activity.

Judicial review was first developed in the United States. Although it does not appear in the U.S. Constitution, Chief Justice John Marshall argued in the 1803 case *Marbury v. Madison* that it was implied in the idea of constitutional supremacy. Despite controversy and occasional challenges, the annulment of the acts of elected officials by appointed judges has become a fundamental feature of government in the United States.

In the United States, controversies over the role of judicial review have often appeared as differences in judicial philosophy. The doctrine of "judicial restraint" argues that judges should restrict themselves to applying the law as they find it. This view is identified with "strict constructivism," the idea that the interpretation of the law should consist only in retrieving the original intentions of those who drafted it. At the opposite extreme is "judicial activism," less a doctrine than the practice of judges who attempt to make policy from the bench by substantively reinterpreting the law. There remains, however, a strong bias against using the courts to legislate, even on the part of activist judges. The Warren Court of the 1950s and 1960s, for example, which expanded the scope of individual rights in advance of and even in opposition to the elected branches of government, argued that it was merely interpreting the underlying principles of the Constitution in light of changed social circumstances.

judiciary   The branch of government responsible for interpreting the law, for resolving legal disputes, and often for determining the legality of legislative or executive actions (see JUDICIAL REVIEW). One of the principal early theorists of the role of the judiciary was Charles-Louis MONTESQUIEU, who held that an independent judiciary was one of the features that distinguished moderate from despotic government. Under Montesquieu's (and later theorists') doctrine of the SEPARATION OF POWERS, the judiciary plays a conservative role by checking the ambitions of the other branches.

Most judiciaries are to a degree insulated from the political process as a means of assuring independence from the other branches of government. Life or long tenure (in the United States), independent budgets (in Great Britain), and self-administering institutions for the training of judges (in much of continental Europe) are some of these measures. These methods are crucial to the legitimacy of modern judiciaries, even where only lip service is paid to the principle—as in many authoritarian regimes. There is also a lively debate within American jurisprudence over the degree to which any interpretation is separable from political values—or should be separable from them.

Juglar cycle   A BUSINESS CYCLE with a period of nine to ten years, named after the French economist Clément Juglar. Juglar emphasized the influence of bank credit in the development of economic crises, and divided the cycle into three periods: prosperity, crisis, and liquidation.

Jung, Carl Gustav   (1875–1961) An eminent psychologist whose theories (collectively known as *Jungian* or *Analytic* psychology) provided a major framework for thinking about personality and the nature of the social bond in the first half of the twentieth century. Jung was born in Switzerland and trained as a medical doctor. By the turn of the century he had moved toward the problems of mental illness and, in this context, encountered Sigmund FREUD's work on dreams and the question of repression. Thereafter, Jung and Freud developed a close relationship, which led to Jung's election as president of the International Psychoanalytic Society in 1911. By 1914, however, Jung had grown increasingly dissatisfied with Freud's emphasis on sexuality as the source of neurosis. A theoretical and ultimately personal dispute led to his break with Freudian PSYCHOANALYSIS.

Unlike Freud, Jung placed considerable emphasis on the religious and mystical dimensions of the human psyche—an area he explored in particular through the analysis of dreams, including his own. Dream analysis led him to his best-known and most controversial theoretical work on the COLLECTIVE UNCONSCIOUS: a deeply buried layer of racial memory that, he argued, played the key role in structuring personality and in reproducing age-old patterns of behavior. The collective unconscious in turn, Jung argued, is composed of *archetypes*, or universal structures of meaning and experience. These, he suggested, are especially visible in mythology and religion.

Individuation, Jung argued, is the process of coming to self-knowledge or wholeness regarding this psychic organization. The goal of Jungian psychotherapy is to overcome neurotic obstacles to this process. Within this framework, Jung also conducted influential work on personality types, distinguishing primarily between *introverts* and *extroverts*. This work opened the door to a long tradition of personality research in SOCIAL PSYCHOLOGY. Jung's theory of the collective unconscious and the increasingly mystical tendencies of his work after World War II have fared less well in the social sciences, but continue to be a point of reference for literary studies. His major works include *Contributions to Analytical Psychology* (1928), *Modern Man in Search of a Soul* (1933), *Civilization in Transition* (1964), and, more comprehensively, a twenty-volume set of collected works (1953–1979).

jural domain and moral domain *Jural* typically refers to the rights and obligations of the legal system, while *moral* refers to those obligations that fall outside them. As used by Meyer FORTES and other, mostly British anthropologists, however, *jural* refers to rules and obligations related to structures of social organization (usually as a function of status or lineage), while *moral* obligations both support and extend beyond that structure (including, primarily, those related to family).

jus sanguinis and jus soli There are two main traditions that inform CITIZENSHIP law in the West: *jus sanguinis*, in which citizenship is determined by that of one or both biological parents, and *jus soli*, in which it is determined by place of birth. France is the classic example of the former; Germany of the latter.

justice One of the central and least agreed-upon ideas in POLITICAL THEORY, generally associated with notions of fairness and right action. Since ARISTOTLE, justice has been studied predominantly under two aspects: *corrective* and *distributive*.

Corrective justice concerns punishment for wrongdoing. Although the forms, degrees, and rationales of punishment are historically and culturally contingent, three general principles of corrective justice are common to most systems: (1) punishment should be reserved for wrongdoers; (2) similar crimes should receive similar penalties; and (3) punishments should be proportional, with more serious crimes accorded harsher penalties. The application of punishment and the evaluation of its effects are the central topics of *penology*.

Distributive justice, in contrast, is primarily concerned with how goods, honors, and obligations are distributed within a community. Commentators such as Michael Walzer (*Spheres of Justice*, 1983) have argued on the basis of the historical diversity of notions of justice that justice is irreducibly plural and specific to particular social practices and understandings. This view, known as *conventionalism*, places the burden of clarifying, realizing, and improving the concept of justice on each community or society. To its critics, conventionalism carries tolerance for different constructions of justice to the point of relativism, and thereby undermines any meaningful conception of the term.

Much of the history of the concept is linked to ideas about NATURAL LAW and divine will. This includes religious moral systems, which identify justice with adherence to God's will, and natural law approaches, such as those of Aristotle, the Stoics, and many early modern thinkers, which argue that justice inheres in nature and is discoverable through reason. Although such views vary widely, they tend to agree that justice derives from a static, eternal, and universal order. Right conduct, in this context, involves adherence to that order.

Modern and secular understandings of justice tend to emphasize the role of rational institutions, such as the STATE, the LAW, or the market, in realizing forms of collective or social justice. Many of these privilege processes of aggregating individual consent or self-interested action into an orderly and inherently just whole. SOCIAL-CONTRACT THEORY is one example; Adam SMITH's "invisible hand," in which the free pursuit of individual interests produce the maximum social benefit, is another. The utilitarian extension of Smith's model of welfare-maximizing agents is a third, based on the identification of justice with "the greatest good of the greatest number" (see UTILITARIANISM).

Modern theories of justice generally combine consideration of the general good with some notion of basic human needs, rights, or reward for merit. While all identify justice with the general principle of fairness (rather than with some substantive way of life), they frequently differ on the relative priority accorded to FREEDOM, EQUALITY, and DEMOCRACY, as well as on whether justice is a starting-point, a procedure, or an outcome. Some, such as Immanuel KANT and more recently John RAWLS, have defined justice in terms of a logical imperative that requires that individuals accord to all others what they themselves regard as fair treatment. Others, such as Ronald Dworkin and Robert Nozick, have followed John LOCKE and other early liberal thinkers in emphasizing the inviolability of certain basic RIGHTS and ENTITLEMENTS (albeit from very different perspectives).

K

Kaldor, Nicholas (1908–1986) Kaldor's contributions to economics range from the MICROECONOMICS of the firm to GROWTH THEORY and monetary and fiscal policy. Most of these are developed in the eight volumes of Kaldor's *Collected Economic Essays* (1960–1980). Among his achievements, Kaldor named the COBWEB THEOREM, introduced the idea of compensation tests into WELFARE ECONOMICS, and clarified the relationship between tariffs and the terms of trade. At the macroeconomic level, Kaldor's growth models had two innovative features: they implied a theory of distribution according to which the overall profit rate in the economy is constrained by the low-profit agricultural sector; and they incorporated a production function in which technical progress depends on learning and, therefore, on the rate of investment. These contributions occupy an important place in the history of modern ECONOMICS.

Born in Budapest, Kaldor studied at the London School of Economics and later became professor of economics at the University of Cambridge. Much of his early work dealt with the economics of the firm and with imperfect competition. While he welcomed the work of Edward Chamberlin and Joan ROBINSON on monopolistic competition, he criticized them for assuming that firms in imperfectly competitive markets face standard demand curves.

Kaldor's early work on growth examined it primarily at the aggregate level, but he later became more interested in the microfoundations of growth. He was among the first of the twentieth-century economists to appreciate the existence of increasing returns to scale both in specific industries and in the macroeconomy. Kaldor believed that technical progress facilitates growth but does not drive it: new knowledge is required to operate plants on a larger scale. The accumulation of physical capital also plays a role.

Increasing returns, however, do not apply to sectors like agriculture and mining. This creates a problem for the growth process, since increased industrial production increases the demand for food and raw materials. Thus, in a closed economy, the growth rate of the primary sectors sets an upper limit on the growth rate of industrial production. The volatility of prices in these sectors also plays an important macroeconomic role.

According to Kaldor, cumulative causation and increasing returns are the chief explanation of why different world regions have followed different growth paths. If a region has a high level of industrial production today, then the presence of increasing returns ensures that this region will continue to be the leader in the future. Similarly, if a region starts off slowly, there is little chance of it breaking this circle of causation. Kaldor believed that the initial stimulus to an economy can be provided by the government through tariffs and subsidies. He advocated such measures for infant industries to help them into the virtuous circle of growth (see INFANT-INDUSTRY ARGUMENT).

Kaldor's views on monetary and fiscal policy are less original than his theory of growth, although they derive from it. He attached little importance to monetary policy but subscribed to the prevalent Keynesian view that effective demand could and should be affected by government expenditure. Yet he also believed that long-term growth and full employment could not be achieved by increasing fiscal deficits. Instead, since higher industrial exports provide the initial stimulus for growth, government policy should be aimed at increasing international competitiveness.

Although he remained a harsh critic of mainstream NEOCLASSICAL ECONOMICS throughout his life, Kaldor's research influenced economic analysis even within neoclassicism. His work is still the starting point of much research on growth, and his involvement in practical affairs regarding taxation, trade policy, and incentives for growth helped consolidate his position as one of the most influential economic thinkers of the twentieth century.

Kalecki, Michal (1899–1970) An economist often regarded as a follower and interpreter of John Maynard KEYNES. Kalecki's work, however, anticipated Keynes's in some important respects. His *Essay on Business Cycle Theory* (1933) theorized the capitalist economy as a demand-determined system three years before the publication of Keynes's *General Theory*.

Kalecki was born in Poland. During the 1930s, he visited Cambridge University, where he established scholarly ties with Piero SRAFFA, Richard Kahn, and especially Joan ROBINSON. He also spent several years in the United States after World War II, until anti-Semitism and McCarthyism prompted him to return to his native Warsaw. Like Keynes, Kalecki searched for an explanation for and solution to the mass unemployment caused by the Great Depression. Unlike Keynes, however, Kalecki's point of departure was not Marshallian EQUILIBRIUM analysis but Karl MARX's theories of capitalist reproduction. Both Kalecki and Keynes reached the conclusion that government intervention was warranted, although Kalecki was more interested in the evolution toward SOCIALISM than the preservation of CAPITALISM.

The starting point of Kalecki's theory is a distinction between the components of national income that actively participate in capitalist production (investment outlays, export surpluses, and budget deficits), and those that passively follow output and employment (workers' consumption). He arrived at the equality between savings and investment, where investment is the active factor and always generates the savings required to finance it. However, he argued that an increase in investment can increase consumption only if there is spare capacity. Kalecki assumed that there is always underutilization of capacity in capitalist economies and that investment therefore determines effective demand. Based on this theory, he attacked the orthodox prescription of reducing unemployment by cutting money wages, arguing that such a measure does not necessarily lower inflation-adjusted real wages and would be harmful if it did, since lower wages mean lower demand and therefore lower employment.

After his return to Poland, Kalecki became increasingly interested in planning and growth. In *Introduction to the Theory of Growth in a Socialist Economy* (1963), he proposed a growth theory somewhat similar to the Harrod–Domar model, stating that the growth rate of national income is determined simultaneously as the sum of the growth rates of employment and labor productivity, as well as the sum of the investment rate and the net improvement in capacity utilization (see GROWTH THEORY).

Kalecki's contribution to economics was a unique mixture of theory and practice. He articulated theories of unemployment and growth and also traveled to Cuba, India, and Israel as a development adviser. Although his theories were not always accepted—even in socialist circles in the West—they were a major influence on DEVELOPMENT policy in the THIRD WORLD.

Kant, Immanuel (1724–1804) A German philosopher of the Enlightenment, Kant also is often considered the first philosopher of MODERNITY—the first to describe the philosophy of the age as a "critical philosophy," directed against all merely inherited conceptions of knowledge and social life. Only from this basis, Kant argued, could philosophy reconstruct knowledge, ethics, and judgment on rational principles. This ambition underwrote nearly all of Kant's mature work—especially his monumental trilogy on the different domains of reason: *The Critique of Pure Reason* (1781), *The Critique of Practical Reason* (1788), and *The Critique of Judgment* (1790).

Kant's work radically challenged both the empiricist and rationalist traditions of inquiry into the nature of human knowledge and experience. Empiricists (mainly George Berkeley, David HUME, and John LOCKE) had treated knowledge primarily as a problem of how human consciousness might reflect the sensory experience of a fundamentally given world. Rationalists (René DESCARTES, Benedict de Spinoza, and Gottfried Wilhelm Leibniz) sought to build outward from fundamental principals of consciousness, such as Descartes's nugget of certainty: "I think, therefore I am." Kant, in turn, treated knowledge as structured *a priori* by certain basic features of the mind, such as the fundamental intuitions of space and time; this entailed a distinction between things as they are for us (phenomena) and things as they are in themselves (noumena). Things in their *phenomenal* aspect appeared to consciousness already structured by the intuitions (and at a different level, by the logical categories) of human thought. This did not exclude the possibility, Kant argued, that things might have other aspects that are imperceptible to human beings—a *noumenal* side that escapes us. Kant's innovative turn toward the analysis of the basic framing structures of the human mind influenced nearly all subsequent inquiries into the status of knowledge and human consciousness and continues to inform theories that accord a central role to the cognitive structuring of human experience and understanding. It became the most influential "idealist" position in modern thought.

The Critique of Pure Reason is the fullest expression of what Kant described as his Copernican revolution in philosophy—and it did, in fact, represent a radical revision of the existing approaches to knowledge. Pure reason, for Kant, described those things that were true without recourse to experience and therefore universal, such as mathematics. It is a critique because it rigorously examines the foundations on which such knowledge can exist.

More direct implications for social science are found in Kant's *Critique of Practical Reason* and *Critique of Judgment*, which address ethics and aesthetics, respectively. In each of these fields, knowledge depends on empirical factors as well as pure reason. In the case of ethics, knowing what is right to do in any particular case requires both knowledge of the case and knowledge of what is correct or proper. Kant placed heavy emphasis on the principle of universalizability, of doing what would always be right to do regardless of circumstances. This yielded his famous concept of the *categorical imperative*, which held that one should act only in ways that one could wish were universal. In a sense, this refashions the Golden Rule (do unto others as you would have others do unto you), a precept of most major religions. It implies that acting on the basis of immediate interest will always fall short of ethical standards, not simply when selfishness is involved but because interests are particular and empirical. Much the same principle was at stake in Kant's notion of "beauty" in *The Critique of Judgment*—only that which produced disinterested pleasure qualified as "beautiful." The rest was merely contingent empirical taste. Here the analogue to the categorical imperative was the notion of an "enlarged sensibility," the capacity to judge not simply from the basis of one's empirical circumstances but from a perspective broadened by taking into account the views and viewpoints of others. One connection to social science involves political decision making, which engages both practical reason and judgment and which faces the question of whether it can transcend merely empirical, particular relations of power and interest. Kant clearly calls for it to do so and to seek the maximally universal good.

Crucial to this notion of the "good" is Kant's understanding of human beings as "ends in themselves." This implied that all human beings have intrinsic value, are due basic respect, and should not be treated as mere objects—and consequently that an instrumental orientation toward human beings is always wrong. Legitimate politics requires that practitioners rise above instrumental purposes and treat individual autonomy as an end in itself. In a just society, therefore, ethical action would be coincident with the LAW, and conscience would be mirrored in the STATE.

Kant's philosophy structured much early debate about the status of the social sciences vis-à-vis the natural sciences. Kantian principles implied that the social sciences could not achieve their distinctive form of knowledge through pure reason, nor should they approach human beings as mere objects of human knowledge. Rather, it was crucial to understand human beings as subjects, potentially autonomous and capable of action. This view shaped the interpretive sociologies of Max WEBER and George SIMMEL. Neo-Kantian philosophy also informed Emile DURKHEIM's concept of a distinct science of society and, especially, his attempt to discern the social sources of the basic categories of mind that Kant had considered *a priori*. See also NEO-KANTIANISM.

Kant was born and spent his life in the German city of Königsberg (now Kaliningrad), where he taught philosophy at the university. He wrote a number of other important works that pursue the themes begun in the three *Critiques*, including *Religion within the Limits of Reason Alone* (1793), *Toward Eternal Peace* (1795), *Metaphysic of Morals* (1797), and *The Conflict of the Faculties* (1798).

Key, V. O. (1908–1963) One of the most influential American political scientists of the mid-twentieth century, Key was known for his broad and practical analyses of the political system of the United States, most particularly its elections. In *Politics, Parties and Pressure Groups* (1942), Key examined the roles of political parties, interest groups, and third-party and independent candidates in American politics. In *Southern Politics in State and Nation* (1949), a groundbreaking study of regional politics, Key explored the issue of RACE as a determinant of election outcomes in the South. In *American State Politics: An Introduction* (1956), he examined the formulation and nature of state parties, including a particular focus on states in which the legislative and executive branches were controlled by different parties. Key also studied a range of related aspects of political systems, including political graft, the administration of federal grants to states, the formulation of PUBLIC OPINION and its effects on government, the role of political activists, and the criteria by which voters elect a president. On this last topic, Key argued that "voters are not fools"—that they generally make rational decisions based on the analysis of past events.

Key was an innovator in the application of statistical data, including survey results, to political science, and he often combined such methods with "elite interviews" of political specialists. He is also associated with the emergence of BEHAVIORALISM in the 1950s. Key taught at the University of California, Los Angeles, Johns Hopkins University, Yale University (where he served as chair of the department of political science), and Harvard University. He was active in the Social Science Research Council and was president of the American Political Science Association. His other major works include *Public Opinion and American Democracy* (1961).

Keynes, John Maynard   (1883–1946) Keynes was probably the twentieth century's most influential economist. His central insights into the role of the government in stabilizing the level of business activity continue to dominate modern thinking about the macroeconomy. Keynes studied at Cambridge University with Alfred MARSHALL and Arthur C. PIGOU. At twenty-eight, he became the editor of the *Economic Journal*. He held various public posts (including service on the governing body of the Bank of England) and wrote extensively as a journalist. Keynes's lasting fame, however, is due primarily to his *General Theory of Employment, Interest and Money*, published in 1936.

Keynes had written several other books before the publication of the *General Theory*, most of which concentrated on practical aspects of public policy. These include *Economic Consequences of Peace* (1919), *Treatise on Probability* (1921), and *A Treatise on Money* (1930). The realities of the Great Depression, however, led Keynes to focus on the means of alleviating unemployment. Keynes observed that classical political economy was concerned primarily with the distribution of the output of the economy, rather than with its amount. This was based on the assumption that the economy always fully employs available resources. Keynes challenged this assumption

and, more broadly, the classical tradition built around it.

The starting point of Keynes's theory is the concept of effective demand—the total proceeds that entrepreneurs expect to receive. This demand in turn implies a certain level of employment—the amount of labor needed to produce the demanded level of output. Because demand, in turn, is determined by the level of NATIONAL INCOME, there is a close relationship between national income and employment. Every dollar spent on final goods and services for either consumption or investment is translated into income. Thus the final determinants of income and employment are the determinants of consumption and investment.

In Keynes's view, people tend to spend a fixed proportion of their income on consumption. Investment spending, on the other hand, is determined by the interest rate at which firms can borrow and by the marginal efficiency of capital—i.e., the expected rate of return on investment. Keynes's main conclusion was that when consumption and investment are inadequate to maintain full employment, the government should add to the income stream by increasing its expenditure, even if this means deficit spending. The effect of this increased government spending on the economy is explained by the MULTIPLIER principle. If the marginal propensity to consume is 75¢ per dollar and the government hires an extra worker at $100, consumption in the economy rises by $75. This 75 percent return, however, does not stop there. It works its way through multiple cycles of production and consumption as workers buy goods whose production underwrites salaries for other workers. Ultimately, the increase in national income and employment derived from a $100 increase in government expenditure is *greater than* $100. Conversely, Keynes argued, an overheated economy could be slowed by reducing government expenditure.

Although there are other implications of the *General Theory*, Keynes's greatest contributions were to discredit the neoclassical notion that reducing wages was a remedy for underemployment and to articulate the central role of government in guiding the economy at a macroeconomic level. Despite neoliberal critiques by monetarists and others, Keynesian principles continue to underpin much of the economic policy of industrialized nations. See also MACROECONOMICS.

Keynesianism   The body of economic thought and policy analysis developed by John Maynard KEYNES and his followers. The principles of Keynesianism were laid forth in Keynes's *The General Theory of Employment, Interest and Money* (1936), a seminal work of economic theory that emphasized the interventionist role of the STATE in stimulating aggregate demand in order to reach a full-employment equilibrium. More generally, Keynes charged the state with responsibility for active management of economic growth—principally through attempts to moderate the swings of business cycles. These priorities reflected a critique of the market/price mechanism as an efficient means of allocating resources. In particular, Keynes argued, there was no automatic tendency toward full employment in a market economy. Unemployment could occur in equilibrium, and the government's job was to correct it.

The practical goals of Keynesianism, then, were to develop monetary and fiscal policies (and other tools of macroeconomic management) that would maintain the economy at or near full employment. The most common version of Keynesian economics is what is known as the Neoclassical–Keynesian synthesis, developed by Paul SAMUELSON, Alvin Hansen, and John R. HICKS. Hicks built the foundations for the modern IS-LM model, which links monetary equilibrium and interest rates with aggregate income and consumption. The IS-LM model remains a standard tool of macroeconomic analysis. See IS-LM ANALYSIS.

Apart from the popular integration with NEOCLASSICAL ECONOMICS, Keynes's economics has developed in two additional directions. *Post-Keynesians* like Joan ROBINSON and Michal KALECKI concentrated on deriving theories of income distribution and capital accumulation from the Keynesian framework and studied its effects on NATIONAL INCOME. Post-Keynesian economics often blends Keynes's models with perspectives from classical POLITICAL ECONOMY, with a focus on market systems in a historical and institutional context. *New Keynesians*, in contrast, are more committed to the neoclassical paradigm, while allowing for market failures and price and wage rigidities that indicate that the economy may not naturally tend toward full employment. The early work in this field focused on the microfoundations that would explain, for example, why firms tend not to reduce wages in bad times, leading to unemployment. Current New Keynesians consider both monetary and fiscal policy to be potent tools of macroeconomic management (unlike Keynes himself, who felt that fiscal policy was more effective), and study the effects on economies with fixed prices and wages. See also BUDGETARY OR FISCAL POLICY; and MACROECONOMICS.

kinked demand curve   A demand curve developed by economist Paul Sweezy in order to explain price rigidities in oligopolistic markets (see OLIGOPOLY AND OLIGOPSONY). It relies on the asymmetric reaction of firms to changes in a single firm's pricing decision. According to Sweezy, each firm believes that a decrease in its price will provoke similar price reduction from other firms, whereas an increase in its price will result in firms maintaining constant prices in order to expand their market shares. This creates a kink in the individual firm's demand curve at the existing price and a discontinuity in its marginal revenue curve. Under these circumstances, shifts in demand and costs can take place without a price change—a form of price rigidity.

kinship   The network of social relationships that structure human reproduction, composed of the roles, rules, and forms of behavior that define relations by blood and marriage. Kinship has been the chief and most enduring subject of ANTHROPOLOGY, dating back as far as Lewis Henry MORGAN's *Systems of Consanguinity and Affinity* (1870). In part, this is due to the preeminence of kin relationships in the preindustrial societies that have traditionally interested anthropologists most. It is also due to the long-standing assumption that the FAMILY is the basis of social organization, whether as the unit of which society is the aggregate or as its developmental kernel, expanding outward through marriage alliances, persisting over time through descent, and abstracting itself into larger forms of political and economic association.

Alliance (marriage) and descent (filiation) are the two main axes of kinship analysis. Relations by marriage are referred to as affinal, while those by blood are consanguineal. Although the number of different possible biological relationships is a human constant, the meaning given those relationships can vary enormously from society to society. Certain relationships will be privileged in one society while others go unrecognized or have no significance. Descent may be reckoned according to the male line (PATRILINEAL DESCENT) or the female line (MATRILINEAL DESCENT); the role of the wife's brothers in raising her children may be highly significant (a feature known as the AVUNCULATE) or totally ignored; the choice of marriage partners may be circumscribed or regulated, and so on through the range of functions and roles that kinship plays in all societies (see SYMMETRICAL EXCHANGE AND ASYMMETRICAL EXCHANGE).

DESCENT THEORY recognizes both unilineal and multilineal systems of descent, the former comprising the large majority of preindustrial societies and divided into patrilineal and matrilineal forms, the latter comprising societies (particularly Polynesian and Southeast Asian societies) in which individuals recognize descent via the mother or father (cognatic or BILATERAL DESCENT).

Within anthropology, the relative importance of alliance and descent has been the subject of considerable debate. Claude LÉVI-STRAUSS is the researcher most responsible for moving structures of alliance to the center of kinship analysis, challenging the descent-oriented arguments of British anthropological work in Africa, particularly E. E. EVANS-PRITCHARD'S work on the Nuer and Meyer FORTES's work on the Tallensi. Another direction of criticism came from American studies of Oceanic societies, which failed to find the unilineal systems of classic descent theory. Indeed, the different theories may in large measure simply reflect the different empirical cases, in which African segmentary lineage systems inform descent theory, and Amerindian and Oceanic cases inform alliance theory.

Outside classic tribal anthropology and especially in the study of modern societies, kinship plays a less central role. Modern societies are modern in part because kin relations have been superseded as the main determinants of social organization by other structures: the market economy, the state, forms of social stratification, and so on. This transition has itself been thematized in a wide range of classic and modern social theory, from theories of modernization to the evolutionary models popular in nineteenth-century anthropology. See MODERNITY.

Klein, Melanie (1882–1960) The founder of OBJECT-RELATIONS THEORY, one of the major traditions of psychoanalytic research after Sigmund FREUD. Although she considered herself faithful to the underlying Freudian theory of the instincts (particularly in relation to the fundamental aggressivity that Freud posited in human personality), Klein rejected much of the Freudian account of child development—especially the OEDIPUS COMPLEX. Instead, she developed a theory of individuation and maturation that proceeds by way of diverse emotional attachments to familial and social "objects," which the child progressively internalizes and distinguishes from the self. In this respect, Klein recognized a continuum in behavior between young, ostensibly pre-Oedipal children and adults. The connections were particularly clear to Klein in the case of psychotics, who seemed to her to share with young children a structure of affect contained between the two poles of *paranoid* and *depressive* anxiety. Paranoid anxiety, Klein argued, arises from the infant's distinctions between good and bad objects (such as the nourishing breast and the milkless breast). Depressive anxiety is the result of the infant's subsequent realization that the good and bad objects are both aspects of the mother. In this context, the infant begins to feel guilt and the desire for restitution—both important social feelings.

Bad objects, Klein argued, are projected on to the external world in some instances and internalized in others, leading to difficulties in the formation of the EGO. The mother plays a crucial role in this development beginning in the first months of life—far earlier than Freudian theory held was relevant. Klein consequently worked with infants who were unanalyzable in Freudian terms—a point that led to a strong disagreement with Anna Freud and an eventual disciplinary break between object-relations theory and EGO PSYCHOLOGY. Klein's work on objects, her analytical techniques, and her theories of sexuality and envy have been central to a large body of psychoanalytic theory and research on child development, including that of Wilfred BION (her student), Donald Woods WINNICOTT, and W. R. D. Fairburn. As an alternative to the Oedipal complex, her work has also had a major impact on feminist theories of identity. One of Klein's major works is *The Psychoanalysis of Children* (1949). Many of her important essays have been published in two collections: *Love, Guilt, Reparation, and Other Works, 1921–1945* (1975) and *Envy, Gratitude and Other Works, 1946–1963* (1975). See also PSYCHOANALYSIS.

Kluckhohn, Clyde (1905–1960) An American anthropologist with broad interests and expertise in a range of fields, including Navajo and Russian society, psychological and physical anthropology, and theories of CULTURE and LINGUISTICS. In his short career, Kluckhohn produced several highly regarded ethnographies of the Navajo and wrote a number of important accounts of ANTHROPOLOGY and the social sciences, including *Mirror for Man* (1949), which argued for the relevance of anthropology in creating a better world. Kluckhohn played a significant institutional role in American anthropology, serving as president of the American Anthropological Association. He was also a central figure in the reintroduction of Franz BOAS's work to American anthropology, although his own work often steps back from Boas's extreme cultural particularism. Kluckhohn's other major works include *The Navaho* (1946) and *Culture and Behavior: Collected Essays* (1961).

knife edge problem   See GROWTH THEORY.

Kniffen, Fred   (1900–1993) The founding figure of American folk geography, Kniffen was an astonishingly productive writer, authoring well over one hundred books on diverse features of folk and rural culture. Kniffen trained with Carl SAUER and Alfred L. KROEBER at the University of California at Berkeley, drawing from the two his strong interest in material culture and considerable expertise with anthropological methods. He was a pioneer in the qualitative study of cultural diffusion and brought a careful eye to differences of style and habits of daily life (see DIFFUSION AND DIFFUSIONISM). Perhaps his best-known study concerns the patterns of diffusion of different types of folk housing. Kniffen spent almost his entire career at Louisiana State University and conducted numerous studies of the Louisiana region and its population. His major works include the seminal essay "Folk Housing: The Key to Diffusion" (1936), *Culture Worlds* (1951, with Richard Russell), and *Louisiana: Its Land and People* (1968).

Koopmans, Tjalling   (1910–1985) An economist and mathematician who made significant contributions to econometric methods, activity analysis (including linear programming), and dynamic optimization. Of these, the most important achievement was probably in econometrics, where he worked out the solution to the identification and estimation problems associated with simultaneous equation systems (with Herman Rubin and Roy Leipnik).

Koopmans was born and educated in the Netherlands; his training lay primarily in mathematical statistical methods with applications in economics. He taught at several universities around the world before accepting a more permanent position on the Cowles Commission for Research in Economics, first at the University of Chicago and then at Yale University. In 1975, he received the Nobel Prize in economics (with Leonid Kantorovich).

Koopmans's doctoral thesis focused on a category of linear regressions in which all variables are subject to measurement error. Later, he turned his attention to simultaneous equation systems—i.e., systems in which equilibrium is determined by both supply and demand equations. The importance of such systems in economics cannot be overemphasized.

There are two problems associated with simultaneous equations: (1) whether the system can be solved (identification) and (2) the inherent bias associated with least squares estimates. An equation is said to be *identified* if the available data allow the estimation of a unique set of parameters for the underlying model. Koopmans and his collaborators found a necessary and sufficient condition for identification (known as the rank condition), as well as another necessary condition, the order condition. In practice, if the order condition is satisfied, the rank condition is likely to be satisfied as well. Koopmans and his colleagues also developed statistical tools for the estimation of simultaneous equations—including the *full information maximum likelihood estimator*, which unlike the more common least squares estimator remains consistent. Later research yielded the *limited information maximum likelihood estimator*, which is computationally less demanding than the full information version. Both remain central to the estimation of systems today.

Koopmans's research in activity analysis, which involves production models that encompass commodities and production processes, led to the 1975 Nobel Prize. He was quick to point out the earlier contributions of Oskar Lange and Abba Lerner, and particularly George Dantzig, who proposed the *simplex* method for solving linear programming problems. Koopmans insisted that Dantzig should have shared the prize.

Some of Koopmans's most important theoretical contributions dealt with optimization over infinite horizons. These include several papers on optimal growth and the problem of the representation of preferences. Koopmans also formalized the concept of impatience (i.e., people prefer to consume now rather than in the future), which follows from postulates about utility over infinite horizons.

Although Koopmans's main contributions were technical, he also involved himself in ethical issues, such as defining optimal growth, and in particular sought a way to bring scientific reason to bear on such problems.

Kristeva, Julia   (1941–) Kristeva's work developed at the intersection of MARXISM, structural LINGUISTICS, and Lacanian psychoanalytic theory (see Jacques LACAN). She is perhaps best known as one of the three French theorists (with Luce Irigaray and Hélène Cixous) whose work sponsored a wave of feminist debates over essentialism and the deconstruction of GENDER in the 1980s and 1990s, although these issues are representative of only a portion of her research (see FEMINISM).

Much of Kristeva's major work has been devoted to analyzing radical or self-subverting modes of subjectivity in literature—a subject she pursued in *Revolution in Poetic Language* and later in *Powers of Horror* ([1980] 1982), which introduced the influential concept of *abjection* to cultural and gender studies. Her subsequent work has devoted greater attention to questions of emotion and mental illness, from the study of melancholia and depression in *Black Sun* ([1987] 1992) to a consideration of the side effects of therapeutic culture in *New Maladies of the Soul* ([1993] 1995). She has also written a semiautobiographical novel, *The Samurai* ([1990] 1992), and a study of immigration and nationalism, *Strangers to Ourselves* ([1988] 1991), which drew on her personal experience of immigration to France from Bulgaria.

Kroeber, Alfred L.   (1876–1960) A student of Franz BOAS and a major American anthropologist during the formative years of the field in the early twentieth century. Kroeber chaired the Department of Anthropology at the University of California at Berkeley for several decades and conducted important work on a wide range of topics, including archaeological reconstructions of cultural timelines in Mexico, Peru, and the American Southwest, analyses of KINSHIP structures and linguistic patterns among Indian tribes of the Southwest, and contributions to PHYSICAL ANTHROPOLOGY and the theory of CULTURE.

Many of these projects have been highly influential in their subfields—particularly the synthesis of his archaeological and linguistic findings in the *Handbook of the Indians of California* (1925). Beyond these specific field contributions, however, Kroeber made numerous methodological innovations that opened doors for other scholars. These include archaeological dating techniques and statistical methods applied to the distribution of linguistic and cultural traits. Kroeber's prominence, however, probably owes most to the sustained reflection on culture that underwrote both his analytical and methodological work. Especially in his early essay, "The Superorganic" (1917), Kroeber contended that culture was a relatively autonomous set of relations that determines the individuals that compose it. This argument set the terms for much of the debate about the definition of culture in the next decades and helped position American cultural anthropology against the emerging British structural-functionalist tradition. His development of the concept of *culture areas* reflected both an interest in deciphering patterns of coherence of cultural traits and a strong belief that such patterns could not be correlated with more general evolutionary schemas (see CULTURE AREA OR CULTURE REGION). This direction of inquiry culminated in his strong defense of cultural anthropology in *The Nature of Culture* (1952), which collected a number of his most important theoretical essays. It also led to a historical overview of theories of culture, *Culture: A Critical Review of Concepts and Definitions* (1952, with Clyde KLUCKHOHN). Kroeber's other important works include *The Arapaho* (1902–1907), *Anthropology* (1923), and *Configurations of Culture Growth* (1944). See also ANTHROPOLOGY.

Kuhn, Thomas   (1922–1996) A physicist turned philosopher of science whose model of scientific revolutions greatly influenced theories of knowledge and social change. Kuhn's major ideas were developed most fully in *The Structure of Scientific Revolutions* (1962). Rather than treat science as the progressive accumulation of knowledge, moving toward an ever more exact knowledge of physical reality, Kuhn proposed that science in any given period operated within a horizon of assumptions—a scientific PARADIGM—that guided the direction of inquiry, determined the standards of truth, and delimited the range of acceptable answers. Kuhn used the term *normal science* to describe scientific research conducted in accordance with the dominant paradigm. Over time, Kuhn believed, paradigms are vulnerable to the accumulation of anomalous findings. Scientific revolutions are begun by work that breaks through the limitations of the current paradigm and accommodates the new information. Paradigm shifts occur when the larger scientific community adopts the new model, although this sometimes takes decades. For Kuhn, ideas from one scientific paradigm were *incommensurable* with those of the next. Propositions framed in terms of one theory, he argued, often cannot be tested effectively in terms of another.

Kuhn's principal example was the Copernican revolution in astronomy—a theory that initially offered no improvement in accuracy over earth-centric Ptolemaic astronomy but that better satisfied the scientific culture's desire for harmony in the heavens. For Kuhn, this transition represented not a closer approach to truth but rather a radically different set of metaphors for humanity's engagement with the world. Over time, these metaphors generated new questions and elicited new kinds of research. In particular, Kuhn argued that the philosophy of science should pursue analytic narratives rather than attempt to specify universal epistemic conditions, and thus be more closely integrated with the history of science.

Kuhn's relativistic conception of science proved both influential and controversial. It directly challenged accepted theories of scientific truth, such as the Vienna Circle's POSITIVISM and Karl Raimund POPPER's more moderate critique of that positivism. Many writers objected to Kuhn's relatively vague definition of paradigm and paradigm shifts, but this flexibility probably aided its adoption into general use. Kuhn's other important works include *The Copernican Revolution* (1957) and *The Essential Tension* (1977).

Kula Ring A system of ritualized exchange of shells practiced among the inhabitants of the islands of Melanesia. The strategies surrounding the exchange allow participants to acquire prestige and to cement relationships with persons on other islands. The Kula Ring became a significant referent for ANTHROPOLOGY after its treatment in seminal works by Bronislaw MALINOWSKI (*Argonauts of the Western Pacific*, 1922) and Marcel MAUSS (*The Gift*, 1990 [1924]).

Kulturkreis In English, the term means *culture-circle* or culture area. It is associated with the theory of cultural diffusion elaborated by the Vienna school of ethnology in the early twentieth century (see DIFFUSION AND DIFFUSIONISM). *Kulturkreis* refers to the idea that cultural and technological development radiates outward from a small number of sites of cultural innovation, sometimes also known as *cultural hearths*.

Kuznets, Simon (1901–1985) In 1971, Kuznets received the Nobel Prize in economics for his comparative study of the growth experience of nations. He also played an important role in developing a framework to systematically measure important aggregate values that provide information about the size of a country's economy.

Born in Russia, Kuznets migrated to the United States and studied at Columbia University. He taught at the University of Pennsylvania, Johns Hopkins University, and Harvard University, and was a member of the research staff at the National Bureau of Economic Research from 1927 to 1961. Kuznets's pioneering research on NATIONAL INCOME and its components preceded his work on growth. Before World War I, little information was available about the size of the economy, because there was no framework for measuring macroeconomic aggregates. Kuznets created the benchmark model by which total output and income could be measured—variously by industry of origin, final product, and type of income. This framework was also used to measure savings, capital formation, and the distribution of income. Kuznets's model thereby laid the foundation for national income statistics, on which most current macroeconomic research depends. It also provided an empirical basis for the Keynesian concepts of consumption, saving, and investment (see KEYNESIANISM). Kuznets's contributions to national income accounts began with *National Income, 1929–1932* (1934) and were extended in several other books.

Kuznets's work on the history of economic growth documents the emergence of what he called "modern economic growth"—first in northwestern Europe in the late eighteenth century, subsequently in southern and eastern Europe, and still later in the European colonies. He pursued this research in several books, including the influential *Modern Economic Growth: Rate, Structure, and Spread* (1966).

According to Kuznets, three conditions set modern growth apart from previous eras: the growth rate of real per-capita income, the industrial and occupational distribution of the labor force, and the form of population settlement. The first—growth—proceeded at a rate of roughly 15 percent per decade in the modern developing economies. The second reflected the shift of a large part of the population toward work in the service sector, including the transportation and distribution of goods. This he linked to the broader shift from a primary sector economy to a network of diversified industries. The third factor was the spatial concentration of population around cities and suburbs, contrasting sharply with the nomadic and village life of previous eras.

Kuznets credited rapid economic growth largely to technological change. The developments in basic science in the late sixteenth century, he argued, facilitated the growth of innovation in the eighteenth century. How-ever, unlike many economists, Kuznets felt it was a mistake to identify the modern era with INDUSTRIALIZATION and CAPITALISM. In most societies, growth was due to the commercialization and modernization of agriculture. Many features of modern growth, too, transcended the particular organization of capitalism common to the Western countries.

Kuznets used little economic theory in this work—here showing the influence of Wesley Clair MITCHELL, who was skeptical about reliance on deductive economic theory and stressed the importance of quantitative facts. This aspect of Kuznets's work contributed significantly to the transformation of economics from a deductive to a primarily quantitative science.

L

labeling theory A school of research on social DEVIANCE that emphasizes (1) the complex factors that come into play in the labeling or identifying of deviant individuals and groups; and (2) the potentially reinforcing effects of that labeling on deviant behavior. Deviance, in this view, is not merely the transgression of a norm, but a process of categorizing behavior in ways that reflect aspects of the social hierarchy, such as CLASS and RACE. Similar behaviors by different groups of youths, for instance, often receive different labels depending on the social backgrounds of those youths. Rowdy behavior can be characterized as simply the sowing of wild oats or as the behavior of hardened teens on the way to criminal careers. Howard Becker's *The Outsiders* (1963) is a classic study of this process; Marlon Brando's fate in the film *The Wild One* offers a more popular illustration. Labeling theory is also interested in the question of who has the power to impose labels, how that power is used, and how labeling conflicts illuminate social divides.

A further issue in labeling theory is the notion that labeling *promotes* individuals' identification with their stigmatized status. Many labeling theorists suggest that labeling contributes to deviant and criminal careers. Edwin Lemert's distinction between *primary* and *secondary deviance*—separating the initial deviant act from the social processes that structure deviant careers—is often considered the source of this assertion. This "career effect" is labeling theory's most controversial claim, particularly among traditional criminologists and social conservatives who view it as placing the blame for criminal or delinquent behavior on the conforming members of society. Such criticisms of labeling theory tend to exaggerate its claims, but do point to the fact that labeling theory offers no real account of the causes of deviant behavior, nor is it relevant to many types of criminal or deviant acts. A different critique of labeling theory from Marxist sociology is that it rarely includes a broader theory of the social divisions that systematically underlie patterns of labeling and deviance, such as class conflict.

Labeling theory emerged in the 1950s. It contributed to a critique of the individualist leanings of much existing criminological research, and benefitted from wider sociological interest in the formation and violation of NORMS. This included norms that defined criminal behavior, to be sure, but also those that identified objects of milder social disapproval, such as some forms of sexual behavior. Labeling theory is also rooted in the tradition of SYMBOLIC INTERACTIONISM, which emphasizes the continuous construction of identity through interpersonal relationships and the importance of the perceptions of others on identity formation. Although labeling theory has greatly declined in importance since the 1970s, many of the issues that it raised continue to underwrite studies of social identity.

labor Generally refers to work in the context of a structure of productive relations, especially, under CAPITALISM, a market in which work can be transacted and contracted. For John LOCKE and many classical political economists, labor was seen as the basic source of value and as the basis of private property distinctions—natural resources and products of the earth were posited as held in common until they were invested with human labor. Karl MARX, while retaining the classical association between labor and value, distinguished between two ways of conceiving labor—first, in its *concrete* aspect, which refers to the forms and goals of specific expenditures of labor power. Such expenditure results in *use value*, reflecting the fact that the product of labor is good for something. Second, there is what Marx called *labor power*, or the abstracted concept of labor that emerges when different forms of labor activity are equated in the marketplace. In this formulation, capitalists hire labor power, and extract labor from it.

In capitalist societies, both of these aspects fall under the category of *wage labor*, or work contracted in a labor market. Classical and

NEOCLASSICAL ECONOMICS concern themselves primarily with this aspect of labor and with the conditions that can cause imbalances in labor supply and demand (see CLASSICAL ECONOMICS). A perfectly functioning labor market, for the neoclassicists, is one that functions transparently, paying a premium for job skills and for difficult work, and permitting workers to move freely between jobs to equilibrate the supply of labor. Obstacles to this exchange create conditions in which labor can be underpaid—this is the neoclassical definition of exploitation. For Marx, the labor relation itself is always a form of exploitation, insofar as surplus value will be extracted from the worker's labor in the form of profit. However, he disagreed with classical economists that this exchange can in any way be unfair, since there is no other determinant of the abstract value of labor outside the exchange itself.

In the 1970s, feminists introduced an influential distinction between wage labor and *domestic labor*—the unpaid but no less socially structured work done primarily by women in the household. This distinction was part of an effort to understand the subordination of women in relation to class divisions, rather than in the classical anthropological terms of male dominance of primitive hunting cultures—the account that both Marx and Friedrich Engels had endorsed.

labor aristocracy   A portion of the working class that is better organized or more highly skilled than the majority of workers, and that consequently is better paid. The concept was developed by Friedrich Engels in his analysis of the relative absence of working-class radicalism in late-nineteenth-century England. In subsequent decades, the role of the labor aristocracy was a recurrent subject of debate among Marxist social theorists.

labor economics   The study of the supply, demand, and pricing of labor as a necessary element or *factor* of production. With regard to demand, labor economics studies how FIRMS develop wage policies that maximize their profits. This includes analysis of hiring and promotion, forms of compensation, and the diverse influences that shape the labor market, such as job mobility and migration.

Some of this research involves modeling different compensation structures and forms of labor-management negotiation. There are *efficiency wage models* (in which higher wages are paid to reduce turnover and shirking), *rent-sharing*

models (where firms share profits with workers), and *firm-union wage bargaining models*, to suggest a few. Empirical studies put such models to the test and seek to determine the relevant parameters that underlie the demand for labor—such as the elasticities and cross-elasticities of labor demand, the relevance of different skills, and the effect of minimum wages on employment.

From the perspective of supply, perhaps the most important development is the HUMAN CAPITAL revolution, associated primarily with Gary BECKER and Jacob Mincer. Their principle innovation was to translate individual decisions regarding labor supply (such as education and the acquisition of skills, job searches, and career choices) into an investment framework that permits analysis of the trade-offs and OPPORTUNITY COSTS of such decisions. This framework involved accommodating rational-choice models of behavior to the high degree of uncertainty about future benefits that such decisions often entail (see RATIONAL-CHOICE THEORY). Improvements in data collection—particularly computerized data sets that provide information on the economic and demographic characteristics of individuals—have contributed to this shift in focus within labor studies from industry to the individual. See also ECONOMICS.

labor theory of value   One of the major economic theories of how commodities in the market are valued, or priced. The labor theory of value was one of the foundations of the classical economic tradition of Adam SMITH, David RICARDO, and later, Karl MARX. It holds that in a competitive market environment, prices are determined principally by the amount of LABOR invested in the production of a GOOD. In the context of individual production, Smith argued, price equals the value of the labor. When capitalists begin to organize the labor of others, however, price includes the profits of the capitalists—the difference between the market price and the cost of wages and inputs. The classical economists generally argued that, over time, the free movement of capital and labor would hold profits to a certain "average" within the economy. Marx, in contrast, held that competition and the escalating cost of improvements in productivity would result in a FALLING RATE OF PROFIT.

In ECONOMICS, the labor theory of value has been largely superseded by a neoclassical approach to price formation that emphasizes the importance of the preferences (or UTILITY) of individuals in determining the value of goods in the marketplace.

labor union In British English, *trade union*. An association of workers that uses collective action to improve its standard of living and working conditions. Historically, a distinction has been drawn between a "trade union," specific to a single line of work, and a "trades union," which cuts across multiple specific occupations. Nascent trade unions emerged first in Britain, in response to the spread of capitalist forms of production during the late seventeenth and eighteenth century, and in the context of the concurrent decline of the guild system, which had organized craft production during the Middle Ages.

The Industrial Revolution of the early nineteenth century dramatically increased the pressure on older models of production. It radically undermined the craft model of production, with its small-scale, artisanal, and relatively autonomous structure, and it vastly expanded the total number of laborers. Trade-union activity took off in the 1830s. Attempts were made to link organizational efforts across trades, resulting in a number of large and, in many cases, international umbrella organizations and congresses, including the Trades Union Congress (1868) and the First and Second Internationals (founded in 1864 and 1889, respectively). In the United States and the rest of Europe, industrial capitalism developed more slowly. By the late nineteenth century, however, the United States had fully entered the industrial age, and unions were organized on a large scale. Groups such as the Knights of Labor (founded in 1869) and later the American Federation of Labor (AFL, founded in 1886) made frequent use of strikes and other actions to assert workers' rights.

Nineteenth-century trade unionism incorporated a diverse range of political positions and maintained a frequently ambivalent relationship to political action. The corporatist visions of early SOCIALISM and later Marxist variants played an important part. Reformist agendas—organized primarily around salary demands and improvements in working conditions—were perennial topics of debate in meetings and congresses, as was the question of whether unions should engage in political activity; this was generally answered in the negative. By the turn of the twentieth century, reformism and the refusal of political action were the bases of increasingly severe splits between radicals and moderates—leading most famously to the Bolshevik break from the reformist politics of the Social Democrats, which eventuated in the successful Bolshevik Revolution in Russia (1917). National differences profoundly affected patterns of labor activism. The British and American unions generally remained closer to their origins in specific trades than their European counterparts. In much of Europe, this produced broader-based, coalitional, and ultimately more politically active unions. SYNDICALISM, which developed in France and was particularly influential in Spain and Italy, continued the model of antipolitical radicalism during the first decades of the twentieth century.

The emergence of the welfare state in developed countries eventually allowed for the institutionalization of industrial relations and routinized patterns of collective bargaining. Post–World War II economic growth in Europe and the United States was largely predicated on this deal between business, labor, and government. Yet the arrangement began to break down in the late 1960s, as economic crises, increasingly mobile CAPITAL, and the broad shift toward service-based and knowledge-based economic activity began to be felt. This has led to a steady decline in union membership and labor's political influence in Western Europe and North America. Since the late 1970s, the rise of NEOLIBERALISM in politics and economic policy (especially under President Ronald Reagan in the United States and Prime Minister Margaret Thatcher in the United Kingdom) also accelerated the decline of union power, which by 2000 accounted for only 15 percent of the U.S. labor force—many of those public employees.

Unions are often credited with a large role in creating the consumer base that underwrote high levels of economic growth during the twentieth century. As capital becomes ever more mobile, companies have shifted production away from countries with high labor costs and complex regulatory structures. The consequences of this fluidity on both developed and developing countries (which maintain their comparative advantage mainly by discouraging labor activism) are a subject of widespread interest and research across a number of social science fields.

Lacan, Jacques (1901–1981) A French psychoanalyst who drew on Sigmund FREUD, Georg HEGEL, and structural LINGUISTICS in developing an original and influential version of psychoanalytic theory (see PSYCHOANALYSIS). Although significant in some areas of psychoanalytic practice,

Lacan's work has had a much greater impact on theories of culture and subjectivity—especially those associated with POSTSTRUCTURALISM, FEMINISM, and CULTURAL STUDIES. Reading Lacan nonetheless poses many difficulties: it is highly complex; it evolved continuously over the thirty-year period of his major work; and above all, it is couched in a cryptic and allusive style that made exegetes out of his major followers. Quite deliberately, Lacan did little to elucidate or even disseminate his ideas much beyond the lectures and seminars that made him famous in the 1960s. His lectures and essays have, however, been collected and published, although only slowly in English.

Lacan's professional trajectory was similarly unorthodox and controversial. Considered a gifted analyst, he became embroiled in conflicts with other members of the Institut Psychoanalytique de Paris. These led to his resignation in 1953—officially over disagreement about the length and structure of analytic sessions (Lacan was known to squeeze sessions into elevator rides). Lacan clarified some of the theoretical issues underlying the break when, in the same year, he founded the Societé Psychoanalytique de Paris and declared the need for a return to Freud's texts—implicitly condemning the dominant analytic tradition of EGO PSYCHOLOGY. The SPP, in turn, suffered a schism in 1963 that resulted in Lacan's departure and in his subsequent creation of the Ecole Freudienne de Paris. Lacan dissolved this organization in 1980.

Much of Lacan's reworking of Freud advances the idea that subjectivity is constituted through a process of division mediated by an externalized image or other—a premise with strong Hegelian overtones. This process is at stake in one of Lacan's most influential developmental concepts: the infant's passage through the *mirror-stage*, in which it comes to understand its body as a singular, unified whole (metaphorically, by seeing its image in a mirror). This process, Lacan argued, effectively constitutes subjectivity through a process of misrecognition—through identification with an ideal that is never identical with bodily experience, and which consequently expresses itself as lack, or incompleteness. In subsequent work, Lacan redescribed this process in linguistic terms. Here he returned to the OEDIPUS COMPLEX but, in a departure from Freud, characterized it as a literalization of a more general process of incorporation of the child into the symbolic world of language. Entry

into the "symbolic" displaced the prelinguistic state of undifferentiated infantile need—a realm that Lacan termed the "imaginary" and identified with the unconscious. The "real," to complete the Lacanian conceptual triad, is the empirical reality on which the symbolic/imaginary division is inscribed, and which is wholly mediated by that division.

Lacan's rapprochement of Freud and structural linguistics has been marginal in psychology since the 1960s, but has proved to be one of the shaping influences on structuralist and poststructuralist thought. It has been highly suggestive for film theorists, feminists (who found uses for Lacan's notion of sexual roles as the products of structured fantasies), and Marxists such as Louis ALTHUSSER (or more recently, Slavoj Žižek), who saw the potential for ideology critique in Lacan's account of linguistic socialization. Lacan's essays and lectures have been published in *Ecrits* (1966), *The Four Fundamental Concepts of Psychoanalysis* (1973), and *The Seminar of Jacques Lacan* (v. 1, 1975; v. 2, 1978).

Laffer curve Illustrates the hypothesis that there is an optimal tax rate that maximizes government tax revenues. The curve is named after its originator, Arthur Laffer, who plotted tax revenues against tax rates as an inverted U-shape. Tax revenues rise initially as the tax rate is raised, but at some point, any additional increase in the tax rate is more than offset by the distortions to the economy caused those by taxes. Thus revenue actually declines as tax rates increase. In the extreme, an income tax rate of 100 percent would yield no revenue at all, as there would be no incentive to work.

The Laffer curve played an important role in the *supply-side* economics of the Reagan administration (1981–1989) as part of an argument that lower income tax rates would raise revenues. There is little empirical evidence, however, to suggest that this occurred.

Lagrangean technique A method for solving constrained optimization problems in economics. In economic models, agents often need to optimize an objective function (e.g., UTILITY or production) that is subject to constraints, such as the consumer's budget constraint. The Lagrangean technique allows the constraint to be added to the optimization problem, so that the problem can be solved by differentiation. The constraint is multiplied by the Langrange multiplier, λ, prior to differentiation. If the partial derivatives with respect to each variable are set to zero, the result is a system of equations that can be solved for the optimal choice under constraint.

lags See LEADS AND LAGS.

Laing, Ronald David (1927–1989) A psychiatrist who became an icon of the sixties counterculture and the leading figure of the ANTI-PSYCHIATRY movement in England and France. Laing specialized in the treatment of schizophrenia, and from the start emphasized empathy with the patient as a means of understanding the peculiar internal logic of the condition. Laing's later work, however, tended to reverse this equation by treating the family as the source of mental illness and society as a form of generalized, repressive madness. Schizophrenia, in this context, constituted a form of immanent critique of society and the family. It was capable, Laing argued, of furnishing a kernel of authentic experience below the collective social neurosis. In this vein, Laing experimented with psychedelic drugs and founded a clinic in which schizophrenia was treated as a form of privileged access to knowledge. His work influenced a broad reaction in England and especially in France to the medicalization of mental illness (the antipsychiatry movement). Later works such as *The Politics of Experience* (1967), however, were strongly marked by his turn toward Indian mysticism—a path that led him ultimately to repudiate many of his key positions regarding the family and psychiatry. Laing's other major works include *The Divided Self* (1960) and *Sanity, Madness and the Family* (1964, with A. A. Esterson).

laissez faire Roughly signifying in French "to let act," laissez faire is an economic doctrine that holds that the economic activity of self-interested individuals in a competitive marketplace maximizes national wealth and social welfare. This implies a minimal role for the government and for centralized decision making. Intervention by the state in matters of economic and (for some advocates) social policy reduces growth by misdirecting resources. An ideal laissez-faire government is limited to creating a proper legal framework for safeguarding property rights, providing for national defense, and maintaining competitive markets by combating noncompetitive and monopolistic practices.

The foundations of laissez-faire economics are visible in the writings of Adam SMITH, David RICARDO, and other classical economists, who were the first to argue for the superiority (and natural basis) of the free market in contrast to forms of state intervention and control—especially the complex restrictions on prices, lending, money supply, and permissible economic activities in eighteenth-century European society. Laissez-faire economics became the dominant ideology of INDUSTRIALIZATION in the nineteenth century, although it integrated the increasingly important role of the state as a guarantor of competition and basic safety standards for workers and consumers. The twentieth century saw a variety of challenges to laissez-faire ideas. MARXISM provided a critique and SOCIALISM a political program that opposed the manifest inequalities that were justified in the name of laissez faire. During the Great Depression of the 1930s, KEYNESIANISM became the dominant capitalist alternative, assigning a strong macroeconomic role to the state in moderating the business cycle and, in this instance, stimulating persistently low aggregate demand. The late-twentieth century saw a return to the prominence of laissez-faire arguments—championed in particular by Milton FRIEDMAN and Friedrich von HAYEK—and a partial dismantling of the Keynesian and social welfare state.

Laissez-faire arguments come in many forms. Nearly all modern economists and politicians allow that the market is the best allocator of most resources and goods. Strong laissez-faire advocates, however, are often vulnerable to the critique that they rely on idealized versions of markets and market behavior that bear little resemblance to historical experience. Problems of social justice in particular tend to be reduced to the question of removing sources of distortion or inefficiency from competitive markets, and take little account of ingrained attitudes or other informal but systemic patterns of discrimination or inequality.

land reform The redistribution of titles to land ownership, particularly by breaking up large holdings in favor of more egalitarian distribution. The post–World War II era saw considerable enthusiasm for land reforms in many former colonies, where small minorities of landowners often held large majorities of the arable land. The success of such reforms has been uneven and is often stymied by the lack of judicial, regulatory, and financial structures that support due process, provide small farmers access to capital, and discourage the reconsolidation of land in the hands of new (or old) elites. Those that have succeeded are credited with providing a foundation for sustainable growth, especially in the East and Southeast Asian economies.

In economic terms, there are two general justifications for land reform. The first stresses the underutilization of land by traditional landlords, the need for rapid growth of food output, and the need for viable rural employment and a healthy consumer class to maintain economic growth. The second justification—essentially a microeconomic neoclassical argument—stresses the superior efficiency of labor-intensive small farmers in land use. According to this view, land redistribution expands the typically scarce supply of capital in rural areas and leads to greater employment of labor, in turn stimulating other markets.

land rent   The classic definition is David RICARDO's: land rent is the portion of the produce of the land that is paid to the landlord for the use of the original and indestructible powers of the soil (*An Essay on the Influence of a Low Price of Corn on the Profits of Stock*, 1815). Ricardian theory argues that rent arises at both the *intensive* and the *extensive* margin of utilization. At the intensive margin, each additional worker adds a smaller amount to total output. Since wages are determined by the marginal product of the last worker employed, the landowner earns a surplus on the total volume of production. Similarly, at the extensive margin, rent is earned on the most productive land as inferior land comes into cultivation. This is because the last unit of land employed has a lower marginal product (is of lower quality) than the first unit.

Marginalist and neoclassical economists, in contrast, viewed rent as the marginal product of land—not as an unearned surplus (see NEOCLASSICAL ECONOMICS). They argued, however, that classical surplus theory is compatible with the marginal theory and that under suitable conditions, the two are equal.

landscape   In common usage, landscape connotes a visual perspective on the land. It has been widely used in GEOGRAPHY in this general sense since the early nineteenth century. The imprecision of this definition for the purposes of research, however, led a number of geographers to specify its meaning for geographical study. The pioneering cultural geographer Carl SAUER was one of these. In the mid-1920s, he attempted to consolidate the field of geography around the concept of *cultural landscape*, or the ways in which human activity contributed to and transformed natural environments. As developed by Sauer's colleagues and students, especially at the Berkeley school of cultural geography, cultural landscape includes the physical impact of human habitation, as well as the beliefs and attitudes that shape a culture's relationship to its environment. The latter often involves distinguishing between objective environmental realities and the perception of those realities—an area of study known as *environmental perception*. This cultural orientation continues to inform much of what geographers mean when they speak about landscapes.

land tenure   The system of laws or customs that governs how people use and inhabit the land. Land tenure has been a major subject of anthropological research because it is frequently crucial to the organization of nonindustrialized societies and is often different from the pattern of public and private ownership established in the industrialized West. See also LAND REFORM.

language   The study of language is pursued in a wide array of contexts that furnish it with very different meanings. This breadth is an indicator of how fundamental language is to both the study of culture and the larger question of what it means to be human.

One of the most persistent classical theories of language holds that the vocabularies of different languages reflect greater or lesser divergence from an original, natural language. This view has been largely rejected by modern linguistics, although the study of change and differentiation among languages remains important. Since Ferdinand de SAUSSURE's pioneering work in the early twentieth century, linguistics has been based on the principle that the relationship of words to their referents is purely conventional—that *signifiers* (or "sound patterns," as Saussure defined them) have no intrinsic relationship to *signifieds* (the mental concepts of things). The pairing of the two constitutes a sign, and signs are only fixed by their relationship to one another. Saussure is generally credited with formalizing this set of insights, and thereby with furnishing not only the basis of modern linguistics but also of subsequent structuralist approaches to CULTURE that exploit the concept of differential systems of meaning (see STRUCTURALISM).

The world's languages also vary enormously in their grammar, although this dimension of language may be less arbitrary. The now widely accepted theories of TRANSFORMATIONAL–GENERATIVE GRAMMAR, associated with Noam

CHOMSKY, suggest that certain capacities or dispositions to the formation of grammar are biological in nature, "hard-wired" into the human brain—although to what degree remains an object of considerable debate. Studies by Phillip Lieberman, John Hawkins, Murray Gell-Mann, and others place emphasis on the development of the human capacity to vocalize a wide and highly differentiated range of sounds, although the gestural languages of the deaf have been shown to replicate nearly all the features and complexity of spoken languages and, in certain respects, can be acquired even earlier than spoken language. All such theories, in the end, need to accommodate the fact that children show a broadly uniform pattern of language acquisition, regardless of the language.

There has been a persistent tension in the study of language between those who treat it as a cognitive science and those who insist on its social, contextual dimension. Modern linguistics in the Chomskyan tradition and the larger issue of language acquisition have emphasized the former, whereas studies of specific languages, their cultural contexts, and linguistic situations more generally (including SEMANTICS, PRAGMATICS, phonemics, ethnographies of language, and structuralism, especially in the anthropological tradition) have emphasized the latter.

Of these areas, pragmatics has produced one of the richest traditions of inquiry, focused on the diverse referential and performative functions of language. C. S. Peirce's work on signs and *indexicality*—the dependence of signs on proximity to the thing referred to—is the origin of this subfield. Pragmatics recognizes that the word "I" changes its referent depending on who is speaking; similarly, the word "here" depends on how the conversation (or text) points to a specific context. Bronislaw MALINOWSKI was one of the first to integrate the study of the contextual effects of language into the study of culture, arguing that in addition to communicating information, language possesses a *conative* function of addressing a listener, an *emotive* function that conveys emotional states, and a *phatic* function that serves to establish and maintain social relations ("hello" and "how are you" generally represent phatic uses of language; see PHATIC COMMUNION). Malinowski's work was elaborated by early linguistic structuralists such as Roman JAKOBSON and Emile Benveniste. In turn, their work had a major impact on the structuralism of Claude LÉVI-STRAUSS and, in

Anglo-American linguistics, the theory of speech-acts proposed by J. L. Austin in the early 1960s. Austin emphasized the ways in which people "do things with words," many of which carry a performative effect distinct from their simple meaning. Naming is an example—the bestowal of a name is different than the use of the same word to describe or invoke an already existing relationship of signifier and signified. Austin's work has influenced both Pierre BOURDIEU's studies of practical action (including speech) and Jürgen HABERMAS's theory of COMMUNICATIVE ACTION. ETHNOMETHODOLOGY and CONVERSATION ANALYSIS share this interest in how speech patterns and habits of language structure activities as fundamental as conversation. SOCIOLINGUISTICS is another area of contextual study that examines (among other things) how linguistic variation correlates with divisions of class, race, gender, or other significant divisions within a community. Many of these studies have emphasized the ways that social inequality produces or authorizes different kinds of speech in specific situations. The term DISCOURSE ANALYSIS is sometimes used to describe this broad turn toward the linguistic analysis of power relations. See also LINGUISTICS.

langue and parole   Concepts introduced by Ferdinand de SAUSSURE in his *Course in General Linguistics* (1916). *Langue* refers to the collectively held system of language and *parole* (French for "word") to an individual utterance within it.

L'Année sociologique   The sociological journal that provided a vehicle and forum for much of the research of Emile DURKHEIM and his followers. Durkheim himself edited the journal between 1896 and 1913. Marcel MAUSS played a prominent role after 1898.

Laski, Harold   (1893–1950) Political theorist Harold Laski was born in Manchester, England, and worked as a journalist before turning to teaching—successively at McGill University, Harvard University, and after 1920 at the London School of Economics. Laski also held high positions in the British Labour Party and the Fabian society (see FABIANISM).

Laski's early writings explore the possibilities of tempering CAPITALISM with elements of SOCIALISM. He was a strong proponent of PLURALISM, challenging the concept of absolute state sovereignty and stressing the value to democracy of independent formal and informal associations that could operate as intermediaries between individuals and the state. Laski held that an absolutely sovereign state was an unaccountable state and that the countervailing influence of organizations such as trade unions and special interest groups made government more responsive to the lives of ordinary citizens. His political objectives were to strengthen such organizations and to decentralize state power.

In the early 1930s, Laski grew increasingly uncertain that such reform was possible. His growing doubt is visible in the progression from *Liberty in the Modern State* (1930) to *Democracy in Crisis* (1931), which evidences Laski's turn to MARXISM. The weakened capitalist democracies, Laski argued, provided a breeding ground for FASCISM. Laski remained opposed to revolutionary action, however, and was convinced that socialism had to prevail through the electoral process. He warned that the capitalist elite would resist this transformation at all cost. Laski became very active in Labour Party politics in the 1940s, and served as Chairman in 1945–1946.

Laski's published works include *Studies in the Problem of Sovereignty* (1917), *The Foundations of Sovereignty* (1921), *The Grammar of Politics* (1925), *The State in Theory and Practice* (1935), *The American Presidency* (1940), *Reflections on the Revolution of Our Time* (1943), and an important account of American society, *American Democracy* (1948).

Lasswell, Harold   (1902–1978) A major figure in the emergence of political psychology and communication studies. Lasswell brought a strong Freudian orientation to the analysis of political leadership and decision making. In *Psychopathology and Politics* (1930), he argued that leaders are driven primarily by psychological motivations rooted in childhood. Understanding politics, therefore, required a psychoanalytic approach to individual leaders, whose motivations could be deciphered and actions predicted. Lasswell pursued this direction of inquiry further in *World Politics and Insecurity* (1935). Together, these studies laid the groundwork for much of the field of political psychology.

Lasswell is perhaps better known for his work on mass communication and his theory of transmission, sometimes called the *hypodermic model* because it conceives the public as the passive receiver of "injected" messages. This work grew out of a series of studies of propaganda and psychological warfare conducted before and during World War II. His was among the first research to address the mass media's potential as an instrument of social control. Lasswell's transmission model is frequently summed up in the phrase, "who says what in which channel, to whom, with what effect," referring to what Lasswell described as the five aspects of any communication: the communicator, the message, the channel (or media), the receiver, and the effect of the message. Lasswell's formula proved highly influential, and versions of it continue to structure a wide range of communications research. In regard to the analysis of the message in particular, Lasswell pioneered a range of statistical techniques that sought to draw conclusions from the incidence of certain types of content, such as particular words or phrases. This became known as CONTENT ANALYSIS.

Lasswell taught political science at the University of Chicago and political science and law at Yale University. He was a prolific writer whose other major works include *Power and Personality* (1948), *Propaganda Technique in the World War* (1972), and *Psychopathology and Politics (1977)*.

latent functions   See MANIFEST FUNCTIONS.

latent status   See STATUS.

law   In general usage, the set of rules established by a political authority in order to govern human affairs within its jurisdiction—often referred to as normative or prescriptive law. In this context, law refers most often to rules made and enforced by the state, rather than to INTERNATIONAL LAW, CUSTOMARY LAW, or religious law (such as the *canon law* established by Christian churches). The two distinct juridical traditions that structure most Western legal systems are COMMON LAW and CIVIL LAW. Western systems generally recognize an internal division among constitutional or basic law (which governs the basic institutions of government and other types of law), private or civil law (concerning relations between citizens), and public law (concerning citizen–state relations), which includes criminal law and ADMINISTRATIVE LAW.

There are three main schools of thought on the origin and nature of law:

1. The doctrine of NATURAL LAW dominated Western jurisprudence and political philosophy until the nineteenth century. It holds that laws draw upon or reflect a permanent, objective order available to humans via reason, divine revelation, or the legacy of a mythical, originary law giver.

The natural law approach has diminished greatly in importance but, for many commentators, remains central to efforts to ground moral critiques of existing law.

2. "Legal positivism," which developed in the nineteenth and early twentieth centuries, holds that law is nothing other than the set of rules that prevail in a particular place and time. It strictly differentiates morality from law, and studies the latter as a formal set of hierarchically ordered rules. Beyond this initial point of agreement, however, many issues divide positive jurisprudence. These include the relative importance accorded coercion and obligation in ensuring obedience to the law, and whether the law can be understood from a purely external, descriptive perspective.

3. There are many historical and sociological theories of law. Early-twentieth-century SOCIOLOGY—especially that of Max WEBER and Emile DURKHEIM—paid considerable attention to law as one of the fundamental dimensions of social organization. For Durkheim, for example, law represented a crystallization of social practices that arose organically from society, as opposed to being ordered from above. "Legal realists" see law as a product and instrument of political struggles. There are also diverse hermeneutic approaches to the law, ranging from "legal evolutionism," which seeks cultural and historical continuity within law, to "legal institutionalism," which treats law as a complex social institution linking abstract normative ideas to concrete actions and organizations. The "critical legal studies" approach emphasizes law's relationship to social hierarchies and power, especially as reflected in divisions of class, race, and gender.

In contrast, *descriptive* or *scientific* law formalizes observed regularities in the natural world. It provides a theoretical basis for predicting certain kinds of carefully specified outcomes (e.g., the law of gravity or the laws of thermodynamics). While social scientists have often claimed to discover laws (e.g., the law of SUPPLY AND DEMAND or the IRON LAW OF OLIGARCHY), the status of these generalizations is a subject of much debate. Few social phenomena are subject to unambiguous description or explanation, and few are as reliably isolable or replicable as natural phenomena. The difference between the two has been a formative problem in the social sciences, from early methodological debates among German philosophers at the turn of the twentieth century (the *METHODENSTREIT*) to more recent poststructuralist and postmodern challenges to POSITIVISM (see POSTMODERNISM; and POSTSTRUCTURALISM).

law and economics movement A relatively recent interdisciplinary movement best known for exploring the use of economic incentives in the adjudication of social issues and questions of public policy. The movement is strongly grounded in rational-choice theories of behavior, although recent advances have begun to explore the implications of BEHAVIORAL ECONOMICS for the practice of law (see RATIONAL-CHOICE THEORY). The COASE THEOREM was a precursor to much of the work in this area. It examined how the proper allocation of property rights might achieve efficient market-based regulation of certain kinds of behavior. The principal jurist associated with the law and economics movement is Richard Posner, who argues that legal remedies should be strongly subject to COST-BENEFIT ANALYSIS and that many issues in which conflicting moral and social values inform decision making should be left to the marketplace—a somewhat notorious example is adoption. EXPECTED UTILITY THEORY has also been used to determine optimal punitive damage awards.

law of one price Holds that the price of a particular good should be the same irrespective of where it is bought or sold. If there are differences in price, rational agents will buy the good where it is cheaper and sell it where it is more expensive—also known as an ARBITRAGE situation. This increases demand (and therefore price) in the first place, and decreases price (by increasing supply) in the second place. This "law" is used in international trade to assert *purchasing power parity*, that is, a given amount of money should be able to buy the same quantity of goods anywhere in the world, after allowing for the exchange rate.

Lazarsfeld, Paul (1901–1976) An Austrian-born sociologist who innovated in many areas of quantitative-research methodology—notably survey and panel techniques—and who specialized in questions of VOTING behavior and mass culture (see PANEL DATA). He is also regarded as a founder of mathematical sociology. Lazarsfeld earned a doctorate in mathematics before turning to the study of SOCIAL PSYCHOLOGY. He become associated with the Institute for Social Research in Frankfurt, Germany (the FRANKFURT SCHOOL) and immigrated to the United States with many of the other Frankfurt school members following Adolf Hitler's rise to power in 1933. In the United States, he became involved in mass-media research and eventually accepted a position in the sociology department at Columbia University. There he founded the Bureau of Applied Research, the first university-based social-survey center in the world.

Although he wrote extensively on methodology, Lazarsfeld is more generally known for his applications of new methods: notably the use of public surveys as a tool of quantitative research. *The People's Choice: How the Voter Makes Up His Mind in a Presidential Campaign* (1944) was the first survey-based analysis of a national election. *Voting* (1954) was similarly a landmark study of voting behavior.

Lazarsfeld also challenged the prevailing view of the mass public as a body of passive recipients of programmed information (a view held by members of the Frankfurt school, among others). In *Personal Influence: The Part Played by People in the Flow of Mass Communications* (1955, with Elihu Katz), he studied the flow of information from source to recipients, finding that media-provided information tends to be distilled through unofficial opinion leaders within communities, who in turn exert influence on other members of the community. These local mediators often had a significant impact on, among other things, voting patterns—a point he had made earlier in somewhat different form in *The People's Choice*.

At Columbia, Lazarsfeld joined with Robert K. MERTON in research collaborations and in the development of a graduate program that did more than any other of the period to combine empirical research with theory and to establish the postwar "mainstream" of American SOCIOLOGY. Lazarsfeld's other major works include *Mathematical Thinking in the Social Sciences* (1954) and *Qualitative Analysis: Historical and Critical Essays* (1971).

LDC   See LESS DEVELOPED COUNTRY (LDC).

Leach, Edmund R.   (1910–1989) An exceptional ethnographer and one of the principal defenders of STRUCTURALISM in England in the 1950s and 1960s. Leach came to ANTHROPOLOGY after having worked for several years in China and the Philippines. He pursued his degree at the London School of Economics under the direction of Raymond William FIRTH, and began fieldwork among the Kachin peoples of Burma

in the late 1930s. When this work was interrupted by World War II, he joined the British Burmese Army. Although Leach completed a manuscript on Kachin society during this service, the manuscript and his materials were lost in the fighting. Leach's reconstruction of this research was published in 1954 under the title *Political Systems of Highland Burma*. The concept of CULTURE that Leach extrapolated from Kachin political life was structured by deep ideological divisions and chronic instability—far from the regulated model of structural FUNCTIONALISM that dominated British social anthropology. Leach was also a careful reader of the political and social content of myths, demonstrating the influence of Claude LÉVI-STRAUSS's *Elementary Structures of Kinship*. In the course of later fieldwork eventually published as *Pul Eliya: A Village in Ceylon* (1961), he took up the question of KINSHIP in relation to economic and political interests.

Leach worked assiduously in these years to promote Lévi-Strauss's work, and structuralism more generally in England, often in running battle with his structural-functionalist colleagues at Cambridge. He produced several theoretical contributions to the field, including the essays collected in *Rethinking Anthropology* (1962), an eponymously titled book on Lévi-Strauss (1970), and *Culture and Communication* (1976).

leads and lags   A variable is said to lead another if it tends to change before the other. In economics, leading variables thereby provide information that may help predict the future values of other variables. This is especially valuable in situations in which predictions cannot be accurately based on the current and past values of the latter variable. Stock market prices are often considered a leading variable of economic growth, insofar as they contain information about the future of the economy that cannot be obtained by looking at the current and past values of economic output.

Lead–lag models are statistical models that map time differences in the spread of certain kinds of phenomena (such as economic booms or diseases) from one region to the next. Lead–lag models are thus implicated in a variety of areas of social research, including studies of cultural diffusion (see DIFFUSION AND DIFFUSIONISM).

learning by doing   The process whereby economic agents gain experience and improve skills through participation in the production process. Such learning increases labor productivity and gives rise to dynamic ECONOMIES OF SCALE. It has been demonstrated empirically that learning by doing accounts for the positive relationship between current labor productivity and past cumulative output or investment. Consequently, learning by doing is often incorporated into economic growth models as a way of explaining or predicting unbounded, endogenous growth without assuming exogenous improvements in technology. Learning by doing may also account for the portion of growth in per capita output (and thus of economic growth) that cannot be attributed entirely to increases in the CAPITAL–LABOR RATIO.

least squares A statistical technique used to determine the best linear or nonlinear regression line. The basic logic of this technique holds that if we want to know what proportion of the change in one variable (for example, output) is due to changes in another (for example, the stock of money), we can plot the output data against the money stock data on a graph, and see whether a straight line can be drawn that approximates the position of the data points. The least squares estimator defines a linear relationship between the two variables such that the sum of the (squared) distances of each data point from the line is minimized. The least squares technique offers the advantages of computational simplicity and optimality properties. Among the latter, the method yields the best linear unbiased estimator (BLUE) in the case of linear regression as well as the maximum likelihood estimator when the error terms in the regression have a normal distribution.

Le Bon, Gustave (1841–1931) A psychologist whose work on crowds influenced subsequent research on COLLECTIVE BEHAVIOR. Le Bon's *The Crowd: A Study of the Popular Mind* (1895) emphasized the irrational nature of crowd behavior and the submergence of individual identity into the "collective mind." Crowd phenomena, he argued, incite primitive, destructive, antisocial feelings that are normally suppressed in moral life. Le Bon also analyzed the process of *social contagion*, through which information or sentiments spread from one person to the next.

A political reactionary in many respects, Le Bon associated his critiques of crowd behavior with his opposition to popular and revolutionary activity, which he regarded as related threats to the civilized order. Le Bon was enormously popular in his time and was considered one of the leading French psychologists. He was also a prolific writer of some forty books. He was, however, marginalized by much of the sociological mainstream in France, especially by Emile DURKHEIM and his followers. Le Bon has benefited from renewed attention in recent years but continues to be remembered primarily for *The Crowd*. His other works include *The Psychology of Socialism* (1898), *Psychological Laws of the Evolution of Peoples* (1894), and *The Psychology of Revolutions* (1912).

Le Chatelier principle A general principle of problem solving in economics that states that additional conditions or constraints on a situation reduce the effect of a shift in one or more parameters. This principle is fundamental to many of the *extremum* or limit-case problems that appear in economics. Prominent examples include Paul SAMUELSON's 1947 demonstration that the elasticities of supply and demand are smaller in the short run than in the long run and that the elasticity of compensated demand is smaller in the presence of rationing than in its absence.

left wing See RIGHT WING AND LEFT WING.

legal pluralism Describes societies in which multiple means of redress or retribution exist, either outside formal legal procedures or in the overlapping sets of legal jurisdications. Legal pluralism is often the norm in colonial and postcolonial societies. The countervailing tendency is *legal centralism*.

legislature The branch of GOVERNMENT responsible for making laws, usually composed of members who are elected by and represent the political community. Modern legislatures evolved from medieval European parliaments—bodies of notables intermittently convened to advise monarchs and approve their policies, especially those concerning taxation. These bodies assumed their present name and most of their modern functions during the struggle between the king and parliament in seventeenth-century England, in which the parliament won legislative power. As democracy became more widespread during the next three centuries, legislatures typically emerged as the seat of popular sovereignty.

Legislatures are now found in all democratic and nearly all nondemocratic governments. Bicameral legislatures (divided into two houses) now outnumber unicameral or one-house legislatures, which tend to exist only in small, centralized countries. Bicameralism developed out of the early modern practice of separately representing the aristocracy and the common people, but is now a preferred means of incorporating the representation of individual states within the national government (as in the United States or Germany), of ensuring a political voice for less populous regions or minority populations, and of acting as a check on government (see CHECKS AND BALANCES). Further important distinctions exist between parliamentary systems (usually derived from the British model, in which the EXECUTIVE is drawn from the legislature) and presidential systems, which follow the principle of SEPARATION OF POWERS. Legislatures also differ in how representatives are elected (see ELECTORAL GEOGRAPHY; and ELECTORAL SYSTEM) and in the PARTY SYSTEMS that have developed within them.

legitimacy The acceptability or appropriateness of a ruler or political regime to its members. Legitimacy is one of the central problems of politics and can be seen as the mirror image of the problem of political obligation or consent. For most of human history, claims to legitimate rule were usually made on religious, traditional, or hereditary grounds. Since the seventeenth century, however, POLITICAL THEORY has sought a rational, secular basis for legitimacy. Two broad approaches have prevailed. Social contract theories, such as those of Thomas HOBBES, John LOCKE, and Jean-Jacques ROUSSEAU, have sought to demonstrate that government is a necessity that people actually or hypothetically consented to at some point in the past (see SOCIAL-CONTRACT THEORY). As long as the regime honors its side of this contract, it is legitimate. Other theories establish "performance criteria" and argue that a government is legitimate as long as it provides certain levels of security, justice, freedom, prosperity, or other political "goods."

These normative theories of legitimacy should be distinguished from social theories that seek to explain why and under what conditions people perceive regimes as legitimate. Here, the abstract moral standard of legitimacy is replaced by an empirical process of "legitimation." This approach was pioneered by Max WEBER, who distinguished between three forms of legitimation of public authority: *traditional authority*, rooted in beliefs and practices that have come to seem part of the natural order; *charismatic authority*, in which followers are attracted to the abilities or personality of a leader; and *rational-legal authority*, based on explicit laws or rules and vested in offices or positions.

While many social scientists have followed Weber's nonevaluative understanding of legitimacy in order to measure and explain POLITICAL BEHAVIOR, others, such as Jürgen HABERMAS, have tried to combine it with a normative standard that modern societies should meet. In *Legitimation Crisis* (1976), Habermas measured legitimacy against citizens' rising expectations. The failure of democracies to live up to these expectations underwrote his demand for greater DEMOCRATIZATION of public life.

leisure Economists traditionally defined leisure in opposition to work and more specifically as a residual of the work day—the time left for idle, unremunerated, unproductive activities. In these terms, it was generally treated as a consumption good—something that could be acquired only by foregoing income, and therefore analogous to a purchase. Gary BECKER ("A Theory of the Allocation of Time," 1965) and Staffan Linder (*The Harried Leisure Class*, 1970) offered an alternative interpretation of leisure that emphasized the duration of the act of consumption. Leisure, in this context, was the time needed to consume the goods and services that individuals purchased with their income. The latter approach was consistent in some respects with sociological investigations of modern leisure. These emphasized historical changes whereby leisure became an increasingly structured activity that no longer existed in clear opposition to the productive process. The FRANKFURT SCHOOL analyses of the emergence of mass culture were perhaps the most pessimistic accounts of this process, seeing modern leisure as fully integrated into and determined (in both duration and form) by the demands of the capitalist economy.

Considerable sociological attention has been paid to the social significance of leisure—perhaps most famously by Thorstein VEBLEN, who treated leisure as a form of competitive display among modern social elites. CULTURAL STUDIES and media studies have also focused attention on the nature of the consumption of leisure goods—in many instances rehabilitating the countercultural significance of leisure and nonwork time from the determinist views of the Frankfurt School.

Leisure has long been an issue in philosophical and political accounts of modernity, particularly those that discuss the Enlightenment goals of liberation from need and increasing freedom to pursue creative and gratifying activities. As many social scientists and social theorists have noted, however, modernity has an uneven record of delivering on this promise. The anthropologist Marshall SAHLINS has argued that agricultural societies generally had a larger portion of leisure time than modern societies, based on the seasonal nature of agricultural work. Another subject of interest to modern researchers (including Linder) has been the question of whether the competitive demands of the (increasingly global) economy have eroded leisure time. A variety of economic and sociological analyses of this question have appeared in recent decades, although general and especially international trends are difficult to establish.

Lenin, Vladimir Ilich (1870–1924) Leading figure of the Bolshevik revolution in 1917 and of the Soviet Union until his death in 1924. Lenin was the architect of the revolutionary-party doctrine that bears his name (LENINISM). He also made a number of other contributions to MARXISM and to theories of imperialism and DEVELOPMENT (see IMPERIALISM AND EMPIRE). In *Imperialism, the Highest Stage of Capitalism* (1916), Lenin explained imperialism as a market-driven form of conquest that was necessary in order to provide an outlet for capitalist overproduction. He also challenged models of development in the colonial world, arguing that the disparities of empire were a functional part of global CAPITALISM. *State and Revolution* (1917) introduced Lenin's theory of the party's mediating role in the transition to COMMUNISM—including both the need to seize state power and the eventual "withering of the state" under communism. His other works include *The Development of Capitalism in Russia* (1899), *What is to be Done* (1902), and *Materialism and Empirio-Criticism* (1908), which advocates scientific materialism and a broad extension of Marxist theory into philosophy and natural science.

Leninism The doctrine of revolution and party organization derived from Vladimir Ilich LENIN's theoretical writings and, perhaps more importantly, from the example Lenin set as leader of the Bolshevik party. Much of this doctrine concerned the central role of the party as an instigator and leader of revolution—especially in countries such as Russia where widespread industrial capitalism and class consciousness, the traditional prerequisites of MARX's theory of revolution, did not exist. For Lenin, the party

was the highly disciplined vanguard of revolution rather than its spontaneous expression. It was responsible for seizing power in order to abolish private property and establish the rule of the working class. Lenin's writing often presents the party as a transitional body that would make way for a fundamentally democratic form of rule—specifically, the workers' *soviets* described in *State and Revolution* (1917). After the Russian revolution, however, Lenin moved to crush the autonomy of the soviets and silence dissent within the party, cementing the party's new role as rulers in the name of the working class. The internally democratic decision-making process that Lenin had made one of the bases of party organization in his early writing (if rarely in practice) was also dropped (see BOLSHEVISM). This revolutionary doctrine is generally known as Marxism–Leninism.

In the end, the official Leninism promoted by Joseph Stalin resolved the contradictions in Lenin's writing and biography in favor of the most authoritarian, state-centered solutions. The strongly internationalist dimension to Lenin's revolutionary theory, articulated in *Imperialism, the Highest Stage of Capitalism* (1916), was subordinated to Stalin's doctrine of "socialism in one country" and to the imperatives of a strongly nationalistic foreign policy. Lenin's late disillusionment with the bureaucratization and irrationality of the state that he had built—a critique that pointedly included Stalin—was suppressed as he became a symbol of legitimation for the Stalinist regime even before his death. Outside the Soviet Union, Lenin's commitment to revolution in the peripheral countries of the capitalist world and his emphasis on the revolutionary potential of peasants provided a compelling organizing model and rhetoric of legitimation for a wide range of anticolonial revolutionary movements. Although certain of these continue in the wake of the collapse of Soviet communism, the high visibility of the Leninist model in the developing world owed much to the bipolar context of the COLD WAR and to the tendency, on both sides, to impose the ideological terms of the great powers on local conflicts.

lens model A social-psychological theory that regards the social perception of uncertain (*distal*) events as dependent upon a process of inference from immediately observable (*proximal*) cues. Given the lack of a one-to-one connection between the two, perceivers must weigh the probabilities that proximal cues signal distal events. The model was developed by Egon Brunswik in *Perception and the Representative Design of Psychological Experiments* (1956).

Social judgment theory is an extension of many of the same principles to the question of judgment and decision making under conditions of uncertainty.

Leontief, Wassily (1906–1999) An economist whose major accomplishment was the invention, development, and application of INPUT–OUTPUT ANALYSIS—a method of analyzing economic productivity by studying the relationships among different sectors. Input–output analysis is rooted in a long algebraic tradition, particularly in work by Georg Frobenius and Oskar Perron, after whom its main theorems are named. However, it was Leontief who first brought their theoretical insights together in a broadly applicable form.

Leontief was born in Russia and earned his doctorate from the University of Berlin. He taught at Harvard University for over forty years before moving to New York University. He was elected President of the American Economic Association in 1970, and received the Nobel Prize in economics in 1973. Leontief's early research included the estimation of elasticities of supply and demand and the use of indifference maps to explain patterns of international trade. Drawing on this work, the term *Leontief preferences* now designates preferences in which positive UTILITY (or well-being) is linked to the consumption of all goods. Leontief's early belief that economic concepts should be observable and measurable led to work on index numbers designed to measure composite concepts like aggregate output. He derived the mathematical conditions under which a single aggregate or index could replace a mass of detailed data without loss of information. Leontief's contribution to input–output analysis was in a similar vein. Among other things, he showed how the coefficients linking different sectors in an economy could be estimated, and proved that these estimates are sufficiently stable to be used in comparative static analyses of different economic policies.

These proposals were, however, difficult to put into practice for several reasons. First, computation of the coefficients involved solving hundreds of simultaneous linear equations. Moreover, data on the inputs used per unit of output in each sector were hard to come by. Finally, the assumption that the coefficients were stable contradicted

the conventional wisdom that factors of production such as labor and capital substitute for each other in response to price changes. Leontief set out to solve some of these problems by constructing the input–output tables himself. By 1941, he had compiled a table with forty-one sectors, which he published in *The Structure of American Economy, 1919–1929*. Within the next few years, the U.S. Bureau of Labor Statistics, with Leontief's help, had constructed a table with four hundred sectors for projecting postwar employment in major industries. Another of his contributions during this time was the so-called LEONTIEF PARADOX. This showed that American exports used more labor per unit of capital than American imports and thereby contradicted the HECKSCHER–OHLIN TRADE THEORY, which suggested that a country favors the export of goods that make use of comparatively abundant inputs.

Throughout his career, Leontief maintained an interest in the estimation of economic concepts, as well as in methods of computation. He oversaw the improvement of his input–output tables but also followed developments in computing to help solve linear systems of equations, from Wilbur's analog equation solver to modern supercomputers. Leontief's success in integrating empirical considerations into a Walrasian system of general equilibrium made him an important contributor to modern economic thought and action.

Leontief paradox A finding by economist Wassily LEONTIEF that, in the American context, international trade runs counter to what is predicted in the HECKSCHER–OHLIN TRADE THEORY. Eli Heckscher and Bertil Ohlin argued that a country privileges the exportation of commodities that make intensive use of the factors of production (such as labor, land, or capital) in which it is comparatively well endowed. This is an extension of the theory of COMPARATIVE ADVANTAGE developed by David RICARDO. Leontief discovered that American exports were more labor intensive than American imports—a paradox in light of the assumption that the United States is comparatively capital abundant and labor poor (*Studies in the Structure of the American Economy*, 1953). Considerable empirical and theoretical work has sought to account for this result, some of which emphasizes technological differences (the Heckscher–Ohlin model assumes uniform technology level among countries), tariffs, and a potential capital bias in American consumption habits. The basic assumption of the comparative abundance of capital in the United States has also been questioned.

less developed country (LDC) A country whose level of economic and social DEVELOPMENT is lower than that of the advanced capitalist West. Like the concept of development on which it is based, the criteria used in identifying these countries has been controversial and to a large extent arbitrary, usually involving a threshold of per-capita gross national product below which countries are considered to be "developing." The designation grew alongside and gradually superseded the attempt to divide countries between a "first" (advanced capitalist), "second" (state socialist), and "third" (poor and developing) world, and inherits most of its problems. Contrary to early versions of MODERNIZATION THEORY, "developing" countries often have little in common besides their relative poverty. A few have developed rapidly—leading to the creation of an intermediate category, "newly industrialized country" (NIC)—while many others have not. Some have managed to escape the "normal" path of development altogether through the windfall of natural resources or by cultivating positions as centers for commerce, finance, or tourism. Despite these problems, the term continues to circulate as a marker of the disparity between rich and poor countries.

levirate A custom that encourages or requires a widow to marry her deceased husband's brother. Levirate marriage is common in patrilineal societies, where ensuring continuity and the retention of property along the male line are social priorities (see PATRILINEAL DESCENT).

Lévi-Strauss, Claude (1908–) Possibly the most influential anthropologist of the post–World War II period, Lévi-Strauss is best known for the development of STRUCTURALISM—a theory of human culture that fuses LINGUISTICS, cognitive theory, ETHNOGRAPHY, and textual analysis. Structuralism reshaped anthropological debates in the 1960s and had a profound impact on philosophy and literary studies, where it contributed to the broad "linguistic turn" toward the study of language's capacities and limitations.

Born in Belgium, Lévi-Strauss received his education in philosophy in France, taught sociology in Brazil, and came to ANTHROPOLOGY by way of reading American ethnographers, particularly Robert H. LOWIE. While teaching sociology at the University of São Paulo in the late 1930s,

he conducted fieldwork among several Brazilian tribes—most famously the Nambikwara. These trips later became the basis of *Tristes Tropiques* (1955), a mixture of ethnography and memoir that continues to be his most widely read work.

Although he returned to France in 1939, Lévi-Strauss fled to New York when war broke out. There he joined a growing group of refugee scholars and artists, including Roman JAKOBSON, who introduced him to the structural linguistic theories that would deeply influence his work. By 1949, he had completed *The Elementary Structures of Kinship*, a sweeping and radical challenge to the theories of KINSHIP articulated by British social anthropologists such as A. R. RADCLIFFE-BROWN. Rather than placing emphasis on relations of descent, Lévi-Strauss privileged marriage, or alliance, as the mechanism of EXOGAMY that underlies human society (see ALLIANCE THEORY). This led to a long-lived and often heated debate within anthropology between descent and alliance theorists—a debate that Lévi-Strauss attempted to trump with his much broader description of the structures underlying alliance. With *The Savage Mind* (1962) and *The Raw and the Cooked* (1964)—the first volume of his larger study, *Mythologiques*—Lévi-Strauss fleshed out a theory of the deeper structure of oppositions and patterns of exchange that informed all language, myth, and social practice. This was structuralism at its most ambitious, proposing a binary structure of human cognition that generated a number of consistent fundamental oppositions: incest–exogamy, raw–cooked, nature–culture, and so on. Much of his later work extended these principles and methods to the study of myth and mythical systems.

Structuralism has met resistance on a number of fronts, not least for its claims of universalism and its difficulty in accounting for historical change. Lévi-Strauss's highly literary style of interpretation has been another point of contention, producing both followers—notably in the SYMBOLIC ANTHROPOLOGY of Clifford GEERTZ and others—and critics who charge him with subjectivism, factual errors, and a lack of clarity. The "poststructuralist" moniker attached to the current generation of theoretical work in the social sciences and humanities reflects the rejection of certain of his claims, but also the vast and often unacknowledged assimilation of his work and methods.

Levy-Bruhl, Lucien (1857–1939) A French philosopher and anthropologist best known for his cognitive theory of the differences between "primitive" and "civilized" thought processes. In a series of books published in the first two decades of the twentieth century, Levy-Bruhl elaborated a distinction between the "primitive mentality" of premodern peoples, characterized by prelogical and mystical reasoning, and "civilized thought" characterized by a rational understanding of cause and effect. This work attracted considerable attention from anthropologists in France and England, who for the most part attacked Levy-Bruhl's research and conclusions. Prominent among them was E. E. EVANS-PRITCHARD, whose work on magic emphasized the complex internal rationality of such systems. In response to these attacks, Levy-Bruhl retreated from many of his positions and proposed a less categorical division between mystical and logical thought. The possibility that significant cognitive differences exist between modern and premodern cultures, as well as between contemporary cultures, reemerged in the post–World War II era as a topic of research in the field of COGNITIVE ANTHROPOLOGY. Levy-Bruhl's major works include *Primitive Mentality* (1928), *Primitives and the Supernatural* (1936), and the posthumously published *Notebooks on Primitive Mentality* (1975).

Lewin, Kurt   (1890–1947) A German psychologist who became one of the founding figures of American SOCIAL PSYCHOLOGY. Like many Jewish intellectuals, Lewin fled Germany upon Adolf Hitler's rise to power in 1933. He held a number of academic posts in the United States and trained many of the prominent social psychologists of the next generation, including Harold Kelley, Albert Pepitone, and John Thibaut.

Lewin is best known for his pioneering experimental methods and for the *field theory* of personality that he developed and revised over the years. Generally speaking, field theory attempted to account for individual behavior in terms of the interaction between perception and the social environment. The intersection of the two, he argued, constituted an individual's "self-awareness field," which could be visually represented in terms of vectors and zones. In this context, Lewin frequently invoked the "life space" of individuals—the sum total of factors that impinged upon and determined individual behavior. His ideas in this area proved influential on a range of other work, including AFFECT CONTROL THEORY and theories of COGNITIVE DISSONANCE.

Lewin pioneered a number of mathematical methods and "topographical" models for describing life spaces, hoping thereby to make social psychology a rigorous science capable of predicting behavior. At the same time, he was a flexible thinker who allowed experimental results to reshape his theories. Lewin was also the founder of group psychology, which at its best prioritized the complexities of human interaction in therapy and social science research. His major works include *A Dynamic Theory of Personality* (1973 [1935]), *Principles of Topological Psychology* (1936), *Resolving Social Conflicts* (1948), and *Field Theory in Social Science* (1951).

Lewis, W. Arthur   (1915–1991) An economist from the West Indies who worked primarily on development economics. His work in this area was enormously influential, if also controversial. In recognition, he was awarded the Nobel Prize in economics in 1979 (with Theodore W. Schulz).

Lewis was educated at the London School of Economics. He later earned a doctorate from the University of London and taught at the University of Manchester. Lewis's most famous work was the 1954 paper "Economic Development with Unlimited Supplies of Labor." This paper describes DUAL ECONOMIES in which small pockets of industry develop in traditional, predominantly rural settings. Lewis argued that such structures had several implications for development: large populations imply disguised unemployment in agriculture, so that the industrial sector commands unlimited supplies of labor as long as it provides the minimum subsistence wage available in agriculture. As industry grows and draws people out of traditional activities, however, the labor supply diminishes. After a point, industry can attract additional labor only by increasing wages.

The features of Lewis's dual economy were widespread in Asia, Africa, and South America. Economic planning in many of these countries was influenced by Lewis's ideas, which were often interpreted as a rationale for a broad strategy of import-competing industrialization. Policies of this kind have fallen into relative disfavor in recent years, however, due to their tendency to create inefficient and uncompetitive industries. Lewis developed most of his important themes in *The Theory of Economic Growth* (1955)—one of the first books to explore development problems in the THIRD WORLD. In addition to these contributions, he served as a development adviser in various institutions, including the United

Nations, and later became president of the Caribbean Development Bank.

lexicographic preference A model of preferences that holds that an individual prefers any allocation of goods that has more of a certain good *x*, regardless of what else is contained in the allocation. Where two allocations have the same amount of *x*, however, the quantities of other goods determine the preference among bundles. The classic example is John RAWLS's theory of JUSTICE, which holds that increases in wealth (generally considered universally desirable) should be preferred only if they improve the situation of the worst-off members of a society. In the event that two allocations leave the worst-off individual equally well off, the second-worst-off person's welfare is to be considered, and so forth. Unlike "well behaved" preferences, lexicographic preferences cannot be represented by a continuous utility function, although they are manageable within a utility-maximization paradigm.

lexicostatistics A statistical method for measuring the relationship between languages, based on the percentage of cognate words that they share. A greater percentage indicates a closer relationship. One application of lexicostatistics is *glottochronology*, which maps these statistical differences onto a timeline in an attempt to establish the period of departure from an original, common language.

liberalism A broad and evolving set of political doctrines associated with opposition to feudal society and the rise of INDIVIDUALISM, democratic institutions, and capitalist economies. Liberalism emerged in western Europe in response to the religious wars of the seventeenth century, when protoliberal theorists such as Thomas HOBBES and John LOCKE argued that freedom of religion, rather than state-imposed religious uniformity, was the only basis for civil peace. Hobbes and Locke also began to articulate the grounds for secular and limited authority and for a civil society of individuals who were free to pursue their private interests—especially trade. Many of these ideas were embodied in the English constitutional monarchy after the 1688 Glorious Revolution. This regime, according to both Locke and Charles-Louis MONTESQUIEU, allowed the greatest scope for individual liberty by combining the RULE OF LAW, LIMITED GOVERNMENT, constitutionalism

(see CONSTITUTION AND CONSTITUTIONALISM), and respect for individual rights.

During the eighteenth and nineteenth centuries, liberalism came to be closely associated with market-based economics and ultimately LAISSEZ-FAIRE capitalism, especially in Great Britain, the United States, and France. Classical economists such as Adam SMITH provided much of the intellectual groundwork for this development by privileging the role of the free, individual economic actor, whose pursuit of private interests collectively achieved the public interest. By the late nineteenth century, however, some "new" or "social" liberals began to follow John Stuart MILL in arguing that individual liberty required the moderation of capitalist inequalities. This division within liberalism has persisted and indeed became entrenched in the distinction between European and American uses of the term—the former favoring free-market principles and a minimal state; the latter relying on the state to ensure equity and the public good. It was also in the context of this individualist, property-centered concept of the public good that SOCIALISM emerged in the early nineteenth century as a distinctive alternative.

Modern liberalism continues to be organized around a number of not-always-harmoniously related principles: the priority of individual rights and freedoms, including broad enfranchisement; the belief that any use of AUTHORITY must be justified; the conviction that ethical choices or ideas of the good life should be left to individuals; the separation of private from public life and the belief that the former should be protected; the belief in the rule of law and the impartiality of the state; and, somewhat more contentiously, faith in human rationality and progress.

Justifications for liberalism have been equally contentious. Early debates circled around the question of inalienable and prepolitical natural rights. Later theorists argued that liberalism was justified simply on the basis of its contribution to public welfare (e.g., UTILITARIANISM). Other issues separate those who view liberalism primarily as a way of preventing social conflict or TYRANNY (initially Hobbes and Locke and, more recently, Isaiah BERLIN) from those who see it as a means of improving human existence (such as Mill or John DEWEY). Still others (notably Immanuel KANT) have sought to logically prove that liberalism is the most rational and just social philosophy.

liberation theology A movement within the Catholic church that fuses theology with secular concerns about social justice. Beginning in the 1960s in Latin America, liberation theology challenged the traditional place of the church as the defender of an extremely inegalitarian social order. It brought tools from Western Marxism to bear on the analysis of that order and reexamined the role of the clergy at the local level. The defining moment of the movement came in 1968 with the writing of the Medellin declaration by the Conference of Latin American Bishops. Toward the end of the twentieth century, it played a less prominent role and was actively discouraged by Pope John Paul II, who reasserted the hierarchical structure of the church.

libertarianism The belief that the role of the state should be minimized in order to create the maximum possible scope for human freedom. It is distinct from anarchism, which advocates the abolition of government (see ANARCHY AND ANARCHISM). Instead, most libertarians accord the highest priority to individual rights, especially the right to property, and recognize that a minimal "night-watchman" state is needed to guarantee these rights. Rights-based libertarianism is best defended in Robert Nozick's *Anarchy, State, and Utopia* (1974). Other varieties include Ayn Rand's ethical defense of rational egoism as the best way of life, Friedrich von HAYEK's pragmatic case that the state should be kept small as a defense against TYRANNY, and Milton FRIEDMAN's celebration of the free market as the fairest and most efficient form of social organization.

liberty See FREEDOM.

life chances A Weberian term that designates a person's chances of acquiring economic, cultural, and social goods. Life chances, Max WEBER observed, are unequally distributed; this inequality provides the basis of his definition of social CLASS.

life course Also *life cycle.* Both terms refer to the culturally defined sequence of stages in human life, rather than to precise periods of years or to biological development. Childhood, adolescence, adulthood, and old age are structured differently in different cultures and may vary considerably in duration. In any given society, specific life stages are associated with sets of STATUSes, ROLEs,

and values. They are similarly accorded different privileges and responsibilities.

life-cycle hypothesis An alternative to the Keynesian CONSUMPTION FUNCTION proposed by Franco Modigliani and Richard Brumberg. Modigliani and Brumberg sought to explain broad regularities in individual consumption over an individual's lifetime (or life cycle). They observed that individuals are net savers during their working years and net *dissavers* before entering the labor force and after retirement. Based on Irving FISHER's model of individual savings decisions, they analyzed savings as a particular case of the general problem of economic choice. In this context, they developed a consumption model in which consumption in each period is seen as a function of the expected value of lifetime wealth (not merely current income). This yields a short-run consumption function that conforms to the Keynesian consumption function, but in which the average propensity to consume shows no tendency to drift downward over time—a difficulty with the Keynesian model that ran largely counter to empirical evidence.

life expectancy The average number of years of life remaining to an individual of a given age. Societal life expectancies are usually reported from birth and strongly correlate with degrees of INDUSTRIALIZATION. They show some variance among the industrialized countries as well. By far the greatest source of variance in life expectancy is infant mortality—a category usually limited to the first year. Social scientists have also sought to explain variations on the basis of class, access to health services, occupation, and other lifestyle issues. According to the *National Vital Statistics Reports* (Vol. 47, No. 9, 1998), in 1996 the average life expectancy in the United States was 76.1 years. This total average contained significantly different results for particular subcategories: the life expectancy for women in 1996 was 79.1 years, for men 73.1. Race, too, plays a considerable role. White women averaged 79.7 years, black women 74.2; white men 73.9, and black men 66.1.

When applied to older populations, life expectancy calculations lengthen, reflecting the fact that the percentage of the population that died before reaching a given age is no longer taken into account. Thus, the life expectancy of fifty-year-olds in 1996 was 29.5 years; for sixty-five-year-olds, 19.5 years. With improvements in health care and nutrition, overall life expectancy continues to lengthen in industrialized countries, dramatically changing population demographics and leading to growing public policy concern with the question of aging.

lifeworld As developed in the phenomenological sociology of Alfred SCHUTZ, the lifeworld is the taken-for-granted stream of everyday routines, interactions, and events that make up individual and social experience. Schutz contrasts it with the highly conceptual world of scientists and social scientists. This distinction has been elaborated by Jürgen HABERMAS in the *Theory of Communicative Action* (1987 [1984]) and other works in order to address what he perceives as the unresolved Weberian paradox of modernity (see Max WEBER). As Habermas conceptualizes it, "society is conceived from the perspective of acting subjects as the lifeworld of a social group. In contrast, from the observer's perspective of someone not involved, society can be conceived only as a system of actions such that each action has a functional significance according to its contribution to the maintenance of the system" (1984: 117). The difference between lifeworld and *system* is thus both a matter of perspective and of scale, since large structures and organizations quickly escape our capacity to engage them personally. The loss of freedom and meaning that Weber attributes to RATIONALIZATION in modern capitalist society, Habermas suggests, is the result of an imbalance between the two dimensions as areas of the lifeworld are rationalized and integrated into larger systems of support and control. Habermas's chief example is the emergence of the welfare state with its strong involvement in family life. Habermas has been criticized for idealizing the lifeworld and neglecting the forms of domination (of women, for example) that have traditionally structured it.

Likert scale Named after psychologist Rensis Likert, the Likert scale is a common survey method that asks respondents to measure the strength of their reactions to a number of statements. Presented with a statement, respondents choose between a scaled range of responses—generally, strong disagreement, disagreement, uncertainty, agreement, and strong agreement (or some equivalent). The responses are assigned ordinal numbers, which make possible analytical methods such as comparison on narrow issues, correlation between issues, and individual or group tallies that reveal information about larger blocks of attitudes or behavior. Such data has proved well suited to FACTOR ANALYSIS, and the Likert scale has become the preferred instrument of large sample survey research in POLITICAL SCIENCE, SOCIOLOGY, psychology, and related disciplines.

liminality A position outside of or between defined states of being. As formulated by the anthropologist Arnold van GENNEP (1909) and later Victor TURNER, liminality refers to the period during rituals of passage in which the subject is held to be in between the categories of normal social life. This is a moment of special importance in many ritual activities and is often accompanied by a suspension or reversal of social norms and values. The term has also been used in CULTURAL STUDIES to refer to the border zones and peripheries of dominant discourses, where the contestation of cultural symbols takes place.

limited government The idea that political power and those who exercise it should be institutionally restrained, usually by the RULE OF LAW or constitutionalism (see CONSTITUTION AND CONSTITUTIONALISM). The principles of limited government were formulated in opposition to ABSOLUTISM by John LOCKE, Charles-Louis MONTESQUIEU, and other Enlightenment political thinkers, but limited government is perhaps best captured by the ancient formula: "a government of laws, not men." As Montesquieu recognized, this principle need not be limited to democratic regimes.

limit pricing A price level that both discourages the entry of potential competitors in a market and allows the incumbent FIRM to earn above-normal profits. The groundbreaking research in this area was done by Bain Sylos-Lambini and Franco Modigliani. Limit-price theory is based on a series of assumptions about the actions of incumbent and entering firms: first, that the incumbent firm is already producing at a level that assures minimum cost, and second, that an entering firm will have higher costs due to smaller output. The entering firm bases its decision on the belief that the incumbent firm will maintain its present level of output and that, under these conditions, there is sufficient residual demand to justify entry. The incumbent firm, however, can anticipate this decision and raise output such that the entering firm can no longer realize a profit. Entry by the second firm causes the price to fall below the firm's average cost of production.

In certain cases, the incumbent firm may be better served by permitting entry, in which case entry is said to be *ineffectively impeded*. Research in this area has involved relaxing the various assumptions set forth in the Bain-Sylos–Modigliani theory, such as the implicit assumption of complete certainty (where the incumbent firm knows the cost function of the potential entrant).

Lindblom, Charles (1917–) A prominent American political economist who specialized in the study of policy making, interest group politics, and democratic governance. Much of Lindblom's work was devoted to analyzing the relationships between government and large interest groups such as unions and corporations, and to understanding the role of government in regulating the relationships between these groups. Bargaining by independent interest groups, Lindblom argued, contributes to effective and accountable democracy. Government serves as both referee and arbitrator in this process and is expected to interfere only as necessary—levying taxes and guaranteeing free trade, for example, in the interests of growth and stability. The great potential for government to be overly sympathetic to the interests of large corporations is checked, in theory, by the democratic principle of "one-man, one-vote," which Lindblom argued ensures that a wide range of interests will be represented in government.

Lindblom's major works include *Politics, Economics and Welfare* (with Robert DAHL, 1953), *The Intelligence of Democracy* (1965), *Politics and Markets* (1977), *Democracy and the Market System* (1988), and *Inquiry and Change: The Troubled Attempt to Understand and Shape Society* (1990).

lineage A group organized on the basis of descent from a common ancestor (called UNILINEAL descent). *Patrilineage* and *matrilineage* designate descent from male and female ancestors respectively (see MATRILINEAL DESCENT; and PATRILINEAL DESCENT).

linear programming A special case of mathematical programming in which the objective function as well as each of the constraints are linear. To illustrate: suppose people require five grams of protein and five grams of calcium in their everyday diet. The two available goods are lentils, which have two grams of protein per ounce and one gram of calcium per ounce, and milk, which has one gram of protein per ounce and two grams of calcium per ounce. Linear programming tells us the least costly combination of these two goods

that gives us the minimum required protein and calcium. Linear programs are solved using the *simplex method*—an algorithm proposed in 1947. Since linear programming models can be large systems with a vast array of variables and constraints, it is necessary to use special software called matrix generators in the model-building process. Perhaps the most famous example of a linear program is Wassily LEONTIEF's input-output analysis in economics (see INPUT–OUTPUT ANALYSIS).

linguistics For much of the early history of the social sciences, linguistics was a method within ANTHROPOLOGY for investigating the social arrangements of different cultures through the particularities of vocabulary and grammar. Comparative and historical linguistics provided a way of indexing the evolution of cultures, and systems of measurement were developed for determining the linguistic "distance" of one culture from another.

In the 1910s, however, Ferdinand de SAUSSURE developed the proposition that language is but one instance of a broader and implicitly cognitive process of signification—rooted in the practice of assigning sounds to things. Saussure's insistence on the purely conventional relationship between "sound patterns" and their associated mental images (in his terms, *signifiers* and *signifieds*) broke with the evolutionary assumption that modern languages bore some relationship to an original, natural language and that they evolved in a linear fashion. This opened the door to anthropological investigations of cognitive functions (of the commonalities and differences in the organization of perception across cultures, for instance—a subject that would become the central concern of COGNITIVE ANTHROPOLOGY), as well as to the discovery of the "structural" function of signification as the basis of social relationships and social distinctions more generally (an avenue pursued by Claude LÉVI-STRAUSS in the development of STRUCTURALISM).

Saussure's work also raised the possibility of studying language as an autonomous science. This autonomy has been a major stake in the evolution of linguistics—especially in the structural linguistics of the 1920s and 1930s. Structural linguistics developed around a number of local "circles" of scholarship—preeminently in Moscow, where the influence of artistic formalism was strong, but also in Prague, where Roman JAKOBSON did much of his pioneering work, and in Geneva, where the implications of Saussure's work were pursued by a number of his students. American linguists such as Alfred L. KROEBER and Edward SAPIR also made important contributions. One major point of differentiation between these schools lies in the question of the independence of linguistic analysis from cultural context. Where Saussure had emphasized the SYNCHRONIC dimension of structural linguistics—taking as its object a snapshot of a language in time—and while formalism supported a model of linguistic analysis in isolation from cultural context, Jakobson and the Prague school made a determined effort to reintegrate the study of context and historical development into the account of linguistic structure.

The turn toward "transformational–generative" models of language, associated with Noam CHOMSKY, gave this process a strongly scientific basis (see TRANSFORMATIONAL-GENERATIVE GRAMMAR). Chomsky proposed a biological or "hard-wired" human competency for grammar that generates all particular grammatical systems. He distinguished three facets of this system: a deep and universal set of grammatical dispositions; a contingent, surface set of particular rules; and the *transformational* rules that mediate between the two. The scientific ambition of Chomskyan linguistics is to explain this deep grammatical structure. The Chomskyan view, or updated versions of it, became the framework of research for much of linguistics as well as related areas of cognitive science.

Linguistics traditionally distinguishes between the units of sound that a given language possesses (PHONEMES) and the system of rules that govern the combinations of those sounds (grammar). Subdisciplines of linguistics include PHONOLOGY, the study of patterns of sound within a given language; SYNTAX, the rules that govern the order of words and the construction of phrases in a language; and SEMANTICS, the study of the meaning of words.

PRAGMATICS, the study of language use and the performative effects of language and speech, has in some respects emerged as a separate and broadly interdisciplinary set of concerns. Here the Chomskyan approach has been of little influence. Pragmatics has a long history originating in the work of C. S. Peirce. Peirce saw that language is not only used but constituted by the situation of its use—as exemplified by terms that have no stable meaning apart from situated acts of reference (such as "here" or "there"). Bronislaw

MALINOWSKI was one of the first to integrate the study of contextual effects of language into the study of CULTURE. His work was elaborated by early linguistic structuralists such as Jakobson and Emile Benveniste. In turn, their work had a major impact on the structuralism of Lévi-Strauss and, in Anglo-American linguistics, the theory of speech-acts proposed by J. L. Austin in the early 1960s. Austin emphasized the ways in which people "do things with words," many of which carry a performative effect distinct from the simple meaning of the words. Naming is an example—the bestowal of a name is different than the use of the same word to describe or invoke an already existing relationship of signifier and signified. Austin's work has influenced both Pierre BOURDIEU's studies of practical action (including speech) and Jürgen HABERMAS's theory of COMMUNICATIVE ACTION. Michael Silverstein has pioneered the related field of *metapragmatics*, the comparative study of how different languages organize pragmatic functions, such as quoting the speech of others or self-reference.

Debates about the relationship between language, society, and ethnographic methods have profoundly shaped anthropology, SOCIOLOGY, and CULTURAL STUDIES in the twentieth century, whether in regard to the relative priority of language in determining world views (see SAPIR-WHORF HYPOTHESIS; and ETHNOSCIENCE), questions about objectivity and interpretation (EMIC AND ETIC), the role of language in social stratification (SOCIOLINGUISTICS), or the merits of different methods of DISCOURSE ANALYSIS. The Chomskyan revolution too, despite its claims for the autonomy of linguistics, has deeply influenced structural and cognitive anthropology.

linkages The most general usage refers to connections between otherwise separate political or social issues. Theories of how and why issues are linked have been pursued in CYBERNETICS and information theory, but these have mostly foundered on the sheer variety and contingency of linkages in political and social life. In a more limited sense, the term often refers to the strategic combination of policy objectives by political actors—visible in, for example, policies that link favorable trade policies to respect for human rights.

In economics, the terms BACKWARD LINKAGES and forward linkages refer to relationships between inputs and outputs in the production process, such that changes in demand for one yield changes in demand for the other. Thus the agro-processing industry has forward linkages to the livestock industry and backward linkages to raw agricultural commodities.

Linton, Ralph (1893–1953) Best known as a cultural anthropologist and member of the CULTURE AND PERSONALITY MOVEMENT of the late 1920s and 1930s. Linton's anthropological interests developed out of an extended archaeological expedition to the Marquesas Islands in Polynesia in 1920–1921—a trip that provided him the material for his dissertation. Subsequent fieldwork in Madagascar led to the publication of his principal ethnographical work, *The Tanala: A Hill Tribe of Madagascar* (1933).

In the mid-1930s in New York, Linton became associated with Abram Kardiner, who had led a number of seminars on the relationship between ANTHROPOLOGY and psychology. Much of Linton's subsequent work addressed a characteristic set of "culture and personality" concerns—especially the attempt to describe broadly applicable and culturally distinct personality types, which Linton characterized initially in terms of different forms of expression of status and later in terms of "modal personalities." Linton elaborated these concerns in *The Study of Man: An Introduction* (1936) and later in *The Cultural Background of Personality* (1945). He is also known for his work on cultural diffusion and ACCULTURATION—here with recourse to the notion of culturally coherent trait complexes, which contain elements that are more or less susceptible to transmission and adoption by other cultures (see DIFFUSION AND DIFFUSIONISM). Linton spent his entire teaching career at Yale University. His later works include *The Tree of Culture* (1955) and *Culture and Mental Disorder* (1956).

Lipset, Seymour Martin (1922–) An American political scientist and sociologist, Lipset has written extensively on labor organization, student movements, the formation and significance of public opinion, and the sociology of ideas. He is perhaps best known, however, for his comparative research on DEMOCRACY, social STRATIFICATION, and social mobility—subjects that form the core of a number of his studies of the United States, Canada, and Europe. He has shown particular interest in the question of the necessary social and historical conditions for stable democracy—most especially, in his view, the prolonged economic development that moderates class divisions and undermines working-class radicalism. The subject of American exceptionalism with respect to Europe has also been a recurring theme in his work—generally conceived in terms of the absence of feudal legacies and the presence of a dominant liberal tradition (most recently in *American Exceptionalism: A Double-Edged Sword*, 1996). This perspective aligns him with much of the "consensus" scholarship of the 1950s, such as that of historians Louis Hartz and Richard Hofstadter. Like Hartz and earlier theorists of the liberal tradition, Lipset emphasizes the degree to which American society performs a delicate balancing act between the conformism of mass society and the divergence of interests—especially class interests—that threaten broader social conflict.

Lipset has taught SOCIOLOGY, POLITICAL SCIENCE, and public policy, holding faculty positions at the University of Toronto, the University of California at Berkeley, Columbia University, Harvard University, Stanford University, and currently, George Mason University. He has served as president of both the American Sociological Association and the American Political Science Association. Lipset's major works include *Social Mobility in Industrialized Society* (1959, with Reinhard BENDIX), *Political Man* (1960), *The First New Nation: The United States in Historical and Comparative Perspective* (1963), *Revolution and Counterrevolution* (1968), *Rebellion in the University* (1972), *Continental Divide: The Values and Institutions of the United States and Canada* (1989), and *Jews and the New American Scene* (1996, with Earl Raab).

liquidity trap A hypothetical situation outlined by John Maynard KEYNES in the *General Theory of Employment, Interest and Money* (1936), whereby an increase in the money supply has no impact on the interest rate. Such an outcome signifies the ineffectiveness of expansionary monetary policies, which are usually undertaken to stimulate aggregate demand (via reductions in the interest rate). In such a case, however, economic agents are willing to hold an unlimited amount of cash.

The liquidity trap occurs when interest rates are very low and bond prices high. Individuals expect an adjustment of both toward more moderate levels, and there is consequently little incentive to hold bonds. Increases in the money supply, under these circumstances, simply add to idle balances and leave the interest rate unaffected.

LM curve   See IS-LM ANALYSIS.

local government   Usually refers to levels of GOVERNMENT beneath the lowest level with constitutionally sovereign power. Thus, American states or German *Länder* are not typically regarded as local governments; county or city governments, in contrast, generally are. Local governments are often favored by advocates of PARTICIPATORY DEMOCRACY and DIRECT DEMOCRACY because of the opportunities they create for citizen involvement in public affairs. Although it is often said that the rise of the NATION-STATE after the late middle ages drastically reduced the scope of local government, in the last quarter of the twentieth century many Western countries have favored the DEVOLUTION of previously centralized powers and functions toward more local levels of decision making.

Systems of local government differ widely in their relationships to the national state. For example, France has regions, provinces or counties, and COMMUNEs beneath the national government, whereas many American states have only counties. As a general rule, local government tends to be stronger in federal rather than UNITARY STATES (e.g., the United States rather than France) and where it is charged with important and expensive services (such as health care, social security, and education in most Scandinavian countries). Political scientists often distinguish between the participatory and administrative aspects of local government: the former tend to be emphasized in relatively decentralized systems such as those of Switzerland and the United States, the latter in centralized systems such as that of France.

location theory   Refers to work that explains the spatial distribution and patterns of economic activity. Interest in this question dates back to the seventeenth century and questions of agricultural land use, but modern inquiries relate mostly to the distribution of industry and the use of resources. Most of the major statements of location theory were produced by economic geographers in the 1940s and 1950s. Many of these were rooted in cost analysis and relied on relatively simplistic models of economic decision making that privileged such variables as distance to market and the availability of resources. This orientation was challenged in the 1960s and 1970s by behavioral geographers, who emphasized the importance of local patterns of economic behavior and ENVIRONMENTAL PERCEPTION on decisions about the location of economic or cultural activity. Similarly, the lack of a historical dimension to many of the early studies was challenged by the growing influence of Marxist analysis, which situated questions of spatial distribution within a broader account of capitalist development.

Locke, John   (1632–1704) An English moral philosopher and political theorist of great range and influence, whose interlocking theory of SOVEREIGNTY, defense of the principles of liberal government, and notion of property set the stage for political and economic liberalism. Locke's insistence that labor was the primary constituent of value opened the door to the classical economic theories of Adam SMITH and Karl MARX. His account of natural rights and revolution was of direct importance to the American Revolution and to subsequent theories of constitutionalism. More generally, Locke was a prominent early champion of EMPIRICISM and the extension of the scientific method to social theory.

In his *Essay Concerning Human Understanding* (1689), Locke made his case for the fundamentally empirical sources of human experience. He argued that knowledge was primarily the perception of "facts" furnished by sensory experience. Human beings learned continually on the basis of that experience, through a process akin to that later specified as "conditioning." Scientific procedures were needed, however, to evaluate the vast realm of human activity that escapes such knowledge and that depends, in greater or lesser degree, on *belief*. The scientific method, therefore, had a strong ethical function in Locke's system, insofar as it applied to nearly all questions of human relations—in fact, he sought to devise a mathematical system for the deduction of ethical principles from a set of natural laws.

The theory of "natural law" underwrites Locke's social theory. Like Thomas HOBBES, he explored the relationship between natural law and society through the metaphor of the social contract (see SOCIAL-CONTRACT THEORY). According to this view, human beings existed prior to society in a natural, independent state; only later did they consent to a system of societal law in order to better pursue their natural rights. Where for Hobbes this natural state included a large measure of brutality and violence, Locke conceived a more peaceful condition, distinguished largely by the absence of property beyond the "ownership" of self: the world was initially given to all. Like Hobbes, Locke believed that humans in this state were fundamentally equal—no divine right over others existed, and no secondary forms of authority (parent–child, master–servant, husband–wife) impinged on the basic political equality of individuals.

Society, Locke argued, is fundamentally tied to the emergence of private property, which develops as people mix their labor (which they do own exclusively) with the land (see PROPERTY AND PROPERTY RIGHTS). This relatively egalitarian process, however, succumbs to the introduction of money, which permits the ownership of property beyond what one individual can personally invest with labor. For Locke, the resulting complexity and inequality requires a system of laws designed to perfect, extend, and adjudicate the right of property. For this purpose, he argued, people submit to a government of their own determination. Locke had little to say about the character of this government, other than that it was constrained by the natural rights of its subjects to life, liberty, and property. Where government overstepped these limits, it became illegitimate; the social contract was broken and the right to reconstitute government returned to the people. For the generations born into an existing society—a recurrent problem for theories of popular sovereignty—Locke articulated a principle of "tacit consent," which, he argued, was granted through any form of participation in that society (not without contortions, he managed to extend his theory even to allow for slavery).

Locke's view of limited government is developed most fully in his *Two Treatises of Government* (1690), a work that fundamentally shaped the tradition of liberal political and economic thought. Locke also wrote an influential defense of religious freedom in which he argued that belief is an essentially individual affair in which the state has no jurisdiction (*A Letter Concerning Toleration*, 1689). Locke's other major works include *Thoughts on Education* (1693) and *On the Reasonableness of Christianity* (1695).

logical positivism   See POSITIVISM.

logit, probit, and tobit models   Techniques used in the statistical analysis of variables whose values are discrete or nonnumerical. Whereas REGRESSION ANALYSIS can incorporate explanatory variables that are dichotomous or categorical in nature, it cannot be used to analyze models where the *dependent variable* is dichotomous, categorical, or qualitative (termed *quantal response*). For example, a decision whether to vote in a given election is a binary one—the dependent variable has only two possible values, yes or no, usually coded numerically as 1 or 0, respectively. Linear regression models are inappropriate for predicting the outcome of such binary choices since the assumptions of the linear regression model are violated: the error terms are heteroskedastic, correlated with the explanatory variables, and the predicted value would not necessarily fall within the logical range of zero to one (see HETEROSKEDASTICITY). Logit and probit models are used to circumvent this problem. Each of these assumes different distributions of the errors—the part of the decision to vote that is not explained by the variables in the regression. The logit model is associated with the cumulative logistic probability function and the probit with the cumulative normal probability function. Dependent variables may also be a mix of discrete and continuous outcomes (for instance, models of markets with price ceilings). Such responses are called *limited responses*. In this case, the tobit model is the appropriate analytical technique. For these models, ordinary linear regression analysis yields biased estimates of the coefficients; therefore, the *maximum likelihood estimation method* is used to yield estimates with desired asymptotic properties.

logocentrism   The tendency in Western philosophy to posit fundamental principles or concepts that anchor philosophical systems and structures of conceptual oppositions. The term implies above all confidence in the strict correlation between language and its referents, which allows terms such as God, being, essence, and so on to serve as fixed points in speculative philosophies. The term is closely associated with Jacques DERRIDA's critique of metaphysics; much of Derrida's work involves deconstructing the nature of these relationships and the authority they claim (see DECONSTRUCTION).

logrolling   The trading of votes between legislators, usually to secure passage of bills that benefit home districts rather than larger constituencies. The term originally referred to the assistance that neighbors provided each other in building log cabins.

Lombroso, Cesare (1836–1909) One of the founders of modern CRIMINOLOGY, Lombroso developed a physiological theory of criminal types based on certain allegedly atavistic physical features, such as a low brow. Lombroso based much of his work on Darwinian evolutionary theory and argued strongly for the hereditary nature of criminal behavior. Twentieth-century SOCIOLOGY and criminology are largely built on the repudiation of such views and are primarily concerned with the analysis of social factors that influence behavior.

longitudinal analysis The analysis of statistical data collected over time, either continuously or at specific intervals. Longitudinal analysis is primarily a method for studying social processes and patterns of change that cannot be approached on the basis of cross-sectional data—i.e., data collected at a single instance in time (see CROSS-SECTIONAL ANALYSIS).

Panel studies are a common form of longitudinal analysis that involves gathering data from the same subjects at repeated intervals. Longitudinal research involves numerous difficulties, not least that of maintaining the integrity of the original sample. Subjects included in a panel study may lose interest, move, or die, and thereby affect sample size and continuity. As the famous Hawthorne investigations show, the fact of being a subject of research may itself affect subjects' behavior, as can the experience of repeated interviews or surveys (see HAWTHORNE EFFECT). To minimize some of these problems, researchers make use of *dynamic sample panels* or *repeated cross-sectional surveys*. In a dynamic sample panel, new subjects are added to the panel to compensate for sample deterioration. In a repeated cross-sectional survey, a new sample is drawn at each measurement point.

In some fields, longitudinal analysis is improved by the growing availability of streams of "real-time" data over extended periods. Rather than looking at stock prices at intervals, for example, one might study the totality of trading over a period of time.

longitudinal effect Refers to changes within a COHORT that are attributable to aging, such as changing preoccupations with school, careers, family life, retirement, and so on. Longitudinal effects are distinguished from *cohort effects*, which reflect the impact of major shared historical experiences on the values and attitudes of members of a cohort and which may differ widely from one cohort to the next.

long run and short run Refers to distant and immediate timeframes of action, respectively. In economics, the terms refer specifically to the ability of an economic system to adapt over time. By definition, the "short run" refers to the period before slow-moving variables (like the capital stock) can be adjusted. In this context, markets and prices may be unstable. In the long run—defined as long enough for all variables to adjust—equilibria are thought to reflect underlying market valuations. The economist Alfred MARSHALL first distinguished between the two types of variables—those that adjust quickly and those that do not. Because of these differences, Marshall argued, unusual profits and losses are possible in the short run, as not all variables are adjustable. In the long run, on the other hand, all factors are variable and there is sufficient time to adapt the structure of fixed capital goods. Prices guarantee "normal PROFITS," and speculative or entrepreneurial profits are reduced to zero.

There is no guarantee that processes of short-run change will ever settle long enough to reach a long-run equilibrium. As John Maynard KEYNES famously quipped, "In the long run, we are all dead" (*A Tract on Monetary Reform*, 1924).

looking-glass self See Charles Horton COOLEY; and SELF.

Lorenz curve A graph of the percentage share of income held by households (on the *y*-axis) against the percentage share of these households in the population arranged in order of increasing wealth (on the *x*-axis). Thus the *x*-axis measures income-distribution percentiles (poorest 10 percent of households, poorest 40 percent, etc.). This results in a curve, bowed inward toward the lower right-hand corner, that illustrates the disparity of income distribution. The more equally income is distributed among households, the closer the Lorenz curve is to the 45-degree line. The Lorenz curve is used to calculate one of the most common measures of income distribution, the GINI COEFFICIENT.

Lowie, Robert H. (1883–1957) One of the first students of Franz BOAS, Lowie played an important role in institutionalizing ANTHROPOLOGY in the United States and in shaping its orientation toward CULTURE. For the first half of the century, he was also the principal authority on the mythology and KINSHIP structures of the Plains Indians, and produced a number of important ethnographic studies. Chief among these was *Primitive Society* (1920), which directly challenged the paradigm of societal evolution developed by Lewis Henry MORGAN and other ethnologists in the nineteenth century. This critique revealed the strict empiricism and aversion to grand theories that would guide Lowie's career and ultimately dominate American anthropology for a generation.

Lowie addressed a range of other topics in his writing, including the history of anthropology, the philosophy of science, the politicization of the academy, the origins of the state in primitive societies, and the character of the German people. Although his involvement with this last subject was a direct response to the exigencies of World War II, it also reflected a deep preoccupation with Germany, European culture, and the Enlightenment that Lowie traced to his childhood in Vienna.

Lowie began his career as a curator of the American Museum of Natural History, which sponsored much of his early fieldwork. He spent most of his career in the Department of Anthropology at the University of California at Berkeley, which he co-chaired with Alfred L. KROEBER. His other major works include *Culture and Ethnology* (1917), *The Origin of the State* (1927), *Are We Civilized: Human Culture in Perspective* (1929), *The History of Ethnological Theory* (1937), *Indians of the Plains* (1954), and *Toward Understanding Germany* (1954).

Luhmann, Niklas (1927–1998) A German sociologist whose SYSTEM(S) THEORY constitutes one of the major contributions to sociological thought in the postwar era. Luhmann was a prolific writer of over forty books. Enormously influential in Germany and much of the world, he has nonetheless received relatively little attention in Anglophone countries, perhaps due to the highly abstract character of much of his writing. Luhmann's contribution to systems theory builds on Talcott PARSONS's theory of the "functional specialization" of various subsystems in society. His later work, however, represents a critique of Parsons—especially the role that Parsons accorded action.

Luhmann's seminal *The Differentiation of Society* (1982) conceived society as composed entirely of communication and the subsystems that organize it, rather than as a network of human actors.

These systems emerge in order to reduce the complexity of the environment—partly through the imposition of binary distinctions. All of these subsystems are self-referential, self-enclosed, and equipped with their own "codes" of communication that hinge on certain basic oppositions, such as property and nonproperty in the economic subsystem, or legal and illegal in the legal subsystem. Luhmann called this process of internal production AUTOPOIESIS and argued that these operating logics lie outside the realm of willful human action. Thus, Luhmann denied the possibility of external intervention to change the subsystemic rules of the game. Human beings as actors are relegated to the "environment" that forms the backdrop of the system. Consequently, society is an autonomous network of systems that escapes any larger efforts to steer it by leveraging one system against another. This was a theme of Luhmann's debate with Jürgen HABERMAS over technology and the question of whether technological change could be subjected to social control without being stymied. Unlike Habermas, Luhmann had little hope for redeeming or recovering control of modernity. In *Risk: A Sociological Theory* (1993), Luhmann emphasizes the historical dimension of this process, arguing that modernity is described by the transition from "danger" to "risk." Danger, in this context, refers to hazards that the individual or collective actor cannot control, whereas risk refers to an environment defined by human actors.

Luhmann's other works include *Observations on Modernity* (1988), *Ecological Communication* (1989), and *Social Systems* (1995).

Lukács, Georg (1885–1971) A Hungarian Marxist philosopher and literary critic whose work inaugurated the turn toward Hegelian MARXISM in the West. With *History and Class Consciousness* (1923), Lukács challenged the scientific positivism and historical determinism prevalent in Marxist thought since Friedrich Engels and dominant in Communist Party doctrine of the period. Moreover, he reconstructed Karl MARX's concept of ALIENATION as the fundamental condition of humanity in capitalist society.

Alienation had played an important role in Marx's early work, especially the *Economic and Philosophical Manuscripts of 1844*, but these writings remained unpublished and were all but unknown until the early 1930s. For Lukács, alienation highlighted the crucial role of working-class consciousness: in capitalist society, he argued, only the position of the working class offered a standpoint for critique radical enough to break through the REIFICATION and FALSE CONSCIOUSNESS of capitalist relations. Only the working class—or theorists adopting the standpoint of the working class—was capable of synthesizing theory and practice into the totality of PRAXIS, which alone could achieve a true grasp of history and bring about revolutionary change. Against prevailing Marxist theory, Lukács argued that the contradictions of capitalism would not in and of themselves create the conditions necessary for revolution. In addition, he argued that the PROLETARIAT had only in certain cases achieved this necessary consciousness. His suggestion that revolutionary change depended on theory as well as practical experience opened the door to Leninist interpretations of the role of the Communist Party (see LENINISM).

Lukács's views were apostasy to much of the Communist orthodoxy but found a very sympathetic ear in the work of FRANKFURT SCHOOL critical theorists and French existentialists. His literary criticism also left a complex and influential legacy: Early works such as *Theory of the Novel* (1916) provide a broad and decidedly un-Marxist account of the fundamentally alienated quality of modernity, which the novel tries to recuperate. His later work represents an attempt to theorize the relationship between narrative and historical processes; *The Historical Novel* (1937), in particular, is notable both for its veiled critique of Soviet realism and its attack on modernism.

Lukács spent much of the 1930s and 1940s in the Soviet Union, including a short period in prison. After the war, he returned to Hungary and served briefly as Minister of Culture under the Nagy government until the Soviet invasion of 1956. Recurrently, he seems to have suppressed the nonorthodox side of his intellectual views in favor of remaining loyal to the Communist Party. This resulted in several public retractions and a number of internal tensions in his work.

Lukács's other major works include *The Young Hegel* (1948), *The Meaning of Contemporary Realism* (1963), and *The Specificity of the Aesthetic* (1963).

lumpenproletariat   According to Karl MARX, the lumpenproletariat is the "refuse of all classes"—an underclass defined by its marginality with respect to the principal social division of capitalist society between the workers (or PROLETARIAT) and the BOURGEOISIE. Unlike the other marginal groups that Marx identified (such as the peasantry or the *petite bourgeoisie*) the lumpenproletariat lacks any relationship to the means of production. The concept later became important in analyzing the composition and appeal of fascist movements.

lump sum tax   A fixed-sum tax assessed on each taxpayer, also called a head tax or a POLL TAX. The attractive feature of such taxes is that they are not distortionary—i.e., taxpayers cannot reduce their liability by changing their behavior, and therefore the taxes create no economic distortions in labor or investment activity. The disadvantage of lump sum taxes is that they impose an unequal relative burden on taxpayers. Thus they are rarely used as primary systems of taxation (see TAXES AND TAXATION).

Lyotard, Jean-François   (1924–1998) A French philosopher and social theorist best known in the Anglophone world for his role in debates about POSTMODERNISM. Much of this prominence is due to the appearance of *The Postmodern Condition* in English (1979), which offered a clear and in some respects deceptively simple claim about the differences between the modern and postmodern at a time when the battle lines surrounding postmodernism were still being drawn. For Lyotard, the distinction turns largely on his account of a broad transformation in the status of knowledge. The modern, he argued, refers to forms of knowledge that legitimize themselves in terms of larger *metadiscourses*, such as the grand nineteenth-century theories of historical progress (primarily Hegelianism and Marxism) or the universal truth claims that form the basis of religion and the scientific tradition. Lyotard argued that such exclusive concepts of truth led toward the totalitarian and exterminatory social solutions of the twentieth century, which sought to eliminate difference at the human level. Echoing Friedrich NIETZSCHE, Lyotard argued that these truth discourses have encountered their limitations and thereby lost their authority. The postmodern condition is what survives this process, defined by Lyotard as "incredulity towards metanarratives."

The emergence of a social realm characterized by diverse, inevitably partial, often incommensurable, and sometimes competing "language games" allows Lyotard to elaborate an ethics of postmodernism based on a rejection of the totalizing impulse. Injustice, especially in later works such as *The Differend* (1984), becomes identified with the subordination of one discourse to another. Human freedom, similarly, consists in finding new ways to play these games—especially inventing new moves that thwart the tendency toward determination by the games. Here, too, Lyotard relies on a concept of aesthetics for theorizing the nature of imaginative play and for reflecting upon the open-endedness of such games.

Such considerations represent a departure from Lyotard's political radicalism of the 1950s and 1960s, when he was a member of the Marxist group "Socialism or Barbarism," a prominent defender of the Algerian revolution, and a participant in the revolutionary turmoil of May 1968. His major philosophical works all postdate this period and include *Libidinal Economy* (1974), *Just Gaming* (1979, with Jean-Loup Thébaud), *The Inhuman: Reflections on Time* (1988), and *Political Writings* (1993).

M

Machiavelli, Niccolò (1469–1526) The first major political philosopher of the Renaissance and still a primary source for arguments in favor of political REALISM. Unlike much of the classical and modern tradition of political thought, Machiavelli was less concerned with theorizing the legitimate basis of political power than with exploring the methods of effective statecraft. His justification of amoral state power—including the use of deceit and violence when it serves the interest of the state—made him notorious in both his time and ours, although the details of Machiavelli's arguments are often overlooked.

Machiavelli's best-known work is unquestionably *The Prince* (1513)—a guide to statecraft written to restore him to the good graces of the Medici rulers of Florence, who had tortured and exiled him for participation in the political opposition. Machiavelli's larger motive was the unification of Italy, which at the time was a fractious group of city-states at the mercy of larger powers. This goal was informed by what he termed the "effective truth" (*verita effettuale*) of politics: the ideal state was not possible, and the failure to employ ruthless means weakened those in power. Machiavelli was not, however, an advocate of TYRANNY, and he argued that effective leadership involved promoting prosperity and respecting private property and tradition. He claimed that rulers are not free, as individuals, from moral standards but are given the freedom to violate conventional morality on the state's behalf. Cruelty and violence, therefore, might in this respect be compatible with honor and the public good. This is the logic underlying Machiavelli's claim that "when the act accuses him, the outcome should excuse him"—often translated as "the end justifies the means."

Machiavelli's other major work, *Discourses on the First Ten Books of Titus Livius* (1532), shifts the emphasis from the ruler to the importance of civic duty in a REPUBLIC. Although he viewed liberty as essential to a successful republic, he argued that leaders must also ensure civic virtue in order to prevent corruption and the dissolution of the state. To this end, he advocated a blend of ARISTOCRACY and DEMOCRACY that would emphasize the participation of the citizenry and the advancement of general over personal interests. Key to this effort was the continued struggle for control over other states: dominance alone, he argued, brings security to the state. Equally important, this vying for power requires a strong citizen military, which ensures a close connection between the people and the state.

MacIntyre, Alasdair (1929–) An American ethical philosopher strongly associated with COMMUNITARIANISM. The guiding theme of much of MacIntyre's work is the disintegration of the framework of values through which modern individuals understand their lives and orient their actions. MacIntyre attributes much of this decline to the triumph of a highly segmented society guided (though not united) by bureaucratic rationality and to the associated rise of liberal pluralism as a way of legitimizing the lack of shared values and experiences. For MacIntyre, ethical systems are necessarily rooted in shared values and community structures. This means that ethical systems may differ from one another—the pluralist point that MacIntyre retains—but also that commonality is necessary at the societal level if society is to function as more than a venue for alienated individualism. Pluralism in itself, he suggests, provides no basis for ethics.

MacIntyre criticizes the Enlightenment philosophies of Immanuel KANT and the Utilitarians for their attachment to universal and abstract moral imperatives, independent of tradition and/or community support; these posit the self as, at least potentially, a creation of pure rationality divorced from its own history (see UTILITARIANISM). MacIntyre consistently argues against such claims and embeds the notion of rationality within tradition itself: only those traditions reflexive enough to question their own notions of truth and justice merit the claim to rationality. *After Virtue: A Study in Moral Theory* (1981) is MacIntyre's most influential account of this fragmentation, and also of its main counterexample: the organic values of community that structured the civic life of ancient Greece. These presented a common idea about the good life in which citizens participated. MacIntyre views selfhood as a reflexive capacity for viewing one's life story as a part of this wider narrative of community life. It is here, too, that he argues that the classical ideal might have lessons for modern society, reinvesting the concepts of virtue and shared societal goals and implementing them practically through schools and other broad-based institutions.

MacIntyre elaborated these themes in *Whose Justice? Which Rationality* (1988) and *Three Rival Versions of Moral Inquiry* (1990)—the latter an examination of Enlightenment morality and its Nietzschean and poststructuralist critiques (see POSTSTRUCTURALISM). Although MacIntyre's early work was strongly inflected by a Marxist understanding of capitalist development and ALIENATION, he has increasingly looked to Roman Catholicism as a basis for social critique and communitarian alternatives.

Mackinder, Halford J. (1861–1947) Mackinder was one of the most influential British political geographers of the early twentieth century, largely based on his formulation of the HEARTLAND THEORY of geopolitical dominance. Initially proposed in a 1904 lecture on the relationship between Europe and Asia, Mackinder argued that the *heartland*, comprising the interior of Eurasia, benefited from a number of strategic advantages over the *rimland*, comprising the coastal areas of Europe, the Mediterranean, and Asia. These included a central location and relative immunity to Western naval power, from which he concluded that world domination could be achieved by a Eurasian power capable of unifying the heartland. The leading contender for such domination, Mackinder believed, was Russia, which by the turn of the twentieth century had accomplished much of this task of unification. The Bolshevik Revolution in 1917 and German interest in eastward expansion guaranteed Mackinder's work a wide audience and long shelf life well into the twentieth century, in spite of what many geographers came to see as its overreliance on environmental and technological determinism.

Mackinder was a major figure in the establishment of academic GEOGRAPHY in Great Britain, both in the Royal Geographic Society and at the University of Oxford, where his efforts led to the creation of the School of Geography in 1899. He lectured frequently and made influential arguments in favor of unifying human and physical geography. He also served as a member of Parliament and participated in the post–World War I repartitioning of Europe. His major works include the essays "The Scope and Methods of Geography" (1887), "The Geographical Pivot of History" (1904), which articulated heartland theory, and several books including *Britain and the British Seas* (1902) and *Democratic Ideals and Reality* (1919).

macroeconomics The branch of economics that analyzes the national economy at an aggregate level—in contrast to MICROECONOMICS, which concerns itself primarily with the economic decisions of individuals and firms. Macroeconomics emerged as a distinct area of economic and policy research in the 1930s, primarily in the context of John Maynard KEYNES's groundbreaking *General Theory of Employment, Interest, and Money* (1936). It integrated the classical economic concern with national income—conceived primarily in terms of gains and losses from foreign trade—into a much more comprehensive account of the relationships among INTEREST RATES, government expenditure, aggregate demand, INFLATION, and employment (see AGGREGATE DEMAND FUNCTION). Because government expenditure and interest rates are controllable through policy decisions, it opened the door to a range of policy options for steering the economy through the upturns and downturns of the business cycle—most immediately the Great Depression.

For Keynes, the severity and length of the Depression was largely a function of inadequate aggregate demand. Keynesian macroeconomics, therefore, focuses on BUDGETARY OR FISCAL POLICY, which can be adjusted in response to shifts in demand (see KEYNESIAN ECONOMICS). Keynesian thinking guided macroeconomic policy in the United States and other developed nations for much of the post–World War II period. The emergence of high inflation and high unemployment in the early 1970s, however, ran counter to Keynesian predictions, and lent weight to a "monetarist" critique of Keynesianism associated most strongly with Milton FRIEDMAN. MONETARISM developed out of dissatisfaction with Keynesian assumptions about the inflexibility of prices and wages, and suggested that government intervention would only displace private activity. Instead, monetarists argued that aggregate variables could be managed through the manipulation of interest rates, which determine the cost of consumption and investment.

Active monetary intervention presupposes that economic actors can be fooled in the short term with regard to prices. Expectations are held to adjust over time, rather than in immediate response to policy changes. The RATIONAL EXPECTATIONS revolution, led by Robert Lucas in the 1970s, broke with this assumption by arguing that actors generally incorporate rational expectations about changes in economic variables into their decisions (an increase in government spending, for example, would rationally be assumed to be paid for by an increase in taxes). All monetary and fiscal policy, given this assumption, is ineffective: only *unexpected* changes, such as price shocks, can impact real aggregate variables. Lucas's *New Classical* perspective had a strong impact on economics in the 1970s and 1980s, but subsequent empirical research has suggested limitations to the rational expectations hypothesis, particularly in regard to wage and price stickiness. No real consensus has emerged on this point, and continuing disagreements about basic macroeconomic assumptions have led to a fracturing of the field. In practice, government inaction has proved to be the least politically tenable strategy, leading to an often *ad hoc* blend of Keynesian and Monetarist strategies.

Recently, macroeconomic analysis has incorporated a wide range of work on institutions and microeconomic behavior into models of aggregate economic activity. This has taken many forms. *Positive political economy* has examined the incentives of politicians and central bankers to manipulate the economy. Consumption theory now challenges the *representative agent* theory in an effort to better understand how individual decisions aggregate into macroeconomic outcomes. The *New Keynesian* school has become interested in how price and wage stickiness can be derived within the neoclassical framework of firm and consumer behavior. And the recent theory of *Real Business Cycles* has sought to explain fluctuations in the macroeconomy within the rational expectations paradigm.

macro-micro analysis See POLITICAL SOCIOLOGY.

macrosociology and microsociology A loose but commonly used distinction between sociological approaches that analyze social systems or populations on a large scale or at a high level of abstraction (*macrosociology*) and those that deal primarily with individuals, face-to-face relationships, and the construction of meaning (*microsociology*). The distinction can be applied to a range of related methodological differences in the social sciences, such as the distinction between *structure* and AGENCY. Anthony GIDDENS's theory of STRUCTURATION and Pierre BOURDIEU's practice theory are among the more prominent recent attempts to integrate the two perspectives (see PRACTICE AND PRACTICE THEORY). Jürgen HABERMAS argues that the difference of perspective is not a contradiction to be overcome but a necessary feature of social science.

MAD Mutually Assured Destruction. See ARMS RACE.

magic A focus of anthropological research since the pioneering work of Edward Burnett TYLOR (*Primitive Culture*, 1871) and James FRAZER (*The Golden Bough*, 1890). Tylor and Frazer made scientific critiques of the practice of magic. They recognized the systematic character of many magical systems but described them as irrational or primitive worldviews based on false associations. Frazer's enormously influential account described magic as a stage in cultural evolution that was superseded by RELIGION and, ultimately, science. He introduced a distinction between *homeopathic magic*, in which power is based on resemblance between things, and *contagious magic*, in which power is a function of past proximity to an object.

Since then, the distinction between magic and religion has been repeatedly examined—among others, by Emile DURKHEIM in *The Elemetary Forms of Religious Life* (1915), who described magic as an individual practice distinct from the social dimension of religion. The scientific dismissal of magic as irrational and ineffective has also been the subject of considerable debate, beginning with Durkheim's view of magic as an irrational practice that nonetheless functioned as a powerful mechanism of social integration. Bronislaw MALINOWSKI took a different functionalist view in describing magic as a psychological supplement to limited practical or technical skills ("Magic, Science and Religion," 1925). The major challenge to the Durkheimian functional model came from E. E. EVANS-PRITCHARD, who argued in *Witchcraft, Oracles and Magic among the Azande* (1937) that magic is generally a coherent, rigorous, and internally rational system of thought. Among the Azande, Evans-Pritchard contended, magic does not replace mundane cause-and-effect rationality but provides a framework for explaining the arbitrary dimensions of good and bad fortune. Debates over the rationality and social functions of magical beliefs continued in the late-twentieth-century context of poststructural challenges to the truth claims of science. See also MANA.

Maine, Henry James Sumner   (1822–1888) One of the major figures of nineteenth-century ANTHROPOLOGY and an innovator in comparative legal history. His classic study, *Ancient Law: Its Connection with the Early History of Societies* (1861), provided an influential account of the emergence of "progressive," or modern, societies from primitive ones in terms of the evolution of legal systems. Drawing a line from early primitive groups through Greece, Rome, and modern societies, Maine described a transition from systems based on family groups, status relations, and private law to systems that privileged the state, criminal law, and contractual relations between individuals. Maine was not a strict evolutionist, however, and believed that for most societies there was little actual development along this path. Maine's work, like that of most early social-evolutionary theorists, was rejected by the social and cultural anthropology of the early part of the twentieth century—especially as newer paradigms of cultural diffusion, historical particularism, and functionalism emerged that better accommodated the vast increase in data from anthropological fieldwork. This dismissal was partly redressed in the 1950s and 1960s, however, when cultural evolutionary paradigms benefited from renewed interest.

Mair, Lucy Philip   (1901–1986) A prominent British anthropologist who specialized in social change in African tribal, colonial, and postcolonial societies. Mair was educated at the University of Cambridge and taught at the London School of Economics in the late 1920s, where she participated in the seminars of Bronislaw MALINOWSKI. Despite Malinowski's considerable influence, Mair's work is remarkable for its consistent refusal of the timeless, ahistorical approach of much of British social anthropology—including that of Malinowski—which tended to ignore the context of colonialism, modernization, and historical change. Mair refused the notion of a purely academic ANTHROPOLOGY geared toward scientific research; rather, she was concerned with the practical potential and consequences of anthropological work. Much of her research, therefore, was oriented toward problems of colonial administration, which might be solved through better understanding of the governed societies. At the same time, she was highly critical of the structural condescension of the colonial regimes and of the failure of the developed nations to recognize the significance of decolonization. Mair was a clear writer whose treatments and syntheses of diverse topics in anthropology earned her a wide audience. Her major works include *Primitive Government* (1962), *New Nations* (1963), *Anthropology and Social Change* (1968), and *Anthropology and Development* (1984).

majority rule   The principle that a majority has the right to make decisions that are binding on the whole. In some contents, the term refers more broadly to universal enfranchisement and elected government. More specific usage distinguishes between two types of majorities: *absolute* majorities, where winning requires receiving more than half the votes cast, and *simple* majorities, or *plurality*, where the recipient of the most votes wins, even when this falls below 50 percent. Majority rule has been criticized on several grounds. First, in elections with simple majority rule and more than two candidates, the winning side may be opposed by an absolute majority (the combined vote for other options). Absolute majority systems do not have this drawback, but may systematically exclude smaller parties from power and leave minorities with limited means of redress when their rights are threatened. This is the principle behind fear of the "tyranny of the majority," described by James Madison in the late eighteenth century, Alexis de TOCQUEVILLE in the nineteenth century, and the liberal tradition of political thought more generally (see LIBERALISM).

Madison's solution in *The Federalist* (1788) was to argue that the SEPARATION OF POWERS, FEDERALISM, and the doctrine of CHECKS AND BALANCES would limit the power of majoritarianism. Tocqueville's contribution was to warn against the decline of CIVIL SOCIETY, which engages individuals in diverse group activities and allegiances, and guards against the sweeping force of mass, majoritarian opinion. While most democratic states have not gone as far as the

United States in creating institutional obstacles to majority rule, many ensure that certain citizens' rights are constitutionally protected, and many empower an independent judiciary to check executive and legislative power. Additionally, some countries guarantee minority representation in legislative bodies through *proportional representation*. All such protections can prove ineffectual, however, in the face of determined majorities.

Absolute majority rules are employed by many countries in electing chief executives, and by Australia and France for legislative elections. Australia uses an alternative vote system in which voters rank the candidates, while France and a number of other countries hold a second ballot between the top candidates if no candidate wins an absolute majority on the first. See also ELECTORAL SYSTEM.

maladaptation See PREADAPTATION.

Malinowski, Bronislaw (1884–1942) Born in Krakow, Malinowski became one of the founding figures of British social ANTHROPOLOGY. With A. R. Richards, he shaped the functionalist agenda that dominated British anthropology for a generation (see FUNCTIONALISM). More importantly, he helped to make FIELDWORK—the intensive study of small groups—the keystone of modern anthropological research.

Malinowski formulated his research methodology in the course of several expeditions to the Australian Papua colonies—trips that also furnished him his great ethnographic subject: the Trobriand Islanders. His studies of these relatively contained populations over long periods of time marked a departure from the short-duration, often interpreter-dependent survey techniques of such leading anthropologists as W. H. R. RIVERS. More than a question of improved methods, however, Malinowski saw in fieldwork a comprehensive critique of the goals of anthropological study. In his major ethnographic works, he challenged the validity of the evolutionary historical models and cross-cultural schemata that dominated the field in his day—interpretations that the survey methods had been designed to support. Instead, he emphasized the "synchronic" analysis of a single society, understood as a functionally integrated whole. This perspective echoed Emile DURKHEIM's view of society as a set of interrelated parts that contributed to the functioning of the whole, as well as the rationalism of such nineteenth-century intellectuals as James FRAZER

and William JAMES, who emphasized the material and psychological sources of spiritual beliefs. Based on this work, Malinowski developed a series of operating premises: society was organized so as to meet the material and psychological needs of its individuals; this organization was fundamentally rational and instrumental; and careful fieldwork could reveal its structure. In so doing, he inaugurated a range of inquiries into the structure of KINSHIP, political authority, and religious systems that would become the hallmarks of British social anthropology.

Although Malinowski was somewhat more flexible in his practices than other functionalists, such as A. R. Richards, the collective functionalist rejection of historical analysis came to be perceived as a serious weakness by the 1950s. In particular, synchronic analysis provided little leverage on the problem of social change—an increasingly glaring problem as decolonization and modernization gained momentum. Similarly, Malinowski's beliefs in the universality of the monogamous (nuclear) family unit and the strictly instrumental character of CULTURE have been largely abandoned. Many of Malinowski's insights into patterns of kinship, sexuality, MAGIC, and MYTH, however, have entered the canon of anthropological thought, and the Trobriand Islander ethnographies, especially *Argonauts of the Western Pacific* (1922), are still widely read.

Malinowski's other major works include *The Family Among the Australian Aborigines* (1913), *Crime and Custom in Savage Society* (1926), *The Sexual Life of Savages* (1929), *Coral Gardens and Their Magic* (1935), and *A Scientific Theory of Culture* (1944).

Malthusian population theory See Thomas Robert MALTHUS.

Malthus, Thomas Robert (1766–1834) A British clergyman and political economist whose work was an early response to the adverse effects of the industrial revolution—primarily unemployment, disease, poverty, and high tax rates. It was in this context that he developed the theory of population growth that bears his name. Malthus argued that populations would grow geometrically until "natural" checks such as famine, plague, and war reestablished an equilibrium.

Malthus's work—especially the famous *An Essay on the Principle of Population as It Affects the Future Improvement of Society* (1798; rev.

ed. 1803)—was in many respects a critique of the optimistic social philosophies of William Godwin and the Marquis de CONDORCET. The meliorating welfare programs of Condorcet would not address the problem of population growth, Malthus argued, but merely remove one of its natural checks—starvation. Similarly, Godwin's egalitarian society would provide more food for the masses and spur an even greater increase in population.

Malthus initially held that population grew at a geometric rate (1, 2, 4, 8, ...) while subsistence or food grew at an arithmetic rate (1, 2, 3, 4, ...). His later versions no longer insisted on this but remained firm on the basic propositions: population is constrained by subsistence and it increases whenever subsistence increases, unless prevented by either positive or preventive checks. Positive checks such as war or natural disaster increase the death rate, while preventive checks such as abstinence reduce the birth rate. The basis of Malthus's theory of population lay in the law of diminishing returns. If an increase in the labor and capital used on a plot of land produces a less than proportionate increase in output, then it becomes increasingly difficult to provide food for a growing population. This application is similar to David RICARDO's theory of differential rent.

Malthus's other contribution to classical political economy was the theory of gluts. This amounted to a critique of Ricardo's and J. B. Say's assertions that the excessive accumulation of capital is impossible because overproduction is impossible. In his *Principles of Political Economy* (1820), Malthus shows that demand may be inadequate to absorb the output of a capitalist economy. The LABOR THEORY OF VALUE implies that unless wages in capitalist production are less than the output of the worker, there will be no profit. Consequently, the worker cannot buy all he or she has produced. Unless either capitalists or landlords agree to consume more than they produce, markets will eventually produce gluts. Malthus supported Britain's landlord-friendly Corn Laws on these grounds, and he recommended occasional increases in government spending to clear commodity gluts.

Malthus's legacy is unusual in that his most celebrated insight, the theory of population, is widely disputed today, while his lesser-known theory of gluts is more relevant today than in his time. Although there are some prominent neo-Malthusians, most analysts hold that advances in technology, changes in industrial structure, and better social infrastructure have obviated or at least greatly deferred the law of diminishing returns; improvements in family planning also challenge Malthus's assumptions. In the end, Malthus remains one of the most original contributors to the classical tradition of POLITICAL ECONOMY.

mana A generic term for the supernatural substance that, according to some Melanesian and Polynesian religious systems, permeates the universe. Although the specific function of mana varies, it is by definition the most fundamental spiritual force—the source of life and power, spread in varying amounts among the different types of beings in nature (rocks, plants, animals, etc.). In ANTHROPOLOGY, the concept of *mana* has played an important role in evolutionary theories of religion—in particular, Robert Marrett's proposition of a stage of spiritual development prior to the personalized spirits and ghosts of ANIMISM (*The Threshold of Religion*, 1909).

managerial revolution Refers to the split, dating to the late nineteenth century, between the ownership and management of corporations. The emergence of the *managerial class*, with specific credentials and training, profoundly changed the organization of corporate activity and signaled the decline of family-organized CAPITALISM. In its place emerged dispersed, share-based models of ownership. Managerial capitalism attracted considerable sociological interest to the new structures of economic and social organization. Key issues include the different patterns of accumulation, investment, and incentive that accompany the shift away from familial control (intersecting organization theory and AGENCY THEORY), as well as the role of the managerial revolution in creating the American middle class. The concept of the managerial revolution is generally credited to sociologist James Burnham and in particular to his work of that name (1941).

manifest functions Social functions of behavior or action that are recognized and intended by actors—for example, the solidarity-building function of a rally. Robert K. MERTON distinguished these from latent functions, which go unrecognized by actors or supplement the official functions associated with an activity.

Mannheim, Karl (1893–1947) A Hungarian philosopher and sociologist best known for his work on the "sociology of knowledge," or *Wissensoziologie*. Against positivistic concepts of knowledge, which privilege the accumulation of objective facts or logical certainties (see POSITIVISM), Mannheim insisted on the importance of context and the place of the knower. Knowledge, he argued, is shaped by particular times and places—a condition that makes strict truth claims impossible and comparisons difficult.

In his best known work, *Ideology and Utopia* (1929), Mannheim combined this situational perspective with a Weberian analysis of social divisions (see Max WEBER). Knowledge, he argued, depended heavily on and tended to align with patterns of CLASS and STATUS. He also recognized the significance of age distinctions in the differential construction of knowledge.

Influenced by Karl MARX's analysis of class, Mannheim argued that conflict between the BOURGEOISIE and the PROLETARIAT went beyond the issue of economic disparity. He insisted that persons were "existentially connected" to their class and that this connection had a broad impact on belief systems and methods of interpreting reality. Each class, Mannheim explained, held its own *Weltanschauung* ("WORLDVIEW") composed of values, interests, and beliefs. Mannheim suggested that all such views were nonetheless incomplete and one-sided and that they could be understood only in relation to the holder's own *Weltanschauung*. Reconciling competing worldviews requires a "dynamic synthesis," which Mannheim argued was within the grasp of an impartial "free intelligentsia." Through this process, he argued, social science could arrive at a scientific, objective set of principles applicable to all societies—an extension of reason with implications for social justice and the social order. He consequently viewed this synthesis as a responsibility incumbent on social scientists and intellectuals.

Mannheim moved to Great Britain following Adolf Hitler's rise to power in 1933. There, he turned to the analysis of the structures underlying more immediate social and political conflict, such as the nature of agreement and disagreement and the methods through which people arrive at consensus. He also turned his attention to education, arguing that modern society required more specialized training. He emphasized, too, the importance of social planning, including the concept of "planning for freedom" as a way of addressing the threat of TOTALITARIANISM.

Mannheim's other major works include *Freedom, Power, and Democratic Planning* (1950) and *Essays on the Sociology of Culture* (1956).

Maoism   A theory and practice of revolution developed by Mao Zedong (1893–1976), leader of the Chinese Communist Party (CCP) from 1934 until his death in 1976. Maoism differs from classical MARXISM in several respects—especially in the role it accords the peasantry. Whereas Karl MARX and later Vladimir Ilich LENIN viewed the industrial working classes and tightly organized Communist parties as the primary sources of revolutionary action, Mao emphasized the revolutionary potential of the peasantry. This was a necessary accommodation of revolutionary theory to predominantly rural China; it was also a practical necessity for the Red Army after its defeat by Nationalist forces in 1934 (resulting in the Long March) and later during the Japanese occupation.

According to Mao, the Party could succeed only by expressing the collective will of the mass of common people; the job of Party leaders was to systematize the collective wisdom and propagate it (see GENERAL WILL). For this reason, Mao discouraged internal social differentiation and individualism (whence the importance of a uniform style of dress, the so-called "Mao jacket"). Mao held that errant individuals could be "re-educated," and he encouraged collective efforts to identify and root out dissent—especially through group meetings devoted to self-criticism. Mao's faith in mass action inspired two attempts at large-scale social engineering, the Great Leap Forward (1958–1959) and the Cultural Revolution (1966–1969). The Great Leap tried to harness revolutionary fervor to the task of rapid industrialization. It was notorious for promoting absurdly high production goals for steel, wheat, and other goods, with little regard to economic realities. The project caused severe economic dislocation and contributed to a famine in which some twenty-five million people died. The Cultural Revolution began as an internal purge of the CCP leadership—partly rooted in Mao's fear that mass participation was giving way to bureaucracy and ideological moderation. The attack on bourgeois and antirevolutionary elements spread across China and plunged the country into chaos—driven largely by the brutal Red Guard. The Cultural Revolution was reined in only after massive intervention by the army.

Maoism influenced a number of other third-world revolutionary movements and elements of the radical left in the West, especially in the 1960s. Its influence is far weaker today. In China, the Party's recent leadership continues to officially revere Mao, while acknowledging that he made a number of major mistakes. They have progressively distanced themselves from his radical vision of SOCIALISM, to the point of undertaking a slow, state-directed transition to CAPITALISM in the past two decades. This transition, and the fall of Soviet socialism, has meant the effective end of Maoism as a revolutionary philosophy—if not in all cases as a practical guide to revolutionary tactics.

March, James G. (1931–) An American sociologist best known for his work on organizations and especially his contributions to the approach known as the New Institutionalism. Institutions figure centrally in March's accounts of social, economic, and political behavior as mechanisms for simplifying the complex social environment. They structure courses of action and influence individual preferences; they also help interpret the past and shape expectations. March and his frequent collaborator Johan P. Olsen thus position themselves against the strong individualism that underlies much political and sociological theory—especially the view that institutions merely embody existing patterns of interest or group power. His approach also allows for a considerable degree of leverage on social problems at the level of institutional form—indeed, the search for better institutions underlies part of his inquiry into the nature of democratic governance. March has studied diverse kinds of institutions, from universities to forms of democratic rule; he has paid particular attention to risk taking, decision making, learning, and leadership within them.

March spent much of his career at Stanford University. His major works include *Leadership and Ambiguity* (1974), *Decisions and Organizations* (1988), *Rediscovering Institutions* (1989), *A Primer on Decision Making* (1994), *Democratic Governance* (1995), and *The Pursuit of Intelligence in Organizations* (1998).

Marcuse, Herbert (1898–1979) A philosopher and key member of the FRANKFURT SCHOOL, Marcuse made diverse contributions to critical theory. With Theodor ADORNO and Max HORKHEIMER, he pioneered the Frankfurt school's critique of instrumental reason; later, he pursued an innovative integration of MARXISM and Freudian psychology, which had a major impact on student radicalism in the 1960s.

Marcuse studied with Martin HEIDEGGER and Edmund Husserl—influences that shaped his early efforts to reconcile existential PHENOMENOLOGY and Marxism. In the course of his association with Horkheimer and Adorno in the 1930s, Marcuse developed an interest in the recently published early works of Karl MARX, and he participated in the renewal of interest in Georg HEGEL—a touchstone of much of the Frankfurt school's work of the period. Marcuse differed from Horkheimer and Adorno, however, in according much more importance to Marx's notion of demystification. Much of this thinking found expression in Marcuse's own *Reason and Revolution* (1941).

Marcuse's later work is characterized, above all, by his effort to explore the revolutionary potential of Sigmund FREUD's work. *Eros*, the free condition of pleasure, occupied much the same place in Marcuse's schema as *reason* did for the other Frankfurt theorists. Society suppressed Eros through the organization of unpleasant labor and replaced it with regimented forms of amusement and entertainment. Revolution, consequently, could be conceived in libidinal terms as a "desublimation" of the instincts and a recovery of pleasure—a prospect that, given humanity's technical mastery over nature, need no longer imply the breakdown of society. *Eros and Civilization* (1955) is the chief document of this revolutionary program, although attention to the suppression of pleasure finds its way into most of Marcuse's analyses of modern society during the 1950s and 1960s.

Marcuse was one of the few Frankfurt school figures to take an active role in the radicalism of the 1960s. The explosion of social demands and the attacks on traditional Western work ethics and sexual mores seemed confirmation of the social and psychological contradictions that Marcuse had identified. *One-Dimensional Man* (1964), an analysis of the disintegration of viable opposition to the social order, became a popular text of the student movement. Although Marcuse was circumspect about the revolutionary potential of the students, he did see reason to place hope in the anticolonial movements of the third world. His other major works include *Negations* (1963), *An Essay on Liberation* (1969), and *Five Lectures* (1970).

marginal analysis In economics and increasingly in other social science disciplines, formal models of choice presume that decision makers maximize an *objective function*—consumers maximize UTILITY, firms maximize PROFITS, and politicians maximize votes or campaign contributions. Decisions are usually constrained because choices imply costs (monetary and otherwise), and decision makers have limited resources. *Marginal analysis* is a technique for evaluating the optimal decision under such conditions. Consider a politician trying to allocate her time in pursuit of campaign contributions for her electoral race. Some donors are easier (and wealthier) targets than others, and logically she pursues those with the greatest value first. As long as the expected contribution is at least as large as the value of the time she must spend to secure it, she will pursue that donor. Marginal analysis determines her optimal stopping point—when the expected incremental change in contributions is just small enough so that the incremental cost (her time) outweighs the benefit. Likewise, a firm trying to decide how much labor to hire will continue to employ workers as long as the value of what they produce is at least as much as the wage they must be paid to produce it. Their productivity is measured at the margin—how much would an additional employee produce? Because it is assumed that the *marginal productivity of labor* declines (with a fixed set of investments in factories, etc.), there will be a point when hiring an additional worker will cost more than he would produce in revenue for the firm. The golden rule in marginal analysis is that the optimal decision is where marginal cost equals the marginal benefit.

marginalism See   NEOCLASSICAL ECONO-MICS.

marginal propensity to consume The relationship between a change in income and the change in expenditure on consumption. The MPC is critical in determining how much of a boost an economy will get from an increase in government spending or a cut in taxes. If individuals tend to consume all of an increase in income (MPC close to one), then the additional income from a tax cut will be plowed back into the economy, creating a multiplier effect. If consumers tend to save most of an income increase, then the multiplier effect is much smaller. The propensity of individuals to consume an increase in income depends on many demographic factors—how close they are to retirement, etc.—but also depends on whether they perceive the change in income to be *temporary* or *permanent*. If the change is seen as permanent—such as a salary increase—the MPC

is expected to be much higher than if the income shock is temporary.

market economy A system of exchange based on private ownership of the means of production and on the laws of supply and demand. Market economies rely heavily on self-regulation: prices are set by the demand for a particular good or service and by its relative scarcity. In principle, self-regulation implies that the role for government can be limited to facilitation, such as guaranteeing that property rights and contracts are upheld and that the preconditions of economic exchange are in place (for example, MONEY, and agreed-upon weights and measures). No active intervention in production decisions or the allocation of resources is necessary.

In practice, market economies exist at the intersection of the private and public sectors, and governments typically engage in a wide variety of regulatory activities: (1) to control market externalities such as pollution; (2) to direct market activity in view of social or political objectives; (3) to maintain the principles of fair competition; and (4) to manage economic growth in the face of BUSINESS CYCLES, supply shocks, and other forms of instability. Fiscal and MONETARY POLICY are the major tools of government action at this level (see BUDGETARY OR FISCAL POLICY). Government action also extends to the provision and administration of PUBLIC GOODS, such as security, health care, education, and INFRASTRUCTURE (e.g., roads and water).

Socialist societies, which privilege government ownership of the means of production, have relied to varying degrees on markets to allocate distribution and sometimes to influence production decisions.

market failure Generally, markets are considered to be functioning well when certain basic conditions are met: (1) there are a large number of buyers and sellers on each side, such that no one can unilaterally influence prices; (2) there is *perfect information*, so that the value of the product or service is common knowledge; (3) there are no constraints on new sellers to enter the market or on sellers to exit; and (4) there are no costs or benefits that accrue to third parties (EXTERNALITIES, such as pollution). More generally, markets usually need an institutional structure in order to function, such as enforceable contract laws and property rights (see PROPERTY AND PROPERTY RIGHTS). If any of these elements are missing, markets may not operate efficiently or they may not operate at all. Such cases are described as *market failures*.

Where the institutional structure is lacking or related markets are also failing, market failures can often be corrected by *completing* markets—i.e., creating contingent markets where there are informational asymmetries, property-right markets for public goods, and polluting-rights markets for externalities. In cases where market failures result from too little competition, there may be no market-based solutions available. In the case of *natural monopolies*, where production costs are such that it would be inefficient to have more than one firm, the solution is usually to regulate prices or output (see MONOPOLY).

market socialism   An attempt to reconcile the advantages of the market as a system of exchange with social ownership of the means of production. One prominent variant involves the cooperative ownership of productive enterprises, which are then encouraged to compete with each other as a way of stimulating production and the efficient exchange and distribution of goods. Supply and demand determine prices and the state intervenes only at the margin. Both Yugoslavia and Hungary introduced this form of market socialism in the 1960s.

market structure   Refers to the number and characteristics of sellers and buyers in a market. With respect to sellers, economists distinguish between *monopolistic* markets, in which there is one seller who controls the price; *oligopolistic* markets with a small number of sellers, each of whom has some degree of influence over price; and *perfectly competitive* market structures with many sellers, such that none influence the market price. Similar classifications are made on the basis of the number of buyers: *monopsony* describes a market with single buyer, *oligopsony* a market with few buyers. Many analyses of market structure also incorporate information about the competitive characteristics of markets, including product differentiation across firms, market share, and cost structure.

marriage systems   Marriage has been an enduring subject of social research because it appears to be a universal human institution: some form of marriage system is present in all observed human societies. Efforts to specify what marriage consists of or what social functions it performs have met with difficulty, however, because of the diversity of marriage forms. Marriage may be

central to the establishment of a new household (part of systems of NEOLOCAL RESIDENCE or PATRILOCAL RESIDENCE) or to the process of child rearing; elaborate rules may specify available marriage partners (EXOGAMY; HYPERGAMY AND HYPOGAMY); and marriage practices may deviate from the convention of one man and one woman.

The centrality of marriage systems in explaining broader social arrangements has been a subject of considerable debate within ANTHROPOLOGY, pitting those who see marriage as the basic associative social bond (see ALLIANCE THEORY) against those who accord the priority in social organization to systems of descent (see DESCENT THEORY). Although this debate has lost intensity since the 1970s, alliance and descent still constitute the main axes of KINSHIP studies of premodern societies.

In modern societies, marriage (and kinship more generally) plays a much less significant role in structuring social and political life. Nonetheless, the history of the Western institution of marriage and the family has been the subject of considerable sociohistorical research. The radical transformation of these institutions since the mid-twentieth century—following gains in equality for women, the availability of birth control, changes in the nature of domestic labor, and the decline of the normative structures that influenced marriage choices—has attracted considerable attention from sociologists. In the West, the critique of marriage as a patriarchal institution has played a major role in feminist debates about life opportunities and norms for women. While diverse in their objectives, these approaches are consistent in treating marriage as, above all, a socially shaped institution that affects and is affected by changes in other areas of economic, family, and social life.

Marsh, George Perkins   (1801–1882) An American geographer whose work on the limits of natural resources had a major impact on the study of human GEOGRAPHY and on the conservation movement in the United States. Much of this work was based on Marsh's observation of deforestation in the Northeast, especially in his home state of Vermont. Marsh was sensitive to the human transformation of the landscape and championed the idea that the exploitation of natural resources required careful management and active conservation. These themes were developed in his best-known and most influential work, *Man and Nature: or, Physical Geography as Modified by*

Human Action (1864). Never an academic geographer, Marsh was primarily a lawyer and politician. He served several terms in the U.S. Congress in the 1840s and later held diplomatic posts in Turkey and Italy.

Marshall, Alfred (1842–1924) The most influential figure in the marginalist tradition of British economics. Marshall sought to combine the basic principles of the classical tradition with the new insights of marginalism—primarily by asserting that value is determined by both UTILITY and the cost of production. He is also credited with being one of the founders of NEOCLASSICAL ECONOMICS. Among his more specific contributions, Marshall popularized diagrammatic treatments of mathematical issues in economics, thereby contributing to both theory and methodology.

Marshall was trained in mathematics and physics and only later in economics. Despite this background, he was skeptical about the use of mathematical techniques in economic analysis. In *Principles of Economics* (1890), he defined economics as "the study of mankind in the ordinary business of life." For him, economic laws were social laws, not natural ones; they described the results of individual action motivated by the pursuit of happiness. Marshall's views were much less dogmatic than those of most other marginalists, and his ideas allowed for small departures from perfect competition that remain central to neoclassical thought.

According to Marshall, demand and supply can be conceived of as the two blades of a pair of scissors: each blade plays a role in cutting. Demand for a good is based on the law of diminishing marginal utility, and the amount of money a person is willing to pay reflects his or her utility at the *margin* (see MARGINAL ANALYSIS). It is the existence of this measure, Marshall argued, that makes economics more exact than other social sciences. One of Marshall's principal achievements was the diagrammatic and mathematical analysis of the *elasticity of demand*, which describes the sensitivity of demand to price changes. This has proved an invaluable tool for many kinds of economic analysis, such as determining the effects of taxes on different goods. Unlike most marginalists, Marshall considered supply—as determined by the cost of production—a central component of economic analysis. Since the amount produced depends on the effort of workers, supply increases as prices (and therefore wages) increase. Marshall

was the first to recognize that market price is determined by the interaction of demand and supply and that there is an important temporal dimension to this process. In general, the shorter the time period considered, the greater the effect of demand on price. The longer the period, the bigger the effect of the cost of production, and therefore of supply. This is because changes in the cost of production take longer to affect the economy than do changes in demand.

Marshall's work concentrated on *partial equilibrium*: it looked at only one sector of the economy at a time. For this reason, he had little to say about aggregate economic issues like business cycles. Still, the methodological tools he introduced, such as the diagrammatic determination of market price and the concept of the representative firm (which is neither the most efficient nor the most inefficient in its market) have shaped aggregate analysis as well.

Marshall, Thomas H. (1893–1982) A British sociologist best known for his work on citizenship and social policy. Marshall's broadest contribution to this subject is *Class, Citizenship and Social Development* (1963)—a historical account of the development of citizenship and the notion of RIGHTS from the eighteenth century to the twentieth. Marshall identified a progression from constitutional rights to electoral rights to welfare rights, and a corresponding shift in the locus of those rights from courts to legislatures to the welfare state. His *Social Policy* (1965) examined the evolution of welfare from 1890 to 1945 in the context of the expansion of the concept of welfare rights. In *The Right to Welfare and Other Essays* (1981), Marshall addressed a broader set of issues, exploring what he saw as contradictory relationship between welfare and DEMOCRACY. Throughout, Marshall stressed the practical, policy aspects of his work, as well as the larger potential of SOCIOLOGY to unify diverse areas of knowledge.

martial law The temporary resort to military rule and the suspension of constitutional principles during wartime and other exceptional circumstances. See also EMERGENCY POWERS.

Marx, Karl (1818–1883) A German philosopher, economist, social scientist, and revolutionary who developed the most influential critique of CAPITALISM in modern times. Marx studied law, history, and philosophy at several German universities and initially found work as a journalist. His critical political and economic writings soon earned him expulsion from Germany, how-ever. He moved to Paris in 1843, where he met Friedrich Engels, with whom he formed a lifelong intellectual collaboration. Forced to move again, he settled in England.

At its broadest, Marx's work provided a pow-erful and, for many, compelling account of the development of modern society—one that derived its urgency from the massive transfor-mative effects of industrial capitalism and the impoverishment of large sectors of the new work-ing class. Marx rooted this critique in a materialist sociological and historical methodology, which carries his name and which helped shape the development of the social sciences and other humanistic fields. His theory incorporated aspects of the German idealist philosophical tradition, including Immanuel KANT's notion of *critique* (in which science advanced partly by a thoroughgo-ing examination of the conditions of knowledge) and Georg HEGEL's approach to *dialectical* reason, in which human existence and knowledge are treated as essentially social and historical.

Marx's early work is especially notable for its emphasis on the ALIENATION or estrangement of humans from one another, from their processes of work, from the world they create, and from their very humanness. This alienation becomes especially acute under capitalism, as workers suffered not only poverty but also the loss of their ability to guide their own productive work. Their work also becomes less social than that of earlier craft producers. This results in not only unhappiness but also mystification and vulnerability to ideological domination—notably to treatments of private property as "natural" and to a doctrine of individualism that obscures what workers share. The most significant of these writings are *The German Ideology* (1846, with Engels) and *The Economic and Philosophical Manuscripts of 1844* (published only in the 1930s). When this work became known in the twentieth century, it led to a renewal of Western Marxism and to a Marxist critique of existing communist regimes (see Antonio GRAMSCI).

Marx's early thought built on Hegel's phi-losophy of history and, especially, on his use of philosophy as a vehicle for social critique. Together with other "Young Hegelians," Marx accepted Hegel's insistence that all reality was historical but did not adopt his profound con-servatism. Influenced by Ludwig Feuerbach, Marx developed a critique of Hegel that incorporated

Hegel's dialectical method, his emphasis on his-torical change, and his approach to totality—but that inverted Hegel's ontology. Where Hegel had treated Spirit (or Reason) as the basis of all reality, Marx insisted on practical, material conditions as the necessary source of human reality; he argued that Reason developed out of the human strug-gle to survive and surmount mere biological and physical necessity.

Marx saw history as shaped by successive stages of this struggle, which was always a social, not merely individual, process. Its dominant feature was class struggle, the confrontation between the defenders of the status quo in any historical period and those who sought to transform it and transcend its limits. The revolutionary class of one period was commonly the conservative class of the next. Thus, Marx held that the bourgeoisie was the most revolutionary class the world had yet seen, having produced the technological and economic innovations that overturned the preindustrial world. Yet capitalism had its own internal contradictions and limitations—most basically its need to exploit workers in order to produce profits and new accumulation of capital. This meant that workers would be poor because their wages would be driven down by competition and the introduction of labor-saving machinery. It also meant that capitalism would experience recurrent crises, in which technological advances made possible vastly greater production, but with a distribution of income so unequal that markets would prove inadequate. When capitalists tried to hold this system together, they became conservative. Workers therefore had an interest in creating a society in which wealth would be more equally distributed and productivity would be oriented to human needs. This was SOCIALISM.

Marx argued that, in this sense, human beings created their own history, but never under condi-tions of their choosing. The historical conditions of class struggle—and also of technology and social institutions—determined the possibilities open at any one time. Marx's most important tool for describing the possibilities and limits of each historical period was the MODE OF PRODUCTION, which signified not only the dominant tech-nology but also the whole pattern of social organization, property relations, and economic institutions. Each mode of production entailed specific relations of production—thus feudalism was dependent on military relations for social order and on religion for a legitimating ideol-ogy. Capitalist relations turned first and foremost on the distinction between those who owned the means of production (the capitalists, or bourgeoisie) and those who did not (the workers, or PROLETARIAT); class conflict was the inevitable result. Yet capitalism also had a dominant ideology that helped to legitimize it and minimize conflict. Central to this was a form of possessive individualism that implied that differences in property were natural and just and that workers (as well as capitalists) should compete with one another rather than unite in class struggle or more limited forms of cooperation, such as LABOR UNIONS or consumer organizations.

Marx's primary mature statement of his economic theory was *Das Kapital* (*Capital*, 3 vols., 1867, 1885, 1893), subtitled "a critique of political economy." This reflected his intensive engagement with the classical economic tradition of Adam SMITH and David RICARDO. Marx took up and revised the LABOR THEORY OF VALUE that underlay their work, similarly arguing that human labor was the source of the value of produced goods but adding a distinction between mere work as such and labor power that was quantified and sold as a commodity. Capital could thus buy labor without dealing with workers as whole human beings; living labor was thereby combined with past labor, which was embodied in equipment used to produce commodities for sale (as distinct from producing directly for use). Capital could grow only by extracting SURPLUS VALUE from labor by paying workers less than the value of their contributions to the production process. Such a system would inevitably drive down wages and immiserate workers. This system was internally contradictory, however, because those very workers were also the consumers who made up part of the market for the goods produced. Marx demonstrated that capitalist productive capacity would therefore outstrip purchasing power. He also expected profit rates to fall as automation diminished the contribution of exploitable living labor to the production process—an aspect of his theory that remains controversial.

Marx never completed the synthetic political theory he intended to produce as a complement to *Capital*. His political ideas are known mainly from his writings of the late 1840s and the 1850s, which focused largely on practical problems of political organizing and on the European political crises of 1848. These include *The Poverty of Philosophy* (1847, an attack on the socialism of Pierre-Joseph PROUDHON), the *Communist Manifesto*

(1848, with Engels), *The Class Struggles in France* (1850), and an analysis of the failure of the 1848 revolution in France, *The Eighteenth Brumaire of Louis Napoleon* (1852).

Marxism Karl MARX and his collaborator Friedrich Engels produced the dominant critical account of CAPITALISM in the nineteenth century. More broadly, they elaborated a theory of human history and modernity, structured around the Industrial Revolution and the social transformations it occasioned. Collectively, this work became known as Marxism.

Through the work of their inheritors, Marxism furnished the major twentieth-century vehicle for radical utopian political aspirations. The impact of Marx and Engels's work on political and social thought is consequently enormous, both in terms of its systematic challenge to political and economic LIBERALISM and the influence of its methodologies and analytical perspectives on the study of society more generally.

The great majority of Marx's work was devoted to analyzing the emergence and organization of capitalist society. He made comparatively little effort to formalize the philosophical, cultural, or revolutionary implications of his positions. Beginning with Engels, however, Marxism began to develop into a much more extensively elaborated "worldview." Marxism was taken into areas that Marx himself had consigned largely to drafts and notes (such as its intellectual debts to Georg HEGEL) or treated only peripherally, such as revolutionary action, the transition to COMMUNISM, and theories of cultural production.

Engels was a strong proponent of the scientific validity of Marxism—a claim he developed into the doctrine of HISTORICAL MATERIALISM. For Engels, the term referenced the entire Marxist "science of history," starting with the priority assigned to economic organization as the determining cause of all social development, including political and cultural life. This relationship had been implicit in much of Marx's work—especially his well-known claim that the economic *base* determined the political, legal, and cultural *superstructure*. It was, moreover, the basis of Marx's larger account of human history, which periodized of societal development in terms of changes in the dominant MODE OF PRODUCTION. A change in the mode of production implied change in the technological and social framework that structured economic activity in a given society, and more precisely in the way that SURPLUS VALUE (or value beyond subsistence needs) was extracted from the labor process. The mode of production included, too, the class distinctions that emerged with respect to control of the means of production—distinctions between serf and lord in feudal society and between worker and bourgeois under capitalism. For Marx and Engels, these class interests were irreconcilable short of revolution and guaranteed to intensify as capital consolidated into fewer and fewer hands.

Emphasis on class conflict and scientific validity formed the doctrinal core of the Second and Third Internationals (the coordinating bodies for international socialism, founded in 1889 and 1919, respectively), as well as the official Marxism in the communist countries. Insofar as it was promoted as a science, however, there remained a tension between Marxism's analytical and revolutionary dimensions. Marxism had a strong influence on the emerging social sciences in the early twentieth century—visible in the prewar work of the Austro-Marxists (Max Adler, Otto Bauer, Karl Renner, and Rudolf Hilferding, among others), as well as on the sociological tradition of Max WEBER and Emile DURKHEIM. These included diverse responses to, qualifications of, and variations on Marx's account of the central place of economic regimes in explaining societal development and organization. As an interpretive framework, Marxism had become unavoidable.

The challenges facing revolutionary Marxism, however, were different. If communism was predicated on the prior concentration of capital and the development of the means of production, as Marx argued, then the role of Communist parties in most countries was uncertain. Revolution in countries where capitalism remained underdeveloped was theoretically impossible. Although revolutionaries such as Vladimir Ilich LENIN, Georgi V. Plekhanov, and later Mao Zedong defended the scientific grounding of Marxism, they were not content with the slow path of historical inevitability that Marx had outlined, with its necessary route through capitalist development. Lenin, in particular, circumvented this problem by proposing a much greater role for the party in creating and leading revolution. This party-centered revolutionary theory became known as Marxism–Leninism (see LENINISM).

Beginning in the 1920s, the rigidity of scientific Marxism produced a range of dissenting humanist approaches—initially in the work

of Georg LUKÁCS, Karl Korsch, and Antonio GRAMSCI. These writers brought Marxist analysis into areas of cultural production, IDEOLOGY, and aesthetics, for which scientific Marxism had little use. By the 1930s, moreover, the rise of FASCISM and Stalinism had obliged a major reconsideration of both the role of class struggle and the dynamics of revolution in the West. The most significant response to this dilemma was the emergence of the FRANKFURT SCHOOL—a group that included Max HORKHEIMER, Theodor ADORNO, Walter BENJAMIN, Herbert MARCUSE, and later Jürgen HABERMAS. These theorists situated the disastrous fascist and communist projects within a broader critique of modern society rooted, as Horkheimer and Adorno argued, in the triumph of instrumental reason. Collectively, they presented modern society as a total system that integrated the state, capitalism, and the CULTURE INDUSTRY.

Another prominent direction of Marxism in the West involved the critique of Stalin and Leninist revolutionary practices on the part of an increasingly independent Eurocommunist movement. Although the dissolution of the Soviet Union and the capitalist transition of many of the remaining Communist regimes has all but ended Marxism as a significant force for revolutionary change, many of the assumptions of Marxist analysis—especially the centrality of economic factors—have diffused to the point of ubiquity in the social sciences. Marxism remains an especially strong influence on theories of social constructivism and histories of human subjectivity.

masculinity   The forms of behavior associated with the male sex, as opposed to the biological difference that defines the sexes. Masculinity is primarily a cultural product; it exhibits a great deal of variation among and often within cultures, where its specific requirements and normative power may vary. The cultural production of masculinity has been a subject of widespread interest in SOCIOLOGY and CULTURAL STUDIES in recent years, following the broad turn toward issues of SEXUALITY and GENDER inaugurated by FEMINISM and continued recently by gay studies. Some of the traditional notions of aggressivity, competitiveness, and sexual promiscuity that structure many concepts of masculinity have also been the subject of sociobiological research. The exact line between biological and cultural sources of behavior, as well as the effects and variability of such biological factors, remains a subject of considerable interest and debate among researchers.

mass society   A description of modern, industrial society as a mass of undifferentiated and alienated individuals. Mass society became an object of concern in the early nineteenth century and initially reflected a shift in the nature of elitist fears for the body politic. Where the "tyranny of the majority" once expressed fears of disruptive mobs and demagogic rule, the new forces of modernization implied stronger leveling tendencies that threatened to eliminate the values traditionally identified with social aristocracy—especially excellence and individuality. Fear of the mob gave way to fear of the conformist, degraded mass.

Although much of this early work was broadly liberal in character—Alexis de TOCQUEVILLE is the principal example—it proved eminently compatible with certain forms of elitism and CONSERVATIVISM (see ELITE AND ELITISM). Conservative accounts, such as José ORTEGA Y GASSETT's *Revolt of the Masses* (1930), typically focused on the intellectual and cultural poverty of mass society, in which judgment sinks to the lowest common denominator. This was (and is) sometimes accompanied by contempt for broad-based democracy and nostalgia for a more hierarchical social order—views that Fascist movements in the 1920s and 1930s were quick to appropriate, as happened with the work of Gaetano MOSCA and Vilfredo PARETO.

Marxist and renewed liberal versions of mass-society critique emerged largely in response to Europe's authoritarian turn in the 1930s. In an effort to explain the appeal of NAZISM, FASCISM, and COMMUNISM, liberal social scientists such as David RIESMAN *(The Lonely Crowd*, 1950) and William Kornhauser (*The Politics of Mass Society*, 1960) emphasized the decline of traditional religious and moral attachments, and the rise of sophisticated propaganda techniques that could manipulate the mass and achieve consent. The Marxist FRANKFURT SCHOOL contended as early as the 1940s that a mass society of alienated individuals was the inevitable product of a CULTURE INDUSTRY that served the interests of capitalism.

These generally monolithic views of mass culture have been superseded by a range of newer approaches. CULTURAL STUDIES have devoted considerable attention to the segmentation of markets and cultural niches in modern society,

and to the diversity of practices of interpretation that render direct, mass manipulation difficult. This more supple model of IDEOLOGY has, to a degree, been corroborated in recent research on Nazi and Soviet TOTALITARIANISM, which challenges the model of mass indoctrination that supported much of the early work on the subject. Resistance to authoritarian regimes since the 1960s, moreover, has frequently been grounded in elements of mass culture, complicating notions about the political implications of mass society and the technologies of mass culture.

master status   The status position that provides the basic structure of an individual's social identity and that dominates in instances of conflicts between statuses. An individual's master status may be rooted in occupation, race, or sex; it may be dependent upon age, appearance, illness, or any other central feature of a person's place in society. Moreover, it may change with time. The concept was developed initially by sociologist Everett Hughes in his studies of the significance of race in American society, and it has played a part in subsequent research on status and roles since the 1950s.

mater   See *PATER AND MATER.*

material culture   The totality of objects produced within a given CULTURE, including technological, artistic, and ritualistic artifacts. In methodological terms, material culture is especially central to ARCHAEOLOGY and related anthropological subfields where other types of data are lacking. Since the 1960s, the study of material culture has also become an important subfield of historical research.

materialism   In common usage, *materialism* describes the privileging of material comforts over spiritual, ethical, and philosophical concerns. In its philosophical sense, *materialism* holds that speculative thought, social processes, and institutions are directly shaped by the physical world; as such, materialism takes issue with IDEALISM—the belief that external reality cannot be understood apart from consciousness, or, more radically, that some ideas or categories of understanding exist prior to experience. The roots of materialist thought can be traced to India in the seventh century BCE and to ancient Greece (as represented in the thought of Leucippus, Democritus, and Epicurus). The Early

Modern version of materialism is attributed primarily to Thomas HOBBES, who used principles of mechanics and geometry to ground his philosophical system. Later works by David HUME and John LOCKE are important contributions to the materialist tradition, while critiques by George Berkeley and Immanuel KANT contributed some of the key texts of idealism. The debate between materialism and idealism formed a central dialectic in modern thought that continues to this day.

In social thought, a significant turn in this debate was Ludwig Feuerbach and Karl MARX's contestation of Georg HEGEL's philosophy of history. Hegel claimed to have privileged neither the subject (as in the transcendental idealism of Kant) nor the object (as in the empiricist or materialist traditions). He claimed that the development of consciousness and knowledge evolved immanently through the material conditions of history, while at the same time determining them. Marx, drawing on Feuerbach, claimed to have "stood Hegel on his head, or rather, on his feet" by arguing that changes in material conditions—most importantly in the modes of economic production—led to changes in speculative thought (as well as in legal and political systems, aesthetics, ethics, and all manner of social relations). Whether or how these "superstructural" elements in turn alter the material "base" of historical development has been at the core of debates between various schools of Marxist thought ever since (see Louis ALTHUSSER, DIALECTICAL MATERIALISM, Antonio GRAMSCI, and HISTORICAL MATERIALISM). The Marxist turn also gave rise to a lasting subfield in SOCIOLOGY—the sociology of knowledge (see Karl MANNHEIM). In the theory and practice of non-Marxist social science, the materialist perspective has been carried forward by various schools of BEHAVIORISM, POSITIVISM, and REALISM; it has been most directly opposed by NEO-KANTIANISM and POSTMODERNISM.

matriarchy   A society in which women exercise political and/or social dominance. Several nineteenth-century theories of societal evolution claimed that matriarchy (sometimes known as *mother right*) was one of the earliest stages of societal development and that it was succeeded by *patriarchy*, although this schema no longer has much currency. It is worth noting that matriarchy does not imply MATRILINEAL DESCENT (a kinship system that accords privileges according

to descent along the female line) or that matrilineal societies are matriarchies.

matrifocal   Or mother-centered. Refers to a family structure in which the mother plays a dominant role.

matrilateral   Describes relations on the mother's side of the family. Distinct from *matrilineal*, which refers more specifically to a line of descent or inheritance through women.

matrilateral cross-cousin marriage   The marriage rule in some societies that prescribes the marriage of a man to his mother's brother's daughter, or inversely, a woman to her father's sister's son. Once thought by anthropologists to be a widely followed prescription in some marriage systems, matrilateral cross-cousin marriage is now recognized to be, in most such cases, an ideal that does not reflect the actual choices of most marriage partners.

matrilineal descent   Descent or inheritance through the female line.

Mauss, Marcel   (1872–1950) One of the major figures of twentieth-century ANTHROPOLOGY in spite of the fact that he never received a doctorate, had no regular teaching position for most of his career, conducted no fieldwork, and published no book-length studies of his own. His influence lay, rather, in a number of brilliant essays spread across a wide range of topics and in his leading role among the collaborators and students of Emile DURKHEIM, the dominant French sociologist of the early part of the century and Mauss's uncle. Much of this work centered around Durkheim's journal, *Année sociologique*, in which he played a prominent role after 1898. Later in his career he became an institution-building figure in his own right, cofounding the Institut d'Ethnologie and gaining admittance to the Collège de France.

In these diverse capacities, Mauss published hundreds of book reviews, facilitated the work of other social scientists, and taught many of the best students of the next generation of French social scientists, including Claude LÉVI-STRAUSS, Louis DUMONT, and Roger Bastide. His writing extended many of the functionalist insights of Durkheim and, in turn, made significant contributions to the FUNCTIONALISM of Bronislaw MALINOWSKI and A. R. RADCLIFFE-BROWN.

Mauss's early work focused primarily on comparative religion—a field to which he contributed a number of seminal essays on SACRIFICE, MAGIC, and primitive forms of CLASSIFICATION.

After Durkheim's death in 1917, Mauss became the principle representative of Durkheimian social science. He focused increasingly on broad issues of social organization and the integration of different dimensions of social research—particularly at the intersection of ETHNOLOGY and SOCIOLOGY. The best known of these contributions is "The Gift" (1925), which analyzed the forms of obligation inherent in primitive and modern systems of exchange, and emphasized the role of exchange in producing social cohesion. His account of the category of the person also achieved wide recognition, and exemplified the neo-Kantian dimension of Durkheimian sociology (see NEO-KANTIANISM).

McDonaldization   A term coined by the sociologist George Ritzer to describe the particular form of RATIONALIZATION and standardization that structures increasingly large areas of social life in the United States and the world more generally (*The McDonaldization of Society*, 1993). McDonald's, Ritzer argued, pioneered the application of Fordist principles of scientific management and homogenization to the service industry, in a form that has been adopted by a growing range of service providers, from journalism to education (see FORDISM). A standardized, widely available but low-quality product becomes the norm, differentiated largely on the basis of advertising. Ritzer's theory draws heavily on Max WEBER's notion of rationalization and on recent work on post-Fordism. It also shares ground with FRANKFURT SCHOOL critiques of mass culture.

McLuhan, Marshall   (1911–1980) McLuhan reached a large audience in the 1950s and 1960s with his theories about the relationship between media technologies and CULTURE. At the broadest level, he believed that the direction of social development and the nature of human experience—up to and including the organization of the senses—was largely determined by the dominant media technologies of the age. It is in this respect, as a general determinant of social possibilities, that "the medium is the message"—the medium carries with it certain possibilities and limits of expression.

McLuhan identified three major historical shifts in media technologies: (1) the invention of the phonetic alphabet, which elevated the written word to prominence in human society; (2) the development of the Gutenberg printing press with movable type, which, he argued, contained the kernel of the principle of mass production; and (3) electronic communication, beginning with the telegraph, which he claimed restored a powerfully sensual dimension to communication. This last point was the basis of his unusual comparison between television as a medium that engaged the imagination and extended the human senses and *print*, with its rational, linear constraints. He argued further that television was a "cool" or participatory medium, as distinct from "hot" media, which excluded the possibility of audience response.

For McLuhan, the proliferation of electronic media in the modern era had a profound internationalizing effect, creating, in another of his well-known phrases, a "global village" of shared information—if in obvious ways not always shared interests. McLuhan's major works include *The Mechanical Bride* (1951), *The Gutenberg Galaxy* (1962), *Understanding Media* (1964), and *The Global Village* (1989).

Mead, George Herbert   (1863–1931) An American sociologist and philosopher who sought to combine BEHAVIORISM and PRAGMATISM in the study of human interactions. Mead's early work was strongly behaviorist in its emphasis on the direct observation of external behavior and, more generally, on the processes by which behavior was learned. He was also among the central protagonists of pragmatism, together with William JAMES, John DEWEY, and C. S. PEIRCE. This side of his work grew in prominence and engaged him in the study of symbolic communication, which required interpretation that went beyond the strictures of behaviorism. It laid the foundation for SYMBOLIC INTERACTIONISM, although the label was introduced by his students. It also influenced other theoretical approaches to communication and the construction of knowledge through social experience, including ETHNOMETHODOLOGY. During his career, Mead published numerous articles but no books. After his death, some of his students assembled four books from his lectures and drafts, including the influential *Mind, Self, and Society* (1934).

In this and other works, Mead developed a systematic theory of the *self* that emphasized the centrality of the reflexive capacity of human beings. He rejected the notion that the self is something possessed innately and focused instead on how it develops in and through social processes. Mead distinguished two stages through which the self develops in response to interactions with others: (1) childhood is marked by a *play stage*, in which children learn to adopt the attitudes of specific others—playing the role of a parent or a fireman, for example; (2) this is followed by a *game stage*, in which children begin to generalize from specific others to the broader attitudes of the community or society. Children thus begin to understand their selves as defined in relation to a generalized, societal other. This *generalized other* represents the organized attitudes of the whole community, permitting children to think about what people in general will think about their actions. In this way, children can assess themselves in terms of cultural norms and values. For Mead, human behavior was thus always under a certain internalized supervision, regardless of the presence or absence of specific others.

In conceiving these processes, Mead distinguished between two aspects of the self: the "I" and the "me." The distinction can be conceived, in part, as separating the self as the subject of action from the self as the object of action (inscribed in and acted upon by the social world). The "I" is the spontaneous and creative power, while the "me" is the reflexive self (the socialized aspect of the self that situates action within a context of perceived expectations). Mead did not consider the "I" or "me" as discrete entities but as constantly interacting phases of the same social process of self-construction. His emphasis on this perpetual construction, reinforcement, and internalization of expectations became the cornerstone of the symbolic interactionist tradition in SOCIOLOGY.

Most of Mead's career was spent at the University of Chicago, where he influenced the generation of sociologists that dominated American sociology during the 1920s and 1930s (see CHICAGO SCHOOL OF SOCIOLOGY). Mead's other major works include *The Philosophy of the Present* (1932), *Movements of Thought in the Nineteenth Century* (1936), and *The Philosophy of the Act* (1938).

Mead, Margaret (1901–1978) A student of Franz BOAS at Columbia University and the lead-

ing figure of the CULTURE AND PERSONALITY MOVEMENT in ANTHROPOLOGY during the 1920s and 1930s. Mead gained a wide popular audience with her anthropological studies of adolescence, sexuality, and socialization in Pacific basin societies. Chief of these were *Coming of Age in Samoa* (1928), *Growing Up in New Guinea* (1930), and *Sex and Temperament in Three Primitive Societies* (1935), which emphasized the primacy of CULTURE over biology in organizing patterns of social life related to sexuality and maturation. Her work owed its popularity not only to its accessible style but also to the ways in which she used her findings to comment on the cultural patterns of American social life. In the same period, she conducted pioneering ethnographic work in Bali (with Gregory BATESON) that integrated traditional ethnographic methods with photography, film, and the analysis of music and dance. By 1940, her ethnographic work was largely over. During World War II, she became involved in a variety of government-sponsored, war-related research projects, including what would prove a long-running study of diet and international DEVELOPMENT. After the war, her continued interest in patterns of personality and her disinclination to further fieldwork led her into collaboration with Ruth Fulton BENEDICT, whose Research in Contemporary Cultures program was promoting the study of national character and personality types in societies "at a distance," when more direct means of study were difficult or impossible.

Mead became an increasingly public figure, lecturing frequently, writing a monthly magazine column, participating in working groups, and testifying before Congressional committees. She worked as a curator at the American Museum of Natural History in New York, taught graduate courses at Columbia University, and continued to publish. With *Culture and Commitment* (1978), she established herself as an authority on relations between the generations. Mead's work continues to be popular and, especially following challenges to her conclusions about Samoan society by Derek Freeman (1983), the subject of considerable academic debate. Mead's other major works include *And Keep Your Powder Dry: An Anthropologist Looks at America* (1942), *Male and Female* (1949), *New Lives for Old: Cultural Transformations, Manus, 1928–1953* (1956), *Ruth Benedict* (1974), and her autobiography *Blackberry Winter* (1972).

measurement The gathering of empirical data on the values of indicators that represent underlying concepts or analytic variables. Inflation, for example, may be measured by gathering data on the prices of each of several specific goods. In this case the prices are the indicators, and the specific records of them the measurements. As the example suggests, measurement involves two challenges: fitting the indicators appropriately to the concepts, and gathering sufficiently accurate data. Data on the price of cars or gasoline alone, for example, may not provide a good measurement of overall inflation and may need to be complemented by data on other kinds of goods, such as food, clothing, or housing. Moreover, price data may be very precise (if it is collected frequently for a representative sample of transactions, for example) or vague, if, for instance, it is collected for purchases made only during summer sales.

Measurement is thus a key concern for empirical social science. Greater precision is often sought by quantification—assigning numerical values to data—but this is not always possible. Thus, some measurements note only qualitative distinctions (like differences in color). Even quantitative measurements may be limited to nonnumerical relationships (like larger or smaller), although more accurate measurement is usually sought. Every method of measuring, however, introduces its own potential biases or limits. Researchers need to choose not only appropriate methods of empirical observation but also appropriate methods of assigning numerical values.

Statisticians usually distinguish between four main types of numerical scale: nominal, ordinal, interval, and ratio scales. In a *nominal scale*, numbers provide a way of distinguishing between observations—but have no *cardinal*, or real, value. The key feature of an *ordinal scale* is sequence, exemplified by techniques that rank preferences among things. Both nominal and ordinal scales measure *qualitative* differences, which generally cannot be assigned meaningful numerical values.

An *interval scale* is an ordinal scale in which the numbers do indicate specific magnitudes, such as equal units. Fahrenheit and Celsius temperature is measured on an interval scale. *Ratio scales* include a zero point that permits the proper ratios of values to be maintained. In such cases, the value 1 represents a tenth of the value 10, and 10 a tenth of the value 100. This is not true of temperature (with the exception of the Kelvin scale). The measurements of weight and distance are the most common examples of ratio scales.

Measurement also raises questions about RELIABILITY and VALIDITY. The first refers to the ability to accurately repeat the results of an experiment or research project; the second, to the appropriate fit of the indicator measured to the analytic variable or concept and to the appropriateness of the methods of measurement to the subject under study. The choice of scale can have a major effect on both questions—especially when highly qualitative issues (such as attitude research) are approached with higher-order quantitative methods. A wide range of research techniques and statistical methods exist, too, for controlling and analyzing the VARIABILITY of results.

mechanical model and statistical model A distinction drawn by Claude LÉVI-STRAUSS between two modes of analysis that differ primarily in the scale on which they treat a topic. A mechanical model, according to Lévi-Strauss, is composed of the specific mechanisms (marriage rules, taboos, etc.) that adequately describe a situation; a statistical model, in contrast, is a mode of abstraction that is appropriate when simpler rules are nonexistent or more difficult to observe (such as contemporary marriage patterns).

mechanical solidarity As defined by Emile DURKHEIM, the form of social solidarity associated with small-scale, premodern societies that have relatively little differentiation of labor. As a consequence, such societies are also characterized by a high degree of uniformity. This uniformity implies both a relative independence of the social units from one another (in the case, for example, of subsistence farming) and, at the same time, a strong group consciousness. For Durkheim, modernity can be measured, in part, by the transition from mechanical solidarity to ORGANIC SOLIDARITY. The latter characterizes modern, highly differentiated societies in which social solidarity derives from the interdependence of the parts.

median voter theorem Also Black's Theorem. For a set of choices on which a group will vote, the theorem demonstrates that the choice preferred by a majority of voters over all other choices will be the choice preferred by the *median voter*. As the name implies, there is a requirement that the voters can be positioned according to their preferences. Additionally, the choices must be orderable along a single dimension, such that for every voter, preferences are *single-peaked*. In other words, voters' valuations of the choices decline on either side of their most-preferred option. If this condition holds, then the choice most preferred by the median voter will be preferred by a majority of voters over all other choices. The intuition is fairly clear in the case of the ideological spectrum from liberal to conservative: Assume that each voter has an optimal ideological preference for his candidate, and that candidates who are either more or less conservative are less attractive than one who represents this ideological *ideal point.* (That is, we assume that the attractiveness of a candidate falls the further away—in either direction—he or she is from the voter's ideal.) If we arrange voters according to their ideological ideals, a candidate whose position matches the ideal of the median voter would be undefeatable in a two-way contest. The median-voter theorem strongly predicts that candidates will tend toward positions in the political center.

mediation Intervention aimed at resolving conflicts through negotiation. Mediation differs from *arbitration* in that there is no previous agreement between the parties in dispute to accept the recommendation of the mediator. Mediation can be requested by the antagonists or volunteered by a third party. In international disputes, mediators may be representatives of states or international organizations such as the United Nations. Mediation is also commonly used to resolve industrial conflicts between labor and management.

medicalization The process of identification of an undesirable social condition or mental state as a medical problem subject to treatment. Studies of medicalization point to the historical and cultural specificity of many "diseases," such as—at different times—alcoholism, homosexuality, juvenile delinquency, and depression.

melting pot A widely used metaphor for the process of assimilation of diverse ethnic groups into the mainstream of American society. The term is drawn from the title of a play by Israel Zangwill (1909), and the concept quickly became a central part of the representation of American society at home and abroad. Nonetheless, research on immigration, ETHNICITY, and RACE has drawn attention to its many limitations—especially the implication of a seamless process of integration

into a singular American culture, and the elision of large minority groups that neither immigrated nor met with easy integration, such as African Americans and Mexican Americans.

mental map Popularized by the geographer Peter Gould in the mid-1960s, mental maps are a way of representing the perceptions and images that people have of other places—in the case of Gould's major study, of regions of the United States. Gould argued that studying such perceptions was crucial to understanding the decisions that people made with regard to space and location. He argued further that empirical studies could reveal the character of these maps and that these could be statistically extended to larger, collective levels. The notion of mental maps has achieved considerable currency in the field of BEHAVIORAL GEOGRAPHY, although some of the larger claims made by Gould and others for their utility have generated debate, especially regarding their analytical purchase on actual behavior. The term ENVIRONMENTAL PERCEPTION is also used to designate this subjective experience of place, although usually with reference to other concepts in geography, such as *landscape.*

The term *cognitive map* has been used in a related sense to describe the points of reference—not only spatial but potentially including things, images, and ideas—that orient people in their daily lives. This concept also has roots in human GEOGRAPHY, although it has achieved wider circulation in recent arguments about the dislocating effects of POSTMODERNISM.

mercantilism A diffuse but important school of economic thought that guided much of European economic development from the mid-sixteenth to the mid-eighteenth century. Mercantilism was strongly associated with the emerging commercial classes (whence the name), which sought to influence state policy in ways that would bolster manufacturing and exports, and limit imports. Early versions tended to equate national wealth with holdings in gold, and thereby justified export policies that would boost the inflow of precious metals. These included tariffs on imports and low-interest rates for business loans. Conversely, they discouraged extractive industries, such as agriculture. Mercantilist policies also had an important political dimension in their support for population growth, which would both depress wages and fill the armies of acquisitive monarchs, and in the establishment of the colonial system as a massive for-profit enterprise.

Mercantilist policies were widely, though haphazardly, implemented throughout Europe in the seventeenth and early eighteenth centuries. By the late eighteenth century, however, a new generation of economic thought had coalesced around a critique of the intellectual foundations and political cronyism of mercantilism. This became known as CLASSICAL ECONOMICS, associated primarily with Adam SMITH and David RICARDO. As Smith pointed out, mercantilism postulated a zero-sum game of international trade, in which one nation's gain was another's loss. It actively encouraged government intervention in support of industry—sometimes through general policy measures but often through inside deals that accorded monopoly rights to individuals, especially in the area of trade. Domestic consumption was viewed as a *wealth-decreasing* activity, providing a justification for low wages. The inflationary effect of increasing specie inflow on prices was ignored. These issues underwrote the classical tradition's support for free trade and its vision of sustained economic growth, in which all partners in the international trade system could benefit.

merger   The process by which two or more corporations become one. Mergers may be of several types: *horizontal* (between competitors), *vertical* (between a supplier and its customer), *conglomerate* (between companies with no complementary markets or production processes), and *hostile* (a stronger business absorbs another against its will). The motives for mergers are diverse and include monopolistic efforts to reduce competition, cost reduction through ECONOMIES OF SCALE, diversification to reduce a firm's dependence on its existing line of business, the favorable capital-market treatment accorded to larger firms, and the desire to revive or rejuvenate failing businesses by the infusion of new management and personnel. The methods of effecting mergers also vary. Usually, one of the corporations buys the property and stock of the other(s). In other cases, the merging companies exchange bonds or options.

meritocracy   A social system in which STATUS reflects talent and effort rather than inheritance or identity categories such as CLASS, GENDER, or RACE. Although the term was popularized by the sociologist Michael Young in the 1960s, the concept is an old one. It was anticipated as early

as PLATO's *Republic* and gained new impetus from the rise of INDIVIDUALISM in the modern era. Meritocracy emphasizes equality of opportunity and generally the value of competition, but it has no particular investment in the equality of outcome. In fact, most advocates expect and defend at least some inequality of outcome, based on differences in talents and effort. In this context, economic and occupational research in sociology has addressed the question of the extent to which actual inequality reflects merit. It has proved difficult to establish a shared definition of merit, however, and to measure actual merit under many circumstances.

A major argument in favor of meritocracy is that it is assures a high degree of SOCIAL MOBILITY, as talent is permitted to rise to the top. The idea of advancement based on merit, however, presumes some independent criteria of judgment. Modern societies commonly use educational credentials and standardized tests as proxies for merit. In his classic book, *The Rise of the Meritocracy* (1958), Young asked whether some societies were, in fact, moving toward a system of rule by the highly educated, and whether this was inherently more just than other systems of distributing social power. This raises two distinct questions. First, are aptitude tests and/or success in school valid measures of merit; second, are there other factors besides intelligence and hard work that determine who succeeds in school?

Questions about the VALIDITY of such measures are troubling on several grounds. Notably, it is doubtful that there is a single phenomenon of intelligence that equips people equally for the many different kinds of work they might do or the decisions they might make—aesthetic, political, moral, technical, and the like. Relatedly, it is not clear why intelligence or achievement in school should outweigh on-the-job performance, or willingness to work hard.

Education research, especially, has focused on the external factors that contribute to success in school. Many of these studies have shown that CULTURE, family, and social networks play a large role in determining a student's commitment to schooling and, consequently, shape outcomes. The quality of schools frequently shows strong correlation with income, and the sense of future opportunities, which underlies academic investment, may similarly vary. Many critics of meritocracy focus on the ways in which meritocratic systems disguise persistent forms of discrimination by class, race, and other sources of social stratification. This often occurs by means of disadvantages in background, which are then reproduced and reinforced through the schools. This view of meritocracy is strongly associated with Pierre BOURDIEU, although it is held by other contemporary critics of structural inequality as well.

Despite the difficulties associated with actual attempts to ensure meritocracy, the idea remains a powerful social ideal in the modern world. In many respects, the critiques offered by researchers such as Bourdieu retain this ideal and amount to demonstrations that meritocracy has not been achieved. The question of whether there could ever be a completely valid and context-independent measure of merit is perhaps more fundamentally troubling. Theorists are also troubled by the question of whether the distribution of social status solely on the basis of merit would be just, even if it could be measured. One reason is that it is not clear how much inequality in rewards or power should follow from any particular difference in ability or effort. The idea of meritocracy offers an account of who should be on top in society—but not of how unequal society should be.

Merriam, Charles Edward (1874–1953) An American political scientist, reformer, and late in his career, pioneer of BEHAVIORALISM in the social sciences. Merriam devoted much of his career to studying and attempting to reform city politics in Chicago—largely as a Progressive determined to modernize the city's institutions and eliminate the forms of systemic corruption that dominated Chicago politics. He was an alderman for six years and ran for mayor (unsuccessfully) on the Republican ticket in 1911. In later years, he held positions on federal government research committees, including the Research Committee on Social Trends and the President's Committee of Administrative Management (under Presidents Herbert Hoover and Franklin Delano Roosevelt, respectively).

For Merriam, behavioralism involved a "tendential" approach to analyzing political behavior that avoided some of the determinism common in other behavioralist claims. Merriam argued that generalizations about political behavior could be drawn from observation, but that these were restricted to outlining the range of possible outcomes—no fully determining explanations or evolutionary models were possible. Methodologically, Merriam advocated the use of a wide range of techniques developed in diverse fields, from

SOCIOLOGY to psychology to the natural sciences. His own research was marked by a strong emphasis on methodological rigor and empirical validation. This is especially visible in *Political Power* (1934), an application of European theories of political organization to American democracy, and in the more theoretical *Systematic Politics* (1945), an analysis of the organizational basis and systemic nature of political behavior in American society.

Merriam spent some forty years teaching political science at the University of Chicago, until his retirement in 1940. He helped to found the Social Science Research Council and had a profound influence on a number of political scientists of the next generation, including Walter Lippman, Harold LASSWELL, Herbert Croly, and V. O. KEY. Merriam's other important works include *American Political Ideals: Studies in the Development of American Political Thought, 1865–1917* (1920), *New Aspects of Politics* (1925), *Chicago: A More Intimate View of Urban Politics* (1929), and *The Making of Citizens: A Comparative Study of Methods of Civic Training* (1931).

Merton, Robert K. (1910–) One of the most influential American sociologists and a leader in modern science studies. Merton's contributions to sociological thought are diverse, though broadly influenced by the FUNCTIONALISM of the 1940s and 1950s. Although he had been influenced by the sociologist Talcott PARSONS since his student days at Harvard University, Merton argued that functionalism in the dominant Parsonian style was rigid and overly ambitious in its theoretical claims. He therefore developed a more flexible mode of functionalist analysis that sought to accommodate different and not always reducible "levels" of analysis (often called "structural-functionalism," and in some ways similar to the anthropological approach that used the same label). This flexibility took many forms, including differentiating among cultural, social, and psychological issues, distinguishing between manifest (intentional) and latent (unintentional) functions, and allowing that some practices were dysfunctional or destructive of social equilibrium.

Much of Merton's work was an exploration of the "unintended consequences" generated by social structures. Perhaps his most influential analysis in this regard was his typology of forms of DEVIANCE. The American emphasis on success, he observed, conflicted with unevenly distributed opportunities for social advancement. Those who had aspirations but not the means to achieve them experienced psychological strain that led to four potential responses: *innovation*, by which Merton meant criminal activity, cheating, or other unsanctioned means of achieving success; *ritualism*, typified by bureaucratic ossification and superconformity; *retreatism*, on the part of those who drop out of the struggle for success; and *rebellion* or other movements to effect social change. Merton's research on organizations and bureaucracy developed a similar point, arguing that the structure of bureaucracy encourages inflexibility and a strong tendency toward self-perpetuation—sometimes at the expense of the social function it is intended to serve. His interest in self-fulfilling prophecies also belongs to this set of concerns (see SELF-FULFILLING PROPHECY).

Merton was active in a number of other areas. With Paul LAZARSFELD at Columbia University, he produced innovative studies of the effects of the mass media, especially in regard to its role in strengthening the economic status quo and established social norms. Together they pioneered new research methodologies, including the "focus group," and built a tradition that sought close connections between theory and empirical research. In this context, Merton famously argued for *middle-range theories*, which he held should fill the gap between the sweeping and often highly abstract theory of sociologists such as Parsons and the undertheorized empirical work of much of American sociology (see MIDDLE RANGE, THEORY OF THE). For Merton, theories of the middle range should be informed by empirical data but also be generalizable to a wide range of situations; they should not attempt to theorize all of social life but rather, specific, widely recurrent patterns that occur in a variety of contexts.

Merton was also an influential researcher, teacher, and theory-builder in the sociology of science. His *Science, Technology and Society in Seventeenth Century England* (1935) was one of the founding works in the field. Although he built on and participated in broad interdisciplinary relationships (starting with George Sarton and Pitirim SOROKIN), Merton helped distinguish the sociology of science from historical and philosophical approaches to the subject. His work on science addressed many themes, including the shaping of scientific careers and the construction of reputations. He also sought to distinguish the contexts in which ideas first appear from those in which they take hold and become influential.

Although he was the author or coauthor of several books, Merton is best known for polished, meticulous, and impressively clear essays; the most renowned are collected in *Social Theory and Social Structure* (1949).

mestizo Originally, a person of mixed Spanish and Indian blood in Latin America—the product of *mestizaje*, "racial mixing." The term is now sometimes used to refer more generally to racially mixed persons. *Ladino* is the common Central American equivalent.

metacommunication Gregory BATESON's term for the dimension of human communication that involves setting the terms through which communication is to occur. In other words, *metacommunication* is "the reflection upon or framing of communication that accompanies communication." The concept is similar to Roman JAKOBSON's notion of PHATIC COMMUNION.

Methodenstreit Refers to a debate among German scholars in the decades prior to World War I regarding the methodological differences between the natural sciences (*Naturwissenschaften*) and the social or historical sciences (*Geisteswissenschaften*). One of the touchstones of this debate was the distinction between nomothetic and ideographic methods, first articulated by the philosopher Wilhelm Wildebrand (see IDEOGRAPHIC SCIENCE AND NOMOTHETIC SCIENCE). The former refers to the search for general laws of nature or society, the latter to the study of specific and unique events, such as historical writing or biography. The philosopher Wilhelm DILTHEY, in contrast, defended a more familiar division of the social and natural sciences based on a distinction between their objects of study. Max WEBER also participated in these debates, and drew from them his extensive use and defense of IDEAL TYPES. See also *GEISTESWISSENSCHAFTEN AND NATURWISSENSCHAFTEN*.

methodological individualism See INDIVIDUALISM.

Michels, Robert (1876–1936) A German sociologist known best for his work on what he called the "iron law of oligarchy," which holds that oligarchical structures eventually dominate any political organization, no matter what its political orientation. Michels developed this set of ideas in his influential *Political Parties* (1911), a study of the left-wing Social Democratic Party in Germany. His argument combined an analysis of specific empirical circumstances with a more general argument based on the implications of numbers alone—the larger an organization, the smaller the proportion of top leaders and the greater their distance from the "masses." Michels emphasized the process whereby the rank-and-file members of the party are gradually marginalized by a party bureaucracy that seeks to perpetuate its organizational structure. In many cases, he argued, the party comes to resist social change that threatens its operating rationale or structure. It becomes increasingly guided by the self-interest of the leaders (through a process of "embourgeoisement") and by intellectuals whose goals often differ from those of the majority of the members. Although he argued that such processes characterized all organizations, he was especially concerned with the decline of the revolutionary potential of left-wing parties; in this, he emerged as a radical counterpart to other contemporary theorists of elite rule, such as Vilfredo PARETO and Gaetano MOSCA, who reached many of the same conclusions in more overtly conservative terms. Michels eventually became more sympathetic to such positions, however, and expressed some approval of the Fascist party in Italy, where he accepted a university position.

Michels addressed a range of other subjects in his writing, although never as influentially. This included research on mass society, morality, NATIONALISM, and the role of intellectuals. Some of this work has been collected and translated into English as *First Lectures in Political Sociology* (1949).

microeconomics Studies the decisions of individuals and firms in markets for goods, materials, and services, as well as their strategic interaction in both market and nonmarket environments. Modern economic research is usually categorized into microeconomic and macroeconomic domains—the latter distinguished by its focus on the aggregate variables affecting the national economy, especially consumption, investment, inflation, government expenditure, and interest rates (see MACROECONOMICS). The division between microeconomics and macroeconomics primarily reflects a difference in the scale of analysis: the aggregation of microeconomic activity broadly defines the macroeconomy. In practice, the methods of microeconomics and macroeconomics differ: macroeconomics works with aggregated empirical data and models of aggregate interactions rather than with individual production and consumption functions, although modern macroeconomic theory is grounded in microeconomic foundations.

Microeconomic analysis tends to restrict its object of inquiry to individualized production and consumption decisions—typically holding constant the role of economy-wide institutions, such as the government.

Microeconomics pursues many of the classical economic concerns with supply, demand, and equilibria in markets, and is generally based on the neoclassical paradigm of maximizing behavior: maximization of profits by producers and suppliers of goods, and maximization of utility by purchasers and consumers (see NEOCLASSICAL ECONOMICS). Microeconomics, consequently, is centrally concerned with the analysis of prices (determined by the intersection of supply and demand curves) and more broadly the allocation of resources—consumption and savings decisions of consumers, production decisions by firms, and so on. Generally, the neoclassical foundation of microeconomic analysis suggests that such choices are governed by equating marginal cost with marginal benefit (see MARGINAL ANALYSIS). Consumers will purchase a good up to the point where the cost exceeds the added value of the additional good; producers will produce up to the point where costs exceed the added income derived from the sale of the good.

middle range, theory of the A concept developed by Robert K. MERTON to fill a gap between the sweeping and often highly abstract theory of such sociologists as Talcott PARSONS and the undertheorized empirical work of much of American sociology. According to Merton, theories of the middle range should be informed by empirical data but be generalizable to a wide range of situations. They should not attempt to theorize all of social life but rather specific, widely recurrent patterns that occur in different contexts. Merton offered several theories of the middle range on such topics as REFERENCE GROUPS, DEVIANCE, and BUREAUCRACY.

migration A central preoccupation of SOCIOLOGY, human GEOGRAPHY, and other fields that treat the subjects of immigration and diasporic experiences. Migration refers most generally to patterns of movement from one place to another. There are several important concepts in migration study. A *migration region* is a bounded geographical area within which there is considerable migratory movement. The movement of nomadic groups, regulated by seasonal or other changes in subsistence patterns, generally falls into this category. *Chain migration* is a process of continuous migration from one place to another over time, such as the disproportionate settlement of certain regions of the United States by immigrants from particular areas of Europe. *Return migration* describes the reverse of this process: the return of relocated members of groups (especially ethnic groups) to their homelands. Emigration and immigration are forms of migration defined by PUSH-AND-PULL FACTORS in their countries of origin and destination, respectively. Such factors can be economic, political, cultural, or environmental in nature; they can exist between countries, as much of the modern history of immigration has shown, or within regions, as in the case of the post–World War II migration of African Americans from the rural South to Northern cities.

One important tendency in the recent sociology of immigration has been to treat both sides of the migratory experience as parts of an integrated whole, with effects in both societies. This permits a less ethnocentric view of what determines the social trajectory and social condition of immigrant groups. Diasporic studies, paradigmatically of the African and Jewish experiences, have also been a major contemporary avenue of migration research, integrating questions of population and cultural diffusion, as well as cultural syncretism and the persistence of group identity.

Milgram, Stanley (1933–1984) An American social psychologist best known for his experiments on obedience to AUTHORITY. These revealed the astonishing degree to which authority figures could produce compliance among members of the general public in what they believed to be acts of cruelty and torture. The experiments placed subjects in the position of administering progressively higher electrical shocks to a second person (an accomplice of Milgram, who feigned the appropriate responses) when that person failed to respond correctly in a series of memory tests. As the level of the shocks increased, the subject was pressured by the experimenter to continue. On average, 65 percent of subjects continued to the maximum level of "punishment" (some 450 simulated volts) in the face of protests and ultimately signs of agony on the part of the "learner." Milgram performed numerous variations of this experiment in order to isolate the variables that affected compliance: distance of the authority figure, distance of the victim, signs of resistance, and so on. The experiments themselves were controversial for the mental anguish they inflicted on their

subjects and, for a time, earned Milgram suspension from the American Psychological Society. Yet they have proved enormously influential both in challenging the view that perpetrators of cruelty and atrocities are monsters and in understanding the nature of crimes that demand complicity and participation by large sectors of society, such as GENOCIDE.

Milgram was expert in conceiving simple experiments that revealed unexpected dimensions of the social bond. He originated the idea that everyone in the United States was linked by, at the time, at most five degrees of separation. He studied variations in how different cities were perceived and examined differences in interpersonal behavior in cities and small towns. Milgram's major works include *Television and Anti-Social Behavior* (1973) and *Obedience to Authority* (1974). Many of his essays and short studies were collected in *The Small World* (1989) and *The Individual in a Social World* (1992).

military-industrial complex (MIC) A term first used by U.S. President Dwight D. Eisenhower, in his 1961 farewell address, to describe the alliance between the military, government officials, and corporate elites. Eisenhower warned that the confluence of interests in these three groups had accelerated the militarization of peacetime civilian society (see IRON TRIANGLE). The term was quickly appropriated by critics of the U.S. defense industry, who argued that increased government spending on defense diverted funds away from needed social programs and heightened the ARMS RACE with the Soviet Union. In the post–COLD WAR era, analysts point to continued high levels of U.S. defense spending as evidence of the distortions caused by the military-industrial complex. In Britain, France, Russia, China, Israel, and Brazil, MICs are associated with a burgeoning arms trade with developing countries. Defenders of the military-industrial complex point out that it is a crucial source of technological innovation (e.g., in computers and aviation) and that military expenditures help counterbalance economic downturns, both at the national and local level.

Mill, John Stuart (1806–1873) A British philosopher, social scientist, reformer, and humanist who elaborated the social and economic dimensions of UTILITARIANISM. Son of the economist James Mill, John was educated from childhood to be the successor and intellectual inheritor of Jeremy BENTHAM, the utilitarian philosopher and Mill's godfather. Mill achieved this goal in many respects, although he developed a more supple brand of utilitarianism that integrated historical and cultural factors into the question of how individuals calculated their self-interest.

Mills wrote on a wide range of issues, from philosophy to logic, government, women's rights, and POLITICAL ECONOMY. His *System of Logic, Ratiocinative and Deductive* (1843) provided what some consider to be the most important contribution to social science methodology prior to Emile DURKHEIM's *The Rules of Sociological Method* (1895), primarily due to its rigorous attempt to separate out valid from invalid forms of deduction as the basis for "a general science of man in society."

On Liberty (1859) is Mill's most significant work of political theory, outlining a version of LIBERALISM that he believed would best guarantee utilitarian principles. Chief among his stipulations were the maximum freedom of thought, speech, association, and lifestyle consistent with the equal exercise of those rights by others. *Utilitarianism* (1861) explained more of Mill's general theory of value and ethics and argued that happiness and unhappiness constituted the most appropriate standard for right and wrong—again provided such choices were consistent with respect for the same privilege in others. Mill specified, however, that some forms of happiness are more valuable than others and thereby set up a moral distinction between different pursuits. In *The Subjection of Women* (1869), Mill argued for the emancipation of women and established himself as a leading liberal feminist of his time.

Mill was also the last great classical economist (see CLASSICAL ECONOMICS). His *Principles of Political Economy with Some of Their Applications to Social Philosophy* (1848) was the leading textbook in the field for more than forty years. In general, Mill considered himself a socialist and favored a more equitable distribution of property. Nonetheless, he believed that production and distribution were unrelated. This view challenged David RICARDO's idea that "laws of distribution" determined the fortunes of an economy, as well as Karl MARX's ideas about the necessity for reorganization of the relations of production. Like Adam SMITH and Ricardo, Mill believed in the long-run tendency of the profit rate to fall. However—against the classicists—he argued that the profit rate was determined by the people's willingness to accumulate and by the security of investments. With continuing social and economic progress, the economy tends toward a stationary state, which Mill considered preferable to the classical portrait of permanent self-interested struggle. Consistent with his broader view of utilitarian behavior, Mill also challenged the strict classical faith in the individual capacity for rational self-interest in the marketplace.

Mill's other major works include *Essays on Some Unsettled Questions of Political Economy* (1844), *Considerations on Representative Government* (1860), and *Examination of Sir William Hamilton's Philosophy* (1865). He was also influential in introducing Alexis de TOCQUEVILLE's work to English-language readers.

millenarianism or millennialism   The belief in an end time or transfiguration that leads to the perfection or salvation of humanity. The terms draw most directly on a prophecy in Chapter 20 of the New Testament's *Book of Revelation*, which announces that Jesus' second coming will inaugurate a thousand-year period of divine rule (although the idea also has roots in Jewish and, later, Islamic thought as well). Because the prophecy promises a period of tribulation before the Second Coming, some believers, called *premillenarians*, associate the advent of the millennium with revolution and cataclysmic social change. Although biblical premillenarianism is linked most strongly to Christian sects, premillenarian strains are visible in many broad-based secular movements as well, from Nazi anticipations of a thousand-year Reich to the Marxist predictions of a history-ending proletarian revolution (see COMMUNISM; and NAZISM).

Postmillenarianists take a less apocalyptic view of the end of history: here the emphasis is on historical progress toward a state of perfection and the gradual victory of good over evil. Disasters and cataclysms play a role in many versions (as trials, proofs, or punishments), but less centrally than in premillenarianism. Postmillenarian currents run throughout the Enlightenment doctrine of the perfectability of humankind, and in the many political and philosophical movements that carry it forward—Progressivism, SOCIAL DEMOCRACY, and others.

Comparative study of millenarian social and religious movements suggests that there are a number of precipitating factors that at least partially account for phases of rapid growth and decline. Common to many millenarian movements is the experience of crisis, often stemming from culture shock as societies modernize, or as they come into contact with cultures significantly different from their own (see IMPERIALISM AND EMPIRE).

Mills, C. Wright (1916–1962) An American sociologist best known for his studies of STRATIFICATION and sociological method. Mills's *The Power Elite* (1956) and *The Sociological Imagination* (1959), in particular, continue to be influential. He also cultivated, and to a degree achieved, a role as a public intellectual engaged with the major political issues of the day. In this vein, he wrote two books aimed at the general public, *The Causes of World War Three* (1958) and *Listen Yankee* (1961)—the latter a defense of the Cuban revolution as an experimental third way between COMMUNISM and CAPITALISM.

In emphasizing social conflict and stratification, Mills drew heavily upon Karl MARX and Max WEBER. Karl MANNHEIM and the philosophical pragmatism of C. S. PEIRCE also strongly informed his approach. Mills was nominally and somewhat loosely a Marxist—only late in his life did he describe himself as a "plain Marxist." Throughout his career, however, he was a radical and a provacateur who challenged the antidemocratic concentration of power in American society. *The Power Elite* was the most emphatic of these efforts and remains a remarkably powerful description of the small, interlocking group of corporate executives, government officials, and military leaders that, Mills argued, held effective control of major social and political decision making in the United States.

The Sociological Imagination was a more general call for sociological humanism. The title refers to the ability to see through the surface of isolated personal experiences to perceive the underlying social issues. For Mills, it was the essential sociological talent—the ability to see connections and patterns. Mills positioned this account against the "abstracted empiricism" that he associated with the sociologist Talcott PARSONS and other representatives of "grand theory."

As one of the most prominent left-wing intellectuals of his day—and one of the few radicals with a major university appointment—Mills was an important influence on the New Left of the 1960s. A significant part of the Mills legend involves his volatile personality and his constant professional (or, defenders would say, political) difficulties with colleagues and administrators at Columbia University, where he taught from 1945

until his death in 1962. Mills's other major works include *The New Men of Power* (1948), *White Collar* (1951), a study of the middle class, and *The Marxists* (1962).

minimax theorem   States that there is always a rational solution to a precisely defined conflict between two people with opposing interests. Such a conflict is often referred to as a two-person zero-sum game (see ZERO-SUM GAMES). The solution is rational in that both players believe they are doing the best they can, given the nature of the conflict. Proved by John von NEUMANN in 1928, it is one of the most celebrated theorems of GAME THEORY.

minimum efficient scale   Refers to the least quantity that can be produced in a cost-minimizing way. For example, a factory may produce most cheaply at full capacity, so that any level of production using less than one factory would not be efficient. But two factories could produce larger quantities equally cheaply.

minister   In a parliamentary system, a minister is a member of the LEGISLATURE who serves as an EXECUTIVE official. Foremost among government ministers is the head of government, called the prime minister, premier, or chancellor. He or she appoints the government's executive body, the CABINET, generally subject to the approval by the lower house of the legislature. A minister's executive role involves advising the head of government, organizing the business of the legislature, and overseeing the work of a ministry or department (ministers "without portfolio" lack a department of their own and assist heads of government). Ministers are also primarily responsible for writing new legislation and steering it through the legislature. As governments have expanded into more policy areas, and as policymaking and implementation have grown more complex, this formal model has given way to an informal reliance on civil servants to perform many, if not most, ministerial duties. Democratic theorists often contend that too many of the traditional functions of executive and legislative government have been ceded to bureaucrats.

minority government   A GOVERNMENT that has the support of less than half the members of the LEGISLATURE. Minority governments are often politically unstable because they can be toppled by a united opposition. The absence of a legislative majority also commonly leads to difficulty in passing policy initiatives into law. In both cases, coalitions and swing votes play an important role.

minority group   A social group or category of people who are stigmatized and/or discriminated against on the basis of that identity. The term generally refers to situations in which such groups are numerical minorities with respect to dominant cultural or ethnic majorities. Yet it sometimes includes all groups that suffer from disparities of power or unequal treatment, such as women, who constitute a numerical majority in the United States.

mirror stage   A developmental stage in Lacanian psychoanalysis in which the infant gradually begins to understand itself as possessing a delimited and unified body, distinct from the world around it. Jacques LACAN explained this process through the example of a child's discovery of its image in a mirror—the initial recognition of itself as a discrete being—although he emphasized that this mirroring need not be literally conceived. For Lacan, the mirror stage occurs between the ages of six months and eighteen months, during which the infant begins to be inscribed into the world of selfhood, difference, and symbolic behavior—ultimately language. See also PSYCHOANALYSIS.

Mises, Ludwig von   (1881–1973) An economist of the Austrian school who built on the foundations laid by Eugen von Böhm-Bawerk and Carl von Menger. Von Mises's greatest contribution was to complete a neo-Austrian integration of MICROECONOMICS and MACROECONOMICS, especially in relation to the theory of money.

Born in Austria-Hungary, von Mises received his Ph.D. from and subsequently taught at the University of Vienna. The rise of NAZISM prompted him to relocate, first to the Graduate Institute of International Studies in Geneva, and then to New York University.

Von Mises's first important work was *The Theory of Money and Credit* (1912), in which he demonstrated how the marginal utility of money (in relation to the utilities of other goods and to the money supply) determines its "price." Austrian economists had struggled with the idea that money has a price, since it is typically demanded not for its own utility but in order to purchase other goods. Von Mises showed that every unit of money that people hold is derived from a nonmonetary commodity that does have value, and that money provides the means of translating that value into purchasing power. His analysis also asserted the *nonneutrality* of money—refuting the conclusions of CLASSICAL ECONOMICS on this question and anticipating the work of John Maynard KEYNES. In the same context, he revived David RICARDO's proposition that there is no unique optimal level of money supply. Because money is only a medium of exchange, a rise in the total quantity of money reduces the purchasing power of each unit but does *not* affect the economy in other ways. This led von Mises to condemn as inflationary the banking practice of holding only a fraction of deposits as reserves. Instead, he advocated a banking system based on 100 percent reserves.

One of von Mises's most notable contributions was his theory of the BUSINESS CYCLE. Von Mises asserted that the cycle is driven by the inflationary expansion of credit. This artificially lowers interest rates, inducing overinvestment in capital goods and underinvestment in consumption. Any reduction in credit reveals this imbalance, and a period of liquidation follows. In this process, the credit distortion is eliminated and the economy is restored to its original state. Although von Mises's theory attracted attention as a possible explanation of the Great Depression, much of his work was overshadowed by the KEYNESIAN ECONOMICS revolution of the 1930s. Nonetheless, he influenced many economists in Europe and the United States, among them the most famous proponent of the Austrian school, Friedrich von HAYEK.

misogyny   The hatred of women. Misogyny plays a central role in many feminist accounts of patriarchy (see FEMINISM). Major theorists of misogyny and its social consequences include Kate Millet, Adrienne Rich, and Andrea Dworkin.

Mitchell, Wesley Clair   (1874–1948) The youngest of the founders of the institutionalist school in economics, which argued—against the neoclassicists—that social institutions played a central role in shaping economic behavior. While Thorstein VEBLEN spelled out the institutionalist philosophy and John R. COMMONS focused on the social reforms implied therein, Mitchell provided institutionalism a more formal, empirical basis—especially through his analysis of the BUSINESS CYCLE.

Mitchell was born in Illinois and studied at the University of Chicago. He taught at several universities, including the University of Chicago, the University of California–Berkeley, Columbia University, and the New School for Social Research. Unlike many economists of his time, Mitchell believed that economics was a science of human behavior rather than of wealth. Against the increasingly abstract modeling of the neoclassical school (see NEOCLASSICAL ECONOMICS), he advocated using statistical research to understand and develop solutions to social problems. Toward this end, Mitchell founded the National Bureau of Economic Research, which continues to produce important empirical research.

Mitchell developed an extensive statistical analysis of the business cycle that supported and strengthened Veblen's pioneering work (much of which was based on speculation). According to Mitchell, the most serious economic problem was the recurring imbalance between production and distribution. While scientific advances had revolutionized the nature and capabilities of production, the methods of distribution had changed much less. Imbalances in this area lead to gluts in the market and to the underutilization of resources. Another dimension of this problem, Mitchell argued, was the lack of effective coordination among firms. While profit maximization guides coordination within a firm, broader coordination is the result of natural selection in the struggle for economic survival. Mitchell claimed that frequent crises and depressions constituted proof that this process was defective. The solution, he argued, was national planning of a kind that would counter the adverse effects of business fluctuations while preserving economic freedom.

Mitchell's account of the business cycle is developed mostly in two books, *Business Cycles and their Causes* (1913) and *Business Cycles: The Problem and Its Setting* (1927). He agreed with the general view that the chief motivation of business activity was profit maximization, but he argued that this was suspended during crises, when solvency became the main objective. He argued further that fluctuations are systematically generated within the economy—not by exogenous disturbances, as many economists believed. The economy, overall, is both dynamic and evolutionary: it experiences cumulative changes as it passes from one cycle to the next.

Business cycles sweep through the modern economy, Mitchell argued, because of the high degree of interdependence among firms. At the bottom of a depression, the first signs of revival generate optimism among entrepreneurs; anticipated profits rise, and production increases throughout the economy. As new capital is commissioned and new plants are built, however, the pressure on resources in the economy leads to rising costs of production. This reduces net profits in the later stages of prosperity. Lower profits presage financial difficulties in all sectors of the economy, and firms reduce production in order to remain solvent. This is the beginning of the next downturn. Eventually, recession produces efforts to cut waste and eliminate inefficient businesses. This reduces costs, increases anticipated profits, and points the way to recovery.

mixed government   A form of rule that combines elements of monarchic, aristocratic, oligarchic, and democratic government. Mixed government was the classical solution endorsed by PLATO, ARISTOTLE, and Niccolò MACHIAVELLI to the threat of domination of the state by one class or person. Each argued that the concentration of power in any one class or person would lead to abuses and produce resentment among the other classes. The only effective check on power, in this context, was to grant a share of it to each class. Modern systems of SEPARATION OF POWERS preserve this principle.

mixed strategy   In GAME THEORY, a *mixed strategy* involves making use of more than one action with a positive probability. That is, rather than choose a single strategic option, a player in a game would randomize his or her choices among several viable options. A *pure strategy*, in contrast, involves staying with one course of action.

MNC (multinational corporation)   See CAPITALISM; and MULTINATIONAL.

M'Naghten rule   The classic criteria for insanity in criminology. The M'Naghten rule holds that a person is legally insane if he or she cannot tell right from wrong at the time of the offense. The rule derives from the 1843 murder trial of Daniel M'Naghten in Great Britain.

mobilization   Two general definitions apply: (1) Preparation for war, including calling reserves to active duty, placing armed forces on a state of alert, shifting economies to a war footing, and where necessary, implementing a draft; and (2) The organization of political action on a large scale. The American civil rights movement of the 1950s and 1960s and the international antinuclear movement of the 1970s and 1980s are examples of the latter. Studies of mobilization tend to focus either on human participants or on the resources necessary to their collective action.

mode of production   A fundamental concept in Marxist thought, *mode of production* refers to both the skills and technologies available to a given society and to the way in which the labor process is organized. Together, these factors determine the way in which SURPLUS VALUE, or value beyond the needs of subsistence, is extracted from the labor process. Although never strictly defined by Karl MARX, the term plays a crucial role in his effort to differentiate historical epochs in terms of their economic organization. Marx noted wide historical variations in these arrangements, and he identified a number of distinct modes of production: PRIMITIVE COMMUNISM, SLAVERY, the ASIATIC MODE OF PRODUCTION, FEUDALISM, CAPITALISM, and COMMUNISM. In all cases, Marx argued, the mode of production fundamentally determines the other dimensions of social organization: it is "the real foundation on which rise legal and political superstructures and to which correspond definite forms of social consciousness" (*A Contribution to the Critique of Political Economy*, 1859). This is the essence of Marx's claim that the economic "base" determines the cultural and political "superstructure"—a relationship that has been widely debated within and outside the Marxist tradition. The dominant tendency, from Max WEBER to such relatively classical Marxists as Louis ALTHUSSER, has been to revise the strict determinism implicit in Marx's argument. Both Weber and Althusser ascribed various kinds and degrees of AUTONOMY to other dimensions of society—although for Althusser such autonomy was only relative and, in the last instance, remained subject to economic determination. This potential autonomy and even reciprocity has had profound implications for Marxist-inspired notions of social change, which placed the onus of social transformation on changing the mode of production. See also CAPITALISM; and BASE AND SUPERSTRUCTURE.

modernity   Theories of modernity generally plot a shift from the traditional European societies of the Middle Ages to the political, cultural, and economic forms that characterize Western and, arguably, industrialized society more generally in the present day. For many writers, this process implies a dramatic transformation of beliefs about the SELF, expectations of the future, and understandings of human potentialities. What precisely defines modernity, however, has been a matter of nearly constant debate among social theorists and is arguably the core question underlying the rise of social science itself. Michel FOUCAULT's answer to this question takes the questioning itself—the interrogation of our condition *as modern*—as the fundamental feature of modernity. Foucault traces this sensibility back to the late eighteenth century and especially to its expression in the work of Immanuel KANT. More conventional answers tend to identify the rise of a number of key modern features in the course of the seventeenth century: the discourse of reason and rationality, with the concomitant growth of science; the emergence of industrial production and CAPITALISM, accompanied by greater social mobility, an emerging BOURGEOISIE, and the spread of literacy; the consolidation of NATION-STATES, state bureaucracies, and the shift of political legitimacy from divine monarchical rule toward the sovereignty of the people; the secularization of society and the retreat of religious worldviews; and the development of a new fabric of selfhood rooted in concepts of individuality, autonomy, and freedom. Whether all of the elements of modernity still pertain and whether they can be grasped in a systematic way are questions that have been at the center of debates about postmodernity (see POSTMODERNISM). Some theories treat postmodernity as an epoch that replaces modernity, while others challenge the classic theoretical attempts to conceive modernity as a coherent project or unified set of historical tendencies.

Although the terms have been used interchangeably by some writers, "modernity" is distinct from the related terms *modernization* and *modernism*. Modernization is the closer of the two in meaning, generally referring to the process of transformation of technologies, economies, and institutions in the modern period. It is not typically used to refer to the philosophical and humanistic dimensions of modernity. The term *modernism*, in contrast, refers primarily to the literary and artistic developments of the late nineteenth and early twentieth century—quintessentially those projects that isolated and experimented with the problem of form. It has also been used to describe the preoccupation with authenticity that characterizes much of the philosophy and social theory of the period and/or the pursuit of novelty as a basic value orientation.

modernization theory The dominant explanation in the 1950s and 1960s of how broad-based economic and social DEVELOPMENT occurs. Modernization theory explained development as the result of the systematic RATIONALIZATION of a society's technology, social structure, and values. The development of a dynamic market-based economy was also accorded a large role in this process as a generator of wealth at the societal level and as a distributor of wealth across the society. Modernization theory informed much of the economic policy of the industrialized West toward developing countries in the post–World War II era.

Although modernization theory was a broad and often internally contentious school of thought, it revolved around two core issues. First, most proponents believed that modernization involved a series of societal stages, beginning with traditional societies and ending with the "age of high mass consumption," in W. W. ROSTOW's typology (*Stages of Economic Growth: A Non-Communist Manifesto*, 1990 [1960]). Scholars debated which aspects of modernization drove the others, but there was general agreement that technology, social structure, and values were closely interrelated. For this reason, policy applications frequently prioritized the broad-based development of physical infrastructure, political institutions, and education. In theory, these would catalyze a process of self-sustaining development of all dimensions of social and economic life.

Modernization theory often schematized the differences between traditional and modern societies—although again there were many debates over particulars. Traditional societies were generally identified with some combination of religiosity, rural life, limited technology, low social mobility, ascribed wealth, arbitrary and ineffective political power, and diffuseness of social, economic, and political roles. Modern societies displayed higher levels of secularization, urbanization, science and technology, education, social mobility, achieved wealth, democratic government and the rule of law, and role specialization and differentiation. Such distinctions often implied psychological parallels: the modern individual was empathetic, oriented toward achievement and mobility, open to diverse interests and social settings, and possessed of "ego flexibility."

The world contained societies at many stages along this continuum.

Contemporary historical research has tended to complicate such accounts of modernization—in part by demonstrating the variety of distinct paths to development in European history. Many social scientists now also speak of multiple modernities as a way of appreciating the often striking differences between developed countries, as well as the disparities of uneven development within countries. This has undermined the notion that the rationalization of certain dimensions of society necessarily entails rationalization of others. Japan, for example, is notable for the persistence of a traditional culture of ascribed status within a modern industrial economy. There are numerous cases in which urbanization and growing literacy have led to *increased* religiosity—as in the case of fundamentalist Islam among the emerging Arab middle class. Nonetheless, few would dispute that modernization is a process that contains important patterns and relationships among its several facets. The interdependence of economic development and political development continues to be an important subject of research, as is the question of convergence in occupational patterns and industrial structures among industrialized societies.

In the 1960s and 1970s, *dependency theory* and later WORLD-SYSTEMS THEORY (associated with Immanuel WALLERSTEIN) emerged as powerful critiques of many of the assumptions of modernization theory. Both treated modernization theory's schematic approach to societies as largely irrelevant to the problems of underdevelopment. Dependency theory tended to focus on patterns of co-optation between first- and third- world political and business elites, in which development created unbalanced growth that enriched multinational corporations and their local clients but left the vast majority of the population with declining standards of living. World-systems theory explained modernization and underdevelopment in terms of a global capitalist system of core and peripheral nations (see CORE-PERIPHERY MODELS). Both asserted that modernization theory "blamed the victim" by exporting features of Western societies to countries where they were inappropriate—especially via foreign-aid projects and private development—while ignoring the systematic exploitation of those countries by multinational capitalism.

Most of the countries that were poor when modernization theory was conceived have remained so—despite interventions to increase education and political capacity, or to improve the infrastructural basis for urbanization and industrialization. Dependency and world-systems explanations seemed to provide an adequate explanation of that outcome. In the 1990s, however, modernization theory was partially rehabilitated due to the failure of many of the policies associated with the Dependency school (e.g., import substitution, protectionism, AUTARKY) and the dramatic successes of East Asian newly industrializing nations. In this context, many academics and policymakers embraced development strategies linked to participation in a growing global economy. This has refocused attention on endogenous variables such as physical infrastructure and political capacity (sound fiscal management, CIVIL SOCIETY, governance) that ostensibly help poor countries to participate effectively in a global market. Among the new features is widespread recognition that fair terms of trade between developing and developed nations are crucial to development. The new consensus also reflects a shift away from grandiose modernizing projects, such as huge dams or highway systems, in favor of programs aimed at increasing literacy and health. This has led to a version of modernization theory that is much more attuned to the local conditions and social context of development—although this is often submerged in the free-market and capital-investment agendas of major international players such as the International Monetary Fund. See also DEPENDENCY.

moiety   Describes the division of a society into two halves, organized by separate LINEAGES. Such structures have been observed in aboriginal Australian and South American tribal societies. They usually involve a principle of EXOGAMY—members of one moiety marry those of the other. The term itself derives from the French *moitié*, meaning "half."

monarchy   A state in which sovereignty is permanently vested in a single person—typically a king, emperor, or other figure. Although monarchy is generally associated with hereditary rule, this is a variable practice that in Europe took centuries to establish. European monarchs were originally far more circumscribed by other centers of power—especially the church and the quasi-independent ARISTOCRACY. Succession could, and often did, result in struggles among aristocratic contenders. Where political regimes were stable, European monarchs relied on a code

of honor that bound aristocrats and royalty in a web of mutual obligations and preferments. As Charles-Louis MONTESQUIEU observed, this same code encouraged aristocrats to limit the power of their leaders in order to protect time-honored rights and privileges. As the European monarchical system gradually consolidated its power in the Medieval and Renaissance periods, it reduced the independence of the aristocracy, elaborated the doctrine of the divine authority of kings, and marginalized the role of the church in secular affairs. The absolute monarchy instituted by Louis XIV in France completed this centralization of power and achieved the identification of the king with the state itself. The disintegration of the lower tiers of aristocratic authority that accompanied this centralization ultimately isolated many monarchical regimes from forms of popular support—as Louis XVI discovered in 1789.

Monarchy was the principal target of the democratizing wave that swept Europe in the nineteenth and twentieth centuries. Nearly all were abolished in the successive rounds of war and revolution, from the French Revolution and the Napoleonic Wars, to the revolutions of 1848, to World War I. Modern despots and dictators reproduce many of the structures of authority of the old monarchical systems, but almost always rely on popular rhetorics of legitimation that bear little resemblance to the aristocratic rights of kings. Even where monarchies were preserved or reinstated, they were reduced to a limited, constitutional mode in which real authority was shared or, as is most often the case today, assigned to other governmental institutions, such as parliament. Most contemporary monarchs serve as symbolic heads of their respective states and have very little true political power. See also ABSOLUTISM.

monetarism   A school of economic thought that holds that the quantity of MONEY in the economy has a major influence on economic activity and the price level. For monetarists, it follows that the best instrument of macroeconomic control is central bank control of the money supply. Monetarism is frequently associated with Milton FRIEDMAN and his influential study *The Quantity Theory of Money—A Restatement* (1963). Friedman argued that monetary policy was superior to Keynesian fiscal measures for stabilizing aggregate demand (see KEYNESIAN ECONOMICS). He proposed that government budget deficits be financed by issuing new money and that budget surpluses be used to reduce the money supply. Such countercyclical variation, he claimed, would help stabilize the economy.

In its early phase, monetarism was considered an extension of the *quantity theory of money*, which holds that changes in nominal prices reflect changes in the money stock and in the velocity of circulation of money (the ratio of aggregate expenditures to the money stock). Monetarists recognized, however, that these are only short-run effects. In the long run, output is determined only by real (nonmonetary) factors and the velocity of circulation is stable. For this reason, control of the money supply provides a tool against INFLATION—the rise in nominal prices.

Analysis of U.S. data confirmed the existence of a stable relationship between the money stock and aggregate expenditures. In contrast, the Keynesian theory of a stable relationship between consumption and income could not be proved empirically. A more novel claim of monetarism is that the money supply has a stronger permanent effect on GNP (gross national product) than fiscal variables—a view supported empirically by economists at the U.S. Federal Reserve Bank. Monetarists argue that although budget deficits and surpluses can affect the demand for money, such effects are small given the low interest elasticity of money demand. Government spending simply crowds out private spending, with the result that deficit spending has little effect on aggregate demand.

For monetarists, monetary policy does not suffer this limitation: money, they argue, is a commodity that is substitutable for a wide range of other commodities and financial assets, with the result that monetary policy has a direct effect on aggregate demand. This contradicts the Keynesian view that the effect of monetary policy is largely limited to financial assets, which generate at most a weak effect on aggregate demand. The monetarist link between money balances and aggregate demand is often called the *real balance effect*. It implies that if there is an optimal or desired level of real balances (the ratio of private money holdings to the price level), then an increase in the money supply will induce individuals to spend the excess money. This will raise the price level (and only the price level if the economy is at its full-employment level) and thus lower real balances. Changes in output and employment will occur in the short run, but the long-run effect will be neutral.

Most monetarists argue however, that given the lags involved in monetary effects and the lack of perfect foresight, it is difficult to correctly time countercyclical monetary policy. They believe that the private economy is basically stable and that an active monetary policy exacerbates, rather than smoothes, economic fluctuations. A stable monetary growth rate (as opposed to discretionary monetary policy) would avoid monetary sources of disturbances and insulate the economy from ill-conceived and badly timed government actions—the principle sources of instability in most monetarist accounts. Monetarism thus generally rejects attempts to reduce short-run fluctuations in economic activity. See MONETARY POLICY.

monetary base   Also, *high-powered money*. A term used to denote the monetary liabilities of a CENTRAL BANK. It consists of cash in the hands of the public and the cash reserves of the banking sector at the central bank. It is so called because it forms the base on which the larger superstructure of convertible bank deposits is built. A change in the quantity of these assets produces a larger than proportionate change in the bank-deposit component of the money stock; this is the effect of the credit or money MULTIPLIER. For example, when the central bank sells an asset through an open-market operation, the buyer pays the central bank with a check on his or her own bank, thereby reducing that bank's balance with the central bank. Since the central bank usually stipulates a minimum ratio of cash reserves at the central bank to demand deposits, this bank must sell an asset in order to restore its depleted cash balance. The second purchaser, in turn, pays by check from another bank and in the process transfers the cash shortage from the first bank to the second. In this way, the multiplier process continues and the initial open-market sale by the central bank causes a more than proportionate fall in bank assets and deposits—and hence, in the money supply.

monetary policy   Refers to government actions that change the cost of money and credit, usually implemented through the central bank for the purpose of stabilizing economic activity.

The main instrument of monetary policy is the ability to change the cost of credit, which influences many aspects of the economy. Raising interest rates will raise the cost of borrowing money (as well as the payoff to saving). This discourages consumption and investment and slows down economic activity. Central banks have a number of tools for controlling interest rates: buying and selling government bonds; changing the requirements for banks to hold cash reserves; and changing the rate at which they lend to private financial institutions, among others.

Governments can also increase the supply of money. Printing more money is now generally thought to have no bearing on the long-run economy, but may temporarily provide a short-run increase in economic output. See INFLATION for an extended discussion of the effects of continuous increases in the money supply.

money Anything that is widely accepted in economic transactions and in the settlement of debts serves the primary purpose of money as a medium of exchange. Money is also a medium of account, in that the prices and values of all other goods and services are expressed in terms of accounting units of money. Finally, money is a "store of value," held as part of an individual's assets.

Economists sometimes distinguish between FIAT MONEY, or money whose status derives from legal enactment, and *commodity money*, which has intrinsic worth as a commodity even without its legal status as tender. Paper notes are the chief example of fiat money—nearly worthless without their legal status.

money demand Refers to the amount of cash that individuals wish to hold, as opposed to holding wealth in other forms of assets. *Money*, in this context, usually refers to cash and checking accounts. Generally, the attraction of holding money is its *transaction value*. Money serves as a medium of exchange, and therefore allows one to purchase goods and services. There may also be speculative motives for holding money, if one expects that less-liquid assets will be more attractive to purchase in the future. At the same time, holding money is costly. It has no intrinsic value, and in holding cash, one gives up the opportunity to earn interest on other forms of wealth, such as bonds. Furthermore, inflation erodes the value of cash. During periods of high inflation, people will choose to hold less cash.

The aggregate quantity of money demanded is an important macroeconomic variable: if growth in supply outpaces growth in demand, inflation will rise. See also MONETARY POLICY.

money illusion A term that describes the failure of economic agents to distinguish between *real* and *nominal* changes in the value of money. For example, a change in both nominal wages and prices that leaves real wages unchanged should not affect the labor-supply decision of an individual. If it does, then the individual is said to be suffering from money illusion. Such illusion violates the so-called *homogeneity postulate*, which states that the demand and supply functions should be homogeneous of degree zero (i.e., they should depend on relative prices and not on absolute prices).

monogenism The doctrine that humanity has a single origin and constitutes a single species. The contrasting term is *polygenism*—the claim of separate origins for the different races. Debate between monogenists and polygenists played a crucial role in the emergence of ANTHROPOLOGY in the late nineteenth century. In the course of these debates, polygenism was marginalized, and anthropology became a field organized around monogenist principles. Monogenism made possible not only serious cross-cultural study but also evolutionary theories of society rooted in the assumption that CULTURE, not human capacities, was the primary variable. The sweeping theories of societal evolution that dominated nineteenth-century anthropology are the major legacy of this debate, and monogenism remains an implicit or explicit assumption of almost all anthropological work. See also ETHNOLOGY; and EVOLUTION AND EVOLUTIONISM.

monopolistic competition A theory developed concurrently by Edward Chamberlin (*The Theory of Monopolistic Competition*, 1933) and Joan ROBINSON (*The Economics of Imperfect Competition*, 1933) to address the divergence of actual markets from models of PERFECT COMPETITION or MONOPOLY. Monopolistic competition describes a market in which there are a large number of sellers who produce similar but differentiated products. Such products are *imperfect substitutes* for each other. In this context, each firm is a monopolist for its own particular product and faces a downward-sloping demand curve. Yet free entry into the market precludes the existence of supernormal or above-average profits. Short-run positive profits are bid away by the entry of new firms into the industry. In comparison to perfect competition, however, long-run equilibrium does not occur at the minimum of the long-run average cost curve: each firm produces its desired output level at more than the minimum cost. In this sense, monopolistic competition is inefficient.

monopoly A market with a single seller of a product for which there are no substitutes. Monopoly is thus the antithesis of PERFECT COMPETITION. Monopolies may arise out of grants of exclusive privilege by government (copyright or patent privileges), through business arrangements that limit competition in production or prices, or through exclusive control of a natural resource or technique.

A monopolistic firm can affect the price of its product by curtailing or expanding its production—also known as *monopoly power* in the market. Monopolists maximize profits by setting marginal revenue equal to marginal cost. In this case, the quantity sold is lower and the price is higher than under conditions of perfect competition. The monopolist can earn above-average or *supernormal* profits in these circumstances, even in the long run.

Although the greater virtues of competitive markets is a point of broad consensus among contemporary economists and policymakers, regulated monopolies have played an important role in many areas—especially in the provision of PUBLIC GOODS, such as energy, water, and mass transportation. Although competitive markets may provide lower overall costs to consumers, there is no guarantee that they will provide equitable treatment—especially in contexts where the provision of goods is more expensive, such as electricity or phone service in rural areas. Other economists argue that there are situations in which monopolies are the most efficient, inexpensive, and innovative producers of goods and services. Three advantages are cited: (1) natural economies of scale may yield lower costs of production when a single firm produces all the output. These *natural monopolies* sometimes occur when overhead or startup costs represent a high proportion of total costs; (2) monopoly firms may be more likely to speculate on expensive development of new technologies because there are no competitors to copy their innovations; and (3) monopoly firms have access to the financing typically required for innovative research and development. The question of innovation remains controversial and forms the basis of a number of prominent recent antitrust actions.

monotheism Generally speaking, the belief in one god. The concept has a long and somewhat checkered history in historical and anthropological debates about religion. Early evolutionary theorists (Edward Burnett TYLOR, Wilhelm Schmidt) argued that monotheism was a late stage in the development of religious thought, proper to relatively advanced or complex societies. Strict definition of the concept, however, has proved elusive, since religions such as Hinduism and Buddhism do not readily conform to either monotheistic or polytheistic criteria, and since even religions conventionally understood as monotheistic, such as Christianity, leave room for competing or secondary deities (such as Satan or the angels).

Monte Carlo method A method of repeated simulation of a stochastic model in order to investigate the properties of statistical techniques applied to it (see STOCHASTIC MODELS). The Monte Carlo method uses a hypothetical economic model with known parameters to generate artificial data (using random-number generators that mimic the random processes believed to generate the economic data). The techniques under investigation are applied to these artificial data sets to provide samples of inference. Since all aspects of the data are known, the reliability of the techniques and their performance under certain conditions can be gauged. The Monte Carlo procedure is adopted when analytical derivations of finite sample properties appear unfeasible.

Montesquieu, Charles-Louis de Secondat, Baron de (1689–1755) A major political philosopher, historian, and novelist of the French Enlightenment, often regarded as a founder of the social sciences. Montesquieu's claim to this last title rests primarily on *The Spirit of the Laws* (1748), an attempt to address the subjects of government, law, virtue, and human happiness through a broad comparative analysis of different nations and forms of government. Montesquieu built on the social contract tradition of Thomas HOBBES and John LOCKE by extrapolating human society from a primary "state of nature" (see SOCIAL-CONTRACT THEORY). He departed from them, however, in arguing that this transition could tell us little about the forms of government that were appropriate to a given people. No general or universal statements about government were possible, because human intelligence was limited by a diverse array of factors and was generally stirred into action only by the specific challenges of the environment. The "spirit of the laws" proper to each nation, consequently, depended on the ways in which the influences of local culture, mores, geography, and climate shaped human needs. Montesquieu nonetheless discerned three basic types of government: despotic, republican, and monarchical—founded on fear, virtue, and honor, respectively. He viewed despotism as an unjustifiable assault on natural law (defined by basic human needs such as self-protection) and therefore devoted most of his energies to analyzing the qualities of the potentially legitimate forms: republics and monarchies.

Montesquieu treated *virtue* as a corporate and conformist quality that tempered individual interest in the name of the state. He viewed *honor* as based on a clear sense of social difference that promoted individuality as well as hierarchy. Both virtue and honor were positive qualities, although in *The Spirit of the Laws* he gradually built a case against the conformist tendencies of the former. The best of both qualities, he argued, were found in England, where the pursuit of commerce and constitutional monarchy had achieved something like a happy balance between the two. Commerce, Montesquieu proposed, directed self-interest toward collective, national ambitions, while reducing the necessary conformism of virtue; moreover, it worked against prejudice and superstition, and instilled a general sense of fairness. The constitution, in turn, introduced a notion of SEPARATION OF POWERS that maintained the distinctions of rank while avoiding the dangers of monarchical power. Montesquieu believed that the value of commerce might be relatively easy to bring to France, although he did not have much hope for transplanting constitutional rule. The doctrine of the "separation of powers"—referring to the independence of the king, Parliament, and the judiciary from each other—proved to be the most important of Montesquieu's political legacies. It directly influenced the model of internal checks and balances among the three branches of government developed in the Constitution of the United States (1787–1789), as well as in the French constitution of 1791.

Montesquieu's other major work includes an epistolary novel, *The Persian Letters* (1721), which satirized the manners and the social and political institutions of France from the perspective of two traveling Persian gentlemen. Also prior to *The Spirit of the Laws*, Montesquieu wrote a history of Rome entitled *Considerations on the Causes of the Greatness of the Romans and Their Decline* (1734), which explored the relationship between republican virtue and self-interest. His work was perhaps most directly influential on Alexis de TOCQUEVILLE and, later, Emile DURKHEIM.

Moore, Barrington, Jr. (1913–) A major figure in comparative historical sociology, Moore devoted much of his career to the historical analysis of systems of government—especially the factors that influenced the emergence of democratic and totalitarian regimes (see DEMOCRATIZATION; and TOTALITARIANISM). His best-known work is *Social Origins of Dictatorship and Democracy* (1968), which examines the relationship between class structures and the formation of modern states. In his analyses of England, France, the United States, India, Japan, and China, Moore distinguished different forms of revolutionary action, including democratic "revolution from below," fascist "revolution from above," and communist revolution, which theoretically confronted both bourgeois and state power with a united peasantry.

Moore wrote that the democratic traditions of the United States, Britain, and France were largely dependent on the historical experience of bourgeois democratic revolutions, which had successfully destroyed FEUDALISM. Where feudal structures remained, revolution took an authoritarian direction, leading to FASCISM in Germany and Japan and to COMMUNISM in Russia and China. Moore also took pains to specify the nature of democratic government, which he characterized as the replacement of arbitrary by rational rule and the reliance on popular participation in the articulation of rules and laws.

Moore was a specialist of the USSR, and he contributed greatly to research on Soviet Communism. His *Soviet Politics: The Dilemma of Power* (1950) and *Terror and Progress: USSR* (1954) developed a functionalist analysis of the countervailing forces of totalitarianism and industrialization in post-revolutionary Russia. He suggested that the demands of industrialization had overwhelmed the ideal of a truly socialist society and precluded its development. Moore has also studied ethical issues, such as human cruelty (*Reflections on the Causes of Human Misery*, 1972) and the relationship between political authority and dissent (*Injustice*, 1978). Other works include *Political Power and Social Theory* (1958), *Critique of Pure Tolerance* (1965), and *Moral Purity and Persecution in History* (2000).

moral domain   See JURAL DOMAIN AND MOR-
AL DOMAIN.

moral hazard   Refers to the possibility that
policies or decisions may create incentives for
undesirable behavior. Moral hazards often arise
where the monitoring of contracts is difficult (see
AGENCY THEORY) or where policies diminish the
risks associated with certain kinds of behavior.

In economics, the term refers more technically
to situations in which economic agents do
not enjoy the full benefits of their actions or,
alternatively, fail to bear the full consequences
of them. This may arise from uncertainty in
decision making or from incomplete contractual
relationships. The presence of moral hazard
implies that the equilibrium governing individual
choices may be inefficient or, in the extreme
case, nonexistent. For example, bankruptcy laws
shelter those who take economic risks from
the full consequences of those risks: it provides
economic agents the option of defaulting on
debts. As a result, bankruptcy laws may encourage
too much risk taking. Similarly, auto insurance
coverage reduces the costs to individuals of
having accidents, presumably giving them an
incentive to drive less carefully. In this context,
insurance companies are constrained by being
unable to monitor the driving of the insured.
As a result, contracts covering such relationships
tend to be incomplete, especially when agents are
risk averse or when full responsibility for actions
cannot be assigned to a single agent.

mores   Cultural norms that articulate the most
basic social values about appropriate behavior and
that carry a strong sanction if violated. The nearly
universal prohibition against incest is an example.
Waving goodbye, on the other hand, is a lesser
norm—sometimes characterized as belonging to
the FOLKWAYS of a group or community. See also
DEVIANCE; and NORMS.

Morgan, Lewis Henry   (1818–1881) One of
the pioneers of modern ANTHROPOLOGY, Morgan
practically invented the field of KINSHIP studies
and became one of the most prominent theorists
of linear social evolution. He produced some of
the earliest and most valuable ethnographic studies of American Indian tribes—particularly the
Iroquois—which continue to be a point of reference for contemporary research. In addition, he
was an important figure in the institutionalization
of anthropology in the United States, creating the

anthropology section of the American Association for the Advancement of Science in 1875 and
becoming president of that organization in 1879.

Morgan was also entirely self-taught in these
matters. He conducted his research when his
legal career permitted it, mostly in the context
of a secret society that he formed with several
friends and modeled on the Iroquois League—a
confederation of Indian tribes. This research
eventuated in the ethnographic study *League of
the Ho-dé-no-sau-nee, or Iroquois* (1851), which
traced the significance of matrilineal descent
in the Iroquois political structure and living
arrangements.

By the 1860s, Morgan had accumulated a fortune that permitted him to retire and pursue his
research at his leisure. He continued to study
the question of kinship classification, discovering
unexpected similarities among some tribes and
even among different peoples of North America,
Asia, and the South Pacific. This data convinced
Morgan that kinship classification was an effective
means of analyzing and demonstrating relationships between groups on a global scale—a case
he made at length in *Systems of Consanguinity
and Affinity of the Human Family* (1871). The
key to demonstrating these relationships was the
notion of linear societal evolution, which allowed
Morgan to locate differences in kinship structure along a single line of historical progression.
This trajectory became the subject of his final
major work, *Ancient Society, or Researches in the
Lines of Human Progress from Savagery through Barbarism to Civilization* (1877), which became one
of the most influential statements of nineteenth-
century social evolutionary theory. Other writing
by Morgan includes *Houses and House-life of the
American Aborigines* (1881) and several ventures
into animal psychology, including *The American
Beaver and His Works* (1868).

Morgenthau, Hans   (1904–1980) A German-
born American political scientist, best known
as an advocate of REALISM in international
relations. Morgenthau's work, especially *Politics
among Nations* (1948), profoundly influenced
the field of INTERNATIONAL RELATIONS and the
American foreign-policy establishment. Realism,
as articulated by Morgenthau, involves the
recognition that the primary activity of both
individuals and nations is the pursuit of power.
All politics, he argued, can be reduced to "keeping
power, increasing power, and demonstrating
power." All societies, similarly, are in the process

of preparing for war, waging war, or recovering from war.

Morgenthau believed that politics in general and foreign policy in particular are determined by objective laws that can be uncovered through the study of human nature. As such, one can establish rational theories regarding the conduct of policy. Morgenthau recognized, however, that rational self-interest did not always guide international policy and that the resulting instability had in many cases been moderated by an underlying moral order—such as that which characterized the European-led world order of the seventeenth, eighteenth, and nineteenth centuries. Morgenthau stressed that a pluralistic view of human nature is required that included the recognition of this subjective moral dimension. Nonetheless, he was skeptical of foreign policy based on moral foundations—even on such values as peace—and argued for an enlightened and moderate understanding of national self-interest. In time, he hoped, a world government might supplant the competitive struggle among nations.

Morgenthau is often criticized and defended as a pure realist—an advocate of the self-interested pursuit of national power. This is certainly the side of Morgenthau's work that has had the greatest impact, but it neglects Morgenthau's emphasis on the need for underlying norms and his case for moving beyond the current international system. Morgenthau came to the United States from Germany in 1937 and spent his career at the University of Chicago. His other writing includes *Scientific Man vs. Power Politics* (1946) and *Politics of the 20th Century* (1962).

morphemes   Basic grammatical components of words that are used consistently (e.g., prefixes, stems, and suffixes). The concept has been an important tool in the structural linguistics of Roman JAKOBSON and others—especially in the effort to map the basic structures of difference within languages. See also LINGUISTICS.

mortality   The incidence of death, generally used by demographers and geographers as an aggregate statistic in population studies. Many circumstances affect mortality rates, but the most widely significant is age. Population studies often stratify mortality rates to account for the pronounced differences associated with early infancy and old age. Mortality rates for middle-aged populations, consequently, may be comparatively low. Since everyone dies at some point, the crude mortality rate is not very helpful analytically; the age-adjusted rate is more significant. Mortality rates are one of the principal determinants of population size, and play a key role in theories of the DEMOGRAPHIC TRANSITION between underdeveloped and developed societies.

Mosca, Gaetano   (1858–1941) An Italian political theorist known primarily for his theory of political elites. Mosca's most influential work was *The Ruling Class* (1896), which developed the argument that all societies, regardless of their organization or ideological claims, are ruled by small elites. Elite rule was not a positive goal for Mosca, but an inevitability rooted in the dynamics of large groups and parties. The best government, as he saw it, imposed clear rules on the behavior of its elite, including especially a powerful and active judiciary. Mosca was critical of MARXISM for ignoring the inevitability of domination; he also argued against totalizing theories of history. At the same time, he was critical of liberals for believing that INDUSTRIALIZATION would close the gap between the ruling elite and the masses, and he rejected efforts to transform elite rule into a basis for AUTHORITARIANISM. This last point was particularly visible in Mosca's antipathy for the Fascists, although they appropriated his notions of elite rule as a justification for power (as they did with his Italian contemporary, Vilfredo PARETO).

Like Pareto, Mosca emphasized the utility of social mobility and circulation in making elites more heterogeneous and in countering the tendency toward the bureaucratization and centralization of the ruling class. He thought that broad-based democratization was a bad idea and was scornful of popular leaders who secured mass support through "political formulae"—although he also argued that any successful elite was necessarily sensitive to popular issues. The key to success for any particular ruling elite was, in the end, its superior organization, without which it would soon be replaced by another. In addition to his work in political philosophy, Mosca was a jurist, politician, and administrator (all prior to the era of Fascist rule).

mother right   An early term for MATRIARCHY. From the German, *Mutterrecht*.

multicollinearity   An analytic problem that arises when two or more independent or explanatory variables in REGRESSION ANALYSIS are highly correlated with one another. The existence of multicollinearity reduces the precision with which parameters can be estimated and increases the variability of the estimates of those parameters.

multiculturalism   As a descriptive term, multiculturalism refers to the coexistence of people with many cultural identities in a common state, society, or community. As a prescriptive term, it is associated with the belief that racial, ethnic, and other groups should maintain their distinctive cultures within society yet live together with mutual tolerance and respect. Advocates of multiculturalism often propose going beyond traditional liberal principles of tolerance for members of other groups toward acknowledgment of their positive value.

The development of multiculturalism as an intellectual theme and social movement has been most prominent in the United States—although it has spread rapidly to other countries. Debates over the content of education in the 1970s and 1980s were pivotal in this process. These centered primarily around multiculturalist arguments for expanding the curricula to include the history and work of marginalized groups (e.g., African Americans, Native Americans, women, immigrants—and later Hispanics, Asians, gays, lesbians, and other minorities). They also urged enlarging the canon of "great works" to include texts originating outside the Western tradition. Perhaps most controversially, multiculturalism has been associated with campus movements to ban offensive speech, and with a much-maligned (and frequently exaggerated) drive for "politically correct" language and behavior (see political correctness).

Although debates in the U.S. educational arena were the most conspicuous sign of multiculturalism's growing influence during the 1980s and 1990s, the broader and deeper themes of inclusion and difference also pervaded transnational political and social discourse. In both Australia and Canada, multiculturalism has been institutionalized in laws that regulate relations among immigrant groups and between ethnocultural minorities and the majority culture. In a number of cases, group-specific rights have been established for the preservation of minority cultures.

Opposition to multiculturalism has come from many sides. Liberals and conservatives have claimed that multiculturalism's celebration of difference and its relativization of the Western tradition threaten social and political cohesion and encourage separatism among groups. Some have argued for a return to traditional liberal

individualism and to a renewed assimilationist ideal or transcultural humanism to buttress liberal society and its institutions (see LIBERALISM). Multiculturalism has undergone a number of internal critiques as well, especially regarding the essentialism implicit in many forms of group identification and the challenge it poses to strongly constructivist accounts of social identity. Some have charged that excessive emphasis on the representation of different groups undermines coalition building.

Despite these misgivings, multiculturalism has had a lasting effect on global political and social practices. In some respects, the battle is over: the educational curricula of many countries now include more attention to the contributions of the diverse groups that compose them (and human society more generally). The success of multicultural discourse in many societies reflects, in part, the unavoidable facts of massive international migration, cross-national integration (e.g., European unification), and lingering questions about the citizenship and autonomy of aboriginal groups.

multilateralism   A form of cooperation and conflict management among three or more states in such areas as international trade, disarmament, security, global environmental policy, and monetary relations. Early examples of multilateralism include the nineteenth-century Concert system (a loose group of European powers that regulated international disputes in the wake of the Napoleonic wars), maintenance of the gold standard, and initiatives to promote free trade. These comprised broad frameworks of rules and norms that governed interactions between states and nonstate actors. In the twentieth century, as the number of countries has grown and interdependence increased, informal multilateral regimes have frequently been supplanted by formal organizations such as the League of Nations, the United Nations (UN), the North Atlantic Treaty Organization (NATO), the World Trade Organization (WTO), and the International Monetary Fund (IMF). These organizations seek to structure interstate relations through mutually acceptable rules and principles and by resolving disputes through bargaining.

multinational   Commonly applied to corporations or organizations that have production facilities or branches in several countries. The rise of multinational capitalism has been a major subject of historical sociology—especially the work of the ANNALES SCHOOL and WORLD-SYSTEMS THEORY. See also GLOBALIZATION; and TRANSNATIONALISM.

multiple-indicator models The practice of using several different indicators of a latent or difficult-to-measure variable in order to enhance the validity of an analysis. Since each indicator is based on a different OPERATIONALIZATION of the conceptual variable, such models reduce potential bias. See also TRIANGULATION.

multiple-nuclei theory A theory of patterns of urban land use proposed by Chauncey Harris and Edward Ullman in 1945. The core of multiple-nuclei theory is the observation that different activities (industry, retailing, residence) have different locational priorities and special needs, such as access to transportation networks, water power, or residential areas. These needs will govern their distribution, Harris and Ullman argued, tending toward the creation of distinct nuclei, or clusters, for particular activities. Multiple-nuclei theory was one of three major models of urban land use to be developed in the period. The others are CONCENTRIC-ZONE THEORY and SECTOR THEORY.

multiplier Describes the disproportionate effect of changes in government spending, private investment, or other forms of expenditure in the economy. Increased expenditure generates a greater-than-equal change in national income because of the way that added money circulates through several rounds of wages, consumption, and investment. The multiplier most commonly describes the ratio of the change in national income to the initial change.

The *multiplier effect* occurs through the following process: expenditure raises employment and income in the capital-goods sector. Of the resulting rise in wages and profits, part is saved and the rest is spent on consumption goods. The greater the marginal propensity to consume, the greater the increase in demand for consumption goods produced in the capital-goods sector. This gives rise to a second round of increases in income and, subsequently, consumption. This cycle continues, and a smaller part of income is passed on at each stage. In time, the rise in income will be a multiple of the initial increase in investment expenditure. The ratio of the two changes—the multiplier—will be larger than one. The multiplier for an open economy (one that trades with other countries) is usually smaller than for a closed economy, because part of the increase in income is spent on imports, which does not raise domestic income and employment.

The term "multiplier" is used in a number of analogous contexts. The money multiplier, for example, describes ratio of the change in the money supply due to a change in excess reserves in the banking system. If the central bank buys bonds, it injects cash into the economy. That money, deposited in banks, gives them an excess of cash relative to their required reserves. They can then loan out the excess, which itself will be deposited in a bank. Thus, the same cash makes several trips through the banking system, multiplying the initial central bank action. The upper limit on the multiplier is just the inverse of the required reserve ratio for banks, but the actual multiplying effect may be reduced if banks decide to hold excess reserves or individuals choose to hold cash.

multipolar See BALANCE OF POWER.

Mundell–Fleming model An extension of the traditional IS-LM model to the open economy, developed by Robert Mundell and J. M. Fleming (see IS-LM ANALYSIS). It has been used to show the effects of monetary and fiscal policies on the exchange rate and on national income under a variety of exchange-rate regimes. The model has been the starting point for subsequent work in open-economy MACROECONOMICS and exchange-rate determination.

mutually assured destruction (MAD) See ARMS RACE.

Myrdal, Gunnar (1898–1987) An influential Swedish economist and political sociologist, perhaps best known for his pioneering book on American democracy and race relations, *The American Dilemma* (1944, with R. M. E. Sterner and Arnold Rose). *The American Dilemma* provided the most thorough analysis of racism and its consequences in the United States to date, and called upon Americans to resolve the contradiction between their racialized society and democratic political ideals. It played a major role in the civil rights movement and helped initiate wider research on the subject of race in American society.

Myrdal was also one of the best-known members of the Stockholm school of economics, which developed an analysis of the macroeconomy that anticipated the work of John Maynard KEYNES in many respects. One of Myrdal's important contributions to the Keynesian revolution was the distinction between *ex ante* and *ex post* aggregates, published three years before Keynes's *General Theory (1936)*. *Ex ante* analysis examines how expectations affect the magnitude of a variable, while *ex post* analysis explains the possible divergence between the expected and actual values of the variable.

Myrdal also produced important work on international development issues and advocated a larger role for government in poor countries. He observed that the gap between rich and poor countries was increasing as poor countries remained poor. Standard economic theory, he argued, was unable to explain this trend. Myrdal believed that this stagnation was due to cumulative causation: less food, poor health, and low working capacity prevent poor countries from breaking the vicious circle of poverty. He argued that orthodox economics had diverted attention from the problems of distribution toward questions of production and exchange. Assumptions like perfect competition and stable equilibrium helped economists avoid the issue of growing inequality. NEOCLASSICAL ECONOMICS, especially, prioritized free trade for poor and rich countries alike. Myrdal felt that such conclusions merely increased the advantages of the industrial nations.

Myrdal's own recommendation was to expand the role of government in poor countries to better manage and increase the rate of growth. This included restrictions on foreign trade in order to preserve foreign-exchange reserves, the protection of infant industries, and public operation of utilities that are crucial for growth. He also advocated land reform. Myrdal believed that these measures would ultimately encourage private enterprise.

Myrdal envisioned a world in which equality of opportunity would be realized on an international scale. He viewed the movement toward welfare states in the richer countries as an essential part of this process. *Crisis in the Population Question* (1934), *Rich Lands and Poor* (1957), and *Beyond the Welfare State* (1960) are his best-known explorations of these themes.

myth Generally refers to stories that contribute to the elaboration of a cosmological system and to a cohesive social identity—e.g., accounts of origins, explanations of values and taboos, and narrative legitimations of authority. Myth is frequently opposed to *history*—to events that can be dated or located in a chronological relationship to the present. Yet the analysis of mythologies across cultures has shown these to be guidelines rather than rules, and there is a long tradition of debate within ANTHROPOLOGY about the place of myth within society. Bronislaw MALINOWSKI is associated with the functionalist view that myth is an instrument of social cohesion—one that links tradition to cosmology. Claude LÉVI-STRAUSS is largely responsible for the structuralist approach to myth as a network of interchangeable narrative elements (mythemes) that reveal the basic oppositions that organize a given culture (endogamy and exogamy, animal and vegetable, raw and cooked, and so on).

Roland BARTHES gave the term a different and highly influential inflection in his book *Mythologies* (1957). For Barthes, myths are the codes that underlie the imagery and practices of much of contemporary CULTURE. Their primary function is to lend the appearance of universality to otherwise contingent cultural beliefs. In this respect, myth occupies much the same place in Barthes's work as IDEOLOGY in the writing of Antonio GRAMSCI and Louis ALTHUSSER: it naturalizes and secures consent for the status quo.

N

Nadel, Siegfried Frederick (1903–1956) An anthropologist noted both for important contributions to the ETHNOGRAPHY of African societies—particularly in Nigeria and the Sudan—and for theoretical work on social structure, individual psychology, and the social sciences. Nadel was born in Vienna, where he trained in psychology and philosophy. He studied ANTHROPOLOGY at the London School of Economics with Bronislaw MALINOWSKI and occupied posts at the University of Durham and the Australian National University. Nadel's principal theoretical works are *The Foundations of Social Anthropology* (1951) and *The Theory of Social Structure* (1957), both of which explored the relationship between individual behavior and SOCIAL STRUCTURE. In particular, the 1957 book proposes a complex dynamic between individual actors, social roles, and the various forms of social, cultural, and economic capital that structure those roles. It has been very influential in the development of network approaches to social structure, including the work of sociologist Harrison White. More generally, the two studies articulated Nadel's larger goal of treating anthropology as an explanatory science linked to the other sciences. Nadel's other major works include *A Black Byzantium: The Kingdom of Nupe in Nigeria* (1942) and *The Nuba: An Anthropological Study of the Hill Tribes in Kordofan* (1947).

NAIRU The nonaccelerating inflation rate of unemployment. Also the *natural rate of unemployment*. Refers to the lowest level of UNEMPLOYMENT an economy can sustain without causing inflation due to wage pressures. Because job markets have a certain degree of friction—owing to the search time needed to find new jobs and similar phenomena—an economy without any unemployment would be one with constantly increasing wages, as firms had to lure workers from existing jobs. Increased wages imply inflationary pressure in the form of increased costs of goods and services.

narrative analysis An approach to the analysis and interpretation of historical events that emphasizes temporal sequence and the historically embedded relationships among the parts. Traditionally considered the province of historians and literary scholars, narrative analysis has attracted considerable recent attention from sociologists. Some researchers focus on formal methods for analyzing the structure of narratives, independent of context. Other proponents hold that because narratives are sensitive to historical contexts and contingencies, they require historically specific explanations. Critics have countered that narrative explanation cannot produce general theory. The terms of the debate ultimately rest on unresolvable disagreements over what constitutes a good explanation. (For a recent enactment of this long debate, see the symposium on historical sociology and RATIONAL-CHOICE THEORY in the *American Journal of Sociology*, Vol. 104, 1998.)

Nash, John (1928–) Mathematician and economist best known for his contributions to GAME THEORY. Nash's interest in games developed at Princeton University, where the two founders of the field, John von NEUMANN and Oskar Morgenstern, were pursuing their work. Von Neumann and Morgenstern had analyzed rivalries in which one party's gain was the other's loss. Yet in economics and most real-world problems, both parties in a game can gain. Nash overcame this limitation of game theory by showing that stable solutions of this kind can exist. This result, known as the NASH EQUILIBRIUM, helped change game theory from an arcane field of mathematics into an indispensable tool for analyzing strategic behavior, ranging from the COLD WAR to business competition. "The Bargaining Problem" (1950) and "Non-Cooperative Games" (1951) are Nash's most influential publications in this field.

As a mathematician, Nash made significant discoveries related to manifolds and real algebraic varieties. He also independently proved Luitzen Brouwer's fixed-point theorem. In the late 1950s, however, Nash developed paranoid schizophrenia, which kept him institutionalized for most of his adult life and prevented him from realizing the potential evident in his early work. The illness began to subside in the late 1980s, and Nash was able to resume his work at Princeton. He was awarded the Nobel Prize in economics in 1994 for his work on game theory, together with John Harsanyi and Reinhard Selten.

Nash equilibrium   The basic solution concept of noncooperative GAME THEORY. Its current formalization and usage was developed by the economist John NASH ("The Bargaining Problem," 1950; "Non-Cooperative Games, 1951), although its origin can be traced back to Augustin COURNOT's 1838 analyses of equilibria in games between two duopolists (Cournot's equilibrium has been shown to be identical to the Nash equilibrium). The Nash equilibrium describes a game situation in which no player has an incentive to unilaterally deviate from the strategies that he or she is currently pursuing. In other words, no single player can obtain higher payoffs by changing strategies, as long as the others stick to the strategies that they have chosen. Nash showed that such equilibria always exist in games with a finite number of players, when each has recourse to only a finite number of actions. This statement is subject to the caveat that the players have the ability to randomize their strategies or play mixed strategies. In the absence of the possibility of collusion among players, the optimizing qualities of Nash equilibria imply that it is *self-enforcing*. With collusion, however, coalitions or subsets might be able to collectively implement strategies more advantageous to certain members of the group.

The concept of the Nash equilibrium has since been extended to games with an infinite number of players and/or strategies, although in some cases the existence of an equilibrium is not guaranteed. In addition, a number of games have multiple Nash equilibria, motivating research into questions of equilibrium selection. Resolutions of this problem include informal notions such as Thomas Schelling's focal points and Reinhard Selten's formal theories of perfection. John Harsanyi has analyzed and sought to extend the concept of Nash equilibria to games where information is

imperfect, that is, where knowledge about preferences, abilities, and even the rules of the game is unevenly distributed ("Games with Incomplete Information Played by Bayesian Players, Parts I, II and III").

nation   See NATIONALISM; and NATION-STATE.

national income   The income accruing to a nation by virtue of its productive activities. In measuring national income, one of the common approaches involves the concept of the gross domestic product (GDP)—the unduplicated value of all goods and services produced in the domestic economy. The gross national product (GNP) differs from GDP in that it includes net-factor incomes from abroad. The concept of *unduplicated value* specifies that total income must be estimated without double counting the value of goods—i.e., when they are produced and then again in subsequent products for which they serve as materials or inputs. One way of avoiding double counting is to total all goods and services that enter *final demand*, which is generally defined as capital formation (capital goods as well as changes in capital stocks), private consumption, and public consumption (government expenditure on police, defense, hospitals, and so on). It is also necessary to add exports and subtract imports—exports are produced domestically but consumed by foreigners; and imports, while part of domestic consumption, are produced abroad. A distinction is also made between gross and net national product. The latter takes into account the depreciation of capital goods that are used or used up in the production process. Net national product is thus the income available to the economy after some portion has been set aside in order to maintain the capital stock intact. The accounting principles that are applied in the measurement and estimation of national income are termed *national income accounting*.

nationalism   Narrowly conceived, nationalism is a bias in favor of one's own nation. It may be manifested in sentiments, social movements, or state policies. More generally, nationalism refers to a way of constructing large-scale and especially political identities on the basis of cultural, linguistic, territorial, historical, and/or racial claims. Nationalists often employ images of KINSHIP and descent, although no nations are simply direct extensions of family relations.

While nationalism is often presented as the expression of a pre-existing, even primordial nation, recent social research has tended to emphasize its status as a discourse employed in the construction of nations. Nationalist rhetoric has several characteristic tropes: claims to sovereignty and/or governmental legitimacy in the name of the people of a nation; claims that the unity of a people reflects its enduring common culture; claims that the members of a group cannot realize their personal freedom unless the group enjoys political self-determination; demands that members of a putative nation adhere to some common standard of behavior; calls for the limitation of immigration, imported goods, or foreign investment; and insistence that a nation be treated as equal to all others (see Calhoun, *Nationalism*, 1997). Yet none of these tropes is a sufficient criterion of definition. Nationalism is a heterogeneous set of nation-oriented idioms and practices that vary according to circumstances but that are joined in an international discourse that legitimizes particularistic claims.

In its modern form, nationalism developed in connection with the consolidation of modern STATE—especially as the state penetrated into everyday life and unified populations. Nationalism does not presuppose an existing state, however, and it flourishes among many groups that aspire to independence and statehood. It is also expressed in calls for stronger national cohesion, culture, or identity. Such movements shape much of popular and scholarly attention to the term. Nationalism and national identities are not limited to political goals, however, or to relations to states. Writers may be concerned with having "national" readerships but not with whether those readers have state power; the nationalism of soccer fans may sometimes have political implications, but it does not stem entirely from political sources; and aboriginal groups may use nationalist rhetoric to seek special recognition without seeking to form states or to secede.

Researchers have offered diverse explanations of nationalism. To cite a few of the major research orientations, nationalism has been described as: (1) a product of enduring ethnic identities (Anthony Smith and John Hutcheson); (2) the result of political and cultural changes associated with industrialization (Ernest GELLNER, Eric Hobsbawm); (3) a form of separatist response to unequal economic development (Michael Hechter); (4) an outlet for the status anxiety and *ressentiment* of new elites (Liah Greenfield); and

(5) an ideological complement to state building (Charles TILLY and Michael Mann, among many others). Although part of the attraction of such theories is their apparent causal parsimony, they do not cumulate in a general theory or a single history of nationalism. This reflects the fundamentally heterogeneous nature of the object.

Nationalism is implicated in many forms of social practice, ranging from the benign (the waving of flags and singing of national anthems) to the terrifying (GENOCIDE). The distinction between *civic* and *ethnic* nationalism is sometimes employed to account for these differences. Civic nationalism is understood to be rooted in legitimate membership in a constituted political state; members of nations are understood first and foremost through their political identities as citizens. In its "ethnic" form, national identity is defined on the basis of cultural or ethnic criteria distinct from, and arguably prior to, political citizenship. Civic nationalism is generally held to be more inclusive, less inclined to stigmatize outsiders, and less prone to violent struggles over the stabilization of one or another particular definition of national identity.

National consolidation has almost always been a conflict-ridden process. This is true not only of the emerging states of the Balkans, sub-Saharan Africa, or Asia but also of states now thought of as stable democracies. Moreover, although the distinction between civic and ethnic nationalism is meaningful, it rarely implies unequivocal distinctions among countries. France, frequently cited as the paradigm of civic nationalism, has had a persistent and sometimes strongly ethnicized tradition of *la patrie*. Germany, which for most of its history refused citizenship to those without German "blood," has possessed elements of civic nationalism since its inception.

One of the major tensions in the literature on nationalism opposes "constructivists" (or "instrumentalists") to "primordialists." Primordialists hold that nations are based on traditions and ethnic identities that are ancient or natural, or that at least predate political mobilization. Conversely, constructivists emphasize the historical and social processes by which nations are created. Among the latter, Eric Hobsbawm and Terrence Ranger argue that this "invention" of nations can be traced to elites who seek to secure their power by mobilizing followers. In contrast, historical research by Anthony Smith and others shows noteworthy continuities between modern national cultures and their antecedents. While even these traditions are "created," in the sense that they are reshaped for contemporary purposes, what gives tradition its force is not its antiquity but its immediacy and givenness. Some nationalist self-understandings may be historically dubious, yet very real as aspects of lived experience and as bases for action. More generally, as Benedict Anderson has argued, national communities are always products of the collective imagination. The idea of the nation is circulated by the media and made possible by specific forms of representation, such as museums and censuses, rather than simply found (see IMAGINED COMMUNITY). The opposition between primordiality and "mere invention" thus leaves open a wide range of historical modes within which national and other traditions can exert real force.

Ethnic conflicts, the discourse of national identity, and the practical power of nationalist mobilizations continue to play a large role in the world, despite the confidence of many earlier social scientists that nationalist forces were in decline. In the wake of communism's collapse, nationalism and ethnic conflict appeared as primary issues in the realignment of eastern European and post-Soviet politics and identity. Nationalist appeals also fuel ethnic separatism, from Quebec to the postcolonial states of Africa. In other contexts, it figures in movements to integrate disparate populations, as in twentieth-century Arab nationalism and nineteenth-century German nationalism. In many parts of the world, nationalism continues to underwrite resistance to GLOBALIZATION. At the same time, transnational relations are assuming new importance—European integration is perhaps the most dramatic example—and postnational institutions such as the World Court or European Union are becoming meaningful mechanisms of governance and even bases of identity for many groups (see TRANSNATIONALISM).

nation-state   The conjoining of political institutions and collective identity in a single sovereign unit. In the modern era, the link between STATE and nation has increasingly become the *sine qua non* of political legitimacy: nationhood is confirmed and realized in an independent state. Foreign rule, in this context, becomes illegitimate (whence the complicated rationales for COLONIALISM and empire rooted in "civilizing" missions and other forms of benevolence; see IMPERIALISM AND EMPIRE). The conjuncture of state and nation also became

an assumption of most social science, and it provided the basic unit of comparative analysis.

Prior to the late eighteenth century, strong conceptions of national unity were unusual. What unity there was derived, in most cases, from long and violent processes of state consolidation and attendant forms of cultural homogenization. These continued well into the nineteenth century in much of Europe and continue elsewhere today. The construction of France from a range of fractious, semi-independent regions and the imposition of the French language across them all provide a prominent example. The desirability of such a situation, however, was not a given; the most successful political enterprises of the age were *empires*—states that encompassed many nations or peoples.

The ubiquity of the nation-state as both an empirical reality and an ideological construct is the consequence of the spread of this model. Increasingly, nations were viewed as natural entities that had a right to self-determination—a principle made explicit in the early twentieth century by Vladimir Ilich LENIN, Woodrow Wilson, and other theorists of the postimperial world. In practice, this meant privileging some claims to national identity over others, especially in multiethnic or other composite states (this is often a source of tension and has produced some spectacular failures—the contemporary case of Yugoslavia is an example). Many scholars see GLOBALIZATION at the economic and, more slowly, political levels as a direct threat to the relevance of the nation-state and the notion of self-determination that underlies it. See also TRANSNATIONALISM.

nativism   A strong form of ETHNOCENTRISM, generally directed against immigrants as the alleged causes of larger socioeconomic problems. There have been several periods of virulent nativism in the United States, although it is rarely absent from populist political discourse. The high point of nativism was in the 1920s, with the broad political and cultural turn against the wave of immigration from southern and eastern Europe. On the history of American nativism, see especially John Higham's *Strangers in the Land: Patterns of American Nativism 1860–1925* (1955).

naturalism   In the social sciences, naturalism describes the position that social science is or should be a natural science, devoted to the same goal of determining positive laws (in this case about social behavior), and drawing on the same methodologies of experimentation, prediction, verification, and so on. There are, however, a number of variations on this position—from those who see social life as a direct extension of the natural world and, consequently, as subject to the same kinds of claims and certainties, to those like Emile DURKHEIM who argued that social processes were of an order distinct from natural processes but nonetheless open to truth-oriented, empirical methods. Naturalism is generally opposed by the broad range of theories and methods that approach social research as primarily an interpretive process, as well as by those that give priority to cultural and historical context over generalizable social laws.

naturalization See CITIZENSHIP.

natural law Universal law that governs both nature and human affairs.

Although the natural law tradition has roots in ancient Greece, it was first codified in Roman law under the categories of *jus naturale* ("natural law") and *jus gentium* ("the laws of nations"), and contrasted with *jus civile* ("CIVIL LAW"). Roman jurists understood natural law as the universally applicable expression of right reason, eternal and unchanging. Natural law provided a guide to proper action—it underwrote ethical behavior, as well as social divisions between "natural" categories, such as the roles of the two sexes and the differences between children and adults.

Early Christian theologians interpreted natural law as the expression of God's will, revealed to human beings through an act of grace. Thomas Aquinas's synthesis of Christian faith and Aristotelian philosophy informed his description of natural law as divine reason accessible to human beings through their natural reason. This conviction of a superior, harmonious, but ultimately accessible order continued to underwrite secularized accounts of nature as a body of universal laws discernable through human reason.

The secularization of Western societies during the seventeenth and eighteenth centuries undermined long-standing assumptions about the discernability of universal moral imperatives derived from either heaven or nature. Serious doubts regarding the validity of natural law doctrines date from this period (see Hugo GROTIUS). Nonetheless, natural law typically provides an absolute and (on its own terms) indisputable grounding for positions—especially in contrast to the *positive* law generated by the conventional or legal sovereignty of the state. For this reason, natural law has continued to play a role in some political philosophy—such as the SOCIAL-CONTRACT THEORY of Thomas HOBBES and in more recent efforts to theorize human rights outside the limits of individual state prerogatives. See also LAW; and RIGHTS.

natural rights See RIGHTS.

nature versus nurture debate A debate about the sources of human behavior that generally opposes cultural or environmental explanations (nurture) to those that emphasize biological or otherwise inherited traits. Nature versus nurture figures prominently in a number of fields of social research and public policy, especially in regard to DEVIANCE and criminality, GENDER and SEXUALITY, and education. Although the modern social sciences emerged largely in opposition to the crude racial biologism of the nineteenth century, important areas of human life are clearly shaped by biological processes (such as maturation) and biological difference (such as sexual difference). How and where these lines are drawn is almost always controversial and affects larger social perspectives on freedom, equality, and responsibility.

Naturwissenschaften See *GEISTESWISSEN-SCHAFTEN AND NATURWISSENSCHAFTEN.*

Nazism The political ideology and program of the National Socialist German Workers Party—better known as the Nazi party. The Nazi party was founded in 1919 in partial emulation of the Italian Fascist party (see FASCISM). In 1933, the Nazis and their allies received more than 50 percent of the vote in what proved to be the final election of the Weimar Republic (the Nazis alone polled 44.5 percent). Under Adolf Hitler, the German government became known as the Third Reich. Hitler ruled from 1933 until its defeat by the Allied forces in 1945.

As a political ideology, Nazism combined a number of contradictory principles. From German Romanticism and post-Romantic sources (Richard Wagner; Friedrich NIETZSCHE) it inherited a disdain for the Enlightenment values of rationality, EGALITARIANISM, DEMOCRACY, and the organization of society according to universal laws. In contrast, Nazism stressed the irrational nature of power, the duty of the individual to submit to the authority of the state, the inequality of men, Aryan bloodlines as the basis of citizenship, and the organic and primordial nature of the German nation. At the same time, Nazism extolled the virtues of pseudoscientific theories such as SOCIAL DARWINISM and eugenics. Moreover, it pursued its own obsessions with order and efficiency, most notoriously through the methodical extermination of Jews, Gypsies, homosexuals, and other "subhumans" during World War II.

Although Nazism was conservative in its emphasis on Germany's glorious past and in its condemnation of LIBERALISM, MARXISM, and SOCIAL DEMOCRACY, it was revolutionary in its ambition to sweep away the social and political structures of the old Germany and to construct the new order of the Third Reich. Nonetheless, much of its agenda was *ad hoc* or opportunistic. Although Nazism vilified industrialists and financiers, it supported private ownership of industry within the context of a command economy—"national socialism." Although it vehemently denounced Marxism and social democracy, Nazism embraced both CORPORATISM, where workers' interests were represented within the state apparatus, and massive state intervention in economic planning. Although Nazism extolled the exceptional individual who lives beyond good and evil, it insisted on absolute obedience to the Führer and terrorized those who resisted.

Nazism's success as a social movement was rooted in the lower middle class but extended into the organized working class and educated sectors of the population. The manifest failure of both leftist working-class opposition to Nazism and the liberal-democratic institutions of the Weimar Republic led to intense efforts to explain the appeal and broader context of Nazism—in many cases on the part of German social scientists who had emigrated to the United States before the war. This group included William Kornhauser, Hannah ARENDT, Max HORKHEIMER, Theodor ADORNO, Erich FROMM, and others. Nazi Germany became, for many of these writers, a case study of the pathological condition of modern society, viewed variously as a nihilistic outcome of CAPITALISM and MASS SOCIETY or as the breakdown of the traditional structures of bourgeois personality. Others preferred simply to villainize the Nazi regime—to hold them out as examples of exceptional and unprecedented evil. There have also been extensive debates about the role and complicity of the broader German population, in regard to which theories of evil become harder to sustain. One of the more recent and controversial entrants into this debate is Daniel Goldhagen, who argues that a long tradition of German antisemitism helps to explain widespread participation in the Holocaust (*Hitler's Willing Executioners*, 1996).

Many scholars have debated whether Nazism's internal contradictions would have eventually caused its downfall; Arendt prominently made this case. In the end, it was the projection of the Nazi vision beyond its borders that threw the world into war and provided the more immediate cause of Nazism's destruction.

negotiated order   Describes the process of collective construction and definition of a particular social order, such as the hierarchical structure of an organization. The concept is generally associated with the work of Anselm Strauss, particularly *Negotiations* (1978), although similar ideas can be found in a range of other sociological sources. Strauss argued that rather than treating organizational structures as rule based, self-evident, and permanently binding, it is important to understand the dynamic in which structures are developed and reproduced through the "testing out" of actions and the feedback of others. The concept of negotiated order is rooted in Strauss's version of SYMBOLIC INTERACTIONISM, which emphasizes the role of the relationships among actors in defining particular situations or contexts.

neighborhood effect   Changes in behavior attributed to local interactions, such as the rapid spread of cultural innovations at the local level.

neoclassical economics   Also *marginalist economics*. The dominant tradition of economic theory throughout most of the twentieth century, especially in the United States. Neoclassical economics concerns itself primarily with the allocation of resources and goods in the economy, above all through the operation of markets. Neoclassical models privilege a range of methodological perspectives and assumptions, especially regarding the autonomy of individual economic actors (methodological individualism), the utility-maximizing behavior of individuals (or FIRMS) based on marginal theories of production and distribution, and the possibility of perfectly competitive equilibrium in markets. The term *neoclassical* was first used by Thorstein VEBLEN (*The Preconceptions of Economic Science*, 1900) to characterize Alfred MARSHALL's account of supply and demand equilibria and his methodology for analyzing economic decisions at the "margin" of profitability or added *utility*. After World War II, the term came to describe marginalist theory in general.

The marginalists, John Bates Clark, Alfred Marshall, Leon WALRAS, William Stanley JEVONS, Knut WICKSELL, Philip Wicksteed, and Eugen Böhm-Bawerk, extended and improved upon the basic foundations of CLASSICAL ECONOMICS, deriving prices from consideration of the *marginal utility* of additional consumption by individuals and the *marginal productivity* of additional materials in the production process (see MARGINAL ANALYSIS). In both cases, a point is reached at which the cost of additional consumption or production exceeds its value or utility. This point determines the price of goods and factors of production (such as labor or raw materials). The marginal theory of prices marked a clear break with the classical economic tradition and, in particular, with the LABOR THEORY OF VALUE, which held the prices of goods and materials to be determined primarily by the quantity of labor invested in their production.

Some neoclassical models rely on strongly naturalized accounts of rational choice, in which it is assumed that individuals always seek to maximize their utility in price and purchasing decisions (see RATIONAL-CHOICE THEORY). Others adopt a more flexible position, arguing only that markets operate, on the whole, *as if* that were true. In either case, neoclassical innovations paved the way for a strongly mathematical and often highly abstract tradition of economic theory that tended to reject social constructivist views of human subjectivity and the structural features of social and economic life (such as CLASS, institutions, or other arrangements of power). Neoclassical scholarship often legitimates itself on the grounds that, unlike politically vested schools of economic thought such as MARXISM, it represents a fundamentally scientific discipline (see POSITIVISM).

What ultimately distinguishes the neoclassical approach from others is not only the foundation of individual maximizing behavior but also a strong belief that markets are the most efficient means of allocating goods under most circumstances. Government, under these circumstances, is accorded a relatively minor role in economic affairs—often limited to ensuring that markets operate properly, especially in regard to guaranteeing competition. The neoclassical paradigm nonetheless encompasses a wide variety of economic theories. The most strident form has long been associated with the University of Chicago,

which has been the source of several neoclassical movements, from the Monetarism of the 1960s (of which Milton FRIEDMAN is the best-known example) to the New Institutionalism of the 1990s (see CHICAGO SCHOOL OF ECONOMICS). Chicago school economists have an unusually high degree of faith in the core assumptions of neoclassical theory and have also been centrally involved in exporting the paradigm to other disciplines, notably SOCIOLOGY, LAW, and POLITICAL SCIENCE.

neocorporatism See CORPORATISM.

neo-Kantianism Attempts to further develop the themes of Immanuel KANT's late eighteenth-century philosophical work. Much contemporary liberal political thought is at least partially neo-Kantian in its emphasis on universality and the freedom and autonomy of agents. Neo-Kantianism was widely influential on late nineteenth- and early twentieth-century social science, including the work of Georg SIMMEL, Max WEBER, and Emile DURKHEIM. An important feature of neo-Kantianism, in this regard, was the effort to separate the social sciences from the natural sciences—the subject of a well-known debate in Germany known as the *METHODENSTREIT*. Views differed on the strict nature of this separation, and different elements of Kantian thought found their way into different aspects of methodological and sociological theory. Among the most important of these was Kant's distinction between different forms of reason. Pure reason, Kant argued, was the basis for scientific knowledge of the objective world and mathematics. Practical reason, in contrast, informed judgments in aesthetics, ethics, and politics. Heinrich Rickert's distinction between IDEOGRAPHIC SCIENCE AND NOMOTHETIC SCIENCE drew strongly on this distinction—the former concerned with the particular historical significance of human action and the latter with generalizable laws. Rickert also drew on Kant to emphasize the way in which human beings organized and sorted their experience of the world through *a priori* structures of mind and to mount a critique of POSITIVISM—the notion that things exist only insofar as they are observable. Kant's analytically approachable account of human experience also opened the door to the interpretive sociologies of Weber and Simmel. In addition, it inspired Durkheim's notion of a distinct science of society. His *Elementary Forms of Religious Life* (1912) included an attempt to trace the social origins of the basic Kantian categories of mind or knowledge. Elements of Kantian philosophy were also incorporated into FRANKFURT SCHOOL critical theory. Building on this foundation, Jürgen HABERMAS developed a strongly neo-Kantian social and ethical theory. Cognitive science, too, has been influenced by Kantian ideas—especially Kant's attempts to isolate the universal structures of perception and consciousness.

neoliberalism   A political label with multiple meanings, neoliberalism is primarily associated with the goal of reducing the role of the STATE in social and economic affairs. This is the main source of continuity with earlier versions of LIBERALISM. The term is also associated with the study of patterns of cooperation between states and other international actors (see INTERNATIONAL RELATIONS).

Three versions of social and economic neoliberalism can be distinguished. One is associated with reformist members of center-left parties in advanced industrial nations. Stressing continuity with traditional left-wing party concerns, such as social JUSTICE, TOLERATION, and MULTICULTURALISM, these neoliberals nonetheless favor reducing the role of the state in areas of fiscal policy and welfare, and generally seek solutions for social problems in the engine of economic growth. In many countries, the electoral success of such agendas has effectively challenged the connection between left-leaning parties and long-standing constituencies such as LABOR UNIONS.

A second version of neoliberalism evinces less concern with social justice and more emphatically embraces the goal of minimal government—at least in regard to the twentieth-century expansion of the regulatory and welfare state. Strongly associated with the Reagan and Thatcher years in the United States and Great Britain, this form of neoliberalism stresses the primacy of free-market principles—especially the belief that capital and labor should be allowed to move freely within a self-regulating market. It relies on a social philosophy of individual responsibility and, correspondingly, de-emphasizes the significance of structural social effects, such as those related to CLASS or POVERTY. Neoliberalism in this sense has been translated into a range of policy initiatives or—in some cases—retreats from existing government responsibilities. It has broadly challenged the role of organized labor, pursued free trade and policies to enhance capital mobility, sought the deregulation of

industry and markets, privatized institutions that provide public goods (e.g., electricity, water), cut funding for social services (while shifting responsibility from the community to individuals and voluntary associations), and sought reduction in taxes. As intellectual cousins, both versions of neoliberalism have succeeded in shifting political discourse and debate to the right in Western countries and have in some degree stigmatized the traditional social democratic welfare state. They have also significantly weakened the position of labor, both domestically and internationally (see WELFARE ECONOMICS).

A third, related version of neoliberalism is associated with measures to promote economic globalization and has been pursued by such multilateral institutions as the World Bank, the International Monetary Fund, and the World Trade Organization during the 1980s and 1990s. By setting the conditions by which developing nations can pay their debts, the international lending community has forcefully advocated a diminished role for the state and established a framework for the effective functioning of the global market. Bearing a close resemblance to the Reagan/Thatcher agenda, these "structural adjustment" programs have sought to limit developing states to ensuring that (a) individual rights and the rule of law are upheld and protected; (b) principles of fair competition are observed; (c) public goods necessary for facilitating economic transactions are available (i.e., infrastructure like roads and water provision); and (d) the appropriate conditions for trade are established by sound fiscal and monetary policy (e.g., balanced budgets, monetary stabilization). In practical terms, this has meant the retrenchment of the state in most developing countries through privatization, tax cuts, the scaling back or elimination of social programs, and a loosening of regulations on industry and commerce. Responsibility for collective goods such as health, nutrition, education, housing, and occupational training have in many cases been transferred from the state to the market or to an international, nongovernmental charity sector. Many of these efforts have resulted in unprecedented levels of aggregate growth, as well as unprecedented levels of inequality and poverty. Recognizing that the benefits of these transformations have been mostly restricted to a narrow elite, some proponents of international neoliberalism have began to advocate a more moderate position that allows for a greater role for the state as an investor in human capital and as a force for mitigating the effects of economic dislocations.

In international relations, neoliberalism signifies the idea that states can and often do cooperate despite belonging to an essentially anarchic, self-help oriented international community. Neoliberals claim that the security concerns of states can be addressed through the institutionalization of mutually beneficial arrangements, such as treaties, conventions, and other forms of international agreement. Neoliberalism also holds that increasing levels of transnationalism and interdependence require a shift away from statecentric approaches in international relations toward mixedactor models capable of recognizing and understanding the roles played by MULTINATIONAL corporations (MNCs), NONGOVERNMENTAL ORGANIZATIONS (NGOs), and other NONSTATE ACTORS.

Neolithic Or "New Stone Age," usually designates a level of human cultural development characterized by ground and polished stone tools, agriculture, animal domestication, and accompanying forms of social organization.

neolocal residence A social convention that governs postmarital residence in many societies. It specifies that newly married couples create a new household in a new locale, separate from the parents on either side. Alternatives include matrilocal and PATRILOCAL RESIDENCE.

nesting In INTERNATIONAL RELATIONS, *nesting* refers to the way in which mutually beneficial economic relations among advanced industrial democracies are situated within more encompassing political and strategic structures or alliances. Nesting deepens cooperative relations by providing greater opportunities for bargaining; states can afford to accept a less advantageous outcome in particular situations if they are confident that they will be compensated elsewhere.

network analysis Although the term circulates in a variety of contexts, *network analysis* proper emerged in the 1950s out of dissatisfaction with the institutional focus of structural functionalism (see FUNCTIONALISM; and SOCIAL STRUCTURE). Its proponents attempted to complicate the static conception of social organization implicit in much structural functionalism by looking at informal, transient forms of association, such as the flow of gossip, the mobilization of social movements and political campaigns, and the maintenance of patron–client relations. Such

networks are groups of persons who do not necessarily know each other or share anything outside the organizing criteria of the network. Early network analysis differentiated between two types of groups: those organized around a particular person, termed an *action set* or *egocentric network*; and those with a more general purpose or a diffuse, sometimes ideological structure, termed a *quasi group*.

Network analysis has roots in British social anthropology and is particularly associated with J. Clyde Mitchell and John Barnes. Many recent practitioners—especially among American sociologists—have shifted the focus from situated action to formal theories of social structures (influenced by Siegfried Frederick NADEL). Much of this work integrates the social theory and analytic techniques of Harrison White.

Neumann, John von (1903–1957) Although primarily a mathematician, von Neumann's contributions to GAME THEORY has had a major impact on the social sciences—especially in economics. Game theory makes it possible to formulate and solve complex problems involving strategic behavior. The game theoretic approach is now widespread in the study of industrial organization, the economics of research and development, political economy, and a number of other fields.

John (or Jansci) von Neumann was born in Budapest and published his first mathematical paper when he was eighteen. He studied in Berlin, where he developed an important connection to David Hilbert, an outstanding German mathematician. Hilbert's interest in the axiomatization of mathematics captured von Neumann's interest and led to his famous 1928 paper on the axiomatization of set theory. Von Neumann visited Princeton University as a lecturer in 1930, and stayed on as a professor at the Institute for Advanced Study. Oskar Morgenstern arrived at Princeton eight years later, eager to work with von Neumann on connecting game theory to economics. The result of this collaboration was the seminal work, *The Theory of Games and Economic Behavior* (1944).

Von Neumann's 1928 paper made three principle advances. First, he formulated a restricted version of an *extensive form game*, where all possible moves by each player are spelled out, and each player either knows nothing or everything about the previous moves made by others. Second, he proved the MINIMAX THEOREM for two-person zero-sum games, which showed that a normal form game can be solved for the optimal mixed strategies of both players, as well as for the value of the game. Third, he defined the characteristic function for (and the solution of) three-person zero-sum games in normal form; this last result helped generalize the minimax theorem to games involving more than two people.

Von Neumann's 1928 conclusions had assumed that the players possessed complete or no information. In contrast, the 1944 *Theory of Games* extends these results to cases in which players have limited information about one another's previous strategies. Moreover, it replaced the monetary value of a game outcome with UTILITY—thus addressing Daniel Bernoulli's objection that a dollar is not worth the same to a rich man and a poor man. The most significant contribution of *The Theory of Games* is the focus on *n-person* games, which allowed the analysis of coalitions and other strategic behavior that arise in interactions among several parties—this helped make game theory of practical use to economics and to other fields with indeterminate numbers of players.

Von Neumann also developed an equilibrium model of a growing economy—the first input–output model that allowed for expansion. Although only three of his publications relate directly to economics, these were highly influential and earned von Neumann a place among the leading economic theorists of the twentieth century.

neutrality of money The proposition that the nominal quantity of money in the economy affects only the level of prices and not the level of real output and other real variables. A one-time increase in the quantity of money, in this case, would raise nominal prices and nominal wages proportionately but would leave all real variables unchanged. The neutrality of money is based on the assumption that individuals are not subject to the MONEY ILLUSION, so that an equal proportional change in all nominal variables leaves behavior unchanged. Money is said to be *superneutral* if a change in the growth of the money supply does not affect real variables. While there exists a firm theoretical basis for the neutrality of money, no such basis exists for long-run superneutrality.

New Ethnography Often used interchangeably with ETHNOSCIENCE and COGNITIVE ANTHROPOLOGY, New Ethnography investigates differences in systems of classification among cultures in order to understand the "knowledge systems" that underlie specific forms of cultural activity. This perspective grew out of the 1950s and 1960s convergence of ANTHROPOLOGY and LINGUISTICS—particularly the theory of TRANSFORMATIONAL–GENERATIVE GRAMMAR developed by Noam CHOMSKY. New Ethnography proposed that analysis of the systems of classification used by different cultures was not only feasible but analytically necessary to rigorous ethnographic observation. The heyday of New Ethnography was the mid-1960s, which saw the publication of major work by Ward Goodenough, Harold Conklin, and Charles Frake—but many of its issues and methods continue to be explored in the subfield of cognitive anthropology.

new social movements (NSMs) See SOCIAL MOVEMENTS.

NGO See NONGOVERNMENTAL ORGANIZATION (NGO).

Nietzsche, Friedrich (1844–1900) A late nineteenth-century German philosopher whose work has been of preeminent importance to a wide range of twentieth-century traditions, from critical theory to existentialism, POSTSTRUCTURALISM, and POSTMODERNISM. Nietzsche was a prolific writer, but he experienced poor health and ultimately suffered a complete mental breakdown in 1889. In the seventeen years preceding that breakdown, however, Nietzsche developed a highly original critical account of Western metaphysics and Christian morality, as well as a radical psychology that introduced many of the themes of repression that would later be developed in Sigmund FREUD's work. Nietzsche's early writing shows the influence of the philosopher Arthur Schopenhauer—especially in the attention he gives to the problem of avoiding despair in a world emptied of transcendental values. He also flirted with (and ultimately rejected) the German cultural nationalism of Richard Wagner, whose work he admired. In time, Nietzsche developed an increasingly assertive theory of the human capacity to create its own values—as exemplified by the figure of the *Übermensch*, or "superman," and as explored through parables such as *Thus Spake Zarathustra* (1883–1891).

Ultimately, Nietzsche came to conceive human existence in terms of a "will-to-power" that structured all human relations and the search for knowledge. Moral systems that sought to mitigate or condemn this will as "evil," he argued, made weakness a virtue and operated against life. Such systems were forces of repression that twisted humanity away from its open, expressive, creative possibilities. He saw Judaism as the original form of this "trick," although he argued that anti-life morality had culminated in the self-sacrificing aspects of Christianity. At the same time, however, he saw that Christianity had set in motion a powerful will-to-truth—initially oriented by the question of knowing God but increasingly rationalized into the pursuit of scientific knowledge. This fundamentally theological ambition, Nietzsche argued, progressively undermined its own basis in transcendental values and diminished the margin for any divine foundation or source of truth. This was the context of Nietzsche's famous declaration of the "death of God." The progressive devaluing of the world, Nietzsche asserted, constituted the crisis of modernity and created the opportunity—even the necessity—for a new kind of man, the autonomous, value-creating *Übermensch*.

Many of these ideas, very selectively read, were employed in justifying the German national will-to-power—first during World War I and then by the Nazis, who admired (and exaggerated) Nietzsche's philosophical antisemitism, borrowed his messianism, and emphasized his suggestive links between the "superman" and German racial ideologies. Much of this was orchestrated after Nietzsche's death by his sister, Elizabeth, who developed into a fervent Nazi and a skilled promoter of her brother's fame. Nonetheless, Nietzsche continued to have a major influence on critical German philosophy and social theory in the 1920s and 1930s—from Max WEBER's account of RATIONALIZATION and SECULARIZATION, to Martin HEIDEGGER's attempt to bring metaphysics to a close, to the FRANKFURT SCHOOL's critique of instrumental reason.

In the 1960s, Nietzsche's work became a fundamental resource for French poststructuralism. It influenced Michel FOUCAULT's genealogical methodology and his equation of knowledge and power, as well as a number of theories of postmodernism (see Jean-François LYOTARD). Nietzsche remains one of the most widely read and misunderstood modern philosophers—in part, because of his accessible and usually polemical style, which avoided (and critiqued) the dense exposition of systems of thought that dominated the metaphysical tradition. Nietzsche's major works include *The Birth of Tragedy* (1872), *The Gay Science* (1882), *Thus Spake Zarathustra* (1883–1891), *Beyond Good and Evil* (1886), *On the Genealogy of Morals* (1887), *The Twilight of the Idols* (1889), and *The Antichrist* (1895).

Nisbet, Robert A. (1913–1996) A sociologist known primarily for his analysis of the decline of community in modern society and his defense of traditionalism. Nisbet's most influential work was *The Quest for Community* (1953), an account of the breakdown of the "intermediate" institutions, such as family and church, which he argued structured and gave purpose to individuals' lives. Drawing on Alexis de TOCQUEVILLE, he traced much of this decline to the rise of the centralized bureaucratic state, which increasingly reduced society to a collection of atomized individuals. Nisbet viewed the classic sociological tradition as deeply concerned with this transition—a theme he developed at length in *The Sociological Tradition* (1967) and other works. *The Social Bond* (1970) and *Prejudices* (1982) explored other aspects of this loss of community.

Nisbet conceived his work as an attempt to overcome the critical vocabularies of Left and Right. Although his language of "community" did find resonance on the Left, especially among later communitarian thinkers (see COMMUNITARIANISM), his strong defense of traditional structures of authority and his particular fondness for medieval society made him much more amenable to American conservatives, who adopted him as an intellectual spokesperson. Nisbet devoted much of his later work to exploring the relationship between tradition and social change, primarily in *Tradition and Revolt* (1968) and *History and the Idea of Progress* (1980). His *Social Change and History* (1969) combined this theme with a critique of evolutionary thought. He also edited a number of important collections, including *Emile Durkheim* (1965), *Contemporary Social Problems* (1961, with Robert K. MERTON), and *A History of Sociological Analysis* (1980, with Tom Bottomore).

nominal scale   See MEASUREMENT.

nominal wages See WAGES, NOMINAL AND REAL.

nomothetic science   See IDEOGRAPHIC SCIENCE AND NOMOTHETIC SCIENCE.

noncooperative games   See GAME THEORY.

nongovernmental   organization   (NGO)
As commonly understood, a not-for-profit organization that is institutionally separate from the state (although in a literal sense businesses are also nongovernmental organizations). NGOs vary widely in their goals and sources of support but most attempt to influence government policy by setting agendas, participating in negotiations, conferring legitimacy on or publicly contesting government actions, and implementing programs.

At one end of the spectrum lie NGOs that are concerned with social change. These operate both within and across national borders and advocate a variety of goals, including the protection of human rights (Amnesty International, Human Rights Watch) and the environment (Greenpeace, Friends of the Earth, EarthAction), alleviating famine (Oxfam), refugee assistance (International Rescue Committee), and narrower issues such as the banning of antipersonnel landmines (through a coalition of some 350 NGOs). These groups tend to operate independently of, if not at odds with, national governments. They receive funding from philanthropic foundations, membership fees, and mass solicitations. A hybrid form of NGO is involved extensively in development efforts in the THIRD WORLD; this category includes independent international and indigenous organizations, as well as a growing number that provide services on behalf of donor programs. These often receive significant state funding but generally maintain at least nominal independence in their constitutions and regulations (see Terje Tvedt, *Angels of Mercy or Development Diplomats?*, 1998).

At the other end of the spectrum are NGOs that are closely tied to business interests. Some are "voluntary" wings of for-profit firms that seek to win government contracts or confer NGO legitimacy on various commercial projects (e.g., National Wetlands Coalition, a pro–wetlands-development organization, or Consumer Alert, an anti–product-safety-regulations group). Others are membership organizations that facilitate business by setting standards or arbitrating conflicts.

NGOs greatly increased in number and power during the twentieth century. According to the *Yearbook of International Associations*, there were 176 international NGOs in 1909; by 2000, the number had increased to 26,000. L. M. Salamon has called this development "a global associational revolution that may prove to be as significant to the late twentieth century as the rise of the nation-state was to the late nineteenth" ("The Rise of the Nonprofit Sector," 1994). Insofar as most NGOs do not pursue clearly state-defined or for-profit agendas, they are part of the broader development of international CIVIL SOCIETY—a proliferating network of organizations, institutions, movements, and individual activists, whose ties are not reducible to state action or markets. See also GLOBALIZATION; and TRANSNATIONALISM.

nonpecuniary   economy See   PECUNIARY ECONOMIES AND NONPECUNIARY ECONOMIES.

nonprice competition In markets for differentiated goods, firms may compete on grounds other than price. They may seek to increase market share through advertising, product differentiation, improvements in product quality, customer services, and so on. Historically, nonprice competition has arisen where variations in prices are impossible—often when there is price regulation that prevents price competition.

nonsatiation The assumption that consumers always prefer more of any good or service to less. Nonsatiated preferences are a common assumption in economic models of consumer behavior. They imply that the marginal utility of a good is always positive, that is, as the consumption of the good increases, the individual derives higher UTILITY (or well-being). See also MARGINAL ANALYSIS.

nonstate actors A broad category of actors in global politics who represent interests and exert influence on issues but who do not exhibit the distinguishing STATE characteristics of legal sovereignty and control of territory and people. This includes various INTERNATIONAL ORGANIZATIONS such as the United Nations and the North Atlantic Treaty Organization (NATO), many private multinational corporations, mercenary armies, and myriad NONGOVERNMENTAL ORGANIZATIONS (NGOs). The growth and increased importance of nonstate actors in world affairs since World War II constitutes a significant change in INTERNATIONAL RELATIONS. In political science, it has occasioned a major revision of REALISM, with its state-centric notions of global power. Neoliberal and neorealist perspectives concede the mixed-actor model and acknowledge that both state and nonstate actors form part of an increasingly interdependent world with multiple channels of contact among societies. Differences center around the degree to which state actors are perceived as losing their autonomy in the conduct of foreign affairs, as nonstate actors pursue their own agendas and successfully avoid state efforts to control them. See also GLOBALIZATION; INTERDEPENDENCE; and TRANSNATIONALISM.

nontradable goods See TRADABLE COMMO-DITIES AND NONTRADABLE COMMODITIES.

nonunilineal descent Systems of descent or inheritance that do not distinguish between or selectively privilege descendants of the mother and father (unlike UNILINEAL descent systems). Nonunilineal systems have been designated by a variety of terms, including cognatic, ambilineal, bilineal, and BILATERAL DESCENT. See also DESCENT THEORY.

NORC National Opinion Research Center. A public-interest survey research organization founded in 1941 and based, since 1947, at the University of Chicago. NORC is best known for the General Social Survey (GSS)—a large-scale, ongoing survey of attitudes and social practices in the United States.

normative theory Involves evaluations of what "should be" as distinct from descriptions of "what is." The latter is often termed *positive* theory. Much of the social-science tradition has been structured by the exclusion of normative analysis, which is often viewed as dependent upon subjective values and therefore more properly the subject of politics or individual preference. This distinction is often linked to controversial claims about the objectivity of social science—particularly the degree to which social scientists can escape their own culture's basic normative assumptions. Many draw on Max WEBER in arguing that, at the limit, positive theory is a goal of research rather than a clear dividing line between types of analysis. A prominent critique of this distinction comes out of the Marxist tradition, which holds that knowledge is inevitably the product of social factors (such as CLASS) and that it is always engaged in the legitimation or contestation of particular regimes of power. See also OBJECTIVITY; and THEORY.

norms Explicit or implicit social expectations and informal rules that derive from and operationalize societal values. Unlike values, norms prescribe and regulate specific forms of behavior. Americans may hug a close acquaintance, whereas the French may exchange a kiss on each cheek. These are different norms that operationalize similar values regarding the expression of warm feelings in greeting or taking leave of a friend.

Norms play a major role in the functionalist and structural-functionalist traditions, in which they bear a large part of the burden of explaining social integration (see FUNCTIONALISM). The work of Emile DURKHEIM and later Talcott PARSONS is especially influential in this regard. Other prominent research on norms focuses on DEVIANCE and SOCIAL CONTROL. The former is often conceived as the violation of norms; the latter as the set of techniques and pressures that assure compliance with them. There is also a diverse tradition of empirical research on SOCIALIZATION that resists the compliance/deviance model by emphasizing the divergence of ordinary behavior from official norms. Alfred Kinsey's studies of sexual behavior in the United States are a prominent example of how norms may bear relatively little relation to actual practices.

Pierre BOURDIEU's practice theory focuses especially on the margin of improvisation implicit in any structure of norms, and it emphasizes the degree to which norms are evoked or activated only in the context of concrete experience. Bourdieu's work and that of other recent theorists of normative structures has tended to dispute the Parsonian presentation of society as a relatively static structure of successfully regulative norms. Norms, in much of this work, are not merely regulatory structures, but codes that play a role in forms of social conflict. Widely accepted norms constitute avenues of legitimacy for some groups; others will succeed in contesting or changing norms in pursuit of their interests. This has been a major element of critiques of structural-functionalism leveled by advocates of more conflictual models of group behavior (CONFLICT THEORY), as well as by Marxist social theorists.

The contestation and invention of norms has also been used to describe the mechanism of collective action. In *Collective Behavior* (1957), Ralph Turner and Lewis Killian argued that individuals in uncertain situations look to one another for cues to appropriate behavior based on earlier experience and expectations. This process of interaction eventually leads to the emergence of new norms that guide action in these particular circumstances.

NSM New social movement. See SOCIAL MOVEMENTS.

numeraire In general equilibrium analysis, the numeraire is a commodity in terms of which all other goods are valued. Precious metals such as gold are the classic numeraire goods, although the principle extends to MONEY more generally, which may be conceived as a good as well as a medium of exchange. In contrast, any good may serve as a unit of account.

Nurkse, Ragnar (1907–1959) An economist whose work examined and sought solutions for the vicious circle of poverty in underdeveloped countries, which he viewed as linked to insufficient investment. Nurkse contended that investment is subject to external economies of scale—that is, the more investment there is, the more profitable further investment becomes. Contrary to neoclassical claims, Nurske argued that poor countries might never follow the development path of the industrialized countries because they might never attract enough capital to fuel the development cycle. The gap between rich and poor countries, in this case, would only increase.

Nurkse was born in Estonia, emigrated to Canada, and spent much of his abbreviated career at Columbia University in New York. The vicious circle of poverty that he identified in *Problems of Capital Formation in Underdeveloped Countries* (1953) describes a number of interlocking disincentives to investment, saving, and capital formation. He saw that the small size of domestic markets is one hindrance to growth in underdeveloped economies; the organization of those economies around the export of raw materials is another. Nurkse argued that this particular source of income would decline as industrial improvements in the richer countries reduced the demand for raw materials.

According to Nurkse, poor countries needed to gear industry toward supplying the home market. He recognized, however, that impoverished farmers cannot afford manufactured goods and that food production is often insufficient to feed the new industrial workers. The success of industrialization, therefore, requires the simultaneous transformation of domestic agriculture and industry. The latter, in turn, needs to be diversified, since the output of any single industry cannot generate sufficient demand for its own product. Only coordinated action can break the vicious circle.

Nurkse saw such coordination as the logical responsibility of government. Collective action was required to enforce compulsory saving, as well as to coordinate investment. Proponents of the theory of LINKAGES, or "unbalanced" growth, have criticized Nurkse's insistence that development must occur along a broad front, and state-centered industrialization has fallen out of favor. Yet there remains no broad consensus about the proper formula for development in the many regions of the world where poverty remains entrenched, and Nurkse's work continues to play a role.

O

Oakeshott, Michael (1901–1990) A British political philosopher known for his critique of rationalist thought in politics and for his defense of TRADITION. These made Oakeshott one of the leading theoreticians of political conservatism in the 1960s and 1970s, although his political views draw on a broader, holistic account of human experience developed in his earlier work, especially the Hegelian-influenced *Experience and Its Modes* (1933).

Oakeshott distinguished between four dominant "modes" of experience, each of which constitutes a vision of reality from a particular perspective: practice, science, history, and poetry. Oakeshott was highly critical of efforts to impose singular views of human experience, particularly on the part of scientific rationalism. The consequences of such monopolization were especially serious in the area of politics. In *Rationalism and Politics* (1962), Oakeshott argued that nearly all politics in post-Renaissance Europe had committed the rationalist error of trying to improve the human condition through the application of a "formula" based on abstract ideas. Such schemes left little margin for the transmission of practices from generation to generation, which for Oakeshott defined a responsible political tradition. Oakeshott argued for a much narrower conception of politics, limited to working within the margins of a legitimate political order based on law and tradition. Later work, such as *On Human Conduct* (1975), was partly devoted to exploring the forms of behavior and deliberation appropriate to this vision of politics.

Oakeshott spent much of his career at the London School of Economics. His other important works include *Social and Political Doctrine of Contemporary Europe* (1941), *Hobbes on Civil Association* (1975), and *On History and Other Essays* (1983).

obedience A subject of considerable interest in the 1960s and 1970s, especially in the wake of Hannah ARENDT's account of the trial of former Nazi official Adolf Eichmann, *Eichmann in Jerusalem* (1963), and Stanley MILGRAM's pathbreaking experimental studies in obedience, collected in *Obedience to Authority* (1974). Both works challenged the widespread assumption that the perpetrators of acts of barbarity or cruelty were monsters or, in some fashion, pathological. The efficiency with which Eichmann coordinated the Nazi GENOCIDE suggested a different model: the mild bureaucratic personality, conscientiously fulfilling its responsibilities. This was source of Arendt's well-known phrase "the banality of evil." Such observations tallied with some of the FRANKFURT SCHOOL's earlier work on the AUTHORITARIAN PERSONALITY as a product of modernity, but not with the narrower attempts by Theodor ADORNO and others to create a personality profile of the authoritarian subject.

Milgram's controlled experiments went further, revealing the astonishing degree to which authority could produce compliance among members of the general public in acts of torture. His experiments placed subjects in the position of administering progressively higher electrical shocks to a second person (an accomplice of Milgram's, who feigned the appropriate responses) when that person failed to respond correctly to a series of tests of memory. As the level of the shocks increased, the experimenter pressured the subject to continue. On average, 65 percent of subjects continued to the maximum level (some 450 simulated volts) in the face of protests and ultimately (feigned) signs of agony on the part of the "learner." Milgram performed numerous variations of this experiment in order to isolate the significant variables in compliance: distance of the authority figure, distance of the victim, signs of resistance, and so on. The experiments were controversial for the mental anguish they inflicted on the subjects, but they have proved enormously influential in understanding the nature of crimes that demanded complicity or participation by large sectors of society.

objectivity The value said to structure most social science research; it implies primarily the absence of researcher bias but also the correspondence of findings to the real world. These different connotations of the term raise a number of fundamental questions about the goals and methods of research: (1) Does the social world have a fixed reality independent of our conceptions of it? This question pits POSITIVISM against the many types of research that emphasize the role of cognitive, cultural, or linguistic structures as the mediators of experience and the constituent features of social reality; (2) a corollary to the first question: Is it possible to produce universal knowledge claims about social systems that are analogous to those claims in the natural sciences? In other words, can social research be said to be "true" in any strong sense, or is it inevitably locked into a series of approximations and debatable opinions; (3) from a methodological standpoint, What are the consequences of detachment or close involvement in the social phenomena under study? This has been a crucial subject in SOCIOLOGY and especially ANTHROPOLOGY, where differences between qualitative and quantitative work are sharp and where the barriers of cultural difference are often high; and (4) Is it possible to keep research procedures free from bias? How can one minimize the tendency of questioners to solicit or steer respondents toward preconceived answers?

A host of diverging and rival answers exist for each of these questions, and it is unrealistic to hope for some final consensus. Much depends on the significance accorded language or symbolic behavior as a mediator of experience and as an inevitably unreliable or partial medium of communication. This has been one of the key contributions of modern philosophy to recent debates in the social sciences—following the so-called linguistic turn of both continental and Anglo-American philosophy in the mid-twentieth century. The question remains central, too, to debates about POSTSTRUCTURALISM and POSTMODERNISM. See also DECONSTRUCTION.

Following the example of the scientific method, positivist scholars tend to advocate a detached attitude toward research. For many others, Max WEBER's concept of *value relevance* provides a guiding principle; he argued that it is all but impossible for researchers to keep their values from entering into observations and analyses. The very process of selecting a research topic, for example, is influenced by researchers' personal backgrounds, interests, and experiences. More radical than Weber's position are the variety of interventionist approaches to social research, which promote the empowerment of subordinate or oppressed social groups.

On the question of bias, Weber again provides an influential example. Although he believed in the principle of value relevance, he also maintained that *value neutrality* should be upheld in the research process; this means that once the research begins, researchers should not let their personal values influence the collection and analysis of data, and they should not hide or change research findings that are contrary to their beliefs or expectations. At this point, the question is no longer confined to the issue of objectivity but involves complex ethical issues as well.

object-relations theory   A major tradition of psychoanalytic research associated primarily with Melanie KLEIN, Wilfred BION, Donald Woods WINNICOTT, W. R. D. Fairburn, and colleagues at London's Tavistock Institute. As developed by Klein, object-relations theory broke with the Freudian sexual drama of identity and child development—in particular the mother-father-child triangle of the Oedipal model—in favor of a notion of individuation and maturation (see Sigmund FREUD; and OEDIPUS COMPLEX). This proceeds by way of diverse emotional attachments to familial and social "objects," which the child progressively internalizes and distinguishes from the self. Klein recognized a continuum in behavior from young, ostensibly pre-Oedipal children to adults. The connections were particularly clear to Klein in the case of psychotics, which led her to propose a universal structure of affect contained between the two poles of paranoid and depressive anxiety. Klein's work on the infant's relationship with its mother was particularly influential in this regard and had a major impact on subsequent feminist theories of identity.

Bion (one of Klein's students), Winnicott, and Fairburn each elaborated on and revised Klein's insights. Bion, in the course of research on schizophrenia, argued strongly for the mother's role in teaching techniques to moderate the paranoid and depressive positions—a role that, when successful, resulted in the relatively complete socialization of the child. He also pioneered group research and group therapy, analyzing the ways in which members of a new group went through stages of resistance and bonding that reflected inner needs and patterns of object relations. Fairburn's research focused primarily on reconceptualizing Freud's theory of the pleasure-seeking libido as a fundamental drive for attachment to objects, leading to a reconfiguration of the Freudian id-ego-superego model. Winnicott also emphasized the importance of the early relationship with the mother and developed an innovative theory of *transitional objects* (such as favorite toys or a blanket), through which the child begins to differentiate external and internal, self and not-self, and to develop competencies for the use of symbols.

The principal competitor to object-relations theory was the EGO PSYCHOLOGY associated with Anna Freud and later with Heinz Hartmann and Edith Jacobson. Klein and Anna Freud strongly disagreed about child development and observational techniques, which resulted in a long (and to a degree still significant) disciplinary schism. See also PSYCHOANALYSIS.

obligation, political   Refers to the nature and degree of individual compliance with a political system, including its laws. Political obligation was an important subject of Classical political thought—perhaps most famously in PLATO's dialogues on the relationship between individual conscience and duty to the *polis*. Greek and Roman forms of citizenship were diverse but often implied a complex web of obligations that went far beyond simple obedience to the laws and included participation in government and in the army in times of danger.

As the feudal system of medieval Europe began to decline, the concept of political obligation returned to prominence. A wide range of forces contributed to renew the problem of the individual's relationship to the STATE—the resurrection of Roman republican traditions, challenges to ecclesiastic authority, the emergence of commercial elites eager for a share of power, and encompassing all, the developing sense of the relative autonomy of individuals as free agents (see BOURGEOISIE; and INDIVIDUALISM). Rather than a divinely given social order, new theories sought a basis for society order in a hypothesized originary moment of individual consent. Consent theories stressed that political obligation was rational, voluntary, and usually subject to a tacit social contract between individuals and society or the state (see SOCIAL-CONTRACT THEORY). Some theorists specified two contracts—one establishing society by agreement among citizens, the other establishing political obligation by agreement between citizens and the state or ruler. Thomas HOBBES (*Leviathan*, 1651), John LOCKE

(*Second Treatise of Government*, 1690), and Jean-Jacques ROUSSEAU (*The Social Contract*, 1772) figure prominently in this tradition.

In the long run, contract theory proved inadequate as a practical basis for political obligation. Social contracts were conjectural rather than historical. They were based on what reasonable people would have, but not on what they had actually agreed to in any meaningful way. To bind successive generations to a political regime with a hypothetical contract proved unrealistic, as did the expectation that citizens would reference that contract in determining whether to continue or abandon their political obligations. A variety of other theories of obligation and consent have sought to address these weaknesses, including UTILITARIANISM (people obey the state because it is beneficial to them), moral gratitude (people obey the state because it takes care of them), and the just state (the state deserves obedience because its institutions, procedures, and measures are just). Reformulations of consent theory have also surfaced, such as John Plamenatz's *Consent, Freedom, and Political Obligation* (1968), which derives broad political obligations from the act of VOTING.

Some traditions of political thought reject the idea of political obligation. Anarchism maintains that states and political institutions are always coercive and, therefore, never binding (see ANARCHY AND ANARCHISM). The broad tradition of critical theory and Marxist-influenced political science views political obligation as primarily a matter of class-based identification with political authority, rather than as a calculation by each citizen of his or her duty to the state.

In contrast, several theoretical literatures have continued to explore the grounds and limitations of political obligation. COMMUNITARIANISM employs the language of *civil* and *moral* obligation in examining the relative balance of RIGHTS and duties in contemporary society. Theories of civic nationalism hold that the ties of collective sentiment—national ties—justify state demands on citizens (see NATIONALISM). Rational-choice theorists continue to scrutinize the *value* of compliance and the problem of FREE RIDERS in the provision of PUBLIC GOODS (see RATIONAL-CHOICE THEORY).

Oedipus complex   For Sigmund FREUD and for much of the psychoanalytic tradition he inspired, the Oedipus complex is the main framework for understanding human sexual development and

SOCIALIZATION. The Oedipus myth, which Freud proposed in 1910 as the central metaphor for this process, recapitulates the basic emotional conflicts that Freud attributed to early childhood: love for the mother and hostility toward the father. For the child, the father represents the realization that the mother's desires are not wholly directed toward it. The father breaks the privileged bond between child and mother. For boys, this occurs fundamentally through the threat of castration—a threat that reproduces paternal authority and sets the child on the road toward finding a mother-substitute. For girls, the process is much less clear and far more controversial, involving resentment of the mother and the transfer of desire to the father or father-figure. Here, "penis-envy" plays a determining role: the successfully "oedipalized" woman seeks a phallus-substitute by having a child of her own.

The Oedipus complex has been an enduring subject of interest in psychology, social theory, and FEMINISM—the last in no small part because Freud relegated female sexuality to a secondary effect of male sexuality. Some of the most interesting of this work treats the Oedipus complex as less a universal of human development—Freud's position—than a socializing structure largely specific to capitalist society (see FRANKFURT SCHOOL; and Gilles DELEUZE).

offer curve   Also *reciprocal demand curve*. Introduced by the economist Alfred MARSHALL and popularized by Francis EDGEWORTH, an offer curve is a popular diagrammatic device used in general EQUILIBRIUM two-country models of international trade. Any point on a country's offer curve indicates the quantity of exports it is willing to offer to obtain a certain quantity of imports from the other country. The point where the offer curves of the two countries intersect is the point where the quantity offered by each country exactly matches the quantity demanded by the other country. This is the point of equilibrium. The magnitude of trade at this level determines the TERMS OF TRADE for each country.

Okun's law   Economist Arthur Okun observed a statistical regularity in the relationship between the change in the employment rate in an economy and the degree to which current real output (GDP) growth exceeded *potential* real output growth, usually assumed to be 3 percent per year. In an economic boom, GDP might grow at 6 percent per year, and the change in the employment rate was observed to be roughly one-third of the growth gap—one-third of 3 percent, or 1 percentage point. Okun's law thus gives a rough estimate of the change in the employment rate through economic growth cycles.

oligarchy   Rule by the few. PLATO and ARISTOTLE were among the first political philosophers to recognize oligarchy as a basic category of government, typically distinguished from rule by the one (MONARCHY) and rule by the many (DEMOCRACY). For Aristotle, oligarchy was distinguished further as a degenerate form of ARISTOCRACY, in which the few rule only in their own interests.

Oligarchy continues to be a subject of interest for modern political theorists—especially as revised and reexamined by early twentieth-century theorists of elites such as Robert MICHELS, Gaetano MOSCA, and Vilfredo PARETO (see ELITE AND ELITISM). These theorists argued that elite rule was a natural outcome of large-scale organization and that oligarchy in some form was an inevitability (see in particular Michels' IRON LAW OF OLIGARCHY). Others have observed that in societies without strong distinctions of rank, oligarchy gravitates toward plutocracy: rule based on wealth.

oligopoly and oligopsony   A market with a small number of sellers and a large number of buyers is called an *oligopoly*. Less common is *oligopsony*—a market in which a few buyers confront a large number of sellers. Both permit strategic behavior on the part of the small group to increase its leverage vis-à-vis the larger group of buyers or suppliers. In practice, this means that oligopolists can restrict output to keep prices and profits above their unrestricted, perfectly competitive level. Oligopsonists, similarly, can conspire to purchase below the competitive price.

Oligopoly is a relatively common example of IMPERFECT COMPETITION and thus an important subject of economic analysis. In general, the fewer the competitors, the greater the control of the oligopolistic group over supply and price. Successful oligopolistic practices require some means of ensuring compliance with the production or price restrictions. This is the challenge facing CARTELS, and the nature of such agreements has been a frequent concern of GAME THEORY. The extreme case, in which there is one supplier, is called MONOPOLY. Two suppliers constitute DUOPOLY.

Olson, Mancur (1932–1998) An American economist who developed a provocative critique of theories of collective action and an influential analysis of lobbying, both in *Logic of Collective Action* (1965). Olson sought an answer to why majority interests in a society (such as the interest of the poor in redistributing wealth) do not generally carry the day. He pointed out that small groups, mobilized in defense of their direct interests, tend to be more efficient at collective action than large, dispersed groups—in large part because members of small groups are more accountable to one another for the defense of their interests. For this reason, business leaders and the wealthy are better able to gain collective goods than workers or social-movement activists. Likewise, the ability of merchants to control prices is a declining function of the number of participants in a market (but usually exceeds the countervailing power of consumers).

To overcome the effects of size, large-scale groups need either a means of discipline over members or some form of "selective incentive" (e.g., the fear of ostracism for nonparticipation). In general, however, Olson argued that the benefits of large-scale collective action are small relative to the costs of participation, so that wherever large populations stand to benefit from a collective good, most potential beneficiaries will not become activists. They will instead wait and hope to benefit from the efforts of those who do become active. Olson popularized the term FREE RIDERS to describe those who benefit from the collective action of others. Such actors thereby optimize self-interest by making gains without any expenditure of time, effort, or money. Olson's views were provocative because they asserted that lack of participation was in fact a rational decision—even where collective action would bring collective benefits. He thus ran counter to much of the democratic pluralist account of groups and social interests, as well as to the prevailing arguments about social movements.

Olson extended many of his ideas to the problem of national economies in *The Rise and Decline of Nations* (1982), in which he argued that lobbying structures tend to calcify over time, resulting in poor allocation of resources. Democratic stability therefore tended toward economic stagnation and decline, as was visible, he suggested, in Britain. Olson's other work includes *Power and Prosperity* (1996), an analysis of the capitalist transition in Russia and the other former socialist countries.

one-dimensional man The title and central concept of an influential study of modern society by critical theorist Herbert MARCUSE (1964). One-dimensionality refers to the progressive closing off of the possibility of radical difference and opposition in modern society. This occurs at the level of social groups (with the decline of working-class radicalism) and, much more insidiously, at the level of thought itself, which increasingly operates within preformed channels of consumer choice and superficial difference. Such a society absorbs and neutralizes dissent, and thereby loses its capacity for critical reflection on the goals of society and the possibility of radical change. The end of this dialectical capacity for reflection signals the collapse of "two-dimensional" man into one-dimensional man—a figure dominated by the singular mode of instrumental rationality that characterizes modern CAPITALISM. On the basis of this work and his earlier *Eros and Civilization* (1955), Marcuse became a major icon of the 1960s counterculture.

one-party state A STATE in which a single political party maintains a MONOPOLY on power (sometimes referred to as a single-party system). Political scientists generally recognize two variants of the one-party state. The first type is characterized by elite membership, centralized organization, and the fusion of the party with the government. Most communist regimes developed along these lines (see COMMUNISM). The second type is associated mainly with regimes on the African continent and is based on mass membership, loose organization, and party dominance of government organs.

There are a number of other distinctive forms of one-party rule, including theocracies such the Taliban regime in Afghanistan, military-led governments, traditional monarchies (e.g., Saudi Arabia and other Gulf states), and façade-liberal, or directed, democracies where, despite the appearances of pluralist democracy, a single party or ruler dominates the government and undermines competition from other elites (e.g., Mexico until the 1990s, Singapore, Egypt). Although such regimes permit little or no open opposition, struggles do occur between factions within the ruling elite.

In China, the Communist party has held a virtual monopoly on political power through its control of the police and military, patronage networks, administrative organs, trade unions, and media. Nationalist appeals have helped link the fate of the party to that of the nation. Although this model lost legitimacy and collapsed in the Soviet Union and in many of its allied countries, one-party communist states have also survived in Cuba, Vietnam, and North Korea.

In Africa, the heyday of one-party states followed the period of European decolonization. Many of these played an important role in integrating diverse social and tribal groups into national life. The remaining African one-party states still employ this argument to justify their hold on power. Leaders of Eritrea and Uganda, for example, argue that multiparty systems divert attention from the national good and encourage competition among ethnic subgroups. Elsewhere, there is widespread agreement that single-party control has transformed governments into predators that have drained their countries of resources. Official corruption, attributable to a lack of governmental accountability, is widely perceived as a root cause of the economic malaise that has lowered standards of living since independence. By the early 1990s, this view, combined with pressure from the international lending community and examples of democratization in other regions of the world, led to a series of democratic transitions and reform throughout Africa. The consolidation of these reforms is far from guaranteed, however, and many African states continue to struggle with issues of nationality and ethnicity, as well as with the challenges of underdevelopment (see DEVELOPMENT).

open-market operations A transaction undertaken by a CENTRAL BANK in the market for securities or foreign exchange that has the effect of increasing or decreasing reserves in the banking system. It is one of the instruments available to a central bank that affects the cost and availability of bank reserves and hence the amount of money in the economy. Open-market operations can be used in the short run to stabilize output fluctuations and in the long run to control INFLATION.

open society Austrian philosopher Karl Raimund POPPER's label, borrowed from Henri Bergson, for a social and political system based on belief in the plurality of truth, scientific innovation, individual freedom, and the RULE OF LAW. According to Popper, open societies deal with social problems through piecemeal reform rather than through wholesale social engineering. In so doing, they maintain a healthy respect for individual rights and impose strict limits on the powers of the state. Conversely, closed societies pursue reform at virtually any cost and attempt to achieve an ideal social order through censorship, propaganda, economic AUTARKY, anti-individualism, and strict limits on scientific and intellectual innovation. In *The Open Society and Its Enemies* (1945), Popper identified PLATO, Georg HEGEL, and Karl MARX as the philosophical enemies of the open society, arguing that their belief in ultimate truth and utopian schemes for social improvement contained the seeds of TOTALITARIANISM.

operationalization The process of transforming an abstract concept or theory into an empirical, testable subject of research. Proper operationalization is therefore crucial to obtaining relevant results and is especially at stake in the formulation of research methods. In sociological research based on surveys or interviews, for example, the construction of the line of questioning is essential. To operationalize a theory about happiness, for example, it may be relevant to try to distinguish degrees of happiness or its context or frequency. Bad operationalization can introduce the researcher's preconceptions or biases into the data or generate responses that do not adequately test the theory in question. In contrast, successful operationalizations (resulting in *operational definitions*) have a high degree of VALIDITY and RELIABILITY.

opportunity cost The worth placed on the second-best choice or opportunity, representing the benefits forgone by making a different choice. Opportunity cost plays a major role in many forms of economic analysis, because it represents the *real* cost of things. LEISURE, for example, may be perceived to be a free good, but in economic analysis the cost of leisure is the money that could have been earned by working. Likewise, positive accounting profits are not necessarily *economic* profits, because all investments have an opportunity cost. If an investment in a firm earns 5 percent, but a government bond pays 6 percent (the opportunity cost), then the investment has generated an economic loss.

options Contracts or securities that give their owner the right to buy or sell an asset at a specified price on or before a specified date. The price is called the *exercise price* or the *strike price*, and the specified date is called the *expiration date*. A contract to sell is called a *put option*, and a contract to buy, a *call option*. In the United States, options may be exercised at any time on or before the expiration date. A European option can be exercised only at maturity. The owner of a call option does not receive any dividends paid by the common stock or have any other rights of ownership until the option is exercised. The owner of the put option has the right to sell on similar terms. When options are first written, the strike price is usually set near or equal to the currently prevailing stock price. The option is then said to be "at-the-money." As the stock prices changes, the option will become either "in-the-money" or "out-of-the-money." A call option is in-the-money when the stock price is above the strike price; it is out-of-the-money when the stock price is below the strike price. The most popular option-pricing model is that of Fischer Black and Myron Scholes in "The Pricing of Options and Corporate Liabilities," which determines the equilibrium option price according to the principle that there should be no ARBITRAGE opportunities in the market.

ordinal scale See MEASUREMENT.

ordinal utility See CARDINAL AND ORDINAL UTILITY.

ordinary least squares In economics, the technique most commonly used in REGRESSION ANALYSIS to estimate parameters. This procedure minimizes the sum of the squares of the distances between the data points and the estimated regression function (these distances are referred to as *residuals*). Under certain conditions, this technique produces the *best linear unbiased estimators* (BLUE) of the parameters.

organic analogy An analogy between social and natural systems. PLATO's analogy between the healthy individual and the well-run state is an example, and many others can be found in classical and modern social theory.

organic solidarity For Emile DURKHEIM, the mode of social solidarity that characterizes modern, highly differentiated societies. It describes a situation in which each part of the society is dependent on the other parts, thus forming an organic whole. In Durkheim's schema, organic solidarity contrasts with MECHANICAL SOLIDARITY, in which solidarity is based on the uniformity and therefore interchangeability of the parts. Agricultural and premodern societies are characterized by mechanical solidarity.

organization man A concept introduced by the sociologist William Foote Whyte in his popular book of that title (1956). The organization man, Whyte argued, was a new personality type characteristic of the highly conformist bureaucratic structure and internal culture of large corporations. The lives of organization men were completely shaped by the company and demanded total commitment—at the expense of external networks of family, friends, and community. The emergence of organization man correlated with the trend toward isolated, homogenized suburban living and, for Whyte, thwarted the competitive individualism at the heart of the official American value system.

organizations Although potentially inclusive of all forms of organized groups, the term refers especially to relatively formal and complex structures with clearly demarcated identities and purposes—such as corporations or bureaucracies. *Organization theory* underpins a wide range of sociological and economic research into management techniques and the organizational structure of FIRMS. Much of organization theory is focused on aspects of the problem of efficiency. The development of corporations and bureaucratic structures has historically been treated as a way of efficiently meeting the challenges of coordinating the complex and varied aspects of modern production and administration. The work of Frederick Taylor oriented much of the early activity in organizational research: his methods of SCIENTIFIC MANAGEMENT promised to allow managers to determine the most efficient division and organization of tasks, based on time and motion studies and, later, on inquiries into forms of surveillance and incentive (see HAWTHORNE EFFECT). Max WEBER pioneered much of the study of bureaucratic structures, which he understood to be driven largely by the imperative of efficiency. At the same time, he argued that bureaucracy was subject to a range of internal counterpressures, such as hierarchical rigidity and the emergence of strong tendencies of self-perpetuation, which potentially threatened the performance of productive or administrative tasks.

Much of the organization theory of the 1950s and 1960s was shaped by functionalist and systems models of analysis, notably that of Talcott PARSONS. Following Parsons, all organizations can be treated as relatively coherent and bounded systems that perform sets of functions and are structured to meet certain goals: reproduction, the management of internal stresses, and the necessity of confronting exogenous change. Peter BLAU led a shift in research toward the study of the internal structures of organizations, without making functionalist assumptions. Still later research in POPULATION ecology studied patterns in whole fields of organizations; this work completed the separation between sociological theories of organization and psychological theories of behavior in organizations (which flourished especially in business schools).

In the late twentieth century, there has been significant debate regarding the inevitability of the particular forms of economic organization that dominate industrial societies. CONTINGENCY THEORY emerged as a challenge to the unilinear notions of efficiency promoted by scientific management. It emphasized the ways in which the relative stability of technologies and markets plays a strong determining role in the nature of the leadership and internal organization of firms. AGENCY THEORY looks at the diverse ways in which services are contracted and provided among buyers and sellers or employers and employees. Considerable historical research has been done on the effect of political and cultural factors in shaping the direction of economic organization—again calling into question the assumption that efficiency has been the driving rational force beyond economic and socioeconomic transformations. This has given rise to a new wave of institutionalist analyses of organizations. A closely related field is the economic theory of the firm (see FIRM, THEORY OF THE).

Oriental despotism A term applied to the tyrannical, highly centralized, and bureaucratized regimes that tended to emerge in societies where the control of water and irrigation was the basis of political authority, such as the ancient civilizations of Mesopotamia, Egypt, India, China, Mesoamerica, and Andean America. These are also frequently described as HYDRAULIC SOCIETIES. The concept of Oriental despotism is closely related to Karl MARX's concept of an ASIATIC MODE OF PRODUCTION, which similarly focused on the role and control of water.

The major modern theorizer of both Oriental despotism and hydraulic society was Karl Wittfogel, a specialist on China and a member of the FRANKFURT SCHOOL. Although Wittfogel's research and contentions are controversial, they have contributed to a significant wave of research since the 1950s on state formation and societal evolution.

orientalism The current use of the term draws heavily on Edward Said's account of Western scholarly practices of exoticizing the East (and especially the Middle East), while neglecting considerations of power (*Orientalism*, 1978). Orientalist accounts, he argued, reduce the East to a wild, disorganized, and exotic locale, where the mysticism of the Orient is set against the putatively superior reason and detachment of the Occident. By characterizing Eastern cultures in inferior terms, Orientalists lent moral justification to Western imperialism (see IMPERIALISM AND EMPIRE). Said thus identifies a discourse of power embedded in a "neutral" tradition of scholarly thinking. He warns that Orientalism continues to pervade the way the industrialized West thinks about developing countries. The concept has had a significant impact on cultural research and has come to represent any discourse that constructs the "other" from a position of hegemony.

Ortega y Gassett, José (1883–1955) Spanish philosopher and man of letters, Ortega y Gassett was an enormously prolific writer and a dominant figure in Spanish intellectual life throughout most of his career. He founded and edited a number of journals and wrote many of his most significant pieces for newspapers. Ortega y Gassett addressed a wide range of philosophical, literary, and political themes but is most often associated with his attack on mass society and his defense of aristocratic values—most prominently in *The Revolt of the Masses* (1929). There, he developed what was in many respects a classic liberal critique of EGALITARIANISM and the tyranny of the majority—a tyranny realized, he argued, in the communist and fascist regimes. Ortega y Gassett asserted the fundamental inequality of human beings and argued for the necessity of intellectual elites. Only the latter, he argued, could preserve the aristocratic values of excellence and individuality on which civilization was based.

In his philosophical writing, Ortega y Gassett described individual existence as a "vital project" that unfolded within its historical circumstances. He wrote important works of literary criticism and was acclaimed for his elegant and accessible style as an essayist. Ortega y Gassett was also active in politics—aligned with the liberals during the 1920s and 1930s and later with the Republican side during the Spanish Civil War (1936–1939). He went into exile during World War II, returned to Spain in 1948, and founded the Institute of Humanities in Madrid.

His other important works include *The Modern Theme* (1923), *The Dehumanization of Art* (1925), and *Toward a Philosophy of History* (1941).

out-group homogeneity   The phenomenon by which a group is perceived as more coherent and homogeneous by people outside the group, regardless of the perceptions of the *in-group*.

overdetermination   Originally used by Sigmund FREUD to signify the way in which a symbol or act may have more than one meaning or cause. The term was subsequently imported into social science by the Marxist philosopher Louis ALTHUSSER (*For Marx*, 1966), who used it to describe multiple, simultaneous, and interpenetrating historical causation. While embracing a "materialist" version of MARXISM, Althusser distanced himself from arguments for the strict economic determinism of other dimensions of society. The classic Marxist relationship between the economic base and the superstructure of political, cultural, and social practices, he argued, is too complicated to be reduced to simple "determination" of the latter by the former (see BASE AND SUPERSTRUCTURE). A mode of production makes possible (and may be bolstered by) diverse ideologies and interests. In practice, therefore, it will generally be impossible to identify one cause as crucial, because many causes are operative and supply more than enough determination to explain a given situation. Removing one of them would not necessarily change that situation. Althusser also argued that the superstructure interacts reflexively with the economic base, such that changes in the dominant ideology, for example, can affect relations of production. Political practices and cultural patterns are subject to the same dynamics—indeed, they are the "conditions of existence" of modes of production as much as modes of production are "in the last instance" determinative of ideologies and political practices. In practical application, for Althusser, this meant that social transformation depends on more than the overthrow of capitalist economic structures; there must be a "ruptural unity" in the overdetermined, reflexive interaction of economic, ideological, cultural, and political structures.

overlapping-generations model   Introduced by the economist Paul SAMUELSON in 1958, the overlapping-generations model allowed economic models to move beyond the artificial assumption that all agents lived contemporaneously. Instead, each generation is held to live for two periods, so that the old of one generation exist simultaneously with the young of the next. Samuelson's model has become the basis of a general-equilibrium optimization model with multiple commodities and many agents. It adheres to the methodological assumptions of the neoclassical model of agent optimization, market clearing, and rational expectations. A vast literature on MACROECONOMICS, public finance, business-cycle theory, and monetary economics makes use of this model, often employing longer lifespans and more overlap between generations. Overlapping-generation models differ from the standard ARROW–DEBREU MODELS of general equilibria in that there may exist multiple equilibria and that these equilibria need not be PARETO OPTIMAL.

overshooting   A "jump" in the value of an economic variable above or below its steady state or EQUILIBRIUM value in response to a shock (such as a sudden change in the money supply). Overshooting is a common feature of asset prices, and figures especially in foreign-exchange markets. This reflects the fact that asset prices such as the EXCHANGE RATE are highly flexible, whereas the prices of goods and services are sticky and slow to adjust. Thus the exchange rate can change in the short run, while in the long run the nominal exchange rate and the international commodity price ratio will change in the same proportion as the initial increase in money supply (see LONG RUN AND SHORT RUN). Overshooting is thus a short-term effect and has no consequences for economic variables in the long term.

P

Paleolithic The "Old Stone Age," identified by John Lubbock (*Prehistoric Times*, 1865). The term designates the earliest human cultural era, characterized by hunting and gathering societies that used chipped and flaked stone tools. It includes such early hominids as Australopithecines and the first varieties of the genus *Homo*. It was followed by the Mesolithic and the NEOLITHIC eras.

panel data Data on a cross section of individuals, firms, or countries sampled at regular intervals of time. Panel data sets are particularly useful where continuous longitudinal data sets (data collected over time) are hard to obtain, and they are critical for testing models of behavior over time. See also LONGITUDINAL ANALYSIS.

panopticon A model prison developed by the nineteenth-century English jurist Jeremy BENTHAM. Bentham's panopticon was a circular ring of cells surrounding a central observation tower. The novelty of his concept was that it involved controlling convicts through the potential for constant observation rather than force: the central tower was opaque, and prisoners could never be certain whether they were being watched. Bentham argued that under these circumstances prisoners would police themselves, and that in the extreme, cells would not need doors. The concept provided an early foundation for behaviorist psychology and informed, in part, B. F. SKINNER's *Walden Two* (1948) (see BEHAVIORISM). It was borrowed and extended by Michel FOUCAULT in *Discipline and Punish* (1975) to characterize the diffuse forms of social control that structure many aspects of modern society. According to Foucault, the panoptic principle is at work in all forms of surveillance and monitoring, from schools to hospitals, army barracks, and factories. As with Bentham's panopticon, Foucault argued that the larger social objective is to internalize discipline so that force is no longer necessary.

paradigm Associated in the social sciences primarily with Thomas KUHN's *The Structure of Scientific Revolutions* (1961), the term refers to the general set of assumptions, questions, and methods that structures a field of inquiry at any given time. Together, these define the boundaries of what Kuhn called "normal science." Paradigm shifts occur, he suggested, when the accumulation of anomalies and contradictions within a given paradigm furnishes the basis for breakthrough research, which then leads to the consolidation of a new scientific paradigm. As Kuhn argued, this process is rarely simple or sudden: the larger implications of such research may take generations to be widely appreciated. He argued further that paradigms are basically "incommensurable"—each is structured by a distinct logic that guides inquiry, determines the standards of truth, and delimits the range of acceptable answers.

Although Kuhn applied the notion of paradigms to the physical sciences, the concept is often applied to systems of thought more generally. Kuhn's account has been criticized as overly vague, however, and debate continues about the usefulness and specificity of the concept. The strong relativism implicit in Kuhn's challenge to more conventional models of scientific progress has also been a source of controversy.

The term *paradigmatic* is also used in STRUCTURALISM and in structuralist LINGUISTICS. As defined by Louis Hjelmslev, linguistic usage refers to a class or category of elements, such as the parts of speech. Paradigmatic, in this context, is contrasted with *syntagmatic*, which designates the rules or structures (such as grammar) that organize the paradigmatic elements. See also SYNTAGMATIC AND PARADIGMATIC.

paradox of voting A circular voting outcome that precludes a majority winner. In the simplest example with three candidates, A is preferred to B, B is preferred to C, and C is preferred to A. Each candidate thus has a claim to be a majority winner, but no candidate can defeat all the others. The paradox of voting occurs when preferences are not *single peaked*, that is, when there is no way to rank A, B, and C along a single dimension for each voter. Where preferences are single peaked, a single choice that can defeat all others is guaranteed. The paradox of voting was originally identified by the Marquis de CONDORCET. See also MEDIAN VOTER THEOREM.

parallel cousins Cousins related through a same-sex sibling bond, usually through the father's brother. CROSS COUSINS are related through an opposite-sex sibling bond, usually the mother's brother.

Pareto, Vilfredo (1848–1923) An Italian economist, sociologist, and political theorist. Pareto's importance to modern economic analysis is difficult to overstate. His preference-based theory of utility (which substituted ranked, or *ordinal*, preferences for quantitative, or *cardinal*, measures of preference) is the foundation of nearly all subsequent economic models. The concept of *Pareto optimality*—an equilibrium situation from which any deviation results in a loss of welfare for at least some people—is the cornerstone of WELFARE ECONOMICS (see PARETO OPTIMAL).

In *Mind and Society: Treatise on General Sociology* (1916 [1936]), Pareto distinguished between the rational behavior of economic actors and the often illogical, sentiment-driven motives for action in other areas of social life. Unlike narrow economic behavior, social behavior was shaped by what Pareto called *residues* and *derivations*. *Residues* were basic human capacities, such as the ability to link unrelated elements together (combination) or the tendency to preserve such links (persistence). *Derivations* were arguments used to rationalize the opinions produced by the residues, such as the recourse to TRADITION, AUTHORITY, or other legitimizing rhetorics. Pareto used this structure to distinguish ECONOMICS from SOCIOLOGY. Combined with his ideas about EQUILIBRIUM, it also informed his theory of the circulation of elites.

Pareto placed great emphasis on the role of competition among social and political elites. Some elites were better suited to preserving social arrangements—these were "lions," in whom the residue of persistence dominated; others were better able to adapt to change and new demands—these were the "foxes," strong in the residue of combination. These complementary qualities resulted in an alternation of power that occurred as changing circumstances unsuited the ruling group for the present needs of society. Pareto thus recommended that ruling groups remain open to new talent from below but also that they be ruthless in maintaining their hold on power, so as to prove their fitness. Pareto's view that society was dominated by competition among divided elites also underwrote his attack on MARXISM in *Les systemes socialistes* (1902, untranslated), which argued against any privileged place for class conflict in modern society.

In general, Pareto came down on the side of traditional authority in his analyses of the contemporary political scene. *The Transformation of Democracy* (1920) condemned rule by a new generation of corrupt plutocrats and proved congenial to the emerging Italian Fascist party, as did his attacks on socialist doctrines (although Pareto was never comfortable with the Fascists and did not live much beyond their ascension to power). Pareto's other major works include *The Rise and Fall of the Elites* (1901) and *Manual of Political Economy* (1906).

Pareto optimal Defined by the economist Vilfredo PARETO as a situation in which society's resources and output are allocated in such a fashion that no reallocation can make at least one individual better off while all others remain at least as well off as before. If such a reallocation is possible, it is said to be a "Pareto improvement" or "Pareto superior" to the original situation.

Pareto showed that competitive equilibrium and use of the price mechanism would yield a Pareto optimal allocation of resources. This provided a concrete theoretical grounding of Adam SMITH's notion of the INVISIBLE HAND and the idea that free trade (between individuals as well as between countries) is socially beneficial. Pareto's proposition was later proved mathematically by Kenneth ARROW and Gerard Debreu in a formulation that came to be known as the FUNDAMENTAL THEOREMS OF WELFARE. The fact that competitive market equilibrium is Pareto efficient has often been used to argue against governmental intervention in markets and for LAISSEZ-FAIRE policies more generally.

The concept of Pareto efficiency holds beyond market applications, however, and is useful in any situation in which interpersonal utility comparisons cannot be made. Because it requires only that individuals judge their own situations, it allows some (often limited) welfare comparison of outcomes without requiring the weighing of some individuals' gains against others' losses.

Park, Robert Ezra (1864–1944) One of the founders and leading sociologists of the CHICAGO

SCHOOL OF SOCIOLOGY, Park played a large role in the emergence of urban sociology, the study of race and immigration, and more generally the field of HUMAN ECOLOGY, which, he argued, encompassed them all. Never a prolific writer, Park was an influential contributor to and sponsor of the work of others—especially the generation of University of Chicago sociologists that came to prominence in the 1920s and 1930s.

At various times, Park studied with John DEWEY, William JAMES, and Georg SIMMEL; their influences are visible in his work. Much of his professional life was spent in journalism and in various forms of activism on behalf of African Americans (he worked for many years with Booker T. Washington). Park had little formal training in sociology and began his career in academia at the age of fifty. With his students at the University of Chicago, Park emphasized the study of urban life and race relations. Methodologically, he stressed the need for empirical research—especially PARTICIPANT OBSERVATION. Park produced a number of important articles but was perhaps best known for the textbook he wrote with Ernest W. Burgess, *Introduction to the Science of Sociology* (1921). With Burgess, he coined the term *human ecology* to describe the systematic study of human relations in the social environment, especially in relation to the patterns of territorial distribution and adaptation of human populations—an interpretive framework that he borrowed from plant and animal ecology.

For Park, society involved this distribution and adaptation of groups and, more generally, the process of social control that organized and integrated them. Within this framework, he argued that four basic principles shaped human relations: competition, conflict, assimilation, and accommodation. *Competition* was the primary force, although the inevitable interdependence of a complex society also often gave rise to unintended cooperation, referred to as "competitive cooperation." Society, in turn, contained numerous *conflicts* that the processes of social control integrated more or less successfully. Park explored accommodation and assimilation primarily in his influential analysis of the differences between immigrant groups and African Americans. *Assimilation* occurred as immigrants integrated into the dominant culture and became indistinguishable from it. *Accommodation* described a situation in which the subordinate group merely adapted to the conditions of the dominant culture.

parole   See LANGUE AND PAROLE.

parsimony   The principle that the simplest solution among models with equivalent results is the best. Put differently, the best model is the one that explains a phenomenon with the fewest variables or parameters.

Parsons, Talcott   (1902–1979) An American sociologist whose functionalist perspective became a dominant sociological paradigm in the 1950s and 1960s (see FUNCTIONALISM). While teaching at Harvard University, Parsons worked toward a unified theory of social systems based on the functional analysis of SOCIAL STRUCTURES—a methodology derived primarily from Emile DURKHEIM and Max WEBER. Against theories that emphasized conflict as the fundamental condition of society, Parsons emphasized the role that shared norms and values (and the process of SOCIALIZATION to those norms and values) played in the operation and stable reproduction of the social order.

Parsons's work was shaped by his studies in the history of social theory. He was active in facilitating the translation of Weber's work, and it was Weber who perhaps most influenced his theory of action. Parsons's first major statement of his perspective came in *The Structure of Social Action* (1937). There, he presented Weber, Durkheim, Vilfredo PARETO, and Alfred MARSHALL as contributors to the development of a "voluntaristic theory of social action," which Parsons saw himself as advancing. His influence also grew out of his editing activities and through his promotion of certain directions in European social theory. These efforts shaped the canonical education of American sociologists for generations—not least by locating Karl MARX outside the core works of the canon.

In *The Social System* (1951), Parsons argued that within a social environment, individuals were presented a limited number of choices and that these choices were informed by social values and norms. The behaviors and choices that maximized individual satisfaction defined the status roles that structured social systems. The social system had its own needs and requirements (an argument taken from Durkheim), and individuals furthered its existence through socialization, or adoption of the system's norms and values. Parsons devised an elaborate model to illustrate the hierarchy of systems and subsystems, in which the survival of each system depended on a number of functional requirements. The AGIL schema (*adaptation*, *goal attainment*, *integration*, and *latency*) was his best known model of how such systems worked: each social system contains subsystems that, respectively, adapt to the physical world (the economy), manage resources to achieve its goals (politics), develop a successful internal organization for managing conflicts (social control), and maintain equilibrium (socialization).

The subsystems that perform these functions, moreover, are not static. Societies progressively differentiate themselves in order to better meet their basic functional needs. Here Parsons drew parallels between social and biological systems—a field he called *evolutionary sociology*. If differentiation creates a greater capacity for adaptation to the environment, Parsons also recognized that it places greater stress on the integrative dimension of social order, creating a greater need for mechanisms of inclusion. This was met, he argued, by a concomitant process of generalization of the values and norms of society to permit broader participation. In his later work, Parsons focused more on evolution and on the capacity of culture to guide social integration.

Following Durkheim, Parsons argued that social subsystems were EMERGENT PROPERTIES, or aspects of social organization that cannot be reduced to attributes or actions of individuals. Nonetheless, Parsons continued to join functional analysis to an ACTION THEORY that was meant to account for the behavior of individuals within structures in a nondeterministic fashion. Parsons's emphasis on the *action frame of reference* was one of the most influential efforts to reconcile the concepts of action (including rational action) and social structure. He treated social structure as a set of abstracted and aggregated norms rooted in patterns of individual interaction; these norms, in turn, contextualize and inform subsequent interactions. Individuals benefit, Parsons suggested, from the recognition from others that normative action bestows. Here, Parsons relied on a concept of individual adaptativeness to society drawn from EGO PSYCHOLOGY.

Parsons made major contributions to a wide range of other theoretical and empirical areas, from introducing the concept of the *sick role* in medical sociology to linking sociology with SYSTEM(S) THEORY and PSYCHOANALYSIS. He was the founder of the Department of Social Relations at Harvard University, an influential attempt to overcome disciplinary divisions in social science. Parsons's other works include *Towards a General Theory of Action* (1951, with Edward Shils), *Societies: Evolutionary and Comparative Perspectives* (1966), and *The System of Modern Societies* (1971).

By the 1960s, Parsons's minimization of social conflict began to seem a conservative or status quo position—incapable especially of dealing with the dimension of social change. His work was widely criticized on this basis. Nonetheless, it remained perhaps the single most influential and comprehensive theoretical statement produced in American sociology. In addition to shaping work directly in the functionalist and systems theoretical traditions, it exerted an influence so pervasive as to pass unnoticed in many of the basic projects of contemporary sociology. It has also been important to other theorists, including some, such as Jürgen HABERMAS, who work within more critical traditions.

partial equilibrium analysis The study of markets for specific commodities or factors of production in isolation from other commodities or factors. Developed by the economist Alfred MARSHALL, this approach contrasts with general equilibrium analysis, which considers all markets simultaneously and recognizes this interdependence.

participant observation A method of research in ANTHROPOLOGY that involves extended immersion in a culture and participation in its day-to-day activities. Originally associated with and promoted by Franz BOAS and Bronislaw MALINOWSKI in the 1910s and 1920s, participant observation quickly became a basic component of American and British anthropological FIELDWORK and ethnography. It led, at first, to work in societies that were small, stable, and without written languages. Such contexts maximized the strengths of participant observation and minimized its weaknesses. As anthropology has shifted toward larger-scale, literate, and even modern societies, the limitations of participant observation have become greater and its objectivity has been challenged.

The difficulty of negotiating the relationship between participating and observing has been a subject of lengthy debate among anthropologists since the 1940s. The assumed objectivity of the observer has been subjected to challenges from poststructuralist, postmodern, and postcolonial critics, who have called into question all claims of neutrality. Positivists, too, have criticized participant observation for its lack of demonstrable or scientific standards. Neither of these criticisms are likely to abolish participant observation or fieldwork, but the debate goes some way toward discouraging complacency and, in the long run, contributes to the necessary questioning and reshaping of anthropological methods.

participatory democracy Emphasizes the direct and active participation of citizens in political institutions. Participatory democracy has traditionally been associated with small republics or communities where citizens can engage in face-to-face deliberations. Athenian democracy provides the classical example in which office holders were drawn from the citizen body; the New England town meeting is the most common American referent. Such models have usually been regarded as impractical for large-scale, modern democracies. In these, *representative* structures have supplanted direct participation in most respects (see REPRESENTATION). Referenda and other forms of DIRECT DEMOCRACY meet some of the participatory criteria, but are frequently criticized for their detachment from the institutional and deliberative aspects of decision making. In response, modern participatory democrats generally advocate the decentralization of power to localities where direct participation in institutions of power is a possibility. Some advocates claim normative benefits for participatory democracy, including reduced public estrangement from power and increased concern for collective problems. See, for example, Carol Pateman's *Participation and Democratic Theory* (1970).

In some contexts, participatory democracy extends into the economic realm in support of workplace democracy, COOPERATIVES, and other forms of consumer and worker empowerment. Participatory democracy also shares ground with other democratic reform movements, including COMMUNITARIANISM and DELIBERATIVE DEMOCRACY.

partition The division of a state or territory into two or more independent, self-governing entities. Partition is generally either a last resort in conflicts or a form of institutionalization and normalization of conflict—as in the case of the several Cold War–related partitions of states. Many contemporary states are the products of partition—North and South Korea, India and Pakistan, and formerly East and West Germany. The causes of partition are diverse, ranging from

the postwar arrangements between the victors to internal religious or ethnic differences (Ireland and Northern Ireland; Cyprus).

party, political In democratic societies, parties are organizations that link actors in CIVIL SOCIETY to the formal structures of government. Political parties typically form around groups that share values, interests, or backgrounds. They are primarily vehicles for expressing and advancing their members' interests—either through control of political office or by less direct influence on government policy. As such, they straddle the boundary between civil society and the STATE and are sometimes considered essential to this relationship. The term can also imply undesirable factionalism, however—as in the usually negative connotation of the cognate term "partisan."

The modern political party emerged in the course of seventeenth- and eighteenth-century state formation in Europe. As European monarchs expanded their territories and consolidated their control, they struck bargains with members of the nobility and clergy. Frequently, both groups were granted formal consultative powers in exchange for their cooperation. Assemblies and parliaments became the forums in which the representatives of all groups met—the Crown, the landed interests, and the clergy. The earliest parties grew out of rivalries within this structure. Supporters of the king clashed with parliamentarians who had other loyalties or policy goals. Increasingly, these disputes reflected salient social and economic divides—notably between emerging commercial interests and the "country" parties linked to traditional agriculture. In Great Britain, this opposition became instantiated in the division between Whigs and Tories.

In the nineteenth century, the expansion of the franchise and the extension of parliamentary representation to a wider but still limited array of social groups encouraged the establishment of distinctive parties with more clearly defined positions. *Liberal* and *conservative* divisions took form during this period—the former associated with the growing capitalist class (see BOURGEOISIE); the latter with the landowning aristocracy and, in Catholic countries, with the church. In Great Britain, these interests mapped onto preexisting divisions between Whigs and Tories. These *cadre parties* remained elitist, with membership and participation limited to men of wealth and social standing.

Mass parties emerged as suffrage rights were extended to larger segments of the working class (and later to women). These parties originated mostly on the left—the Labour party in Great Britain and Socialist parties on the European continent were among the first true mass parties. Facing the challenge of mobilizing millions of new voters, they borrowed organizational strategies from labor unions and, over time, became highly structured, centralized, and ideologically oriented. Center and right-wing parties in Europe soon followed in abandoning the cadre structure in the pursuit of a mass electorate (the Liberal party in Great Britain is a notable exception).

In the United States, a number of factors encouraged a more dispersed form of party control. The late nineteenth-century Democratic and Republican parties continued to function much like cadre parties, even as they organized on a mass basis for national elections. One consequence was the much-remarked-upon pattern of local CLIENTALISM and PATRONAGE, often called "machine politics" (see POLITICAL MACHINE). Twentieth-century reforms, notably the emergence of the primary system, were designed to undermine this tendency. Yet the American party system remains rooted in decentralized, state-level organizations. American parties are also less ideological than those of Europe. The Democratic and Republican parties are sometimes referred to as "catch-all" parties: each integrates a wide range of interests into a relatively centrist party platform.

One area of current research focuses on the transformation of European-style mass parties into American-style catch-all parties. Researchers have noted that longstanding social democratic parties have had to modify their appeals as the traditional working-class declines. To remain competitive, social democratic parties have had to search for votes elsewhere, particularly from the middle class. This has prompted many parties on the left to adopt catch-all strategies that place less emphasis on ideology. Some right-leaning parties have pursued similar transformations.

New party orientations, sometimes based on "postmaterialist" values such as ecology and pacifism, have also compelled traditional mass parties to alter their platforms. Perhaps the most significant new factor, however, is the growth of the mass media, with its attendant pollsters, public-relations consultants, and advertising costs. The mass media have tended to erode party power by creating other avenues for reaching the public. In this environment, many politicians can afford to act as quasi-independent operators, with relatively few debts or obligations to the party hierarchy.

Undemocratic regimes present other types of party. Communist and later Fascist parties sought monopolies on power—in large measure by eliminating other organized interests and bases for opposition (see COMMUNISM; FASCISM; and NAZISM). This was the political foundation of modern TOTALITARIANISM. In the developing world, many of the colonial independence movements also rejected competitive democratic systems, preferring ONE-PARTY STATE structures that could better face the challenges of development and Cold War rivalries. While one-party states still dominate parts of Africa and Asia, there has been movement toward more pluralistic party systems. See also DEMOCRACY; ELECTORAL SYSTEM; and PARTY SYSTEM.

party system Governs the roles and relationships among the political parties in a pluralist society. The study of party systems has been strongly influenced by Maurice Duverger's distinction between two-party and multiparty systems. Two-party systems feature major parties of roughly the same size, each with a strong chance of winning a general election. Multiparty systems are composed of more than two parties, and often feature small parties at the margins of a group of larger, governing parties. Because single parties can rarely muster a majority of the vote in such circumstances, COALITION GOVERNMENTs are a common outcome. Different ELECTORAL SYSTEMS have a major impact on the party system: proportional representation usually allows small parties to participate in a significant way. Simple majority, single-ballot electoral systems, on the other hand, generally prevent the formation of smaller parties, resulting in two-party systems.

Britain and the United States are usually described as two-party systems; Italy and France are examples of the multiparty model. However, the distinction often fails to capture some of the variation visible in these systems. Britain, for example, features a significant third party: the Liberal Democrats. Some political scientists have revised Duverger's typology to address these situations. Giovanni Sartori has suggested counting only those parties capable of winning parliamentary representation and affecting coalition governments. Jean Blondel has defined two-party systems as those in which two major parties together gain 90 percent or more of the popular vote. He defines multiparty systems, in contrast, as those in which the two largest parties gain no more than 60 percent of the vote. Blondel also specified "two-plus-one" party systems to account for countries in which a third smaller party plays a stable role (e.g., Germany).

pastoral nomads   Groups that live primarily by animal husbandry and that move regularly according to the dictates of the season or herd movement. This combination of major traits has often been designated a "type" of society in ANTHROPOLOGY, since various forms of pastoral nomadism have been common worldwide. Recent research has tended to dispute the purity of these traits, as well as the presumed autonomy of a pastoral nomadic MODE OF PRODUCTION. Many such societies have been shown to engage in forms of agriculture, and the relationships between pastoral nomadic societies and sedentary ones, especially in the context of COLONIALISM and state formation, is inevitably complex.

patents   A temporary grant of MONOPOLY rights over an innovation or an invention. Patents run for twenty years in most European countries and for seventeen years in the United States. Patent protection is intended to provide incentives for research, although it implies a corresponding monopoly cost to society.

pater **and** ***mater***   From Roman law, *pater* (Lat. "father") is used to distinguish between the socially recognized father and the biological father (the *genitor*). The female equivalents are *mater* (Lat. "mother") and *genetrix*.

patriarchy   Literally, "rule by the father," but now widely used to designate societies or situations in which men play the dominant roles. The term came into use in nineteenth-century theories of social evolution as part of a debate about whether human society was patriarchal or matriarchal in origin. Common to both positions was the association of patriarchy with the emergence of modern systems of private property (Friedrich Engels) and law (Sigmund FREUD). These have remained compelling associations for many feminist scholars, who see in patriarchal domination a basis for the economic and political divisions of modern societies.

patrilineal   In KINSHIP relations, a system that privileges descent through the male line—both for male and female offspring.

patrilocal residence   A marriage rule in which the newly married couple lives with or near the husband's family. The term VIRILOCAL is used synonymously.

patronage   The granting of offices, employment, contracts, franchises, licenses, and other special favors to allies. Modern patronage is most often associated with the *spoils system* in politics, in which a victorious party confers offices and other rewards on its supporters. See also POLITICAL MACHINE.

patron–client relations   See CLIENTALISM.

peasantry   No consensus definition of peasantry exists, but anthropologists have tended to stress its agrarian character, household-level subsistence economy, and relationship to a larger state system or urban elite that dominates it politically, economically, and culturally. Although long considered a principal category of social organization, peasantry has only in recent decades become a major subject of social science research—especially in ANTHROPOLOGY. Early ETHNOLOGY and ethnography around the turn of the twentieth century tended to prefer the comparative social and economic autonomy of tribal societies over the complex relationships of dependence and subordination characteristic of peasant societies. This situation did not begin to change until the 1930s and 1940s with the work of Robert REDFIELD, Conrad Arensberg, and others. It was not until the late 1960s that peasants and peasantry began to receive widespread, interdisciplinary attention.

Redfield's FOLK–URBAN CONTINUUM provides a model for understanding the contact between relatively isolated peasant communities and the cultural traditions and technologies produced in modern cities. As with many other attempts to establish general societal typologies, however, ongoing research has tended to complicate matters by demonstrating the diversity of peasant societies and peasant modes of production, both historically and geographically.

pecuniary economies and nonpecuniary economies   ECONOMIES OF SCALE may be internal or external to a FIRM. In turn, each of these may be classified as pecuniary or nonpecuniary. Pecuniary internal economies of scale occur when a firm can negotiate lower prices for inputs bought in large quantities. Nonpecuniary internal economies result from the fuller utilization of *lumpy* inputs, such as buildings, machinery, and the like. Both reduce cost per unit as output expands.

Nonpecuniary external economies exist when there is technological interdependence between firms, such that it is impossible to specify one firm's production function without knowing the inputs or outputs of other firms. An example of this would be two oil wells on a single oilfield: the yield of each well depends on the output of the other. Pecuniary external economies are those that are dependent on the general development of the industry or on advances made by subsidiary industries.

Peirce, C. S. (1839–1914) An American philosopher credited with laying the groundwork for PRAGMATISM and for an early theory of semiotics (see SEMIOTICS AND SEMIOLOGY). Peirce also contributed to an astonishing number of other fields, from logic to experimental psychology, astronomy, and cartography. He was educated as a chemist and spent most of his career as a member of the U.S. Coast and Geodetic Survey (1860–1891). Except for a brief time at Johns Hopkins University, he never held a teaching position and never found employment as a philosopher.

Peirce consistently sought to apply the scientific method to philosophical problems. His early work focused on an antifoundationalist critique of René DESCARTES—especially Descartes's attempt to ground knowledge in individual consciousness. Against the Cartesians, Peirce argued that knowledge is implicated in a triadic system of meaning that involves the sign, its object, and an "interpretant" that determines what that relationship means. Like later models of structural linguistics elaborated by Ferdinand de SAUSSURE and others, Peirce viewed this triadic relationship as an interlocking network that encompassed all language: the interpretant is always another sign, resulting in a purely relational structure of meaning. Unlike most subsequent structural accounts, however, Peirce argued that language had effects: it structured forms of conduct and experience. In this respect, language was performative and real, rather than a purely symbolic mediation of the world.

Peirce viewed language as one aspect of a larger triadic structure of possible relationships to the world. He distinguished between Firstness (feeling), Secondness (reaction), and Thirdness (habit or generalization). Collectively, these relationships defined the field of *semeiotics* (spelled *semiotics* in most modern linguistic usage). Truth, in this context, was not something that could be fixed within inevitably shifting fields of meaning but did reside in the act of putting meaning to use. In "The Fixation of Belief" (1877) and "How to Make Our Ideas Clear" (1878), Peirce argued that validation through experimentation and action is the only criteria of truth and that even this is limited to advancing provisional beliefs on which we can base further action. The scientific method, in the end, provides the best method for collectively converging on stable beliefs. This theory of truth as *contingent upon its usefulness* was Peirce's major contribution to the pragmatism of William JAMES, John DEWEY, and later figures, although Peirce remained far more concerned with logic than with action or society.

perfect competition   A market structure characterized by (1) many small firms producing homogeneous products; (2) perfect information throughout the market about prices and production; and (3) no impediments to the entry or exit of firms (such as start-up costs). Individuals and firms, in such conditions, exercise no influence on price via their production and consumption decisions—in other words, there is no MONOPOLY power in the market. Further, the free entry and exit of firms implies that all firms earn only normal PROFITS in the long run, sufficient to convince them to stay in the market. Higher short-run profits are possible, but these induce other firms to enter the market until exceptional (or *supernormal*) profits are competed away. By the same token, losses drive competitors from the market until normal profitability is restored. While real markets rarely demonstrate such features, perfect competition plays a key role as a benchmark for efficiency in economic theory. This follows from the demonstration that market allocation under perfect competition is PARETO OPTIMAL—no one can increase profits without someone losing. Perfect competition is thus the limit case of the general theory of markets.

perfect foresight   The assumption that individuals make correct and precise predictions about the future value of variables (i.e., there is no uncertainty). Perfect foresight is a theoretical assumption used in dynamic economic models in order to assure EQUILIBRIUM solutions.

performance principle   A utilitarian principle of distributive JUSTICE that holds that rewards should be distributed on the basis of performance alone. The concept is frequently discussed in the sociology of sports. See also UTILITARIANISM.

person One of the foundational insights of modern SOCIOLOGY and ANTHROPOLOGY is that experiences and conceptions of personhood differ widely, both within and across cultures. The sociologists Emile DURKHEIM and Marcel MAUSS were among the first to attempt a major contextualization of different concepts of personhood, initially by invoking *person* as a basic category of human thought shaped by variable structures of law and morality. Psychological anthropology, particularly the American CULTURE AND PERSONALITY MOVEMENT of the 1920s and 1930s, further pursued study of the relations among individual consciousnesses, types of personality, and broad cultural patterns.

Basic conceptions, experiences, and normative values of personhood also vary historically. Charles Taylor's *Sources of the Self* (1989) provides a major account of this historical development in the West. Such approaches to personhood challenge versions of social science that assume the human individual to be an equivalent unit across cultures.

phatic communion Bronislaw MALINOWSKI's term for speech intended to create and maintain social relations, rather than to exchange useful information. Greetings, pleasantries, and chitchat generally fall into this category.

phenomenology A philosophical movement with origins in the early twentieth-century work of the German philosopher Edmund Husserl. Phenomenology studies the basic structures of consciousness—especially the tools and practical knowledge that underwrite action and intention at a fundamental level. These structures govern consciousness, ways of categorizing "external" objects and phenomena, and types of action. Analyzing them required, Husserl argued, a "bracketing" of the problem of the real existence of objects or other persons in order to focus on the internal processes of consciousness—an analytical step termed *phenomenological reduction*. Phenomenological reduction became a subject of considerable debate among later phenomenologists, who accorded a greater role to processes of interaction with the environment.

Martin HEIDEGGER and Jean-Paul SARTRE, among other philosophers, were greatly influenced by Husserl and by the phenomenological approach more generally. In the social sciences, phenomenology has at times had strong affinities with cognitive psychology and the other cognitive sciences—indeed the work of Maurice Merleau-Ponty relied heavily upon cognitive research on the differentiation of colors and sensations. Phenomenology has also played a role in SOCIOLOGY, initially through the work of Husserl's student Alfred SCHUTZ in the 1930s, and later through that of Peter Burger and Thomas Luckmann. For Schutz, phenomenology provided the necessary basis of any more abstract discussion of social structures or influences—following a distinction between first-order typifications (or basic, taken-for-granted forms of experience and action) and second-order typifications (which integrate more complex information about the world on a broader scale). Schutz also emphasized the fundamental way in which language and symbolic behavior shape experience, thereby providing a bridge between phenomenology and SYMBOLIC INTERACTIONISM. Berger and Luckmann (*The Social Construction of Reality*, 1966) showed similar priorities, if somewhat different methods, in arguing for the rootedness of social structures and social analysis in the forms of typification that underlie the practical, problem-solving forms of everyday knowledge.

Phillips curve Originally, the Phillips curve traced the negative relationship between the rate of change in nominal wages and the rate of UNEMPLOYMENT. Later versions of the curve depicted the trade-off between inflation and unemployment—that is, reducing INFLATION results in higher unemployment. This inverse relationship was described by A. W. Phillips in 1957 on the basis of studies of long-term wage and employment data in the United Kingdom. He further observed that the rate of unemployment required to hold down the level of wage inflation to the normal or accustomed rate is positive (2 to 3 percent in his data), and that this had not changed over a century of observation.

The Phillips curve remains controversial among economists, but most today accept the idea that there is a short-run trade-off between inflation and unemployment. The common explanation underlying this trade-off is that prices are sticky and slow to adjust. Suppose, for example, that the government reduces the quantity of money in the economy. In the long run, the only result of this policy change will be an equivalent fall in all nominal wages and prices—a demonstration of the NEUTRALITY OF

MONEY. Yet not all prices and wages adjust immediately, with the result that such policies will have a short-run effect that differs from the long-run effects. A drop in the money supply while wages and prices remain rigid implies lower spending and sales. This, in turn, causes firms to lay off workers. Thus, the reduction in the money supply lowers inflation but temporarily raises unemployment. Fiscal and monetary policy are commonly used to manipulate this relationship. In the long run, however, all prices adjust and the economy returns to the natural rate of unemployment, which reflects the permanence of structural and frictional forces in the economy. In the long run, therefore, the Phillips curve is vertical at the natural rate of unemployment, and the margin of action for fiscal and monetary policy is zero.

A more recent modification of the Phillips curve demonstrates the relationship between the unemployment rate and the *change* in the rate of inflation. The assumption is that individuals will adjust to any constant increase in the money supply, and that therefore even the short-run economic impact will disappear as people adjust to chronic inflation. Under such assumptions, unemployment can be lowered below the natural rate only if people are surprised—that is, the *rate* of money growth must keep increasing, creating *accelerating* inflation. For this reason, the natural rate of unemployment is also known as NAIRU—the nonaccelerating inflation rate of unemployment.

phonemes The smallest units of sound in a language that create differences of meaning. Phonemic status is determined comparatively: for example, the sounds /s/ and /t/ are phonemes in English, visible in the fact that "sail" and "tail" have different meanings; but other differences in sound may convey no difference in meaning, such as aspirated or unaspirated versions of /p/, as well as the /s/ or /z/ sound in making plural forms of words. Differences of this kind are called ALLOPHONES. The anthropologist Edward SAPIR was the first to propose that languages could be mapped in terms of their phonemic systems. See also LINGUISTICS.

phonetics The study of human (linguistic) sound patterns independent of their context in a specific language, generally by mapping and measuring linguistic sounds according to objective criteria. Phonetics is thus distinct from

phonemics—the study of the relationship of sound to meaning within a given linguistic context.

phonology The study of the patterns of sound within a given language, including both PHONETICS (the mapping of sound patterns) and phonemics (the attempt to find the smallest meaningful differences of sound—PHONEMES—within a language).

phratry A form of organization or relation between a group of clans or other nominally related KINSHIP groups. Phratry often revolves around a common narrative of origins, such as a claim of descent from a common ancestor, as among some extended tribal societies. The term was introduced into ANTHROPOLOGY in the nineteenth century by Lewis Henry MORGAN.

phrenology A long held but specious theory that human personality and character traits can be determined by examining the shape and features of the face and skull. Phrenology was influential in the emergence of the early social sciences during the nineteenth century, especially in regard to the project of establishing social and racial types through studies of the physiognomy of criminals. Although PHYSICAL ANTHROPOLOGY continues to use measurements as a way of tracing and categorizing human populations, both ancient and modern, the link between physical and moral qualities was repudiated by the mainstream of twentieth-century science and social science.

physical anthropology Inquires into biological and physical explanations of human culture and physical variation—both ancient and modern. It integrates a wide range of research areas, including the study of human biology, human evolution, paleoanthropology, demographics, comparative research on other primates, and issues related to ecological adaptation. Early physical anthropology relied heavily on ANTHROPOMETRY, the study of physical measurements of individuals and groups. It tended to focus on isolating racial characteristics and racial identities, often in the service of colonial and imperial projects.

The repudiation of RACE as a major determinant of human behavior by social and cultural anthropologists around the turn of the twentieth century (preeminently by Franz BOAS) led to the separation of physical anthropology into a distinct subfield within American anthropology. Although modern physical anthropology largely repudiates race as a meaningful way of categorizing populations, periodic attempts to reinvigorate the link between race and CULTURE have remained a substantial burden on the discipline. For this reason, the term *biological anthropology* is sometimes preferred.

Physiocrats A group of mid-eighteenth-century French thinkers who developed the first formal school of economic thought. Physiocrats stressed a number of points: (1) the importance of the agricultural sector, which they regarded as the only source of wealth; (2) the sterility of trade and industry, in contrast to prevailing mercantilist thinking (see MERCANTILISM) and subsequent classical accounts of the LABOR THEORY OF VALUE; (3) the subjection of economics to natural laws—whence the name Physiocrat, or "rule by nature."

From these principles flowed a number of theories and recommendations. Perhaps the most significant was the insistence that taxes be limited to a single tax on agricultural profits, or *rent*. This implied abolishing taxes on the peasantry and on commercial activity—the latter justified on the grounds that trade and industry only reformulated existing wealth. In François QUESNAY's view, this would lead to greater investment by farmers in productivity, higher profits for landowners, and ultimately increased tax revenues for government. This last point justified lowering the overall tax burden on agriculture, which they believed had become unprofitable in the eighteenth century. It also implied a strong interest in agricultural improvement.

The Physiocrats' concept of natural law underwrote a strong belief in free trade and LAISSEZ FAIRE. The economy functioned best (and prices reached their "natural" level) when it followed its natural course, without interference or regulation. This represented a significant departure from the pervasive government involvement in all areas of eighteenth-century economic life, and constituted one of the chief legacies of the Physiocrats to Adam SMITH and the classical tradition.

Quesnay was the leading Physiocrat, although the group counted a number of other prominent figures, including Victor de Mirabeau. Although their view of trade and industry as sterile activities diminished their relevance to the next century of economic thought, they nonetheless produced pioneering work on the concepts of surplus, rent, and capital, and laid much of the foundation for CLASSICAL ECONOMICS.

Piaget, Jean (1896–1980) A Swiss psychologist whose theories of child development and human intelligence shaped thinking on the subjects for decades. Based largely on studies of his own three children, Piaget argued that interaction with the environment was the main stimulus to cognitive development. He asserted that development was a process of constant *adaptation*, of finding new ways to balance the *assimilation* of new experience to existing patterns of action, and of *accommodation* or revision of those patterns in function of environmental demands. Maturation, for Piaget, involved reaching higher states of equilibrium between assimilation and accommodation. Piaget identified several major stages in this process—each associated with the development and internalization of different types of logical operation: (1) the *sensorimotor* intelligence characteristic of early infancy, in which the world is progressively differentiated into discrete objects and logical, externalized actions; (2) the long period of childhood, dominated by the passage from *preoperational* to *concrete operations*, by which Piaget meant the facility for translating knowledge and experience into logical categories; and (3) a *formal operational* stage, dominated by the achievement of abstract thought and logic that are independent from immediate experience.

By the 1950s, Piaget extended these theories toward a more general consideration of the developmental bases of human intelligence—a subject he called *genetic epistemology*. Piaget treated intelligence as primarily an adaptation to the environment at the biological level. This work challenged much of the prevailing research in cognitive and linguistic theory (such as the SAPIR-WHORF HYPOTHESIS, a model of linguistic determinism), including Noam CHOMSKY's assumptions about the "hard-wired" characteristics of the human intelligence. Piaget's major works include *The Language and Thought of the Child* (1923 [1926]), *The Origin of Intelligence in the Child* (1936 [1952]), *The Principles of Genetic Epistemology* (1970 [1972]), *Biology and Knowledge* (1967 [1971]), and *The Development of Thought* (1975 [1977]).

picaresque organization A relatively enduring form of criminal organization, characterized by a single leader and the distribution of profits through a system of rank. Gangs and pirates are often picaresque organizations.

pidgin languages Simplified languages used for communication between different established language groups, often in the context of trade. Pidgin languages are distinguished from *creole* languages, which—though also hybrids—are used as primary languages and so demonstrate greater complexity.

Pigou, Arthur C. (1877–1959) A leading neoclassical economist noted for his formal analysis of the methods of increasing economic welfare—most famously in *The Economics of Welfare* (1920). Like Alfred MARSHALL, Pigou was concerned with POVERTY and inequality. Unlike his neoclassical predecessors, however, he believed that private and social interests could diverge.

Theorizing the difference between social and private marginal benefits and costs was probably Pigou's most significant achievement. *Private marginal cost* is the expense incurred by the producer in producing an additional unit. *Social marginal cost* is the cost borne by society in order to produce that unit (as opposed to producing something else). Similarly, *private marginal benefit* is measured by the price received by the producer, while *social marginal benefit* refers to the benefit to society. Whenever private costs (or benefits) are different from social costs (or benefits), private and social interests diverge. In other words, total social welfare is not equal to the sum of all individuals' welfare.

The simplest example of such a case occurs when the production of a good involves harmful emissions into the environment, or when, conversely, the expansion of one firm reduces the cost for other firms in an industry. In the first case, social costs exceed private costs; in the second, social benefits exceed private benefits. Pigou recognized that monopolistic competition was another source of divergence between private and social interests. In such situations, the economy can experience too little investment in social infrastructure, such as hospitals and schools. In Pigou's opinion, this was one justification for government intervention; another stems from what Pigou argued was the shortsighted behavior of most individuals, who tend to prefer present to future satisfaction. For Pigou, this meant that people save too little, leading to low investment and limited creation of new capital. They also consume natural resources quickly and wastefully.

Pigou concluded that consumption taxes were needed to counter both tendencies.

Since firms are driven by self-interest, Pigou believed that LAISSEZ FAIRE was justified where private and social interests coincided. Where they diverged, however, government intervention was required to ensure that social welfare took precedence. Unlike many economists of his time, Pigou believed that interpersonal comparisons could be made between people with similar ethnic backgrounds. On this basis, he thought it possible to make value judgments about relative welfare and to set practical guidelines for government action.

Pigou succeeded Marshall in the chair of political economy at the University of Cambridge and remained there until his retirement in 1943.

Pigou effect Also *real-balance effect*. A change in the demand for commodities associated with a change in real balances (the quantity of money held by individuals in the economy, divided by the price level). Extending work by John Maynard KEYNES, the economist Arthur C. PIGOU argued that an increase in the real value of money balances directly increases the aggregate demand for goods. Pigou's rationale was that individuals save in order to accumulate a certain amount of wealth *relative to their income*, and that saving therefore depends inversely on the ratio of wealth to income. Thus, an increase in real balances raises the ratio of wealth to income, which causes a decrease in savings and an increase in the demand for consumption goods. This direct effect on consumption demand was termed the *Pigou effect*. Pigou's argument implied that if a country is caught in a liquidity trap (where monetary policy is powerless), there is nonetheless a price level that generates a full-employment level of aggregate demand.

Pigouvian taxes Taxes enacted to correct for the effects of negative EXTERNALITIES—the harmful consequences of economic (or potentially other) activity on the well-being of others. Pollution is a prominent example of a negative externality. Arthur C. PIGOU (1877–1959) was an early advocate of such corrective taxes, which are theoretically more efficient in producing the desired welfare result than equivalent legal sanctions.

pilot study A small-scale test of a research project to evaluate its design. Pilot studies are frequently conducted in order to minimize the risks (and correct for potential errors) involved in large-scale survey research or other types of labor intensive fieldwork.

planned economy   See CENTRAL PLANNING.

Plato   (428/7–348/7 BCE) Plato inaugurated the Western metaphysical tradition and fundamentally shaped the study of ethics, POLITICS, and science. He occupied a pivotal position in Greek philosophy: it is largely through his writing that we have information about Socrates, his teacher. In turn, Plato directly shaped much of the philosophical inquiry of the next centuries through his own influential pupils, especially ARISTOTLE, and through the Academy he founded.

Plato's writing consists of some thirty-six clearly attributable texts, nearly all of them in the form of philosophical dialogues. Plato himself never appears in these dialogues—a fact that has given rise to a long and probably unresolvable debate about his precise views on many subjects. Plato frequently used Socrates as a protagonist, including in the remarkable account of the trial and death of Socrates in the *Apology* and in *Crito*. Socrates often seems to be a surrogate for Platonic ideas, but the outcome of many of the exchanges is indecisive. In addition, most scholars recognize a significant philosophical and thematic shift between the early and late dialogues, although again some doubt exists about the order of the texts. The early texts—generally understood as including the *Apology*, *Crito*, *Ion*, *Charmides*, *Cratylus*, *Gorgias*, *Meno*, *Protagoras*, *Symposium*, *Phaedrus*, and *Republic*—are largely devoted to exploring ethical issues, conceived broadly to include piety, beauty, temperance, virtue, political obligation, JUSTICE, and the nature of the good, and the related question of how these values can be transmitted. All of these dialogues find Socrates arguing against proponents of alternative ethical systems—from Gorgias' equation of rhetoric and truth to Protagoras' defense of the values of the polis to the roundtable discussion of love found in the *Symposium*. Socrates, in the dialogues, generally rejects commonsense ethical views as unreflective and relativistic ethics as logically fallible. Plato employed both strategies to prove the necessity of his metaphysical doctrine of "Forms" or "Ideas"—the belief that physical objects, values, and qualities are only imperfect projections of their idealized forms, which exist in a higher realm. Thus any particular triangle is the concrete representation of the complete and perfect idea of a triangle. Similarly, particular good acts or notions of the good are derivative of a pure idea of the Good, which orients all ethical behavior. Philosophy, in this context, is the search for understanding of these ideas. Grasping and contemplating them is the highest human pursuit.

Plato's early dialogues introduce several other key Platonic doctrines: notably the tripartite theory of the soul, comprising reason, the appetite, and the will. This provided the basis for a theory of individual virtue—defined as the proper balance between the three parts—and for a general subordination of the appetites and will to reason. Plato applied this to the model of the just society famously elaborated in the *Republic*. The ideal republic, Socrates argues in the dialogue, is based on a division of the population into three castes—statesmen, workers, and soldiers—with the latter two subordinated to a philosopher-king drawn from the first. The dialogues also imply Plato's belief in the immortality of the soul and in a notion of learning as "recollection"—both concepts closely tied to the incorporeality and persistence of the "Forms." Many of Plato's later dialogues, including the *Sophist*, *Statesman*, *Laws*, *Philebus*, and *Timaeus*, have an ambiguous or oblique relationship to these ideas. The subject of logic comes to the fore in the *Sophist* and several others dialogues; the *Laws* provides a much more practical, if also more authoritarian, alternative to the *Republic* in matters of government and constitutionalism; and the *Timaeus* presents a complicated cosmology, partly based on geometric forms. Whatever this shift signifies, Plato's strong commitment to dialectical reasoning—understood as the movement toward truth by way of argument and counterargument—established a method of inquiry that continues to underpin broad areas of philosophical and scientific thought.

Platonic idealism, especially as reworked by neo-Platonists such as Plotinus, was influential in early Christianity. In Saint AUGUSTINE, for example, it informs an account of the radical separation of this world and its institutions from the perfect "City of God." More generally, Plato's thought has shaped rationalist approaches of all kinds that assert the power of reason to understand the underlying structures of human consciousness, society, and history.

plebiscite   See DIRECT DEMOCRACY.

pluralism   Most commonly describes a society in which political power is dispersed among different groups. The problem of incorporating distinct group interests into a unified political structure runs through much of the Western tradition of political thought—from PLATO and ARISTOTLE to Charles-Louis MONTESQUIEU and early American republican reflections on the SEPARATION OF POWERS. Modern theories of pluralism by Harold LASKI and others developed in the context of narrower research trends—especially in reaction to the dominant tradition of legalistic studies of the STATE, which often failed to recognize the role of group differences in the political process. Gaetano MOSCA's argument in favor of the "circulation of elites" (and elite theory more generally) also played a contributing role (see ELITE AND ELITISM).

As normative theory, pluralist accounts have often been preoccupied with the atomization of social ties and the centralization of power in MASS SOCIETY. They frequently present the dispersal of power among different groups as a counterweight to those tendencies. As descriptive theory, they emphasize the extent to which politics is driven by the competition for power and influence among groups. Such ideas informed a significant body of sociological and political analysis of American pluralism in the 1950s and 1960s, including work by Robert DAHL (*Who Governs?*, 1961) and Nelson Polsby (*Community, Power and Political Theory*, 1963). In these accounts, the state is represented as primarily a neutral umpire that weighs the merits of competing claims—satisfying some and mediating among others. These accounts also tend to describe power as widely dispersed among social groups, such that no single group can dictate outcomes according to its narrow interests: the state is in some measure permeable to all. This pluralist thesis has been supported by numerous empirical studies, especially in the United States. A prescriptive version of pluralism became popular during the fall of the communist states in Eastern Europe and the Soviet Union (see CIVIL SOCIETY) and has remained an attractive response to the increasingly multicultural reality of social and political relations in a globally integrated world (see MULTICULTURALISM).

Critics of pluralist political models dispute its central tenets. Neo-Marxists and some elite theorists (such as C. Wright MILLS) argue that entrenched economic interests hold power disproportionately. They argue that capitalist elites do not need to visibly dominate day-to-day politics because their interests are satisfied in the very institutions of liberal societies, which

discourage or marginalize strongly dissenting forms of political mobilization; this has a variety of methodological implications, including a general case that power should be studied not just in the formal arena of political activity but also around issues that *fail* to reach the agendas of political decision makers. The media's role in maintaining a broad hegemonic consensus on capitalism has also been a fertile avenue of research in this area.

A related critique of pluralist theories comes from those who argue that states do not simply respond to demands emanating from society but rather are autonomous actors that can act independently of the wishes of social groups. Foreign policy is the area most often presented as a zone of state autonomy, although such cases have also been made in regard to aspects of social-welfare policy.

plurality rule   A system of decision making or voting in which the winner is the choice ranked first by the most voters. Such a system is used in some governmental elections, but is open to the criticism that it considers only the top choice of every voter—not the ranking of possible alternatives. Where there are more than two choices or candidates, the plurality rule does not guarantee a majority decision. See also ELECTORAL SYSTEM; and MAJORITY RULE.

plural societies   Societies composed of multiple ethnic, racial, religious, national, tribal, and/or linguistic groups that retain their cultural identities and social networks but participate in shared political and economic systems. The negotiation of conflict between groups within plural societies has been a prominent topic of political and social analysis (see CONFLICT THEORY). Where multiple groups have access to power, the term PLURALISM is generally used. See also MULTICULTURALISM.

polarization   In politics, an increasingly stark and antagonistic division between political parties, groups, or viewpoints, and the accompanying decline of moderate or centrist positions that normally mediate those differences.

police state   A state in which the police and/or military exercise unlimited power and dominate the political system. Terror, secrecy, surveillance, detention, torture, and executions are used to crush dissent and prevent organized opposition. The term was initially used to describe Germany society under Nazi rule. See also NAZISM; and TOTALITARIANISM.

polis The form of political community associated with the Ancient Greek city-states. The polis was based above all on a concept of citizenship as the foundation of the social, political, and military order. This implied legal equality among all men with citizen status—generally property holders—and diverse responsibilities to the state, especially in times of war. The polis accommodated forms of democratic rule, as in Classical Athens, but also other forms of government.

political behavior A key term in many behavioralist approaches to political science that refers to the observable activity of voters, lobbyists, politicians, parties, and other political actors (see BEHAVIORALISM). Research on VOTING, political participation, and the role of POLITICAL CULTURE—often based on statistical analyses of surveys and opinion polls—underlies most behavioralist attempts to make the study of politics a systematic and scientifically valid enterprise.

political culture Refers to the attitudes, beliefs, and values that underlie a society's political system—a subject associated especially with Gabriel Almond and Sydney VERBA's classic, *The Civic Culture* (1963). Political culture, in this sense, is embedded in a range of phenomena, from national anthems and memorials honoring soldiers to widely held beliefs concerning equality or freedom of speech (see NATIONALISM). It includes historical myths about nations, patterns of parental discipline, and the sense of personal efficacy that one learns as a child.

Much of the work in this area has been shaped by Almond and Verba's interest in the nature of citizens' dispositions toward their political systems—in particular those that might explain the success or failure of democratic regimes. Their comparative methodology has been influential, if also difficult to reproduce due to its extensive comparativism. *The Civic Culture* is based on parallel studies of the United States, Great Britain, Germany, Italy, and Mexico. Political socialization—the way that political culture is formed and reproduced over time—has also been a significant and clearly related subject of research, as have the cleavages within political cultures that distinguish mass politics from that of elites, national political culture from regional, ethnic, CLASS, or occupational groupings, and even the political system from the "cultural"

strata itself—as in many socialist regimes where the official ideology only imperfectly intersected older patterns of beliefs and values.

Skeptics have complained that the political-culture approach treats culture as a fixed entity that affects politics but remains unaffected in the process. Much political activity—for example, that associated with new SOCIAL MOVEMENTS and IDENTITY POLITICS—seeks explicitly to change political culture. Indeed, as Margaret Somers has shown, the term itself has undergone a variety of changes in usage, reflecting the shifting relationships between politics and culture in both POLITICAL THEORY and common usage. Another frequent criticism is that reliance on SURVEY RESEARCH and statistical methods in comparative studies of political culture distorts results because people in different cultures interpret identical questions differently. Much, though not all, of the recent work on political culture has relied on ethnographic fieldwork and textual interpretation, rather than on the survey methods that dominated earlier approaches (see CULTURE; and ETHNOGRAPHY).

political economy The study of economic production and its relation to society and the activities of the state. Until the mid-nineteenth century, political economy was the preferred term for the study of economics in general. It was introduced by Antoine de Monchréstien in 1615 and gained wide exposure in England with the publication of James Steuart's *Inquiry into the Principles of Political Economy* (1767). The first school of political economy centered around the work of François QUESNAY (1694–1774), Louis XV's personal physician. Quesnay and the French PHYSIOCRATS argued that national prosperity depended not only on the accumulation of wealth through trade—the basis of mercantilist economic thought—but also on a successful agricultural sector.

What is now referred to as classical political economy grew out of the Scottish Enlightenment—especially through the work of Adam Ferguson, David HUME, and, most notably, Adam SMITH. Smith's *Wealth of Nations* (1776) set the terms for much subsequent discussion of the creation of wealth and the role of the state in the economy. The key to national economic prosperity, Smith argued, was the unimpeded functioning of markets, which simultaneously satisfied the needs of both individuals and the larger community. His central claim was that disparate individual interests and actions were harmonized through the marketplace—a notion famously expressed as the working of an "invisible hand." Both the principle of harmonization and the corresponding nominal role for the state (termed LAISSEZ FAIRE) have been influential in economics and in liberal social theory more generally. They underwrite a broad understanding of the relationship between the individual, society, and the state that is firmly rooted in the priority of economic activity. Subsequent classical political economy, such as David RICARDO's *Principles of Political Economy and Taxation* (1817), buttressed these views with more sophisticated analysis of formal laws of profit, wages, and the distribution of RENT. See also CLASSICAL ECONOMICS.

Although in many respects the last of the classical economists, Karl MARX argued against the tendency of political economy to treat the market—and especially the market in labor—as universal and thus deducible from general principles. Instead, he argued that it reflected a particular historical mode of production—CAPITALISM. Marx also criticized the concept of the harmonization of interests, arguing that capitalism was based on a fundamental class conflict between workers and the BOURGEOISIE (or capitalist class), who expropriated surplus value from the labor of the workers. Marx thereby refused the sharp separation of the economy and the state, and argued that the state embodied the interests of the capitalist class. This tradition of political economy survived in Marxist thought, although it was not greatly extended until the 1960s and 1970s, when it anchored a strong interdisciplinary approach that combined economic, sociological, and political perspectives in the analysis of capitalism—especially in the developing world. DEPENDENCY theory and WORLD-SYSTEMS THEORY are the most prominent among these.

From the late nineteenth century forward, economics became a more autonomous and formalized field with respect to politics (see NEOCLASSICAL ECONOMICS). Nonetheless, institutionalist and later Keynesian approaches (especially in the post–World War II decades) sustained the link between the economy and the activities of the state (see Keynesianism). Political economy also proved durable in Europe, where it had strong connections to the study of law and history. Increasingly, political economy has come to be associated with comparative POLITICAL SCIENCE—although SOCIOLOGY continues to play a role. A variety of methodologies and perspectives inform this development, from RATIONAL-CHOICE THEORY, to COST-BENEFIT ANALYSIS, to models of public choice and social choice (see PUBLIC-CHOICE THEORY; and SOCIAL-CHOICE THEORY).

political geography The study of the spatial dimension of politics and political institutions. Many of the key concerns of political geography were formulated by Charles-Louis MONTESQUIEU, who speculated at length about the link between climate and political regimes. Subsequent political geography continued to examine the effects of climate and environmental factors on politics, as well as the political significance of borders and other territorial features of states. Although the field was partially discredited by the Nazi infatuation with *Geopolitik*, political geography has experienced a renaissance since the 1970s, especially in relation to the study of subnational political units such as regions and cities, the consequences of GLOBALIZATION, and the emergence of new NATION-STATES. See also GEOGRAPHY; and GEOPOLITICS.

politically incorrect A form of condemnation of opinions, ideas, speech, cultural goods, or behavior according to political criteria—most often for failure to conform to the constellation of IDENTITY POLITICS concerns that became prominent on U.S. college campuses in the 1980s. The term has roots in MAOISM, where it was the doctrinaire form of condemnation of subversive or nonconforming ideas during the Cultural Revolution (1966–1969). It resurfaced in the mid-1980s among left-wing college students and activists in the United States, for whom it signified lack of conformity to a broad multicultural and feminist agenda located in part in struggles over the right of groups to name themselves in neutral or valorizing ways. Political correctness, in contrast, implied sensitivity in matters of race, gender, age, and sexuality, the elimination of stereotypes and hurtful language through the use of speech codes, and the removal of inappropriate references in school texts. Although such use was often ironic, the concept was quickly taken up by conservatives as a way of ridiculing attempts to police language, change curricula, and interrogate patterns of discrimination in daily life. Opponents of political correctness claim, above all, that it stifles freedom of speech and promotes censorship. See also MULTICULTURALISM.

political machine A hierarchically structured political party organization led by a "boss" or narrow group of leaders. Political machines were important actors in American electoral politics at both the state and local levels throughout much of the late nineteenth and early twentieth centuries. They persist in some U.S. locales, but with a much-reduced hold on political life. Political machines generally operate according to the spoils system: PATRONAGE appointments are awarded to party workers whose chief task is to persuade constituents in their respective districts to vote along party lines. Party operatives secure votes by extending bribes and favors to prospective supporters.

The waves of immigration that arrived in New York, Boston, and Chicago at the turn of the twentieth century were crucial to the development and maintenance of these systems. Political machines provided the newcomers with desperately needed social services in exchange for their support at the polls. In many respects, political machines operated as primitive welfare organizations where official, state-sponsored entities had not yet emerged. The impact of political machines waned as Progressive-era reforms (1880–1920) took hold in the areas of political appointment and voter registration. New Deal ENTITLEMENTS in the 1930s and the expansion of the American welfare state after World War II also did much to limit the welfare role of machines. Immigration restrictions passed in the early 1920s also removed an important source of new clients for party bosses. Political machines remain central to many democratic societies. The PRI party in Mexico, for example, maintained its monopoly on power for over seventy years through organized systems of patronage and control, despite formal multiparty DEMOCRACY. Similar ruling-party structures exist in Japan and, until recently, in Taiwan. See also CLIENTALISM; and NEOLIBERALISM.

political psychology Overlapping the field of SOCIAL PSYCHOLOGY, political psychology emphasizes the psychological dimension of POLITICAL BEHAVIOR and values. It includes a variety of methods and objects of analysis: the psychobiography of political leaders, studies of the personality structures that correspond to fascist or authoritarian belief systems (see Theodor ADORNO), and inquiries into the "post-material" bases of identity politics. Attitude surveys have also been frequently used to examine the connections among personality factors, demographic and population variables (e.g., ethnicity, religion, class), and dispositions toward participation and party preference.

political science Broadly conceived, the study of the institutions of government and the activity of politics. In this sense, political science dates back to the systematic study of states and the social order in ancient Greece. In a more narrow academic sense, political science is a relatively recent and largely American disciplinary formation that builds on and has become synonymous with that tradition. From ARISTOTLE forward, political science has both examined the operation of specific governmental institutions and offered *normative* theories of politics directed toward the improvement of state or society. This long-standing division of the field into descriptive or positive concerns and normative ones has persisted even as political science has grown to include the study of diverse processes, structures, and informal sites of political activity.

The "empirical" wing of the discipline includes comparative politics (see COMPARATIVE GOVERNMENT AND COMPARATIVE POLITICS), INTERNATIONAL RELATIONS, public policy, POLITICAL BEHAVIOR, and public administration. Most countries also treat their national politics as a distinct subfield, as in the United States. Theoretical political science or POLITICAL THEORY encompasses the history of political thought, the study of ethical and moral questions in politics (sometimes called *political philosophy* or *normative political theory*), the logic of social-scientific inquiry, the construction of generalizations based on the observation of political behavior and the formal modeling of political behavior (the latter two sometimes called *empirical political theory*).

There have been numerous attempts to unify the field around a common set of assumptions or methods. The broad consolidation of BEHAVIORALISM in the years following World War II is the most prominent and, for a time, successful example. Although diverse in its formulations, behavioralism coalesced around the desire for more scientific explanations of political behavior that could inform policy. It was based, in large part, on a critique of older descriptive research methods—especially those viewed as qualitative, particularist, or not readily applicable to the real world. It departed in particular from the study of constitutions and constitutional processes—partly in recognition of the routine divergence of political behavior from formal structures and rules (see CONSTITUTION AND CONSTITUTIONALISM). Behavioralism dominated the field from the late 1950s to the early 1970s and innovated in a number of areas—perhaps most significantly in moving beyond institutions toward the consideration of other processes and structures that affect politics (e.g., CLASS, ETHNICITY). No longer strictly identified with the state, behavioralism broadened its conception of politics to include, in David EASTON's words, the "authoritative allocation of resources" in the community, however and wherever it occurred (*The Political System*, 1953). New methodologies also played an important role, including the development of survey research and quantitative methods.

The "behavioral revolution" was also exported to other countries, where political science was typically a less autonomous field. In this context, behavioralism provided a means of separating the empirical study of political behavior from the legal, historical, economic, governmental, and philosophical concerns that traditionally informed the study of politics. Behavioralism's influence began to wane in the late 1960s, as it faced growing criticism on a number of fronts. These included (1) the renewal of conflict-based approaches to politics—in many cases responding to the new forms of social and political unrest in the United States and abroad, and in some cases reflecting the renewed influence of MARXISM; (2) critiques of behavioralism's scientific methodology, which lacked an account of how values informed research and the interpretation of "facts"; (3) a related critique of the lack of reliably predictive results in behavioralist research; and (4) resistance to the reduction of states and individuals to passive intersections of societal processes and structures.

More recently, proponents of RATIONAL-CHOICE THEORY have renewed some of the scientific ambitions of behavioralism by applying methods rooted in NEOCLASSICAL ECONOMICS, UTILITARIANISM, and GAME THEORY to the study of government and politics. Like behavioralism, rational choice groups together a range of positions, but generally seeks to ground explanations in the choices of individual actors (a.k.a. methodological individualism). In most versions, individuals are assumed to maximize their self-interest wherever possible. The attractiveness of this approach is that it marries a sophisticated, deductive

methodology—putatively more scientific than the "barefoot empiricism" of survey research—to a view of the reasonable individual engaged in making choices among alternatives. This went some way toward returning human agency to the study of political science. Rational-choice methodologies continue to play a prominent role in American political science, though less so abroad. Although sophisticated rational-choice models have paid attention to questions of historical change, cultural difference, and the historically variable content of rationality itself, there remains a significant fault line within the discipline that divides its practitioners from a range of mostly qualitative, historical, and theoretical traditions. These include diverse contributions from critical theory (see FRANKFURT SCHOOL) and POSTSTRUCTURALISM, as well as a range of interdisciplinary subfields that link politics to other methodologies or social realms: POLITICAL PSYCHOLOGY, POLITICAL GEOGRAPHY, POLITICAL SOCIOLOGY, political theory, and so on. See also POLITICS.

political sociology   A subfield of POLITICAL SCIENCE and SOCIOLOGY that studies relations between political institutions and social structures. Although diverse in its formulations and methods, political sociology has an identifiable set of core concerns: the rise of industrial CAPITALISM and its social and political repercussions, the role of BUREAUCRACY in modern states, considerations of the social bases of liberal DEMOCRACY, and the role of political parties and elites in modern political systems. Comparative methodologies have also played a prominent role. Much of this tradition dates back to the nineteenth- and early twentieth-century work of Karl MARX, Alexis de TOCQUEVILLE, Max WEBER, Emile DURKHEIM, Vilfredo PARETO, Gaetano MOSCA, and Robert MICHELS.

The post–World War II era marked a resurgence in political sociology, based in part on the work of Seymour Martin LIPSET, Stein Rokkan, S. N. Eisenstadt, and Morris JANOWITZ. Much of their research and writing focused on how shifts in social structure associated with advanced industrial capitalism affected political institutions—both in the established industrial societies of the North and in the newly industrializing societies of the South. The field of political sociology has continued to flourish and has expanded to include studies of the rise and relative decline of welfare states, transitions from authoritarian to democratic rule, and the role of ethnicity and nationalism in politics. Much of the field is concerned with broad institutional patterns or movements, often studied comparatively and/or historically. At the same time, political sociology also includes studies of specific processes (e.g., how legislative committees work) and joins with POLITICAL PSYCHOLOGY in survey research on political attitudes.

political theory   The study of underlying rules or regularities in politics. Political theory is usually pursued at a level of abstraction from immediate empirical data. All political analysis, however, relies on theoretical assumptions or generalizations about the salient factors that structure political activity. Where these are closely derived from empirical data, the term *empirical political theory* is sometimes used. *Formal political theory* (or "positive political theory"), in contrast, refers to the abstract modeling of the behavior of political actors in particular situations (such as voters in elections). The application of GAME THEORY or RATIONAL-CHOICE THEORY to political situations is an example of formal political theory.

Most often, however, political theory refers to the exploration of normative issues in politics—paradigmatically questions about the nature of the "good" society and how it might be achieved. In this context, it includes the history of political thought, efforts to clarify political concepts, and explorations of ethical and moral questions. Much of the tradition of political thought from PLATO to modern figures such as Michel FOUCAULT belongs in this category and much of it lies close to the philosophical tradition, where answers to basic questions about human life were traditionally sought. As in the philosophical tradition, however, the nature of the questions asked has changed over time. The main issue for classical political theory—beginning in ancient Greece, carried through in the social contract theorists of the Enlightenment, and continuing in present-day liberal political thought—was not merely to analyze how power was used, but to ask how political institutions might best harness it to collective ends. The LEGITIMACY of political institutions was a fundamental concern, along with related issues of JUSTICE, FREEDOM, and SOVEREIGNTY. For moderns from Karl MARX to Friedrich NIETZSCHE to Foucault, in contrast, the question of power is more complicated—linked to historical trajectories of social development and to a concept of the individual that is as much *produced* by as *subject to* political power. Although this represents a critique of the earlier tradition—especially its liberal versions—the critical turn in political theory did not thereby do away with the problems of authority and justice that preoccupied the liberal tradition. To a considerable degree, therefore, the two traditions coexist today and, at their best, inform one another. See also THEORY.

politicization   The process through which certain issues become objects of public contention and debate, and are thereby legitimated as concerns of the state or political realm. Politicization is therefore generally a contentious process, insofar as it introduces new demands for resources, justice, or recognition. The politicization of diverse aspects of social life has been a prominent feature of nineteenth- and twentieth-century POLITICS, including such areas as employment and the conditions of work, the social and political status of putatively inferior groups, the relationships of production and consumption to the environment, relations within the family, education, and a range of other areas of social life once widely assumed to be ordered by nature or outside the purview of the state.

politics   Broadly, the ways in which people gain, use, and lose POWER. Ancient Greek thought and its heirs also stress a view of politics as constitutive of legitimate social life, insofar as it provides ways for individuals to express their opinions, influence each other, and build institutions. Most modern usage prioritizes the activity of STATES—whether action between states or the processes of reconciling diverse interests within them. The latter responsibility includes deliberation over means and ends, as well as the implementation of collective decisions. Some perspectives take the state as the central actor, possessing potentially independent prerogatives and goals (the traditions of GEOPOLITICS and *realpolitik* operate within this framework); others look to the process by which groups and interests (both inside and outside the state) negotiate and vie for control.

Defining what counts as political has always been inseparable from the question of how societies govern themselves. It has been particularly important for the development of liberal-democratic societies, which provide institutional frameworks for resolving certain kinds of conflict. Liberal-democratic traditions originally endorsed an extremely limited notion of the political that ruled out interference in large areas of social and economic life. Many social movements and political philosophies have contested these limits—from franchise movements on behalf of excluded groups, to populist movements that support farmers in times of crisis, to MARXISM, FEMINISM, and environmentalism, which have in many respects sought a more pervasive definition of politics that includes economic production, the family, and the ecosystem. Totalitarian regimes have taken the opposite tack in crushing opportunities and structures for meaningful political contestation (see TOTALITARIANISM). In practice, this has required a vast extension of the definition of the political into all forms of symbolic and covert dissent from the regime. For these reasons, drawing the borders of the political is, in many respects, the fundamental political activity—a view held by Hannah ARENDT and a number of other philosophers of the public sphere (see PUBLIC SPHERE AND PRIVATE SPHERE).

Not all accounts of politics restrict it to the essentially instrumental function of mediating conflicts, ensuring order, and distributing resources. Politics may also be conceived as having an expressive dimension, in which the process of collective participation and deliberation is seen as a good in itself. Drawing on ARISTOTLE and theories of the Greek polis, Arendt, Carol Pateman, and others argue that human life is fulfilled through active participation in the definition and construction of the social world—quintessentially political activities—and that this process involves recognizing the perspectives of others and experiencing, at first hand, the interdependence and cooperative dimension of society.

On a somewhat different level lie certain poststructuralist views of power, associated especially with Michel FOUCAULT, that argue for a still more pervasive understanding of politics as diffuse in everyday practices, identities, and technologies (see POSTSTRUCTURALISM). Martin HEIDEGGER argued a similar point in asserting that modern technology has a politics insofar as it creates an instrumental relationship to the world that permits certain kinds of knowledge and action while foreclosing others. Such views inform broad critiques of the trajectory of MODERNITY but are often difficult to reconcile with narrower views of politics rooted in institutions and social action.

polity   1. A politically organized society. In this sense, the term is used interchangeably with government, regime, and political system. 2. As conceived by ARISTOTLE in *The Politics*, a constitutional arrangement mixing OLIGARCHY and DEMOCRACY and directed toward the common good.

Pollack, Friedrich   (1894–1970) A German political economist and critical theorist. Pollack was a member of the FRANKFURT SCHOOL known best for his study of economic planning in the Soviet Union and for developing the notion of STATE CAPITALISM. He was born in Freiburg, earned a doctorate in economics, and fled to the United States in the 1930s with many of his Frankfurt School colleagues when the Nazi party came to power in Germany.

Pollack's *Experiments in the Planned Economy in the Soviet Union, 1917–1927* (1928) was a critical, though sympathetic, account of the challenges of centralized planning faced by the Soviets during the decade following the Russian Revolution. Pollack later coined the term *state capitalism* (in an essay of that name, 1942), to describe state-owned and -directed economies—primarily the Soviet Union but also (and more controversially) Nazi Germany. The term was later often applied to socialist-bloc economies in general. For Pollack, the term called into question the differences between the ostensibly competing socialist and capitalist models of economic organization. In all cases, including democratic and totalitarian varieties, a ruling class of bureaucrats and managers emerged that exercised de facto control of the nation and the economy.

Throughout the 1930s, Pollack argued against treating the Soviet economy as a radically different economic model—or even as a transitional form. He argued that state control of the economy was not a stage on the road to socialism but, rather, a new social form in which the monopoly power of late capitalism was appropriated by the state in order to suppress the growing contradictions of the system. Economic planning, forced employment, technological innovation, and a large, surplus-absorbing military sector, Pollack argued, provided a durable set of techniques that could prolong capitalism, perhaps indefinitely. Pollack and other Frankfurt school members also recognized strong state-capitalist tendencies in the initiatives of the New Deal, and they eventually moved toward a broader critique of the instrumental rationality that underlay all the modern, exploitative state forms. By the late 1930s, Pollack's ideas were part of a debate within the Frankfurt school over whether a "private" capitalist economy still existed in Nazi Germany.

His principal opponent in this debate was Franz Neumann, author of the major study of Nazism, *Behemoth* (1942). Pollack participated in a number of other Frankfurt school initiatives, including the series *Studies in Prejudice*. After World War II, he returned to Frankfurt with Max HORKHEIMER and Theodor ADORNO.

poll tax   See LUMP-SUM TAX.

pollution and purity   In many societies, concepts of *purity* and *pollution* form the basis of a system of distinctions that regulates behavior and determines status. Such concepts typically focus on questions of what touches, enters, or leaves the human body. Thus, food preparation, defecation, menstruation, sex, and childbirth tend to be special occasions for concern and danger. Pollution can be physical or spiritual, temporary or permanent, and thus can serve as a powerful determinant of social status. The caste system of India is a prominent example. There, a traditional, elaborate scale of pollution and purity determines not only the division of labor but the rules of conduct between the castes. The importance of such systems was recognized quite early in ANTHROPOLOGY through the work of W. Robertson Smith, James FRAZER, and Emile DURKHEIM. Contemporary research into pollution and purity has been broadly influenced by Mary DOUGLAS's *Purity and Danger* (1966).

polyandry   A marriage system that allows a woman to have more than one husband. Polyandry's most common form is *fraternal* or *Adelphic* polyandry—the marriage of one woman to a group of brothers, usually to preserve scarce family resources (polyandry in Tibet follows this pattern). It may also imply a shared or group concept of paternity. Such polyandry is sometimes serial rather than simultaneous—implying marriage to a second brother following the death of the first.

polyarchy   Literally, many rulers. The term is used by political scientists to classify modern representative democracies in which popular power over officials is widely, but not equally, shared. Accordingly, polyarchies are distinguished from both ancient and idealized versions of DEMOCRACY. Characteristic features of polyarchy include institutional arrangements that encourage consultation, widespread opportunities for political participation, genuine competition among organized interest groups, and constitutionally protected democratic rights for all citizens. Robert DAHL has noted that polyarchy thrives in societies that have reached a rough consensus on the rules of governmental procedure, the legitimate scope of political activity, and the range of available policy options (*A Preface to Democratic Theory*, 1956).

polygamy   A marriage system that permits the taking of either several husbands (POLYANDRY) or several wives (POLYGYNY).

polygyny   A form of marriage in which a man takes several wives. Polygyny is a common feature of societies where there is sharp age stratification. It typically has a strong economic and political function in the establishment of alliance and descent ties among groups.

polytheism   The worship of or belief in more than one god. Polytheism is generally contrasted to MONOTHEISM—the worship of one god—although the diversity of supernatural forces and beings in many monotheistic religions (such as Christianity) complicates this distinction. Polytheism was a key subject of nineteenth-century theories of religious and cultural evolution, and it figured prominently in the work of Edward Burnett TYLOR, Herbert SPENCER, and others. Most of these early social theorists described polytheism as an intermediate stage between primitive ANIMISM or ancestor worship and the development of monotheism. Although such linear evolutionary models were discredited by Franz BOAS and others in the first decades of the twentieth century, study of the polytheistic structure of many of the world's religions remains strong in several disciplines.

pooling equilibrium and separating equilibrium   Equilibria that arise in economic interactions in the presence of incomplete information, where one side of the market has more information than the other side. For example, a FIRM would like to hire the most productive individual, but information about the individual's productivity is not directly observable. In such a scenario, the individual may attempt to signal his or her potential productivity by means of some costly signal, such as the acquisition of education. In such a situation, if all individuals find it optimal to acquire the same level of education, the equilibrium is termed a *pooling equilibrium*. As a result, the firms are unable to infer the productivity levels of the individuals based on their decisions. If individuals with different underlying potential productivity levels find it optimal to acquire different amounts of education, their productivity types are revealed. This is termed a *separating equilibrium*.

Popper, Karl Raimund   (1902–1994) An Austrian philosopher best known for his contributions to the philosophy of science, including debates over the status of the social sciences. Popper developed an influential critique of the inductive method in science (the belief that observations lead to generalizations that can be proved through experiment). In this, he largely agreed with David HUME's critique of EMPIRICISM—that the logic of causality in inductive reasoning was faulty because no amount of experimentation could definitively prove a hypothesis. Hume was widely read as threatening the foundations of science, particularly with regard to the potential for science to unify reason and empirical research. Although a supporter of science, Popper rejected this ambition. Rather, he argued that the best that scientific claims could aspire to was a kind of provisional validity in the absence of falsification and that science should therefore be driven by the generation and falsification of hypotheses. In this regard, it was less the accumulation of truths than the elimination of errors that marked progress. Popper developed these ideas in *The Logic of Scientific Discovery* (1934 [1959]) and further in *Conjectures and Refutations* (1963).

Popper applied much the same criteria to problems of politics and the state. He argued strongly against social theories that monopolized the notion of truth or the concept of the good life. The best state, Popper argued in *The Open Society and Its Enemies* (1945), was one that left room for the criticism of its own actions and policies—and the adoption, as necessary, of new courses of action. The best society, in this respect, was an "open society" that was maintained on the basis of the "piecemeal social engineering" of many individuals; this implied the rejection of large-scale social experimentation in favor of continuously monitored, small-scale policies that were open to criticism, change, and improvement. In practice, he suggested, these goals were best met by democratic systems. A similar rejection of historical determinism underwrote his critique of philosophies of history—especially those of Georg HEGEL and Karl MARX—in *The Poverty of Historicism* (1957).

Popper's theory of knowledge has had a broad impact on a range of fields outside the philosophy of science, from economics to art history. In later work such as *Objective Knowledge* (1972), Popper continued to explore the nature of knowledge claims and forms of causality. He also wrote *Quantum Theory and the Schism in Physics* (1982), which describes the early twentieth-century discoveries that split classical physics from the new field of quantum mechanics.

population   In statistics, a population refers to the total set of elements of interest in a given study. Generally, studies involve only a SAMPLING drawn from a given population; if the study is properly constructed, the results from the sample may be extended to the larger population. Populations are either finite or infinite; the latter is often applicable to processes for which no fixed population exists—such as the study of traffic flows. The term *universe* is sometimes used synonymously with population.

populism   In the United States, *populism* was a late nineteenth-century agrarian social movement that organized farmers, ran candidates for president (1892, 1896), and fought for a number of political and economic reforms—including the shift to a silver-based currency, greater accountability of elected officials, and more protection from monopolistic businesses (such as the railroads). The term has been used in reference to other agrarian-based political movements as well.

More generally, *populism* has come to designate a mode of political rhetoric that privileges the collective action of the people against elitist threats. There are both left-wing and right-wing versions of populism—although a frequent component of both is the refusal of overtly ideological positions. Populist politics, consequently, shows considerable variation. Some versions have worked to create broad coalitions across traditional social divisions of class and race; others have used ethnic and racial scapegoats as the glue to bond a more narrowly defined in-group. Many are highly personalistic in their structures of AUTHORITY, leading to frequent accusations of demagoguery against their leaders; many appeal strongly to NATIONALISM or to ostensibly traditional values.

Populism is quintessentially an outsider rhetoric, dependent on real or at least posited distance from institutionalized politics. It is almost always associated with forms of mass politics and, at its most democratic, with reforms that promote greater inclusion and accountability in the political process. Most research on populism agrees that it is in large measure a response to the social transformations that accompany economic modernization. INDUSTRIALIZATION has produced populist movements throughout the world, from the most advanced industrial democracies to the poorest developing states. Populist activity is usually directed against the agents of authority and change—impersonal state bureaucracies, industrial capitalists, purveyors of modern tastes and worldviews—or against minority scapegoats who are blamed for such change. This interpretation is most useful in accounting for the rise of nineteenth-century populist movements in the United States and in Russia. It is less helpful in understanding developments in Latin America in the twentieth century, where populist movements such as Peronism embraced economic modernization. Populism is also a frequent component of other ideologies and movements. Indeed, all appeals to the unity and innate good sense of the people or the masses are populist to some degree.

positivism   A philosophical and social scientific doctrine that upholds the primacy of sense experience and empirical evidence as the basis for knowledge and research. The term was coined by Auguste COMTE to emphasize the doctrine's rejection of value judgments, its privileging of observable facts and relationships, and the application of knowledge gained by this approach to the improvement of human society. *Logical positivism*, associated with the Vienna Circle philosophers of science of the early twentieth century, describes a similar concept of scientific certainty that relies more on logical deduction and less on empirical induction. These two dimensions have often been confused in debates about whether the social sciences should be made more scientific. Positivism has been used since either as an epithet or mark of distinction by scholars who have differed on what constitutes acceptable social-science research and theory. Critics of empiricist positivism have held that its single-minded search for "brute facts" stands in the way of understanding the complexity of social reality, where CULTURE and consciousness are primary. They have also argued that values, culture, LANGUAGE, and intentionality constitute an ineradicable mediation of the "facts." Positivists have countered by criticizing the imprecision of qualitative approaches, which rarely permit empirical verification, and they reaffirm Comte's faith in the gradual improvement of the world through the application of verifiable social-scientific laws. Positivism's empiricism and value neutrality have also come under sustained scrutiny in the work of Thomas KUHN, Paul K. FEYERABEND, W. V. O. Quine, and other

philosophers of science, leading to a situation in contemporary social science best characterized as methodological pluralism. To varying degrees, most social scientists now agree that knowledge in their fields is generated by the continual interplay of personal experience, values, theories, hypotheses, and logical models, as well as empirical evidence generated by a variety of methodological approaches, from ETHNOGRAPHY to statistical analyses.

possibilism   A critique of environmental determinism that was initially developed in the work of Paul VIDAL DE LA BLACHE and other French geographers in the early twentieth century. Possibilism emphasizes the range of possible strategies of cultural adaptation to given environmental conditions and the resulting impossibility of speaking of strict environmental DETERMINISM. Societies, possibilists argue, do not merely reflect their environmental conditions but adapt to them in historically contingent and often widely varying ways. Moreover, as societies advance technologically, they may achieve more or less autonomy from environmental demands. American geography developed a strong possibilist orientation with the work of Richard Hartshorne, Carl SAUER, and Robert Platt in the 1930s and 1940s. Although the term is not universally used, most modern geography adheres to possibilism's basic tenets.

postcolonialism   A catchall term for the range of artistic movements, political projects, and research agendas that have developed in reference to the end of the European colonial system (see COLONIALISM). There is no strict consensus about what constitutes the postcolonial situation: neocolonial and dependency relations have in many cases survived the transition to political independence in the former colonies, and there are few postcolonial problems that do not have roots in the colonial era. Debate, too, surrounds the question of whether productive generalizations can be drawn across the borders of nation, RACE, and imperial context. Many efforts have been made to establish broader postcolonial identities: the political and literary *Negritude* movement of the 1930s, patronized by Leopold Senghor, Aimée Cesaire, and other Africanist intellectuals, attempted to create a sense of identity rooted in the African diaspora. Diverse strains of revolutionary MARXISM, too, have tried to translate the logic of CLASS into the typically unindustrialized colonial situation.

Vladimir Ilich LENIN, in *Imperialism, the Highest Stage of Capitalism* (1916), was one of the first to attempt to reconcile underdevelopment with Marxist revolution—first and foremost in the Russian context, but eventually, he argued, in the vulnerable colonial periphery of the capitalist system.

Inevitably, postcolonialism intersects with the study of the NATION-STATE and emergent NATIONALISM—the chief political and ideological works-in-progress of nearly all postcolonial societies. Although Lenin was a strong critic of the national model as an obstacle to world COMMUNISM, national consciousness has been fundamental to decolonization—if also deeply ambivalent in its effects. Perhaps the most influential theorist of decolonization and revolution was Franz FANON, a psychologist and participant in the Algerian war of independence in the late 1950s and early 1960s. Fanon treated nationalism as the necessary vehicle of collective mobilization and liberation—the only available one in the context of a colonial society stripped of other psychological resources. He played on the analogy between subjected nations and subjected classes, inaugurating a broad tradition of crossover analyses of different forms of subjugation. More recent criticism in this vein has addressed the persistence of structural inequality within postcolonial societies, with examinations of the relationship between the colonial past, national projects, and the reproduction of traditional forms of gender, ethnic, and caste discrimination. The concept of the SUBALTERN, drawn from descriptions of the CASTE system of India, has become a widely used tool for comparing structures of internal discrimination across national lines and between the first world and third world.

Since the 1960s, postcolonialism has become an institutionalized if still highly diverse field of study in Western universities, intersecting with CULTURAL STUDIES, FEMINISM, and more traditional areas of the social sciences, history and literary studies. Among other consequences, this position of distance and relative privilege has produced a strong tradition of inquiry into the role of intellectuals in speaking for and addressing postcolonial situations. With *Orientalism* (1978), Edward Said inaugurated a prominent and closely related direction of research on how Western representations of the East as a perpetual "other" contributed to the ideological matrix of colonialism. Concern with the power and limits of colonial discourse continues to inform a large segment of contemporary postcolonial scholarship, including that of Homi Bhabha and Gayatri Spivak. Drawing heavily on Michel FOUCAULT and Jacques DERRIDA, respectively, their scholarship is indicative of the ways in which postcolonial studies integrates a wide range of poststructural, neo-Marxist, and psychoanalytic paradigms (see POSTSTRUCTURALISM; and PSYCHOANALYSIS). Others have placed a greater emphasis on social history—notably the subaltern studies group in India and political analysts such as James Scott.

postindustrial society A term coined by Daniel BELL and expanded upon at length in his *The Coming of Post-Industrial Society* (1974). Bell predicted a society in which technological advances shifted the economy away from the production of goods in factories toward the provision of services. The primary sectors of the fully developed service economy, Bell argued, were the health industry, educational and research institutions, and government. He claimed that this shift would improve the social status of professionals and technicians, resulting in a new and dominant intellectual class. It would also marginalize and shrink the industrial working class. At the center of this transformation was theoretical knowledge: the production of goods would be increasingly reliant on science (e.g., computers, not steel), economic management would be carried out via modeling and forecasting, research and development would become key priorities in most sectors of the economy, and use of computers in everyday work would be extensive.

While other social scientists have echoed Bell's predictions (John Kenneth GALBRAITH, Jacques Ellul, Alain Touraine), there is continued debate over whether the recognizable shift in the West toward a service economy has created a discreet class of knowledge workers and whether the political and economic power of that group has substantially increased. To date, most jobs created in the service economy have been low paying and few have significant advancement potential. In some sectors, however, knowledge-based jobs (e.g., in information technology) have also became remarkable generators of wealth.

One significant shift accompanying the transition to postindustrialism may lie in generational value structures. Ronald Inglehart, in *Culture Shift in Advanced Industrial Society* (1990), has argued that the rise of postindustrial society produces an attendant shift from materialist to *postmaterialist* values. According to Inglehart, improvements in overall standards of living and levels of education in postindustrial societies have made materialist concerns about personal security and economic well-being less pronounced. In this context, postmaterialist values, such as care for the environment and personal autonomy, become more salient. Some evidence for postmaterialist values can be seen in the recent decline of traditional social democratic political parties and in the founding of new-issue political groups, such as the European Green parties. Whether this is a cumulative or a temporary change is subject to dispute, and few would argue that economic materialism is in any danger of disappearing.

postmarital residence An important variable in marriage systems and, consequently, in theories that explain social structure as a function of marriage alliances (see ALLIANCE THEORY). Postmarital residence refers to whether a newly married couple will live with or near the wife's family (matrilocal or UXORILOCAL RESIDENCE), the husband's family (VIRILOCAL or PATRILOCAL RESIDENCE), with or near either (ambilocal), or in a new place altogether (NEOLOCAL RESIDENCE).

postmodernism Originally an architectural design movement rooted in the reaction to the extreme functionalism of the Bauhaus school. Since the 1970s, the term has come into much wider use to designate a range of artistic styles, philosophical and critical positions, and sociological descriptions of contemporary society that postulate a break with either modernism as an aesthetic movement or, more broadly, modernity as a historically distinct era of human society and experience.

Defining postmodernism is complicated by the different inflections given a number of related and cognate terms, especially *postmodernity*, which implies modernity as a foil, rather than the narrower field of artistic modernism, and POSTSTRUCTURALISM, which marks a divide in critical perspectives that is frequently aligned with postmodernism. One result of this lack of precision is that the term is often criticized or resisted by writers whose work is identified with various postmodernist trends (such as Michel FOUCAULT and Jacques DERRIDA).

At its lowest common denominator, postmodernism implies a shift away from the conditions that informed or structured a variously "modern" past. When applied to questions of artistic or literary practices, postmodernist critics often cite the breakdown of historically conditioned styles, and the resulting transformation of techniques and even the content of works and texts into a kind of toolbox, available for mixing, juxtaposition, and reproduction at the artist's or writer's discretion. The terms *pastiche* and *intertexuality* are sometimes used in reference to these practices.

This artistic postmodernism is often correlated with the elaboration, beginning in the 1960s, of a broadly Nietzschean critique of metaphysics, modernity, and humanism—an undertaking initially dominated by French philosophers and social theorists. This orientation has formed the basis of many of the claims for the existence of a peculiarly postmodern condition, whether characterized by the dissolution of the rational, enlightenment view of the human subject, the end of grand narratives of progress or religion (Jean-François LYOTARD), the progressive undermining of truth discourses, or the reduction of experience to a realm of simulacra, "hyperreality" (Jean BAUDRILLARD), and superficial affect (Fredric Jameson). Other, more sociologically inclined critics have made economic cases for postmodernism based on the decline of the industrial economy—typically the Fordist model—and the rise, variously, of the information economy, new models of "flexible accumulation," consumer capitalism, and economic globalization (e.g., Daniel BELL, David HARVEY, Alvin Toffler; see also FORDISM; and POSTINDUSTRIAL SOCIETY). It is important to note that for almost all these writers, the economic, discursive, and aesthetic dimensions of this process are intimately linked—in fact, the breakdown of the divisions between them often serves to define the phenomenon.

Postmodernism has been criticized variously as a concept that sets up a false opposition with the modern, as a doctrine that undercuts the possibility of rational judgment, and as an abdication of the critic's responsibility to systematically analyze the world around us. Jürgen HABERMAS's critique of postmodernism (1987) brings together many of these objections, and has been particularly influential in debates in the social sciences. Yet it should be noted that these criticisms also come from defenders and even innovators of the concept. As a catchall term for a range of positions and agendas, postmodernism is internally contradictory and perhaps unable to provide adequate articulations between the many different registers in which it operates. Nonetheless, it has dramatically altered debates about knowledge and subjectivity in the social sciences, especially in fields like ANTHROPOLOGY, where the positivism implicit in many versions of ethnographic research has been called into question (among others, by James Clifford) and where the reflexive critique of ethnographic practice has become prevalent.

poststructuralism Like POSTMODERNISM, poststructuralism begs the question of how it differs from its predecessor, STRUCTURALISM. There is no single answer to this question, but there are a number of influential critical relationships to structuralism that are generally considered to have problematized it in productive ways. At the risk of being reductive, these can be divided into two broad strategies: historicizations of the subject, exemplified by the work of Michel FOUCAULT; and challenges to the linguistic essentialism implicit in some structuralist accounts, exemplified by the work of Jacques DERRIDA. Although poststructuralism is also often associated with the critique of subjectivity, in this respect it simply continues the strong attack on notions of free will, rational choice, and intentionality that is implicit in structuralism. Like structuralism, poststructuralism attributes subjectivity and meaning to systems of differential relations, such as language or power; beyond that, poststructuralism seeks to explain the generation of those structures, either in terms of historical change or of deeper linguistic and experiential realities.

Poststructuralists have undertaken epistemological inquiries while rejecting the philosophy of consciousness on which conventional EPISTEMOLOGY is based. Much of this work emphasizes the mutual complicity of power and knowledge. Foucault's history of humanism in *The Order of Things* (1966 [1970]) is one such attempt, positing not only an epochal shift in the definition of the human in the course of the eighteenth century but a variety of ways in which different historical formations of knowledge (EPISTEMES) carry residual and anticipatory elements of one another. Foucault thus follows in the footsteps of Friedrich NIETZSCHE's historical genealogy of the human—perhaps the defining influence on poststructural debate—and, by emphasizing the permeability of these epochal boundaries, undercuts the implicit structuralism of his own account.

Derrida, in contrast, has undertaken a more direct criticism of the structuralism developed by Claude LÉVI-STRAUSS, arguing that the fundamental oppositions that Lévi-Strauss placed at the source of cultural activity (left vs. right, raw vs. cooked, the incest taboo) are themselves contingent and unstable products of an endless process of differentiation—*différance*—that constitutes structure, identity, and opposition. This emphasis on the dialectical relationship of identity and difference and the inevitable imprecision or failure of signifying acts has been central to attempts to think about the postmodern condition. For Derrida, however, deconstruction is largely a theoretical innovation: the only thing new about this condition is our recognition of it.

Foucault's later work and the work of Pierre BOURDIEU develop a more sociological set of poststructural positions. Somewhat analogous to Derrida's efforts find a "differential" substructure to language and drawing on Nietzsche's concept of the will to power, they attempt to understand the microlevel of power that is constitutive of larger social, state, and economic formations. Both emphasize the process of negotiation or resistance that enters into every act and, thus, challenge the tendency to view structure as a transparent mechanism of determination. Bourdieu, moreover, has integrated a wide range of empirical techniques into this analytical framework. His work constitutes perhaps the most developed attempt to bring poststructuralism into the social sciences. The work of Anthony GIDDENS has also figured prominently in this regard.

potlatch A term applied to a ceremonial form of gift exchange found in many cultures in which social status is derived from the extravagance of one's gift giving—or in some cases, the destruction of one's wealth. The word derives from the ceremonies of Pacific Northwest Indians, first studied in detail around the turn of the twentieth century by Franz BOAS. New research has elaborated the political, social, and ecological dimensions of potlatch ceremonies and has challenged the traditional view that they constitute irrational behavior in a subsistence culture. See also EXCHANGE.

poverty A condition of absolute or relative deprivation of material and cultural resources. The term *absolute poverty* refers to the condition in which the basic resources necessary to sustain life are lacking; *relative poverty* is the lack of resources in comparison with other members of a given society.

Poverty is conventionally measured by income, although a number of studies have called attention to the distinct importance of wealth—or its absence. The concept of the *poverty line*, first introduced by Charles Booth (*The Life and Labour of the People in London*, 1889–1903), reflects calculations about the money required for subsistence living—including housing, food, and other necessities. The poverty line can be calculated in different ways, and the methodology used is a source of regular controversy. The U.S. government has set the poverty line at around $15,000 (1999) for a family of four. Yet the poverty line does not reflect regional or local differences in the cost of living, which can dramatically affect purchasing power.

Eradicating poverty was one of the major goals of post–World War II politics in the United States and other Western industrialized countries. It gave rise to initiatives such as U.S. President Lyndon B. Johnson's "War on Poverty" during the 1960s and to the rapid expansion of the welfare state in the United States and Europe. Although such programs often succeeded in reducing levels of poverty, the economic crises of the 1970s and the political turn against the activist welfare state in the 1980s (in both the United States and Great Britain) reversed some of these gains. By the 1990s, poverty hovered around 15 percent of the U.S. population. Some of these policy shifts reflect changes in the politically dominant explanations of the sources of poverty. The emergence of urban, industrial poverty in the nineteenth century set the stage for two broadly competing explanations: one viewed poverty as a consequence of structural economic factors, and therefore as potentially remediable through political action; the other treated poverty as a sign of personal failure or inadequacy, and as a necessary outcome of a competitive marketplace that rewards talent and effort.

Explanations of poverty consequently vary a great deal and are often highly politicized. Many debates center around populations that are disproportionately represented among the poor, such as a number of racial and ethnic groups in the United States, but also women, who suffer poverty in higher percentages than men. Especially controversial, in this regard, are the long-term poor, who rely heavily on government services and show little economic mobility as a group. For decades, race and heredity were widely accepted as sufficient explanation of such patterns. Although that view is widely discredited

in the modern social sciences, it continues to inform some sociological literature, including Richard Herrnstein and Charles Murray's recent *The Bell Curve: Intelligence and Class Structure in American Life* (1994).

Some sociologists emphasize the psychological component of poverty, especially what Michael Harrington described as persistent "attitudes of defeat and pessimism" (1962). Poverty, in such a context, becomes self-reinforcing, and persons become unable to take advantage of new opportunities. This pattern of reinforcement is at stake in *culture-of-poverty* arguments, which draw on and extend Oscar Lewis's work (*The Culture of Poverty*, 1966). Lewis and others maintain that concentrated, long-term poverty produces its own cultural values and goals, which differ from those of the economic mainstream and which discourage entrepreneurialism, hard work, and investments in social-mobility factors, such as education.

Other sociologists downplay the significance of multigenerational poverty in American society. In *The American Occupational Structure* (1967), Peter Blau and Otis Duncan found considerable intergenerational socioeconomic mobility in the United States and little evidence for a vicious cycle of poverty. Their *status-attainment* argument inaugurated an influential line of research that sought to explain the sources of poverty in terms of social-structural factors, not individual weaknesses or cultural deficiencies. This structural perspective has roots in the classical Marxist account of social inequality as an endemic feature of capitalist society. Recent accounts of intergenerational poverty include the resources model (Gary BECKER, *Human Capital*, 1993), the correlated-disadvantaged model (Robert Haveman, Barbara Wolfe, and James Spalding, "Childhood Events and Circumstances Influencing High School Completion," 1991), the welfare-culture model (Lawrence M. Mead, *The New Politics of Poverty: The Nonworking Poor in America*, 1992) and the UNDERCLASS model (Julius Wilson, *The Truly Disadvantaged*, 1987).

In developed economies, poverty is more likely to be relative than absolute, in that basic needs are met even for the poor. In less developed countries, poverty is also likely to be absolute. Lack of adequate nutrition, housing, and health care are primary concerns, especially lack of food. Adequate food, health, and basic education have all been consistently demonstrated to be important foundations for economic development. Empirically, growth in per capita income does not necessarily mean that the poor are also gaining, nor does it account for geographical disparities in growth. Much of the recent research on economic development has focused on the degree to which policies aimed at economic growth improve incomes of the poor, and how to target growth strategies more effectively to alleviate poverty.

power   Perhaps the most canonical definition is Max WEBER's, which asserts that *power* is "the ability to exert control over people, even against their will." For Weber, power is basic to the organization of social action and the pursuit of interests. Consequently, it is the key to understanding the diverse forms of social STRATIFICATION, which include *class* divisions (reflecting the unequal distribution of economic power), *status* differences that cut across lines of economic power (such as education or prestige), and party differences (by which Weber meant differences in access to larger forms of institutional power, such as corporations or the state). Where power is accepted as legitimate and requires no direct coercion, Weber argued, it is better described as AUTHORITY. In conceiving society as a plural realm of different power relations, Weber set the terms for a wide range of social science research agendas—including those that emphasize the capacity of groups or individuals to pursue their interests and affect others, those that study the distinction between legitimate and illegitimate power, and those that map lines of social stratification, forms of conflict, and the mechanisms of societal integration.

In American SOCIOLOGY and POLITICAL SCIENCE, questions of interest, political power, and political participation are the basis for a long tradition of research. C. Wright MILLS's account of the POWER ELITE that dominated American society works within these parameters (*The Power Elite*, 1959), as do Robert DAHL's conclusions about the basic pluralism of American politics (*Who Governs: Democracy and Power in an American City*, 1961).

Nonetheless, the strong Weberian bias toward AGENCY—to conceiving power as *A*'s ability to affect *B*—was resisted by a broad tradition of philosophical and critical theory that emphasized the deployment of power in the service of social systems beyond any particular agent's interests or intentions. Aspects of this can be found in Weber's account of BUREAUCRACY and RATIONALIZATION, as well as in the FRANKFURT SCHOOL's critiques of modernity. Perhaps the most influential inheritor of this critical tradition is Michel FOUCAULT, who treated power as not merely a matter of capacities or constraints on individual action but as the medium of all social difference. For Foucault, power constructs human subjectivity at a fundamental level and creates the conditions under which certain kinds of agency become equated with power, freedom, and constraint. A common critique leveled against this deeply poststructural conception of power is that its very ubiquity makes it of little analytical value (see POSTSTRUCTURALISM). If all relations are power relations and if power underlies even our basic frameworks for understanding and interpreting social life, then we risk losing the basis for positive social critique and social change. Such issues have animated much of the controversy over the implications of poststructuralist criticism and POSTMODERNISM in the social sciences.

Another departure from the Weberian view of "power over" others concerns its inherently conflictual view of social life. The functionalist tradition represented by Talcott PARSONS minimizes this in favor of understanding power as the capacity to mobilize resources to attain collective goals. From this perspective, the state is not primarily an institution that monopolizes the legitimate use of force (the Weberian definition) but one that serves an integrative social function by "building the power of individuals and subcollectivities into a coherent system of legitimized authority where power is fused with collective responsibility" (Parsons, *The Social System*, 1951: 127).

Both the conflict and integrationist approaches have been criticized for polarizing the distinction between agency and structure—among others by such poststructuralist sociologists as Anthony GIDDENS. Others have followed Foucault in critiquing the essentialist core—the individual or the social structure—of which power is then said to be a property. Research on the nature of social power and its empirical, specific instances continues within a rich set of traditions in the social sciences. Power is likely to remain a highly contentious and central term—not least because different understandings of the concept suggest different ways of analyzing and interpreting the social world and human activity.

power-control theory   A theory of delinquency that ascribes the different observed propensities for deviant behavior in boys and girls to differences in parental control. John Hagan, in *Structural Criminology* (1989), suggests that not only do girls experience greater parental control of their behavior, leaving them less margin for DEVIANCE, but that this distinction is further skewed within traditional male-dominated or patriarchal families. Feminist scholars have criticized power-control theory for its implicit argument that the increased participation of mothers in the labor force (signaling the breakdown of traditional family norms) is a cause of increased delinquency among girls.

power elite A term introduced by the sociologist C. Wright MILLS (*The Power Elite*, 1959) to describe the small interlocking group of corporate executives, government officials, and military leaders that, he argued, held effective control of major social and political decision making in the United States. This group, Mills argued, generally operated in the interests of what he called "military capitalism," but it was not identical with the capitalist class and was capable of acting against that class's short-term interests. Mills's power elite was broadly unified in terms of social, educational, and ethnic background—typified, if no longer as strongly characterized, by the Ivy League–educated Eastern Protestant elite. His analysis generated a long debate and a considerable secondary literature in American SOCIOLOGY. It also contributed to a significant and, in some respects, ongoing social debate—especially following President Dwight D. Eisenhower's parting warning about the MILITARY-INDUSTRIAL COMPLEX in 1961.

power sharing The practice of distributing offices of political power to different constituencies in a society—often where societies are marked by deep religious, ideological, linguistic, cultural, or ethnic cleavages. In parliamentary systems, this may be achieved through forms of COALITION GOVERNMENT, which include leaders from all significant factions. In presidential systems, the presidency may alternate between representatives of the groups or may be shared among them. Power may also be dispersed by guaranteeing a certain number or percentage of seats in the legislature to each group. Power-sharing systems are generally contrasted with majoritarian, noncoalition systems, such as those based

on the British WESTMINSTER MODEL. See also ELECTORAL SYSTEM.

practice and practice theory *Practice* is what people do, as distinct from what they say they do, or what the larger societal norms or structures identified by social scientists imply they usually do. Concern with practice emerged as a response to the functionalist orientations of Emile DURKHEIM, A. R. RADCLIFFE-BROWN, and others, which in outlining the major structures of social organization did little to account for the widespread divergence of individual behavior from the stated norms. There are several versions of this approach in SOCIOLOGY and ANTHROPOLOGY, from TRANSACTIONALISM, which emphasizes rational-choice assumptions and methodological individualism, to the SYMBOLIC ANTHROPOLOGY of Clifford GEERTZ and others, which emphasizes the variability of individual (and anthropological) interpretative practices, to Anthony GIDDENS's sociological theory of structuration.

The term *practice theory*, however, is usually associated with the work of Pierre BOURDIEU, who places at the center of his critical agenda the relationship among stated norms, more or less objective structures, and divergent individual strategies. The main theoretical element of Bourdieu's argument is his distinction between the space of improvisational, if still broadly normative action (the HABITUS) and the more entrenched set of unconscious cultural ideals that constitute the limits of individual strategizing (the *doxa*). His attempt to provide a framework for reconciling debates about rational and determined aspects of social and individual behavior has been important to a wide range of contemporary research.

praetorianism Originally descriptive of military rule in ancient Rome, the term now refers more generally to military intervention in politics. Modern praetorianism usually develops where political and social institutions have failed to provide a stable structure for channeling political participation and mediating social conflicts. In this context, civil society disintegrates and social groups begin to polarize. Military rule is often perceived as a solution to this crisis and can often temporarily command high levels of popular support. The absence of institutional mechanisms for sustaining popular support, however, tends to isolate such regimes and reproduce the oppositional relationship between state and society. This often results in additional instability, which rationalizes continued military rule and greater repressive measures. Escaping this political double-bind is one of the main challenges facing post-praetorian democracies—especially in Latin America, where military rule was common until the 1980s, and where continued economic instability imposes high political costs on elected governments.

pragmatics The branch of LINGUISTICS that studies how language is used and how it functions in context, particularly in regard to its performative effects. Pragmatics is thus distinguished from SEMANTICS, which focuses on the *referential* function of language, or the meaning of words irrespective of context. C. S. PEIRCE's work on signs and *indexicality*—the dependence of signs on proximity to the thing referred to—is the origin of pragmatics. For instance, the word *I* changes its referent depending on who is speaking; the word *here* on how the conversation (or text) points to a specific context.

The anthropologist Bronislaw MALINOWSKI was one of the first to integrate the study of the contextual effects of language into the study of CULTURE, arguing that in addition to communicating information, language possessed a *conative* function of addressing a listener, an *emotive* function that conveyed emotional states, and a *phatic* function that served to establish and maintain social relations ("Hello," or "How's the weather?"; see PHATIC COMMUNION). Malinowski's work was elaborated by early linguistic structuralists, such as Roman JAKOBSON and Emile Benveniste. In turn, their work had a major impact on the STRUCTURALISM of Claude LÉVI-STRAUSS and, in British and American linguistics, the theory of speech acts proposed by J. L. Austin in the early 1960s. Austin emphasized the ways in which people "do things with words," many of which carry a performative effect distinct from the simple meaning of the words. Naming, for example, is a performance that is distinct from describing or invoking an already existing relationship of signifier and signified. Austin's work has influenced both Pierre BOURDIEU's studies of practical action (including speech) and Jürgen HABERMAS's theory of communicative action.

Metapragmatics (associated especially with Michael Silverstein) is the branch of anthropological linguistics that studies cross-cultural variation in the way communicative pragmatics is organized (e.g., how self-reference is accomplished or how a story that reports the speech of others is narrated).

pragmatism A school of philosophy associated primarily with C. S. PEIRCE, William JAMES, John DEWEY, and peripherally with such figures as George Herbert MEAD, F. C. S. Schiller, and more recently Richard Rorty. At its broadest, pragmatism was a reaction against the dominant idealist tradition in philosophy, which conceived truth as an abstract, systematic, and logically consistent reflection of reality. Against this tradition, pragmatists argued that philosophy should abandon its search for transcendent knowledge and turn to considerations of human action in the world. Against metaphysical concepts of truth, pragmatists generally held that the consequences of action alone confirm or deny the validity of ideas. For pragmatists, knowledge and truth serve as changing standards for intelligent action, and not as fixed ends. Truth is above all a provisional construct that serves as a tool of a fundamentally future-oriented and outer-directed human intellect.

The early pragmatists took these ideas in different directions. The originator of the term, Peirce, was interested primarily in putting scientific practice on a sounder footing and more generally in the clarification of ideas. Toward this end, he sought a more adequate concept of language as an interconnected medium of instrumental relationships between persons and things, thus laying the groundwork for semiotics (see SEMIOTICS AND SEMIOLOGY). James, who popularized the term, was far more interested in connecting the instrumental conception of truth to other areas of human experience, such as beliefs, values, and forms of satisfaction. It is James who bears the brunt of most critiques of pragmatism for his tendency to justify any belief on the grounds of its usefulness (including religious belief), and for the ways in which his instrumental logic approximated the needs of the American business class. Dewey made pragmatism the basis of a much broader philosophy of experience and society (which he generally called INSTRUMENTALISM), rooted in the practice of critical thinking and oriented toward social progress. Dewey's pragmatic approach to education, for example, emphasized the acquisition of processes of critical thinking and evaluation over wrote learning or specific content. A pragmatic understanding of democracy emphasized the power of individuals to pursue creative solutions to problems and to explore notions of the good in relative autonomy from larger structures of power and interest. Mead, for his part, turned pragmatic principles toward a socially constructed and maintained theory of *mind*.

Pragmatism shared ground with other twentieth-century philosophies of action and critiques of metaphysics, including Henri Bergson's vitalism, Edmund Husserl's PHENOMENOLOGY, and the existentialism of Jean-Paul SARTRE and Maurice Merleau-Ponty. It has also had an impact on the philosophy of science, especially among the "logical empiricists," P. W. Bridgman and Rudolf Carnap, and in work by Ludwig WITTGENSTEIN and W. V. Quine. Since the 1970s, pragmatism has experienced a revival because of its affinities with poststructuralist critiques of truth and its reformulation—especially in Dewey—of democratic and egalitarian social goals in light of that critique (see POSTSTRUCTURALISM). Richard Rorty is the standard-bearer of this version of pragmatist thought, although his attempts to reconcile a radically plural concept of truth with a functioning democratic society have proved controversial.

praxis ARISTOTLE distinguished between three basic forms of human activity: *praxis*—action which is an end in itself, including the domains of ethics and politics; *poiesis*—goal-oriented action, including action that produces things; and *theoria*—the production of truth. This framework structured most scientific and philosophical inquiry from the Classical era through Georg HEGEL, who continued to endorse a distinction between practical and theoretical knowledge. It was substantially revised by nineteenth-century post-Hegelian thinkers—especially Karl MARX—who rejected the Hegelian effort to recover the unity of practical and theoretical knowledge at a higher level of speculative reality. Instead, Marx suggested that *praxis* was itself the goal of philosophy. Marx offered no strict and consistent definition of the term, but used it to designate the creative activity through which human beings made and shaped their world. *Praxis*, in this sense, is the species-specific activity of human beings—the creative activity that marks their freedom from the work or labor done out of strict necessity. Marx's goal, then, was not speculative truth but rather a reorganization of society in order to free the human capacity for *praxis*. Much of the subsequent Marxist tradition

has followed this lead, reproducing the constitutive tension within MARXISM between social science and social revolution.

preadaptation Refers to adaptive traits that a group may possess before it migrates to another area. The most common form involves migration to an area with similar climate or ecology, where earlier strategies of adaptation continue to function. Instances in which such migration proved disastrously misinformed are termed *maladaptation*.

Prebisch, Raul (1901–1986) An Argentine economist and diplomat associated with the development of DEPENDENCY theory in the 1960s. Prebisch helped redefine the terms in which first-world and third-world economic relations are discussed. As director of the Economic Commission for Latin America and as founder and first secretary general of the United Nations Conference on Trade and Development (UNCTAD), Prebisch gained an international reputation as an advocate of economic reform in third-world countries (mainly in Latin America), especially in their relations with the industrialized first world. Beginning with *The Economic Development of Latin America and its Principal Problems* (1949), Prebisch argued that despite the fact that incomes were rising worldwide, the impoverishment of "peripheral" countries was growing worse relative to the developed "central" countries. Prebisch attributed much of this to the growing imbalance in trade—based largely on the export of agricultural products and natural resources to the developed world and on the import of finished industrial goods from the developed world. The solution, he believed, was third-world industrialization.

In *Towards a Dynamic Development Policy for Latin America* (1963), Prebisch outlined the elements of dependency theory. The shift toward capital-intensive manufacturing (which put the capital-poor, labor-rich peripheral nations at a greater disadvantage) played a significant role, as did the concentration of wealth and power in the hands of a local elite while conditions for the majority grew worse. From his leadership position at UNCTAD, Prebisch called for greater cooperation among third-world nations, for democratically directed industrialization, and for reforms to benefit those still struggling to make a living in agriculture, including greater access to first-world markets and more equitable commodity-price agreements.

Prebisch's ideas had a major effect on economic and development policy in the 1960s. In later years, uneven, poorly planned, and often highly subsidized industrialization created its own systematic problems. By the 1990s, dependency theory had been largely supplanted by neoliberal programs of monetary stabilization, privatization, and government austerity. Nonetheless, the conditions that Prebisch identified persist throughout much of the underdeveloped world, and they are the subject of his continued research in *Peripheral Capitalism* (1981) and other works.

Prebisch–Singer hypothesis One of the most widely discussed and influential theories regarding the *terms of trade* and DEVELOPMENT in developing countries. Advanced by Raul PREBISCH and Hans Singer in the 1950s, the theory predicts the long-term deterioration of the terms of trade in developing countries—that is, a long-term fall in the prices of the primary goods exported by developing countries (generally agricultural goods and natural resources) in relation to the prices of manufactured goods imported from developed countries.

The hypothesis is based on a number of observations about the demand for goods and the organization of the labor market. First, primary product exports have a low *income elasticity of demand*. This means that a drop in prices will not significantly increase demand, so that export revenues decline as the price falls. In contrast, manufactured goods have a high income elasticity of demand, meaning that demand is more responsive to changes in income.

Prebisch and Singer argued that, in developed countries with well-organized labor, increased productivity generally results in rising wages, whereas in developing countries, it results in lower prices. For this reason, developing countries experience deteriorating terms of trade over time. Moreover, this produces a trade deficit, which accelerates the deterioration.

Based on this reasoning, many developing countries resisted open-trade policies and actively engaged in *import-substituting industrialization*. This was true particularly in the post–World War II period, during which many European colonies achieved independence. Such policies run contrary to the doctrine of COMPARATIVE ADVANTAGE, which stresses that countries should specialize in the production of commodities for which they have a *relative* advantage in costs of production. Some economists have questioned the theoretical and empirical basis

of the Prebisch–Singer hypothesis—challenging, for example, the choice of the base period, which is vital in determining whether the terms of trade have moved against developing countries. The picture is further complicated by the diversity of developing-country economies: many are importers of agricultural commodities and exporters of manufactured goods.

predatory pricing The practice of lowering prices to a point where neither the instigating FIRM nor its competitor can make any profits. Such price cutting is inconsistent with maximizing profits in the short run but, in the longer term, can drive competition out of the market or into bankruptcy. This is regarded as detrimental to consumer welfare and is often subject to antitrust action.

Although predatory pricing is a risky and costly strategy for firms, it is not uncommon, especially in relatively unregulated international markets and where firms seek to protect a dominant market position against new entrants.

present value The worth of a future stream of returns or costs in terms of their value today. The present value is calculated by discounting future returns or costs at the interest rate for the relevant period.

pressure group Any interest group or organization established to influence government and affect decisions about public policy. Pressure groups are distinct from political parties, whose main goal is to nominate and assist candidates to become members of the government. Such groups take a variety of forms, from LABOR UNIONS and business associations, to environmental and consumer groups, to single-issue groups such as Mothers Against Drunk Driving (MADD). Pressure groups with mass memberships can exert influence by leveraging large blocks of votes for or against particular candidates for office. They can lobby members of legislative assemblies through the provision of information, and to varying degrees shape and channel PUBLIC OPINION. In some countries, they can also directly fund candidacies and purchase access to leaders. Debates in the United States over campaign reform reflect the wide latitude that such groups enjoy.

There are a variety of accounts of the role of pressure groups in American politics and in democratic societies more generally. C. Wright MILLS, for one, argued that a mostly unelected POWER ELITE controls public decision making on most issues of importance in the United States. Pluralist perspectives, such as that of Robert DAHL, stress the permeability of democratic politics to multiple pressure groups. Pressure groups differ from most social movements in their greater level of organization and greater access to resources, especially money. CORPORATISM is a political arrangement in which pressure groups are granted formal, institutionalized access to the decision making process.

prestation   Marcel MAUSS's term for the larger context or "total social phenomenon" of gift giving and EXCHANGE.

prestige   A major differentiating factor among occupations and social positions; consequently, an important aspect of structures of social STRATIFICATION. The forms and uses of prestige have been of enormous interest to social scientists—especially sociologists and anthropologists. In modern societies, prestige is a form of status that overlaps but rarely corresponds exactly to other forms of power, such as wealth or political influence. Prestige related to educational accomplishments is a notable example. Such distinctions are the subject of Max WEBER's well-known discussion of the different registers of social stratification, and they have generated a subfield of SOCIOLOGY (and to a lesser degree, ECONOMICS) devoted to studying occupational choices and the relative exchangeability of prestige for other forms of power (on this subject, the work of Pierre BOURDIEU is especially important).

In premodern societies, prestige or honor frequently plays a dominant role, and correlates closely with forms of social and political authority. This has made prestige a central topic of anthropological research, especially within the tradition of social ANTHROPOLOGY.

price discrimination   The charging of different prices to different categories of consumers. Price discrimination is attractive to firms because it permits profits to rise above the level implied by a single or uniform price. Discriminating prices are not only closer to the highest price a particular consumer is prepared to pay (her "reservation price") but also make it possible to serve customers who would buy only at a lower price. Price discrimination works, however, only to the extent that (1) arbitrage is impossible (there is no possibility that a buyer will resell the product); (2) buyers have varied demands and abilities

to pay; and (3) the firm can identify different segments of the market.

price effect   The effect of a change in the price of a particular commodity on the demand for that commodity. The price effect can be separated into the substitution effect and the INCOME EFFECT—in the former case, demand changes because the good's price has changed relative to other goods; in the latter, demand changes because the change in price has affected the consumer's purchasing power (see SUBSTITUTES).

primary groups and secondary groups   A distinction drawn by the sociologist Charles Horton COOLEY between two categories of relationship. Primary groups and secondary groups are differentiated by the degree of face-to-face interaction, affective ties, and mutual identification among individuals that bind them. *Primary groups* include the family and circles of close friends. They play a major role in the formation of personal identities and produce strong senses of common collective identity. *Secondary groups* are typified by voluntary associations of persons who may have little or no direct contact; they are therefore comparatively fragile and less likely to cement strong loyalties or durable social bonds. Cooley's distinction belongs to a group of influential sociological accounts of differences in social scale and the passage from COMMUNITY to larger levels of social organization. Ferdinand TÖNNIES's distinction between *GEMEINSCHAFT AND GESELLSCHAFT* is analogous in many respects. See also INDIRECT RELATIONSHIPS.

primary institutions and secondary institutions   A distinction between those institutions that shape the "basic personality" of a group (primary institutions) and those institutions that derive from that basic personality (secondary institutions). The terms were introduced by Abram Kardiner, a contributor to the CULTURE AND PERSONALITY MOVEMENT, which tried to bridge psychology and the analysis of larger social patterns and institutions.

primate city   A city that dominates the economic and political life of a country, usually containing a large percentage of the country's population.

primitive   Once a ubiquitous term in evolutionary models of human society, it was retired from general use in the social sciences as evolutionary models fell out of favor and as anthropologists reacted against the sometimes pejorative implications of the term (see EVOLUTION AND EVOLUTIONISM). Moreover, the general disciplinary division between the "primitive" subjects of ANTHROPOLOGY and the "modern" subjects of SOCIOLOGY has blurred as anthropology expanded to include contemporary industrialized societies, and as sociological methods found a place in the study of nonindustrialized or historically distant cultures. The disappearance of the term has not meant the disappearance of the features it once described; now often termed *premodern*, they include a range of distinctions regarding social complexity, political organization, and religious development. Debate continues about how to characterize and evaluate these different dimensions of social organization, and more sophisticated and flexible evolutionary models have proved valuable to contemporary anthropology. See also COMPLEX SOCIETY.

primitive accumulation See ACCUMULATION OF CAPITAL.

primitive communism Initially popularized by Jean-Jacques ROUSSEAU and early modern writers of imagined travelogs, *primitive communism* was conceived as a form of utopian social order—simple in its needs and uncorrupted by conflicts over property or struggles between competing interests. Friedrich Engels provided the dominant modern version in the nineteenth century, characterizing it as the earliest MODE OF PRODUCTION—one that precedes significant social stratification. In this view, primitive communism is characterized by the absence of private property, class divisions, and authoritarian rule. Low productivity and the resulting meager surpluses are another feature.

primitive mentality Against such early anthropologists as James FRAZER and Edward Burnett TYLOR (who argued that human beings in all societies fundamentally share the same cognitive processes), Lucien LÉVY-BRUHL posited a distinction between "primitive" and "civilized" mentalities. He distinguished the *primitive* on the basis of such features as "mystical reasoning" (the failure to distinguish between natural and supernatural) and a "pre-logical" understanding of causation. These categories received considerable attention in the 1910s and 1920s, but they have not stood up to anthropological scrutiny and Lévy-Bruhl himself

backed away from them in his later work. Still, the question of cognitive differences between cultures is very much alive in the fields of COGNITIVE ANTHROPOLOGY and LINGUISTICS.

primogeniture A rule of inheritance that privileges the first-born child—in most cases, the first-born son.

principal and agent An *agent* is a person who is employed to perform an act on behalf of another—the *principal*. For example, managers in a FIRM act as agents of the directors, who in turn are agents of the shareholders of the firm. An agent as such cannot delegate tasks or responsibilities—but it is possible for an individual to be both agent and principal. AGENCY THEORY is concerned with the economic analysis of the contractual relationships between principals and agents. It focuses especially on situations in which an individual's actions can be neither observed nor perfectly inferred on the basis of observed variables. For example, the director of the firm can observe only the output of the firm but not the actual effort made by the manager.

Prisoner's Dilemma The best-known example from GAME THEORY, which illustrates how people behave in strategic situations. The Prisoner's Dilemma is based on some version of the following situation: two men have been arrested and are suspected of burglary. The police do not have evidence to convict them unless one or the other confesses to the crime; however, they do have enough evidence to convict them of a minor felony if neither confesses. This conviction carries a sentence of a year in prison. The two prisoners are not permitted to communicate and each is told the following: if both confess, then both get eight years of prison time; if one confesses and implicates his partner (who does not confess), he is set free while the partner receives twenty years in prison; if neither confesses, they both go to prison for a year.

In the language of game theory, confession is considered the *dominant strategy* for each prisoner. Each can rationally reason that (1) if the other does not confess, his own confession results in freedom; alternatively, (2) if the other confesses, the best strategy is still to confess, since this will reduce the sentence from twenty to eight years. Therefore, confession is the best strategy regardless of what the other person does. Yet this rationality prevents the best collective outcome—no confession by either prisoner and two one-year sentences. The Prisoner's Dilemma, therefore, illustrates the divergence between individual and collective rationality, and the difficulty of maintaining cooperation in strategic situations. The situation in which both prisoners confess is termed the *noncooperative Nash equilibrium*; if neither confesses, the result is cooperative, but it is not an equilibrium, because knowledge of the silence of the other would normally result in a confession.

Many social situations resemble the Prisoner's Dilemma in that one observes a similar friction between individually rational and socially optimal outcomes. The nuclear arms race between the United States and the Soviet Union or price wars between two duopolists are conspicuous examples. In each case, self-interest prevents cooperation and leads to an inferior outcome for all concerned parties. The Prisoner's Dilemma has been extensively used in experimental economics to gather data and to develop theories of behavior. The dynamics of repeated play of the Prisoner's Dilemma have also generated considerable interest. While a tacit agreement to cooperate may seem rational in iterated play of this game, if the game is played a finite number of times, the only rational strategy is to confess every time. This logic of backward induction, however, cannot be applied when the number of rounds of play are infinite, unknown, or determined probabilistically. With an infinitely repeated Prisoner's Dilemma, it is possible to sustain cooperation by threats of punishment if one player chooses the noncooperative action of confessing. The *folk theorem*, so called because it was proved so many times, has demonstrated the range of infinite games that can sustain cooperative behavior as an equilibrium.

The Prisoner's Dilemma can be generalized to situations with more than two players—it then becomes a version of the *Tragedy of the Commons*. In this variation, it is in each farmer's interest to add one more cow to a communal grazing pasture, but if each farmer takes such self-interested action, the land becomes overgrazed to the detriment of all farmers. Here, too, there exists a conflict between cooperative and competitive action.

private sphere   See PUBLIC SPHERE AND PRIVATE SPHERE.

privatization   The sale of public assets or the practice of contracting out their management to the private sector. Privatization is a means of diminishing the role of government in the economy. It is contrasted with *socialization* or *nationalization*, in which economic resources are taken out of private hands and controlled or managed by the government. Government control of parts of the economy was a central feature of socialist economic policies in the twentieth century and of development policy in many areas of the nonindustrialized world—especially in the decades after World War II. Nearly all states maintain some public control of services that are considered public goods or rights, reflecting the difficulty of guaranteeing universal provision of certain goods and services through the marketplace. Utilities (water, electricity, telephone service) have generally fallen into this category, as have some larger public goods such as health care and defense.

Privatization emerged as a powerful ideological counterforce to the welfare state in the late 1970s and 1980s—initially in conservative circles but increasingly among social democratic and left-leaning parties as well. This reflected the rising political fortunes of economic NEOLIBERALISM. Today, most economists and policymakers tend to accept the argument that markets are more efficient allocators of many scarce resources. Most also agree that public management tends toward rigidity and inefficiency—not least because the government is obliged to cover all losses. For these reasons, privatization has been encouraged by the World Bank and other institutions as a response to the problem of stagnant, debt-ridden, state-owned enterprises—although the cost of such adjustment is often high and the benefits uncertain. See also PUBLIC OWNERSHIP.

probabilism   A theoretical position in human GEOGRAPHY from the late 1950s and 1960s that sought a middle ground between ENVIRONMENTAL DETERMINISM and some of the more voluntaristic elements of POSSIBILISM (which emphasized the diversity of potential cultural adaptations to a given set of environmental conditions). Probabilism does not deny such diverse possibilities but emphasizes that some will be more probable than others.

probit models   See LOGIT, PROBIT, AND TOBIT MODELS.

product cycle   The cycle through which goods pass following their introduction, from new to mature to standardized. In their early stages, new products tend to be unstandardized as producers experiment with production processes, designs, and inputs. In this stage, suppliers generally cannot determine the optimal location and scale of production or the optimum sale price; consequently, product differentiation among various suppliers is high. In later stages, the product becomes more standardized, production and location decisions become more certain, and production moves to countries with cheaper labor and other inputs. Such cycles have characterized the development of many products. The semiconductor industry is a prominent example—developed originally in the United States and subsequently relocated to Asian countries once mass-production techniques became standardized.

product differentiation If FIRMS produce goods that are similar but differentiated, the goods are imperfect substitutes for one another. In such cases, each firm has some monopoly power over its own product. This monopoly power, in turn, provides an incentive for firms to differentiate their goods. On the demand side, consumers are assumed to perceive goods as a collection of characteristics that the goods possess; each consumer is assumed to have a preferred mix of characteristics. Consumers choose the goods by balancing prices and perceived qualities. Cars are an example of such commodities. In other cases, consumers are assumed to have homogenous preferences but have a taste for variety—they prefer one unit of each of n different goods to n units of a single good. Books and movies fall into this category.

production, relations of A key concept in Karl MARX's theory of capitalist development that refers to the social relations between capitalist owners and workers in the production process. For Marx, the relations of production in capitalist society take the form of the exploitation of workers by capitalists. This structure of conflict and domination provides the economic base of capitalist society and determines all other aspects of political, cultural, and religious life (what Marx referred to as the relationship between BASE AND SUPERSTRUCTURE). See also MARXISM; and MODE OF PRODUCTION.

production function Production is the act of transforming inputs (labor, capital, land, etc.) into outputs (or finished goods). The relationship between the quantity of inputs used to make a good and the quantity of output of that good constitutes the production function. The production function has the general form

$$Q = f(L, K, \ldots)$$

where Q is output, L is labor input, K is capital input and where other inputs may also be used. Generally, output increases with the quantity of inputs, and there may be scope for substituting one input for another. For example, a sweater could be knitted by hand with no machinery, or could be knitted on a knitting machine. Some versions—such as the Cobb–Douglas or CES PRODUCTION FUNCTIONS—specify the degree to which factors can be substituted for one another, as well as the *returns to scale* (see COBB-DOUGLAS PRODUCTION FUNCTION). A production function that specifies that a doubling of all inputs will double the quantity produced exhibits *constant returns to scale*. Increasing and decreasing returns are also possible.

Although economists typically speak of the production function of a FIRM, it is also possible to characterize a nation's output as a function of its resources. Such a production function is referred to as an *aggregate production function* and has the same general form as the one above. Q, in this case, refers to gross domestic (or national) product, L to the total labor force in the country, and K to the entire capital stock in the country.

production possibility frontier Also PPF, or *transformation frontier*. A graph showing the various combinations of output that an economy can produce, given the available factors of production (labor, capital, land, etc.) and the available production technology. The classic two-good example illustrates the trade-off between producing guns and butter. An alternative interpretation of the PPF is that it shows the OPPORTUNITY COST of one good measured in terms of the other good. If the economy is on the PPF, it is said to be *efficient* in the sense that all factors of production are being fully utilized. The output of one good can be expanded only by reducing the output of the other. An inefficient outcome would lie at a point *inside* the frontier where not all resources are fully employed—here it is possible to expand the output of both goods.

profane The mundane or ordinary; sometimes the defiled. The term acquired a special significance in the study of religion in the wake of Emile DURKHEIM's *The Elementary Forms of Religious Life* (1915 [1912]), which drew an important distinction between the sacred and the profane domains of society. For Durkheim, the ritual separation of the sacred from the profane provided the basis of RELIGION. See also SACRED.

profession and professionalization In the nineteenth century, professions and professional organizations emerged from a variety of traditionally learned occupations—generally those that required substantial theoretical knowledge and training, such as medicine, law, and science. *Professionalization* describes the process of consolidation of diverse practitioners under a set of homogeneous norms or rules, including the emergence of standards of certification, credentialization, ethics, the development of self-governing associations, and the pursuit of legal recognition and protection.

These structures, the relative autonomy of professional work, and the high degree of prestige generally attached to professional activities differentiates professions from other forms of work and worker organization. Nonetheless, a number of tendencies in medicine and other professional fields have increasingly blurred these distinctions, as physicians, for example, become subordinate to larger bureaucratic structures of decision making or as faculty consider unionization. A large body of sociological research has studied the organization and role of professions in modern society. Andrew Abbott's *The System of Professions* (1988) is a prominent example that emphasizes the degree to which the process of professionalization is structured by interprofessional competition and conflict.

profits For a firm, profits equal total revenue less the total costs of production. Costs include both explicit costs, such as that of hiring labor, as well as implicit or OPPORTUNITY COSTs that represent the profits that would have been earned by using resources differently. The recognition of opportunity costs distinguishes the economist's concept of profit from the accounting definition of profits.

Economists also distinguish between *normal profits* and *supernormal profits*. Normal profits are the minimum that is required to induce a firm to continue to operate. In this case, total revenue just equals the opportunity cost of the firm's activity. Profits that exceed the opportunity cost are referred to as supernormal profits. Any number of short-term factors can generate supernormal profits, but most economists hold that in competitive markets, competition between firms erodes supernormal profits in the long run.

profit maximization A firm's profits are maximized when marginal revenue (the revenue gained from the production of another unit) exactly equals marginal cost (or the cost of production of that unit). As long as the revenue gained from an additional unit of output exceeds its cost, the firm has an interest in continuing production. See also MARGINAL ANALYSIS; and NEOCLASSICAL ECONOMICS.

projection In statistical research, a projection is a prediction about the future. In PSYCHOANALYSIS, projection is one of the EGO's defense mechanisms, which involves attributing one's own feelings and/or impulses to other persons.

proletariat Synonymous with the "working class" in Marxist accounts of CAPITALISM. Members of the proletariat must sell their labor to survive, and they generally accumulate little capital beyond the skills with which they work. In this they are distinguished from the BOURGEOISIE, or capitalist class. See also CLASS; and MARXISM.

property and property rights The legal relationship that governs the control and use of goods and resources. The configuration of property and property rights shows considerable historical and cross-cultural variation. Generally, property rights have been extensively elaborated only where goods are *rivalrous* (i.e., where one person's use impedes another's). Consequently, property rights have closely tracked with technological and social developments that put pressure on new or existing resources. This need not imply private-property rights—indeed many societies have been organized on principles of collective or state-owned property. Most research on the emergence of modern Western society, however, accords a major role to the growth of a strong and extendable concept of *private property*—not only as a prerequisite of economic development, but as the basis of a system of political rights and as a foundation for INDIVIDUALISM. A long liberal tradition of political and economic thought followed John LOCKE in treating private property as a natural right on the same level as life and liberty. The socialist and Marxist traditions placed even greater emphasis on the role of private property in the development and maintenance of capitalist society—though they saw it as the basis of a form of exploitation that worsened despite formal economic and political liberties. For this reason, Marx made the abolition of private property the chief goal of revolution.

In this context, theories of the origin of property have been extremely important. Perhaps the most influential version is Locke's account of how the world was originally held in common, then gradually expropriated by individuals through the application of their labor. No theory of property emerged in a vacuum, however; all situated themselves in relation to an existing social order, and thus all were entangled in issues of political legitimacy, social and economic justice. While few scholars disputed the right to personal property, many debates have focused on how far property rights extend beyond the direct possession of goods. For Locke, this extension was the source of inequality and injustice, and thus the main reason for the establishment of government. The growth of CAPITALISM created new mechanisms of extended ownership and new forms of accumulation of wealth. Some Utilitarian thinkers responded by rejecting the notion of an absolute right of property in favor of determining what best serves the social good. Such arguments were key to the extension of property rights to ideas and inventions through the mechanism of copyright and patent law. These granted temporary monopolies over such non-material goods in order to provide incentives for their production.

More recently, property rights have been explored as a potentially efficient means of regulating certain kinds of activities, such as polluting. Environmentally friendly companies, the theory goes, will profit from this arrangement by selling their pollution credits to less efficient companies. Well-defined and enforced property rights are increasingly viewed as a critical institutional prerequisite of economic growth—an issue with continued relevance in the developing world, where it implies the need for accompanying political DEVELOPMENT.

The specification of private property rights also usually necessitates clearer rules for other forms of property, such as public or common property (see PUBLIC GOODS). These face different challenges. The *Tragedy of the Commons*—the overuse of commonly held goods—is perhaps the best-known dilemma (see COMMON-PROPERTY RIGHTS). Modern forms of communal and cooperatively owned property nonetheless thrive in some circumstances (see COOPERATIVES).

proportional representation See ELECTORAL SYSTEM.

prospect theory A social-psychological theory of decision making under conditions of risk and uncertainty, developed by Daniel Kahneman and Amos Tversky. Prospect theory analyzes the biases and interpretive strategies that shape people's choices in the face of uncertain outcomes. It helps to illuminate experimental results that show that individuals often make divergent choices in situations that are substantively identical but framed differently.

Prospect theory has identified four significant tendencies in how individuals construe choices: (1) the *certainty effect*, which refers to the tendency to give greater weight to certain outcomes than to uncertain outcomes; (2) the *isolation effect*, which describes the tendency to emphasize the differences between choices over their common elements; and (3) the *reflection effect*, which describes the observed preference for guaranteed small gains over uncertain large gains, and conversely for uncertain large losses over small certain losses. This implies that the value function is concave for gains but convex for losses; (4) the observation that small probabilities are overweighted, which may help to explain the popularity of lottery tickets.

protectionism A trade policy that restricts the importation of goods and services into a country. Protectionism is a strategy for shielding domestic producers from foreign competition through the imposition of tariffs, quotas, or nontariff barriers. See also FREE TRADE AND PROTECTIONISM.

Protestant ethic In Max WEBER's influential analysis of the origins of CAPITALISM, *The Protestant Ethic and the Spirit of Capitalism* (1905), the Protestant ethic describes the set of ascetic Protestant values (rooted in Calvinism) that influenced the growth of capitalism in early modern Europe. These include the acceptance of work and accumulation as a duty, strong individualism (particularly in the matter of salvation or self-worth), the rational organization of conduct, and the rejection of hedonistic pleasures.

Weber argued that three central concepts in Protestantism—predestination, the unknowability of God, and the notion of calling—linked it psychologically to the rational characteristics of capitalism. The Calvinist doctrine of predestination held that only a small number of people were chosen for salvation, and that there was no earthly way of distinguishing among them because God's motives were beyond human comprehension. Weber contended that this uncertainty was a hard burden for Calvinists to bear, and that they compensated by seeking personal assurance of salvation through hard work in the service of God. Such work was implied in the idea of individual *calling*, the belief that God assigns individuals tasks or occupations. The pursuit of one's calling required a methodical and disciplined conduct of everyday life; this represented, for Weber, the incipient value of the RATIONALIZATION of conduct that he considered central to the capitalist spirit. In particular, the Protestant ethic discouraged consumption and luxury and encouraged investment and the careful calculation of returns. Like Friedrich NIETZSCHE, Weber believed that although this spirit of rationalization emerged from religion, it was ultimately destructive of religious values. The asceticism of the early Protestants was materialist and worldly, not other-worldly.

Weber's account of the religious preconditions of capitalism is frequently read as a critique of the strong economic determinism of MARXISM, which treats religious and other cultural formations as derived from the economic base. Nonetheless, Weber integrated much of the Marxist account and viewed class structure as one of the fundamental features of capitalism. The Protestant-ethic argument has been a controversial subject in historical and sociological scholarship, not least for its marginalization of both Roman Catholicism in Europe and the role of increased consumption—contrary to the ascetic spirit—in fueling the expansion of capital.

Proudhon, Pierre-Joseph (1809–1865) A French editor, politician, and social theorist who contributed greatly to the development of SOCIALISM and whose work is the cornerstone of much of modern anarchism (see ANARCHY AND ANARCHISM). Proudhon's first book, *What is Property* (1840), set the terms of the critique of property relations, social organization, and social injustice that would occupy him for the rest of his life. In it he drew a basic distinction between personal *possession* (which he defended as basic to freedom) and *property* (or personally controlled means of production used to extract profit from the labor of others). A society that protected property, in this respect, protected exploitation—indeed Proudhon reached the famous conclusion, "Property is theft." The

proper goal of society, rather, was to assure the right of access to the means of production as an extension of the right to life itself. For Proudhon, this implied a form of communal living, in which individuals are guided by the desire for unfettered self-expression and collective justice. It further implied a borderless Europe, free of government and structured law. Proudhon argued that government functioned, by definition, through coercion and constraint—and as such thwarted the human spirit and precluded any genuine sense of community. Instead, power would be held and wielded locally in a highly decentralized system of political democracy and interestless banking. Toward these ends, Proudhon called for revolutionary action. He had an enormous influence on the radicalism of 1848 and served, during that period, as a member of the French Constituent Assembly.

Mutualism is the term Proudhon gave to this vision of social organization. Central to mutualism is a notion of moral responsibility and cooperation in the context of mutually agreed upon rules and principles. If individuals were truly allowed to think and choose for themselves, Proudhon believed, they would do so with equal measures of self-interest and moral restraint. Still, some maintenance of order would be necessary, and Proudhon insisted on a regulatory structure that would ensure that all individuals were permitted to equitably bargain for their needs. Some degree of self-sufficiency would also be necessary, as would a division of labor and a balance of power.

Proudhon's other influential writings are *A General Idea of the Revolution in the Nineteenth Century* (1851), *On Justice in the Revolution and the Church* (1858), and *The Principle of Federation* (1863).

proxemics A term coined by anthropologist Edward T. Hall in 1963 to describe the study of interpersonal distances. Proxemics now refers broadly to the active use people make of the spatial context in which social interactions occur. It addresses issues such as crowding, territoriality, privacy, and personal space.

PSID Panel Study of Income Dynamics. The major data set on income stratification and related demographic information in the United States. The PSID was launched in 1968 and is now conducted biennially. It is based at the University of Michigan.

psychoanalysis Initially, the set of theories and practices pioneered by Sigmund FREUD in the late nineteenth century for the treatment of mental illness. Although both theory and practice underwent considerable change during the course of Freud's research, two basic tenets remained consistent: the theory of repressed affect, in which mental illness is the symptom of a past traumatic experience that remains blocked from consciousness; and a conversation-based therapeutic approach, in which patient and analyst attempt to recover that trauma from the distortions and displacements that mediate its expression. In principle, the cure involves arriving at a successful interpretation that is accepted by the patient, although the complexity and potential for deception within that process is such that the nature of the endgame remains a constant issue in psychoanalytic practice.

Freud frequently revised and elaborated his theories of the unconscious—from early notions of the accumulation and discharge of tension, to the tripartite division into ID, EGO, and SUPEREGO, to the developmental theory of the OEDIPUS COMPLEX, and finally to notions of life drives and death drives that underwrote all biological life and shaped civilization. Psychoanalysis also produced a number of dissenting schools in its first decades. Carl Gustav JUNG broke with Freud in 1914, largely over Jung's dissatisfaction with Freud's emphasis on sexuality as the source of neurosis. Jung developed a number of theoretical tools to explain the process of individuation and the broad commonalities of myth, culture, and religion across human society—a commonality he attributed to a COLLECTIVE UNCONSCIOUS. Although very popular in their day, Jung's theories have had a larger impact in ANTHROPOLOGY and literary study than in clinical psychoanalysis. The most prominent of the dissenting clinical forms was OBJECT-RELATIONS THEORY, associated with Melanie KLEIN, Wilfred BION, Donald Woods WINNICOTT, and W. R. D. Fairburn. Object-relations theory broke with the Freudian sexual drama of identity—and especially the mother-father-child triangle of the Oedipal model—in favor of a notion of individuation and maturation that proceeds by way of diverse attachments to familial and social "objects," which the child progressively internalizes and distinguishes from the self. Klein's work on the infant's relationship with its mother

was particularly influential in this regard and had a major impact on subsequent feminist theories of identity. The principal competitor to object-relations theory was EGO PSYCHOLOGY, associated with Anna Freud, and later Heinz Hartmann and Edith Jacobson. Klein and Anna Freud strongly disagreed about child development and observational techniques, leading to a long (and to a degree still significant) disciplinary schism. Unlike object-relations theory, ego psychology remained close to Freud's theory of the instincts while emphasizing ego defenses and the possibility of a broader, less vexed accommodation of the psyche to societal demands.

Psychoanalysis has become influential in literary and CULTURAL STUDIES, although this comes at a time when it has lost standing as a specific explanatory theory in psychology and psychiatry. Much of this influence is due to the encounter of Freudian psychoanalytic theory and structural linguistics in the work of Jacques LACAN, who recast the Oedipal model of child development in the terms of a socializing fall into language.

These varied concepts have had a major impact on the social sciences, contributing new dimensions to the study of CULTURE at both the macro level of social structure and the micro level of individual behavior. Perhaps the most basic contribution is the general idea that human behavior is internally complex and even contradictory. Freud's divided psyche challenged simpler atomistic notions of persons as unitary "actors" or "points" in a system of behavior. More broadly, the outlines of Freud's work have become part of the modern, Western worldview, providing a widely accepted language for explaining behavior and feelings. See also CULTURE AND PERSONALITY MOVEMENT.

psychological anthropology The observation that different cultures have different ways of thinking dates back to the turn of the twentieth century, especially to debates about the existence of a PRIMITIVE MENTALITY in premodern societies, but anthropology's most significant engagement with psychology reflects the encounter with Freudian PSYCHOANALYSIS—particularly Freud's attempts to theorize the links between psychology and culture in *Totem and Taboo* (1913 [1950]), *Civilization and its Discontents* (1929 [1930]), and other late works. The CULTURE AND PERSONALITY movement, formed by students of Franz BOAS in the 1920s, led the way in investigating the relationship between psychological development and modes of socialization—prototypically in Margaret MEAD's comparative studies of childhood and Ruth Fulton BENEDICT's identification of culturally specific psychological "patterns." Subsequent directions of research have opened up a much wider range of issues, from the development of structures of cognition (COGNITIVE ANTHROPOLOGY), to the universalizing psychological claims of STRUCTURALISM, the border between culture and physiology (SOCIOBIOLOGY), and the critique of the privilege accorded Western psychological models in postcolonial and poststructural debates.

public administration (1) A state's public bureaucracy, the institutional arrangements devised to administer public services. (2) A subdiscipline of POLITICAL SCIENCE that focuses on the study of public bureaucracy through institutional analysis and the evaluation of public policy.

public-choice theory Studies the behavior of actors in political systems using models of individual maximizing behavior. James Buchanan and Gordon Tullock are generally credited with establishing the subfield with their book *The Calculus of Consent* (1962). Buchanan and Tullock broke with the assumption that politicians are driven primarily by ideological motivations or are concerned with the welfare of society as a whole. Rather, they assumed a primary self-interest, operating in situations of complex and often contradictory objectives—fundraising, satisfying competing interest groups, reelection, and so on. While most work in public-choice theory has been directed toward explaining political behavior, some researchers have sought to apply it to improving systems of governance, based on positive information about how procedures and policies actually function. This normative component is usually referred to as the *theory of constitutions*. See also RATIONAL-CHOICE THEORY.

public goods Two characteristics distinguish public goods from private goods: they are not *excludable*, and they have low *rivalry of consumption*. A good is said to be excludable when individuals can be prevented from using it. Rivalry of consumption refers to the degree to which one person's consumption of a good prevents another from consuming it. For example, one person's use of a pair of shoes prevents others from using them, while a person's enjoyment of

an outdoor concert prevents no one else from enjoying it. The simplest definition of a public good is that it is nonrivalrous. Often, public goods are nonexcludable as well, but not necessarily. An example of a *pure* public good is national defense—it is impossible to exclude individuals of a country from benefiting from national defense, and the consumption benefits of each individual do not depend on the consumption benefits of others. Note that a public good is not the same thing as a publicly provided good, although the nature of public goods means that governments often must provide them because the market will not. The government also provides many *private goods*.

Some goods that may be regarded as public goods do possess rivalry characteristics. Roads and bridges have *low rivalry*, provided that traffic is limited. Beyond a certain point, however, congestion begins to impose a cost on users and the nonrivalry characteristic no longer applies. The *Tragedy of the Commons* is an example used to illustrate the problem of exhaustible public goods.

When public goods are nonexcludable, they are unlikely to be adequately furnished by the marketplace. No firm can earn money if consumption does not depend on purchasing the product. At the same time, goods with low rivalry have essentially zero marginal cost of production. The socially efficient level of production, in this case, is far greater (and at a far lower price) than a private firm would find profitable. As a result, public goods are traditionally provided by the government, and financed with tax money.

public opinion For most modern commentators, the term refers to views held by a significant portion of the population on topics of public concern. Although the power of public opinion in politics has been recognized in various forms since classical times, the modern concept is closely tied to two developments: the emergence of representative systems of government, in which legitimacy is rooted in the capacity of institutions to reflect or weigh the wishes of larger bodies of constituents, and the development of finance markets, where evaluations of the collective opinions of participants became necessary to effective action. Both contexts informed theories of political LIBERALISM and related concepts of the public sphere, which conceive public opinion as emerging out of free debate in a "marketplace" of ideas, and therefore as, at least potentially, a form of rational consensus (see PUBLIC SPHERE AND PRIVATE SPHERE).

The dominant eighteenth-century usage emphasized open expression and debate, contrasting free public opinion to absolutist repression. At the same time, it generally treated public opinion as a consensus formed on the basis of reasoned judgment. "Opinion" was something less than knowledge but, especially where it had been tested in public discourse, it was more than simply sentiment and it gained truth-value from reflexive examination. Various euphemisms like "informed opinion" and "responsible opinion," however, reflected both a bias in favor of the opinions of elites and anxiety about the possibly disruptive opinions of the masses. This anxiety came increasingly to the fore during the nineteenth century. Both Alexis de TOCQUEVILLE (*Democracy in America*, v. 2, 1840) and John Stuart MILL (*On Liberty*, 1859) contrasted public opinion to reasoned knowledge; Mill especially worried about "collective mediocrity," in which the opinions of the debased masses would triumph over scientific reason. Where advocates of the public sphere saw rational-critical discourse producing unity, critics saw mass opinion reflecting psychosocial pressures for conformity. Implicitly, they associated reason with individuals rather than any collective process. The distinction between "public" and "crowd" or "mass" was lost in such views. See MASS SOCIETY.

Commentators have routinely disagreed about the inclusiveness and unity of public opinion. Eighteenth-century accounts were often narrow in their definitions of which opinions mattered—consistent, in this respect, with existing restrictions on political participation. Increasingly, however, the idea of the public was reformulated as an inclusive, nationally bounded entity that legitimized or challenged the state through the expression of a singular will—as in Jean-Jacques ROUSSEAU's account of the GENERAL WILL. This singular notion of public opinion continues to shape much popular use of the term—although as the French Revolution demonstrated, unanimity was difficult to find and even harder to create. The reluctance of many social scientists to use the term in an analytical sense reflects the recognition that democratic societies are composed of a plurality of opinions and publics. Where broad consensus on certain issues does exist, there is disagreement about the significance of those views.

Modern research on public opinion tends in several directions: some researchers emphasize the role of the mass media and other technologies in disseminating views and creating consensus. The critical theory of the FRANKFURT SCHOOL, the sociology of Harold LASSWELL, and a variety of more recent approaches within CULTURAL STUDIES take up these issues. Walter Lippman and others helped make the shaping and manipulation of public opinion an acknowledged feature of both politics and marketing. Public opinion, in this context, has become largely equated with the findings of polling techniques—especially as developed by George GALLUP in the 1930s. A second direction looks at how opinions spread through and mobilize communities, including political communities such as interest groups or unions. Pluralist accounts of American politics by Robert DAHL and others emphasize the capacity of such communities of opinion to mobilize political power. The cultural Marxism of Antonio GRAMSCI examines similar practices in relation to forms of SOCIAL CONTROL and hegemony. Public-sphere theorists such as Jürgen HABERMAS represent a third direction, which seeks to redeem the early liberal notion of public opinion as the product of rational discourse among citizens from the diverse large-scale interests that dominate it.

public ownership The ownership and operation of productive enterprises by the state—generally because such enterprises are considered fundamental to the public interest (such as the provision of water or electricity) or because of the difficulty of pursuing some kinds of targeted objectives through the marketplace (such as rapid industrialization). See also PRIVATIZATION; and PROPERTY AND PROPERTY RIGHTS.

public sphere and private sphere The modern public sphere has two related meanings: it refers both to the open discussion among members of a collectivity about their common concerns and to the activities of the state that are central to defining that community. This double notion has its parallel in the private sphere. The private is simultaneously that which lies outside the purview of the state and that which concerns personal ends distinct from the public good—the *res publica* or matters of legitimate public concern.

The earliest discussions of the division between public and private spheres date to ancient Greece, where *public* referred to the realm of politics and *private* to the areas of family and economic life. Modern political theorists returned to the notion of the public in their efforts to theorize democratic rule. From the eighteenth century forward, liberal political theory has attributed a range of democratic functions to the public sphere: the business of weighing and formulating opinion, discussing and redefining the meaning of politics, and compelling the state to justify its actions.

Jürgen HABERMAS is perhaps the foremost contemporary theorist of these political functions. His early historical inquiry into the structural transformation of the public sphere since the eighteenth century has been central to nearly all subsequent debates ([1962] 1989). For Habermas, the basic political question that the public sphere raises is how to promote widespread and more or less egalitarian participation in rational-critical discourse about the proper ends of society. The public sphere, he argues, was created largely for the purposes of addressing the state and the sorts of public issues on which state policy might bear. It is based on (1) a notion of the public good as distinct from private interest; (2) social institutions, like private property, that empower individuals to participate independently in the public sphere; and (3) forms of private life, notably the family, that prepare individuals to act as autonomous, rational-critical subjects in the public sphere. A central paradox and weakness—not just in Habermas's theory but in the liberal conception that it analyzes and partially incorporates—arises from the implication that the public sphere depends on an organization of private, prepolitical life that enables and encourages citizens to rise above private identities and concerns. Habermas and other critical celebrants of the eighteenth-century public sphere have been especially criticized on this ground by feminist scholars, who draw attention to the historically strong gender division between public and private realms on which male political freedom rested.

Another influential modern theorist of the public sphere was Hannah ARENDT, who focused on the capacity of action in public to create the world that citizens share in common (*The Human Condition*, 1958). Arendt drew on both ancient Greek and Revolutionary-era American sources in developing a vision of public life as central to a republic's moral community. Similar notions of a vibrant republican public sphere have had a major influence in American historical studies—particularly in the work J. G. A. Pocock, Bernard Bailyn, and Gordon Wood. Like Arendt, these "republican synthesis" scholars emphasize the ephemeral nature of republicanism and the rapid emergence in the nineteenth century of a variously liberal, national, and representative (rather than participatory) model of the public sphere. They join a broad current of thought on both the Left and Right that deplores the modern decline of the public sphere—a phenomenon generally associated with the rise of particular interests at the expense of concern for the general good, as well as the deterioration of rational public discourse about public affairs. New scholarship has gone some way, however, in challenging this treatment of the republican era as a golden age.

Contemporary research on the public sphere turns on a number of important issues: the breadth of political participation, the existence of multiple or overlapping public spheres, the impact of new communications media, and the quality of rational-critical discourse and its relationship to culture-forming activities. These issues also inform discussions about the international public sphere, which emphasize such themes as human rights, democratization, and capital and financial flows. The basic question of the public sphere—to what extent can collective discourse determine the conditions of social life—is crucial to emerging research in this area.

purchasing power parity States that the exchange rate between two countries' currencies equals the ratio of the currencies' respective purchasing powers, as measured by the price of a typical basket of consumption goods. The purchasing power parity theory predicts that a fall in a country's purchasing power, as reflected in a rise in its price level, will cause a proportional currency depreciation in the foreign-exchange market. It follows that a rise in the foreign price level will cause a proportional appreciation in the domestic currency. This is referred to as the "strong" or "absolute" version of purchasing power parity. Its basis lies in the *law of one price*, which states that in competitive markets free of transport costs, barriers to trade, and other frictions, identical goods must sell for the same price when their prices are expressed in the same currency units. Prices will tend to be equalized through spatial arbitrage.

The conditions mentioned above are necessarily ideal. Markets are not perfectly competitive; information costs and impediments to trade hinder the spatial equalization of prices. Further, prices may be sticky and slow to adjust in the short run. Despite this, the common currency prices of any good in the different locations should be closely related and, indeed, arbitraged.

Another version of purchasing power parity is known as *relative* purchasing power parity. It states that the percentage change in the exchange rate between two currencies over some period equals the difference between the percentage change in the national price levels. Relative purchasing power parity is important because it may be valid even when absolute purchasing power parity is not. If the factors causing deviations from purchasing power parity are stable over time, percentage changes in relative price levels can still approximate percentage changes in exchange rates.

Empirically, the evidence in favor of purchasing power parity is weak. Even the law of one price does not fare well. Manufactured goods that are similar to one another are sold at widely differing prices in various international markets; however, purchasing power parity remains a good benchmark by which to judge whether an exchange rate is overvalued or undervalued.

purity   See POLLUTION AND PURITY.

push-and-pull factors   In the study of migration, *push factors* are those that encourage a population to leave its home, *pull factors* are those that draw a population to another area or place.

putty-clay or putty-putty   See CLAY-CLAY.

Q

***q*-theory of investment** See INVESTMENT.

qualitative response models See DISCRETE-CHOICE MODELS.

quango A term used especially in England to designate *quasi-nongovernmental organizations*—bodies appointed and funded by the state that enjoy operational independence. Quangos perform diverse administrative, advisory, and regulatory functions. Some critics argue that quangos compromise democratic principles because they are not directly accountable to the public. This has given rise to fears of an unelected "quangocracy."

quality theory of money See DEMAND FOR MONEY.

quasi rent The return on a good or factor of production, over and above its OPPORTUNITY COST, when the good or factor is temporarily in short supply. In the long run, supply can be reduced or increased; quasi rent disappears and the return on the good or factor equals its opportunity cost. Alfred MARSHALL used this concept in determining the price of capital in the short run, when supply is fixed.

Quesnay, François (1694–1774) The court physician of Louis XV of France and the founder of the PHYSIOCRATS—a school of economic thought that preceded the CLASSICAL ECONOMICS of Adam SMITH and David RICARDO. Quesnay believed that the circulation of wealth and goods in the economy was similar to the circulation of blood in the body and that, like the physical world, the economy was subject to natural, discoverable laws. For Quesnay, this implied a minimal role for government in facilitating the functioning of those laws—in sharp contrast to the protectionist policies of mercantilist thought (see MERCANTILISM).

Quesnay's *Tableau Economique* (1758) presented the first systematic analysis of the macroeconomy, depicted as a circular flow of goods and money through a perfectly competitive market. Perhaps the most important feature of this model was the distinction between *productive* and *sterile* labor—labor that produces output in excess of what it consumes and labor that merely reformulates existing wealth. The Physiocrats believed that only agriculture was productive in this sense.

The most significant aspect of *Tableau Economique* is its analysis of the circulation of this surplus, or *produit net*, throughout the economy. Farmers who cultivate the land produce food and raw materials for manufacture. Part of this is deducted to account for the farmer's consumption and the cost of seeds. Of the remaining output, part is paid as RENT to the proprietors (the king, the church, and all other landowners). The proprietors then buy food from the farmers and manufactured goods from the sterile class (artisans, merchants, etc.). The sterile class uses its income to buy food and raw materials for manufacture. This analysis comes close to a theory of VALUE, and it was probably the inspiration for the LABOR THEORY OF VALUE and the definition of surplus developed by the classical economists; Quesnay, however, did not take that step.

Like the classicists after him, Quesnay subscribed to a cost-of-production theory of price and considered labor the source of all value. He also recognized that competition resulted in a market price that was independent of the buyers or sellers. This view is similar to the neoclassical views of Alfred MARSHALL and others, but Quesnay thought that the value of goods to individuals provided the motive only for exchange; it did not influence price. Ultimately, the Physiocrats' belief that industry and trade were sterile activities proved unacceptable to the next generation, which witnessed the explosive development of both.

quorum The minimum number of people who must be present at a meeting to transact official business and make votes valid, usually established by procedural rules.

quota In economics, a restriction on the quantity of goods that may be produced or purchased—most commonly used in reference to quantitative restrictions on the volume of imported goods. *Quotas* may also refer to the minimum required levels of production, especially in planned economies (see CENTRAL PLANNING). Quotas are also common elements of AFFIRMATIVE ACTION policies. In this context, they entail setting aside a certain number or percentage of job positions (or contracts, or other resources) for members of historically disadvantaged groups.

R

---

race Prior to the nineteenth century, the term *race* was frequently interchangeable with "people" and connoted the mix of national and ethnic distinctions that separated, for example, the English from the French or the Germans. In the course of the nineteenth century, *race* acquired an increasingly biological definition, which was buttressed by a range of scientific, anthropological, and historical research. Much of the early anthropological tradition focused on making the proper racial distinctions among human societies—often with a strong hierarchical impulse rooted in theories of societal evolution and differential racial capacities. These were consistent, in many respects, with the colonial projects of the European powers and with the internal need to justify racial hierarchies in countries like the United States. Modern ANTHROPOLOGY emerged in the course of a protracted debate on this subject—pitting *monogenists*, who viewed humanity as comprising a single and generally equal race, against *polygenists*, who viewed the different races as akin to different species. The monogenist perspective dominated in the late nineteenth century, and the great formative works of modern SOCIOLOGY and anthropology generally endorsed the view that race was primarily a social construct that corresponded poorly with observed differences in physiology or appearance—above all, skin color. The work of the anthropologist Franz BOAS, himself versed and interested in physiometric techniques, was central to this repudiation of race as a natural category. In sociology, the study of race was profoundly influenced by the model of assimilation proposed by Chicago school scholars such as Robert Ezra PARK, who conceived a gradual, irrevocable process of homogenization of cultural differences (of immigrants and racial minorities) into the American mainstream (see CHICAGO SCHOOL OF SOCIOLOGY).

Today, social scientists (and increasingly biologists drawing on genetic research) generally hold that the notion of a sharp biological differentiation of humanity into distinct races is misleading. While there are biological differences among people, they are not primarily organized into racial categories. Nevertheless, social relations do often reflect historical racial distinctions. Race may thus be unreal in biological terms but real in social experience, complicating attempts to move beyond the use of superficial physical characteristics to organize social life.

The modern sociology of race addresses a broad range of issues regarding the construction and perception of racial categories; the consequences of racial stratification (how economic, political, and social status varies among different racial and ethnic groups); and the means of bringing equality of opportunity and other forms of social justice across racial lines. Much of this work also deals with the complexities of categorical distinctions between race and ETHNICITY (a term some social scientists find less problematic), as well as with the arbitrary and often flexible operation of racial categories and the hard aggregate differences in socioeconomic and cultural status that nonetheless accompany them. Attempts to explain the relatively high rate of POVERTY among African Americans in the United States on the basis of a self-reinforcing *culture of poverty*, for example, have proved controversial—especially when they seem to reintroduce value judgments about cultural norms that apply widely to the African-American population. Covertly biologized arguments about the racial component of poverty also continue to play a role in social-scientific and public debate, as in Richard Herrnstein and Charles Murray's *The Bell Curve: Intelligence and Class Structure in American Life* (1994). Marxist accounts have traditionally treated race as a secondary product of class relations and racism as an ideological strategy designed to thwart the natural alliance of working-class blacks and whites. A more recent Marxist theory of racial formation by Michael Omi and Howard Winant (*Racial Formation in the United States*, 1989), however, uses Antonio GRAMSCI's model of hegemonic struggle to describe the dynamic movement of racial categories, notions of justice and redress, and the

---

larger democratic and capitalist values that have shaped them.

racism   A form of prejudice based on the belief that certain racial groups are inherently superior to others. Racist discourse generally attributes such characteristics to biology, although cultural and historical arguments may also come into play. Such prejudice has in many cases grounded broader social and legal forms of discrimination, such as SLAVERY and, later, segregation in the United States.

Racism has been the subject of extensive research in the social sciences, from studies of its impact on the psychology of its victims to quantitative research on the forms of social stratification it sustains. Most recognize that racism is not a monolithic, unchanging, or unidirectional phenomena, and that perceptions of racism depend greatly on one's location in a racial system. This explains broad differences, for example, in black and white views of the role of race in the United States: blacks tend to see race as a central and systemic feature of American life, while whites tend to downplay its significance. See also RACE.

Radcliffe-Brown, A. R.   (1881–1955) One of the founding figures and leading proponents of British social ANTHROPOLOGY. Radcliffe-Brown is credited with developing structural functionalism—an approach to the study of society that focuses on the relations among social institutions (inheritance, ritual, marriage, etc.) and their integration into the larger economic and political framework. This perspective owed much to Emile DURKHEIM'S concept of FUNCTIONALISM, which Radcliffe-Brown assimilated in the 1910s. It demonstrated a number of important differences, however, from the functionalism of Bronislaw MALINOWSKI, which subordinated institutions to the primacy of individual psychological and biological needs.

Radcliffe-Brown emphasized general laws and structures and attempted to establish a unified and scientific approach to human society. Eventually, this placed him at odds with anthropologists who saw their work as a fundamentally humanistic endeavor, such as E. E. EVANS-PRITCHARD. The scientific character that Radcliffe-Brown attributed to structural functionalism also justified a strong comparative focus with roots in the grand comparative tradition of nineteenth-century anthropology. These commitments were very much in evidence in Radcliffe-Brown's most influential study, *The Social Organization of Australian Tribes* (1930–1931), which attempted to synthesize and relate the dramatic social differences observed among Australian aboriginal societies.

Radcliffe-Brown was never a prolific writer, but he became an enormously successful ambassador for social anthropology, teaching for extended periods in Australia, South Africa, and the United States. Although many of his scientific claims have been disproved or rejected, he was a central figure in the institutionalization of the discipline and in debates over its role. His other important works include *The Andaman Islanders* (1922), *Structure and Function in Primitive Society* (1952), and the volume edited with Daryll FORDE, *African Systems of Kinship and Marriage* (1950).

ramage   A term used primarily in ethnographies of Polynesian societies, *ramage* refers to the internal hierarchical structure of LINEAGES common in those societies. Where ramage exists, both MATRILINEAL DESCENT and PATRILINEAL DESCENT may be recognized but accorded different value.

random variables   Variables whose value is a numerical outcome of a random phenomenon. Such variables typically derive their value from a probability distribution, which describes the range and likelihood of certain values. Random variables are *discrete* when they take only a finite number of possible values, or *continuous* where they can represent all values within a given interval of numbers.

random walk   In statistics, a variable is said to "follow a random walk" when the current value of the variable is equal to its most recent value plus a random element.

range   See VARIABILITY.

ranked societies   Societies of moderate complexity, in which members occupy distinct ranks within a common structure of KINSHIP. CHIEFDOMS and BIGMAN societies are ranked societies. The term is associated with the evolutionary schema presented in Morton Fried's *The Evolution of Political Society* (1967).

rational-choice theory   The analysis of human action on the basis of individual strategic choices, generally predicated on treating individuals as rational maximizers of their interests. Rational-choice theory underlies most work in ECONOMICS and a considerable body of research in the other social sciences—especially in SOCIOLOGY and POLITICAL SCIENCE.

Rational-choice theory treats individuals as the basic unit of analysis, and individual choices and decisions as the foundation of larger economic and social phenomena. Put differently, it seeks to decompose social phenomena into sequences of individual actions. Generally, rational-choice theorists assume that individuals consistently behave rationally in choosing the most efficient means to a desired end or ends. In this respect, they are assumed to always seek to maximize their *utility*—the standard term in economics for well-being, however specified. Further, individual preferences in most rational-choice models are taken to be given *a priori*, rather than constructed and revised through ongoing social processes. Most work does not attempt to specify those preferences, however, and instead treats them as empirical variables: individual preferences are revealed by individual actions.

Rational-choice approaches tend to set aside culture, psychology, class, group dynamics, or other variables that suggest the divided nature or heterogeneous logic of human experience. In principle, these can be incorporated into analyses, but much of the power and elegance of rational-choice models depends on simplifying assumptions about the character of people and their orientations to action. Likewise, in most rational-choice models, actors are treated as equivalent or the differences among them are presented as attributes of individuals; this contrasts with approaches that focus on larger social relationships of power or on cultural differences. Partly for this reason, and partly because of resistance to its simplifying assumptions, rational choice marks a major methodological and philosophical divide within social science (and especially within sociology and political science).

Nonetheless, much recent work has been done to understand the limits of rational-choice theory's operating parameters—especially in real-world situations, where individuals face decisions under circumstances far different from the classical ideal of a competitive market. In choice situations where actions affect others—where there is the possibility of cooperative, altruistic, or punishing behavior—individual choices often do not seem optimal by any logical utility construction. Also, individuals are often inconsistent in their own choices, indicating that they are influenced by past choices, have problems of self-control, or

are sensitive to framing effects and other manipulations of information. To varying degrees, these behaviors can be explained within the paradigm; but increasingly, decision theorists recognize the importance of norms, rules, and habits for guiding behavior.

Other researchers (especially economists) have taken up the question of complexity and cognitive power. In RATIONAL EXPECTATIONS models, agents form expectations of prices based on expectations of the entire economy. In any complex economy, therefore, rationality implies extensive data gathering and information processing. When the model of perfect competition gives way to markets that are more or less oligopolistic or monopolistic, actors need to know not only prices but also how their actions will change the character of the market. Where prices and actions are interrelated, a truly optimal choice would require a general equilibrium model of the economy—a severe strain on the information gathering and computational abilities of individuals. For this reason, research on SATISFICING and other ways of compensating for complexity and imperfect information has grown in importance in recent years.

Some proponents of the rational-choice approach argue that its assumptions were never meant to characterize the actual decision-making process in such circumstances, but that individuals nonetheless act as if they were calculating optimizers. Milton FRIEDMAN's famous analogy is to the billiards player, who has no knowledge of physics and yet, through practice, achieves what looks like the result of complicated calculations in sinking shots. Others emphasize the importance of recognizing that individuals act within a framework of BOUNDED RATIONALITY—or are rational within certain parameters or contexts. Still, it is possible to devise economic models that are based on other principles. Most macroeconomic models, including Keynesian and monetarist models, are only partly based on rationality postulates (see KEYNESIANISM; and MONETARISM).

rational expectations The assumption that economic actors generally incorporate informed predictions about changes in economic variables into their decisions. While essentially a microeconomic theory of decision making, rational expectations has had its greatest impact in MACROECONOMICS, where it underwrote the New Classical response to Keynesian and monetarist theories of macroeconomic intervention (see KEYNESIANISM). For Robert Lucas and other economists in the 1970s and 1980s, rational expectations implied that people could not be "fooled" by changes in monetary policy, such as a shift in the interest rate. Where earlier models implied a lag in prices based on the persistence of expectations—permitting policy to have a real impact on economic variables in the short run—rational expectations implied that prices would adjust immediately, based on a generally clear understanding of the economy and the consequences of policy shifts. Under these assumptions, monetarist macroeconomic policy was ineffective.

In recent years, empirical research has cast some doubt on the validity of strong rational-expectations claims, leaving room for both monetarist assumptions about the analytical limitations of economic actors (often called BOUNDED RATIONALITY) and to a degree reestablishing Keynesian claims about the stickiness of prices and wages. Lucas himself abandoned much of the rational-expectations model, and no clear consensus exists about this fundamental component of macroeconomic theory. At the same time, the use of rational expectations at the microeconomic level has increased with the growth of GAME THEORY, which presumes rational strategizing. See also EXPECTATIONS; and MICROECONOMICS.

rationalization   In most social science usage, the process by which systematic thought, instrumental reason, measurement, and calculation came to dominate the life of modern societies. Although rationalization has been recognized as a central feature of modern social development since the early Enlightenment—indeed Enlightenment social thinkers were powerful contributors to this process—the concept was most strongly marked by Max WEBER's treatment in the early twentieth century. For Weber, rationalization was a total social process that affected all areas of social life—the economy, POLITICS, BUREAUCRACY, LAW, RELIGION, and science. These developments were interrelated, and progress in one generally spilled over into others. Weber's account of the relationship between the Protestant reformation and early CAPITALISM is perhaps the most famous of these linkages (*The Protestant Ethic and the Spirit of Capitalism*, 1904).

Regarding the emergence of modern capitalism, Weber argued that rationalization involved a number of related processes, including the decline of family control of business and the growth of management practices structured by the calculation of profits and precise accounting

procedures; in politics, it was reflected in the way that organized mass parties supplanted charismatic figures and patron–client relations; in the area of public administration, rationalization meant the spread of bureaucracy and the growing sophistication of managerial techniques, which brought social life increasingly under the control of the modern state; in law, legal-rational principles with universal applicability progressively replaced arbitrary case-law and judicial discretion; in religion, the "disenchantment of the world" signified the decline of religious WORLDVIEWS and practices; in science, individual genius gave way to organized research teams whose members carry out specific tasks at the behest of states and large corporations.

At its core, then, rationalization is a worldview as much as a social process. It is not only the ability to master problems by measurement and calculation, but also an inclination to see problems as subject to this kind of solution. Despite the many ways in which rationalization freed individuals from traditional forms of constraint and want, Weber distinguished between *formal rationalization* and the deeper *substantive irrationality* that characterized many aspects of capitalist society. He feared especially that, divorced from substantive goals, rationalization could be captured by patently irrational or aesthetic visions of politics—a view that anticipated NAZISM by a few short years. Weber also believed that rationalization exacted a price in other ways. The regimentation and disciplinary logic of factory production and bureaucracy imposed itself in other spheres of life and threatened to transform society into an "iron cage." Moreover, the disenchantment of the world meant that modern human beings were deprived of the otherworldly comforts and moral certainties that earlier generations enjoyed.

Weber's analysis of rationalization informed subsequent FRANKFURT SCHOOL critiques of instrumental reason by Max HORKHEIMER, Theodor ADORNO, and others. These placed more hope, at least initially, in the capacity of reason to create substantive, liberatory goals for human society. Later Frankfurt school scholars such as Jürgen HABERMAS and Claus Offe tried to account for different forms of rationality—in part by challenging Weber's view of the reducibility of all social life to instrumental rationality and in part by exploring the possibility of rational principles of moral and political reasoning.

rationed equilibria   Also *non-Walrasian equilibria*. Equlibria in which markets do not clear—that is, where economic agents cannot buy or sell as much as they desire and are thereby constrained (or rationed) in their trades in the market. Walrasian equilibria, in contrast, assumes that agents can exchange as much as they want and that markets clear through price movements (see Leon WALRAS).

rationing A situation in which consumers face constraints on the quantity of goods and services available. This contrasts with the standard theory of consumer behavior, which holds that the only constraint is that of resources—the budget constraint. The prevalence of government-regulated rationing in Britain during World War II led to a great deal of theoretical and empirical work on the implications of quantity rationing. The dominant assumption has been that any restriction on consumers can only reduce welfare, although more recent behavioral work has challenged this idea.

ratio scale See MEASUREMENT.

Ratzel, Friedrich (1844–1904) One of the founders of modern political GEOGRAPHY in Germany, Ratzel's contributions are diverse. He was a strong advocate of ENVIRONMENTAL DETERMINISM in explaining the course and character of civilizations. He also promoted an influential theory of the state as an organic entity, which must expand or die for lack of new resources. In this context, he coined the term *Lebensraum* ("living room"), which was to have a profound influence on German expansionism in the twentieth century. Ratzel traveled widely in North America and produced an important work of regional geography, *Die Vereinigten Staaten von Nord-Amerika* (The United States of North America, 1878). His other major works include the two-volume *Anthrogeographie, oder Grundzüge der Anwendung der Erdkunde auf die Geschichte* (Anthropology, or the Basic Elements of the Application of Geography to History, 1882–1891).

Rawls, John (1921–) An American political philosopher whose work has profoundly shaped contemporary debates about social justice. Rawls's essential contributions in this regard are *A Theory of Justice* (1971) and the elaboration and revision of those ideas in *Political Liberalism* (1993). In the first work, Rawls sought to logically determine the structure of a just society by asking what social principles people would agree upon if they argued from a hypothetical "original position," in which they had no knowledge of their identities, social positions, talents, or opinions. Under such conditions, Rawls argued, the utilitarian principle of the greatest good for the greatest number would prove inadequate, insofar as it potentially sacrificed the freedom or well-being of some people for the larger good (see UTILITARIANISM). Instead, he proposed that two general principles of fairness and justice would emerge. First, each person would be accorded equal rights to certain fundamental liberties: freedom of thought, association, movement, and political participation, to the maximal degree that these do not interfere with the enjoyment of the same rights by others. Second, social and economic inequalities would be permissible only if they work to the greatest possible benefit of the least advantaged and are gained under conditions accessible to all. This he termed the *difference principle*. The first principle is generally viewed as the core of Rawls's liberalism: individual freedoms take priority over economic well-being, and broader notions of social solidarity or collective purposes are excluded altogether. The second principle is more clearly egalitarian and consistent with Rawls's preference for a form of democratic SOCIALISM.

The cultural and historical specificity of Rawls's principles has been an issue of concern for many of his critics, and Rawls ultimately retreated from the universalistic implications of *A Theory of Justice* toward a more historical positioning of his work within the democratic political tradition. Rawls's "original position"—although presented as a thought experiment rather than a prescription—has also proved controversial, in part for its implication that uniform rationality and values are disrupted by identity and social issues. Rawls's later work pays more attention to the potential plurality of values that exist in any given polity. His notion of the emergence of common principles through a process of "overlapping consensus" is an attempt to accommodate such plurality.

Rawls's other works include *The Idea of Overlapping Consensus* (1987), in which he develops an approach to reconciling unity and diversity, and *The Law of Peoples* (1999).

reaction formation A psychological defense mechanism whereby people react to unsettling or dangerous feelings by strongly adopting the opposite posture or attitude. Heterosexual posturing on the part of persons who fear homosexuality is the classic psychoanalytic example. Reaction formations have also been used in the sociology of DEVIANCE to explain the emergence of delinquent subcultures.

reaction functions Commonly used in oligopoly theory, reaction functions specify the optimal strategic response of economic agents to the choices made by others (see OLIGOPOLY AND OLIGOPSONY). In studying market behavior of firms, these choices often affect price, quantity, or nonprice variables such as advertising expenditures.

reader-response theory See RECEPTION THEORY AND READER-RESPONSE THEORY.

real-balance effect See PIGOU EFFECT.

realignment See ALIGNMENT.

real income A measure of the goods and services that a person can afford to consume. Real income is nominal income (measured in currency units) divided by the aggregate price level in the economy. The price level is determined as a function of the prices in some base year.

Real income is sometimes used as an indicator of welfare or of productive capacity. An increase in real income implies that the consumer is better off. Moreover, it implies that there has been an outward shift in the PRODUCTION POSSIBILITY FRONTIER for the economy as a whole.

realism A term with distinct meanings in POLITICAL SCIENCE and the philosophy of science. In political science, the term refers to the tradition of "power-politics," which views the international system as a continuous struggle among sovereign countries (see INTERNATIONAL RELATIONS). As a philosophical position, realism holds that the *real* is not limited to either sensory experience or our internally developed ideas. It is thus a refutation of extreme versions of IDEALISM and EMPIRICISM. In the philosophy of science, realism gives theory (and beliefs and conjectures that may not quite add up to theories) standing alongside empirical induction. In most versions, progress in knowledge is held to depend on both new observations and new thought about available observations. In this context, we can analyze as real categories of phenomena whose existence is theoretically necessary but not directly observable.

Realism acknowledges that the real may well exist but may be unalterably mediated by the structures of language or consciousness—a position consistent with much of modern philosophy, from Kantianism to PHENOMENOLOGY to structural and poststructural approaches to knowledge. These mediations, in turn, may be more or less subject to scientific analysis—a position that underlies Emile DURKHEIM's concept of social science. Such questions played an important role in late nineteenth-century accounts of the relationship between the natural and human sciences, especially the German debate about truth claims and methodologies known as the *METHODENSTREIT*. Realism also plays a prominent role in the contemporary philosophy of science, primarily through the work of Roy Bhaskar, where it continues an argument with empiricism regarding the status of speculative scientific claims.

realistic conflict theory A theory of group relations that explains intergroup conflict in terms of competition for limited resources. Associated primarily with Musafer Sherif (*Common Predicament: Social Psychology of Intergroup Conflict and Cooperation*, 1966), realistic conflict theory builds on the observation that in cases where one group's gain depends on another's loss, intergroup competition tends to increase, whereas in cases where intergroup cooperation is a prerequisite for mutual gain, competition between the two groups will tend to decrease. Sherif's work is in part a sociological demonstration of the cooperative and noncooperative dimensions of GAME THEORY.

reality principle The survival-oriented awareness that Sigmund FREUD associated with the EGO—the choice-making, rational part of the psyche. The reality principle is often described as the process of adaptation of mental life to environmental threats and physiological needs; in other accounts, it refers to the ego's role in mediating between the instincts (associated with the ID) and the understanding of what is acceptable and possible in reality.

real money balances A measure of the quantity of goods and services that an individual (or economy) commands. Unlike *nominal money balances*, it reflects the basic assumption that individuals are free of MONEY ILLUSION and care only about the purchasing power of their money.

realpolitik See INTERNATIONAL RELATIONS.

real versus nominal In all circumstances where economic concerns must be valued, using current prices provides only a *nominal* value. That is, it tells you the value of income, goods, etc., only in terms of today's valuations. Valuing income in terms of the goods that it can purchase, however, provides the basis for comparison across time, region, or countries, where goods may have different costs. This is an example of measuring REAL INCOME. Alternatively, *real values* use a standard of pricing—such as a price index—to convert nominal values to a common standard.

reapportionment See APPORTIONMENT.

recall See DIRECT DEMOCRACY.

reception theory and reader-response theory Related theoretical arguments about the construction of meaning by readers or, more generally, by viewers or consumers of information and cultural goods. Reception theory opposes traditional views of signification that privilege strong concepts of authorial intention and the related view that meaning inheres in texts. Both of these views situate the reader as the recipient of fixed, intentional meaning. Instead, reception theory emphasizes the range of possible "positions" that a reader may occupy with respect to a text. Certain of these positions correspond to an intended audience and require a set of *competencies* in the expectations of the genre or complicity in suspending critical judgment. Others may be critical or dissenting positions that emerge at the margins of reading publics.

The term *reception theory* is sometimes reserved for the orientation that Hans Robert Jauss, Wolfgang Iser, and other European literary theorists have given this set of issues, which tends to emphasize literary aesthetics. Many of the same themes have been pursued by *reader-response* and audience theorists in English-speaking countries—primarily within CULTURAL STUDIES, where it represents a critique of both the literary aestheticism of New Criticism and the seamless theories of cultural manipulation developed by the FRANKFURT SCHOOL. These themes have underwritten a wide range of research and in many cases integrate a strong sociological focus—from Stuart HALL's work on television reception, to Stanley Fish's concept of interpretive communities, to Janice Radway's survey studies of structures of value among readers of romance novels.

Redfield, Robert (1897–1958) A specialist of peasant communities and the effects of modernization, Redfield published a number of influential ethnographies of Mexican villages in the Yucatán Peninsula. He also introduced several important concepts for theorizing the relationship between developed and underdeveloped areas, notably the FOLK-URBAN CONTINUUM and the distinction between GREAT AND LITTLE TRADITIONS. Redfield's Yucatán studies made an additional, if unintended, contribution to the field after Oscar Lewis published a different set of conclusions based on later research in the same community. The discrepancies between their studies touched off a debate among anthropologists about the subjectivity of ethnographic work and the value of repeated study of the same group. Throughout his career, Redfield was an advocate of expanding ANTHROPOLOGY beyond its traditional focus on premodern societies, in recognition of the importance of contact between societies characterized by different degrees of modernization and urbanization. His major works include *The Folk Culture of the Yucatan* (1941) and *Peasant Society and Culture* (1956).

redistribution A shift in the distribution of income or wealth, generally as a means of pursuing egalitarian goals or of assisting disadvantaged sections of the population. The most common tools of redistribution are taxes on income, wealth, and commodities; transfer payments, such as pension and social security; and the provision of PUBLIC GOODS, such as public services and national defense. Other measures include price controls, rent controls, minimum-wage legislation, and the rationing of goods and services. At the societal level, the challenge is not merely to achieve a more equitable distribution of wealth, but to increase wealth so that redistribution is not simply a zero-sum game in which one person's gain is another's loss. For this reason, equity considerations cannot be divorced from issues of how income and wealth are generated. Government action can also privilege the redistribution of "opportunity," as in the case of subsidies for education. See also FUNDAMENTAL THEOREMS OF WELFARE; GROWTH THEORY; and JUSTICE.

reference group Any group whose standards serve an individual as a basis for evaluating aspects of his or her own life, regardless of whether the individual is part of that group. The concept was introduced by Herbert Hyman in "The Psychology of Status" (1942) and has since become important in a range of sociological research. For functionalists such as Robert K. MERTON and Alice Kitt, reference groups provide normative standards that serve as mechanisms of social integration. A person, for example, may seek to emulate the behavior of a social elite that he or she respects or a professional elite to which he or she belongs. Reference groups may operate negatively, as well, when groups define their behavior through opposition to the norms of another group. Research has also shown that reference groups play an important role in individual or group evaluations of their conditions of life. The sense of deprivation or social inequality, for example, exists primarily in relation to other groups whose condition is perceived to be superior or easier. A central work in this line of inquiry is Merton and Kitt's "Contribution to the Theory of Reference Group Behavior" (1950).

The symbolic interactionist tradition has developed a somewhat different concept of reference group, related to George Herbert MEAD's idea of the *generalized other* (see SYMBOLIC INTERACTIONISM). In this context, reference groups play a crucial role in constructing the sense of SELF—initially through the mediation of parents, later peers, and eventually through the generalized perspective of society itself toward which individuals direct their behavior. Other work has retained a focus on particular reference groups, seeking to understand the distinct social worlds that inform different aspects of people's lives. Such work approaches society as a set of separate but overlapping spheres of identification or norms, and individuals as complexly positioned and defined in relation to, potentially, several at once. The difficulty of specifying how and which groups influence aspects of a person's beliefs or sense of self is a persistent challenge in reference-group research.

referendum   See DIRECT DEMOCRACY.

reflexive modernization   A concept associated with the MODERNIZATION THEORY of Ulrich Beck and the structuration theory of Anthony GIDDENS. Beck periodizes modernization into a *simple* form, associated with INDUSTRIALIZATION and the distribution of goods, and a *reflexive* form that emphasizes the growing scientific, administrative, and social task of coping with earlier effects of modernization. Modernity thereby becomes defined by the management of risks that

it itself has created. Beck also accords considerable importance to the decline of traditional registers of ascribed identity (e.g., class) and the transfer of responsibility for identity formation from social groups to individuals (see Beck's *Risk Society: Towards a New Modernity*, 1992).

reflexivity   One of the constitutive problems of modern philosophy and social science, rooted in the question of whether and how persons can know the world with any certainty. Although its philosophical origins lie in Ancient Greek thought, modern reflection on this question derives primarily from the work of René DESCARTES, who argued that the basic kernel of certainty derives from consciousness turning back upon itself to recognize its own existence: "I think, therefore I am." This concept of reflection as a basic operation of thought informed the dialectical tradition of Georg HEGEL, Karl MARX, and more recently *critical theory*, which treats reflexivity as the basis of critique and, consequently, as the only way to understand history and society. Contemporary philosophers such as Michel FOUCAULT and Jürgen HABERMAS go further in identifying reflexivity with MODERNITY itself, drawing on Immanuel KANT's eighteenth-century description of modernity as the era of inquiry into the conditions of the present. In a related context, reflexivity often designates the process of *interiorization*—the interest in and interrogation of one's own interior life—that many historians and social theorists associate with modern selfhood.

In the social sciences, *reflexivity* often refers more narrowly to the problem of accounting for the role of social scientists as participants in the cultures they study. Beyond the question of the personal biases that may affect research, social scientists need reflexive awareness of their impact on the objects of study. An anthropologist, for example, is not a neutral factor in a peasant village. More generally, the position of social scientists as knowledge producers is always defined by larger institutions, structures of value, and concepts of truth—all of which change over time, however slowly. Reflexive approaches frequently come into conflict, therefore, with the forms of POSITIVISM that continue to underwrite much social-scientific research. Positivism assumes the impartial, objective, and detached role of the social scientist with respect to the subject matter. It implies an understanding of reality as given—awaiting the truth-revealing methods of the scientist.

Recently, social science practice has itself become an object of reflexive analysis. Such research often emphasizes the socioeconomic issues, political conditions, and other practical circumstances that shape the history and institutions of social science. Alvin Ward GOULDNER was a particularly strong advocate of such inquiry, especially in *The Coming Crisis of Western Sociology* (1970). Harold GARFINKEL and Pierre BOURDIEU have similarly insisted that SOCIOLOGY is a necessary subject of sociological investigation—Garfinkel through a general equation of sociological methods with "popular" methods of explaining social phenomena; Bourdieu by bridging the gap between objective and subjective approaches, and by carefully accounting for the place of the sociologist as an interested observer—a process he calls "participant objectivation."

refugee   According to the 1951 United Nations Convention Relating to the Status of Refugees, a *refugee* is any person forced to live outside his or her country of origin because of fear of persecution by reason of RACE, RELIGION, nationality, or membership in a particular social or political group.

The question of who meets these criteria has become highly politicized. Refugee status is generally privileged over immigrant status and offers greater opportunities for citizenship in the host country. Refugee policies have also become targets of criticism because of the disruption that refugees sometimes bring to economic, class, and ethnic relations in the host countries. Relations between host countries and countries of origin may also be strained. Policy and public discourse is consequently shaped by contrary forces: on one side, growing humanitarian concern for displaced persons; on the other, restrictive interpretations of refugee status in the name of national interest. Humanitarians have criticized the UN definition for requiring evidence of persecution and for being excessively narrow. They note that refugees are also produced by interstate and civil wars, environmental crises, civil disorder, and government programs that violate rights without involving persecution *per se*. Other criteria—such as the inability of a state to protect its citizens from public disorder or to provide subsistence—have also been advanced for determining refugee status. Nonetheless, most definitions maintain distinctions between refugees and internally displaced persons, economic migrants, and environmental refugees fleeing natural disasters. Because the narrow definition of refugee status is politically useful to many countries, it is likely to persist.

regime   Used interchangeably with "government" to denote an organized system of rule (e.g., ARISTOCRACY, MONARCHY, DEMOCRACY). The term is also sometimes used in place of "administration" to refer to a specific government in office. *Regime* can also signify a broad framework of rules and norms that govern a particular issue, such as security, intellectual property, or the environment.

regional economics   The study of the spatial distribution of production and population within a national economy and the accompanying variation in levels of economic performance. A region is similar to a nation in that it trades with the rest of the world and has its own particular resource endowments and comparative advantages. The important distinction between the two is that labor can move freely between the various regions within a nation but cannot do so across national boundaries. Moreover, a region, unlike a nation, cannot undertake independent monetary and trade policies. Therefore, while international trade theory concerns itself with exchange rates, tariffs, and monetary policies, the major policy concerns of regional economics are the effects of local taxation and expenditure policies, as well as efforts to influence the distribution of activities across regions.

A further distinction can be drawn between regional MACROECONOMICS and regional MICROECONOMICS. The former compares economic growth, unemployment levels, and the mobility of factors of production (such as labor and capital) across regions. Its emergence as a field of research may be traced to political concern with regional disparities in economic performance and prosperity. The latter is more concerned with the location and interaction of particular economic activities, and it incorporates an explicit treatment of the influence of space and distance on such activities (see LOCATION THEORY).

regionalism   Consciousness of the distinct identity and interests of people residing within a bounded territory, whether in terms of social or political identity or as a framework for research. Regions are not naturally given, although geographical features and related social patterns (such as the predominance of certain kinds of agriculture or the ease of communication) play a central role. In a more fundamental sense, regions are the product of symbolic processes that render a certain territory distinctive in cultural, political, or ethnic terms, either from the inside or the outside. This process can involve (1) districts within states, (2) territories cutting across parts of multiple states, and (3) areas uniting contiguous states. The southwestern United States, the Basque lands of France and Spain, and Southeast Asia are each regions in these terms, although of somewhat different sorts.

With regard to state politics, *regionalism* refers to the process by which regional groups articulate specific needs. Governments with strong regional constituencies generally must take steps to accommodate those needs. Where such integration breaks down, regional identity can take a separatist and, in some cases, nationalist turn. A variety of political systems exist that recognize and institutionalize the role of regional power. Empire was one early form—distinct, in part, because it rejected the attempt to forge a singular national entity. The modern federation of states is another. FEDERALISM is a form of split sovereignty that accords a zone of political control to regional authorities; it is in this respect distinct from the decentralization of power undertaken by some unitary states.

regression analysis A statistical tool for understanding how one quantity is influenced by another. The former is called the *dependent variable* and the latter the *independent variable*. The fundamentals of regression analysis were developed by Francis Galton and Karl Pearson. For any given value of an independent variable, the value of the dependent variable is uncertain. Regression analysis determines our "best guess" of that value—its EXPECTED VALUE or *mean*. Regression in its simplest form is written as

$$yi = \alpha + \beta x_i + \varepsilon_I$$

where y is the dependent variable, x is an independent variable, β is the regression coefficient, and ε is a random error term. The regression coefficients are the unknown parameters of the relationship between x and y. In this example, the predicted relationship is linear, and β is the slope of the regression line.

Once the parameter β has been estimated, predicted values of the dependent variable can be calculated by using the values of independent variables. The differences between the estimated values and the actual values of the dependent variable are known as *residuals*.

Regression residuals are useful measures of the fit between the estimated regression line and the data. A good regression equation is one that helps explain a large proportion of the variance of y. Large residuals imply a poor fit, while small residuals imply a good fit.

The ORDINARY LEAST SQUARES (OLS) estimator is a tool that generates a set of values of the parameters that minimizes the sum of the squared residuals. Of all the estimators that are linear and that yield unbiased estimates, it yields the minimum VARIANCE. In other words, OLS estimates are the *best linear unbiased estimates* (BLUE).

Classical linear regression models rest on five assumptions: (1) the dependent variable can be calculated as a linear function of a specific set of independent variables and as a disturbance term; (2) the error has a zero expected value, that is, $E(\varepsilon) = 0$; (3) the error terms have constant variance for all the observations, that is, $E(\varepsilon^2) = \sigma^2$; (4) the random variables ε_i are statistically independent of each other, that is, $E(\varepsilon_i, \varepsilon_j) = 0$ for all $i \neq j$; and (5) the number of observations is greater than the number of independent variables, and there is no exact linear relationship between the independent variables.

If these assumptions are changed in various ways, the OLS estimator will no longer be the optimal or BLUE estimator. If the error term has a constant variance (as assumed above), it is called *homoskedastic*; if the error variance is itself variable, the error is *heteroskedastic* (see HETEROSKEDASTICITY). Further, if the error terms corresponding to different observations are correlated, they are called *autocorrelated* error terms. (This is common with time-series data.) If two or more independent variables are approximately linearly related in the sample data, then there is a problem of MULTICOLLINEARITY. Statistical analysis can test whether the standard assumptions hold. Where any of the above problems appear, new estimators are needed.

regulation Broadly, the creation of formal standards and codes of conduct for private enterprise and behavior—generally by GOVERNMENT. Although STATES have always been in the business of controlling and sanctioning aspects of economic activity and forms of behavior, the modern regulatory state emerged as a reaction to the LAISSEZ-FAIRE capitalism of the late nineteenth century—especially in the context of the Progressive movement in the United States (1880–1920). Regulation, in this sense, was intended both to preserve the marketplace against anticompetitive practices and to ensure that markets respected certain notions of public welfare. Major targets of regulatory activity include MONOPOLY practices, the provision of PUBLIC GOODS (such as electricity, communication, and transportation), workers' and consumers' health and safety, environmental protection, rules for borrowers and private investors, and fairness-in-hiring practices. A wide range of "private" behavior has also become subject to regulatory regimes, such as smoking, the availability of abortion, and marriage.

Drawing on Max WEBER and other theorists of RATIONALIZATION, many scholars have viewed the growth of regulatory structures and related bureaucracies during the twentieth century as a key aspect of modernization (see MODERNIZATION THEORY). This inevitability is not without its critics—especially on the part of defenders of the free-market, who view regulation as an undesirable distortion of market efficiency. Since the late 1970s, *deregulation* has been a prominent policy objective in the United States, Great Britain, and increasingly elsewhere—especially in relation to traditionally regulated industries such as telecommunications and transportation.

regulation school   A group of French political economists and economic historians that has produced influential work on the stages of capitalist development and the logic of its periodic crises and transformations. The regulation school consolidated in the 1970s around a significant revision of the Marxist theory of capitalist accumulation. Of most importance, it abandoned MARXISM as revolutionary teleology and incorporated a much more flexible understanding of the evolution of both *regimes of accumulation* (consisting of the particular technological and social organization of production) and *modes of regulation* (the institutional structures that govern the relationship between labor and capital and that situate the national economy within the larger international economic structure).

The regulation school introduced a number of important distinctions that allowed it to differentiate between periods of capitalist organization. The first was the distinction between extensive and intensive regimes of accumulation. *Extensive accumulation* describes labor-intensive production, in which growth is achieved by adding laborers or lengthening and/or intensifying the work day. *Intensive accumulation* reflects a shift toward industrial production and the growth of investment in productivity-enhancing technologies.

The second distinction was between *competitive* and *monopoly* modes of regulation—the latter reflecting interlocking relationships among corporations, the rise of SCIENTIFIC MANAGEMENT, the determination of wages by collective bargaining, and the emergence of an elaborate governmental structure to govern and moderate those relationships. Whereas the nineteenth century was largely dominated by the shift from extensive to intensive accumulation, the twentieth was primarily about the shift from competitive to monopoly regulation, resulting in the stage of capitalist development known (following Antonio GRAMSCI) as FORDISM. The regulation school is also well known for theorizing the contemporary decline of the Fordist model, resulting in what some call post-Fordism or flexible accumulation; post-Fordism continues to be a subject of considerable debate in economics and political economy. The principle French regulationist is Michel Aglietta, but regulationist themes quickly spread in the 1970s into American and British ECONOMICS, SOCIOLOGY, and POLITICAL SCIENCE.

Reich, Wilhelm   (1897–1957) An Austrian psychologist who emphasized the importance of the development during childhood of psychological defenses against internal and external threats. These, he argued, were the determinants of *character*—the durable organization of affect and action. This dimension of Reich's work was influential in the development of *ego-analysis*, with its emphasis on defense mechanisms. Reich also pioneered the integration of MARXISM and PSYCHOANALYSIS in the 1920s and 1930s. This work earned him expulsion from both the Communist party and the International Psychoanalytic Association in the early 1930s, but it had a profound impact on the subsequent work of the FRANKFURT SCHOOL and that of other Marxist-oriented social psychologists.

Reich's major contribution in this area was to extend the discussion of sexual repression beyond its usual Freudian coordinates in the family triangle toward an account of the psychological demands of capitalist reproduction. CAPITALISM, he argued, especially in its fascist phase, required massive sublimation of the libido and a careful channeling of desire (for which the family was largely responsible). Reich thus became an early advocate of sexual liberation (which he accorded revolutionary potential), as well as of more practical measures, such as sexual education.

Reich fled the rise of FASCISM in Austria and eventually moved to the United States, where his work took a bizarre turn toward a theory of universal life energy contained in particles he called *orgones*. He developed a theory of human sexuality based on the characteristics of these orgones, and he eventually built and marketed a device called the "orgone energy accumulator," which he claimed possessed therapeutic powers in the treatment of mental illness. The accumulator eventually ran afoul of the U.S. Food and Drug Administration. Reich's refusal to stop distributing the device landed him in prison, where he died in 1957. Reich's major works include *The Function of the Orgasm* (1927), *The Mass Psychology of Fascism* (1934 [1970]), and *Character Analysis* (1934, 1935 [1961]).

reification   The process by which persons cease to understand society as the product of their own labor and actions and come to credit it with autonomous existence and the power to dominate them. The concept was central to Georg LUKÁCS's reconstruction of the foundations of Marxist theory in *History and Class Consciousness* (1923) and is closely related to Karl MARX's concepts of ALIENATION and COMMODITY FETISHISM.

reintegrative shaming   An approach to reintegrating criminals back into society after they have been punished for their crimes. Developed by John Braithwaite in *Crime, Shame and Reintegration* (1989), reintegrative shaming emphasizes the reacceptance of and respect for the person by the community after punishment. The approach is influenced by studies of cultural attitudes in non-Western societies such as Japan, where concern for social solidarity leads to the relatively low stigmatization of offenders.

relative autonomy   A concept introduced by the Marxist philosopher Louis ALTHUSSER to explain the relationships among the economic, political, and ideological dimensions of society. Relative autonomy signifies that none of these realms can be strictly reduced to the others—or strictly determined by the others. This challenged the Marxist theoretical orthodoxy, which held that the political and ideological realms were determined by the economic base. Althusser did little to specify or describe this relative autonomy, however, and was inclined to accord economic factors a determining role "in the last instance."

relative deprivation   See DEPRIVATION.

reliability   The degree to which a research technique or experiment yields the same results over repeated attempts and by different researchers. Reliability is distinct from VALIDITY, which concerns whether a technique is an appropriate measure of the phenomenon in question. In the social sciences, reliability often raises informational problems, insofar as the knowledge gained by the subjects can skew results. See also MEASUREMENT.

religion   According to Emile DURKHEIM's classic definition in *Elementary Forms of Religious Life* ([1912] 1965), *religion* is simultaneously a social institution, consisting of a system of beliefs and practices related to sacred things, and a moral community that serves to unite its members. In emphasizing this unifying function, Durkheim established a broad tradition of inquiry into the functional dimension of religious life—above all its role in integrating individuals into the larger social collectivity (see FUNCTIONALISM).

Max WEBER is the second foundational figure in the modern sociological and historical study of religion, although his contributions are more diverse. Weber argued for a broad understanding of religion as any systematic attempt to answer fundamental moral or existential questions about human life, such as those related to birth, death, good, evil, and suffering. In this context, Weber undertook a comparative study of world religions that focused on general attitudes toward the world and beliefs about salvation. He also pursued historical studies that examined the relationship between religion and other areas of human activity. Chief among these is *The Protestant Ethic and the Spirit of Capitalism* (1905), in which Weber argued that the rational principles and rationalizing impulse underlying CAPITALISM originated in Calvinist doctrines. In his comparative studies of world religions, Weber pushed this rationalization thesis further, proposing that the process of RATIONALIZATION of various spheres of social life, including economic, political, aesthetic, sexual, and intellectual life, was simultaneously a process of SECULARIZATION—of the "disenchantment" of the modern world.

Durkheim and Weber's accounts of religion represented a sharp turn away from the prevailing concerns of nineteenth-century research—especially the evolutionary schemas of religious development common in ANTHROPOLOGY. The evolutionary theories of major anthropologists of religion, such as Edward Burnett TYLOR and R. R. Marrett, were based on linear models of religious (and societal) development (see EVOLUTION AND EVOLUTIONISM). They were greatly concerned to specify the origins of religion in ANIMISM and other concepts of primitive supernatural belief, and to trace religious development through to modern forms of MONOTHEISM. Many of these models were organized by a strong Enlightenment sense of religion as an irrational practice, soon to be superseded by scientific or philosophical reason. Where Weber retained this secularization thesis in many respects, he greatly complicated the relationship between the two ostensibly separate domains. The secularization thesis proved enormously durable, but it became vulnerable to criticism from sociologists as new research demonstrated the continuing centrality of religious belief, practices, and organizations in contemporary social life. As measured by such things as church attendance or adherence to unambiguously religious beliefs, it is by no means clear that secularization is a dominant trend or that there is a correlation between secularization and other aspects of societal rationalization or modernity. The United States, for example, routinely shows high levels of religious identification and practice compared to other industrialized countries.

In addition to the traditional focus on organized religion, sociologists and anthropologists also now study a wide range of related topics, including comparisons of religious and secular belief systems, religious movements, CIVIL RELIGIONS (see Robert Bellah, *The Broken Covenant*, 1975), and more broadly the cultural structures that provide transcendent frameworks of meaning for individuals (see Thomas Luckmann's *The Invisible Religion*, 1963). The relationships between religion and other strong sources of collective identification and practice, such as NATIONALISM, have also been explored in some detail.

RATIONAL-CHOICE THEORY has also generated new approaches to the study of religion—in part by postulating that individuals engage in religious activities in much the same way as in economic activities: they balance the costs and benefits of participation and seek to maximize their gains. Within a given religion this may involve finding cheaper, symbolic substitutes for costly forms of religious ritual; in a religiously plural society, it may involve shifts in membership toward the religion with the greatest satisfactions and fewest burdens. In this context, religion operates as a market for transcendental goods, such as the afterlife or divine justice, as well as for worldly benefits, such as social status and social networks. Laurence Iannaccone, Stephen Warner, and Rodney Stark are often associated with this perspective.

rent   Payment for the use of a resource such as labor, land, or capital. To early economists such as David RICARDO, *rent* meant payment for the "uses of the original and indestructible powers of the soil." Subsequently, it was recognized that the supply of land was relatively insensitive to price (i.e., the elasticity of supply of land was near zero). In this context, the term *economic rent* was introduced to describe payment for any resource whose availability is insensitive to its price. Because virtually every resource is unresponsive to a change in price for at least a short period of time, resources can earn high returns in the short term. Economic rent in this sense is similar to the concept of QUASI RENT, developed by Alfred MARSHALL (1920), which describes profitability in supply-constrained, short-run situations. Another category of rent is *differential rent*, according to which equivalent resources earn different returns in their best alternative uses.

rent-seeking activities   Nonproductive activities pursued by economic agents in the effort to obtain *economic rents* (above average profits) for themselves. Usually *rent seeking* refers to attempts to use government regulation to create barriers to competition, or to secure favored status such as exclusive production rights. Lobbying for trade protection and making campaign contributions to secure government contracts are examples. Rent-seeking activities are distinguished from other profit-motivated behavior in that they do not add to the economic pie, but rather seek to secure a larger slice at someone else's expense. (A counterexample is research that leads to patentable processes, which would generate rents but also add to productive activity.) Thus any resources spent on rent seeking are wasted in aggregate economic terms.

representation   To stand for, symbolize, or act on behalf of a person, group, or thing. The term is used in a wide array of contexts with different meanings. In the social sciences, two broad traditions of inquiry into representation stand out: (1) the nature of *symbolic representation*, or the relationship between language and reality; and (2) the proper understanding of *political representation*, or how individuals should stand for larger groups or constituencies in democratic systems.

The question of how words represent things is among the oldest in LINGUISTICS, dating back to PLATO's theory of a natural correspondence between words and things. The modern structural linguistics of Ferdinand de SAUSSURE, Roman JAKOBSON, and others broke with this assertion. Saussure treated language as an arbitrary network of signifiers, defined not by any intrinsic relation to their objects but by their difference from other signifiers. Philosophies of consciousness have raised similar issues regarding the relationship between sensory experience and the real: do the senses represent reality to consciousness, or is sensory data the fundamental reality itself? Both questions have implications for social science investments in OBJECTIVITY and truth. Postmodern and poststructuralist tendencies in social science have undermined the conventional relationship between observer and reality—not least through the DECONSTRUCTION of the truth claims of language (see POSTMODERNISM; and POSTSTRUCTURALISM). Although this has not proved fatal to social science, the core activities of description, explanation, and theory construction are now generally pursued with greater self-consciousness than in the past.

The nature of representation in democratic politics is an old subject of debate that dates back to the eighteenth century. At stake is whether election to office implies a responsibility to represent the opinions of a constituency or party, or whether it authorizes the representative to act independently or in accordance with the more general public interest. Among the strongest early statements on this subject was Edmund BURKE's defense of the independence of representatives, on the grounds that individual conscience provided the best basis for political judgment. He believed that this would deter parochial interests from obstructing the general interests of the community. Defenders of the opposing view—that representation implies a specific mandate from electors—argue for a more organic link between people and their representatives. Yet this raises a host of questions about how views are to be aggregated and measured, and whether the voters for the opposition are thereby deprived of representation.

Although few people today hold a strict view of electoral mandates, a closely related debate continues to shape electoral politics in the United States and other pluralist societies. On one side is a *descriptive* notion of representation, which implies that a representative body should proportionately reflect the salient identity categories in society—RACE, GENDER, ETHNICITY, and so on (see Anne Phillips, *The Politics of Presence*, 1995). This view privileges the idea that different identity groups produce different interests and perspectives, and that a just model of representation incorporates this diversity. On the other side is the notion of *substantive* representation, which holds that individuals are capable of understanding and representing the interests of people who differ from them (see Hanna F. Pitkin, *The Concept of Representation*, 1967).

Among the chief objections to descriptive representation is that it reinforces group essentialism and falsely asserts the homogeneity of interests within those groups. Substantive models run into the difficulty that identity categories *do* play an important role in the political landscape and that members of certain minorities suffer effective exclusion from power. This problem is particularly acute in countries where representation is based on simple-majority, winner-take-all, single-member districts, such as the United States. This weakness underlies the use of *proportional representation* and other electoral mechanisms in other countries (see ELECTORAL SYSTEM).

Some strands of democratic theory offer a deeper critique of representative government itself. One of the earliest and most effective of these critics was Jean-Jacques ROUSSEAU, who held that individuals could never legitimately delegate their SOVEREIGNTY to others. Rousseau emphasized that representative democracy allows for only a brief moment of actual popular sovereignty when citizens select their representatives. Between elections, citizens are effectively subjects of a sovereign power lodged elsewhere. Rousseau's critique is preserved in contemporary arguments for PARTICIPATORY DEMOCRACY and DIRECT DEMOCRACY, which hold that continuous engagement in the political process is necessary for the preservation of individual autonomy and the accountability of the state.

republic   Most definitions specify a constitutionally limited, representative government in which SOVEREIGNTY resides in the electorate. Republican government, in this context, is often contrasted with DEMOCRACY—especially where the latter implies MAJORITY RULE and direct or plebiscitary decision making by the people. The distinction between the two has played a large role in the history of American government. Fears of the TYRANNY of the majority structured many early debates about the Constitution, and the original franchise was kept narrow in an effort to limit participation to the social elite.

Other points of contrast emerge in some accounts of republican government and the associated political culture of *republicanism*. An important tradition of historical and sociological research on the public sphere has explored the differences between republican political culture and the variously liberal, democratic, and nationalist political culture that succeeded it in the nineteenth century (see PUBLIC SPHERE AND PRIVATE SPHERE). These accounts tend to emphasize the value of deliberation about public matters among equals in CIVIL SOCIETY, in contrast to the emergence of mass publics that are fed opinions by the media. They emphasize the notion of republican virtue—the effort to rise above personal interests in seeking the public good—in opposition to the liberal notion of government as a mediator and a check on individual interests. Jürgen HABERMAS, Hannah ARENDT, and Gordon Wood are associated with this tradition of research.

The term is also used more loosely in a range of other contexts. Republican thought drew on the experience and political theory of Ancient Greece, which explored many variations on republican and democratic forms of government. Although the historical parallels are limited, PLATO and ARISTOTLE elaborated similar fears of popular or mob rule. Aristotle also contributed a famous "law" of small republics that shaped much eighteenth-century reflection on the question: deliberation among social equals, he argued, required a degree of face-to-face contact that made large republics untenable.

reservation price The price below which the owner of a GOOD or FACTOR OF PRODUCTION will choose not to sell.

retreatism An element in Robert K. MERTON's well-known typology of forms of individual adaptation to the dominant goals of a given society. These forms reflect, in many respects, a reformulation of Emile DURKHEIM's concept of ANOMIE. In Merton's view, all people internalize the goals of their culture, as well as the legitimate ways of attaining them. In the United States, Merton argued, financial success is the dominant goal. Anomie occurs because the legitimate opportunities for realizing such goals are limited or mostly restricted to certain classes. Under such

conditions, individuals may seek alternative ways to achieve those goals—or, they may abandon societal goals altogether. *Retreatism* refers to this last possibility and signifies the many ways of "dropping out" of society.

The other four types of individual social adaptation, Merton argued, are conformity, innovation, ritualism, and rebellion. In cases of *conformity*, individuals continue to seek culturally approved goals by approved means, despite the discrepancy between expectations and opportunities. *Innovation* refers to the pursuit of culturally approved goals by disapproved (including illegal) means. *Ritualism* refers to excessively rigid conformity to approved goals and means, even to the neglect of the actual results; inefficient bureaucrats who adhere rigidly to the rules are the classic example of ritualism. *Rebellion* refers to the rejection of approved goals and means in favor of new ones. See Merton's *Social Theory and Social Structure* (1968).

returns to scale Describes the proportional relationship between the outputs of a production process and changes in the level of inputs—or a change in the scale of production. The production function exhibits *constant returns to scale* if doubling all inputs doubles the quantity of output. There are increasing returns to scale if doubling all inputs raises output by more than double. Analogously, decreasing returns to scale implies that doubling all inputs results in less than double the quantity of output.

revealed-preference theory The economic study of consumer tastes as determined by actual choices rather than assumptions about underlying *preferences*. The advantage of this approach is that consumer choices are observable whereas preferences are not. Revealed-preference theory was introduced by Paul SAMUELSON ("Consumption Theory in Terms of Revealed Preference," 1948).

A consumption bundle X is said to be *revealed preferred* to another bundle Y if the consumer chooses X when Y is also affordable. Revealed-preference theory is based on a few axioms, the most famous of which is the Weak Axiom of Revealed Preference (WARP). WARP is a form of consistency requirement that states that if X is revealed preferred to Y—in the sense discussed above—then Y can never be revealed preferred to X. In other words, economic actors are rational in the sense that they are consistent in their preferences. Modern microeconomic theory has drawn heavily on Samuelson's original insights—especially in regard to consumer choices (see MICROECONOMICS).

reverse discrimination See DISCRIMINATION.

revitalization movement Usually (but not exclusively) refers to religious movements that seek to radically transform their societies. The term generally implies a number of related characteristics: millenarianism, charismatic organization by or around a prophetic figure, conversion experiences, and a context of social crisis in which the movement becomes resonant (see MILLENARIANISM OR MILLENNIALISM). The best known of these is the Ghost Dance ritual that spread through many American Indian tribes in the late nineteenth century. Such movements tend to be short lived or periodic in nature. Their charismatic structure and millennial energies generally cannot sustain a high level of mobilization over time. When they do succeed, they tend to undergo a process of routinization and institutionalization that brings them closer to the organization of a sect or RELIGION.

revolution The transformation of an established order—most often conceived in political terms and identified with such rapid, tumultuous events as the French Revolution (1789) and the Bolshevik Revolution (1917), but also used to describe long-term processes of social and economic change, such as the Industrial Revolution. There have been many theories but little general agreement about what constitutes or causes revolution. This includes attempts to explain how revolutions differ from rebellions, uprisings, coups d'état, or other expressions of political or social discontent.

Many of these questions are visible in the long tradition of distinguishing political from social revolutions. *Political revolutions* involve the replacement of one form of government by another—the American Revolution is the classic example. *Social revolutions* are more far reaching and involve the simultaneous transformation of both the regime and its attendant social order. The most prominent theorist of the latter type was Karl MARX. According to Marx, social revolutions are the result of changes in the MODE OF PRODUCTION, which generate new classes that threaten the established order. Thus, in the French Revolution, the capitalist BOURGEOISIE overturned the aristocratic social order associated with FEUDALISM. In time, Marx argued, the exploited but growing working class would rise against the bourgeoisie. He devoted a number of works to exploring the social and political dynamics of this process, which he saw as manifestations of underlying economic forces. *The 18th Brumaire of Louis Bonaparte* (1852) was perhaps the most influential of these. It introduced the issues of CLASS CONSCIOUSNESS, class fragmentation, and bourgeois co-optation that subsequently informed much of the Marxist debate about revolution. Questions about the continuity between pre- and post-revolutionary societies also played a part in Marx's analysis but figured much more centrally in Alexis de TOCQUEVILLE's influential 1856 study, *The Old Regime and the French Revolution*. Tocqueville's analysis of bureaucratic continuity was later echoed in Leon Trotsky's critique of the Soviet state (see TROTSKYISM) and in more recent analyses of the breakdown of COMMUNISM.

Professional revolutionaries proved unwilling to wait for the development of the social and historical conditions identified by Marx. Vladimir Ilich LENIN and Mao Zedong made the most influential revisions of Marxist revolutionary theory by recasting the role of the Communist party and its leadership. Lenin, in particular, stressed the role of the party vanguard in fomenting and leading revolutions (see LENINISM). Mao's reflections on guerrilla warfare and the role of the peasantry addressed the problem of revolution in underdeveloped societies (see MAOISM).

Sociologists and political scientists have usually taken different approaches in studying the causes of revolution. Proponents of MODERNIZATION THEORY in the 1950s and 1960s generally maintained that revolutions occur in countries where INDUSTRIALIZATION has dissolved long-standing social bonds, prompting mass disaffection and social instability. Refinements to the modernization thesis have emphasized the effects of the rapid mobilization and politicization of disaffected groups, which can lead to the institutional paralysis of the state and to its vulnerability to mass action. Relative deprivation in situations of rationing or economic crisis has also been advanced as a general condition for revolution, although work by Charles TILLY and others (1975) has challenged that explanation. Most critics of the modernization approach have argued that it is too general to provide much purchase on the diversity of revolutionary experiences—for example, the prominent role that elites often play in revolutionary situations. Few generalizations about composition of revolutionary movements hold up against comparative study. Participation by the military, peasants, revolutionary and moderate parties, unions, commercial elites, and other groups raises distinct and historically embedded issues. Research on the particular ideologies and strategies of revolutionary leaders and movements has also tended to avoid broad generalizations.

Some recent approaches have nonetheless tried to account for this diversity—from Tilly's model of "resource mobilization" to social-structural analyses of revolution such as Theda Skocpol's *States and Social Revolutions* (1979). Unlike much earlier scholarship, Skocpol accords an important role to international conflict, which can tip the scales against social orders with weak central bureaucracies and underdeveloped agricultural sectors. Skocpol's structural account has been criticized, in turn, on the grounds that it pays inadequate attention to the role of revolutionaries and ideological factors.

Other methodologies have also contributed to this discussion. Demographic analysis can shed light on revolutionary situations, as Jack Goldstone has demonstrated in his analysis of the ways in which population patterns shaped prices, labor markets, and state finances (*Revolutions and Rebellions in the Early Modern World*, 1991). Discourse analysis has shaped understanding of the role of language and ideology and has often overlapped with attention to gender, as in Lynn Hunt's *The Family Romance of the French Revolution* (1992). The differences between early modern revolutions, anticolonial revolutions, and recent anticommunist revolutions have also been a major subject of inquiry. So, too, is the question of whether the social and economic dislocations associated with GLOBALIZATION will produce a new cycle of broad-based, radical unrest.

Ricardian equivalence theorem   Also Barro-Ricardian equivalence theorem. The proposition that consumer spending or capital formation is unaffected by the choice between taxes or bonds (debt) to finance government spending. Suppose the government collects taxes of $100 per capita instead of issuing bonds of the same amount. If consumers can borrow $100 to pay the higher taxes, the results are the same in both cases, since debt finance leads to higher public borrowing, and tax finance leads to higher private borrowing. Under appropriate conditions, it makes no difference whether the borrowing takes place in the private sector or in the public sector. Another way of justifying the equivalence is that tax-financed government expenditure involves taxes today, whereas debt-financed government expenditure involves taxes in the future, since the government finances future interest (and principal) payments through taxes. Both have the same present value and thus have equivalent effects on consumption and capital formation. This argument depends on a number of assumptions, the most crucial of which are infinite-planning horizons (individuals with their finite horizons cannot leave negative bequests for their heirs), foresight on the part of the private sector, LUMP SUM TAXes, and a complete set of competitive markets. The empirical tests of this proposition have yielded mixed results, and the concept remains a subject of some controversy.

Ricardo, David   (1772–1823) Possibly the most influential economist of the classical school (see CLASSICAL ECONOMICS). Ricardo's rigorous deductive method superseded the less formal style associated with Adam SMITH. His interest in relative values focused attention on the determination of individual prices and set the stage for work on the problem of equilibrium. His main achievements, consequently, lie primarily in the areas of value theory and distribution theory.

Ricardo was born into a family of merchants and eventually made his fortune in the stock market. Although he became a rich landowner, his strong advocacy of economic and political liberalization frequently ran against the interests of that group. His numerous political causes included parliamentary reform, religious freedom, and a tax on capital, as well as free-market arguments against poor relief.

Ricardo spent much of his abbreviated career as an economist trying to formulate an infallible theory of value, based on the exchange ratios between commodities and a complicated attempt to compare the labor inputs required to produce different goods. In this he extended the LABOR THEORY OF VALUE to capitalist society (a step Smith had not taken) in a way that would have a profound influence on another great classicist, Karl MARX. Ricardo recognized that, in capitalist production, the wage reflects only a portion of the value of the labor invested in production, and that the capitalist appropriates the remainder—the surplus value.

Ricardo's work on differential RENT was another major advance in economic theory. He pointed out that the cost of production is lower for land of better quality; however, the price of output must be high enough to cover the cost of production of the worst piece of land. Thus better land earns a rent, or *surplus*, over its cost of production. This view implies a conflict of interests between landlords and the rest of society. As the population rises, the increased demand for food causes rising food prices. At the same time, land of poorer and poorer quality is brought into production. This means that rents rise, even though wages and profits fall. Ricardo opposed England's Corn Laws on these grounds. He argued that better technology and the import of cheap food would partially alleviate this problem, but he shared his friend Thomas Robert MALTHUS's longer-term pessimism about the relationship between population growth and average output per worker.

Perhaps the most enduring and influential idea attributed to Ricardo is the theory of COMPARATIVE ADVANTAGE. Conventional analyses of trade recognized that things that are cheaper to produce at home will be exported to other countries, while things that are cheaper to produce abroad will be imported from other countries. Ricardo's insight was that trade will also occur and be beneficial whenever there are international differences in *relative* costs of production, vis-à-vis other goods. Ricardo has been criticized for basing this theory on a flawed labor theory of value and for assuming full employment in the economy. Still, his theory of comparative advantage was an improvement on Smith's theory of absolute advantage, and it provided a framework for thinking about the gains from free trade. Ricardo also developed a theory of money and advocated a return to the GOLD STANDARD. His main work was *Principles of Political Economy and Taxation* (1817).

Riesman, David (1909–) Primarily a sociologist, Reisman was one of the most influential analysts of American culture in the 1950s and early 1960s. He is best known for his popular and controversial book *The Lonely Crowd: A Study of the Changing American Character* (1950; with Nathan Glazer and Reuel Denney).

Reisman obtained a bachelor's degree in biochemical science and later a degree in law, which he practiced and taught for several years. During World War II, Reisman developed interests in SOCIAL PSYCHOLOGY and PSYCHOANALYSIS—primarily through the influence of Erich FROMM. After the war, he obtained a position in the sociology department at the University of Chicago, then in 1958 moved to Harvard University, where he remained for the rest of his career.

Reisman's interest in the psychological characteristics of modern society informed much of *The Lonely Crowd*. He developed a historical typology of personality, distinguishing among premodern "tradition-directed" character; "inner-directed character," centered around private life, the family, and internalized adult authority; and "outer-directed character," shaped largely by peer groups (Riesman referred to them as "retailers" of cultural information). These peer groups, in turn, are influenced by the mass media (the "wholesalers"). American society, he argued, was once rooted in inner-directed character but has increasingly moved toward outer-directedness. Especially among the middle class, superficial group adherence and generalized ALIENATION were becoming the norm. Society became a "lonely crowd."

Reisman was one of the early theorists of mass culture and mass consumption, and he drew attention to the effects of television, cinema, magazines, and the pervasive role of advertising and marketing. Yet he was not wholly negative in his appraisal of these phenomena (as most of the FRANKFURT SCHOOL theorists had been). If mass communication diminished people's sense of place and made culture more homogeneous, it also made the world more accessible. Riesman analyzed these themes further in *Faces in the Crowd: Individual Studies in Character and Politics* (1952; with Nathan Glazer) and *Individualism Reconsidered* (1954).

Riesman's later work deals primarily with the expansion, professionalization, democratization, and reform of higher education. His academic studies (including *The Academic Revolution*, 1968, with Christopher Jencks) have been influential. He has also been an outspoken critic of the nuclear-arms race, and he cofounded the modern Committees of Correspondence—a group dedicated to fostering and informing public debate on nuclear weaponry. Reisman's other published works include *Conversations in Japan: Modernization, Politics and Culture* (1967) and *On Higher Education* (1980).

rights Legitimate claims, liberties, or powers—originally conceived in terms of individual protections against the government but now widely invoked wherever political, economic, or social actors seek to define their place in society. In most usage, *human rights* are understood to be universal to all people, while *civil rights* are understood to be contingent on membership in a specific STATE or society (although ideally each state would also recognize and protect all human rights).

The Western democratic political tradition has often been characterized in terms of the development and expansion of systems of enforceable individual rights. This structure was initially outlined in the SOCIAL-CONTRACT THEORY of John LOCKE, Jean-Jacques ROUSSEAU, and others. It was later institutionalized in documents such as the U.S. Declaration of Independence (1776), the Bill of Rights (1791), and the French Declaration of the Rights of Man (1789). Subsequently, it was made visible in traditions of constitutionalism and in the array of social movements that fought to expand the scope of political and social rights on behalf of excluded groups (the propertyless, women, minorities, and so on). These assertions of rights had a predominantly negative character: they posited the individual's freedom from forms of oppression or arbitrary authority. It is this perspective that informed the famous enumeration of the rights to "life, liberty and the pursuit of happiness" in the Declaration of Independence—a variation on Locke's earlier conception of natural rights to life, liberty, and property. It also underwrote rights of participation in the polity, in which the people (however narrowly qualified) had rights to free speech, to congregate, to vote, and to present themselves for office—all aspects of the larger and often complicated concept of self-determination.

Running throughout these rights debates— and still an unresolved issue in many contexts—is the question of the source of rights. Are rights "inalienable" gifts of nature (i.e., natural or human rights) or are they political and social—a set of conventions embedded in and dependent on society. Natural rights doctrines developed out of Greco-Roman and, more directly, Christian NATURAL LAW traditions that described the natural limits of human conduct and duties. Natural rights, from this perspective, are inalienable and prepolitical. They are founded on an authority that, in principle, antedates and/or transcends society. One of the central implications of this distinction is that rights anchored in convention may apply only to members of a specific polity (like the right to vote in a given country). The Declaration of Independence follows this line in basing most of its political claims on the rights of British subjects. Natural rights, in contrast, are universal in character and thus theoretically transcend the prerogatives of states and the particularities of cultures. In contemporary debates, this sometimes places human-rights advocates at odds with defenders of local cultural or political traditions, which also claim rights to self-determination and autonomy.

Two major considerations enter into any such discussion: (1) the ultimate reliance of rights on a legal structure of enforcement; and (2) the historically evolving nature of rights claims. The first point is central to the emergence of modern human rights discourse—itself a twentieth-century articulation of universalist political and social rights claims that date back to the Declaration of the Rights of Man. International support for certain basic rights has become a priority for a number of international associations and conventions—especially, since 1945, the United Nations. Anticolonial movements and the creation of an international legal framework for judging the organizers of the Holocaust also contributed to universalistic rights discourse, as have diverse movements for equal political and social rights within polities—the civil rights movement in the United States and the women's rights movement among them. By the 1970s, human rights had begun to have a significant impact on state behavior—competing, in some cases, with dominant ideas of political REALISM or *Realpolitik*. NONGOVERNMENTAL ORGANIZATIONS (NGOs) such as Amnesty International played an increasingly significant role in bringing human rights abuses to world attention. While the content of much of this rights discourse reproduced traditional concerns with state power and individual protections—most prominently freedom from torture, arbitrary detention, and other forms of abuse—it also overlapped other forms of rights that have emerged since the nineteenth century.

Economic and social rights are the main foci of this development. Economic rights began to be defined and demanded in nineteenth-century MARXISM, SOCIALISM, and SYNDICALISM, and later more formally developed in the emergence of the modern welfare state; they include such nominally or explicitly defined rights as a living wage, health care, job security, education, leisure, and retirement benefits. Social rights emerged in the diverse bids for equality that underwrote parts of the women's movement and other struggles for minority inclusion. Often evoking notions of dignity, respect, or difference, social rights have generally been more difficult to obtain (and in many cases to define) than the array of established political or civil rights. Since the 1960s and 1970s, there have been further and not always compatible pressures for other kinds of rights—especially as globalization results in more extensive ties between countries and groups. These include the rights to cultural difference and the preservation of the environment.

right wing and left wing   A way of describing political orientations that dates back to the seating arrangement in the French constituent assembly in the early days of the revolution (1789). Jacobin radicals sat on the left side of the King; moderates sat in the center; and royalists and clerical members sat on the right. The terms passed into general use to refer to the opposition between the egalitarian, democratic, and anticlerical views of many reformers and radicals, and the defense of aristocratic and clerical privileges by conservatives (see CONSERVATISM; and LIBERALISM).

Although the terms continue to be widely used, their content has changed. Where economic liberalization—especially free trade—was once a radical proposition in many contexts, it has migrated to the right. Left-wing agendas are generally much more tied to forms of state regulation and intervention in economic life—reflecting the modern pursuit of egalitarian goals with the tools of the welfare state (see SOCIALISM). The polarization of politics by communist and later fascist movements also informs these labels—although not without important ambiguities. The specific content of the terms also depends heavily on cultural context: the political spectrum in France lies, in many respects, to the left of that of the United States on most issues.

Riker, William   (1921–1993) An American political scientist known for his contributions to RATIONAL-CHOICE THEORY and coalition theory. In his best-known work, *Liberalism against Populism* (1982), Riker presented American history in terms of a "structure-induced equilibrium" that reflected the cyclical movement of societies in response to inevitable political instability. He argued that, in a democratic society, no political party can remain permanently in office because there can be no platform of policies that is impervious to challenge. Challengers will consistently

be able to piece together alternative platforms that garner a majority. In the end, the countervailing forces of political parties, special-interest groups, and other mainstream institutions maintain this cyclical balance. Riker's other major works include *Democracy in the United States* (1965) and *The Art of Political Manipulation* (1986).

risk   Generally, the chances of malign events or uncertainty of outcome. Risk may or may not be quantifiable in terms of specific likelihoods of outcomes, but its most common use implies that the underlying probabilities of various outcomes are known. These probabilities may either be objectively specified, as in the case of a lottery, or may reflect an individual's private subjective beliefs. A common mathematical measure of risk is the *variance* of the outcome: $\sigma^2 = E[x-E(x)]^2$, where E denotes mathematical expectation. Generally, the higher the variance, the wider the range of possible outcomes, which corresponds with higher risk. The tractability and statistical properties of this formal representation of risk has led to its widespread use since the 1950s.

Attempts to estimate risk are basic to insurance and actuarial analysis, where profits in the industry are determined by how often uncertain events occur. Firms also seek to assess risk as part of their business strategies. Individuals are usually assumed to be *risk averse* and thus likely to purchase insurance and seek other ways of reducing their personal risk (see RISK AVERSION). An influential body of research in SOCIOLOGY and ANTHROPOLOGY (notably by Ulrich Beck and Mary DOUGLAS) addresses cultural and historical variation in how agents assess risk and to what extent their actions are guided by understandings or analyses of risks. Modern Western societies are sometimes characterized as highly oriented to risk (as distinct, for example, from an orientation to fate or more traditionally defined notions of danger).

risk aversion   In economics, a person is *risk averse* if he or she prefers to forgo a risky investment in favor of a payment equal or lower in value to the fair value of the investment. For example, in a lottery with a 50 percent chance of winning nothing and a 50 percent chance of winning $100, the fair value is $50. The risk averse person will prefer a payment of $50 or less to participation in the lottery. The more risk averse, the lower that acceptable payment—the CERTAINTY EQUIVALENT—will be. The analogous terms are *risk neutral* and *risk loving*.

Individuals are generally considered to be risk averse, in part due to the diminishing *marginal utility* of income (e.g., the first $50 provides more utility or well-being than the second $50).

risky shift   The tendency for a group to make more risky decisions than individuals might make in isolation. Also known as *group polarization*.

rites of passage   A ritual by means of which a person passes from one social status to another. In his classic account, Arnold van GENNEP identifies three moments proper to rites of passage: a phase of separation from the original status, a privileged moment of LIMINALITY in which roles are suspended or reversed, and a phase of reincorporation into the social order. Initiation rites, in this respect, are often considered a subset of rites of passage.

Ritter, Carl   (1779–1859) Considered, with Alexander von HUMBOLDT, to be the founder of modern GEOGRAPHY. Ritter pioneered the study of the spatial patterns of human behavior—a subject that would become the central preoccupation of human geography. He believed that such behavior is governed by objective laws that can be scientifically determined. In practice, however, he tended to emphasize the need for a holistic understanding of human occupancy of the earth before undertaking to specify such laws. Ritter's methodology and patience is visible in his best-known work: the monumental, nineteen-volume, and at his death still incomplete *Earth Science in Relation to Nature and the History of Man* (*Die Erdkunde*), which appeared between 1822 and 1859. Ritter was appointed to the chair of geography at the University of Berlin in 1820, where he taught and lectured for nearly forty years. He also played a central role in the consolidation of geography as an academic discipline in Germany. His other work includes the two-volume *Europa* (1804, 1807).

ritual   Repeatable patterns of behavior that carry complex meanings, especially when shared within a group and related to basic themes of group culture. The study of ritual is at the heart of much anthropological research and, like so many key terms, resists strict definition. Anthropologists tend to identify ritual with formalized behavior, whether in the broad sense of a basic form of human expression, or more narrowly in opposition to mere ceremony, PROFANE (secular) activities, MYTH, or instrumental behavior.

Emile DURKHEIM inaugurated one of the most durable lines of inquiry with his strong functionalist argument that ritual constitutes the basic mechanism and expression of social solidarity. This insight informed much of the subsequent British social anthropological treatment of ritual, from Bronislaw MALINOWSKI to A. R. RADCLIFFE-BROWN and Meyer FORTES, who found in ritual the privileged moment of visibility of the social order. Other major approaches to ritual emphasize the complexity and layered quality of the ritual act and its symbols. Victor Turner's *The Forest of Symbols* (1967) has been highly influential in this respect. Such approaches tend to focus on the ways that ritual functions at the psychological level, whether as a resource against illness or danger, or as a means of knitting together diverse natural and social elements into a coherent WORLDVIEW.

ritualism   Generally, behavior with a strong emphasis on RITUAL, often with the connotation that this is overly rigid or out of proportion to underlying religious or other conviction. Ritualism is also one of sociologist Robert K. MERTON's five types of individual adaptation to cultural goals in the absence of the legitimate means of achieving them. In this context, it refers to the rigid adherence to rules characteristic of bureaucracies. See also RETREATISM.

ritual kinship   A privileged social relationship established by RITUAL, such as that of godparents or fraternal orders.

Rivers, W. H. R.   (1864–1922) Trained as a physician and probably best known as a psychologist, Rivers was also an influential figure in early twentieth-century ANTHROPOLOGY. While serving as chief psychologist for the Torres Strait Expedition of 1898, Rivers developed the enormously influential "genealogical method" of analyzing kinship, and a variety of psychological techniques for studying the relationship between social behavior and environmental adaptation. The expedition also did much to establish the centrality of FIELDWORK to anthropological study.

Although Rivers never held a position in anthropology, he trained or mentored several of the great anthropologists of the next generation, including A. R. RADCLIFFE-BROWN and Bronislaw MALINOWSKI. His anthropological work included several ethnological surveys in Melanesia, which resulted in *The History of Melanesian Society* (1914), and participation in debates over social evolution and later diffusion (see

DIFFUSION AND DIFFUSIONISM; and EVOLUTION AND EVOLUTIONISM). Yet it was as a psychologist that he achieved public renown, first through the treatment of victims of "shell shock" during World War I and later as an interpreter and proponent of Freudian psychology (see PSYCHOANALYSIS). His other major anthropological works include *Kinship and Social Organization* (1914), *Dreams and Primitive Culture* (1917–1918), and *Social Organization* (1924).

Robinson, Joan (1903–1983) A British economist who contributed to the theory of imperfect competition, to Keynesian economics, to work on economic development and international trade, and to the revival (among economists) of interest in Karl MARX. *The Economics of Imperfect Competition* (1933) was the first of Robinson's major works. There she extended Piero SRAFFA's insights about monopolistic competition to a variety of related cases, such as markets in which producers sell products that are slightly different from one another. She explored the implication of such differentiation on the traditional theory of the FIRM and also investigated the concept of monopsony—a situation in which there are many sellers and one buyer.

Despite the innovations of this work and the controversy it fostered, Robinson did not pursue it. She soon discovered KEYNESIANISM and became one of its major theorists, defenders, and popularizers. *The Accumulation of Capital* (1956) is the most ambitious of the books she wrote on Keynesian theory. Its principal achievement is to extend Keynesianism toward long-run issues of growth and capital accumulation—a traditional weakness of Keynesian theory. Robinson also influenced Michal KALECKI and Marxist analyses of reproduction. In concert with other economists at the University of Cambridge, her work on growth led to a general break with many of the assumptions of American neo-Keynesians and to the emergence of a distinct school known as Cambridge Keynesianism or Cambridge growth theory.

In her later work, Robinson turned toward a number of methodological issues in economics and continued her general criticisms of neoclassical and equilibrium theory. Her other writing includes *Essay on Marxian Economics* (1942).

Rogers, Carl (1902–1987) A psychologist and the originator of a number of widely used therapeutic methods and concepts, including person-centered counseling (*Client-Centered Therapy*,

1951) and the therapeutic objectives of personal growth and self-actualization. Rogers's approach was phenomenological and humanistic; it prioritized the uniqueness of individual perceptions of the world and limited the role of the psychologist to supporting and clarifying that perspective. Rogers extended his ideas into group therapy and education. His other major works include *Freedom to Learn* (1969) and *Encounter Groups* (1970). See also PHENOMENOLOGY; and SOCIAL PSYCHOLOGY.

role The behavior expected of individuals who occupy a specific STATUS or, metaphorically, the part each person is called on to play in the social drama, together with its attendant privileges and responsibilities. A role is the dynamic or behavioral aspect of status and is a sort of script for acting in appropriate ways. There is always some tension between the actual performance of a role and the expectations others may hold for it. The word role is used mainly to refer to the typical expectations, rather than the individual enactments. As each individual has multiple statuses, so each has multiple roles. *Role strain* arises when two or more roles associated with one status are in tension—a student monitor may be torn between loyalties to teacher and students. *Role conflict* arises from tensions between roles associated with two or more statuses—such as the common dilemma facing working mothers.

Role theories tend to divide into top-down approaches, which associate roles with positions in the larger social structure, and bottom-up approaches, which emphasize the interactive, performative, and frequently flexible dimension of roles and *role-taking*. Structural functionalists such as the anthropologist Ralph LINTON and sociologist Talcott PARSONS were innovators of the top-down approach. They focused on roles as relatively fixed bundles of expectations, responsibilities, and relationships that indicate an individual's place in the social structure. From this perspective, society functions in large part through the process of socializing its members into various roles. Those who fail to perform them face societal disapproval or are subject to various kinds of sanction. In this regard, functionalist perspectives can account for deviant behavior (see DEVIANCE), but they leave very little room for individual creativity or the negotiation of NORMS.

Bottom-up theories include the SYMBOLIC INTERACTIONISM of George Herbert MEAD and the DRAMATURGICAL APPROACH of Erving GOFFMAN; both emphasize the individual's active part in the interpretation, performance, and negotiation of roles. By focusing on the creative aspect of social interactions, they recognize that individuals rarely just follow their roles; rather, they are always actively involved in making and managing them. Both sociological and psychological factors come into play in such decisions. Goffman's concept of *role distance* opens up some of this complexity in suggesting that because people occupy multiple roles, they are rarely completely engaged in any single one. Instead, they maintain a variety of forms and degrees of distance from their roles, which in turn informs how they perform them.

Consistent with the general turn away from structural functionalism, role theory no longer occupies the central place in SOCIOLOGY that it held in the mid-twentieth century. The issues underlying performative versions of role theory have continued to inform sociological research, however, if not always in a direct line from Mead and Goffman. Poststructuralist theories of power and social reproduction frequently treat individual behavior as highly coded and socially determined, and they have made the question of individual improvisation or the margin of indeterminacy accorded individuals a central issue. The influential work of Pierre BOURDIEU is broadly oriented by these concerns, as are Michel FOUCAULT's inquiries into the constitutive effects of power and the disciplinary nature of a wide array of modern institutions.

Media studies have also taken an interest in the part played by television and other mass media in the reproduction of social roles. This is highly visible in early FRANKFURT SCHOOL critiques of the CULTURE INDUSTRY, and it played an important role in feminist debates about GENDER norms and social attitudes toward women. Theories of education, child development, and adolescence have also devoted considerable attention to the question of *role models*—persons who represent broader sets of social values and provide ideal enactments of those values.

Rostow, W. W. (1916–) An economist known for his work on growth and DEVELOPMENT. Rostow's views on the subject were very different from those of his contemporaries Ragnar NURKSE and Gunnar MYRDAL, who advocated a balanced approach to growth across many sectors of the economy. Rostow argued instead that different sectors in the economy are characterized by different growth rates and that overall growth is based on the rapid expansion of key sectors that can pull the rest of the economy up with them. Rostow developed this argument primarily in *The Stages of Economic Growth* (1960), which presented a historical account of the transition from traditional to modern societies. This involved a series of stages: the emergence of preconditions for economic *take-off*, the take-off itself, the drive to maturity, and finally arrival in the era of mass consumption. His approach is similar to earlier evolutionary theories of societal development by anthropologists and economists—among others, Adam SMITH, who identified hunting, pastoral, agricultural, commercial, and manufacturing stages.

A traditional society, Rostow argued, is characterized by low productivity and production techniques based on pre-Newtonian science and technology. The second stage of growth involves the transition to modern science, which is increasingly exploited for the benefit of the economy. New opportunities present themselves, and enterprising people come forward to capitalize on them. Trade and investment expand, and early industries develop. These, Rostow argued, are the preconditions for take-off. The take-off itself requires investment in infrastructure, a spurt in industrial and agricultural innovation, and the emergence of a social group that identifies itself with the modernization of the economy. New industries expand as profit rates rise, and a large proportion of profits are reinvested. There is also technical progress in agriculture, which allows food production to keep pace with the demands of the industrial sector.

According to Rostow, it takes about sixty years for a new industrial state to mature. This period is depicted as a time of sustained growth. New technology diffuses throughout the economy, and the economy widens and deepens its scope of activity. Production becomes increasingly routinized. This is followed by an interval in which consumption shifts toward durable goods and services. Expenditure on nonnecessities rises as purchasing power increases. There is also a rise in the percentage of the population living in cities, as well as in the percentage of workers in the service sector.

Rostow's theory of growth has been criticized for being relevant for only today's industrialized countries. This is somewhat mitigated by the fact that at the center of this system are humans who have complex objectives. As one or the other of these objectives becomes important, society moves from one stage to the next. This evolutionary approach to growth attracted considerable attention and marked one side—known as MODERNIZATION THEORY—of a postwar controversy about the best path to development in the THIRD WORLD.

Rostow was educated at Yale University, taught at the Massachusetts Institute of Technology, and served as a consultant to the Eisenhower administration. He looked back on much of his earlier development theory in *Rich Countries and Poor Countries* (1987).

Rousseau, Jean-Jacques (1709–1778) A French philosopher who profoundly shaped eighteenth-century thought on a number of fronts, including education, religion, music, and especially ideas of the person and theories of society and the state. Rousseau was both a radical individualist and an advocate of an extreme notion of social unity (the GENERAL WILL). The link between the two is his critique of society as a corrupting influence that estranges people from their own nature and from harmonious social relations. This link also exists between Rousseau's social-psychological thought and his political theory. Rousseau was one of the principal theorists (with Thomas HOBBES and John LOCKE) of the "social contract"—an account of the origins of society rooted in a foundational moment of individual consent to government and of transfer of individual rights to the state. Rousseau's emphasis on popular sovereignty and the supremacy of the "general will" of the people in this process deeply marked the French Revolution, as well as many subsequent theories of social and political equality.

Basic to Rousseau's thought was a defense of nature against the claims both of society and instrumental reason. In this, he anticipated the Romantic reaction to dominant currents of the Enlightenment. In particular, he played a pivotal role in developing the modern ideal of expressive individualism and the notion of an interior self. Much of his criticism of society focused on the duplicity of hiding this self and the damage done to it by attempts to conform to social roles. Rousseau's thought, in this context, helped to pioneer the critique of ALIENATION; this rested not only on psychological arguments but also on his criticism of private-property relations as a root cause of social division.

Although Rousseau was born in Geneva, Switzerland, his intellectual milieu was Paris of the 1740s and 1750s—the center of Enlightenment thought. There, Rousseau met Denis Diderot, Jean Le Rond D'Alembert, and many of the Encyclopedists. He contributed articles on music and political economy to Diderot's *Encyclopédie* (28 vols., 1751–1772), but criticized Enlightenment claims for scientific and human progress. His first and second *Discours*—*On the Sciences and Arts* (1750) and *On the Origins of Inequality* (1775)—argued strongly for the superiority of an ostensible "natural" state of humanity that existed prior to the development of society and the state. Society, he claimed, was a corrupting influence that had replaced the original simplicity and generalized sympathy of human life with complexity and conflict rooted in the emergence of property, the division of labor, class divisions, and the state. He made clear that knowledge about society was to be counted among the corrupting influences, although, as many commentators have pointed out, his second discourse is a remarkable example of social analysis.

Rousseau's *The Social Contract* (1762) begins from the rather different premise that society is a means of freeing humanity from the dangers of the state of nature, but that this potential had been squandered. He argued that the solution to humanity's unhappy condition might therefore be found within society, through a more harmonious accommodation between the individual and the collective will.

Rousseau's model society was based on the principle of popular sovereignty, which held that the only legitimate government was one based on the wills of its members. Insofar as government and its laws reflect that will, the individual will and the general will coincide. This coincidence required that individuals follow not their private interests but the general good. He also advocated the creation of a CIVIL RELIGION that could support this system of values. Rousseau recognized, however, that achieving a society ordered on these principles was difficult; in practice, few people acted in accordance with the general will. To escape this difficulty, Rousseau posited an enlightened transitional figure—the *legislator*—who would transform society and its laws. The ideas of the legislator and the supremacy of the general will have remained controversial. Some claimed to see in them justification for the violence of the French Revolution. Rousseau's confidence that liberty could be guaranteed by an unmediated relationship between citizens and the state has also proved contentious—especially within the liberal tradition concerned with the counterweight and deliberative space provided by "intermediary" structures. Ultimately, Rousseau had little to say about the ideal form of government, and he admitted that both democratic and monarchical solutions existed to the problem of the general will. He was less ambivalent about the rule of law and the equality of all citizens before the state; these, he argued, were the necessary foundations of freedom within society.

Rousseau left other important works—notably his reflections on education, *Emile* (1762); his pioneering work of autobiography and psychological introspection, *Confessions* (1770); and his *Letter to d'Alembert* (1758), which argued against Voltaire's ideas on the theater. He was a controversial figure in both life and in death; for many, his reputation remained tied, for better or for worse, to the French Revolution that his work arguably foreshadowed and to a degree theorized. At the same time, Rousseauian "naturalism" has shaped much modern thought and recurrent social movements, including elements of 1960s counterculture.

routinization Max WEBER's term for the inevitable transformation of charismatic leadership into institutional authority—whether through the creation of a new bureaucracy that formalizes the charismatic leader's principles or through a return to the tradition that the charismatic leader disrupted.

rule of law The principle that power should be exercised according to mutually understood rules and procedures that are applicable to all members of a polity, including officers of the state. The rule of law requires an independent JUDICIARY capable of enforcing laws against even the highest-ranking agents of the state. For this reason, it is closely associated in the Western political tradition with the doctrine of the SEPARATION OF POWERS. Although the rule of law is not limited to DEMOCRACY, it is an important condition for it and thus plays a large part in studies of DEMOCRATIZATION. See also LAW.

Rybczynski theorem See HECKSCHER-OHLIN TRADE THEORY.

S

sacred Emile DURKHEIM gave the term its strongest sociological inflection in *The Elementary Forms of the Religious Life* (1915), arguing that the *sacred* is that which is separated from the PROFANE (the ordinary world) by ritual—and that this distinction forms the basis of religious systems. Durkheim focused on the function of the sacred in legitimating and integrating the social order—as do symbolic anthropologists such as Clifford GEERTZ.

sacrifice The ritual offering of an animal or, in some cases, a person or goods to a deity or spirit. Sacrifice is a means of defining the relationship between the human and the divine, although the wide range of functions, activities, and strategies that such practices encompass make stricter definitions problematic. The classic functionalist arguments of Emile DURKHEIM and his inheritors focused on sacrifice as an aspect of religious ritual, which serves to divide the SACRED from the PROFANE and to maintain social solidarity. Numerous other frameworks for studying sacrificial acts have been proposed over the years, from the question of *commensality*, or sharing a meal with the gods, to logics of exchange and reciprocity, including bargaining and the substitution of symbolic or "cheaper" sacrifices. An important theme is the question of whether sacrifice depends on or produces transcendence of the limits of everyday life—a *liminal* experience, in the terms of Arnold van GENNEP.

Sahlins, Marshall (1930–) A leading contemporary anthropologist whose work on premodern economies and the impact of European expansion on indigenous cultures has been influential in academic and popular circles. Much of Sahlins's work seeks to challenge complacent notions of progress, cultural superiority, and privileged anthropological access to knowledge about other cultures. He is perhaps best known for an argument about the "original affluent societies," advanced in *Stone Age Economics* (1972). Sahlins proposed that if affluence is measured in leisure

time and the degree to which wants are met—as it frequently is in sociological and economic research from Thorstein VEBLEN forward—then hunter-gatherer societies have a strong claim to affluence because they generally possessed a larger portion of leisure time than their more economically advanced agricultural neighbors. More recently, Sahlins has been a key developer of structuralist anthropology and a pioneer in relating this form of cultural analysis to historical change.

Sahlins has produced significant ethnological and historical work on societies in Hawaii, Fiji, New Guinea, and Turkey. His other major works include *Evolution and Culture* (1960), *Culture and Practical Reason* (1976), and *How "Natives" Think* (1995).

Saint-Simon, Claude-Henri de Rouvroy, Comte de (1760–1825) A French aristocrat and eclectic social theorist who laid the foundations for much of the nineteenth-century socialist tradition. Saint-Simon is best known as a utopian thinker who actively pursued the Enlightenment goals of scientific reason and the application of scientific knowledge to the study and organization of society. He was a strong opponent of aristocratic privilege, a defender of republicanism, and—no less fervently—a Roman Catholic who argued that the combination of technology, reason, and enlightened religious faith would guide mankind out of the age of feudalism and toward a just and progressive society.

Saint-Simon was a prescient observer of the growth of industrial society and he predicted the dramatic impact of industrialization on traditional beliefs and forms of social organization. He sought to meet this challenge by studying and planning for the complete reorganization of European society along modern, scientific principles. He called this work "social physiology"—the study of the nature and basic organization of society. In this context he is often recognized as one of the founders of the modern social sciences. Perhaps his most direct influence was on his secretary, Auguste COMTE, who adapted Saint-Simon's notions of discernable social laws and technocratic rule to his own social philosophy, POSITIVISM.

Saint-Simon argued in favor of a meritocratic but highly ordered social hierarchy. He advocated industrialization and viewed science as the engine of social reform and general prosperity. Although his work is frequently associated with the wave of small communes that applied his principles, Saint-Simon was not a collectivist in regard to private property—indeed, he defended it on the meritocratic principle of just rewards. Although he recognized class struggle as one of the principal social ills, he argued that it would disappear as all members of society became productively employed in a social order structured for the greater good. The role of government in such a society would be minimized, and the combination of meritocracy, technological society, and republicanism would result in rule by experts. Toward these ends, Saint-Simon advocated the replacement of the European nation-states by a European republic.

Saint-Simon came to be regarded as a founder of SOCIALISM—a view held by Karl MARX among others. By the mid-nineteenth century, Saint-Simonian societies of various kinds dotted the social and political landscape. Saint-Simon's social thought is elaborated primarily in *The Reorganization of European Society* (1814). His ideas regarding an enlightened Roman Catholicism oriented toward social justice have also proved influential, especially in twentieth-century LIBERATION THEOLOGY. These are presented in *New Christianity* (1825).

salvage ethnography Generally associated with the ANTHROPOLOGY of Franz BOAS and his students among the American Indians around the turn of the twentieth century, salvage ethnography is an explicit attempt to document the rituals, practices, and myths of cultures facing extinction from dislocation or modernization. Because the objects of such study are often already gone, it relies heavily on second-hand accounts and reminiscences rather than on direct or PARTICIPANT OBSERVATION.

sampling In social research, the use of a small set of a population to represent the total population, generally because of the prohibitive cost of collecting information from a large group. There are a variety of sampling techniques applicable to different kinds of groups. The chief principle underlying all sampling methods is that the sample is *randomly* determined in order to minimize the risk of selection biases. The RELIABILITY of a sample can be evaluated by looking at the standard deviation of the distribution of data. In general, the standard error decreases as the size of the sample increases.

Samuelson, Paul (1915–) An economist whose contributions range from consumer theory and trade to MACROECONOMICS and finance. Samuelson figured prominently in the reemergence of NEOCLASSICAL ECONOMICS in the post–World War II era and bears much of the responsibility for moving economic methodology from Alfred MARSHALL's diagrammatic methods to present-day quantitative reasoning.

Samuelson earned his bachelor's degree from the University of Chicago. He went on to graduate studies at Harvard University at a time when the revolutions in Keynesian economics and monopolistic competition were reshaping economic orthodoxies. One of his earliest and most significant contributions to economic theory was *Foundations of Economic Analysis* (1947)—an attempt to derive empirically meaningful propositions about comparative equilibrium from the neoclassical principle of maximization. One of the achievements of this book was the elaboration of REVEALED-PREFERENCE THEORY—Samuelson's major contribution to consumer theory. Revealed-preference theory imposes conditions on the observed (or revealed) choices of individuals, rather than postulating utility functions or preference orderings in abstraction from observed behavior. The key condition is the *weak axiom of revealed preference*, which requires that if an individual chooses consumption bundle A when he can afford to buy B, then he will never choose B when he can afford A. As long as this condition is satisfied, most of the demand conditions implied by utility theory can be derived. The theory of revealed preference plays an important role in linking demand theory, index numbers, and welfare economics.

Samuelson also contributed to capital theory, finance, and the theory of general equilibrium. While his microeconomic research showed a definite neoclassical bent, his work in macroeconomics reflected a more mixed approach. In fact, many regard Samuelson's greatest contribution to be the *neoclassical synthesis*—the view that monetary *and* fiscal policy can be used to keep the economy at close to full employment and that the mix of policies determines the rate of investment.

This was the dominant view on macroeconomic policy in the 1950s and 1960s. Its acceptance was aided by the popularity of Samuelson's textbook, *Economics* (1948, and many subsequent revised editions), which continues to be widely read.

Among Samuelson's other accomplishments are the STOLPER-SAMUELSON THEOREM, which analyzes the consequences of tariffs in international trade, and the *multiplier-accelerator*—a macroeconomic model that relates consumption, investment, and output. One of the often-cited shortcomings of Samuelson's approach to macroeconomics is his disregard for the microeconomic foundations of macroeconomic phenomena. He justified this by arguing that aggregate demand, not wages and prices, is the key determinant of output. Samuelson's contributions were recognized with the Nobel Prize in economics in 1970.

sanctions In sociology, the term most commonly refers to forms of punishment for deviant behavior. Sociologists often distinguish between *informal sanctions*—the casual expressions of disapproval or pressures for conformity that occur in many aspects of daily life—and *formal sanctions*, which imply official, institutional procedures for assuring compliance. Sanctions can be either positive or negative. Positive sanctions can consist of informal rewards for conformity (such as a thumbs up or similarly casual sign of approval) or formal rewards (such as titles, prizes, awards, and other forms of official approval). Negative sanctions involve informal punishments for failing to conform, including ridicule, verbal or emotional abuse, and ostracism, as well as formal penalties based on written laws or rules.

In INTERNATIONAL RELATIONS, the term has a more specific meaning that refers to punitive measures taken by states against other states. Such sanctions are generally economic in nature and involve the restriction of imports or exports to or from the targeted country. They are generally conceived of as a form of political intervention short of military action, although this line grows thin in cases where sanctions are applied with military force, as in blockades. Sanctions have been an important tool for international organizations like the United Nations, and they can only be effective (short of expensive and generally short-term unilateral military blockades, as during the Cuban missile crisis) where substantial cooperation exists among countries. Without such cooperation, economic activity can be redirected through nonparticipating countries or black markets. Multilateral support of sanctions is therefore a key element in the doctrine and system of *collective security*. There is, however, considerable debate about the usefulness of such sanctions, especially in comparison to other forms of international pressure and engagement. Critics point out that sanctions are blunt instruments that may have devastating consequences for the general population without necessarily damaging or influencing the targeted regime. Proponents argue that when sanctions are effective, even to a minor degree, they demonstrate their value over more expensive or interventionist methods. Since there is little consistency in the application of sanctions, however, the advantages and disadvantages are often overshadowed by other political concerns. U.S. debate about China policy in the 1990s dramatized these issues and was resolved in favor of economic engagement. Cuba, however, continues to be subject to U.S. sanctions, although these have been undermined by lack of international support.

Sapir, Edward (1884–1939) One of Franz BOAS's eminent students, Sapir was a brilliant linguist as well as an anthropologist, and he contributed greatly to developing connections between the two fields. In the 1910s and 1920s, Sapir conducted extensive fieldwork among American Indian tribes of the Pacific Northwest and published a number of studies of tribal languages that remain classics of the genre. Generalizing from this work, he developed a system of classification of North American Indian languages.

Sapir also published widely on general LINGUISTICS, including the enormously influential *Language* (1921), which prefigured many of the insights of structural linguistics. After accepting a position at the University of Chicago in 1925, he turned his attention to the relationship between language, culture, and psychology. With Margaret MEAD and Ruth Fulton BENEDICT, he founded the CULTURE AND PERSONALITY MOVEMENT, which attempted to integrate developments in psychology, child development, and the anthropological study of cultural variation. Sapir's work in this area was realized mainly through a number of articles on the relationship between cultural traits and individual personality. Whether this writing implies the SAPIR-WHORF HYPOTHESIS regarding the linguistic determination of structures of thought (later developed by his student Benjamin Lee Whorf) remains a subject of debate.

Sapir–Whorf hypothesis The proposition that differences in the structures of languages produce differences in the thought structures of their speakers. It is sometimes credited solely to Benjamin Lee Whorf, a student of Edward SAPIR and the principal exponent of the theory. Although most modern anthropology assumes a certain amount of linguistic relativism and recognizes the impact of language on the way people perceive the world, Whorf held this position *in extremis*, arguing that differences in linguistic systems produced potentially radical differences in the structure of thought. Much of this argument focused on the ostensible distinction between concrete and abstract language, which Whorf used to differentiate American Indian languages and modern English. Whorf's claims have been challenged by much subsequent linguistic theory, particularly the TRANSFORMATIONAL-GENERATIVE GRAMMAR of Noam CHOMSKY and others, which posits a commonality of basic language structures (and therefore cognitive structures) among human beings. Nonetheless, questions remain about the extent to which linguistic variation shapes cultural difference and differences in human experience. Do the Inuit experience snow differently than Vermonters because they have more words to describe its varying qualities? See also COGNITIVE ANTHROPOLOGY; and LINGUISTICS.

Sartre, Jean-Paul (1905–1980) A French philosopher, novelist, playwright, and public intellectual of enormous stature from the 1930s on. Sartre's early philosophical writing was strongly shaped by the PHENOMENOLOGY of Edmund Husserl and Martin HEIDEGGER—primarily in its concern for the relationship of human consciousness to the material, external world. Sartre not only denied that consciousness constituted an essence (as René DESCARTES had argued in the seventeenth century), but that it was precisely "nothingness"—a capacity for negation that propelled consciousness into the future and conferred on human beings a fundamental existential freedom. This freedom was the main philosophical and ethical preoccupation of Sartre's early work—best represented in *Being and Nothingness* (1943), the philosophical treatise he wrote during the war. There, Sartre controversially proclaimed an irreducible human freedom of choice, even under

extreme circumstances, although he did not deny that choices could be influenced and shaped by circumstances. Relatedly, he argued that this freedom confers a heavy responsibility on the individual to recognize the self as a process of constant invention and, conversely, to avoid the "bad faith" of refusing responsibility for one's actions or character. In this context, Sartre refused Sigmund FREUD's concept of the *unconscious*, and articulated an existential psychology based instead on the notion of a character-forming "original choice."

In addition to the facticity of ourselves and our past actions (our *being-in-itself*), and the constant creative forward movement of our freedom (our *being-for-itself*), Sartre argued that there is a *being-for-others* that reflects the power of others over our conception of self. Sartre generally presented this as a power for stigmatization and constraint—indeed, it underlies the famous comment from his play *No Exit* (1943) that "hell is other people."

Sartre's experience in the war left him far more politicized than *Being and Nothingness* suggests. After the war, he became a leading and controversial figure on the French left, frequently supporting the Communist party and taking an active part in the major political struggles of the day. In *The Critique of Dialectical Reason* (1958–1959), Sartre sought to bridge existentialism and MARXISM. Much of this turned on an attempt to compare what he described as the thin sociality of bourgeois society—the accidental commonality of purpose he called "seriality"—to the revolutionary power of the "group in fusion," which uses its freedom on behalf of historical change. He also hoped to overcome the traditional divide between structural approaches to social analysis and historical, or "situated," approaches. The massive *Critique of Dialectical Reason* was widely criticized, not least because Sartre's commitment to existential freedom ran counter to emerging structural (and poststructural) approaches to subjectivity. Existentialism's dominant place in the post–World War II intellectual and philosophical scene faded quickly, although Sartre continued to exercise enormous personal authority.

Sartre was a prolific and successful writer in many genres. His major literary works include *Nausea* (1938), *Saint Genet* (1953), *The Words* (1964), and *The Idiot of the Family* (1971–1972), a study of Flaubert. He refused the Nobel Prize in Literature in 1964.

satiation   The state of having had enough of a particular good. In economics, satiation is reached when the consumption of an additional unit yields no additional UTILITY, that is, the marginal utility is zero.

satisficing   An agent is said to *satisfice* when his choice of an alternative (among the options available) meets or exceeds some specified criteria but is not guaranteed to be in any sense optimal or best. In "A Behavioral Model of Rational Choice" (1955), Herbert Simon proposed satisficing as an alternative to maximization behavior—the choice of the option that best satisfies one's preferences. Satisficing behavior arises when a decision maker, faced with a choice, either finds it impossible to maximize or finds the cost of doing so too high. This can occur for a variety of reasons, such as when there is too much information to analyze or when the cost of acquiring information is high. Searching out the full range of options and attempting to calculate their advantages and disadvantages can consume time and other resources. Individuals acting in their own behalf or as managers of firms may choose the best among a narrower range of possibilities or the first course of action that satisfies a number of constraints.

Sauer, Carl   (1889–1975) The principal figure in the development of CULTURAL GEOGRAPHY in the United States. Sauer placed human interaction with the natural environment at the center of his work, thereby explicitly challenging the dominant paradigm of environmental determinism. In a series of influential essays, books, and addresses from the 1920s forward, Sauer attempted to consolidate geography around the concept of *cultural landscape*, which referred to the ways in which human activity contributed to and transformed natural environments. This perspective, as well as Sauer's interest in premodern societies, owed much to his association with the anthropologist Alfred L. KROEBER, who, like Sauer, arrived at the University of California at Berkeley in the 1920s. Sauer's work and growing influence led directly to the foundation of the Berkeley school of cultural geography, where he remained for more than fifty years—most of that time as its director.

As developed by Sauer, his colleagues, and his students, cultural geography pays close attention to the beliefs and attitudes that shape a culture's relationship to its environment. Studying beliefs often involves distinguishing between objective environmental realities and the perception of those realities—an area of research known as *environmental perception*. This humanist and often highly interpretive form of geography came under pressure in the 1960s from a range of quantitative methods, which resulted in a reevaluation of some of the Berkeley school's conclusions and more generally a fragmentation of the field. Nonetheless, Sauer's culturalist perspective remains a major orientation and has informed such recent reformulations as the "new cultural geography" of the 1980s.

Sauer played a major institutional role in mid-twentieth century geography, serving twice as president of the Association of American Geographers and training several generations of cultural geographers, including Fred KNIFFEN, Wilbur Zelinsky, and Yi Fu TUAN. He wrote on a wide array of subjects, from the origins of agriculture to the processes of exploration and colonization of the New World. Sauer's major works include *Agricultural Origins and Dispersals* (1952) and a number of seminal essays, including "The Morphology of Landscape" (1925) and "The Agency of Man on Earth" (1956).

Saussure, Ferdinand de   (1857–1913) Possibly the most important linguist of the twentieth century, Saussure elaborated the basic principles of SEMIOTICS and structural LINGUISTICS—a set of ideas that have had an enormous impact on the social sciences and on cultural theory more generally. Yet Saussure never produced a general statement of his linguistic theory. Although two early books on comparative grammar and Indo-European grammar established his reputation as a brilliant linguist, his important theoretical work is contained only in a slim volume posthumously assembled from notes taken by students during his lectures at the University of Geneva; this was the *Course in General Linguistics* (1915).

Saussure's structural linguistics is rooted in a number of fundamental and now commonly used conceptual distinctions. Perhaps most significant with respect to the practice of linguistics before Saussure is his distinction between diachronic and synchronic analysis. *Diachronic analysis* addresses change through time, a perspective Saussure associated with the classic subject of nineteenth-century grammarians: shifts in usage, meaning, and grammatical structure within languages. *Synchronic analysis*, in contrast, explicitly rejects the historical dimension of change. Instead, it treats a cross section of language at a moment in time and, in so doing, reveals the "principle of organization" that structures the language.

From this methodological basis, Saussure argued that the relationship of words to their referents is purely conventional—that a *signifier* (or sound pattern, which can be represented as a word) has no intrinsic relationship to its *signified* (the concept of the thing—in his central example, a tree). This *concept of the thing* is not the thing itself—the question of thought's relationship to material reality is an ontological question that Saussure thought unnecessary to the study of language. The pairing of signifier with signified forms a *sign*, and language is a differentiated system of signs that take their meaning only from their relationship with one another. Saussure further distinguished this total system of signs (*langue*) from individual speech (*parole*), which represents a singular expression of the larger rules and possibilities of the language.

A final important aspect of Saussurean linguistics is the distinction between syntagmatic and associative relationships. *Syntagmatic relationships* exist between specific words in a given sentence or speech act; they are governed by grammatical rules. *Associative relationships* are those that place a given word in a more general category of subjects: that is, politics may be associatively related to elections, government, legislation, and so on.

Saussure's work has been a key element in the broader "linguistic turn" of the humanities and the social sciences during the second half of the twentieth century, reflecting the paramount place language has acquired in theorizing and understanding practices of interpretation, the workings of ideology and cultural codes, and, more broadly, the operations of identity and difference. Saussure's work has become one of the theoretical touchstones of twentieth-century thought, visible in Claude LÉVI-STRAUSS's anthropological STRUCTURALISM, Louis ALTHUSSER's structural-Marxism, Jacques DERRIDA's DECONSTRUCTION, and a range of other projects, methodologies, and orientations.

Say's law   Most succinctly, the principle that "supply creates its own demand." Say's law postulates that the production of output tends to create purchasing power, and this purchasing power is equal to the value of the output. Attributed to Jean Baptiste Say (1767–1832), it exposed the weakness of the common assumption that economic growth had an upper boundary

beyond which there would be no means of purchasing the additional output.

Schmitt, Karl   (1888–1985) A German political theorist and one of the most influential critics of liberal democracy during the Weimar Republic (1919–1933). In his major work, *The Concept of the Political* (1932), Schmitt argued that the essential feature of politics is decision making in a political field structured by binary relationships of friend and foe—a doctrine he termed *decisionism*. Politics is therefore a fundamentally hostile activity—a constant mobilization of the mass against its enemies, both internal and external. It is manifestly not, Schmitt argued, about ideas or social ends. His work is in many respects a disillusioned settling of accounts with the major political ideologies of the nineteenth century.

Democratic institutions, Schmitt held, tend to paralyze the political process by interfering with the charismatic leaders who can best conduct decisionist politics. For this reason, Schmitt supported AUTHORITARIANISM and ultimately became a supporter of the Nazi party. His work was broadly discredited after World War II, but it has become the object of renewed attention by scholars working on SOVEREIGNTY and LAW. Schmitt's other work includes *Political Romanticism* (1919).

Schumpeter, Joseph   (1883–1950) An influential economist who explored the underlying structures of capitalist growth. CAPITALISM, Schumpeter argued, advances by way of a process of "creative destruction," loosely tied to cycles of prosperity and decline, and largely dependent on the energy of society's entrepreneurs. The key to economic change, in Schumpeter's model, is innovation. This includes, but is not restricted to, the invention of new products or processes. Entrepreneurs introduce innovations, and thereby figure centrally in the process of change. Owners, shareholders, and managers of firms, he argued, are not necessarily part of this group.

Schumpeter maintained that, *ceteris paribus*, the economy tends toward a static EQUILIBRIUM, in which production and profits stagnate. Entrepreneurs break this tendency by introducing profit-increasing innovations. This is not, however, a steady process. Innovations often come in clusters, tied to breakthrough technologies or ideas. The most adventurous entrepreneurs create a favorable climate for others to follow; investment, prices, and incomes rise, and the economy prospers. Yet rising prices deter further investment, and competition from new products make older forms of production unprofitable; this produces a downturn. In this way, the BUSINESS CYCLE is tied to the process of adaptation to innovation and change. The same process that causes growth in the long run causes fluctuations in the short run.

Like many political economists who lived through the years between the world wars, Schumpeter believed that capitalism was in a state of decline. Yet, he rejected most of the available accounts of this decline: David RICARDO's theory of diminishing returns, Thomas Robert MALTHUS's theory of population crisis, and both the Marxian and Keynesian theories of stagnation. He argued instead that there were three main trends that worked against capitalism. First, the role of entrepreneurs was becoming obsolete. Trained specialists were increasingly responsible for technological innovation, which was being rationalized into a routine procedure. As this occurred, entrepreneurs were reduced to wage earners and lost their incentive to innovate. Next, the core groups that defended capitalism were weakening. Small entrepreneurs were being swallowed by big business, thereby shifting ownership toward shareholders whose investment in the system was less direct. In addition, capitalism produces intellectuals and other groups that have a vested interest in social unrest. Finally, he held that the institutional framework of capitalism was crumbling. Schumpeter illustrated this by pointing to the post–World War II policies of European governments. High and progressive taxation, he argued, was thwarting private accumulation and investment; public expenditure was dramatically growing, labor legislation had tilted the balance of power away from entrepreneurs, and big business was increasingly constrained by regulation. According to Schumpeter, this increasing dependence on government would lead to "guided capitalism" and finally to "state capitalism."

Schumpeter's theory remains strongly within the classical tradition. His signal achievement was to link business cycles to the process of capitalist development. This theory, particularly the notion of creative destruction, has been revived in recent work on growth. Schumpeter studied law and economics at the University of Vienna and later taught at the University of Bonn and at Harvard University. He also served as president of the American Economic Association. His major works include *The Theory of Economic Development* (1912), *Capitalism, Socialism and Democracy* (1942), and *History of Economic Analysis* (1954).

Schutz, Alfred (1899–1959) An Austrian sociologist who bridged the gap between the phenomenological study of everyday life and the analysis of higher-order social relations (see PHENOMENOLOGY). Schutz was educated at the University of Vienna and pursued a dual career as a banker and phenomenologist—drawing, in the latter role, on the work of Edmund Husserl and Max WEBER. Schutz immigrated to the United States in 1939, where he continued his financial career. Only in 1952 did he take a permanent teaching position at the New School for Social Research in New York.

Schutz took Husserl's emphasis on the phenomenology of individual consciousness in the direction of intersubjective experience. He was interested, above all, in the phenomenological and symbolic shaping of ordinary daily experience—the *social construction of reality* that underlies the experience of the self and social identity. For Schutz, the *lifeworld* was made up of the taken-for-granted stream of everyday routines, interactions, and events. These experiences produce and, in turn, are negotiated by way of what Schutz called *commonsense knowledge*—a level of practical, routine, naturalized knowledge. Schutz argued that this type of knowledge was the necessary basis of any more abstract discussion of social structures or influences—following a distinction between *first-order typifications* (or basic, taken-for-granted forms of experience and action) and *second-order typifications* (which integrate more complex information about the world on a broader scale). The task of the sociologist was to construct "second order" meanings, or abstract, analytical models of the social world, although only for heuristic purposes. This occasioned a well-known dispute with Talcott PARSONS, the patron of abstract sociological theory in the 1940s and 1950s.

Schutz also emphasized the fundamental way in which language and symbolic behavior shape experience, thereby providing a bridge between phenomenology and interpretive sociology, including SYMBOLIC INTERACTIONISM. The task of the sociologist, he said, was to create models of social action that reconstruct particular actions, primarily through the device of IDEAL TYPES. This methodology aligned Schutz's work with Weber's, and in this connection he had a strong influence on Harold Garfinkel's

ETHNOMETHODOLOGY as well as on Peter Berger and Thomas Luckman's work, especially *The Social Construction of Reality* (1966). His notion of the lifeworld also figures prominently in Jürgen HABERMAS's theory of COMMUNICATIVE ACTION.

Schutz's major works include *The Phenomenology of the Social World* (1932) and several posthumous publications (largely facilitated by Luckman)—*Collected Papers* (1971) and *The Structures of the Life-World* (1974).

scientific management   A broad program for reorganizing the workplace through the application of "scientific" methods to the study of management and the work process. Scientific management, sometimes called Taylorism in recognition of its American innovator and promoter Frederick Winslow Taylor (1856–1915), revolutionized industrial production in the late nineteenth and early twentieth century. Most famously, it pioneered the use of time-and-motion studies to analyze and break down the tasks of individual workers into faster, smaller, repetitive steps. The more efficient use of time was one goal of this greater division of labor. The DESKILLING of work—permitting the hiring of lower paid, unskilled workers—was another, although Taylor believed that a system of production incentives would result in a more equitable distribution of profits than the existing wage model. Implicit in scientific management was the goal of complete control over the work process by a new category of managers. Scientific management thus gave a major impetus to the rise of the managerial class—a group that did not, in itself, own capital. Scientific management systematically undercut the older industrial model of skilled work and workplace solidarity; consequently, it was vigorously opposed by most labor groups. It was resisted, too, for reflecting a view of workers as little more than machines and for failing to understand the social dimension of work. Nonetheless, scientific management was broadly incorporated into the Fordist model of assembly-line production. It soon became the dominant factor in industrial relations and continues to shape the workplace today.

scientific method   In the social sciences, the scientific method refers to research methodologies that pursue verifiable knowledge through the analysis of empirical data. In practice, the validity of different research methodologies has always been a matter of contention. The issues underlying such debates are diverse. They concern, for example, whether and how data can be collected and measured without bias, whether and how research can (or should) be value free, whether there are general laws that govern society or individual behavior, and what counts as a causal explanation or a valid theory—to indicate only some of the most general issues. See also THEORY.

search theory   In economics, the analysis of resource allocation when agents are imperfectly informed about their trading opportunities and have to incur *search costs* in order to find trading partners. This is in contrast to Walrasian analysis, which presumes instantaneous and costless coordination of trade (see Leon WALRAS). Often applied to labor markets, search theory addresses the question of when to accept an existing option (a job or employee, for example) that has arisen. Doing so provides the immediate benefit of the deal, but further searching might provide a better offer or match.

secession   The voluntary withdrawal of a state or province from a larger state structure, such as a federation or empire. Secession aims at securing sovereign statehood and self-government for the breakaway community or, in some cases, absorption into a neighboring ethnic "kin" state. If secession is acceptable to both sides, a negotiated division of the country is possible. An example is the "Velvet Divorce" that led to the establishment of the Czech and Slovak Republics after the 1992 breakup of Czechoslovakia. Conversely, secession may prompt conflict and violence, as leaders of the larger state attempt to block the division of the country through the use of military force. This outcome is more common and was exemplified by the secession of the eleven Confederate States of America, which precipitated the American Civil War (1861–1865). The 1991 break-up of the Yugoslav Federation also culminated in war, as what remained of the central government sought to forcefully block the secession of Croatia, Slovenia, and Bosnia-Herzegovina. Some constitutions include provisions for the political secession of regions or groups, including procedures and criteria for considering secessionist proposals. See also SEPARATISM.

secondary analysis   The analysis of data gathered by others, such as government institutions, as distinct from the analysis of data collected by the researchers themselves.

secondary groups See PRIMARY GROUPS AND SECONDARY GROUPS.

secondary institutions See PRIMARY INSTITUTIONS AND SECONDARY INSTITUTIONS.

second best, theory of In economics, the postulate that if one of the conditions of Pareto optimality cannot be fulfilled (for example, due to an EXTERNALITY in the production or consumption of a particular good), then the best attainable or second-best situation can be achieved only by departing from the other Paretian conditions as well (see PARETO OPTIMAL). Formulated by Richard Lipsey and Kevin Lancaster in 1956, it overturned the conventional wisdom of pursuing Paretian conditions in a piecemeal fashion and in other markets, after they have been violated in a particular market. This theory has seen wide application in welfare analysis, the theory of public finance, and international trade policy.

second-price auction See AUCTIONS.

sector theory Like MULTIPLE-NUCLEI THEORY and CONCENTRIC ZONE THEORY, sector theory describes patterns of urban land use. Introduced by Homer Hoyt in 1939, it postulates that zones devoted to particular activities (industry, retailing, working-class residence, upper-class residence, etc.) are roughly wedge-shaped and extend outward from a central business district. Hoyt argued that the largest determining factor in this distribution was the upper class, whose residency needs exercised a powerful influence on the location of undesirable neighbors, such as industry and the poor. The theory also accorded a large role to transportation infrastructures, since the expansion of a given sector could occur at the periphery of the city. Like most attempts to model land use, sector theory is more useful as an attempt to specify some of the forces driving development than as a reliable predictor of actual urban development. Subsequent attempts to revise or build upon the insights of sector theory have challenged Hoyt's strong assumption that decisions about development are guided by rational choice and that economic actors outside the upper class play comparatively insignificant roles.

secularization The process by which sacred beliefs are weakened over time, RELIGION becomes less influential in social life, and scientific and other rationalist worldviews come to dominate both the understanding of nature and social life. Secularization has played a prominent role in most accounts of modernization and MODERNITY. In the West, these tend to emphasize the transition from a Christian worldview, which described the social and natural world as reflections of divine will, to a progressively human-centered worldview, which required logical, verifiable knowledge about the world. Max WEBER produced one of the most powerful accounts of secularization in his studies of world religions, arguing that secularization in modern societies was paralleled by a broad and diverse process of RATIONALIZATION in other spheres of social activity, including economic, political, aesthetic, sexual, and intellectual life. Like Friedrich NIETZSCHE before him and a number of later social theorists, Weber attributed important aspects of this process to developments that were in themselves religious—particularly the role of the Protestant reformation in launching capitalist accumulation in Europe. These same theological impulses—the will to truth and the desire for a more immediate relationship with God—eventually turn inquiry against religious structures of authority and knowledge.

Many recent scholars have seen this as either too categorical a view of the process of secularization or as too dismissive of the ways in which other value systems come to perform many of the same functions as religion. Robert Bellah's notion of the American CIVIL RELIGION provides one prominent alternative, as do studies of the relationship between religion and nationalism more generally. Moreover, degrees of religious affiliation vary greatly in modern societies—from strong majorities in the United States to relatively small minorities in France or Scandinavia. The growth of religious fundamentalisms, too, has become a major subject of study in the context of structural inequalities in processes of globalization, as well as in social contexts where stronger structures of values emerge in the face of rapid change and growing multicultural pressures. In short, generalizations about the decline of religion in either public or private life have proved difficult to sustain. Nonetheless, in many settings religion is accorded a highly circumscribed role, as in the relatively strict modern separation of spiritual matters from technical or economic ones.

segmentary-lineage systems A model of social organization based on a branching system of KINSHIP descent, first described by E. E. EVANS-PRITCHARD in his classic study *The Nuer* (1940). Lineage segments form CORPORATE GROUPS, each defined by a common ancestor. Within a lineage, the unity of larger groups is defined by more distant common ancestry; smaller groups are distinguished by common ancestors unique to that segment. Living adults may thus be differentiated by the identities of their fathers, while at the same time being unified by a common grandfather. For large groups, the *apical ancestor* who defines the group may be several generations distant. Segmentary systems commonly reckon some ten to twelve generations of ancestry, which define the major lineage segments into which the society is divided. A sliding scale of identity governs interpersonal relations, with the relevant group identity for conflict or alliance defined by the largest segment that distinguishes two parties and the smallest group that unifies them.

The result, Evans-Pritchard argued, is a system in which any dispute immediately implies a set of familial alliances and oppositions, rallying the nearest relations around each party and expanding the alliance outward to include others (depending on how members trace their descent along the family tree and how far back the point of commonality lies). The segmentary model loosely describes many African societies, but also proved to be an idealization that did not precisely explain the patterns of alliance in actual conflicts. Nonetheless, the segmentary system does help to explain social solidarity and conflict resolution in societies without formal political organization. While segmentary-lineage systems exist outside Africa, they usually offer less complete explanations of social relations.

segregation The physical and/or social separation of different groups within a society, of which the best-known instances are racial and sexual segregation. Segregation may be *de jure* (mandated by law) or *de facto*, operating through mechanisms such as social norms, economic stratification, or specific qualifications for work. Racial segregation in the United States has been supported by both *de jure* and *de facto* mechanisms over time, although contemporary segregation mainly evidences the latter—including economic factors, forms of unofficial coercion, and the strong sense of group identity that generally structures racial and ethnic membership. Sexual segregation is in many respects the most pervasive and naturalized form of the practice in many societies, underlying separate facilities for men and women, as well as many broader assumptions about the spheres of activity "appropriate" to each sex.

Desegregation has been a major subject of public-policy discussions since the end of *de jure* segregation in the United States. Many of the specific measures used to achieve this goal, such as school busing and AFFIRMATIVE ACTION, have been controversial.

seigniorage Under the gold standard, gold could be brought to a mint and converted to coin. A small levy, or seigniorage, was generally paid to the ruler for this privilege. Today, the term refers to the difference between the face value of the currency and its lower cost of production—a difference that represents profit for the money printer (the government).

self One's sense of possessing a distinct and relatively stable identity, separate from the external world and from other people. The sense of self is the product both of natural processes of maturation and of the process of socialization in which maturation is inscribed.

A sociological perspective on the self emerged in the early part of the twentieth century in the work of Charles Horton COOLEY and George Herbert MEAD. Drawing on his experiences with his own children, Cooley developed the concept of the *looking-glass self*, which asserted that individuals are profoundly affected in their own actions by the way they imagine that others see them. For Cooley, this mirroring effect extends to our apprehensions about our "appearance, manners, aims, deeds, character, friends, and so on" (*Human Nature and the Social Order*, 1902/1964: p. 169).

Mead developed a more systematic theory of the self that, while in some respects a critique of Cooley, shared his sense of the centrality of the reflexive capacity of human beings. He was interested particularly in the ways in which the self is developed in and through social processes, rejecting the notion that the self is something possessed innately or at birth. Mead distinguished two stages through which the self develops in response to interactions with others. The first is a *play stage*, in which children learn to adopt the attitudes of specific others—playing the role of a parent or a fireman, for example. This is followed by a *game stage*, in which children begin to generalize from specific others to the broader attitudes of the community or society. They begin to understand their selves as defined in relation to a generalized, societal other. The internalization of this perspective marks the complete maturation of the self.

In conceiving these processes, Mead distinguished between two aspects of the self: the "I" and the "me." The "I" is the self as the author or subject of action; the "me" is the self as the object of action, inscribed in and acted upon by the social world. The "I" is the spontaneous and creative power, while the "me" is the reflexive self—the socialized aspect of the self that situates action within a context of perceived expectations. Mead did not consider the "I" or "me" as discrete entities but as constantly interacting phases of the same social process of self-construction. Mead's emphasis on this perpetual construction, reinforcement, and internalization of expectations (developed primarily in *Mind, Self and Society*, 1934/1962) became the cornerstone of the symbolic interactionist tradition in sociology (see SYMBOLIC INTERACTIONISM).

Many contemporary empirical studies of the self focus on differences in the process of socialization across class, gender, race, and ethnic lines. These works draw attention to the limitations of Cooley and Mead's conceptions of the self—especially their neglect of the impact of different social contexts on its development.

More broadly, there is a long tradition in modern social theory in which the concept of self is linked to individualism, personhood, and identity, and made to bear the primary burden of explaining the condition and consequences of modernity. Partly a critique and partly an extension of the Enlightenment view of man as a rational actor, this tradition has persistently sought to historicize conceptions of the self and individuality. It runs through the classic works of Karl MARX, Max WEBER, and Emile DURKHEIM to those of their contemporary critical inheritors, including Michel FOUCAULT, Jürgen HABERMAS, Charles Taylor, and Anthony GIDDENS.

self-actualization A theory of the hierarchy of human needs that posits a necessary progression from physiological needs to the need for security, love, status, and *actualization*—the self-reflexive desire to maximize one's potential. The theory of self-actualization is credited primarily to the American psychologist Abraham Maslow.

self-concept Refers to what people think they are, as distinct from their actual personality characteristics. The sociologist Morris Rosenberg defines self-concept as "the totality of the individual's thoughts and feelings having reference to himself as an object" (*Conceiving the Self*, 1979). Empirical studies of self-concept often employ the Twenty Statements Test (TST). This technique asks respondents to write twenty statements in answer to the question: Who am I? Content-analysis of the results suggests that individuals' self-concepts are multidimensional and tend to be organized around their social roles. The notion of *self-image* is similar but more colloquial and imprecise—although initially it focused literally on people's sense of their physical appearance.

self-determination The notion of collective self-determination operates by analogy to ideas of individual freedom and autonomy. It usually refers to the process by which nations or national minorities acquire statehood or political independence. By extension, it refers to the freedom of a sovereign state to determine its own form of government and set its own policies. As a political ideal, self-determination has provided a powerful rationale for the break-up of Europe's colonial system since the eighteenth century—beginning with the American colonies that formed the United States. In practice, however, claims for self-determination are frequently linked to ethnic particularism—based on the close association between the idea of the NATION and that of unified peoples or cultures. In this context, the logic of self-determination has few limits and can prove antithetical to the democratic principles on which it is based. The breakup of Yugoslavia provides a prominent example. See NATIONALISM.

self-efficacy theory A theory of motivational psychology that relates people's beliefs about their capabilities to their performance of tasks and life achievement. The theory is rooted in the observation that people who strongly believe in their personal capabilities tend to perform better and achieve more, whereas people who doubt their capabilities shy away from difficult tasks and tend to achieve less. The sense of self-efficacy is based on past experience, observations of the behavior of other people, and feedback from others. Self-efficacy theory is associated primarily with the work of Albert Bandura (*Social Foundations of Thought and Action*, 1986).

self-fulfilling prophecy A prediction that becomes true because people act as if it is true. The rumor of a bank failure that leads to a run on the bank is an example. This notion of the thin line between people's perceptions of an event and its reality runs throughout much of the sociological and philosophical tradition. As William Isaac THOMAS suggested, that which people believe to be true becomes true for the purposes of their action. Robert K. MERTON helped to theorize this "Thomas principle" and introduced the term *self-fulfilling prophecy* into modern sociology (in *Social Theory and Social Structure*, 1957). Self-fulfilling prophecies have been the subject of a wide range of empirical work, particularly in educational settings, where differences in expectations frequently lead to differences in performance.

A related concept is the *self-destroying prophecy*, which describes the potentially perverse impact of a widely disseminated prediction. Predictions of huge crowds at a public event, for example, can dissuade people from attending and result in a small crowd.

self-image See SELF-CONCEPT.

self-presentation Refers to an individual's efforts to present a self acceptable to others in the context of social interactions. The concept was elaborated by Erving GOFFMAN in his classic *The Presentation of Self in Everyday Life* (1959). Goffman argued that individuals are usually successful in this process, which is why social interactions usually proceed in a routine and regular fashion. On some occasions, however, disturbances occur that undermine individuals' performances. For this reason, individuals, like actors, often consciously manage their own impressions as well as the responses of the audience.

Strategies of self-presentation, *self-monitoring*, and *impression management* vary with the nature of the "stage" on which an individual performs. Thus, people dress differently on different occasions; they follow different scripts when talking to different audiences. These variations have been the subject of considerable sociological research, as have the differences in abilities or skills that people bring to these strategic decisions. An influential empirical study in this respect is Arlie

Hochschild's *The Managed Heart: Commercialization of Human Feeling* (1983), which examines the negative consequences of impression management on the emotional life of individuals in the workplace.

self-report study Any form of research based on self-reported data—that is, data "volunteered" by the target population. In the United States, self-report studies were introduced into criminology in the 1940s and 1950s as an alternative to the analysis of data from the police and the Federal Bureau of Investigation—until then the primary source of crime statistics. Police reports, in particular, were widely criticized for focusing on street crime while excluding white-collar, economically motivated, or politically motivated crime. Self-report studies ask respondents to identify the kinds of illegal activities in which they have participated—generally based on a list of choices. Despite the obvious risk that respondents will underreport and/or distort their activities, self-report studies have proved better suited to measuring some forms of deviance than police reports, such as minor offenses among adolescents. Self-report studies have also proved useful in a variety of social–psychological studies, especially those in which the monitoring of subjective feelings or states is at issue.

semantics The branch of linguistics concerned with the study of what words mean. Historically, semantics has dominated the study of language and played a major role in anthropological and other comparative investigations of CULTURE. Its focus on the referential function of language—the question of content or of information communicated, regardless of context—has been challenged by the study of context-dependent or performative dimensions of language, a field generally known as PRAGMATICS. See also COMPONENTIAL ANALYSIS.

semiotics and semiology Often used interchangeably, the terms refer to the study of systems of signs—above all in regard to language but with consequences in other areas of cultural theory, where questions of interpretation are paramount. Although semiotics has deep roots in Western philosophy, it received its major modern formulations around the turn of the twentieth century in the work of the Swiss linguist Ferdinand de SAUSSURE and the American philosopher C. S. PEIRCE. Saussure described language as a system of *signifiers* (or sound patterns, which can be represented as words) and *signifieds* (or the mental concepts of material things, such as the concept of a tree). The pairing of these two components constitutes a *sign*—what Saussure somewhat paradoxically described as an "acoustic image." Saussure challenged theories of natural language by suggesting that signs depended not on the thing signified but only on their relationship to other signs. In other words, the system of signs is conventional and arbitrary, rather than rooted in a natural relationship between language and things. Language is structured, therefore, by oppositions and differential relationships among signs.

This insight had a profound effect on LIN-GUISTICS, as well as on the study of mythology, folklore, and a range of other forms of highly structured cultural activity. Claude LÉVI-STRAUSS carried this structural principle toward one of its limits with the theory of STRUCTURALISM, which sought to explain the sources of primitive social organization on the basis of certain fundamental organizing oppositions: raw versus cooked, left versus right, exogamy versus endogamy, and so on.

Semiology, in contrast, became a major term in cultural theory following Roland BARTHES's work of the 1950s and 1960s. His *Elements of Semiology* (1964 [1967]) provided a theoretical context for his practice of decoding the content of cultural signs and locating these significations within larger structures of *myth*. Barthes used the terms *connotative* and *denotative* to refer to the manifest and latent levels of signification in these myths. His version of semiology was influential on a range of culture and media studies in the 1970s and 1980s.

Peirce inaugurated a somewhat independent line of semiological inquiry that emphasized a third position, the "interpretant" in the process of signification. In this way, he addressed the question of how systems of signs were mobilized in communicative acts that were themselves dependent on logical structures. This gave rise to a largely British and American tradition of SPEECH-ACT THEORY and communications theory. It was also part of the more general philosophical movement known as PRAGMATISM. Communications theory and pragmatism have been of considerable importance in the social sciences, especially through their offshoot, the sociological theory of SYMBOLIC INTERACTIONISM.

Semple, Ellen Churchill (1863–1932) An important American geographer and one of the most prominent women in any academic field in the United States in the 1910s and 1920s. Semple studied at Vassar College and then in Germany with the geographer Friedrich RATZEL, where she acquired a strong grounding in theories of ENVIRONMENTAL DETERMINISM. Returning to the United States, Semple worked largely within Ratzel's conceptual framework of *Anthropogeographie*, although she rejected his other notions about the state as an organic entity. Semple wrote on many subjects and regions, from Alaskan Indians, to the study of oceans and mountain passes, to Japanese agriculture. She also wrote a number of comparative studies of religion that explored the thesis that the environment was the main determinant of religious forms. These studies reached both a scholarly and popular audience, and they helped elevate Semple to prominence in the field. In recognition of this position, she was elected president of the Association of American Geographers in 1921. Semple's major works include *American History in its Geographic Conditions* (1903), *Influences of Geographic Environment* (1911), which did much to disseminate Ratzel's theories in the United States, and, culminating much of the work of her later years, *The Geography of the Mediterranean Region: Its Relation to Ancient History* (1931).

separation of powers A doctrine prescribing the establishment of separate branches of government, with clearly defined and limited powers. According to its most eminent proponent, Charles-Louis de MONTESQUIEU (*The Spirit of the Laws*, 1748), the separation of legislative, EXECUTIVE, and judicial powers diminishes the threat of despotism—the absolute control of the state by a single person, party, or faction. Montesquieu's formulation of the separation of powers doctrine has been a touchstone for much of the tradition of constitutionalism—perhaps most prominently in the newly independent American states in the 1780s, where it informed the thinking of the constitutional Framers. The U.S. Constitution is generally recognized as a strong expression of the separation of powers doctrine in that it establishes the complete independence of the executive, legislative, and judicial functions while maintaining overlapping powers among them to ensure that they check and balance each other. The Framers also instituted a separation of powers between the federal and state governments. Critics note that the division of sovereignty among a government's branches and/or levels diminishes its dynamism and accountability. See also CHECKS AND BALANCES; and JUDICIAL REVIEW.

separatism Stresses resistance to integration within a society or culture on the part of a people or other group. In the extreme, separatism can involve secession from a state and the establishment of independent countries. In some cases, the goal of separatism is absorption into ethnic "kin" states.

Some forms of separatism do not involve the state, *per se*, but rather relationships between groups within society. Thus, some versions of radical lesbianism advocate withdrawing from all relations with men, and black separatism often involves withdrawing from functional integration in white-dominated economies, including integrated schools and neighborhoods. See also NATIONALISM; and NATION-STATE.

sequent occupance In geography, a theory of the changes in human occupancy of an area over generations, rooted in an analogy to plant succession. The model examines how the occupancy of one generation changes the landscape in a way that prepares the conditions for the different types of occupancy of successive generations. Although the concept has various antecedents in physical geography, it was named and popularized in human geography by Derwent Whittlesley in 1929. The theory proved a durable alternative to theories of ENVIRONMENTAL DETERMINISM throughout the 1930s and 1940s, although it has since fallen out of general use.

serial correlation Also *autocorrelation*. A statistical problem in which the current value of a variable (or the error term in a regression) is correlated with its own past values. The term *autocorrelation* is used when observations come from cross-section data; the term *serial correlation* is used with data over time or time-series data. Under autocorrelation, the residual for one observation is correlated with the other observations. As a result, the ORDINARY LEAST SQUARES estimate no longer has desirable properties in terms of efficiency—that is, it no longer has minimum variance. Special tests (such as the Durbin-Watson test) exist for determining serial correlation, and econometric procedures may be used to restore the efficiency of the estimates. See also CORRELATION ANALYSIS; and REGRESSION ANALYSIS.

sex Refers to the biological differences between male and female, especially those directly related to reproduction and erotic pleasure. Sex is distinct from GENDER, which refers to the culturally and socially produced distinctions between men and women, broadly organized by the terms MASCULINITY and FEMININITY. Nonetheless, there is considerable debate about where, precisely, the line between natural and cultural tendencies lies—particularly surrounding questions of cognitive differences, sexual behavior, and maturation.

For much of the late nineteenth and twentieth centuries, sex was the province of two research agendas: psychology and the empirical investigation of sexual practices, both often conducted under the aegis of DEVIANCE or of mental illness. The differences between men and women have been a famous subject of contention among psychologists, many of whom treated women's psychological make-up as a kind of failed or inferior variant of the male psyche. Sigmund FREUD's work on female psychology has become notorious in this regard.

Sociological interest in these questions arrived in the 1960s, in step with the growth of modern feminism and the structural economic changes that brought large numbers of women into the workplace. Sociological studies of sex and gender are generally concerned with the consequences of sex and/or gender differences on the division of labor and patterns of social inequality. These target the social institutions and processes that have traditionally (and with a remarkable degree of cross-cultural consistency) consigned women to secondary roles in society and deprived them of equal treatment and equal opportunities. See also SEXUALITY.

sexuality Refers to the reproductive and erotic dimensions of human life, at once physical and culturally constructed. Freudian psychology was perhaps the dominant force in shaping modern perspectives on sexuality, exerting an influence that extended well beyond the audience of academic and professional psychologists. Freud treated sexuality as the motive force behind the formation of the psyche and nearly all subsequent adult behavior—although other psychological schools, such as OBJECT-RELATIONS THEORY, took issue with this prioritization. Although Freudianism underwrote several interdisciplinary attempts to bridge psychology and the other social sciences, sexuality was generally studied by sociologists and anthropologists only insofar as it intersected with social institutions, such as marriage and motherhood. The vast outpouring of professional and lay interest in sexuality visible since the nineteenth century was not primarily social scientific in nature, although psychologists such as Richard Krafft-Ebing collected broad data about sexual practices.

Although sexuality has traditionally been the object of strong feelings about what constitutes *natural* behavior, it has been substantially redefined since the 1960s as a subject with a complicated and shifting history. For Michel FOUCAULT, whose writing has probably had the greatest influence on this new orientation, *sexuality* is "the name that can be given to a historical construct: not a furtive reality that is difficult to grasp, but a great surface network in which the stimulation of bodies, the intensification of pleasures, the incitement to discourse, the formation of special knowledges, the strengthening of controls and resistances, are linked to one another, in accordance with a few major strategies of knowledge and power" (*The History of Sexuality*, vol. 1, 1978, pp. 105–106).

As a result of new critical examinations of sexuality, coupled with the powerful feminist and gay/lesbian movements of the late twentieth century, the once strictly guarded boundaries between "normal" and "perverse" sexuality have been undermined. In many respects, this is a logical extension of the culturalist and comparativist values of sociology and anthropology, which emphasize and examine the socially constructed nature of seemingly natural institutions. These changes have made possible a powerful critique of the existing sexual order. As Anthony GIDDENS argues in *The Transformation of Intimacy* (1992), the separation of sexuality from reproduction and marriage, and the breakdown of traditional sexual boundaries amount to a radical democratization of intimacy. In this process, sexuality becomes an aspect of the broader reflexive project of self-fashioning.

Many of these investigations deal with the question of sexual orientation—a subject that confronts most of the values that structure sexual activity: procreation, pleasure, and love. The division of sexuality into two dichotomous poles, heterosexuality and homosexuality, has similarly been historicized and challenged. Studies of sexual orientation often disagree about how heterosexuality and homosexuality develop. A current debate pits advocates of a biological disposition for homosexuality (e.g., Dean Hamer and Peter Copeland), against such scholars as Eve Kosofsky-Sedgwick, who emphasize

how cultural factors shape sexual orientations and identities. Such disagreement mirrors the familiar and unresolved NATURE VERSUS NURTURE DEBATE about the line between inheritance and environment.

sexual selection   A basic tenet of evolutionary biology that holds that certain features in animal species are favored through a process of selective mating. Sexual selection occurs when a trait provides an advantage in attracting mates. Two forms of sexual selection are distinguished: intersexual and intrasexual selection. In *intersexual selection*, a trait gains an advantage because it is attractive to the opposite sex. In *intrasexual selection*, a trait helps an individual compete with same-sex rivals.

shadow pricing   An imputed valuation of a good or service that either has no market price or for which the SOCIAL COSTS AND SOCIAL BENEFITS do not coincide with the private costs and private benefits. When a government evaluates a project it estimates the social costs and benefits of the project (all indirect costs and benefits are also accounted for). This may differ significantly from the hypothetical market cost of a project. These prices are termed *shadow prices* or *accounting prices*. If the government is concerned only with efficiency—and if there are no EXTERNALITIES—then shadow and market prices coincide. In addition, if the economy is not in competitive equilibrium, there is a case for using shadow prices instead of market prices.

shamanism   A socioreligious system in which certain individuals (shamans) are credited with powers over the physical and spiritual world, often in a context of ecstatic and temporary embodiment of the divinity. Shamans play an interstitial role, mediating between different dimensions of reality. Shamanism had a prominent place in nineteenth-century social theory as an evolutionary stage between magic and religion. Because versions of shamanism are common to a wide range of cultures, it remains a subject of widespread interest.

Shapley value   A solution concept in CO-OPERATIVE GAMES that measures the value of each player by his contributions to various coalitions of players. The Shapley value of each player is the expected marginal contribution of that player. Put differently, it measures how the worth of a coalition changes when a particular player participates in it, then averages this value across all possible coalitions that could form in the game. The Shapley value of the game is a unique payoff vector, assigning to each player an expected marginal contribution. It has the advantage of being a reasonably easy way to calculate an individual's contribution to a group effort. The sum of the individual values exactly equals the value of the game itself.

The Shapley value has been used in models of taxation, in allocating joint costs, and in the study of voting power and other political mechanisms. In political contexts, the Shapley value (also called the Shapley–Shubik index) has been used as an objective measure of the political power of individuals and political parties or coalitions.

sharecropping   A form of land tenancy in which the landlord allows the tenant to use a portion of land in return for a portion of the output (the share). Such an institutional arrangement is common in many parts of the world, especially in less developed countries. Early research on sharecropping provided the basic paradigm for studying a wider class of relationships known as PRINCIPAL AND AGENT problems.

shock therapy   In economics, the term usually refers to radical economic reforms aimed at speeding the transition from a planned economy to a market-oriented economy. Most versions of shock therapy involve some combination of rapid PRIVATIZATION of public enterprises, withdrawal of state subsidies to firms, termination of wage and price controls, implementation of deflationary monetary policies, and elimination of tariffs and other barriers to foreign trade. The merits of shock therapy have been a subject of considerable debate. Proponents argue that it represents a faster and more definitive path to CAPITALISM and to integration into the global economy than piecemeal or incremental reform—albeit at a high initial cost in terms of economic and social dislocation. Critics of shock therapy draw attention to the political and social consequences of radical economic disruption in emerging democracies, including unemployment, lower wages, the concentration of wealth in new elites, and increased opportunities for corruption—especially where the institutions of state and civil society, such as an independent judiciary and press, are too weak to monitor or check the process. In these circumstances, rapid, chaotic change can imperil the broader process of DEMOCRATIZATION.

Shock therapy was implemented in post-Communist Poland and Russia during the early 1990s. While Poland's experience has been widely judged a success, the results of the Russian experiment have been far more uncertain. China has also played an important role in these debates as an example of an incremental transition to capitalism.

short-run equilibrium   See LONG RUN AND SHORT RUN.

sib   A generally obsolete word for clan or, in American ANTHROPOLOGY, a group of clans. Sometimes also used as an abbreviation of *sibling*.

sick role   A conception of illness as comprising a set of responsibilities and modes of expected behavior—in short, a role. The concept of the sick role was developed by Talcott PARSONS, who identified four major components: (1) exemption from social responsibilities, which must be authorized by a proper authority such as a doctor; (2) exemption from blame for the illness; (3) a responsibility to get better, since sickness is socially undesirable; and (4) an expectation that the sick person will seek outside medical help and follow any prescriptions or advice. Parsons's criteria have been widely criticized as being too rigid and narrow in application. Nonetheless, he succeeded in raising questions about the social management of illness, especially on the part of health professionals. Variations on these themes continue to inform much of the contemporary sociology of medicine and the study of health and illness.

signaling models   Models that show how potential gains from trade can be realized even in the presence of ASYMMETRIC INFORMATION—a situation in which one side of the market has more information about product quality or can take actions that are not observable to the other side of the market. Signaling models generally make the assumption that buyers can only observe the average quality of the goods they purchase. In such cases, they will be willing to pay a price that reflects their estimates of the average. As a result, sellers of high-quality products may be better off withdrawing from the market. This is the problem of the *market for lemons*, in which bad products chase good ones from the market. The assumption is that there is no credible way for the high-quality sellers to declare their quality.

Low-quality sellers can simply claim the same thing.

Signaling is a solution to this problem of credibility. If high-quality sellers can find some activity that they can undertake at a lower cost than lower-quality sellers, it may benefit them to do so in order to signal their higher quality. Offering a lifetime warranty is an example. This behavior will serve as a meaningful signal of high-quality goods only if the lower-quality sellers cannot profitably replicate it. Buyers will learn that the signal is associated with higher quality and will be willing to pay a premium price. Such signaling needs to be differentially costly for the two types of producers, so that they each optimally choose different behavior. Otherwise, the information content is lost. Signaling models have been used to analyze education as a signal of productivity, coinsurance in insurance markets, aversion to risk, and investment opportunities.

Simmel, Georg (1858–1918) A German philosopher and sociologist of remarkable range, both in subject matter and methodology. Simmel is often ranked with Emile DURKHEIM and Max WEBER among the founders of modern sociology, although his influence has been more episodic and his legacy is more difficult to characterize. Simmel wrote prolifically on modernity and modern life, money, religion, the philosophy of art and culture, and epistemology—the last especially in relation to Immanuel KANT. Although late in life he claimed that his research was organized above all by an inquiry into the conditions of modern individuality, most commentators have found his work hard to classify. Apart from the difficulty raised by the shear breadth of his interests, Simmel refused to systematize his thought or remain within clearly defined disciplinary boundaries. He moved easily between sociology, psychology, and economics. He drew creatively on MARXISM and on NEO-KANTIANISM—the first underlying his critique of capitalist modernization and the second a variety of epistemological insights, including the groundwork of his FORMAL SOCIOLOGY. Simmel was also a master of the short, idiosyncratic essay form, rooted in the concrete particulars of an experience or situation; "The Metropolis and Mental Life" and "The Stranger" (both included in *Sociology: Investigations on the Forms of Sociation*, 1908) are the most famous of these.

The combination of Simmel's Jewish parentage and intellectual adventurousness made for a difficult university career in turn-of-the-century Berlin—this despite the support of such prominent colleagues as Weber and Heinrich Rickert. Simmel consequently spent much of his career in a variety of junior positions at the University of Berlin until he was granted a full professorship at the University of Strasbourg (France) in 1914.

Simmel is best known for his "formal sociology," or investigation of what he called the forms of "sociation." Formal sociology is an attempt to determine the basic forms of social interaction that underlie more complex forms and contexts of social behavior. Working from neo-Kantian principles, Simmel sought to reduce social encounters to their simplest arrangements, such as the possibilities for alliance and mediation that emerge in the transition from two-person groups to three-person groups. These contributed to what he called the "geometry" of human relations. Central to this geometry were distinctions between the basic modes of interaction that inform group situations (e.g., cooperation, competition, and conflict), as well as the complementary study of social types such as the stranger. Much of Simmel's work was oriented by his theory of modern alienation, which drew on Karl MARX and highlighted the role of commodity fetishism and the money economy in objectifying social relations; this is especially visible in his influential study, *The Philosophy of Money* (1900), a philosophical reflection of the social impact of the money economy and the operation of money as a dominant social "form."

Simmel had a major impact on subsequent German social theory and American sociology, especially Georg LUKÁCS in the former case and Robert Ezra PARK in the latter. Park and his colleague Ernest Burgess closely modeled their own urban research on Simmel's sociology of the city and, in so doing, shaped much of the agenda of the CHICAGO SCHOOL OF SOCIOLOGY during the 1920s and 1930s. Symbolic interactionists and microsociologists, such as Erving GOFFMAN, were also influenced by Simmel's theory of social interaction and his emphasis on the structure of face-to-face encounters. Simmel's analyses of social conflict were crucial bases for the development of a tradition of conflict analysis within FUNCTIONALISM during the 1950s and 1960s (especially by Lewis Coser in sociology and Max GLUCKMAN in anthropology). More recently, Peter BLAU's effort to develop a social theory based purely on number and other formal classifications has acknowledged a basic debt to Simmel.

Other important works by Simmel include *Philosophische Kultur* (1911), *Hauptprobleme der Philosophie* (1911), *Fundamental Questions of Sociology* (1917), and *Lebensanschauung* (1918), as well as monographs on Kant, Goethe, and Rembrandt.

simulacrum   A concept associated primarily with Jean BAUDRILLARD's contention that modern capitalism has emptied out the category of the authentic or real experience, leaving only simulacra, or simulations of the real. The simulacrum, however, is not a false representation—it is not opposed to the real or the authentic in the way that an *imitation* is. Rather it reflects the disappearance of the opposition between representations and reality. For Baudrillard, the simulacrum becomes the essential metaphor of society because social activity and the experience of self have become inseparable from their representations. Simulacra, nonetheless, remain efficacious. The 1991 Gulf War, both conducted and observed by television (at least for the Americans), is Baudrillard's recent and most controversial example of this efficacy.

SIT   See SOCIAL-IDENTITY THEORY.

situational status   A status that exists only as long as an individual is in a particular situation and performing the role associated with it. "Passenger" is a situational status that implies certain goals and forms of behavior—prescriptions that end when the person leaves the situation.

situationists   A group of French social theorists who broke with the doctrines of French communism and pursued a more radical project of critique and revolutionary activity in the 1950s and 1960s. Drawing upon the artistic movements of early twentieth-century Dadaism and Surrealism, as well as on anarchist theories of political action, the situationists extended Karl MARX's critique of alienation and paralleled some of the FRANKFURT SCHOOL conclusions about mass publics and the totalizing tendencies of capitalism. The leader of the situationists was Guy Debord, author of *The Society of the Spectacle* (1967). Many other Leftist intellectuals disaffected with the Communist party also had connections with the group, such as Jean-François LYOTARD and Jean BAUDRILLARD. The situationists advocated abolishing the division between life and art—drawing in part on the sociology of daily life pioneered by Henri Lefebvre. They played a leading role in the social turmoil in Paris in 1968, but

fell victim to much of the disillusionment with revolutionary action that followed.

Skinner, B. F.   (1904–1990) Probably the most influential experimental psychologist of the postwar period, Burrhus Frederic Skinner was the chief proponent of radical BEHAVIORISM—the study of environmental determinants of behavior. Skinner extended the work of earlier behaviorists, such as Ivan Pavlov and John Watson, who established the principle of conditioned response in laboratory experiments on animals. Although Skinner similarly used positive and negative reinforcement to train animals to perform complex actions—notably through the choices presented an animal within a "Skinner box"—he was much more interested in the consequences of behaviorism for human society. In this direction, Skinner argued not only that responses could be conditioned—a principle that has become the basis of innumerable therapeutic and learning methodologies—but also that conditioned behavior could become a stimulus to further behavioral change. Skinner outlined his goals for such social conditioning in a utopian novel, *Walden Two* (1948), which presented a thoroughly ordered society based entirely on principles of positive reinforcement (rather than punishment). Throughout, he remained a radical proponent of the plasticity of human behavior and a critic of what he considered fetishized intrinsic human values and concepts of character—subjects he addressed in *Beyond Freedom and Dignity* (1971). Skinner's work reached a wide audience and remains a powerful influence within SOCIAL PSYCHOLOGY and SOCIOLOGY. His other major works include *The Behavior of Organisms* (1938) and *Verbal Behavior* (1957).

slavery   An institutional system of bondage practiced in many societies and in a variety of forms. In ancient societies, slavery had a strong political component and was frequently a consequence of conquest, often of whole defeated peoples. Slaves in ancient Greece and Rome might thus possess varying degrees of education and perform different social roles, though without rights. Most research into slavery emphasizes its economic role: slavery was often the defining element of systems of production—typically in labor-intensive premodern and agricultural societies. Although *serfdom* and *indentured labor* possess many of the same qualities as slavery (and are sometimes considered variants), they usually do not involve the more extreme removal from society characteristic of modern slavery—what Orlando Patterson has called "social death" ("Slavery and Social Death," 1982). The extreme reduction of humans to property associated with New World slavery is generally termed *chattel slavery*. It was distinguished by a system of organized capture of individuals in Africa, transportation for sale as slaves, and subsequent treatment as items of personal property, which could be bought and sold. It was further accompanied by the general stigmatization of Africans as racial inferiors, and by the rationalization of slavery on the basis of an increasingly elaborate racial "science." Early work in physical anthropology was not infrequently organized around such goals—although the modern social sciences came to reject racial arguments about character and society.

The categorical "either/or" distinctions among races were perhaps most extreme in the United States. In Latin America, where slavery was similarly widespread, such distinctions were more flexible; it was sometimes possible to buy one's way out of slavery and a much greater degree of mixing among African, Indian, and Spanish (or Portuguese) populations occurred. Some scholars have argued that Latin American slavery was in some ways a gentler institution than its American counterpart—certainly it was more diverse and in many cases less socially and ideologically entrenched. In the United States, the social legacy of slavery also continues to be a major public and sociological preoccupation, inasmuch as the end of slavery in no way ended the systemic forms of discrimination and inequality that defined (and continue to define) the lives of most African Americans. See RACE.

Smelser, Neil J.   (1930–) A prominent American sociologist of institutions and collective behavior. Smelser has also made important contributions to social and economic history—especially in relation to the Industrial Revolution in Britain—and has worked to bridge the gap between psychoanalytic and sociological perspectives.

Smelser's sociological work is most closely aligned with the structural-functionalism of Talcott PARSONS, with whom he wrote *Economy and Society* (1956), a defining text of economic sociology and structural-functional theory. Parsons and Smelser conceived of society as a system composed of different "subsystems," which perform different functions. The economy is preeminent among these and is broadly responsible for the task of "adaptation" to the environment.

Smelser and Parsons also made an influential case for money as a "generalized medium of exchange" between the subsystems and challenged the attempt to base all economics on a microeconomic notion of disembedded, strategic individual action. Smelser continued to pursue these themes in *Social Change in the Industrial Revolution* (1959), where he applied the theory of "structural differentiation" to institutional development during the Industrial Revolution in Britain.

In *Theory of Collective Behavior* (1962), Smelser developed perhaps the most influential functionalist interpretation of social movements. He argued that under conditions of rapid social change precipitated by such "master processes" as economic development, severe "strain" undermines the value consensus in society and gives rise to collective protest. He emphasized the role of *structural conduciveness*, the economic and social conditions that legitimate collective and potentially extralegal behavior; *precipitating factors*, which crystallize collective sentiment—as in the case of the police beating that preceded the Los Angeles riots in 1992; and the counteraction by forces of SOCIAL CONTROL. His work informed a variety of subsequent research in this area and continues to play an important part in conceptions of collective action. See also COLLECTIVE BEHAVIOR.

Smelser is also a practicing psychoanalyst and has worked to reconcile the psychological emphasis on personality and behavior with social-structural accounts of function and role. His recent *The Social Edges of Psychoanalysis* (1999) is the most developed of his work in this area. Smelser's other works include *Sociology of Economic Life* (1963), *Comparative Methods in the Social Sciences* (1976), *Handbook of Sociology* (1988), *Social Paralysis and Social Change* (1991), *Effective Committee Service* (1993), and *Handbook of Economic Sociology* (edited with Richard Swedberg, 1994). Smelser spent much of his career at the University of California at Berkeley, and has served as director of the Center for Advanced Study in the Behavioral Sciences at Stanford University.

Smith, Adam   (1723–1790) The founder of the classical school of economics and, for many, modern economics itself. His monumental work, *An Inquiry into the Nature and Causes of the Wealth of Nations* (1776) went through five editions during his lifetime. Smith's overarching contribution was the theory and political logic of LAISSEZ FAIRE—the principle that society's interest is best served by the free pursuit of individual interests. As a political doctrine, laissez faire stipulated minimal or no intervention by government in the economy. Smith conceived of the market as an "invisible hand" that allocated rewards and punishments to economic actors in accordance with the merits of their actions. This was the foundation of the modern idea of the economy as a self-regulating system.

Smith studied at the University of Oxford and later returned to his native Glasgow as a professor of logic. In 1759, he published the *Theory of Moral Sentiments*, which marked a shift in his interests from ethics to economics. *The Wealth of Nations*, published in 1776, was a vigorous attack on MERCANTILISM—the dominant economic theory of the day. In contrast to the mercantilists, Smith argued that the wealth of a nation rose and fell with that of its neighbors and trading partners. He therefore defended foreign trade as a means of overcoming the narrowness of the domestic market and of promoting a more efficient division of labor.

The basis of Smith's work, like that of the PHYSIOCRATS and mercantilists before him, was an inquiry into the source of wealth. Unlike earlier thinkers, Smith understood wealth as based largely on the productivity of a nation's labor and the amount of productive labor employed. Productivity, in turn, is determined by the division of labor, which is limited by the size of the market. Only the cost of production—wages, rent, and profit—determines value in the long run. The "natural price" of a good reflects these costs. Actual or market price, however, will fluctuate around the natural price depending on short-run imbalances in demand and supply.

Smith also established the classical bias against according a major role to MONEY. Money facilitates the circulation of goods, Smith believed, but revenue is generated only by production. In contrast to the mercantilists, therefore, Smith believed that paper money would do just as well as gold or silver and cost less. By providing paper money, banks would save the labor required to produce gold coin and bullion and free it for other productive activities.

Smith's emphasis on the importance and effects of the division of labor has generated confusion about his commitment to the LABOR THEORY OF VALUE. While at one point he concluded that labor is the real measure of the exchange value of a commodity, he later measured the value of a commodity in terms of both the amount of labor it can command in exchange and the amount of labor required to produce it. This raises the difficulty of equating the products of labor of different individuals, since each commands a certain amount of another's labor in exchange. Later classicists such as David RICARDO chose one or the other explanation, and tried to rationalize the disharmonious elements in Smith's theory of value.

In spite of this and other contradictions in Smith's work, it is hard to imagine the development of economic theory without him. Smith's theory of development was the first systematic analysis of where and how conflicts of social interest arise. More importantly, Smith mapped out the terrain of economic analysis—production, value, distribution—in a way that has guided all subsequent economic thought. See CLASSICAL ECONOMICS.

Smith, Dorothy Elizabeth   (1926–) A sociologist whose work helped define the first wave of modern feminist social science in the 1970s. Smith conducted empirical research on the social dimensions of psychiatric issues and also helped launch a rethinking of interviews and other sociological methods as forms of interaction.

Smith argued for the uniqueness of the standpoint of women as subjects of sociological research and as sociologists working in a male-dominated field. In both cases, she argued, the experience (and consequently, standpoint) of women was systematically neglected or marginalized (see STANDPOINT THEORY). Smith turned this problem around, drawing on Karl MARX and the ethnomethodological tradition of Harold GARFINKEL to argue that this marginality offered a privileged perspective from which to analyze contemporary social relations (see ETHNOMETHODOLOGY). Experience, in this context, became a means of asserting truth claims against the dominant culture, as well as against the postmodern tendencies that have recently sought to undercut such claims. Smith has resisted the universalizing or biologizing claims of much early feminism, instead emphasizing women's distinctive position in social relations. She has also stressed the commonalities produced by shared forms of oppression, especially among women who are separated by group differences but also including men who experience certain kinds of structural social subordination. This has underwritten an emphasis on issue-based and coalitional agendas in her work.

Smith's later work has built upon and broadened this set of issues. In *The Everyday Life as Problematic: A Feminist Sociology* (1987), she argued that sociological inquiry should turn its attention to the local and everyday level in explaining how individual experiences are mediated by supralocal ideas and practices and, more generally, how the everyday world of experience is molded by social relations of power. In *Conceptual Practices of Power: A Feminist Sociology of Knowledge* (1990), Smith extended this approach toward an analysis of the "conceptual practices of power" that underlie and legitimize the social order and the views of its privileged members.

Smith's work frequently returns to the inclusive and exclusive practices that define discursive fields—especially the social sciences. She argues that the dominant frameworks of sociological thought tend to reproduce the concerns and ideas of a white, male-dominated, and largely European intelligentsia. Much of her recent work has implicitly integrated the success of feminism in establishing itself as a legitimate standpoint within the academy. Her *Writing the Social: Critique, Theory and Investigations* (1999) examines the consequences of this success in focusing on the question of "intertextuality"—the dominant culture's strategies of capture of alternative viewpoints. Smith was born in the United Kingdom, was educated at the University of California at Berkeley, and has spent much of her career affiliated with the University of Toronto.

snob effect A countertendency to the rise in demand for a product as its price falls, due to efforts of some consumers to differentiate themselves from the majority trend. The aggregate demand curve, in such cases, turns out to be steeper than expected. GIFFEN GOODS and the prestige goods discussed by Thorstein VEBLEN obey a similar principle.

sociability A central concept in Georg SIMMEL's formal sociology, which refers to any form of social interaction that exists primarily for its own sake. A common example of sociability is a party, where participants interact neither for instrumental purposes nor entirely from personal and subjective motives. Rather, an individual "enters the form of sociability equipped only with the capacities, attractions, and interests with which his pure humanness provides him" (*The Sociology of Georg Simmel*, 1950, pp. 46–47). Since sociability is typically disinterested and impersonal, Simmel called it the "play-form" of social interaction. It is a "game" that involves equals, and hence is democratic in nature. Simmel did point out, however, that although sociability has neither objective purpose nor intrinsic results, it has a definite role in social life in that it indirectly influences more serious endeavors. The more serious person, Simmel argued, derives from sociability a feeling of liberation and relief, because the practical tasks of life are sublimated.

social capital Interpersonal networks that provide people with resources or status, which they can exploit in other areas of social life and potentially leverage in the pursuit of economic or cultural capital. The principal example is educational accomplishment. Pierre BOURDIEU defines social capital as "the actual or potential resources which are linked to possession of a durable network of more or less institutionalized relationships of mutual acquaintance or recognition" ("The Forms of Capital," 1985). Families and communities are generally the levels on which social capital is constructed. Communities of professional or social elites make different resources available than working-class or ethnic communities. The concept of social capital has attracted considerable attention from contemporary social scientists, partly due to the influence of Bourdieu's writings on the reproduction of various forms of capital and partly because of its affinities with existing sociological concepts and theories, such as social resources, social exchange, and social networks.

The idea of social capital has been linked more generally to the notion of noneconomic resources. While Bourdieu's research has focused on strategies of accumulation of capital and the reproduction of inequality, others have treated social capital as a basis for social solidarity and as a collective resource that makes trust possible—as in Robert Putnam and Francis Fukuyama's account of community and civil society. In these conceptions, social capital is neither possessed nor accumulated by individuals but rather is held by a social group. Social capital is thus envisioned as a productive variable that facilitates development and democracy. James Coleman has sought to bridge the two sorts of accounts through RATIONAL-CHOICE THEORY. Social capital has also been brought to bear on the question of family support and on benefits mediated by extrafamilial networks. As Alejandro Portes recently noted, there may be negative consequences of social capital, including restricted access to opportunities, restrictions on individual freedoms, excessive claims on group members, and downward-leveling norms.

social-choice theory   Developed in its modern form by the economist Kenneth ARROW (*Social Choice and Individual Values*, 1951), social-choice theory deals with the aggregation of individual preferences into larger social judgments or choices. The cornerstone of this research is ARROW'S IMPOSSIBILITY THEOREM, which asserts that no perfect mechanism exists for social choice in a pluralistic society. Arrow defined five conditions that he felt were normatively essential to any preference-aggregation procedure—among them "non-dictatorship" (that social choice shall not be determined by one individual's preferences) and "positive responsiveness" (if an increasing number of people prefer one choice to another, the social judgment does not move in the opposite direction). Arrow's theorem demonstrated that, where all possible tastes are allowed, there is no way to aggregate preferences into a coherent social choice. A broad literature has developed around variations and modifications of this theorem, without substantially challenging its conclusions. Other topics include the manipulation of voting procedures, in which individuals vote differently from what their preferences dictate (potentially for strategic reasons); the debate on CARDINAL AND ORDINAL UTILITY and compensation tests that bypass the need for UTILITY comparisons; and notions of fairness, EQUITY, and nonutility information, such as the consideration of liberty and rights. The Marquis de CONDORCET'S PARADOX OF VOTING was an early articulation of certain of these difficulties. See also COMPENSATION PRINCIPLE.

social-comparison theory   Initially formulated in 1954 by Leon Festinger to explain why people rely on other people to evaluate their own attitudes and abilities. The theory has three basic premises: (1) individuals need to evaluate their own attitudes and abilities; (2) individuals will compare themselves to others in the absence of objective and nonsocial means of self-evaluation; and (3) in comparing themselves to others, individuals tend to choose for comparison those people whose attitudes and abilities are close to their own. In the hands of other scholars, the theory has been applied to the analysis of intragroup and intergroup relations. See also REFERENCE GROUP; SELF; and SYMBOLIC INTERACTIONISM.

social-contract theory   A tradition of political theory concerned with understanding the relationship between individuals and the STATE—conceived as a "social contract"—as well as the basis and limits of legitimate state power. Its classic formulations are those of Thomas HOBBES, John LOCKE, and Jean-Jacques ROUSSEAU—although a number of its themes extend back to ancient Greek political thought and forward into nineteenth- and twentieth-century versions of LIBERALISM.

Early social-contract theories focused on explaining the origins of society—generally conceived as a moment of collective consent to sovereign authority that replaces the natural, isolated state of individuals. These were not, in most cases, literal propositions about historical origins, but were rather thought experiments that enabled political philosophers to describe the social order as founded on popular consent. In its day, this radical proposition ran strongly counter to the divine justification of the social order associated with MONARCHY—although it implied no necessary contradiction of the principle of monarchical rule, as both Hobbes and Locke understood.

The major theorists differed widely about the motivations and functions of the social order—and consequently about the nature of legitimate political authority. For Hobbes, the natural order was characterized by a brutal "war of all against all." In this context, individuals give up some of their natural rights to the sovereign in return for social rights, above all the protection of the law. The sovereign exercises absolute and legitimate power, revocable only when the life of the individual is threatened.

Locke took a more benign view of the human condition and conceived society less as the product of fear than of the inevitable conflicts that accompanied the development of private property. Social complexity and inequality required a system of laws designed to perfect, extend, and adjudicate the rights of property. For this purpose, persons submit to a government of their own determination. Locke had little to say about the character of this government, other than that it was constrained by the natural rights of its subjects: life, liberty, and property. Where it overstepped these limits, it became illegitimate—the social contract was broken and the right to reconstitute government returned to the people. Locke's ideas proved central to the American Revolution and to the emergence of liberal forms of democratic rule.

Rousseau gave social-contract theory an explicitly utopian turn by invoking the notion of the

GENERAL WILL as a heretofore unmet condition of political legitimacy. The general will implied not only unanimity with regard to major social and political issues but also the transcendence of mere agreement among individuals (the *will of all*) in the creation of a larger collective subjectivity. As the French Revolution demonstrated, this could easily serve as a rationale for exterminatory political violence—a charge that has followed Rousseau ever since. More generally, he is credited with emphasizing the unmediated bond between individual and state that underwrites modern NATIONALISM.

Social-contract theory exerts less direct influence in social science today, although it continues to shape popular understanding of constitutionalism and LEGITIMACY. It is closely related to some rational-choice theories of the origin of social bonds and groups (e.g., Michael Hechter's theory of group solidarity). The most influential modern incarnation of social-contract thought is found in John RAWLS's *A Theory of Justice* (1971). Rawls proposes a thought experiment that asks individuals to choose the kind of society they would prefer given the assumption of a "VEIL OF IGNORANCE"—none could know beforehand the place they would occupy within the society. Rawls's work has generated renewed interest in social-contract theory and in abstract principles of justice and legitimacy. See also CONSTITUTION AND CONSTITUTIONALISM; OBLIGATION, POLITICAL; and RATIONAL-CHOICE THEORY.

social control   The mechanisms by which social norms are upheld and enforced. In general, social scientists distinguish between two forms of social control: SOCIALIZATION and the use of SANCTIONS. Socialization refers to the process of internalizing norms and values. Through socialization, individuals learn to identify with their society and commit themselves to a set of legitimized goals. A stable, enduring society is one in which mechanisms of socialization are effective—partly because sanctions (imposed controls or punishments) are relatively expensive and inefficient. Socialization has played a central part in the functionalist tradition, from Emile DURKHEIM to Talcott PARSONS. It has also been at stake (with different vocabularies) in the tradition of critical theory, running from the FRANKFURT SCHOOL through French POSTSTRUCTURALISM—the latter especially in the work of Michel FOUCAULT.

For the Frankfurt school and the body of Marxist theory it intersects, social control is not merely an abstract process of social integration but an *interested* one, which either directly serves elites or reflects the specific imperatives of given social systems, such as capitalism. For Foucault, social control often appears as the defining feature of society, and socialization as a ubiquitous process that does not merely bring individuals into compliance but constructs the self around particular values and roles. Foucault's *Discipline and Punish* (1975) is a major source of this influential conception of social control.

Many studies of social control focus on the use of sanctions as a means of maintaining order and punishing nonconforming behavior. Sociologists often distinguish between *informal sanctions* (the casual expressions of disapproval or pressures for conformity that occur in many aspects of daily life) and *formal sanctions* (those that imply official, institutional procedures for assuring compliance). Sociologists and criminologists (such as Travis Hirschi) draw a strong connection between the absence of effective means of socialization and the incidence of deviant behavior (see DEVIANCE). These are frequently correlated with poverty and the breakdown of social institutions, as much of the classic urban research of the CHICAGO SCHOOL OF SOCIOLOGY described.

social costs and social benefits   Any action entails private costs and private benefits to the individual who initiates the action. It may also entail costs and benefits that are not borne by the individual—termed *external costs* and *external benefits*. The sum of private and external costs is termed the *social cost. Social benefits* similarly reflect the sum of private and external benefits. Thus, social costs reflect the cost to everyone in society, while private costs include costs only to parties in the transaction. Examples where social costs differ from private costs include pollution or deaths caused by drunken driving. An example where the social benefit exceeds the private benefit is the positive spillover effects of research and development.

One of the chief topics of *social cost–benefit analysis* is market failure—the inability to achieve Pareto efficiency in a market (see PARETO OPTIMAL). In the presence of EXTERNALITIES such as transaction costs, social costs and benefits fail to coincide with private costs and benefits, and the market fails to maximize social WELFARE. Taxes, subsidies, and other forms of regulation or intervention are frequently used to correct such inefficiencies. See also COST–BENEFIT ANALYSIS.

social Darwinism   A body of late nineteenth-century social theory that applied evolutionary work on natural selection to the analysis of human society. Although Charles Darwin's insights shaped this effort, he kept a distance from it—despite the appropriation of his famous name. Equally influential and more directly involved were Herbert SPENCER in Britain and William Griffith SUMNER in the United States. It was Spencer who coined the phrase "the survival of the fittest" to explain the evolution of human society, according to which individuals who were better suited to the environment survived and prospered while the ill-adapted perished. Because it credited social elites with natural superiority, social Darwinism became an enormously popular rationalization of social inequality, whether organized along lines of class, race, or ethnicity. In the work of Sumner and his American colleagues, it served to justify the ruthless capitalism of the Robber Baron era.

Social Darwinism always had more currency in popular discourse than in the social sciences, where forms of natural and/or biological determinism were widely challenged. While Spencer and Sumner were serious scholars, many advocates of social Darwinism were unambiguously ideological. Outside the British–American world, social Darwinism found a receptive audience in societies such as Japan and China, where it gave theoretical impetus to emerging nationalist movements.

Social Darwinism should be distinguished from Talcott PARSONS's concept of *evolutionary sociology*, which emphasizes the functional integration of various elements of the social system in the development of human societies, and from other more rigorous efforts to apply evolutionary theory to social analysis, from Spencer to Gerhard Lenski and Leslie A. WHITE. It should also be distinguished from contemporary sociobiology, although there are a number of similarities.

social democracy   A political tradition dating back to the mid-nineteenth century that focused on the pursuit of SOCIALISM by democratic means. Early social democrats accepted Karl MARX's critique of CAPITALISM but generally rejected his claim that socialism could win only through violent revolution. Early social-democratic parties, such as the German SPD, enjoyed considerable success and were emulated by other left-wing politicians and activists. The British Labour Party, the Canadian NDP, and the French Socialist Party are all heirs to the social-democratic tradition. The end of the COLD WAR, the decline of industrial labor, the rise of NEOLIBERALISM, and the discrediting of MARXISM as a mass ideology have led to revisions of the agenda and rhetoric of many social-democratic parties. Public ownership and strong support for labor unions—once a hallmark of social-democratic politics—have given way in many instances to appeals to middle-class, white-collar voters.

social disorganization   The breakdown of social institutions, frequently associated with poverty. Social disorganization was first explored by the urban sociologists of the CHICAGO SCHOOL OF SOCIOLOGY, especially by Clifford Shaw and Henry McKay, who analyzed it by correlating rates of truancy, tuberculosis, infant mortality, mental disorder, adult crime, and juvenile delinquency in the poorest areas of the city.

social facts   Emile DURKHEIM's term for the enduring aspects of social life that shape or constrain individual action. In *The Rules of Sociological Method* (1895, 1964), Durkheim used the concept to clarify the subject matter of sociology and to delimit its field of investigation. He was concerned to distinguish sociology from the introspective theorizing of Auguste COMTE, from the grand synthesis of Herbert SPENCER, and from the concern with mental states characteristic of psychology. By treating social facts as "things" external to the individual, Durkheim put sociology on a strongly empirical footing. He also specified that they exercised a coercive power over individuals. Later, he revised this strong objectivism by suggesting that social facts had to be capable of being internalized.

Durkheim distinguished two broad categories of social facts, material and nonmaterial. The structural components of society, such as the church and the state, are examples of material social facts. Nonmaterial social facts include morality, the collective conscience, collective representations, and social currents (see COLLECTIVE CONSCIOUSNESS). Durkheim's major substantive studies are all concerned with nonmaterial social facts: especially social integration in *Suicide* (1893) and social solidarity in *The Division of Labor in Society* (1897).

social formation A Marxist term designating the arrangement of economic, political, and ideological relations that determines the MODE OF PRODUCTION and all other aspects of social life. It is usually associated with the structuralist MARXISM of Louis ALTHUSSER, who introduced the term as a replacement for what he perceived as the overly humanistic connotations of SOCIETY. Although Althusser hoped thereby to draw attention to the structural determination of much of social life by these arrangements, social formation is effectively synonymous with society in most usages.

social-identity theory (SIT) A social psychological theory of identity formation that privileges the role of large group identities in forming individuals' concepts of self. It has been used, in particular, to examine the formation and forms of adherence to national and ethnic groups.

socialism A form of social organization that prioritizes the common ownership of property and the collective control of economic production. Socialism emerged from a diverse array of social experiments and doctrines developed in the 1820s. These reflected both excitement about the possibilities of a rational, ordered, industrial society, and growing concern about the actual effects of INDUSTRIALIZATION under the conditions of private accumulation and market CAPITALISM. In its early decades, socialism was associated primarily with British and French thinkers—especially Robert Owen, Charles Fourier, Pierre-Joseph PROUDHON, and Claude-Henri SAINT-SIMON. These writers outlined principles for the reorganization of society along collectivist lines—although they differed on important issues such as centralized versus decentralized control, the role of private property, the degree of EGALITARIANISM, and the organization of family and community life. During its first decades, socialism was pursued primarily by small, utopian communities that drew inspiration from the writings of Saint-Simon or Owen.

The transformation of socialism into a political doctrine occurred in the 1850s, 1860s, and 1870s—especially as Karl MARX and Friedrich Engels developed their own account of socialism as the outcome of a revolutionary class struggle between workers and capitalists. Although they called this doctrine COMMUNISM as a way of distinguishing it from the utopian socialist groups, *socialism* remained the more common term. By the late nineteenth century, socialism had developed into a political doctrine associated with newly formed trade unions and mass political parties (e.g., the Social Democratic Party in Germany and the Labour Party in Britain). These groups supported diverse views of socialism, from the incremental and ameliorative goals of many trade unionists to the radical, revolutionary agendas of Marx, Engels, and the anarchists. These divisions became increasingly pronounced over time. Moderates like Karl Kautsky and Eduard Berstein advocated working for socialism within the democratic political process (a model increasingly known as SOCIAL DEMOCRACY). Others, such as Vladimir Ilich LENIN, advocated violent revolution. The Bolshevik Revolution of 1917 and the end of World War I marked the definitive split between the two. Communist parties in the Soviet Union and Europe dismissed the more moderate socialist parties and pursued, for the most part, a separate path; the installation of communist regimes in Eastern Europe after World War II solidified this division. The nominally socialist parties, in turn, became increasingly identified with the expansion of the capitalist welfare state.

This situation continued to evolve in the post–World War II era. In the 1970s, western European communist parties abandoned their revolutionary goals and embraced democratic strategies, resulting in a Eurocommunism that resembled earlier social-democratic configurations—although the two political tendencies remained distinct. The rise of neoliberal agendas and, by 1991, the disintegration of communism produced a centrist turn in most social democratic parties. Noncommunist socialist parties remain prominent in many countries in European and the rest of the world. Most now pursue agendas associated with increasing social welfare rather than fundamental economic transformations. See also FABIANISM; and NEOLIBERALISM.

socialization Usually, the process through which individuals internalize the values, beliefs, and norms of a society and learn to function as its members. Socialization can refer to narrower processes of group formation and integration—in accordance, for example, with occupational or ethnic groups. It can also be treated as a more fundamental process of acquisition of the basic cognitive and psychological requisites for social life, such as language.

Different conceptions of the self also play an important role. Socialization can be conceived primarily in terms of the roles to which a basically autonomous individual subscribes or as a fundamental process of constitution of the self—a self whose sense of autonomy is the product of its place in an extensive network of power. The work of Michel FOUCAULT exemplifies the latter view. Much of the early research on socialization dealt with childhood and maturation—clear instances in which the learning of social norms is central. Yet socialization is an ongoing process insofar as individuals adopt or acquire different roles in the course of their lives.

Socialization was one of the primary concerns of the functionalist tradition in sociology and anthropology, which strongly emphasized its role in the operation and stable reproduction of the social order (see FUNCTIONALISM). Talcott PARSONS spoke for many functionalists in describing socialization as "the learning of any orientations of functional significance to the operation of a system of complementary role-expectations." There has been considerable debate, however, about the degree to which socialization is accurately conceived as a top-down process, functioning in the service of social-structural forces. In most top-down accounts, socialization is described as a process that fits individuals into fixed roles. Much of the functionalist tradition follows this lead. An alternative tradition—represented by SYMBOLIC INTERACTIONISM and the more voluntaristic elements of ROLE theory—emphasizes the active part that individuals play in meeting, negotiating, and redefining their social roles. In this context, socialization appears as a much more flexible and less strongly determined process. Other critiques of functionalism have similar consequences for how we think about socialization—notably critiques of the notion of a singular, consensual society that smoothly organizes the socialization of its members.

Sociologists draw a number of distinctions between types of socialization. The process of internalizing norms and values that are different from those held in the past is often called *resocialization*. *Anticipatory socialization* refers to the practicing of roles that will be assumed in the future, as when children take care of baby dolls.

social-judgment theory   See LENS MODEL.

social mobility   The movement of individuals within a social hierarchy—conceived by some sociologists in terms of occupational mobility and by others in terms of more complex structures of CLASS. Social mobility is usually defined in terms of intergenerational mobility, although some research on the *intragenerational* mobility of individuals exists. Societies differ in the degree to which they permit or facilitate changes in status. Where class structures penetrate deeply into social life, social mobility may be relatively limited. Such are the findings of many comparative studies of mobility in Europe (where class identification and stratification remains relatively strong) and in the United States (where class distinctions are less visible and pervasive). Many researchers have also tried to measure the effect of the apparent *decline* of class structures on mobility, as the industrial basis of modern class identity loses its dominance. Here the results are ambivalent: major recent studies by John Goldthorpe and others suggest that there has been little measurable increase in social mobility.

A further complication is that increases and decreases in social mobility are often the result of structural changes in the economy, which may increase or decrease the number of jobs in a given category. The emergence of the middle and managerial classes in the late nineteenth and twentieth centuries is frequently associated with the generic expectation of social mobility in the United States known as the American Dream. Such factors can operate in the opposite direction as well, as evidenced by widespread concern over the decline in high-paying industrial jobs in the industrialized Western countries. The perception of new prosperity in the United States during the 1980s and much of the 1990s in many respects hid a dramatic redistribution of wealth and opportunity: the percentage of both rich and poor increased at the expense of the middle class and the most prosperous sectors of the working class. How these factors affect mobility in both the long and short run is a subject of considerable debate, and empirical findings are often dependent on the methodologies employed.

Social mobility was a subject of interest to a number of nineteenth-century social theorists, although the topic did not become a distinct subject of research until the publication of Pitirim SOROKIN's pioneering *Social Mobility* (1927). Sorokin maintained that social mobility was primarily evidenced by movement from one occupation to another, and that such mobility was crucial to the proper functioning of society, insofar as it rewarded talent. This occupation-based notion proved extremely influential and led to a variety of hierarchical models of occupations based on such variables as income and prestige. The most important of these was *The American Occupational Structure* (1967) by Peter BLAU and Otis Duncan, which distinguished seventeen occupational categories and examined intergenerational mobility between fathers and sons. They found evidence of a high degree of upward mobility in American society, caused by the expansion of opportunity in higher-level occupations, lower fertility rates among occupants of those positions, and a contraction of opportunity in lower-level occupations. Mobility, for Blau and Duncan, was thus strongly determined by large-scale changes in occupational structures.

Other studies identified different tendencies and obstacles to mobility. David Glass's *Social Mobility in Britain* (1949) found that there was considerable mobility from father's occupation to son's occupation but also a significant barrier between manual and nonmanual occupations. This finding was later generalized by Seymour Martin LIPSET and Reinhard BENDIX in *Social Mobility in Industrial Society* (1959).

The occupational model has been criticized on a variety of grounds. The hierarchy of professions that structures it frequently seems arbitrary—especially among radically different professions that provide similar incomes. Many sociologists have preferred to reformulate notions of class, denoting similar relationships to the labor market, to account for the relatively common occurrence of small intergenerational movements in occupation and the relatively rare instances of dramatic changes in status. Goldthorpe's work is influential in this regard and has analyzed mobility within classes as well as between them. Feminist critiques of the male-centered bias of occupational sociology have also figured prominently since the 1970s, leading to attempts to reexamine mobility from the perspective of families as well as individuals and women as well as men. Most of the earlier research was restricted to male mobility because men most consistently fit into the occupational categories associated with paid employment.

social movements Collective attempts to bring about or resist social change that emerge and operate mainly outside institutionalized political processes—although they themselves may be highly organized. Concentrated attention to social movements is relatively recent in the social sciences, dating back only to the 1950s. Nonetheless, this research draws on and in many respects differentiates itself from a long and diverse tradition of investigating social change and collective identities—including the pivotal MARXIST tradition with its analysis of class conflict, work on crowd behavior, and studies of mass movements, such as the FRANKFURT SCHOOL's investigations of FASCISM and AUTHORITARIANISM in the 1930s and 1940s. The term was originally used in the singular by nineteenth-century reformists and socialists in reference the expected convergence of forces for social change.

Social movements can be narrow in scope, targeting particular social issues such as drunk driving or electoral reform, or they can reflect major social divisions within society, such as the labor, civil rights, and women's movements. In both cases, they generally emerge around issues that institutionalized political processes have failed to adequately address. Social movements often operate in an uneasy dialectic with institutionalized political processes. In most democratic societies, they are primarily reformist in nature, seeking recognition by and integration into institutional politics. Many social scientists treat this as a fundamental feature of democratic politics—part of the formation and recognition of new needs and social goals. Where institutions are too rigid or too tied to narrow social interests or, alternatively, where demands are too sweeping to be accommodated by existing political institutions, social movements can become radicalized and revolutionary. Marxist revolutionary theory was predicated on the radicalizing effect of ostensibly unassimilable social contradictions, especially the impoverishment of a growing portion of society under the industrial system.

The modern sociology of social movements has devoted considerable energy to understanding how such movements emerge and develop. The wide historical variations in social movements—including the veritable explosion of such activity in the 1960s—led to a number of relatively distinct theories of social-movement formation. One strong school of thought, prevalent in the 1950s and much of the 1960s, integrated theories of MASS SOCIETY, STATUS INCONSISTENCY, relative DEPRIVATION, and COLLECTIVE BEHAVIOR to explore the notion that "structural social pathologies" cause disruptive psychological states (such as ALIENATION) that prompt organization among the affected sectors of the population. Neil SMELSER's *Theory of Collective Behavior* (1963) is a celebrated example of this type. James Davies's account of the explosive potential of rising expectations and reversals of fortune is another, based on a broad historical and comparative account of social unrest.

Critics of deprivation-based or structural-conflict theories of social movements argue that such factors are inadequate in and of themselves. There are many examples of deprivation, inequality, and discontent in society that produce no organized social movements. These critics have pointed to the need for *resource mobilization* on the part of disaffected groups—including tangible assets such as money and access to mass communication, human skills such as leadership, and other factors such as the degree of interpersonal connection between the potential members. Doug McAdam, John McCarthy, Mayer Zald, and Charles TILLY are among the major advocates of such models. A closely related theory, associated especially with Sidney Tarrow, argues that structures of political opportunity determine the incidence of movement activity. In this context, the *absence* of repression and the pursuit of new allies by existing parties are important factors.

Social movements and theories about social movements have to contend with the well-known *free-rider problem*, which describes the fact that individuals may not take part in risky social action if they believe they can benefit from it without participating (see FREE RIDERS). In his classic study, *The Logic of Collective Action* (1965), Mancur OLSON proposes that movements succeed in part by offering members selective incentives beyond the goals of the movement itself, such as the satisfactions of group solidarity or participation in festive public events. A large body of recent research has explored this question, partly in order to tackle the theoretical problems of group integration and free riders and partly to explain certain apparently new features of recent social movements. This identity-oriented scholarship emerged in the late 1970s and the 1980s, especially in Europe, where it is associated with Alain Touraine and Alberto Melucci—although its main themes have received considerable attention in the United States as well. This research emphasizes that individual participation in collective action is not driven merely by self-interest. Participation is also oriented to achieving solidarity, recognition, and personal expression. These are crucial to a strong sense of personal identity, which needs to be constantly negotiated, constructed, and created in social processes. For individual actors, therefore, the meaning of collective action lies, in large part, in the process of participation itself. Although a range of recent scholarship has questioned the degree to which such investments are in any sense *new*, these themes have become especially important to what many sociologists identify as the *new social movements* (NSMs) that have dominated American and (to a lesser extent) European political culture since the 1960s. These include the organized struggles of ethnic and racial minorities, the women's movement, and more recently the gay-rights movement, to cite only some of the largest. New social movements are sometimes distinguished from the class-based movements of earlier periods in the attention they give to struggles for symbolic resources, such as meaning, recognition, autonomy, and identity. Craig Calhoun and others have argued that the contrast to the mature labor movement of the 1950s is strongest precisely because that movement was no longer new and had become highly institutionalized. Symbolic and identity issues, in this account, are not new to social movements but are distinctive of all social movements during their early phases. In addition, some earlier periods show movement forms and concerns similar to those that emerged in the 1960s—and that similarly contrast with the heyday of class movements and organized labor.

social networks See NETWORK ANALYSIS.

social organization A general term for all patterns of relationship and structures in social life, especially when seen in macrosociological perspective, or as phenomena independent of psychology. It is also one of the three areas into which mid-twentieth-century SOCIOLOGY was often (if arbitrarily) divided, along with SOCIAL PSYCHOLOGY and demography. See also SOCIAL STRUCTURE; and SOCIETY.

social psychology As a discipline, social psychology is largely an American phenomenon, with roots in the study of the ATTITUDES and processes of SOCIALIZATION of immigrants who arrived in the early twentieth century. It was only in the 1930s that the field acquired institutional legitimacy and coherence around a set of experimental principles. This process was greatly boosted by the arrival of a wave of European psychologists fleeing Germany and World War II. German psychologist Kurt LEWIN, a pioneer in the area of personality research and experimental methods, became something of a founding figure of American social psychology. With other experimental psychologists, such as F. W. Allport, Gordon ALLPORT, and Leon Festinger, the field consolidated around the principles of BEHAVIORISM, which studied changes in attitudes or behavior in the face of experimental manipulation. This emphasis on the plasticity of individual psychology and the reliability of laboratory experimentation—visible, for example, in Stanley MILGRAM's famous studies of AUTHORITY—continues to represent the mainstream of social-psychological research.

There is also, however, a more sociological tradition of social psychology that eschews laboratory methods in favor of fieldwork and survey-based research. This lineage includes the pioneering work of Erving GOFFMAN, George Herbert MEAD, and George HOMANS, as well as the FRANKFURT SCHOOL synthesis of MARXISM and PSYCHOANALYSIS undertaken by Erich FROMM, Paul LAZARSFELD, Theodor ADORNO, and others—another product of German exile to the United States. Much of this work moved beyond the methodological individualism of the experimental tradition toward the problem of larger dynamics of social behavior at the level of groups and organizations. Postwar European social psychology retains a much stronger interest in this area of research than its American counterpart.

From the 1930s through the 1960s, much of the work of both traditions was orientated toward examining the psychological bases of democratic and totalitarian societies. Recent research displays a greater distance from these concerns, as well as the rapid development of cognitive science. As in other fields, the experimental methods of social psychology have been the subject of much debate in recent years. The laboratory has come to be understood as less a replica of the social world than an extension of it—complicating claims to generalization. The false pretenses that structure much social psychological experimentation on human subjects have also come under fire. As in other fields, the best work has integrated these critiques.

social referencing In psychological studies, social referencing refers to an individual's ability to decide how to respond to ambiguous situations through the recognition of facial expressions.

social-resources theory A theory of status attainment that combines social exchange theory and NETWORK ANALYSIS. It builds on the assumption that social resources, both material and symbolic, can be accessed and used to attain instrumental goals, such as finding a job. As formulated by Nan Lin ("Social Resources and Instrumental Action," 1982), the theory correlates a number of variables regarding resources, starting position, and social ties with outcomes. See also STATUS-ATTAINMENT THEORY.

social stratification See STRATIFICATION.

social structure The most basic, enduring, and determinative patterns in social life. SOCIOLOGY and ANTHROPOLOGY are broadly oriented by the goal of understanding systematic relationships and regularities among social phenomena—indeed their history is in no small part the history of methods and developments in the study of such structures. The concern for structures is, however, sometimes distinguished from concern for process or action, and is thus not necessarily equivalent to the whole concern of either discipline. Moreover, there are important differences between those who privilege cultural factors and those who privilege more material factors in their accounts of social structure.

One of the earliest and most comprehensive accounts of social structure was furnished by MARXISM, which related the diverse arenas of political, cultural, and religious life to an underlying economic structure, or MODE OF PRODUCTION. The economic base substantially determined the cultural and political superstructure, Karl MARX argued, and revolutionary change became possible as social contradictions in the economic base grew more intense. This was the logic of CLASS STRUGGLE. Subsequent Marxist accounts, such as Louis ALTHUSSER's, provided a more complex account of this relationship that asserted the RELATIVE AUTONOMY of cultural and political institutions, and only a general determination "in the last instance" by economic factors.

Emile DURKHEIM, drawing on the analogies between biological and social systems popularized by Herbert SPENCER and others, introduced what would become perhaps the most widespread means of understanding and analyzing social structure in the social sciences. For Durkheim, the common denominator among diverse social institutions and practices was their role in assuring the *functional integration* of society—the assimilation of diverse parts into a unified and self-reproducing whole. FUNCTIONALISM, following Durkheim, became the dominant paradigm of anthropological and sociological research in the early to mid-twentieth century. Here the basic structure of a society was conceived as a pattern of differentiation into parts or subsystems. In this context, Durkheim distinguished two forms of structural relationship: MECHANICAL SOLIDARITY and ORGANIC SOLIDARITY. The former describes structures that unite similar parts through a shared culture; the latter describes differentiated parts united through exchange and material interdependence.

Durkheim's heirs in anthropology developed the analysis of social structure beyond this simple distinction by studying relatively stable and apparently basic patterns in social relations. KINSHIP, for example, was analyzed in terms of both the creation of corporate groups through descent and the formation of alliances through marriage. While the functional perspective remained influential, increasing attention was paid to structural analysis in its own right, and especially to the varying forms of structure revealed by research into different societies. *Structural functionalism* became a term for research that distinguished inquiry into structures of social organization from inquiry into their purposes or possible functional integration. In British anthropology, this became the dominant approach following the work of A. R. RADCLIFFE-BROWN. In sociology, it is associated with Robert K. MERTON and his students, in contrast to the attempts at a grand functionalist synthesis by Talcott PARSONS.

A further distinction within studies of social structure developed between those who emphasized the abstract or ideal forms of organization and those who focused on actually existing patterns. Radcliffe-Brown contrasted structural form and social structure in this context; Raymond William FIRTH distinguished social structure from SOCIAL ORGANIZATION, meaning much the same thing. The terminological confusion reflected a debate about the extent to which abstract forms did or did not shape actual patterns of relationships. This has been a persistent concern in studies of social structure. In the 1960s, it was manifested in an anthropological argument over the question of whether social structure involved *models of* actual relations or *models for* such relations—and, relatedly, whether social structure was mainly in the heads of social scientists

or of those studied. British social anthropology focused especially on concrete patterns of relationships, while French anthropology took a more formal tack, especially under the influence of Claude LÉVI-STRAUSS's STRUCTURALISM. American anthropology, meanwhile, contributed a tradition of systematic comparative analysis closer to the French in its emphasis on cultural form but attempting more concrete and even quantitative analysis of variations. The work of George P. Murdock was pivotal, especially with the creation of the Human Relations Area Files at Yale University (1949) and the Ethnographic Atlas (1962). This linked anthropology to a tradition of comparative sociology, including both evolutionists like Spencer and opponents of evolutionism like Pitirim SOROKIN, and including more recent figures such as Michael Mann, who has studied the structural forms of power relations and the historical order in which those forms appear.

Contemporary theorists of social structure continue to mean different things by the term. Some follow Marx in trying to identify basic dimensions of social organization that explain the other dimensions. Although they may disagree about what those dimensions are, most emphasize either economic production or political power. Others follow Lévi-Strauss in seeking logical order in cultural structures. Still others, notably Peter BLAU, follow Georg SIMMEL in attempting to base a formal theory of social structure on numerical patterns in relationships—analyzing, for example, the ways in which factors like group size shape intergroup relations. Perhaps the most influential approach in sociology is NETWORK ANALYSIS. Rooted in British social anthropology, network analysis has also been influenced by Lévi-Strauss's structuralism; it attempts to combine attention to form and concrete actuality, often by using computer algorithms to search for patterns in concrete relations. One key insight offered by Harrison White is that patterns are often identified not only with existing connections, but also with the absence of possible connections; this means that simple empirical induction from concrete relationships can never yield a full picture of social structure. Also important was the anthropologist Siegfried Frederick NADEL's distinction of *category* (or grouping on the basis of similar attributes) from *network* (or grouping on the basis of social connections). This in turn led back to Durkheim and to the distinction in kinship studies between CLANS and their components—LINEAGE and marital alliances.

Strong programs of structural analysis (like White's network theory) sometimes seek to include questions of process and agency within the realm of structure. Others see these as complimentary concerns or as bases for opposing perspectives. There is considerable debate over whether it is possible to integrate structural and action-oriented analysis in a single theoretical perspective and, if so, which dimension (if either) should have priority. This has given rise to a long-running structure-agency debate over the relative autonomy of individual action, the extent to which structures are creations of such action, and the question of whether either the "objectivist" perspective associated with structuralism or the "subjectivist" perspective associated with action research are adequate. The most influential attempts to combine structure and agency are Anthony GIDDENS's theory of STRUCTURATION and Pierre BOURDIEU's practice theory. Giddens emphasizes the duality of structure and agency, in the sense that structures and agency cannot be conceived apart from one another. This permits him to argue that structures are neither independent of actors nor determining of their behavior, but rather sets of rules and competencies on which actors draw, and which, in the aggregate, they reproduce. Giddens's analysis, in this respect, closely parallels Jacques DERRIDA's DECONSTRUCTION of the binaries that underlie classic sociological and anthropological reasoning—notably the universalizing tendencies of Lévi-Strauss's structuralism.

Bourdieu's practice theory also seeks a more supple account of structure as embedded in, rather than determinative of, individual behavior. The key concept in his account is that of HABITUS—a system of general, generative schemes that are both durable and transposable, function unconsciously, and take place within a structured space of possibilities. Within the habitus, individuals improvise—they excel or fail and conform or deviate, depending on factors that cohere (and are reproduced) in the aggregate but not in the particular.

social welfare The well-being of society or the community at large. In economic terms, social welfare is an aggregation of the welfare or utility of the individual members of the society. See also UTILITY; and UTILITY FUNCTION.

social-welfare function A mathematical representation of society's well-being, incorporating all variables that affect welfare. The first social-welfare function was proposed by Jeremy BENTHAM and consisted simply of the sum of individual welfares. This model assumed that *utility* (the economic term for well-being) was *cardinal* (or quantifiable) and that it was therefore possible to compare utility between individuals (see CARDINAL AND ORDINAL UTILITY). Interpersonal comparisons of utility, however, proved extremely difficult to establish and constituted a major weakness of the Benthamite model.

This criticism led to a reformulation of the social-welfare function on the basis of *ordinal* utilities, where only the individual *ranking* of different social preferences is relevant—there is no pretense of quantification. The concepts of Pareto optimality and optimal resource allocation were applied to this context, but the strict Pareto condition that no one be made worse off posed major obstacles for economic policy, which almost always makes some individuals better off at a cost to others.

Two general attempts were made to circumvent these difficulties. The first suggested that a valid criterion for decision making might be the willingness of gainers to compensate losers—the principle of *compensation tests*. If the monetary value to the winners is greater than the monetary cost to the losers, then, in principle, winners can pay losers and still create a Pareto improvement. The second was the introduction of the Bergson–Samuelson social-welfare function, which stated that unanimous individual preferences for a particular social state could be taken as the corresponding social (collective) preference for that state. These preferences, it was argued, could be represented as real values in a larger welfare function. The well-known ARROW'S IMPOSSIBILITY THEOREM, however, established that the construction of a social preference ordering from individual preferences was impossible if the social ordering was to satisfy the Pareto criterion—a condition still stipulated by Bergson–Samuelson.

society Used to describe both the general phenomenon of social life and the specific units into which social life is organized. Thus, all human beings live in society—their lives are social and involve relationships to others. At the same time, a person may be said to be a member of one society and not another. In the latter sense, the idea of a society takes on notions of boundedness, cultural distinctiveness, and often self-sufficiency. These are at best relative, however, and may be misleading. Thus, Charles

TILLY has criticized this notion of a bounded, internally integrated and externally discrete society as one of social science's "pernicious postulates"; in its origins and persistence, it reflects the prominence of NATIONALISM as a way of understanding human identity and the NATION-STATE as a basic organizational unit of modern life. Research comparing "societies" thus often actually compares data on different states (territories and populations organized under a common government). In practice, how close-knit, culturally similar, or economically autonomous the people of any one state are is subject to empirical variation. The ideal of the nation-state suggests both a distinction and a one-to-one match: the nation is the society distinct from the state, but properly matched to it. This usage informs the idea of "the people" implied in democratic self-government. It signifies a social sphere distinct from the political institution of the state.

Society contrasted to the state is commonly known as *civil society*, yet this is a recent distinction formed in the seventeenth and eighteenth century. Prior to this separation, there was no firm distinction between political and social realms. The ancient Greek conception of the *polis*, for example, clearly referred to both, and ARISTOTLE's description of man as a *zoon politicon* did not mean a narrowly "political animal" in the modern sense, but more generally a "social animal." It was only in the course of early modern reflection on the origins of the social order and the nature of the state—quintessentially in the writings of John LOCKE, Thomas Paine, Adam SMITH, and Adam Ferguson—that civil society came to be seen as a sphere distinct from the state that needed to be defended against possible encroachments. This drew on older roots, including the freedoms claimed by medieval cities and the distinction of civil law from criminal law (in which civil law governs relations formed voluntarily among individuals and criminal law the claims of the whole society against malefactors). The crucial innovation of the Early Modern era was to understand society as at least potentially self-organizing, rather than organized only by rulers. This was exemplified by the market but not limited to it. It formed one basis for understanding society as a distinct object of analysis, not reducible to either state or individual. People formed society impersonally, as actors in markets, and more personally as parties to contracts. The idea of

civil society also suggested that communication among members might be the basis for self-conscious decisions about how to pursue the public good. See PUBLIC SPHERE; and PRIVATE SPHERE.

Similar ideas were taken up by Auguste COMTE and Herbert SPENCER as they sought to establish SOCIOLOGY as a separate science in the mid-nineteenth century. Comte and Spencer insisted that society was not the sum of individuals but a distinctive entity that transcended the individual members. This conception of society was developed systematically by Emile DURKHEIM, who emphasized society's objective existence external to individuals and frequently constraining on them. Society, as such, came to be seen as an entity in its own right, independent of the actions of the individuals that composed it. This tension between society and the individual has been a central methodological and perspectival problem for sociology ever since Durkheim.

One more terminological opposition has been formative for the idea of society: the contrast of society to COMMUNITY (understood as structured by personal, face-to-face, close-knit relations and shaped by TRADITION). This contrast describes society as the realm of large-scale social integration, impersonally joining strangers to one another, allowing greater individual autonomy, and relying on rational choice and contract. Ferdinand TÖNNIES famously articulated this contrast with the terms *GEMEINSCHAFT AND GESELLSCHAFT* ("community" and "society," respectively, although *gesellschaft* is sometimes translated as "association"); Tönnies saw the latter as superseding the former, but others would suggest that the two coexist as distinct forms of social integration.

sociobiology A field of study that uses biological methods to understand social life and that often asserts the biological determination of social patterns. Attempts to determine how much behavior is learned and how much is biologically determined have a long history in the social sciences and a long association with evolutionary theory (see EVOLUTION AND EVOLUTIONISM; and ETHNOLOGY). At its most general, this is often called the NATURE VERSUS NURTURE DEBATE. The term *sociobiology*, first coined in E. O. Wilson's book of that name (1975), recapitulates many of these interests. Sociobiologists attempt to account for social behavior and norms (for example, the INCEST TABOO or cross-cousin marriage) in evolutionary terms—as the product of processes of natural selection and survival of the fittest. What counts as "selection" and "fitness" in the context of relatively abstract or symbolic social behavior has been the subject of considerable debate, but the general framework of Darwinian science provides the field its operating assumptions and strongly functionalist orientation. Sociobiology is sometimes extended to include all analysis of direct genetic determination of human social behavior or organization. A strong objection to sociobiology has come from anthropologists such as Marshall SAHLINS, who argue that biological causality is too general to explain the diversity and normative functions of culture. See also FUNCTIONALISM; and PHYSICAL ANTHROPOLOGY.

sociolinguistics The study of how linguistic variation correlates with CLASS, RACE, GENDER, or other significant divisions within a community. The term is used to describe a range of techniques in linguistic, ethnomethodological, and conversation analysis that emerged in the 1950s. More recent versions by John Gumperz (1982) and others have tended to emphasize the ways that social inequality produces or authorizes different kinds of speech in specific situations. The term DISCOURSE ANALYSIS is often used to describe this broad turn toward the linguistic analysis of power relations. See also ETHNOMETHODOLOGY; and LINGUISTICS.

sociological imagination From C. Wright MILLS's book of that name (1959), the sociological imagination refers to the ability to see past the surface of isolated personal experiences and perceive the underlying social issues. For Mills, it was the essential sociological talent—the ability to see connections and patterns.

sociology The scientific study of SOCIETY, including patterns of social relationships, social action, and culture. The term *sociology* was first used by Auguste COMTE in the 1830s to propose a synthetic science that would unite all knowledge about human activity. While few contemporary sociologists are fully Comtean in their ambitions, the discipline remains broad, seeking to relate different aspects of social life and overlapping with other social and behavioral sciences.

Sociology developed initially in response to social changes in early modern Europe. Most important were the growth of states, exploration and colonization, and the industrial revolution. Each of these created demands for knowledge about social organization. States used censuses, new statistical techniques, and other kinds of sociological research to gather better data about their populations, develop improved administrative operations, and even motivate citizens in times of war. Colonial powers drew on sociology (and, even more, on its close relative ANTHROPOLOGY) in their administrative work. Capitalist firms sought better knowledge of markets and consumer tastes and also information about how to organize and motivate employees. At the same time that powerful elites drew on the new discipline of sociology, sociologists were driven by their own curiosities and concerns to develop deeper understanding of the nature of modern society. Some privileged inquiry into forms of state rule; others examined the processes and conditions of social change, including revolution. New knowledge of the diversity of human cultures and social organizations challenged European sociologists to see their own societies as embodying only some of the many possibilities for human life and to study the patterns that differentiated these possibilities. Perhaps most importantly, the rise of large-scale markets, capitalist enterprises, and industrial organization based on ever-improving technologies transformed everyday social life in Europe and eventually in all the world. Sociologists took up the study of factories, business organizations, and other changes that accompanied industrial revolution: urbanization, migration, new patterns of inequality, and new family structures.

These changes were sometimes summed up in the notion of a transition from traditional to modern society. How did the emerging social order of NATION-STATES and CAPITALISM differ from feudal society in Europe (see FEUDALISM), and how did European culture and society differ from those of the rest of the world? How did expectations of continuing change—and indeed, progress—come to be institutionalized? Could growth—of populations, wealth, or knowledge—continue indefinitely? What were the implications of increasing individual freedom of choice? In taking up questions like the last, sociologists sought to make a more empirical science of issues that had long animated philosophies of history. Especially since the Protestant Reformation, scholars had recognized the growth of INDIVIDUALISM and debated its implications.

While psychology grew in part as a reflection of the concern for individuals as such, sociology sought to examine the social sources that shaped individual life. The two were joined in SOCIAL PSYCHOLOGY—including studies of the way individual psychology and social relations interacted in the formation of groups. Like all the social and behavioral sciences, both were also influenced by the secularization that accompanied individualism—understanding of the human world as a product of human action.

Sociology shares common seventeenth- and eighteenth-century roots with ECONOMICS and POLITICAL SCIENCE. While economics came increasingly to focus on the self-regulating characteristics of markets (and on the modeling of individual choices), sociology emphasized the specific institutional forms that organized not only economic life but all of society. Likewise, political science specialized in the understanding of states and their domestic and international power, while sociology focused more on the patterns of social organization and social change within states—or across state boundaries. Disciplinary boundaries were still minimal in the nineteenth century, when, for example, the evolutionary theorist Herbert SPENCER was a leader in contemporary biological, psychological, economic, and political science as well as a founder of sociology. He coined the phrase "survival of the fittest," which was immediately applied to both biological evolution and market competition. Likewise, Karl MARX worked simultaneously on what we would now call sociology, political science, and economics. Indeed, his theory of capitalism showed the limits of efforts to fully separate the three perspectives, since social relations, power structures, and economic exchanges always influence each other.

Nonetheless, each of the social sciences took on an increasingly distinct disciplinary character during the late nineteenth and early twentieth centuries. Journals and university departments devoted specifically to sociology began to proliferate in the 1890s. The most influential sociologists of this period were Emile DURKHEIM in France, Max WEBER in Germany, and a group known as the "Chicago school" in the United States, including Albion Small, Robert Ezra PARK, and George Herbert MEAD (see CHICAGO SCHOOL OF SOCIOLOGY). In each of these countries, as well as in Britain (and soon after in Italy and elsewhere), degree programs and research training specifically in sociology began to be institutionalized.

The end of the nineteenth and beginning of the twentieth centuries was also the occasion for an influential conflict over the relationship between "natural" and "cultural" sciences. Known as the *METHODENSTREIT* because its German version was especially prominent, this debate pitted those who thought that "objective" natural science methods could handle all aspects of human behavior research against those who thought that "interpretative" methods were needed to deal with CULTURE and meaningful human action. While some disciplines fit more or less clearly on one side or the other, sociology was distinctively split by this debate and remains a field in which "objectivistic" and "interpretative" methods are both prominent. Although their positions are complex and difficult to categorize, Durkheim has been taken as a key defender of "objectivistic" sociology, linked to the natural sciences, and Weber and Mead as advocates for a more "interpretative" sociology with ties to the humanities as well as the sciences.

During the twentieth century, sociology spread throughout the world, developing some distinctive features in different national and regional settings. Latin Americans, for example, were especially active in bringing sociology to bear in research on DEVELOPMENT and underdevelopment (see, for example, Fernando HENRIQUE CARDOSO). East Europeans did pioneering work on the social psychology of class relations and on the relations between state and civil society. American research was more often quantitative than its British counterparts, and less influenced by philosophy than the French.

During the third quarter of the twentieth century, the functionalist perspective became a dominant orientation in American sociology, primarily through the work of Talcott PARSONS, Robert K. MERTON (under the name of *structural functionalism*), and their followers. By the 1970s, Parsonian FUNCTIONALISM had been widely rejected, although its approach to information and processes of feedback received renewed attention in contemporary SYSTEM(S) THEORY. Various approaches to interpretive sociology have always been prominent, SYMBOLIC INTERACTIONISM perhaps most so. Marx's work received renewed attention when functionalism came under attack; it shaped such new orientations as WORLD-SYSTEMS THEORY. Critical social theory, also influenced by Marx as well as by Weber and Sigmund FREUD, became prominent in the mid-twentieth-century work of the FRANKFURT SCHOOL and, more recently, in that of Jürgen HABERMAS and other inheritors of this tradition. Microeconomics informed the development of RATIONAL-CHOICE THEORY, which applied economic models of maximizing behavior to social phenomena and introduced more sociological analysis into economic reasoning.

Contemporary sociology has also been subdivided into a wide range of specialized fields of research and theory, including interpersonal relations, marriage and the family, SOCIAL MOVEMENTS, GENDER, economic sociology, formal organizations, professions, health, STRATIFICATION and inequality, RACE and ETHNICITY, and dozens more (the American Sociological Association has more than forty sections devoted to different subfields). It includes community studies, international comparisons, and studies of globalization and the world system. Sociology is equally heterogeneous with regard to research methods, which include CENSUSes, surveys, analyses of secondary data sources (those collected for other purposes), ETHNOGRAPHY, interviews, textual analyses, historical research, and experiments. Likewise, sociological theory still shows the imprint of such founding figures as Marx, Weber, and Durkheim; of renewed interest in other early sociologists like Georg SIMMEL and Marcel MAUSS; and of continued innovation.

The high level of internal differentiation of sociology makes it a hard field to summarize and makes the formation of intellectual consensus difficult. At the same time, it provides openings for a wide variety of analytic approaches and for creative interdisciplinary relationships. Sociology has been unusually open to first-generation scientists and intellectuals drawn from historically dominated groups—workers, ethnic minorities, women. Each of these has broadened the sociological perspective and kept it from simply representing one dominant WORLDVIEW. Sociology is recurrently shaped by efforts to make it more scientific, more practical, or more theoretical. Each of these tendencies is influential, but sociology remains enduringly a discipline in which relations are forged between natural science and humanistic concerns, practical engagements and an abstract desire for knowledge, theory, and research.

soft currency   National currency that is exchanged only with difficulty. Soft-currency countries typically have minimal exchange reserves and BALANCE OF PAYMENTS deficits. Generally, these currencies are not held as foreign reserves by other countries. This is in contrast to hard currencies, which may be exchanged for other currencies without restriction and are universally acceptable in international transactions. The U.S. dollar is an example of a hard currency.

solidarity   Describes the cohesion of individuals within social groups—literally, the extent to which groups are "solid." The study of solidarity is often associated with Emile DURKHEIM, who distinguished in *The Division of Labor in Society* (1893 [1964]) between two types: mechanical and organic solidarity. MECHANICAL SOLIDARITY is characteristic of the relatively undifferentiated social structures of premodern societies, where members were bound together by shared values, beliefs, and customs, and were generally engaged in the same activities. ORGANIC SOLIDARITY is more characteristic of modern, industrial societies, where people are bound together by a high degree of functional interdependence based on a complex division of labor. The sociologist Talcott PARSONS influentially expanded Durkheim's account, emphasizing the role that normative consensus plays in creating solidarity.

Group solidarity and the diverse factors that impact it continue to be a common subject of both empirical and theoretical work in SOCIOLOGY. The idea of solidarity need not imply harmony, although it is sometimes used that way (especially following Parsons). It does imply social integration and is sometimes simply subsumed under that term.

Solow, Robert   (1924–) An economist known mainly for his model of growth in the neoclassical context of full employment and for his contributions to capital theory. Solow was educated at Harvard University and teaches at the Massachusetts Institute of Technology. He received the Nobel Prize in Economics in 1987.

Although he has researched and published in a number of areas, his largest contributions are generally considered to be "A Contribution to the Theory of Growth" (1956) and "Technical

Change and the Aggregate Production Function'' (1957). In the 1956 paper, he postulated a theory of growth that is considered the first neoclassical version of the classic Harrod–Domar model. In this model, capital and labor substitute for each other in production, thus leading to the possibility of a growth path where both factors are fully employed. It has been criticized insofar as it takes growth to be essentially an exogenous phenomenon—rising either with increases in the exogenously given savings rate or with improvements in technology. The 1957 paper marked the birth of *growth accounting*, the study of how much each factor of production contributes to growth in an accounting sense. The difference between the actual growth rate and the sum of growth attributable to labor and capital must, by definition, be due to improvements in technology. This is termed the *Solow residual*. This paper led to a number of estimates of the production function that seek to determine the role of technology in growth. Both papers have become classics and serve as benchmarks in GROWTH THEORY.

Solow later discussed the capital embodiment hypothesis and, in particular, the role of vintage capital, or the significance of different generations of machines at work at the same time. Technical change is said to be embodied in capital if it takes the form of new machines, which suggests that technical change and capital are not independent sources of growth. In other words, technical progress is impossible without investment in new capital. This represented a break, in certain respects, with his earlier conclusions and inspired a large literature on vintage capital. Solow also analyzed how the rate of return on capital is determined. In *Capital Theory and the Rate of Return* (1963), he argued that this is the most important question in capital theory—allying himself in this regard with Paul SAMUELSON against Joan ROBINSON and Nicholas KALDOR in the "Cambridge" debates about growth. Solow remains a spirited contributor to macroeconomic literature, including commentary on new growth theory, which rejects many of the premises of his own work.

Sorokin, Pitirim (1889–1968) A Russian-born sociologist who pioneered the study of SOCIAL MOBILITY and later developed a broadly synthetic and typological approach to the study of CULTURE, which he called *integralism*.

In Russia, Sorokin had been a politically active Menshevik and participant in the Provisional Russian Government prior to the October Revolution. He had frequent troubles with Tsarist and later Communist officials, and in 1922 was forced into exile—ultimately to the United States. In 1930, he became the chair of the newly established Harvard University Department of Sociology and later directed the Harvard Research Center in Creative Altruism. There he played a major institutional role in mid-twentieth-century American sociology.

Sorokin was an encyclopedic intellectual and a prolific writer. Counting his years in Russia, he wrote some thirty-five books on a wide range of subjects, including art, agriculture, penology, American–Soviet relations, work, and social STRATIFICATION. This diversity reflected Sorokin's belief that the study of societies could not be reduced to narrow topics or methodologies. His most influential work is *Social Mobility* (1927), in which he studied the "vertical channels" of movement within society that allowed it to allocate talent efficiently. Unlike some later functionalist accounts of SOCIAL MOBILITY and structures of reward, however, he recognized the advantages that social stratification accorded the successful in perpetuating and transmitting their positions.

The four-volume *Social and Cultural Dynamics* (1937–1941) is Sorokin's major attempt to synthesize and historicize his diverse interests into a broad theory of culture. Here he distinguished between ideational, sensate, and idealistic cultures—the first organized by spiritual principles, the second by materialist, tangible goals, and the third integrating elements of both. Sorokin saw Western modernity as the long progress and ultimately destructive undoing of sensate culture, as materialism became increasingly alienating and hostile to spiritual qualities. His hopes for the future rested on the emergence of an idealistic culture (akin to fifth-century B.C.E. Athens) that balanced both. Sorokin's other works include *The Sociology of Revolution* (1925), in which he analyzed the Russian Revolution, *Contemporary Sociological Theory* (1928), *Rural Sociology* (1930), *Fads and Foibles in Modern Sociology and Related Sciences* (1956), and *Sociological Theories of Today* (1966).

sororate A custom that dictates that upon the death of a wife, the husband marries the wife's sister. Sororate marriage is relatively common in African tribal societies.

sovereignty Final and absolute authority within a political community—originally ascribed to the king, and now more generally to the STATE or to the citizens (*popular sovereignty*). Although Roman law developed a concept of the sovereign power of the emperor, modern Western reflections on sovereignty emerged only as the religious structure of worldly authority began to crumble during the Renaissance. The first modern account of sovereignty is usually credited to the sixteenth-century French political philosopher Jean BODIN, who argued that all political communities need a single, final, and legitimate source of power, whether located in the king, the ARISTOCRACY, or the people. The classic social contract tradition of Thomas HOBBES, John LOCKE, and Jean-Jacques ROUSSEAU is the core of the sovereignty tradition in Western political thought (see SOCIAL-CONTRACT THEORY). Hobbes and Rousseau are often contrasted as the theorists of state sovereignty and popular sovereignty, respectively; Locke offered perhaps the most influential account in treating the state as constituted by a loan of authority from the inalienably sovereign people, contingent on its faithfulness to the people's interests.

Such accounts are concerned primarily with the question of internal sovereignty. For Hobbes and others there was also a fundamental need for *external* sovereignty, or formal independence in the conduct of international affairs. External sovereignty describes the autonomy of the state to act and pursue its interests within the interstate system, which has historically lacked a sovereign authority of its own. While all states are nominally equal with regard to their sovereign status, real power is unevenly distributed. Security, for example, is usually a collective concern—the product of alliances and coalitions. Differences in size, population, resources, and government create disparities in the power of states to act. Recent trends toward economic and political interdependence on the international level have undermined sovereignty in some respects—a subject of special interest to research on GLOBALIZATION. Perhaps the most impressive example of such a process is the European Union, in which individual member states have surrendered an array of traditional sovereign powers to a nascent international government, including control over monetary policy and some control over borders and labor laws.

The proliferation of human rights covenants and the deepening of international legal norms have also led to questions about the practical limits of internal sovereignty. While these changes may signal a shift in the quality and status of sovereignty, the concept is far from anachronistic and continues to structure contemporary politics within, among, and between states. See also ANARCHY AND ANARCHISM; and INTERNATIONAL LAW.

spatial analysis   To a degree, a subject coterminous with modern geography, reflecting a change in the emphasis of geographical study from descriptive accounts of differences between areas (a subject known as AREAL DIFFERENTIATION) to accounts of regularities in the spatial distribution of economic activity, populations, land use, and other dimensions of human activity. Although the beginnings of this disciplinary transition are visible in Richard Hartshorne's seminal work of the late 1930s and, more generally, in the variety of zonal theories of urban and agricultural land use developed since Johann von Thünen's concentric-ring theory of the 1820s, the boom period in spatial analysis and related questions of LOCATION THEORY was the 1950s and 1960s. See also VON THÜNEN MODEL.

specie-flow mechanism   A financial tool designed to eliminate deficits or surpluses in the BALANCE OF PAYMENTS through induced flows of gold, or specie. The classic exposition of this mechanism was David HUME's simple application of the quantity theory of money to an international trade setting in his 1752 essay, "Of the Balance of Trade." According to Hume, a fall in a country's money stock leads to a fall in domestic prices, which makes its goods cheaper relative to the goods of other countries. This country's imports then fall and exports increase, leading to a favorable trade balance. As gold flows into the country to finance this trade balance, prices in this country rise until the international price differences and trade imbalances are eliminated. In EQUILIBRIUM, the distribution of gold among countries yields price levels consistent with equilibrium in the balance of trade. This conclusion, that trade imbalances are eventually eliminated through the flow of specie, contrasted with the mercantilist position that stipulated the persistent promotion of export surpluses and the indefinite accumulation of gold. The specie-flow mechanism was posited in terms of changes in price levels; subsequently, exact conditions were established that are sufficient to ensure that the gold flow and the concomitant price changes do in fact equilibrate the balance of trade. This is known as the *Marshall–Lerner condition*, which holds that given initially balanced trade and infinite supply elasticities, the sum of the elasticity of demand for a country's exports plus its elasticity of demand for imports will be greater than one. If this condition holds, then price changes will establish a trade balance.

speech-accommodation theory Also known as *communication-accommodation theory*. First developed by Howard Giles and Nikolas Coupland in *Language: Contexts and Consequences* (1991), this psycholinguistic theory analyzes the ways in which individuals in social interactions converge or diverge with respect to their forms or styles of speech. It suggests that speakers are motivated under certain circumstances to adjust their speech styles in order to fulfill identity expectations. *Convergence* is defined as "a strategy whereby individuals adapt to each other's communicative behaviors in terms of a wide range of linguistic/prosodic/nonvocal features including speech rate, pausal phenomena and utterance length, phonological variants, smiling, gaze, and so on" (Giles and Coupland, 1991: p.35). *Divergence* refers to "the way in which speakers accentuate speech and nonverbal differences between themselves and others" (Giles and Coupland, 1991: p.36). Convergence is seen as expressing a desire for social integration; divergence, as serving the function of promoting social distance. See also SOCIOLINGUISTICS.

speech-act theory A philosophical and linguistic investigation of the *performative* dimension of language. This includes the question of what language accomplishes in ordinary circumstances, such as conferring a new status (through naming) or asserting that something is true. Performative functions are distinct from *semantic* functions, the communication of meaning. Speech-act theory draws on Ludwig WITTGENSTEIN's philosophy of language, and it is closely associated with the work of John Searle and J. L. Austin in the 1960s. It has had a significant impact on Pierre BOURDIEU's theory of practice, Jürgen HABERMAS's theory of COMMUNICATIVE ACTION, Jacques DERRIDA's theory of DECONSTRUCTION, the linguistic anthropology of Dell Hymes, and related subfields of LINGUISTICS. See also PRAGMATICS; and SOCIOLINGUISTICS.

Spencer, Herbert (1820–1903) A British philosopher and scientist who developed a unified theory of biological, psychological, and social evolution. Spencer's ideas were enormously popular (if also frequently misunderstood), and they strongly influenced the emerging social and biological sciences of the nineteenth century.

Based on the observation that organisms grow in complexity in response to their changing environment, Spencer argued that human societies and individuals pursue an analogous path of adaptation to their conditions by differentiating and integrating new functions or specializations. The basis of this process, Spencer held, was the "survival of the fittest" (a phrase that Charles Darwin later borrowed), which referred to the process by which some adaptations prospered while others failed. This theory of differentiation and integration influenced later functionalist approaches to society—initially that of Emile DURKHEIM and especially that of Talcott PARSONS. In the mid-twentieth century, Parsons worked toward a similarly unified theory of functional evolution that encompassed both biological and social development.

Spencer, in his account of social development, argued that nineteenth-century Europe was in a state of transition between a "militarist" and an "industrial" stage of society. Although he is often credited with originating the extreme claims of SOCIAL DARWINISM and the *laissez-faire* vision of government that would give social evolution free rein, Spencer strongly believed that violent competition would become obsolete as the industrial model developed. Industrialism, he argued, implied increasing reliance on cooperation and the coordination of individual efforts. State intervention in the marketplace, he held, only gets in the way of this natural process.

Spencer received no higher education and began his career as a railway engineer. He later worked as a journalist before establishing himself as an independent scholar. Spencer devoted much of his career to his multivolume *System of Synthetic Philosophy* (1862–1896), although his shorter works have generally received more attention. These include *Social Statics* (1850), *The Principles of Psychology* (1855), *First Principles* (1862), *The Study of Sociology* (1873), and *Principles of Sociology* (1874), as well as several works of biology.

spillover A concept employed in neofunctionalist analyses of political integration. According to neofunctionalists, the integration of governmental activities leads to new sets of goals, whose satisfaction requires further integration. Spillover has been used to explain the evolution of the European Union (EU).

spot markets Markets in which commodity or currency contracts are traded for immediate delivery (on the "spot"). In practice, spot contracts are delivered within one or two business days. This is in contrast to *forward markets*, where contracts call for delivery at a future date of a specified amount of the currency or good in question. The prices applicable to spot-market transactions are called spot prices for goods and spot exchange rates for currencies.

Sraffa, Piero (1898–1983) An economist who was one of the earliest and most influential critics of NEOCLASSICAL ECONOMICS—especially in regard to the central role that neoclassicists accorded PERFECT COMPETITION. Sraffa pointed out that in some industries, the unit costs of production can fall as the scale of production increases. This may be the result of economies of scale internal to a firm or caused by the fact that the fixed overhead costs are spread over a larger number of units. Falling costs of production are incompatible with perfect competition because they favor the single largest producer. For this reason, a theory of IMPERFECT COMPETITION was needed.

Sraffa's approach involved breaking down one of the main tenets of perfect competition: the homogeneity of sellers. He noted that in many industries where competitive conditions seem to prevail, some producers enjoy certain MONOPOLY-like privileges. Sraffa linked this to technological issues, which do not always spread evenly or quickly among producers. Nonetheless, he argued that a situation with heterogeneous producers and decreasing costs might result in a determinate equilibrium. This insight was extended by Joan ROBINSON, Edward Chamberlin, and others at the University of Cambridge. A large body of subsequent economic research, especially in the analysis of technology, assumes monopolistic competition of this kind. Sraffa's attention to the need for an alternative to perfect competition eventually led to a methodological revolution within neoclassical economics.

stabilization policy Deliberate changes in government fiscal and monetary policy designed to stabilize the economy, often when INFLATION is very high, debts cannot be repaid, or output is falling sharply. Objectives of stabilization policies

include maintaining economic growth, slowing inflation, recovering equilibrium in the BALANCE OF PAYMENTS, and stabilizing currency values. Usually, such policies have distributional consequences, and often there are trade-offs among objectives. For example, stopping high inflation without causing a recession is notoriously difficult.

stagflation The simultaneous occurrence of accelerating INFLATION, rising UNEMPLOYMENT, and declining productivity growth (stagnation). Until the 1970s, it was widely believed that rates of unemployment and inflation were inversely related—a relationship described by the PHILLIPS CURVE. High rates of unemployment and excess capacity were associated with low rates of wage and price inflation. After 1974, however, rising rates of unemployment were accompanied by accelerating rates of inflation, whence the neologism *stagflation*. Because the traditional Keynesian economics response to inflation—contractionary aggregate demand policies—proved ineffective in this context, a collective revaluation of Keynesian remedies for problems of excess capacity and inflation became necessary. What later became clear is that the oil crises of the 1970s were a *supply shock*, and that attempts to reduce aggregate demand could alleviate inflation only at a further cost to output. Rising oil prices produced a problematic change in the costs of production, one that could be remedied only over time as businesses adopted new technologies (and, in practice, as OPEC lost control of prices).

stalking horse A candidate for public office who acts as a decoy for a potentially stronger, but as yet unannounced candidate. The term was originally used to describe a hunter's use of a horse as camouflage when stalking game.

standard deviation and standard error A statistical measure, *standard deviation* describes the degree of deviation of a set of values in a distribution from the *mean* of those values. In statistical terms, it is calculated by adding up the square of the deviation of each individual value (a total known as the *sum of squares* or SSTO) and dividing by the number of values in order to obtain an average. This is known as the VARIANCE. Where all values are equal, the variance is zero. The standard deviation is obtained by taking the square root of the variance.

The *standard error* is an application of the standard deviation to the problem of measuring the accuracy of a single sample in a data set.

standardization The imposition of uniformity on a good or measure, generally in cases where data or products are unique or produced according to different criteria. This informs the commonplace meaning of the term in reference to industrial production and the emergence of uniform production standards for goods. Standardization has a related meaning in statistical research, where it is often necessary to compare either different sets of data or the frequency of some event of interest across multiple populations. Standardization provides a way of adjusting raw rates to eliminate the influence of distorting factors. Raw rates are generally converted to a common measure, such as a decimal representation, which allows for more direct comparison.

standpoint theory Holds that different individuals or groups in society possess significantly different perspectives (or standpoints) that shape their views of reality. Standpoint theory usually involves claims that some standpoint should be privileged over others, at least for analytic problems. This idea has a long philosophical pedigree dating back to critiques of Enlightenment universalism.

One of the premises of Enlightenment philosophy, articulated by René DESCARTES and others, was that knowledge had to be freed from the constraints and distortions of perspective; truth had to be based on pure reason. For some later philosophers, this implied a "view from nowhere." Such critics argued that all knowledge reflected the position (in space, time, and social relations) of the observer. Karl MARX, for one, assigned a prominent role to economic status in determining forms of thought and selfhood. More particularly, he accorded an analytical privilege to the proletariat based on its subordination—a capacity to grasp the underlying structures of the social order. Georg LUKÁCS famously described this as the standpoint of the proletariat, which he argued enabled insight into processes of social transformation.

Much of the contemporary work in standpoint theory is associated with the feminist scholarship of Dorothy Smith and Sandra Harding—both of whom continue to strongly engage these Marxist concerns (as well as, in Smith's case, the ETHNOMETHODOLOGY of Harold GARFINKEL).

Their work addresses the question of a privileged perspective for subordinated groups, especially women, as well as the practical political question of how to reconcile shared forms of oppression with the diversity of women's experiences—diversity that may not necessarily produce shared understandings of women's condition or shared interests in combating structures of patriarchy. This resistance to the universalizing or biologizing claims of much early feminism represents a significant turn within feminism and feminist theory since the 1980s. It involves the recognition, too, of the advantages of issue-based or coalitional agendas, which may include other groups who experience similar forms of subordination. Much of the work in this area draws on a strong Marxist tradition of ideology critique and demystification, which seeks to unmask forms of consent to the patriarchal social order.

Standpoint theory has its critics. Many of these argue that, at least in its extreme forms, standpoint theory leads to a problematic relativism—an inability to defend a statement as generally true. Many also suggest that any proposed categorical basis for a collective standpoint (for example, women) hides or even represses a plurality of specific perspectives (for example, those of black women, poor women, victims of sexual violence, etc). The claimed unity of the standpoint thus dissolves. Researchers who agree that knowledge is dependent on perspective therefore often seek to minimize this problem by emphasizing intersubjective communication as a way of reaching shared understanding. Jürgen HABERMAS is a notable example. Others accept the inevitability of standpoint but refuse to privilege any in particular (a position sometimes called *perspectivism*).

state Following Max WEBER's influential definition, a set of institutions that possesses a monopoly on rule-making and the legitimate use of force within a bounded territory—powers collectively termed SOVEREIGNTY. Although the term often refers broadly to all institutions of government or rule—ancient and modern—the modern state system is characterized by a number of features that consolidated first in western Europe beginning in the fifteenth century. Initially, this involved the centralization of power and the delineation of political boundaries, as European monarchs gradually defeated or co-opted other sources of power, such as the church and lesser nobility. In place of the fragmented system of feudal rule, with its often-indistinct territorial claims, large, unitary states with extensive control over bounded territories emerged. This process culminated in the highly centralized and increasingly bureaucratized forms of absolute monarchical rule of the seventeenth and eighteenth centuries. Processes of cultural homogenization (especially of language) and regional assimilation also figured prominently, leading to the gradual naturalization of the concept of cultural or ethnic identity and territorial nationhood. Centralized states both fostered and benefited from this homogenization, insofar as it created stronger ties of loyalty and facilitated increasingly complex administrative tasks.

Changes in political thought were closely related to these developments—especially in regard to changing conceptions of legitimate state power. The broad Enlightenment claim that authority should be subject to reason undermined the doctrine of divine rule and gradually relocated sovereignty from the monarch to the people. Much of this trajectory is visible in the classic social contract tradition—beginning with Thomas HOBBES's absolutist theory of monarchy and in a sense culminating with Jean-Jacques ROUSSEAU's absolutist theory of popular sovereignty (see SOCIAL-CONTRACT THEORY).

The gradual shift from monarchical rule to democratic rule in the late eighteenth and nineteenth centuries obscured a number of important continuities in state development—especially in regard to bureaucratic and administrative functions. By the late nineteenth century, successful states possessed a remarkably consistent set of basic features. Sovereignty and clearly demarcated borders were requisite, as were the abilities to tax inhabitants effectively and to regulate significant areas of social and economic life. These powers relied on increasingly elaborate forms of data collection and identification, from the census to citizenship rules and passports. They also required more extensive forms of social control and integration, such as civil police forces, public schools, mandatory military service, and standardized cultures and languages. Permanent diplomatic embassies staffed by trained civil servants allowed for more complex and routinized interstate relations. By the end of the nineteenth century, the modern state had become the dominant form of political organization in Europe. By the middle of the twentieth, the same could be said for the rest of the world.

The state has been the subject of numerous modern traditions of inquiry. The internal composition of states—for example, the division into EXECUTIVE, legislative, and judicial branches, as well as often-separate military and police functions—has informed studies of tension and conflict within states. A great number of variables come into play in these contexts: state power may be more or less dispersed; states may be more or less limited in their power to control society; and they may be more or less permeable to social forces. The strong Marxist tradition of state analysis tends to treat these tensions as epiphenomena of the fundamental subservience of the state to modern CAPITALISM (see Antonio GRAMSCI and Louis ALTHUSSER). The much-commented-upon decline of the state in the face of transnational capitalism and the related tendency toward the devolution of centralized state power has not fundamentally contradicted this view (see Miliband, *The State in Capitalist Society*, 1969; Poulantzas, *Political Power and Social Classes*, 1968).

The distinction between the state and SOCIETY—a term that signifies primarily economic and social relations—has underwritten other directions of inquiry, especially the long liberal tradition that has sought to minimize state interference in social and economic life. The relationship of the state to the public sphere or to CIVIL SOCIETY, as sites of extra-institutional engagement with matters of public interest, has also been the subject of considerable attention in analyses of the trajectory of state development by Jürgen HABERMAS and others (see PUBLIC SPHERE AND PRIVATE SPHERE). There is also a long anti-liberal tradition—running from such early modern figures as Jean BODIN and Thomas HOBBES to Georg HEGEL, Karl SCHMITT, and various twentieth-century architects of authoritarian and totalitarian rule—that emphasizes the supremacy of the state to society (see TOTALITARIANISM).

One of the more influential recent accounts of this relationship (associated primarily with Theda Skocpol) emphasizes the AUTONOMY of the state vis-à-vis social forces. Drawing on the work of Weber and Otto HINTZE, Skocpol has suggested that the state is neither the product of a bargain struck between rulers and ruled nor the tool of capitalist interests, but primarily an abstract and impersonal set of institutions governed by legal-rational rules of bureaucracy and standing above all other organizations and social groups (Evans,

Rueschemeyer, Skocpol, *Bringing the State Back In*, 1985).

state capitalism A phrase coined by the German sociologist and FRANKFURT SCHOOL member Friedrich POLLACK to describe the state-owned and directed economy of the Soviet Union. The term was later often applied to the socialist-bloc economies in general. As developed by Pollack, the concept called into question the nature of the economic differences between the ostensibly competing models of SOCIALISM and CAPITALISM.

Throughout the 1930s, Pollack argued against treating the Soviet economy as a radically new economic system or even a transitional form. State control of the economy, he argued, was not a stage on the road to socialism but rather a social form in which the monopoly power of late capitalism was appropriated by the state in order to suppress the contradictions of the system. Economic planning, forced employment, techno-logical innovation, and a large, surplus-absorbing military sector, Pollack argued, provided a durable set of techniques that could prolong the new social order, perhaps indefinitely. Pollack and other Frankfurt school members also recognized strong state-capitalist tendencies in the initiatives of the New Deal.

statistical model See MECHANICAL MODEL AND STATISTICAL MODEL.

status Most commonly linked with the term *role* to encompass all culturally prescribed rights and duties inherent in social positions, whatever their origins. This usage was pioneered by the anthropologist Ralph LINTON (*The Study of Man*, 1936).

Historically, status referred to legally enforce-able delineations of rights, obligations, superi-ority, or inferiority, on the basis of inheritance or honor. Sir Henry James Sumner MAINE thus famously distinguished status-based societies from those based on contract (with a presumed equality between parties). Max WEBER developed this line of analysis in describing status as any specific "positive or negative, social estimation of honor"—a definition closely linked with the concept of prestige (*Economy and Society*, 1922). Weber's concept of status informed his inquiry into different modes of STRATIFICATION—the forms of enduring inequality that structure a society. He drew a basic distinction between ASCRIBED STATUS, or status assigned at birth,

and ACHIEVED STATUS acquired through accom-plishments, career, or other forms of contingent social distinction. The CASTE system of India, SLAVERY, and the three *estates* of European feu-dal society are examples of systems of ascribed status. The meritocratic ideal of most modern societies exemplifies achieved status. Weber rec-ognized that status groups were defined through positive and negative privileges, and that these, in turn, were defended or reinforced through visible cultural differences and practices. For this rea-son, he argued, status groups were more visible in preindustrial societies, where exclusive cultural practices could be more strictly controlled. In this context, Weber mapped the ascribed/achieved distinction onto a historical distinction between status societies and modern *class societies*, where status groups no longer overwhelmingly fix and dominate individual lives.

Sociology and anthropology have long been concerned with questions of status. Since the 1960s, STATUS-ATTAINMENT THEORY, empha-sizing social mobility and perceptions of relative socioeconomic status, has been an important sub-ject of sociological inquiry. The concept of STATUS INCONSISTENCY, based on the recognition of multiple and not always exchangeable registers of status, has been a resource for work on DEVIANCE and social change. Recently, some analysts have used the concept of *status injury* to describe dam-age to someone's dignity (e.g., by a racist slur), whether or not it has material consequences.

status-attainment theory A tradition of re-search in American sociology that analyzes stan-dards of achievement, forms of prestige, and the larger question of SOCIAL MOBILITY. Much of this work has sought to relate perceptions of socioeconomic status to the realities of edu-cational levels, occupations, and incomes—in many instances through quantitative methods that relate different forms and degrees of prestige. Status-attainment theory has also placed consid-erable emphasis on determining the importance of these diverse factors in determining possibili-ties for social advancement, including especially the parents' socioeconomic status.

Status-attainment theory became a sociologi-cal preoccupation in the 1960s, following a major study of generational mobility and occupational prestige by Peter BLAU and Otis Duncan (*The American Occupational Structure*, 1967). This study, and several that followed, emphasized the signif-icance of education and certain aspects of family background for social mobility. Such findings set off a long debate about the degree to which the United States was a meritocratic society—a debate that continues to this day in academic, popular, and policy circles. Recent research on status achievement has become closely tied to methodological advances and somewhat distant from broader theoretical questions.

status inconsistency A lack of correlation between different measures of status, such as wealth and educational level. The sociologist Gerhard Lenski argued that such inconsistency—in the case, for example, of low-paid but highly educated and prestigious professors—leads to perceived deprivation and resentment. Status inconsistency frequently follows broader lines of social stratification, such as race and gender, and produces pressures for what Lenski called *status crystallization*, via either forms of social change or individual efforts to translate one form of status into another. George HOMANS designated similar issues with the term *social certitude*. The concept of *status frustration*, important in strain theories of DEVIANCE, also covers similar ground (see STRAIN THEORY).

status offenses Behavior that is considered illegal only for specified categories of people. For example, school children can be charged with truancy, but not adults. Status offenses play a role in the sociology of DEVIANCE.

status set Per Robert K. MERTON's usage in *Social Theory and Social Structure* (1957), *status set* refers to the different social statuses (or roles) that individuals possess. For example, a single person might be simultaneously a student, a musician, a daughter, and a Hispanic. See also STATUS.

stem family A family type organized around the transmission of property from one generation to the next. Associated with European patterns of landholding, the salient features of stem families are the selection of one heir to inherit the bulk of an estate, and the presence of the heir (typically a son) as the head of the family's household until succession occurs.

Steward, Julian (1902–1972) An American anthropologist and central figure in the development of cultural ecology. Steward trained at the University of California at Berkeley with Alfred L. KROEBER and Robert Lowie (both students of Franz BOAS, and strong proponents of Boasian cultural anthropology), as well as with

Carl SAUER, the leading American cultural geographer of the period. Steward developed strong interests in environmental adaptation and cultural evolution—subjects that ran counter to the dominant Boasian emphasis on HISTORICAL PARTICULARISM and patterns of cultural diffusion (see DIFFUSION AND DIFFUSIONISM). Environmental adaptation became an issue in the context of his research among the Shoshone and Paiute, both desert Indian societies in which the relationship to the environment was of paramount importance. Steward held that the key determining factors in such societies were the environment and the available subsistence technologies, which together determined the dominant form of labor. The form of labor, in turn, structured many of the social institutions and cultural practices.

Steward also pursued comparisons between cultures that shared certain environmental and technological constraints. Such comparison revealed a process of "multilineal evolution"—the set of available responses to specific environmental challenges. By carefully circumscribing his comparisons, Steward avoided the sweeping unilinear evolutionary models of nineteenth-century anthropology. He sought to demonstrate, rather, the diversity of paths from simple to complex societies. Later in his career, Steward turned these techniques to the study of modern, complex societies, such as Puerto Rico. He also became a major proponent of AREA STUDIES.

Steward edited a number of major studies, including the six-volume *Handbook of South American Indians* (1946–1959), and the three-volume *Contemporary Change in Traditional Societies* (1967). He is the author of *Area Research: Theory and Practice* (1950), *The People of Puerto Rico* (1956), and, with Louis Faron, *Native Peoples of South America* (1959).

stigma According to Erving GOFFMAN—its principal sociological theorist—*stigmas* are visible or invisible social distinctions that disqualify individuals or social groups from full social acceptance. Goffman distinguished between physical stigmas such as obesity or handicaps, moral stigmas such as homosexuality, and tribal stigmas that affect ethnic or national groups. His work contributed to the large body of sociological research on labeling and DEVIANCE in the 1950s and 1960s.

stochastic models Statistical models that address processes of change or uncertainty over time. These play a prominent role in some areas of economics and risk assessment. Stochastic noise is the fluctuation around a trend (e.g., the daily ups and downs of the stock market), as distinct from the long-term trend line.

Stolper–Samuelson theorem See HECKSCHER-OHLIN TRADE THEORY.

strain theory An explanation of DEVIANCE as the result of stress and frustration. Strain theory is rooted in Emile DURKHEIM's notion of ANOMIE and was elaborated by Robert K. MERTON in his famous typology of modes of adaptation. Strain, in this context, is usually attributed to structural social and psychological factors. One of the principal examples is *status frustration*, which Albert Cohen studied as a function of the gap between norms of success and the legitimate means of achieving them. Strain theory implicitly assumes that delinquency is located primarily among the lower strata of society—an assumption that has been widely attacked by criminological studies based on self-report data.

stratification The systemic forms of inequality that divide societies and broadly impact occupational and social status. Stratification may take many forms based on wealth, gender, age, ethnicity, or some other form of distinction. Stratification is consequently a central concern of economic, anthropological, and especially sociological research. It involves not only the forms of discrimination or differential treatment that stand in the way of egalitarianism but also the larger system of rewards that structures the economy and the social order. Studies of stratification trace the evolution and reproduction of these systems; they document the ways in which groups maintain or change their positions within them; and they seek to understand the consequences of these processes for the social order.

In small-scale and low-technology societies, inequality is limited by low levels of accumulated wealth and usually organized in terms of age, gender, and KINSHIP position. This minimizes the formation of enduringly unequal groups—youths will become elders, for example.

By contrast, larger-scale, wealthier societies are more likely to be stratified into enduringly reproduced groups or classes. While Karl MARX described all history as the history of class struggle, others distinguish CLASS as one specific form of stratification among others. Sociologists commonly identify three major forms of stratification in complex societies: CASTE systems, with rigid borders, highly differentiated statuses, and little possibility of mobility (the caste system of India is one example; slave and/or racially segregated societies are another); the system of *estates* characteristic of European feudal societies, which distinguished between the clergy, the nobility, and the broad category of peasants, merchants, and artisans; and *class systems*, more common in modern societies. Max WEBER and later Talcott PARSONS described the first two systems as dominated by ASCRIBED STATUS, or status into which one is born. Class systems, in contrast, provided a greater margin for ACHIEVED STATUS. The contemporaneous rise of the meritocratic ideal places a premium on achievement, in spite of the many economic, cultural, and institutional pressures that assure the general reproduction of structures of inequality.

Sociologists, especially in the United States, have devoted a great deal of attention to the question of social mobility. Despite the meritocratic ideal, the preponderance of research suggests that mobility patterns are primarily determined by structural factors, such as changes in occupational opportunities or fertility rates (Blau and Duncan, *The American Occupational Structure*, 1967). Furthermore, there is strong evidence that significant social mobility among the social strata is more the exception than the rule (this is more strongly the case in Europe, where stratification is more determining of life chances than in the United States). Systems of stratification tend to reproduce themselves: children from families of a particular social class tend to follow the occupational trajectories typical of their class background.

To a considerable extent, the history of sociology is the history of efforts to explain historical and actual stratification and to develop means of addressing social inequalities. MARXISM, with its theory of class stratification based on ownership of capital and its program of revolution, is one of the most prominent approaches. Weber, in contrast, contended that in modern societies there were sources of stratification other than the relationship to capital, and that not all forms of stratification aligned with one another. He defined class in terms of "life-chances," but he also stressed the partial autonomy of power—particularly the bureaucratic power so influential in modern society. In this respect,

Weber anticipated the restratification of communist societies along lines of access to bureaucratic power. In addition, he proposed the concept of *status group* to describe groups whose prestige derives from cultural rather than economic or political factors. Perhaps the most significant contemporary analyst of this dimension of stratification is Pierre BOURDIEU, who emphasizes the role of "cultural capital" in the negotiation of class positions.

Marx's and Weber's theories of stratification are examples of CONFLICT THEORY, insofar as they see society as an arena in which people compete for power, wealth, and prestige. In contrast, Herbert SPENCER and Emile DURKHEIM argued that some degree of inequality contributes to the functional integration of society. This view was extended by Kingsley Davis and Wilbert Moore in an influential article, "Some Principles of Stratification" (1945). Davis and Moore argued that all societies need some means of motivating their most competent workers to fill important and difficult occupations. This motivational problem is addressed by fashioning a hierarchy of rewards that privileges functionally important positions. Social inequality is therefore functionally necessary, because a society that fails to motivate people to perform important jobs risks collapse. Critics were quick to argue that this functionalist view neglected the question of power within systems of stratification, and that it legitimized existing inequality. This long-running exchange became known as the DAVIS-MOORE DEBATE, although it has faded in importance with the decline of FUNCTIONALISM and the rise of Marxist and poststructuralist accounts of power and IDEOLOGY.

Strauss, Leo (1899–1973) A German-born philosopher and political theorist who produced the most significant school of conservative political philosophy in the post–World War II era. Strauss shared much of post-Nietzschean philosophy's preoccupation with *nihilism*, the progressive undermining of transcendental and fixed values of all kinds by rationalist inquiry. Strauss argued that this crisis had bankrupted liberalism and led to popular experiments with totalitarian rule (see TOTALITARIANISM). Fundamentally, he accepted the nihilistic "truth" of modern philosophy and all its implications: that there was no God, that morality is relative, and that natural rights are a fiction. Where Strauss parted ways with Martin HEIDEGGER, Jean-Paul SARTRE, and other Nietzscheans was in arguing that this truth

should have been reserved for philosophers, and conversely that society is dependent upon a structure of uninterrogated basic values. Strauss thus asserted the essential falseness of religion or patriotism, but he defended them on the grounds of their salutary public effects.

Strauss anchored his argument in an unusual reading of the classical tradition of political philosophy that remains controversial, even among some Straussians. The core of this analysis was his reading of PLATO in *The City and Man* (1964), in which he distinguished between the "exoteric," or public meaning, of Plato's writings and its "esoteric," or private meaning. The exoteric Plato was the metaphysician—the theorist of the "Ideas" and the immortal soul. The esoteric Plato was the philosopher who recognized that the truth needed to be hidden—that society, as Plato made clear in the *Republic*, had to be based on a lie. Strauss argued, in other words, that the truth that there was no truth was the rightful property of philosophers alone, and that modern philosophy had gone wrong precisely in democratizing this insight. In so doing, it had lost its capacity to reflect on the basic question of what constitutes the good society—an activity that requires a backdrop of values that are not understood merely as historically contingent or the product of will. Here lies the logic of Strauss's defense of natural rights as a necessary support for law.

Strauss was of Jewish origin and fled the rise of Adolph Hitler in 1932. He went first to France, later to England, and finally to the United States in 1938, where he joined the New School for Social Research in New York. In 1949, he accepted an appointment at the University of Chicago, where he spent the remainder of his career. His work has had a significant impact on a generation of Straussian political and social theorists, including Alan Bloom and Harry Jaffa. Strauss's other important works include *The Political Philosophy of Hobbes* (1936), *Persecution and Art of Writing* (1952), *Thoughts on Machiavelli* (1958), *On Tyranny* (1968), and *Liberalism: Ancient and Modern* (1968).

structural differentiation See COMPLEX SOCIETY.

structural-functionalism See FUNCTIONALISM; and SOCIAL STRUCTURE.

structuralism A general theory of culture and method of analysis developed by Claude LÉVI-STRAUSS in the 1950s and 1960s. Structuralism's origins lie in the social theories of Emile

DURKHEIM and Marcel MAUSS, and in the structural linguistics of Ferdinand de SAUSSURE.

The principles of structural linguistics reached Lévi-Strauss by way of Roman JAKOBSON, a prominent linguist encountered by Lévi-Strauss while both were in exile in New York during World War II. Also available to Lévi-Strauss for the first time was the vast and largely unanalyzed record of American Indian myths and legends collected by Franz BOAS and his students. Structuralism emerged at the intersection of these two research traditions, as Lévi-Strauss took up the study of myth as a differential network that reflected certain basic, deeply rooted cultural binaries: raw and cooked, left and right, nature and culture, man and woman, and so on. For Lévi-Strauss, these distinctions provided the larger structure and language—the fuller set of possibilities—to which particular myths or cultural forms gave expression. Myth reflected, he argued, a universal process of human thought and apprehension of the world—a way of ordering things and experience by way of differences and binary distinctions. By means of this ontological claim, structuralism became a general theory that encompassed not only MYTH but also CULTURE. Lévi-Strauss explored this analogy in the classic anthropological context of KINSHIP. His particular contribution was to found the tradition of ALLIANCE THEORY, which explained social organization in terms of marriage rules rather than rules of descent. His structuralism also integrated a range of contemporary work on information and systems theory, and thereby staked a claim to scientific rigor and proof.

Lévi-Strauss published major works of structuralist anthropology throughout the 1960s. In the same period, the structuralist label was somewhat loosely extended to a wider group of French intellectuals (Louis ALTHUSSER, Roland BARTHES, Jacques LACAN, Michel FOUCAULT), who proposed similarly revisionist frameworks for understanding human history, psychology, and behavior. POSTSTRUCTURALISM takes its distance from the universalizing and relatively static nature of many of these claims, especially those of Lévi-Strauss, but the line between the two is often a matter of opinion: both tend to emphasize transpersonal systems that shape human subjectivity. Although many of the claims for structuralism within anthropology and linguistics have been challenged—by the rise of an even more universalizing Chomskyan linguistics (see Noam CHOMSKY), on the one hand, and by a general concern for the internal limits of interpretation on the other—structuralism in both its broad and narrow sense remains important to a wide range of contemporary social theory.

structural strain   See STRAIN THEORY.

structural unemployment   See UNEMPLOYMENT.

structural violence   Most often used to describe forms of institutionalized social injustice, *structural violence* is a terminological attempt to move beyond the commonsense understanding of violence as the individual use of bodily force. "Structural," in this context, calls attention to the violence that inheres in some social roles, norms, and patterns, as well as to the persistence and durability of those patterns. It also draws attention to the political dimensions of violence (as in government-sponsored systems of apartheid or ethnic discrimination) and to the ways in which discriminatory patterns of social behavior (e.g., racism) can persist without explicit expression in institutional practices. The term also frequently references a broader conception of violence that includes harm to the dignity and freedom of individuals.

structuration   Associated primarily with the sociologist Anthony GIDDENS, structuration theory steps back from the long debate within the social sciences over the relative priority of SOCIAL STRUCTURE and individual AGENCY. Rather than choose sides, Giddens argues that structures and agency cannot be conceived of apart from one another. Structures are neither independent of actors nor determining of their behavior but are rather a set of rules and competencies upon which actors draw and which, in the aggregate, they tend to reproduce over time. Put differently, social structures are not simply "facts" that constrain human action—they exist only insofar as they are recognized by agents.

The theoretical underpinnings of this work parallel, in many respects, Jacques DERRIDA's DECONSTRUCTION of the binary concepts that underlie classic sociological and anthropological reasoning—notably the universalizing tendencies of the STRUCTURALISM of Claude LÉVI-STRAUSS. Like many POSTSTRUCTURALIST theorists of social structure (Pierre BOURDIEU is another), Giddens recognizes the importance of the historical dimension of social change, and the difficulty of integrating it into an account that seems to accord individuals only a margin of improvisation within a relatively stable set of rules. Although his later work contains many elements of a historical sociology, a full account of how societies change remains elusive in this research. The theory of structuration is also open to the criticism, in Margaret Archer's view, that it conflates two analytically distinct levels of social life. For the present, these are ongoing debates that testify to the influence of structuration theory and to its engagement with the larger challenges of social analysis. The theory of structuration is developed most fully in Giddens's *Central Problems in Social Theory* (1979) and *The Constitution of Society: Outline of the Theory of Structuration* (1984).

structures of feeling A key and recurring term in Raymond WILLIAMS's studies of culture, *structures of feeling* refers to the general organization of emotion and experience in a given period—especially as developed along generational lines. It describes the ways in which common values or shared generational experiences shape subjective experience. For Williams, certain social practices, works of art, and literature are the principle records of such structures. Although the term has obvious affinities with the concept of IDEOLOGY, Williams initially argued that structures of feeling belong to the level of "formative processes" that shape experience—not, in his view, to the more developed structures and social positions that characterize ideology. Although he maintained this general distinction in later work, such as *Marxism and Literature* (1971), he did allow that structures of feeling had an important class component. This bracketing of ideology from experience placed Williams at odds with many of the structuralist and poststructuralist accounts of subjectivity that came to dominate CULTURAL STUDIES. Williams's Marxist humanism and sociological orientation provided an alternative to this tradition in both cultural and literary studies.

stylized facts A concept attributed to Nicholas KALDOR and often employed by economists in theoretical model building. Kaldor argued that economists should be free to start off with a "stylized" view or a broad summary of the facts that were to be explained by a theoretical model. Specifically, he suggested that modelers should concentrate on general tendencies and ignore details that introduce insignificant but complex variables into calculations. Such assumptions underlie all economic modeling, in one form or another; at the same time, they furnish a perpetual source of debate and a frequent basis for challenging the validity of economic models.

subaltern One who occupies a subordinate or lower position in a social hierarchy, whether based on property, CASTE, ETHNICITY, or other criteria. The term has become prominent in studies of the structural subordination of certain groups in India's caste system. *Subaltern studies* has come to designate a movement of primarily Marxist scholars of South Asia, who prioritize inquiry into these largely disempowered, politically voiceless populations. Many of these draw on Antonio GRAMSCI's early use of the term in his description of the disorganized sectors of the working class. From these sources, *subaltern* has come into wider and somewhat controversial use in CULTURAL STUDIES as a way of referring to other situations of social subordination, such as those of minority groups in Western societies.

subculture A set of distinctive norms, values, artifacts, language, symbols, or forms of knowledge that a particular social group uses to distinguish itself from the dominant culture. Subcultures are both a manifestation of social diversity and a potential source of social conflict, conservatism, or change. Much of the early sociological work on subcultures focused on questions of DEVIANCE and criminality in relation to working-class and middle-class values. Albert Cohen, Richard Cloward, Lloyd Ohlin, and other American sociologists emphasized the alternate forms of STATUS that subcultures provided for groups whose access to economic or other "legitimate" forms of achievement was limited. Such research focused on inner-city youths and institutionally defined populations, such as prisoners. Some versions of subculture research within CRIMINOLOGY have argued for the existence of *subcultures of violence*; these correlate certain cultural characteristics within a community to the incidence of violent crime. This is an area of considerable controversy, however, and arguments in favor of strong correlations have not received widespread support.

The notion of subcultures was strongly inflected in the 1970s by the study of British youth movements, which had achieved a certain degree of social and stylistic coherence. For British CULTURAL STUDIES, these groups complicated the model of CLASS antagonism that had driven much of the early work on popular culture, insofar as one of their chief features was opposition to the working class. The term *subculture* has since entered much wider use, extending to forms of consumerism, fashion, and fandom. Recent work has also paid more attention to subcultural stratification along gender and racial lines.

Countercultures are sometimes seen as a subset of subcultures, in which a particular group explicitly challenges or seeks to change aspects of the dominant culture. In the United States, the 1960s and 1970s were a time of strong *countercultural* activity.

subject Very generally, the person considered as actor rather than the object of action. The term is sometimes used interchangeably with *individual* or *person* in social and cultural theory; however, it has a more distinct meaning that reflects the broad shift in modern social thought toward socially constructed or historically situated conceptions of selfhood. At its most general, this shift represents a critique of the classic liberal humanist idea of the self as naturally autonomous, self-contained, and abstract—a notion with deep and extensive roots in Western thought. The use of the term *subject*, in this context, implies recognition of the contingency of this development, and permits the subject to become, in effect, an object of analysis. This recognition inaugurates the full range of nineteenth- and twentieth-century theories of the subject, from MARXISM to PRAGMATISM, PSYCHOANALYSIS, STRUCTURALISM, existentialism, FEMINISM, and many other theoretical perspectives. Crucial to many of these analyses is a rethinking of the autonomous individual as either socially constructed (rather than natural) or as an ideological fiction or image in discourse. Karl MARX, for example, treated individualism as a basic element of bourgeois ideology—crucial to the naturalization of private property, liberalism, and capitalist enterprise. For Sigmund FREUD, it is an illusion that only approximates the outcome of the OEDIPUS COMPLEX and covers the fundamental divide of consciousness from the unconscious. In the context of many theories of gender and racial identity, it is a rhetoric of privilege traditionally stratified by sex and skin color. For Michel FOUCAULT, it is part of the discursive formation of modernity, albeit an unstable part that generates new positions and oppositions.

As many social theorists have recognized, if our concept of self is embedded in social institutions and practices, then it presents a moving target as those institutions and practices change. Such change is very much at stake in theories of epochal historical change, and most recently in POSTMODERNISM, which generally correlates the revolutions in culture and technology of the past decades with a broad shift in human sensibilities. For most social scientists, the reciprocity between subjectivity and social structure opens the door to social relationships of great complexity; it raises questions concerning social reproduction, individual agency, and the nature of social change. Still, this relationship can easily be reduced to determinism, as reflected in social engineering of all kinds, from conservative efforts to legislate ostensibly natural modes of behavior to revolutionary efforts to create persons fit for new societies.

sublimation In Freudian PSYCHOANALYSIS, the redirection of libidinal energy toward socially acceptable or constructive ends. Sublimation plays an important role in Sigmund FREUD's account of creativity and artistic production.

subsidiarity A doctrine holding that higher levels of an organizational hierarchy should refrain from assuming responsibility for tasks that can be successfully accomplished by subordinate units. The doctrine of subsidiarity is commonly associated with the European Union (EU); tasks that cannot be discharged by member states are handed up to the EU's central administrative bodies. Conversely, the principle limits the EU to those functions that cannot be carried out by member states.

subsidy A payment made by the government (or private individuals) to producers or consumers of a particular good or service. A subsidy is a negative tax and has the same effect of introducing a wedge between the prices paid by the buyers and the prices received by the sellers. Subsidies generally target particular economic and social objectives, such as improving the competitiveness of domestic producers in international markets.

subsistence The minimum level of wages and/or consumption necessary to ensure survival and the basic necessities of life. CLASSICAL ECONOMICS assumed that subsistence was the natural level of wages in the long run, as population pressures drove wages down.

substitutes A good is a *substitute* for another good if it can be consumed in its stead. *Perfect* substitutes are goods that are completely interchangeable—such as nickels and dimes. More generally, substitutability refers to the degree to which goods are consumed instead of one another—measured by *cross-price* ELASTICITY. When goods are substitutes, a price increase for one good (for example, butter) leads to an increase in demand for another (for example, margarine). See also COMPLEMENTS.

succession In politics, the process by which one leader succeeds another. The existence of rules or customs governing succession is one of the basic requisites of stable regimes or states. Elections perform this function, as does hereditary succession. Regimes that lack clearly prescribed rules of succession are prone to crisis when their leaders die, resign, or are deposed.

sucker effect A group dynamic that occurs in the context of differential and/or unfair treatment of members of a group—generally in regard to rewards. The most common consequence is reduced effort on the part of those members who perceive themselves as "suckers," or victims, of that treatment.

suffrage The right to participate in public deliberations and to vote in referenda and elections. Suffrage has been a subject of protracted political and social struggle since the emergence of democratic states in the late eighteenth century. Restrictive definitions of who can vote or fully participate—based on property ownership, gender, race, and other criteria—have been broadly challenged and discredited. Universal suffrage, granted to all citizens of a state, is now the norm.

Noncitizen residents, such as immigrants, refugees, and illegal aliens, are usually denied suffrage or granted only limited participation (for example, in local elections). Incarcerated criminals are another excluded category in many countries, including the United States (as determined by state law). The term *suffrage movement* usually refers to the struggle that led to the extension of the voting franchise to women in the late nineteenth and early twentieth centuries—especially in the United States (1920) and Britain (completed by 1928). This was earlier than in many other countries (Switzerland accorded the vote to women only in 1971); woman suffrage is still a subject of contention in some Islamic societies. See also CITIZENSHIP; and VOTING.

suicide The ending of one's own life, either by choice or as a knowing by-product of other actions, became a major topic of sociological inquiry following Emile DURKHEIM's classic study *Suicide* (1897). By seeking a social explanation for a quintessentially private and—as frequently understood—pathological phenomenon, Durkheim produced an early and major demonstration of the goals and methods of sociological research.

In approaching the subject, Durkheim related types and rates of suicide to the degree of social integration of a society or subgroup. In this, he specifically challenged the earlier theory of Gabriel Tarde, which attributed suicide to a process of "social imitation" of influential models. Durkheim avoided the questions of specific intent and psychological motivation. Instead, he studied suicide rates. These were, he argued, SOCIAL FACTS that needed to be explained by other social facts, such as collective sentiments. In this context, he classified suicides into four categories linked to different levels of social integration and social (or normative) regulation. Social integration, for Durkheim, referred both to the degree to which collective sentiments were shared by the community and the way that individuals were bound to one another. Within this parameter, Durkheim distinguished *egoistic suicide*, which occurs when individuals are poorly integrated into society, from *altruistic suicide*, which occurs when social integration is unusually strong (as in suicide over matters of honor or as elements of ritual). Social regulation, in contrast, describes the degree to which individual behavior is subject to constraint. Here Durkheim distinguished *anomic suicide*, which occurs when there is a breakdown of social regulation, from *fatalistic suicide*, the product of excessive social regulation (as among prisoners).

Although Durkheim's study has been profoundly influential in sociology, it has also been widely criticized, and many of its specific findings have been rejected. Some of these critiques challenge Durkheim's implicit universalism by emphasizing the highly variable significance of suicide in different societies. Some have taken issue with Durkheim's use of data. Still others have found empirical support for competing explanations such as the imitation theory, which Durkheim rejected; David Phillips, for example, has demonstrated that suicide rates rise after highly publicized celebrity suicides.

Sullivan, Harry Stack (1892–1949) An American psychiatrist whose work with schizophrenics in the 1920s led to a relatively independent direction of psychoanalytic research, termed *interpersonal psychoanalysis*. In contrast to the depth model of Freudian PSYCHOANALYSIS, with its emphasis on repression, Sullivan studied the ways in which personality was a product of interpersonal relations—responsive to context and developing through time. In this, he was part of a broader "social" turn in psychoanalysis that included Alfred Adler, Karen HORNEY, and Erich FROMM. A number of social scientists interested in issues of culture and personality, including Talcott PARSONS, collaborated with Sullivan and his colleagues at the William Alonson White Institute.

Sullivan's attempts to understand the meaning of schizophrenic symptoms in the context of the therapeutic relationship proved influential on later analyses of schizophrenia by Ronald David LAING and others, and they continue to inform *existential–phenomenological psychology* and clinical practice more generally.

Sumner, William Graham   (1840–1910) An American sociologist who was one of the most prominent turn-of-the-century advocates of SOCIAL DARWINISM and laissez-faire government in the United States. Sumner's major scholarly work was *Folkways* (1907), an evolutionary study of the origin of social customs and laws. In it, he drew an influential distinction between *folkways* (informal, noncoercive conventions, learned through socialization) and *mores* (more binding conventions, backed by sanctions). These were part of a general approach to the study of society and social behavior that Sumner called "ethology." Sumner also coined the term *ethnocentrism* (the assumed superiority of one's own group vis-à-vis other groups).

Sumner was strongly influenced by Herbert SPENCER's social evolutionism, which he viewed as a unilinear and irreversible master logic of history. Sumner also adopted and, to a degree, distorted the strong Darwinism that characterized some of Spencer's claims about the social dimension of this process—in particular arguing that society was inevitably and ideally an arena for the "survival of the fittest." These views played an important part in late nineteenth- and early twentieth-century debates about poverty, equality, and the role of the state.

Sumner taught at Yale University and served as the president of the American Sociological Society from 1908 to 1910.

sum of squares   See VARIANCE.

sunspots   In economics, the term *sunspots* refers to *extrinsic* forms of coordination of the plans of individual market participants and, therefore, to sources of market uncertainty that are neither transmitted by nor attributable to market fundamentals. This is in contrast to *intrinsic market uncertainty*, which is transmitted through such market fundamentals as endowments, technology, and preferences. The weather is an example of extrinsic market uncertainty that produces coordinated action.

superego   Sigmund FREUD's principle account of the human psyche distinguishes between the EGO, ID, and *superego*. The superego is the product of the internalization of moral inhibitions and societal ideals—initially through the child's attempts to please its parents. Ultimately, it reflects the child's identification with social models and ideals. The superego then acts as an internal controlling agency, producing feelings of guilt and censoring socially unacceptable feelings and desires. This role places it in direct conflict with the *id*—the seat of primal human drives. Developmentally, the superego begins to form between the ages of three and five—a period seen as crucial to the process of SOCIALIZATION. See also REALITY PRINCIPLE.

superneutrality   See NEUTRALITY OF MONEY.

supernormal profits   See PROFITS.

superorganic   Coined by Herbert SPENCER but given its anthropological stamp by Alfred L. KROEBER in 1917, the term describes CULTURE as a supra-individual system of relations that exists primarily beyond the control of the individuals who compose it. Although Kroeber's initial targets were the "organic" evolutionary models and racial determinisms of the day, the concept anticipated many of the concerns of modern social theory; it was one of the first theoretical claims for the relative autonomy of culture from individual agency or thought.

superpower   Used to describe the United States and the Soviet Union during the COLD WAR—a period in which competition between the two nations dominated international politics. Military power and influence over a network of allied states were the primary measures of superpower status. The break-up of the Soviet Union in 1991 left the United States as only remaining superpower, although the nature of its dominance is no longer as clear. See also THIRD WORLD.

superstructure   In Marxist thought, superstructure refers to the political, legal, religious, and cultural institutions that rest upon and are determined by the economic *base*, or MODE OF PRODUCTION. See also BASE AND SUPERSTRUCTURE; and MARXISM.

supply and demand The principle that the combined forces of market supply and market demand uniquely determine the price of a good. Because the supply of a good generally increases as price rises, while demand for a good decreases as price rises, there is only one price where supply equals demand. Thus the value of all goods and services is determined by intersection of the two.

supply function A model of the factors that determine the supply of a good—primarily price. The relationship between the quantity supplied and the price, holding all other determinants constant, is termed the *supply curve*. The broader supply function for a market takes into account profit maximization by the supplier (given different potential prices) and UTILITY maximization by consumers.

supply-side economics A school of economic thought anchored in the belief that lower tax rates fuel economic expansion. The theory holds that a reduction in taxes will increase the aggregate supply of goods by encouraging production, providing greater incentives to work, and stimulating the savings and investment needed to support business growth. Supply-side economics focuses on the impediments to supply and the efficient use of the factors of production, rather than on the level of effective demand, as in conventional Keynesian macroeconomics. Increased supply is also seen as a means to restrain inflation, as greater production puts downward pressure on prices. A still more unusual argument of supply-side economists is that the prosperity generated by tax cuts will offset the lower tax rates. Supply-side found a modern champion in Arthur Laffer, whose LAFFER CURVE (relating lower tax rates to higher tax revenues) provided much of the rationale for U.S. President Ronald Reagan's 1981 tax-cut program. See KEYNESIANISM; and MACROECONOMICS.

supranational Laws or institutions that supersede the authority of the state. A supranational organization is formed by states that have agreed to transfer certain rulemaking prerogatives to a higher, central authority. In so doing, members of these organizations give up their sovereign jurisdiction in these specific areas. The European Union (EU) is one of the clearest examples of a supranational organization. EU member states are no longer the sole sources of sovereign power within their borders. Rather, the EU—acting through the Council of Ministers or the European Court of Justice—has the power to make laws that can be imposed on member states. The loss in individual member states' sovereignty is, proponents claim, offset by the advantages of being a part of a powerful political and economic entity that can successfully compete with other states or supranational organizations.

surplus value In the Marxist analysis of capitalist economies, surplus value refers to the difference between the costs of production (including capital investment and wages, or *constant* and *variable* CAPITAL) and the exchange value (price) of the final product. This difference is expropriated by the capitalist and forms the basis of profit and capital accumulation. Karl MARX distinguished between absolute and relative surplus value, the former created by lengthening the workday or increasing its intensity, the latter by improving technology or other means of production to extract more product from the same amount of labor.

survey research One of the basic research methodologies in the social sciences, survey research typically refers to work based on questionnaires or interviews. The vast majority of contemporary survey work also depends on SAMPLING—the use of a well-chosen small population to gather data that will represent a larger population. A survey that attempts to reach an entire population is called a CENSUS. For most purposes, sample surveys are more accurate. Surveys have the great advantage of permitting data collection from large groups, which tends to minimize the risk of skewed results. Data can also be carefully controlled to allow for reliable statistical inference.

Surveys are useful in a wide range of research projects that seek objective data (for example, on income or education) and/or information about subjective opinions, such as the prestige of different occupations or preferences in an election. They are vulnerable, however, to a range of distortions inherent to the data-gathering process, from the necessity of prior construction of the path of questioning to the tendency of respondents to conform to perceived social norms. Care is thus needed in the formulation of individual questions and protocols for the selection of samples, in the assessment of patterns of response, and in the interpretation of results.

Ideally, both questions and protocols are tested before use.

The gathering of survey data has become highly specialized and has undergone numerous technical refinements in order to ensure high levels of reliability. Nonetheless, critics often raise questions of VALIDITY, contending that surveys too often rely on simplistic indicators for complex analytical variables. While they are a key source of quantitative data, many argue for complementing them with richer qualitative data.

swidden agriculture The technical term for slash-and-burn agriculture—the process of burning away and clearing relatively small areas of tropical vegetation before planting. Swidden agriculture is associated primarily with the conversion of tropical forests to arable land.

swing vote A measure of the shift in strength between two political parties in the course of successive elections. The *swing vote* is based on the average of the winning party's gain and the losing party's loss. It is often used as a simple predictive tool in countries with majority or plurality ELECTORAL SYSTEMS, where two main parties vie for power. The term is also used to refer to an aggregate of undecided voters large enough to "swing" an election in a party's favor, if it is captured as a block.

symbol Generally designates the combination of a *sign* (a word, graphic, gesture, image, etc.) with its *meaning* (tree, honesty, patriotism, etc.), although there is considerable variation in usage. Symbols are purely conventional objects used to organize and represent concepts and things. They are also the structural units of meaning and therefore are sometimes treated as the constitutive units of CULTURE; in this broad sense, LANGUAGE is a subset of symbolic behavior.

Particularly central or powerful symbols are a subject of interest in many areas of the social sciences, from the study of general principles of language and culture to the particular forms and uses of political symbolism. In ANTHROPOLOGY, the concept of symbol is often reserved for usages that evoke the sacred or that are productive of an indefinite range of meanings, rather than strictly limited to a single aspect of reference (like a *sign*). Symbols are often central to struggles for power, insofar as they are a means of forging and defining group identities. The concept of *symbolic violence* was introduced by Pierre BOURDIEU to designate the stakes in some struggles over the categories of knowledge and social organization. More generally, the concept designates the deliberate appropriation, distortion, or desecration of the symbols of a particular group by its opponents or enemies.

symbolic anthropology Anthropological interest in the study of SYMBOLS dates back to the late nineteenth century, when the dense symbolism of RITUAL and MYTH provided the basis for a number of influential accounts of what Lucien LEVY-BRUHL called PRIMITIVE MENTALITY; Edward Burnett TYLOR's *Primitive Culture* (1871) is perhaps the most prominent. Twentieth-century ANTHROPOLOGY, however, developed largely in opposition to the ethnocentrism and evolutionary assumptions of many of those early perspectives. The rise of FUNCTIONALISM in the 1920s, with its emphasis on political structure and KINSHIP, also tended to displace symbolism from the ethnographic agenda.

The modern movement loosely known as *symbolic anthropology* dates to the 1960s, particularly to the work of Clifford GEERTZ, David Schneider, and Victor TURNER. These anthropologists reexamined symbolism in its specific cultural contexts, treating symbols as belonging to the relatively autonomous network of meanings that comprise a given culture. Symbolic anthropology thus called for careful attention to the details of symbolism and to the multiple levels on which a symbol might signify. Geertz outlined these goals in his case for THICK DESCRIPTION, which he promoted as a methodology and goal of ethnography. These writers brought to the study of symbols a variety of different relationships to STRUCTURALISM and functionalism, but they shared a faith in the power of interpretation to trace the complexities of symbolism, even in contexts where such reconstructions demanded a high degree of speculation. Much of the thrust of poststructuralist anthropology has been to challenge this assumption of neutral interpretation. Other difficulties include the question of how to account for historical change within a symbolic network. Despite these and other objections, the general concerns of symbolic anthropology remain very much alive, and Geertz's emphasis on ETHNOGRAPHY as a narrative practice has had a significant influence outside the field of anthropology.

symbolic capital Resources available to a social actor on the basis of prestige or recognition, which function as an authoritative embodiment of cultural value. A war hero, for example, may have symbolic capital in the context of running for political office. The concept was developed by Pierre BOURDIEU in an extension of Max WEBER's analysis of STATUS. It is part of Bourdieu's account of the convertibility of different forms of CAPITAL (including economic and cultural forms). See also CULTURAL CAPITAL.

symbolic interactionism A school of sociological research oriented by the proposition that human behavior is determined not only by the objective facts of a situation but also by the meanings that people attribute to them through the use of symbols. Symbolic interactionism also emphasizes the significance of social roles in the formation of the SELF, and it privileges the study of everyday interactions over large-scale social structures. It bears the strong imprint of George Herbert MEAD's theories of the self and social roles, as well as the influence of early cultural sociologists such as Georg SIMMEL. As a research program, it coalesced at the University of Chicago in the 1920s and 1930s around Mead, William Isaac THOMAS, and Herbert Blumer, who introduced the term in 1937.

Thomas provides one of the most concise statements of the privilege the group accorded symbolic relations: "If men define situations as real, then they are real in their consequences" (*The Child in America*, 1928). Thomas, like Mead, emphasized the importance of the intersubjective construction of social life: individuals learn what behavior and events mean through interaction with others. Because the thoughts and feelings of others are not directly accessible, however, persons communicate through symbols—words, gestures, facial expressions, and other sounds and actions that have common, widely understood interpretations. In this sense, Mead argued, human behavior is shaped by symbolic interaction.

Symbolic interactionism returned to prominence in the 1960s, partly as a reaction to the dominance of FUNCTIONALISM and SYSTEM(S) THEORY—especially the highly abstract version associated with Talcott PARSONS. It also became closely identified with ethnographic field research—as contrasted to survey-based research. The movement's broad emphasis on symbols, interpretation, and personal interactions, in turn, contributed to the development of a variety of research subfields in areas where roles carry particular weight in determining interpersonal

dynamics. These have included the study of careers, DEVIANCE, pedagogy, learning, and the doctor–patient relationship. While early symbolic interactionist theories were criticized for neglecting large-scale structural concerns, more recent work has attempted to integrate such perspectives. As a result of these efforts at renewal, symbolic interactionism remains a major orientation within contemporary SOCIOLOGY.

symmetrical exchange and asymmetrical exchange *Symmetrical exchange* describes a marriage system in which the men of one group may marry the women of a second group, and vice versa. *Asymmetrical exchange* reflects an element of nonreciprocity, as when men from one group are barred from marrying women of a second group and must seek wives from a third group. In such systems, there emerges a distinction between wife-givers and wife-takers.

symptomatic reading An interpretive strategy developed by Louis ALTHUSSER and Etienne Balibar in *Reading Capital* (1965), which argues for separating the *latent* content from the *manifest* or surface content of a text. Symptomatic reading explores that which is ruled out by the structure of an argument and is thus a method for illuminating the ideological structure of texts. The notion draws on Sigmund FREUD's strategy for interpreting dreams and was popular in the 1960s and 1970s among Marxist cultural theorists.

synchronic Analysis that excludes or minimizes the dimension of historical change. Structuralist and functionalist accounts of society are generally synchronic, insofar as they ascribe SOCIAL STRUCTURE to sets of stable oppositions or functions. DIACHRONIC analysis is the historical, temporal counterpart. See also FUNCTIONALISM; and STRUCTURALISM.

syncretism The blending or amalgamation of two or more traditions. The term is often used in the comparative study of religion, but can also apply to languages or cultures.

syndicalism A radical form of LABOR activism that privileged direct action by workers over coalition building or political activity. Syndicalism relied on strikes and, above all, on the project of the "general strike" involving all workers as a form of collective refusal of the system. It rejected the goal of appropriating or engaging the power of the STATE, whether with revolutionary or reformist intentions, and emphasized worker control of the workplace. Syndicalism emerged in France in the late nineteenth century, where it flourished until the 1930s. It also played a major role in the Spanish and Italian labor movements of that period. In the United States, it was represented chiefly by the Industrial Workers of the World (IWW), which staged a number of successful strike actions, especially among its core areas in the mining and timber industries on the West Coast. IWW influence peaked during World War I and was violently suppressed in its wake, as part of the larger state-supported, antilabor backlash of the early 1920s. See also CLASS; and LABOR UNION.

synnomie   Introduced by criminologist Freda Adler to describe the condition of social solidarity prevalent in societies with low crime rates. For Adler, *synnomie* is the opposite of ANOMIE.

syntagmatic and paradigmatic   For Ferdinand de SAUSSURE and other theorists of structural LINGUISTICS, the terms designate two axes of language: *syntagmatic* refers to the rules that govern the order of words, such as grammar or poetic principles of sonority; *paradigmatic* refers to distinctions among a category of words or objects, such as the different nouns that may occupy a given place in a sentence.

syntax   The rules that govern the order of words and the construction of phrases in a language. Distinguished from SEMANTICS, or the study of the meaning of words. See also LINGUISTICS.

system(s) theory   Generally, any attempt to model the complex relationships among variables in biological, ecological, or social systems. Although the practice of drawing analogies between social and biological systems is ancient, systems theory in modern social science has generally involved extending a set of abstract principles from biological to social systems. The roots of this method lie in the work of Herbert SPENCER and Vilfredo PARETO, as well as in more properly biological research, such as Alfred Lotka's *Elements of Physical Biology* (1925). Modern systems theory grew rapidly after World War II with the development of CYBERNETICS (by Norbert Weiner) and a variety of computer-modeling techniques. Many advocates saw it as a possible means of unifying the different sciences. At the heart of cybernetics were the ideas of control, communications, and especially self-regulation through feedback and response. Much systems theory was closely tied to applied mathematics and through this has influenced economics.

Another type of systems theory in the social sciences traces its origins to Talcott PARSONS, who analyzed social systems as assemblages of internally ordered functions that maintain equilibrium in the face of external constraints and pressures. Largely on the basis of Parsons's work, this set of principles became the core of an influential *system approach* to the social sciences in the 1950s and 1960s. Perhaps the best-known aspect of this work is the set of *functional prerequisites* that Parsons argued characterized all self-maintaining systems: what he called the "AGIL sub-systems," consisting of (A) *a*daptation, (G) *g*oal-attainment, (I) *i*ntegration, and (L) *l*atency (the process of socialization that maintains the systemic pattern). As with many versions of FUNCTIONALISM, the model was adept at describing the structure of a social system, but it provided little analytical purchase on the dynamics of conflict and social change. This is one of the recurrent criticisms directed at system approaches. System approaches also have to adequately deal with the problem of spiraling complexity—of deciding what lies inside and outside the system model.

Systems theory is attracting renewed attention from social theorists of many persuasions. Cybernetic theories that focus on communication and information as a system of flows and controls have become prominent in a number of fields. The most influential systems theorist in recent years was Niklas LUHMANN, who conceived *society* as composed entirely of communications and the subsystems that organize them (rather than as a network of human actors). For Luhmann, these systems emerge in order to reduce the complexity of the environment—partly through the imposition of binary distinctions. Systems theory has also contributed to the neofunctionalism of Jeffrey Alexander and to Jürgen HABERMAS's theory of communicative action—including his fundamental distinction between *system* and LIFE-WORLD.

T

taboo Also *tabu*. The ritual avoidance of a person, place, or thing. The word *taboo* is Polynesian in origin, but it has come to designate prohibitions in many cultures. The concept has figured prominently in the anthropological tradition, enlisted variously in evolutionary, functionalist, psychological, symbolic, sociobiological, and structuralist accounts of CULTURE. For social theorists such as Sigmund FREUD and Claude LÉVI-STRAUSS, the INCEST TABOO is the inaugural social fact—basic to establishing the bonds of society around the principle of law (Freud) and marriage alliance (Lévi-Strauss).

targets and instruments *Targets* are numerical values of economic variables; they designate the goals of economic policy. *Instruments* are the means used to achieve these goals. Examples of target variables include the rate of UNEMPLOYMENT, the BALANCE OF PAYMENTS surplus, the government budget deficit, and the rate of inflation. Examples of instruments are direct and indirect taxes, interest rates, government expenditures, and working hours per week.

tariffs Taxes imposed on imports of foreign goods and, less often, on exports of goods and services. A tariff is *specific* when it is levied as a fixed sum per unit of merchandise; it is *ad valorem* when levied as a percentage of a good's value. Tariffs have a long history as a source of government revenue, and a large body of economic thought has been devoted to establishing the effects of tariffs on the larger economy.

Tariffs on imports raise the domestic price of those goods, shift demand to domestic substitutes, and increase the profitability of the import-competing domestic sector. While tariffs generate revenues, they reduce the purchasing power of income over imports. Consumers lose, while government and producers gain. Under certain circumstances, the gains can outweigh the losses, but generally, tariffs are considered to be welfare-reducing. Despite the strong welfare arguments against them, tariffs have a range of political and economic rationales, including protection from DUMPING and the defense of infant industries. See also INFANT-INDUSTRY ARGUMENT; and PROTECTIONISM.

tatonnement As described by the economist Leon WALRAS, the process by which markets find their way to equilibrium. Walras viewed tatonnement as a gradual calibration of supply and demand through prices. When prices are too high, too few people buy; when prices are too low, there is excess demand. Walras argued that markets clear as if led by an auctioneer, negotiating prices until the number of buyers matches the number of sellers. See also AUCTIONEER, WALRASIAN.

taxes and taxation Taxes serve a variety of purposes—most immediately as the primary source of government revenue. Taxes are also tools of macroeconomic policy, insofar as they can affect levels of disposable income, investment, or other economic variables (see MACROECONOMICS). They are also a means of pursuing social policies, such as discouraging consumption of certain goods by raising the cost of purchase, or by changing the distribution of income in a society.

Many different kinds of taxes have been developed to achieve these diverse ends. Economists draw a basic distinction between *direct taxes* and *indirect taxes*. Direct taxes are paid by the person or organization taxed, as in the case of income taxes or capital gains taxes. Indirect taxes involve shifting the payment from the taxed entity to someone else, usually to the final consumers of goods. These include taxes on manufacturers, wholesalers, and retailers, which are shifted (through increased prices) partially or wholly to the final consumers. Excise duties, sales taxes, and VALUE-ADDED TAXES are examples. Such taxes may excise a certain amount per unit of the commodity concerned (termed *specific taxes*) or they may target a percentage of the final retail price (called an *ad valorem tax*). By altering relative prices, indirect taxes distort consumer choices and are said to impose a deadweight loss on consumers—a loss over and above the tax revenue derived by the governments. This distortion reflects the incomplete nature of most indirect taxes: a uniform tax on *all* goods and services would leave relative prices unchanged and avoid distortionary effects. Such uniformity would be simpler to administer but would eliminate other uses of indirect taxes. In particular, indirect taxes can be used to correct for the presence of EXTERNALITIES (such as market dominance by a single agent) that arise in consumption or production.

Economists also distinguish between progressive, proportional, and regressive taxation, terms that refer to the potential for differentiating the burden of taxation by income. With *progressive* taxes, high-income taxpayers pay a larger fraction of their income than do lower-income taxpayers (i.e., the marginal tax rate increases with income). *Proportional* taxes claim the same fraction of income from taxpayers, regardless of income. *Regressive* taxes burden high-income taxpayers less (as a fraction of income) than lower-income taxpayers, although high-income taxpayers may still pay more in absolute terms. Income taxes are generally progressive, while sales taxes are usually regressive, insofar as the poor spend a larger fraction of their income on consumption.

Taxes differ in their effects depending on whether they target capital, income, wealth, or transactions. Many of these effects are subjects of considerable disagreement among economists. Taxes on capital are among the most controversial, especially among neoclassical economists (see NEOCLASSICAL ECONOMICS). In most neoclassical models, taxes on capital are held to reduce the net flow of savings and have a negative effect on capital accumulation, leading to lower levels of overall economic growth. Output and consumption are also lower in the long-run steady state. These conclusions suggest that, in the long run, the most efficient tax rate on capital value is zero.

Income taxes are a form of direct tax imposed on the income of individuals rather than on their transactions. Over time, income taxes have grown in importance and now represent the single most important revenue source in most developed countries. Their principal advantage is that they constitute a potentially progressive, broad-based tax structure that can address social concerns for equity more fairly than other methods, such

as a combination of indirect (and generally regressive) taxes on transactions or consumption. Economists have devoted considerable energy to the question of the optimal progressivity of income taxes. One of the most widely invoked principles is that the tax burden should rise with income so as to exact a comparable sacrifice in terms of UTILITY, or well-being. Others emphasize that income taxes are by nature distortionary with regard to individual choices between labor and leisure. Higher income taxes diminish the value of labor relative to leisure and thereby shift the aggregate labor supply in the economy.

Wealth taxes are levied on the net assets of individuals, based on the principle that ownership of wealth constitutes taxable capacity over and above the income that it generates. The case for wealth taxes is usually based on concerns for equity and equality, although they can also be used to alter the attractiveness of different assets. Examples of wealth taxes include property taxes (most commonly on land), estate taxes (on bequests and inheritances), capital levies (one time taxes on existing wealth), and net-worth taxes (annual taxes on personal net worth).

Taylorism See SCIENTIFIC MANAGEMENT.

technocracy Rule by experts in technology and the applied sciences. Originally coined by William H. Smyth in 1919, the term became a short-lived political cause in the 1920s, reflecting broader concern that modern industrial society had become too complex for traditional forms of elected leadership. Technocratic assumptions played a large role in the expansion of the administrative state during the Progressive era and then, to a greater degree, during the New Deal and World War II—both of which required the large-scale coordination of resources and technical expertise. The term resurfaced in the 1960s as part of a critique of those same features of modern technological society—initially by French intellectuals such as Jacques Ellul (*The Technological Society*, 1964) and Jean Meynaud. Reversing the original valence of the term, Ellul and Meynaud warned against the growing role of technocrats who were neither elected nor equipped with sufficient moral imagination to wield power responsibly and responsively to the needs of society. Other critics have challenged the ways in which technical rationales supplant political decision-making in areas such as nuclear power, employment, or health policy. Jürgen HABERMAS and other advocates of an invigorated public sphere have warned against this "colonization" of social life by technical logics and have argued that many technical issues are quintessentially political questions, involving the principles by which societies choose to live (Habermas, *Toward a Rational Society: Student Protest, Science and Politics*, 1971). See also PUBLIC SPHERE AND PRIVATE SPHERE.

technological progress, biased and unbiased   Technological progress is a central element of economic growth that enables more output to be produced from unchanged quantities of labor and capital in the production process. *Biased* technological progress is commonly classified as labor saving or capital saving. Inventions that do not save relatively more of either input are described as *unbiased* or neutral technological progress.

There are three rival definitions of unbiased technological progress, proposed, respectively, by John R. HICKS (1932), Roy HARROD (1942), and Robert SOLOW (1969). Hicks argued that technological progress is neutral (*Hicks neutral*) if it increases the productivity of all factors proportionately. Harrod defined an innovation as neutral (*Harrod neutral*) if it raises output in the same way as an increase in the stock of labor. Finally, Solow defined an innovation as neutral (*Solow neutral*) if it increases output in the same way as an increase in the stock of capital.

In neoclassical growth models, Harrod neutrality of technological progress is a necessary condition for steady state growth, that is, a situation in which output and capital grow at the same rate in the long run. Empirical evidence on the long-term growth experience of the United States and other developed countries has tended to support this use, indicating that per capita growth rates can be positive and trendless over long periods of time.

technology   The whole range of means by which humans act on their environments or seek to transcend the limits of their natural capacities. Technology thus includes the production and improvement of material goods, transport, and communication. In this broad usage, language is a technology. Most usage is narrower, however, stressing the human use of implements, machines, and electronic devices, as well as the knowledge required for this use.

Late nineteenth- and early twentieth-century debates about technological innovation focused on two alternative models: social evolution and diffusion (see DIFFUSION AND DIFFUSIONISM;

and EVOLUTION AND EVOLUTIONISM). Evolutionary theory tried to demonstrate the existence of coherent trajectories of technological and social development. It postulated that each society passed through stages defined either by technologies themselves (Stone Age, Bronze Age, etc.) or by forms of social organization that required or exploited different technological bases (nomadic, pastoral, industrial, etc.). Such evolutionary models implied a broadly independent process of technological innovation, in which technological progress operated along parallel tracks in different societies. The diffusionist model, in contrast, viewed technological development as a process of outward expansion from a center of innovation (a cultural hearth, or *KULTURKREIS* in German), much like ripples in a pool.

By the mid-twentieth century, anthropological investigations tended to focus on the more complex relationship of techniques to issues of social organization and ECOLOGY, whether in a determining role (*technological determinism*) or in a dynamic relationship with other social or environmental variables.

teknonymy   The custom of referring to a person by way of his or her relationship to a child. Thus, instead of using a personal name, the person is referred to as "mother of X," "father of X," and so on. Teknonymy is common in Southeast Asia.

teleology   From the Greek *telos*, meaning "end," teleology is the study of ends or final results. A theory is teleological when it conceives activity or development in terms of progress toward a final goal or outcome. In the West, the concept is rooted in religious narratives, but the modern social sciences have also been shaped by the need to attribute a direction or purpose to social life.

Teleological reasoning structures a broad range of social theories: Hegelian and Marxist philosophies of history were strongly teleological in their commitment to transcendence of the social order; moreover, they directly confronted the problem of how to situate human social diversity in the context of a larger historical design (see Georg HEGEL; and MARXISM). So, too, were the nineteenth-century evolutionary theories of August COMTE and Herbert SPENCER, which held that human society naturally tends to move to higher levels of civilization. FUNCTIONALISM, in contrast, evinces a more common and modern teleological structure, which views diverse social activities in terms of their contributions to a larger, integrated social process; put differently, it establishes the functional social order as the *telos* of action and behavior.

terms of trade   The most common conception is the ratio of the price index of exportables to the price index of importables—called either the *commodity* or the *net barter* terms of trade. This measures the number of units of an importable good obtainable by a unit of an exportable good. The *gross terms of trade* can be found by dividing the volume of imports by the volume of exports, which equals the commodity terms of trade only if trade is balanced (i.e., imports and exports are equal). The *income terms of trade* measures the purchasing power of exports and corresponds to the commodity terms of trade multiplied by the volume of exports; this equals the volume of imports if trade is balanced, but it exceeds or falls short of it to the degree that there is a surplus or deficit. In other words, it is the level of imports that can be sustained by current export earnings. The *factoral terms of trade* refers to the average or marginal productivity of a factor (such as labor or capital) in the export sector, in terms of the imported good at the commodity terms of trade.

Alfred MARSHALL made use of OFFER CURVES to represent the excess demand and supply of each good in a two-country framework and, thereby, to determine the terms of trade. The equilibrium value, under these circumstances, lies at the intersection of two offer curves, provided world-excess supply for each good is zero. Modern economic theory makes an important distinction between the size of the players in international trade: for small open economies that cannot influence world prices, the terms of trade are *exogenously given*; in the case of large economies that do exercise some control over world supply, demand, and/or price, the terms of trade are *endogenously determined* as a function of preferences, labor and capital endowments, and coefficients of production. Countries have a strong interest in changes in the terms of trade, since a rise in the commodity terms of trade implies that a given quantity of exports now commands a larger volume of imports. Such changes can positively affect the standard of living in a country. In general, exogenous improvements in the terms of trade raise social welfare, except where there are domestic distortions, such as monopoly or monopsony power in factor markets. Improvement in the terms of trade as a consequence of endogenous

shocks, such as a change in tastes, technology, or factor endowments, may or may not enhance welfare, but their full effects cannot be inferred from changes in the terms of trade.

thanatomia   Death following sorcery or the violation of a TABOO. Physical death, in such cases, often follows a symbolic "social death," in which the person is treated as dead by his kin and ceases to eat or drink.

theocracy   From the Greek signifying "the rule of god." The term was introduced by the Roman-Jewish historian Josephus (38–c.100 CE) to describe the ancient Hebrew constitution and the role of Mosaic law. Since then, the term has applied to REGIMES founded on priestly rule—either by the conjoining of secular and religious leadership or the institutionalization of revealed religious codes. Examples of theocratic states include the Papal States, Calvin's Geneva, the Taliban's Afghanistan, and the Islamic Republic of Iran.

theory   In the most general sense, an orderly system of knowledge. The proper scope of theory and its relationship to empirical data have been widely debated in the social sciences. Consequently, there are many definitions of theory, models of theory building, and criteria of validity. The root of the term lies in ARISTOTLE's distinction of knowledge pursued purely for the sake of understanding from other forms of knowledge, especially in regard to things that either cannot change or that exist separately from human beings (including physics and mathematics). *Practical* knowledge, in contrast, focuses on producing valid judgment in changeable activities, such as politics and ethics. *Poesis* refers to knowledge made manifest in producing something (i.e., craft skill). Aristotle's typology informed an enduring distinction between theory, produced from a contemplative or objective orientation, and practical reason, embedded in the relationship of an actor to the world. Philosophy claimed dominance in the realm of theory, and purported to give an all-encompassing account of reality. Such theories were in principle true, although potentially disconnected from many matters of everyday concern. This gave rise to the saying that a thing may be true in theory but not in practice.

Science, in contrast, arose from attempts to make things work in practice and from efforts to correct theory with the results of empirical observations. It was then a short step to two of the three main modern understandings of theory: the view of theory as conjecture to be tested and either confirmed or refuted, and the view of theory as a summary of all that had been found to be true so far. The third sense emerged later: theory began to be understood as the source of concepts and the connections among them that made it possible to produce hypotheses, identify confirmations or refutations, and thus understand discrete phenomena as related. This third sense was clarified when David HUME demonstrated that observation enabled only knowledge of correlation, not causation.

The social sciences have produced all three sorts of "theories," and they have been bedeviled by the failure to keep them conceptually distinct. Some social scientists have wished to build knowledge on as purely empirical grounds as possible; these empiricists have tried to restrict theory to inventories and structures of tested and confirmed propositions—that is, to facts. This has the virtue of requiring careful elaboration of what is said to be known and on what basis, but it fails to make sense of the generation of new propositions or even the role of theory in constituting a sufficient common language for determining what counts as a valid proposition or empirical test.

A second group of theorists has concentrated on the perfection of abstract systems of propositions, including the definitions necessary to make sense of them. These may be improved by testing, but they gain much of their persuasive force through completeness of elaboration, elegance, and parsimony. Formal theory of this sort is dominant in economics, where it is commonly expressed in sophisticated mathematical forms. It appears also in other disciplines, both in similarly formal RATIONAL-CHOICE THEORY and in less formally expressed theories like Talcott PARSONS's or Niklas LUHMANN's versions of SYSTEM(S) THEORY, which are driven by similar aspirations and criteria of judgment.

The third kind of theory is often produced by the same social scientists as the second, although it also has its specialists. Thus, Robert K. MERTON may have had Parsons in mind when he called for a distinction between theories proper (by which he meant formal, abstract theories of the second sort) and *theoretical orientations* (by which he meant the third). Colloquially, many social scientists reproduce this distinction by distinguishing between lower case "theories" and upper case "Theory." These orientations shape not only the interpretation of data, but the direction and methodologies of research. Many theoretical debates are, in fact, debates between theoretical orientations in this third sense, and they are thus not strictly resolvable by empirical research findings. Arguments between Marxists and functionalists, or between liberals and communitarians, or between advocates of neoclassical economic theory and analysts of transaction costs are generally of this sort.

POSITIVISM has become a label for attempts to combine empirical certainty with theoretical comprehensiveness. Merton called for separating the comprehensive goals proper to orientations from the more narrowly explanatory project of theories. Theories, he held, needed to be more than mere hypotheses but less than global systems. In order to achieve parsimony and elegance, and also to be empirically corrigible (if not perfectly testable), theories should work at a middle range, mediating between specific research results and broader orientations (see MIDDLE RANGE, THEORY OF THE). While Merton's argument has been influential and widely praised, it has not succeeded in clearing up all confusion. The main reason is that theories, in the sense of orderly systems of propositions, depend heavily on the prior role of theoretical orientations to establish a general sense of how the world works, what counts as evidence, how terms should be understood, and so on.

Perhaps the simplest way of thinking about the issue is to see that people may evaluate theories on the basis of different criteria. Some want high reliability and closeness to the data. Some want elegance and parsimony, explaining as much as possible on a narrow base of assumption. Others want synthesis, bringing the maximum range of knowledge into one framework, even at the expense of parsimony. Finally, some want social theory to be as objective as possible, while others want it to be engaged in changing the world.

All of the above discussion concerns *empirical theory*, that is, theory that purports to explain how the world works. In some areas of social science, *normative theory* is also important. Normative theory assesses questions of how society should be organized or how people should act. It is concerned with issues of the good or of justice rather than with truth or falsehood (although normative theory also depends on background assumptions about how the world actually works). Some theories (and debates) concern both empirical explanation and moral order; LIBERALISM, COMMUNITARIANISM, UTILITARIANISM, and MARXISM all exemplify this. These are broad theoretical orientations, to transplant Merton's term from empirical to normative theory. Within each, there are also more specific theories, such as the communitarian theory of group rights or the liberal theory of free speech.

In both normative and empirical realms, a large part of what theory offers is systematicity—the attempt to understand how different propositions (factual or normative) relate to each other. The truth of some propositions may depend on others, or on mere assumptions. Theory examines such dependencies. The value of concepts depends on the clarity and coherence of their formulation and their adequacy to their conceptual frameworks. Theory helps us to understand the world and our own choices better, but never perfectly. As a result, there are always multiple theories in the social sciences. These produce arguments, but even more importantly, they offer the capacity to clarify what is at stake in arguments.

theory-laden Refers to propositions that are only true in the context of a given theory. Such propositions are contrasted to *objective* or *theory-neutral* propositions, although the distinction is challenged by thinkers like Thomas KUHN, who argue that all science is discursively constructed and thus that there are no perfectly neutral propositions. POSTSTRUCTURALISM offers a similar critique.

thick description Proposed by Clifford GEERTZ in *The Interpretation of Cultures* (1973), the term refers to an ethnographic method that privileges sensitivity to detail and the multiple significations that an activity, event, or SYMBOL may bear. It implies not merely description but also the interpretation of the relationship between symbol and context on a potentially large number of levels. Geertz distinguishes this practice from the broad comparative analysis characteristic of much social and structuralist anthropology, which claims to discover a single language or matrix for the interpretation of phenomena across a wide range of cultures. In this, thick description reclaims some of Franz BOAS's concern with the particularity and incommensurability of cultures.

third world Originally introduced in the late 1940s to describe European countries that might remain neutral in the COLD WAR between the United States and the Soviet Union. The term was reformulated by the United Nations to describe the economically underdeveloped countries of the world—especially in Latin America, Africa, and parts of Asia. These were differentiated from the advanced industrial capitalist societies of the *first world* (the United States, Western Europe, and Japan, most prominently) and from the socialist industrial planned economies of the *second world* (the Soviet Union and its Eastern European satellites). Because of this mix of political and economic criteria, the "third world" has always been a catchall category that included oil-rich states with high per capita incomes, unevenly developed countries such as Brazil and India, and the most impoverished, underdeveloped nations. This imprecision has become more striking with the end of the Cold War, which dissolved the political matrix in which the term made most sense. Development issues, moreover, have become more complex in the context of rapid GLOBALIZATION and the breakup of the Soviet Bloc. Former socialist countries have not, in most cases, made easy transitions to CAPITALISM, and some have fallen into economic distress (e.g., Russia and Romania). In contrast, several historically underdeveloped countries have profited by globalization and have moved closer to the developed world—if often with considerable internal disparities (e.g., Malaysia and Brazil). Because of these issues, the term is less commonly used by specialists of political and development issues, but it continues to circulate in popular usage.

Thomas, William Isaac (1863–1947) One of the founding members of the CHICAGO SCHOOL OF SOCIOLOGY at the University of Chicago. Thomas is most often remembered for his work on the "definition of the situation"—the way in which persons subjectively construct the meaning of social situations, sometimes with little connection to the "objective" facts. In his succinct and oft-quoted description of this process, Thomas noted that "If men define situations as real, they are real in their consequences."

Thomas worked primarily on immigration and urban issues. His major work is *The Polish Peasant in Europe and America* (1918–1921, with Florian Znaniecki), a pathbreaking study of immigration, SOCIALIZATION, and ETHNICITY. He also served a term as president of the American Sociological Association (1927).

Thompson, Edward Palmer (1924–1993) A historian of eighteenth- and nineteenth-century England, Thompson was one of the first writers to emphasize the recovery of the history of social actors who had been marginalized by traditional historiography—in his best-known work, the diverse craft, guild, and small-industry workers who mounted the early resistance to capitalist industrialization and who contributed visions of social and economic organization to socialism and other radical movements (*The Making of the English Working Class*, 1963). Thompson's book had a major impact on social history and historical sociology, opening up new topics of study and promoting a highly integrated view of culture. Working against the dominant narratives of industrialization, he emphasized the forms of local agency of small social actors—investigating criminality, local rituals and practices, food riots, and other forms of popular protest. In this context, Thompson famously described class as a "happening" rather than a fixed structure.

The Making of the English Working Class was also one of the crucial early contributions to the CULTURAL STUDIES movement, then in its formative years at the University of Birmingham. Thompson's relatively supple MARXISM and interest in working-class culture aligned his work with that of contemporaries Richard HOGGART, then director of the Birmingham school, and Raymond WILLIAMS. Together, they set the main direction of cultural studies in the 1960s. In the 1970s, Thompson became a strong critic of emerging trends in cultural theory, particularly the hyperabstraction and risk of political disengagement he found in POSTSTRUCTURALISM. This led him to a restatement of the political stakes of historical research in *The Poverty of Theory* (1978). Throughout his career, Thompson wrote in a manner accessible to a broad readership. This, like the years he spent teaching adults in worker-education programs, reflected his commitment to the intellectual potential of ordinary citizens and to a broadly democratic emancipatory radicalism. These commitments affirm his membership in a lineage of English radicals (about whom he also wrote) that runs from William Blake to John Ruskin and William Morris.

In addition to his historical writing, Thompson was also a founder and, briefly, editor of the *New Left Review* in the early 1960s. He also intervened directly in a wide range of contemporary political debates, from university management in *Warwick University, Inc.* (1970) to nuclear disarmament in *Writing by Candlelight* (1980). His other major works include *William Morris: Romantic to Revolutionary* (1955), *Whigs and Hunters: The Origin of the Black Act* (1975), and *Witness Against the Beast: William Blake and the Moral Law* (1993).

tight money A phase of monetary policy in which the supply of credit is restricted and interest rates are high; the term refers to the tightness of the supply of money relative to demand. Tight-money policies are adopted to reduce the level or growth of aggregate demand and to curtail inflationary pressures in the economy.

Tilly, Charles (1926–) An American historical sociologist best known for his work on the relationship between collective action and long-term social transformations in France, particularly with respect to INDUSTRIALIZATION, urbanization, and the growth of the STATE. Against prevailing assumptions about the disorganized character of much nineteenth-century social unrest, Tilly emphasized the strategic dimension of protest movements, labor activism, and small-scale insurrections. Tilly has been a key analyst of transformations in state power and their implications for popular politics, as well as of the importance of warfare as an agent of social change (including state-making). He has also been an influential methodologist. His major works include *The Vendée* (1964), *The Rebellious Century, 1830–1930* (1975, with Louise and Richard Tilly), *From Mobilization to Revolution* (1978), *As Sociology Meets History* (1981), *Big Structures, Large Processes, Huge Comparisons* (1985), *Coercion Capital and European States. AD 990–1990* (1990), *Durable Inequality* (1998), and *From Contention To Democracy* (1998, with Marco Giugni and Doug McAdam).

time inconsistency Also *dynamic inconsistency*. Refers to the divergence of a policy choice from optimality over time. Consider a policy established today that needs to be implemented over several years. Such plans are generally optimal from the perspective of today's policymakers (for example, the decision to delay a tax increase). For a plan to be dynamically consistent, however, it must be optimal at each point in the future as well, especially if future policymakers have to implement those stages. The same notion holds for individual decisions. Dynamic consistency is equivalent to the notion of *subgame perfection* in GAME THEORY.

The problem and its implications have been the subject of extensive research since Finn Kydland and Edward Prescott (1977) demonstrated that optimal macroeconomic policies can be dynamically inconsistent. If so, they are not currently credible either, because in the future the policies will not be carried out.

time preference The general principle that people prefer goods available for use in the present to goods available for use in the future. This preference is rooted in a variety of possible factors: the risk of death, the presence of myopia on the part of economic agents, or individual expectations of greater wealth in the future—all of which would raise the value of present consumption relative to future consumption. Such considerations lead economic agents to discount future costs and benefits by a subjective discount factor, known as the *rate* of time preference. This is especially prevalent with regard to the time value of MONEY, since money in hand may be invested and increase, while money paid in the future cannot and is subject to possible inflation.

time series analysis The study of the dependence of observations at different points in time. Any series of observations that is temporally ordered may be called a *time series*, but generally the term is used for observations that are frequent and regular enough to generate a continuous variable. Various economic variables such as GNP (gross national product) and prices are observed over time, and time series analysis concerns itself with the relationships among the current and past values of one or more of them. Time series analysis is used for forecasting the future values of variables, for analyzing the cyclical properties of economic variables, for the description of economic variables that exhibit seasonal and periodic fluctuations, and for constructing dynamic econometric models.

time–space compression Geographer David HARVEY's term for the increasingly rapid transfer of information and capital in postmodern society—a development that suppresses the once fundamental and ubiquitous social realities of distance and delay for much of the industrialized world. Time–space compression, for Harvey, is a fundamental experiential and social feature of

POSTMODERNISM. See Harvey's *The Condition of Postmodernity* (1989).

timocracy Used by PLATO in *The Republic* to describe an ideal state structured around aristocratic honor, bravery, and military virtue. Sparta was Plato's example of a timocratic state. ARISTOTLE uses the term somewhat differently to describe a state in which property confers civic honor and political power.

Tinbergen, Jan   (1903–1994) Primarily a theoretical statistician, Tinbergen made numerous contributions to the applied econometric analysis of the dynamics of modern economies. These contributions earned him the first Nobel Prize in economics in 1969 (shared with Ragnar FRISCH).

Tinbergen was born in the Netherlands and studied mathematical physics at Leiden University. He later became professor of economics at the Netherlands School of Economics. His first major publications dealt with theoretical issues in dynamics, such as the COBWEB THEOREM and "shipbuilding cycles." From a theoretical point of view, Tinbergen introduced a system that accommodated both discrete changes in time (difference equations) as well as continuous change (differential equations). His innovative tool played an important role in Frisch's theory of cycles and Michal KALECKI's macrodynamic model.

Tinbergen is best known for his work on economy-wide models. He established his reputation in this area with "An Economic Policy for 1936" (1959)—a quantitative analysis of the Dutch economy. Tinbergen was soon invited by the League of Nations to expand this model as part of its project on business cycles. This work comprised two parts: (1) an exposition of the correct statistical method to use in analyzing investment fluctuations; and (2) a statistical analysis of business cycles in the United States from 1919 to 1932. John Maynard KEYNES wrote a famous review of the first part in which he criticized Tinbergen's methods. Nevertheless, Tinbergen's approach to economy-wide quantitative models became quite influential.

As early as 1942, Tinbergen wrote a paper considered by many to have anticipated Robert SOLOW's growth model—although it did not attract much attention at the time. In later years, Tinbergen focused on the growth problems of developing countries, as well as on the effects of changes in income distribution. He also served as an adviser to several national governments, including his own. While Tinbergen's efforts in these fields lacked the originality of his earlier theoretical work, his emphasis on empirical methods and quantitative study of the economy helped steer economics away from the deductive practices that had dominated in the nineteenth century.

tobit models   See LOGIT, PROBIT, AND TOBIT MODELS.

Tocqueville, Alexis de   (1805–1859) French politician, historian, sociologist, and political scientist who profoundly shaped debates about LIBERALISM and EQUALITY in the nineteenth century, especially through his study of American DEMOCRACY. Tocqueville was rediscovered in the twentieth century as a prescient critic of state power and remains one of the foremost influences on democratic theory.

Tocqueville was born and raised in an aristocratic family deeply marked by the violence of the French Revolution and the turmoil of the Napoleonic Wars. He sought a career in politics, studied law, and initially served as a magistrate in Versailles. With the July Revolution of 1830, family loyalties to the deposed Bourbon monarchs made Tocqueville's position precarious—although he was himself close to the liberals. Partly to escape these uncertainties, he obtained permission to study prison reform in the United States with his lifelong friend Gustave de Beaumont. Their nine-month trip during 1831 and 1832 furnished Tocqueville not only with the material for *On the Penitentiary System in the United States and Its Application in France* (1833, with Beaumont) but also with notes toward a much broader study of American democracy and society. On his return to France, Tocqueville resigned from the magistracy and devoted himself to writing *Democracy in America* (1835, 1840).

Tocqueville believed that *equality* was the great social and political idea of the age and that the modern era could be interpreted in terms of its progress. Liberal victories during the July Revolution seemed further confirmation of this. Although Tocqueville initially looked to England as a model of equality within a structure of monarchical rule, he became increasingly convinced that the United States was the most advanced example of this global tendency.

Tocqueville's essential concerns in *Democracy in America* were the fate of democratic societies and the lessons that the American experience might offer the French. In the first volume,

he offered a remarkable analysis of American society and character that remains a touchstone of historical research. The equality of condition enjoyed by Americans, he argued, made for a superficial diversity of views and beliefs but also a strong conformity in mores, which posed a risk to the freedoms that democratic government and social equality made possible. In the second volume, Tocqueville expanded on the dangers of democratic equality. Carried to extremes, he argued, it led toward a debased and isolated individualism, in which rivalry among neighbors undermined community and made each feel weak and in want of support. Tocqueville lamented the loss of "intermediary" structures between the individual and the American state—a buffering role once played by corporate structures and the aristocracy—and he feared that individuals would seek support from the state instead of from one another. The state would grow as it became the singular power in society and the necessary guarantor of equality; individuals, in such circumstances, would lose the ability to challenge the state. Eventually, the state might come to seem an essential support for individualism. The result, Tocqueville suggested, would be a form of gentle, democratic tyranny. It remained to be seen whether the loose federal structure of American government and the American traditions of local and self-rule would provide an adequate check on these tendencies.

Tocqueville reentered politics in 1839 and became a deputy in the assembly. He played an active role in the political turmoil following the Revolution of 1848, siding with the liberal BOURGEOISIE against the demands of the working class and, later, opposing the coup of Louis Napoléon. Napoléon's victory forced Tocqueville out of politics, and he retreated back into research, this time on the qualities and defects of the *ancien régime* and its continuities with the new one. The result was another celebrated study, *The Old Regime and the French Revolution* (1856). Tocqueville suffered long periods of poor health and nervous exhaustion; he suffered a fatal collapse at the age of 54.

Tocqueville's attention to the dangers of conformity and the expansion of the state seemed obsolete to many social theorists by the end of the nineteenth century, as class struggle intensified and as progressive movements sought out government solutions to social and economic ills. However, he was rediscovered as a defender of liberal democracy in the post–World War II era by English and American scholars who were critical of TOTALITARIANISM and fearful of the decline of democratic culture at home. More recently, his work has influenced some versions of COMMUNITARIANISM.

toleration The recognition of or respect for others' opinions, beliefs, or practices, by those who do not share them. The modern idea of *toleration* emerged as a response to the religious controversies that wracked post-Reformation Europe, and played a fundamental role in emerging liberal discourse on the relationship between the state and society. John LOCKE's *Letter Concerning Toleration* (1689) is perhaps the key document in this development. There, Locke argued that states should refrain from passing judgment on the truth of competing religious doctrines and simply uphold public order and citizens' rights. Over time, this principle was extended into other areas of moral controversy. In *On Liberty* (1859), John Stuart MILL defended toleration on the grounds that it engenders the free expression of opinions. According to Mill, the airing of what some consider heretical doctrines in an open public sphere prompts debate and deliberation, which eventually fosters genuine knowledge.

In modern liberal theory, the principle of state neutrality with regard to a wide range of beliefs and practices is central. There is considerable disagreement, however, about the meaningful limits of toleration in a liberal society—especially where individuals or groups challenge the core principles of LIBERALISM or pluralist conceptions of society (see PLURALISM). MULTICULTURALISM, although concerned primarily with lifestyle issues that traditionally fall within the liberal conception of tolerance, has been a source of debate—in particular for those who equate the liberal democratic tradition with certain cultural or ethnic foundations. Some argue, in this context, that neutrality on many points is equivalent to moral relativism and that the values of liberal (or Western) society are substantive and universalizable, rather than simply formal, procedural, and local. Herbert MARCUSE, in his influential critique of "repressive tolerance" (1969), argued that the tolerance espoused by modern liberalism was above all a form of neutralization of radical dissent. It was incompatible, he argued, with a more genuine notion of tolerance rooted in principles of social and economic justice.

Tönnies, Ferdinand (1855–1936) A German sociologist who developed one of the early and most influential conceptual distinctions between traditional and modern forms of social organization, *Gemeinschaft* (community) and *Gesellschaft* (society, or association) (see GEMEINSCHAFT AND GESELLSCHAFT). Tönnies also played a major institution-building role in German SOCIOLOGY, cofounding the German Sociological Association (1909, with Georg SIMMEL, Max WEBER, Werner Sombart, and others).

Tönnies's account of *Gemeinschaft* and *Gesellschaft* in the book of that name (1887) was one of a number of turn-of-the-century attempts to theorize the specificity of the modern. For Tönnies, *Gemeinschaft* describes a situation in which common values, aspirations, roles, and sometimes common ancestry are the dominant social forces. Individuals are embedded in and supported by a strong social network of friends and relatives, with whom they build close and emotional ties through face-to-face interactions. Status is usually ascribed at birth, geographic mobility is often limited, and individuals associate their identities with their places in the community. *Gesellschaft*, in contrast, expresses the turn toward urban, industrial styles of life and to the patterns of calculated, rationalized behavior that increasingly underlie daily activity. Relationships between and among individuals tend to be more superficial, impersonal, and anonymous, as reflected in the diminished role of shared values, backgrounds, norms, and attitudes. Even work roles do not provide a common ground, since urbanization calls for both increased specialization and mobility.

Tönnies's distinction was primarily a historical one, but it also reflected a distinction between two forms of human will. *Gemeinschaft*, he argued, is characterized by the *Wessenwill* ("essential will"), an organic and habitual or instinctive force, whereas *Gesellschaft* is marked by the *Kurwille* ("rational will"), which is deliberate and instrumental. In general, Tönnies lamented the dissolution of community life and the development of modern individualism. He argued that life in modern cities is too often reduced to a strict regimen of industrial discipline, "low pleasures," and the resulting decay of CULTURE. Tönnies hoped that a reintroduction of community spirit might salvage this situation. He did not conceive of this simply as a return to *Gemeinschaft*, however, but as the development of public opinion as a rational collective judgment on basic normative issues. In his *Kritik der öffentlichen Meinung* (*Critique of Public Opinion*, 1922, never fully translated into

English), Tönnies presented the public as an intellectual community, created among dispersed persons on the basis of communication and shared knowledge.

Tönnies worked and actively researched in a number of other areas, including the editing and commentary of Thomas HOBBES's work, the philosophy of law, and political reform—although nowhere with comparable effect. His last years were distinguished by his active stand against NAZISM, which cost him his professorship at the University of Kiel.

total factor productivity Growth-accounting procedures in economics have been unable to fully explain actual growth performance on the basis of the two key contributors: capital and labor. That part of the growth of output that remains unaccounted for after determining the contribution of labor and capital is referred to as *total factor productivity growth*. It is alternatively referred to as technical progress or increased efficiency and is often attributed to the inadequacy of current economic theory and measurements.

total institution A closed social system, such as a prison or mental hospital, where people are isolated from society and subject to a highly regimented existence. Erving GOFFMAN introduced the term in *Asylums* (1961) and placed particular emphasis on how life in such institutions is structured around principles of bureaucratic control. He focused also on the internal culture of inmates, which reflects processes of adaptation and resistance. Goffman recognized the relevance of the concept to a wide range of institutions, from monastic orders to concentration camps.

totalitarianism An extreme form of DICTATORSHIP characterized primarily by its ambition to control all aspects of individual and social behavior, although other features, such as large-scale social engineering and utopian agendas, mass politics organized around a single party, organized terror, and personality cults, play a part in some accounts. Totalitarianism is distinct, in these respects, from most earlier forms of TYRANNY, dictatorship, and ABSOLUTISM, which, while concerned with monopolizing political power, were rarely as comprehensive in their domination of other realms of social and economic life. Early connotations were somewhat broader—the term was applied in the 1920s to

a number of right-wing regimes, including Fascist Italy. Nazi Germany (1933–1945), however, provides the most enduring vision of totalitarianism, later extended to include Stalinism in the Soviet Union (1929–1956) and a number of other communist regimes (e.g., North Korea).

Totalitarianism is a distinctly twentieth-century phenomenon, marked by a strong relationship to modern technology, particularly in the field of communications. Totalitarian regimes were among the first to recognize and exploit the power of mass media, such as radio and film. They also took advantage of innovations in bureaucratic organization to track and administer society and to support secret police forces used to terrorize actual and potential dissenters. The completeness of such systems was a key subject of early debates about totalitarianism. The FRANKFURT SCHOOL's pioneering analyses of Nazi Germany set the terms for much of this research, via studies of the psychological matrix of authoritarianism (see Theodor ADORNO) and the terroristic organization of political authority (Franz Neumann). Many commentators saw the new technologies of social control as guarantees of the permanence of these regimes (for example, George Orwell); many viewed the attack on all forms of social bond outside the state as resulting in a fundamentally altered, conformist human subject. Hannah ARENDT, in her influential analysis, *Totalitarianism* (1951), both developed and critiqued this tradition by presenting the systematic reduction of politics to material concerns as fundamentally destructive of the capacity to reproduce public life. Continuities between ideas of "social engineering" in modern social thought and the extreme forms these took in Nazi Germany are also stressed by Zygmunt Bauman in *Modernity and the Holocaust* (1991).

American COLD WAR scholarship—especially that of Zbigniew Brzezinski, Carl Friedrich, and Jane Kirkpatrick—turned the discussion from Nazi Germany to the Soviet Union. Much of this work sharpened assumptions about the fundamental stability of the totalitarian regimes and their diametric opposition to Western democracy. Kirkpatrick, in particular, developed a controversial distinction between totalitarian and authoritarian regimes that emphasized the implacability and special oppressiveness of the former and that implicitly justified American support, where necessary, for the latter. This monolithic view began to change in the 1970s and 1980s, especially among scholars of the Soviet Union. These began to question whether complete control was ever possible, much less achieved. Contemporary accounts of Soviet politics call attention to the competition between various internal centers of power, such as industrial sectors, the regional governments, and the military, and to the pervasive separation of public acts of conformity from private life. Research on this subject—including continued interest in the dynamics of Nazi rule—continues to animate debates in history and political science.

total war See WAR.

totemism A form of identification between KINSHIP groups and certain animals or natural phenomena. Totemism has been extensively debated in anthropology and has played a key role in theories about the origins of religion (Emile DURKHEIM), law (Sigmund FREUD), and the regulation of kin identity and EXOGAMY (Claude LÉVI-STRAUSS). Totems symbolically condense a wide range of societal distinctions and rules, including those involving food, sex, the economy, kinship, and the line between the SACRED and the PROFANE.

tradable commodities and nontradable commodities *Tradable commodities* are those goods and services for which there exist international markets. *Nontradable commodities* are those for which there are only domestic markets. The distinction of goods and services into "tradable" and "nontradable" is a distinguishing feature of models of international trade. Certain commodities may be nontradable either intrinsically (because they do not travel well; land, for example) or because they are unprofitable to trade, given the costs of transportation or the imposition of tariffs and quotas.

trade union See LABOR UNION.

tradition Generally refers to persistent cultural patterns that evoke or testify to continuity with the past. In principle, these can be of almost any kind: beliefs, customs, knowledge, or values. Some accounts of tradition stress actual continuity with the past; others stress the belief that certain practices are legitimate or proper because of their antiquity. Such venerable traditions may actually be relatively new or flexible, yet they may appear to social actors as "that which we have always done."

The concept of tradition has a long and varied history in the social sciences. It was first shaped by European Enlightenment skepticism toward religion and other inherited knowledge, with its call to test all claims against standards of reason and evidence. In this context, tradition became an inferior basis for claims to knowledge. This usage soon generated the opposition of "traditional" with "modern," as well as the disadvantageous comparison of the former to the latter. Increasingly, traditional cultures became identified with resistance to change, while the modern was largely defined by its orientation to progress. This view figured in anthropological studies of communities in transition or crisis. Much of the early twentieth-century anthropological theory of MODERNIZATION, from Franz BOAS to Robert REDFIELD, uses some version of this oppositional framework. Redfield went further in describing an opposition between the Great traditions of urban elites and the Little traditions of local and/or oral knowledge and custom (see GREAT AND LITTLE TRADITIONS).

Tradition was also given a particular inflection by research that sought to recover the ostensibly untainted experience of premodern peoples. In this context, tradition was difficult to distinguish from CULTURE, insofar as cultural features that existed independent of contact with the West or other external influences constituted, in effect, both tradition and the original culture. This notion of tradition was rooted in a concept of authenticity that demanded constant triage to separate out traditional elements from new or imported practices, and it lent itself to popular acts of "rediscovery" of traditions that had long since disappeared from contemporary practice. Early ETHNOLOGY was dominated by this perspective, and it continues to characterize a great deal of popular discourse on tradition.

Since the 1960s, there has been a broad turn toward interrogating the authenticity of tradition. Historians such as Eric Hobsbawm, Terrence Ranger, Edward Spicer, and Raymond WILLIAMS have looked at the historical pressures that foster the conscious elaboration of tradition, particularly the relativization of worldviews and competition among groups. The high valuation of tradition occurs, many of these scholars suggest, after the emergence of PLURALISM and conscious reflection upon group identity. These writers have also emphasized the instrumental value of tradition, whether as a means of investing actors or social goals with legitimacy or as a means of resisting (or, less often, facilitating) social change.

Most scholars now avoid the dichotomy between traditional and modern, suggesting among other things that it obscures the level of change in so-called traditional societies. Tradition may be better seen as a process in which culture is continuously renewed with reference to the past. In this sense, even modern scientific fields are often described as embodying different traditions, since no knowledge is passed on purely on the basis of reason and logic without involving some level of less explicit culture. A scientific tradition, thus, may include a particular structure of prestige within subfields or certain preconceptions about appropriate problems for inquiry.

transactionalism A theory of political action that analyzes the formation of political groups and social hierarchies in terms of the individual relations between leaders and their clients. Transactionalism was developed by Fredrik Barth in *Political Leadership among the Swat Pathans* (1959) and achieved considerable currency in the 1970s. It presumes a widely generalizable, cross-cultural framework of rational choice and methodological individualism—assumptions that tend to divide social theorists, and that have been the basis of criticism of the theory. See also RATIONAL-CHOICE THEORY.

transaction costs A catchall for heterogeneous costs that arise in economic activity. In many deals, parties have to find each other, communicate, measure and inspect the goods that are to be purchased, draw up the contract using lawyers, keep records, and so on. In some cases, compliance needs to be enforced through legal action. All these entail costs in terms of real resources and time, termed *transaction costs*. The reality of these costs contrasts with the frequent assumption of a perfectly clearing, frictionless market.

Transaction costs reduce the volume of transactions and provide incentives to individuals to economize and bundle their transactions. This idea has been used to explain the establishment and organization of firms (see Ronald COASE, 1937), and it has also played a major role in explaining the demand for money (see W. J. Baumol, 1952; James Tobin, 1956). The establishment of firms internalized some transactions and thereby obviated the need to incur the transaction costs of both price and market mechanisms in those cases. Similarly, cash balances are held because the costs of buying and selling assets are too high, compared to the yield on cash for short holding periods. Transaction costs inevitably reduce welfare by suppressing mutually beneficial transactions and by using up resources.

transculturation Also ACCULTURATION. Cultural change resulting from contact between cultures.

transference In PSYCHOANALYSIS, the process whereby the patient's relationship to the therapist reproduces aspects of the patient's neurosis. In its classic form, the patient invests the relationship with the therapist with feelings of love, fear, loyalty, hatred, or other emotion, that draw upon the crucial childhood or familial situations that form the core of the neurosis. Sigmund FREUD was the first to realize that the patient's transference was a repetition of "repressed material," and that it thereby provided a key subject of the analysis itself. The analysis of the transference might then allow the patient to consign the neurotic investment to the past, breaking its hold on present emotional life. Nonetheless, transference has always been an extremely difficult area for psychoanalysis, not least because of the risk of countertransference on the part of the analyst.

transfer payments A payment in which the payer receives nothing valuable in exchange—as distinct from an exchange transaction in which both parties stand to benefit. Government payments for retirement or poverty assistance are the classic examples of transfer payments. Transfers can also be made between individuals and between countries. Generally, transfers differ from gifts in that they serve specific social objectives, such as equity.

transfer pricing Prices attached by a business enterprise to transactions between its affiliates or divisions. They are used to value internal transfers of goods, technology, financial and other services, as well as for internal management control and the monitoring of the performance of various operating divisions. Transfer pricing is also frequently employed by multinational corporations in order to minimize tax liabilities.

transfer problem Describes the adverse secondary effects of large transfer payments between countries, such as reparation payments. In addition to the cost of the payment, the paying country will suffer a secondary burden in the form of a decline in its international TERMS OF TRADE. This secondary burden might be so large as to reduce the value of traded goods produced in the affected country to an amount less than the required transfer. In 1919, Germany was required to make reparations to the European powers as a condition of the Treaty of Versailles. Initially, Germany's capacity to pay was assessed on the basis of constant international prices. John Maynard KEYNES (1929) was the first to identify the transfer problem in the German case. Many of Keynes's fears were borne out as Germany suffered hyperinflation in the 1920s. The relationship between transfer payments and terms of trade subsequently became an important subject of economic research.

transformational–generative grammar   A theory of language developed by Noam CHOMSKY in the late 1950s that holds that humans have a biological or "hard-wired" competency for grammar that generates all particular grammatical systems. Chomsky distinguished between a deep universal set of grammatical dispositions, a contingent surface set, and the *transformational* rules that mediate between the two. The scientific ambition of transformational LINGUISTICS is twofold: to explain this deep grammatical structure, enabling the formulation of a "universal grammar"; and to produce grammars of specific languages consistent with the universal grammar. Although the system has been substantially revised by Chomsky and others through the years, some version of transformational–generative grammar underlies most contemporary research in linguistics.

The scientific goals of transformational–generative grammar have been the basis of claims that language is autonomous from its cultural or semantic context. This tendency has been much criticized by those who see Chomsky's work as inattentive to the cultural diversity, practical nature, and context specificity of language use. Nonetheless, transformational–generative grammar has found a wide audience in other areas of the social sciences, especially among structural and cognitive anthropologists.

transformation problem   The problem in Marxian economics of deriving a unique set of prices from labor inputs. The transformation problem arose from the attempt to show that the LABOR THEORY OF VALUE is consistent with the money prices of exchange. Marx argued that prices are transformed values and that profit is redistributed surplus value. The equality of these aggregates was used to argue that nothing had been created or destroyed in the transformation

from value to prices and that only a redistribution had occurred.

transhumance   Seasonal movement of a population from one region to another so as to benefit from differences in ECOLOGY. The term typically refers to the movement of livestock or to the pastoral and/or nomadic cultures that follow or facilitate such movement.

transitional objects   Privileged objects (such as toys or a blanket) that help a child adapt to the constraints of reality. Associated with OBJECT-RELATIONS THEORY and the work of Donald Woods WINNICOTT in particular.

transnationalism   Refers to activities that cross state boundaries, such as human migration, the flow of ideas and information, and movements of money and credit. The term is often used in preference to "international" to distinguish such phenomena from interstate political relations.

Transnational flows are not new; the trans-Atlantic migrations of the nineteenth century and the spread of NATIONALISM, COMMUNISM, and other political ideologies are notable examples. More recent innovations in the fields of communications and transportation have vastly expanded and intensified transnational activities. Multinational corporations (MNCs)—incorporated in a "home" state and operating with subsidiaries in "host" states—are among the most visible transnational actors. Others include such internationally active organizations as the Roman Catholic church and the Palestine Liberation Organization (PLO). Transnational flows are often cited as threats to the political and economic self-determination of NATION-STATES, particularly in the fields of macroeconomic policy and immigration—although this is not always easy to establish empirically. See also GLOBALIZATION.

triangulation   A way of assuring the validity of research results through the use of different research methods and approaches. Methodological triangulation involves the use of multiple methods in the analysis of the same set of data. Theoretical triangulation involves the use of multiple theoretical perspectives. Data triangulation means that data are gathered using multiple sampling strategies. In investigator triangulation, more than one investigator is used in the field situation. The strongest form of triangulation is *multiple triangulation*, which brings to bear all four varieties at once. See also MULTIPLE-INDICATOR MODELS.

tribes Tribes have been at the center of anthropological research since its inception, and anthropologists have spent nearly as long trying to determine the distinguishing characteristics of this favored subject. Nineteenth-century anthropologists, such as Lewis Henry MORGAN and Henry James Sumner MAINE, tended to equate tribes with the absence of political institutions or contractual relations. Subsequent research complicated such models, even while, in some cases, retaining their evolutionary underpinnings. In *Primitive Social Organization* (1962), Elmer Service proposed an influential evolutionary framework, based on a schema of political organization that distinguished bands, TRIBES, CHIEFDOMS, and STATEs. Others have suggested that tribes are, to a degree, the products of state consolidation, even prior to European colonization. Certainly there is no tribal situation today that does not negotiate its relationship to or distance from states. With these limitations in view, some anthropologists prefer the broader term ETHNICITY, although the history of many groups is so coded in the language of tribes that this terminological importation raises yet another set of categorizing problems.

Trotskyism A tradition of Marxist theory and revolutionary practice associated with Leon Trotsky (1879–1940). In the 1920s, Trotsky elaborated a series of critiques of the increasingly authoritarian, nationalistic, and bureaucratic structure of then-emerging Soviet COMMUNISM, especially as Joseph Stalin consolidated his power. The core of Trotskyism is the commitment to "permanent revolution," based in Trotsky's contention that Russian socialism was feasible only if the revolutionary process continued elsewhere. The broader implication of this position was that socialism was possible only with the complete defeat of CAPITALISM. Permanent (i.e., ongoing international) revolution challenged the creation of ever stronger Soviet state authority and the stabilization of control in a class of state officials. Stalin's explicit rejection of both critiques (the former on nationalist grounds) led to Trotsky's exile from the Soviet Union and his eventual assassination by Stalinist agents in Mexico in 1940. Trotskyist currents within MARXISM in the West continued to emphasize this international dimension of revolutionary struggle and provided tools for understanding the bureaucratic authoritarianism,

disastrous social engineering, and imperialism of the Stalinist and post-Stalinist state.

Truman, David (1913–) A prominent scholar of political parties, lobbying, and interest groups in the United States, as well as one of the early and most influential promoters of BEHAVIORALISM in political science. Truman's *The Governmental Process* (1951) largely invented the "group behavioral" approach to American politics. He argued that public policy is not an expression of a neutral "public good" or the result of the capture of the process by a minority but the product of diverse groups acting in their own interests. Truman focused on the strategies that political groups utilize in pursuing those interests and on their relative efficacy in capturing government attention. The American political system, Truman argued, is basically open to contestation and competition among groups; moreover, group interactions, rather than individual politicians, are the determining factors in policymaking. For Truman, the United States is thus a predominantly pluralist political system, in which no group can dominate policy completely for its own ends or ignore public opinion for long. In this context, parties and interest groups operate on different levels—the first geared toward electoral results, the second toward policy. *The Congressional Party* (1959) brought a similar analytical framework to the subject of congressional elections, specifically to the problem of how candidates accommodate the diverse interests of their backers and constituents. Truman argued that the dominant strategy was a form of strategic triangulation among those interests and that the results tended strongly toward centrism within the parties.

Truman was a strong advocate of the empirical and, whenever possible, scientific study of political behavior. He placed an emphasis on rigorous, "value free," highly quantitative methods. These became hallmarks of the behavioral approach that dominated American political science in the 1950s, 1960s, and 1970s.

Truman spent much of the latter part of his career as president of Mount Holyoke College in Massachusetts. His other important work includes *Congress and America's Future* (1965).

Tuan, Yi Fu (1930–) One of the leading cultural geographers of the late twentieth century. Tuan was born in China, educated at the University of Oxford, and pursued doctoral work at the University of California at Berkeley—the center of CULTURAL GEOGRAPHY in the United States under Carl SAUER. Tuan's early work dealt primarily with physical geography, especially the geomorphology of the American West. In the 1960s, he began to engage directly the cultural issues for which he became well known. In several important works, Tuan revisited and rearticulated many of the major concepts of cultural geography, from the concept of place (in *Space and Place: The Perspectives of Experience*, 1977) to *environmental perception*—the study of cultural ideas and human perceptions of the land. A wide-ranging thinker, Tuan has also turned this perspective toward the questions of architecture and morality. His other major works include *Man and Nature* (1971), *Topophilia: A Study of Environmental Perception* (1974), *Landscape of Fear* (1980), and *Morality and Imagination: Paradoxes of Progress* (1989).

Turner, Victor (1920–1983) A leading anthropologist in the study of ritual and a proponent of SYMBOLIC ANTHROPOLOGY in the late 1960s and 1970s. Although educated in the British functionalist school of A. R. RADCLIFFE-BROWN and Max GLUCKMAN, Turner's research among the Ndembu in Central Africa led him to focus increasingly on the complex symbolism of Ndembu collective rituals. In *The Forest of Symbols* (1967), *The Ritual Process* (1969), and other works, Turner made use of Arnold van GENNEP's classic study of "rites of passage" to articulate a more general structure to collective rituals. He emphasized the importance of the transcendent or "liminal" moment, in which the social order is suspended or inverted for the subject or group. Such suspensions, Turner argued, produce a sense of solidarity (or *communitas*), which, despite its ambiguity, serves to reinforce the link between ritual participants and the larger community.

Turner's contribution to symbolic anthropology stems largely from his vivid ethnographic style and confidently speculative interpretations—characteristics that aligned him with such anthropologists as Clifford GEERTZ and David Schneider in privileging the role of the author-ethnographer. Turner's other major works include *The Drums of Affliction* (1968), *Dramas, Fields and Metaphors* (1972), and *Revelation and Divination in Ndembu Ritual* (1975).

turnout The number or percentage of eligible voters who cast ballots in an election. Political scientists have devoted considerable attention to the study of voter turnout, especially in the United States, where turnout is low with respect to other developed democratic societies (in the 1990s, slightly below 50 percent in most national elections and far lower in most state and local elections). A variety of competing explanations for low voter turnout circulate in popular and academic discourse, including voter apathy, voter satisfaction, feelings of disempowerment, and the difficulty of voting. Some states, such as Australia, address this problem through mandatory voting. Some political scientists argue that modest turnout is actually beneficial, in that it reflects informed opinion and signals general support for the government. See also DEMOCRACY; ELECTORAL SYSTEM; and VOTING.

turnpike theory A class of propositions in GROWTH THEORY, concerned with the convergence or the closeness of the economy's optimal growth paths to maximal BALANCED GROWTH paths. The term *turnpike* was coined by Robert Dorfman, Paul SAMUELSON, and Robert SOLOW in *Linear Programming and Economic Analysis* (1958) and is used to signify efficient capital accumulation.

Tylor, Edward Burnett (1832–1917) Tylor can, with considerable justification, be called the founder of modern ANTHROPOLOGY, having developed the theory of social evolution that dominated the field in its first half century. His seminal two-volume work *Primitive Culture* (1871) contains not only an elaborate theory of societal progression through a series of evolutionary stages but also a response to one of the chief challenges to evolutionary theory in his "doctrine of survivals," which explained how characteristics of earlier societal stages were sometimes preserved in living cultures. *Primitive Culture* also contributed to what would become a long-running anthropological debate about the origins of religion, positing an evolutionary progression from ANIMISM to MONOTHEISM.

Tylor had no academic training, but achieved wide recognition in British academic circles and played a crucial role in the institutionalization of anthropology as a field of research. He was appointed to the University of Oxford, elected to the British Royal Society, and served several terms as president of various anthropological associations. Tylor wrote numerous articles but only two other major anthropological works: *Researches into the Early History of Mankind and the Development of Civilization* (1861) and his textbook, *Anthropology: An Introduction to the Study of Man and Civilization* (1881).

tyranny From the Greek *turannos*, meaning "absolute ruler." Initially the term described the rule of a single individual, whether by force or with the tacit or formal consent of the people. By the fifth century BCE, tyranny had acquired its more familiar association: unjust, illegitimate, and lawless rule. PLATO and ARISTOTLE described tyranny as a corrupt form of MONARCHY, in which the society serves the tyrant's ambition and egotism. The term still carries these connotations and is sometimes used to characterize societies in which individuals or single parties rule without regard to the rule of law.

U

ultimogeniture A rule designating the last born (usually, the last-born son) as the successor or heir to property.

unbalanced growth See BALANCED GROWTH; and GROWTH THEORY.

uncertainty Exists when a particular decision can give rise to more than one possible consequence or outcome. Uncertainty has been a topic of persistent interest in ECONOMICS.

There are various categories of economic uncertainty. Sources of *exogenous* uncertainty include consumers' tastes, firm technologies, the weather—all those factors not strictly derived from market exchange. *Endogenous* uncertainty is a function of the operation of the economic system and of the decisions of economic agents—a buyer may face uncertainty in finding a seller (or vice versa); both may be uncertain about the terms of the trade, and so on. Policy uncertainty arises from the margin of unpredictability inherent in decisions about complex and interrelated systems, such as taxes, interest rates, or the provision of public goods. See also RISK.

unconscious Although the concept has many antecedents in Western philosophy, it was Sigmund FREUD who first systematically sought to distinguish between *consciousness*, the *preconscious* (denoting information available but not immediately present in consciousness) and the *unconscious* (a broad realm of the psyche hidden from conscious processes). Although Freud's thinking on the subject evolved considerably during the course of his work, he maintained that what divided the conscious from the unconscious was a mechanism of *repression* that blocked socially unacceptable impulses, wishes, and traumatic experiences from conscious realization. Nonetheless, he argued that the relationship between consciousness and the unconscious was porous and dynamic: the unconscious shaped behavior outside of conscious intention. Freudian "slips" and TRANSFERENCE are examples. Although the manifestations of the unconscious opened it to

study, Freud was highly sensitive to the processes of *condensation* and *displacement*—forms of camouflage and distortion—that repression imposes on unconscious material. Much of Freud's work in this area derived from his study of dreams, where the barriers between the conscious and unconscious were lower than in waking life. In Freud's later work, the term *unconscious* is largely superseded by the notion of the ID—an element of the tripartite division of the psyche into *id, ego,* and *superego.* See also PSYCHOANALYSIS.

underclass Close to the Marxist notion of the LUMPENPROLETARIAT, the term designates people without the means or opportunity for effective legal participation in society. The underclass is thus situated below the working class, which, although exploited, is able to participate in economic reproduction, rather than subsisting on government subsidies, charity, or crime. The emergence of an underclass of structurally unemployed persons—often concentrated in minority groups—has been widely debated in recent years, especially in American urban SOCIOLOGY. Definitions of the underclass vary. Nearly all stress the lack of employment opportunities. This has to do not only with an absolute job shortage, but with a mismatch of skills to opportunities, exacerbated by rising demands for formal education and declining demands for manual labor.

One key part of contemporary sociological debates about the underclass involves the cultural reproduction of structural features of poverty and dependency—single motherhood, criminality, the devaluation of education, and so on—over and above the relative absence of steady employment. Many of these issues are condensed in the controversy surrounding the notion of a *culture of poverty,* animated by Charles Murray and William Julius Wilson among others. Arguments about the underclass have been used to justify an array of policy initiatives from benign neglect of the poor to radical social intervention. The concept has been extended to analyses of the structural subordination of women, and it has come into use in other societies—Britain, in particular—where long-term unemployment has become acute.

underdevelopment See DEVELOPMENT; LESS DEVELOPED COUNTRY (LDC); and MODERNIZATION THEORY.

unemployment The economic definition includes all jobless individuals who are seeking employment. It does not include individuals who choose not to work or who have given up looking for work.

Unemployment may be classified into different types according to its sources. *Frictional unemployment* arises when an individual is temporarily unemployed between jobs. *Structural unemployment* occurs when people find that their skills are obsolete as production and consumption shifts away from certain activities. *Technological unemployment* arises from the adoption of labor-saving techniques as the economy grows. *Seasonal unemployment* occurs in industries such as agriculture or tourism, which exhibit a seasonal pattern of work.

It is generally accepted that there will always be at least some unemployment, even in a healthy economy and without labor-market constraints. Workers find themselves between jobs (frictional unemployment), and the shifting nature of technology means that some structural unemployment may also be unavoidable. This level of unavoidable unemployment is what economists call the *natural rate of unemployment*, or the nonaccelerating inflation rate of unemployment (NAIRU). It is the rate of unemployment that is sustainable in the long-run without inducing increasing inflation. The NAIRU is dependent on historical, economic, technological, and cultural factors, and therefore does not correspond to any particular rate of inflation. In the U.S. economy, it has historically been thought to be about 6 percent, although in the 1990s, unemployment rates were below 5 percent for extended periods without any notable inflation.

Unemployment is usually analyzed using the competitive market framework. In general, unemployment arises if the real wage rate is set at a level where the supply of labor exceeds demand. Over time, the real wage rate should fall, raising the demand for labor, until equilibrium is reestablished. The real wage rate may fail to adjust, however, for a variety of reasons. An imperfectly competitive labor market is one source of rigidity: there may be inequalities of information among different sectors regarding the labor market, firms with monopoly power may shift the balance of power between labor and management, and so on. These factors tend to raise the level of unemployment. There is much debate about whether minimum-wage legislation substantially increases unemployment, but from a theoretical perspective, any price floor can create a disequilibrium in the market. More recently, the theory of *efficiency wages* has argued that workers are more productive if firms maintain wages above the market-clearing level. One version holds that if unemployment is too low, the cost of losing a job is minimal; thus workers have little incentive to perform well in their current jobs. Other models stress the good will engendered among employees when firms pay higher-than-market wages. See also NAIRU.

uneven development A concept developed by Vladimir Ilich LENIN and Leon Trotsky to describe the way in which CAPITALISM fosters industrial development in some areas and retards it in others, in accordance with the larger needs of an increasingly global capitalist system. The concept has been especially significant to analyses of the persistence of premodern elements in modernizing societies, as well as to studies of colonialism and neodependency. See also CENTER–PERIPHERY AND CORE–PERIPHERY; and DEVELOPMENT.

unicameralism See LEGISLATURE.

unilineal Describes a system of descent that privileges either the male line or the female line. See also DESCENT THEORY.

unintended consequences One of the core insights of sociology is that the purposes of agents do not exhaust the meaning or results of their actions. The "unintended consequences of purposive social action" (as Robert K. MERTON phrased it in 1936) may diverge from the conscious intentions of a group. Markets provide a common example in that they are created by multiple individual acts of buying and selling without collective or broader intention.

union See LABOR UNION.

unitary state A country in which local governments exercise only those powers granted to them by the central government. Under a unitary system, local governments are more accurately thought of as administrative units of the central government. Such states differ from federal states, in which SOVEREIGNTY is divided between the national government and the regional governments. See also FEDERALISM.

unobtrusive measures Methods for obtaining data without the knowledge of the subject. Unobtrusive measures are important in cases where knowledge of the study is likely to produce changes in the nature of the responses, as in surveys of sexual or petty criminal behavior. Deception as to the object of the study is one such measure. Secret observation is another.

urban economics The analysis of economic activity in towns and cities, most frequently in terms of the spatial distribution of populations. In its practical applications, urban economics evaluates policies designed to change the distribution of populations and economic activity within cities, between cities, and between urban and rural areas. This often involves the study of MARKET FAILURES that arise from EXTERNALITIES such as traffic congestion, pollution, and the provision of PUBLIC GOODS. Urban economics also contributes to design policies that improve non-coordinated allocative decisions in urban areas.

Urban economics relies on a variety of sector and zone models from LOCATION THEORY in mapping the distribution of populations and economic activity—the latter, in particular, in relation to the criteria firms use in their location decisions (see SECTOR THEORY). It has also explored the relationship between city size, productivity, and productive specializations.

In the United States, the decentralization of activity within urban areas has been accompanied by the concentration of low-income groups in the central cities. There are two general explanations of this suburbanization of metropolitan areas: one is based on pull factors, such as technological change, decreasing transportation costs, increased use of automobiles, rising real income, and population growth (sometimes known as the *monocentric* model); the other emphasizes socio-economic and quality-of-life issues, such as lower suburban tax rates, high urban crime rates, congestion, pollution, poor city schools, and declining central city neighborhoods.

Much of urban economics privileges these relationships between changes in income and spatial decisions; the costs and benefits of decentralization; and the tendencies that encourage recentalization and redevelopment of long-neglected central cities. New research has emphasized such factors as climate and the interaction between economies and diseconomies of scale.

urbanism The way(s) of life characteristic of cities. The linked phenomena of urbanization and MODERNIZATION furnished SOCIOLOGY with one of its great subjects in the nineteenth and the early twentieth century, and they have remained at the center of a variety of social-science agendas. Explosive growth in population and the large-scale shift from small, traditional communities to large, anonymous, highly differentiated cities provided the frame of reference for the classic work of Emile DURKHEIM, Ferdinand TÖNNIES, and Georg SIMMEL on the nature of the social bond, as well as much of the rich tradition of modernity critique inaugurated by Karl MARX, Friedrich NIETZSCHE, and Sigmund FREUD. There has been a correspondingly vast body of research on the new characteristics of urban life, a subject pioneered by Friedrich Engels and Simmel and later extended to large-scale empirical studies by members of the CHICAGO SCHOOL OF SOCIOLOGY in the 1920s—notably Louis Wirth. This direction of inquiry integrated theories of urban geography, which divided the city into functionally defined areas and sought to explain vectors of development (see LOCATION THEORY). A new wave of urban research in the 1970s and 1980s (exemplified by the geographer David HARVEY and the sociologists Richard Sennett and Manuel Castells) both recovered Marxist insights and drew upon a range of new theoretical perspectives and sociological objects, such as theories of DEVELOPMENT, modernization, state power, aesthetics, and new social movements.

urban morphology Refers to the shape of a city, including its architecture, layout of streets, and different densities of habitation. It is often distinguished in urban studies from FUNCTIONAL ZONATION—the pattern of land use in a city.

utilitarianism A school of moral philosophy best known for the principle that social decisions should be based on a maximization of sum total of the happiness (or UTILITY) of individuals—"the greatest happiness of the greatest number," in Jeremy BENTHAM's famous phrase. This social logic derives from a more basic understanding of the good as identical with the decisions of welfare-maximizing individuals: the good is whatever makes one happy—or in early "hedonistic" versions, gives pleasure. Utilitarianism was thus preeminently a practical theory—less concerned with the motives or the intrinsic value of an action than with its consequences. Through the work of Bentham and John Stuart MILL, utilitarianism became associated with a broad agenda of social reform, especially in regard to the extension of social and political equality to all members of society. For Mill and some later welfare economists, it also justified policies of income redistribution, insofar as a poor person would gain far more utility from a given sum than a rich person would lose by relinquishing it.

Utilitarianism's model of individual decision-making and aggregate social good drew upon and extended principles of POLITICAL ECONOMY. It also drew heavily upon the tradition of British empiricism associated with David HUME. Utilitarianism has had its greatest impact in ECONOMICS, where the principle of utility became the basis of theories of social welfare and marginal choice. Here, some of the limitations of early utilitarian calculations became apparent. Where Bentham initially equated utility with the maximization of pleasure and the minimization of pain, Mill recognized the challenge of equating forms of utility across different individuals or groups. He drew value distinctions between different forms of welfare in an effort to sharpen utilitarianism's social engagement, and he never abandoned the search for a basis for INTERPERSONAL UTILITY COMPARISONS. Subsequent utilitarian thought, especially in economics, has taken a more circumspect position on utility, seeking proxies, such as willingness-to-pay (in money), as indicators of individual valuation of social choices.

utility In economics, utility is synonymous with satisfaction or well-being. This use of the term goes back to Jeremy BENTHAM, who first argued that social welfare should be conceived of as the sum of individual welfare, or utility. It signifies a more structured definition than simple happiness or well-being, in that *utility* is seen as measurable or quantifiable in some way.

A major early debate in utility theory concerned the quantifiable measurement of utility, pitting theorists who argued for a cardinal definition (quantifiable in units termed *utils*) against defenders of ordinal utility, based solely on the relative values or ranking of preferences (see CARDINAL AND ORDINAL UTILITY). Cardinal utility was desirable for two reasons: it would allow comparisons across individuals, and it would therefore permit social welfare to be measured as an aggregation of individual utilities.

The difficulty of comparing the value of different kinds of well-being to different individuals proved insurmountable in all but carefully circumscribed cases (such as those in which utility can be directly equated with money).

Since the 1930s, most work on utility has been based on ordinal principles, although they more commonly allow for utility to be proxied by *willingness to pay*, and compare valuations across individuals. Without such proxies, the only possible welfare comparisons are those between *Pareto efficient* outcomes (where no actor can be made better off without making another actor worse off) and those that are Pareto inefficient (see PARETO OPTIMAL). The development of the theory of *revealed preference* has also played an important role; rather that measuring preferences directly, relative utility is *revealed* by the choices that individuals make. Thus, if an individual has a choice between coffee and tea and chooses the latter, it can be asserted that tea provides greater utility.

utility comparisons See INTERPERSONAL UTILITY COMPARISONS.

utility function A mathematical representation of consumer preferences for goods and services. Although there are no logical restrictions on the form of the function or its components, it is generally assumed that marginal utility decreases—that is, individuals derive less additional pleasure from each additional amount of a good consumed. This diminishing marginal utility implies that the utility function is concave and that individuals are risk averse (see RISK AVERSION).

utility maximization One of the basic tenets of modern MICROECONOMICS is that individuals seek to maximize utility—or make themselves as happy as possible. Utility can come from any source, but there is usually a presumption that the more goods an individual consumes, the less marginal (additional) utility he or she receives from additional quantities. Thus, the marginal utility of consumption is positive but decreasing. To maximize utility, the consumer chooses to consume as long as the additional cost is less than or equal to the additional benefit. More formally, the maximizing individual consumes to the point where marginal cost equals marginal benefit.

The idea that consumers behave in this way has been the subject of much controversy. In the weakest interpretation, few would argue with the notion that individuals faced with a set of options will choose what they prefer. However, theories of BOUNDED RATIONALITY, dynamic inconsistency, and mental accounting, among others, suggest that individuals do not (and perhaps cannot) consistently maximize. Individuals may satisfice (choosing acceptable, rather than optimal, options); they may make decisions they will later reverse; and they may process information in ways that lead to consistently sub-optimal decisions (see SATISFICING). Defenders of maximizing behavior counter that individuals learn from their mistakes and that given repeated opportunities to make choices, consumers will come closer and closer to the maximization model. Milton FRIEDMAN offered the now-famous analogy of a game of billiards: the expert billiards player does not need to know the physics involved, but he plays *as if* he does, because he has learned from experience.

EXPECTED UTILITY THEORY addresses the related issue of how rational people make decisions in the absence of certainty about the consequences of their actions. Developed largely by John von NEUMANN and Oskar Morgenstern (*The Theory of Games and Economic Behavior*, 1944), the theory posits a utility function that—provided certain framing conditions are met—represents the process of rational choice among actions whose outcomes differ in probability. Virtually all research in the field of risk and uncertainty works within this framework, including analyses of wealth levels, consumption bundles, and time streams of consumption.

utopia From the Greek words *utopos* ("no place") and *eutopia* ("good place"). A utopia is an ideal society free of the defects of existing societies. The description of utopias has been a classic mode of reflection on politics and society, dating back to the ideal republic developed by PLATO. Utopias have often been imaginatively put forward as a way of criticizing contemporary society. Sir Thomas More was a pioneer in this genre, offering in *Utopia* (1516) an imaginary island society where social, political, and economic arrangements were founded on equality and

JUSTICE—qualities whose conspicuous absence from contemporary England becomes the point of the comparison. Utopian ideals have figured in the work of a number of theologians and philosophers, including Saint AUGUSTINE and Francis Bacon.

Utopian speculation took on a different character in the industrial age. Especially for Romantic writers, industrial society presented a fall from nature and wholeness into a fragmented and alienated existence. Romantics theorized forms of transcendence of this state on both the individual and the social level—often through the vehicle of poetics or art. Socialists such as Charles Fourier and Robert Owen pursued complex alternative arrangements of production and social organization. In COMMUNISM, Karl MARX and Friedrich Engels developed their own utopian vision of society.

Utopias have a poor record when carried into practice. Central to many modern versions is the transformation of not only external arrangements but also human character at a more fundamental level—something that has proved extremely difficult to achieve. The worst of these efforts have turned to social engineering on a massive scale—for example, the collectivization of agriculture in the Soviet Union, the racial program of the Third Reich, and the Chinese Cultural Revolution—and to political repression and extermination when such measures meet inevitable resistance. These experiences have largely discredited utopianism as a political agenda.

More productively, utopian thought raises the question of the limits of change in society; it continues to be a basic, if seldom avowed, critical mode for posing normative questions about the direction of social change. Dystopias (Greek, *bad places*) often play an analogous role as a cautionary analytical mode.

uxorilocal residence A rule that dictates that a married couple take up residence with or near the wife's family. The practice is more commonly called *matrilocal* residence; it contrasts with *virilocal* or PATRILOCAL RESIDENCE, which indicates the priority of the husband's family.

V

validity With regard to any study or analysis, validity refers to the degree to which the analysis is properly conceived to address the subject of study. Validity is therefore different from *accuracy* or RELIABILITY: studies may be flawlessly conducted (accurate) and results may be repeatable (reliable), but the methods may nonetheless be inappropriate for achieving the desired results. An adequate measurement must be both reliable and valid.

value CLASSICAL ECONOMICS distinguished among *use value* (or how useful an item is to a given person or situation), *exchange value* (which reflects its price on the market), and *labor value* (which reflects the amount of human effort invested in its production). In principle, labor value was held to explain exchange value, although this proved hard to demonstrate. Karl MARX contributed the further notion of SURPLUS VALUE, which reflects the difference between the price of the good over the cost of labor and raw materials. Surplus value, appropriated by the capitalist, becomes the mechanism of the reproduction and expansion of CAPITAL. Marx also stressed that the production of value in capitalism depended not just on labor as such—work—but on labor power made into a commodity as workers sold their human capacities in quantified units in capitalist labor markets. The concern for the sources of economic value continues to motivate research in ECONOMICS and POLITICAL ECONOMY.

Sociologists and anthropologists often have a completely different understanding of value. They generally speak of social or cultural values as mechanisms of solidarity and collective identity. The sociologist Talcott PARSONS based his influential account of the dynamic between solidarity and heterogeneity around the notion of a deep level of shared values that permits relatively wide variance at the level of attitudes and ideas. The question of SOCIALIZATION, or the reproduction of values—fundamental to any account of the persistence of a society or culture over time—has also been central to modern SOCIOLOGY and ANTHROPOLOGY.

Values have also been at the center of a long methodological debate in the social sciences over the degree to which social science is subject to determination by the social-value system in which it is conducted. Perhaps the dominant figure in this debate was Max WEBER, who defended the principle of *value relevance*—a scientific approach to the analysis of values that seeks to avoid reproducing the values of the scientist. Positivist social science defends a still stronger version of objectivity, *value neutrality*, which tends to treat values as extrinsic to proper scientific procedure. These debates have been animated in recent years by the turn toward POSTSTRUCTURALISM and POSTMODERNISM in the social sciences, which openly challenge claims to objectivity.

value-added tax Also VAT. A tax upon a FIRM's contribution to the market value of the goods or services it produces (as measured by subtracting the value of production inputs from outputs). Unlike most sales taxes, VATs are neutral in that they do not target specific economic activities and avoid multiple taxation of the same input. They are also often defended as more efficient and conducive to growth than profit-based forms of corporate taxation. See also TAXES AND TAXATION.

variability There are a number of measures of the variability of the observations in a data set. The most common are the *range*, the *interquartile range*, the VARIANCE, the standard deviation, and the *coefficient of variation* (see STANDARD DEVIATION AND STANDARD ERROR). The *range* of a data set is the difference between the largest and the smallest observations. While useful in some cases, it does not capture the characteristics of data sets well if some observations fall well outside the majority grouping. The *interquartile range* is sometimes used to correct for this limitation; it uses a trimmed data set in which the smallest 25 percent and the largest 25 percent of observations are removed, providing a measure of the variability of the middle 50 percent of the observations.

The most commonly used measure of variability is *variance*, obtained by adding up the square of the deviation of each individual value from the mean of the values (a total known as the *sum of squares* or SSTO) and dividing by the total number of values. Where all values are equal, the variance is zero. In contrast, the greater the variability of the observations in a data set, the greater the variance. The square root of this value is called the *standard deviation*—a measure of the absolute variability in a data set. The most commonly used measure of relative variability is the *coefficient of variation*, which is the ratio of the standard deviation to the mean expressed as a percentage (denoted by C).

variable costs   Costs that vary with the level of output (e.g., labor costs). In the short run, some costs are fixed (such as rental costs for land or the cost of a factory) while others are variable. In the long run, all costs are variable.

variance   Describes the degree of deviation of a set of values in a distribution from the mean of those values. In statistical terms, it is calculated by adding up the square of the deviation of each individual value from the mean value (a total termed the *sum of squares* or SSTO) and dividing by the number of values in order to obtain an average. Where all values are equal, the variance is zero. The square root of this value is called the standard deviation (see STANDARD DEVIATION AND STANDARD ERROR).

ANOVA (*analysis of variance*) is a statistical procedure that measures the significance of variables in situations where there are multiple variables or subgroups. It involves analyzing variance comparatively across groups distinguishable on the basis of whether they share or do not share the particular variable in question. In principle, a variable is significant if the comparison of unlike groups reveals a large difference in variance compared to the like groups.

Veblen, Thorstein   (1857–1929) An American economist and sociologist who pioneered the study of LEISURE and consumption. Veblen also founded the *institutionalist school* in economics, which undertook the first major critique of NEOCLASSICAL ECONOMICS. Against the neoclassical orthodoxy, which viewed the pursuit of self-interest as the principal motive of people's behavior, Velden believed that economic outcomes are shaped in large part by social institutions, which introduce other motivations into human activity; moreover, these institutions are historical and evolve over time.

Veblen was one of the few prominent American economists at the turn of the century. He taught at several universities and became the editor of the *Journal of Political Economy*, although he never reached the rank of full professor. He died in 1929, a few weeks before his dire predictions about the inflated stock market were realized. *The Theory of the Leisure Class* (1899) was Veblen's first and by far most popular book, mostly for its provocative treatment of leisure and consumption as forms of competitive display among social elites. Although Veblen's commentary was directed against the new capitalist leisure class of the late nineteenth century, his argument was couched in anthropological terms that drew parallels to tribal POTLATCH practices and to a more general human need for "invidious comparison."

Veblen was highly critical of entrepreneurialism, which he believed destroyed the rewards of workmanship and gave undue priority to profit. He also emphasized the role of credit in the capitalist economy, which allows some firms to take greater advantage of profit opportunities. This potential figured prominently in Veblen's theory of the BUSINESS CYCLE, which viewed expansion of credit as a cause of rising prices for capital goods, which in turn act as collateral for further credit. Ultimately, a discrepancy emerges between the price of the collateral and the "value" of the physical capital goods. This leads to periodic liquidation, canceled credit, and reduced output. More workers are employed during the upswing, but real wages fall as prices rise.

Veblen thought that SOCIALISM might be a solution to this problem, but he was not a socialist himself. Instead, he advocated a form of technocratic rule that he thought would prove more objective than the perspectives of capital or labor. Veblen was fundamentally a pessimist, however, and his attempt to resolve these problems was half-hearted. His contribution to economics is primarily a theory of crisis and change rather than a set of potential solutions. His contribution to SOCIOLOGY and later CULTURAL STUDIES is perhaps more significant—especially his rich and innovative exploration of the dynamic between consumption and class.

Veblen effect   Named after Thorstein VEBLEN, the Veblen effect describes a situation in which a fall in the price of a good is interpreted as a reduction in quality, causing consumers to buy less of it. As a result, the market demand curve is steeper than would otherwise be expected.

veil of ignorance   A concept developed by John RAWLS in his theory of JUSTICE (*A Theory of Justice*, 1971). Rawls posits an imaginary "original position," in which individuals are asked to choose what sort of social order they would prefer. Fairness, Rawls argues, dictates that they do so from behind a *veil of ignorance*, without knowledge of their abilities or future status. Rawls argues that this will ensure the choice of a system that maximizes the chances of happiness for all individuals, regardless of their place in society. The veil of ignorance, for Rawls, is therefore the key to consensus on a singular and universal concept of justice—and thus also the basis of a just and stable constitutional regime.

velocity of circulation   The average number of times a given sum of money changes hands within a specific time period. Velocity of circulation is designated as *V* in the equation of exchange

$$MV \equiv PT$$

where *M* is the stock of money, *P* is the price level, and *T* is the volume of transactions. This identity defines *V* as PT/M, that is, the ratio of a flow of payments to the stock of money. This identity also serves for the quantity theory of money and implies that, with both *V* and *T* held constant, an increase in *M* implies a proportionate increase in *P*. In other words, printing money in excess of demand causes inflation.

vent for surplus   First proposed by Adam SMITH, the theory of vent for surplus asserts that international trade allows for the fuller use of economic resources than closed, domestic trade. By extension, it implies that closed economies are likely to possess underutilized surplus resources. Trade, in this context, brings not only direct gains in the form of cheaper imports but also indirect gains through the structural reorganization of the economy—improved transport and communications, the export-financed provision of public goods, and the development of traditional agricultural sectors. The gains from trade

thus include *allocative efficiency gains* from productive specialization as well as *output gains* in the export sector, without a corresponding contraction in the output for domestic consumption. See also COMPARATIVE ADVANTAGE.

Verba, Sidney   (1932–) An American political scientist who has studied comparative politics, political participation, and civic culture. Verba was also a major innovator of survey research and statistical techniques. Many of his contributions are contained in his influential study *Civic Culture* (1963, with Gabriel Almond)—a systematic, cross-national survey of citizen attitudes regarding democratic participation and public life. In many respects, this work set the standard for behavioral research on VOTING and other forms of political participation (see BEHAVIORALISM); it also showed the way toward overcoming the national framework that had traditionally limited empirical research.

Much of Verba's later work expands on these themes and continues the comparative project of *Civic Culture*. *Participation and Social Equality* (1978) was a seven-country comparison of the major features of civic participation, including voting, campaign activity, and communal activity. *Voice and Equality: Voluntarism in American Politics* (1995, with Kay Schlozman and Henry Brady) focused on American political participation and on the influence on public policy of religious and other nonpolitical associations. *Equality in America: A View from the Top* (1985) looks at how equality is valued in different spheres of American life.

Verba's more recent work on methodology emphasizes the importance of rigorous research design in quantitative and qualitative studies. His *Designing Social Enquiry* (1994, with Gary King and Robert O. Keohane) is a prominent, if also controversial, statement of these views. Verba's other important works include *Small Groups and Political Behavior* (1961), *Caste, Race and Politics: A Comparison of India and the United States* (1971), *Participation and Political Equality* (1978), *The Changing American Voter* (1976, with Norman Nie), and *Elites and the Idea of Equality* (1987).

verstehen   German word usually translated as "understanding" or "interpretive understanding." *Verstehen* is central to Max WEBER's concept of the social sciences as a field that relies not only on mechanistic or external models (i.e., those of the natural sciences) but also on understanding the motives and values of actors. While scientific methodologies can describe action, he argued, they cannot decipher the meaning of socially embedded, contextualized behavior.

There is little disagreement today that interpretation plays a role in social analysis, although the margin accorded it varies and does not always include the kind of empathic projection into the lives of others that Weber advocated. Similarly, the relationship of interpretation to objective social rules and to empirical verification remains a subject of theoretical and methodological debate. Although the concept of *verstehen* has shaped much of this debate, Weber's own imprecision with the term has proved problematic. In particular, Weber gestured toward the conflation of *verstehen* with the analysis of causes of action—a subject that has generated considerable speculation about Weber's intentions but little clarity as to the advantages and limitations of his approach.

vertical integration   A situation in which the activities of a firm extend over more than one successive stage in the production process. *Forward* and *backward* vertical integration describe the incorporation of successive or prior stages of the production process, respectively. For example, an automaker that begins to produce its own tires would be integrating backwards—taking on the production of inputs. Vertical integration can be undertaken for strategic reasons, such as raising barriers to entry by competitors. Vertical integration may also be explained in terms of the existence of TRANSACTION COSTS, which may be reduced by integrating transactions into a larger corporate structure (rather than conducting them in the market).

veto   A Latin word meaning "I forbid." The veto is the power to block the passage of a legislative bill or a policy proposal. It is common to many forms of democratic constitutional government and generally resides with the EXECUTIVE branch. The U.S. president has veto power, but it can be overruled by a two-thirds majority vote in Congress. See also SEPARATION OF POWERS.

vicious cycles   Any self-reinforcing, harmful, or undesirable process. In economics, it refers to a trap of low-income equilibrium. When a country's total income is quite low, all available resources go toward current consumption, leaving no resources for savings. Because growth depends critically on investment, the absence of savings means there is no growth. Yet without economic growth, incomes are stagnant. Thus the economy remains stuck in its low-income state.

Vico, Giambattista   (1668–1744) An Italian philosopher who pioneered the historical analysis of human nature and knowledge—later known as HISTORICISM. His work was largely ignored during his lifetime, but his ideas, especially those developed in *The New Science* (1725, substantially revised in 1730), attracted growing attention as history began to be seen as a powerful explanatory framework for the study of society. Much of the historiography and philosophy of history of the nineteenth century owes a debt to Vico, and he remains a figure of interest to materialist and other historically minded scholars.

Vico's epistemological radicalism lies in his argument that truth is made rather than found, and that therefore a strong conception of science—based on the knowledge of causes—was possible only in the realm of human action. For Vico, this included history, government, mathematics, and ethics. In contrast, truth was not possible in the natural sciences, where knowledge reflected only a more or less profound "consciousness" of pre-existing relationships. Only God, as the creator of the world, could have a truly scientific knowledge of the natural world.

In asserting the priority of the human-made or historical world, Vico challenged the dominant Cartesian project of founding knowledge on deductive, rational principles (see René DESCARTES). Similarly, he positioned himself against contemporary assertions of a universal or unchanging human nature. Vico argued (influenced by ARISTOTLE) that human nature changes just as societies do, and that such change can be expressed as a cyclical movement through distinct historical stages. Each society passes, he wrote, through an "age of the gods," during which it emerges from a bestial condition through the creation of myths and gods, which then rule human action. This is followed by the "age of heroes," during which institutions are formed and society becomes stratified into classes, largely through the actions of great personalities who embody the virtues of the age. The last stage is the "age of men," during which social distinctions are effaced and the power of the divine recedes. Here, society falls into luxury and decadence—and risks disintegration. In this progression, Vico payed particular attention to the role and status of religion, which he considered a central force in human history. The inevitability of this trajectory, however, made his work controversial in seventeenth-century Italy, and cost him the support of his patron, Cardinal Corsini. Vico did, however, leave open the possibility that divine providence might intervene to end this cyclical process.

Vico taught rhetoric at the University of Naples for much of his career. His other works include the influential *Autobiography* (1728–1731) and "On the Method of the Studies of Our Time" (1709).

Vidal de la Blache, Paul (1845–1918) The dominant figure in human GEOGRAPHY in France at the turn of the twentieth century, Vidal de la Blache was a prolific writer, a major institutional force at both the Ecole Normale Supérieure and the Sorbonne, and the teacher of a generation of major French geographers, including Albert Demangeon, Maximillian Sorre, and Lucien Gallois. His views were shaped largely by dissatisfaction with the environmental determinism that dominated nineteenth-century geography, particularly as articulated by the German geographer Friedrich RATZEL. Instead, Vidal de la Blache proposed the doctrine of POSSIBILISM, which holds that a set of environmental conditions can give rise to different cultural responses. This contingency, he argued, necessitated much closer attention to history and a narrower focus on places than was usual in the human geography of the day, which often drew its comparisons at the level of civilizations.

Vidal de la Blache's priorities strongly marked the next generation of French geographers, who not only inherited many of the theoretical and methodological preoccupations of his work but also finished projects that he had sketched or left incomplete at his death. These included the *Principes de géographie humaine* (1922), assembled posthumously by Emmanuel de Martonne from Vidal de la Blache's notes and articles, and the massive *Géographie universelle* (1927–1948) undertaken by Lucien Gallois, his successor at the Sorbonne. Vidal de la Blache's major works include *Etats et nations de l'Europe* (1889), *Tableau de la géographie de la France* (1903), and *La France de l'est* (1917).

virilocal A social rule that dictates that a married couple should take up residence with or near the husband's family. Also known as *patrilocal* and contrasted to *uxorilocal* or *matrilocal* residence, which indicates the priority of the wife's family.

virtual community Community mediated by the Internet or other electronic communication technologies—an increasingly important form of indirect social relationship. Such relations are "virtual" in the sense that they generally involve no face-to-face contact or physical gathering of members. They merit consideration as "communities" because large groups of individuals may be linked together to share information, ideas, feelings, and desires (although strong arguments distinguish them from local face-to-face communities). The most influential account is Howard Reingold's *Virtual Communities: Homesteading on the Electronic Frontier* (1993).

voice Widely used to describe the articulation of demands for redress or recognition by marginalized or dissatisfied groups. Political scientist Albert O. Hirschman (*Exit, Voice, and Loyalty*, 1970) has characterized this in terms of a market situation: where exit costs are low, actors can abandon a product, firm, or other unsatisfactory situation. Where exit costs are high or where other factors, such as loyalty, come into play, actors make use of their voices.

voluntary export restraints Also VER. A voluntarily limit set on exports by producers in a particular country, intended to forestall or prevent protectionist measures in the importing country. For example, Japanese automobile companies imposed quantitative restraints on car exports to the United States in the 1980s in order to preempt protectionist action by the U.S. government. Such measures are often seen as less costly and more flexible than formal import tariffs.

von Neumann–Morgenstern utility function   See EXPECTED UTILITY THEORY.

Von Thünen model One of the earliest abstract models of land use, proposed in the 1820s by German landowner Johann von Thünen. Von Thünen modeled agricultural land use as a function of distance from a central market. He posited a series of concentric rings around the market, each devoted to a different agricultural activity. Proximity to the center correlated with higher intensity of agriculture and higher perishability of its products. The model had a major influence on later studies of the spatial distribution of economic activity, including the structurally similar CONCENTRIC ZONE THEORY.

voting The expression of preference among contending proposals or candidates. Many different kinds of voting systems exist—both in terms of the form of the voting (show of hands, secret ballot, and so on) and the nature of the selection process (winner-take-all majority voting, proportional voting, ranked voting, etc.). Secret ballots have become a ubiquitous feature of democratic systems as a way of ensuring the free expression of choice. Voting rights have also been one of the major axes of social reform in the nineteenth and twentieth centuries, as the originally narrow franchise of most liberal-democratic societies was progressively extended to excluded groups—especially women, minorities, and those without property (see SUFFRAGE).

Patterns of voting and voting behavior have been central topics of political science since the 1940s. Practices of *strategic voting*, in which individuals vote not according to their preferences but in order to deceive other voters or to manipulate the final outcome, also figure prominently. Ranked voting systems, in particular, allow a significant margin for strategic behavior. In this context, social scientists distinguish between *sophisticated* voting strategies and *sincere* voting strategies and study the ways in which these strategies affect outcomes. See also DEMOCRACY; and ELECTORAL SYSTEM.

W

wage discrimination Describes a situation in which equally productive workers are paid different wages. This implies that not all workers are paid according to their *marginal product* (i.e., their real wages are not equal to the additional output that is produced by that worker).

wage-fund doctrine The idea that wages for productive activities are paid out of a fixed fund of capital. The wage-fund doctrine was developed in the eighteenth-century writings of Richard Cantillon, François QUESNAY, David HUME, A. R. J. Turgot, and Adam SMITH. Equilibrium wages are determined by the supply of and demand for labor—with demand depending on the size of the wage fund and supply on the population of the country. Thus, the classical economists suggested that the wage rate was determined by the ratio of the wage fund to the labor force.

wage–push inflation A variant of COST-PUSH INFLATION that attributes the origin of inflationary pressures in the economy to increases in nominal wages, generally through trade union pressure in the labor market or very low levels of unemployment. Wage increases raise the cost of producing goods, as well as increasing demand (through higher incomes). Both effects contribute to upward pressure on prices.

wages, nominal and real The return to labor in the production process; it may be denoted either in terms of monetary units (nominal wages) or expressed in terms of purchasing power (real wages). Real wages are simply money wages deflated by a price index—an appropriately weighted average of prices of all goods and services.

The classical economists analyzed the determination of wages in terms of the subsistence level of wages and the WAGE-FUND DOCTRINE. According to this theory, real wages are pushed down to the subsistence level by population pressures. If wages move above or below that level, population changes will equilibrate the supply of labor

(either through starvation or increased reproduction) until supply and demand again coincide at the subsistence-level wage. Wage funds or "the funds destined for the employment of labor," in their view, could only be increased through a rise in the savings of the propertied classes. Yet it soon became apparent that productivity increases could counter population pressure. From the nineteenth century onward, real wages rose, despite the rising in population of Europe and the United States.

This rise prompted a rethinking of wage doctrines in the late nineteenth century by such neoclassical economists as J. B. Clark and Alfred MARSHALL. They argued that real wages were determined by the *marginal product of labor*—the point of equality between the additional cost of employing labor and additional revenues generated (see MARGINAL ANALYSIS). Institutional economists have criticized this emphasis on optimizing behavior and the exclusion of political, social, and institutional factors in wage determination. Contemporary neoclassical approaches have responded to many of these objections and have been enriched by developments in HUMAN CAPITAL theory and the economics of information.

Wallerstein, Immanuel (1930–) Historical sociologist known primarily for his pioneering work on WORLD-SYSTEMS THEORY—the historical study of the emergence of global relations of economic and political power. World-systems theory grew out of Wallerstein's early work on African development, which he came to see as inextricable from a larger international economic and political order. Methodologically, it was shaped by the great interdisciplinary syntheses of the ANNALES SCHOOL historians, especially Fernand BRAUDEL. Wallerstein investigated the origins and trajectory of this world order in his three volume *The Modern World-System* (1974, 1980, 1988)—a richly detailed, interdisciplinary work that integrates POLITICAL SCIENCE, ECONOMICS, history, SOCIOLOGY, and GEOGRAPHY.

Wallerstein locates the origin of the modern world system in the emergence of the capitalist economy in northwestern Europe in the sixteenth century—initially in Holland and later in England. In the course of this development, the European empires progressively extended their economic and political reach across the world. The governments of the core countries began to be administered more efficiently, and a geographic division of labor emerged that foreshadowed the Industrial Revolution and the entrenchment of a stratified economic world order. Wallerstein described this stratification in terms of the distinction between core, periphery, and semiperiphery. The development of peripheral countries became increasingly structured by demands from the core countries for agricultural and raw materials, while the core countries produced finished goods and retained all profits. Wallerstein further distinguished between world empires and world economies: while empires seek to maintain comprehensive control over their dominions, world economies are concerned only with control of markets and resources. One conclusion is that world economies are thereby more stable than empires. The second and third volumes of *The Modern World-System* carry this account further, tracing the international implications of the Industrial Revolution through to the emergence of the United States as a superpower in the post–World War II era.

In *After Liberalism* (1995), Wallerstein speculates about the future development of the world system—a topic and responsibility he refers to as "utopistics." The chief determinants of this future, Wallerstein argues, are the exhaustion of natural resources and the completed integration of the peripheral countries into the industrial labor force—thereby ending the supply of cheap labor that has driven the movements of capital since the 1940s. Whether this spells catastrophe or a new democratic opening depends on the degree to which new economic structures "internalize" their costs, such as pollution and the exploitation of "free" resources. Another key theme of Wallerstein's later work is the historical development of the social sciences. Among other things, he has analyzed the arbitrariness of disciplinary divisions, as well as the possibility of new forms of interdisciplinary integration.

Wallerstein was a professor of sociology at the State University of New York at Binghamton from 1976 to 2000, where he served as director of the Fernand Braudel Center for the Study of Economies, Historical Systems and Civilizations. He then moved to Yale University. Wallerstein's other published works include *The Capitalist World Economy* (1979), *Historical Capitalism* (1983), and *Unthinking Social Science* (1991).

Walras, Leon   (1834–1910) One of the founders of the marginalist school in economics and very likely the most influential of them. Much of Walras's methodology and many of his ideas have continued currency in modern economics.

Like much of the classical tradition, Walras argued that self-interest was the principal motive of economic activity. Like his fellow marginalist, William Stanley JEVONS, he developed mathematical models for converting self-interest into a quantifiable and manipulable object of scientific research. Walras was also influenced by Augustin COURNOT—a connection that likely helped him integrate his utility theory of value with a formal theory of market equilibrium.

In his *Eléments d'économie politique pure* (1889), Walras proposed his version of the marginal utility doctrine and his theories of exchange and production. Walras is best known, however, for his description of how EQUILIBRIUM is achieved in a competitive market. He made use of a fictional device for this purpose: the auctioneer. In a Walrasian auction, the auctioneer calls out a price, after which individuals declare how much they want to buy or sell. If demand is greater than supply, the auctioneer calls out a higher price; if demand is less than supply, he calls out a lower price. This *tatonnement* process continues until demand and supply are equated at the announced price. One implication of this model is that it forbids exchange at nonequilibrium prices. Walras also addressed the problem of a general exchange equilibrium, which requires the analysis of the relationships among all variables in an economy. To this end, he introduced the concept of a NUMERAIRE good—a benchmark against which the prices of other goods are compared. If the number of goods in an economy is also known, Walras claimed, then there is a determinate solution to this general equilibrium system. See also AUCTIONEER, WALRASIAN.

Walras's theory of production was an application of his method of general equilibrium to factor markets (labor, capital, etc.). His approach has been criticized for its naiveté regarding exchange outside equilibrium conditions, which occurs frequently in the real world, and for abandoning the attempt to derive prices from a more fundamental notion of value. The latter criticism is aimed at Walras's attempt to express general equilibrium in a series of equations where prices, rather than quantities, are the independent variables. Despite these criticisms, the Walrasian system of general equilibrium remains the benchmark for microeconomic analysis today. See also MICROECONOMICS.

war The use of military force to resolve disputes between STATES or between groups within a SOCIETY (civil war)—a definition close to Carl von Clausewitz's famous characterization of *war* as "the continuation of politics by other means" (*On War*, 1832). Wars have shaped state boundaries, political systems, and to various degrees the social organization of most of the world's societies. They have played important roles in processes of state formation and NATION building on a variety of levels, from the direct question of demarcating or unifying territories, to the creation of national solidarity in the face of common enemies, to the diverse forms of modernization and innovation incumbent on effective military power.

War is a diverse phenomenon that runs throughout human history. The capacity for fielding armies has almost always played a large role in defining the social and political order, from the militarized citizenry of the Greek city-states, to nomadic armies of conquest, to the military function of the nobility in feudal Europe. Total war—entailing the broad mobilization of a society's human, economic, and financial resources—is a distinctly modern phenomenon credited to Napoleon Bonaparte and more broadly to the Napoleonic Wars (1802–1814). The Industrial Revolution further transformed the way that war is waged, not only in terms of the routinization of technological innovation (in weaponry, in transportation, in communications, and so on) but also in the way that the economy is assimilated to the war effort.

The modern era has spawned a variety of forms of more limited conflict, including guerrilla wars that involve unconventional forces and strategies geared toward attrition or political concession. Euphemisms such as "police action" (used during the Korean War) or "humanitarian intervention" (as in the Balkans) sketch out a middle ground in which war is very much in evidence to the inhabitants of the conflict zones but minimized for diverse reasons on the international scene.

Historians, political scientists, psychologists, and anthropologists have proposed myriad explanations of the causes of war, from innate human aggression, to rational struggles over resources, to the lack of a sovereign power at the interstate level. At the same time, war (and preparations for war) is seen as a major factor shaping social change. Modernization has been claimed as both a deterrent to war and as an explanation of its novel, total character. The 1990s conflict in the Balkans dented one casual but indicative modernization thesis: the NATO bombing of Belgrade was the first armed conflict between countries that possessed McDonald's restaurants.

war crimes A class of crimes determined by international agreement or convention to exceed the bounds of acceptable military operations. These typically include GENOCIDE, systemic rape, the mistreatment of prisoners, and (somewhat controversially) the targeting or forcible deportation of civilian populations. War crimes are sometimes conflated with the broader category of "crimes against humanity," which represents an attempt to promote durable and neutral standards of conduct that can be universally enforced.

Perhaps the most famous war crimes trials were held in Nuremberg after the Allied victory in World War II. The International Military Tribunal issued indictments against twenty-four German officials and officers, twenty-two of whom were found guilty. The International Military Tribunal for the Far East similarly indicted twenty-five Japanese officers and found all guilty of war crimes. More recently, tribunals convened under the authority of the United Nations Security Council have charged individuals with war crimes during civil wars in the former Yugoslavia and in Rwanda. Although conducting war crimes trials has generally been a privilege of the victor in war, there are ongoing attempts to establish a permanent and independent international criminal court. These efforts generate opposition on the part of states that fear the implicit threat to their national sovereignty. Many states (including the United States) also resist the criminalization of practices of war that have become ubiquitous—such as attacks on economic and industrial infrastructure, in which civilians are also killed.

wealth effect Also *PIGOU EFFECT* and *real-balance effect*. The wealth effect refers to the increase in aggregate consumption that follows an increase in real money balances. When prices fall during times of insufficient aggregate demand, the real wealth of individuals increases, consumption expenditure increases, and aggregate demand rises toward full-employment levels. This can result either from a fall in the general level of prices or through an increase in nominal money balances. The wealth effect was postulated by Arthur C. PIGOU and Don Patinkin as a way of circumventing the underemployment equilibrium developed by John Maynard KEYNES.

Weber, Alfred (1868–1958) Brother of sociologist Max WEBER, Alfred was a prominent geographer who spent most of his career at the University of Heidelberg. Weber's most significant contribution was his aptly titled *Theory of Industrial Location*, originally published in 1909. He argued that decisions about industrial location are largely driven by attempts to minimize costs; they thus take into account such issues as access to markets and available sources of labor and raw materials. Weber's model of the relationships between these factors laid the groundwork for industrial spatial analysis, which remains a common topic in contemporary geography. He also undertook a broad sociology of knowledge that examined the relationship between civilization and science: *Kulturgeschichte als Kultursoziologie* (1935).

Weber, Max (1864–1920) German sociologist—and social scientist, more broadly—who made essential contributions to the study of politics, the state, economic history, organizations, law, religion, music, and diverse other topics. Weber's work was strongly interdisciplinary and deeply grounded in comparative history. He moved easily between ancient and modern civilizations, Western and Eastern religions, history and SOCIOLOGY, and theoretical work and empirical case studies. Although Weber made important and innovative contributions to the study of many cultures, his comparative research was oriented largely to the task of analyzing the specificity, contingency, and historical trajectory of Western modernity. Like Karl MARX, Weber recognized capitalist industrialization as a dominant feature of this process. Unlike Marx, he argued that economic change was but one feature of a broader process of RATIONALIZATION of human activity visible in all areas of social life, including production techniques, forms of administration, belief systems, and social norms. This analysis of rationalization—integrating aspects of both Marx's and Friedrich NIETZSCHE's accounts of modernity—was basic to many of Weber's historical and sociological inquiries, especially in regard to organizational forms (such as BUREAUCRACY), social STRATIFICATION, and world religions.

Weber was also a central figure in the METHODENSTREIT, a set of turn-of-the-century debates about the epistemological goals and methodologies of the social sciences—especially in relation to the natural sciences and the prospect of establishing objective laws of social behavior. In this, he was strongly marked by neo-Kantian idealism and the work of Wilhelm DILTHEY, which emphasized the place of the human sciences in understanding motives and values (see NEO-KANTIANISM). Unlike the natural sciences, Weber argued, the social sciences were structured by the problem of VERSTEHEN (usually translated as "understanding" or "interpretive understanding"). The social sciences relied not only on mechanistic or external models (comparable to those of the natural sciences), but, more fundamentally, on efforts to understand the motives and values of actors. While objective scientific methodologies can describe behavior—and Weber called for empirical research in that regard—they cannot fully account for action. This is so because action is undertaken by individuals on the basis of their meaningful understanding of the world. Sociology, for Weber, therefore inevitably required interpretive inquiry into the sources and logic of individuals' actions.

Because interpretative researchers had to focus on values, it was all the more important that they keep their own values distinct from their research projects. This injunction gave rise to important but frequently confused arguments over "value-freedom" and "value-relevance." Weber argued that it was all but impossible for researchers to keep their values from entering into observations and analyses. The very process of selecting a research topic was likely to be influenced by the researcher's personal background, interests, and experiences. Weber maintained, however, that "value-neutrality" should be a goal of the research process; this meant that once the research began, researchers should not let their personal values influence the collection and analysis of data and they should not hide or change research findings that were contrary to their beliefs or expectations. Social science, therefore, could aspire to a kind of objectivity through its openness to criticism. This was not the objectivity of natural laws but of a consensus-building process within the field that depended on the collective and ethical action of its members.

Weber's views contrasted with those of Emile DURKHEIM, arguably the other founding figure of modern sociology and an advocate of a positivistic approach to social knowledge (see POSITIVISM). They differed, too, in the level of analysis that they privileged. Where Durkheim argued for a strong concept of SOCIAL STRUCTURE that existed outside the decisions or actions of the individuals who composed it, Weber's emphasis on the subjective meaning that actors attach to their action implied an individual focus, often described as ACTION THEORY. Social action, for Weber, implied a meaningful orientation to others that defines and informs the act (as distinguished from mere cause-and-effect observations of behavior). When Weber conceived of higher orders of organization and structure, he relied on the notion of the IDEAL TYPE as a tool for generalizing patterns of human behavior. This condensed a set of commonly recurring characteristics but in no way implied strict or exhaustive correspondence to reality. Weber distinguished four ideal types of social action: *traditional action,* justified as a repetition of the past; *affective action,* geared toward the expression of emotion; *value-oriented action,* in which the performance is taken as an end in itself; and *instrumental action* or means–ends rationality, in which actors pursue their economic or other interests. Any specific action might involve one or more of these rationales.

For Weber, POWER—the ability to exert control over people, even against their will—is basic to the organization of social action and the pursuit of interests. Consequently, power is the key to understanding the diverse forms of social stratification, which include *class* divisions (reflecting the unequal distribution of economic power and life chances), *status* differences (which cut across lines of economic power, and include education or prestige), and *party* differences (by which Weber meant differences in access to larger forms of institutional power, such as corporations or the state). Where power is accepted as legitimate and requires no direct coercion, Weber argued, it is better described as *AUTHORITY.* Here, too, Weber distinguished among different types: *traditional authority* is rooted in beliefs and practices that have come to seem part of the natural order; *charismatic authority* rests solely on the perceived personal qualities of individual leaders and the receptivity of followers; and *rational-legal authority* derives from explicit laws or rules and is vested in offices or positions. Weber viewed the trajectory of the West as largely defined by the shift from traditional to rational-legal authority, mediated

by charismatic transitions such as the Protestant Reformation (led by Martin Luther). Weber had strong misgivings about the direction of this shift and envisioned an increasingly bureaucratized future with a diminishing margin for democracy and individual autonomy. This was the context of Weber's famous description of modernity as an "iron-cage."

Weber's best-known work, *The Protestant Ethic and the Spirit of Capitalism* (1905), addresses this transition. The Protestant ethic, for Weber, was the set of ascetic Protestant values (rooted in Calvinism) that had influenced the growth of CAPITALISM in early modern Europe. Weber's account of the religious preconditions of capitalism is frequently read as a critique of the strong economic determinism of MARXISM, which treats religious and other cultural formations as derived from the economic base. Like Nietzsche, Weber saw the particular forms of Western rationality and selfhood as deeply rooted in religion. In his comparative studies of world religions, he argued that the process of rationalization of various spheres of social life occurred simultaneously with the process of secularization—the "disenchantment" of the modern world. His comparative works on world religion generally support this argument and explain in detail how religious barriers to the development of a certain kind of instrumental rationality produced other economic and political outcomes. In one example, he contrasted what he saw as the other-worldly asceticism of Buddhism with the inner-worldly asceticism of Protestant Christianity to help explain why capitalism developed in the West.

Weber was intensely interested in social plurality—the diversity of social forms. Social systems and historical development were defined not in terms of a singular logic or a deterministic set of factors but in terms of a frequently complex array of values, none of which fully determined the others. In conceiving society as a plural realm of different power relations and values, Weber set the terms for a wide range of social science research agendas—including those that emphasized the capacity of groups or individuals to pursue their interests and affect others, those that studied the distinction between legitimate and illegitimate power, and those that mapped the lines of social stratification, the forms of conflict around them, and the mechanisms of societal integration.

Given Weber's importance, it took an inordinately long time for his work to be adequately translated into English; a complete version of the seminal *Economy and Society* (1921), for example, was not available until 1968. Similar difficulties plagued the translation of his studies of Chinese and Indian religions, originally part of the larger *Economic Ethics of the World Religions* (1922).

welfare economics A field of economics that grew out of the debate between proponents of LAISSEZ FAIRE and proponents of government intervention. Laissez-faire proponents generally hold that the best government is one that governs least and that the invisible hand of markets transforms the self-interest of individual economic actors into the common good. In contrast, interventionists believe that markets are less than perfect and are frequently characterized by monopoly power, MARKET FAILURE, and informational asymmetries that cripple competition. Welfare economists use mathematical tools to analyze whether free markets achieve *socially* optimal outcomes.

The theoretical side of welfare economics is organized around three main propositions—the first two are the FUNDAMENTAL THEOREMS OF WELFARE economics and the third is ARROW'S IMPOSSIBILITY THEOREM. The first theorem asserts that an economy with competitive buyers and sellers attains a PARETO OPTIMAL outcome—that is, there exist no feasible alternatives that improve the welfare of some without reducing the welfare of others. The second theorem states that any Pareto optimal equilibrium can be achieved via the competitive mechanism, provided appropriate lump-sum taxes and transfers are imposed on individuals and firms. This means that the common good can be achieved by modifying the operations of markets. These two theorems both revised and supported Adam SMITH's classical argument that markets have the ability to achieve a "first-best" outcome without the guiding hand of a central planner.

In theory, a SOCIAL-WELFARE FUNCTION would use aggregated individual preferences to resolve questions about distributions of resources and wealth—especially questions that are not approachable using the Pareto criterion. Arrow's impossibility theorem, however, showed that such aggregation is not possible if the social-welfare function is to satisfy certain reasonable criteria. By extension, there is no *logically infallible*

way of solving the problem of the distribution or redistribution of resources and wealth.

Weltanschauung See WORLDVIEW.

Westminster model A democratic political system patterned after the British Parliament. Under the Westminster model, popularly elected members of a parliament's lower house hold extensive legislative powers. The prime minister and members of the CABINET are drawn from the LEGISLATURE, either from the dominant party, in cases of MAJORITY RULE, or from members of parties making up a COALITION GOVERNMENT. Under the Westminster form of government, the legislature's upper house has little real power and typically operates as a legitimizing body limited to suggesting revisions to legislation drawn up by the lower house. See also GOVERNMENT.

whip A member of a LEGISLATURE from either the majority or minority political party who assists the leadership in maintaining party unity and discipline. Whips canvass colleagues for their opinions, remind them to be present for important votes, and urge them to cast their ballots according to the party line.

White, Leslie A. (1900–1975) An American anthropologist best known for his rehabilitation of the theory of societal evolution, which had been marginalized in twentieth-century ANTHROPOLOGY by Franz BOAS and his students. Revising the HISTORICAL PARTICULARISM of the Boasian school, which broadly rejected cross-cultural comparison, White developed a grand evolutionary schema similar to that of nineteenth-century anthropologist Lewis Henry MORGAN. In *The Science of Culture* (1949) and *The Evolution of Culture* (1959), White defended and refined the evolutionary paradigm and, in the latter work, proposed per-capita energy expenditure as a viable measure of societal development.

White worked in other areas of anthropology as well. He was an active ethnographer and ultimately published five studies of the Pueblo Indians. He also defended a symbolic approach to CULTURE, termed "culturology," that held that culture was composed entirely of symbolic structures that surpassed their particular manifestations. His other major works include *The Social Organization of Ethnological Theory* (1966) and *The Concept of Culture* (1973).

Wicksell, Knut   (1851–1926) A monetary theorist in the marginalist tradition considered to be an important forerunner of John Maynard KEYNES. Wicksell was among the first to use monetary theory to analyze the working of the economy as a whole, rather than at the level of individual purchasing decisions. He made three major contributions to economic theory: an analysis of how interest rates affect EQUILIBRIUM prices, a study of how the government or CENTRAL BANK can achieve price stability, and an approach to monetary phenomena based on aggregate supply and demand.

With regard to interest rates and price stability, Wicksell demonstrated how upward deviation in the bank rate from the equilibrium interest rate can lead to INFLATION. The possibility of inflation creates a role for the government and the central bank in maintaining price stability. Wicksell advocated government supervision of interest and discount rates to minimize bank-created inflationary pressure. He argued that the monetary authority should raise interest rates if prices begin to rise and lower them if prices begin to fall. This is the operating principle of many central banks today, including the Federal Reserve Bank of the United States.

Wicksell also analyzed the relationship between aggregate savings and investment in the economy. He was concerned with the tendency of bank-financed new investment to divert land and labor away from the production of consumer goods and toward the production of capital goods. This reduces the supply of consumer goods, while demand increases as the new investment bids up the prices of land and labor. The resulting price rise implies that the real value of physical capital purchased by the loan is smaller than planned. As the rise in prices constricts consumption, forced saving occurs, which effectively finances the new investment.

Wicksell's greatest contribution was to have integrated the microeconomic insights of the marginalist tradition—the marginal productivity theory and price theory—into macroeconomic theory (see MACROECONOMICS; and MICROECONOMICS). His most significant works are *Interest and Prices* (1898) and *Lectures on Political Economy* (1906). Keynes recognized Wicksell as a precursor, and he followed up many of Wicksell's ideas in developing his own *general theory* of the economy, which brought macroeconomics into its own.

Wildavsky, Aaron   (1931–1995) An American political scientist whose contributions span a number of fields, including the analysis of the national budget, the presidency, risk policy, and cultural theory.

The U.S. political budgetary process was an area of persistent concern for Wildavsky, first in *The Politics of the Budgetary Process* (1964), which emphasized the struggle among diverse social and political actors over budgetary allocation, and later in *The New Politics of the Budgetary Process* (1988), which reformulated his original notion of struggle in terms of wider culture clashes among different lifestyles. Budgeting thereby provided a window on larger social priorities, the mechanisms of PLURALISM, and the sociopolitical structure of the local and national levels. Wildavsky argued that national budgeting is essentially a top-down process, in which a central authority makes allocations based on a conception of the national interest. A bottom-up process, he suggested, would better serve democratic ideals but would likely render the overall process uncontrollable. The efficacy of this allocation process, therefore, has much to do with political leadership—an issue explored in Wildavsky's *Dilemmas of Presidential Leadership: From Washington to Lincoln* (1989, with Richard Ellis). There, Wildavsky presented the U.S. presidency as a coalition-building office that is shaped by a complex dynamic of cultural needs, collective perceptions of the polity, and political rhetoric.

Wildavsky also made important contributions to research on RISK. In *Risk and Culture* (1982, with Mary DOUGLAS), *Searching for Safety* (1988), and *The Rise of Radical Egalitarianism* (1991), he described modernity as largely defined by a preoccupation with safety and increasingly vexed by the new risks that safety measures often entail. Risk, in this context, becomes a relative idea that reflects trade-offs between different kinds of benefits and dangers. The public perception of risk, he argued, is thus a cultural construct that depends on time and place, and on management by government agencies or political groups.

Wildavsky's other work is diverse and includes *Leadership in a Small Town* (1964), *Speaking Truth to Power: The Art and Craft of Policy Analysis* (1979), *Craftways: The Organization of Scholarly Work* (1989), and *The Beleaguered Presidency* (1991).

Williams, Raymond   (1921–1988) A cultural theorist of great range and influence, Williams moved easily between history, literary criticism, the sociology of culture, and by the 1970s, the analysis of technology and the mass media. His early works, *Culture and Society: 1780–1950* (1958) and *The Long Revolution* (1961), were sustained explorations of the concepts of CULTURE and TRADITION that analyzed the relationships between material production, social transformation, and aesthetic developments in Great Britain. For Williams, tradition was not a fixed object but a process of selection and reinvention shaped by present needs and sensibilities. Culture, in turn, was an integrated whole—"a whole way of life"—that required analysis of both its material conditions and symbolic forms. These inquiries proved highly influential on the emerging CULTURAL STUDIES movement, then centered around the University of Birmingham in England. Williams's approach to culture—at once textual and materialist—resonated strongly with that of Richard HOGGART (director of the Birmingham school) and Edward Palmer THOMPSON, an innovative historian of the eighteenth century and the working class. Together, these three writers shaped the Marxist orientation, interdisciplinarity, and preoccupation with popular culture that dominated cultural studies through the mid-1970s.

By the 1970s, Williams described this orientation as CULTURAL MATERIALISM and aligned it with Antonio GRAMSCI's theory of HEGEMONY, which described the form of legitimation pursued by the ruling class. Hegemony involved not direct coercion but actively managed consent that frequently took the form of struggles over the meaning of cultural symbols and social vocabularies. Williams's close attention to the history of pivotal terms, such as culture, DEMOCRACY, and CLASS—leading to his seminal exposition, *Keywords* (1976)—was very much in this spirit in its attempt to trace the major points of hegemonic conflict. In the same period, Williams began to explore the hegemonic implications of the mass media, with particular concern for the ways in which specific technologies (such as television) penetrated and structured daily life. This work culminated in *Television, Technology and Cultural Form* (1974), which, along with Stuart HALL's essay "The Television Discourse—Encoding/Decoding" (1973), helped open the floodgates of modern media studies.

Williams's other important works include *Problems in Materialism and Culture* (1980) and *Towards 2000* (1983).

winner's curse   Occurs in auctions when the true value of the item for sale is not known and the winner has overvalued the item. For example, an expanse of land may be known to have oil, but the actual value of the oil is open to speculation. Each bidder will make a best guess as to the true value, based on available information. But if the information gives only a probabilistic value, then the winner of the auction will almost certainly have overestimated the true value of the oil field—the winner is the one who guessed highest, and if the guesses are correct only on average, then the highest guess is too high. Having won the auction, the winner can expect to lose money on the venture.

Winnicott, Donald Woods   (1896–1971) A British psychoanalyst and pediatrician who was one of the principal contributors to OBJECT-RELATIONS THEORY. Winnicott emphasized the importance of the early relationship between the child and mother (or caregiver) in the creation of a healthy or *true self*—especially in the first months of infancy. The mother, he said, is responsible for providing the child a *holding environment*, in which the child can dispossess itself of its initial sense of omnipotence—of needs instantly met—without trauma; Winnicott called this role that of the *good-enough mother*. The failure to provide such an environment leads to the creation of a *false self*, which Winnicott held responsible for a variety of neuroses and failures of SOCIALIZATION. Winnicott also proposed an influential theory of TRANSITIONAL OBJECTS (such as favorite toys or a blanket), through which the child begins to differentiate external and internal, self and not-self, and to develop competencies for the use of symbols.

Many of these ideas resonated with those of Melanie KLEIN and other object-relations theorists, who together had rejected the Freudian account of child development—especially the primal sexual triangle of the OEDIPUS COMPLEX. Like that of other object-relations theorists, Winnicott's work supported a much more continuous understanding of the process of personality formation, in which the symbolic roles of mother and father did not wholly determine psychological development. Winnicott's major works include *The Child, the Family and the Outside World* (1964), *Playing and Reality* (1971), *Deprivation and*

Delinquency (1984), and *Home Is Where We Start From* (1990).

witchcraft   Much of the pioneering anthropological work on witchcraft was done in Africa by British social anthropologists. These scholars tended to follow E. E. EVANS-PRITCHARD's 1937 distinction between *witchcraft* and *sorcery*—the former a hereditary power to cause injury, the latter a set of learned skills put to the same purpose. This distinction has proved to be widespread in human society but not universal. It did, however, give a strong functionalist stamp to the study of witchcraft, which credited it with a range of nonoccult social functions, from assimilating unexplained events, to establishing the boundaries between normal and transgressive behavior, to building solidarity in certain social movements. See also MAGIC.

Wittgenstein, Ludwig   (1889–1951) A Viennese-born philosopher of LANGUAGE and one of the pivotal philosophers of the twentieth century. Wittgenstein's work on the rootedness of language in everyday use has had a profound effect on the study of experience, CULTURE, and knowledge. It is a keystone of the broad linguistic turn of post–World War II philosophical and cultural analysis. Nonetheless, Wittgenstein is perhaps best known for his early *Tractatus Logico-Philosophicus* (1921), which develops a very different concept of language. There, Wittgenstein argued that the only language that could be said to be true or false was language limited to narrow factual statements. The rest—including all assertions about ethics or ends and even theories about the relationship of words to reality such as the *Tractatus*—were, strictly speaking, meaningless. The *Tractatus* was often interpreted as a defense of the truth-value of science and as an attack on other claims for value, although it has also been read as a defense of the realm of ethical judgment. In any event, it was an important influence on the logical POSITIVISM of the Vienna Circle of philosophers of science.

In his later work, Wittgenstein abandoned this purist concept of language and argued instead for a plural notion of the diverse "language games" that structure human activity—including the sciences. These games and the rules that organize them, he argued, are purely conventional, learned, and generally unquestioned. Language, in this context, has no truth content but acquires efficacy in its *use* or applicability to daily life. He thereby argued against abstract philosophizing that distanced itself from these uses.

Wittgenstein's work has been influential in both SOCIOLOGY and ANTHROPOLOGY. It was the basis for Peter Winch's *The Idea of a Social Science* (1958), which challenged the notion that there could be a science of social phenomena, since these were inevitably implicated in language games. This anticipated aspects of later poststructuralist arguments (see POSTSTRUCTURALISM). Wittgenstein's work also proved central to debates about rationality and the question of whether cross-cultural comparison could be neutral and/or reliably verified.

Wittgenstein's major study of these themes is *Investigations* (1953, posthumous). His other works include *On Certainty* (1969, posthumous) and *Culture and Value* (1977, posthumous). Wittgenstein spent much of his career at Cambridge University.

Wolin, Sheldon   (1922–) An American political scientist whose work has explored the nature of POLITICS, POWER, and the public realm. Wolin works in a tradition of political theory marked by the problem of demarcating the space of political life in relation to private, economic, and state activities. He has been especially concerned with the problem of connecting the activity of politics to the pursuit of visions of the good life and the good society. In *Politics and Vision* (1960), Wolin traced the ways in which this issue has been historically and culturally shaped as far back as PLATO. The particular malaise of the late modern era, he argued, involves the depoliticization of the public sphere and the subordination of collective deliberation on communal concerns to the organizational prerogatives of power, objectivity, and mechanical rationality—especially in their modern bureaucratic form (see PUBLIC SPHERE AND PRIVATE SPHERE; and RATIONALIZATION).

Wolin describes much of this trajectory in his collection of essays, *The Presence of the Past* (1989). Here he focused on the experience of democratic action and on the threats posed to civic cooperation by state encroachment on the public sphere. He based much of this argument on his reading of the U.S. Constitution, which he argued favored a centralized state that could subordinate local structures of power (states and local governments). In his view, the U.S. Constitution was intended as a modernizing and centralizing force, directed against a decentralized and feudal tradition of politics. Yet it set into motion forces that far outstripped this goal. State power continued to evolve and grow in new ways, especially during the vast bureaucratic expansion associated with the New Deal, the welfare state, and the development of the United States into a global military power—whence the domination of the political process, according to Wolin, by new state imperatives regarding regulation, welfare, and empire. The result, he argued, is a political-economic megastate, directed by opaque, undemocratic, and largely unaccountable bureaucracies.

Wolin's interest in restoring a viable political sphere aligns his work with that of Hannah ARENDT and Jürgen HABERMAS. His other important works include *Hobbes and the Epic Tradition of Political Theory* (1970) and *The Berkeley Rebellion and Beyond* (1970, with J. H. Schaar).

work   See LABOR; and WORK ORIENTATION.

work orientation   Refers to the values, expectations, and feelings that workers bring to the work situation. The subject has been of long-term interest to sociologists as a variable in social and economic stratification and as an element in rational choice debates about the values that govern professional choices (see RATIONAL-CHOICE THEORY). Not surprisingly, forms of work motivation and satisfaction vary widely, often as a function of the level of professional expertise and prestige associated with the task. Such findings have been enlisted in a range of sociological and applied projects, from efficiency studies to mappings of ideological formations.

There are other approaches that, to a degree, cut across the question of social stratification. John Goldthorpe and David Lockwood, for example, conducted a number of well-known studies that emphasized three general orientations to work: (1) an *instrumental* logic, which sees work primarily in terms of income and the workplace as discrete from other areas of social life; (2) a *bureaucratic* logic, which emphasizes service to an organization, security of employment, and relative continuity between work and self-identity; and (3) a *solidaristic* orientation, which stresses satisfaction with work and a strong continuity between the workplace, self-identity, and community. Among professionals where a high degree of job choice exists, they were able to observe a process of self-selection into different types of work.

world-systems theory   Provides an account of the transnational development of CAPITALISM and a theory of the global structure of inequality among nations. Along with DEPENDENCY theory, it challenged the prevailing modernization theories of the 1960s, which proposed that the less developed countries could follow the same path to development as the highly industrialized Western countries. World-systems theorists argued that this underestimated the interconnection of the global economy and the advantages that early leadership conferred on the rich countries.

Rooted in MARXISM and in the historical research of the ANNALES SCHOOL, world-systems theory is associated primarily with the work of the sociologist-historian Immanuel WALLERSTEIN. Following Wallerstein, it generally distinguishes three classes of economic positions in the world of transnational capitalism: the core, the periphery, and the semiperiphery. The core of the global economy consists of the world's most powerful industrial nations, including the United States, most West European nations, and Japan. The core nations provide the management and technology for the production of the world's goods, and they reap most of the profits. The periphery of the global economy consists primarily of the THIRD WORLD nations, which export agricultural products and raw materials—generally on terms set by the core nations. For Wallerstein, these differences have profound political consequences that reverse the premodern model of empire—based largely on political uniformity—and challenge the model of democratization promoted by the West. Stable, democratic regimes, Wallerstein argues, are built on the dominant, diversified economies of the core nations. Peripheral nations, in contrast, remain dependent on the core nations for manufactured goods, aid, expertise, and a range of other services—a relationship that takes precedence over the question of political autonomy and political freedom. Wallerstein also identifies a category of semiperipheral countries that share elements of both core and periphery. These are actively involved in the world system but have only limited influence in it. They may also move up and down in the system, depending on how well they compete in world markets. Turkey, Mexico, and the newly industrialized countries in Asia belong to this group. A country's opportunities for development depend largely on its position in the world system.

World-systems theory has been criticized for depicting the global economic system in terms of a unified theory of capitalism that downplays the historical and cultural differences of developing countries. It has also been criticized for neglecting the fact that the populations of core nations do not necessarily benefit equally from their dominant position—in other words, core–periphery distinctions may exist internally as well as externally (e.g., the persistence of an underclass in many industrialized nations). Nonetheless, the model was among the first to insist on the truly international dimension of capitalism and the limitations of prevailing notions of dependency and neocolonialism.

worldview   From the German *Weltanschauung*, worldview refers to the total system of values and beliefs that characterize a given culture or group. The notion of singular and unified structures of value and belief has been important to a number of traditions within the social sciences—including the CULTURE AND PERSONALITY MOVEMENT; a variety of developmental and evolutionary cultural theories (such as Robert REDFIELD's concept of the FOLK-URBAN CONTINUUM); and in much sociological work on the attitudes and beliefs of specific groups. Many of the more categorical claims made for worldviews, however, have drawn criticism from scholars who reject the monolithic concept of CULTURE implicit in the term.

Worsley, Peter   (1924–) A British sociologist and anthropologist best known for his work on developing societies, the sociology of knowledge, medical sociology, and MARXISM. Worsley spent much of his career at the University of Manchester and served as president of the British Sociological Association from 1971 to 1974.

Worsley's first book, *The Trumpet Shall Sound* (1957), was an anthropological study of the CARGO CULTS that emerged in New Guinea after World War II—an "indigenous" response to the end of the vast military-supply operations that flooded many Pacific islands with Western goods. Worsley was distinctive in arguing for the prepolitical content of these "revivalistic movements." The cargo cults, he claimed, provided ways of coping with modernization and colonialism prior to the development of global political awareness and organization for independence.

Worsley has also made significant contributions in the area of development studies. His *Three Worlds: Culture and World Development* (1984) situated the problem of underdevelopment within a broad historical and cultural context. While integrating elements of neo-Marxist theories of underdevelopment, Worsley criticized the economic determinism of much of that work. He argued instead that economic underdevelopment needed to be understood as embedded within a wider social and cultural matrix. Worsley has also addressed some of the classic issues in the sociology of knowledge. *Knowledges: Culture, Counterculture and Subculture* (1997) seeks to relativize knowledge systems and thereby transcend the rigid boundary between scientific and nonscientific knowledge. To that end, Worsley analyzed the scientificity of knowledge in non-Western societies, especially among the Australian aborigines, and also examined the coexistence of iconic and scientific knowledge claims in the West.

Worsley's other publications include *The Third World* (1964), *Inside China* (1975), and *Marx and Marxism* (1982).

Wundt, Wilhelm   (1832–1920) Considered by many to be the father of experimental psychology, Wundt was a strong proponent of bringing scientific methods to bear on the question of behavior and its environmental determinants (an orientation then known as *associationism*, which would survive in modern BEHAVIORISM). He was trained as a medical doctor and held a chair in philosophy at the University of Leipzig, where he established the first laboratory for psychological studies and one of the first journals to publish research in the field. Part of the contemporary interest of Wundt's work is that he brought a historical and voluntarist dimension to the question of learning and conditioned response that would largely disappear from subsequent behavioral and experimental research. He believed that the missing component in deterministic accounts of behavior was the human capacity for *apperception*—a term with roots in the work of Gottfried Leibniz and Immanuel KANT—which described the synthetic, creative response of the human mind to the environment. The mind, Wundt argued, could produce responses that were not a direct or predictable result of external stimuli. He also accorded a much greater role than most psychologists to history and CULTURE—a subject on which he wrote at length. Wundt was a prolific writer whose works include *Principles of Physiological Psychology* (1904), *Elements of Folk Psychology* ([1912] 1916), and *The Language of Gestures* (1973).

X

X-efficiency A situation in which a firm fails to produce in the least-costly manner. Many theories of the causes of X-efficiency use postulates that depart from those employed in standard economic analysis. For one, they may relax the profit-maximizing behavior assumed by microeconomic analysis. Rather, they assume that decisions are guided by habits, conventions, moral imperatives, and emulation, none of which is of a maximizing nature. Often, contracts between workers and employers are not fully specified; workers have discretion with regard to their effort, and employers have discretion with regard to wages and work conditions. The theory also assumes that there is inertia in the decision-making process and that changes in the independent variables are not always reflected in changes in the dependent variables. For this reason, innovations may not be introduced when it is optimal to do so. Thus, two identical plants in two locations (such as a Ford Motor plant in the United Kingdom and in Germany), using the same labor and equipment may exhibit different output and productivity levels, because technologies or the conventions regarding effort are different in the two countries.

Y

---

yield The annual return on a security as a percentage of its current market price. Yields may be calculated either on the basis of net profits (termed *earnings yield*) or on the basis of declared dividends (termed *dividend yields*). The dividend yield is normally lower than the earnings yield because of retained profits.

Z

Zeitgeist   German, meaning "spirit of the age." The term *Zeitgeist* is associated most strongly with Georg HEGEL's philosophy of history, which accorded different modes of realizing the progress of a universal Spirit to different historical eras. More generally, the term has come to signify any particularly salient quality or sensibility of a period.

zero-sum games   Games in which the payoffs to the players in any outcome add up to a constant. In other words, one player's gain is the others' loss. Zero-sum games are a polar case within noncooperative games. Payoffs may be positively correlated, such that what is good for one player is good for all (a *coordination game*), or there may be a combination of aligned and opposed interests. Zero-sum games are sometimes used outside economics to model situations in which actors compete against one another for scarce resources.

zonal model   See CONCENTRIC ZONE THEORY.

BIBLIOGRAPHY

Abbott, Andrew. *The System of Professions: An Essay on the Division of Expert Labor*. Chicago: University of Chicago Press, 1988.

Addams, Jane. *Democracy and Social Ethics*. New York: Macmillan, 1902.

———. *Newer Ideals of Peace*. New York: Macmillan, 1907.

———. *Twenty Years at Hull-House*. New York: Macmillan, 1910.

Adorno, Theodor. *Aesthetic Theory*. Edited by Gretel Adorno and Rolf Tiedemann. Translated from German by C. Lenhardt. London: Routledge and Kegan Paul, 1984. Originally published as *Asthetische Theorie* (Frankfurt am Main: Suhrkamp, 1970).

———. *Minima Moralia: Reflections from Damaged Life*. Translated from German by E. F. N. Jephcott. London: New Left Books, 1974. Originally published as *Minima Moralia: Reflexionen aus dem beschadigten Leben* (Berlin: Suhrkamp Verlag, 1951).

———. *Negative Dialectics*. Translated from German by E. B. Ashton. New York: Seabury Press, 1973. Originally published as *Negative Dialektik* (Frankfurt am Main: Suhrkamp, 1966).

———. *Prisms*. Translated from German by Samuel and Sherry Weber. London: Spearman, 1967. Originally published as *Prismen: Kulturkritik und Gesellschaft* (Berlin: Suhrkamp Verlag, 1955).

Adorno, Theodor, E. F. Brunswik, D. J. Levinson, and R. N. Sanford. *The Authoritarian Personality: Studies in Prejudice*. New York: Harper and Row, 1950.

Alchian, Armenia. "Uncertainty, Evolution and Economic Theory." *The Journal of Political Economy* 58.3 (Jun. 1950): 211–221.

Alchian, Armenia, and Harold Demsetz. "Production, Information Costs, and Economic Organization." *American Economic Review* 62.5 (Dec. 1972): 777–799.

Alexander, Sidney. "The Effects of Devaluation on a Trade Balance." *IMF Staff Papers* 3 (Apr. 1952): 359–373.

Allais, Maurice. *Economie et intêret: Presentation nouvelle des problemes fondamentaux relatifs au role economiques du taux de l'interet et de leurs solutions*. 2 vols. Paris: Librairie des Publications Officielles, 1947.

———. *À la recherche d'une discipline économique, première partie: L'économie pur*. N.p: Saint-Cloud, 1943.

Allport, Gordon. *The Nature of Prejudice*. Cambridge, Mass.: Addison-Wesley, 1953.

———. *Pattern and Growth in Personality*. New York: Holt, Rinehart and Winston, 1961.

———. *Personality and Social Encounter*. Boston: Beacon Press, 1960.

Allport, G. W., and L. Postman. *The Psychology of Rumor*. New York: Holt, 1947.

Almond, Gabriel A., and Sidney Verba. *The Civic Culture: Political Attitudes and Democracy in Five Nations*. Princeton, N.J.: Princeton University Press, 1963.

Althusser, Louis. *Essays in Self-Criticism*. Translated from French by Grahame Lock. London: New Left Books, 1976. Originally published as *Elements d'autocritique* (Paris: Hachette, 1974).

———. *For Marx*. Translated from French by Ben Brewster. New York: Pantheon, 1969. Originally published as *Pour Marx* (Paris: Maspero, 1966).

———. *The Future Lasts a Long Time and The Facts*. Edited by Olivier Corpet and Yann Moulier Boutang. Translated from French by Richard Veasey. London: Chatto and Windus, 1993. Originally published as *L'avenir dure longtemps: Suivi de les faits* (Paris: Stock/IMEC, 1992).

———. "Ideology and Ideological State Apparatuses (Notes Toward an Investigation)." In *Lenin and Philosophy and Other Essays*. Translated from French by Ben Brewster. London: New Left Books, 1971. Originally published as *Lenine et la philosophie* (Paris: F. Maspero, 1969).

———. *Lenin and Philosophy and Other Essays*. Translated from French by Ben Brewster. London: New Left Books, 1971. Originally published as *Lenine et la philosophie* (Paris: F. Maspero, 1969).

Althusser, Louis, and Etienne Balibar. *Reading Capital*. Translated from French by Ben Brewster. London: New Left Books, 1970. Originally published as *Lire "Le capital"* (Paris: F. Maspero, 1965).

American Journal of Sociology. Chicago: University of Chicago Press, 1895–.

Anderson, Benedict. *Imagined Communities: Reflections on the Origin and Spread of Nationalism*. London: Verso, 1983.

Annales d'Histoire Economique et Sociale. Paris: A. Colin, 1929–1938.

Aoki, M., ed. *The Economic Analysis of the Japanese Firm*. Amsterdam: Elsevier, 1984.

Arendt, Hannah. *Between Past and Future: Eight Exercises in Political Theory*. New York: Viking Press, 1968.

———. *Eichmann in Jerusalem: A Report on the Banality of Evil*. New York: Viking Press, 1963.

———. *The Human Condition.* Chicago: University of Chicago Press, 1958.

———. *The Life of the Mind.* 2 vols. Edited by Mary McCarthy. New York: Harcourt Brace Jovanovich, 1978.

———. *Men in Dark Times.* New York: Harcourt, Brace and World, 1968.

———. *On Revolution.* New York: Viking Press, 1963.

———. *The Origins of Totalitarianism.* New York: Harcourt, Brace, 1951.

Aristotle. *The Athenian Constitution: The Eudemian Ethics: On Virtues and Vices.* Translated from Greek by H. Rackham. Cambridge, Mass.: Harvard University Press, 1992.

———. *Constitution of the Athenians, by the Old Oligarch and by Aristotle: A New Interpretation by Livio Catullo Stecchini.* Glencoe, Ill.: Free Press, 1950.

———. *The Metaphysics.* Translated from Greek by Hugh Tredennick. Cambridge, Mass.: Harvard University Press, 1969–1975.

———. *Nicomachean Ethics.* Translated from Greek by Terence Irwin. Indianapolis, Ind.: Hackett, 1985.

———. *The Politics.* Translated from Greek by William Ellis. Buffalo, N.Y.: Prometheus Books, 1986.

Aron, Raymond. *Clausewitz: Philosopher of War.* Translated from French by Christine Booker and Norman Stone. London: Routledge and Kegan Paul, 1983. Originally published as *Penser la guerre, Clausewitz* (Paris: Gallimard, 1976).

———. *Democracy and Totalitarianism.* Translated from French by Valence Ionescu. London: Weidenfeld and Nicolson, 1968. Originally published as *Démocratie et totalitarisme* (vol. 3 of *Sociologie des sociétés industrielles*) (Paris: Gallimard, 1965).

———. *Eighteen Lectures on Industrial Society.* Translated from French by M. K. Bottomore. London: Weidenfeld and Nicolson, 1967. Originally published as *Dix-huit leçons sur la société industrielle* (Paris: Gallimard, 1962).

———. *German Sociology.* Translated from French by Mary and Thomas Bottomore. Glencoe, Ill.: Free Press, 1957. Originally published as *Sociologie allemande contemporaine* (Paris: F. Alcan, 1935).

———. *Main Currents in Sociological Thought.* 2 vols. Translated from French by Richard Howard and Helen Weaver. New York: Basic Books, 1965–1967. Originally published as *Etapes de la pensée sociologique. Montesquieu. Comte. Marx. Tocqueville. Durkheim. Pareto. Weber* (Paris: Gallimard, 1967).

———. *The Opium of the Intellectuals.* Translated from French by Terence Kilmartin. Garden City, N.Y.: Doubleday, 1957. Originally published as *L'Opium des intellectuels* (Paris: Calmann-Lévy, 1955).

———. *Peace and War: A Theory of International Relations.* Translated from French by Richard Howard and Annette Baker Fox. Garden City, N.Y.: Doubleday, 1966. Originally published as *Paix et guerre entre les nations* (Paris: Calmann-Lévy, 1962).

———. *Progress and Disillusion: The Dialectics of Modern Society.* New York: New American Library, 1968. Originally published as *Les désillusions du progrès, essai sur la dialectique de la modernité* (Paris: Calmann-Lévy, 1969).

Arrow, Kenneth J. *Social Choice and Individual Values.* New York: Wiley, 1951.

Arrow, Kenneth, H. B. Chenery, B. S. Minhas, and R. M. Solow. "Capital-Labor Substitution and Economic Efficiency." *Review of Economics and Statistics* 53 (Aug. 1961): 225–251.

Augustine, Saint. *Confessions.* Translated from Latin by R. S. Pine-Coffin. Harmondsworth: Penguin, 1961.

———. *The Literal Meaning of Genesis.* 2 vols. Translated from Latin by John Hammond Taylor. New York: Newman Press, 1982.

———. *On the City of God.* Translated from Latin by John Healey. London: J. M. Dent, 1931.

———. *The Trinity.* Translated from Latin by Stephen McKenna. Washington, D.C.: Catholic University of America Press, 1963.

Bachelard, Gaston. *The New Scientific Spirit.* Translated from French by Arthur Goldhammer. Boston: Beacon Press, 1984. Originally published as *Le nouvel esprit scientifique* (Paris: Librairie Felix Alcan, 1934).

———. *The Poetics of Space.* Translated from French by Maria Jolas. Boston: Beacon Press, 1969. Originally published as *La poétique de l'espace* (Paris: Presses Universitaires de France, 1957).

———. *The Psychoanalysis of Fire.* Translated from French by A. C. Ross. Boston: Beacon Press, 1964. Originally published as *Le psychanalyse du feu* (Paris: Gallimard, 1932).

Bakhtin, Mikhail. *Problems of Dostoevsky's Poetics.* Translated from Russian by R. Rotsel. Ann Arbor, Mich.: Ardis, 1973. Originally published as *Problemy tvorchestva Dostoevskogo* (Leningrad: Priboi, 1929).

———. *Rabelais and His World.* Translated from Russian by Helene Iswolsky. Cambridge, Mass.: MIT Press, 1968. Originally published as *Tvorchestvo Fransua Rable i narodnaia Kul'tura srednevekov'ia i Renessansa* (Moskow: Khudozh. lit-ra, 1965).

———. *Statism and Anarchy.* Translated from Russian and edited by M. S. Shatz. New York: Cambridge University Press, 1990. Originally published as *Gosudarstvennost' i anarkhiia* (1873).

Baltzell E. Digby. *Philadelphia Gentlemen.* New York: Free Press, 1966.

———. *The Protestant Establishment.* New York: Random House, 1966.

Bandura, Albert. *Social Foundations of Thought and Action: A Social Cognitive Theory.* Englewood Cliffs, N.J.: Prentice-Hall, 1986.

Barth, Fredrik. *Political Leadership among the Swat Pathans*. London: University of London, Athlone Press, 1959.

Barthes, Roland. *Camera Lucida: Reflections on Photography*. Translated from French by Richard Howard. New York: Hill and Wang, 1981. Originally published as *La chambre claire: Note sur la photographie* (Paris: Cahiers du Cinema, 1980).

———. *Elements of Semiology*. Translated from French by Annette Lavers and Colin Smith. London: Jonathan Cape, 1967. Originally published as *Elements de semiologie* (Paris: Editions du Seuil, 1964).

———. *Mythologies*. Translated from French by Annette Lavers. London: Paladin, 1973. Originally published as *Mythologies* (Paris: Editions du Seuil, 1957).

———. *S/Z*. Translated from French by Richard Miller. London: Jonathan Cape, 1975. Originally published as *S/Z* (Paris: Editions du Seuil, 1970).

———. *Writing Degree Zero*. Translated from French by Annette Lavers and Colin Smith. London: Jonathan Cape, 1967. Originally published as *Le degre zéro de l'écriture* (Paris: Editions de Seuil, 1953).

Bateson, Gregory. *Mind and Nature: A Necessary Unity*. New York: E.P. Dutton, 1979.

———. *Naven: A Survey of the Problems Suggested by a Composite Picture of the Culture of a New Guinea Tribe Drawn from Three Points of View*. Cambridge: Cambridge University Press, 1936.

———. *Steps to an Ecology of Mind*. New York: Ballantine, 1972.

Bateson, Gregory, and Margaret Mead. *Balinese Character: A Photographic Analysis*. New York: The New York Academy of Sciences, 1942.

Baudrillard, Jean. *The Consumer Society: Myths and Structures*. Translated from French by Chris Turner. London: Sage, 1998. Originally published as *La société de consommation: Ses mythes, ses structures* (Paris: S.G.P.P., 1970).

———. *For a Critique of the Political Economy of the Sign*. Translated from French by Charles Levin. St. Louis, Mo.: Telos Press, 1981. Originally published as *Pour une critique de l'économie politique du signe* (Paris: Gallimard, 1972).

———. *Forget Foucault*. Translator unknown. New York: Semiotext(e), 1987. Originally published as *Oublier Foucault* (Paris: Editions Galilee, 1977).

———. *The Mirror of Production*. Translated from French by Mark Poster. St. Louis, Mo.: Telos Press, 1975. Originally published as *Le miroir de la production; ou, L'illusion critique du materialisme historique* (Tournai, Belgium: Casterman, 1973).

———. *Simulations*. Translated from French by Paul Foss, Paul Patton, and Philip Beitchman. New York: Semiotext(e), Inc., 1983. Originally published as *Simulations* (Paris: Galilée, 1981).

———. *The Transparency of Evil: Essays on Extreme Phenomena*. Translated from French by James Benedict. London: Verso, 1993. Originally published as *La transparence du mal: Essai sur les phenomenes extremes* (Paris: Galilee, 1990).

Bauman, Zygmunt. *Modernity and the Holocaust*. Ithaca, N.Y.: Cornell University Press, 1989.

Baumol, W. J. "The Transactions Demand for Cash: An Inventory Theoretical Approach." *Quarterly Journal of Economics* 66 (Nov. 1952): 545–556.

Beard, Charles A. *American City Government*. 1912. Reprint, New York: Arno Press, 1970.

———. *A Charter for the Social Sciences in the Schools*. New York: Scribners, 1932.

———. *An Economic Interpretation of the Constitution of the United States*. 1913. Reprint, New York: Macmillan, 1925.

———. *Economic Origins of Jeffersonian Democracy*. New York: Macmillan, 1915.

———. *The Industrial Revolution*. London: Sonnenschein, 1901.

———. *The Supreme Court and the Constitution*. New York: Macmillan, 1912.

Beard, Charles A., and Mary R. Beard. *The Rise of American Civilization*. 2 vols. New York: Macmillan, 1927.

Beaumont, Gustave de, and Alexis de Tocqueville. *On the Penitentiary System in the United States and Its Application in France*. Translated from French by Francis Lieber. Philadelphia: Carey, Lea and Blanchard, 1833. Originally published as *Du système pénitentiaire aux Etats-Unis, et de son application en France; suivi d'un appendice sur les colonies penales et de notes statistiques* (Paris: H. Fournier jeune, 1833).

Beauvoir, Simone de. *All Said and Done*. Translated from French by Patrick O'Brian. New York: Putnam, 1974. Originally published as *Tout compte fait* (Paris: Gallimard, 1972).

———. *The Ethics of Ambiguity*. Translated from French by Bernard Frechtman. New York: Philosophical Library, 1948. Originally published as *Pour une morale de l'ambiguité* (Paris: Gallimard, 1947).

———. *The Second Sex*. 2 vols. Translated from French by H. M. Parshley. New York: Knopf, 1952. Originally published as *Le deuxième sexe* (Paris: Gallimard, 1949).

———. *The Mandarins*. Translated from French by Leonard M. Friedman. Cleveland, Ohio: World, 1956. Originally published as *Les mandarins* (Paris: Gallimard, 1954).

———. *Memoirs of a Dutiful Daughter*. Translated from French by James Kirkup. Cleveland, Ohio: World, 1959. Originally published as *Memoires d'une jeune fille rangée* (Paris: Gallimard, 1958).

———. *Pyrrhus et Cineas*. Paris: Gallimard, 1944.

———. *The Woman Destroyed*. Translated from French by Patrick O'Brian. New York: Putnam, 1969. Originally published as *La femme rompue: L'age de discretion: Monologue* (Paris: Gallimard, 1967).

Beck, Ulrich. *Risk Society: Towards a New Modernity.* London: Sage, 1992.

Becker, Gary S. *The Economics of Discrimination.* Chicago: University of Chicago Press, 1957.

———. *Human Capital: A Theoretical and Empirical Analysis, with Special Reference to Education.* New York: Columbia University Press, 1964.

———. "A Theory of the Allocation of Time." *Economic Journal* 75 (1965): 493–517.

Becker, Howard S. *Art Worlds.* Berkeley: University of California Press, 1982.

———. *Outsiders: Studies in the Sociology of Deviance.* New York: Free Press, 1963.

Becker, Howard S., ed. *The Other Side: Perspectives on Deviance.* New York: The Free Press, 1964.

Becker, Howard S., Blanche Geer, and Everett Hughes. *Making the Grade.* New York: Wiley, 1968.

Becker, Howard S., Blanche Geer, Everett Hughes, and Anselm Strauss. *Boys in White: Student Culture in Medical School.* Chicago: University of Chicago Press, 1961.

Bell, Daniel. *The Coming of Post-Industrial Society.* New York: Basic Books, 1973.

———. *Communitarianism and Its Critics.* Oxford: Clarendon Press, 1993.

———. *The Cultural Contradictions of Capitalism.* New York: Basic Books, 1976.

———. *The End of Ideology: On the Exhaustion of Political Ideas in the Fifties.* Glencoe, Ill.: Free Press, 1960.

———. *Marxian Socialism in the United States.* Princeton, N. J.: Princeton University Press, 1967. First published in 1952 as chapter 6 of *Socialism and American Life* (Princeton Studies in American Civilization, no. 4), edited by Donald Drew Egbert and Stow Persons.

———. *The New American Right.* New York: Criterion Books, 1955.

———. *The Radical Right.* Garden City, N.Y.: Doubleday, 1963.

———. *The Reforming of General Education: The Columbia College Experience in Its National Setting.* Foreword by David B. Truman. New York: Columbia University Press, 1966.

Bellah, Robert N. *Beyond Belief: Essays on Religion in a Post-Traditional World.* New York: Harper and Row, 1970.

———. *The Broken Covenant.* Chicago: The University of Chicago Press, 1975.

Bendix, Reinhard. *Embattled Reason: Essays on Social Knowledge.* New York: Oxford University Press, 1970.

———. *Kings or People: Power and the Mandate to Rule.* Berkeley: University of California Press, 1980.

———. *Max Weber: An Intellectual Portrait.* New York: Doubleday, 1960.

———. *Nation Building and Citizenship.* New York: Wiley, 1964.

———. *Social Science and the Distrust of Reason.* Berkeley: University of California Press, 1951.

———. *State and Society.* Boston: Little, Brown, 1968.

———. *Work and Authority in Industry: Ideologies of Management in the Course of Industrialization.* New York: Wiley, 1956.

Bendix, Reinhard, and Seymour M. Lipset, eds. *Class, Status and Power.* New York: Free Press, 1966.

Benedict, Ruth Fulton. *The Chrysanthemum and the Sword: Patterns of Japanese Culture.* Boston: Houghton Mifflin, 1946.

———. *Patterns of Culture.* Boston and New York: Houghton Mifflin, 1934.

———. *Race: Science and Politics.* New York: Modern Age, 1940.

———. *Tales of the Cochiti Indians.* 1931. Reprint, St. Clair Shores, Mich.: Scholarly Press, 1976.

———. *Zuni Mythology.* 1935. Reprint, New York: AMS Press, 1969.

Benedict, Ruth Fulton, and Gene Weltfish. *The Races of Mankind.* New York: Public Affairs Committee, 1943.

Benjamin, Walter. *The Arcades Project.* Translated from German by Howard Eiland and Kevin McLaughlin. Cambridge, Mass.: Belknap Press of Harvard University Press, 1999. Originally published as *Das Passagen-Werk* (Frankfurt am Main: Suhrkamp, 1982).

———. *Illuminations.* Translated from German by Harry Zohn. Edited by Hannah Arendt. New York: Schocken Books, 1968. Originally published as *Illuminationen: Ausgewahlte Schriften* (Frankfurt am Main: Suhrkamp, 1955).

———. *Reflections.* Translated from German by E. Jephcott. New York: Harcourt Brace Jovanovich, 1978.

———. *Understanding Brecht.* Translated from German by Anna Bostock. London: Verso, 1983. Originally published as *Versuche uber Brecht* (Frankfurt am Main: Suhrkamp, 1966).

Bentham, Jeremy. *The Constitutional Code.* 1822–. Reprint, vol. I, edited by F. Rosen and J. H. Burns. Oxford: Clarendon Press, 1983.

———. *A Fragment on Government.* London: T. Payne, P. Elmsly, and E. Brooke, 1776.

———. "Indirect Legislation." In *Selections,* edited by Mary Peter Mack. New York: Pegasus Books, 1969.

———. *An Introduction to the Principles of Morals and Legislation.* 1780. Reprint, Oxford: Clarendon Press, 1876.

———. *The Limits of Jurisprudence Defined.* Edited by Chares Warren Everett. New York: Columbia University Press, 1945.

Bentley, Arthur F. *The Process of Government: A Study of Social Pressures.* Chicago: University of Chicago Press, 1908.

Berelson, Bernard R., Paul F. Lazarsfeld, and William McPhee. *Voting.* Chicago: University of Chicago Press, 1954.

Berger, Peter L., and Thomas Luckmann. *The Sociological Construction of Reality*. New York: Doubleday, 1966.

Berlin, Brent, and Paul Kay. *Basic Color Terms: Their Universality and Evolution*. Berkeley and Los Angeles: University of California Press, 1969.

Berlin, Isaiah. *Against the Current: Essays in the History of Ideas*. London: Hogarth Press, 1979.

————. *The Age of Enlightenment: The 18th Century Philosophers, Selected*. New York: New American Library, 1956.

————. *The Crooked Timber of Humanity: Chapters in the History of Ideas*. Edited by Henry Hardy. London: John Murray, 1990.

————. *The Hedgehog and the Fox: An Essay on Tolstoy's View of History*. New York: Simon and Schuster, 1953.

————. *Karl Marx: His Life and Environment*. 1939. Reprint, Oxford: Oxford University Press, 1963.

————. *Personal Impressions*. Edited by Henry Hardy. New York: Viking Press, 1981.

————. *Russian Thinkers*. Edited by Henry Hardy and Aileen Kelly. New York: Viking Press, 1978.

————. "Two Concepts of Liberty." In *Four Essays on Liberty*. Oxford: Oxford University Press, 1969.

————. *Vico and Herder: Two Studies in the History of Ideas*. London: Hogarth Press, 1976.

Berry, Brian J. *Geography of Market Centers and Retail Distribution*. Englewood Cliffs, N.J.: Prentice-Hall, 1967.

————. *The Human Consequences of Urbanization*. New York: St. Martin's Press, 1973.

Berry, Brian J., and Frank E. Horton, eds. *Geographic Perspectives on Urban Systems*. Englewood Cliffs, N.J.: Prentice-Hall, 1970.

Bertrand, Joseph. "Theorie Mathématique de la Richesse Sociale." *Journal des Savants* 67 (1883): 499–508. Translated from French by James W. Friedman as *Cournot Oligopoly*. Cambridge: Cambridge University Press, 1988.

Bettelheim, Bruno. *Symbolic Wounds: Puberty Rites and the Envious Male*. London: Thames and Hudson, 1955.

Bhagwati, Jagdish. "Immiserizing Growth: A Geometrical Note." *Review of Economic Studies* 25 (June 1958): 201–205.

Bion, Wilfred. *Attention and Interpretation*. London: Tavistock, 1970.

————. *Elements of Psychoanalysis*. London: William Heinemann, 1963.

————. *Experiences in Groups*. London: Tavistock, 1961.

————. *Transformations*. London: William Heinemann, 1963.

Black, Fischer, and Myron Scholes. "The Pricing of Options and Corporate Liabilities." *Journal of Political Economy* 81 (1973): 637–654.

Blau, Peter M. *The Dynamics of Bureaucracy: A Study of Interpersonal Relations in Two Government Agencies*. Chicago: University of Chicago Press, 1955.

————. *Exchange and Power in Social Life*. New York: Wiley, 1964.

————. *Inequality and Heterogeneity: A Primitive Theory of Social Structure*. New York: Free Press, 1977.

Blau, Peter M., and Otis Dudley Duncan. *The American Occupational Structure*. New York: Wiley, 1967.

Blau, Peter M., and Richard A. Schoenherr. *The Structure of Organizations*. New York: Basic Books, 1971.

Blau, Peter M., and Joseph Schwartz. *Cross-Cutting Social Circles: Testing a Macrostructural Theory of Inter-Group Relations*. New York: Academic Press, 1983.

Blau, Peter M., and W. Richard Scott. *Formal Organizations: A Comparative Approach*. San Francisco: Chandler, 1962.

Bloch, Marc. *Feudal Society*. 2 vols. Translated from French by L. A. Manyon. Chicago: University of Chicago Press, 1961. Originally published as *La société féodale: La formation des liens de dépendance* (Paris: A. Michel, 1939).

Bloch, Marc. *French Rural History: An Essay on Its Basic Characteristics*. Translated from French by Janet Sondheimer. Berkeley: University of California Press, 1966. Originally published as *Les caracteres originaux de l'histoire rurale française* (Cambridge, Mass.: Harvard University Press, 1931).

————. *The Historian's Craft*. Translated from French by Peter Putnam. New York: Knopf, 1953. Originally published as *Apologie pour l'histoire: ou métier d'historien* (Paris: Librairie Armand Colin, 1949).

————. *The Royal Touch: Sacred Monarchy and Scrofula in England and France*. 1924. Translated from French by J. E. Anderson. London: Routledge and Kegan Paul, 1973. Originally published as *Les rois thaumaturges: Etude sur le caractere surnaturel attribué à la puissance royale, particulierement en France et en Angleterre* (Strasbourg: Librairie Istra, 1924).

————. *Strange Defeat: A Statement of Evidence Written in 1940*. Translated from French by Gerard Hopkins. Cambridge: Oxford University Press, 1949. Originally published as *L'étrange défaite: temoignage écrit en 1940* (Paris: Société des Editions Franc-tireur, 1946).

Blumer, Herbert. "Collective Behavior." In *New Outline of the Principles of Sociology*, edited by A. M. Lee. 1939. Reprint, New York: Barnes and Noble, 1951.

————. *Symbolic Interactionism*. Englewood Cliffs, N.J.: Prentice-Hall, 1969.

Boas, Franz. *Kwakiutl Culture as Reflected in Mythology*. New York: G. B. Stechert, 1935.

————. "The Limitations of the Comparative Method in Anthropology." *Science* n.s. 4 (1896): 901–908.

————. *The Mind of Primitive Man*. New York: Free Press, 1911.

———. *Primitive Art.* Cambridge, Mass.: Harvard University Press, 1927.

———. *Race, Language, and Culture.* New York: Macmillan, 1940.

———. *The Social Organization and Secret Societies of the Kwakiutl Indians.* Washington, D.C.: Government Printing Office, 1897.

Boas, Franz, ed. *General Anthropology.* Contributions by Ruth Benedict, Franz Boas, Ruth Bunzel, others. Boston: D. C. Heath, 1938.

Bodin, Jean. *Colloquium of the Seven about Secrets of the Sublime.* Translated from Latin and edited by M. L. Daniels Kuntz. Princeton, N.J.: Princeton University Press, 1975. Originally published from the manuscript of 1588 as *Colloquium heptaplomeres de rerum sublimium arcanis abditis* (Paris: Suerini Megaloburgiensium, 1857).

———. *Method for the Easy Comprehension of History.* Edited and translated from Latin by B. Reynolds. New York: Norton, 1966. Originally published as *Methodus ad facilem historiarum cognitionem* (Paris: Apud Martinum Iuvenem, 1566).

———. *The Response of Jean Bodin to the Paradoxes of Malestroit, and the Paradoxes.* Translated from French by G. A. Moore. Washington, D.C.: Country Dollar Press, 1946. Originally published as *Réponse aux paradoxes de M. de Malestroit, touchant le fait des monnaies et l'eneherissement de toutes choses* (1568).

———. *Six Books of the Commonwealth.* Edited by K. McRae. Cambridge, Mass.: Harvard University Press, 1962. Originally published as *Les six livres de la Republique* (Paris: Chez Iacques du Puys, 1576).

Boeke, J. H. *Economics and Economic Policy of Dual Societies as Exemplified in Indonesia.* New York: Institute of Pacific Relations, 1953.

Böhm-Bawerk, Eugen von. *Positive Theory of Capital,* vol. 2 of *Capital and Interest* (3 vols. bound as one). Translated from German by George D. Huncke and Hans F. Sennholz. South Holland, Ill.: Libertarian Press, 1959. Originally published as *Positive Theorie des Kapitales* (Innsbruck: Wagner, 1889).

Booth, Charles. *The Life and Labor of the People in London.* 9 vols. London and New York: Macmillan, 1892–1897.

Bourdieu, Pierre. *Distinction: A Social Critique of the Judgment of Taste.* Translated from French by Richard Nice. Cambridge, Mass.: Harvard University Press, 1984. Originally published as *La distinction: Critique sociale du jugement* (Paris: Editions de Minuit, 1979).

———. *The Field of Cultural Reproduction: Essays on Art and Literature.* Edited by Randal Johnson. New York: Columbia University Press, 1993.

———. *The Forms of Capital.* In *Handbook of Theory and Research for the Sociology of Education,* edited by J. Richardson. New York: Greenwood Press, 1986.

———. *The Logic of Practice.* Translated from French by Richard Nice. Stanford, Calif.: Stanford University Press, 1980. Originally published as *Le sens pratique* (Paris: Editions de Minuit, 1980).

———. *Outline of a Theory of Practice.* Translated from French by Richard Nice. Cambridge: Cambridge University Press, 1977. Originally published as *Esquisse d'une théorie de la pratique: Precédé de trois études d'ethnologie kabyle* (Geneva and Paris: Droz, 1972).

Bourdieu, Pierre, ed. *La misère du monde.* Paris: Seuil, 1993.

Bourdieu, Pierre, and Jean-Claude Passeron. *Reproduction in Education, Culture and Society.* 1970. Translated from French by Richard Nice. London: Sage, 1990. Originally published as *La reproduction: Elements pour une théorie du systeme d'enseignement* (Paris: Editions de Minuit, 1970).

Braithwaite, John. *Crime, Shame and Reintegration.* 1923. Reprint, Cambridge: Cambridge University Press, 1989.

Braudel, Fernand. *Civilization and Capitalism: 15th–18th Century.* 3 vols. Translated from French by Siân Reynolds. London: HarperCollins, 1985. Originally published as *Civilisation materielle, économie et capitalisme: Xve–XVIIIe siècle* (Paris: A. Colin, 1979).

———. *The Identity of France.* 2 vols. Translated from French by Siân Reynolds. New York: Harper and Row, 1988. Originally published as *L'identité de la France* (Paris: Arthaud: Flammarion, 1986).

———. *The Mediterranean and the Mediterranean World in the Age of Philip II.* 2 vols. Translated from French by Siân Reynolds. London: Collins, 1972–1973. Originally published as *Méditerranée et le monde méditerranéen à l'époque de Philippe II* (Paris: A. Colin, 1949).

Braverman, Harry. *Labor and Monopoly Capital: The Degradation of Work in the Twentieth Century.* New York: Monthly Review Press, 1974.

Brownmiller, Susan. *Against Our Will: Men, Women, and Rape.* New York: Simon and Schuster, 1975.

Brunswik, Egon. *Perception and the Representative Design of Psychological Experiments.* Berkeley: University of California Press, 1956.

Buchanan, James M., and Gordon Tullock. *The Calculus of Consent: Logical Foundations of Constitutional Democracy.* Ann Arbor: University of Michigan Press, 1962.

Burke, Edmund. *A Philosophical Enquiry into the Origin of Our Ideas of the Sublime and the Beautiful.* [1757.] Edited by Adam Philips. Oxford: Oxford University Press, 1990.

———. *Present Discontents.* New York: Maynard, Merrill, 1893. Originally published as *Thoughts on the Causes of the Present Discontent* (1769).

———. *Reflections on the Revolution in France.* London: Penguin Classics, 1968. Originally published in London: J. Dodsley, 1790.

———. *Thoughts on French Affairs.* Vol. 4 of *The Works of the Right Honourable Edmund Burke.* 12 vols. London: John C. Nimmo, 1899. Originally published in London: F. & C. Rivington, 1791.

Burnham, James. *The Managerial Revolution: What is Happening in the World.* New York: John Day, 1941.

Calhoun, Craig. "The Infrastructure of Modernity: Indirect Social Relationships, Information Technology, and Social Integration." In *Social Change and Modernity* edited by Hans Haferkamp and Neil J. Smelser, 205–236. Berkeley: University of California Press, 1992.

Cardoso, Fernando, Martin Carnoy, Manuel Castells, and Stephen S. Cohen. *The New Global Economy in the Information Age: Reflections on Our Changing World.* University Park: Pennsylvania State University Press, 1993.

Cardoso, Fernando, and Enzo Faletto. *Dependency and Development in Latin America.* 1967. Reprint, Berkeley: University of California Press, 1979.

Castoriadis, Cornelius. *The Imaginary Institution of Society.* Translated from French by Kathleen Blamey. Cambridge, Mass.: MIT Press, 1987. Originally published as *Institution imaginaire de la société* (Paris: Seuil, 1975).

———. *World in Fragments: Writings on Politics, Society, Psychoanalysis, and the Imagination.* Translated from French and edited by David Ames Curtis. Stanford, Calif.: Stanford University Press, 1997. Originally published as *Le monde morcelé* (Paris: Seuil, 1990).

Chamberlin, Edward. *The Theory of Monopolistic Competition.* Cambridge, Mass.: Harvard University Press, 1933.

Chatterjee, Partha. *Nationalist Thought and the Colonial World: A Derivative Discourse?* London: Zed Books, 1986.

Chomsky, Noam. *Aspects of the Theory of Syntax.* Cambridge, Mass.: MIT Press, 1965.

———. *Cartesian Linguistics: A Chapter in the History of Rationalist Thought.* New York: Harper and Row, 1966.

———. *Language and the Mind.* New York: Harcourt Brace Jovanovich, 1968

———. *Syntactic Structures.* The Hague: Mouton, 1957.

Chomsky, Noam, and Edward S. Herman. *Manufacturing Consent: The Political Economy of the Mass Media.* New York: Pantheon, 1988.

Christaller, Walter. *Southern Places in Central Germany.* 1934. Translated from German by Carlisle W. Baskin. Englewood Cliffs, N.J., Prentice-Hall, 1966.

Clark, J. B. *The Distribution of Wealth: A Theory of Wages, Interest and Profits.* 1899. Reprint, New York: Macmillan, 1927.

Clausewitz, Carl von. *On War.* Translated from German and edited by Michael Howard and Peter Paret. Princeton, N.J.: Princeton University Press, 1984. Originally published as *Vom Kriege,* 1832.

Clifford, James. *The Predicament of Culture: Twentieth-Century Ethnography, Literature, and Art.* Cambridge, Mass.: Harvard University Press, 1988.

Cloward, Richard A., and Lloyd E. Ohlin. *Delinquency and Opportunity: A Theory of Delinquent Gangs.* New York: Free Press, 1960.

Clower, Robert. *A Reconsideration of the Microfoundations of Monetary Theory.* 1967. Republished as chapter 5 in *Money and Markets: Essays by Robert W. Clower,* edited by D. A. Walker. Cambridge: Cambridge University Press, 1984.

Coase, Ronald H. "The Nature of the Firm." *Economica* n.s. 4 (1937): 385–405.

———. "The Problem of Social Cost." *The Journal of Law and Economics* 3 (1960): 1–44.

Cohen, Stanley. *Folk Devils and Moral Panics.* London: Macgibbon and Kee, 1972.

Coleman, James S. *The Adolescent Society.* New York: Free Press, 1961.

———. *Community Conflict.* Glencoe, Ill.: Free Press, 1957.

———. *Equality of Educational Opportunity.* Washington, D.C.: U.S. Government Printing Office, 1966.

———. *Foundations of Social Theory.* Cambridge, Mass.: Harvard University Press, 1990.

———. *Introduction to Mathematical Sociology.* New York: Free Press of Glencoe, 1964.

———. *The Mathematics of Collective Action.* Chicago: Aldine, 1973.

———. *Youth: Transition to Adulthood* (Report of the Panel on Youth of the President's Science Advisory Committee). Chicago: University of Chicago Press, 1974.

Coleman, James S., and Thomas Hoffer. *Public and Private High School: The Impact of Communities.* New York: Basic Books, 1987.

Coleman, James S., Thomas Hoffer, and Sally Kilgore. *High School Achievement: Public, Catholic, and Private Schools Compared.* New York: Basic Books, 1982.

Coleman, James S., and Torsten Husén. *Becoming Adult in a Changing Society.* Paris and Washington, D.C.: Organisation for Economic Co-operation and Development/OECD Publications and Information Centre, 1985.

Coleman, James S., Elihu Katz, and Herbert Menzel. *Medical Innovation: A Diffusion Study.* Indianapolis, Ind.: Bobbs-Merrill, 1966.

Commons, John R. *A History of Labor in the United States.* 4 vols. New York: Macmillan, 1918–1935.

———. *Institutional Economics.* New York: Macmillan, 1934.

———. *Legal Foundations of Capitalism.* New York: Macmillan, 1924.

———. *Myself.* New York: Macmillan, 1934.

Comte, Auguste. *The Positive Philosophy.* 6 vols. New York: AMS Press, 1974. Originally published as *Cours de philosophie positive* (Paris: Bachelier, 1830–1842).

Condorcet, Marie-Jean-Antoine-Nicolas de Caritat, Marquis de. *Sketch for a Historical Picture of the Progress of the Human Mind.* Translated from French by June Barraclough. London: Weidenfeld and Nicolson, 1955. Originally published as *Esquisse d'un tableau historique des progres de l'esprit humain* (Paris: M.me Condorcet and Daunou, 1795).

Constant, Benjamin. "The Liberty of the Ancients Compared with That of the Moderns." 1819. Republished in *The Political Writings of Benjamin Constant,* edited by Biancamaria Fontana. Cambridge: Cambridge University Press, 1988.

Cooley, Charles Horton. *Human Nature and the Social Order.* New York: Schocken, 1964 (New York: Scribners, 1902.)

———. *Life and the Student: Roadside Notes on Human Nature, Society, and Letters.* New York: Knopf, 1927.

———. *Social Organization: A Study of the Larger Mind.* New York: Scribners, 1909.

———. *Social Progress.* New York: Scribners, 1918.

Coser, Lewis. *The Functions of Social Conflict.* New York: Free Press, 1956.

Cournot, Antoine Augustin. *Researches into the Mathematical Principles of the Theory of Wealth.* Translated from French by N. T. Bacon. New York: Macmillan, 1897, 1927. Originally published as *Recherches sur les principes mathematiques de la theorie des richesses* (Paris: L. Hachette, 1838).

Crozier, Michael. *The Bureaucratic Phenomenon.* Chicago: University of Chicago Press, 1964.

Cyert, R. M., and J. G. March. *A Behavioral Theory of the Firm.* Englewood Cliffs, N.J.: Prentice-Hall, 1963.

Dahl, Robert. *After the Revolution? Authority in a Good Society.* New Haven, Conn.: Yale University Press, 1970.

———. *Democracy and Its Critics.* New Haven, Conn.: Yale University Press, 1989.

———. *On Democracy.* New Haven, Conn.: Yale University Press, 1998.

———. *Dilemmas of Pluralist Democracy: Autonomy vs. Control.* New Haven, Conn.: Yale University Press, 1982.

———. *Polyarchy, Participation and Opposition.* New Haven, Conn.: Yale University Press, 1971.

———. *A Preface to Democratic Theory.* Chicago: University of Chicago Press, 1956.

———. *A Preface to Economic Democracy.* Berkeley: University of California Press, 1985.

———. *Who Governs? Democracy and Power in an American City.* New Haven, Conn.: Yale University Press, 1961.

Dahl, Robert, and Charles Lindblom. *Politics, Economics and Welfare.* New York: Harper, 1953.

Dahl, Robert, and Edward Tufte. *Size and Democracy.* Stanford, Calif.: Stanford University Press, 1973.

Dahrendorf, Ralf. *Class and Class Conflict in Industrial Society.* Stanford, Calif.: Stanford University Press, 1959.

Darwin, Charles. *On the Origin of the Species.* New York: New York University Press, 1988. Originally published Condon: J. Murray, 1859.

Davis, Kingsley. *Human Society.* New York: Macmillan, 1949.

———. *The Population of India and Pakistan.* Princeton, N.J.: Princeton University Press, 1951.

———. *World Urbanization 1950–1970.* 2 vols. Berkeley: Institute of International Studies, University of California, 1969–1972.

Davis, Kingsley, ed. *A Crowding Hemisphere: Population Change in the Americas. Annals of the American Academy of Political and Social Science* 316 (Mar. 1958).

Davis, Kingsley, and Wilbert E. Moore. "Some Principles of Stratification." *American Sociological Review* 10 (Apr. 1945): 242–249.

Day, Richard Hollis, and E. Herbert Tinney. "How to Cooperate in Business without Really Trying: A Learning Model of Decentralized Decision Making." *Journal of Political Economy* 76 (Jul. 1968): 583–600.

Debord, Guy. *The Society of the Spectacle.* Translated from French by Donald Nicholson-Smith. New York: Zone Books, 1994. Originally published as *La société du spectacle* (Paris: Buchet/Chastel, 1967).

Deleuze, Gilles. *Difference and Repetition.* Translated from French by Paul Patton. New York: Columbia University Press, 1994. Originally published as *Difference et repetition* (Paris: Presses Universitaires de France, 1968).

———. *The Logic of Sense.* Translated from French by Mark Lester and Charles Stivale. New York: Columbia University Press, 1990. Originally published as *Logique du sens* (Paris: Editions de Minuit, 1969).

Deleuze, Gilles, and Félix Guattari. *Anti-Oedipus: Capitalism and Schizophrenia.* Translated from French by Helen R. Lane, Robert Hurley, and Mark Seem. Minneapolis: University of Minnesota Press, 1986. Originally published as *Capitalisme et schizophrenie: L'anti-Oedipe* (Paris: Editions de Minuit, 1972).

———. *A Thousand Plateaus: Capitalism and Schizophrenia.* Translated from French by Brian Massumi. Minneapolis: University of Minnesota Press, 1987. Originally published as *Capitalisme et schizophrenie: Mille plateaux* (Paris: Editions de Minuit, 1980).

———. *What Is Philosophy?* Translated from French by Hugh Tomlinson and Graham Burchell. New York: Columbia University Press, 1994. Originally published as *Qu'est-ce que la philosophie?* (Paris: Editions de Minuit, 1991).

Derrida, Jacques. *Of Grammatology.* Translated from French by Gayatri Chakravorty Spivak. Baltimore,

Md.: Johns Hopkins University Press, 1976. Originally published as *De la grammatologie* (Paris: Editions de Minuit, 1967).

———. *The Margins of Philosophy.* Translated from French by Alan Bass. Brighton and Chicago: Harvester Press/University of Chicago Press, 1982. Originally published as *Marges de la philosophie* (Paris: Editions de Minuit, 1972).

———. *Specters of Marx: The State of the Debt, the Work of Mourning, and the New International.* Translated from French by Peggy Kamuf. London: Routledge, 1994. Originally published as *Spectres de Marx: L'etat de la dette, le travail du deuil et la nouvelle Internationale* (Paris: Editions Galilee, 1993).

———. *Writing and Difference.* Translated from French by Alan Bass. Chicago: University of Chicago Press, 1978. Originally published as *Ecriture et la difference* (Paris: Editions du Seuil, 1967).

Descartes, René. *Discourse on Method and Other Writings.* Translated from French by F. E. Sutcliffe. Harmondsworth: Penguin, 1968. Originally published as *Discours de la methode pour bien conduire sa raison, et chercher la verité dans les sciences. Plus La dioptrique. Les meteores. Et La geometrie. Qui sont des essais de cete methode* (Leiden, Holland: I. Maire, 1637).

———. *Meditations on First Philosophy.* Translated from Latin by John Cottingham. New York: Cambridge University Press, 1986. Originally published as *Regulae ad directionem ingenii* (1641).

———. *Le Monde, ou, Traité de la Lumière.* Translated from French by Michael Sean Mahoney. New York: Abaris Books, 1977. Originally published as *Traité du monde ou de la lumière* (Paris: Clerselier, 1664).

———. *The Passions of the Soul.* Translated from French by Stephen Voss. Indianapolis, Ind.: Hackett, 1989. Originally published as *Les passions de l'ame* (Paris: Henry Le Gras, 1649).

———. *The Principles of Philosophy.* Translated from Latin by Valentine Rodger Miller and Reese P. Miller. Dordrecht/Boston/London: D. Reidel, 1983. Originally published as *Principia philosophiae* (Amsterdam: Apud Ludovicum Elzevirium, 1644).

Deutsch, Karl. *The Analysis of International Relations.* Englewood Cliffs, N.J.: Prentice-Hall, 1968.

———. *Nationalism and Social Communication: An Inquiry into the Foundations of Nationality.* Cambridge, Mass. and New York: MIT and Wiley, 1953.

———. *The Nerves of Government: Models of Political Communication and Control.* London: Free Press of Glencoe, 1963.

———. *Political Community at the International Level: Problems of Definition and Measurement.* Garden City, N.Y.: Doubleday, 1954.

———. *Politics and Government: How People Decide Their Fate.* New York: Houghton Mifflin, 1970.

———. *Tides among Nations.* New York: Free Press, 1979.

Dewey, John. *Art as Experience.* New York: Minton, Balch, 1934.

———. *Democracy and Education: An Introduction to the Philosophy of Education.* New York: Macmillan, 1916.

———. *Freedom and Culture.* New York: Putnam, 1939.

———. *The Quest for Certainty: A Study of the Relation of Knowledge and Action.* New York: Minton, Balch, 1929.

———. *Reconstruction in Philosophy.* New York: Holt, 1920.

Dilthey, Wilhelm. "On the Construction of the Historical World in Human Studies." In *Selected Writings,* edited, translated from German, and introduced by H. P. Rickman. Cambridge: Cambridge University Press, 1976. Originally published as *Der Aufbau der geschichtlichen Welt in den Geisteswissenschaften* (1910).

———. *The Essence of Philosophy.* Translated from German by Stephen A. Emery and William T. Emery. Chapel Hill: University of North Carolina Press, 1954. Originally published as *Systematische Philosophie* (1907).

———. *Introduction to Human Sciences.* Edited by Rudolf A. Makkreel and Frithjof Rodi. Princeton, N.J.: Princeton University Press, 1989. Originally published as "Einleitung in die Geisteswissenschaften. Versuch einer Grundlegung für das Studium der Gesellshaft und Geschichte." In *Gesammelte Schriften.* Bd 1. Stuttgart and Göttingen: Teubner, 1993.

———. *Meaning in History: W. Dilthey's Thoughts on History and Society.* Edited by H. P. Rickman. London: Allen and Unwin, 1961.

Dobb, Maurice. *Political Economy and Capitalism: Some Essays in Economic Tradition.* London: Routledge, 1937.

———. *Studies in the Development of Capitalism.* London: Routledge, 1946.

Domar, Evsey. "Capital Expansion, Rate of Growth, and Employment." *Econometrica* 14 (Apr. 1946): 137–147.

———. "Expansion and Employment." *American Economic Review* 37.1 (Mar. 1947): 34–55. Reprinted in *Macroeconomic Theory: Selected Readings,* edited by Harold R. Williams and John D. Huffnagle. Englewood Cliffs, N.J.: Prentice-Hall, 1969.

Dorfman, Robert, Paul A. Samuelson, and Robert M. Solow. *Linear Programming and Economic Analysis.* New York: McGraw-Hill, 1958.

Douglas, Mary. *How Institutions Think.* Syracuse, N.Y.: Syracuse University Press, 1986.

———. *Natural Symbols: Explorations in Cosmology.* New York: Pantheon, 1970.

———. *Purity and Danger: An Analysis of Concepts of Pollution and Taboo.* New York: Praeger, 1966.

Douglas, Mary, ed. *Witchcraft: Confessions and Accusations*. London and New York: Tavistock, 1970.

Douglas, Mary, and Baron Isherwood. *The World of Goods: Towards an Anthropology of Consumption*. New York: Basic Books, 1979.

Douglas, Mary, and Aaron Wildavsky. *Risk and Culture: An Essay on the Selection of Technical and Environmental Dangers*. Berkeley: University of California Press, 1982.

Dubois, W. E. B. *Black Reconstruction in America*. New York: Atheneum/Macmillan, 1992. Originally published as *Black Reconstruction* (New York: Harcourt, Brace, 1935).

———. *Darkwater: Voices from within the Veil*. 1920. Reprint, New York: Schocken Books, 1969.

———. *Dusk of Dawn*. Millwood, N.Y.: Kraus-Thomson Organization, 1975. Originally published by Harcourt, Brace, 1940.

———. *The Souls of Black Folk*. 1903. Reprint, New York: New American Library, 1969.

Dubois, W. E. B., and Guy B. Johnson. *Encyclopedia of the Negro: Preparatory Volume with Reference Lists and Reports*. New York: Phelps-Stokes Fund, 1945.

Duesenberry, James. "Income-Consumption Relations and Their Implications." In *Income, Employment and Public Policy: Essays in Honor of Alvin H. Hansen*, edited by L. Metzler et al. New York: Norton, 1948.

Dumont, Louis. *Affinity as a Value: Marriage Alliance in South India, with Comparative Essays on Australia*. Chicago: University of Chicago Press, 1983.

———. *Essays on Individualism: Modern Ideology in Anthropological Perspective*. 1983. Reprint, Chicago: University of Chicago Press, 1986.

———. *Homo Aequalis*. Paris: Gallimard, 1976. Translated from French as *From Mandeville to Marx: The Genesis and Triumph of Economic Ideology* (Chicago: University of Chicago Press, 1977).

———. *Homo Hierarchicus: Essai sur le Système des Castes*. Paris: Gallimard, 1967. Translated from French by Mark Sainsbury as *Homo Hierarchicus: An Essay on the Caste System* (Chicago: University of Chicago Press, 1970).

———. *A South Indian Subcast: Social Organization and Religion of the Pramalai Kallar*. 1957. Reprint, Delhi: Oxford University Press.

Durkheim, Emile. *Contributions to L'Année Sociologique*. Edited by Yash Nandan. Translated from French by John French et al. New York: Free Press, 1980. Originally published in *L'année sociologique* (Paris: Presses Universitaires de France, 1940–1949).

———. *The Division of Labor in Society*. Translated from French by George Simpson. New York: Macmillan, 1933. Originally published as *De la division du travail social étude sur l'organisation des sociétés superieures* (Paris: F. Alcan, 1893).

———. *The Elementary Forms of Religious Life: A Study in Religious Sociology*. Translated from French by J. W. Swain. London and New York: Allen and Unwin/Macmillan, 1915. Originally published as *Formes elementaires de la vie religieuse* (1912).

———. *Moral Education*. 1925. Translated from French by E. K. Wilson and H. Schnurer. Glencoe, Ill.: Free Press, 1961. Originally published as *L'education morale* (Paris: F. Alcan, 1925).

———. *The Rules of Sociological Method*. 1895. Translated from French by Sarah A. Solovay and John H. Mueller. New York: Free Press of Glencoe, 1964. Originally published as *Les règles de la methode sociologique* (Paris: 1910).

———. *Suicide: A Study of Sociology*. Translated from French by J. A. Spaulding and G. Simpson. New York: Free Press, 1951. Originally published as *Suicide, étude de sociologie* (Paris: F. Alcan, 1897).

Durkheim, Emile, and Marcel Mauss. *Primitive Classification*. Translated from French by Rodney Needham. Chicago: University of Chicago Press, 1963. Originally published as "De quelques formes primitives de classification" in *L'année sociologique* (1901–1902).

Easton, David. *A Framework for Political Analysis*. Englewood Cliffs, N.J.: Prentice-Hall, 1965.

———. *The Political System: An Inquiry into the State of Political Science*. New York: Knopf, 1953.

———. *A Systems Analysis of Political Life*. New York: Wiley, 1965.

———. *Varieties of Political Theory*. Englewood Cliffs, N.J.: Prentice-Hall, 1966.

Easton, David, John G. Gunnell, and Michael B. Stein, eds. *Regime and Discipline: Democracy and the Development of Political Science*. Ann Arbor: University of Michigan Press, 1995.

Econometrica. Published by the Econometric Society. Evanston, Ill.: Northwestern University Economics Department, 1933–.

Economic Journal. Published by the Royal Economic Society. Oxford: Blackwell, 1891–.

Edgeworth F. "The Pure Theory of Taxation." *Economic Journal* 7 (1897): 46–70, 226–238.

Elias, Norbert. *The Civilizing Process*. 2 vols. Translated from German by Edmund Jephcott. New York: Urizen Books, 1978. Originally published as *Uber den Prozess der Zivilisation; Soziogenetische und Psychogenetische Untersuchungen* (Basel: Haus zum Falken, 1939).

———. *The Court Society*. Translated from German by Edmund Jephcott. New York: Pantheon, 1983. Originally published as *Die hofische Gesellschaft: Untersuchungen zur Soziologie des Konigtums und der hofischen Aristokratie, mit einer Einleitung: Soziologie und Geschichtswissenschaft* (Neuwied: Luchterhand, 1969).

———. *Involvement and Detachment*. Translated from German by Edmund Jephcott. New York: Blackwell, 1987. Originally published as *Engagement und Distanzierung* (Frankfurt am Main: Suhrkamp, 1983).

———. *The Loneliness of the Dying*. Translated from German by Edmund Jephcott. Oxford and New York: Blackwell, 1985. Originally published as *Uber die Einsamkeit der Sterbenden in unseren Tagen* (Frankfurt am Main: Suhrkamp, 1982).

———. *Time: An Essay*. Translated from German by Edmund Jephcott. Oxford and Cambridge, Mass.: Blackwell, 1992. Originally published as *Uber die Zeit* (Frankfurt am Main: Suhrkamp, 1984).

———. *What is Sociology?* Translated from German by Stephen Mennell and Grace Morrissey. Foreword by Reinhard Bendix. London: Hutchinson, 1978. Originally published as *Was ist Soziologie?* (Munich: Juventa, 1970).

Ellul, Jacques. *The Technological Society*. Translated from French by John Wilkinson. Introduction by Robert K. Merton. New York: Vintage Books, 1964. Originally published as *La technique; ou, L'en jeu du siècle* (Paris: A. Colin, 1954).

Encyclopédie. 1751–1772. Reprinted as *L'Encyclopédie*, edited by Jeanne Charpentier and Michel Charpentier. Paris: Éditions Bordas, 1967.

Engels, Friedrich. *Anti-Duhring*. Translated from German by Emile Burns. Edited by C. P. Dutt. New York: International, 1939. Originally published as *Herrn Eugen Duhrings Umwalzung der Wissenschaft "Anti-Duhring"* (1877–1878).

———. *Socialism: Utopian and Scientific*. Translated from German by Edward Aveling. Chicago: C. H. Kerr, 1908. Originally published as *Die Entwicklung des Sozialismus von der Utopie zur Wissenschaft* (Berlin: Verlag der expedition des "Vorwarts" *Berliner Volksblatt*, 1891).

Erikson, Erik. *Childhood and Society*. New York: Norton, 1950.

———. *Gandhi's Truth: On the Origins of Militant Nonviolence*. New York: Norton, 1969.

———. *Identity: Youth and Crisis*. New York: Norton, 1968.

———. *The Life Cycle Completed*. New York: Norton, 1982.

———. *Young Man Luther: A Study in Psychoanalysis and History*. New York: Norton, 1958.

Etzioni, Amitai. *The Active Society*. New York: Free Press, 1968.

———. *The New Golden Rule: Community and Morality in a Democratic Society*. New York: Basic Books, 1996.

Evans, Peter B., Dietrich Ruescherneyer, and Theda Skocpol, eds. *Bringing the State Back In*. New York: Cambridge University Press, 1985.

Evans-Pritchard, E. E. *Kinship and Marriage among the Nuer*. Oxford: Clarendon Press, 1951.

———. *The Nuer: A Description of the Modes of Livelihood and Political Institutions of a Nilotic People*. Oxford: Clarendon Press, 1940.

———. *Nuer Religion*. Oxford: Clarendon Press, 1956.

———. *The Sanusi of Cyrenaica*. Oxford: Clarendon Press, 1949.

———. *Witchcraft, Oracles and Magic among the Azande*. Oxford: Clarendon Press, 1937.

Eysenck, Hans. *The Biological Basis of Personality*. Springfield, Ill.: Thomas, 1967.

———. *Crime and Personality*. Boston: Houghton Mifflin, 1964.

———. *The IQ Argument: Race, Intelligence, and Education*. New York: Library Press, 1971.

———. *The Scientific Study of Personality*. London: Routledge and Kegan Paul, 1952.

Eysenck, Hans, ed. *A Model for Personality*. New York: Springer, 1981.

Eysenck, Hans, and David W. Fulker. *The Structure and Measurement of Intelligence*. Berlin: Springer-Verlag, 1979.

Fanon, Frantz. *Black Skin, White Masks*. Translated from French by Charles Lam Markmann. New York: Grove Press, 1967. Originally published as *Peau noire, masques blancs* (Paris: Editions du Seuil, 1952).

———. *A Dying Colonialism or Year Five of the Algerian Revolution*. Translated from French by Haakon Chevalier. New York: Grove Press, 1965. Originally published as *An V de la Révolution algerienne* (Paris: F. Maspero, 1959).

———. *Toward the African Revolution: Political Essays*. Translated from French by Haakon Chevalier. New York: Grove Press, 1967. Originally published as *Pour la révolution africaine: Ecrits politiques* (Paris: F. Maspero, 1964).

———. *The Wretched of the Earth*. Preface by Jean-Paul Sartre. Translated from French by Constance Farrington. New York: Grove Press, 1963. Originally published as *Les damnes de la terre* (Paris: F. Maspero, 1961).

Festinger, Leon, and J. M. Carlsmith. A Theory of Cognitive Dissonance. Evanston, Ill.: Row, Peterson, 1957.

Feyerabend, Paul K. *Against Method: Outline of an Anarchistic Theory of Knowledge*. London: New Left Books, 1975.

———. *Science in a Free Society*. London: New Left Books, 1978.

Firth, Raymond William. *Elements of Social Organization*. London: Watts, 1951.

———. *Essays on Social Organization and Values*. London: Athlone Press, 1964.

———. *Malay Fishermen: Their Peasant Economy*. London: Kegan Paul, Trench, Trubner, 1946.

———. *Social Change in Tikopia: Re-study of a Polynesian Community after a Generation*. London: Allen and Unwin, 1959.

———. *Symbols, Public and Private*. Ithaca, N.Y.: Cornell University Press, 1973.

———. *We, the Tikopia: A Sociological Study of Kinship in Primitive Polynesia*. 1936. Reprint, London: Allen and Unwin, 1957.

Firth, Raymond William, ed. *Themes in Economic Anthropology*. London: Tavistock, 1967.

Fisher, Irving. *100% Money*. New York: Adelphi, 1936.

——. *The Nature of Capital and Income*. New York: Macmillan, 1906.

——. *The Purchasing Power of Money*. New York: Macmillan, 1911.

——. *Stabilizing the Dollar: A Plan to Stabilize the General Price Level without Fixing Individual Prices*. New York: Macmillan, 1920.

Fishlow, Albert. *American Railroads and the Transformation of the Ante-Bellum Economy*. Cambridge, Mass.: Harvard University Press, 1965.

Fogel, Robert. *Railroads and American Economic Growth: Essays in Econometric History*. Baltimore, Md.: Johns Hopkins University Press, 1964.

Forde, C. Daryll. *The Context of Belief: A Consideration of Fetishism among the Yako*. Liverpool: Liverpool University Press, 1958.

——. *Habitat, Economy and Society*. London: Methuen, 1934.

——. *Marriage and Family among the Yakö in Southeastern Nigeria*. London: Lund, Humphries, 1941.

——. *Yakö Studies*. London and New York: Published for the International African Institute by the Oxford University Press, 1964.

Fortes, Meyer. *The Dynamics of Clanship among the Tallensi, Being the First Part of an Analysis of the Social Structure of a Trans-Volta Tribe*. 2 parts. 1945. Reprint, Oosterhout, the Netherlands and London: Anthropological Publications/Oxford University Press, 1967.

——. *Kinship and the Social Order*. Chicago: Aldine, 1969.

——. *Oedipus and Job in West African Religion*. Cambridge: Cambridge University Press, 1959.

——. *Time and Social Structure and Other Essays*. London: University of London, Athlone Press, 1970.

——. *The Web of Kinship among the Tallensi*. London: Oxford University Press, 1949.

Fortes, Meyer, and E. E. Evans-Pritchard, eds. *African Political Systems*. London: Oxford University Press, 1940.

Foucault, Michel. *The Archaeology of Knowledge*. Translated from French by A. M. Sheridan Smith. New York: Pantheon, 1972. Originally published as *L'Archeologie du savoir* (Paris: Gallimard, 1969).

——. *The Birth of the Clinic: An Archaeology of Medical Perception*. 1963. Translated from French by A. M. Sheridan-Smith. New York and London: Pantheon/Tavistock, 1973. Originally published as *Naissance de la clinique: Une archeologie du regard medical* (Paris: Presses Universitaires de France, 1963).

——. *Discipline and Punish: The Birth of the Prison*. Translated from French by A. Sheridan. Harmondsworth: Penguin, 1979. Originally published as *Surveiller et punir: Naissance de la prison* (Paris: Gallimard, 1975).

——. *The History of Sexuality*: Vol. 1: *An Introduction*. Translated from French by Robert Hurley. New York: Vintage Books, 1978. Originally published as *Histoire de la sexualité* (Paris: Gallimard, 1976–).

——. *Madness and Civilization: A History of Insanity in the Age of Reason*. Translated from French by Richard Howard. New York: Vintage Books, 1965. Originally published as *Histoire de la folie à l'age classique* (Paris: Librairie Plon, 1961).

——. *The Order of Things: An Archaeology of the Human Sciences*. Translator unknown. New York: Vintage Books, 1970. Originally published as *Les mots et les choses: Une archeologie des sciences humaines* (Paris: Gallimard, 1966).

——. *Power/Knowledge: Selected Interviews and Other Writings, 1972–1977*. Edited by Colin Gordon. Translated from French by Colin Gordon et al. New York: Pantheon Books, 1980.

Frank, André Gunder. *Capitalism and Underdevelopment in Latin America: Historical Studies of Chile and Brazil*. New York: Monthly Review Press, 1967.

——. *Dependent Accumulation and Underdevelopment*. London: Macmillan, 1978.

——. *Latin America: Underdevelopment or Revolution: Essays on the Development of Underdevelopment and the Immediate Enemy*. New York: Monthly Review Press, 1969.

——. *Reflections on the World Economic Crisis*. New York: Monthly Review Press, 1981.

——. *Reorient: Global Economy in the Asian Age*. Berkeley: University of California Press, 1998.

——. *World Accumulation 1492–1789*. New York: Monthly Review Press, 1978.

Frazer, James. *The Golden Bough: A Study in Magic and Religion*. 1890. Reprint, London: Macmillan, 1911–1915.

Freeman, Derek. *Margaret Mead and Samoa: The Making and Unmaking of an Anthropological Myth*. Cambridge, Mass.: Harvard University Press, 1983.

Freud, Sigmund. "Beyond the Pleasure Principle." In *The Standard Edition of the Complete Psychological Works of Sigmund Freud* (Vol. 18), edited and translated from German by James Strachey. London: Hogarth Press, 1953. Originally published as *Jenseits des Lustprinzips* (Vienna: Internationaler Psychoanalytischer Verlag, 1920).

——. *Civilization and Its Discontents*. 1929. Translated from German by James Strachey. London: The Institute of Psycho-Analysis, 1930. Originally published as *Das Unbehagen in der Kultur* (Vienna: Internationaler psychoanalytischer Verlag, 1930).

——. *The Ego and the Id*. Translated from German by Joan Riviere. London: Hogarth Press and the Institute of Psycho-analysis, 1927. Originally published as *Das Ich und das Es* (Vienna: Internationaler Psychoanalytischer Verlag, 1923).

——. *The Future of an Illusion*. Translated from German by James Strachey. New York: Norton, 1961. Originally published as *Die Zukunft einer*

Illusion (Leipzig/Vienna/Zurich: Internationaler Psychoanalytischer Verlag, 1927).

————. *Group Psychology and the Analysis of the Ego.* Translated from German by James Strachey. London: The International Psycho-Analytical Press, 1922. Originally published as *Massenpsychologie und Ich-Analyse* (Vienna: Internationaler Psychoanalytischer Verlag, 1921).

————. *Interpretation of Dreams.* Translated from German and edited by James Strachey. New York: Basic Books, 1955. Originally published as *Die Traumdeutung*(Leipzig and Vienna: F. Deuticke, 1900).

————. *Jokes and Their Relation to the Unconscious.* Translated from German and edited by James Strachey. New York: Norton, 1960. Originally published as *Der Witz und seine Beziehung zum Unbewussten* (Vienna: F. Deuticke, 1905).

————. *Moses and Monotheism.* Translated from German by Katherine Jones. New York: Knopf, 1939. Originally published as *Mann Moses und die monotheistische Religion* (1938).

————. *On Dreams.* Translated from German by James Strachey. New York: Norton, 1963. Originally published as *Uber den Traum* (Wiesbaden: J. F. Bergmann, 1901).

————. *The Psychopathology of Everyday Life.* Translated from German by Alan Tyson. Edited and introduced by James Strachey. New York: Norton, 1965. Originally published as *Zur Psychopathologie des Alltagslebens* (Berlin: S. Karger, 1904).

————. "Three Essays on the Theory of Sexuality." In *The Standard Edition of the Complete Psychological Works of Sigmund Freud* (Vol. 7). Translated from German and edited by James Strachey. London: Hogarth Press, 1981. Originally published in 1905 as "Drei Abhandlungen zur Sexualtheorie" (Three Contributions to the Sexual Theory), later translated as "Three Essays on the Theory of Sexuality."

————. *Totem and Taboo: Some Points of Agreement between the Mental Lives of Savages and Neurotics.* Translated from German by J. Strachey. New York: Norton, 1950. Originally published as *Totem und Tabu: Einige Ubereinstimmungen im Seelenleben der Wilden und der Neurotiker* (Leipzig: H. Heller, 1913).

Fried, Morton. *The Evolution of Political Society: An Essay in Political Anthropology.* New York: Random House, 1967.

Friedan, Betty. *The Feminine Mystique.* New York: Norton, 1963.

Friedman, Milton. *Essays in Positive Economics.* Chicago: University of Chicago Press, 1953.

————. "The Quantity Theory of Money—A Restatement." In *Studies in the Quantity Theory of Money.* Chicago: University of Chicago Press, 1956.

————. "The Role of Monetary Policy." *American Economic Review* 58 (Mar. 1968): 1–17.

————. *A Theory of the Consumption Function.* Princeton, N.J.: Princeton University Press, 1957.

Friedman, Milton, ed. *Studies in the Quantity Theory of Money.* Chicago: University of Chicago Press, 1956.

Friedman, Milton, and Anna Schwartz. *A Monetary History of the United States, 1867–1960.* Princeton N.J.: Princeton University Press, 1963.

Fromm, Erich. *The Anatomy of Human Destructiveness.* New York: Holt, Rinehart and Winston, 1973.

————. *The Art of Loving.* New York: Harper, 1956.

————. *The Crisis of Psychoanalysis.* New York: Holt, Rinehart and Winston, 1970.

————. *Escape from Freedom.* New York: Farrar and Rinehart, 1941.

Galbraith, John Kenneth. *The Affluent Society.* Boston: Houghton Mifflin, 1958.

————. *The Age of Uncertainty.* Boston: Houghton Mifflin, 1977.

————. *American Capitalism: The Concept of Countervailing Power.* Boston: Houghton Mifflin, 1952.

————. *Money, Whence It Came, Where It Went.* Boston: Houghton Mifflin, 1975.

————. *The New Industrial State.* Boston: Houghton Mifflin, 1967.

Gallup, George. *The Pulse of Democracy.* New York: Simon and Schuster, 1940.

Galton, F. *Hereditary Genius: An Inquiry into Its Laws and Consequences.* London: Macmillan, 1869.

Garfinkel, Harold. *Ethnomethodological Studies of Work.* London: Routledge and Kegan Paul, 1986.

————. *Studies in Ethnomethodology.* Englewood Cliffs, N.J.: Prentice-Hall, 1967.

Geddes, Patrick. *Cities in Evolution.* London: Williams and Norgate, 1915.

Geertz, Clifford. *After the Fact: Two Countries, Four Decades, One Anthropologist.* Cambridge, Mass.: Harvard University Press, 1995.

————. *Agricultural Involution: The Process of Ecological Change in Indonesia.* Berkeley: University of California Press, 1963.

————. *The Interpretation of Cultures: Selected Essays.* New York: Basic Books, 1973.

————. *Islam Observed: Religious Development in Morocco and Indonesia.* New Haven, Conn.: Yale University Press, 1968.

————. *Local Knowledge: Further Essays in Interpretive Anthropology.* New York: Basic Books, 1983.

————. *The Religion of Java.* Glencoe, Ill.: Free Press, 1960.

————. *Work and Lives: The Anthropologist as Author.* Stanford, Calif.: Stanford University Press, 1988.

Gellner, Ernest André. *Conditions of Liberty: Civil Society and Its Rivals.* London: Hamish Hamilton, 1994.

————. *Muslim Society.* Cambridge: Cambridge University Press, 1981.

————. *Nations and Nationalism.* Ithaca, N.Y.: Cornell University Press, 1983.

——. *Saints of the Atlas*. London: Weidenfeld and Nicolson, 1969.

——. *Words and Things: A Critical Account of Linguistic Philosophy and a Study in Ideology*. Boston: Beacon Press, 1959.

Gellner, Ernest André, and Charles Micaud, eds. *Arabs and Berbers: From Tribe to Nation in North Africa*. London: Duckworth, 1973.

Gellner, Ernest André, and John Waterbury, eds. *Patrons and Clients in Mediterranean Societies*. London and Hanover, N.H.: Duckworth/Center for Mediterranean Studies of the American Universities Field Staff, 1977.

Gennep, Arnold van. *Manuel de Folklore Français Contemporain*. 9 vols. Paris: A. Picard, 1937–.

——. *Rites of Passage*. Translated from French by M. B. Vizedon, and G. L. Caffee. Reprint, Chicago: University of Chicago Press, 1960. Originally published as *Les rites de passage étude systematique des rites de la porte et du seuil, de l'hospitalité, de l'adoption, de la grossesse et de l'accouchement, de la naissance, de l'enfance, de la puberté, de l'initiation, de l'ordination, du couronnement des fiançailles et du mariage, des funerailles, des saisons, etc.* (Paris: E. Nourry, 1909).

Gerth, Hans H. "The Nazi Party: Its Leadership and Composition." *American Journal of Sociology* 44.4 (1940): 517–541.

Gerth, Hans, trans. *Religion of China: Confucianism and Taoism*. New York: The Free Press, 1951.

Gerth, Hans H., and Don Martindale, trans. *Ancient Judaism*. New York: The Free Press, 1952.

——. *The Religion of India: Buddhism and Hinduism*. New York: The Free Press, 1958.

Gerth, Hans H., and C. Wright Mills. *Character and Social Structure: The Psychology of Social Institutions*. New York: Harcourt, Brace, 1953.

Gerth, Hans H., and C. Wright Mills, trans. and eds. *From Max Weber: Essays in Sociology*. New York: Oxford University Press, 1946.

Giddens, Anthony. *Capitalism and Modern Social Theory*. Cambridge: Cambridge University Press, 1971.

——. *Central Problems in Social Theory: Action, Structure and Contradiction in Social Analysis*. London: Macmillan, 1979.

——. *The Consequences of Modernity*. Stanford, Calif.: Stanford University Press, 1990.

——. *The Constitution of Society: Outline of the Theory of Structuration*. Cambridge: Polity Press, 1984.

——. *Emile Durkheim*. London and New York: Fontana/Penguin, 1978.

——. *Modernity and Self Identity: Self and Society in the Late Modern Age*. Cambridge: Polity Press, 1991

——. *The Nation-State and Violence*. Cambridge: Polity Press, 1985.

——. *New Rules of Sociological Method*. New York: Basic Books, 1976.

——. *Politics and Sociology in the Thought of Max Weber*. London: Macmillan, 1972.

——. *The Third Way and Its Critics*. Malden, Mass.: Polity Press, 2000.

——. *The Third Way: The Renewal of Social Democracy*. Cambridge: Polity Press, 1998.

——. *The Transformation of Intimacy: Sexuality, Love and Eroticism in Modern Societies*. Cambridge: Polity Press, 1992.

Giles H., and N. Coupland. *Language: Contexts and Consequences*. Pacific Grove, Calif.: Brooks/Cole, 1991.

Gilligan C. *In a Different Voice: Psychological Theory and Women's Development*. Cambridge, Mass.: Harvard University Press, 1982.

Glass, David V., ed. *Social Mobility in Britain*. London: Routledge and Kegan Paul, 1954.

Gluckman, Max. *Custom and Conflict in Africa*. Oxford: Blackwell, 1955.

——. *Order and Rebellion in Tribal Africa: Collected Essays*. London: Cohen and West, 1963.

——. *Politics, Law and Ritual in Tribal Society*. Chicago: Aldine, 1965.

Goffman, Erving. *Asylums*. Chicago: Aldine, 1961.

——. *Behavior in Public Places: Notes on the Social Organization of Gatherings*. New York: Free Press of Glencoe, 1963.

——. *Encounters: Two Studies in the Sociology of Interaction*. Indianapolis, Ind.: Bobbs-Merrill, 1961.

——. *Forms of Talk*. Philadelphia: University of Pennsylvania Press, 1981.

——. *Frame Analysis: An Essay on the Organization of Experience*. Cambridge, Mass.: Harvard University Press, 1974.

——. "The Nature of Deference and Demeanor." *American Anthropologist* 58 (1956): 473–499.

——. *The Presentation of Self in Everyday Life*. Garden City, N.Y: Doubleday, 1959.

——. *Relations in Public: Microstudies of the Public Order*. New York: Basic Books, 1971.

Goldhagen, Daniel Jonah. *Hitler's Willing Executioners: Ordinary Germans and the Holocaust*. New York: Knopf, 1996.

Goldstone, Jack A. *Revolution and Rebellion in the Early Modern World*. Berkeley: University of California Press, 1991.

Gorz, André. *Farewell to the Working Class: An Essay on Post-Industrial Socialism*. Boston: South End Press, 1982.

Gottman, Jean. *A Geography of Europe*. New York: Holt, 1950.

——. *Megalopolis: The Urbanized Northeastern Seaboard of the United States*. New York: Twentieth Century Fund, 1961.

Gottman, Jean, and Robert Harper, eds. *Metropolis on the Move: Geographers Look at Urban Sprawl*. New York: Wiley, 1967.

Gouldner, Alvin W. *Against Fragmentation: The Origins of Marxism and the Sociology of Intellectuals.* New York: Oxford University Press, 1985.

———. *The Coming Crisis of Western Sociology.* New York: Basic Books, 1970.

———. *The Dialectic of Ideology and Technology: The Origins, Grammar, and Future of Ideology.* New York: Seabury Press, 1976.

———. *Enter Plato: Classical Greece and the Origins of Social Theory.* New York: Basic Books, 1965.

———. *The Future of Intellectuals and the Rise of the New Class: A Frame of Reference, Theses, Conjectures, Arguments, and an Historical Perspective on the Role of Intellectuals and Intelligentsia in the International Class Contest of the Modern Era.* New York: Seabury Press, 1979.

———. *Patterns of Industrial Bureaucracy.* Glencoe, Ill.: Free Press, 1954.

———. *Two Marxisms: Contradictions and Anomalies in the Development of Theory.* New York: Seabury Press, 1980.

———. *Wildcat Strike.* Yellow Springs, Ohio: Antioch Press, 1954.

Gouldner, Alvin W., and Richard A. Peterson. *Notes on Technology and the Moral Order.* Indianapolis, Ind.: Bobbs-Merrill, 1962.

Gramsci, Antonio. *Prison Notebooks.* Edited by Joseph Buttigieg. Translated from Italian by Joseph Buttigieg and Antonio Callari. New York: Columbia University Press, 1992. Originally published as *Quaderni del carcere* (Rome: Editori Riuniti, 1971).

Grotius, Hugo. *Commentary on the Law of Prize and Booty.* Translated from Latin by G. L. Williams and W. H. Zeydel. Oxford: Clarendon Press, 1950. Originally titled *De jure praedae commentarius* (1604–1605).

———. *The Rights of War and Peace: Including the Law of Nature and of Nations.* Translated from Latin by A. C. Campbell. Introduction by David J. Hill. New York: M. W. Dunne, 1901. Originally published as *De jure belli ac pacis libri tres,* 1625.

———. *True Religion.* Translated from Latin. New York: DaCapo, 1971. Originally published as *De veritate religionis Christianæ (True Religion Explained, and Defended against the Archenemies Thereof in the Times)* (London: R. Royston, 1632).

Guattari, Félix. *L'inconscient machinique: Essais de schizo-analyse.* Paris: Recherches, 1979.

———. *Molecular Revolution: Psychiatry and Politics.* Translated from French by Rosemary Sheed. Harmondsworth and New York: Penguin, 1984. Originally published as *Psychanalyse et transversalite; essais d'analyse institutionnelle* (Paris: Maspero, 1972) and *La revolution moleculaire* (Fontenay-sous-Bois: Editions Recherches, 1977).

———. *Les trois ecologies.* Paris: Galilée, 1989.

Guinier, Lani. *The Tyranny of the Majority: Fundamental Fairness in Representative Democracy.* New York: Free Press, 1994.

Gumperz, John. *Discourse Strategies.* Cambridge: Cambridge University Press, 1982.

Gumperz, John J., ed. *Language and Social Identity.* New York: Cambridge University Press, 1982.

Gurvitch, Georges. *Déterminisme sociaux et liberté humaine: Vers l'étude sociologique des cheminements de la liberté.* Paris: Presses Universitaires de France, 1955.

———. *Dialectique et Sociologie.* Paris: Flammarion, 1962.

———. *Sociology of Law.* New York: Philosophical Library and Alliance Book Corporation, 1942.

———. *The Spectrum of Social Time.* Translated from French and edited by Myrtle Korenbaum and Phillip Bosserman. Dordrecht, the Netherlands: D. Reidel, 1964. Originally published as *La multiplicite des temps sociaux* (1958).

Habermas, Jürgen. *Between Facts and Norms.* Cambridge: Polity Press, 1996.

———. *Knowledge and Human Interests.* Translated from German by Jeremy Shapiro. Boston: Beacon Press, 1971. Originally published as *Erkenntnis und Interesse* (Frankfurt am Main: Suhrkamp, 1968).

———. *Legitimation Crisis.* Translated from German by T. McCarthy. Boston: Beacon Press, 1975. Originally published as *Legitimationsprobleme im Spatkapitalismus* (Frankfurt am Main: Suhrkamp, 1973).

———. *On the Logic of the Social Sciences.* Cambridge, Mass.: MIT Press, 1988.

———. *The Inclusion of the Other: Studies in Political Theory.* Cambridge, Mass.: MIT Press, 1998.

———. *The Philosophical Discourse of Modernity: Twelve Lectures.* Translated from German by Frederick Lawrence. Cambridge, Mass.: MIT Press, 1987. Originally published as *Der Philosophische Diskurs der Moderne: Zwolf Vorlesungen* (Frankfurt am Main: Suhrkamp, 1985).

———. *The Structural Transformation of the Public Sphere.* Translated from German by T. Burger. Cambridge, Mass.: MIT Press, 1989. Originally published as *Strukturwandel der Offentlichkeit Untersuchungen zu einer Kategorie der burgerlichen Gesellschaft* (Neuweid: H. Luchterhand, 1962).

———. *The Theory of Communicative Action.* 2 vols. Translated from German by T. McCarthy. Vol. 1, Boston: Beacon Press, 1984. Vol. 2, Cambridge: Polity Press, 1987. Originally published as *Theorie des kommunikativen Handelns* (Frankfurt am Main: Suhrkamp, 1981).

———. *Towards a Rational Society: Student Protest, Science and Politics.* Translated from German by Jeremy J. Shapiro. Boston: Beacon Press, 1970. Originally published in *Protestbewegung und Hochschulreform* (Frankfurt am Main: Suhrkamp, 1969) and in *Technik und Wissenschaft als "Ideologie"* (Frankfurt am Main: Suhrkamp, 1968).

Hagan, John. *Structural Criminology.* New Brunswick, N.J.: Rutgers University Press, 1989.

Haggard, Stephan. *Pathways from the Periphery: The Politics of Growth in the Newly Industrializing Countries*. Ithaca, N.Y.: Cornell University Press, 1990.

Hall, Stuart. "Cultural Studies: Two Paradigms." *Media, Culture and Society* 2 (1980): 57–72.

———. *The Hard Road to Renewal: Thatcherism and the Crisis of the Left*. London and New York: Verso, 1988.

———. "The Television Discourse—Encoding/ Decoding." In *Culture, Media, Language: Working Papers in Cultural Studies, 1972–79*, Centre for Contemporary Cultural Studies. London: Hutchinson, 1973.

Hall, Stuart, and Tony Jefferson, eds. *Resistance through Rituals: Youth Subcultures in Post-War Britain*. London: Hutchinson, 1976.

Hamilton, Alexander, James Madison, and John Jay. *The Federalist Papers*. New York: New American Library, 1961. Based on the original McLean edition of 1788.

Harrington, Michael. *The Other Avenue*. New York: Macmillan, 1962.

Harris, Marvin. *Cannibals and Kings: The Origins of Cultures*. New York: Random House, 1977.

———. *Cultural Materialism: The Struggle for a Science of Culture*. New York: Random House, 1979.

———. *Good to Eat: Riddles of Food and Culture*. New York: Simon and Schuster, 1985.

———. *Patterns of Race in the Americas*. New York: Walker, 1964.

———. *The Rise of Anthropological Theory: A History of Theories of Culture*. New York: Thomas Y. Crowell, 1968.

———. *Theories of Culture in Postmodern Times*. Walnut Creek, Calif: AltaMira Press, 1999.

Harrod, Roy. "An Essay in Dynamic Theory." *Economic Journal* 49 (Mar. 1939): 14–33.

———. "Notes on Supply." *Economic Journal* 40 (Jun. 1930): 233–241.

———. *The Trade Cycle: An Essay*. Oxford: Clarendon Press, 1936.

Harsanyi, John. "Games with Incomplete Information Played by Bayesian Players, Parts I, II and III." *Management Science* 14 (1968): 159–182, 320–334, 486–502.

Hartshorne, Richard. *The Nature of Geography*. London: John Murray, 1959. Originally published in Lancaster, Penn.: Association of American Geographers, 1939.

Harvey, David. *The Condition of Postmodernity: An Enquiry into the Origins of Cultural Change*. New York: Blackwell, 1989.

———. *Explanation in Geography*. London: Edward Arnold, 1969.

———. *Justice, Nature and the Geography of Difference*. Cambridge, Mass.: Blackwell, 1996.

———. *The Limits to Capital*. Chicago and Oxford: University of Chicago Press/Blackwell, 1982.

———. *Social Justice and the City*. Baltimore, Md.: Johns Hopkins University Press, 1973.

———. *The Urbanization of Capital: Studies in the History and Theory of Capitalist Urbanization*. Baltimore, Md.: Johns Hopkins University Press, 1985.

Haveman, Robert, Barbara Wolfe, and James Spaulding. "Childhood Events and Circumstances Influencing High School Completion." *Demography* 28.1 (1991): 133–157.

Hayek, Friedrich von. *The Counter-Revolution of Science: Studies on the Abuse of Reason*. Glencoe, Ill.: Free Press, 1952.

———. *The Pure Theory of Capital*. Chicago: University of Chicago Press, 1941.

Hegel, Georg Wilhelm Friedrich. *Encyclopedia of Philosophy*. Translated from German and annotated by Gustav Emil Mueller. New York, Philosophical Library, 1959. Originally published as *Encyklopadie der philosophischen Wissenschaften im Grundrisse* (Heidelberg: A. Oswald, 1817–1827; Heidelberg: Verwaltung des Osswald'schen Verlags [C. F. Winter], 1830).

———. *Hegel's Philosophy of Right*. Translated from German by T. M. Knox. Oxford: Clarendon Press, 1942. Originally published as *Grundlinien der Philosophie des Rechts* (Berlin: In der Nicolaischen Buchhandlung, 1821).

———. *Hegel's Science of Logic*. 2 vols. Translated from German by W. H. Johnston and L. G. Struthers. London: Allen and Unwin; New York: Macmillan, 1929. Originally published as *Wissenschaft der Logik* (Nurnberg: J. L. Schrag, 1812–1816).

———. *The Phenomenology of Mind*. 2 vols. Translated from German by J. B. Baillie. New York: Macmillan, 1910. Originally published as *System der Wissenschaft: Erster Theil, Die Phanomenologie des Geistes* (Bamberg and Wurzburg: Bey Joseph Anton Goebhardt, 1807).

Heidegger, Martin. *Being and Time*. Translated from German by John MacQuarrie and Edward Robinson. London, SCM Press, 1962. Originally published as *Sein und Zeit* (Halle: M. Niemeyer, 1929).

———. *An Introduction to Metaphysics*. Translated from German by Ralph Manheim. New Haven, Conn.: Yale University Press, 1959. Originally published as *Einfuhrung in die Metaphysik* (Tübingen: M. Niemeyer, 1953).

———. *The Question Concerning Technology and Other Essays*. Translated from German by William Lovitt. New York: Garland, 1977. Originally published in *Holzwege* (Frankfurt am Main: V. Klostermann, 1950), and *Vortrage und Aufsatze* (Pfullingen: G. Neske, 1954), and *Die Technik und die Kehre* (Pfullingen: Neske, 1962).

Held, David. *Democracy and the Global Order: From the Modern State to Cosmopolitan Governance*. Cambridge: Polity Press, 1995.

Herrnstein, Richard, and Charles Murray. *The Bell Curve: Intelligence and Class Structure in American Life*. New York: Free Press, 1994.

Hershberg, Eric. "Social Science and Development." In *International Encyclopedia of the Social and Behavioral Sciences*, edited by Neil J. Smelser and Paul B. Bates. New York: Elsevier, 2001.

Herskovits, Melville J. *Acculturation: The Study of Culture Contact*. New York: J. J. Augustin, 1938.

———. "The Cattle Complex in East Africa." *American Anthropologist* 28 (1926): 230–272, 361–380, 494–528, 633–664.

———. *Dahomey: An Ancient West African Kingdom*. New York: J. J. Augustin, 1938.

———. *The Economic Life of Primitive Peoples*. New York: Knopf, 1940.

———. *Man and His Works: The Science of Cultural Anthropology*. New York: Knopf, 1948.

———. *The Myth of the Negro Past*. New York: Harper and Brothers, 1941.

Herskovits, Melville J., and Frances S. Herskovits. *The American Negro: A Study in Racial Crossing*. Bloomington, Ind.: University Press, 1928.

Herskovits, Melville J., M. H. Segall, and D. T. Campbell. *The Human Factor in Changing Africa*. New York: Knopf, 1962.

Hicks, John R. *Capital and Growth*. New York: Oxford University Press, 1965.

———. "Mr. Keynes and the 'Classics': A Suggested Interpretation." *Econometrica* 5 (1937): 147–159.

———. *The Theory of Wages*. London: Macmillan, 1932.

———. *Value and Capital: An Inquiry into Some Fundamental Principles of Economic Theory*. Oxford: Clarendon Press, 1946.

Higham, John. *Strangers in the Land: Patterns of American Nativism 1860–1925*. New Brunswick, N.J.: Rutgers University Press, 1955.

Hilferding, Rudolf. *Finance Capital: A Study of the Latest Phase of Capitalist Development*. Edited by Tom Bottomore. London: Routledge and Kegan Paul, 1981. Originally published in 1910.

Hintze, Otto. *Geist und Epochen der Preussischen Geschichte*. Leipzig: Koehler und Amelang, 1943.

———. *Soziologie und Geschichte*. Göttingen: Vandenhoeck und Ruprecht, 1943.

———. *Staat und Verfassung*. Göttingen: Vandenhoeck und Ruprecht, 1962.

Hirschman, Albert. *Exit, Voice, Loyalty: Responses to Decline in Firms, Organizations, and States*. Cambridge, Mass.: Harvard University Press, 1970.

Hobbes, Thomas. *A Dialogue between a Philosopher and a Student of the Common Laws of England*. Edited by Joseph Cropsey. Chicago: University of Chicago Press, 1997. Originally published in 1681.

———. *De Cive*. Edited by Howard Warrender. Oxford: Clarendon Press, 1983. Originally published in Latin as *Elementorum philosophiae sectio tertia de cive* (1642).

———. *The Elements of Law, Natural and Politic*. Edited by Ferdinand Tönnies. 2d ed., new intro. M. M. Goldsmith. London: Cass, 1969. Originally published in 1650.

———. *Leviathan*. Reprint, London: Dent, 1983. Originally published in 1651.

Hobsbawm, Eric, and Terence Ranger. *The Invention of Tradition*. New York: Cambridge University Press, 1983.

Hobson, John. *Imperialism*. 1902. Reprint, London: Allen and Unwin, 1938.

Hochschild, Arlie Russell. *The Managed Heart: Commercialization of Human Feeling*. Berkeley: University of California Press, 1983.

Hoggart, Richard. *Speaking to Each Other: Essays*. New York: Oxford University Press, 1970.

———. *The Uses of Literacy: Aspects of Working-Class Life with Special References to Publications and Entertainments*. London: Chatto and Windus, 1957.

———. *The Way We Live Now*. London: Chatto and Windus, 1995.

Homans, George. *Certainties and Doubts: Collected Papers, 1962–1985*. New Brunswick, N.J.: Transaction Books, 1987.

———. *Coming to My Senses: The Autobiography of a Sociologist*. New Brunswick, N.J.: Transaction Books, 1984.

———. *English Villagers of the Thirteenth Century*. Cambridge, Mass.: Harvard University Press, 1941.

———. *The Human Group*. New York: Harcourt, Brace, 1950.

———. *The Nature of Social Science*. New York: Harcourt, Brace, 1967.

———. *Sentiments and Activities: Essays in Social Science*. New York: Free Press, 1962.

———. *Social Behavior: Its Elementary Forms*. New York: Harcourt, Brace, 1961.

Horkheimer, Max. *Critical Theory: Selected Essays*. Translated from German by Matthew J. O'Connell and others. New York: Herder and Herder, 1972. Originally published as *Kritische Theorie: Eine Dokumentation* (Frankfurt am Main: S. Fischer, 1968).

———. "Traditional and Critical Theory." In *Critical Theory: Selected Essays*. Translated from German by Matthew J. O'Connell and others. New York: Herder and Herder, 1972. Originally published as *Kritische Theorie: Eine Dokumentation* (Frankfurt am Main: S. Fischer, 1968).

———. *The Eclipse of Reason*. New York: Oxford University Press, 1947.

Horkheimer, Max, and Theodor Adorno. *Dialectic of Enlightenment*. Translated from German by John Cumming. New York: Herder and Herder, 1972. Originally published as *Dialektik der Aufklarung: Philosophische Fragmente* (Amsterdam: Querido, 1947).

Horkheimer, Max, and Samuel H. Flowerman, eds. *Studies in Prejudice*. New York: American Jewish Committee (Harper & Brothers), 1949–1950.

Horney, Karen. *Feminine Psychology*. Edited and with an introduction by Harold Kelman. New York: Norton, 1967.

———. *Neurosis and Human Growth: The Struggle Toward Self-Realization*. New York: Norton, 1950.

———. *The Neurotic Personality of Our Time*. New York: Norton, 1937.

———. *Self-Analysis*. New York: Norton, 1942.

Hotelling, Harold. "Stability in Competition." *Economic Journal* 39.1 (1929): 41–57.

Humboldt, Alexander von. *Kosmos: A Sketch of a Physical Description of the Universe*. 4 vols. Translated from German by E. C. Otté. New York: Harper, 1870–1872. Originally published as *Kosmos. Entwurf einer physischen Weltbeschreibung* (Stuttgart and Tübingen: Cotta, 1845–1862).

Humboldt, Alexander von, and Aime Bonpland. *Personal Narrative of Travels to the Equinoctial Regions of America during the Years 1799–1804*. 13 vols. Translated from French and edited by Thomasina Ross. London: G. Routledge, 1851. Originally published as *Voyage aux regions equinoxiales du nouveau continent, fait en 1799, 1800, 1801, 1802, 1803 et 1804* (Paris: F. Schoell, 1810–1834).

Hume, David. *A Treatise of Human Nature*. 1739–1740. Reprint, 3 vols., edited by L. A. Selby-Bigge. Oxford: Clarendon Press, 1896.

———. *History of England from the Invasion of Julius Caeser* [sic]*to the Abdication of James the Second, 1688*. 1763. Reprint, New York: G. P. Putnam and Sons, 1871.

———. *Inquiry Concerning the Principles of Morals*. 1751. Reprint, New York: Liberal Arts Press, 1957.

———. *My Own Life. The Writings of David Hume*. Edited by James Fieser. Internet Release, 1995. Originally published in *The Scots Magazine*, January 1777, Vol. 39, pp. 1–7.

———. *The Natural History of Religion*. Reprint, Stanford, Calif.: Stanford University Press, 1957. Originally published in 1755.

———. *Political Discourses*. Edinburgh: Printed by R. Fleming, for A. Kincaid and A. Donaldson, 1752.

Hunt, Lynn Avery. *The Family Romance of the French Revolution*. Berkeley: University of California Press, 1992.

Huntington, Ellsworth. *Civilization and Climate*. New Haven, Conn.: Yale University Press, 1915.

———. *The Human Habitat*. New York: D. Van Nostrand, 1927.

———. *The Pulse of Asia: A Journey in Central Asia Illustrating the Geographic Basis of History*. Boston and New York: Houghton Mifflin, 1907.

Huntington, Samuel. *Political Order in Changing Societies*. New Haven, Conn.: Yale University Press, 1968.

Hurwicz, Leonid. "On Informationally Decentralized Systems." In *Decision and Organization*, edited by C. B. McGuire and R. Radner. North-Holland: Elsevier, 1972.

Hyman, Herbert. "Psychology of Status." *Archives of Psychology* 269 (1942): 5–28.

Inglehart, Ronald. *Culture Shift in Advanced Industrial Society*. Princeton, N.J.: Princeton University Press, 1990.

Jakobson, Roman. *On Language*. Edited by Linda R. Waugh and Monique Monville-Burston. Cambridge, Mass.: Harvard University Press, 1990.

———. *Selected Writings*. 6 vols. The Hague: Mouton, 1962–1982.

James, C. L. R. *Beyond a Boundary*. London: Hutchinson, 1963.

———. *The Black Jacobins: Toussaint Louverture and the San Domingo Revolution*. New York: The Dial Press, 1938.

———. *Notes on Dialectics: Hegel, Marx, Lenin*. 1948. Reprint, London: Allison and Busby, 1980.

———. *World Revolution, 1917–1936: The Rise and Fall of the Communist International*. Westport, Conn.: Hyperion Press, 1973.

James, William. *Essays in Radical Empiricism: A Pluralistic Universe*. 1909. Reprint, New York: Longmans, Green, 1958.

———. *Pragmatism*. 1907. Reprint, Cambridge, Mass.: Harvard University Press, 1975.

———. *The Principles of Psychology*. New York: Holt, 1890.

———. *Some Problems in Philosophy*. 1911. Reprint, Cambridge, Mass.: Harvard University Press, 1979.

———. *The Varieties of Religious Experience: A Study in Human Nature*. 1902. Reprint, London and New York: Longmans, Green, 1906.

———. *The Will to Believe, and Other Essays in Popular Philosophy*. 1897. Reprint, New York: Longmans, Green, 1899.

Janowitz, Morris. *The Last Half-Century: Societal Change and Politics in America*. Chicago: University of Chicago Press, 1978.

———. *Political Conflict*. Chicago: Quadrangle Books, 1970.

———. *The Professional Soldier: A Social and Political Portrait*. New York: Free Press, 1960.

———. *The Reconstruction of Patriotism: Education for Civic Consciousness*. Chicago: University of Chicago Press, 1983.

———. *Social Control of the Welfare State*. New York: Elsevier, 1976.

Janowitz, Morris, and Bruno Bettleheim. *Dynamics of Prejudice: A Psychological and Sociological Study of Veterans*. New York: Harper, 1950.

Jevons, William Stanley. *The Theory of Political Economy*. London: Macmillan, 1871.

Johnson, Harry G. *Economic Policies Toward Less Developed Countries*. Washington, D.C.: Brookings, 1967.

Journal of American Folk-Lore. Boston and New York: Published for the American Folk-lore Society by Houghton Mifflin, 1888–.

Journal of Political Economy. Chicago: University of Chicago Press, 1892–.

Jung, Carl Gustav. *Civilization in Transition*. New York: Pantheon, 1964.

———. *Collected Works*. 20 vols. Edited by Herbert Read, Michael Fordham, and Gerhard Adler. New York: Pantheon, 1953–1979.

———. *Contributions to Analytical Psychology*. 8 vols. Collection of essays translated from German by Helton Godwin Baynes and Cary F. Baynes. New York: Harcourt, Brace, 1928.

———. *Modern Man in Search of a Soul*. Collection of essays translated from German by W. S. Dell and Cary F. Baynes. New York: Harcourt, Brace, and World, 1933.

———. *Psychological Types*. Revision by R. F. C. Hull of the translation from German by H. G. Baynes. Princeton, N.J.: Princeton University Press, 1971. Originally published as *Psychologische Typen* (Zurich: Rascher, 1921).

Kaldor, Nicholas. *Collected Economic Essays* (1960–1980). 8 vols. New York: Holmes and Meier, 1980.

Kalecki, Michal. *Introduction to the Theory of Growth in a Socialist Economy*. Translated from Polish by Zdzislaw Sadowski. New York: A. M. Kelley, 1969. Originally published as *Zarys teorii wzrostu gospodarki socjalistycznej* (Warsaw: Panstwowe Wydawn. Naukowe, 1963).

———. *Studies in the Theory of Business Cycles, 1933–1939*. Translated from Polish by Ada Kalecka. Oxford: Blackwell, 1966. Originally published as *Proba teorji konjunktury* (Warsaw: Instytut Badania Konjunktur Gospodarczych i cen, 1933).

Kant, Immanuel. *The Conflict of the Faculties*. Translated from German by Mary J. Gregor. New York: Abaris Books, 1979. Originally published as *Der Streit der Facultaten in drey Abschnitten* (Konigsberg: N.p., 1798).

———. *The Critique of Judgment*. Translated from German by Werner S. Pluhar. Indianapolis, Ind.: Hackett, 1987. Originally published as *Kritik der Urteilskraft* (1790).

———. *Critique of Pure Reason*. Translated from German by Norman Kemp Smith. London: Macmillan, 1929. Originally published as *Kritik der reinen Vernunft Riga* (Verlegts: Johann Friedrich Hartknoch, 1781).

———. *The Metaphysics of Morals*. 2 vols. Translated from German by John Ladd. Indianapolis, Ind.: Bobbs-Merrill, 1965–. Originally published as *Die Metaphysik der Sitten* (Konigsberg: Bey Friedrich Nicolovius, 1797).

———. *Principles of Lawful Politics: Immanuel Kant's Philosophic Draft Toward Eternal Peace*. Translated from German by Wolfgang Schwarz. Originally published as *Zum ewigen Frieden* (Konigsberg: Bey Friedrich Nicolovius, 1796).

———. *Religion within the Limits of Reason Alone*. Translated from German by Theodore M. Greene and Hoyt H. Hudson. Chicago: The Open Court Publishing Company, 1934. Originally published as *Die Religion innerhalb der Grenzen der blossen Vernunft* (Konigsberg: Bey Friedrich Nicolovius, 1794).

Kardiner, Abram, and Ralph Linton. *The Individual and His Society: The Psychodynamics of Primitive Social Organization*. New York: Columbia University Press, 1939.

Keohane, Robert O., and Joseph S. Nye. *Power and Interdependence: World Politics in Transition*. Boston: Little, Brown, 1977.

Key, V. O. *American State Politics: An Introduction*. New York: Knopf, 1956.

———. *Politics, Parties and Pressure Groups*. New York: Thomas Y. Crowell, 1942.

———. *Public Opinion and American Democracy*. New York: Knopf, 1961.

———. *The Responsible Electorate*. New York: Random House, 1968.

———. *Southern Politics in State and Nation*. Knoxville: University of Tennessee Press, 1949.

Keynes, John Maynard. *The Economic Consequences of the Peace*. London: Macmillan, 1919.

———. *General Theory of Employment, Interest and Money*. London: Macmillan, 1936.

———. *How to Pay for the War: A Radical Plan for the Chancellor of the Exchequer*. New York: Harcourt, Brace, 1940.

———. "A Rejoinder to Ohlin's *The Reparation Problem*." *Economic Journal* 39 (1929): 404–408.

———. *A Tract on Monetary Reform*. Amherst N.Y.: Prometheus Books, 1999. Originally published London: Macmillan, 1924.

———. *A Treatise on Money*. London: Macmillan, 1930.

———. *Treatise on Probability*. London: Macmillan, 1921.

Kinsey, A. C., W. B. Pomeroy, and C. E. Martin. *Sexual Behavior in the Human Male*. Philadelphia: W. B. Saunders, 1948.

Kinsey, A. C., W. B. Pomeroy, C. E. Martin, and P. H. Gebhard. *Sexual Behavior in the Human Female*. Philadelphia: W. B. Saunders, 1953.

Klein, Melanie. *Envy and Gratitude and Other Works, 1946–1963*. New York: Delacorte Press/S. Lawrence, 1975.

———. *Love, Guilt, and Reparation and Other Works, 1921–1945*. New York: Delacorte Press/S. Lawrence, 1975.

———. *The Psycho-analysis of Children*. Translated from German by Alix Strachey. London: Hogarth Press and the Institute of Psycho-analysis, 1949. Originally published as *Die Psychoanalyse des Kindes* (Vienna: Internationaler Psychoanalytischer Verlag, 1932).

Kluckhohn, Clyde. *Mirror for Man: The Relation of Anthropology to Modern Life*. New York: Whittlesey House, 1949.

Kluckhohn, Clyde, and Dorothea Leighton. *The Navaho*. Cambridge, Mass.: Harvard University Press, 1946.

Kluckhohn, Richard, ed. *Culture and Behavior: Collected Essays of Clyde Kluckhohn*. New York: Free Press of Glencoe, 1962.

Kniffen, Fred B. "Folk Housing: Key to Diffusion." *Annals of the Association of American Geographers* 55 (1965): 549–577.

———. *Louisiana: Its Land and People*. Baton Rouge: Louisiana State University Press, 1968.

Knight, Frank H. *Risk, Uncertainty and Profit*. Boston: Houghton Mifflin, 1933.

Koopmans, Tjalling, ed. *Statistical Inference in Dynamic Economic Models*. Cowles Commission Monograph no. 10. New York: Wiley, 1950.

Kornhauser, William. *The Politics of Mass Society*. London: Routledge and Kegan Paul, 1960.

Kristeva, Julia. *Black Sun: Depression and Melancholy*. Translated from French by Leon Roudiez. New York: Columbia University Press, 1989. Originally published as *Soleil noir: Depression et melancolie* (Paris: Gallimard, 1987).

———. *New Maladies of the Soul*. Translated from French by Ross Guberman. New York: Columbia University Press, 1995. Originally published as *Les nouvelles maladies de l'âme* (Paris: Fayard, 1993).

———. *Powers of Horror: An Essay on Abjection*. Translated from French by Leon Roudiez. New York: Columbia University Press, 1982. Originally published as *Pouvoirs de l'horreur: Essai sur l'abjection* (Paris: Editions du Seuil, 1980).

———. *Revolution in Poetic Language*. Translated from French by Margaret Waller. New York: Columbia University Press, 1984. Originally published as *La révolution du langage poétique: l'avant-garde à la fin du XIXe siècle, Lautréamont et Mallarmé* (Paris: Editions du Seuil, 1974).

———. *Strangers to Ourselves*. Translated from French by Leon Roudiez. New York: Columbia University Press, 1991. Originally published as *Etrangers à nous-mêmes* (Paris: Fayard, 1988).

———. *Tales of Love*. Translated from French by Leon Roudiez. New York: Columbia University Press, 1987. Originally published as *Histoires d'amour* (Paris: Denoel, 1983).

———. *The Samurai: A Novel*. New York: Columbia University Press, 1992. Originally published as *Les samourais: Roman* (Paris: Fayard, 1990).

Kroeber, Alfred L. *Anthropology*. New York: Harcourt, Brace, 1923.

———. "The Arapaho." *Bulletin of the American Museum of Natural History* 18 (1902–1907): part 1, 1–150; part 2, 151–230; part 3, 231–278; part 4, 279–454.

———. *Area and Climax*. Berkeley: University of California Press, 1936.

———. *Configurations of Culture Growth*. Berkeley: University of California Press, 1944.

———. *Cultural and Natural Areas of Native North America*. Berkeley: University of California Press, 1939.

———. *Handbook of the Indians of California*. Washington, D.C.: U.S. Government Printing Office, 1925.

———. *The Nature of Culture*. Chicago: University of Chicago Press, 1952.

———. "The Superorganic." *American Anthropologist* 19 (1917): 163–213.

Kroeber, Alfred L., Clyde Kluckhohn, Wayne Untereiner, and Alfred G. Meyer. *Culture: A Critical Review of Concepts and Definitions*. Cambridge, Mass.: The Peabody Museum of Archaeology and Ethnology, Harvard University, 1952.

Kuhn, Thomas S. *The Copernican Revolution: Planetary Astronomy in the Development of Western Thought*. Cambridge, Mass.: Harvard University Press, 1957.

———. *The Essential Tension: Selected Studies in Scientific Tradition and Change*. Chicago: University of Chicago Press, 1977.

———. *The Structure of Scientific Revolutions*. Chicago: University of Chicago Press, 1962.

Kuznets, Simon. *Modern Economic Growth: Rate, Structure, and Spread*. New Haven, Conn.: Yale University Press, 1966.

———. *National Income, 1929–1932*. New York: National Bureau of Economic Research, 1934.

Kydland, Finn E., and Edward C. Prescott. "Rules Rather Than Discretion: The Inconsistency of Optimal Plans." *Journal of Political Economy* 85.3 (1977): 473–491.

L'Année Sociologique. Paris: Felix Alcan, 1898–1927. Paris: Presses Universitaires de France, 1949–.

Lacan, Jacques. *Ecrits*. Paris: Editions du Seuil, 1966.

———. *The Four Fundamental Concepts of Psychoanalysis*. Edited by Jacques-Alain Miller. Translated from French by Alan Sheridan. New York: Norton, 1981. Originally published as *Le séminaire de Jacques Lacan, Livre XI, Les quatre concepts fondamentaux de la psychanalyse* (Paris: Editions du Seuil, 1973).

———. *The Seminar of Jacques Lacan*. 2 vols. Edited by Jacques-Alain Miller. Translated from French by John Forrester. Cambridge and New York: Cambridge University Press, 1988. Originally published as *Le séminaire de Jacques Lacan* (Paris: Editions du Seuil, 1975–).

Laing, Ronald David. *The Divided Self: An Existential Study in Sanity and Madness*. Middlesex: Penguin, 1960.

———. *The Politics of Experience*. New York: Pantheon, 1967.

Laing, Ronald David, and A. A. Esterson. *Sanity, Madness and the Family*. London: Tavistock, 1964.

Laski, Harold. *The American Democracy: A Commentary and an Interpretation.* New York: Viking Press, 1948.

———. *The American Presidency: An Interpretation.* Westport, Conn.: Greenwood Press, 1940.

———. *Democracy in Crisis.* Chapel Hill: The University of North Carolina Press, 1933.

———. *The Foundations of Sovereignty.* New York: Harcourt, Brace, 1921.

———. *A Grammar of Politics.* London: Allen and Unwin, 1925.

———. *Liberty in the Modern State.* London: Faber and Faber, 1930.

———. *Reflections on the Revolution of Our Time.* New York: Viking Press, 1943.

———. *The State in Theory and Practice.* New York: Viking Press, 1935.

———. *Studies in the Problem of Sovereignty.* New Haven, Conn.: Yale University Press, 1917.

Lasswell, Harold. *Power and Personality.* New York: Norton, 1948.

———. *Propaganda Technique in the World War.* New York: Knopf, 1927.

———. *Psychopathology and Politics.* 1930. Reprint, Chicago: University of Chicago Press, 1977.

———. *World Politics and Insecurity.* New York and London: Whittlesey House/McGraw-Hill, 1935.

Lasswell, Harold, and Abraham Kaplan. *Power and Society.* New Haven, Conn.: Yale University Press, 1968.

Lazarsfeld, Paul. *Mathematical Thinking in the Social Sciences.* Glencoe, Ill.: Free Press, 1954.

———. *Qualitative Analysis: Historical and Critical Essays.* Boston: Allyn and Bacon, 1972.

Lazarsfeld, Paul, Bernard Berelson, and Hazel Gaudet. *The People's Choice: How the Voter Makes Up His Mind in a Presidential Campaign.* New York: Columbia University Press, 1944.

Lazarsfeld, Paul, and Elihu Katz. *Personal Influence: The Part Played by People in the Flow of Mass Communications.* Glencoe, Ill.: Free Press, 1955.

Le Bon, Gustave. *Les lois psychologiques de l'evolution des peuples* (Paris: F. Alcan, 1894).

———. *The Crowd: A Study of the Popular Mind.* New York: Viking Press, 1960. Originally published as *Psychologie des foules* (Paris: F. Alcan, 1895).

———. *The Psychology of Socialism.* Wells, Vt.: Fraser Publishing, 1965. Originally published as *Psychologie du socialisme* (Paris: Alcan, 1898).

———. *La révolution française et la psychologie des révolutions.* Paris: E. Flammarion, 1912.

Leach, Edmund R. *Claude Lévi-Strauss.* New York: Viking Press, 1970.

———. *Culture and Communication, The Logic by Which Symbols Are Connected: An Introduction to the Use of Structuralist Analysis in Social Anthropology.* Cambridge: Cambridge University Press, 1976.

———. *Political Systems of Highland Burma: A Study of Kachin Social Structure.* Cambridge, Mass.: Harvard University Press, 1954.

———. *Pul Eliya, A Village in Ceylon: A Study of Land Tenure and Kinship.* Cambridge, Mass.: Harvard University Press, 1961.

———. *Rethinking Anthropology.* London: Athlone Press, 1961.

Lemkin, Raphael. *Axis Rule in Occupied Europe: Laws of Occupation, Analysis of Government, Proposals for Redress.* Washington, D.C.: Carnegie Endowment for International Peace, Division of International Law, 1944.

Lenin, Vladimir Ilich. *The Development of Capitalism in Russia.* 1899. Translation of *Razvitie kapitalizma v Rossii.* Moscow: Progress Publishers, 1967.

———. *Imperialism, the Highest Stage of Capitalism: A Popular Outline.* 1916. Reprint, New York: International, 1933. Originally published as *Imperializm, kak noveishii etap kapitalizm: Populiarnyi ocherk* (Moskow, 1916).

———. *Materialism and Empirio-Criticism: Critical Comments on a Reactionary Philosophy.* 1908. Translation of *Materializm i empiriokrititsizm.* Moscow: Foreign Languages Publishing House, 1947.

———. *State and Revolution: Marxist Teaching about the Theory of the State and the Tasks of the Proletariat in the Revolution.* New York: International, 1932. Originally published as *Gosudarstvo i revoliutsiia: Uchenie marksizma o gosudarstvie i zadachi proletariata v revoliutsii* (Russian Socialist Federation, 1919).

———. *What is to be Done.* 1902. Translated from Russian by S. V. and Patricia Utechin. Oxford: Clarendon Press, 1963. Originally published as *Chto dielat'.*

Lenski, Gerhard. "Status Inconsistency and the Vote: A Four Nation Test." *American Sociological Review* 32 (Apr. 1967): 298–301.

Leontief, Wassily. *The Structure of the American Economy, 1919–1929: An Empirical Application of Equilibrium Analysis.* Cambridge, Mass.: Harvard University Press, 1941.

Leontief, Wassily, et al. *Studies in the Structure of the American Economy: Theoretical and Empirical Explorations in Input–Output Analysis.* New York: Oxford University Press, 1953.

Lévi-Strauss, Claude. *Elementary Structures of Kinship,* rev. ed. Edited by Rodney Needham. Translated from French by James Harle Bell, John Richard von Sturmer, and Rodney Needham. Boston: Beacon Press, 1969. Originally published as *Les structures élémentaires de la parenté* (Paris: Presses Universitaires de France, 1949).

———. *Introduction to the Science of Mythology.* 4 vols. Translated from French by John and Doreen Weightman. New York: Harper and Row, 1969. Originally published as *Mythologiques* (Paris: Plon, 1964–1971).

———. *The Raw and the Cooked.* Translated from French by John and Doreen Weightman. New

York: Harper and Row, 1969. Originally published as *Le cru et le cuit* (Paris: Plon, 1964).

———. *Tristes Tropiques*. Translated from French by John Russell. New York, Criterion Books, 1961. Originally published as *Tristes tropiques* (Paris: Plon, 1955).

———. *The Savage Mind*. Chicago: University of Chicago Press, 1966. Originally published as *La pensée sauvage* (Paris: Plon, 1962).

Lévy-Bruhl, Lucien. *How Natives Think*. Translated from French by Lillian A. Clare. New York: Washington Square Press, 1966. Originally published as *Fonctions mentales dans les sociétés inférieures* (Paris: F. Alcan, 1910).

———. *Notebooks on Primitive Mentality*. Translated from French by Peter Rivière. Oxford: Blackwell, 1975. Originally published as *Les carnets* (Paris: Presses Universitaires de France, 1949).

———. *Primitive Mentality*. Translated from French by Lilian A. Clare. New York: Macmillan, 1923. Originally published as *La mentalité primitive* (Paris: Librairie Felix Alcan, 1922).

———. *Primitives and the Supernatural*. Translated from French by Lilian A. Clare. New York: E. P. Dutton, 1935. Originally published as *Le surnaturel et la nature dans la mentalité primitive* (Paris: F. Alcan, 1931).

Lewin, Kurt. *A Dynamic Theory of Personality: Selected Papers*. Translated from German by Donald K. Adams and Karl E. Zener. New York and London: McGraw-Hill, 1935.

———. *Field Theory in Social Science: Selected Theoretical Papers*. Edited by Dorwin Cartwright. New York: Harper, 1951.

———. *Principles of Topological Psychology*. Translated from German by Fritz Heider and Grace M. Heider. New York: McGraw-Hill, 1936.

———. *Resolving Social Conflicts: Selected Papers on Group Dynamics*. Edited by Gertrud Weiss Lewin. New York: Harper, 1948.

Lewis, H. Gregg. *Unionism and Relative Wages in the United States*. Chicago: University of Chicago Press, 1963.

———. *Union Relative Wage Effects: A Survey*. Chicago: University of Chicago Press, 1986.

Lewis, Oscar. "The Culture of Poverty." *Scientific American* 215.4 (Oct. 1966): 19–25.

Lewis, W. Arthur. "Economic Development with Unlimited Supplies of Labor." *The Manchester School* 22 (May 1954): 139–191.

———. *The Theory of Economic Growth*. London: Allen and Unwin, 1955.

Lin, Nan. "Social Resources and Instrumental Action." In *Social Structure and Network Analysis*, edited by Peter V. Marsden and Nan Lin. Beverly Hills, Calif: Sage, 1982.

Lindblom, Charles. *Democracy and the Market System*. Oslo: Norwegian University Press, 1988.

———. *Inquiry and Change: The Troubled Attempt to Understand and Shape Society*. New Haven, Conn.: Yale University Press, 1990.

———. *The Intelligence of Democracy*. New York: The Free Press, 1965.

———. *Politics and Markets: The World's Political Economic Systems*. New York: Basic Books, 1977.

Linder, Staffan. *The Harried Leisure Class*. New York: Columbia University Press, 1970.

Lintner, John. "The Valuation of Risk Assets and the Selection of Risky Investments in Stock Portfolios and Capital Budgets." *Review of Economics and Statistics* 47.1 (1965): 13–37;

———. "Security Prices, Risk, and Maximal Gains from Diversification." *Journal of Finance* 20.4 (1965): 587–615.

Linton, Ralph. *The Cultural Background of Personality*. New York: Appleton-Century, 1945.

———. *Culture and Mental Disorders*. Edited by George Devereux. Springfield, Ill.: Thomas, 1956.

———. *The Study of Man: An Introduction*. New York: Appleton-Century-Crofts, 1936.

———. *The Tanala: A Hill Tribe of Madagascar*. Chicago: Field Museum of Natural History, 1933.

———. *The Tree of Culture*. New York: Knopf, 1955.

Lipset, Seymour Martin. *American Exceptionalism: A Double-Edged Sword*. New York: Norton, 1996.

———. *Continental Divide: The Values and Institutions of the United States and Canada*. New York: Routledge, 1990.

———. *The First New Nation: The United States in Historical and Comparative Perspective*. New York: Basic Books, 1963.

———. *Political Man: The Social Bases of Politics*. New York: Doubleday, 1960.

———. *Rebellion in the University*. Boston: Little, Brown, 1972.

———. *Revolution and Counterrevolution*. New York: Basic Books, 1968.

———. *Union Democracy: The Internal Politics of the International Typographical Union*. Glencoe, Ill.: Free Press, 1956.

Lipset, Seymour Martin, and Reinhard Bendix. *Social Mobility in Industrial Society*. Berkeley: University of California Press, 1959.

Lipset, Seymour Martin, and Earl Raab. *Jews and the New American Scene*. Cambridge, Mass.: Harvard University Press, 1995.

Lipset, Seymour Martin, and Stein Rokkan, eds. *Party Systems and Voter Alignments*. New York: Free Press, 1967.

Lipset, Seymour Martin, and Sheldon S. Wolin, eds. *The Berkeley Student Revolt*. Garden City, N.Y.: Doubleday, 1965.

Lipsey, Richard, and Kevin Lancaster. "The General Theory of Second Best." *Review of Economic Studies* 24 (Oct. 1956): 11–32.

Locke, John. *A Letter Concerning Toleration*. Revised and edited with variants and an introduction by Mario Montuori. The Hague: M. Nijhoff,

1963. Originally published in Latin as *Epistola de tolerantia ad clarissimum virum* (Goudae: Apud Justum ab Hoeve, 1689).

———. *Essay Concerning Human Understanding* (1689). 2 vols. Abridged and edited by A. S. Pringle-Pattison. Reprint, Oxford: Clarendon Press, 1924.

———. "An Essay Concerning the True Original Extent and End of Civil Government" (1690). In *The English Philosophers from Bacon to Mill*, edited by Edwin A. Burtt. New York: Modern Library, 1939.

———. *Of Civil Government, Second Essay* (1690). Chicago: H. Regnery, 1955.

———. *The Reasonableness of Christianity, as Delivered in the Scriptures*. London: Printed for Awnsham and John Churchill, 1695.

———. *Some Thoughts Concerning Education*. London: Printed for Awnsham and John Churchill, 1693.

———. *Two Treatises of Government*. London: Printed for Awnsham Churchill, 1690.

Lorenz, K. *On Aggression*. New York: Harcourt, Brace, and World, 1966.

Lotka, Alfred. *Elements of Physical Biology*. Baltimore, Md.: Williams and Wilkins, 1925.

Lowie, Robert H. *Are We Civilized: Human Culture in Perspective*. New York: Harcourt, Brace, 1929.

———. *Culture and Ethnology*. New York: McMurtrie, 1917.

———. *The History of Ethnological Theory*. New York: Boni and Liveright, 1934.

———. *Indians of the Plains*. New York: McGraw-Hill, 1954.

———. *The Origin of the State*. New York: Harcourt, Brace, 1927.

———. *Primitive Society*. New York: Liveright, 1920.

———. *Toward Understanding Germany*. Chicago: University of Chicago Press, 1954.

Lubbock, Sir John. *Prehistoric Times as Illustrated by Ancient Remains and the Manners and Customs of Modern Savages*. London: Williams and Norgate, 1865.

Lucas, Robert. "Expectations and the Neutrality of Money." *Journal of Economic Theory* 4.2 (1972): 103–124.

Luckmann, Thomas. *The Invisible Religion: The Problem of Religion in Modern Society*. New York: Macmillan, 1967. Originally published as *Das Problem der Religion in der modernen Gesellschaft: Institution, Person, und Weltanschauung* (Freiburg: Rombach, 1963).

Luhmann, Niklas. *The Differentiation of Society*. Translated from German by Stephen Holmes and Charles Larmore. New York: Columbia University Press, 1982. Originally published as *Soziologische Aufklärung* (Cologne: Westdeustscher Verlag, 1970).

———. *Ecological Communication*. Translated from German by John Bednarz Jr. Chicago: University of Chicago Press, 1989. Originally published

as *Okologische Kommunikation: Kann die moderne Gesellschaft sich auf okologische Gefahrdungen einstellen?* (Opladen: Westdeutscher Verlag, 1986.)

———. *Observations on Modernity*. Translated from German by William Whobrey. Stanford, Calif.: Stanford University Press, 1998. Originally published as *Beobachtungen der Moderne* (Opladen: Westdeutscher Verlag, 1992).

———. *Risk: A Sociological Theory*. Translated from German by Rhodes Barrett. New York: A. de Gruyter, 1993. Originally published as *Soziologie des Risikos* (Berlin and New York: W. de Gruyter, 1991).

———. *Social Systems*. Translated from German by John Bednarz Jr., with Dirk Baecker. Stanford, Calif.: Stanford University Press, 1995. Originally published as *Soziale Systeme: Grundriss einer allgemeinen Theorie* (Frankfurt am Main: Suhrkamp, 1984).

Lukács, Gyorgy. *A Defence of History and Class Consciousness: Tailism and the Dialectic*. Translated from German by Esther Leslie. London and New York: Verso, 2000. Originally published as *Chvostismus und Dialektik* (1923).

———. *The Historical Novel*. Translated from German by Hannah and Stanley Mitchell. London: Merlin Press, 1962. Originally published as *Tortenelmi regeny* (1937).

———. *The Meaning of Contemporary Realism*. Translated from German by John Mander and Necke Mander. London: Merlin Press, 1963. Originally published as *Wider den missverstandenen Realismus* (Hamburg: Claassen, 1958).

———. *The Theory of the Novel: A Historico-Philosophical Essay on the Forms of Great Epic Literature*. Translated from German by Anna Bostock. Cambridge, Mass.: MIT Press, 1971. Originally published as *Die Theorie des Romans: Ein Geschichtsphilosophischer Versuch uber die Formen der grossen Epik* (Berlin: P. Cassirer, 1920).

———. *Asthetik* (Neuwied am Rhein: Luchterhand, 1963).

———. *The Young Hegel: Studies in the Relations between Dialectics and Economics*. Translated from German by Rodney Livingstone. Cambridge, Mass.: MIT Press, 1975. Originally published as *Der junge Hegel: Über die Beziehungen von Dialektik und Oekonomie* (Zurich and Vienna: Europa Verlag, 1948).

Lukes, S. Power. *A Radical View*. London: Macmillan, 1974.

Lyotard, Jean-François. *The Differend: Phrases in Dispute*. Translated from French by Georges Van Den Abbeele. Minneapolis: University of Minnesota Press, 1988. Originally published as *Le differend* (Paris: Minuit, 1983).

———. *The Inhuman: Reflections on Time*. Translated from French by Geoffrey Bennington and Rachel Bowlby. Stanford, Calif.: Stanford University Press, 1991. Originally published as *L'inhumain:*

Causeries sur le temps (Paris: Editions Galilee, 1988).

———. *Libidinal Economy*. Translated from French by Iain Hamilton Grant. Bloomington: Indiana University Press, 1993. Originally published as *Economie libidinale* (Paris: Editions de Minuit, 1974).

———. *Political Writings*. Translated from French by Bill Readings and Kevin Paul Geiman. Minneapolis and London: University of Minnesota Press, 1993.

———. *The Postmodern Condition: A Report on Knowledge*. Translated from French by Geoff Bennington and Brian Massumi. Minneapolis: University of Minnesota Press, 1984. Originally published as *La condition postmoderne: Rapport sur le savoir* (Paris: Editions de Minuit, 1979).

Lyotard, Jean-François, and Jean-Loup Thébaud. *Just Gaming*. Translated from French by Brian Massumi. Minneapolis: University of Minnesota Press, 1985. Originally published as *Au juste* (1979).

Machiavelli, Niccolò. *Discourses on the First Decade of Titus Livius*. Translated from Italian by Ninian Hill Thomson. London: K. Paul, Trench, 1883. Originally published as *Discorsi di Nicolò Machiavelli . . . sopra la prima deca di Tito Livio, a Zanobi Bvondelmonti, et a Cosimo Rvcellai . . . .* (Rome: A. Blado, 1531).

———. *The Prince*. Translated from Italian by W. K. Marriott. London: J. M. Dent, 1920. Originally published as *Il principe* (1513).

MacIntyre, Alisdair. *After Virtue: A Study in Moral Theory*. Notre Dame, Ind.: University of Notre Dame Press, 1981.

———. *Three Rival Versions of Moral Inquiry: Encyclopaedia, Genealogy, and Tradition: Being Gifford Lectures Delivered in the University of Edinburgh in 1988*. Notre Dame, Ind.: University of Notre Dame Press, 1990.

———. *Whose Justice? Which Rationality?* Notre Dame, Ind.: University of Notre Dame Press, 1988.

Mackinder, Halford J. *Britain and the British Seas*. New York: D. Appleton, 1902.

———. *Democratic Ideals and Reality: A Study in the Politics of Reconstruction*. London: Constable, 1919.

———. "The Geographical Pivot of History." *Geographical Journal* 23 (1904): 421–437.

———. "On the Scope and Methods of Geography." In *Democratic Ideals and Reality* (1919). New York: Norton, 1962.

Madison, James. *The Federalist: A Collection of Essays, Written in Favour of the New Constitution, as Agreed upon by the Federal Convention, September 17, 1787*. 2 vols. New York: J. and A. M'Lean, 1788.

Maine, Henry James Sumner. *Ancient Law: Its Connection with the Early History of Society and Its Relation to Modern Ideas*. London: J. Murray, 1861.

Mair, Lucy Philip. *Anthropology and Development*. London: Macmillan, 1984.

———. *Anthropology and Social Change*. London: Athlone Press/Humanities Press, 1969.

———. *New Nations*. Chicago: University of Chicago Press, 1963.

———. *Primitive Government*. Baltimore, Md.: Penguin, 1962.

Malinowski, Bronislaw. *Argonauts of the Western Pacific: An Account of Native Enterprise and Adventure in the Archipelagoes of Melanesian New Guinea*. London: G. Routledge and Sons, 1922.

———. *Coral Gardens and Their Magic: A Study of the Methods of Tilling the Soil and of Agricultural Rites in the Trobriand Islands*. New York: American Book Company, 1935.

———. *Crime and Custom in Savage Society*. London: Routledge and Kegan Paul, 1926.

———. *Magic, Science and Religion and Other Essays*. 1925. Reprint, New York: Doubleday, 1954.

———. *The Family among the Australian Aborigines: A Sociological Study*. London: University of London Press, 1913.

———. *A Scientific Theory of Culture and Other Essays*. Chapel Hill, N.C.: The University of North Carolina Press, 1944.

———. *The Sexual Life of Savages in North-Western Melanesia: An Ethnographic Account of Courtship, Marriage, and Family Life among the Natives of the Trobriand Islands, British New Guinea*. New York: Halcyon House, 1929.

Malthus, Thomas Robert. *Essay on the Principles of Population as It Affects the Future Improvement of Society with Remarks on the Speculations of Mr. Godwin, M. Condorcet and Other Writers* (1798). London: Macmillan, 1926.

Mannheim, Karl. *Essays on the Sociology of Culture*. Edited by Ernest Manheim and Paul Kecskemeti. London: Routledge and Kegan Paul, 1956.

———. *Freedom, Power, and Democratic Planning*. New York: Oxford University Press, 1950.

———. *Ideology and Utopia: An Introduction to the Sociology of Knowledge*. Translated from German by Louis Wirth and Edward Shils. New York: Harcourt, Brace, and World, 1936. Originally published as *Ideologie und Utopie* (1929).

———. *Man and Society*. Translated from German by Edward Shils. New York: Harcourt, Brace, 1940. Originally published as *Mensch und Gesellschaft im Zeitalter des Umbaus*. (Leiden, the Netherlands: A. W. Sijthoff, 1935).

March, James G. *Decisions and Organizations*. New York: Blackwell, 1988.

———. *Democratic Governance*. New York: Free Press, 1995.

———. *A Primer on Decision Making: How Decisions Happen*. New York: Free Press, 1994.

———. *The Pursuit of Organizational Intelligence*. Malden, Mass.: Blackwell, 1999.

March, James G., and Cohen M. D. *Leadership and Ambiguity: The American College President.* New York: McGraw-Hill, 1974.

March, James G., and Johan P. Olsen. *Rediscovering Institutions: The Organizational Basis of Politics.* New York: Free Press, 1989.

Marcuse, Herbert. *Eros and Civilization: A Philosophical Inquiry into Freud.* Boston: Beacon Press, 1955.

———. *An Essay on Liberation.* Boston: Beacon Press, 1969.

———. *Five Lectures: Psychoanalysis, Politics, and Utopia.* Translations from German by Jeremy J. Shapiro and Shierry M. Weber. Boston: Beacon Press, 1970.

———. *Negations: Essays in Critical Theory.* Translated from German by Jeremy J. Shapiro. Boston: Beacon Press, 1968.

———. *One-Dimensional Man: Studies in the Ideology of Advanced Industrial Society.* Boston: Beacon Press, 1964.

———. *Reason and Revolution: Hegel and the Rise of Social Theory.* London: Oxford University Press, 1941.

———. Marcuse, Herbert. "Repressive Tolerance." In *A Critique of Pure Tolerance*, edited by Robert Paul Wolff, Barrington Moore Jr., and Herbert Marcuse. London: Jonathan Cape, 1969.

Marrett, R. R. *The Threshold of Religion.* London: Methuen, 1909.

Marsh, George Perkins. *Man and Nature: or, Physical Geography as Modified by Human Action.* New York: Charles Scribner, 1864.

———. *Principles of Economics*, Vol 1. London: Macmillan, 1890.

Marshall, Thomas H. *Class, Citizenship and Social Development: Essays.* Garden City, N.Y.: Doubleday, 1964.

———. *Social Policy.* London: Hutchinson, 1965.

———. *The Right to Welfare and Other Essays.* New York: Free Press, 1981.

Marx, Karl. *The Eighteenth Brumaire of Louis Bonaparte.* Translated from German by Daniel De Leon. Chicago: Charles H. Kerr, 1907. Originally published as *Der Aschtzehnte Brumaire des Louis Bonaparte* (1852).

———. *Capital: A Critique of Political Economy.* 2 vols. Translated from German by B. Fowkes. New York: E. P. Dutton, 1930. Originally published as *Das Kapital.* 3 vols. (1867–1894).

———. *The Civil War in France.* New York: International, 1940. Originally published as *Der Bürgerkrieg in Frankreich* (Leipzig: Franke's Verlag, n.d.)

———. *The Class Struggles in France.* Translated from German by Henry Kuhn. New York: New York Labor News Company, 1924. Originally published as *Klassenkampfe in Frankenreich 1848–1850* (1850).

———. *Contribution to the Critique of Political Economy.* Translated from German by S. W. Ryazanskaya. New York: International, 1970. Originally published as *Zur Kritik der politischen Ökonomie* (1859).

———. *Economic and Philosophical Manuscripts of 1844.* In *Marx-Engels Collected Works Volume 3.* Translated from German by Andy Blunden. N.p.: Progress Publishers, 1932.

———. *The Poverty of Philosophy, Being a Translation of the Misere de la philosophie (A Reply to "La philosophie de la misere" of M. Proudhon).* Preface by Friedrich Engels. 1848 speech translated from German by H. Quelch. Chicago: C. H. Kerr, 1934.

Marx, Karl, and Friedrich Engels. *Communist Manifesto.* Edited and annotated by Frederick Engels. New York: New York Labor News, 1948. Originally published as *Manifest der Kommunistischen Partei* (London: Gedruckt in der Office der "Bildungs-Gesellschaft fur Arbeiter," 1848).

———. *German Ideology: Including Theses on Feuerbach and Introduction to The Critique of Political Economy.* Amherst, N.Y.: Prometheus Books, 1998. Originally published as *Die deutsche Ideologie: Kritik der neuesten deutschen Philosophie in ihren Reprasentanten, Feuerbach, B. Bauer und Stirner, und des deutschen Sozialismus in seinen verschiedenen Propheten, 1845–1846* (1846).

———. *The Holy Family: Or Critique of Critical Criticism against Bruno Bauer and Company.* Translated from German by R. Dixon. Moscow: Foreign Languages Publishing House, 1956. Originally published as *Die heilige familie: oder, Kritik der kritischen kritik* (Frankfurt am Main: Literarische Anstalt [J. Rutten], 1845).

Maslow, A. H. *Motivation and Personality.* New York: Harper and Row, 1954.

Mauss, Marcel. *The Gift: Forms and Functions of Exchange in Archaic Societies.* Translated from French by Ian Cunnison. New York: Norton, 1967. Originally published as *Essai sur le Don, Forme et Raison de l'Echange dans les Sociétés archaiques* (Paris: Alcan, 1925).

McLuhan, Marshall. *The Global Village: Transformations in World Life and Media in the 21st Century.* New York: Oxford University Press, 1989.

———. *The Gutenberg Galaxy: The Making of Typographic Man.* Toronto: University of Toronto Press, 1962.

———. *The Mechanical Bride: Folklore of Industrial Man.* New York: Vanguard Press, 1951.

———. *Understanding Media: The Extensions of Man.* New York: McGraw-Hill, 1964.

Mead, George Herbert. *Mind, Self and Society: From the Standpoint of a Social Behaviorist.* Chicago: University of Chicago Press, 1934.

———. *Movements of Thought in the Nineteenth Century.* Edited by Merritt H. Moore. Chicago: University of Chicago Press, 1936.

———. *The Philosophy of the Act.* Edited by Charles W. Morris, John M. Brewster, Albert M. Dunham, and

David L. Miller. Chicago: University of Chicago Press, 1938.

———. *The Philosophy of the Present.* Edited by Arthur E. Murphy. Chicago: Open Court, 1932.

Mead, Lawrence M. *The New Politics of Poverty: The Nonworking Poor in America.* New York: Basic Books, 1992.

Mead, Margaret. *And Keep Your Powder Dry: An Anthropologist Looks at America.* New York: William Morrow, 1942.

———. *Blackberry Winter: My Earlier Years.* New York: William Morrow, 1972.

———. *Coming of Age in Samoa: A Psychological Study of Primitive Youth for Western Civilisation.* New York: William Morrow, 1928.

———. *Culture and Commitment: The New Relationships between the Generations in the 1970s.* New York: Columbia University Press, 1978.

———. *Growing Up in New Guinea: A Comparative Study of Primitive Education.* New York: William Morrow, 1930.

———. *Male and Female: A Study of the Sexes in a Changing World.* New York: William Morrow, 1949.

———. *New Lives for Old: Cultural Transformations, Manus, 1928-1953.* New York: William Morrow, 1956.

———. *Ruth Benedict.* New York: Columbia University Press, 1974.

———. *Sex and Temperament in Three Primitive Societies.* 1935. Reprint, New York: William Morrow, 1963.

Medvedev, Pavel, and Mikhail Bakhtin. *The Formal Method in Literary Scholarship: A Critical Introduction to Sociological Poetics.* Translated from Russian by Albert Wehrle. Baltimore, Md.: Johns Hopkins University Press, 1973. Originally published as *Formal'nyi metod v literaturovedenii* (1928).

Merriam, Charles Edward. *American Political Ideas: Studies in the Development of American Political Thought, 1865-1917.* New York: Macmillan, 1920.

———. *Chicago: A More Intimate View of Urban Politics.* New York: Macmillan, 1929.

———. *The Making of Citizens: A Comparative Study of Methods of Civic Training.* Chicago: University of Chicago Press, 1931.

———. *New Aspects of Politics.* Chicago: University of Chicago Press, 1925.

———. *Political Power: Its Composition and Incidence.* New York and London: Whittlesey House, McGraw-Hill, 1934.

———. *Systematic Politics.* Chicago: University of Chicago Press, 1945.

Merton, Robert K. *Science, Technology and Society in Seventeenth Century England.* Bruges, Belgium: Saint Catherine Press, 1938.

———. "Social Structure and Anomie." *American Sociological Review* 3 (1938): 672–682.

———. "Social Structure and Anomie: Revisions and Extensions." In *The Family,* edited by Ruth Anshen. New York: Harper Brothers, 1949.

———. *Social Theory and Social Structure: Toward the Codification of Theory and Research.* Glencoe, Ill.: Free Press, 1949. Reprints, New York: Free Press of Glencoe, 1957, 1968.

———. "The Unanticipated Consequences of Purposive Social Action." *American Sociological Review* 1 (1936): 894–904.

Merton, Robert K., and Alice Kitt. "Contributions to the Theory of Reference Group Behavior." In *Continuities in Social Research: Studies in the Scope and Method of "The American Soldier,"* edited by Robert K. Merton and Paul F. Lazarsfeld. Glencoe, Ill.: Free Press, 1950.

Merton, Robert, and Robert Nisbet. *Contemporary Social Problems: An Introduction to the Sociology of Deviant Behavior and Social Disorganization.* New York: Harcourt, Brace, and World, 1961.

Michels, Robert. *First Lectures in Political Sociology.* Translated from Italian by A. de Grazia. Minneapolis: University of Minnesota Press, 1949. Originally published as *Corso di sociologia politica* (Milan: Instituto Editoriale Scientifico, 1927).

———. *Political Parties: A Sociological Study of the Oligarchical Tendencies of Modern Democracy.* Translated from German by Eden and Cedar Paul. New York: Collier Books, 1962. Originally published as *Zur Sociologie des Parteiwesens* (1911).

Milgram, Stanley. *Obedience to Authority: An Experimental View.* New York: Harper and Row, 1974.

———. *The Individual in a Social World: Essays and Experiments.* Edited by John Sabini and Maury Silver. New York: McGraw-Hill, 1992.

———. *The Small World.* Norwood, N.J.: Ablex, 1989.

Milgram, Stanley, and R. Lance Shotland. *Television and Anti-Social Behavior: Field Experiments.* New York: Academic Press, 1973.

Miliband, R. *The State in Capitalist Society.* London: Weidenfeld and Nicolson, 1969.

Mill, James. *Elements of Political Economy.* London: Baldwin, Cradock, and Joy, 1821.

Mill, John Stuart. *Considerations on Representative Government.* London: Parker, Son, and Bourn, 1861.

———. *Essays on Some Unsettled Questions of Political Economy.* London: J. W. Parker, 1844.

———. *Examination of Sir William Hamilton's Philosophy and of the Principal Philosophical Questions Discussed in His Writings.* London: Longman, Green, Longman, Roberts and Green, 1865.

———. *On Liberty.* London: J. W. Parker, 1859.

———. *Principles of Political Economy with Some of Their Applications to Social Philosophy.* 2 vols. London: J. W. Parker, 1848.

———. *A System of Logic, Ratiocinative and Inductive: Being a Connected View of the Principles of Evidence, and the Methods of Scientific Investigation.* London: J. W. Parker, 1843.

———. *The Subjection of Women.* London: Longmans, Green, Reader, and Dyer, 1869.

———. *Utilitarianism.* London: Parker, Son, and Bourn, 1863.

Mills, Charles Wright. *The Causes of World War Three.* New York: Simon and Schuster, 1958.

———. *Listen Yankee: The Revolution in Cuba.* New York: McGraw-Hill, 1960.

———. *The Marxists.* New York: Dell, 1962.

———. *The New Men of Power: America's Labor Leaders.* New York: Harcourt, Brace, 1948.

———. *The Power Elite.* New York: Oxford University Press, 1956.

———. *Power, Politics and People.* Edited by I. L. Horowitz. New York: Oxford University Press, 1963.

———. *The Sociological Imagination.* New York: Oxford University Press, 1959.

———. *White Collar.* New York: Oxford University Press, 1951.

Mises, Ludwig von. *The Theory of Money and Credit.* Translated from German by H. E. Batson. Indianapolis, Ind.: Liberty Classics, 1980. Originally published as *Theorie des Geldes und der Umlaufsmittel* (Munich, Leipzig: Duncker and Humblot, 1912).

Mitchell, Wesley Clair. *Business Cycles and Their Causes.* Berkeley: University of California Press, 1913.

———. *Business Cycles: The Problem and Its Setting.* New York: National Bureau of Economic Research, 1927.

Modigliani F., and R. Brumberg. "Utility Analysis and the Consumption Function: An Interpretation of Cross-Section Data." In *Post-Keynesian Economics*, edited by K. K. Kurihara. New Brunswick, N.J.: Rutgers University Press, 1954.

Montesquieu, Charles Louis de Secondat, Baron de. *Considerations on the Causes of the Greatness of the Romans and Their Decline.* Translated from French by David Lowenthal. Ithaca, N.Y.: Cornell University Press, 1965. Originally published as *Consideration sur les causes de la grandeur des Romains et de leur decadance* (Amsterdam: Chez Jaques [sic] Desbordes, 1734).

———. *The Persian Letters.* Translated from French by George R. Healy. Indianapolis, Ind.: Bobbs-Merrill, 1964. Originally published as *Lettres persanes* (Cologne: Chez Pierre Marteau, 1721).

———. *The Spirit of the Laws.* Translated from French by Thomas Nugent. New York: Hafner, 1949. Originally published as *De l'esprit des lois: ou Du rapport que les loix doivent avoir avec la constitution de chaque gouvernement, les moeurs, le climat, la religion, le commerce, etc.; a quoi l'auteur a ajouté. Des recherches nouvelles sur les loix romaines touchant les successions, sur les loix françoises, et sur les loix féodales* (Geneva: Chez Barillot, et fils, 1748).

Moore, Jr., Barrington. *Injustice: The Social Bases of Obedience and Revolt.* White Plains, N.Y.: M. E. Sharpe, 1978.).

———. *Moral Purity and Persecution in History.* Princeton, N.J.: Princeton University Press, 2000.

———. *Political Power and Social Theory: Six Studies.* Cambridge, Mass.: Harvard University Press, 1958.

———. *Reflections on the Causes of Human Misery and upon Certain Proposals to Eliminate Them.* Boston: Beacon Press, 1972.

———. *Social Origins of Dictatorship and Democracy: Lord and Peasant in the Making of the Modern World.* Boston: Beacon Press, 1966.

———. *Soviet Politics: The Dilemma of Power: The Role of Ideas in Social Change.* Cambridge, Mass.: Harvard University Press, 1950.

———. *Terror and Progress: USSR: Some Sources of Change and Stability in the Soviet Dictatorship.* Cambridge, Mass.: Harvard University Press, 1954.

Morgan, Lewis Henry. *Ancient Society, or Researches in the Lines of Human Progress from Savagery through Barbarism to Civilization* (1877). Tucson: University of Arizona Press, 1985.

———. *Houses and House-life of the American Aborigines.* Washington, D.C.: U.S. Government Printing Office, 1881.

———. *League of the Ho-dé-no-sau-nee, or Iroquois.* Rochester, N.Y.: Sage and Brother, 1851. Republished as *League of the Iroquois* (New York: Corinth, 1961).

———. *The American Beaver and His Works.* Philadelphia: J. B. Lippincott, 1868.

———. "Systems of Consanguinity and Affinity of the Human Family." In *Smithsonian Contributions to Knowledge* vol. 17, no. 218. Washington, D.C.: Smithsonian, 1871.

Morgenthau, Hans. *Politics among Nations: The Struggle for Power and Peace.* New York: Knopf, 1948.

———. *Politics in the Twentieth Century.* Chicago: University of Chicago Press, 1962.

———. *Scientific Man vs. Power Politics.* Chicago: University of Chicago Press, 1946.

Mosca, Gaetano. *The Ruling Class.* Edited by Arthur Livingston. Translated from Italian by Hannah D. Kahn. New York: McGraw-Hill, 1939. Originally published as *Elementi di scienza politica* (Rome: Bocca, 1896).

Mulvey, Laura. "Visual Pleasure and Narrative Cinema." *Screen* 16.3 (Fall 1975): 7.

Mundell, Robert. *The International Monetary System, Conflict and Reform.* Montreal: Canadian Trade Committee, Private Planning Association of Canada, 1965.

Myrdal, Alva, and Gunnar Myrdal. *Kris i befolkningsfrågan* (Crisis in the Population Question). Stockholm: Bonnier, 1934.

Myrdal, Gunnar. *Beyond the Welfare State: Economic Planning and Its International Implications.* New Haven, Conn.: Yale University Press, 1960.

————. *Rich Lands and Poor: The Road to World Prosperity.* New York: Harper, 1957. Republished as *Economic Theory and Underdeveloped Regions* (New York: Harper and Row, 1971).

Myrdal, Gunnar, R. M. E. Sterner, and Arnold Rose. *An American Dilemma: The Negro Problem and Modern Democracy.* New York: Harper and Row, 1944.

Nadel, Siegfried Frederick. *A Black Byzantium: The Kingdom of Nupe in Nigeria.* London and New York: Published for the International Institute of African Languages and Cultures by the Oxford University Press, 1942.

————. *The Foundations of Social Anthropology.* London: Cohen and West, 1951.

————. *The Nuba: An Anthropological Study of the Hill Tribes in Kordofan.* London and New York: Oxford University Press, 1947.

————. *Nupe Religion.* London: Routledge and Kegan Paul, 1954.

————. *The Theory of Social Structure.* Glencoe, Ill.: Free Press, 1957.

Nash, John. "Equilibrium Points in n-Person Games." *Proceedings of the National Academy of Science* 36 (1950–1951): 48–49.

————. "The Bargaining Problem." *Econometrica* 18 (1950): 128–140.

————. "Non-Cooperative Games." *Annals of Mathematics* 54 (1951): 286–295.

Neumann, Franz. *Behemoth: The Structure and Practice of National Socialism.* Toronto and New York: Oxford University Press, 1942.

Nie, Norman H., Sidney Verba, and John R. Petrocik. *The Changing American Voter.* Cambridge, Mass.: Harvard University Press, 1976.

Nietzsche, Friedrich. *The Antichrist.* Translated from German and introduced by H. L. Mencken. Torrance, Calif.: Noontide Press, 1980. Originally published as *Antichrist* (1895).

————. *Beyond Good and Evil: Prelude to a Philosophy of the Future.* Translated from German by Marianne Cowan. Chicago: Gateway Editions, distributed by H. Regnery, 1955. Originally published as *Jenseits von Gut und Bose: Vorspiel einer Philosophie der Zukunft* (Leipzig: C. G. Naumann, 1886).

————. *The Birth of Tragedy and the Genealogy of Morals.* Translated from German by Francis Golffing. Garden City, N.Y.: Doubleday, 1956. Originally published as *Die Geburt der Tragodie aus dem Geiste der Musik* (Leipzig: E. W. Fritzsch, 1872).

————. *The Gay Science.* Translated from German by Walter Kaufmann. New York: Vintage Books, 1974. Originally published as *Die frohliche Wissenschaft* (New York: E. Steiger, 1882).

————. *On the Genealogy of Morals.* Translated from German by Walter Kaufmann and R. J. Hollingdale. New York: Vintage Books, 1967. Originally published as *Zur Genealogie der Moral: Eine Streitschrift* (Leipzig: C. G. Naumann, 1887).

————. *The Twilight of the Idols, or, How to Philosophize with the Hammer.* Translated from German by Richard Polt. Indianapolis, Ind.: Hackett Publishing, 1997. Originally published as *Götzendämmerung* (1889).

————. *Thus Spake Zarathustra.* 4 vols. Translated from German by Thomas Common. New York: Modern Library, 1954. Originally published as *Also sprach Zarathustra: Ein Buch fur Alle und Keinen* (Leipzig: E. W. Fritzsch, 1883–1891).

Nisbet, Robert A. *Emile Durkheim.* Englewood Cliffs, N.J.: Prentice-Hall, 1965.

————. *History of the Idea of Progress.* New York: Basic Books, 1980.

————. *Prejudices: A Philosophical Dictionary.* Cambridge, Mass.: Harvard University Press, 1982.

————. *The Quest for Community.* London and New York: Oxford University Press, 1953.

————. *The Social Bond: An Introduction to the Study of Society.* New York: Knopf, 1970.

————. *Social Change and History.* London: Heinemann, 1966.

————. *The Sociological Tradition.* New York: Basic Books, 1966.

————. *Tradition and Revolt.* New York: Random House, 1968.

Nisbet, Robert A., and Tom Bottomore, eds. *A History of Sociological Analysis.* New York: Basic Books, 1978.

Nozick, Robert. *Anarchy, State, and Utopia.* New York: Basic Books, 1974.

Nurkse, Ragnar. *Problems of Capital Formation in Underdeveloped Countries.* New York: Oxford University Press, 1953.

Oakeshott, Michael. *Experience and Its Modes.* Cambridge: Cambridge University Press, 1933.

————. *Hobbes on Civil Association.* Berkeley: University of California Press, 1975.

————. *On History and Other Essays.* Totowa, N.J.: Barnes and Noble, 1983.

————. *On Human Conduct.* Oxford: Clarendon Press, 1975.

————. *Rationalism and Politics, and Other Essays.* New York: Basic Books, 1962.

————. *The Social and Political Doctrine of Contemporary Europe.* Cambridge: Cambridge University Press, 1939.

Olson, Jr., Mancur. *The Logic of Collective Action: Public Goods and the Theory of Groups.* Cambridge, Mass.: Harvard University Press, 1965.

————. *Power and Prosperity: Outgrowing Communist and Capitalist Dictatorships.* 1996. Reprint, New York: Basic Books, 2000.

———. *The Rise and Decline of Nations: Economic Growth, Stagflation, and Social Rigidities.* New Haven, Conn.: Yale University Press, 1982.

Omi, Michael, and Howard Winant. *Racial Formation in the United States: From the Sixties to the Eighties.* London: Routledge, 1987.

Ortega y Gassett, José. *The Dehumanization of Art, and Other Essays on Art, Culture, and Literature.* Translated from Spanish by Albert Lee McVitty. Princeton, N.J.: Princeton University Press, 1948. Originally published as *La deshumanizacion del arte. Ideas sobre la novela.* (Madrid: Revista de Occidente, 1928).

———. *The Modern Theme.* Translated from Spanish by James Cleugh. New York: Norton, 1933. Originally published as *El tema de nuestro tiempo* (1923).

———. *The Revolt of the Masses.* Edited by Kenneth Moore. Translated from Spanish, annotated, and with an introduction by Anthony Kerrigan. Notre Dame, Ind.: University of Notre Dame Press, 1985. Originally published as *La rebelión de las masas* (Madrid: Revista de Occidente, 1930).

———. *Toward a Philosophy of History.* Translated from Spanish by Helene Weyl. New York: Norton, 1941.

Paine, Thomas. *The Rights of Man.* 2 vols. Boston: N.p., 1791–1792.

Pareto, Vilfredo. *Les systemes socialistes.* Geneva: Librarie Droz, 1965. Originally published as 2 volumes. Paris: Giard and Brière, 1902–1903.

———. *Manual of Political Economy.* Translated from Italian by Ann S. Schwier. Edited by Ann S. Schwier and Alfred N. Page. New York: A. M. Kelley, 1971. Originally published as *Manuale di economia politica* (1906).

———. *Mind and Society: Treatise on General Sociology.* 4 vols. Translated from Italian by A. Bongiorno and A. Livingston. New York: Harcourt, Brace, 1935. Originally published as *Trattato di sociologia generale* (Florence: G. Barbera, 1916).

———. *The Rise and Fall of the Elites.* New York: Arno Press, 1968. Originally published as "Applicazione di teorie sociologiche," in *Revista Italiana di sociologia* (1901): 402–456.

———. *The Transformation of Democracy.* Edited by Charles H. Powers. Translated from Italian by Renata Girola. New Brunswick, N.J.: Transaction Books, 1984. Originally published as *Trasformazione della democrazia* (1920).

Park, Robert Ezra, and Ernest W. Burgess. *Introduction to the Science of Sociology.* Chicago: University of Chicago Press, 1921.

Parsons, Talcott. *Politics and Social Structure.* New York: Free Press, 1969.

———. *The Social System.* Glencoe, Ill.: Free Press, 1951.

———. *Societies: Evolutionary and Comparative Perspectives.* Englewood Cliffs, N.J.: Prentice-Hall, 1966.

———. *The Structure of Social Action.* 1937. Reprint, New York: Free Press, 1968.

———. *The System of Modern Societies.* Englewood Cliffs, N.J.: Prentice-Hall, 1971.

Parsons, Talcott, and Edward Shils. *Towards a General Theory of Action.* New York: Harper Torchbooks, 1951.

Parsons, Talcott, and Neil J. Smelser. *Economy and Society: A Study in the Integration of Economic and Social Theory.* New York: Free Press, 1965.

Partisan Review. New York: John Reed Club, 1934–1935.

Pateman, Carol. *Participation and Democratic Theory.* Cambridge: Cambridge University Press, 1970.

Patterson, Orlando. *Freedom in the Making of Western Culture,* Vol. 1. 2 vols. (Vol. 2 in press) New York: Basic Books, 1991.

———. *Slavery and Social Death: A Comparative Study.* Cambridge, Mass.: Harvard University Press, 1982.

Pavlov, I. P. *Conditioned Reflexes: An Investigation of the Physiological Activity of the Cerebral Cortex.* Translated from Russian by G. V. Anrep. London: Oxford University Press, 1927. Originally published as *Dvadtsatiletnii opyt obektivnogo izucheniia vysshei nervnoi deiatel'nosti zhivotnykh* (1923).

Peirce, Charles Sanders. "The Fixation of Belief." *Popular Science Monthly* 12 (Nov. 1877): 1–15.

———. "How to Make Our Ideas Clear." *Popular Science Monthly* 12 (Jan. 1878): 286–302.

Phelps, E. S. "Phillips Curves, Expectations of Inflation, and Optimal Unemployment over Time." *Economica* 34 (1968): 254–281.

Phillips, Anne. *The Politics of Presence.* New York: Oxford University Press, 1995.

Piaget, Jean. *Biology and Knowledge: An Essay on the Relations between Organic Regulations and Cognitive Processes.* Translated from French by Beatrix Walsh. Chicago: University of Chicago Press, 1971. Originally published as *Biologie et connaissance: Essai sur les relations entre les régulations organiques et les processus cognitifs* (Paris: Gallimard, 1967).

———. *The Child's Conception of Physical Causality.* Translated from French by Marjorie Gabain. New York, Harcourt, Brace, 1930. Originally published as *La causalité physique chez l'enfant, avec le concours de dix-sept collaborateurs* (Paris: Librairie Felix Alcan, 1927).

———. *The Child's Conception of the World.* Translated from French by Joan and Andrew Tomlinson. New York: Humanities Press, 1951. Originally published as *Representation du monde chez l'enfant* (Paris: PUF, 1926).

———. *The Construction of Reality in the Child.* Translated from French by Margaret Cook. New York: Basic Books, 1954. Originally published as *La construction du reel chez l'enfant* (Neuchâtel, Switzerland: Delachaux et Niestlé, 1937).

——. *The Development of Thought: Equilibration of Cognitive Structures*. Translated from French by Arnold Rosin. New York: Viking Press, 1977. Originally published as *L'équilibration des structures cognitives: Problème central du développement* (Paris: Presses Universitaires de France, 1975).

——. *The Language and Thought of the Child*. Translated from French by Marjorie Warden. New York: Harcourt, Brace, 1926. Originally published as *Langage et la pensée chez l'enfant* (Paris: Delachaux et Niestlé, 1923).

——. *The Moral Judgment of the Child*. Translated from French by Marjorie Gabain. London: K. Paul, Trench, Trubner, 1932. Originally published as *Le jugement moral chez l'enfant. Avec le concours de sept collaborateurs*. Nouvelle ed. (Paris: Presses Universitaires de France, 1956).

——. *The Origin of Intelligence in the Child*. Translated from French by Margaret Cook. London: Routledge and Kegan Paul, 1953. Originally published as *Naissance de l'intelligence chez l'enfant* (Geneva: Delachaux et Niestlé, 1936).

——. *The Principles of Genetic Epistemology*. Translated from French by Wolfe Mays. New York: Basic Books, 1972. Originally published as *L'Epistémologie génétique* (Paris: Presses Universitaires de France, 1970).

Pigou, Arthur. *The Economics of Welfare*. London: Macmillan, 1920.

Pike, Kenneth. *Language in Relation to a Unified Theory of the Structure of Human Behavior*. Vol. 1. 3 vols. Glendale, Calif.: Summer Institute of Linguistics, 1954.

Pitkin, Hanna F. *The Concept of Representation*. Berkeley: University of California Press, 1967.

Plamenatz, John P. *Consent, Freedom, and Political Obligation*. 2d ed. London and New York: Oxford University Press, 1968. Originally published in 1938.

Plato. *Plato: Works*. 10 vols. Translated from Greek by H. N. Fowler. New York: G. P. Putnam, 1914–1929.

——. *The Republic*. Translated from Greek by Robin Waterfield. Oxford: Oxford University Press, 1993.

Podgorecki, Adam, et al. *Knowledge and Opinion about Law*. London: M. Robertson, 1973.

Polanyi, Karl. *The Great Transformation: The Political and Economic Origins of Our Time*. Boston: Beacon Press, 2001. Originally published: New York: Farrar and Rinehart, 1944 and reprinted in Boston: Beacon Press, 1957.

Polanyi, Karl, Conrad M. Arensberg, and Harry W. Pearson, eds. *Trade and Market in the Early Empires; Economies in History and Theory*. Glencoe, Ill.: Free Press, 1957.

Pollock, Friedrich. *Die planwirtschaftlichen Versuche in der Sowjetunion, 1917–1927*. Leipzig: C. L. Hirschfeld, 1929.

Polsby, Nelson. *Community, Power and Political Theory*. New Haven, Conn.: Yale University Press, 1963.

Popper, Karl Raimund. *Conjectures and Refutations: The Growth of Scientific Knowledge*. New York: Basic Books, 1962.

——. *Objective Knowledge: An Evolutionary Approach*. Oxford: Clarendon Press, 1972.

——. *The Logic of Scientific Discovery*. Translated from German by Popper, et al. London: Hutchinson, 1959. Originally published as *Logik der Forschung; Zur Erkenntnistheorie der modernen Naturwissenschaft* (Vienna: J. Springer, 1935).

——. *The Open Society and Its Enemies*. London: G. Routledge and Sons, 1945.

——. *The Poverty of Historicism*. London: Routledge and Kegan Paul, 1957.

——. *Quantum Theory and the Schism in Physics*. London: Hutchinson, 1982.

Poulantzas, Nicos. *Political Power and Social Classes*. Translated from French by Timothy O'Hagan. London: Verso Editions, 1978. Originally published as *Pouvoir politique et classes sociales de l'etat capitaliste* (Paris: F. Maspero, 1968).

Prebisch, Raul. *Capitalismo Periférico—Crisis y Transformación*. Mexico City: Fondo de Cultura Económica, 1981.

——. *The Economic Development of Latin America and Its Principal Problems*. New York: United Nations, 1950.

——. *Towards a Dynamic Development Policy for Latin America*. New York: United Nations, 1963.

Proudhon, Pierre-Joseph. *A General Idea of the Revolution in the Nineteenth Century*. Translated from French by John Beverley Robinson. New York: Haskell House, 1969. Originally published as *Idée générale de la révolution au XIXe siècle (Choix d'etudes sur la pratique revolutionnaire et industrielle)* (Paris: Garnier Frères, 1851).

——. *La justice dans la revolution et dans l'eglise*. 1858. 4 vols. (Paris: Fayard, 1988–1990).

——. *The Principle of Federation*. Translated from French by Richard Vernon. Toronto and Buffalo: University of Toronto Press, 1979. Originally published as *Du principe federatif et de la necessité de reconstituer le parti de la revolution* (Paris: E. Dentu, 1863).

——. *What is Property?* Edited and translated from French by Donald R. Kelley and Bonnie G. Smith. Cambridge and New York: Cambridge University Press, 1994. Originally published as *Qu'est-ce que la propriété? ou, Recherches sur le principe du droit et du gouvernement*, vol. 1:*mémoire* (Paris: Garnier Frères, Libraries, 1848).

Quesnay, François. *Tableau économique*. Edited, with new material, translations from French, and notes by Marguerite Kuczynski and Ronald L. Meek. London: Macmillan; New York: A. M. Kelley for the Royal Economic Society and the American

Economic Association, 1972. Originally published as *Tableau économique* (1758).

Radcliffe-Brown, A. R. *The Andaman Islanders*. New York: Free Press, 1964. Originally published in 1922.

———. "On the Concept of Function in Social Science." *American Anthropologist* 37 (1935): 392–402.

———. "The Social Organization of Australian Tribes." *The Oceania Monographs* (1930–1931): 134–163, 2062–46, 322–341, 426–456.

Radcliffe-Brown, A. R., ed. *Structure and Function in Primitive Society*. New York: Free Press, 1965. Originally published in 1935.

———. "On Joking Relationships." In *Structure and Function in Primitive Society*. 1935. Reprint, New York: Free Press, 1965. Originally published in 1935.

Radcliffe-Brown, A. R., and Daryll Forde, eds. *African Systems of Kinship and Marriage*. London: Oxford University Press, 1950.

Ratzel, Friedrich. *Anthropogeographie oder Grundzüge der Anwendung der Erdkunde auf die Geschichte* (Anthropology, or the basic elements of the application of geography to history). 2 vols. Stuttgart: J. Engelhorn, 1882.

———. *Die Vereinigten Staaten von Nord-Amerika* (The United States of North America). 2 vols. Munich: R. Oldenbourg, 1878–1880.

Rawls, John. "The Idea of Overlapping Consensus." *Oxford Journal of Legal Studies* 7 (1987): 1–25.

———. *Law of Peoples*. Cambridge, Mass.: Harvard University Press, 1999.

———. *Political Liberalism*. New York: Columbia University Press, 1993.

———. *A Theory of Justice*. Cambridge, Mass.: The Belknap Press of Harvard University Press, 1971.

Redfield, Robert. *The Folk Culture of the Yucatan*. Chicago: University of Chicago Press, 1941.

———. *Peasant Society and Culture: An Anthropological Approach to Civilization*. Chicago: University of Chicago Press, 1956.

Reich, Wilhelm. *Character-Analysis: Principles and Technique for Psychoanalysts in Practice and in Training*. Translated from German by Theodore P. Wolfe. New York: Orgone Institute Press, 1945. Originally published as *Charakteranalyse* (Cologne: Kiepenheuer and Witsch, 1934).

———. *The Function of the Orgasm: Sex-Economic Problems of Biological Energy*. 8 vols. Translated from German by Theodore P. Wolfe. New York: Noonday Press, 1961. Originally published as *Die Funktion des Orgasmus: Zur Psychopathologie und zur Soziologie des Geschlechtslebens* in *Neue Arbeiten zur ärztlichen Psychoanalyse*, no. 6 (Leipzig: Internationaler Psychoanalytischer Verlag, 1927).

———. *The Mass Psychology of Fascism*. Translated from German by Vincent R. Carfagno. New York: Farrar, Straus and Giroux, 1970. Originally published as *Massenpsychologie des Faschismus: Zur Sexualökonomie der politischen Reaktion und zur proletarischen Sexualpolitik* (Copenhagen: Verlag für Sexualpolitik, 1933).

Reingold, Howard. *The Virtual Community: Homesteading on the Electronic Frontier*. New York: HarperPerennial, 1993.

Ricardo, David. *An Essay on the Influence of a Low Price of Corn on the Profits of Stock: Showing the Inexpediency of Restrictions on Importation; with Remarks on Mr. Malthus' Two Last Publications: "An Inquiry into the Nature and Progress of Rent"* and *"The Grounds for an Opinion on the Policy of Restricting the Importation of Foreign Corn."* London: John Murray, 1815.

Riesman, David. *Principles of Political Economy and Taxation*. London: John Murray, 1817.

———. *Individualism Reconsidered, and Other Essays*. Glencoe, Ill.: Free Press, 1954.

———. *On Higher Education: The Academic Enterprise in an Era of Rising Student Consumerism*. San Francisco: Jossey-Bass, 1980.

Riesman, David, and Nathan Glazer. *Faces in the Crowd: Individual Studies in Character and Politics*. New Haven, Conn.: Yale University Press, 1952.

Riesman, David, Nathan Glazer, and Reuel Denney. *The Lonely Crowd: A Study of the Changing American Character*. New Haven, Conn.: Yale University Press, 1950.

Riesman, David, and Evelyn Thompson Riesman. *Conversations in Japan: Modernization, Politics and Culture*. New York: Basic Books, 1967.

Riker, William. *The Art of Political Manipulation*. New Haven: Yale University Press, 1986.

———. *Democracy in the United States*. New York: Macmillan, 1965.

———. *Liberalism against Populism: A Confrontation between the Theory of Democracy and the Theory of Social Choice*. San Francisco: W. H. Freeman, 1982.

———. *The Theory of Political Coalitions*. New Haven, Conn.: Yale University Press, 1962.

Ritter, Carl. *Die Erdkunde im Verhältniss zur Natur und zur Geschichte des Menschen: Oder allgemeine vergleichende Geographie, als sichere Grundlage des Studiums und Unterrichts in physikalischen und historischen Wissenschaften*. 2 vols. Berlin: G. Reimer, 1822–1859.

Ritzer, George. *The McDonaldization of Society*. Newbury Park, Calif.: Pine Forge Press, 1993.

Rivers, W. H. R. *Dreams and Primitive Culture: A Lecture Delivered in the John Rylands Library on the 10th April, 1918*. London: Longmans, Green, 1917–1918.

———. *The History of Melanesian Society*. Cambridge: Cambridge University Press, 1914.

———. *Kinship and Social Organization*. London: Constable, 1914.

———. *Social Organization*. Edited by W. J. Perry. London: Kegan Paul, Trench, Trubner, 1924.

Robinson, Joan. *The Accumulation of Capital*. London: Macmillan, 1956.

——. *The Economics of Imperfect Competition*. London: Macmillan, 1933.

——. *An Essay on Marxian Economics*. London: Macmillan, 1942.

Rogers, Carl. *Carl Rogers on Encounter Groups*. New York: Harper and Row, 1970.

——. *Client-Centered Therapy: Its Current Practice, Implications, and Theory*. With chapters contributed by Elaine Dorfman, Thomas Gordon, and Nicholas Hobbs. Boston: Houghton Mifflin, 1951.

——. *Freedom to Learn: A View of What Education Might Become*. Columbus, Ohio: C. E. Merrill, 1969.

Rosenau, Pauline Marie. *Post-Modernism and the Social Sciences: Insights, Inroads, Intrusions*. Princeton, N.J.: Princeton University Press, 1992.

Rosenberg, Morris. *Conceiving the Self*. New York: Basic Books, 1979.

Rosenstein-Rodan, Paul. "Problems of Industrialization of Eastern and South-Eastern Europe." *Economic Journal* 53 (Jun.–Sept. 1943): 202–211.

Rostow, Walt Whitman. *Rich Countries and Poor Countries: Reflections on the Past, Lessons for the Future*. Boulder, Colo.: Westview Press, 1987.

——. *Stages of Economic Growth: A Non-Communist Manifesto*. New York: Cambridge University Press, 1960. Rev. ed., 1990.

Rousseau, Jean-Jacques. *The Confessions; and Correspondence, Including the Letters to Malesherbes*. Translated from French by Christopher Kelly. Edited by Christopher Kelly, Roger D. Masters, and Peter G. Stillman. Hanover, N.H.: Published by University Press of New England (for) Dartmouth College, 1995. Originally published as *Confessions* (Geneva: N.p., 1770).

——. *Discourse on the Origin of Inequality*. Translated from French by Franklin Philip. Edited by Patrick Coleman. Oxford and New York: Oxford University Press, 1994. Originally published as *Discours sur l'origine et les fondements de l'inégalité parmi les hommes* (Amsterdam: Chez Marc Michel Rey, 1755).

——. *Emile*. 4 vols. Translated from French by Barbara Foxley. New York: E. P. Dutton, 1974. Originally published as *Emile, ou, De l'education* (Amsterdam: N.p., 1762).

——. *Discours sur les sciences et les arts. The first and second discourses*. Edited by Roger D. Masters. Translated from French by Roger D. Masters and Judith R. Masters. New York: St. Martin's Press, 1964. Originally published as *Discours qui a remporté le prix a l'Academie de Dijon en l'année 1750: Sur cette question proposée par la même academie: si le rétablissement des sciences et des arts a contribué à épurer les moeurs* (Geneva: Chez Barillot et fils, 1750).

——. *Politics and the Arts: Letter to M. D'Alembert on the Theatre*. Translated from French by Allan Bloom. Ithaca, N.Y.: Cornell University Press, 1960. Originally published as *J. J. Rousseau citoyen de Geneve, a Mr. d'Alembert . . . : Sur son article Geneve dans le VIIme volume de l'Encyclope et particulierement sur le projet d'etablir un theatre de comedie en cette ville . . . .* (Amsterdam: Chez Marc Michel Rey, 1758).

——. *The Social Contract, and Discourses*. Translated from French by G. D. H. Cole. New York: E. P. Dutton, 1950. Originally published as *Contrat social; ou, Principes du droit politique. Précédé de discours, lettre a D'Alembert sur les spectacles et suivi de considérations sur le gouvernement de Pologne et la réforme projetée en avril 1772. Lettre a M. De Beaumont, Archevéque de Paris* (Paris: Librairie Garnier Frères, 1762).

Russell, Richard J., and Fred B. Kniffen. *Culture Worlds*. New York: Macmillan, 1951.

Rybczynski, T. M. "Factor Endowments and Relative Commodity Prices." *Economica* 22 (1955): 336–341.

Sahlins, Marshall. *Culture and Practical Reason*. Chicago: University of Chicago Press, 1976.

——. *How "Natives" Think about Captain Cook, for Example*. Chicago: University of Chicago Press, 1995.

——. *Stone Age Economics*. New York: Aldine de Gruyter, 1972.

——. "Poor Man, Rich Man, Big Man, Chief: Political Types in Melanesia and Polynesia." *Comparative Studies in Society and History* 5.3 (1963): 285–303.

Sahlins, Marshall, and Elman R. Service, eds. *Evolution and Culture*. Ann Arbor: University of Michigan Press, 1960.

Said, Edward. *Orientalism*. London: Routledge and Kegan Paul, 1978.

Saint-Simon, Claude-Henri de Rouvroy. *De la réorganisation de la société européenne, ou de la nécessité et des moyens de rassembler les peuples de l'Europe en un seul corps politique en conservant à chacun son indépendance nationale, par M. le comté de Saint-Simon et par A. Thierry, son élève. (Octobre 1814)*. 1814. Reprint, Paris: Les Presses Françaises, 1925.

——. *New Christianity*. Translated from French by the Rev. J. E. Smith. London: B. D. Cousins and P. Wilson, 1834. Originally published as *Nouveau christianisme: Dialogues entre un conservateur et un novateur. Premier dialogue* (Paris: Bossange père, 1825).

Salamon, L. M. "The Rise of the Nonprofit Sector." *Foreign Affairs* 73.4 (Jul./Aug. 1994): 111–124.

Samuelson, Paul A. "Consumption Theory in Terms of Revealed Preference." *Economica* 15 (Nov. 1948): 243–253.

——. *Economics*. New York: McGraw-Hill, 1948.

——. *The Foundations of Economic Analysis*. Cambridge, Mass.: Harvard University Press, 1947.

———. "An Exact Consumption Loan Model with or without the Social Contrivance of Money." *Journal of Political Economy* 66 (1958): 467–482.

Sandmo, Agnar. 1971. "On the Theory of the Competitive Firm under Price Uncertainty." *American Economic Review* 61 (1971): 65–73.

Sapir, Edward. *Language*. New York: Harcourt, Brace, 1921.

Sartre, Jean-Paul. *Being and Nothingness: An Essay on Phenomenological Ontology*. Translated from French by Hazel E. Barnes. Secaucus, N.J.: Citadel Press, 1956. Originally published as *L'être et le néant, essai d'ontologie phénoménologique* (Paris: Gallimard, 1943).

———. *The Critique of Dialectical Reason: Theory of Practical Ensembles*. Translated from French by Alan Sheridan-Smith. Edited by Jonathan Rée. London: Verso, 1976. Originally published as *Critique de la raison dialectique, précédé de Question de méthode* (Paris: Gallimard, 1960).

———. *The Family Idiot: Gustave Flaubert, 1821–1857*. 5 vols. Translated from French by Carol Cosman. Chicago: University of Chicago Press, 1981–1993. Originally published as *L'idiot de la famille; Gustave Flaubert de 1821 à 1857* (Paris: Gallimard, 1971–).

———. *Nausea*. Translated from French by Lloyd Alexander. New York: New Directions, 1964. Originally published as *La nausée* (Paris: Gallimard, 1938).

———. *No Exit and Three Other Plays*. Translated from French by Stuart Gilbert. New York: Vintage Books, 1989. Originally published as *Huis clos: pièce en un acte* (Paris: Gallimard, 1945).

———. *Saint Genet, Actor and Martyr*. Translated from French by Bernard Frechtman. New York: Braziller, 1963. Originally published as *Saint Genêt, comédien et martyr* (Paris: Gallimard, 1952).

———. *The Words*. Translated from French by Bernard Frechtman. New York: Braziller, 1964. Originally published as *Les mots* (Paris: Gallimard, 1964).

Sauer, Carl. "The Agency of Man on Earth." In *Man's Role in Changing the Face of the Earth*, edited by William L. Thomas Jr. Chicago: University of Chicago Press, 1956.

———. *Agricultural Origins and Dispersals*. New York: American Geographical Society, 1952.

———. "The Morphology of Landscape." *University of California Publications in Geography* 2 (1925): 19–54.

Saussure, Ferdinand de. *Course in General Linguistics*. Translated from French by Wade Baskin. Edited by Charles Bally and Albert Sechehaye. New York: Philosophical Library, 1959. Originally published as *Cours de linguistique générale* (Paris: Payot, 1915).

Savage, L. J. *The Foundations of Statistics*. New York: Wiley, 1954.

Schelling, Thomas. *The Strategy of Conflict*. Cambridge, Mass: Harvard University Press, 1960.

Schmitt, Karl. *The Concept of the Political*. Translated from German by George Schwab. New Brunswick, N.J.: Rutgers University Press, 1976. Originally published as *Der Begriff des Politischen* (Hamburg: Hanseatische Verlagsanstalt, 1933).

———. *Political Romanticism*. Translated from German by Guy Oakes. Cambridge, Mass.: MIT Press, 1986. Originally published as *Politische Romantik* (Munich: Duncker und Humblot, 1919).

Schumpeter, Joseph A. *Capitalism, Socialism, and Democracy*. New York: Harper and Brothers, 1942. Originally published as *Kapitalismus, Sozialismus und Demokratie* (Tübingen: Francke, 1942).

———. *History of Economic Analysis*. New York: Oxford University Press, 1954. Published in German as *Geschichte der ökonomischen Analyse* (Göttingen: Vandenhoeck und Ruprecht, 1965).

———. *The Theory of Economic Development*. Translated from German by Redvers Opie. New York: Oxford University Press, 1961. Originally published as *Theorie der wirtschaftlichen Entwicklung* (Leipzig: Duncker und Humblot, 1912).

Schutz, Alfred. *Collected Papers*. 4 vols. Edited by Maurice Natanson. The Hague: M. Nijhoff, 1962–1966.

———. *The Phenomenology of the Social World*. Translated by George Walsh and Frederick Lehnert. Evanston, Ill.: Northwestern University Press, 1967. Originally published as *Der sinnhafte Aufbau der sozialen Welt: Eine Einleitung in die Verstehende Soziologie* (Vienna: J. Springer, 1932).

Schutz, Alfred, and Thomas Luckmann. *The Structures of the Life-World*. 2 vols. Translated from German by Richard M. Zaner and H. Tristram Engelhardt Jr. Evanston, Ill.: Northwestern University Press, 1973–1989. Published in German as *Strukturen der Lebenswelt* (Neuwied: H. Luchterhand, 1975).

Selten, Reinhard. "Reexamination of the Perfectness Concept for Equilibrium Points in Extensive Games." *International Journal of Game Theory* 4.1 (1975): 25–55. Reprinted in *Classics in Game Theory*, edited by H. W. Kuhn. Princeton, N.J.: Princeton University Press, 1997.

———. "Spieltheoretische Behandlung eines Oligopolmodells mit Nachfragetragheit." *Zeitschrift fur die gesamte Staatswissenschaft* 121 (1965): 301–324, 667–689.

Semple, Ellen Churchill. *American History in Its Geographic Conditions*. Boston: Houghton Mifflin, 1903.

———. *The Geography of the Mediterranean Region: Its Relation to Ancient History*. New York: H. Holt, 1931.

———. *Influences of Geographic Environment*. New York: H. Holt, 1911.

Service, Elman R. *Primitive Social Organization: An Evolutionary Perspective*. New York: Random House, 1962.

Sharpe, William. "Capital Asset Prices: A Theory of Market Equilibrium under Conditions of Risk." *Journal of Finance* 19 (1964): 425–442.

Sherif, M. *Common Predicament: Social Psychology of Intergroup Conflict and Cooperation.* Boston: Houghton Mifflin, 1966.

Sidrauski, M. "Rational Choice and Patterns of Growth in a Monetary Economy." *American Economic Review* 57 (1967): 534–544.

Simmel, Georg. "The Metropolis and Mental Life." In *The Sociology of Georg Simmel,* translated from German and edited by Kurt Wolff. New York: Free Press, 1950. Originally published as *Die Grosstadte und das Geistesleben* (1902–1903).

———. *The Sociology of Georg Simmel.* Translated from German and edited by Kurt Wolff. New York: Free Press, 1950. Original German essays include *Die Grosstadte und das Geistesleben* (1902–1903) and *Soziologie: Untersuchungen über die formen der vergesellschaftung* (Leipzig: Duncker und Humblot, 1908).

———. "The Stranger." In *The Sociology of Georg Simmel,* translated from German and edited by Kurt Wolff. New York: Free Press, 1950. Originally published in *Soziologie. Untersuchungen über die Formen der Vergesellschaftung* (Berlin: Duncker und Humblot, 1908).

———. *Grundfragen der Soziologie (Individuum und Gesellschaft).* Berlin and Leipzig: G. J. Göshen, 1917.

———. *Hauptprobleme der Philosophie.* Leipzig: G. J. Göschen, 1910.

———. *Lebensanschauung: Vier metaphysische Kapitel.* Munich and Leipzig: Duncker und Humblot, 1918.

———. *Philosophische Kultur: Gesammelte Essais.* Leipzig: W. Klinkhardt, 1911.

———. *The Philosophy of Money.* Translated from German by Tom Bottomore and David Frisby. London and Boston: Routledge and Kegan Paul, 1978. Originally published as *Philosophie des Geldes* (Leipzig: Duncker und Humblot, 1900).

Simon, Herbert. "A Behavioral Model of Rational Choice." *Quarterly Journal of Economics* LXIX (Feb. 1955): 95–118.

———. "A Comparison of Game Theory and Learning Theory." *Psychometrika* 21 (1956): 267–272.

———. *Models of Man.* New York: Wiley, 1956.

———. "Rational Choice and the Structure of the Environment." *Psychological Review* 63 (1956): 129–138.

Simon, Herbert, with R. M. Cyert and D. B. Trow. "Observation of a Business Decision." *Journal of Business* 29 (1956): 237–248.

Skinner, Burhus Frederic. *The Behavior of Organisms: An Experimental Analysis.* New York and London: Appleton-Century, 1938.

———. *Beyond Freedom and Dignity.* New York: Knopf, 1971.

———. *Science and Human Behavior.* New York: Macmillan, 1953.

———. *Verbal Behavior.* Englewood Cliffs, N.J.: Prentice-Hall, 1957.

———. *Walden Two.* New York: Macmillan, 1948.

Skocpol, Theda. *States and Social Revolutions: A Comparative Analysis of France, Russia, and China.* New York: Cambridge University Press, 1979.

Smelser, Neil J. *Comparative Methods in the Social Sciences.* Englewood Cliffs, N.J.: Prentice-Hall, 1976.

———. *Effective Committee Service.* Newbury Park, Calif.: Sage, 1993.

———. *Social Change in the Industrial Revolution: An Application of Theory to the British Cotton Industry.* Chicago: University of Chicago Press, 1959.

———. *The Social Edges of Psychoanalysis.* Berkeley: University of California Press, 1998.

———. *Social Paralysis and Social Change: British Working-Class Education in the Nineteenth Century.* Berkeley: University of California Press, 1991.

———. *Sociology of Economic Life.* Englewood Cliffs, N.J.: Prentice-Hall, 1963.

———. *Theory of Collective Behavior.* New York: Free Press of Glencoe, 1963.

Smelser, Neil J., ed. *Handbook of Sociology.* Newbury Park, Calif.: Sage, 1986.

Smelser, Neil J., and Richard Swedberg, eds. *Handbook of Economic Sociology.* Princeton, N.J.: Princeton University Press, 1994.

Smith, Adam. *An Inquiry into the Nature and Causes of the Wealth of Nations.* Chicago: University of Chicago Press, 1976. Originally published in 1776.

———. *Theory of Moral Sentiments.* Indianapolis, Ind.: Liberty Classics, 1976. Originally published in 1759.

Smith, Dorothy Elizabeth. *Conceptual Practices of Power: A Feminist Sociology of Knowledge.* Boston: Northeastern University Press, 1990.

———. *The Everyday Life as Problematic: A Feminist Sociology.* Boston: Northeastern University Press, 1987.

———. *Writing the Social: Critique, Theory and Investigations.* Toronto and Buffalo: University of Toronto Press, 1998.

Solow, Robert. *Capital Theory and the Rate of Return.* Amsterdam: North-Holland, 1963.

———. "A Contribution to the Theory of Growth." *Quarterly Journal of Economics* 70 (1956): 65–94.

———. *Growth Theory: An Exposition.* Oxford: Oxford University Press, 1969.

———. "Technical Change and the Aggregate Production Function." *Review of Economics and Statistics* 39.3 (Aug. 1957): 312–320.

Somers, Margaret R. "Symposium on Historical Sociology and Rational Choice Theory." *American Journal of Sociology* 104 (1998): 722–871.

Sorokin, Pitirim. *Contemporary Sociological Theories.* New York and London: Harper and Brothers, 1928.

——. *Fads and Foibles in Modern Sociology and Related Sciences.* Chicago: H. Regnery, 1956.

——. *Social and Cultural Dynamics.* 4 vols. New York: Bedminster Press, 1937.

——. *Social Mobility.* New York: Harper and Brothers, 1927.

——. *Sociological Theories of Today.* New York, Harper and Row, 1966.

——. *The Sociology of Revolution.* Philadelphia and London: J. B. Lippincott, 1925.

Sorokin, Pitirim, Carle C. Zimmerman, and Charles J. Galpin, eds. *A Systematic Source Book in Rural Sociology.* Minneapolis: University of Minnesota Press, 1930–1932.

Spencer, Herbert. *The Evolution of Society: Selections from Herbert Spencer's Principles of Sociology.* Edited by Robert L. Carneiro. Chicago: University of Chicago Press, 1967.

——. *First Principles.* 1862. Reprint, New York: A. L. Burt, 1880.

——. *The Principles of Psychology.* 1855. Reprint, Farnborough, England: Gregg International, 1970.

——. *Principles of Sociology.* 2 vols. 1874. Reprint, New York and London: D. Appleton, 1885.

——. *Social Statics: The Conditions Essential to Human Happiness Specified, and the First of Them Developed.* New York: Robert Schalkenbach Foundation, 1954. Originally published in 1850.

——. *The Study of Sociology.* Boston: Routledge and Kegan Paul, 1873.

——. *System of Synthetic Philosophy.* 9 vols. New York: D. Appleton, 1862–1896.

Stackelberg, Heinrich von. *Marktform und Gleichgewicht.* Vienna and Berlin: J. Springer, 1934.

Steuart, James. *An Inquiry into the Principles of Political Economy.* 2 vols. 1767. Reprint, edited by Andrew S. Skinner. Chicago: University of Chicago Press, 1966.

Steward, Julian. *Area Research: Theory and Practice.* New York: Social Science Research Council, 1950.

——. *Theory of Culture Change: The Methodology of Multilinear Evolution.* 1936. Reprint, Urbana: University of Illinois Press, 1955.

Steward, Julian, ed. *Contemporary Change in Traditional Societies.* 3 vols. Urbana: University of Illinois Press, 1967.

——. *Handbook of South American Indians.* 6 vols. Prepared in cooperation with the United States Department of State as a project of the Interdepartmental Committee on Cultural and Scientific Cooperation. Washington, D.C.: U.S. Government Printing Office, 1946–1959.

Steward, Julian, and Louis Faron. *Native Peoples of South America.* New York: McGraw-Hill, 1959.

Steward, Julian, et al. *The People of Puerto Rico: A Study in Social Anthropology.* Urbana: University of Illinois Press, 1956.

Stolper, Wolfgang, and Paul Samuelson. "Protection and Real Wages." *Review of Economic Studies* 9.1 (Nov. 1941): 58–73.

Strauss, Anselm. *Negotiations: Varieties, Contexts, Processes, and Social Order.* San Francisco: Jossey-Bass, 1978.

Strauss, Leo. *The City and Man.* Chicago: Rand McNally, 1964.

——. *Liberalism: Ancient and Modern.* New York: Basic Books, 1968.

——. *On Tyranny.* New York: Free Press of Glencoe, 1963.

——. *Persecution and the Art of Writing.* Glencoe, Ill.: Free Press, 1952.

——. *The Political Philosophy of Hobbes: Its Basis and Its Genesis.* Translated from the German manuscript by Elsa M. Sinclair. Oxford: Clarendon Press, 1936.

——. *Thoughts on Machiavelli.* Glencoe, Ill.: The Free Press, 1958.

Sumner, William G. *Folkways.* Boston: Ginn, 1906.

Sumner, William G., and Albert G. Keller. *The Science of Society.* New Haven, Conn.: Yale University Press, 1927.

Tannen, Deborah. *You Just Don't Understand: Women and Men in Conversation.* New York: Ballantine, 1990.

Taylor, Charles. *The Ethics of Authenticity.* Cambridge, Mass.: Harvard University Press, 1992.

——. *The Explanation of Behavior.* New York: Routledge and Kegan Paul, 1964.

——. *Hegel.* New York: Cambridge University Press, 1975.

——. *Hegel and Modern Society.* New York: Cambridge University Press, 1979.

——. *Human Agency and Language.* New York: Cambridge University Press, 1985.

——. "Modes of Civil Society. Public Culture." *Bulletin of the Center for Transnational Cultural Studies* 3.1 (Fall 1990): 95–118.

——. *Philosophical Arguments.* Cambridge, Mass.: Harvard University Press, 1995.

——. *Reconciling the Solitudes: Essays in Canadian Federalism and Nationalism.* Edited by Guy Laforest. Montreal and Buffalo: McGill–Queen's University Press, 1993.

——. *Sources of the Self: The Making of the Modern Identity.* Cambridge, Mass.: Harvard University Press, 1989.

——. "What's Wrong with Negative Liberty?" In *The Idea of Freedom: Essays in Honor of Isaiah Berlin,* edited by Allan Ryan. New York: Oxford University Press, 1979.

Taylor, Charles, et al. *Multiculturalism: Examining the Politics of Recognition.* Edited by Amy Gutmann. Princeton, N.J.: Princeton University Press, 1994.

The New Leader. New York: American Labor Conference on International Affairs, 1935–.

Thomas, William Isaac. *The Child in America*. New York: Knopf, 1928.

Thomas, William Isaac, and Florian Znaniecki. *The Polish Peasant in Europe and America*. 5 vols. Chicago: University of Chicago Press, 1918–1920.

Thompson, Edward Palmer. *The Making of the English Working Class*. New York: Vintage Books, 1963.

———. *Whigs and Hunters: The Origin of the Black Act*. New York: Pantheon Books, 1975.

———. *William Morris: Romantic to Revolutionary*. London: Lawrence and Wishart, 1955.

———. *Witness against the Beast: William Blake and the Moral Law*. New York: New Press, distributed by Norton, 1993.

———. *Writing by Candlelight*. London: Merlin, 1980.

Thompson, Edward Palmer, ed. *Warwick University Ltd.: Industry, Management and the Universities*. Harmondsworth: Penguin, 1970.

Tilly, Charles. *As Sociology Meets History*. New York: Academic Press, 1981.

———. *From Mobilization to Revolution*. Reading, Mass.: Addison-Wesley, 1978.

———. *The Vendée*. Cambridge, Mass.: Harvard University Press, 1964.

Tilly, Charles, Louise Tilly, and Richard Tilly. *The Rebellious Century, 1830–1930*. Cambridge, Mass.: Harvard University Press, 1975.

Tinbergen, Jan. "An Economic Policy for 1936." In *Jan Tinbergen: Selected Papers*, edited by L. Klaasen et al. Amsterdam: North-Holland, 1959.

Tobin, James. "Liquidity Preference as Behavior Towards Risk." *Review of Economic Studies* 25.4 (Feb. 1958): 65–86.

———. "The Interest-Elasticity of the Transactions Demand for Cash." *Review of Economics and Statistics* 38.3 (Aug. 1956): 241–247.

———. "Money and Economic Growth. "*Econometrica* 33.4 (1965): 671–684.

Tocqueville, Alexis de. *Democracy in America*. 2 vols. Translated from French by Henry Reeve. New York: J. and H. G. Langley, 1841. Originally published as *De la démocratie en Amérique* (Brussels: L. Hauman et Cie., 1835).

———. *The Old Regime and the French Revolution*. Translated from French by John Bonner. New York: Harper and Brothers, 1856. Originally published as *L'ancien régime et la Révolution* (Paris: Michel Levy Frères, 1856).

Tönnies, Ferdinand. *Community and Society*. Translated from German and edited by Charles P. Loomis. New York: Harper and Row, 1957. Originally published as *Gemeinschaft und Gesellschaft* (Reislad and Leipzig: N.p., 1887).

———. *Kritik der öffentlichen Meinung*. Berlin: Aalen, Nachdruck der Ausgabe, 1922.

Touraine, Alain. *The Post-Industrial Society: Tomorrow's Social History: Classes, Conflicts and Culture in the Programmed Society*. Translated from French by Leonard F. X. Mayhew. New York: Random House, 1971. Originally published as *La Société post-industrielle* (Paris: Denoël, 1969).

Truman, David. *The Congressional Party: A Case Study*. New York: Wiley, 1959.

———. *The Government Process: Political Interests and Public Opinion*. Westport, Conn.: Greenwood Press, 1951.

Truman, David, ed. *Congress and America's Future*. Englewood Cliffs, N.J.: Prentice-Hall, 1965.

Tuan, Yi Fu. *Landscapes of Fear*. New York: Pantheon, 1979.

———. *Man and Nature*. Washington, D.C.: Association of American Geographers, Commission on College Geography, 1971.

———. *Morality and Imagination: Paradoxes of Progress*. Madison: University of Wisconsin Press, 1989.

———. *Space and Place: The Perspectives of Experience*. Minneapolis: University of Minnesota Press, 1977.

———. *Topophilia: A Study of Environmental Perception, Attitudes, and Values*. Englewood Cliffs, N.J.: Prentice-Hall, 1974.

Turner, Ralph H., and Lewis M. Killian. *Collective Behavior*. Englewood Cliffs, N.J.: Prentice-Hall, 1972.

Turner, Victor. *Dramas, Fields and Metaphors: Symbolic Action in Human Society*. Ithaca, N.Y.: Cornell University Press, 1974.

———. *The Drums of Affliction: A Study of Religious Processes among the Ndembu of Zambia*. Oxford: Clarendon Press, 1968.

———. *The Forest of Symbols: Aspects of Ndembu Ritual*. Ithaca, N.Y.: Cornell University Press, 1967.

———. *Revelation and Divination in Ndembu Ritual*. Ithaca, N.Y.: Cornell University Press, 1975.

———. *The Ritual Process: Structure and Anti-Structure*. Chicago: Aldine, 1969.

Tvedt, Terje. *Angels of Mercy or Development Diplomats? NGOs and Foreign Aid*. Trenton, N.J.: Africa World Press, 1998.

Tylor, Sir Edward Burnett. *Anthropology: An Introduction to the Study of Man and Civilization*. New York, D. Appleton, 1881.

———. *Primitive Culture: Researches into the Development of Mythology, Philosophy, Religion, Language, Art and Custom*. London: John Murray, 1871.

———. *Researches into the Early History of Mankind and the Development of Civilization*. 1861. Reprint, London: John Murray, 1865.

Veblen, Thorstein. "The Preconceptions of Economic Science, Part 3." *The Quarterly Journal of Economics* 14.2 (1900): 240–269.

———. *The Theory of the Leisure Class: An Economic Study of Institutions*. New York: Macmillan, 1899.

Verba, Sidney. *Small Groups and Political Behavior: A Study of Leadership*. Princeton, N.J.: Princeton University Press, 1961.

Verba, Sidney, Bashiruddin Ahmed, and Anil Bhatt. *Caste, Race and Politics: A Comparison of India and the United States.* Beverly Hills, Calif.: Sage, 1971.

Verba, Sidney, Steven Kelman, et al. *Elites and the Idea of Equality: A Comparison of Japan, Sweden, and the United States.* Cambridge, Mass.: Harvard University Press, 1987.

Verba, Sidney, Gary King, and Robert O. Keohane. *Designing Social Enquiry: Scientific Inference in Qualitative Research.* Princeton, N.J.: Princeton University Press, 1994.

Verba, Sidney, Norman H. Nie, and Jae-on Kim. *Participation and Political Equality: A Seven-Nation Comparison.* Cambridge and New York: Cambridge University Press, 1978.

Verba, Sidney, and Gary R. Orren. *Equality in America: The View from the Top.* Cambridge, Mass.: Harvard University Press, 1985.

Verba, Sidney, Kay Schlozman, and Henry Brady. *Voice and Equality: Civic Voluntarism in American Politics.* Cambridge, Mass.: Harvard University Press, 1995.

Vico, Giambattista. *The Autobiography of Giambattista Vico.* Translated from Italian by Max Harold Fisch and Thomas Goddard Bergin. Ithaca, N.Y.: Cornell University Press, 1944. Originally published as "Vita di G. B. Vico scritta da se medesimo." In *Raccolta di opuscoli scientifici e filologici* (Venice: Angelo Calogerà, 1728).

———. *The New Science of Giambattista Vico.* 2 vols. Translated from Italian by Thomas Goddard Bergin and Max Harold Fisch. Ithaca, N.Y.: Cornell University Press, 1968. Originally published as *Principi di una scienza nuova intorno alla natura della nazioni per la quale si ritruovano i principi di altro sistema del diritto naturale delle genti all'eminentiss, principe Lorenzo Corsini amplissimo cardinale dedicati* (Naples: F. Mosca, 1725).

———. *On the Study Methods of Our Time.* Translated from Latin by Elio Gianturco. Indianapolis, Ind.: Bobbs-Merrill, 1965. Originally published as *De nostri temporis studiorum ratione* (Naples: Typis Felicis Mosca, 1709).

Vidal de la Blache, Paul. *Etats et nations de l'Europe: Autour de la France.* Edited by C. Delagrave. Paris: N.p., 1889.

———. *La France de l'Est (Lorraine-Alsace).* Paris: A. Colin, 1917.

———. *Principles of Human Geography.* Edited by Emmanuel de Martonne. Translated from French by Millicent Todd Bingham. New York: H. Holt, 1926. Originally published as *Principes de géographie humaine publiés d'apres les manuscrits de l'auteur* (Paris: A. Colin, 1922).

———. *Tableau de la géographie de la France.* Paris: Librairie Hachette, 1911. Originally published in 1903.

Vidal de la Blache, Paul, and Lucien Gallois, eds. *Géographie Universelle.* 15 vols. Paris: A. Colin, 1927–1948.

Volosinov, V. N. *Marxism and the Philosophy of Language.* Translated from Russian by Ladislav Matejka and I. R. Titunik. Cambridge, Mass.: Harvard University Press, 1973. Originally published as *Marksizm i filosofiia iazyka; osnovnye problemy sotsiologicheskogo metoda v nauke o iazyke* (Leningrad: Priboi, 1930).

Von Neumann, John, and Oskar Morgenstern. *The Theory of Games and Economic Behavior.* 1944. Reprint, Princeton, N.J.: Princeton University Press, 1947.

Wallerstein, Immanuel. *After Liberalism.* New York: New Press, distributed by Norton, 1995.

———. *The Capitalist World Economy: Essays.* Cambridge and New York: Cambridge University Press, 1979.

———. *Historical Capitalism.* London: Verso, 1983.

———. *The Modern World System.* 3 vols. Vol. 1: New York: Academic Press, 1974. Vol. 2: New York: Cambridge University Press, 1984. Vol. 3: New York: Cambridge University Press, 1988.

———. *Unthinking Social Science: The Limits of Nineteenth-Century Paradigms.* Cambridge, Mass.: Polity Press, in association with B. Blackwell, 1991.

Walras, Leon. *Elements of Pure Economics.* Translated from French by William Jaffe. London: Published for the American Economic Association and the Royal Economic Society by Allen and Unwin, 1954. Originally published as *Éléments d'économie politique pure; ou, Théorie de la richesse sociale* (Lausanne: F. Rouge, 1889).

Walzer, Michael. *Spheres of Justice: A Defense of Pluralism and Equality.* New York: Basic Books, 1983.

Watson, J. B. *Behaviorism.* New York: Norton, 1925.

Weber, Alfred. *Kulturgeschichte als Kultursoziologie.* Leiden, the Netherlands: A. W. Sijthoff, 1935.

———. *Theory of the Location of Industries.* Translated from German by Carl J. Friedrich. New York, Russell and Russell, 1971. Originally published as *Reine Theorie des Standorts* (Tübingen: Universitat Tübingen, 1909).

Weber, Max. *Economy and Society: An Outline of Interpretive Sociology.* Translated from German by E. Fischoff. Edited by Guenther Roth and Claus Wittich. New York: Bedminster Press, 1968. Originally published as *Wirtschaft und Gesellschaft: Grundriss der verstehenden Soziologie* (Tübingen: N.p., 1922).

———. *The Protestant Ethic and the Spirit of Capitalism.* Translated from German by Talcott Parsons. New York: Scribners, 1958. Originally published as *Die protestantische Ethik und der "Geist" des Kapitalismus* (Leipzig: J.C.B. Mohr (P. Siebeck): 1904).

———. "Politics as a Vocation." In *From Max Weber: Essays in Sociology,* edited by H. H. Gerth and C. Wright Mills. London: Routledge and Kegan Paul, 1948.

——. "Science as a Vocation." In *From Max Weber: Essays in Sociology*, edited by H. H. Gerth and C. Wright Mills. London: Routledge and Kegan Paul, 1948.

Weiner, N. *Cybernetics*. Cambridge, Mass.: MIT Press, 1948.

White, Leslie A. *The Concept of Cultural Systems*. New York: Columbia University Press, 1975.

——. *The Evolution of Culture: The Development of Civilization to the Fall of Rome*. New York: McGraw-Hill, 1959.

——. *The Science of Culture: A Study of Man and Civilization*. New York: Farrar, Straus, 1949.

——. *The Social Organization of Ethnological Theory: Monograph in Cultural Anthropology*. Houston, Tex.: William Marsh Rice University, 1966.

White, Leslie A., and Beth Dillingham. *The Concept of Culture*. Minneapolis, Minn.: Burgess, 1973.

Whorf, Benjamin Lee. *Language, Thought and Reality*. Cambridge, Mass.: MIT Press, 1956.

Whyte, William H. *Organization Man*. New York: Doubleday, 1956.

Wicksell, Knut. *Interest and Prices: A Study of the Causes Regulating the Value of Money*. Translated from German by R. F. Kahn. London: Published on behalf of the Royal Economic Society by Macmillan and Co., Limited, 1936. Originally published as *Geldzins und Güterpreise. Eine Studie uber die den Tauschwert des Geldes bestimmenden ursachen* (Jena: G. Fischer, 1898).

——. *Lectures on Political Economy*. 2 vols. Translated from Swedish by E. Classen and edited by Lionel Robbins. New York: Macmillan, 1934–1935. Originally published as *Forelasingar i nationalekonomi* (1901–1906).

Wicksteed, P. H. *An Essay on the Co-ordination of the Laws of Distribution*. London: Macmillan, 1894.

Wildavsky, Aaron. *The Beleaguered Presidency*. New Brunswick, N.J.: Transaction Publishers, 1991.

——. *Budgeting: A Comparative Theory of Budgetary Processes*. Boston: Little, Brown, 1975.

——. *Craftways: On the Organization of Scholarly Work*. New Brunswick, N.J.: Transaction Publishers, 1989.

——. *Dixon-Yates: A Study in Power Politics*. New Haven, Conn.: Yale University Press, 1962.

——. *Leadership in a Small Town*. Totowa, N.J.: Bedminster Press, 1964.

——. *The New Politics of the Budgetary Process*. Glenview, Ill.: Scott, Foresman, 1988.

——. *The Politics of the Budgetary Process*. Boston: Little, Brown, 1964.

——. *Revolt against the Masses and Other Essays in Politics and Public Policy*. New York: Basic Books, 1971.

——. *The Rise of Radical Egalitarianism*. Washington, D.C.: American University Press, 1991.

——. *Searching for Safety*. New Brunswick, N.J.: Transaction Books, 1988.

——. *Speaking Truth to Power: The Art and Craft of Policy Analysis*. Boston: Little, Brown, 1979.

Wildavsky, Aaron, and Mary Douglas. *Risk and Culture: An Essay on the Selection of Technical and Environmental Dangers*. Berkeley: University of California Press, 1982.

Wildavsky, Aaron, and Richard Ellis. *Dilemmas of Presidential Leadership: From Washington to Lincoln*. New Brunswick, N.J.: Transaction Publishers, 1989.

Williams, Raymond. *Culture*. Glasgow: Fontana, 1981.

——. *Culture and Society: 1780–1950*. New York: Columbia University Press, 1958.

——. *Keywords: A Vocabulary of Culture and Society*. New York: Oxford University Press, 1976.

——. *The Long Revolution*. New York: Columbia University Press, 1961.

——. *Marxism and Literature*. Oxford: Oxford University Press, 1977.

——. *Problems in Materialism and Culture: Selected Essays*. London: Verso Press, 1980.

——. *Television, Technology and Cultural Form*. New York: Schocken Books, 1974.

——. *The Year 2000*. New York: Pantheon Books, 1983.

Williamson, O. E. *The Economic Institutions of Capitalism*. New York: The Free Press, 1985.

Wilson, E. O. *Sociobiology: The New Synthesis*. Cambridge, Mass.: Belknap Press of Harvard University Press, 1975.

Wilson, Julius. *The Truly Disadvantaged: The Inner City, the Underclass and Public Policy*. Chicago: University of Chicago Press, 1987.

Winnicott, Donald Woods. *The Child, the Family, and the Outside World*. Baltimore, Md.: Penguin, 1964.

——. *Home Is Where We Start From: Essays by a Psychoanalyst*. Edited by C. Winnicott. New York: Norton, 1986. Reprint, London: Penguin, 1990.

——. *Playing and Reality*. London: Tavistock, 1971.

Wissler, Clark. *The Relation of Nature to Man in Aboriginal America*. New York: Oxford University Press, 1926.

Wittfogel, Karl. *Oriental Despotism*. New Haven, Conn.: Yale University Press, 1957.

Wittgenstein, Ludwig. *Culture and Value*. Edited by G. H. von Wright in collaboration with Heikki Nyman. Translated from German by Peter Winch. Oxford: Blackwell, 1980. Originally published as *Vermischte Bemerkungen: Eine Auswahl aus dem Nachlass* (Frankfurt am Main: Suhrkamp, 1977).

——. *On Certainty*. Edited by G. E. M. Anscombe and G. H. von Wright. Translated from German by Denis Paul and G. E. M. Anscombe. San Francisco: Arion Press, 1991. Originally published as *Über Gewissheit*.

——. *Philosophical Investigations*. Translated from German by G. E. M. Anscombe. Oxford: B. Blackwell, 1953. Originally published as *Philosophische Untersuchungen*.

————. *Tractatus Logico-Philosophicus.* Translated from German by D. F. Pears and B. F. McGuinness. London: Routledge and Kegan Paul, 1974. Originally published as *Logisch-philosophische Abhandlung.*

Wolff, Robert Paul, Barrington Moore Jr., and Herbert Marcuse. *A Critique of Pure Tolerance.* Boston: Beacon Press, 1965.

Wolin, Sheldon. *Hobbes and the Epic Tradition of Political Theory.* Los Angeles: William Andrews Clark Memorial Library, University of California–Los Angeles, 1970.

————. *Politics and Vision: Continuity and Innovation in Western Political Thought.* Boston: Little, Brown, 1960.

————. *The Presence of the Past: Essays on the State and the Constitution.* Baltimore, Md.: Johns Hopkins University Press, 1989.

Wolin, Sheldon, and John H. Schaar. *The Berkeley Rebellion and Beyond: Essays on Politics and Education in the Technological Society.* New York: New York Review, distributed by Vintage Books, 1970.

Wollstonecraft, Mary. *A Vindication of the Rights of Woman: With Strictures on Political and Moral Subjects.* 2d ed. London: J. Johnson, 1792.

Worsley, Peter. *Inside China.* London: A. Lane, 1974.

————. *Knowledges: Culture, Counterculture and Subculture.* New York: New Press, 1997.

————. *Marx and Marxism.* London and New York: Tavistock, 1982.

————. *The Third World.* Chicago: University of Chicago Press, 1964.

————. *Three Worlds: Culture and World Development.* London: Weidenfeld and Nicolson, 1984.

————. *The Trumpet Shall Sound: A Study of "Cargo" Cults in Melanesia.* London: MacGibbon and Kee, 1957.

Wundt, Wilhelm. *Elements of Folk Psychology: Outlines of a Psychological History of the Development of Mankind.* Translated from German by Edward Leroy Schaub. New York: Macmillan, 1916. Originally published as *Elemente der Völkerpsychologie. Grundlinien einer psychologischen Entwicklungsgeschichte der Menschheit* (Leipzig: Alfred Kröner Verlag, 1912).

————. *The Language of Gestures.* The Hague, the Netherlands: Mouton, 1973. Originally published as *Völkerpsychologie: Eine Untersuchung der Ent-Wicklungsgesetze von Sprache, Mythus und Sitte,* vol. 1, part 1 (Leipzig, W. Engelmann, 1904–1923).

————. *Principles of Physiological Psychology.* Translated from German by Edward Bradford Titchener. New York: Macmillan, 1904. Originally published as *Grundzuge der physiologischen Psychologie* (Leipzig: Engelmann, 1874).

Young, Michael. *The Rise of the Meritocracy.* London: Thames and Hudson, 1958.

Zangwill, Israel. *The Melting Pot: Drama in Four Acts.* New York: Macmillan, 1939. Originally published in 1909.